BUSINESS AND LAW
FOR THE SHIPMASTER

Form No. 9

CERTIFICATE OF BRITISH REGISTRY

PARTICULARS OF SHIP

SIGNAL — Top — G / 2nd — O / 3rd — X / Silent — S

Official Number	Name of Ship	No., Year and Port of Registry	No., Year and Port of previous Registry (if any)
343017	Wild Auk	582 in 1971 London	

Whether a Sailing, Steam or Motor Ship; if Steam or Motor, how propelled	Where Built	When Built	Name and Address of Builders
Motor Ship Single Screw	Bergen	1971	A.S. Bergens Mekaniske Verksteder Bergen. Norway.

		Length from fore-part of stem, to the aft side of the head of the stern-post / fore side of the rudder stock	FEET 492	TENTHS 6.0
Number of Decks .... Four		Main breadth to outside of plating	70	0.0
Number of Masts .... One and three twin derrick posts		Depth in hold from tonnage deck to ceiling amidships	26 insulation 9.0	
Rigged .... Not		Depth in hold from upper deck to insulation amidships, in the case of two decks and upwards	37	5.0
Stem .... Raked		Depth from upper deck at side amidships to bottom of keel	41	8.0
Stern .... Transom		Round of beam on upper deck	1	3.0
Build .... Carvel		Length of engine-room (if any)	78	7.5
Framework and description of vessel .... Steel Cargo				
Number of Bulkheads .... Seven watertight				

PARTICULARS OF PROPELLING ENGINES, &c. (IF ANY), as supplied by Builders, Owners, or Engine Makers.

No. of sets of Engine	Description of Engine	When made	Name and Address of Makers	Reciprocating Engines No. of cylinders in each set	Diameter of cylinders	Rotary Engines No. of cylinders in each set	N.H.P. B.H.P. I.H.P. Estimated Speed of Ship
One	Internal Combustion Direct Acting	Engines 1971	Engines Nylands Verksted Oslo I, Norway	Nine	740mm		3107 17400
No. of Boilers One	Description .. Oil Fired Waste heat Number .. One One Loaded pressure 7kg/cm² 7kg/cm²	Boilers 1971	Boilers Oil Fired :- Aalborg Vaerft A/S, Aalborg, Denmark. Waste heat :- Nylands Verksted Oslo I, Norway		Length of Stroke 1600 mm		18900 22.0 knots

PARTICULARS OF TONNAGE

The tonnages of this ship in accordance with her British Tonnage Certificate are:—

GROSS TONNAGE .... 9709·34 .... tons (27477·43 cubic metres)

REGISTER TONNAGE .... 5429·26 .... tons (15364·51 cubic metres)

This ship is assigned with a tonnage mark on each side of the ship which is 164½ inches below the upper deck line and when this mark is submerged the above tonnages are applicable.

When the tonnage mark is NOT submerged the following tonnages are applicable:—

GROSS TONNAGE .... 7290·34 .... tons (20631·66 cubic metres)

REGISTER TONNAGE .... 3255·89 .... tons (9214·17 cubic metres)

Delete if not applicable

A detailed summary of the tonnages for this ship is shown on The British Tonnage Certificate.

The number of seamen and apprentices for whom accommodation is certified 35

I, the undersigned, Registrar of British Ships at the Port of London, hereby certify that the Ship, the Description of which is prefixed to this my Certificate, has been duly surveyed, and that the above Description is in accordance with the Register Book; that Harold Dorkins whose Certificate of Competency or Service is No. 77309, is the Master of the said Ship; and that the Name, Residence and Description of the Owner, and Number of Sixty-fourth Shares held by it, are as follows:—

Name, Residence, and Occupation of the Owner.	Number of Sixty-fourth Shares.
Federal Steam Navigation Company Limited having its principal place of business at P & O Building, Leadenhall Street, E.C.3, in the City of London	Sixty-four

Dated at H.M. Custom House, London the 17th day of December One thousand nine hundred and seventy one

Assistant Registrar of British Ships.

Reproduced by kind permission of the Federal Steam Navigation Company Ltd.

Certificate of Registry of m.v. "Wild Auk".

BUSINESS AND LAW
FOR
THE SHIPMASTER

BY

F. N. HOPKINS, M.R.Inst.Nav.

(Extra Master)

REVISED BY

G. G. WATKINS

(Extra Master)

GLASGOW

BROWN, SON & FERGUSON, LTD.

NAUTICAL PUBLISHERS

4-10 DARNLEY STREET

Second Edition	–	–	– 1966
Third Edition	–	–	– 1974
Fourth Edition	–	–	– 1977
Fifth Edition	–	–	– 1979
Sixth Edition	–	–	– 1982

ISBN 0 85174 434 6 (Sixth Edition)
ISBN 0 85174 349 8 (Fifth Edition)

© 1982 Brown, Son & Ferguson Ltd., Glasgow, G41 2SD
Printed and Made in Great Britain

PREFACE TO SIXTH EDITION

THE main changes that have had to be made since the last edition are due to the bringing into force of the SOLAS Convention 1974 in May 1980 followed by the Protocol to that Convention one year later. The M.S. Act 1979 has also introduced changes particularly to matters concerning United Kingdom pilotage, offences by seamen, and the Athens Convention relating to Carriage of Passengers. Some changes have been made to the chapter on carriage of goods and I have tried to 'slim' the book by removing the Marine Insurance Act 1906, the M.S. Act 1970 and the Collision Regulations 1972 from the Appendix. Unless otherwise stated, I have endeavoured to state the legal position as at 1st September 1981.

G. G. WATKINS

SIDCUP, SEPTEMBER 1981

ACKNOWLEDGEMENTS

FOR supplying documents and giving permission to reproduce them the author tenders his sincere thanks and acknowledges his indebtedness to:—

The Controller of Her Majesty's Stationery Office.
Publishers of Lloyd's Nautical Yearbook.
Lloyd's Register of Shipping.
The Institute of London Underwriters.
The Federal Steam Navigation Company Limited.
Trinity House Lighthouse Service.
The Port of London Authority.
The General Council of British Shipping.
The Baltic and International Maritime Conference (BIMCO).
The International Association of Independent Tanker Owners (INTERTANKO).

For kindly responding to requests for information on various topics the author also expresses his grateful thanks to:—

The Director of The Seafarers' Education Service.
The Secretary of The Merchant Navy Training Board.
The Secretary of The General Council of British Shipping.
The Secretary of The Royal Thames Yacht Club.
The Registrar General of Shipping and Seamen.
The Federal Maritime Commission, Washington, D.C.
The Head of the Department of Maritime Law and Economics, United States Merchant Marine Academy.
The Head of Department, City of London Polytechnic School of Navigation.
The Indo-China Steam Navigation Company Limited.

AUTHOR'S NOTES

1. WHILST every care has been taken to avoid mistakes and to give up-to-date information, should any faults be found the author would greatly appreciate the publishers' attention being drawn to them so that they may be rectified in the future. Suggestions for improvements will also be gratefully accepted.

2. Unless the context indicates otherwise, any references to the Board of Trade or to the Department of Trade and Industry which remain should be taken as though they were references to the Department of Trade (D.o.T.). References to the Secretary of State, unless otherwise stated, mean the Secretary of State, Department of Trade.

3. On 22nd May 1982 the Inter-Governmental Maritime Consultative Organisation (IMCO) changed its name to the International Maritime Organisation (IMO). After that date, unless the context indicates otherwise, references to IMCO which have not been altered should be taken as though they were references to the organisation's new name.

LIST OF DOCUMENTS REPRODUCED

CONTENTS

xi

CHAPTER I

INFORMATION ABOUT LAW

Introduction. Throughout this book references will have to be made to certain Acts of Parliament and to numerous rules and regulations. That being so, it would seem that no apology is needed for beginning with a brief account of how our laws are made, administered and enforced, together with some explanation of those legal terms which are so often being brought to the notice of ship-masters and their officers.

Readers should understand that this has not been written by a lawyer and is not intended for students of law who have at their disposal a full range of excellent text-books written by highly qualified law experts. The purpose of this opening chapter is simply to place at the disposal of young shipmasters and those who aspire to command some information about law which may assist them to a better understanding of the many problems they may be faced with in the course of their careers. Teaching experience over a long period has convinced the author that a lack of at least some know-ledge of this kind can be a considerable handicap whilst, on the other hand, it seems highly probable that those who are better informed will be likely to recognise more readily the circumstances in which assistance from a qualified legal adviser is really necessary. That is the answer to any possible criticism to the effect that learning about the law might, to misquote the title of a well-known book, tempt "every man to be his own lawyer"—a possibly disastrous policy.

It is hardly necessary to add that no sympathy for "sea lawyers" is implied. They are better left ashore.

ENGLISH LAW

Making of Law. Reference to Appendix I of this book will show that the preamble to the Carriage of Goods by Sea Act, 1971, is concluded by the words: "Be it enacted by the Queen's most Excellent Majesty, by and with the advice and consent of the Lords Spiritual and Temporal, and Commons, in this present Parliament assembled, and by the authority of the same, as follows . . ." Then follow the various sections of the Act and the appended Schedule of Rules.

Although the theory of English law is that all justice proceeds from the Sovereign, this is a reminder—though one is scarcely needed—that the reigning monarch cannot make laws by himself but is obliged to have the advice and consent of Parliament and to

1

give his Royal Assent to all Acts of Parliament. The Lords Spiritual are the archbishops and some of the bishops, whilst the Lords Temporal are the hereditary and life peers, and they collectively form the House of Lords. The Commons are the House of Commons, containing the elected representatives of the various parliamentary constituencies throughout England, Scotland and Northern Ireland. England, for this purpose, includes Wales. Although Scotland sends members of Parliament to the House of Commons, Scottish law is different from English law, and in many respects the country is governed differently. Northern Ireland not only sends members of Parliament to the House of Commons, but also normally has a Parliament of its own (The Stormont) which, owing to the current state of emergency in the province, is for the time being in abeyance.

The law which the courts have to interpret, and upon which the rights of individuals are founded, consists of the Common Law of England, the Rules of Equity, and the Statute Law.

The Common Law. This consists of the law which has developed from and been founded upon ancient usage or Custom of the Realm as recognised by the courts. In their decisions, the courts professed to be declaring and explaining the Common Law as it had always existed, but in practice their decisions often created the law and established precedents for future guidance. In other words, cases were decided in accordance with the manner in which similar cases had been decided in the past. Hence, Common Law is referred to as "Case Law" or "Law of Precedent" and it is binding on every court having a jurisdiction inferior to that of the court which gave the original decision. Even courts of equal jurisdiction usually follow the earlier decision, particularly if it is of long standing and has never been questioned. Much Common Law has, in relatively recent times, been incorporated into statutes passed by Parliament. For example, the Marine Insurance Act, 1906, to which reference is made in Chapter 14, did not create any new law but merely codified the then existing law.

Rules of Equity. Since the Common Law was understood to be based entirely on custom and precedent, in order to bring an action at Common Law, it was necessary to show that the cause of complaint was governed by some established precedent or custom, failing which the Common Law courts could give no remedy. Because of this there arose a special class of pleaders, whose particular skill consisted of drafting the form of a plaint so that it should come within the scope of some precedent. However, there was always a fiction that the Sovereign, as the fount of all justice, was in possession of certain principles of law unknown to the Common Law judges, by the application of which he was able to mitigate the harshness of the Common Law and give relief where none was available at Common Law. Such principles were administered by the King's Chancery by the Chancellor and his assistants who, being ecclesiastics, actually applied the rules of Roman Law in which they were all well versed. These rules were the rules of Equity and were supplementary to, rather than contradictory of, the rules of Common Law. Various Judicature Acts, now consolidated by the Supreme Court of Judicature Act, 1925, have diminished the importance of the distinction between Courts of Law and Courts of Equity, although a distinction between law and equity still remains. Today the Common Law Courts are able to give equitable relief and the Chancery Division of the High Court can give Common Law remedies. That is to say that the Judicature Acts have abolished a system of having separate courts of law and equity and have provided for the convenient administration of both in the one court. To take a simple illustration of the distinction between law and equity, consider the example of a trust where property has been conveyed to one person to be held in trust by him for another. The Common Law says that A is the owner of the property. Equity supplements the law by saying that whilst it is a fact that A is the legal owner, he holds the property on trust for B. Obviously, the two sets of rights, legal and equitable, can be administered just as well in one court as in two. A "bond" provides a further example. A bond is a promise under seal to pay a sum of money as a penalty for the non-performance of some condition which is the real object of the bond. At Common Law, the entire sum named was held to be payable on breach of the condition; but at Equity, no more could be recovered than the amount of the damage actually sustained by the breach of the condition, and this is all that can now be recovered.

Statute Law. This consists of the various Acts of Parliament which are passed from time to time. These may create new law or may either declare or overrule the existing Common Law.

In the sphere of private law there are three classes of statutes of particular importance, viz.:—

1. The type of statute such as the Marine Insurance Act 1906, which takes a branch of the law developed by a long series of court decisions and casts the outcome of a mass of cases into the form of principles set out in the sections of an Act of Parliament.

2. Statutes such as the Conveyancing Act, 1881, which aimed at codifying the labours of conveyancers by importing into all documents of a certain class the provisions which are common form in all well drawn instruments of that class.

3. The statute which deals with an isolated point of private law where, for instance, a rule has become established by court decisions which is recognised to work injustice but which cannot be altered by the courts in view of the doctrine of binding precedent.

Statute has played a considerable part in the development of private law, but it is in the field of public law that its action is most in evidence. Modern social services would be impossible without the existence of those new public authorities with powers far more extensive than the prerogative powers allowed to the Government by Common Law. It was inevitable, therefore, that Acts of Parliament should have appeared, one after another, in rapid succession during the nineteenth and twentieth centuries.

Many Acts of Parliament are extremely complicated, and some consideration will now be given to the manner in which an Act comes into being.

Bills may be rejected by Parliament, and those that are passed are frequently amended during their passage through Parliament. However, Parliament does not itself draft the bills which it considers. Generally, statutes amending private law have been drafted by distinguished lawyers, sometimes on their own initiative, though more frequently at the instance of the Chancellor or of a committee which has reported in favour of a change in the law. Most of the more recent statutes which deal with public law, on the other hand, have been drafted by a body of civil servants called the Parliamentary Counsel to the Treasury, working in collaboration with the civil servants of the particular ministry concerned. The "Bill", which has put into a proper form the suggestions originally made for a new Act of Parliament, is then introduced into the House of Commons, by the minister concerned and certain other members of his party, whose names will appear on the back of the bill to signify their approval of it. It is then given what is called a "first reading", which means that it is printed and made available for all members of Parliament to consider. In course of time it comes forward for a "second reading", at which stage the Minister will address the House to explain the bill and the reasons for wanting it passed. It is then debated under the chairmanship of the Speaker and put to the vote. Assuming that a majority of the members of the House of Commons vote in favour of the bill, it will then be referred to Committee. The Committee may be the whole House of Commons sitting in Committee, or a smaller number of members chosen from the different parties in the House in proportion to the strength of each party. The function of the Committee is to consider the bill clause by clause, but there may be an arrangement known as the "guillotine" limiting the time for discussion of any clause. The bill having been considered in detail in Committee, with or without additions or amendments, it is then reported to the House of Commons. After the report, it is given a "third reading" and then sent to the House of Lords.

Procedure in the House of Lords is different from that in the House of Commons, but all that need be said here is that if the former decide to make changes in the bill, they could send it back in its altered form to the House of Commons who might accept the changes or make other suggestions and ask the House of Lords to accept those. If agreement between the two Houses cannot be reached the House of Commons might wait until the next Session and send the bill again to the Lords. If by sending up a bill three times in three successive Sessions the House of Commons keeps on asking for it, the bill will become law, even though the House of Lords rejects it every time. Thus, although the House of Lords can delay a bill becoming law, they cannot in the long run prevent it.

The final stage before a bill becomes law is the receiving of the Royal Assent. This is quite formal and is usually given by the Queen signing a Commission telling three members of the House of Lords to assent on Her Majesty's behalf. They send for the Commons to attend in the House of Lords where the former are told "La Reine le veult" (The Queen wills it).

In the case of a Money Bill the House of Lords has no power to alter or delay it. The House of Commons alone is the body which passes Acts of Parliament for raising taxes. Hence, the preamble to a Finance Act is worded in a special way and the Royal Assent takes a different and more elaborate form compared with that quoted above.

Regulations. Many modern Acts of Parliament deal with matters so complex that it would be impossible for Parliament to devote sufficient time to the arrangement of all details. Accordingly, a practice has grown up whereby an Act authorises the appropriate Minister to make regulations about details; and if any person breaks one or other of those regulations, he will have committed an offence in just the same way as if he had been in breach of the Act itself. Regulations made pursuant to Acts of Parliament are issued in the form of Statutory Instruments and there are in force many thousands of them. This will not be surprising to anyone who has considered, for example, the Merchant Shipping Act, 1979. Whilst Parliament is, quite rightly, deeply concerned with the general principles of safety of life at sea, it is no more than logical to accept that the regulation concerning, say, the frequency of the testing of ships' reserve radio transmitters should be left to the recommendation of the appropriate civil servants of the Department of Trade.

Courts of Law. The English Courts of Law are divided broadly into criminal courts and civil courts, though there is some overlapping which will be apparent from what follows.

Police—Crime—Criminal Courts. As long ago as 1829, the Metropolitan Police Force was created by an Act of Parliament and placed under the direct control of the Home Secretary. A few years later, the Municipal Corporations Act provided for the establishment in municipal boroughs of a force of constables appointed by and partly under the authority of a Watch Committee of the borough council, and at about the same time the City of London acquired its own police force. In 1856 the establishment of a similar force in each county was made obligatory on the county justices, though in 1888 control of county police passed out of the hands of the justices and was vested in a Standing Joint Committee consisting of (a) representatives of the then newly-formed county councils and (b) representatives of Quarter Sessions. The Home Secretary has no direct control over county and borough police as he still has over the Metropolitan Police, but his indirect control over them is considerable for the reason that a large proportion of the cost of their maintenance is supplied by grants from the central government, which can be withheld in the event of standards of efficiency falling below what is required by the Home Office. Moreover, since 1919 the Home Secretary has been empowered to make the necessary regulations to ensure uniformity in the pay and conditions of service in all police forces throughout England and Wales. Whilst the chief duty of the police is to prevent the commission of crimes and apprehend suspected criminals, it is well known that they have many additional duties, not the least of which nowadays is traffic control. In recent years a number of borough police forces have been merged in the surrounding or adjacent county force as part of a policy to reduce the number of separate constabularies in order to increase the efficiency of police organisation throughout the country.

A *crime* may be defined as an act forbidden by law under pain of punishment, being an offence or injury which is not only a wrong to an individual but a wrong done to the community. Thus, a crime is distinguished from a *tort*, which is an injury or wrong suffered by one person at the hands of another, irrespective of any contract between them. *Breach of contract* is further distinguished by there being a contract in existence. If A deliberately and maliciously breaks B's shop window, that is a crime. If A carelessly and accidentally breaks B's window, that is a tort. If A enters into a contract to supply B with certain goods on or before a certain date and, the contract not being frustrated, he fails to fulfil his bargain, then there is a breach of contract. Torts and breaches of contract which may be subject to actions for damages are matters for civil proceedings and will be referred to again later.

Crimes in English law are divisible into indictable offences and summary offences. The former, which admit of trial by jury, were, prior to 1967, further subdivided into felonies and misdemeanours. The Criminal Law Act 1967, however, abolished this distinction. Power to arrest a felon was given not only to constables but also to private citizens but in the case of misdemeanour no one could arrest an offender without a magistrate's warrant except in certain particular cases. Under the new Act powers of summary arrest apply to offences for which the sentence is fixed by law or for which a person (not previously convicted) may under or by virtue of any enactment be sentenced to imprisonment for a term of five years, and to attempts to commit any such offence. Any such offence or attempt is known as an "arrestable offence". Any person may arrest without warrant anyone who is, or with reasonable cause is suspected to be, in the act of committing an arrestable offence. Where an arrestable offence has been committed any person may arrest without warrant anyone who is reasonably suspected to be guilty of the offence. Similar powers of arrest are, of course, given to a constable who is further empowered to enter (if need be, by force) and search any place where the offender is reasonably suspected to be. A person may use such force as is reasonable in the circumstances in the prevention of crime, or in effecting or assisting in the lawful arrest of offenders, suspected offenders, or persons unlawfully at large. Penalties, consisting of imprisonment for a number of years, can be imposed on persons found guilty of assisting offenders. There are also penalties for concealing offences, giving false information and causing wasteful employment of the police.

The first step in the prosecution of any offence, indictable or summary, is normally either the placing of an information before a magistrate by some person acquainted with the facts who may or may not be the injured party, or the arrest of the accused by a constable or a private individual without any preliminary information followed by a charge against the arrested person when in custody. On receipt of the information the magistrate generally issues a summons requiring the accused to attend, but in the case of a grave charge made under oath he may issue a warrant to a constable for the accused to be arrested and taken into custody. In the case of a non-indictable offence, enforcement of attendance by mere summons is most frequent. At one time there were strict rules of venue under which the accused had to be tried in the county where the crime was alleged to have been committed, but now-a-days he can be tried in the county or place where he is held in custody.

Magistrate's Court of Summary Jurisdiction. This is otherwise known as a Court of Petty Sessions, or a Police Court, but the latter name is apt to be misleading because the primary function of the police is to act in their capacity as witnesses. The Police Court in any town is quite distinct from the Police Station. Except in London and some large towns, administration of justice in these courts is still in the hands of justices of the peace who, with certain exceptions, are appointed by the Crown on the advice of the Lord Chancellor—the head of all judges, magistrates and lawyers. In selecting county justices the Lord Chancellor usually accepts the recommendation of the Lord Lieutenant of the county, who is assisted by a selection committee. In the case of borough justices recommendations are received from the advisory committee of the borough. It should be mentioned that many persons who have no intention of sitting as magistrates are appointed justices in recognition of their services to the community. Despite the importance of the work of those who do sit, J.P.'s are not required to have an expert knowledge of the law and they receive no remuneration for the work they do. It was only as recently as 1949, that powers were given to pay them their expenses, and even more recently that provision was made for all J.P.'s to have an adequate amount of legal training. It is now considered desirable that more good candidates for appointment to the bench should be selected from the wage-earning sections of the population, and with this object in view magistrates have become entitled to subsistence allowances in certain circumstances and allowances for loss of earnings. Their retiring age has been lowered from 75 to 70. There must always be at least two J.P.'s to hear a case, one of whom acts as chairman and takes the lead. A Clerk of Court, who is normally a qualified solicitor, is present to assist the justices and inform them on points of law. In London a system has long been established of having qualified and salaried magistrates known as "stipendiaries". The Metropolitan Police Courts are staffed by magistrates, each of whom sits alone with powers that elsewhere can be exercised only by two lay justices sitting together. This system has never been compulsorily extended to the rest of the country, but any borough or populous urban district willing to pay his salary may obtain the appointment by the Crown of a barrister of at least seven years' standing to serve as a stipendiary magistrate for the district.

Proceedings in a magistrate's court differ according to whether the accused is to be tried summarily or by a jury.

For procedural purposes the Criminal Law Act 1977 further classified offences by establishing the following modes of trial:—

    (i) offences triable only summarily;
    (ii) offences triable either summarily or on indictment;
    (iii) offences triable only on indictment.

Summary offences, which are the more numerous and less serious than indictable offences, are tried by magistrates. If the defendant pleads guilty, the court may convict him without hearing evidence. Attendance is enforced, as previously stated, by summons or arrest, with or without warrant. After hearing each side and witnesses, the magistrates can convict or discharge the defendant. On conviction they can punish the defendant by imposing a fine, or a short term of imprisonment; or they can defer sentence for up to six months to take account of the conduct of the defendant after conviction; or they can commit the defendant to the Crown Court for sentence.

The mode of trial for offences triable either way is laid down in the 1977 Act. Magistrates listen to representations made to them by each side and then take account of the nature of the case, whether the circumstances make the case one of a serious character, the punishment they have power to inflict and any other circumstances which appear to make it more suitable for trial one way or the other. If the magistrates decide that the case should be tried summarily, they explain this to the defendant and ask him whether he consents to be tried summarily or wishes to be tried by jury. If he agrees to be tried summarily they proceed with summary trial; if he does not agree, they consider the evidence as examining magistrates, and if satisfied that it is sufficient, commit the defendant for trial at the Crown Court. Summary proceedings for an indictable offence under the M.S. Acts can be commenced at any time after the offence was committed. Proceedings for summary offences should be started within six months of the offence being committed, or if one or both parties are out of the U.K. during that time, within two months after they both arrive and are within the U.K. and so that summary conviction is obtained within three years of the offence being committed.

Where the accused is to be tried on indictment, the magistrates conduct a preliminary examination to decide whether there is a strong enough case to justify them in committing the accused for trial. The procedure is now regulated by the Magistrates' Courts Act, 1952. This Act makes it essential for the accused to be present at the enquiry and to have the opportunity of cross-examining the witnesses against him. He may be represented by solicitor or counsel. In practice the enquiry is conducted in public, though this is not necessary. The accused is not asked whether he is guilty or not guilty. The case is opened by the prosecutor, who will be the private individual who laid the information, or a police officer if the police initiated the prosecution. In either case the prosecutor may appear by solicitor or counsel. The prosecutor calls his witnesses to be examined, cross-examined, and re-examined. The clerk to the justices takes down the evidence which, after being signed by the witnesses, is read over to the accused. Then the magistrates explain to the accused the nature of the charge against him, tell him that he can call his own witnesses and give evidence himself if he wishes. The accused will be warned that if he desires to make a statement, anything he says will be taken down and used in evidence at the trial. Any statement he makes is taken down and signed by the magistrates. He, if he chooses to give evidence, and any witness he may call are then examined in the same way as the witnesses for the prosecution, such evidence being recorded and signed. The accused's solicitor or counsel may address the court on his behalf. The magistrates, after considering all the evidence, may decide there is no case for trial; but if they decide otherwise, they will also determine at which particular Crown Court the accused should be tried, and whether he should be let out on bail or be remanded in custody until the date of the trial. The granting or withholding of bail is entirely at the discretion of the justices, but usually when the accused has an established address and is not a notorious character bail will be allowed. If bail is refused, there remains a right of application for it to the Queen's Bench Division of the High Court. Finally, the magistrates will bind over the prosecutor to prefer an indictment against the prisoner, and bind over the witnesses for both parties to attend the trial. They may also, in appropriate circumstances, assign legal aid to the accused under the Legal

Aid Act, 1974. The question of legal aid in criminal proceedings including the provisions as to legal aid orders, the circumstances in which legal aid may be given, the liability for contributions, the computation of resources, the payment of costs of legal aid, and many other relevant matters, is fully dealt with in the above Act.

Although the greater proportion of the work done by the justices in petty sessions is the holding of preliminary examinations and summary trials, much of it does not come under the heading of "criminal" justice at all. Before the nineteenth century a great part of local government was in the hands of the justices and, though most of it is now performed by elected councils, some administrative functions are still exercised by magistrates. Licensing is a case in point. Further, some proceedings taken by J.P.'s are definitely civil proceedings; for instance, separation or maintenance orders. Others, such as infringements of local bye-laws, are matters not generally regarded as crimes, although technically subject to criminal proceedings.

After an accused has been committed for trial, a bill of indictment is preferred against him by the prosecutor. At this stage, the issue is between the Crown and the prisoner—Regina *v.* B, not A *v.* B—and Her Majesty's Attorney-General has power to stop any prosecution by entering what is called a *nolle prosequi*. However, the prosecution, in the name of the Queen, is not normally carried on by agents of the central government but either by private individuals or local chief constables. The Director of Public Prosecutions is an official appointed to advise private prosecutors and chief constables on the conduct of cases and to undertake himself the prosecution of important cases on behalf of the State, but only a relatively small proportion of persons tried on indictment are, in fact, prosecuted by that official. Whoever does prosecute must cause a bill of indictment to be drawn up, setting out the charges against the accused. The signature of the appropriate officer of the Crown Court converts the bill of indictment into an indictment which the court can try.

All proceedings on indictment are now brought before the Crown Court. A magistrates' court committing a person for trial is required to specify the place at which he is to be tried having regard to (*a*) the convenience of the defence, prosecution and witnesses, (*b*) the expediting of the trial, (*c*) any direction given by or on behalf of the Lord Chief Justice with the concurrence of the Lord Chancellor.

If the defendant or the prosecutor is dissatisfied with the place of trial as fixed by the magistrates' court he may apply to the Crown Court for a direction varying the place of trial and that court, having taken the matter into consideration, may comply or give some other direction as it thinks fit.

The Supreme Court. This consists of the Court of Appeal and the High Court together with the Crown Court established by the

Courts Act 1971. Sittings of the High Court may be hald, and any other business of the High Court may be conducted, at any place in England or Wales. Subject to rules of court the places at which, and the times when, the High Court sits outside the Royal Courts of Justice are determined in accordance with directions given by or on behalf of the Lord Chancellor.

The Crown Court. All Courts of Assize and Courts of Quarter Sessions were abolished by the Courts Act 1971 and are replaced by Crown Courts. The Act provides that there shall be a Crown Court in England and Wales which shall be a superior court of record. The jurisdiction and powers of the Crown Court are exercised by (a) any judge of the High Court, or (b) any Circuit judge or Recorder, or (c) subject to certain provisions a judge of the High Court, Circuit judge or Recorder sitting with justices of the peace.

This reform has been described by a former Lord Chancellor as the greatest in the administration of justice this century, and possibly the greatest in legal history. Courts of Assize began in the reign of Henry II and quarter sessions go back to the early Middle Ages but, in these days of expanding populations frequently shifted away from assize towns and concentrated in new centres, the vast increase in crime and the great extension of legal aid put the courts under intense pressure. With so many lengthy contested cases untried, prisoners were being kept in gaol for unduly long periods or were waiting on bail many months with prosecutions hanging over their heads. Civil cases at assizes were being subjected to mounting delay as it was the practice for judges to deal with them at the end of their lists. From 1966 to 1969 a Royal Commission headed by Lord Beeching conducted a study which showed beyond doubt that the old system was out of date, time wasting and inefficient. The Commission therefore proposed a new system of Crown Courts administered under the Lord Chancellor's Office and sitting at convenient centres of population. The Courts Act 1971, which stemmed from the Beeching report, provides that the Crown Court while normally sitting at designated centres for ease of communication, has power as stated above to hear cases anywhere in England and Wales.

For the purpose of the new Crown Courts England and Wales are divided into six circuits which conform mainly, though with some adjustments, to the former assize circuits. The Crown Courts are divided into three tiers. At "first tier" centres High Court judges try civil cases as well as the most serious criminal cases such as murder, manslaughter and rape. According to its seriousness other criminal work is divided between a new category of Circuit judges and part-time recorders sitting alone or with not less than two and not more than four J.P.'s. The Circuit judges referred to are made up of present county court and Old Bailey judges, the recorders of Liverpool and Manchester Crown Courts and former full-time chairmen of quarter sessions. The so-called "second tier" courts can deal with the less serious cases of murder, rape, arson, etc., whilst the "third tier" takes over all those criminal cases that were formerly within the jurisdiction of quarter sessions.

Offences are now classified as follows:—

Class One, which includes treason, murder and genocide, will be tried by a High Court judge;

Class Two, including manslaughter, rape, sedition, mutiny, piracy and offences under the Geneva Conventions Act, will be tried by a High Court judge unless released by him to a Circuit judge or recorder;

Class Three, lesser indictable offences, will be tried by a High Court judge, Circuit judge or recorder; and

Class Four, which includes some indictable offences, and offences which could have been tried summarily by magistrates, will normally be tried by a Circuit judge or recorder.

Magistrates committing persons for trial, besides being able to specify the most convenient location of the Crown Court where the case can be heard, are also able to indicate that in their view a particular case in Class Four should be tried by a High Court judge. Such cases would include those where widespread public concern is involved or where the accused owes a duty to the public.

The Courts Act 1971 provides that Her Majesty may from time to time appoint as Circuit judge, to serve in the Crown Court and county courts, such qualified persons as may be recommended to Her by the Lord Chancellor. The maximum number shall be such as may be determined from time to time by the Lord Chancellor with the concurrence of the Minister for the Civil Service. No person shall be qualified to be appointed a Circuit judge unless he is a barrister of at least ten years' standing or a Recorder who has held that office for at least five years. Subject to certain exceptions a Circuit judge is required to vacate his office at the end of the completed year of service in which he attains the age of seventy-two. So long as he holds his office no Circuit judge is permitted to practise as a barrister or act for any remuneration to himself as arbitrator or referee or be directly or indirectly concerned as a conveyancer, notary public or solicitor.

The Act also provides that Her Majesty may from time to time appoint qualified persons, to be known as Recorders, to act as part-time judges of the Crown Court. Every such appointment must be of a person recommended by the Lord Chancellor and no person is qualified unless he is a barrister or solicitor of at least ten years' standing. Neither the initial term for which a Recorder is appointed nor any extension thereof may continue after the end of the completed year of service in which the Recorder attains the age of seventy-two.

For the first time in the course of our legal history the way is now open for solicitors to achieve high judicial office. As indicated above, solicitors as well as barristers are now eligible for appointment to the part-time recorderships and, after five years of such experience, they can be selected as full-time Circuit judges.

As well as simplifying the structure of the courts the Act is designed to reduce delays through its fundamental reform of court administration. A unified court service is set up embracing the High Court, Crown Courts and County Courts under the central control of the Lord Chancellor's Department. The Department of the Environment has become responsible for court buildings, judges' lodgings and other necessary accommodation. The only exception to this is in the City of London where the City Corporation continues to provide for the Old Bailey and the Mayor's and City of London Court. The latter, which as it was constituted before the commencement of the Act has been abolished, still retains its name as the local county court for the City of London and now has a reduced jurisdiction confined to county court business only.

Circuit administrators have been appointed in each of the six circuits and they, working with the High Court judges nominated to supervise each circuit, are responsible to the Lord Chancellor for preventing the build-up of delays, ensuring that judges are available where needed, organising efficient court services, and arranging instruction for lay magistrates.

The Central Criminal Court ("Old Bailey"). This court was established in 1834 as the seat of criminal assizes for the Metropolitan area and takes trials of indictments of persons committed from petty sessions in London, Middlesex and other parts of southeast England. The judges include the Recorder of London and the Common Serjeant (both of whom became Circuit judges under the 1971 Act), the judge of the City of London Court, and the High Court judges. To deal more effectively with the increasing number of cases tried at this court the Old Bailey building has recently undergone extensive reconstruction and enlargement. It is now possible for as many as twelve courts to sit simultaneously.

Crown Court procedure is broadly on the following lines. The defendant is arraigned at the bar of the court and pleads to the indictment. The jury is empanelled and sworn in after their names have been read out and the prisoner asked whether he objects to any of them. Counsel for the prosecution states his case and calls witnesses. Each witness enters the witness box in turn, takes the oath, and answers questions. Counsel for the defence then cross-examines those witnesses. Counsel for the defence then states his case and calls his witnesses, including the defendant himself if he chooses to give evidence. Counsel for the prosecution then cross-examines the witnesses for the defence. Copies of depositions made by witnesses at the preliminary enquiry will have been supplied to the court and to the prisoner, but, except in the case of unavoidable absence of witnesses, such depositions cannot be used at the trial;

the witnesses must be called in person. Counsel for the prosecution is not permitted to comment on the fact that the prisoner has not chosen to submit himself to cross-examination, but the judge or recorder may do so in his summing up. When the evidence is completed and the speeches of counsel are ended the summing up takes place and the jury retire to consider their verdict. Formerly the verdict had to be unanimous but the Criminal Justice Act 1967 makes majority verdicts allowable although a special procedure is necessary to prevent it becoming known that a "not guilty" verdict was by a majority. In all criminal cases a verdict of 10 jurors can be accepted from juries of 12 or 11, and the verdict of 9 if there are 10 jurors. Should the jury or the necessary majority of them fail to agree, they will be discharged and the prisoner remanded for a new trial. The Attorney-General may, however, enter a *nolle prosequi*. When the jury is ready they are asked whether they find the prisoner guilty or not guilty, and the foreman of the jury replies on their behalf. If a verdict of guilty is returned, then—and not till then— the judge or recorder calls for the police officer in charge of the case and asks for the previous history of the defendant. Finally sentence is given. The punishment of a person found guilty of a criminal offence may be imprisonment or fine, but in some cases, particularly where the prisoner is a first offender, he may be given a suspended sentence, discharged absolutely or conditionally, or placed on probation. Where a person who has attained the age of seventeen is convicted of an offence punishable with imprisonment the court, instead of dealing with him in any other way, may make an order, referred to as a "community service order", requiring him to perform unpaid work for such number of hours (being in the aggregate not less than forty nor more than two hundred and forty) as may be specified in the order. The court may not make a community service order unless the offender consents and the court has been notified by the Secretary of State that arrangements exist for persons who reside in the petty sessions area in which the offender resides to perform work under such orders. The court must also be satisfied from a probation officer's report about the offender and his circumstances that he is a suitable person to perform work under such an order, and that provision can be made under the arrangements for him to do so.

Court of Appeal (Criminal Division). This consists of the Lord Chief Justice of England, the Lords Justices of Appeal and any judge of the High Court asked to sit by the Lord Chief Justice. In practice, the Lord Chief Justice and two puisne (or lesser) judges generally constitute the Court, but in important cases there may be five or even seven judges. The Court has no jurisdiction to hear appeals from petty sessions or appeals by the Crown against acquittals, but any person convicted on indictment has absolute right of appeal to this Court on any question of law and, with the leave of the trial judge or the judge of the Court of Appeal, the right to appeal on any question of fact or of mixed law and fact. There is also right of appeal to this Court against a sentence, provided that the Court gives leave to appeal and the sentence was one given in the discretion of the trial judge and not a sentence fixed by statute. Unless a substantial miscarriage of justice has occurred, the Court is not bound to allow the appeal, even though the appellant may be technically in the right. The Court has no power to grant a new trial unless the original trial was completely abortive, and in the case of an appeal against sentence the Court may not only reduce the sentence, or confirm it, but may also increase it. The establishment of the Court of Appeal has rendered the use of the royal prerogative of mercy less necessary than it was formerly, but many cases still arise where, on the advice of the Home Secretary, the royal prerogative is exercised and results in either free pardon or mitigation of sentence.

The House of Lords. Although the decision of the Court of Appeal (Criminal Division) is generally final, a further appeal to the House of Lords is available to either the Crown or the prisoner, if the Attorney-General certifies that a point of law of exceptional importance is raised.

In principle, all the peers of Parliament are eligible to hear appeals but, in practice, appeals are heard only by the Lords of Appeal in Ordinary. These are the Lord Chancellor and nine salaried life-peers who hold, or have held, high judicial office. It is customary for two of them to be Scottish lawyers, on account of the fact that the House hears appeals from the Court of Session in Scotland. Appeals from the Court of Appeal in Northern Ireland are also brought to the House. Arguments in appeals are heard in a Committee Room, though the decision of the House is given in the Chamber and observes the forms of a sitting. A quorum of three is essential. Judgments are couched in the form of speeches addressed to the House and at the conclusion of them the Chancellor or the senior Law Lord present puts the matter formally to the vote of the House. (That is why a House of Lords decision is always cited in court as "the speech of Lord . . .").

Juvenile Courts. This brief description of criminal courts would not be complete without some mention of offences committed by "children" from ten to fourteen years of age, or "young persons" between fourteen and seventeen. If a child is charged with an indictable offence, other than homicide, he must be tried summarily, unless charged jointly with someone who is not a child and who is committed for trial. A young person charged with an indictable offence, other than homicide, may be tried summarily if he gives his consent. Unless the juvenile is charged jointly with an adult, he is tried in a special juvenile court set up under the Children and Young Persons Act, 1933. Such courts must be held at a different time or in a different place from the ordinary court. Juvenile court justices are drawn from a panel of specially qualified magistrates and not more than three, one of whom is generally a woman, sit at a time. Although the general public are not allowed in court, press representatives are admitted, and the parents or guardians of the juvenile offender must be present. Where the offender was found guilty the magistrates, under the 1933 Act, could discharge him (absolutely or conditionally), or place him on probation. Alternatively, they could impose a fine which they could order the parent or guardian to pay, or send the juvenile to an approved school, or commit him to the care of a "fit person". They could not send him to prison. However, under the Children and Young Persons Act which came into force in 1971 many of the powers previously held by magistrates were transferred to the social services departments of local authorities. For example, the magistrates lost the right to send a child to an approved school and, if they feel that children should be given special supervision or custodial treatment, all they can do is to place them in the care of a local authority whose social workers then decide what should happen to the child.

For persons between seventeen and twenty-one found guilty of serious offences, there are the well-known Borstal Institutions, several of which have been established in different parts of the country.

Civil Courts. The principal civil courts are the County Courts, the Supreme Court of Judicature with its two branches, the High Court of Justice and the Court of Appeal, and the House of Lords.

County Courts. The name is of great antiquity, but these courts were instituted in their present form in 1846, since when, however, various Acts of Parliament have added considerably to their original jurisdiction. Such jurisdiction now includes:—

1. Actions founded on contract or tort where the debt or damages claimed does not exceed £2000 unless the parties agree to waive the limit.

2. Actions for the recovery of land or in which the title to an hereditament is in question where neither annual value nor rent payable exceeds £1000.

3. An equity jurisdiction up to £15,000 in respect of claims under various heads.

4. In some county courts an admiralty jurisdiction mostly limited to claims not exceeding £5000, but in salvage claims up to £15,000.

5. Probate jurisdiction where personal estate is estimated to be less than £15,000.

6. Arbitration, if the sum does not exceed £200.

Any common law, equity, or admiralty proceedings otherwise within the jurisdiction of the Court can, if the parties agree, be determined in a county court, even though the sum in dispute exceeds the statutory minimum. An action commenced in the High Court which might have been brought in a county court can be transferred by the former to the latter. Further, if an action within the jurisdiction of a county court is fought out in the High Court, the successful litigant may be deprived of costs or at least recover costs only on the county court scale.

The jurisdiction mentioned above accounts for only a portion of the volume of work which comes before county courts, as they are entrusted with special jurisdiction in a great variety of matters under numerous Acts of Parliament. The principal county courts possess local jurisdiction in bankruptcy (unlimited) and in the windings-up of companies where paid-up capital does not exceed £120,000.

Proceedings are fairly simple. There need be no pleadings, parties can be represented by solicitors and not by counsel, and there is rarely a jury. Appeals go before the divisional courts of the High Court or, except in certain cases, may go direct to the Court of Appeal.

The County court judge presides in each court in his district. In addition, each county court has its registrar who is a solicitor of at least seven years' standing. The registrar, who has a staff of assistants under him, acts as clerk of the court, entering all plaints and recording and executing the judgments. Section 20 of the Courts Act 1971 provides that every Circuit judge shall, by virtue of his office, be capable of sitting as a judge for any county court district in England and Wales, and the Lord Chancellor shall assign one or more Circuit judges to each district and may from time to time vary the assignment of Circuit judges among the districts. Subject to any directions given by or on behalf of the Lord Chancellor in any case where more than one Circuit judge is assigned to a district under the above provision, any function conferred by or under the County Courts Act 1959 on the judge for a district may be exercised by any of the Circuit judges for the time being assigned to that district.

The following, that is—

> every judge of the Court of Appeal,
> every judge of the High Court,
> every Recorder,

shall, by virtue of his office, be capable of sitting as a judge for any county court district in England and Wales and if he consents to do so shall sit as a judge at such times and on such occasions as the Lord Chancellor considers desirable.

Notwithstanding that he is not for the time being assigned to a particular district, a Circuit judge—

> (a) shall sit as a judge of that district at such times and on such occasions as the Lord Chancellor may direct; and
> (b) may sit as a judge of that district in any case where it appears to him that the judge of that district is not, or none of the judges of that district is, available to deal with the case.

All appointments of temporary and deputy judges of county courts have been terminated.

Apart from the question of judges as outlined above, the Courts Act 1971 leaves county courts unaffected and they continue unchanged.

The High Court of Justice. The High Court is part of the Supreme Court of Justice which now consists of the Court of Appeal, the High Court and the Crown Court. Following the passing of the Administration of Justice Act 1970 the High Court was re-arranged into the Queen's Bench Division, the Chancery Division and the Family Division. The High Court sits in London at the Royal Courts of Justice, but there are also High Court sittings in Circuit Courts at twenty-four provincial centres where High Court judges are present continuously or for long periods.

Queen's Bench Division. The Lord Chief Justice of England and a number of puisne judges constitute this division, which deals with most business actions, including actions arising out of contract or tort. A special court known as the Commercial Court sits in the Queen's Bench Division to hear cases arising out of the ordinary transactions of merchants and traders, including the construction of documents (such as bills of lading, charter-parties, insurance policies, etc.), mercantile usages, and so on. Procedure is of a more summary nature than in the Queen's Bench Division proper, and a decision as to whether a case shall go to this Court is made by the Master. Admiralty jurisdiction is part of the work of the Division where an Admiralty Court staffed by High Court puisne judges nominated by the Lord Chancellor deals with actions related to shipping, principally damages arising out of collision cases and salvage awards. These arrangements ensure that shipping and commercial matters are dealt with by specialist judges and are not just part of the ordinary work of the division to be taken by any judge who is available. There are eight Masters of the Queen's Bench Division of the High Court, of whom the senior is the Queen's Remembrancer (head of the official staff of the Revenue side of the Queen's Bench Division). Another is the Master of the Crown Office. The functions of the Masters, who are all barristers, are various; one of them being to sit in chambers in the Division and deal (subject to an appeal to a judge) with the preliminary stages in an action.

Except in special cases, it is within the discretion of the Court whether a trial in the Queen's Bench Division shall be with or without a jury, and the general tendency is for such discretion to be exercised against trial by jury. In cases of libel, slander, malicious prosecution, false imprisonment, however, a jury must be granted if either side applies for it. Also, whenever fraud is alleged, trial must be by jury if the party against whom it is alleged applies for it. But even in these cases a jury will not be granted if the Court thinks that prolonged investigations, that cannot be conveniently made by a jury, are likely to be involved.

Chancery Division. The Lord Chancellor and a number of puisne judges constitute the Chancery Division, which deals with litigation in respect of trusts, partnerships, patents and copyrights, as well as other matters. Bankruptcy proceedings and the winding-up of companies are also within the jurisdiction of this Division. There are eight Masters, who are solicitors appointed by the Lord Chancellor. Their functions include dealing with the preliminary stages of proceedings and the accounts and enquiries therein entailed. They do not have the independent jurisdiction possessed in certain cases by the Masters of the Queen's Bench Division, but make orders in the name of the judge, so that any party can claim to bring any point before the judge himself. Actions brought in this Division are tried by a judge without jury.

Family Division. In this Division of the High Court there is a President assisted by a number of puisne judges. It deals with all High Court business which concerns marriage, family property and children, including adoption and wardship.

Divisional Courts. A Divisional Court is a court consisting of two or more judges of the High Court of Justice to hear and determine appeals from Judges in Chambers, appeals from inferior tribunals, and other matters defined by the Judicature Acts. It should be noted that in all other cases High Court Judges act alone.

Court of Appeal (Civil Division). This court consists of the Lord Chancellor as President, the Lord Chief Justice, the Master of the Rolls, the President of the Family Division and a number of other judges. These are known as the Lords Justices of Appeal. The court deals with appeals on law or fact from any division of the High Court, from a County Court, or from orders of Judges in Chambers on matters which have arisen before trial. The court may uphold or reverse the decision of the lower court, or substitute another judgement. In some circumstances it may order a new trial. Three Lords Justices are usually necessary to form a court, but sometimes five or even seven judges sit.

House of Lords. This is the highest Court of Justice, the composition of which has already been referred to. To this Court all final appeals are taken from the Court of Appeal in England, the Court of Session in Scotland, and the Court of Appeal in Northern Ireland. An appeal can be brought only with the leave of either the Court of Appeal or the House of Lords. As previously mentioned, at least three Law Lords are necessary to form a court. If, when there are more than three, they are evenly divided in opinion, the decision given in the Court of Appeal will prevail.

The Privy Council. There is another tribunal known as the Judicial Committee of the Privy Council, which acts as the Supreme Judicial Authority of dependencies in the Commonwealth. In the form of petitions to the Crown appeals may be brought to the Committee from Consular Courts, Courts of Vice-Admiralty and the Courts of certain members of the Commonwealth. The jurisdiction of the Privy Council in relation to domestic matters includes consideration of petitions for the granting of charters incorporating new boroughs, and the hearing of final appeals in ecclesiastical cases. Further, the Crown may specially refer to the Judicial Committee any matter which it thinks fit for such a reference. The Committee is composed largely of the Lords of Appeal in Ordinary, but those Dominion members of the Committee who happen to be in London from time to time may form part of the board. Judges of the High Court and the Scottish Court of Session are often made Privy Councillors on their retirement from the bench and give their services voluntarily, when required, as members of the Committee. A quorum of three is essential.

Court of Justice of the European Community. On 1 January 1973 the United Kingdom became a member of the European Community. The European Communities Act 1972 enables the Government to make orders and regulations to give effect to the country's obligations as a member of the Community; and it alters existing United Kingdom law to take account of specific Community obligations.

Community law is normally applied by the domestic courts of the member countries so that the English, Scottish and Northern Ireland legal systems remain intact and their courts continue to operate as before. In the event of conflict however, Community law prevails over domestic law by virtue of the European Communities Act 1972.

Under the Community treaties the Court of Justice of the European Community interprets and adjudicates on the meanings of the treaties and of any measures taken under them by the Council of Ministers and the Commission. It hears complaints and appeals brought by or against Community institutions, member states or individuals, and it gives preliminary rulings on questions referred to it by courts in the member states. Therefore questions of validity and interpretation may be referred to it by United Kingdom courts and they must be so referred when the question arises in a court or tribunal from which there is no appeal. The Court of Justice makes then a preliminary ruling on the question which is binding on the national court which is left to apply the law and decide the case. The Court of Justice has nine judges assisted by four advocates-general.

OTHER COURTS

Courts Martial. These are principally regulated by the Naval Discipline Act, 1866, and the Army Discipline and Regulations Acts, 1879 and 1881. As the raising and keeping of a standing army within the United Kingdom in peace time without the consent of

Parliament is illegal, it is expressly enacted by Parliament that the above-mentioned Acts shall not come into force, except in pursuance of an Annual Act of Parliament. Accordingly, the Army and Air Force (Annual) Act is passed anew every session, empowering the Sovereign to make articles of war and rules of procedure and to convene, and grant authority to convene, Courts Martial with jurisdiction to try and punish offences according to such articles and rules. The Courts Martial Appeals Court exercises appellate jurisdiction over Naval, Military and Air Force Courts Martial. Applications for leave to appeal must be made to the Registrar. The Court must allow an appeal if they think the finding of the Court Martial is unreasonable, or cannot be supported by the evidence, or is wrong in law, or if there has been a miscarriage of justice. The Court consists of three judges of the Queen's Bench Division of the High Court and procedure is similar to that of the Court of Appeal (Criminal Division).

Coroners' Courts. The holding of a coroner's inquest, that is the investigation of the circumstances of death, is the function of a coroner's court which, though it may be held in an ordinary Police Court, has nothing to do with Petty Sessions. A Coroner is a salaried official appointed by a Town or County Council. He must be a barrister or solicitor or a qualified medical practitioner of not less than five years' standing. When he is informed that a dead body is lying within his jurisdiction and he has reasonable cause to suspect that the person died a violent or unnatural death, or died suddenly from unknown causes, or died in prison, or died in such other circumstances as to require an inquest, it is his duty to hold an inquest. In certain cases a jury must be summoned. These are (1) when the death occurred in prison, (2) when the death was due to an accident, (3) when death was due to a notifiable disease, (4) when death occurred in circumstances prejudicial to public health or public safety. In all other cases, although a jury may be summoned, the coroner has power to sit without a jury. A coroner's jury consists of not less than seven nor more than eleven "good and lawful men" (which nowadays includes women), and, although the inquiry is public, it has been held that a person having no interest in the case may be expelled. After hearing the evidence, the jury give their verdict. In case of failure to agree, so long as the minority is not more than two, the majority verdict is accepted. Otherwise the coroner must discharge the jury, summon another, and proceed as though the former proceedings had not taken place.

The Home Secretary announced in August 1975 that the Government had accepted some recommendations made by the Brodrick Committee. Coroners have been given complete discretion whether or not to hold an inquest, except in cases of homicide, deaths of persons in legal custody and deaths of unidentified persons. The

B

duty of a coroner's jury to name a person it finds responsible for murder or manslaughter, and the coroner's obligation to commit that person for trial, has also been abolished.

JURIES

The jury is a very old English institution but, as stated earlier, trial by jury in civil cases has been very much on the decline in recent years. The function of the jury in a criminal case is to decide whether the prisoner is guilty or not guilty, and in a civil case to decide questions of fact. In a civil case, if the trial is by jury, the judge, at the conclusion of the hearing, sums up the facts to them and gives them the necessary directions as to the law applicable to the case. The jury may be asked to give a general verdict for one side or the other or, in a complicated case, a special verdict on particular questions of fact left to them by the judge. When the jury have returned their verdict, the judge has to give judgment.

A county court jury consists of eight persons. Elsewhere the number of jurors is generally twelve, with the exception of the coroner's jury mentioned above.

Every person, unless he is ineligible, disqualified or excusable as of right, is qualified to serve as a juror and is liable to attend for jury service when summoned if (a) he is for the time being registered as a parliamentary or local government elector and is not less than eighteen nor more than sixty-five years of age; and (b) he has been ordinarily resident in the United Kingdom, the Channel Islands or the Isle of Man for any period of at least five years since attaining the age of thirteen.

Persons are not summoned to serve on a jury or inquest more than once in any one year unless all the persons on the list have already been summoned during that year. Jurors who have given their service in a prolonged and difficult case are often excused from further service for a stated period of time or sometimes for life.

A written summons sent to any person is accompanied by details of the provisions for eligibility, disqualifications and excusals as of right. A person receiving a summons is asked to complete a form telling the court whether he or she is qualified for jury service, and, if so, whether it is the person's wish to be excused 'as of right' or for any other reason. If a person summoned has some physical disability or has insufficient understanding of English which puts his capacity to serve in doubt he may be brought before a judge who will determine whether or not he should act as a juror. Any person who serves as a juror is entitled to receive payment, at the prescribed rates, by way of allowance for travelling and subsistence and any other financial loss suffered such as loss of earnings or national insurance benefit.

Persons ineligible, disqualified or excused from jury service include:—

(a) Ineligible.
    (i) the judiciary;
    (ii) others concerned with the administration of justice, including barristers and solicitors;
    (iii) the clergy;
    (iv) the mentally ill.

(b) Disqualified.
    (i) a person who has at any time been sentenced to life imprisonment or for a term of five years or more;
    (ii) a person who at any time in the past ten years has served a prison sentence of three months or more or has been detained in a borstal institution.

(c) Excusal of right.
    (i) members and officers of both houses of parliament;
    (ii) serving members of the armed forces;
    (iii) practising members of medical and other similar professions such as dentists, nurses, midwives, etc.

(d) Excusal for good cause.
    Persons suffering from serious ill health, or having insufficient understanding of the English language.

(e) Excusal for previous jury service.
    Persons who have undertaken jury service within the previous two years.

LAW OFFICERS AND PUBLIC OFFICIALS

Attorney-General. The principal law officer of the Crown and legal adviser to the Government of the day who is chosen from among Queen's Counsel, usually from those sitting in the House of Commons.

Solicitor-General. One of the law officers of the Crown and legal adviser to the Government of the day, ranking after the Attorney-General (in Scotland after the Lord Advocate), who is also chosen from among Queen's Counsel sitting in the House of Commons.

Master of the Rolls. One of the senior judges of the Court of Appeal, in which he sits *ex officio*. He is also Keeper of the Records preserved in the Record Office.

Admiralty Marshal. An officer of the Queen's Bench Division of the High Court. One of his functions is to take into his custody maritime property placed under arrest pending an Admiralty action *in rem* against the property. Such an action is commenced by a writ of summons *in rem* prepared by the plaintiff or his solicitor. In collision damage and salvage cases the writ must be issued within two years of the date when the damage was caused or the salvage service rendered.

The plaintiff having procured the issue of a writ, or his solicitor, may apply (even before the service of the writ) at the Admiralty Registry in London or at the district registry office where the action has been commenced for a warrant for the arrest of the property against which the action has been brought. A warrant will not be issued until an affidavit by the party applying (or his agent) has been filed and an undertaking in writing lodged to pay the fees and expenses of the Admiralty Marshal. The warrant is ordinarily issued as a matter of course, unless a caveat against an arrest has been entered. A party, by filing a proper notice signed by himself or his solicitor giving an undertaking to enter an appearance in any action which may be commenced against the property, the arrest of which it is desired to prevent, and an undertaking to give bail in a stated sum, may cause a caveat to be entered. This does not prevent a warrant for the arrest of the property being taken out, but any person who causes the arrest of property protected by caveat is liable to have the warrant discharged and to be condemned in costs and damages, unless he proves sufficient reason for having taken out the warrant.

If no caveat has been entered, or if a warrant has been taken out in any case, the plaintiff, after the warrant has been issued, must leave it with a notice for its execution in the Admiralty Registry for service by the Admiralty Marshal or his substitute. In practice no delay takes place, as the Collector of Customs at the port where the property is to be arrested acts as a substitute for the Admiralty Marshal.

Service of the warrant can be effected at any time within twelve months of its date and, if the property to be arrested is a ship, freight or cargo on board, service must be effected by nailing or affixing the original warrant for a short period of time on the mainmast or on the single mast of the vessel and afterwards replacing the original with a true copy.

A shipkeeper is put in possession, under the authority of the Admiralty Marshal, during the time the ship is under arrest, and any person breaking the arrest or interfering with property under arrest is guilty of contempt of court and liable to attachment. By the mere arrest of a ship the Admiralty Marshal gains custody, though not possession, and, subject to his control, all previously existing possessory rights continue to exist.

Barrister. A barrister-at-law is a person who, having been "called to the Bar" at one of the Inns of Court (Lincoln's Inn, Inner Temple, Middle Temple, Gray's Inn), is entitled, with other barristers, to the right of audience and advocacy in the Superior Courts, viz., Courts of the Sovereign as originally settled at Westminster and distinguished from inferior courts having only local jurisdiction and which are subject to control by the Superior

Courts. Barristers practise also in chambers as conveyancing counsel, draftsmen of pleadings, and in other capacities.

Queen's Counsel. The title given to leading barristers as a mark of distinction which gives them precedence over what is called the "junior bar". The Queen's Counsel wears a silk gown instead of a stuff gown, sits within the Bar of the Court, and always has a junior to assist him. The junior counsel does the preliminary work in an action, advises whether the action should be brought, drafts the pleadings, advises on evidence, and so on, while the actual case in court is primarily conducted by the Queen's Counsel. Barristers receive their appointment as Queen's Counsel by Letters Patent under the Great Seal issued on the advice of the Chancellor—a process known as "taking silk".

Solicitors and the Law Society. A solicitor is a person admitted to practise as a legal adviser to persons seeking his services and as an advocate in those courts where barristers do not have exclusive rights of audience. The solicitor is an officer of the Supreme Court, but has no right of audience there in open court unless he holds a recordership or, when the time comes, he has been appointed as a Circuit judge. He has, however, a right of audience in chambers in the High Court and in county courts and petty sessions. Besides conducting litigation personally for his client, he employs and instructs counsel, where necessary, and advises clients in various kinds of non-litigious legal business. The scale of solicitors' charges is laid down by statute, and a client who so desires can have his solicitor's costs taxed by one of the taxing masters of the court.

The Law Society, although a voluntary association to which solicitors may belong or not as they choose, has been entrusted by Parliament with control over all solicitors, including those who are not members of the Society. Before a person can practise as a solicitor, he must obtain from the Law Society a certificate of having passed the final examination and apply to have his name placed on the Roll of Solicitors. The Society provides for, and controls, the education of articled clerks and holds the examinations which qualify for admission to the Roll. The Lord Chancellor nominates a number of leading members of the profession who are members of the Council of the Society to form what is known as the Discipline Committee of the Law Society. This Committee has the task of investigating charges of professional misconduct brought against solicitors and, subject to appeal to the High Court, has powers to strike a solicitor off the Roll or suspend him from practice.

Taxing Masters. Officials whose duty it is to tax the costs of all proceedings in the Queen's Bench and Chancery Divisions of the High Court. More often than not a judgment in favour of one or other of the parties to an action includes an order that the successful party be paid by the other party his "taxed costs" of the action.

The taxing master hears the solicitors for both parties and decides what costs were reasonably incurred by the successful party in bringing or defending the action. Expenses incurred by the successful party prior to the commencement of the action are usually excluded and those incurred subsequently are restricted by the taxing master to a strict minimum. It is, therefore, generally the case that the costs which the successful party will have to pay to his own solicitor will be substantially higher than the amount recoverable from the losing party.

Official Referees. Permanent officers attached to the Supreme Court for the trial of such questions as shall be directed to be tried by them.

Notary Public. A public official admitted and enrolled as prescribed by Act of Parliament who "notes" matters which are of public concern. Originally the notary was an official of the ecclesiastical courts who drafted and authenticated documents to be used in the international world of the Western Church. In many countries abroad, the practice of having documents notorially certified spread from the ecclesiastical world to the commercial world, and in those countries the practice is still carried on. In England the practice did not develop to anything like the same extent, but there are a number of "notaries public" to be found in some of the seaport towns and they are still appointed, as they always have been, by the Master of the Faculties of the Archbishop of Canterbury. The modern notary is generally a solicitor who attests deeds and other documents, bills of exchange in particular, so as to enable recovery to be effected in another country. Further reference to notaries is made in Chapter 5 in connection with the noting of protests by shipmasters.

Official Receiver. A person appointed by the Board of Trade and attached to a court having bankruptcy jurisdiction to act as the receiver of the property of a person against whom a receiving order in bankruptcy may be made. He is also appointed to act as provisional liquidator in the case of a company against which a compulsory winding-up order is made.

Receiver. A person appointed by the court, or by an individual, to take possession of property for its protection, or to receive rents and profits arising from property and apply them as directed.

Tipstaff. An officer of the court whose duty it is to arrest persons guilty of contempt of court.

SOME LEGAL TERMS

Court of Record. A court whose proceedings are officially recorded and preserved as evidence.

Summons. A citation to appear in answer to a complaint or representation made according to law. It is the first stage of proceedings in an inferior court.

27

Originating Summons. A method of commencing proceedings in the High Court without the issue of a writ. The main differences between an originating summons and an action are that there are no pleadings in it, evidence is given in the first instance on affidavit instead of orally (though a deponent is liable to be cross-examined on his affidavit), and that it first comes on in chambers, where it may be finally disposed of. In the Chancery Division originating summonses involving the exercise of judicial discretion are heard privately in chambers, either by a Master or, if necessary, by the judge. Those involving questions of law are adjourned by the Master into court for argument before the judge. This procedure is relatively speedy and inexpensive and is widely used in connection with many matters, for example, applications for the foreclosure of mortgages.

Writ of Summons. A document issued in the name of the Queen by which an action in the Superior Courts is commenced, and distinguished from a plaint or summons in a county or other inferior court. It calls upon the defendant to cause an appearance to the action to be entered for him within eight days of service, and in default of compliance the plaintiff may proceed to judgment and execution.

Execution. The final process of an action whereby the judgment is enforced.

Plaintiff. A complainant or prosecutor or person who brings a suit against another person.

Defendant. A person who is summoned into court to answer some charge.

Petition. Another method of initiating proceedings in the High Court. In a petition the petitioner sets out the facts of his case in numbered paragraphs and concludes with a prayer that the court will make the order suggested. Procedure by petition is used in the Chancery Division in certain cases. For example, a company obtains leave to reduce its capital by petition, and creditors apply to the court by petition to wind up a company that has become insolvent. In the Family Division petitions are used in application for divorce.

Affidavit. A statement in writing and on oath, sworn before a person having authority to administer oaths.

Deposition. The evidence of a witness reduced to writing.

Caveat. A process to stop procedure.

Attachment. Apprehension, especially for contempt of court. It also applies to the seizure of goods or estate to secure a debt or demand. Seizure of the goods of foreigners to satisfy creditors is called a foreign-attachment.

Nolle prosequi. To be unwilling to prosecute.

Prima facie. (Literally) at first glance. (Law) a case apparently established by the evidence.

Bail. Surety given by one person, under pain of forfeiture of a stated sum of money should the surety fail, for the appearance in court of another person who is charged with an offence. Sometimes an accused is remanded in his own surety.

Injunction. An order of the court restraining a person, permanently or for a specified period of time, from doing a certain act or commanding him to perform a certain act. The main principle on which an injunction is given is that the awarding of damages would not suffice to do justice. It is often preferable to obtain an order to stop a person committing a certain kind of act once and for all rather than to have to bring repeated actions for damages. Orders to restrain a tenant in possession from "committing waste", to restrain a defendant from publishing libel, or continuing a nuisance, or using another person's trade mark, and so on, are examples of injunctions.

Easement. A right enjoyed by one proprietor over the property or estate of another. A right of way is an example.

International Law. The law which is recognised as between one nation and another or between several nations.

Municipal Law. The internal law of the State as opposed to International Law. (Not the law relating to local municipal authorities.)

Power of Attorney. An authority under seal given by one person to another authorising the latter to act on behalf of the former.

Estoppel. A rule of evidence whereby, in certain circumstances, a party to an action is prevented from making allegations which are contrary to that which has already been decided against him, or to that which he himself has represented to be the fact.

Right in rem. A right of action against property, *i.e.*, against the *thing* itself, irrespective of who owns it, in which the claimant is enabled to have the property arrested and detained until his claim has been adjudicated upon. In Chapter 2 reference is made to the distinction between statutory rights *in rem* and maritime liens.

Right in personam. A right of action other than a right *in rem*, *i.e.*, a right against a person. A seaman who has a claim for wages has a right *in personam* against the owner of the ship in which the wages were earned. In addition, he has a maritime lien (*see* Chapter 2) against the ship itself.

Without Prejudice. Without impairing any pre-existing right.

Force majeure. Supreme power, or (in appropriate contexts) circumstances beyond one's control.

False Pretences. A charge arising where goods or money are fraudulently obtained from the owner in circumstances which do not amount to larceny.

Larceny. Simple theft, or the taking of a person's goods without his consent with the intention of permanently depriving him of them.

Conversion. The converting by a person to his own use of the goods of another.

Tortfeasor. A person who commits a tort.

MERCHANT SHIPPING ACTS

In 1895 the then existing Shipping Acts were repealed and replaced by the Merchant Shipping Act, 1894. This Act, now referred to as the principal Act, not only consolidated the earlier Acts but included a number of amendments. Since that date changing conditions have made necessary the creation of many other statutes, of which those still wholly or partly in force today are:—

M.S. Act, 1897, extending the powers of detention for unsafety due to undermanning.

M.S. (Mercantile Marine Fund) Act, 1898, which—amongst other things—abolished the Mercantile Marine Fund and instituted the General Lighthouse Fund.

M.S. (Liability of Shipowners and Others) Act, 1900.

M.S. Act, 1906, which made a substantial number of amendments to the principal Act in connection with safety, passenger and emigrant ships, seamen's food, relief and repatriation of seamen left abroad, and many other matters. Many sections of this Act were repealed by the M.S. Act, 1970.

M.S. Act, 1911, which extended the jurisdiction of certain British Courts in foreign countries.

Maritime Conventions Act, 1911, dealing with collision and salvage.

Pilotage Act, 1913.

M.S. (Amendment) Act, 1920.

M.S. (Scottish Fishing Boats) Act, 1920.

M.S. Act, 1921, dealing with unsafe lighters.

M.S. (Equivalent Provisions) Act, 1925, exempting foreign ships and ships registered out of the United Kingdom from certain provisions of the M.S. Acts.

M.S. (Safety and Load Line Conventions) Act, 1932, many sections of which have since been repealed by the M.S. (Safety Convention) Act, 1949, and the M.S. (Load Lines) Act, 1967.

Pilotage Authorities (Limitations of Liability) Act, 1936.

Merchant Shipping Act, 1948.

M.S. (Safety Convention) Act, 1949, covering the construction and equipment of ships, safety certificates, and various provisions for furthering safety of life at sea. Some sections of this Act are repealed or amended by the M.S. Acts, 1970 and 1979.

M.S. Act, 1950, which introduced new rules relating to accommodation in fishing boats, and is partly repealed by the M.S. Act 1970.

M.S. (Liability of Shipowners and Others) Act, 1958.

M.S. Act, 1964, which is concerned with the application of the Act of 1949 to the 1960 Safety Convention. It deals with new requirements for cargo ships, damage control and life-saving appliances, radio installations and certificates, and certain other matters including an extension of the duty to report dangers to navigation.

Shipping Contracts and Commercial Documents Act, 1964.

M.S. Act, 1965, which deals with the measurement of tonnage.

M.S. (Load Lines) Act, 1967, which makes further provisions as to load lines and related matters.

Anchor and Chain Cables Act, 1967.

M.S. Act, 1970, which gives effect to recommendations contained in the Pearson Report of March 1967 and replaces Part II and much of Part VI of the Principal Act.

M.S. (Oil Pollution) Act, 1971.

M.S. Act, 1974.

M.S. (Safety Convention) Act, 1977.

M.S. Act, 1979.

M.S. Act, 1981.

There are certain other enactments which, though not Merchant Shipping Acts, are to a greater or less extent concerned with matters affecting shipping. These include:—

Ships and Aircraft (Transfer Restrictions) Act, 1939.

Crown Proceedings Act, 1947.

National Insurance (Industrial Injuries) Acts, 1946-53.

Clean Air Act, 1956.

Administration of Justice Act, 1956.

Prevention of Oil Pollution Act, 1971.

Carriage of Goods by Sea Act, 1971.

Immigration Act, 1971.

Social Security Acts 1973 and 1975.

Dumping at Sea Act, 1974.

LEGAL PROCEEDINGS AS PROVIDED FOR BY MERCHANT SHIPPING ACTS

(References to quarter sessions or assizes should now be taken to be references to the Crown Court, references to the Board of Trade to be references to the Department of Trade, and references to misdemeanours or felonies to be references to indictable offences.)

On account of the special nature of the shipping industry, and the world-wide scattering of ships and seamen, it has been found necessary to supplement the ordinary rules of procedure as laid down by the Magistrates' Courts Acts and other statutes by a number of special provisions. These form the subject matter of Part XIII of the principal Act, which should, of course, be consulted for details. Here it will be sufficient to mention a few particular items only.

Prosecution of Offences. Subject to any special provisions of the Act, an offence declared to be a misdemeanour is punishable by a fine and by imprisonment not exceeding two years, but the offence may be prosecuted summarily and, if it is, the punishment is fixed at imprisonment for a term not exceeding six months and with a fine not exceeding £1000. Further, an offence under the Act made punishable by imprisonment not exceeding six months or fine not exceeding £1000 must be prosecuted summarily.

Any offence committed or fine recoverable under a bye-law made in pursuance of the Act may be prosecuted or recovered in the same manner as an offence or fine under the Act.

Application of Magistrates' Courts Acts. These Acts shall, so far as applicable, apply to any proceeding under the Merchant Shipping Act before a summary court, whether connected with an offence punishable on summary conviction or not, and also to the trial of any case before one J.P. where, under the Act, such a justice may try the case.

Where any sum may be recovered *as a fine*, that sum, if recoverable before a summary court, shall in England be recovered as a civil debt as provided by the Magistates' Courts Acts. (For example, pilotage dues have been made recoverable "in the same manner as fines"). Being in the nature of civil debts, and not fines imposed as punishment for offences, these sums can be recovered as civil debts. The debtor is not liable to imprisonment in default of payment, unless proof of means to pay has been given.

Appeals. A person convicted summarily can appeal to the Crown Court against sentence if he pleaded guilty, or against conviction or sentence if he pleaded not guilty. Further, any person party to proceedings before a magistrates' court can question the decision on the ground that it is wrong in law, or that it is in excess of the jurisdiction, by applying to the magistrates to "state a case" for the opinion of the Divisional Court of the Queen's Bench, on the question of law or jurisdiction.

Time Limit for Summary Proceedings. In general, neither a conviction for an offence nor an order for payment of money shall be made under this Act in any summary proceeding instituted in the

United Kingdom, unless it is commenced within six months after the commission of the offence or after the cause of complaint arises, or, if both or either of the parties are then out of the United Kingdom, unless it is commenced, in the case of a summary conviction within two months, and in the case of a summary order within six months, after they both first arrive, or be at one time, in the United Kingdom, and, in the case of a summary conviction, before the expiration of three years beginning with the date on which the offence was committed. The above restrictions are not to apply to summary proceedings for an indictable offence. (s.42 (1), M.S. Act, 1979.)

Jurisdiction. For the purpose of giving jurisdiction, every offence shall be deemed to have been committed and every cause of complaint to have arisen either in the actual place of occurrence or in any place in which the offender or person complained against may be. It is a basic principle of international law that no state can legislate outside its territorial jurisdiction, except for its own subjects. Whilst there is much uncertainty about the territorial limits of various countries, our own Territorial Waters Jurisdiction Act deals in terms of a limit of three nautical miles from the coast measured from the low water mark.

Jurisdiction over Ships Lying off the Coasts. Where any district within which any court or magistrate has jurisdiction is situated on the coast of any sea, or abutting on or projecting into any bay, channel, lake, river, or other navigable water, every such court or magistrate shall have jurisdiction over any vessel on or lying or passing off that coast, or being in or near that bay, channel, etc., and over all persons on board or belonging to that vessel. (It may be noted that in certain cases passengers have been held to be "persons belonging to" a ship, but it does not follow that they necessarily would be in all cases.)

Jurisdiction in Case of Offences on Board Ship. Where any British subject is charged with the commission of any offence on board any British ship on the high seas or in any foreign port or on board any foreign ship to which he does not belong, or where a person not being a British subject is charged with the commission of any offence on board any British ship on the high seas, and that person is found within the jurisdiction of any court in Her Majesty's dominions which would have had cognizance of the offence if it had been committed on board a British ship within the limits of its ordinary jurisdiction, that court shall have jurisdiction to try the offence as if it had been so committed. (It has been held that a person is "found within the jurisdiction" if he be brought within it, even against his will.)

Offences Committed at Foreign Ports by Persons Belonging to British Ships. All offences committed ashore or afloat out of Her Majesty's dominions by any master, seaman, or apprentice who is at the time of the offence, or was within three months previously, employed in any British ship are within Admiralty jurisdiction.

Conveyance of Offenders and Witnesses to United Kingdom. Whenever a complaint is made to a British consular officer (*a*) that an offence against property or person has been committed, ashore or afloat, at a place out of Her Majesty's dominions by any master or seaman, who at the time of the offence, or within three months previously, was employed in any British ship, or (*b*) that an offence on the high seas has been committed by any master or seaman, belonging to a British ship, that consular officer may inquire into the case upon oath and take steps to place the offender under restraint to be sent in safe custody to the United Kingdom or to any British possession to be proceeded against in court.

The consular officer may order the master of any British ship bound to the United Kingdom or to a British possession to provide passage and subsistence to the offender and witnesses. The master is not required to receive more than one offender for every 100 tons of the ship's registered tonnage, or more than one witness for every 50 tons. The consular officer shall endorse particulars of those sent upon the ship's agreement. On arrival in the United Kingdom or British possession the master of the conveying ship shall give the offender into police custody to be taken before a magistrate, who shall deal with the matter as in cases of offences committed upon the high seas. Failure to carry any offender or witness or failure to deliver an offender into police custody as above is an offence punishable by a fine not exceeding £1000. The expense of imprisoning and conveying an offender where not paid as part of the costs of prosecution is payable out of public funds.

Depositions to be Received in Evidence when Witness Cannot be Produced. Whenever in the course of any legal proceeding instituted in Her Majesty's dominions before a judge, magistrate, or other person authorised by law or by consent of parties to receive evidence the testimony of a witness is required, then upon due proof that the witness cannot be found in the place where the proceedings are to be instituted, any deposition he may have previously made upon oath before any judge, magistrate, or consular officer shall be admissible in evidence, provided that:—

(*a*) if made in the United Kingdom, it shall not be admissible in any proceeding instituted in the United Kingdom;

(*b*) if made in any British possession, it shall not be admissible in any proceeding instituted in that possession;

(*c*) if the proceeding is criminal, it shall not be admissible unless made in the presence of the person accused.

The deposition shall be authenticated by the judge or other person before whom it is made who shall certify, if the fact is so, that the accused was present.

N.B.—Under the National Insurance (Industrial Injuries) Acts it is provided that, for the purpose of any claim for injury benefit by or in respect of a mariner, depositions may be made:—

(*a*) in any part of Her Majesty's dominions before a judge or magistrate or Mercantile Marine Superintendent;

(*b*) in a foreign country before a British consular officer.

Detention of Ship. Where under the Merchant Shipping Act a ship is to be or may be detained, any commissioned officer on full pay in the naval or military service of Her Majesty, any officer of the Dept. of Trade, any officer of Customs, or any British consular officer may detain the ship. If after detention, or after service of the detention order on the master, the ship proceeds to sea before being properly released, the master is liable on indictment to a fine or on summary conviction to a fine not exceeding £1000, so also is the owner or other person who sends the ship to sea if party to the offence.

If a ship proceeding in defiance of a detention order takes the detaining officer or any D.o.T. surveyor or Customs officer to sea, the owner and master shall be liable to pay all expenses incidental thereto and on conviction on indictment to a fine or on summary conviction to a fine not exceeding £1000.

An officer of Customs may refuse clearance or transire to a ship ordered to be detained. Where the Act provides that a ship may be detained until a document is produced to the proper officer of Customs, the term "proper officer" means, generally, the officer able to grant clearance or transire.

N.B.—The above has been extended to apply to the detention of a ship under a number of other statutes.

Distress on Ship. Where a court or magistrate has power to order payment of seamen's wages, fines or other monies, then if the party directed to pay is the master or owner of a ship, and payment is not made as prescribed in the order, the court or magistrate may, in addition to other powers they may have to compel payment, direct the amount remaining unpaid to be levied by distress or poinding and sale of the ship, her tackle, furniture and apparel.

Admissibility of Documents in Evidence. Where a document is by the Act declared to be admissible in evidence, such document shall, on its production from proper custody, be admissible in evidence in any court or before any person authorised to receive evidence. Proved copies of such documents are also admissible in evidence.

The officer to whose custody the original document was entrusted shall furnish a certified copy or extract to any person applying on payment of a fee. Further, a person shall be entitled to have (*a*) a certified copy of particulars entered in a register book on the registry of a ship, and a certified statement showing the ownership of the ship; and (b) a certified copy of any declaration, or document, a copy of which is made evidence by the Act, on payment of a fee.

Wilfully certifying a document as a true copy or extract knowing the same not to be true is a misdemeanour punishable by imprisonment for a term not exceeding eighteen months. Forging the seal, stamp or signature of a document, and tendering such a document knowing it to be false, are offences, each punishable by imprisonment for a term not exceeding seven years.

Service of Documents. Where for the purposes of the Act a document is to be served on a person, that document may be served:—

(a) in any case by delivering a copy personally to the person to be served, or leaving it at his last place of abode; and

(b) if it is to be served on the master of a ship, where there is one, or on a person belonging to a ship, by leaving it for him on board with the person who is, or appears to be, in command or charge of the ship; and

(c))if it is to be served on the master of a ship, where there is no master, the ship being in the United Kingdom, on the managing owner of the ship. If there is no managing owner, it should be served on some agent of the owner residing in the United Kingdom. If no agent can be found, then it should be served by affixing a copy to the mast of the ship.

If any person obstructs the serving on the master of a ship of any document under the provisions of the Act relating to the detention of ships as unseaworthy, that person is liable on conviction on indictment to a fine or on summary conviction to a fine not exceeding £1000, and if the owner or master of the ship is party or privy to the obstruction, he shall be guilty of misdemeanour.

Application of Penalties. Where any court or magistrate imposes a fine under the Act for which no specific application is provided, the court or magistrate may direct the whole or part of it to be applied in compensating any person for wrong or damage sustained by the act or default in respect of which the fine is imposed.

Subject to such directions or to any specific application, all fines recovered in the United Kingdom shall be paid into the Exchequer, and those recovered in a British possession paid into the public treasury of that possession.

Legal Proceedings in Scotland and Prosecution of Offences in the Colonies. Other sections of Part XII of the principal Act make special provisions for procedure under Scottish law. It is also provided that any offence under the Act shall, in any British possession, be punishable by any court or magistrate by whom an offence of a like character is ordinarily punishable, or in such other manner as may be determined by any Act or ordinance having the force of law in that possession.

ADMINISTRATION OF JUSTICE ACT, 1956

One of the several purposes of this Act is to amend the law relating to Admiralty jurisdiction, legal proceedings in connection with ships and aircraft and the arrest of ships and other property. Part I of the Act, which is the part concerned with these matters, provides as follows:—

1. (1) The Admiralty jurisdiction of the High Court shall be as follows, that is to say, jurisdiction to hear and determine any of the following questions or claims:—

(a) any claim to the possession or ownership of a ship or to the ownership of any share therein;

(b) any question arising between the co-owners of a ship as to possession, employment or earnings of that ship;

(c) any claim in respect of a mortgage or of a charge on a ship or any share therein;

(d) any claim for damage done by a ship;

(e) any claim for damage received by a ship;

(f) any claim for loss of life or personal injury sustained in consequence of any defect in a ship or in her apparel or equipment, or of the wrongful act, neglect or default of the owners, charterers or persons in possession or control of a ship or of the master or crew thereof or oɪ any other person for whose wrongful acts, neglects or defaults the owners, charterers or persons in possession or control of a ship are responsible, being an act, neglect or default in the navigation or management of the ship, in the loading, carriage or discharge of goods on, in or from the ship or in the embarkation, carriage or disembarkation of persons on, in or from the ship;

(g) any claim for loss of or damage to goods carried in a ship;

(h) any claim arising out of any agreement relating to the carriage of goods in a ship or to the use or hire of a ship;

(j) any claim in the nature of salvage (including any claim arising by virtue of the application, by or under section fifty-one of the Civil Aviation, 1949, Act of the law relating to salvage to aircraft and their apparel and cargo);

(k) any claim in the nature of towage in respect of a ship or an aircraft;

(l) any claim in the nature of pilotage in respect of a ship or an aircraft;

(m) any claim in respect of goods or materials supplied to a ship for her operation or maintenance;

(n) any claim in respect of the construction, repair or equipment of a ship or dock charges or dues;

(o) any claim by a master or member of the crew of a ship for wages and any claim by or in respect of a master or member of the crew of a ship for any money or property which, under the provisions of the Merchant Shipping Acts, 1894 to 1954, is recoverable as wages or in the court and in the manner in which wages may be recovered;

(p) any claim by a master, shipper, charterer or agent in respect of disbursements made on account of a ship;

(q) any claim arising out of an act which is or is claimed to be a general average act;

(r) any claim arising out of bottomry;

(s) any claim for the forfeiture or condemnation of a ship or of goods which are being or have been carried, or have been attempted to be carried, in a ship, or for the restoration of a ship or any such goods after seizure, or for droits of Admiralty*;

together with any other jurisdiction which either was vested in the High Court of Admiralty immediately before the date of the commencement of the Supreme Court of Judicature Act, 1873 (that is to say, the first day of November, 1875), or is conferred by or under an Act which came into operation on or after that date on the High Court as being a court with Admiralty jurisdiction and any other jurisdiction connected with ships or aircraft vested in the High Court apart from this section which is for the time being assigned by rules of court to the Queen's Bench Division and directed by rules to be exercised by the Admiralty Court.

(2) The jurisdiction of the High Court under paragraph (b) of subsection (1) of this section includes power to settle any account outstanding and unsettled between the parties in relation to the ship, and to direct that the ship, or any share thereof, shall be sold, and to make such other order as the court thinks fit.

(3) The reference in paragraph (j) of subsection (1) of this section to claims in the nature of salvage includes a reference to such claims for services rendered in saving life from a ship or aircraft or in preserving cargo, apparel or wreck as, under sections 544 to 546 of the Merchant Shipping Act, 1894, or any Order in Council made under section 51 of the Civil Aviation Act, 1949, are authorised to be made in connection with a ship or an aircraft.

(4) The preceding provisions of this section apply:—

(a) in relation to all ships or aircraft, whether British or not and whether registered or not and wherever the residence or domicile of their owners may be;

(b) in relation to all claims, wheresoever arising (including, in the case of cargo or wreck salvage, claims in respect of cargo or wreck found on land); and

(c) so far as they relate to mortgages and charges, to all mortgages and charges, whether registered or not and whether legal or equitable, including mortgages and charges created under foreign law;

---

* Droits of Admiralty are rights to the property of enemies, proceeds of wrecks, etc., which go into the public treasury.

provided that nothing in this subsection shall be construed as extending the cases in which money or property is recoverable under any of the provisions of the Merchant Shipping Acts, 1894 to 1954.

2.   This section has been repealed and largely re-enacted as s.56 of the County Courts Act, 1959. (see end of this section)

3.   (1) Subject to the provisions of the next following section the Admiralty jurisdiction of the High Court, may in all cases be invoked by an action *in personam*.

(2) The Admiralty jurisdiction of the High Court may in the cases mentioned in paragraphs (*a*) to (*c*) and (*s*) of subsection (1) of section one of this Act be invoked by an action *in rem* against the ship or property in question.

(3) In any case in which there is a maritime lien or other charge on any ship, aircraft or other property for the amount claimed, the Admiralty jurisdiction of the High Court, may be invoked by an action *in rem* against that ship, aircraft or property.

(4) In the case of any such claim as is mentioned in paragraphs (*d*) to (*r*) of subsection (1) of section one of this Act, being a claim arising in connection with a ship, where the person who would be liable on the claim in an action *in personam* was, when the cause of action arose, the owner or charterer of, or in possession or in control of, the ship, the Admiralty jurisdiction of the High Court may (whether the claim gives rise to a maritime lien on the ship or not) be invoked by an action *in rem* against:—

(*a*) that ship, if at the time when the action is brought it is beneficially owned as respects all the shares therein by that person; or

(*b*) any other ship which, at the time when the action is brought is beneficially owned as aforesaid.

(5) In the case of a claim in the nature of towage or pilotage in respect of an aircraft, the Admiralty jurisdiction of the High Court may be invoked by an action *in rem* against that aircraft if at the time when the action is brought it is beneficially owned by the person who would be liable on the claim in an action *in personam*.

(6) Notwithstanding anything in the preceding provisions of this section, the Admiralty jurisdiction of the High Court shall not be invoked by an action *in rem* in the case of any such claim as is mentioned in paragraph (*o*) of subsection (1) of section one of this Act unless the claim relates wholly or partly to wages (including any sum allotted out of wages or adjudged by a superintendent to be due by way of wages).

(7) Where, in the exercise of its Admiralty jurisdiction, the High Court orders any ship, aircraft or other property to be sold, the court shall have jurisdiction to hear and determine any question arising as to the title to the proceeds of sale.

(8) In determining for the purposes of subsections (4) and (5) of this section whether a person would be liable on a claim *in personam* it shall be assumed that he has his habitual residence or a place of business within England and Wales.

4. (1) No court in England and Wales shall entertain an action *in personam* to enforce a claim to which this section applies unless:—

(*a*) the defendant has his habitual residence or a place of business within England and Wales; or

(*b*) the cause of the action arose within inland waters of England and Wales or within the limits of a port of England and Wales; or

(*c*) an action arising out of the same incident or series of incidents is proceeding in the court or has been heard and determined in the court.

In this subsection:—

"inland waters" includes any part of the sea adjacent to the coast of the United Kingdom certified by the Secretary of State to be waters falling by international law to be treated as within the territorial sovereignty of Her Majesty apart for the operation of that law in relation to territorial waters;

"port" means any port, harbour, river, estuary, haven, dock, canal, or other place so long as a person or body or persons is empowered by or under an Act to make charges in respect of ships entering it or using the facilities therein, and "limits of a port" means the limits thereof as fixed by or under the Act in question or, as the case may be, by the relevent charter or custom;

"charges" means any charges with the exception of light dues, local light dues and any other charges in respect of light-houses, buoys or beacons and of charges in respect of pilotage.

(2) No court in England and Wales shall entertain an action *in personam* to enforce a claim to which this section applies until any proceedings previously brought by the plaintiff in any court outside England and Wales against the same defendant in respect of the same incident or series of incidents have been discontinued or otherwise come to an end.

(3) The preceding provisions of this section shall apply to counter-claims (not being counter-claims in proceedings arising out of the same incident or series of incidents) as they apply to actions *in personam*, but as if the references to the plaintiff and the defendant were respectively references to the plaintiff on the counter-claim and the defendant to the counter-claim.

(4) The preceding provisions of this section shall not apply to any action or counter-claim if the defendant thereto submits or has agreed to submit to the jurisdiction of the court.

(5) Subject to the provisions of subsection (2) of this section the High Court shall have jurisdiction to entertain an action *in*

personam to enforce a claim to which this section applies whenever any of the conditions specified in paragraphs (*a*) to (*c*) of subsection (1) of this section are satisfied, and the rules of court relating to the service of process outside the jurisdiction shall make such provision as may appear to the rule-making authority to be appropriate having regard to the provisions of this subsection.

(6) Nothing in this section shall prevent an action or counter-claim which is brought in accordance with the provisions of this section in the High Court being transferred, in accordance with the enactments in that behalf, to some other court.

(7) The claims to which this section applies are claims for damage, loss of life or personal injury arising out of a collision between ships or out of the carrying out of or omission to carry out a manoeuvre in the case of one or more of two or more ships or out of non-compliance, on the part of one or more of two or more ships, with the collision regulations.

(8) For the avoidance of doubt it is hereby declared that this section applies in relation to the jurisdiction of any court not being Admiralty jurisdiction, as well as in relation to its Admiralty jurisdiction, if any.

5.   (1) Repealed.

(2) Nothing in this Part of this Act shall be construed as limiting the jurisdiction of the court to refuse to entertain an action for wages by the master or a member of the crew of a ship, not being a British ship.

6. No court in England and Wales shall have jurisdiction to determine any claim or question certified by the Secretary of State to be a claim or question which, under the Rhine Navigation Convention, falls to be determined in accordance with the provisions thereof and any proceedings to enforce such a claim which are commenced in any such court shall be set aside.

7.   (1) Nothing in this Part of this Act affects the provisions of section 552 of the Merchant Shipping Act, 1894 (which relates to the power of a receiver of wreck to detain a ship in respect of a salvage claim).

(2) The provisions of sections one to three of this Act shall, as respects the High Court, have effect in lieu of sections 22 and 33 of the Supreme Court of Judicature (Consolidation) Act, 1925, and those Acts, and in particular by any provision of the first-mentioned Act referring to the Admiralty jurisdiction of the High Court, shall be construed accordingly.

(3) Nothing in this Part of this Act shall authorise proceedings *in rem* in respect of any claim against the Crown, or the arrest, detention or sale of any of Her Majesty's ships or Her Majesty's aircraft, or of any cargo or other property belonging to the Crown.

In this subsection "Her Majesty's ships" and "Her Majesty's

aircraft" have the meanings assigned to them by subsection (2) of section 38 of the Crown Proceedings Act, 1947.

8. (1) In this Part of this Act, unless the context otherwise requires:—

"ship" includes any description of vessel used in navigation;

"goods" includes baggage;

"collision regulations" means regulations under section 418 of the Merchant Shipping Act, 1894, or any such rules as are mentioned in subsection (1) of section 421 of that Act or any rules made under subsection (2) of the said section 421;

"master" has the same meaning as in the Merchant Shipping Act, 1894, and accordingly includes every person (except a pilot) having command or charge of a ship;

"towage" and "pilotage", in relation to an aircraft, mean towage and pilotage while the aircraft is waterborne;

"the Rhine Navigation Convention" means the Convention of the seventh of October, 1868, as revised by any subsequent Convention.

(2) Nothing in any provision in this Part of this Act or in any repeal consequential thereon shall affect proceedings in respect of any cause of action arising before the coming into operation thereof.

N.B.—Part V of the Act deals with Admiralty jurisdiction and arrestment of ships in Scotland. Part I of the First Schedule deals with Admiralty jurisdiction and other provisions as to ships in respect of the provisions applicable to Northern Ireland.

Certain County Courts have Admiralty jurisdiction, their powers being defined in sections 56 to 61 of the County Courts Act, 1959, the gist of which is as follows:—

56. (1) Subject to the limitations of amount specified in subsection (2) of this section, an Admiralty county court shall have the following jurisdiction, that is to say, jurisdiction to hear and determine any of the claims as are mentioned in paragraphs (*d*) to (*p*) of subsection (1) of section 1 of the Administration of Justice Act, 1956, and sub-sections (3) and (4) of that section shall, with the necessary modifications, have effect in relation to them.

(2) The limitations of amount referred to in sub-section (1) of this section are as follows, that is to say, that the court shall not have jurisdiction to hear and determine any claim mentioned in the said sub-section (1) for an amount exceeding £5000, except in the case of a claim in the nature of salvage where the value of the property saved does not exceed £15,000.

(3) and (4). Have the same effect as sub-section (3) and (4) (*a*) and (*b*), and the proviso, of section 1 of the Administration of Justice Act, 1956.

(5) If, as respects any proceedings as to any such claim as is mentioned in sub-section (1) of this section, the parties agree, by a

memorandum, signed by them or by their respective solicitors or agents, that a particular county court specified in the memorandum shall have jurisdiction in the proceedings, that court shall, notwithstanding anything in sub-section (2) of this section or in any rules made under sub-section (3) of section 102 of this Act, for prescribing the courts in which proceedings shall be brought, have jurisdiction to hear and determine the proceedings accordingly.

(6) Nothing in this section shall be taken to affect the jurisdiction of any county court to hear and determine any proceedings in which it has jurisdiction by virtue of section 39 or 41 of this Act.

(7) Nothing in this section, or in section 55 of this Act, or any order made thereunder, shall be taken to confer on a county court the jurisdiction of a Prize Court within the meaning of the Naval Prize Acts, 1864 to 1916.

57.   This section provides for the mode of exercise of Admiralty jurisdiction in county courts and with the substitution of the words county court for High Court where appropriate, reads the same as section 3 (excluding sub-section (2) of the Administration of Justice Act, 1956.

58.   Provides for the transfer of Admiralty proceedings from a county court to the High Court under certain circumstances.

59.   Where an action has commenced in the High Court, this section allows any party to apply to the High Court for the claim and/or counterclaim to be transferred to an Admiralty county court, and the court or judge may, if it or he thinks fit, so order. Where any action is transferred in this way, any vessel or other property which has been arrested is to remain in the custody of the Admiralty Marshal, who is to comply with any orders made by the county court. (Subject to any directions of the High Court.)

60.   This section defines the circumstances when either no costs, or alternatively limited costs, shall be payable to a successful plaintiff where an action commenced in the High Court which could have been commenced in the county court.

61.   Nothing in the provisions shall, limit the jurisdiction of a county court to refuse an action for wages by the crew of a non-British ship; or, affect the provisions of the M.S. Acts, 1894, relating to the power of a receiver of wreck to detain a ship in respect of a salvage claim; or, authorise proceedings *in rem* in respect of any claim against the Crown, or the arrest, detention or sale of any of H.M. ships or aircraft, or any cargo or other property.

ORDERS IN COUNCIL

Where Her Majesty has power under an Act of Parliament to make an Order in Council, Her Majesty may from time to time make that Order in Council, and by Order in Council revoke, alter, or add to any Order so made.

Every Order in Council is required to be published in the *London Gazette* and laid before both Houses of Parliament within one month after it is made if Parliament be then sitting, or if not, within one month after the next meeting of Parliament.

Subject to any special provisions otherwise, an Order in Council takes effect from the date of its publication or any later date mentioned in the Order as if it were enacted by Parliament.

D.O.T. SURVEYORS

The Merchant Shipping Acts give powers to the Department of Trade to appoint and control surveyors of ships. The persons appointed are:—

Principal officers (in connection with the survey of ships and matters incidental thereto).

Ship surveyors.

Nautical surveyors (some of whom also act as examiners of masters and mates).

Engineer surveyors (some of whom act as examiners of engineers).

Radio surveyors.

The powers of a D.o.T. surveyor may be summarised as follows.

A surveyor may board any steamship at reasonable times and inspect the ship or any part thereof, or machinery, boats, equipment, or articles on board, or any certificates of the master, mate, or engineer to which the Act and associated regulations apply, without unnecessarily detaining or delaying the ship. If in consequence of any accident or for any other reason they consider it necessary, surveyors may require the ship to be docked for hull survey. The penalty for obstructing a surveyor in the execution of his duties, or failing to comply with a requirement to take a ship into dock for survey, is a fine not exceeding £1000.

D.O.T. INSPECTORS

The Department may also appoint any person as an inspector to report on:—

(a) the nature and cause of any accident or damage sustained or caused by any ship;

(b) whether the provisions of the Merchant Shipping Acts and associated regulations or the terms of any approval, licence, consent, direction or exemption given by such regulations have been complied with;

(c) whether the hull and machinery of any steamship are sufficient and in good condition.

An inspector and any person having the powers of an inspector may:—

(a) at any reasonable time, (or at any time if the situation is or may be dangerous) enter any premises in the United Kingdom, or board a ship registered in the United Kingdom anywhere, and any other ship when in United Kingdom territorial waters, in order to perform his functions as an inspector and to make an examination and investigation as he considers necessary;

(b) direct that such premises or ship are to be left undisturbed for as long as necessary to make his examination;

(c) take measurements, photographs, make recordings, and take samples of articles, substances and the atmosphere in or near the ship;

(d) cause articles to be dismantled and subjected to tests;

(e) require the production of books or documents for inspection or copying;

(f) require any person to attend at a specified place and time to answer questions and certify to the truth of his answers;

(g) require any person to assist him with respect to any matters within that person's control or for which that person has responsibilities.

Nothing in the above provisions authorises any person unnecessarily to prevent a ship from proceeding on a voyage.

No person can be compelled to produce a document which he would on grounds of legal professional privilege be entitled to withhold on an order for discovery in a High Court action.

A person who attends at a specified place to answer questions and give assistance is entitled to claim expenses as prescribed by regulations.

A person who wilfully obstructs an inspector, or does not comply with a requirement without reasonable excuse, or makes a statement or signs a declaration which he knows is false, or recklessly makes a statement or signs a declaration which is false, is guilty of an offence and liable on summary conviction to a fine not exceeding £1000 or, on conviction on indictment, to imprisonment for not exceeding two years or a fine or both.

SPECIAL SHIPPING INQUIRIES AND COURTS

Inquiries and investigations now regulated by the Merchant Shipping Act 1970 are:—

Inquiry into the fitness or conduct of an officer.

Disqualification of the holder of a certificate other than an officer's.

Inquiry into the fitness or conduct of a seaman other than an officer.

Preliminary inquiry into a shipping casualty.

Formal investigation into a shipping casualty.

Re-hearing of and appeal from an inquiry or investigation.

Inquiries into deaths of crew members and others.

Still regulated by the Merchant Shipping Act 1894 are:—

Courts of Survey.

Reference of difficult cases to scientific referees.

Preliminary Inquiry. Section 55 of the 1970 Act states:—

(1) Where any of the following casualties has occurred, that is to say:—

(a) the loss or presumed loss, stranding, grounding, abandonment of or damage to a ship; or

(b) a loss of life or serious personal injury caused by fire on board or by any accident to ship or ship's boat, or by any accident occurring on board a ship or ship's boat; or

(c) any damage caused by a ship;

and, at the time it occurred, the ship was registered in the United Kingdom or the ship or boat was in the United Kingdom or the territorial waters thereof, the Department of Trade:—

(i) may cause a preliminary inquiry into the casualty to be held by a person appointed for the purpose by the Department; and

(ii) may (whether or not a preliminary inquiry into the casualty has been held) cause a formal investigation into the casualty to be held, if in England, Wales or Northern Ireland, by a wreck commissioner and, if in Scotland, by the sheriff.

(2) A person appointed under this section to hold a preliminary inquiry shall for the purpose of the inquiry have the powers conferred on an inspector by section 27 of the M.S. Act, 1979.

Following a report of a casualty received by them, directly or indirectly, the D.o.T. may call for a more detailed account on the appropriate WRE 1 form. The form is completed by a receiver of wreck from information given to him by the master of the ship. It is important that every question asked on this form should be completely answered and, in the case of a relatively small matter, that may be as far as the inquiry will go. If questions are left unanswered, or are inadequately answered, or if for other reasons further probing appears to be necessary, depositions from the master and members of the crew will be taken by the receiver of wreck who, for technical reasons, will be assisted by one or more D.o.T. surveyors. These depositions should be completed before being sworn, and no alterations should afterwards be made by the officer of Customs or Coastguard or other person holding the inquiry.

A preliminary inquiry is for departmental purposes and the results thereof are not made public.

Formal Investigation. Section 56 of the 1970 Act states:—

(1) A wreck commissioner or sheriff holding a formal investigation into a casualty under section 55 of this Act shall conduct it in accordance with rules under section 58(1) of this Act, and those rules shall require the assistance of one or more assessors and, if any question as to the cancellation or suspension of an officer's certificate is likely to arise, the assistance of not less than two assessors.

(2) Subsections (1), (3) and (4) of section 77 of the Magistrates'

Courts Act 1952 (which provide for the attendance of witnesses and the production of evidence) shall apply in relation to a formal investigation held by a wreck commissioner as if the wreck commissioner were a magistrates' court and the investigation a complaint; and the wreck commissioner shall have power to administer oaths for the purposes of the investigation.

(3) Where a formal investigation is held in Scotland the sheriff shall, subject to any rules made under section 58(1) of this Act, dispose of it as a summary application, and, subject to section 57 of this Act, his decision on the investigation shall be final.

(4) If as a result of the investigation the wreck commissioner or sheriff is satisfied, with respect to any officer, of any of the matters mentioned in paragraphs (a) to (c) of section 52(1) of this Act and, if it is a matter mentioned in paragraph (a) or (b) of that section, is further satisfied that it caused or contributed to the casualty, he may cancel or suspend any certificate issued to the officer under section 43 of this Act or censure him; and if he cancels or suspends the certificate the officer shall deliver it forthwith to him or to the Department of Trade.

(5) The wreck commissioner or sheriff may make such order with regard to the costs of the investigation as he thinks just and shall make a report on the case to the D.o.T.

(6) Any costs which a person is ordered to pay under the preceding subsection may be recovered from him by the D.o.T.

(7) (This deals with the application of this section to Northern Ireland.)

Rules as to inquiries, etc. Section 58 of the 1970 Act empowers the D.o.T. to make rules for the conduct of inquiries, formal investigations, and for the conduct of any re-hearing which is not held by the High Court or Court of Session. Such rules may provide for the appointment and summoning of assessors, the manner in which facts may be proved, the persons allowed to appear, and the notices to be given to persons affected. Rules of court made for the purpose of re-hearings held by the High Court, or of appeals to the High Court may require the court (subject to any exceptions allowed) to hold a re-hearing or hear an appeal with the assistance of one or more assessors.

In practice a formal investigation which, unlike a preliminary inquiry, is a public inquiry, will be held in addition to or instead of a preliminary inquiry in any of the following circumstances:—

(a) if the preliminary inquiry is not sufficient;
(b) if it appears likely to lead to the prevention of similar casualties in the future;
(c) usually where there has been loss of life;
(d) if the casualty has given rise to a substantial amount of public attention or to a disturbance of public confidence;

(e) if there has been default or negligence on the part of the master or officers;

(f) If a certificate of competency is likely to be dealt with.

A court holding a formal investigation is a technical court and, accordingly, each assessor must sign its report or sign his dissent therefrom. The court has no power to deal with a certificate of competency unless at least one assessor concurs in its findings.

The court may make such order as it thinks fit respecting the costs of the investigation, though the D.o.T. may themselves pay the costs if they think fit to do so. If a charge is made against any person, that person shall have an opportunity of making a defence.

The investigation must be held in some town hall, Crown or county court, public building, or other suitable place, but not in an ordinary police court, unless no other place is available.

An outline of the proceedings is as follows.

The papers relating to the case are sent to the Treasury Solicitor who prepares an "Order for a Formal Investigation".

The Home Secretary appoints the wreck commissioner and the assessors. The date and place of the hearing are arranged. The place chosen will generally be that most convenient for the majority of witnesses, or the ship's home port. The parties to the case and the interested organisations are informed.

Copies of documents are prepared, which will include the statement of the case, log entries, calculations (if required) pertinent to such matters as stability or flooding, and the list of questions on which it is desired to ask the opinion of the court. The final question will always be: "Was the casualty due to any wrongful act or default of the master or other person?"

Notice of the investigation is then addressed to the parties to the case accompanied by the statement of the case, a statement of the documents to be produced, and the list of questions. No certificate of competency can be dealt with until this is done.

Whilst the D.o.T. have the management of the case, they are not in any sense prosecutors, and any charges made against persons are purely and solely in the interests of safety of life at sea.

All parties to the case can be, and are advised to be, represented. They can cross-examine all witnesses, produce their own, and recall others. As soon as the parties have been notified as above, the case can proceed, even though all the parties are not present.

In England, Wales and Ireland, the court preserves an informal appearance, no wigs or gowns being worn, and any witness may be present throughout the hearing. In Scotland, however, more formality is observed and witnesses are not allowed to be present throughout.

The case is opened by the D.o.T. to introduce the parties and their representatives. The D.o.T. themselves are represented by the Treasury Solicitor or by a barrister of the Admiralty Bar (often a Q.C. with a junior). Anyone can apply to be a party, even while the case is in progress, and the court will not refuse an application unless it is considered to have been made for some ulterior purpose unconnected with the case and of no help to the investigation.

The statement of the case is read and documents, some of which may require to be proved true, are produced. The witnesses are then called in convenient order to take the oath. The wreck commissioner and assessors have, apart from what they may have read in the press, no previous knowledge of the case and are not sent notices.

The D.o.T. representative reads the questions, with any amendments, and that completes the Department's case.

Each party in turn then calls its witnesses. Representatives of the parties are then invited to address the court, the D.o.T. representative last. He must sum up the evidence fairly and impartially and state whether the Department puts the blame for the casualty on any person and whether they recommend that a certificate should be dealt with. The Department cannot be neutral in this respect.

Time is then allowed for the court to issue its findings and, when this is done, the findings are communicated to the Treasury Solicitor and a press notice is put out. If a certificate is dealt with, the report must be read in open court; otherwise, it may be sent direct to the Home Secretary. Finally, a copy of the report goes to the D.o.T., is published, and put on sale.

Any cancellation or suspension of a certificate of competency may be followed by the issue of one of a lower grade.

Although a court holding a formal investigation into a shipping casualty is not in the ordinary sense a penal court it does have power, purely in the interests of safety of life at sea, to impose certain punishments. These can be summed up as follows:—

(1) Cancellation of a certificate of competency.
(2) Suspension of a certificate of competency.
(3) Requiring a party to bear all or part of the costs of the case.
(4) Censure.
(5) Admonishment (or censure in mild degree).

Investigation in a British Possession Abroad. This can take place if a ship suffers a casualty, or if a charge of misconduct is made against a person on board, when the ship is (a) within the territorial waters of the possession, or (b) is bound to a port in that possession, and, in any case, if the ship is registered in that possession.

Investigation in the Dominions. Cancellation or suspension of a certificate of competency affects its validity only in the local waters of the Dominion, but other administrations may extend the cancellation or suspension to their waters.

Inquiry into Fitness or Conduct of Officer. Section 52 of the 1970 Act provides as follows:—

(1) If it appears to the D.o.T. that an officer—

(a) is unfit to discharge his duties, whether by reason of incompetence or misconduct or for any other reason; or

(b) has been sriously negligent in the discharge of his duties; or

(c) has failed to comply with the provisions of section 422 of the M.S. Act 1894 (duty to give assistance and information after collision);

the D.o.T. may cause an inquiry to be held by one or more persons appointed by them and, if they do so, may, if they think fit, suspend, pending the outcome of the inquiry, any certificate issued to the officer in pursuance of section 43 of this Act and require the officer to deliver it to them.

(2) Where a certificate issued to an officer has been suspended under subsection (1) of this section the suspension may, on the application of the officer, be terminated by the High Court, or if the inquiry is held in Scotland, by the Court of Session, and the decision of the court on such an application shall be final.

(3) An inquiry under this section shall be conducted in accordance with rules made under section 58(1) of this Act and those rules shall require the persons holding the inquiry to hold it with the assistance of one or more assessors.

(4) The persons holding an inquiry under this section into the fitness or conduct of an officer—

(a) may, if satisfied of any of the matters mentioned in paragraphs (a) to (c) of subsection (1) of this section, cancel or suspend any certificate issued to him under section 43 of this Act or censure him;

(b) may make such order with regard to costs of the inquiry as they think just; and

(c) shall make a report on the case to the D.o.T.;

and if the certificate is cancelled or suspended the officer (unless he has delivered it to the D.o.T. in pursuance of subsection (1) of this section) shall deliver it forthwith to the persons holding the inquiry or to the D.o.T.

(5) Any costs which a person is ordered to pay under subsection (4)(b) of this section may be recovered from him by the D.o.T.

Disqualification of Holder of Certificate other than Officer's. Section 53 of the 1970 Act states:—

(1) Where it appears to the D.o.T. that a person who is the holder of a certificate to which this section applies is unfit to be the holder of such a certificate, whether by reason of incompetence or misconduct or for any other reason, they may give him notice in writing that they are considering the suspension or cancellation of the certificate.

(2) The notice must state the reasons why it appears to the

D.o.T. that that person is unfit to be the holder of such a certificate and must state that within a period specified in the notice, or such longer period as the D.o.T. may allow, he may make written representations to the D.o.T. or claim to make oral representations to the Department.

(3) After considering any representations made in pursuance of the preceding subsection, the D.o.T. shall decide whether or not to suspend or cancel the certificate and shall give the holder of it written notice of their decision.

(4) Where the decision is to suspend or cancel the certificate the notice shall state the date from which the cancellation is to take effect, or the date from which and the period for which the suspension is to take effect, and shall require the holder to deliver the certificate to the Department not later than the date so specified unless before that date he has required the case to be dealt with by an inquiry under section 54 of this Act.

(5) Where, before the date specified in the notice, he requires the case to be dealt with by such an inquiry, then, unless he withdraws the requirement, the suspension or cancellation shall not take effect except as ordered in pursuance of the inquiry.

(6) The D.o.T. may make regulations prescribing the procedure to be followed with respect to the making and consideration of representations in pursuance of this section, the form of any notice to be given under this section and the period to be specified in any such notice as the period within which any steps are to be taken.

(7) This section applies to every certificate issued under section 50 of this Act (which deals with special certificates of competency) and to any certificate issued under section 43 of this Act (see Chapter 4) other than one certifying that a person is qualified as an officer.

Inquiry into Fitness or Conduct of Seaman other than Officer. Section 54 of the 1970 Act provides:—

(1) Where a person has, before the date mentioned in section 53(4) of this Act, required his case to be dealt with by an inquiry under this section the D.o.T. shall cause an inquiry to be held by one or more persons appointed by them.

(2) An inquiry under this section shall be conducted in accordance with rules made under section 58(1) of this Act and those rules shall require the persons holding the inquiry to hold it with the assistance of one or more assessors.

(3) The persons holding an inquiry under this section—

(a) may confirm the decision of the D.o.T. and cancel or suspend the certificate accordingly;

(b) may, where the decision was to cancel the certificate, suspend it instead;

(c) may, where the decision was to suspend the certificate, suspend it for a different period;

(*d*) may, instead of confirming the decision of the D.o.T., censure the holder of the certificate or take no further action;

(*e*) may make such order with regard to the costs of the inquiry as they think just; and

(*f*) shall make a report on the case to the D.o.T.;

and if the certificate is cancelled or suspended it shall be delivered forthwith to the persons holding the inquiry or to the D.o.T.

(4) Any costs which a person is ordered to pay under subsection (3)(*e*) of this section may be recovered from him by the D.o.T.

Failure to Deliver Cancelled or Suspended Certificate. Section 59 of the 1970 Act states:—

If a person fails to deliver a certificate as required under sections 52, 53, 54 or 56 of this Act he shall be liable on summary conviction to a fine not exceeding £200.

Power to Restore Certificate. Section 60 of the 1970 Act provides:—

Where a certificate has been cancelled or suspended under this Act or under section 478 of the M.S. Act 1894 (relating to the authority of a colonial court to make inquiries into shipping casualties and conduct of officers), the D.o.T., if of opinion that the justice of the case requires it, may re-issue the certificate or, as the case may be, reduce the period of suspension and return the certificate, or may grant a new certificate of the same or a lower grade in place of the cancelled or suspended certificate.

Inquiries into Deaths of Crew Members and Others. Section 61 of the 1970 Act states:—

(1) Subject to subsection (4) of this section, where—

(*a*) any person dies in a ship registered in the United Kingdom; or in a boat or liferaft from such a ship; or

(*b*) the master of or a seaman employed in such a ship dies in a country outside the United Kingdom;

an inquiry into the cause of the death shall be held by a superintendent or proper officer at the next port where the ship calls after the death and where there is a superintendent or proper officer, or at such other place as the D.o.T. may direct.

(1A) Subject to subsection 4 of this section, where it appears to the Secretary of State that—

(*a*) in consequence of an injury sustained or a disease contracted by a person, when he was the master of or a seaman employed in a ship registered in the United Kingdom, he ceased to be employed in the ship and subsequently died; and

(*b*) the death occurred in a country outside the United Kingdom during the period of one year beginning with the day when he so ceased, the Secretary of State may arrange for an inquiry into the cause of the death to be held by a superintendent or proper officer.

(1B) Subject to subsection 4 of this section, where it appears to the Secretary of State that a person may—

(a) have died in a ship registered in the United Kingdom or in a boat or liferaft from such a ship; or

(b) have been lost from such a ship, boat or liferaft and have died in consequence of having been so lost,

the Secretary of State may arrange for an inquiry to be held by a superintendent or proper officer into whether the person died as aforesaid and, if the superintendent or officer finds that he did, into the cause of the death.

(2) The superintendent or proper officer holding the inquiry shall for the purpose of the inquiry have the powers conferred on an inspector by section 27 of the M.S. Act, 1979.

(3) The person holding the inquiry shall make a report of his findings to the D.o.T. and the Department shall make a copy of the report available:—

(a) if the person to whom the report relates was employed in the ship and a person was named as his next of kin in the crew agreement or list of the crew in which the name of the person to whom the report relates last appeared, to the person so named;

(b) in any case, to any person requesting it who appears to the D.o.T. to be interested.

(4) No inquiry shall be held under this section in a case where, in England, Wales or Northern Ireland, a coroner's inquest is to be held or, in Scotland, an inquiry is to be held under the Fatal Accidents Inquiry (Scotland) Act 1895 or the Fatal Accidents and Sudden Deaths Inquiry (Scotland) Act 1906.

Re-hearing of and Appeal from Inquiries and Investigations. These matters are now regulated by section 57 of the M.S. Act 1970 which provides as follows:—

(1) Where an inquiry or formal investigation has been held under the preceding provisions of this Act the D.o.T. may order the whole or part of the case to be re-heard, and shall do so:—

(a) if new and important evidence which could not be produced at the inquiry or investigation has been discovered; or

(b) if there appear to the D.o.T. to be other grounds for suspecting that a miscarriage of justice may have occurred.

(2) An order under subsection (1) of this section may provide for the re-hearing to be as follows:—

(a) if the inquiry or investigation was held in England, Wales or Northern Ireland, by the persons who held it, by a wreck commissioner or by the High Court;

(*b*) if it was held in Scotland, by the persons who held it, by the sheriff or by the Court of Session.

(3) Any re-hearing under this section which is not held by the High Court or the Court of Session shall be conducted in accordance with rules made under section 58(1) of this Act; and section 56 of this Act shall apply in relation to a re-hearing of an investigation by a wreck commissioner or sheriff as it applies in relation to the holding of an investigation.

(4) Where the persons holding the inquiry or investigation have decided to cancel or suspend the certificate of any person or have found any person at fault, then, if no application for an order under subsection (1) of this section has been made or such an application has been refused, that person or any other person who, having an interest in the inquiry or investigation, has appeared at the hearing and is affected by the decision or finding, may appeal to the High Court or the Court of Session, according as the inquiry or investigation was held in England, Wales or Northern Ireland or in Scotland.

COURTS OF SURVEY

The Rules of the Court of Survey, 1876, are published by H.M. Stationery Office. Copies are kept at the office of the registrar of every Court of Survey and at every custom house and mercantile marine office. They may be perused at such places by the master or owner of any ship which may be provisionally detained under the Merchant Shipping Act and by anyone deputed by him.

A notice is required to be put up in some conspicuous place in every custom house and mercantile marine office, containing the name of the registrar of the Court of Survey for that district and the ddress of his office.

Where the owner or master of a ship desires to appeal to a Court of Survey, he shall file at the office of the registrar of the Court of Survey for the London district, or for the district where the ship is, a notice in a prescribed form. Immediately upon the filing of the notice of appeal the registrar shall communicate the fact to the D.o.T., who shall then inform him whether the appeal is to be heard by a wreck commissioner, and, if so, on what day. If the D.o.T. decides against a hearing by a wreck commissioner, the registrar shall ascertain which of the other judges of the Court will hear the appeal, and on what day. If practicable, the Court shall be summoned on a day not later than fourteen days from the filing of the notice of appeal.

The district of the Court of Survey for London includes the City of London, the districts of all Metropolitan County Courts, and the districts of certain County Courts in Kent, Essex and Surrey. The district of any other Court of Survey in England is the district of the County Court of the place at which the Court of Survey is

C

held. In Scotland and Ireland the district is the district of the Port of Customs of the place at which the Court is held.

A list of the judges of Courts of Survey in England is printed annually in *The Law List*. Those for Scotland and Ireland are listed in the Rules of the Court of Survey. The Rules provide that the wreck commissioner shall be a judge of every Court of Survey in the United Kingdom.

The registrar of the Court of Survey for London is specially appointed. The registrar of any other Court of Survey in England is the registrar of the County Court of the place at which the Court of Survey is held.

A right of appeal to a Court of Survey is granted to the owner or master of a ship:—

(1) when a surveyor refuses to give a declaration of survey in respect of a passenger steamer (but not if the surveyor has been accompanied by a person appointed by the shipowner and the two are in agreement);

(2) when a ship is refused a certificate as to lights and fog signals;

(3) when an order has been given to detain a ship as unsafe:

(4) when a ship is refused a safety certificate.

In accordance with the principal Act:—

1. The Court shall consist of a judge sitting with two assessors.

2. The judge shall be summoned from a list approved by the Home Secretary; but if the D.o.T. think it expedient, the judge shall be a wreck commissioner.

3. The assessors shall be persons of nautical, engineering or other special skill, one of whom shall be appointed by the D.o.T., and the other summoned by the registrar out of a list of persons nominated by a body of local shipowners or merchants approved by the Home Secretary; but where there is no list he shall be appointed by the judge.

4. Every case shall be heard in open court.

5. The judge may appoint a competent person (or persons) to survey the ship and report to the Court.

6. The judge, an assessor, or any person appointed by the judge may board and inspect the ship, its machinery and equipment and cargo, and may require cargo or ballast to be removed. The penalty for impeding survey is a fine not exceeding £1000.

7. The judge may order the release or final detention of the ship, but one assessor must concur in an order for final detention.

8. The owner and master of the ship or any person appointed by them may attend at every inspection or survey.

9. The judge shall send a report to the D.o.T. and each assessor must sign it or sign his dissent therefrom.

SCIENTIFIC REFEREES

If the D.o.T. are of the opinion that an appeal to a court of survey involves a question of contruction or design or of scientific difficulty or important principle, they may refer the matter to one or more scientific referees chosen out of a list approved by the Home Secretary and having the special qualifications necessary for the particular case. The referees may be selected by agreement between the appellant and the Department, but failing such agreement the Home Secretary will appoint them.

If the appellant requires it, and gives security for costs, the case shall be referred to a scientific referee (or referees), who shall have the same powers as a judge of a court of survey.

CHAPTER 2

LIENS, CONTRACTS, ARBITRATION AND AGENCY

LIENS

A LIEN is a form of remedy which is available to a person in certain circumstances, entitling him to enforce the satisfaction of a claim.

There are three classes of liens, viz.:—

1. Possessory liens, subdivided into (a) particular liens, and (b) general liens.
2. Maritime liens.
3. Equitable liens.

POSSESSORY LIENS (PARTICULAR)

A particular lien is the right of a person in possession of goods to retain possession of them until payment has been made by their real owner of any sum due in respect of those goods. Such a lien arises (i) when the person in possession has bestowed labour, skill or expense in altering or improving the goods, (ii) where the person in possession has been obliged to receive the goods or render the service which has given rise to the lien, (iii) where the person in possession has saved the goods from loss at sea or capture by an enemy.

Such lien cannot arise until the work contracted for has actually been performed; but if the owner of the goods prevents the work from being completed, the lien attaches for the work actually done.

At common law, a person enforcing a particular lien has no right to sell the goods. He may retain them until his charges are settled, and once he parts with either actual or constructive possession of the goods his right of lien is lost. In certain circumstances, however, the possessor may have a statutory right to sell the goods. Such a right is granted by a section of the Merchant Shipping Act dealing with delivery of goods, details of which will be found in Chapter 9.

The most common cases of particular liens are:—

(a) the common law lien of a carrier on the goods he carries for his charge for carriage (e.g., shipowner's lien on cargo for freight);
(b) tradesmen's liens in respect of labour expended for reward on goods;
(c) the lien of an unpaid seller of goods;
(d) warehousemen's liens on goods for their services for reward in connection with the goods.

SHIPOWNERS' POSSESSORY LIENS

At common law, a shipowner has a lien on the cargo carried on board his ship for:—

1. Freight.
2. Cargo's contribution in general average.
3. Salvage expenditure.

Possessory liens on cargo for charges other than the above must be specifically contracted for.

Freight. The common law lien on cargo for freight only arises when the freight is due on delivery of the cargo. Obviously no lien can arise in connection with freight that is payable in advance, or where a contract provides for freight to be payable after delivery. In the latter case delivery must be made before the freight can be demanded, and in the event of such freight remaining unpaid when due the carrier would have to seek some other remedy for its recovery.

In exercising his lien for freight the shipowner may lawfully retain all the goods for which freight is payable, and that is so even though the value of the goods exceeds the freight due. He may, however, if he wishes, merely retain sufficent of the goods to give adequate security for the freight due on them all. Where a number of bills of lading have been issued in respect of one shipment and the various bills have been endorsed to different consignees, the shipowner has a separate lien under each B/L extending only to the freight due under each particular bill. The shipowner cannot exercise his lien on goods carried under one B/L in respect of freight due from the holder of another B/L. Nevertheless, if several B's/L issued in pursuance of the same agreement between shipper and carrier are all endorsed to the same person, the carrier may retain goods shipped under one of those bills in exercise of his lien for the freight due under them all. Further, the lien for freight applies only to the freight due on the particular goods carried; it cannot be exercised in respect of a payment due from the owner of the goods under some other transaction.

General Average. The lien on cargo for general average charges can be exercised only by the shipowner in possession of the goods and, where necessary, it is his duty to other cargo owners to protect their interests by retaining possession of any goods in respect of which a contribution in G/A is outstanding. However, owing to the difficulty of assessing the amount of such contributions and the time required for general average adjustment, it is not usual for shipowners to avail themselves of the right of lien in these circumstances. The customary procedure is for the goods to be delivered in exchange for the security afforded by a general average bond, a general average deposit, or both. Further reference to this is made in Chapter 14.

Salvage. Whenever salvage expenditure has been incurred by a shipowner for the preservation of ship and cargo, he has a lien on the cargo for its proportion so long as the salvage was not made necessary by neglect or default of the shipowner himself.

Demurrage and Detention. A lien on cargo for demurrage exists only when the contract of affreightment expressly gives one. Where a charter-party does provide one, that lien does not extend to damages for detention at the loading port when a fixed number of demurrage days have been agreed and the ship is detained after the lay days and demurrage days have expired. To give the shipowner full protection, it would be necessary to stipulate in the C/P that the ship is to have a lien on cargo for demurrage *and* detention. Liens for demurrage and detention expressly given by a charter-party do not hold good against a bill of lading holder, unless they are specifically incorporated in the B/L. It has been held that the words "all other conditions . . . as per charter-party" are sufficient to incorporate in the B/L all liens expressly provided by the C/P.

Deadfreight. As deadfreight is payable, in respect of space which has been booked but not used, no common law lien for it can arise. There are no goods which the shipowner can retain by way of exercising a lien. All the same, it is quite common for a C/P to give an express lien for deadfreight, and such a lien, evidently, can be exercised only by refusing delivery of goods which have been carried to enforce payment of the deadfreight chargeable in respect of goods which have not been carried. Where an express lien for deadfreight exists, it applies not only where the entire cargo is carried at the same rate of freight but also where different parcels are carried at different rates.

Voyage Chartered Ships. The shipowner's lien for freight and other charges on goods shipped under a B/L on a chartered ship may, according to circumstances, apply to the freight due under the C/P or to the freight due under the B/L. The following appear to be established rulings.

1. If the consignee is the charterer, or charterer's agent, he is bound by the lien for freight due under the C/P and by express liens given by the C/P for other charges. But if it be found that the shipowner and the charterer-cum-consignee intended that the C/P should be varied by the B/L (and such an intention can only be found where the charterer is not only the shipper but also the consignee), then the lien extends only to the B/L freight. The consignee will, in any case, be bound by liens expressly given in the C/P, provided they are clearly incorporated in the B/L.

2. If the consignee is an agent of the shipper who is not the charterer, or if the consignee is an indorsee of the B/L, he is bound only by the lien for freight due under the terms of the B/L. Such consignee is also bound by express liens given in the B/L. Express

liens given by the C/P will not bind such consignee, unless they are incorporated in the B/L by the insertion of an adequate clause.

3. A shipper or indorsee of a B/L, even if he is acquainted with the terms of the C/P, will ordinarily be bound only by those C/P terms which are expressly incorporated in the B/L. But if a shipper who does not know the C/P terms is also aware that the master of the chartered ship has no authority to issue a B/L that does not incorporate the liens expressed in the C/P, the shipowner will be able to exercise such liens, in spite of the fact that the B/L has not included them.

Time Chartered Ships. A simple time charter usually contains a clause giving the shipowner a lien on all cargoes and all sub-freights for hire and general average contributions, and giving the charterer a lien on the vessel for all moneys paid in advance and not earned. If the vessel is sub-chartered, the lien on the sub-freight can only be exercised before the sub-freight has been paid to the charterer. In the exercise of such a lien it is considered advisable for the shipowner to give a formal notice to the sub-charterer or consignee requiring him to pay the sum to the owner before payment is made to the charterer or his agent. The notice might take the following form:—

From Shipowner's Agents to Sub-charterers.

s.s. "...................... ...."

Take notice that the sum of £......................hire is due to the owners of the above vessel from the time charterers, Messrs. ....under a time charter, dated

....

We accordingly give you for mal notice that such sum must be paid by you to us on behalf of owners out of any freight or moneys in your hands or due to the time charterers in respect of the current voyage of this ship. Such freight or moneys must not be released by you to the time charterers or their agents until the hire has been paid, and, on behalf of the owners, we must hold you personally liable if this occurs.

Signed..

Agents for..

....Owners.

Demise Chartered Ships. The cargo carried in a ship which has been demised or leased to the charterer is in the charterer's possession, not the shipowner's. Accordingly, no shipowner's lien on such cargo can arise.

Effect of Warehousing Goods. To preserve his lien the shipowner must retain actual or constructive possession of the goods. If they are warehoused with an independent agent the lien is lost, except in the United Kingdom where goods landed to a warehouse because the owner has failed to take delivery remain there subject to lien under the M.S. Act. In all other cases, in order to preserve the lien, goods not retained in the ship must be stored in the ship-owner's name or placed in a warehouse over which the shipowner or his agent has exclusive control.

Abandoned Goods. Since at common law freight is not earned until the goods are delivered at their proper destination, it follows that no lien for freight can exist in a case where goods have been abandoned by the shipowner before their arrival at the agreed destination and afterwards carried on to that destination by a salvor or other third party.

Waiver of Lien. A shipowner will be deemed to have waived his lien on goods for freight if he has accepted a bill of exchange for freight in advance which has not matured by the time of delivery, and this is still the case should the acceptor of the bill be bankrupt at the time of delivery.

POSSESSORY LIENS (GENERAL)

A general lien is the right which arises by custom in certain trades or professions, or by contract, to retain goods not only until any sum due in respect of them is paid; but also in respect of any sum which may be owing by the owner of the goods to the person in possession of them. Examples of general liens are (i) a solicitor's lien over all the papers of his client except his will, (ii) a factor's lien on the goods of his principal. There are many others.

MARITIME LIENS

A maritime lien is a right against a ship and the freight she may be earning at the time which gives a claimant power to have the property arrested and, if necessary, realised so that the proceeds may be applied in satisfaction of a claim.

Such a lien can be enforced, if the ship is within the jurisdiction of the courts of this country, by having her placed under arrest through the offices of the Admiralty Marshal.

A maritime lien provides a most valuable method of enabling an injured party to make the ship itself available as security for his claim for the following reasons. The right exists independently of the possession of the property over which it is claimed, and it continues to attach to the property in the sense that it is unaffected by the change of ownership. The bankruptcy of the shipowner does not affect the lien on the ship itself. The holder of a maritime lien generally has a higher priority than other creditors if the ship has to be sold and the assets distributed. The lien can be enforced by the issue of a writ "in rem" at any time within two years of the lien attaching and, in certain cases, even that period may be extended by the court. A claim against a foreign ship can be enforced if such ship comes within the jurisdiction of the English courts, which is of particular value when proceedings against the owner abroad have failed to provide satisfaction.

Although a maritime lien is a right "in rem", that is a right against the "thing" itself as distinct from a right against the person who owns it, it should be understood that there are other rights "in rem" provided by statute which are not liens. Such rights are intended, in respect of certain transactions, to give a claimant greater protection than he would enjoy if he could do no more than bring a personal claim. Where remuneration is claimed for the building, repairing, equipping, or towing of a ship; or where necessaries have been supplied to a foreign ship; or where the disputed ownership, possession, or mortgage of a vessel is in issue in the Admiralty Court, these statutory rights "in rem" may apply and the ship may be arrested at the suit of the claimant. In these cases, however, the arrest is not with a view to realising the property, but simply to secure its continued presence until the question in dispute has been determined. At one time the opinion was held that these statutory rights giving remedy "in rem" did confer a maritime lien, but the Administration of Justice Act, 1956, makes it clear beyond doubt that they do not. It is this Act which has widened the grounds on which ships can be arrested, and brought Great Britain into line with Continental countries by extending the right of arrest to sister ships (*i.e.*, ships under the same ownership). The difference between statutory right "in rem" and maritime lien has been expressed as follows.

The former can be availed of against the ship and freight on the one hand, and against the cargo on the other, only so long and so far as they continue *at the time of the arrest* to be the property of the person who is personally liable for the damage or breach of duty complained of. By contrast, maritime lien arises the moment the event occurs which creates it. The proceedings "in rem" which perfect the inchoate (*i.e.*, incomplete) right relate back to the time *when it first attached* and the maritime lien travels with the thing into whatsoever possession it may come. The arrest of a vessel under statute is, on the contrary, only one of several alternative proceedings, and no right in or against the ship is created at any time before the arrest.

CLASSIFICATION AND PRIORITY OF MARITIME LIENS

Maritime liens are of two classes, namely (*a*) contractual liens, and (*b*) damage liens.

Contractual liens are those which arise in respect of payment due under some contract. Examples are bottomry, respondentia, salvage, seamen's wages, master's wages, master's claim for wrongful dismissal, and master's claims for disbursements (in so far as the master had authority to pledge the owner's credit). By long established custom a seaman has a lien on the ship for his wages, but apparently the master has not always enjoyed the same right. However, the position as regards the master has been rectified by statute. Section 167 (1) of the principal M.S. Act gave masters the same rights as are enjoyed by a seaman. Although that section is now repealed, the 1970 Act makes similar provision.

There is no lien for either pilotage or towage unless the service becomes merged in a salvage service. Nor is there a lien on a ship for port dues.

Although it is usual to include the salvage lien in this list of contractual liens, it should be noted that, strictly, a salvage service must be a voluntary service so that no contract can exist. In modern practice, however, salvage agreements are always entered into by the parties, and the form of agreement generally used is constructed so as to retain the salvor's right of maritime lien on the property salved.

Damage liens arise principally from collision damage and the following points are important:—

(i) The damage must be done by the ship. (In a particular case the crew of ship "A" cut the cables of ship "B" in order to get to sea. "B" suffered damage in consequence, but her owners had no lien on ship "A".)

(ii) Although the damage must be caused by the ship, the lien does not arise unless in support of a personal action. If lien is claimed, the wrongful act or neglect of the owner or his servant must first be proved.

(iii) Lien can be exercised only within two years of the date of the damage suffered unless the court sees fit to extend the period.

In order of priority contractual liens rank as follows. Salvage obviously comes first, because the successful salvage service has preserved the property which provides the fund out of which other claimants can be paid. On the same principle, if there should be several salvage liens on the same ship at the same time the latest would rank first and the earliest last. Next in order come seamen's wages, and then the wages and other claims of the master. All these are preferred to bottomry but if, before enforcing settlement of their claims, the master and seamen allow the ship to proceed on a new voyage, any bottomry bond entered into on that new voyage would have priority over the previous liens.

Damage liens, even though they arise on different occasions, are treated as being of equal rank, and if the assets are insufficient to satisfy all claims in full the court will distribute them on a rateable basis.

Where there are conflicting claims between contractual liens and damage liens no fixed rule exists as to priority. The court will deal with them on an equitable basis, being guided by the circumstances of the case. Generally, however, the court will be influenced by the following principles. (1) Liens arising from tort should rank prior to those which previously arose from contract. Master and crew, volunteer salvors, and bottomry bond holders are all persons who have concerned themselves with the ship of their own free will, and their claims should be postponed to that of the owner of a ship damaged in a collision which occurred *after* the contractual liens accrued. (2) If the collision damage lien arises first, subsequent contractual liens should take precedence on the grounds that the subsequent services for reward have preserved the fund for the benefit of the collision creditors.

Maritime Lien and Mortgage. If there are claims against a ship giving the right of maritime lien, and there are mortgages on the ship as well, the question of priority again rises. In these circumstances it is ruled that the mortgages must wait until the liens are discharged, as the former are voluntary commercial transactions.

Maritime Lien and Possessory Lien. Suppose a ship on which there are claims giving maritime liens is put under repair, and the ship repairer acquires a possessory lien in respect of his claim for payment for work done. Here again a conflict arises, the settlement of which seems to depend upon the order of events. Since the ship was already encumbered by maritime liens when the repairer admitted her to his yard, his claim will be postponed until the maritime liens have been discharged. On the other hand, the repairer's possessory lien will rank superior to any claims that arise after he has accepted the ship. This point, however, is probably only of academic interest as the possessory lien would be lost if and when the repairer allowed the ship to depart from the area over which he has control.

Maritime Liens and Bills of Sale. Since a maritime lien is transferable with the property it is important that a bill of sale should indicate whether the ship is free from such an encumbrance. If a ship encumbered by maritime lien is sold, the new owner will have to settle the outstanding claim or risk seizure of the vessel which may then be resold by order of the court to satisfy the claim.

EQUITABLE LIENS

An equitable lien may be defined as the right to have certain property applied in a particular manner. Unlike a possessory lien, it exists irrespective of possession and confers on the holder the right to a judicial sale. Liens of this type being really outside the scope of this book, it will suffice to give only one example, viz., the partnership lien. This consists of the right of a partner on dissolution of the partnership to have the firm's property applied in the settlement of the firm's liabilities and any surplus divided among the partners in proper proportions.

CONTRACTS

The general law of contract is a very wide subject and no attempt is being made here to summarise it. Nevertheless, a few remarks about contracts in general are purposely included in the hope that what is said elsewhere in the book about particular forms of contracts will be more easily understood.

Shipmasters have a direct or indirect interest in many forms of contracts such as crew agreements and other contracts of service, charter-parties, bills of lading, contracts for the supply of bunkers, stores and other goods, repair contracts, stevedoring contracts, and others in connection with towage, pilotage, and so on. For this reason it is desirable that they should be to a sufficient extent aware of the law governing the actions of persons who make contracts, and should recognise that lack of knowledge can never be pleaded as an excuse by a person who becomes involved in the law. Where a contract is entered into it is always assumed that the parties to it were aware of, and made allowances for, the legal consequences of any breach of the agreement.

If an agreement is not a contract there is no redress in the event of either party failing to carry it out. On the other hand, where there is a contract a breach of it always gives rise to a legal remedy. Hence it is important to know what agreements the courts will, and will not, regard as contracts. For example, if an agreement contains a clause to the effect that it is to be binding in honour only, the courts would give effect to that clause and no action could be sustained on the agreement.

DEFINITIONS

A **Contract** may be defined as an agreement between two or more persons which may be legally enforced if the law is properly invoked.

A **Voidable Contract** is one which is capable of affirmation or repudiation at the option of one of the parties, *e.g.*, a charter-party giving the charterer the option of cancelling the charter in the event of the ship not arriving at the loading port or delivery port by a stipulated date.

A **Void Contract** is one that is destitute of legal effect, *e.g.*, a contract which is impossible of performance.

An **Illegal Contract** is one which contravenes the law, whether common law or statute law. Whilst it is true that an illegal contract is void, it does not follow that a void contract is necessarily illegal.

An **Unenforceable Contract** is one that is not capable of proof, or one which in defiance or neglect of revenue laws has not been properly stamped (though this may be rectified by paying a fine to the revenue authorities), or one in respect of which legal remedy has been barred by lapse of time.

CLASSES OF CONTRACTS

There are three classes of contracts known, respectively, as (1) contracts of record, (2) speciality contracts, or deeds, (3) simple or parol contracts.

A **Contract of Record** is the obligation which is imposed by the entry in the parchment rolls of the proceedings in a court of record. Such contracts are principally judgments and recognisances. A judgment is an obligation imposed on one party by a court of record in favour of another party. Being an order of the court and an obligation imposed, it is not strictly a contract which rests upon agreement. A recognisance is a contract made with the Sovereign through her Judicial Representative, generally in the nature of a promise to do some particular act or answer to a stated penalty, *e.g.*, an undertaking by a person tried on a criminal charge to come up for judgment if called upon, or a promise to pay a specified sum of money if an accused person out on bail fails to appear at the trial. The terms of such a contract admit of no dispute but are conclusively proved by the record itself.

A **Speciality Contract,** or **Deed,** is a written contract executed under seal and delivered. Both sealing and signature are essential for the proper execution of a deed. Delivery may be actual or constructive, and it is usual for it to be made simultaneously with execution. The party executing touches an affixed wafer with his finger and declares, "I deliver this as my act and deed".

A **Simple Contract** is a contract created by verbal promise, or by writing not under seal, or by implication. Strictly speaking, a parol contract is one entered into by word of mouth but it is customary to use the term to describe simple contracts of all kinds. Most contracts entered into in ordinary commercial transactions are simple contracts. A contract by implication can arise in various ways. By boarding a public vehicle, or hailing a taxicab, a person indicates his intention by mere act so that a contract is implied.

ESSENTIALS OF A VALID CONTRACT

For a contract to be valid there must be:—

(1) Offer and acceptance. There must be a distinct communication by the parties to one another of their intention. It is important to determine from which party the offer emanates. A shopkeeper exhibiting goods for sale in his window, even if they are marked with a price, is not making an offer, but is merely making an invitation to offer.

(2) Genuineness of the consent expressed in the offer and acceptance. It may happen that consent to the agreement may have been so given or obtained that it did not express the true intention of the consenting party. This could arise from mistake, misrepresentation, fraud, duress, or undue influence.

(3) Form or consideration. "Form" means some solemnity attaching to the expression of agreement, as in the execution of a deed. "Consideration" means valuable consideration (in this sense valuable does not mean of high value, but means capable of being valued), and this must consist of

something capable of being estimated in money. Consideration is necessary to the validity of every promise not under
seal. Consideration has been defined as "some right, interest,
profit, or benefit accruing to one party, or some forbearance,
detriment, loss, or responsibility given, suffered, or undertaken by the other".

(4) Capacity of the parties to contract. Certain parties are by
law incapable, wholly or in part, of binding themselves by a
promise, or enforcing a promise made to them. Examples
include enemy aliens, convicts, infants, lunatics, and
drunken persons.

(5) Legality of the object. It may be declared by statute that
a contract is illegal or void, a common instance of such
an illegal contract being one of a gaming nature. Certain
contracts are illegal at common law, *e.g.*, agreement to
commit an indictable offence or a civil wrong, or an agreement contrary to public policy.

(6) Possibility of performance at the time when the contract is
entered into. If a contract is impossible of performance at
the date when it is entered into it is void, but the impossibility
must be complete, and not merely in relation to the party
liable to perform the act or fulfil the promise. Impossibility
may arise prior to, or subsequent to, the formation of the contract and remedies will differ according to circumstances.

Should any of the above elements be lacking the contract will
either be void or voidable, but even if they are all present the
contract may still be unenforceable.

DISCHARGE OF CONTRACT

Contracts may be discharged by agreement, performance,
breach, impossibility, or operation of law.

Discharge by Agreement can take place by (1) waiver, *i.e.*, an
agreement by the parties that they shall no longer be bound by the
contract; (2) by substituted agreement, *e.g.*, where with the consent
of the creditor a new debtor is substituted for an old one; (3) by
condition subsequent, *i.e.*, a provision in the contract that the
fulfilment of a condition, or the occurrence of an event, shall discharge the parties from further liabilities.

Discharge by Performance may be effected by actual performance where each party actually carries out his part of the contract,
or by payment where the liability of one party to the other consists
in the payment of a sum of money.

Discharge by Breach. Breach of contract may take place in the
following ways:—

(1) By renunciation. If one party renounces his liabilities before
the time for performance has come, the other party is discharged if he so pleases, and may at once sue for the breach.

Alternatively, the person entitled to performance may refuse to accept the renunciation, hold the other party to the contract, and institute proceedings if the contract be not duly performed.

(2) By one party through his own act making it impossible to fulfil the contract, in which case the other party may treat the contract as renounced and commence an action at once.

(3) By failure of performance. Where there has been a breach by failure of performance, the injured party may bring an action for such breach, but it depends on the nature of the contract and on the nature of the breach whether the injured party is himself discharged from further performance or not. If the contract requires both parties to perform their respective promises simultaneously, the promises being inter-dependent, breach by one party does discharge the other. However, if the contract consists of a number of divisible promises, partial failure of performance by one party does not necessarily discharge the other party from further performance. The question of degree comes into it. If the breach is of such a serious nature that it goes to the root of the whole contract, the innocent party will be discharged. The same will apply if the act or conduct of one party amounts to an intimation of an intention to abandon or refuse performance of the contract. Where the breach is less serious, the injured party, though able to bring an action for damages will not be liberated from the performance of his own promises.

Those terms of a contract which are so fundamental that they may be said to go to the root of the whole contract are referred to as "conditions", whilst those that are merely collateral to the agreement are referred to as "warranties". Summing up what has been said above, therefore, breach of a condition will give rise to an action for damages and will also discharge the injured party from further performance. Breach of a warranty, on the other hand, gives the injured party a remedy in damages but does not discharge him from further performance. Here it is necessary to point out that the term "warranty" can easily give rise to some confusion as it is used in the Marine Insurance Act in a different sense. Marine insurance warranties, which are explained in Chapter 14, correspond to "conditions" in other contracts, and if such a warranty is broken the insurer is entitled to avoid the policy unless, of course, it contains a clause providing otherwise.

Both conditions and warranties are only parts of a contract and it is often found difficult to determine whether a particular item is a condition or a warranty. The finding will depend on the intention of the parties deduced from the terms of the contract and the subject matter to which it relates.

Conditions may be precedent, concurrent, or subsequent.

A **Condition Precedent** is one which has to be fulfilled before the main purpose of the contract is performed. To take a common example, under the provisons of a voyage charter-party it is a condition precedent to the charterer's obligation to load that the ship shall be arrived, ready and reported on or before the cancelling date. If this is not complied with the charterer may exercise his option to cancel the contract.

A **Condition Concurrent** is one to be performed at the same time as the main agreement. For instance, in the case of a cash sale payment must be made concurrently with the delivery of the goods to the purchaser.

A **Condition Subsequent** is a condition the non-observance of which would entitle the other party to avoid transactions already completed. The "excepted risks" of a charter-party serve as an illustration. The occurrence of an excepted risk releases the ship-owner from the strict performance of the contract. Unjustifiable deviation by the carrier's vessel is an example of a breach of a condition subsequent in a voyage charter-party or a bill of lading.

REMEDIES FOR BREACH OF CONTRACT

(*a*) Where there is a total breach of contract, or a partial breach in circumstances where the injured party is discharged from further performance, the following remedies are available. The injured party may:—

(1) consider the contract discharged by breach, refuse to do any act under the contract himself, and bring an action for damages;

(2) continue to act upon the contract and bring an action for damages;

(3) where he has already performed part of the contract himself, sue on a *quantum meruit*;

(4) apply to the court, where such remedy is appropriate, for a decree of specific performance, or for an injunction.

(*b*) Where a partial breach does not entitle the injured party to be discharged from further performance an action for damages is the only remedy.

DAMAGES

Damages are intended to be in the nature of compensation for loss actually suffered, and accordingly the *measure of damages* is the amount of the loss which the parties contemplated, or might reasonably have contemplated, would *naturally* result from failure to perform the contract. In a contract of sale, for instance, should the buyer fail to take delivery of the goods, the measure of damages in an action by the seller would be the difference between the contract price and the price the seller could obtain in the open market. Even if no damage has resulted from the breach, the plaintiff would still be entitled to a verdict for nominal damages, say one half-penny, or five pence.

Damages for a special loss cannot be recovered unless that is provided for by the terms of the contract or unless the party in breach knew of the special circumstances. Damage which is not the natural and probable result of the breach is regarded as too remote and is not recoverable. Difficulty of assessing damages will not deprive an injured party of his right to recover and he may claim, not only for loss already sustained, but also for prospective loss provided the latter was reasonably within the contemplation of the parties.

The injured party always has a duty to minimise the loss he has sustained. For example, if a person agrees to sell goods to another for £60 and, because the buyer repudiates the contract before delivery, resells them elsewhere for £40 when he could have sold them for £50, the measure of damages will be £10, not £20. To take another example, it has been held that there is always an implied term in a charter-party that if the charterer fails to load a full cargo then the shipowner is entitled to take in a substitute cargo if by doing so he is acting reasonably. The test of reasonableness in such a case is whether the shipowner's action in loading the substituted cargo will mitigate the damages to which the charterer has made himself liable by his failure to load a full cargo.

Damages may be liquidated or unliquidated. "Liquidated damages" means a sum *agreed* by the parties to the contract as an assessment of the loss or damage consequent upon breach. Demurrage is of this nature. An agreement of this kind is frequently the subject of a clause in a contract for the erection of a building, or for the repair of a ship, and similar works, providing for the payment of a stated sum for every day (or other period) of delay beyond an agreed time for the completion of the work.

It should be noted that there is a difference between liquidated damages and a "penalty". The latter is a sum named in a contract to be forfeited in the event of breach, not as an agreed amount of damages, but as security for due performance of the contract. If a contract containing a penalty clause is breached, only the actual loss incurred can be recovered. The so-called penalty clause in a charter-party would not appear by its usual wording to provide for a penalty in the strict sense of the term. One version of this clause, for instance, reads "Penalty for non-performance of this agreement, estimated amount of damages".

SPECIFIC PERFORMANCE

Specific performance is a decree of the court ordering a party to carry out his part of the contract. Such an order is made where the usual remedy of damages would not sufficiently compensate the injured party whose rights can be satisfied by nothing less than the performance of the contract in its precise terms.

QUANTUM MERUIT

In certain cases where a person who has performed a portion of his duties under a contract finds himself unable to complete the whole, he may sue on a *quantum meruit* for the value of the work done. This is possible only where (i) complete performance was prevented by the action of the other party, (ii) the contract is divisible so that a specific portion of the remuneration can be allocated to each portion, (iii) the other party has accepted and retained the benefit of the part performance after the time of completion of the contract has expired. Where a builder had agreed to build a house for a lump sum and abandoned the contract after performing part of the work, it was held that he had no remedy in part payment even though the other party had benefited by the breach. On the other hand, if the other party had repudiated the contract the builder would have been able to sue on a *quantum meruit* for the value of the work done plus the loss of profit consequent on the breach.

BREACH PROCURED BY THIRD PARTY

It is an actionable wrong for one person to induce another to break a contract already entered into if the object of that person is either to injure the person who suffers by the break or to obtain some benefit for himself. But by virtue of the Trades Disputes Act members of a trade union may induce a person to break a contract in contemplation of a trade dispute. In respect of their contracts of service, seamen were not protected by this Act, but Section 42 of the M.S. Act 1970 provides that notwithstanding any notice which, under the crew agreement, a seaman is required to give before he can terminate his employment, he may leave the ship in contemplation or furtherance of an industrial dispute if he gives the master at least 48 hours' notice. Such notice, however, if it is to be effective, can be given only when the ship is securely moored at a safe berth in the United Kingdom. If the notice has not been withdrawn a seaman who has given such notice cannot be compelled to go to sea in the 48 hours following the giving of the notice. The basic principle is that a contract is sacred to the parties to it and no third party has a right to interfere to the detriment of either of them. Merely to induce a person not to enter into a contract is not actionable, but if intimidation is used, or if persons wilfully combine to injure a man in his trade, a wrong is committed and damages may be recoverable.

Discharge by Impossibility of Performance. If a person undertakes to perform an act which is manifestly impossible, there can be no contract. But performance will not be excused unless the act is *generally* impossible and not merely impossible as regards the particular person making the promise. What cannot be done by one person may be done by another.

Where, without the knowledge of either party, performance has already become impossible *at or before* the time of entering into the contract, such contract is void.

Subsequent impossibility, however, is a different matter. Impossibility which arises *after* the contract has been entered into does not excuse a party from his obligation under the contract unless the impossibility is of a kind which amounts to "frustration". Provided that the contract is not frustrated in the strict legal sense of that term, a party must perform what he has promised or be liable in damages, and that is so even though the impossibility has arisen through no fault of his own. Where a person desires to guard against a particular risk it is, therefore, of paramount importance that an appropriate clause should be inserted in the contract, such as the "exceptions" clause in a B/L or a C/P.

Frustration has been defined as "the premature determination of an agreement between parties, lawfully entered into and in course of operation at the time of its premature determination, due to the occurrence of an intervening event or change of circumstances so fundamental as to be regarded by the law as striking at the root of the agreement, and entirely beyond what was contemplated by the parties when they entered into the agreement".

Hence, there is no frustration:—

(1) if the intervening circumstance is one which the law would not regard as so fundamental as to destroy the basis of the agreement;

(2) if the terms of the agreement show that the parties contemplated the possibility of such a circumstance arising;

(3) if one of the parties has deliberately brought about the supervening event by his own choice.

Where a contract is definitely frustrated it is thereupon discharged as regards both parties quite apart from their own volition.

Frustration and consequent release from further performance may arise in the following ways:—

(1) Where a contract is made on the basis of the continued existence of a specific thing, on the continuance of some existing state of affairs, or on the happening of some future event, further performance is excused if the specific thing ceases to exist, the state of affairs ceases to continue, or the event fails to take place.

(2) If the contract is one of *personal service* the death of either party will excuse further performance. Illness or other incapacity will have the same effect so long as the disability is of such a nature as to make performance practically impossible. In respect of other contracts illness is not an excuse, and in case of death the personal representatives of the deceased will be liable for the performance of the contract.

(3) A change in the law which renders further performance illegal will discharge a contract. Frustration of this kind

arises in connection with contracts that cannot be performed on the outbreak of war because they would involve trading with the enemy. The imposition of a rationing system by the government would similarly frustrate a contract for the sale of goods.

Brief reference to a number of decided cases will serve to illustrate some of the rules stated above.

Case I. A contract was made for the use of a music hall on certain days for the purpose of giving concerts and other entertainments. Before the date arrived the hall was destroyed by fire. Further performance of the contract was excused on the grounds that the contract had been made on the basis that the hall would continue to exist.

Case II. A contract was made for the hire of a room and balcony from which to view the Coronation procession of King Edward VII. Owing to the King's illness the procession was abandoned. It was held that the contract had been frustrated because it was to the knowledge of both parties that the holding of the procession was the basis of the contract.

Case III. A pianist was prevented by illness from performing at a concert in accordance with his contract on the appointed day. He was held not to be liable for damages as the contract was deemed to be based on the assumption that the performer would be living and in sufficient health to give his performance.

Case IV. A vessel was chartered to proceed from A to B and there load a cargo for C. On the way to B she stranded on a rocky shore and was badly damaged. After long delay she was refloated and taken back to A where the necessary repairs occupied several months. The court found that the time for repairing the vessel and enabling her to continue the contractual voyage was so long as to frustrate the commercial object of the voyage and that the contract was therefore at an end.

Case V. A ship was chartered to load at a port on the east coast of England a cargo of wool in bales for delivery at a port in Germany. On the day when the master tendered notice of readiness to load all but 167 bales of the intended cargo were destroyed by fire in the warehouse where they were awaiting shipment. The court held in this case that the charter-party was not frustrated because (1) the contract was not for the carriage of the specific goods that were destroyed, (2) the charterers could have performed the contract by getting a cargo from elsewhere, (3) the undamaged cargo which was not *de minimis* (*i.e.*, a mere trifle) could in any case have been shipped.

Where a contract governed by English law has become impossible of performance or has been otherwise frustrated so that the parties are discharged from further performance, the method of settlement of outstanding claims is, in general, subject to the provisions of the Law Reform (Frustrated Contracts) Act, 1943. Details of this Act are purposely omitted here, but it is interesting to note that the Act does not apply to voyage charter-parties, other contracts of carriage of goods by sea, or to contracts of insurance. It does, however, apply to simple time charters and to charters by demise. The reason for excluding contracts of sea carriage from the application of the Act seems to be the undesirability of interfering with the long established practices of maritime law that (i) freight paid in advance is not recoverable in the event of the ship being lost before delivery can be effected, and (ii) that ordinary freight is not earned and payable until the contract is completely performed. Any interference with those rules would involve substantial modification of insurance practice which, it is considered, is better avoided. The application of the Act to time charters has the effect that in most cases hire payable up to the date of frustration, but if hire has already been paid beyond that date the charterer is entitled to recover the balance. This may, however, be subject to the court allowing the shipowner to retain a sum in respect of expenses incurred by him, or benefit bestowed upon the charterer, before the date of frustration for the purpose of performing the contract beyond the date of frustration.

Discharge by Operation of Law. The principal cases arise in connection with merger, bankruptcy, and the application of the provisions of the Limitation Acts, 1939–1975.

By the doctrine of merger, a contract of lower degree is merged into one of higher degree relating to the same matter. Further consideration of this is outside the scope of this book.

When a bankrupt obtains his discharge he is, with certain exceptions, freed from liability in respect of debts payable in the bankruptcy. Although existing or continuous contracts may be adopted by the Trustee, the latter can put an end to contracts of an unprofitable nature by disclaimer.

It is always considered expedient that any right to which a person is entitled should be enforced by bringing an action, if that is necessary, within a reasonable time. For that reason the Limitation Act prescribes the maximum periods within which actions of various kinds must be brought after the cause of action first arose. Actions on simple contracts, for instance, are barred after the lapse of six years.

Variations of a Contract. As a general rule, once the terms of a contract have been agreed they cannot be varied without the consent of the parties, and such consent should be evidenced in the same manner as the original contract. A contract in writing, for instance, can be amended by another written instrument. In this connection it is important that a shipmaster should realise that he cannot vary the terms of a charter-party to which he himself is not a party. Whilst he has a duty, as far as he is able, to see that the terms of such a contract are adhered to, it is not in his power to give the charterer permission to vary the contract in any way.

In a particular case a C/P provided that the ship was to load in a specified number of working days, *i.e.*, Sundays and holidays were not to count as lay days. During loading the charterer approached the master and requested permission for work to be carried on during two days that were not working days. The master granted permission and loading was completed earlier than would otherwise have been the case. The charterer's time sheet showed these two days as holidays and indicated that dispatch money was due to the charterer in respect of the time saved. The master, assuming that the two days in question should have been treated as lay days, protested and the shipowner counter-claimed for demurrage. The dispute eventually became the subject of a High Court action where it was held that the shipowner's counter-claim should prevail. The Court of Appeal upheld this decision, but a further appeal to the House of Lords resulted in the earlier decisions being reversed on the grounds that "in the absence of an express agreement to the contrary the original terms of the charter-party must stand". Had the master insisted on the charterer obtaining permission direct from the shipowner (the charterer bearing the expense of cabling, of course,) the existence of the cablegrams would have provided evidence, in case of dispute, of a supplementary agreement between the actual parties to the contract.

Construction of Contracts. Naturally, there are rules governing the contruction of contracts, but it is feasible to mention only a few of them, as follows:—

1. The language must be construed so as to carry out the intention of the parties as shown by the whole of the terms.

2. Words must be presumed to have their literal meaning but evidence is permissible to show that apparently unambiguous words were used in a special sense. This rule is often applied in mercantile contracts where evidence is adduced to show that by the custom of merchants certain words are used in a technical sense which differs from their usual meanings.

3. Of two possible constructions, one legal and the other illegal, the legal one must be adopted.

4. Words are to be construed most strongly against the party who would benefit by them.

5. A contract must be construed according to the law of the country where it is made unless the intention of the parties that this should not be so is made clear. Rules of evidence and procedure, however, are governed by the law of the country where the action is brought.

6. A contract must be construed in relation to any custom of the trade or custom of the port or locality to which the contract applies. To be enforceable a custom must be lawful, certain, reasonable, consistent, and accepted by the mercantile community. That is

not to say that custom must be regarded as static. As mercantile transactions develop and expand, custom may be extended in conformity therewith.

Unfair Contract Terms Act, 1977. This Act does not deal with unfair contracts as such, but merely with exemption clauses in them which might be unfair. Such clauses are of interest to shipowners and passengers in connection with lawful terms that may be included in passengers' contracts of passage. (*See* Chapter 8.)

ARBITRATION

Many contracts with which shipowners and their masters are concerned, such as bills of lading, charter-parties, salvage agreements, and marine insurance policies, nowadays provide for various litigious matters to be referred to arbitration. Some of the terms used in connection with this method of settling disputes, together with the main advantages and disadvantages of arbitration, the various methods of referring to arbitration, and so on, form the subject matter of this section.

DEFINITIONS

Arbitration consists of the reference of a dispute to one or more independent persons for settlement, instead of to a court of law.

The **Arbitration Agreement** is the agreement between the parties to refer the decision of differences to one or more arbitrators.

The **Reference** is the term which, strictly speaking, denotes the proceedings during arbitration, although the same term is often used to mean the submission.

The **Arbitrator** is the person to whose decision the dispute is referred.

The **Award** is the arbitrator's decision.

The **Umpire** is a person appointed, when reference is to more than one arbitrator, to give a decision when the arbitrators fail to reach agreement.

The **Umpirage** is the umpire's decision.

ADVANTAGES OF ARBITRATION

Avoidance of Publicity. When a court action takes place the court is open to the public and the press so that facts brought out in evidence become public property. Arbitration is conducted privately and the parties are under no obligation to publish information relating to the case.

Informality of Procedure. Arbitration procedure is relatively simple though, naturally, it will vary according to the magnitude and complexity of the issue. In all cases it will be less formal that the fixed procedure of the courts.

Possible Avoidance of the Uncertainty and Expense Involved in **Appeals.** Provided the arbitration reward is good, the result is final and is not subject to appeal and attendant delays.

Saving of Expense. The expenses of a legal action are generally heavy involving, as they do, court fees, solicitors' costs, and fees of counsel. The last mentioned may be a particularly heavy item when it is considered necessary to brief very highly experienced counsel. By comparison the remuneration of arbitrators will generally be much less.

Arbitrator's Special Knowledge. In a dispute involving technical differences an arbitrator having special knowledge of the business concerned may, with advantage, be appointed.

DISADVANTAGES OF ARBITRATION

Possibility of Arbitrator Being Incompetent or Biased. The appointment of a business man might be a disadvantage on account of his not being well versed in the law, whilst the appointment of a lawyer might be unsatisfactory due to his lack of that special knowledge and experience which the nature of the dispute requires. An arbitrator appointed by one party may be biased in favour of that party. If each side appoints its own arbitrator there is a risk that each will regard himself as the advocate of the party who appointed him. It is, of course, possible to eliminate or reduce such risks by nominating some independent person to appoint the arbitrator, and that is frequently done.

An incompetent arbitrator may make a bad award which, on appeal to the court, may be set aside so that the time and money of the parties to the reference will have been spent in vain. A competent but biased arbitrator, on the other hand, may make a final and binding award which is in fact unjust.

POSSIBILITY OF INJUSTICE ARISING FROM INFORMALITY

Informality of procedure has been included among the advantages attaching to arbitration, yet it is possible for it to operate to the disadvantage of one or other of the parties. Whereas the procedure obtaining in a court of law is rigidly defined, procedure in arbitration is, within certain limits, controlled at the discretion of the arbitrator. Misuse of such discretion could give rise to some injustice.

PERSONS ENTITLED TO SUBMIT TO ARBITRATION

Any person, individual or corporate, who is capable of entering into a contract can submit to arbitration. Persons incapable of contracting cannot be bound by a submission. A duly authorised agent may bind his principal by submission to arbitration, and in some cases an implied authority may arise from the nature of the agency.

SUBJECT MATTER OF REFERENCE

With certain exceptions, any matter that might be settled by action between the parties in a court of law may be referred to arbitration. Stated briefly, the exceptions are (1) purely criminal matters, since punishment of a crime can be imposed only in a court of law; (2) matters affecting status, such as suits for dissolution of marriage, or proceedings in bankruptcy.

METHODS OF REFERRING TO ARBITRATION

1. By statute. Under some statutes parties have an option to refer disputes to be settled by arbitration procedure; under some other statutes reference may be compulsory.

2. By order of the court. The Rules of the Supreme Court allow for the exercise of the powers and jurisdiction of the High Court in specified circumstances by official or special referees, masters and registrars. Any type of question emerging before a court may be referred for inquiry. The jurisdiction of the county court as related to arbitration has now been extended so that small consumer claims can be dealt with by registrars.

3. By voluntary submission of the parties verbally at Common Law. The provision of the Arbitration Acts do not apply to submissions of this kind which are subject to a number of relatively serious disadvantages.

4. By arbitration agreement in writing under the Arbitration Acts. Under this agreement known as a "submission" or an arbitration agreement, the parties agree to submit to an arbitration procedure present or future disputes whether an arbitrator is named or not. Such an agreement can be included in an exchange of letters or by telegram. The submission should indicate whether *all* matters of dispute which might arise should be subject to arbitration, and if not, the scope of the arbitration clause should be precisely defined.

The terms of a submission may be altered, with the agreement of the parties, at any time before the arbitrator's decision has been given, but such alteration must be in writing and must be made at the instance of the parties themselves. The arbitrator has no authority to make an amendment.

An agreement which purports to oust the jurisdiction of the court, being contrary to public policy, is illegal and void, but an agreement to refer to arbitration does not generally oust the jurisdiction of the court as it is still open to the parties to take legal proceedings instead of going to arbitration. However, if one party does institute proceedings the court may exercise its powers under the Arbitration Act, 1950, to stay proceedings on the application of the other party. Moreover, if the agreement (like the time charter clause quoted above) provides that reference to arbitration shall be a "condition precedent" to the right to sue, no action can successfully be brought until a reference to arbitration has first taken place for the reason that, by the terms of the agreement itself, no cause of action exists until then.

THE ARBITRATOR

The parties to a reference have an absolutely free choice in the matter of the appointment of an arbitrator. Whether it is better to have a layman or a lawyer is a very open question, and much depends on the particular nature of the reference. The person or persons selected must be appointed in accordance with the provisions of the submission, and where no other method of reference is provided the reference will be to a sole arbitrator.

Where the reference is to a single arbitrator and the parties do not, after differences have arisen, concur in the appointment of an arbitrator, any party may serve upon the other written notice to appoint an arbitrator, and if such appointment is not then made within seven days the court has power under the Arbitration Act to make an appointment.

In any case where an agreement provides for the appointment of an arbitrator or umpire by a person who is neither one of the parties nor an existing arbitrator and that person refuses to make an appointment or fails to make it within the specified or reasonable time, any party to the agreement may serve him written notice to appoint. If the appointment is not made within seven days, the High Court may, on the application of the party who gave notice, appoint an arbitrator or umpire.

Where the reference is to two arbitrators, they must appoint an umpire immediately after they themselves are appointed.

Where the agreement provides for reference to three arbitrators, one to be appointed by each party and the third by the two appointed by the parties, the agreement has effect as if it provided for the appointment of an umpire. If, however, the appointment of three arbitrators is made in any other way they will all three act as arbitrators and the award of any two of them will be binding. The distinction between a third arbitrator and an umpire is an important one. A third arbitrator is one of three who are required to act in concert and whose duties commence forthwith on appointment. An umpire, on the other hand, does not act with the arbitrators but enters upon the reference only when they have disagreed.

If the reference is to two arbitrators, one to be appointed by each party, the failure of one party to make an appointment within seven days after the other party, having appointed his arbitrator, has served notice on the first party to make an appointment, the arbitrator already appointed may then be appointed sole arbitrators. His award will then be binding on both parties as if he had been appointed by their common consent. It is essential, however, that he be actually appointed as sole arbitrator as, otherwise, he would have no authority to proceed alone.

POWERS OF THE ARBITRATOR

Subject to the terms of the submission the arbitrator has power:—

1. to administer oaths;
2. to take affirmations of parties and witnesses;
3. to correct in an award any clerical mistake or error;
4. to require, subject to legal objection, parties and persons claiming through them to produce books, deeds, accounts and other documents which he may require, and do all other things which he may require during the proceedings;
5. with certain exceptions, to order specific performance of a contract;
6. to make an interim award.
7. to make an award on the dispute submitted.
8. To direct to and by whom the costs of the reference and award shall be paid and to tax or settle the amount of costs.

THE UMPIRE

Where the reference is to two arbitrators the submission often provides that in the case of disagreement between them the matter shall be decided by an umpire. Even if the submission omits this provision, it is required by the Arbitration Act that the two arbitrators must appoint an umpire, unless a contrary intention is expressed in the submission.

When called upon to act the umpire must proceed with the reference with all reasonable despatch, failing which either party may apply to the court for his removal.

The umpire has the same powers and duties as the arbitrators and, unless he has sat with the arbitrators throughout the proceedings and made his own notes, he must rehear the matter and examine the parties' witnesses himself. As a general rule he is not allowed to take evidence from the notes of the arbitrators unless the parties so consent, although the arbitrators may give evidence before him. However, in commercial arbitrations there is a recognised practice, which has the approval of the courts, for each arbitrator to state the case for his own party and then submit the evidence to the umpire who finally makes a decision binding on both parties.

PROCEEDINGS AND AWARD

The reference must be conducted in accordance with the terms of the submission. The time and place of the hearing are usually fixed by the arbitrator who also gives the necessary notice to the parties. If a party applies for an extension of time the arbitrator should grant the extension if reasonable. Where a party persistently refuses to appear or produce witnesses, the arbitrator should serve on him a notice marked "peremptory", indicating that in the event of failure to appear on the date fixed by the notice the arbitration will proceed in his absence. Although the proceedings are private, the arbitrator is not justified in excluding genuinely interested persons unreasonably. Whilst the conduct of the proceedings is in the discretion of the arbitrator, it is desirable that the practice of the courts should be followed as far as possible. Further, in arriving at his decision, the arbitrator is bound to observe the rules of law and equity. The Arbitration Act provides that a party may compel the attendance of witnesses and production of documents by subpoena. A party with cause for complaint in the conduct of the proceedings should at once protest and apply to the court for the revocation of the submission or the removal of the arbitrator. If he withdrew from the proceedings or, alternatively, continued to appear without protest he would be placed at a considerable disadvantage.

When the arbitrator is satisfied that he has heard all the evidence the parties are prepared to offer, he should give distinct notice that the proceedings are at an end and that he is prepared to make an award.

Apart from express provision otherwise in the submission no time limit is fixed within which an award must be made, but the arbitrator must use all reasonable despatch. If the submission does provide for a time limit any variation of it can be made only by the parties themselves or by the court. If there is a sole arbitrator, he will make the award. When there are two, they will make the award if they agree, otherwise it will be made by the umpire. If the reference is to three arbitrators in circumstances where none of them becomes an umpire, the award of any two of them is binding. The award requires a revenue stamp and is issued to the party applying for it on payment of the arbitrator's charges. A copy is issued to the other party on application. Unless the submission provides to the contrary, the award will be final and binding although in certain circumstances it may be set aside or referred back. The court may set an award aside if there has been actual or technical misconduct on the part of the arbitrator, if there has been a mistake in law, and for certain other reasons. Even though not set aside, an award may be referred back by the court for reconsideration by the arbitrator in order to correct an error or if fresh evidence has been discovered. When the award is referred back the original powers of the arbitrator are revived, and the original award becomes void unless remitted only for a mendment on some specific point. Should any party refuse to accept the award, the arbitrator may apply to the courts for his decision to be upheld.

ARBITRATOR'S REMUNERATION

Unless the submission expresses a contrary intention, the arbitrator may fix the amount of his fee and include it in his award. If a fee has not been agreed in writing and the arbitrator refuses to deliver his award except on payment, the court may on the application of the party order the fee demanded to be paid into court and demand that it be taxed by the taxing officer. Out of the money paid into court there shall be paid to the arbitrator such sum as may be found reasonable on taxation, and any balance is payable to the applicant. Apart from this provision of the Arbitration Act the arbitrator has a lien on the submission and award for the amount of his charges, but the lien does not extend to documents handed to the arbitrator in the course of the reference.

JUDICIAL REVIEW

The Arbitration Act, 1979 repealed s.21 of the 1950 Act which provided for an arbitrator to make an award in the form of a Special Case for the Court to give its opinion on any question of law. The 1979 Act instead provides for the arbitrator to seek the opinion of the Court during the course of the arbitration where a difficult point of law arises, but the High Court is not to take such an application unless it is satisfied that the determination of the question of law will produce substantial savings in costs to the parties and that the question of law concerned could substantially affect the rights of one or more of the parties.

Also an appeal to the High Court can be made on any question of law arising out of an award, and the High Court may by order confirm, vary or set aside the award, or remit the award to the re-consideration of the arbitrator or umpire together with the court's opinion on the question of law. The arbitrator or umpire shall then, unless the order directs otherwise, make his award within three months of the date of the order.

No appeal lies to the Court of Appeal from a decision of the High Court unless the High Court or the Court of Appeal gives leave and the High Court certifies that the question of law is of general public importance or is one which for some other special reason should be considered.

Parties to so called "International Agreements" are permitted to exclude the right of appeal by entering into an "exclusion agreement", but an exclusion agreement will be effective only if entered into after commencement of arbitration proceedings where the question or claim falls within Admiralty jurisdiction of the High Court, or is a dispute arising out of an insurance contract or a commodity contract.

ARBITRATION CLAUSES IN CONTRACTS
OF CARRIAGE BY SEA

Bills of lading and charter-parties frequently contain clauses to the effect that the parties agree to refer to arbitration disputes arising under the contract. Such clauses are perfectly valid, but what constitutes a "dispute arising under the contract" is a matter deserving of some consideration. If, for instance, one party contends against the other that the contract has never been entered into at all, that is a dispute which cannot go to arbitration under the clause, for the party who denies that he entered into the contract is at the same time denying that he joined in the submission. On similar grounds, if a party alleges that the contract is void, that cannot be a matter for arbitration under the clause, for on the view that the whole contract is void the part (i.e., the submission) must be seen to be void as well.

An arbitration clause may provide that if the claimant fails to appoint an arbitrator within a stipulated time the claim shall be barred absolutely. Generally, this provision is effective, but there are some exceptions. For instance, by the Arbitration Act, 1950, the court may grant an extension of time if of the opinion that undue hardship would otherwise be caused.

No dispute arises within the meaning of the clause where a charterer admits a shipowner's claim for freight but fails to satisfy it. Where a shipowner claimed freight and the charterer, having admitted the claim, sought to set off the amount due against his counter-claim the Court held that failure to appoint an arbitrator within the prescribed time barred the counter-claim but not the claim which was never in issue.

The question may arise as to whether an arbitration clause in a charter-party is imported into a bill of lading when the latter contains an incorporating clause such as "Freight and all other terms, conditions and exceptions, including the negligence clause, as per charter-party". It would seem that it is not, but as between a shipowner and a charterer who is also the shipper and who, in his capacity as shipper, has obtained a bill of lading, the arbitration clause in the charter-party remains effective even though the charter party contains a cesser clause, and even after the bill of lading has been assigned to a third party.

It appears that a merchant has no right to arrest a ship in respect of a dispute arising under a contract which contains an arbitration clause.

AGENCY

An **Agent** may be defined as a person having express or implied authority to represent or to act on behalf of another person, called the **Principal,** with the object of bringing the principal into legal relations with third parties.

Agency, which is the relationship between a principal and his agent, is generally (though not necessarily) created by a contract entered into by them.

Any person who is capable of entering into a contract on his own behalf may do so through an agent, and that is so even if the agent lacks the capacity to contract on his own behalf. However, a legal disability to contract personally cannot be overcome by appointing an agent, as an agent cannot be given powers which the principal himself does not possess.

A **Universal Agent** is one with unrestricted authority to contract on behalf of a principal. Needless to say, such appointments are extremely rare.

A **General Agent** is one with authority to act for his principal in all matters relating to a particular trade or business, or in some other general way.

A **Special Agent** is one given authority to do only some particular act, or to represent his principal in some specific transaction.

A **Mercantile Agent** is defined under the Factors Act as a mercantile agent having, in the customary course of his business as such agent, authority either to sell goods, or to consign goods for the purpose of sale, or to buy goods, or to raise money on the security of goods.

A **Del Credere Agent** is a mercantile agent who, in consideration of a higher rate of remuneration than is otherwise paid, undertakes that persons with whom he enters into contracts on behalf of his principal shall perform those contracts.

A **Factor** is a mercantile agent whose ordinary course of business is to sell or dispose of goods with the possession or control of which he is entrusted by his principal.

A **Broker** is an agent employed to make bargains and contracts of a mercantile character between other parties for a commission commonly called brokerage. The distinction between factors and brokers may be explained by stating that (i) brokers do not have possession of the goods, whereas factors do, (ii) a broker can sell only in the name of his principal, whilst a factor may sell in his own name.

An **Insurance Broker** is an agent employed to arrange a contract of insurance with an underwriter on behalf of his principal. In arranging the insurance the broker is merely an agent, but for the purpose of receiving payment of the money due from the assured and paying it to the underwriter he is a principal.

A **Banker** is the agent of his customer in respect of the customer's right to order the banker to pay cheques drawn on him, and in connection with other acts performed on the customer's behalf, but otherwise the relationship between banker and customer is normally that of debtor and creditor (such roles being reversed when the customer's account becomes overdrawn).

Creation of Agency by Express Appointment. There is no rule that the express appointment of an agent by a principal should take place in any particular form. But if an agent is to be authorised to contract under seal his appointment must be under seal also; in other words, he must be given power of attorney.

Creation of Agency by Implied Appointment. If A assumes to act for B, the assent of B will not be implied merely from his silence or acquiescence, unless the parties are so situated that it may be presumed that A acted on B's authority. In a sale by public auction the auctioneer is primarily the agent of the seller, but after the fall of the hammer he becomes, by implication of law, the agent of the buyer so that his signature binds both parties.

Agency of Necessity. In certain circumstances a person may become the agent of another without appointment, either express or implied. Such an agency is known as an agency of necessity. For example, a shipmaster who, in exceptional circumstances (seldom likely to be met with in modern conditions), pledges the cargo in the ship as security for money advanced to enable him to complete the voyage, is acting as an agent of necessity of the cargo owners. Ordinarily, of course, the master is only the bailee of the cargo, responsible for its custody, care, and proper delivery, but without authority to dispose of it or treat with it in any way.

Appointment by Ratification. Where an act is done in the name of or on behalf of a person without his authority by another person who assumes to act as his agent, the person in whose name or on whose behalf the act is done may, by ratifying the act, make it as valid and effectual as if it had been done originally by his authority. The person doing the act may be an already appointed agent who is exceeding his authority, or he may be a person having no authority to act in any matter at all, but no one other than the person in whose name or on whose behalf the act is done has power to ratify it.

Authority of an Agent. An agent has implied authority to do whatever is necessary for the effectual execution of his express authority. His authority, express or implied, cannot exceed the limits of the powers of his principal. He has implied authority to conform in pursuance of his agency with the usage and custom of the place where he is employed, unless such usage or custom is illegal or unreasonable, or would change the character of the agency.

Duties of an Agent to his Principal. An agent must carry out the terms of his agreement in accordance with the authority conferred upon him, and follow his principal's instructions so far as they are legal. In the absence of express instructions he must act according to custom, if any. If there is no custom he may exercise his proper discretion. He must use all due care, skill and diligence, and must not act in any way that would be inconsistent with his agency. He must pay over to his principal all money received on the latter's behalf, and keep such money and all other property of the principal, while in his custody, separate from his own money and property or that of other persons. He must always be ready with accounts of transactions that arise in the course of his agency, preserve documents relating to his principal's affairs, and produce them when required. He has no right to make profits without the knowledge and consent of his principal, and any so acquired must be paid over to the principal.

Liability to Principal. Apart from the special case of a "del credere" agent, an agent does not generally incur personal liability to his principal in respect of contracts made on the latter's behalf. He does become liable in damages to his principal if he is guilty of a breach of duty. He is not permitted to disclose to third persons confidential information entrusted to him in the course of his duties either during the period of his agency or after its termination.

Rights of an Agent against his Principal. An agent is entitled to remuneration unless he has undertaken to act gratuitously. Where the contract expressly states the remuneration, he is entitled to whatever is agreed upon; otherwise he is entitled to a reasonable remuneration. If the contract provides for the agent to be remunerated by commission it depends upon the precise construction of the contract whether such events have occurred as will entitle the agent to his commission. To claim his reward the agent must show that the transaction was due to his agency. In certain cases, depending on the actual terms of his employment, he may be entitled to commission in respect of transactions that arose after his employment had ceased. But if it can be shown that there is a well-established custom of trade whereby right to commission on business introduced ceases with the termination of the agency, then there will be no right to remuneration on orders executed subsequently. Even if the principal does not benefit from the performance of the agency, the agent is still entitled to remuneration if he has done what he contracted to do.

An agent has a right to be indemnified by his principal against losses, liabilities and expenses properly incurred by him in the course of his agency, and may sue to set off the value of such indemnity against any sum due from him to his principal. Ordinarily an agent has no right of action against his principal in respect of any contract made by him on the principal's behalf, even though the agent has made himself liable upon the contract to the third party. His remedy is simply by way of indemnity. Insurance brokers, however, may sue their principals for premiums in respect

D

of insurances entered into by them on the principal's behalf.

Where goods are legally obtained by an agent in his capacity as such, he has a general or particular lien on them for what is due to him from the principal upon such goods. If he has made himself personally liable for goods purchased on behalf of his principal he may exercise the right of stoppage *in transitu* in the same manner as he would be able to if the relationship between him and his principal were that of seller and buyer, respectively.

Delegation of Agent's Authority. Unless he has the express or implied assent of his principal, an agent has no power to delegate his authority to a deputy or substitute. The assent of the principal may be implied (i) by the custom of the trade or business concerned, (ii) where delegation to a sub-agent is necessary to the proper carrying out of the agency, (iii) in the event of a sudden emergency if there is extreme urgency and the agent is unable to communicate with his principal.

If an agent delegates to a sub-agent he is answerable to the principal for money received by such sub-agent to the use of the principal. He is also responsible to the principal for any loss or damage arising from the negligence, lack of skill, or breach of duty of the sub-agent. Even where an agent has authority to delegate, as a general rule no privity of contract exists between the principal and sub-agent, and the former cannot sue the latter for the negligent performance of his duties. However, if an agent delegates his entire employment to a substitute with the knowledge and consent of the principal, privity of contract may arise between the principal and the substitute and, if such was the intention of the agent and the substitute, the latter will become directly responsible to the principal for the proper performance of his duties.

If a sub-agent is appointed without the assent of the principal, the latter is not bound by the acts of the former.

Master of Chartered Ship—Whose Agent? Where the master is appointed by the shipowner and is, in fact, the latter's servant, all third parties, in the absence of any express notification otherwise, are justified in assuming that he will act as the agent of the shipowner. Where a ship has been chartered to be employed as a general ship, the master may be the agent of the owners or he may be the agent of the charterer. If, under the terms of the C/P, the charterer takes over full control of the ship, the master is generally the agent of the charterer. But this only happens when the charter amounts to a demise of the ship, in which case it is usual for the charterer to appoint his own master anyway. In cases of ambiguity, however, the tendency of the courts has usually been against treating the charter as a demise. The fact that the C/P itself provides that the master shall be the agent of the charterer is not binding on third parties who have had no notice of the fact, and the master in signing B's/L in such circumstances will be deemed to be doing so as agent of the owners who will therefore be rendered liable. A B/L clause stating "all conditions . . . etc., as per C/P" is not sufficient to give constructive notice to a shipper that the C/P makes the master the charterer's agent.

Consignment Clause in Charter-party. A C/P may contain a clause "Ship to employ Charterer's Agents at the port of loading". Where this is the case those agents automatically become the ship's agents when the ship arrives at the port concerned and the ship-owner, as principal, will be responsible for their acts on the ship's behalf, and they will have the usual agents' duty to use all care, skill and diligence in the performance of the agency. They will be mainly concerned with Customs formalities and dealing with port authorities, but not with ship's husbandry or formalities in connection with the crew, unless they are specifically instructed. They have no special jurisdiction over the master who may, and should if he has reason to consider it advisable, himself collect demurrage, advance freight, or other monies that may be due to the ship, and arrange for remission to the owners. Frequently, however, owners have their own agents at the port to whom the master can apply for advice and assistance with regard to customs of the port, supplies of fuel, stores and provisions, and so on, or when difficulties arise.

CHAPTER 3

THE SHIP

REGISTRY

COMPULSORY registration of British ships dates from the Navigation Acts from 1660 onwards. The original purpose was to confine the privileges of certain branches of British trade to vessels owned by British subjects and either built in the British dominions or captured as prize of war. Today, the law still requires that all British ships, with a few exceptions, shall be registered, but the objects of registration have changed with the times. There are nowadays two important points of public policy involved in registration, viz., (1) the question of who may be entitled to the privileges of the British flag, (2) evidence of title to ownership of the ship as property.

There are other advantages associated with registration. For instance, if in a vessel about to proceed beyond United Kingdom territorial waters it is desired to ship bonded or drawback stores, the vessel will have to be entered and cleared outwards at the Customs. This would not be possible without the production of a certificate of registry. In certain circumstances, as described in Chapter 15, the owner of a sea-going ship is permitted to limit his liability when, without his own personal fault or privity, loss of life or injury or loss of or damage to goods occurs for which his ship is responsible. In such cases the maximum liability is related to the tonnage of the ship concerned, so that a certificate of registry would be required in all but a few special cases to establish the appropriate tonnage figures. Future transactions in the ship, *i.e.,* transfers, transmissions, mortgages and the discharge of mortgages, are greatly facilitated by having the ship registered.

Owners' Qualifications. A ship is not deemed to be British unless owned wholly by persons who are (*a*) British subjects, or (*b*) bodies corporate established under and subject to the laws of some part of Her Majesty's dominions and having their principal place of business in those dominions.

British Subject. The term embraces naturalised as well as British-born persons, and all Commonwealth citizens. There are also special provisions enabling citizens of the Republic of Ireland to retain the status of British subjects under certain conditions.

Obligation to Register. Every British ship must be registered, unless exempted. Failure to register a non-exempted ship is not made a punishable offence, but such ship would not be recognised as British and may be detained until the master produces a certificate of registry.

Exempted Ships. There are two classes of ships exempted from the obligation to be registered, viz., (1) ships not exceeding 15 tons burden (*i.e.*, net registered tonnage) employed solely on the rivers or coasts of the United Kingdom or of the British possession in which the managing owners reside; (2) ships not exceeding 30 tons (net) and not having a whole or fixed deck employed solely in fishing or trading coastwise on the shores of Newfoundland, Gulf of St. Lawrence, and adjacent coasts of Canada.

Registrars. The M.S. Act provides for the following persons to be registrars:—

United Kingdom and Isle of Man—The Chief Officer of Customs.
Guernsey and Jersey—The Chief Officer of Customs together with the Governor.
Gibraltar—The Governor or a person appointed by him.
Various other British possessions—The Chief Officer of Customs, or Governor, or person appointed by the Governor.

There are well over one hundred registrars in the British Isles and some two hundred elsewhere.

Register Books. Every registrar must keep a register book with entries made in accordance with the following provisions:—

1. The ship is divided into 64 shares. This dates from 1823, but there seems to be much doubt about the reason for choosing that particular number. It is evidently a very convenient number inasmuch that it has seven factors, including itself and unity. It has been suggested that it may owe its origin to a former system of distributing prize money whereby the amount was first divided into eight shares, some of which were further subdivided into eighths.
2. Not more than 64 individuals or corporations may be registered as owners of one ship at the same time. A member of a company may claim through any registered owner or joint owner.
3. No person may be registered as owner of a fraction of a share. But any number not exceeding 5 may be registered as joint owners of a ship, or a share, or a group of shares.
4. Joint owners are regarded as "one person" and may not dispose of their joint interest in severalty.
5. A corporation may be registered as owner of a ship or share by its corporate name, and since most ships are owned by companies this is nowadays a common practice.

On first registry the register book will show the name of the ship and the name of the port to which she belongs, together with the following information:—

(i) Details of tonnage and build and other particulars descriptive of the identity of the ship as shown in the surveyor's certificate.

(ii) Particulars respecting her origin as stated in the declaration of ownership.

(iii) The name and description of the registered owner and, if more than one, the proportions in which they are interested, *i.e.*, the number of 64ths owned by them.

Further information may be added during the subsequent career of the ship depending on circumstances as shown below:—

(i) If the ship or any share is sold the name of the transferee must be entered. It is the duty of the vendee to register the transfer. Bills of sale are entered in the order of their production to the registrar.

(ii) If a ship or any share is transmitted to a qualified person on the death or bankruptcy of the registered owner, the name of the person entitled to be the owner (or persons, if more than one) under the transmission must be entered.

(iii) Mortgages are entered in the order of their production.

(iv) Discharged mortgages are entered on production of the mortgage deed endorsed with a receipt for the mortgage money.

(v) Transfers and transmissions of mortgages are entered.

(vi) Particulars are entered of registered alterations and the fact of a new certificate of registry being issued or the original certificate endorsed, as the case may be.

(vii) If registry is transferred from one port to another, that must be entered.

(viii) Any change of the ship's name would be entered.

Survey, Measurement and Marking. Prior to registry a ship must be surveyed and measured for tonnage in accordance with the tonnage regulations. Such measurement and survey may be undertaken by a surveyor appointed by an authorised Classification Society instead of by a surveyor of ships. For this purpose Lloyd's Register of Shipping and the British Committees of Bureau Veritas, American Bureau of Shipping, Det norske Veritas and Germanischer Lloyd are authorised Classification Societies. The surveyor grants a certificate specifying the tonnage, build, and other particulars descriptive of the vessel's identity, and this certificate must be delivered to the registrar.

The ship is required to be marked permanently in the following manner:—

(a) The name on each bow, and the name and port of registry on the stern, are to be in white or yellow on a dark ground or

in black on a light ground, the letters being at least one decimetre long and of proportionate breadth. (It is not necessary
for these to be cut into the fabric of the ship. The usual practice is to paint the lettering on the hull or to affix solid lettering.)

(b) The official number and the registered tonnage must be cut
in on the main beam. The "main beam" is nowadays taken
to be the after coaming of the main hatch or, in a tanker,
the dry hatch.

(c) For ships registered before 1st January 1974, the draught
scale on each side of the stem and stern in Roman numerals
or in figures of 6 inches in length must be cut in and painted
in white or yellow on a dark ground or black on a light
ground, or in some other approved way.

(d) Ships registered on or after the above date are to be marked
with a draught scale on each side of the stem and sternpost,
either of decimetres, or of metres and decimetres. The scale
is to be cut in and painted at two-decimetre intervals, the
figures being not less than one decimetre in length. and the
lower line of the figures coinciding with the draught line
indicated. Where the scale is in metres and decimetres, the
capital letter M is to be placed after each metre figure and
the top figures of the scale are to show both the metre and
decimetre figures.

All the above marks must be permanently continued. The
penalty for inaccurate, concealed or defaced marks is a fine not
exceeding £200.

It should be noted that the assignment and marking of load
lines does not enter into registry procedure at all. That is a matter
provided for by the M.S. (Load Lines) Act and is dealt with elsewhere
in this book.

Declaration of Ownership. No person is entitled to be registered
as the owner of a ship or share thereof until he has made and signed
a declaration of ownership containing:—

1. His qualification to own a British ship.
2. A statement of when and where the ship was built. (If the
   ship was foreign built at some place unknown, a statement
   to that effect must be made. In the case of a ship condemned as prize of war, particulars of the condemnation are
   required.)
3. The name of the master.
4. The number of shares of which he is entitled to be registered
   as owner.
5. A declaration that no unqualified person has an interest in
   the ship or share.

Further Evidence required on First Registry. The following
must be produced in addition to the declaration of ownership.

1. If the ship is British built, a **Builder's Certificate** giving particulars of the ship including her estimated tonnage, when, where and for whom she was built; and if there has been a sale, the **Bill of Sale.**

If foreign built, similar evidence is required, or a statement that the builder's certificate cannot be produced, if that is the case.

If the ship has been condemned by a prize court, a copy of the condemnation.

N.B.—A false statement in a bill of sale makes the offender liable to punishment consisting of a fine not exceeding £500.

When all the above evidence has been produced, and provided that all rules have been satisfactorily complied with, the registrar is required to enter the appropriate particulars in his register book.

The Carving Note. When it is proposed to register a ship, the owner or owners, or their accredited and testified agents, must apply to the registrar at the intended port of registry, supporting the application with the documents mentioned above. The registrar then issues to the owner what is usually referred to as a "carving note". This form shows the proposed name of the vessel, the name of the intended port of registry, estimated tonnage, official number, and a request that the necessary markings shall be made. When the ship has been satisfactorily "carved" the D.o.T. surveyor signs the carving note to that effect, and the Department return it to the owner. The latter can then deliver it back to the registrar who, on the strength of it, will issue the Certificate of Registry.

Certificate of Registry. This document contains all the details from the register book, including gross and register tonnage, and the name of the master. The name of the first master is endorsed on the face of the register. Subsequent masters have their names endorsed on the back by a registrar, or British consular officer, or an officer of the Court, according to the circumstances and place of the masters' appointment. The master does *not* sign the register. If the master is a certificated officer the number of his certificate of service or certificate of competency is also endorsed on the certificate of registry.

In the sense that it provides *prima facie* evidence of title to ownership, the certificate of registry is a private document. It is not, however, conclusive evidence, and proof that the owner was in fact an unqualified person would rebut any presumption that the ship was lawfully British. It is also a public document, showing that the ship is entitled to the privileges and subject to the duties of a British ship, and it must be produced on demand by various authorities. It also shows that the master is lawfully appointed. It may be used only for the lawful navigation of the ship, and is not subject to detention by an owner, a mortgagee, or any other person in respect of any claim. The master is the proper person to have custody of the certificate so long as he remains the lawful master.

Use of a certificate not legally granted is an offence rendering the ship liable to forfeiture.

The M.S. Act provides that if a person, whether interested in a ship or not, has the ship's certificate of registry in his possession and refuses to deliver it up to an officer of Customs on the latter's request, a court capable of taking cognisance of the matter may summon that person to appear before it and be examined. Unless it is proved to the satisfaction of the court that there was reasonable cause for refusal to deliver up the certificate, the offender shall be liable to a fine not exceeding £200. If it is proved to the court that the certificate is lost, the person summoned shall be discharged and the court shall certify that the certificate of registry is lost. If the person referred to is proved to have absconded, or if he persists in his refusal to deliver up the certificate, the court shall certify the fact, and the same proceedings may then be taken as in the case of a certificate being lost, mislaid, or destroyed.

Change of Master. When this occurs the succeeding master must have his name endorsed on the certificate of registry by a registrar, consular officer, or court officer.

Change of Ownership must be endorsed by the registrar of the port of registry or elsewhere, and the master, under penalty of £200 (max.), must deliver the certificate for such endorsement. The registrar is obliged to act so as not to detain the ship.

If the Ship is Lost, constructively lost, taken by the enemy in time of war, or transferred or transmitted to an unqualified person, the registrar must be notified and the master must deliver the certificate of registry (unless it is destroyed) to a registrar or consular officer under penalty of £200.

Procedure when Certificate of Registry is Lost. In the event of a ship's certificate of registry being mislaid, lost or destroyed, the registrar of her port of registry is required to grant a new certificate. But if the port, having a British registrar or consular officer, at which the ship is, or first arrives after the event, is not in the United Kingdom or British possession in which the ship is registered. then the master or some other person having knowledge of the facts of the case must make a declaration stating those facts and giving the names and descriptions of the registered owners to the best of his knowledge and belief. The registrar or consular officer is then required to grant a **Provisional Certificate of Registry** which should contain a statement of the circumstances in which it is granted.

Within ten days after the first subsequent arrival of the ship in the United Kingdom or possession in which she is registered the provisional certificate must be delivered up to the registrar of the ship's port of registry who must then grant a new certificate. Failure to comply with this requirement without reasonable cause is an offence punishable by a fine not exceeding £200.

If it is discovered when the ship is at sea that the certificate is not on board, it is possible that a quick recovery may be effected by notifying by radio the ship's agents in the last port of call. If the certificate is still in their hands, or has been left behind at the local consulate or shipping office, the agents may be able to airmail it to the ship's next port of arrival and thereby save the trouble of applying for a provisional certificate. In those cases, probably rare, where a provisional certificate is needed to replace temporarily a mislaid certificate, much trouble can be avoided by having all the information contained in the certificate available in a handy form. For this purpose a photostat copy, or simply a handwritten copy of the document, kept on board at all times, would be of tremendous value.

Ship becoming British-owned in Foreign Port. If a ship becomes British-owned when abroad and not at a port within Her Majesty's dominions, the British Consul may, on the application of the master, grant a provisional certificate of registry stating:—

(a) the name of the ship,
(b) the time and place of purchase and the names of the purchasers,
(c) the name of the master,
(d) the best particulars of tonnage, build and description which are available.

The Consul is required to forward a copy of the provisional certificate to the Registrar General of Shipping and Seamen.

In this case the provisional certificate is valid for six months or until the ship arrives at a port where there is a registrar, whichever happens first.

The usual procedure for obtaining a provisional certificate of registry in a foreign port involves the following.

The previous certificate of registry (*i.e.*, the foreign one) and the bill of sale, or photostat copies of those documents, are taken to the Consul so that the necessary particulars extracted from them can be entered into the provisional certificate.

The declaration of ownership must be made. This could be signed at the foreign port by someone having power of attorney from the owners, but a more practical alternative is for the owner to make his declaration at the port where the ship is to be registered, and for the registrar at that port to cable the Consul at the port where the ship is lying to confirm that the declaration is in his possession. The Consul will also require a letter or cablegram sent on behalf of the Home Office—Radio Regulation Division indicating the radio call sign (signal letters) that has been allocated to the ship. (Although signal letters are allocated by the H.O., application for them should be made to the Registrar General of Shipping and Seamen.) He will, in addition, need a letter or other confirmation from the local Collector of Customs to the effect that the ship's former foreign registry has been cancelled. In some countries, too, a permit from the appropriate government department would be required giving official approval of the "sale of the ship to aliens".

Before the ship sails from the foreign port the master should satisfy himself that the ship is in all respects seaworthy according to British standards, including proper documentation. If the load line certificate, safety and radio certificates, etc., or any of them, are out of date, the necessary surveys should be arranged and the certificates affected endorsed or renewed, as the case may be.

On arrival at the British port where the new certificate of registry is to be issued, the vessel will be surveyed and remeasured, her markings will be checked, and the new official number (and registered tonnage, if changed) will be cut in on the main beam, the old ones being obliterated.

Whilst on passage to the country where she is to be permanently registered, such a provisionally registered ship retains her original official number. Suppose, for example, that the ship's name is "California" and her existing port of registry is New York. The ship, if taken over in Galveston, would be described in the provisional certificate issued by the British Consul in Galveston as the "California" of New York, with the original official number shown. It would, however, be consistent with common practice to paint out New York on the ship's stern, but this does not matter. No rule is being broken if the old port of registry is allowed to remain on the stern until the ship is newly "carved".

If it is intended that the ship's name should be changed at the same time as the change of flag, the owner must arrange with the Secretary of the Marine Division, D.o.T., for the old and new names to be cabled to the British Consul so that he may enter the new name in the provisional certificate. It would seem that much expense and formality are avoided by renaming the ship at this stage instead of deferring it until after the ship has been formally registered.

Temporary Pass. In special circumstances the Commissioners of Customs in the United Kingdom, or the Governor of a British possession, may issue a temporary pass to enable an unregistered ship to proceed to sea from a port in Her Majesty's dominions to another such port (usually for the purpose of undergoing registration survey). Such a pass ranks for the time being as the equivalent of a certificate of registry, thus ensuring for the vessel all the privileges of a British ship, and extending to the owner the provisions of the Acts relating to limitation of liability.

REGISTRATION PROCEDURE IN SPECIAL CASES

(1) Ship built in United Kingdom for First Registry in a Commonwealth Country or British Colony.

In most cases the owner or his agent will apply to the registrar at the port where the ship is built, or to the registrar in London, to have a special pass issued to enable the vessel to sail to the port or country where she is to be registered. If application is made to a provincial registrar, he will forward it to London where the pass will be made out and returned to the provincial registrar for issue to the applicant. Although the usual markings, excluding the port of registry on the stern (and even that may be put in), will probably be made in the United Kingdom, they will not be checked, and no carving note is issued at this stage. On the ship's arrival at the Commonwealth or colonial port where she is to be registered, the local registrar will issue the carving note on the application of the owner or his agent. Thereafter, the local Marine Department surveyors will check the tonnage and markings, endorse the carving note, and return it to the owner. The latter, on delivering it to the local registrar, will be issued with a certificate of registry. This registrar will, as usual, require and retain the declaration of ownership, builder's certificate, and bill of sale (if one).

However, if there is time for the necessary documents to be completed and sent back and forth, it is possible for the ship to be completely registered as a colonial or Commonwealth ship while she is still in the United Kingdom, and this is sometimes done. In such a case the required documents will be delivered to the registrar abroad who will issue a carving note. This, which will indicate the official number and radio call sign allocated, will be sent to the United Kingdom. The ship will be marked, measured and surveyed here, and the carving note will be endorsed and returned to the port of registry abroad. The certificate of registry will be issued abroad and sent to this country in time for the ship to use it before she sails on her maiden voyage.

(2) Ship built or purchased in Foreign Country for Registry in the United Kingdom.

As already stated, the most usual procedure is for the ship to sail furnished with a provisional certificate of registry issued on the master's application by the British Consul. However, it is not necessarily the case that this provisional certificate will be in force until the ship arrives in the United Kingdom. For instance, a ship may be built, say, in Japan to be registered in London. The master may request the Consul at the Japanese port to issue a provisional certificate to enable the ship to go to Australia. Meanwhile, application to register is made in London. While in Australia, marks, tonnage, etc., are checked by the Marine Survey department there, registration is completed in the United Kingdom, and the certificate of registry sent to Australia. The certificate will be delivered to the master on his surrendering the provisional certificate. The ship could, in fact, remain long or altogether absent from the United Kingdom.

Here again it is possible for the ship's United Kingdom registration to be completed whilst she is still in the foreign port, but this takes time and is very seldom convenient except, perhaps, where the ship is being built in some near European continental port.

(3) Ship built or purchased in a British Port abroad for Registry in the United Kingdom.

The procedure is the same as that described in (2) above, except that a temporary pass would be granted by the Commissioners of Customs or the Governor of the British possession instead of a provisional certificate of registry.

Where the duration of such a pass is fixed by reference to the voyage to be undertaken it does not become invalid by reason of no time being mentioned. To obtain the pass the owner would first be required to produce proof of title (by builder's certificate and/or bill of sale) together with a certificate of survey.

In this case, also, United Kingdom registration could be completed while the ship was still at the place of building, if time permitted.

(4) Ship built or purchased in a Foreign Port for Registry in a British Possession abroad.

The procedure is the same as that described in (2) above, calling for the issue of a provisional certificate of registry.

(5) Ship built or purchased in a British Port abroad for Registry in some other British Port abroad.

The procedure is the same as that described in (3) above, calling for the granting of a temporary pass.

(6) Existing Foreign Ship becoming British-owned in the United Kingdom.

When a British ship is sold to a foreign purchaser abroad (which can be done only after a "certificate of sale" has been applied for and granted by the registrar) it is usually the case that the foreign authorities will demand evidence of the closure of the ship's British registration. Similar evidence, however, is not required by a United Kingdom registrar when a ship is bought from a foreigner to be registered in this country. Here the registrar will be satisfied so long as the visa of the British consular officer in the country from which the ship is being purchased appears on the bill of sale.

(7) British-built Ship becoming Foreign-owned after Delivery abroad.

It would seem that a problem has arisen in a case where a ship was built in the United Kingdom for delivery to a foreign purchaser at a foreign port, but which was to remain the property of the builder until she was delivered. It was held in this case that the vessel was not a British ship so as to require to be registered. All the same, it is generally held that the nationality of the owners is the criterion of the nationality of the ship as far as regards the duties and liabilities of the owners and persons belonging to the ship, and that is so even if the ship flies the flag of a foreign country. Presumably, however, there would be nothing to prevent the builder-cum-owner from registering the vessel as a British ship if he thought the circumstances justified such a step, even though not compelled to do so.

REGISTRATION OF GOVERNMENT-OWNED SHIPS

Except where for certain purposes it is specially provided, the M.S. Acts do not apply to ships belonging to Her Majesty. But, by the 1906 Act, Her Majesty may by Order-in-Council make regulations as to the manner in which Government ships may be registered as British ships for the purposes of the M.S. Acts. Government ships are ships not forming part of Her Majesty's Navy which belong to Her Majesty or are held by a person on behalf of or for the benefit of the Crown and which, for that reason, cannot be registered under the principal Act. Post Office cable ships used to be included in that category when the G.P.O. was a department of State, but since it became a Public Corporation such ships require to be registered. A number of such Orders in-Council have been made from time to time enabling Government ships both at home and overseas to be registered.

REGISTRATION OF YACHTS AND FISHING BOATS

Section 2 of the principal Act demands that every British ship, unless exempted, shall be registered, while section 742 defines a "ship" as any vessel used in navigation not propelled by oars. As mentioned earlier, apart from certain Canadian vessels, the only vessels exempted are those under 15 tons solely employed on the coasts and rivers of the United Kingdom or British possession in which the managing owners reside. Accordingly, all yachts over 15 tons are required to be registered, and even those under 15 tons if they depart from the coastal waters of the United Kingdom or country where they are owned. It is well known that a very large number of yachts which ought to be registered are, in fact, unregistered. Such vessels, therefore, are not lawfully recognised as British ships and are deprived of the benefits conferred by the M.S. Acts upon British ships though they remain exposed to the liabilities attaching thereto. The official view appears to be that any attempt to enforce all owners of unregistered yachts to comply with the law relating to registration would be impracticable. Though they are not committing any punishable offence, such owners are liable to make unnecessary difficulties for themselves particularly over such matters as transfer of ownership. They would also be unable, on the occasions when they leave territorial waters, to ship bonded or drawback stores.

Pleasure yachts under 45 feet (13.7 metres) in length overall which are registered will be measured for tonnage under a system introduced in Part 4 of the M.S. (Tonnage) (Amendment) Regulations 1975 as amended. The measurements may now be taken either by a surveyor appointed by an authorised Classification Society, or a measurer appointed by the Royal Yachting Association, or by the Yacht Brokers, Designers and Surveyors Association, or as previously by a D.o.T. surveyor of ships.

What has been said about yachts applies equally to fishing boats. Subject to certain exemptions, every fishing boat is required to be lettered and numbered, to have official papers, and to be entered in the fishing boat register. But these formalities are additional to the requirement under which it is obligatory for all fishing boats to be registered as "ships" unless exempted. So in the event of a fishing boat requiring duty-free stores she would need to be registered as a "ship" and be measured for tonnage in the same way as other registered ships. Her "fishing boat tonnage" would not be acceptable for this purpose.

The M.S. (Unregistered Ships) Regulations 1972. These regulations declare that certain provisions of the M.S. Act 1970 and regulations made thereunder shall extend to British ships which (1) are required to be registered but are not so registered, (2) are not required to be registered because they do not exceed 15 tons burden and are employed solely on the rivers or coasts of the United Kingdom and Republic of Ireland, and to masters and seamen employed in them. Fishing vessels and vessels belonging to a general lighthouse authority are not subject to these regulations.

With regard to ships which are required to be registered, the following sections of the Act apply, viz. 1 to 4, 5 (with a modification), 7 to 14, 21 to 23, 25 to 31, 33 to 35, 37 to 42, 48, 61 to 69, 73, 74 and 76 to 79. The following regulations also apply to them, viz.:—

Crew Agreements, lists of Crew and Discharge of Seamen.
Seamen's Wages and Accounts.
Seamen's Wages (Contributions).
Seamen's Allotments.
Provisions and Water.
Disciplinary Offences.
Repatriation.
Property of Deceased Seamen.
Official Log Books.

With regard to ships which are not required to be registered, the following sections of the Act apply, viz. 27, 39, 40, 42, 61 (with modifications), 62 to 64 and 67. The Repatriation Regulations also apply to them except for regulations 8 to 10.

MORTGAGE OF SHIP OR SHARE

The instrument of mortgage must be in the statutory form as prescribed by the First Schedule to the principal Act, and the mortgage should be registered. If there is more than one mortgage they rank in priority according to their dates of registration, not according to the date of mortgage. Except as far as may be necessary for making the ship or share available as security for the mortgage debt, the mortgagee is not deemed to be the owner of the ship or share which still remains in the ownership of the mortgagor. A mortgagee enjoys a statutory right to dispose of the ship or share in respect of which he is registered but, in practice, he is usually bound by a separate agreement not to do so unless the mortgagor defaults. Transfers and transmissions of mortgages are required to be entered by the registrar in his register book. Transmission of a mortgage is required to be authenticated by a declaration of the person to whom the interest is transmitted in a similar manner to the transmission of ownership.

A shipowner who desires to use his ship (or a share thereof) as security for a mortgage debt usually arranges to mortgage it to a bank.

A registered mortgage is not affected by the bankruptcy of the mortgagor.

A registered owner desirous of disposing, by way of mortgage or sale, of the ship at a place out of the country in which the port of registry is situate may apply to the registrar who may then grant a certificate of mortgage or a certificate of sale. There are various restrictions, however, on the granting of such certificates and an applicant is required to give the registrar certain information for entry into his register book.

Mortgage of Ship to a Bank. A shipowner, or a prospective shipowner, is not always in a position to purchase a vessel outright, pay the cost of any repairs and alterations, equip the vessel for some particular form of employment, and meet all the incidental expenses involved in preparing the ship for a voyage, out of his immediate resources. Hence, it will often occur that a banker is approached to aid the shipowner by accepting the security of the ship in return for a mortgage loan.

As, by the M.S. Act, the mortgagor retains the status of owner, the mortgagee does not incur liabilities to third parties and it is not essential for him to be a British subject.

The banker, naturally, will wish to avoid any necessity of having to enforce the mortgage. Therefore, in deciding whether to accept the security of the ship, he will be influenced not only by the personal integrity of the borrower but also by the general state of shipping and the particular prospects of the mortgagor. He will engage a professional ship valuer to assess the value of the security and, to ensure that the ship substantially maintains its value, he will require that the ship be classed by one of the recognised societies and kept in class through periodic survey and repair. For his further protection the banker will consider it desirable to have a collateral deed of agreement drawn up providing, amongst other things, that the mortgage shall be a security for such sums as the bank may decide to advance from time to time, that the advances shall be payable on demand, that the ship shall retain her British nationality and be registered at a United Kingdom port, and that she shall be kept free of any other charge or maritime lien. Liens arising out of tort, obviously, must be excluded from this provision. It will also be required of the mortgagor that he shall keep the vessel adequately insured and do nothing to render the insurance void or voidable. Such deed will generally provide that the mortgage shall become enforceable (1) should there be a default in the payment of principal or interest, possibly allowing seven days' grace, (2) in the event of breach of covenant (*e.g.*, failure to keep the ship seaworthy, or failure to keep her insured), (3) should the mortgagor become bankrupt or go into liquidation, (4) in the event of the arrest or seizure of the ship, and possibly on the happening of other events.

If the borrower mortgages another one of his ships to the bank it is customary for the collateral deed in respect of the second ship to contain, either directly or by reference, the covenants as in the first collateral deed, and a clause providing that all monies secured by the previous mortgage shall be deemed to be secured on the second vessel also, and *vice versa*. Another clause is necessary to provide that the borrower shall not be entitled to redeem one mortgage without at the same time repaying outstanding amounts in respect of the other.

If the mortgagor is a company the mortgage must be registered with the Registrar of Companies as well as being registered in the Shipping Register. The latter registry is acknowledged by the registrar and endorsed on the mortgage document stating the date and hour of the day when registration was made. A first mortgage will be described in the registrar's memorandum and in the register book as "Mortgage A". Any subsequent ones will be denoted by successive letters of the alphabet. This alphabetical notation can be relied on as evidence that there are no prior encumbrances on the register. The banker will, nevertheless, usually obtain a transcript of the entries in the register. A personal search may be made for a fee of a small sum for each ship inspected, but for a transcript a somewhat larger fee is charged. The latter, however, has the advantage that the details are extracted by experts and are certified as correct by the registrar. Moreover, the M.S. Act provides that the transcript is admissible in evidence in any court. Search of the register may reveal that a certificate of sale or a certificate of mortgage has been issued. The existence of the former would obviously render a proposed mortgage out of the question. The latter would give warning that any mortgage raised in pursuance of the certificate and endorsed thereon by a registrar or British consul would take priority over the one proposed.

The insurance of the ship will normally include the usual marine risks, war risks, and club or mutual insurance, and since it is customary for the ship to be insured by the mortgagor there is a risk that, in the event of total loss of the ship, the proceeds of the insurance will be available for the mortgagor's creditors in general.

To meet this difficulty the banker will probably obtain an undertaking from the underwriters that they will hold the policies and proceeds of claims on behalf of the bank and that the insurers will notify the bank in the event of premiums or calls being unpaid when they fall due.

SHIP'S NAME

The principal Act lays down that a ship shall not be described by any name other than its registered name which cannot be changed without the consent of the D.o.T. To change the name of a ship requires an application in writing and such notice published as the Department may require. Notice of a proposed change is usually published in Lloyd's List and other shipping papers and is displayed in Mercantile Marine Offices and Custom Houses. The notice will include a request that any objection to the proposed name should be notified to the Registrar-General of Shipping and Seamen at Cardiff. When permission is given, the name must be changed forthwith on the bows and stern of the ship and in the certificate of registry. The penalty for non-compliance is a fine not exceeding £200.

A ship having once been registered may not be re-registered under any name other than her original registered name without previous written permission from the D.o.T.

Where a foreign ship becomes British-owned she may not without previous written permission be registered except by the name she bore at the time of her becoming British.

By the 1906 M.S. Act it is provided that the D.o.T. may refuse the registry of any ship by a name that is already the name of a registered British ship or a name so similar as to be calculated to deceive. Amending regulations, dated 1979, modify this, however, with the proviso that they may allow registry by the proposed name if satisfied that the ship is intended to replace another of the same name which within 10 years of the date of the application belonged to the same owner when her British registry was closed, or which within 10 years of the date of the application was sold by the same owner on condition that her name should be changed and her name has been changed. Hence, it is possible for two ships of the same name to be registered as British ships at the same time. Since 1936 yachts have been under the same rules as regards names as commercial ships.

REGISTRY OF ALTERATIONS

If the particulars of a ship's tonnage and description which appear in the register book are altered, the owner must apply for registration of the alteration, or for renewal of registry. Failure to comply is an offence punishable by a fine not exceeding £200 plus £20 for each day of the continuance of the default. If the alteration involves a change in any of the ship's principal dimensions (length, breadth, or depth), or if there is a change of the means of propulsion, registry anew is insisted upon.

REGISTRY ANEW

Where the ownership of a ship is changed, the new owner may have the ship registered anew, but this is not essential. However, renewal of registry would be necessary if a ship reappeared which had been presumed lost and had had her original registry closed in consequence. So it would in the case of a ship, originally British, which had been sold to foreigners and subsequently bought back again. Such registration would entail application to re-use the ship's name, a declaration of ownership, certificate of survey, marking and carving, a certificate of seaworthiness, and payment of fees. The ship would be re-allocated her original official number— so long as a ship remains British that is never changed.

TRANSFER OF REGISTRY

Should an owner wish to transfer the registry of a ship from one port of registry to another, he must first obtain the approval of the D.o.T. Subject to such approval, registry may be transferred from one port to another on application to the registrar of the existing port of registry made by a declaration in writing of all the persons appearing in the register to be interested as owners or mortgagees (without affecting the rights of those persons). On receipt of such application the registrar is required to transmit a notice to the registrar of the intended port of registry with a copy of all particulars relating to the ship and the names of all persons appearing to be interested. The ship's certificate of registry must be delivered up to the registrar either of the existing or intended port of registry, and if to the former, transmitted by him to the latter. On receipt of the documents mentioned, the registrar of the intended port of registry is required to enter in his register book all the particulars and names transmitted to him and grant a fresh certificate of registry. The ship is then considered registered at the new port and the name of that port must be substituted for the former name on the stern of the ship.

It may be asked what advantage there is in transferring a ship's registry from one port to another. Amongst British shipowners there has always been a diversity of practice in respect of where their ships are registered. Some owners, perhaps partly for business and partly for sentimental reasons, prefer to register their vessels at the port where they have always registered them. Some may register them where they are built, and others may adopt still different policies. However, there are no doubt cases where a transfer could be a distinct advantage. Suppose an owner with a fleet of ships all registered, say, at Hull, manages his ships from that port and resides in that neighbourhood. He might purchase as an addition to his fleet an existing ship which is registered at Belfast. Obviously, if he envisages future transactions taking place in respect of that ship, it will be more convenient for him to negotiate through the Hull registrar than to deal at a distance with Belfast where he may not have a permanent agent.

TRANSFERS OF SHIPS

When the ownership of a ship changes as a result of some voluntary act such as sale or deed of gift, the ownership is said to be "transferred". Transfers of ships which require to be registered can only be made by bill of sale. Thus, should a registered ship be "given" by one party to another, the recipient of such gift would have to "purchase" it for some nominal sum—say, 5p—for the purpose of executing a bill of sale. The function of this recording document is similar to the function of a title deed of real property, and it provides the evidence of entitlement on which a registrar can act. If the ship is to be sold to a foreign purchaser the registrar will close the British register. If sold to a British subject the purchaser will be registered as the new owner. The bill of sale must be in the form given in the First Schedule to the principal Act, or as nearly so as possible, showing the names of the parties, the consideration paid together with a receipt, and a description of the identity of the ship conforming to the information contained in the certificate of registry and the surveyor's certificate. It must also show that the vendor covenants with the vendee that he has power to transfer the ship and its equipment, and that the ship is free from encumbrances other than those, if any, which appear by the registry of the ship. The transferee cannot be registered until he has made a **Declaration of Transfer** containing a statement of his qualification to own a British ship.

The transferor signs the Bill of sale, which is exempt from stamp duty, in the presence of a witness or witnesses and with it the ship passes to the purchaser with everything then on board necessary for the prosecution of the voyage, or whatever may afterwards be brought on board to replace what was there originally. The onus is then on the purchaser to have the change of ownership registered, or the ship registered anew, as the case may be, and the fact of this being done will be endorsed by the registrar on the bill of sale so as to show the date and hour of registration. In the event of the ship being disposed of out of the country in which the port of registry is situate, the registered owner must apply for the granting of a certificate of sale.

TRANSMISSION OF SHIPS

Involuntary transfer of the property in a ship through death or bankruptcy, and formerly through marriage, is known as "transmission". (As the result of a long process mainly effected by equity and various statutes culminating in the passing of the Law Reform (Married Women and Tortfeasors) Act, 1935, married women are now able to hold property of their own so that transmissions through marriage are no longer possible.) If the ship or share is transmitted to a qualified person, then after authentication by **Declaration of Transmission** and production of evidence, the change of ownership must be registered in the usual way. It may happen, however, that a ship or share is transmitted to an alien, in which case the law does not permit him to take possession of the property. His proper procedure is to apply, within four weeks after the event which has given rise to the transmission, to the appropriate court (High Court in England) for an order for the sale of the property transmitted. The Court may then make such an order and direct that the proceeds of sale, after deducting the expenses thereof, be paid to the person entitled under the transmission. Since a foreigner cannot execute a bill of sale in respect of a British ship the order of the Court is required to contain a declaration vesting in some person named by the Court the right to transfer the ship or share, and that person becomes lawfully entitled to perform the transfer as if he were the registered owner of the ship or share. If application is not made within the four weeks or such further time (not exceeding one year) as the Court may allow, the property is subject to forfeiture.

Since the vast majority of commercial ships are nowadays owned by limited companies, transmissions of the kind described are seldom likely to occur except, perhaps, in respect of such craft as private yachts. Some special cases of transmissions arose when, through nationalisation, such bodies as the National Coal Board, the British Transport Commission, and the Regional Gas and Electricity Boards took over ships previously belonging to companies.

THE MANAGING OWNER

The principal Act requires that the name and address of the managing owner of every registered ship shall be registered at the Custom House of the port of registry. If there is no managing owner, then there must be registered the name of the ship's husband or other person entrusted with management. Non-compliance with this rule renders the owners liable to a fine not exceeding £200 every time the ship leaves a United Kingdom port.

The term "managing owner" is regarded purely as a commercial term, not as a legal expression. In practice a managing owner may be an actual owner or part owner. On the other hand, he may be a person employed by the owner or owners to manage the ship. It is often the case that a director of a shipping company is registered as managing owner of the company's ships.

NATIONAL CHARACTER AND FLAG

The master of a ship must declare the nationality of the ship before he will be granted clearance or transire by H.M. Customs, and the nationality must be inscribed on the clearance form or transire.

Using the British flag or assuming the British national character on board a ship wholly or partly owned by unqualified persons renders the ship subject to forfeiture, unless it is done to escape capture by an enemy or by a foreign warship in the exercise of a belligerent right.

Concealment of British character or the assumption of foreign character by a British ship similarly renders the ship liable to forfeiture and the master, if he commits or is privy to the commission of the offence, is guilty of an indictable offence.

If an unqualified person acquires otherwise than by transmission any legal or beneficial interest in a ship using the British flag or assuming the British character such interest is subject to forfeiture.

A ship not recognised as British is not entitled to the benefits, privileges, advantages or protection usually enjoyed by British ships, but, as regards the payment of dues, liability to fines and forfeitures and punishment of offences committed on board by persons belonging to the ship, such ship shall be dealt with as if she were recognised as British.

The red ensign without defacement or modification is declared to be the proper national colours for all ships and boats belonging to any British subject except in the case of Her Majesty's ships or boats or those allowed to wear other national colours in pursuance of a warrant.

If a British ship, without warrant, wears any colours except the red ensign or Union Jack with a white border, the owner, master, or other person responsible is liable on conviction on indictment to a fine, or on summary conviction to a fine not exceeding £1000.

Any full-pay commissioned officer of the Royal Navy or military service, or any British officer of customs or consular officer, may board a ship and seize colours hoisted contrary to the Act.

Obligation to display National Colours. The Act provides that national colours must be shown:—

(1) on receiving a signal from one of Her Majesty's ships,

(2) when entering or leaving a foreign port,

(3) in a ship of 50 tons gross or more, when entering or leaving a British port.

The penalty for non-compliance is a fine not exceeding £200, but this does not apply to fishing boats duly lettered and numbered.

It should be noted that the Act does not make any distinction between day and night with respect to the obligation to show colours. The section has often been interpreted, rightly or wrongly, to mean that when entering, or leaving port colours should be displayed whenever there is sufficient light for them to be distinguishable. Nowadays, in view of the fact that floodlighting, searchlights, and other forms of effective illumination may be employed, it would seem to be good practice to comply strictly with the letter of the law and show national colours when entering or leaving port at any hour of the day or night.

The practice of hoisting the red ensign at the fore-yard or other suitable position by foreign ships in British ports, and the flag of the country visited by British ships in foreign ports, seems to be more widespread than it used to be. No official objection is raised to this use of a "courtesy flag" provided, of course, that it is displayed in such a position that it will not give a misleading impression of the nationality of the ship concerned. On at least one occasion recently the master of a ship came under severe criticism in a port abroad for neglecting this "courtesy", but most seamen would probably agree that that is going too far.

BLUE ENSIGN

Regulations for Wearing the Blue Ensign. British merchant ships are allowed to wear the Blue Ensign plain and undefaced, under the authority of a Warrant issued by the Secretary of State for Defence, subject to the following conditions being fulfilled:—

The officer commanding a ship other than a fishing vessel must be an officer on the retired or emergency list of the Royal Navy or a Commonwealth Navy, or an officer on the active or retired lists of any branch of the Reserves of such navies. If the rank held on one of these lists by the officer is below that of Commander, at least one other officer in the ship's company must be an officer on one of the lists mentioned.

Before hoisting the Blue Ensign, the officer commanding the ship must be in possession of a warrant.

The officer in command of a ship who fails to fulfil the above conditions, unless failure is due to death or other circumstances over which he has no control, will no longer be entitled to hoist the Blue Ensign in the ship. The Blue Ensign is in no circumstances to be worn if the officer to whom the warrant was issued is not in command of the ship or if the ship changes to foreign ownership.

Before the Blue Ensign may be hoisted in a vessel other than that

for which the warrant was originally granted but in the same ownership, the officer should report the name, official number, tonnage and
trade of the vessel to the Ministry of Defence.

Officers commanding Her Majesty's ships, British Consuls in
foreign ports and Customs Officers in the Commonwealth, are
empowered to ascertain that ships wearing the Blue Ensign are
provided with warrants, and that the foregoing conditions and
regulations are complied with.

The Captain of one of Her Majesty's ships meeting a ship wearing
the Blue Ensign may, in order to ascertain that these instructions
are being strictly obeyed, send on board at any convenient opportunity an officer not below the rank of Lieutenant. The restriction
as to rank of the boarding officer is in no way to limit or otherwise
affect the authority or the duties of naval officers either under the
Merchant Shipping Acts or in time of war.

If it should be found that although the ship is provided with a
warrant, the above regulations are not complied with, a report
should be made to the Ministry of Defence.

If it is found that the ship is wearing the Blue Ensign without a
warrant, the Blue Ensign should be seized, and the case reported to
the Ministry of Defence.

A list of the officers (with their shipping companies) to whom
warrants have been issued will be prepared annually by the Ministry
of Defence for publication in the Spring Edition of the "Navy List".

Relinquishing the Blue Ensign. The warrant to hoist the Blue
Ensign must be returned by the officer to whom it is granted to the
Ministry of Defence when he ceases (*a*) to command a vessel belonging
to the owners named on the warrant, (*b*) to belong to any of the
naval forces specified above.

The Royal Standard. In the event of a visit by Her Majesty the
Queen to a merchant ship, the appropriate place for the Royal
Standard to be worn is at the mainmast head.

TONNAGE

It is important to distinguish between two entirely different
classes of tonnage figures, viz., (1) those which relate to weight
(actual tons of 2,240 lb. or tonnes of 1,000 kg.), and (2) those which
relate to measurement.

In the former class there are:—

light displacement,
load displacement,
deadweight carrying capacities when loaded to tropical,
summer, and winter load lines respectively.
deadweight at some particular mean draught.
The latter class includes:—

underdeck tonnage,
gross tonnage,
net register tonnage,
Suez Canal tonnage,
Panama Canal tonnage.

Light Displacement is the total weight of the hull, machinery, fittings, spare parts and all permanent equipment, and (in the case of a steamship) water in boilers up to the working level.

Load Displacement is the weight of the ship when loaded to the depth of her seasonal load line. The load displacement at the depth of the summer load line in sea water is the figure normally quoted.

Deadweight Carrying Capacity may be defined as the difference between the light and load displacements, so that for instance:—

> **Tropical Deadweight** is the difference between light displacement and the displacement when submerged in sea water to the depth of the tropical load line.

> **Summer Deadweight, Winter Deadweight** and the deadweights at other assigned load lines may be defined in a similar way.

Deadweight at any particular draught is the difference between the light displacement and the displacement at that draught.

N.B.—Since the light displacement does not include fuel, consumable stores, feed water, and so on, these weights must therefore be included in the deadweight. Hence, the deadweight carrying capacity is not an indiction of the weight of cargo a vessel can lift. Her cargo carrying capacity will be the deadweight less the weights of fuel, stores, etc.

BRITISH TONNAGE

For registration purposes the unit employed in assessing the tonnage of a ship is the "measurement ton" or "register ton" which is 100 cu. ft. (or 2.83 cubic metres) of space, and has nothing to do with weight. A ship's certificate of registry shows gross tonnage and register tonnage, each expressed in both tons and cubic metres. In the case of a ship to which alternative tonnages are assigned these are shown in the same way.

From 1st March 1967, the tonnage of any U.K. registered ship is to be ascertained in accordance with the Merchant Shipping (Tonnage) Regulations, 1967, made by the then B.O.T. under powers conferred by the Merchant Shipping Act, 1965. These Regulations give effect to an I.M.C.O. recommendation with regard to the treatment of shelter deck and certain other spaces for tonnage measurement purposes, thereby providing for the allocation of alternative tonnages or, in certain circumstances if desired, permanently reduced tonnages. This means that the tonnage openings previously required to qualify for reduced tonnage can now be permanently closed for reasons of safety without prejudicing the reduced tonnage.

The M.S. Tonnage Regulations 1967 have been amended by Part 3 of the M.S. (Tonnage) (Amendment) Regulations 1975 (as amended) to provide for the measurement and survey of a ship, for the purpose of ascertaining its tonnage, to be undertaken by a surveyor appointed by an authorised Classification Society instead of by a surveyor of ships. An authorised Classification Society means Lloyd's Register of Shipping, or any one of the British Committees of Bureau Veritas, American Bureau of Shipping, Det norske Veritas and the Germanischer Lloyd. Before his ship can be registered in the United Kingdom, a prospective British shipowner must apply to Lloyd's Register of Shipping or one of the other authorised Societies to have this ship surveyed and measured for tonnage. The Society and its surveyors will then exercise all the functions (except certification of crew accommodation) previously carried out by the D.o.T., and issue the Certificate of British Tonnage on completion of the survey and measurement.

All measurements required by the Regulations must be expressed in feet and decimal fractions of a foot and tonnage (as hitherto) is measured in terms of cubic capacity, 100 cubic feet representing 1 ton.

Certificates. The D.o.T. or the authorised Classification Society issue to the owner of every ship, the tonnage of which has been ascertained in accordance with the Regulations, a Certificate of British Tonnage showing (a) name, port of registry and official number of ship; (b) registered dimensions; (c) gross tonnage and tonnage of each of the components thereof; (d) register tonnage and deductions and allowances made in ascertainment thereof; (e) where applicable particulars of spaces the tonnage of which is excluded in ascertaining reduced or alternative tonnages; (f) the position in which any tonnage mark assigned is to be placed.

There are three forms of these certificates, as follows:—

> Surveys 53 for a ship to which no tonnage mark has been assigned.
>
> Surveys 53A for a ship to which alternative tonnages and a tonnage mark have been assigned.
>
> Surveys 53B for a ship with permanently reduced tonnages and with a tonnage mark placed corresponding to the load line marks which have been assigned on the assumption that the second deck is the freeboard deck. In this case the position of the tonnage mark is in line with the deepest load line to which the ship may be loaded (i.e., normally the tropical fresh water load line).

Gross Tonnage. Subject to the provisions in respect of modified or alternative tonnages, the gross tonnage is the sum of:—

(a) underdeck tonnage;

(b) tonnage of space between second deck and upper deck;

(c) tonnage of permanently closed-in spaces on or above upper deck including breaks situated above the line of the deck but excluding (i) tonnage of hatchways, (ii) tonnage of framed-in spaces on or above upper deck which contain any part of propelling machinery or which light or ventilate such spaces, (iii) other spaces as given in separate list further on;

(d) "excess of hatchways" (*i.e.*, aggregate tonnage of all hatchways less $\frac{1}{2}$ of 1 per cent of gross tonnage excluding such aggregate);

(e) tonnage of framed-in spaces on or above upper deck which contain any part of propelling machinery or which light or ventilate such spaces if (i) owner has made written application for inclusion of such spaces in propelling machinery space, (ii) they are permanently marked to show their purpose and (iii) they are certified by a surveyor of ships as safe, seaworthy, properly constructed, reasonable in extent and unusable for any other purpose.

Permanently Closed-in Spaces on or above Upper Deck. These include:—

(a) Poop, bridge or forecastle, unless opening in end bulkhead extends from deck to deck or for one half or more of breadth of deck in way of bulkhead.

(b) Deckhouse, unless opening in boundary bulkhead extends from deck to deck for one half or more of length of bulkhead and is 4 feet wide or more.

(c) Side to side structure, unless opening in ship's side extends for one half or more of length of space it serves and exceeds in height one third of distance from deck to deck in way of opening or 2 feet 6 inches, whichever is the greater.

(d) Passage way at ship's side, unless it is 4 feet wide or more and open to weather at one or both ends.

(e) Recess, unless it extends from deck to deck for three feet or more of its width and is exposed to weather.

(f) Any space having opening in deck over being a deck exposed to weather, unless area of opening is one quarter or more of deck area over space.

Underdeck Tonnage. This is the sum of (a) tonnage of space below tonnage deck bounded by (i) tonnage deck, (ii) upper surface of double bottom tanks, open floors or ceiling, (iii) inner face of timbers, frames or sparring (with certain limitations in special cases and excluding breaks above line of tonnage deck); (b) tonnage of shaft bossings and appendages forming part of hull below tonnage deck.

Closed-in Spaces on or above Upper Deck not included in Gross Tonnage. These are:—

(*a*) dry cargo space, unless in break above line of upper deck;

(*b*) machinery and condenser space;

(*c*) wheelhouse, chart room, radio and navigational aids spaces;

(*d*) skylights, domes and trunks for light or ventilation;

(*e*) chain lockers, anchor gear and capstan spaces;

(*f*) space for storing safety equipment or batteries;

(*g*) companions and access hatches protecting stairways and openings over stairways;

(*h*) galley and bakery;

(*i*) washing and sanitary accommodation for crew or master;

(*j*) workshops and store rooms for use of pumpmen, engineers, carpenters and boatswains, and lamp room;

(*k*) water ballast tanks not usable for other purposes;

(*l*) shelter space for use free of charge by deck passengers in ships on voyages not exceeding 10 hours duration;

(*m*) sheltered promenade space, glassed in and unfurnished except for deck chairs or portable seating in ships making international voyages.

The above must be certified by a surveyor as reasonable in extent, properly constructed and permanently marked to show their purpose.

Register Tonnage. This is the tonnage obtained by deducting from the gross tonnage (*a*) the tonnage of the spaces listed below, (*b*) the allowance for propelling machinery space. No deduction may be made in respect of any space which has not first been included in the gross tonnage.

Spaces to be Deducted. These are:—

(*a*) master's accommodation;

(*b*) crew accommodation, except space for storage of fresh water and space for storage of provisions, being in the latter case space in excess of 15 per cent of the aggregate of (i) master's accommodation, and (ii) crew accommodation other than space for provisions and water;

(*c*) wheelhouse, chart room, radio and navigational aids spaces;

(*d*) chain lockers, anchor gear and capstan spaces;

(*e*) space for storing safety equipment or batteries;

(*f*) workshops and store rooms for use of pumpmen, electricians, carpenters and boatswains, and lamp-room;

(*g*) donkey engine and boiler spaces if outside propelling machinery space and connected to main pumps;

(h) space occupied by main pumps if outside propelling machinery space;

(i) sail room in sailing ships if not exceeding 2½ per cent of gross tonnage;

(j) water ballast tanks not usable for other purposes so however that the total tonnage to be deducted when added to water ballast spaces not included in gross tonnage does not exceed 19 per cent of gross tonnage.

To qualify for deduction, crew accommodation must comply with the statutes and regulations relating thereto, and other spaces must be certified to be reasonable in extent, properly constructed, and permanently marked to show their purpose.

Allowance for Propelling Machinery Space. For ships propelled by screws this is determined as follows:—

If tonnage of space is 13 per cent or over but less than 20 per cent of gross tonnage, allowance is 32 per cent of gross tonnage.

If tonnage of space is less than 13 per cent of gross tonnage, allowance is that lesser percentage of gross tonnage multiplied by 32/13

If tonnage of space is 20 per cent or more of gross tonnage, allowance is 1¾ times tonnage of space.

For ships propelled by paddle wheels the allowance is determined as follows:—

If tonnage of space is 20 per cent or over but less than 30 per cent of gross tonnage, allowance is 37 per cent of gross tonnage.

If tonnage of space is less than 20 per cent of gross tonnage, allowance is that lesser percentage of gross tonnage multiplied by 37/20.

If tonnage of space is 30 per cent or more of gross tonnage, allowance is 1½ times tonnage of space.

In no case save that of tugs may the allowance exceed 55 per cent of that portion of the tonnage remaining after making the other deductions from gross tonnage. All deductions are subject to the space being certified as adequate and permanently marked to show purpose.

Modified Gross and Register Tonnages. In ships where (a) greater than minimum freeboards have been assigned under the Load Line Rules, (b) the load lines are not higher than they would have been if freeboards and load line positions had been calculated treating the second deck as the freeboard deck, the D.o.T. on the shipowner's application may assign modified gross and register tonnages. These will be ascertained in the normal way except that (i) for references to the upper deck there will be substituted references to the second deck, and (ii) the space between the second deck and the upper deck will not be a component of the gross tonnage. Such ships must be marked on each side with a tonnage mark placed in line with the uppermost load line to which the ship may be loaded, but subject to the foregoing in a position determined in accordance with Schedule 4. (*See* reference to Schedule 4 further on.)

Alternative Tonnages. The D.o.T. may on the shipowner's application assign to the ship as an alternative to its gross and register tonnages ascertained in the normal way the modified tonnages referred to above. In this case also a tonnage mark must be placed on each side of the ship in a position to be determined by reference to Schedule 4 to the Regulations. (*See* reference to Schedule 4 further on). When the ship is so loaded that the tonnage mark is not submerged then the modified tonnages apply. If the mark is submerged then the tonnages obtained in the normal way apply. Thus, such a ship will have two sets of tonnage figures.

Remeasurement of Already Registered Ships. The D.o.T. on the application of the owner of a ship registered under Part I of the Principal Act before the coming into operation of the 1967 Regulations may direct remeasurement of the ship's tonnage. After such remeasurement the ship's certificate of registry must be delivered up to a registrar to be replaced by a new one, and the Register Book will be altered accordingly.

Note:—Reference above to the D.o.T. includes in appropriate cases an authorised Classification Society.

Deck Cargo. Section 85 of the Principal Act provides that if a foreign-going ship carries deck cargo in any uncovered space on deck or in a covered space not included in the register tonnage, dues will be payable thereon. In this connection the M.S. (Tonnage) Regulations, 1967 as amended by the M.S. (Tonnage) (Amendment) Regulations, 1967, provide that where (*a*) a ship has been assigned alternative tonnages, and (*b*) the tonnages applicable are the modified tonnages, no account shall be taken for the purpose of the said section 85 of any space which is included in the larger register tonnage but which is not included in the smaller register tonnage to the extent that the tonnage of such space exceeds the difference between those register tonnages. It is further provided that goods or stores shall not be carried in any permanently closed-in space which has not been included in the registered tonnage other than (*a*) dry cargo spaces; (*b*) workshops or store rooms appropriated for the use of pumpmen, engineers, electricians, carpenters and boatswains; (*c*) the lamp room; or (*d*) double bottom tanks. If goods or stores are carried in contravention of this provision the master and owner of the ship shall each be liable to a fine not exceeding £200.

Meanings of Terms. The following are extracts from that section of the Regulations devoted to interpretation.

"dry cargo space" means space appropriated for the carriage of cargo other than liquid or gaseous matter in bulk;

"propelling machinery space" means space below upper deck (or second deck for modified tonnages purposes) for main or auxiliary machinery, and includes (*a*) ventilation and other trunks, (*b*) boiler space, (*c*) shaft tunnels, (*d*) store rooms and workshops up to a specified limit, (*e*) settling tanks within specified limits, and light and air spaces on or above upper deck if included in gross tonnage at owner's request;

"second deck" means deck next below upper deck;

"tonnage deck" means second deck except in single deck ships in which case it means upper deck;

"upper deck" means uppermost complete deck exposed to sea and weather;

"the principal Act" means Merchant Shipping Act, 1894.

N.B.—Certain details are purposely omitted from some of the above definitions for the sake of simplicity. Readers familiar with the old definition of "tonnage deck" are especially cautioned to note the change introduced by the 1967 Regulations.

Dimensions. For the purpose of ascertaining the underdeck tonnage (by Simpson's first rule) the length of the tonnage deck is measured in a straight line in the middle plane of the ship between the points at the forward and after ends where the underside of the deck meets the inner face of the frames, timbers, or sparring as the case may be. This length is referred to as the "tonnage length".

Depths are measured in the middle plane of the ship from the underside of the tonnage deck to the top of the open floor or double bottom, deducting therefrom the average thickness of ceiling, if fitted, and one third the round of beam (with corrections if the top of the double bottom rises or falls from the middle plane).

Breadths are measured horizontally to the inner face of the timber, frame or sparring, as the case may be.

Tonnage Mark. This consists of a horizontal line 15 inches long and one inch wide upon which for identification purposes is an inverted equilateral triangle, each side 12 inches long and one inch wide, having its apex on the mid-point of the horizontal line. In the case of a ship intended to operate in fresh or tropical waters (not being a ship with modified tonnages only) an additional horizontal line may, on owner's application, be placed above such tonnage mark at a distance of one forty-eighth of the moulded draught to that tonnage mark. This line must be 9 inches long and one inch wide measured from a one inch wide vertical line at the

DIAGRAM (A)

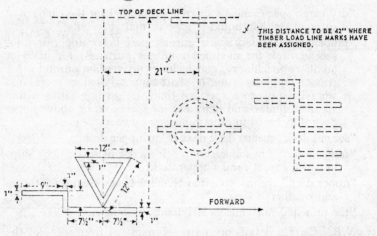

TOP OF DECK LINE

THIS DISTANCE TO BE 42" WHERE TIMBER LOAD LINE MARKS HAVE BEEN ASSIGNED.

21"

12"

1"

9"

1"

12"

1"

7½" 7½" 1"

FORWARD

DIAGRAM (B)

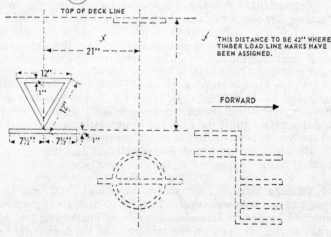

TOP OF DECK LINE

21"

THIS DISTANCE TO BE 42" WHERE TIMBER LOAD LINE MARKS HAVE BEEN ASSIGNED.

12"

1"

12"

FORWARD

7½" 7½" 1"

Dimensions in inches	1"	7½"	9"	12"
Corresponding dimensions in millimetres	25 mm	190 mm	230 mm	300 mm

after end of, and perpendicular to, that tonnage mark. This additional line is taken to be the tonnage mark when the ship is operating in fresh or tropical waters.

The lines and triangle must be painted in white or yellow on a dark ground or black on a light ground, and cut in, centre punched or welded on the ship's sides.

SURVEYS 53 A

UNITED KINGDOM
BRITISH TONNAGE CERTIFICATE

FOR SHIPS TO WHICH A TONNAGE MARK HAS BEEN ASSIGNED

NAME OF SHIP	PORT OF REGISTRY	OFFICIAL NUMBER
WILD AUK	LONDON	343017
REGISTER DIMENSIONS	492.6 ft x 70.0 ft x 26.9 ft	

I, the undersigned Surveyor appointed by the Board of Trade, hereby certify that I have measured the above ship in accordance with Rule I of the Merchant Shipping (Tonnage) Regulations, 1967, and by this Rule:-

When the Tonnage Mark (or the appropriate line for freshwater and/or tropical waters) is submerged the

GROSS TONNAGE   is:- .....9709.34......... tons (......27477.43...... cubic metres) and the

REGISTER TONNAGE is:- .....5429.26......... tons (......15364.81....... cubic metres).

When the Tonnage Mark (or the appropriate line for freshwater and/or tropical waters) is NOT submerged the

GROSS TONNAGE   is:- ....7290.34......... tons (.....20631.66...... cubic metres) and the

REGISTER TONNAGE is:- ....3255.89......... tons (......9214.17....... cubic metres).

A summary of the respective tonnages is given overleaf, together with an account of the spaces which have not been included in the above tonnages.

The TONNAGE MARK is marked on each side of the ship as follows:-

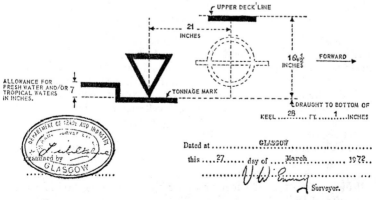

E

Position of Tonnage Marks (Schedule 4). The distance at which the tonnage mark is to be placed below the line where the underside of the second deck stringer plate meets the ship's side plating amidships (or equivalent line if the deck is stepped) is obtained from a Tonnage Mark Table in Schedule 4 to the Regulations. The arguments for finding the distance are Lt and the ratio Lt/Ds.

SUMMARY OF THE PARTICULARS OF TONNAGE

WHEN THE TONNAGE MARK IS SUBMERGED

GROSS TONNAGE		NO. OF TONS	DEDUCTIONS ALLOWED	NO. OF TONS
Under tonnage deck		5856.56	On account of space required for propelling power...	3106.99
Space or spaces between decks		2794.43		
Turret or trunk		—	Master	48.83
Forecastle		—	Crew Accommodation	936.11
Bridge space...		314.99	Navigational Spaces	59.73
UPPER BRIDGE		264.16	Safety Equipment	
Break			Workshops and Storerooms	21.07
Side houses			Donkey Engine and Boiler	
Deck houses		381.08	Pump Rooms...	
... ...			Sail Room	
Spaces for machinery and light and air, under Reg 4 (1) (c) of the Merchant Shipping (Tonnage) Regulations 1967			Water Ballast	107.35
Excess of hatchways		98.12		

	Cubic metres			
GROSS TONNAGE	27477.43	9709.34		
Deductions, as per contra	12112.63	4280.08		
REGISTER TONNAGE	15364.80	5429.26	Total	4280.08

The tonnage of the engine room spaces below the upper deck is ....1567.51......... tons.

The tonnage of the total spaces framed in above the upper deck for propelling machinery and for light and air is .... 367.09 .... tons.

The undermentioned cargo spaces above the upper deck are not included in the above tonnages

Forecastle Length 51.0 ft   88.84 Tons

Lt is the distance in feet on the second deck between the points at the forward and after ends where the underside of the deck meets the inner surface of the frames, ceiling or sparring in the middle plane of the ship (or equivalent length if the deck is stepped).

Ds is the depth in feet amidships from top of keel to the point at which the underside of the second deck stringer plate meets the ship's side plating (or equivalent depth if the deck is stepped).

Values of Lt are given at 10-foot intervals from 220 to 800 feet and Lt/Ds ratios at unit intervals from 12 to 20. For intermediate values the relevant distance is obtained by interpolation or extrapolation and in all cases the distance is corrected to the nearest half-inch. (If Lt is 220 feet or under the distance is 2.0 inches for all values of Lt/Ds.)

Where load lines have been assigned the tonnage mark is placed so that the apex of the triangle is 21 inches abaft the centre of the load line disc. In no case may the tonnage mark be placed above the deepest load line to which the ship may be loaded.

SUMMARY OF THE PARTICULARS OF TONNAGE

WHEN THE TONNAGE MARK IS NOT SUBMERGED

GROSS TONNAGE		NO. OF TONS	DEDUCTIONS ALLOWED	NO. OF TONS
Under tonnage deck		5856.56	On account of space required for propelling power	2988.98
Space or spaces between decks				
Turret or trunk			Master	48.83
Forecastle			Crew Accommodation	936.11
Bridge space		314.99	Navigational Spaces	
Poop Upper Bridge		264.16	Safety Equipment	
Break			Workshops and Storerooms	
Side houses			Donkey Engine and Boiler	
Deck houses		381.08	Pump Rooms...	
... ...			Sail Room	
Spaces for machinery and light and air under Reg 4 (1)(e), of the Merchant Shipping (Tonnage) Regulations 1967		473.55	Water Ballast	60.53
Excess of hatchways				
	Cubic metres			
GROSS TONNAGE	20631.66	7290.34		
Deductions, as per contra	11417.49	4034.45		
REGISTER TONNAGE	9214.17	3255.89	Total	4034.45

The tonnage of the engine room spaces below the second deck is .....1237.57.......... tons.

The tonnage of the total spaces framed in above the second deck for propelling machinery and for light and air is ....473.55............... tons.

The undermentioned cargo spaces above the second deck are not included in the above tonnages.

FORECASTLE	LENGTH	51.0ft	88.84 tons
No 1 Tween Deck	Length	66.5ft	256.94 tons
No 2 "	"	77.6 "	454.39 "
No 3 "	"	65.5 "	417.84 "
No 4 "	"	65.0 "	423.67 "
No 5 "	"	80.2 "	400.91 "

Where load lines have not been assigned the tonnage mark is placed at the middle of the length Lt and in such case the line of the upper deck is shown by a deck line corresponding in form to that required by the Load Line Rules and placed centrally to a vertical line bisecting the triangle of the tonnage mark.

Diagrams A and B. The former illustrates how the tonnage mark appears on a ship to which alternative tonnages have been assigned, whilst the latter shows the appearance of the tonnage mark for ship assigned modified tonnages only.

Tonnage Measurement of Yachts. Part 4 of the M.S. (Tonnage) (Amendment) Regulations 1975 introduced a new system of tonnage measurement for pleasure yachts under 45 feet in length overall which are to be registered under the M.S. Act 1894, and also provided for such measurement to be carried out by surveyors of an authorised Classification Society, or by measurers appointed by the Royal Yachting Association or by the Yacht Brokers, Designers and Surveyors Association, as an alternative to D.o.T. surveyors of ships. After measurement, the tonnage of such a yacht is calculated by multiplying together its overall length, breadth outside of planking and internal depth, and multiplying the resultant figure by .0045. The volume, divided by 100, of any side-to-side break in the line of the deck, is then added to the previous figure to give both the gross and register tonnage of the yacht. In the case of a catamaran or trimaran, the tonnage of each hull is measured separately and the sum of such tonnages is the yacht's tonnage.

INTERNATIONAL CONFERENCE ON TONNAGE MEASUREMENT OF SHIPS, 1969

Recognising that the establishment of a universal system of tonnage measurement for ships engaged on international voyages should constitute an important contribution to maritime transport, a Conference was held in London in June 1969, upon the invitation of the Inter-Governmental Maritime Consultative Organization, for the purpose of drawing up an International Convention on Tonnage Measurement of Ships.

The governments of some forty-eight states were represented by delegations at this Conference, and several others were represented by observers as were some shipping associations and canal authorities.

The Conference adopted three recommendations arising from its deliberations, viz.:—

(1) Acceptance of the International Convention on Tonnage Measurement.
(2) Uses of gross and net tonnages.
(3) Uniform interpretation of definitions of terms.

With the deposit at I.M.C.O. in July 1980 of Japan's instrument of acceptance, this Convention has been ratified by 44 countries whose combined fleets of merchant shipping total 72 per cent of the world's fleet in terms of gross tonnage. In accordance with the terms of Article 17 of the Convention it therefore entered into force on 18 July 1982. It should be noted that it applies immediately only to new ships, existing ships which undergo substantial alterations, and existing ships if their owners so request. For other existing ships it will not apply until 12 years after the above date in 1994.

Definitions. For the purpose of the Convention, unless expressly provided otherwise:

(1) "Regulations" means the Regulations annexed to the Convention;

(2) "Administration" means the Government of the State whose flag the ship is flying;

(3) "international voyage" means a sea voyage from a country to which the Convention applies to a port outside such country, or conversely;

(4) "gross tonnage" means the measure of the overall size of a ship determined in accordance with the provisions of the Convention;

(5) "net tonnage" means the measure of the useful capacity of a ship determined in accordance with the Convention;

(6) "new ship" means a ship the keel of which is laid, or which is at a similar stage of construction, on or after the date of coming into force of the Convention;

(7) "existing ship" means a ship which is not a new ship;

(8) "length" means 96 per cent of the total length on a waterline at 85 per cent of the least moulded depth measured from the top of the keel or the length from the fore side of the stem to the axis of the rudder stock on that waterline, if that be greater. In ships designed with a rake of keel the waterline on which the length is measured shall be parallel to the designed waterline;

(9) "Organization" means the Inter-Governmental Maritime Consultative Organization.

Application.

(1) The Convention shall apply to the following ships engaged on international voyages:

(a) ships registered in countries the Governments of which are Contracting Governments;

(b) ships registered in territories to which the Convention is extended;

(c) unregistered ships flying the flag of a State the Government of which is a Contracting Government.

(2) The Convention shall apply to:

(a) new ships;

(b) existing ships which undergo alterations or modifications which the Administration deems to be a substantial variation in their existing gross tonnage;

(c) existing ships if the owner so requests; and

(d) all existing ships, twelve years after the date on which the Convention comes into force, except that such ships, apart from those mentioned in (b) and (c) of this paragraph, shall retain their then existing tonnages for the purpose of the application to them of relevant requirements under the existing International Conventions.

(3) Existing ships to which the Convention has been applied in accordance with sub-paragraph (2)(c) of this Article shall not

subsequently have their tonnages determined in accordance with the requirements which the Administration applied to ships on international voyages prior to the coming into force of the Convention.

The proviso in paragraph (2)(d) above is intended to eliminate the need for structural alterations to existing ships as a result of an increased tonnage for the purposes of the application of International Conventions relating to safety, such as the International Convention for the Safety of Life at Sea, 1974. For instance, an existing ship of 499 tons gross tonnage under the existing tonnage regulations may continue to be exempt from the 1974 Safety Convention after 12 years from the date of coming into force of the Tonnage Convention. The use of tonnage for other purposes, such as taxes and dues, is not within the scope of the Tonnage Convention and is, therefore, dealt with by Recommendation 2 of that Convention.

Exceptions. The Convention shall not apply to ships of war and ships less than 24 metres in length and nothing within the Convention shall apply to ships solely navigating the Great Lakes of North America, part of the River St. Lawrence, the Caspian Sea or parts of the Plate, Parana and Uruguay Rivers.

Regulations. Annex 1 of the Convention sets out the regulations for determining gross and net tonnages of ships.

Regulation 1 provides that the tonnage of a ship shall consist of gross tonnage and net tonnage which shall be determined in accordance with the provisions of the Regulations. It adds that the tonnages of novel types of craft whose constructural features are such as to render the application of the provisions of the Regulations unreasonable or impracticable shall be as determined by the Administration.

Regulation 2 defines the terms Upper Deck, Moulded Depth, Breadth, Enclosed Spaces, Excluded Spaces, Passenger, Cargo Spaces and Weathertight.

Regulation 3 states that the gross tonnage (GT) of a ship shall be determined by the following formula:

$$GT = K_1 V$$

where: $V =$ Total volume of all enclosed spaces of the ship in cubic metres,

$K_1 = 0.2 + 0.02 \log_{10} V$ (or as tabulated in Appendix 2).

Regulation 4 states that the net tonnage (NT) of a ship shall be determined by the following formula:

$$NT = K_2 V_c \left(\frac{4d}{3D}\right)^2 + K_3 \left(N_1 + \frac{N_2}{10}\right),$$

in which formula:

(a) the factor $\left(\dfrac{4d}{3D}\right)^2$ shall not be taken as greater than unity;

(b) the term $K_2 V_c \left(\dfrac{4d}{3D}\right)^2$ shall not be taken as less than 0.25 GT,

(c) NT shall not be taken as less than 0.30 GT, and in which:

V_c = total volume of cargo spaces in cubic metres,

K_2 = $0.2 + 0.02 \log_{10} V_c$ (or as tabulated in Appendix 2),

K_3 = $1.25 \dfrac{GT + 10{,}000}{10{,}000}$;

D = moulded depth amidships in metres as defined in Regulation 2,

d = moulded draught amidships in metres as defined in paragraph 2 of this Regulation (see below),

N_1 = number of passengers in cabins with not more than 8 berths,

N_2 = number of other passengers,

$N_1 + N_2$ = total number of passengers the ship is permitted to carry as indicated in the ship's passenger certificate; when $N_1 + N_2$ is less than 13, N_1 and N_2 shall be taken as zero,

GT = gross tonnage of the ship as determined in accordance with the provisions of Regulation 3.

The moulded draught (d) referred to above shall be one of the following:

(a) for ships to which the International Convention on Load Lines in force applies, the draught corresponding to the Summer Load Line (other than timber load lines) assigned in accordance with that Convention;

(b) for passenger ships, the draught corresponding to the deepest subdivision load line assigned in accordance with the International Convention for the Safety of Life at Sea in force or other international agreement where applicable;

(c) for ships to which the International Convention on Load Lines does not apply but which have been assigned a load line in compliance with national requirements, the draught corresponding to the summer load line so assigned;

(d) for ships to which no load line has been assigned but the draught of which is restricted in compliance with national requirements, the maximum permitted draught;

(e) for other ships 75 per cent of the moulded depth amidships as defined in Regulation 2.

Regulations 5, 6 and 7 deal respectively with Change of Net Tonnage (when the characteristics of a ship are altered), Calculation of Volumes, and Measurement and Calculation.   Regulation 7 requires measurements used in calculating volumes to be taken to the nearest centimetre or one-twentieth of a foot. (The latter seems rather odd since volumes are to be expressed in cubic metres.)

International Tonnage Certificate. Annex II of the Convention provides a specimen form of the International Tonnage Certificate which, in accordance with Article 9 of the Convention, is required to be drawn up in the official language or languages of the issuing country. If the language used is neither English nor French, the text is to include a translation into one of these languages. The form of certificate is required to correspond to that of the model given in Annex II.

Coming into force. The Convention entered into force on 18 July 1982.

Abandonment of Tonnage Mark. Under the new Convention ships will not have the tonnage mark or dual tonnage. It was the unanimous view of the Conference that the new Convention should not introduce the tonnage mark, but nevertheless the concept of the tonnage mark scheme has been retained in the calculation of net tonnage which varies with the change of ship's draught.

Gross and Net Tonnage Figures. The gross and net tonnages of a ship calculated by the formulae described above will be simply pure numbers and the word "tons" will not be used. For instance, a ship may be stated to have "Gross Tonnage 4567" and, say, "Net Tonnage 1998".

DECK CARGO

If any ship, other than a home trade ship, carries cargo in any uncovered space on deck, or in a covered space which is not included in the registered tonnage, dues will be payable thereon. The master is responsible for seeing that such space is measured by ship's personnel, and the tonnage entered on form D.C.I. or D.C.O., if inward or outward bound respectively. The Declaration, in duplicate, must be handed to a Customs officer for checking, signing and stamping, before discharge, or sailing, respectively. This signed copy must be produced to the Collector of Light Dues when dues are paid. Any deck lading counts for this purpose, whether it earns freight or not, and oil fuel carried in double-bottom tanks must be included.

SUEZ CANAL TONNAGE

Canal transit dues are charged on net tonnage ascertained in accordance with the system of measurement recommended by the International Tonnage Commission assembled at Constantinople in 1873. A shipowner who wishes to have a ship measured under the rules of the Commission and to have a special certificate issued can apply on Form Surveys 6 and pay the required fee to the superintendent of a mercantile marine office. On receipt of the application the surveyor will apply to the Principal Surveyor for Tonnage for the formulae and papers of the previous measurement of the ship. When the measurement is made and the exempted spaces have been marked (in the manner referred to later) the Tonnage Certificate will be issued.

The 100 cu. ft. "ton" is used as the unit of measurement as in British tonnage, but the system of measurement differs in many respects. Hence, for ships intending to navigate the Suez Canal and Danube a special tonnage certificate is required. Any alteration in tonnage after the issue of a certificate is taken into account when assessing the amount of dues payable.

Exempted and deducted spaces may not be used during canal transit for the carriage of passengers, goods, bunker coal or stores. If they are so used the whole of the space is added to the net tonnage permanently and, in the words of the official Rules "can nevermore be exempted from measurement". However, if the ship were sold the new owner could apply to have the space exempted again. It appears that such applications have met with success.

Dues are charged on any double bottom space partly or wholly used to carry bunker or cargo oil, but an exception to the above rule is made in this case and the addition is not permanent.

The Canal authority's officials may verify whether cargo or passengers are being carried in any space not included in the certified net tonnage, also whether spaces which ought to be included in the net tonnage are correctly determined. Ten per cent of the Suez Canal net tonnage is added to that tonnage to take account of containers carried on deck.

Ships not provided with tonnage certificates have a tonnage figure determined provisionally on arrival at the Canal terminus, being measured in conformity with special rules, and this figure remains in force until a proper certificate is tendered on the occasion of a subsequent transit.

Merchant ships not earning freight and carrying only fuel for their own consumption, and their crews, with provisions for the crew are considered as being in ballast. A maximum of 20 tons weight of perishable foodstuffs is allowed, or a volume not exceeding 10 tons measurement. Ships which land passengers or goods before passing through the Canal and picking them up afterwards are not considered to be in ballast. To claim the benefit of the ballast rate fuel must not exceed 125% of the certified engine room space, and should be in proper bunkers, but special permission may be applied for to have fuel on deck or in holds. Steps must be taken so that the total volume of all bunkers on board can be easily ascertained.

On arrival at the Canal terminus a ship must be entered at the Transit Office and dues paid. Information required will be the name and nationality of the ship, name of master, names of owners and charterers, ports of sailing and destination, draught, number of passengers, a statement of the crew, and the capacity of the ship as shown in the Canal Certificate. The master will receive a copy of the Rules of Navigation.

Transit dues are fixed from time to time at so much per ton, and ships in ballast are allowed a substantial reduction. Half dues are charged for half transit, but no further subdivision is allowed and Ismailia is considered to be the half-way mark. Separate pilotage dues are not payable as they are included in the transit dues. Special rates are applicable to vessels towed or convoyed by approved tugs. There are no passenger dues. All dues and charges are payable in advance in cash, and if an amount paid in advance is not sufficient the balance must be made before transit.

SYSTEM OF MEASUREMENT OF
SUEZ CANAL TONNAGE

Underdeck Tonnage. Except in certain special cases this is obtained in the same way as British underdeck tonnage.

Gross Tonnage. This consists of the underdeck tonnage plus every permanent covered and closed-in space on or above the tonnage deck without any exception.

In considering what are covered and closed-in spaces, spaces may be divided into three classes, viz.:—

(a) spaces covered only by planks separated by intervals exceeding one inch,

(b) Spaces in side-to-side erections (in the lowest or any other tier), completely covered but having large openings without coamings at either or both ends,

(c) parts of spaces completely covered, such as shelter decks, open forecastles, bridges and poops.

To claim exemption a space must be exempted in the ship's national tonnage.

Spaces of class (a) are completely exempted.

Spaces of class (b) are named "open" spaces and their partial exclusion is conditional upon the permanent openings at the end of the erection being equal to or greater than one half of the breadth of the deck in the way of them. The part not included in the gross tonnage is that part of the erection not exceeding in length the half breadth of the deck. But if within this limit of length the width of the clear opening is less than the half breadth of the deck, the length of open space allowed is reduced to that part of the length for which the standard breadth is maintained. If coamings are fitted, or if the openings are of less than standard breadth, the whole space is included in the gross tonnage. If two side-to-side erections in the same tier are separated by a distance of less than half the breadth of the deck, they are measured in the gross tonnage whatever the size of openings may be.

Spaces of class (c) are classed as exempted spaces as follows:—

Shelter-deck Spaces. The whole space is included in the gross tonnage except the part immediately abreast of the openings (if any) in the sides of the ship. Such openings must be opposite each other and unclosable. Air spaces within shelter-decks are measured into the engine room space and deducted together with 75% of their volume.

Poops, Bridges, and Forecastles. The exemptions allowed are:—

(a) such length of poop measured from the inside of the stern timber at half height of poop as is equal to 1/10th of the length of the ship;

(b) the portion of the bridge in the way of machinery air spaces, but this may not extend beyond the forward stokehold bulkhead and after engine room bulkhead;

(c) such length of forecastle measured from the inside of the stem at half height of forecastle as is equal to 1/8th of the length of the ship;

(d) in all the above superstructures, those portions in the way of openings in the walls of the ship which are opposite each other and unclosable.

Poop and Bridge combined, or **Forecastle and Bridge combined.** The exemptions consist of:—

(a) that length only which corresponds to the engine and boiler space as in (b) above;

(b) spaces as in (d) above.

If the ship has more than one tier of superstructures, the above exemptions apply in their entirety to the lowest tier only. Tiers above the lowest have exempted only such portions as are in the way of openings in the side plating of the ship which face one another and are not fitted with any means of closing.

N.B.—Cargo or stores *may* be carried in an "open" space provided additional dues are paid thereon, but they *may not* be carried in an "exempted" space. The boundaries of exempted parts of poops and forecastles are required to be marked by a permanently and securely fixed plate on each side of the vessel. The centres of the plates are marked with a star (*) indicating the exact limit of the exempted space in agreement with the particulars on the back of the Canal Tonnage Certificate. The inscription on the plate reads, "This space .... feet in length from the inside of the stem (stern timber) at the half height of the space to this mark, is exempted from Suez Canal tonnage on the ground that no cargo or stores are carried therein". No plates are required in the exempted zone of a bridge space. Means must be provided for gaining access to the exempted parts in the event of adjacent parts being filled with cargo.

Net Tonnage. Deductions allowed in arriving at the net registered tonnage are:—

1. **Propelling Space.** The shipowner may choose the Danube Rule allowing $1\frac{3}{4}$ times the actual engine room for screw steamers, or $1\frac{1}{2}$ times for paddle steamers; or the actual measurement of the engine room plus permanent bunkers. In either case the limit is 50% of the gross tonnage except in tugs. Light and air spaces do not form part of the engine room unless they are situated in a continuous shelter-deck, 'tween-deck, bridge, poop, or other first tier erection.

2. **Crew Spaces** and **Navigation Spaces.** Deductions unde-this head are limited to a maximum of 10% of the gross tonnage, and to be eligible for deduction the spaces must be permanently marked to show the purpose to which they are exclusively appropriated. The spaces include:—

Spaces exclusively occupied by officers and crew.

Captain's accommodation, officers' smoking room, offices for chief officer and chief engineer.

Doctors' cabins (so long as they are actually occupied by doctors), consulting room, hospital, infirmary, surgery, operating room, laboratory.

Wireless operator's cabin, stewards' cabins (if stewards are solely for officers and crew).

Cabins of engineers, storekeepers and water tenders.

Mess rooms (but not if available for passengers).

Lavatories for use of crew only.

Bath rooms (not available to passengers).

Galleys, pantry, scullery, bakery (in non-passenger ship), laundry, drying room, space for heating-boilers, refrigerating machinery (excluding cold storage and store rooms).

Distilling apparatus and disinfecting apparatus.

Wardrobes, oilskin and lifebelt lockers.

Ventilators used neither for cargo nor passengers.

Accommodation for night watchman if signed on and not employed for cargo or passengers, also fire-fighting personnel.

Chart house and Captain's spare room on bridge.

Searchlight space, spaces for submarine telephone, direction finder, sounding gear, gyro-compass, wireless, radar, signal lamps.

Lookout houses, emergency generators, fire-extinguishing installations,

Steering engine house, capstan and anchor gear space.

N.B.—Some of these spaces are exempted in British tonnage, but by the Suez Canal rules they are first included and then deducted. A donkey boiler house in a closed space on the upper deck is not deducted, nor are passengers' galleys, lavatories, W.C.'s, luggage rooms, boatswain's stores, and sail rooms.

PANAMA CANAL TONNAGE

Rules have been adopted by U.S.A. authorities for assessing net or register tonnage for the calculation of tolls and other charges to be paid by trading vessels passing through the Canal, and special certificates are issued setting forth the necessary particulars.

Panama Canal Gross Tonnage. This includes all spaces below the upper deck and all permanently covered or closed-in spaces on or above that deck.

Panama Canal Net Tonnage. This is derived by making deductions from the gross tonnage.

Spaces above the tonnage deck are classed as one or other of:—

    (1) permanent covered and closed-in spaces,
    (2) exempted spaces,
    (3) deducted spaces.

Those defined as (1) form part of the gross tonnage.

Those defined as (2) do not, but the tonnage of the space is recorded on the back of the certificate so that, in the event of the space being used for carriage of cargo when entering the canal, it may readily be assessed for dues. As under the Suez Regulations, certain exempted spaces—if used for cargo, stores or fuel during canal transit—are added to the Canal Tonnage for the rest of the ship's career. This does not apply to open spaces at the ends of permanently covered-in superstructures or spaces covered by a deck supported by stanchions.

Those defined as (3) must first be included in the gross tonnage to be eligible for deduction therefrom, and must be appropriated solely for the purpose specified in the rules.

When the sum of those deducted spaces together with the propelling space is deducted from the gross tonnage, what remains is the net tonnage.

Spaces comprising gross tonnage are all those included in British gross tonnage plus all spaces used or intended for the navigation or the service of the vessel, or for the use or possible use of passengers. Double bottom spaces are exempted from measurement except when used, designated or intended for carrying cargo or fuel. If used for feed water or stores, they are exempted.

Underdeck tonnage is the same as British, but all 'tween-deck spaces between the tonnage deck and the uppermost full-length deck are fully included unless there are openings in the side walls of the ship at least three feet in height. In that case the portion of the 'tween-deck opposite such openings is exempted. Hence, an "open shelter-deck" ship will have only a very small part of the shelter-deck space exempted from measurement.

Spaces within open poops, bridges, forecastles, and other superstructures are excluded from measurement on the same conditions as laid down in the Suez Canal regulations, but the Panama rules do not exempt the zone abreast of the machinery opening in the bridge space, nor spaces in poops or forecastles other than "open" spaces measured in from the ends.

Spaces framed in around funnels and engine casings in the lowest tier of side-to-side erections above the upper deck are included but those above the lowest tier are exempt. Also exempted are companionways, domes, skylights, etc., and double bottom spaces exclusively used for water ballast.

Deducted spaces come under three headings, viz.:—

(a) crew accommodation,
(b) closed-in spaces used in working the ship,
(c) propelling spaces.

Under (a) the deductions are in respect of the total tonnage of spaces for the exclusive use of officers and crew, including clerks, pursers, stewards, and others whose duties are partly or wholly concerned with the care of passengers. Hospitals, mess rooms, bath rooms, washrooms, W.C.'s, lavatories, galleys, bakeries, dynamo, and condenser spaces are included in the deductions.

Under (b) deductions are made of the tonnage of chartroom, wheelhouse, steering gear and capstan spaces, donkey boiler space (if above the upper deck or the boiler is connected with the main pumps), sail room (in sailing ships), boatswain's store, water ballast spaces other than double bottom compartments.

Under (c) the deduction is the space occupied by engines, boilers, settling tanks, lubricating oil tanks, shaft tunnels, light and air spaces below the first tier and space for working the engines. The maximum allowed is 50 per cent of gross tonnage.

Dues are payable on deck cargo.

Warship tolls are based on Displacement tonnage at the time of application for passage through the Canal.

A ship may be measured for Panama Canal tonnage in the United Kingdom at the same time as her national tonnage is measured and the Panama Tonnage Certificate is obtainable here.

CLASSIFICATION

Apart from, and in addition to, official national registration, the vast majority of ships are "classed" or registered with one or other of the Classification Societies or "Shipping Registers". Such registration is not compulsory, but is attended with so many advantages that an unclassed ship is nowadays a comparative rarity. In the absence of these registers much difficulty would be experienced by marine underwriters, chartering brokers, bankers, merchants and shippers, and others who need a ready access to the latest and most reliable information regarding the ships in which they are interested. Shipowners, too, would be at a great disadvantage if there existed no reliable organisation to ensure that their vessels were constructed, repaired, and maintained in accordance with the highest prevailing standards both as regards materials and workmanship no matter in what part of the world such operations take place.

Well over ninety per cent. of British tonnage and more than a third of the world's tonnage is classed in Lloyd's Register of Shipping which, since 1949, has been united with its former rival British register which was known as the British Corporation. Other registers which are recognised by marine underwriters are:—

American Bureau of Shipping.
Bureau Veritas.
Germanischer Lloyd.
Japanese Marine Corporation.
Norske Veritas.
Registro Italiano.

LLOYD'S REGISTER OF SHIPPING

Lloyd's Register of Shipping should not be confused with the Corporation of Lloyd's Underwriters. It is the latter which is familiarly referred to as "Lloyd's of London" and the former which gives point to the expression "A1 at Lloyd's." Though it is probably true to say that the two organisations share a common origin, they have long been distinctly separate entities, although the Underwriters are strongly represented on the Committee of the Society.

Lloyd's Register is an independent authority, non-profit making, and relying entirely for its income on the fees charged for surveys and other services rendered. It is controlled by a committee representing shipowners, ship and engine builders, forgemasters, underwriters, the Institute of London Underwriters, the London General Shipowners' Society, and the technical committees of the Royal Institution of Naval Architects and Shipbuilders.

The various functions of Lloyd's Register of Shipping are:—

(1) The survey and classification of merchant vessels, yachts, tugs, fishing vessels, and other craft.

(2) The publication of:—
Register of Ships, issued annually,
Lloyd's Register of Yachts, published annually,
Register of Ships (Subsidiary Sections),
Register of Offshore Units, Submersibles and Diving Systems,
Rules and Regulations for the Classification of Ships,
Rules for Inland Waterways Vessels,
Rules for Floating Docks,
Rules for Mobile Offshore Units,
Rules for Submersibles and Diving Systems,
Rules for Ships for Liquefied Gases,
Rules for Yachts and Small Craft,

Geometric Properties of Rolled Sections and Built Girders,

Freight Container Certification Scheme,

Refrigerating Machinery Certification Scheme,

List of Approved Welding Consumables for use in Hull Construction,

List of Approved Fuses,

List of Type Tested Circuit-breakers,

Cargo Handling Gear Code,

Rules for the Survey and Classification of Refrigerated Stores,

Provisional Rules for the Application of Glass Reinforced Plastics to Fishing Craft,

Guidance Notes and Requirements for the Classification of Air Cushion Vehicles,

List of Type Approved Control and Electrical Equipment,

Guidance Notes for Lifts in Ships.

(3) Supervision of the testing of anchors and chains under the provisions of the Anchors and Chain Cables Acts.

(4) Supervision of the testing at the places of manufacture of steel for use in the construction of ships and boilers, and of large ship and engine forgings and castings.

(5) The assignment of freeboard to vessels of all types, whether classed or not, under the M.S. (Load Lines) Act and the corresponding statutes of other countries.

(6) The survey of refrigerating machinery and appliances.

(7) The survey and measurement of ships classed with the Society for the purpose of obtaining their tonnages under powers given by the M.S. (Tonnage) (Amendment) Regulations 1975.

The Society also undertakes a large amount of non-marine work chiefly in connection with power stations and oil refineries, and a number of highly specialised Lloyd's surveyors are engaged in ship and machinery research.

Conditions for Classification of Ships. Ships built in accordance with the Society's Rules and Regulations will be assigned a class in the Register Book, and they will continue to be so classed as long as they are found, upon examination at the required surveys, to be maintained in accordance with the rules. Compliance with the Society's requirements for both hull and machinery is a condition for classification.

The Rules are framed on the basis that ships will be properly loaded and handled. They do not, unless stated or implied in the class notation, provide for special distributions or concentrations of loading, but the Committee may require additional strengthening to be fitted in any ship which, in their opinion, would otherwise be subjected to severe stresses due to particular features in the design, or where it is desired to make provision for exceptional loaded or ballast conditions. It is also to be understood that the Rules are framed on the basis that ships will not be operated in environmental conditions more severe than those agreed for the design basis and approval, without the prior agreement of the Society. Any damage, defect or breakdown, which could invalidate the conditions for which a class has been assigned, is to be reported to the Society without delay.

Character Symbols. All ships, when classed will be assigned one or more character symbols. For the majority of ships, the character assigned will be 100A1 or ✠100A1. The character symbols used have the following meanings:—

✠ This mark will be assigned to new ships constructed under the Society's Special Survey, in compliance with the Rules, and to the satisfaction of the Committee.

100 This character figure is assigned to all ships which are considered suitable for sea-going service.

A This character letter is assigned to all ships which have been built or accepted into class in accordance with the Society's Rules and Regulations, and which are maintained in good and efficient condition.

1 This character figure is assigned to ships having on board in good and efficient condition, anchoring and/or mooring equipment in accordance with the Rules.

Where the equipment is found to be seriously deficient in quality or quantity, the ship's class will be liable to be withheld.

Class notations (hull). When considered necessary by the Committee, or when requested by an Owner and agreed to, a class notation will be added to the character of classification assigned to the ship. This class notation will consist of one of, or a combination of, a type notation, a cargo notation, a special duties notation and/or a service restriction notation. For example:—

✠100A1 Oil tanker Baltic service F.P. above 65°C in No. 4 tanks Ice Class 2.

Class notations (machinery). The following class notations may be assigned as appropriate:—

✠LMC Assigned when the propelling and essential auxiliary machinery has been constructed, installed and tested under Society's Special Survey, rules and regulations.

✠LMC Propelling and auxiliary machinery constructed under survey of a recognised authority to rules equivalent to those of the Society. In addition, the whole of the machinery has been installed and tested under the Society's Special Survey in accordance with the Rules.

UMS   Notation assigned when the ship can be operated with the machinery spaces unattended. The control engineering equipment has been arranged, installed and tested in accordance with the Rules.

CCS   Machinery may be operated with continuous supervision from a centralized control station.

IGS   Notation assigned when a ship intended for carriage of oil in bulk, or for carriage of liquid chemicals in bulk, is fitted with an approved system for producing gas for inerting the cargo tanks.

Class notations (refrigerated cargo installations).

✠ Lloyd's RMC   Notation assigned when a refrigerated cargo installation has been constructed, installed and tested under Special Survey in accordance with the Rules.

✠ Lloyd's RMC(LG)   Notation assigned to a classed liquefied gas carrier or tanker, in which reliquefaction or refrigeration equipment is approved and fitted for cargo temperature and pressure control where equipment has been constructed installed and tested in accordance with the Rules.

Special features. When a special feature in the design or construction of a ship or its machinery has been approved, an appropriate class notation may be entered in the Register Book.

Corrosion control. Where an approved method of corrosion control is fitted and an appropriate reduction in scantlings has been permitted, the notation (cc) will be entered in the Register Book.

Strengthening for Navigation in Ice. Where an ice class notation is desired, additional strengthening is to be fitted in accordance with the requirements given in the Rules.

It is the responsibility of the Owner to determine which notation is most suitable for his requirements.

Dredgers, etc. There are special requirements for dredgers, hopper dredgers, sand carriers, hopper barges and reclamation craft. Certain classes and notations are assigned to such ships which are intended to make sea-going voyages either as part of their work or while transferring from one work area to another as part of their normal operations. Other classes are assigned to such ships which are intended to operate a restricted service, and still others for such ships which are intended to operate only within protected waters.

New construction surveys. Materials used in the construction of hulls and machinery or in the repair of ships already classed must be of good quality and free from defects and are to be tested under the supervision of the Society's surveyors. (Lloyd's Surveyors include naval architects, marine engineers, and electrical and metallurgical specialists.) Steel is to be manufactured by an approved process at works recognised by the Committee.

When it is intended to build a ship for classification with the Society, plans and particulars of hull and machinery are required to be submitted through the local surveyors for the approval of the Committee before work is commenced. Any subsequent modifications or additions to scantlings, arrangements, or equipment are also required to be submitted for approval. Where the proposed construction is novel in design or involves the use of unusual material, special tests or examinations before and during service may be required and a suitable notation inserted in the Register Book.

New ships built under special survey are, when classed, entitled to the distinguishing mark ✠ inserted before the character in the Register Book, thus: ✠ 100 A1. In a similar way new machinery contructed under special survey is indicated thus: ✠ L.M.C.

During the construction from the commencement of the work until the completion of the ship and final test of the machinery under working conditions, the surveyors are required to examine the material and workmanship and are to indicate, and require the rectification of, any items not in accordance with the Rules or the approved plans, or any material, workmanship, or arrangement found to be defective or unsatisfactory.

Date of Build. The date of completion of the special survey during construction of ships built under the Society's inspection will normally be taken as the date of build to be entered in the Register Book. If, however, the period between launching and completion or commissioning is, for any reason, unduly prolonged, the dates of launching and completion or commissioning may be separately indicated in the Register Book. If a ship on completion is not immediately put into commission, but is laid up for a period, the Committee may direct an examination of the ship to be made in dry dock by the Society's surveyors. If hull and machinery are reported in all respects free from deterioration the subsequent special survey will date from the time of such examination.

N.B.—The *date of build* for the purpose of Lloyd's Register classification regulations should not be confused with the *year of build* for the purpose of the official registration of ships. The latter is determined by the following rule:—

"If a ship is launched in the first six months of a year, that year is to be inserted in the surveyor's certificate under the heading 'when built'. If launched during the second half of the year, that year should be inserted as the year when built if the ship is either registered or completed in that year, otherwise the following year should be inserted."

Ships not built under Survey. A special set of rules is formulated to be applied to such ships. The application for classification is required to be supported by plans showing the main scantlings and arrangements of the actual ship and any proposed alterations. If such plans cannot be obtained or be prepared by owners, facilities must be given for the Society's surveyors to take the necessary information from the ship. Ships of recent construction receive special consideration.

Periodical Surveys. All steel ships classed with the Society are subject to survey in accordance with the requirements of the Rules. Owners are expected to notify the Society whenever a ship can be examined in dry dock or on a slipway. Ships should be examined in dry dock approximately once every two to two and a half years. The date of the last examination is recorded in the supplement to the Register Book. Annual surveys should, whenever practicable, be held concurrently with statutory annual or other load line surveys.

Special Surveys. These became due at four-yearly intervals, the first 4 years from the date of build or date of Special Survey for Classification, and thereafter 4 years from the date of the previous special survey. When it is inconvenient for owners to fulfil all the requirements of a special survey at its due date, the Committee of the Society will be prepared to consider its postponement, either wholly or in part, provided that the surveyors are afforded an opportunity, about the due date, of assessing the general condition of hull and machinery. For this purpose the Committee will normally call for a general examination of the ship, including drydocking, of sufficient extent to be assured that her condition is satisfactory for the period of grace desired, which is not to exceed 12 months from the due date. Ships which have satisfactorily passed a special survey will have a record entered in the supplement to the Register Book indicating the date and place of such survey.

Continuous Surveys. When, at the request of the owners, it has been agreed by the Committee that the complete survey of the hull may be carried out on the Continuous Survey basis, all compartments of the hull should be opened up for survey and testing in rotation with an interval of 5 years between consecutive examinations of each part. If the examination during Continuous Survey reveals any defects, further parts are to be opened up and examined as considered necessary by the Surveyor. Ships which have satisfactorily completed the cycle will have a record entered in the Supplement to the Register Book indicating the date of completion.

Surveys of Machinery. (This relates to main and auxiliary engines, boilers, essential appliances, pumping arrangements and electrical equipment.) Complete Surveys of machinery become due at four yearly intervals, the first one four years from the date of build or date of first classification recorded in the Register Book, and thereafter four years from the date of the previous Complete Survey. Whether or not they are commenced prior to their due date, they are not to extend over a period greater than 12 months without approval. On satisfactory completion of the survey an appropriate record will be made in the Supplement to the Register Book. When a complete survey of the machinery is not carried out at one time the date recorded in the Supplement will be that on which the major portion of the survey is carried out. If it is found that any part of the machinery should be again examined before the due date of the next survey, a certificate for a limited period will be granted in accordance with the nature of the case.

Continuous Survey of Machinery. When, at the request of owners it has been agreed by the Committee that the complete survey of the machinery may be carried out on the Continuous Survey basis, the various items of machinery should be opened for survey in rotation, so far as practicable, to ensure that the interval between consecutive examinations of each item will not exceed five years. In general, approximately one-fifth of the machinery should be examined each year.

In such cases a record indicating the date of completion of the Continuous Survey cycle will be made in the Supplement to the Register Book.

If any examination during Continuous Survey reveals defects, further parts are to be opened up and examined as considered necessary by the Surveyor and the defects are to be made good to his satisfaction.

Upon application by owners the Committee may agree to an arrangement whereby, subject to certain conditions, some items of machinery may be examined by the Chief Engineer of the ship at ports where the Society is not represented or, where practicable, at sea, and a limited confirmatory survey carried out at the next port of call where an Exclusive Surveyor is available. Particulars of the arrangement may be obtained from the Society's Head Office.

Where an inert gas system is fitted on board a ship, the system is to be surveyed at intervals not exceeding two years.

Regulations relating to Special Hull Surveys. It is not within the purpose of this book to give details of the requirements of the Regulations relating to special hull surveys but, needless to say, such requirements will increase in stringency with the advancing age of the ship. The Regulations give full particulars of what is required in the case of ships under 5 years old. Those together with certain additional requirements apply to ships between 5 and 10 years old, and still further examinations are demanded at the surveys of ships over 10 years old. At the first special survey held after the ship is 24 years old and at every 12 years thereafter, or at the next special survey after the expiration of the latter period, the full requirements for ships over 10 years old have to be complied with together with numerous others. Special rules are laid down for petroleum tankers.

Boiler, Steam Pipes, and Screw Shaft Surveys. Water tube boiler supplying steam to the main propelling machinery (other than cylindrical boilers having corrugated or plain furnaces in conjunction with water tubes) and steam heated steam generators are to be surveyed at two-yearly intervals. All other boilers (except domestic boilers with a heating surface not more than 5 square metres and a working pressure not more than 3·5 bar gauge) are to be surveyed at two-yearly intervals until they are 8 years old and subsequently annually. At intervals of 6 years from the date of build a selected number of main and auxiliary steam pipes supplying steam for essential purposes at sea are to be removed for internal examination and hydraulically tested to twice their working pressure. Screw shafts and tube shafts are to be drawn periodically for examination. Where shafts are fitted with continuous liners or running in oil, and of approved construction, they normally become due for survey at intervals of 5 years for single screw ships and 5 years for ships having two or more screws. All other shafts should be drawn at intervals of 2 years.

Refrigeration. Refrigerated cargo installations which comply with the Rules and are favourably reported on by the surveyors are assigned an appropriate class, which will be retained provided the installation is found in good and efficient condition at the periodical loading port and other surveys provided for by the Rules.

Repairs and Alterations. All repairs to hull, equipment, and machinery required in order that a ship may retain her class are to be carried out under the inspection of, and to the satisfaction of, the Society's surveyors. When effected at a port where there is no Lloyd's surveyor the ship is to be surveyed by one of the Society's surveyors at the earliest opportunity. Plans and particulars of proposed alterations are to be submitted for approval and such alterations carried out under the inspection of, and to the satisfaction of, the Society's surveyors.

Certificates. When the required reports on completion of the special surveys of new ships, or existing ships submitted for classification, have been received from the surveyors and approved by the Committee, certificates of first entry of classification duly signed and countersigned will be issued to the builders or owners. Certificates of class maintenance in respect of completed periodical surveys will also be issued to owners on application. The Society's surveyors are permitted to issue provisional (interim) certificates to enable a classed ship to proceed on her voyage provided that in their opinion she is in a fit and efficient condition. Such certificates embody the surveyors' recommendations for continuance of class but are subject to confirmation by the Committee.

Withdrawal of Class.

1. When the class of a ship, for which the Regulations regarding survey have been complied with, is withdrawn in consequence of a request from the owners, the notation "LR class withdrawn—Owner's request" (with date) is made in the Supplement and, in due course, in the Register Book. After one year the notation will be altered to "Classed LR until" (with date).

2. When the Regulations as regards surveys have not been complied with and the ship thereby is not entitled to retain her class, the class will be withdrawn and the notation "Class withdrawn" (with date) will be made in the Supplement and the notation "LR class withdrawn" (with date) will be made in the next reprint of the Register Book. After one year the notation will be altered to "Classed LR until" (with date).

3. When it is found from reported defects that a ship is not entitled to retain her class, and the owners fail to repair such defects in accordance with requirements the class will be withdrawn and the notation "Class withdrawn—Reported defects" (with date) will be made in the Supplement and the notation "LR class withdrawn—Reported defects" (with date) will be made in the next reprint of the Register Book. After one year the notation will be altered to "Classed LR until" (with date).

4. Where a ship proceeds to sea with less freeboard than that approved by the Committee or where freeboard marks are placed higher on the ship's sides than the position assigned or approved, the ship's class will be liable to be withdrawn.

Extract from Lloyd's Register Book

See page 147.

DIMENSIONS OF SHIPS

MOULDED DIMENSIONS

Length between Perpendiculars (L) is the length on the summer load water-line measured from the fore side of the stem or fore perpendicular to the after side of the stern post or after perpendicular. In a vessel without a stern post it is measured to the fore side of the rudder stock.

Moulded Breadth (B) is the breadth measured over the widest part of the frame at the middle of the length L.

Moulded Depth (D) is the depth measured from the top of the keel to the top of the deck beam at side at the middle of the length L.

CERTIFIED COPY

LLOYD'S REGISTER OF SHIPPING

For The Secretary
LLOYD'S REGISTER
OF SHIPPING.

FOUNDED 1760   RE-CONSTITUTED 1834

S P E C I M E N

Certificate of Class

	Motor Stern Trawler	"ROSLYN 1"

*Official Number*_____ *Port of Registry*_____ Hong Kong_____

Owners   Fishing Enterprises (H.K.) Ltd.

Builders, and where and when built Ferro Cement Marine Construction Ltd., Hong Kong,

January 1972.

REGISTERED TONNAGES	**MOULDED DIMENSIONS**
Gross 164.77	Length 75' 10"
Net	Breadth 22' 0"
	Depth 10' 3"

This is to Certify *that this Ship has been built under the Special Survey of the Surveyors*

*to this Society, and was reported to be, on the*___7th January 1972___

in a fit and efficient condition and in accordance with the Rules; also that she has been CLASSED and entered

in the REGISTER BOOK of this Society, with the Character ✠ 100A1_____

subject to Periodical Surveys as required by the Rules.

Witness my hand,

(Signed) W.T. LEADBETTER   (Signed) A.C. GROVER

Secretary,   Chairman.

*71, Fenchurch Street, London, E.C.3.*___13th October 1972___

Reproduced by kind permission of Lloyd's Register of Shipping

Certificate of Class

LLOYD'S REGISTER OF SHIPPING

CERTIFIED COPY

FOUNDED 1760   RE-CONSTITUTED 1834

LLOYD'S MACHINERY CERTIFICATE
(LMC)

S P E C I M E N

This is to Certify *that the Machinery of this*

Motor Stern Trawler   "ROSLYN 1"

165   *Tons, of*   Hong Kong

has been Specially Surveyed by the Surveyors to this Society during construction at

Abenra

and was reported to be on the 7th January 1972 at Hong Kong

in good working condition.

The Record LMC *has been made in the Register Book, subject to Periodical Surveys as required by the Rules.*

PARTICULARS

Description of Machinery	Oil Engine 4 Stroke Cycle Single Acting With a controllable pitch propeller.	
Makers of Main Engines	Aabenraa Motorfabrik.	
Makers of Main Boilers	—	
Approved pressure of Main Boilers	—	lb. per square inch saturated steam
Steam Temperature	—	lb. per square inch superheated steam
	—	
Approved pressure of Aux./Domestic Boilers	—	lb. per square inch
Approved pressure of Steam Heated Steam Generators	—	lb. per square inch
Approved pressure of Exhaust Gas Economiser	—	lb. per square inch
B.H.P. 480		425 r.p.m. of Engine
Approved total S.H.P. —	—	425 r.p.m. of Propeller

Witness my hand

(Signed) W.T. LEADBETTER   (Signed) A.C. GROVER

Secretary   Chairman

71, Fenchurch Street, London, EC3M 4BS 13th October 1972

Reproduced by kind permission of Lloyd's Register of Shipping

Lloyd's Machinery Certificate (LMC)

LLOYD'S REGISTER OF SHIPPING

To The Secretary
LLOYD'S REGISTER
OF SHIPPING.

SPECIMEN

FOUNDED 1760   RE-CONSTITUTED 1834

CONTINUOUS SURVEY—MACHINERY

No. 722898

71, Fenchurch Street,
LONDON, EC3M 4BS

This is to Certify *that the Machinery of the*

Motorship NIKANNA"

1949 *Tons, of* Piraeus

Built at Gothenburg *in* December, 1929 *has been*

surveyed by the Surveyors to this Society in accordance with the Continuous Survey

requirements and reported to be on the 1st May 1972

in good working condition.

The Record ✠LMC has been maintained in the Register Book

of this Society, subject to the continuance of the survey as required by the Rules, and

the entry CS 2.72 *has been made in the Engine Survey column of the*

Supplement to the Register Book.

Witness my hand

R M Turnbull

(Signed) D.H.G. KIDD.   Chairman of the Classification Committee

Classification Manager

Date of Issue 1st August 1972

This Certificate is issued upon the terms of the Rules and Regulations of the Society, to which Owners are referred, and which provide that:—

"The Committees of the Society use their best endeavours to ensure that the functions of the Society are properly executed, but is is to be understood that neither the Society nor any Member of any of its Committees nor any of its Officers, Servants or Surveyors is under any circumstances whatever to be held responsible or liable for any inaccuracy in any report or certificate issued by the Society or its Surveyors, or in any entry in the Register Book or other publication of the Society, or for any act or omission, default or negligence of any of its Committees or any Member thereof, or of the Surveyors, or other Officers, Servants or Agents of the Society."

N. CS (M) 2m.6.72

Reproduced by kind permission of Lloyd's Register of Shipping

Lloyd's Continuous Survey—Machinery Certificate

LLOYD'S REGISTER OF SHIPPING

Ship's Name SS/MS ....   Gross tons   6389

LR number						Port		Report No.					Recommended survey date

Port: L O N

Recommended A.S. date — Month Year

Report No.: 3 0 0 7 0 4 — Recommended DD date Month Year

Recommended survey date — Month Year: 0 5 7 3

A.L.L. certificate endorsement date — Day Month Year

First date   18.4.73

Last date   2.5.73   Port of Registry   GLASGOW   Date of build   1946-12

<u>S P E C I M E N</u>

This is to Certify that I have surveyed the

above ship on account of <u>Damage</u> to Deck Plating in way of
Port Side forward mast house in way of ventilator coaming to
No.1 Hold.
and that I am transmitting to the Committee of Lloyd's Register of Shipping, London, a report,
stating that all repairs recommended by me have been completed to my satisfaction also that
I am recommending that she be continued as now classed, but subject to all
conditions of class being dealt with as previously recommended.

Surveyor to Lloyd's Register of Shipping   Date   2nd, May 1973

(G.H. ANTIEUL)   KEY TO ABBREVIATIONS

AS	Annual Survey	SS	Hull Special Survey
BS	Biennial Survey	SS(TD)	Hull Special Survey (Thickness determination)
DS	Docking Survey	SS(M)	Hull Special Survey (Modified)
NS	Cargo Battens not fitted (No Sparring)	CSH	Hull Special Survey (Continuous)

This Certificate is issued upon the terms of the Rules and Regulations of the Society, which provide that:—

"The Committees of the Society use their best endeavours to ensure that the functions of the Society are properly executed, but it is to be understood that neither the Society nor any Member of any of its Committees nor any of its Officers, Servants or Surveyors is under any circumstances whatever to be held responsible or liable for any inaccuracy in any report or certificate issued by the Society or its Surveyors, or in any entry in the Register Book or other publication of the Society, or for any act or omission default or negligence of any of its Committees or any Member thereof, or the Surveyors, or other Officers, Servants or Agents of the Society".

Cert. B.

Reproduced by kind permission of Lloyd's Register of Shipping

Lloyd's Continuation of Class Certificate

LLOYD'S REGISTER OF SHIPPING

Ship's Name SS/MS ....   Gross tons   7185

L.R. number	Port	Report No.	Recommended survey date
			Month Year
	L O N	3 0 0 7 6 3	0 5 7 3

First date   2.5.73

Last date   4.5.73   Port of Registry   LONDON   Date of build   1959-7

S P E C I M E N

This is to Certify *that I have surveyed part of the machinery and that all my recommendations have been carried out to my satisfaction. I am reporting accordingly and recommending to the Committee of Lloyd's Register of Shipping that the machinery classification should be retained and the following survey records assigned.,* with fresh record of ABS (ex.g.)05.73 when the safety valves have been set under steam, and CSM (with date) on completion of the survey.

Subject to the following conditions of class detailed below
and/or as previously recommended   Subject to the Port inboard main engine lub. oil pump (temporary repairs in way of air pump) being specially examined and dealt with as necessary by the end of November 1973.

Surveyor to Lloyd's Register of Shipping   Date   10.5.73
(C.D. WILKIE) KEY TO ABBREVIATIONS

ABS	Auxiliary Boiler Survey	MBS	Main Boiler Survey	TS	Tailshaft Survey
CSM	Continuous Survey of Machinery	OF	Fitted for oil fuel (date) FP above 150° F.	TS(CL)	Tailshaft Survey—Continuous Liner
DBS	Domestic Boiler Survey	SGS	Steam Generator Survey	TSN	Tailshaft renewed
ES	Engine Special Survey	SPS	Steampipe Survey	TS(OG)	Tailshaft Survey—Oil Gland

This Certificate is issued upon the terms of the Rules and Regulations of the Society, which provide that:—

"The Committee of the Society use their best endeavours to ensure that the functions of the Society are properly executed, but it is to be understood that neither the Society nor any Member of any of its Committees nor any of its Officers, Servants or Surveyors is under any circumstances whatever to be held responsible or liable for any inaccuracy in any report or certificate issued by the Society or its Surveyors, or in any entry in the Register Book or other publication of the Society, or for any act or omission default or negligence of any of its Committees or any Member thereof, or the Surveyors, or other Officers, Servants or Agents of the Society".

Cert. R.t.

Reproduced by kind permission of Lloyd's Register of Shipping

Lloyd's Interim Certificate of Class

To avoid confusion the name of the deck to which the depth is measured should be stated, *e.g.*, moulded depth to freeboard deck.

REGISTERED DIMENSIONS

These are sometimes called the identification dimensions, and are those stated in the Certificate of Registry for a British ship, being expressed in feet and tenths.

Registered or Identification Length is measured from the fore part of the stem head to the after side of the stern post, or fore side of the rudder stock if there is no stern post.

Registered or Identification Breadth is measured over the outside of the shell plating at the widest part (not necessarily at the middle of the length).

Registered or Identification Depth, or **Depth in Hold,** is measured from the top of the ceiling to the top of the deck beam at the centre line of the vessel at the middle of the length. This depth is measured to the tonnage deck.

The certificate of registry also shows in appropriate cases (*a*) depth in hold from upper deck to ceiling amidships, in the case of three decks and upwards, (*b*) depth from top of deck at side amidships to bottom of keel.

EXTREME DIMENSIONS

Length Overall is the length measured from the foremost point of the stem or figurehead (excluding bowsprit, if any) to the after side of the taffrail, or cruiser stern.

Extreme Breadth is measured over the outside of the shell plating, or rubbing strakes, or paddle sponsons (if any).

Depth is measured from the top of the keel to the top of the deck amidships.

DRAUGHT, FREEBOARD AND TRIM, ETC

Draught (d) is the distance of the lowest point of the keel below the water-line.

Mean Draught is the half sum of the draughts at the forward and after perpendiculars, or at the stem and stern post.

Moulded Draught (δ) is the distance of the top of the keel below the water-line.

Light Draughts are the draughts forward and aft when the vessel is floating complete with water in boilers, but without crew, bunkers, cargo, water ballast, solid ballast, fresh water, stores, or other loads.

Load Draught is the mean draught when the vessel is submerged to the depth of her seasonal load line. The Summer load line draught is the one quoted in Lloyd's Register Book. Tropical, Winter, and Winter North Atlantic load draughts can be deduced from the Summer draught by the application of simple rules (See Chapter 18.)

Bulkhead Draught is the term sometimes used to describe the maximum permissible mean draught for a passenger steamer to which subdivision load lines have been assigned in accordance with the International Convention for the Safety of Life at Sea, 1974.

Freeboard (actual) is the vertical distance of the upper edge of the "deck line" above the existing water-line.

Mean Freeboard is the half sum of the freeboards measured on the port and starboard sides, respectively.

Minimum Seasonal Freeboard is the vertical distance of the upper edge of the "deck line" above the seasonal load line.

Trim is the difference between the forward and after draughts. If the former is the greater the vessel is trimmed "by the head". If the latter is the greater she is trimmed "by the stern". If the forward and after draughts are equal the vessel is said to be "on even keel".

Change of Trim is the sum of the changes of draught forward and aft if one increases and the other decreases as a result of adding, removing, or shifting weight. Should they both increase or both decrease by different amounts, it is the difference of the changes.

Transverse Inclinations. When a vessel is not upright she is said to have a "heel", a "list", or a "loll", according to circumstances. Inclination due to initial negative stability is by general agreement referred to as "loll". On the other hand, the terms "heel" and "list" seem to be used indiscriminately. It would, in the author's opinion, be an advantage if unnecessary confusion were avoided by associating "heel" exclusively with inclinations due to the application of external forces, and "list" with inclinations due to unsymmetrical distribution of weight within the ship.

SALE AND PURCHASE OF SHIPS

In connection with the sale and purchase of a ship the preliminary negotiations may, of course, take a variety of forms depending upon the particular circumstances. Here it will be sufficient to concentrate on a few of the more important aspects common to most cases.

An owner with tonnage to dispose of may insert advertisements in the shipping press, or he may instruct his broker to attempt negotiations with a limited number of possible purchasers. Direct negotiations between seller and buyer are not very usual, the

C. A. E. DEACON **REGISTER OF SHIPS** 1973-74

1 LR Identity No. Call Sign Official No. Navigational aids	2 SHIP'S NAME Former names OWNERS Managers Port of Registry Flag	3 TONS Gross Net Summer Deadwt Gross Net Summer Deadwt	4 CLASSIFICATION Hull Latest SS recorded Machinery Refrigerated cargo installation Equipment letter	5 HULL Date of build Shipbuilders—Place of build Length overall Breadth extreme Draught maximum Length B.P. Breadth moulded Depth moulded Superstructures Decks Riveted/Welded Bulkheads Alterations Rise of floor Keel Water ballast	6 CARGO CAPACITIES/HANDLING Description of ship No. of Passengers No. of Holds & lengths/No. of Cargo tanks Grain/Liquid c.ft. Bale c.ft. Insulated spaces c.ft. Heating coils No. of Hatchways and sizes No. of Winches Cranes/Derricks No./SWL tons	7 MACHINERY Engines Bore and stroke Total horsepower Type Fuel Bunkers (tons) Enginebuilders Where manufactured Boilers Heating surface Pressure Aux. electrical generating plant Special propellers Speed knots
7226810 350678 Esd Rdr RT	C. A. E. DEACON Republic of South Africa (Railways & Harbours Administration) Cape Town S. African	57 9 —	✠100A1 South Africa coasting service within 10 miles offshore ✠LMC EL (A) ¼ "U1	1972-3 Dorman Long (Africa) Ltd.—Drb 66' 5" 17' 11" 6' 1½" 60' 0" 17' 0" 9' 3" 1 dk 5BH rf 24"	M Pilot Cutter	Oil 4SA 6Cy. 7⅞"×8½" sr geared 700bhp Ruston Paxman Diesels Ltd. Cpl 2×25kW 380V 50c/s a.c. Controllable pitch propeller 12k
5056244 Df Esd Pld Rdr RT	C. A. LARSEN Argenbal S.A. Buenos Aires Argentine	428 150 —	✠Classed BC until 5/56	1926-11 Smith's Dock Co. Ltd.—Mdb 156' 10" 27' 7" 14' 0½" 146' 6" 27' 6" 15' 6" 1 dk RW rf 7½"	S Whaler Mchy.aft	C 4Cy. (2) 14½" & (2) 34½"×32½" 2300ihp 211t (o.f) Smith's Dock Co. Ltd. Mdb 14k
5056233	C. C. N. Y. VICTORY 7637 tons gross Built 1945 Bethlehem Fairfield—Bal TYPE VC2-S-AP2 — Dimensions, etc., recorded after ships letter Z United States Department of Commerce					
5058263 CYFV 189414 Df Esd Gc Pld Rdr RTm/h/v	C. D. HOWE Vestgron Mines Ltd. Ottawa Canadian	3628 1871 2935	✠100A1 SS 5/66 with freeboard Str. nav. ice ✠LMC EL u	1950-6 Davie S.B. & R. Co. Ltd.—Lauzon 294' 8" 50' 2" 18' 7¾" 270' 8" 50' 0" 28' 6" B&F156' 2 dks 5BH WB1867t incl. Tunnel tanks 373t DTf166t DTa24t DTm532t	TS Supply Ship 3 Ho 20', 46½', 43½' 2 Ha (stl) (10½'×10½') (22'×18') 1 Ha (w) (13'×18') Cr 1(15) 1(3) 3(1)	S 6Cy. 24½"×20" 8000ihp (o.f) Canadian Vickers Ltd Mtl 2WTB 275lb Spt 220lb hs8714 3×65kW 225V d.c.
6118191 VC3901 154984	C. DE MALOIZE exFort Liberté-71 exMartin S.-62 exDonnacona No. 3-60 Agence Maritime Inc. Quebec Canadian	304 250 —	Classed LR until 8/59	1929 Davie S.B. & Rep. Co. Ltd.—Lauzon 149' 0" 30' 1" 8' 0½" 139' 6" 30' 0" 10' 0" 1 dk R	TM Mchy.aft 1 Ho 83' B.19475	2 Oil 2SA each 4Cy. 255×380 mm NE42 6¼t Fairbanks, Morse & Co. Beloit 7½k
6602271 KGTP 290282 Df Esd Gc Pld Rdr RTm	C. E. DANT States Steamship Co. San Francisco United States	T.Mk 8046 5408 — 12724 9180 14376	AB	1963 National Stl & S.B. Co.—S.Diego 565' 0" 76' 2" —/31' 1½" 535' 0" 76' 0" 44' 6" B64' F152' 2 dks, 3rd dk fwd rf nil	S (12P) Ref pt container ship 6 Ho 47½', 74½', 67½', 67½', 70½', 55½' G.810534 B.737733 In.33068 6 Ha (stl) (17½'×19½') (37½', 37½', 37½', 37½', 37½'×29½') 24W Der 1(50) 4(20) 7(5)	2 S Turb dr geared to sc. shaft 19250shp 3850t (o.f) General Electric Co. Lyn 2×750kW 450V 60c/s a.c. 20k
5058296 ZSBV 152581 Df Esd RTm	C. F. KAYSER Republic of South Africa (Railways & Harbours Administration) Port Elizabeth S. African	601 — —	✠Classed LR until 7/37	1938-9 Lobnitz & Co. Ltd.—Rnf 154' 3" 33' 1" 14' 0" 32' 11" B42' R rf 12"	TS Tug 1 Ho 13' 1 Ha (5½'×6')	T 9Cy. 17" 29" & 48"×30" 236t (c) Lobnitz & Co. Ltd. Rnf 12k
5030286 IKZV 493 Df Esd Pld RT	C. F. O. TONTINI exErnst Gröschel-60 Fratelli Tontini Rome Italian	447 206 —	RI	1949 Rickmers Werft—Bhn 157' 8" 26' 4" 14' 0" 142' 1" 26' 3" 15' 6" F17' RW	M Trawler 1 Ho B.13419 1W	Oil 4SA 6Cy. 370×560 mm 800bhp NE80 Ansaldo Stab. Mecc. Gen 10k
6601069 IKZY 495 Df Esd Gc Pld Rdr RT	C. F. O. TONTINI SECONDO exHans Vom Hoff-63 Fratelli Tontini Rome Italian	630 301 —	RI	1950 Rickmers Werft—Bhn 176-4" 29' 0" 171' 5" 28' 10" 16' 5"	M Trawler 1 Ho B.17796	Oil 4SA 6Cy. 400×580mm 1800bhp NE88 Klöckner-Humboldt-Deutz Kln
6909249 301076 Df Gc Pld Rdr RTm/h	C. G. HOVELMEIER exKos 58-66 Union Whaling Co. Ltd. Durban S. African	626 202 —	NV	1958 A/S Fredrikstad M/V—Fks 172' 0" 29' 8" 151' 4" 29' 6" 16' 0" 1 dk	S Whaler	C 4Cy. (2) 15½" & (2) 37½"×34½" 3000ihp (o.f) Smith's Dk Co. Ltd. Mdb 3×25/30, 25/30, 6/10kW 220V d.c.
6821057 336105	C. H. HORN Poole Harbour Commissioners Poole British	159 134 168		1968 J. W. Cook & Co. (Wivenhoe) Ltd.—Wvn 85' 0" 28' 0" 6' 0" 80' 0" 28' 6" 8' 2" 1 dk rf nil	M Hopper Dredger Mchy.aft 1 Ho 27½' Cr 1(5)	Oil 4SA 5Cy. 5"×5½" 163bhp 4t (d.o) Dorman & Co. Ltd. Stafford 1×3kW 24V 6½k
5068218 WA3882 204466 Df Gc Rdr RT	C. H. McCULLOUGH, Jr. exWard Ames Pickands, Mather & Co. Wilmington, Del United States	5938 4748 10800	AB	1907 Superior S.B. Co.—Superior 540-0" 55' 2" 20' 10½" 530' 10" 56' 0" 30' 8" 1 dk R	S Mchy.aft 4 Ho 18 Ha (stl) (each 11'×37')	Uniflow 3Cy. 28"×36" 3510ihp NE54 Skinner Engine Co. Erie

C. H. McCULLOUGH, Jr. 566

Reproduced by kind permission of Lloyd's Register of Shipping

Extract from Lloyd's Register Book (Register of Ships)

services of a broker generally being considered essential. The seller will furnish the broker with full particulars of the vessel for sale and these will be entered into a form suitable for circulation amongst prospective purchasers. The form may show the name of the vessel or, if the owner does not wish to disclose the name at that stage, merely a folio number. To enable a possible purchaser to decide whether the ship will suit his requirements it is necessary that the particulars form should be very detailed. The kind of information required is indicated in the following list of items:—

Deadweight capacity in tons.
Load draught.
Speed in knots.
Daily consumption of fuel and type of fuel.
Name of builders.
Where and when built.
Principal dimensions.
Gross and net register tonnage.
Type of ship (*e.g.*, open shelter-deck).
Material and rig, whether riveted or welded or both.
Number and type of masts.
Number and arrangement of decks.
Particulars of erections and superstructures.
Height between decks.
Number and capacity of ballast tanks.
Number and capacity of fresh water tanks.
Number of bulkheads.
Number and sizes of hatchways.
Number of holds (and deep tanks, if any).
Grain and bale capacity of each hold, 'tween-deck, and other
    compartments.
Total grain and bale space.
Particulars of passenger accommodation, if any.
Arrangement and capacity of bunkers.
Name of engine builders.
Description of main engines including N.H.P., I.H.P., number
    of cylinders, and length of stroke.
Principal auxiliaries.
Number, age, and description of boilers.
Heating surface and working-pressure of boilers.
Donkey engine and donkey boiler.
Type of steering gear and emergency steering.
Particulars of windlass, winches, and other deck machinery.
Number and S.W. Loads of derricks and/or cranes.
Radio installation and navigational aids installed.
Number of motor and other lifeboats and type of davits.
Where and when the vessel may be inspected.
Price asked.

Other remarks may be appended including, for instance, the
date and place of the last classification survey and class assigned, if
any. As a necessary precaution against the possible effects of
misdescription it is usual to insert a clause to read "These particulars
are believed to be correct but are not guaranteed".

When a possible purchaser comes along who is seriously interested
he may request permission to make an inspection of the vessel, or he
may make an offer "subject to inspection". In the former case it
is probable that only a relatively superficial examination would be

permitted, but when a definite offer has been made a full examination is likely to be agreed to involving the opening up of machinery. The buyer, before making a final decision to purchase, will usually instruct his marine and engineer superintendents or other experts to make a thorough examination of the vessel and report on her condition and capabilities. Some bargaining may ensue before terms and price are finally agreed, and when that stage is reached an agreement of sale will be drawn up, signed, and witnessed.

The details of contracts of sale are naturally subject to considerable variation, but the features described below are common to most.

The agreement indicates that on the date specified "A" has sold and "B" has purchased the vessel (named) of (so many) tons register, and as she now lies with all stores belonging to her on board and on shore for the sum (stated); payment to be made by (person stated) within (so many) days from this date. A deposit of ten per cent. to be paid on account of the purchase money on signing of this contract to (persons stated) to be held by them pending completion of the contract.

At this juncture the buyer will usually have inspected the outside of the hull above water as well as the interior of the vessel and her machinery, but not the ship's bottom. Therefore, a clause in the contract will provide that the purchasers may place the vessel in graving dock at their own risk and expense, and if she be then and there found damaged in the bottom the sellers are to make good the damage or cancel the contract at their option. If they opt to cancel they are to repay all expenses in connection with the docking.

An extremely important clause provides that, on payment of the whole of the purchase money agreed, a legal bill of sale, free from incumbrances, shall be executed to the purchasers at their expense, and the ship and all belonging to her shall be delivered to them. The purchaser of a British registered ship does not obtain a complete title of ownership until the bill of sale has been executed and recorded by the registrar at the ships' port of registry. If the transfer is being arranged by a broker it will be his duty to complete the transfer by seeing that this is promptly carried out.

When the balance of the purchase money has been paid and the bill of sale handed to the buyer the sale is completed, and the seller should guarantee that all debts against the vessel up to the date of completion will be paid prior to delivery of the vessel.

Should the buyer fail to pay the purchase money as agreed, the seller then has the right, by the terms of the contract, to resell the vessel by private or public sale. Moreover, the buyer will forfeit his deposit and will be liable for all loss and expense arising from the resale with interest.

If the seller does not produce the legal bill of sale, or if he fails to deliver the vessel as and when agreed, it is provided by the

F

contract that he shall return the buyer's deposit and, unless the default has arisen from events over which he has no control, be liable for compensation for disappointment and loss of time.

A brokerage clause is generally included, stating the amount of brokerage due, and usually providing for it to be paid by the seller.

As well as the method of sale by private contract, ships can be sold by public auction, but this is comparatively rare except in the case of "forced sale" or in the case of a shipowning company being compulsorily wound up. A reserve price may be put on the vessel at the risk, of course, of the seller being put to considerable expense to no purpose if a sale is not effected. Prospective purchasers may be permitted to inspect the vessel before the date of the auction or, alternatively, the seller may give a guarantee of the particulars of the vessel. In the absence of guarantee or opportunity to inspect, it is evident that buying at auction a vessel to be sold "as she lies" could be a very risky undertaking.

EMPLOYMENT OF SHIPS

It will hardly be necessary to remind readers of this book that a large number of vessels are employed in special ways. For instance, there are fishing vessels, tugs, salvage craft, dredgers, hoppers, ferries, ice-breakers, cable ships, and others, and in an entirely different category certain large vessels designed for the carriage of passengers exclusively either on regular routes or on pleasure cruises. This section on employment, however, is concerned only with the employment of ships as carriers of goods, and in connection therewith it will be convenient to consider separately (a) dry cargo carriers, and (b) bulk liquid carriers.

DRY CARGO CARRIERS

The most common methods of employment are:—

1. Employment of the ship by her owners in a liner trade, *i.e.* "on the berth", or as a combined transport operator carrying containers.
2. Employment of the ship by a demise charterer.
3. Employment of the ship by a charterer under a simple time charter.
4. Ship fixed by her owners for a voyage charter.
5. Ship hired by a charterer for a voyage or for a period of time and sublet in whole or in part to others.

Cargo Liners employed by Owners. A ship employed in this way is generally a unit in a fleet of vessels regularly engaged in a particular trade. The owners are usually a limited company and in many cases, also, members of one or other of the various Liner Conferences. The owners' remuneration consists of the freight earnings which depend on the kind and quantity of cargo carried, supplemented in some cases by passage money if the vessel carries fare-paying passengers as well as goods. All running expenses are paid by the owners who appoint the master and supply the crew. Information of intended sailings is circulated among shippers by means of "sailing cards" and by advertisement in national and local newspapers as well as in "Lloyd's List" and other official publications. The information given will generally include the following items:—

> the name of the ship;
> the port, dock, and berth where the vessel will load;
> the date when she will be ready to receive cargo;
> the closing date (*i.e.*, the date after which goods will not be accepted);
> the expected date of sailing;
> the port, or series of ports, to which the vessel will proceed—possibly indicating that she will call at other named ports if sufficient inducement offers, and possibly reserving the right to vary the route or alter the sailing date with or without notice;
> the name, address, telephone number and telegraphic address of the loading broker to whom requests to book space should be made.

The owner of the ship is also the "carrier" and, as explained in Chapter 9, he will be to a limited extent a common carrier.

In many liner trades in recent years the ship has been employed more and more as part of a combined transport operation for carriage of goods from door to door. The ship is on the container berth for loading for named ports for a limited number of hours or days, but the cargo will be, or will have been, delivered to the ship already pre-packed in standard sized containers which have been loaded either at the goods manufacturers' works, or at the forwarding agents' or shipping company's inland depots, ready to be loaded by special cranes. An alternative to this practice is for the containers to be placed on a trailer and driven on board over a ramp in what is known as a Roll-on/Roll-off (RO-RO) operation.

Door to door container transportation raises a number of legal problems because of the different modes of transport and the different limits of liability for damages provided by the Conventions which apply to road or rail or sea carriage.

Demise Chartered Ship. If the ship is let on demise charter, the charterer appoints the master, supplies the crew, acts as carrier, and takes over the full control of the ship, employing her as if she were a unit of his own fleet. The shipowner's remuneration takes the form of hire money usually fixed at a certain rate per ton of summer deadweight per calendar month, and payable in advance. The owner may retain the right to require the removal of the master and chief engineer, if dissatisfied. The charterer's remuneration is the freight and passage money (if any) earned. When building cost are very high a shipowner with berth commitments he could not otherwise meet may resort to demise chartering in preference to ordering new tonnage. It may sometimes be necessary to demise charter a vessel to replace temporarily a ship that has been lost, or one that is laid up for extensive repairs.

The apportionment of expenses is usually as follows:—

For owner's account:—
> Depreciation.
> Insurance, unless by agreement the charterer insures the vessel.
> Survey prior to delivery.
> Brokerage, if incurred.

For charterer's account:—
> Crew's wages, maintenance, repairs and stores.
> Lubricating oil and water.
> Bunkers, port charges, stevedoring costs, cost of hold cleaning, dunnage, ballast (if any).
> Canal dues, towage, and pilotage.
> Commissions and brokerage on cargo.
> Claims against ship for loss of or damage to cargo.
> All overhead expenses.

N.B.—As far as dry cargo ships are concerned the terms "demise charter" and "bareboat charter" are practically synonymous. However, as pointed out further on, there is an important distinction between the two terms with regard to tanker chartering.

Ship let on Simple Time Charter. In this case the shipowner appoints the master and supplies the crew, and is remunerated by hire money paid, usually, at an agreed rate per month. The charterer, unlike the demise charterer, does not take over full control of the vessel.

Expenses are apportioned as shown below:—

For owner's account:—
> Depreciation.
> Insurance, surveys, and all overheads.
> Crews' wages, provisions, maintenance, repairs and stores.
> Lubricating oil and water, unless otherwise agreed in the C/P.
> Certain claims as agreed.

For charterer's account:—
> Bunkers.
> Port charges.
> Canal dues.
> Stevedoring, hold cleaning, and dunnage.

Ballast (if any).
Water, unless supplied by owners.
Commissions and brokerage on cargo.
Claims not payable by owners under terms of C/P.

Ship fixed for Voyage Charter. Where a ship is fixed to carry a cargo under a voyage charter-party the shipowner appoints the master and crew, and acts as carrier—in this case a private carrier. Most commonly the contract will be for the carriage of a full cargo, but it may be for a part cargo. It may happen, for instance, that part of the space in a general ship is let to a charterer. If a "voyage berth charter" is fixed, the charterer places the ship on the berth as a general ship, in which case the exact nature of the cargo is not known in advance, though the charterer will be liable to the owner for deadfreight if he fails to load a full cargo. The majority of voyage charters, however, are for the carriage of homogeneous cargoes like grain, timber, metallic ores, and so on.

All running expenses are borne by the owners unless the charter-party specifically provides that all or part of the stevedoring charges are to be paid by the charterer. The freight rate agreed will naturally take into account the amount of these charges and by whom they are paid.

The shipowner's remuneration is the freight earned by carrying the cargo. Where the charterer is also the shipper his profit is the difference between the price he pays for the cargo and the price he ultimately sells it for, less expenses. In some cases, however, the charterer may be a broker who has undertaken to find a cargo for the ship to carry. Such a charterer's profit is the excess of the bill of lading freight over the chartered freight which is due from him to the shipowner. According to circumstances, the bill of lading freight will be collected from the consignee of the cargo by the shipowner's agent or by the charterer's agent. In the former case the owner will retain the chartered freight and pay over the surplus to the charterer. In the latter case the agent pays the charter freight to the owner and retains the balance.

Ships habitually employed on voyage charters are referred to as "tramps" as distinct from "liners" employed as general ships on more or less fixed routes.

A voyage charter-party may be arranged to cover two or more voyages.

Subletting. In both time charters and voyage charters it is not uncommon for the contract to be claused to permit the charterers to sublet the vessel in whole or in part on condition that they remain responsible to the shipowner for due performance of the original charter-party. Subletting in the case of a voyage charter usually means that other shippers book space in the ship from the charter instead of directly from the shipowner.

BULK LIQUID CARRIERS

The vast majority of these vessels are designed for the carriage of bulk oil, but besides oil tankers there are other bulk liquid carriers for the transportation of such commodities as molasses and, very recently, so-called liquid gas (gas reduced to a very low temperature so as to liquefy it), and liquid chemicals.

Many oil tankers are owned by the major oil companies and are employed by those companies to carry crude oil from the oil fields to their various refineries, or to carry refined products from the refineries to the marketing depots.

In addition to the above, numerous large tanker fleets are owned by independent shipowners and are chartered by the oil companies under various arrangements as shown below:—

1. Charter for a single voyage.
2. Charter for a stipulated number of consecutive voyages.
3. Charter for consecutive voyages extending over a stipulated period of time.
4. Charter for consecutive voyages extending over a fixed period followed by a time charter for world-wide trading (generally on a long term basis, say, for several years).
5. Time charter for a number of years for world-wide trading for shipments of dirty oil.
6. Time charter for a number of years stipulating a maximum period of clean oil trading.
7. Bareboat charter.
8. Time charter by demise.

Oil companies may sometimes charter each other's tonnage as well as chartering vessels independently owned.

The above references to clean and dirty oil are important on account of the higher rate of corrosion suffered by tankers when carrying clean oils. Owners of newly built tonnage will generally insist that such vessels shall be operated in the clean petroleum trade for a certain maximum period only. For the same reason time charter rates for clean oil carriage are usually somewhat higher than the rates quoted for dirty oil on the same voyage.

Black Oil or **Dirty Oil** includes:—
    crude oil,
    heavy diesel oil,
    fuel and furnace oils,
    some grades of gas oil.

Clean Oil includes:—
    motor and aviation spirit,
    benzine,
    white spirit,
    tractor vaporising oil,

kerosene,
some grades of gas oil,
some grades of high speed diesel oil.

Lubricating Oil is in a class by itself and is usually carried by ships specially built for the purpose.

The distinction between tanker demise and bareboat charters may be briefly explained as follows.

Under a bareboat charter the owner puts the vessel at the disposal of the charterer for a period of time, frequently for a number of years, at an agreed rate of hire. The oil company which has chartered the vessel operate her in the same way as they operate units of their own tanker fleet by appointing their own master and crew and paying all running expenses themselves.

A demise charter-party, however, contains a "management agreement" clause in pursuance of which the owners undertake to operate the vessel on behalf of the charterers in accordance with the charterer's instructions and in return for the annual payment of an agreed management fee. Accordingly, it is the shipowner who appoints master, officers, and crew, equips and supplies the vessel, and arranges for docking, surveys, repairs, and maintenance. The principal reason for this arrangement is that oil companies who find need to charter large numbers of vessels, in addition to operating their own, can take advantage of already existing operating organisations and are spared the difficulty and expense of expanding their own.

CHAPTER 4

MASTER AND CREW

INTRODUCTION

The Merchant Shipping Act 1970. As so much of this Act is concerned with the employment of masters and seamen under crew agreements, together with such topics as engagement and discharge, wages, discipline, manning and so forth, it is felt that this is the right place in this book wherein to make the following introductory comments.

The Pearson Report. A Court of Inquiry set up under Lord Pearson produced its report in March 1967 for submission to the then Minister of Labour. This report, which ran to some 63,000 words, dealt with personnel relations, working conditions, and the pressing need for changes in the Principal Act of 1894. It pointed out that that Act—the longest on the Statute Book—contained much anti-quated legislation dating back to the days of sailing ships and largely illiterate seamen. A new Act, the report suggested, should be free from unnecessary detail and should deal broadly with matters of principle and policy so as to foster rather than inhibit future development. It was recommended that much less use should be made of criminal law and more of civil law, and that many things should be left to industrial negotiation and new contracts between seamen and their employers. Two of the many important points raised were the questions of demarcation and wastage. With regard to the former something had already been done by the introduction, with the agreement of the National Union of Seamen, of all-purposes ratings associated with a special training scheme. Regarding wastage, a sample survey had shown that a third of catering ratings, a quarter of engine-room ratings and a fifth of deck ratings had left the industry after less than a year's service, and it was suggested that such an unsatisfactory state of affairs could be largely remedied by the adoption of many of the reforms recommended and particularly by schemes whereby seamen could spend a greater proportion of their time on leave or under training ashore.

Comments on the new Act. Arising from the above-mentioned report the Merchant Shipping Act 1970 was passed to be brought into force on such date as the Board of Trade (now D.o.T.) may by order made by statutory instrument appoint, and providing that different days may be so appointed for different provisions of the Act. The greater part of it, together with the supporting Regulations, came

156

into force on 1st January 1973 and only sections 6, 50, 51, 87 and 91 now remain to be brought into force, as section 36 giving powers to provide for ship's disciplinary committees will not be implemented.

Extensions of the Act. Under section 92 the D.o.T. may make regulations extending certain provisions of the Act to unregistered British ships and to masters and seamen employed in them with such exceptions, adaptations or modifications as may be specified. Under section 93 Her Majesty may by Order in Council direct that certain provisions of the Act and regulations shall extend, with exceptions, etc. as specified, to ships registered in independent Commonwealth countries and to masters and seamen employed in them. Under section 94 Her Majesty may by Order in Council give, with respect to the Isle of Man, Channel Islands, any colony or any territory outside Her Majesty's dominions in which for the time being Her Majesty has jurisdiction, either or both of the following directions—(i) that specified provisions of the Act and regulations shall apply to ships registered in the territory (with exceptions, etc. as may be specified) as they apply to U.K. registered ships and their crew members; (ii) that such provisions as may be specified shall extend to the territory, with such exceptions, etc. as may be specified in the Order, as part of the law of the territory. For instance, it may well be that proper officers (Shipping Masters or Superintendents) in Commonwealth countries and colonies will when operating under their own legislation continue the practice of attending at the engagement and discharge of crews. It is understood that the Government of Hong Kong does not contemplate introducing the system whereby members of a ship's crew enter into an agreement with the shipowner instead of the master of the ship, though most of the provisions of the M.S. Act 1970 will apply to agreements opened in Hong Kong and legislation is being enacted to incorporate various amendments to the previous Act.

Non-sea-going Ships. The provisions of the Act other than sections 19, 20, 43-60, 88, 90 and 91 do not apply to ships which are not sea-going ships or to masters and seamen employed in them. If such a ship plies, or attempts to ply, without carrying such officers and other seamen as are required under section 43 the owner or master will be liable on conviction on indictment to a fine, and on summary conviction to a fine not exceeding £1000 and the ship may be detained.

Interpretation of the Act. It should be noted that in sections 62 to 66 "seamen" (notwithstanding section 742 of the 1894 Act) includes the master of a ship. Section 97 states, amongst other things, that "ship's boat" includes a life-raft, that references to going to sea include references to going to sea from any country outside the U.K., that a seaman discharged in any country and left there is deemed to be left behind in that country even though the ship remains there, and that references to dying in a ship include references to dying in a ship's boat and to being lost from a ship or ship's boat.

Adaptation to Metric Units. Under section 90 the D.o.T. may by regulations provide for such adaptations of any enactments contained in M.S. Acts as appear to them appropriate for the purpose of replacing references therein to units other than metric units by references to metric units which are either equivalent thereto or such approximations thereto as appear desirable to secure that enactments are expressed in convenient terms.

THE MASTER

Master's Authority. The master of a ship is always authorised to perform whatever acts are ordinarily necessary for the safe and proper prosecution of the voyage with regard to both ship and cargo. As the agent of the shipowner and the bailee of the cargo it behoves him to act as though both were his own uninsured property so as to complete the voyage with the minimum of delay and the minimum of expense. With modern facilities of communication it is not now normally within the authority of the master to act as general agent at ports abroad, to arrange charters and decide the next employment of the ship. Owners have their own agents at most ports abroad to conduct the business of the ship on their behalf and according to their instructions. Moreover, the master's authority is generally defined in and limited by the provisions of printed bills of lading and charter-parties. However, extraordinary circumstances may arise, which (a) extend the authority of the master as agent of the shipowner, and (b) force upon him the rôle of "agent of necessity" of the cargo owners. Such extended authority may give the master powers to order repairs, to raise money for ship's disbursements, to tr anship cargo, to jettison cargo, to have damaged cargo reconditioned or sold, to deviate from the contract route of the voyage, or to enter into a salvage agreement. But before taking it upon himself to act in such capacity, the master must be quite certain that actions taken under such extended authority are absolutely necessary in the interests of the ship and/or cargo, and that it is impossible to communicate with the shipowner or cargo owners in sufficient time to receive their instructions before the time arrives when the necessity to act becomes urgent.

Except perhaps in wartime, circumstances which justify the extension of the master's authority in this way arise only very rarely, and in any case the master's actions must be limited to what is reasonable.

Within certain limits, as explained in the section on bills of lading in Chapter 9, the master has authority to bind the shipowner to the terms of a B/L signed by him on the owner's behalf.

If his ship is being employed under a time charter, the master has no authority to sign drafts for bunkers, stores, or other goods supplied to the ship, which by the terms of the charter-party are for the charterer's account, so as to make the shipowner liable for payment thereof. He should also be careful to exclude his own personal liability. The best way to achieve this is to sign "for and on behalf of Messrs. .... time charterers and for their sole a/c" or "for and on behalf of time charterers without recourse to self or owners."

Master's Liabilities. To such extent as loss occurs through any wrongful or negligent act on his part the master will incur personal liability. For example, if he unjustifiably deviates from the ordinary course of the voyage he will be liable in full to the shipowner for any loss or damage that results therefrom. If he signs B's/L for goods which are not actually on board, and those documents pass into the hands of third parties for good consideration, he will be personally liable to those third parties for whatever loss they sustain by reason of the mis-statement of facts in the B's/L. Further he will be personally liable under all contracts made by him in relation to the employment of the ship and the supply of bunkers, stores, and other necessaries to the ship, unless he specifically excludes such liability at the time of entering into the contract in the manner previously described.

Under section 73 of the M.S.Act 1970, where there has occurred any casualty that may give rise to an inquiry or investigation (see sections 55 and 56 of the Act) the owner or master must, as soon as practicable, and in any case not later than 24 hours after the ship's arrival at the next port, report the casualty to the D.o.T. giving a brief description of it and stating the time and place where it occurred, the name and official number of the ship, its position at the time of the report and the next port of call. Failure to comply without reasonable cause renders the owner or master liable on summary conviction to a fine not exceeding £1000.

Master's Power of Arrest. Under Section 79 of the 1970 Act the master of a U.K. registered ship may cause any person on board to be put under restraint if and for so long as it appears to him necessary or expedient in the interest of safety or for the preservation of good order and discipline on board.

Unauthorised Presence on Board Ship. Where a ship registered in the U.K. or any other country is in a U.K. port and a person who is neither in Her Majesty's service nor authorised by law to do so (*a*) goes on board without the master's consent or that of any authorised person, or (*b*) remains on board after being requested to leave by the master, a constable, a D.o.T. officer or an officer of customs and excise, he will (under section 78) be liable on summary conviction to a fine not exceeding £50.

Relationship with Deck and Engineer Officers. It is obviously in the best interests of the owner that the master should at all times do his utmost to ensure the smooth and efficient working of the ship by acquiring and retaining the confidence and co-operation of his officers. No doubt there are different approaches to this problem as no two people are exactly alike, but the following points are, perhaps, especially worth emphasising. Deck officers should be encouraged to take an active and responsible part in the navigation of the ship and should always be informed well in advance of the master's intentions. Standing orders and night orders should be drawn up clearly and free from ambiguity, and no officer should be allowed the excuse that he was, when in doubt about the ship's position, "afraid to call the master". A good master will always take the view that he would rather be called a dozen times unnecessarily than remain uncalled on the one occasion when his presence on deck was urgently required. But it is most important that his officers should be in no doubt about it. An officer should always understand that when it is necessary or prudent for him to call the master he should first put the ship in a safe position. The master should see that each officer knows what his duties include so that friction due to "interfering in someone else's job" is avoided. Whenever the master goes on the bridge, and particularly in busy waters, he should make clear to the officer of the watch his intention to take over the navigation of the ship, or the contrary, as the case may be. It is not only embarrassing to the officer concerned, but a possible source of danger, if the officer of the watch is uncertain on this point. It should be borne in mind that a young officer may be too diffident to ask the master what the position is. If an officer shows weakness in any aspect of his work it will be more useful to instruct him than to castigate him unduly.

Good relations with the chief engineer and his staff are equally important and to this end the master should always keep the chief engineer informed, as well in advance as possible, of sailing and arrival times, intended changes of speed, and the probable duration of stays in ports and anchorages. The master with the chief engineer's assistance and co-operation should always have accurate knowledge of the quantity of fuel in the bunkers at all times.

Responsibility for Cadets. Deck cadets or trainee deck officers entering the Merchant Navy are required to have a minimum qualification of four specified passes at GCE "O" level; this might be reduced to three in certain circumstances. Before a cadet may qualify for a first Certificate of Competency at either Class 3, 4 or 5 level, he or she must have satisfactorily completed a specified minimum training period recognised by the Department of Trade.

The general scheme of training is an induction course followed by sea service. Two college based phases separated by sea service are then followed before the trainee finally receives the qualification appropriate for his course of training.

It is an essential feature of courses that the student has completed a laid down period of planned training at sea. Proof of the planned training will normally take the form of a Record Book duly completed by masters and officers of ships in which sea service is performed. It is the responsibility of the cadet to make sure that his Record Book is properly maintained and endorsed, and the responsibility of the master and appropriate officers to complete the relevant sections when they are satisfied that the tasks have been properly carried out.

Although the master of a ship which carries cadets will normally delegate the actual training to one or more of his officers, he will have the over-riding responsibility for seeing that the training is properly carried out. He should inspect record books at intervals and should enter any comments he feels to be relevant.

Master's Duties. The interests of the owners, the safety of the ship and cargo, and the welfare of all on board should, it is hardly necessary to say, be the constant concern of the master. Private trading or profit making on his own account are serious breaches of the confidence his employers have obviously placed in him by appointing him to command and the master should never accept gratuities, rebates, commissions, or allowances of any kind without the knowledge and sanction of the owners. In cases where owners give standing instructions to the master, such instructions should be scrupulously observed at all times. Numerous statutory and other duties of the master are mentioned in other parts of this book and the following remarks are intended to cover a few points only.

It is highly important that the owners should be kept promptly and fully informed of all matters that affect their interests, and the master should at the first opportunity send them all relevant information concerning delays or accidents. If the ship is under time charter the master should always advise the owners of the ports which have been nominated by the charterers. Sailings and arrivals should be promptly notified as well as crew changes. In many cases the master will be supplied with the names and addresses of the agents of the owner's Protecting and Indemnity Association at ports abroad. Should serious difficulties arise in connection with ship, cargo, or crew the advice of these agents should be promptly sought. If an accident occurs which is likely to give rise to litigation, reports sent to the owners or their agents will generally have to be produced to the other side. For that reason many owners have special report forms on which masters can report directly to the owners' solicitors. Such documents being "privileged" do not have to be produced in court. Special care is necessary to see that such reports contain a true and accurate account of what occurred, free from all irrelevancies and conjectures. Officers and other members of the crew should be warned to keep their own counsel over matters relating to accidents and not discuss with or give their own version of events to strangers. The master himself, before giving information to solicitors who may visit the ship should make certain that they are "on his side".

Masters should not put their signatures to documents of any kind without first scrutinising them carefully and making sure they are fully understood. It ought not to be necessary to add that signing a blank or incomplete form on the understanding that it will be completed later is something a master should never agree to. This has, in fact, been done on more than one occasion considerably to the owner's detriment.

The master should always satisfy himself that he is furnished with copies of all important regulations, official notices and recommendations, harbour bye-laws, immigration laws, and so on. It is his duty to see that regulations are complied with, particularly those dealing with safety and the prevention of accidents. The Docks (Factory Act) Regulations which apply in the United Kingdom, and corresponding regulations elsewhere, are particularly important as are the rules laid down under the Prevention of Oil Pollution Act and the Clean Air Act. Breaches of statutory regulations not only render the master liable to be fined personally, but if accidents result from such breaches the owners will invariably be faced with successful claims for heavy damages. Stevedores and other contractors who board the ship as "invitees", and persons who come on board as "licensees" for their own private purposes or as guests, are all entitled to adequate protection against pitfalls and traps. Apart from specific regulations the master has a common law duty to provide such protection. Hence the importance of impressing upon officers the necessity to fence open hatchways and manholes, provide safe and secure gangways, attend to moorings, provide the proper lighting of dangerous parts of the ship, and lock doors leading to dangerous compartments when they are not in use. When necessary, strangers should be accompanied about the ship by a responsible member of the crew. It is not sufficient that safety appliances are provided. The master must insist that they are properly used, and it is no defence to show that an unsafe system has been customarily employed for a long period of time without accident. Persistent indulgence in dangerous practices requires repeated warnings; a single warning is not enough. It is in the nature of things that despite all precautions accidents will occur, and if a man is injured on board prompt first aid should be given and, if necessary, his removal to hospital should be arranged without delay. In the interests of the owners they or their agents should be notified at once so that an immediate investigation can be made. If a broken rope, wire, shackle, or other gear has been the cause of the accident the master should see that it is preserved for expert inspection and a record should be made of the names of witnesses. An official log book entry should be made, signed and countersigned, and this is advisable even when the victim of the accident is not a member of the crew.

What constitutes a "safe port" or a "safe berth" and what the master's duty is when ordered to a port or berth which is unsafe are matters dealt with in Chapter 9, but it may happen that a ship is anchored or moored in a safe and satisfactory position when some other ship comes along and fouls the berth by anchoring dangerously close. In these circumstances it is the duty of the master of the first mentioned ship to put the safety of his own vessel above all other considerations. He should, therefore, remove his ship to a safe place and then afterwards take up the issue with the other master and, if there is sufficient reason, request him to move his ship. Refusal to comply with such a request would then be a matter for a report to the harbour authority.

The master should not permit unnecessary overtime working and such overtime as is really necessary must be properly recorded. There are circumstances in which the master can bind his owners to crew wage rates in excess of those originally agreed to, but such circumstances arise only very rarely, say, where the ship has to proceed to a war-infested area.

In his dealings with his owner's agents, charterer's agents, and officials such as port health officers and customs officers—and this is particularly important in foreign ports—the master will invariably find that it is in the interests of the ship and the owners, not to mention his own interests, to leaven any necessary firmness with the utmost politeness and diplomacy and to answer such questions as they have a right to ask willingly and truthfully. Reasonable hospitality, too, can often work wonders. Brusqueness and indifference to other people's feelings have been the cause of many delays and frustrations.

Succession to command in Emergency. In the unfortunate event of the master dying at sea or being left behind unfit at a port abroad, the question arises as to who shall succeed him in command. If the first mate is properly qualified he is without question the proper person to take over for the time being and, in the absence of information from the ship's agents that the owners propose to make different arrangements, he will in the port where the ship is or next arrives make the appropriate reports and get authority to have his name endorsed on the certificate of registry.

MANNING

Manning and Certification. Section 43 of the M.S. Act 1970 as amended by the M.S. Act 1979 gives the D.o.T. power to make regulations specifying the number of qualified officers, cooks and seamen to be carried by ships in various circumstances. The D.o.T. is also given power by s.44 to exempt any ship from any of the requirements of the regulations and such exemption may be confined to a particular period or to one or more particular voyages.

Going to sea undermanned. Section 45 states that if a ship goes to sea or attempts to do so without carrying the required officers and other seamen the owner or master is liable on conviction on indictment to a fine, or on summary conviction to a fine not exceeding £1000, and the ship, if in the U.K., may be detained.

Unqualified Persons going to sea as qualified. If a person goes to sea as a qualified officer or seaman without being qualified for the purposes of s.43 he is liable on conviction to the fines specified in the previous paragraph above.

Certficates of Competency of Officers. In December 1980 the D.o.T. revoked the previous regulations made in 1977 and 1978 and made new regulations to come into operation from 1st September 1981. These are the M.S. (Certification of Deck Officers) Regulations 1980 (SI 1980 No. 2026) and the M.S. (Certification of Marine Engineer Officers) Regulations 1980 (SI 1980 No. 2025). The regulations specify the number of officers holding appropriate certificates to be carried on ships according to their size or power and the trading area in which they operate. The trading areas are each defined in Schedule 2 of the regulations and are named Near Continental, Middle Trade and Unlimited trading areas respectively. The areas defined are shown in the map on page 165. The Unlimited trading area means any location not within the other two defined areas.

Deck Officers. The Deck Officers Regulations require all U.K. ships, and all other ships registered elsewhere which carry passengers between places on the U.K. coast, the Isle of Man and the Channel Islands, or on voyages which begin and end at the same U.K. port without calling elsewhere, and which go to sea beyond the limits of smooth or partially smooth waters, to carry the minimum number of qualified deck officers specified in the following tables A, B and C in accordance with the ship's gross tonnage and trading area. The regulations do not apply to pleasure craft of less than 80 GRT and fishing vessels and the Secretary of State may exempt ships operating in areas specified in Merchant Shipping Notice M.979 from any or all of the requirements and subject to specified conditions. (GRT means Gross Register Tonnage.)

As can be seen from the tables five classes of Certificates of Competency are specified, ranging from Class 1 (Master Mariner) to Class 5. The officer in command of a ship must be either the holder of a Class 1 (Master Mariner) certificate, or be the holder of a certificate of a lower class which has a Command Endorsement. Command Endorsements which can be obtained after appropriate sea time and examination are shown in Tables 3 and 4 and are

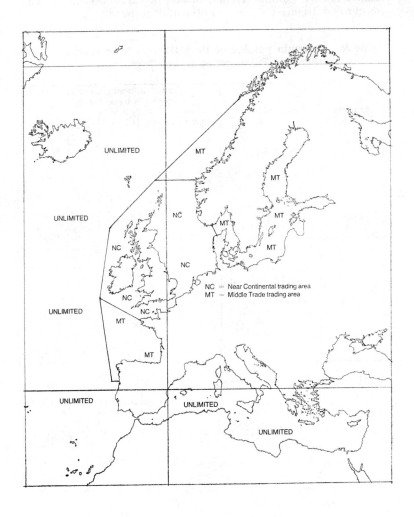

UNLIMITED

MT

MT

NC

MT

MT

UNLIMITED

NC

MT

NC

MT

NC

NC = Near Continental trading area
MT = Middle Trade trading area

UNLIMITED

NC

NC

MT

MT

UNLIMITED

UNLIMITED

UNLIMITED

named Master (Middle Trade), Master (Near Continental), Tugmaster and Tugmaster (Near Continental) respectively.

Table A   Minimum number of Deck Officers to be carried in ships other than Passenger Ships and Tugs.

Trading area	Descriptions of ships	Minimum numbers of certificated officers to be carried				
		Class 1 Cert.	Class 2 Cert.	Class 3 Cert.	Class 4 Cert.	Class 5 Cert.
Unlimited	1,600 GRT & over	1	1	1	1	—
	under 1,600 GRT	1	1	1	—	—
Middle Trade	5,000 GRT & over	1	1	1	1	—
	1,600 GRT but under 5,000 GRT	—	—	1(A)	1(E)	1
	Under 1,600 GRT	—	—	—	2(A)	1
Near Continental	10,000 GRT & over	1	1	1	—	—
	5,000 GRT but under 10,000 GRT	1	—	1(E)	1	—
	1,600 GRT but under 5,000 GRT	—	—	—	2(B)(E)	1
	800 GRT but under 1,600 GRT	—	—	—	—	3(B)
	200 GRT but under 800 GRT	—	—	—	—	2(B) (C)
	under 200 GRT	—	—	—	—	1(D)

In the above table the letters have the meaning:—

(A)   The certificate, or one of the certificates, requires the Master (Middle Trade) endorsement.

(B)   One of the certificates requires the Master (Near Continental) endorsement.

(C)   Offshore supply vessels under 1600 GRT operating in the Near Continental trading area are to carry 3 such officers unless, as specified in M. Notice 781, the crew's workload does not require a third officer.

(D)   The certificate requires the Master (Near Continental) endorsement, and where the duration of the voyage makes a change of watch necessary, an extra Class 5 certificate holder must be carried.

(E)   The second in command, (unless his certificate is endorsed with a command endorsement) must have previously served as officer in charge of a watch on a ship of 200 GRT or more for not less than 18 months.

Table B   Minimum number of Deck Officers to be carried in Passenger Ships (excluding ships with Classes IV, V, VI and VIA Passenger Certificates on voyages in smooth or partially-smooth waters).

Trading area	Description of passenger ships	Minimum number of certificated officers to be carried				
		Class 1 Cert.	Class 2 Cert.	Class 3 Cert.	Class 4 Cert.	Class 5 Cert.
Unlimited or Middle Trade	Any tonnage	1	1	1	1	—
Near Continental	2,000 GRT and over	1	1	—	1	—
	1,000 GRT but under 2,000 GRT	1	—	—	1(Y)	—
	200 GRT but under 1,000 GRT	—	—	—	1(X)	1
	Under 200 GRT	—	—	—	—	1(X)

In the above table the letters have the meaning:—

(X)   The certificate requires the Master (Near Continental) endorsement, and where the duration of the voyage makes a change of watch necessary, an extra Class 5 certificate holder must be carried.

(Y)   The certificate holder, if the ship is of 1600 GRT or more, must have previously served as officer in charge of a watch on a ship of 200 GRT or more for not less than 18 months.

Table C   Minimum number of Deck Officers to be carried in Tugs.

Trading area	Description of tugs	Minimum number of certificated officers to be carried				
		Class 1 Cert.	Class 2 Cert.	Class 3 Cert.	Class 4 Cert.	Class 5 Cert.
Unlimited	Any tug	—	2(a)	1	—	—
Middle Trade	Any tug	—	—	2(a)(c)	1	—
Near Continental	Any tug	—	—	—	—	2(b)(c)

The letters in the above table have the meaning:—

(a)   One of the certificates requires the Tugmaster's command endorsement.

(b)   One of the certificates requires the Tugmaster's (Near Continental) command endorsement.

(c)   The second in command, if the tug is of 1600 GRT or more, (unless his certificate is endorsed with a command endorsement), must have previously served as officer in charge of a watch on a ship of 200 GRT or more for not less than 18 months.

The requirements are basically simple with all ships (with few exceptions) required to carry a specified minimum number of certificated deck officers and the master either holding a Class 1 (Master Mariner) certificate, or, for ships below specified tonnages operating in the Middle and Near Continental trading areas, a certificate of a lower grade which has an appropriate command endorsement.

Some complications are introduced by the fact that before 1st September 1981 many serving officers did not hold, and were not required to hold, certificates under the M.S. Act 1894 (e.g. Home Trade cargo ship masters and mates, and Foreign-going third mates, etc.). Also, for existing holders of M.S. Act 1894 certificates, it is necessary to define equivalents under the new regulations. This is achieved in reg. 5 where Table 1 specifies equivalents to M.S. Act 1894 certificates.

Table 1.   Equivalents to M.S. Act 1894 Certificates.

Class of MSA 1894 certificate	Equivalent class of certificate of competency issued under the Deck Officers Regulations
Master Foreign Going	Class 1 (Master Mariner)
First Mate Foreign Going	Class 2
Second Mate Foreign Going	Class 3
Master Home Trade	Class 1 (or any lower class with a command endorsement issued under these Regulations) in any passenger ship, and in any other ship not exceeding 10,000 GRT, going between locations in the Near Continental trading area; or Class 4 (or any lower class) in any ship going to from or between locations in the combined Middle Trade and Unlimited trading areas
Mate Home Trade	Class 2 (or any lower class) in any passenger ship, and in any other ship not exceeding 10,000 GRT, going between locations in the Near Continental trading area; or Class 4 (or any lower class) in any ship going to from or between locations in the combined Middle Trade and Unlimited trading areas.

Also regulation 5(3) makes the holder of a M.S. Act 1894 certificate with a Middle Trade command endorsement under these regulations eligible to command ships (other than passenger ships) of not more than 10,000 GRT trading in the combined Near Continental and Middle Trade trading areas. Further in addition to the Table 1 equivalents shown above, regulation 5(4) makes a M.S. Act 1894 Mate Home Trade certificate which has a Near Continental command endorsement added under these regulations, equivalent to a Class 4 with command endorsement or a Class 5 with command endorsement in any passenger ship not more than 1,000 GRT, or any other ship not more than 5,000 GRT, trading in the Near Continental trading area.

Certificates of Service (Deck Officer). Regulation 6 provides for an uncertificated officer, or the holder of a certificate issued under

Table 2.   Equivalents to Certificates of Service (Deck Officer).

Certificate of Service (Deck Officer) Capacity in which person has been previously employed	Equivalent class of certificate of competency issued under the Deck Officers Regulations
Master Middle Trade	Class 1 (or any lower class with command endorsement) in ships (other than passenger ships) not exceeding 10,000 GRT going between locations in the combined Near Continental and Middle Trade trading areas.
Mate Middle Trade	Class 2 in ships (other than passenger ships) not exceeding 10,000 GRT going between locations in the combined Near Continental and Middle Trade trading areas.
Third Mate Foreign Going	Class 4 endorsed not as first, second or third in command in ships going to from or between any location.
Master Home Trade (other than passenger ships)	Class 1 (or any lower class with command endorsement) in ships (other than passenger) ships) not exceeding 10,000 GRT going between locations in the Near Continental trading area
Mate Home Trade (other than passenger ships)	Class 3 in ships (other than passenger ships) not exceeding 10,000 GRT going between locations in the Near Continental trading area
Second Mate Home Trade	Class 4 endorsed not as first or second in command in ships not exceeding 10,000 GRT going between locations in the Near Continental trading area
Mate Foreign Going (Tugs)	Class 2 endorsed For Tug Service Only
Second Mate Foreign Going (Tugs)	Class 3 endorsed not as first or second in command and further endorsed For Tug Service Only
Master Home Trade (Tugs)	Class 5 endorsed For Tug Service Only with command endorsement in ships going between locations in the Near Continental trading area
Mate Home Trade (Tugs)	Class 5 endorsed For Tug Service Only in ships going between locations in the Near Continental trading area

the 1980 regulations, or under the M.S. Act 1894, who has served as master or watchkeeping officer on a vessel which did not require the carriage of a certificated officer in that capacity, or who has served on dispensation in a higher capacity than the certificate he holds on Middle Trade voyages, to apply for a Certificate of Service (Deck Officer). To qualify, such an officer must have had sea service before 12 July 1977, have served not less than 3 years as master or officer in any 6 year period ending between 11 July 1977 and 31 August 1981, and shown evidence of 12 months of sea service in U.K. ships in the capacity for which the certificate is claimed.

Command Endorsements. An officer, shown by examination to be competent to command a ship of size and trade described in Table 3, will have his certificate endorsed with a Master (Middle Trade) or Master (Near Continental) Endorsement as appropriate.

Table 3.   Command Endorsements and descriptions of ships to which they apply.

Certificate of Competency (Deck Officer)	Command Endorsement	Description of Ship
Class 2 or Class 3	Master (Middle Trade)	Ships (other than passenger ships) of less than 5,000 GRT going between locations in the combined Near Continental and Middle Trade trading areas
Class 4	Master (Middle Trade)	Ships (other than passenger ships) of less than 1,600 GRT going between locations in the combined Near Continental and Middle Trade trading areas
Class 2, Class 3 or Class 4	Master (Near Continental)	Ships (other than passenger ships) of less than 5,000 GRT going between locations in the Near Continental trading area. Passenger ships of less than 1,000 GRT going between locations in the Near Continental trading area
Class 5	Master (Near Continental)	Ships (other than passenger ships) of less than 1,600 GRT going between locations in the Near Continental trading area. Passenger ships of less than 200 GRT going between locations in the Near Continental trading area

Tugs. Officers who have performed the requisite sea service in tugs will be issued after examination with a Class 2, 3, 4, or 5 certificate as appropriate, endorsed 'For Tug Service Only'. An officer shown by examination to be competent to command a tug of a type described in Table 4, will have his certificate endorsed with a Tugmaster or Tugmaster (Near Continental) endorsement as shown.

Table 4. Tugmaster Command Endorsements and descriptions of tugs to which they apply.

Certificate of Competency (Deck Officer)	Command Endorsement	Description of Tug
Class 2 endorsed For Tug Service Only	Tugmaster	Tugs going to sea from any location
Class 3 endorsed For Tug Service Only	Tugmaster	Tugs going between locations in the combined Near Continental and Middle Trade trading areas
Class 4 or Class 5 endorsed in both cases For Tug Service Only	Tugmaster (Near Continental)	Tugs going between locations in the Near Continental trading area

Marine Engineer Officers. From 1st September 1981, all U.K. ships, and all other ships which carry passengers and go to sea on the voyages described in the Deck Officer Regulations above, having registered power of 350 kilowatts or more, must carry at least a Chief Engineer Officer, a Second Engineer Officer, (except in ships of less than 3,000 kilowatts registered power operating within the Near Continental area) and in addition, every engineer officer in charge of a watch in ships of 750 kilowatts registered power or more must hold an appropriate Class 4 certificate. 'Registered power' means the brake or shaft power specified in the ship's certificate of registry. (i.e. the total continuous rated brake or shaft power of all the propulsion engines.)

Certificates of Competency (Marine Engineer Officer) are issued after examination in four classes numbered 1 to 4. Class 1, 2 and 4 certificates are issued for motor or steam machinery, or combined motor and steam machinery, and Class 3 for motor machinery only.

The minimum classes of certificates to be held by Chief and Second Engineer Officers, depending on the power and trading area for the ship, are shown in Table 5, the letter (e) against a class number indicating that the certificate required must be endorsed with the Chief Engineer Officer service endorsement.

Table 5.   Minimum certification requirements of Engineer Officers.

Area	Registered power (kilowatts) of ships including sail training ships	Required classes of certification	
		Chief Engineer Officer	Second Engineer Officer
Unlimited or Middle Trade	3,000 and over	1	2
	750 or more but under 3,000	2(e)	3
	350 or more but under 750	3(e)	4
Near Continental	6,000 and over	1	2
	3,000 or more but under 6,000	2(e)	3
	750 or more but under 3,000	3(e)	—
	350 or more but under 750	4(e)	—

For the purposes of the above table, an existing 1894 certificate as First Class Engineer or Second Class Engineer is equivalent to a Marine Engineer Officer Class 1 or Marine Engineer Officer Class 2 Certificate with a service endorsement, respectively.

Certificates of Service. An engineer officer who has served in ships prior to 1st September 1981 for similar periods to those specified above in the Deck Officer Regulations and in a capacity where a certificated officer was not required by law to be carried, may be issued, after he has provided satisfactory evidence of service, with a Certificate of Service (Engineer Officer) which indicates the type of machinery, class, trading areas and capacities for which it is eligible.

Chief Engineer Officer Endorsements. The holder of a Class 2, 3 or 4 certificate may have it endorsed 'Chief Engineer Officer' if the Secretary of State is satisfied, after examination, that the officer is competent to be carried as Chief Engineer in ships of specified power and trading areas.

MATTERS AFFECTING BOTH DECK AND ENGINEER OFFICERS

Form, validity etc. of certificates. Certificates are issued in duplicate on payment of the fee (if any), the original being issued to the person entitled to it, and the duplicate being held by the Secretary of State. A certificate is valid for sea-going service only so long as the holder can comply with the standards and conditions as to medical fitness and competency specified by the Secretary of State.

A record of all certificates issued and of all suspensions, cancellations or alterations etc. is kept by the Registrar General of Shipping and Seamen or such other person as the Secretary of State may direct.

Loss of certificate. If a person entitled to a certificate proves to the satisfaction of the Secretary of State that he has, without fault on his part, lost or been deprived of his certificate, the Secretary of State shall, and where he is not so satisfied may, on payment of a fee (if any), cause a copy of the certificate to be issued to him.

Exceptional provisions when a ship may proceed to sea with one deck officer less than the number required. (Regulation 16 in Deck Officer Regulations.) A ship may sail with one certificated deck officer less than the statutory requirements provided the cause of sailing without him is illness, incapacity or other unforeseen circumstance affecting the officer concerned. However, all reasonable steps must have been taken to replace the officer concerned and the maximum period for which a ship shall sail with one officer short shall not exceed:—

(a) 28 days in the case of a ship going to sea from a location beyond the Middle Trade area;

(b) 14 days in the case of a ship of 5,000 GRT and over going to sea from a location beyond the Near Continental area but within the Middle Trade area;

(c) 14 days in the case of a ship under 5,000 GRT going to sea from a location beyond the Near Continental area but within the Middle Trade area;

(d) 7 days in the case of a ship going to sea from a location beyond the United Kingdom but within the Near Continental area and which is required by the regulations to carry not less than three qualified deck officers.

The above concession shall not apply in the case of (c) and (d) above if the vessel is also sailing with one certificated engineer officer less than the number required by the Marine Engineer Officers Regulations. For the concession to apply, the master, when going to sea from the place in question must notify a proper officer of his intention not to carry the qualified officer in question, and make an entry of that notification in the ship's official logbook.

One period of 28, 14 or 7 days as appropriate must not be followed immediately by any further period at sea during which the ship carries one less than the number of qualified officers required by the regulations.

Engineer Officers. Similar provisions apply when a ship is one engineer officer short, but the ship must carry at least one qualified engineer for the provisions to apply.

Ships carrying dangerous cargoes. A ship to which these regulations apply which has a whole or part bulk cargo consisting of:

(*a*) crude liquid petroleum or petroleum products; or
(*b*) liquid chemicals; or
(*c*) liquefied gases;

shall carry as officer in command and as second in command respectively, qualified deck officers whose certificates have been endorsed to show that they have satisfied specified conditions of training and service required by the Secretary of State.

A cargo officer (other than the officers above) responsible for loading, discharging and care in transit or handling of cargo, shall hold a similarly endorsed certificate.

The Chief and Second Engineer Officers, and an engineer cargo officer (if one), must have similar endorsements on their certificates.

For the above purpose:—

'petroleum products' means substances produced directly or indirectly from crude, such as fuels, lubricants, bitumen, wax, industrial spirits and any wide range substance (meaning a substance whose final boiling point at normal atmospheric pressure is more than 50° higher than its initial boiling point) but excluding any product defined as 'liquefied gas'.

'liquefied gas' means any liquefied gas listed in Chapter XIX of the 1976 IMCO publication "Code for the Construction and Equipment of Ships carrying Liquefied Gases in Bulk" as amended by Supplements.

'liquid chemical' means any liquid chemical listed in Chapter VI of the 1980 IMCO publication "Code for the Construction and Equipment of Ships carrying Dangerous Chemicals in Bulk" and any Supplement specified in a Merchant Shipping Notice.

Conditions for the issue of Dangerous Cargo Endorsements. The conditions to be fulfilled before an officer may be issued with an endorsement are detailed in Annex 1 to Merchant Shipping Notice M.952. It will be seen that certain senior officers may qualify on the strength of past service, but all other officers must have completed specialist training ashore, together with a period of shipboard training and/or appropriate sea service. The conditions specified are:—

Six months service as Master, Chief Officer, Chief or Second Engineer in ships carrying the relevant dangerous cargo within the six years period immediately preceding the date of application, and completed before 1 January 1981.

OR

Completion, in each case within the six year period prior to the date of application, of:—

(*a*) a training course on the carriage of the relevant dangerous cargo, either approved by the D.o.T. or conducted between July 1975 and 31 December 1980 in accordance with recommendations in Merchant Shipping Notice No. M.771

and

(*b*) either:—

(i) 14 days ship-board training and 3 months credited ship-board service; or

(ii) 6 months credited ship-board service; or

(iii) 28 days intensive ship-board training approved by the D.o.T.

'Shipboard training' must be in a supernumary capacity in ships carrying cargoes of the type for which the endorsement is sought, or on ballast passages between carrying such cargoes.

'Credited ship-board service' means service in ships carrying any of the three type of cargo requiring an endorsement, but if the cargo is not of the type for which the endorsement is sought such service will count only at half rate up to a maximum of half the amount of such service specified in paragraph (*b*) (i) or (ii) above.

Applicants under the first paragraph above must produce a letter from the Owners; all other applicants must support their application with reports from the Master or Chief Engineer on their ship-board training and service and must produce a college certificate attesting satisfactory completion of their shore-based training course.

Watchkeeping Requirements.

(A) No deck officer is to act as Master or Second in command, and no engineer officer is to act as Chief Engineer or Second Engineer Officer, respectively, unless he holds an appropriate certificate of competency or service. However, in the event of the death or incapacity of the master or second in command, or the chief or second engineer officer while the ship is at sea; or of a ship going to sea without a duly certificated master or second in command, or chief or second engineer officer, because of illness or incapacity or other unforeseen circumstances after all reasonable steps have been taken to secure another officer, a deck officer may act in the capacity of master or second in command, and an engineer in the capacity of chief or second engineer, respectively, until the ship reaches the next intended port of call or during the period of 28, 14 or 7 days allowed by regulation 16 in the exceptional provisions described above.

(B) A ship's master must not permit any deck officer to be in charge of a navigational watch unless he holds a certificate of competency or service of a class required to be held by a deck officer in that ship at that time.

(c) Neither the master nor the chief engineer must permit an engineer to be in charge of a watch in a ship of 750 kilowatt power or more unless he holds a certificate of competency or service of a class required to be held by an engineer in that ship at that time.

(d) An owner must not appoint any deck or engineer officer in a capacity for which he is not duly certificated.

Offences and penalties. Any deck or engineer officer who contravenes (A), any ship's master who contravenes (B) or (C), any chief engineer who contravenes (C) and any owner who contravenes (D) is guilty of an offence and liable on summary conviction to a fine not exceeding £1000 or, on conviction on indictment to imprisonment for a term not exceeding two years and a fine.

If a person makes a statement which he knows to be false or recklessly makes a statement which is false in a material particular for the purpose of obtaining for himself or another person a certificate or other document he shall be liable on summary conviction to a fine not exceeding £1000.

Certificates equivalent to Certificates of Competency. The Secretary of State may specify that a certificate issued by an authority under the laws of a country outside the United Kingdom shall be treated as evidence of the attainment of a standard of competence equivalent to the standard required for the issue of a specified class of certificate under these regulations.

Examination of Aliens. No alien may be examined for a Certificate of Competency (Deck) Class 1 or Class 2, for a Certificate of Competency as Extra Master, or for a Command Endorsement, save in exceptional circumstances. Application for details of such circumstances must be made to the D.o.T.

Certificate of Competency as Ship's Cook. Every United Kingdom ship of 1000 G.R.T. or over (excluding pleasure craft or fishing vessels) which goes to sea beyond the Near Continental trading area and which carries a crew the majority of whom are domiciled in the U.K., must carry a qualified and certificated ship's cook. (See S.I. 1981 No. 1076 and Merchant Shipping Notice No. M. 981).

Certificate of Competency (A.B.). No seaman can be rated as an A.B. in a U.K. registered ship unless he holds a certificate of competency as A.B.

The qualifying examination serves also as the examination for the award of a Certificate of Qualification as Efficient Deck Hand. All seamen of 18 years of age and over may take this examination when they have performed 12 months' service at sea in a deck rating. Four weeks remission of service in respect of pre-sea training is allowed.

No certificate of competency as A.B. will be awarded unless the seaman can prove that he has:—

(1) passed the qualifying examination, which is practical and oral only, not written,
(2) attained the age of 18 years,
(3) performed 36 months' service at sea in a deck rating, subject to remission up to a maximum of 6 months in respect of pre-sea training,
(4) produced a certificate of efficiency as Lifeboatman,
(5) produced a steering certificate.

Because of the number of vessels manned by general purpose ratings, the D.o.T. have made provision for service performed as a general purpose rating to count, in part or in full, towards that qualifying for certificate of competency examination purposes. A seaman who qualifies in other respects may apply to sit the examination for a certificate of competency as A.B. when he has served at sea for a period of at least:—

(a) 12 months in a deck rating; or
(b) 18 months in a general purpose rating (i.e. as a general purpose rating in ship manned by a general purpose or integrated crew); or
(c) between 12 and 18 months, partly in a deck rating and partly in a general purpose rating, such periods to be counted proportionately.

A successful candidate is issued with a certificate of qualification as Efficient Deck Hand. After two years further qualifying sea service either in a deck rating or in a general purpose rating, the certificate of competency as A.B. is issued.

Boys attending the National Sea Training College, Gravesend for a pre-sea training course, may take the qualifying examination at the college before going to sea. Boys who are successful in the examination have their discharge books noted to this effect, and later apply for the issue of an E.D.H. certificate after they have fulfilled all requirements as to age, qualifying service and steering experience.

Certificate of Qualification as E.D.H. Successful candidates at the qualifying examination who do not qualify by length of service for an A.B. certificate are issued with E.D.H. certificates. Possession of this is accepted as proof of having passed the examination when application for the issue of an A.B. certificate is made subsequently.

Certificate of Efficiency as Lifeboatman. Although possession of this certificate is not a requirement for admission to the examination for an A.B. certificate, its possession or otherwise is taken into account by the examiner. Application for both examinations may be made at the same time and both taken together.

Steering Certificate. This must show that, apart from periods of instruction, the seaman has taken turns at the wheel in ships of 100 gross tons or over for periods totalling at least 10 hours. Masters of ships concerned are requested to certify the time spent on this duty until the seaman has completed the minimum period. Steering Certificate forms (Exn. 50G) are obtainable at M.M. Offices.

Loss of E.D.H. or A.B. Certificate. If such a certificate is lost or destroyed the holder is required to notify the Registrar General of Shipping and Seamen without delay, explaining the circumstances. If the Registrar General is satisfied that the certificate is lost he will issue a copy on payment of a small fee. If, however, it is proved that shipwreck or fire on board was the cause of the loss, the copy will be issued free.

Safe Deck Manning. Any person sending a ship to sea is required by law (M.S. Act 1894, s. 458-459 and M.S. Act 1979, s. 44) to ensure that it is seaworthy in respect of manning bearing in mind the nature of the ship's service. The D.o.T. is responsible for ensuring that the law is complied with, and it has powers to detain ships thought to be unsafe due to undermanning. The 1970 Act gave the D.o.T. powers to make regulations requiring U.K. registered ships when putting to sea to have sufficient deck ratings for the safe conduct of the ship. The Department has considered making regulations, but has decided that the required flexibility required by modern conditions can only be achieved by considering ships individually, bearing in mind their construction, equipment and nature of service intended. For the time being the D.o.T. have, after discussions with both sides of the shipping industry, set out in Merchant Shipping Notice No. 798 on an advisory basis the new measures which will be applied to ensure safe conduct of ships.

Notice No. 798 applies to all sea-going merchant ships registered in the United Kingdom with the exception of the following special classes of ships:

(a) Oil rig supply vessels whose manning is dealt with in Notice No. M.781.

(b) Small coasting ships having a gross tonnage not exceeding 350 tons, a summer deadweight of under 425 tons, overall length of not more than 50 metres, and power not exceeding 350 kW. These vessels are the subject of M.794.

(c) Certain ships under 2,500 tons gross tons working within closely defined limits on the U.K. coast, which are to be exempted by the D.o.T. from the M.S. (Certification of Deck Officers) Regulations.

(*d*) Sea-going cadet training ships which are subject to special approval.

To decide the number of seamen required for safety purposes it is necessary to consider the workload of seamen under several headings, such as maintaining a safe bridge watch, mooring the vessel, damage control, the use of fire fighting equipment and life-saving appliances. Having considered the workload separately and collectively, it is then necessary to relate it to a number of men based on an identifiable grading structure of seamen in terms of their skill and experience. For this purpose, M.798 classifies deck ratings of any nationality as follows:

Category I Seaman. Holder of an A.B. Certificate issued by the D.o.T., or a certificate issued by another national maritime administration which is regarded by the D.o.T. as equivalent: or a seaman who is at least 20 years old, has the ability to steer, and can prove at least 42 months' satisfactory service at sea in a deck capacity.

Category II Seaman. Holder of an E.D.H. Certificate issued by the D.o.T. or a D.o.T. recognised equivalent issued by another national administration: or a seaman who is at least 18 years old, has the ability to steer and can prove at least 24 months' satisfactory service at sea in a deck capacity.

Category III Seaman. A person who has successfully completed a course of training and the qualifying examinations as a seaman at a D.o.T. approved nautical training establishment in the U.K. (or at a D.o.T. recognised overseas equivalent), and who can prove 2 months' satisfactory sea service in a deck capacity and who can steer: or a person who has attended such a training course as above, but who has failed to pass the qualifying examinations, and who can prove 4 months' satisfactory sea service in a deck capacity and who can steer: or a person who can prove at least 6 months' satisfactory sea service in a deck capacity who can steer.

Although this covers deck ratings of any nationality, it must be remembered that the crew must be able to understand orders given to them in English or alternatively there must be adequate arrangements for transmitting orders in a language which they have sufficient knowledge. (M.S. Act 1970, s. 48.)

Manning Certificates. It is impracticable to draw up manning scales based on the above principles for general application to all ships and circumstances. Therefore the D.o.T. will, at the request of the owner, state the deck manning for any sea-going U.K. registered merchant ship to comply with the above principles.

Manning will be expressed in terms of the three grades of seamen defined above and will constitute the minimum number of seamen in a deck capacity which should be provided for the ship to be safely manned in the view of the D.o.T. having regard to the nature of service intended.   There will be no provision for substitutions of seamen of lower grade.   Deck cadets will not be included in the manning, nor will the D.o.T. regard them as forming part of manning except in emergency situations of limited duration of which the D.o.T. will be the sole judge.

The manning decided by the D.o.T. will be stated in a Deck Manning Certificate which will be issued to the owner . It should be displayed on board where it can be seen by D.o.T. staff, proper officers and by the crew.   The grading structure defined above will be used to express the safe manning required in ships with General Purpose and Interdepartmental Flexibility agreements.

In the event of any disagreement by owners or official seafarers' representatives with prescribed manning, the D.o.T. will reconsider, revise if justified, but may require a practical demonstration of the ability of the crew to carry out certain essential tasks.

It is important that there should be consultation with the D.o.T. on manning when ships are in the design stage since questions of crew accommodation may have to be considered.   The manning certificate will not be issued until the ship is built.   Application should be made by the owner or a person authorised to act on his behalf, on a form obtainable from any Marine Survey Office or Mercantile Marine Office.   A fee will be charged.   The certificate will be sent to the applicant.

Production of Certificates, etc.   Section 47 states that any person serving or engaged to serve in any ship to which this section applies and holding any certificate or other document which is evidence that he is qualified for the purposes of section 43 shall on demand produce it to any superintendent, surveyor or proper officer and (if he is not himself the master) to the master of the ship; and if he fails to do so without reasonable cause he shall be liable on summary conviction to a fine not exceeding £200.

Engine Room Manning.   A National Maritime Board agreement provides that, subject to its being practicable to provide the necessary accommodation and to the supply of seafarers being available, in foreign-going vessels exceeding 3,000 tons gross there shall be carried as a minimum in each watch, in addition to the engineer officer in charge of the watch, either a junior engineer, or a senior mechanic, or a petty officer, or a motorman grade 1.

Restriction on Employment of Young Persons.   Section 51 lays down that a person under school-leaving age shall not be employed in any U.K. registered ship except as permitted by regulations made by the D.o.T.   These regulations, when made, will prescribe the circumstances in which, and conditions subject to which, persons under school-leaving age may be employed and in what capacities. They will also prescribe the circumstances and capacities in which persons over school-leaving age but under 18 may be employed. If a person is employed in contravention of this section or the relevant regulations the owner or master of the ship will be liable on summary conviction to a fine not exceeding £200.

In the List of Crew a separate list must be made of those under 18 years of age. The standard form of crew agreement provides for this list which must contain (i) reference number in the crew list, (ii) full name, (iii) date of birth, (iv) place of birth, and (v) capacity.

SUPPLY OF SEAMEN

Restrictions on Making Arrangements for Employment of Seamen. Section 6 provides as follows:—

(1) A person shall not for reward make arrangements for finding seamen for persons seeking to employ seamen or for finding employment for seamen, unless—

(a) he is the holder of a licence under this section authorising him to do so or is in the regular employment of the holder of such a licence; or

(b) he is in the regular employment of persons seeking to employ the seamen or makes the arrangements in the course of acting as ship's agent for those persons or is the master of the ship in which the seamen are to serve or an officer acting under his authority; or

(c) the employment is such as is exempted from the provisions of this subsection by regulations made by the D.o.T.

(2) A person shall not demand or directly or indirectly receive from any person any remuneration for providing him with employment as a seaman.

(3) The D.o.T. may grant licences for the purposes of this section for such periods, on such terms and subject to such conditions, including conditions providing for revocation, as they think fit.

(4) If a person acts in contravention of subsection (1) or (2) he shall be liable on summary conviction to a fine not exceeding £50.

Licences to Supply Seamen. Hitherto, persons who held these licences have been the committees of management or captain-superintendents of certain nautical training establishments, officials of the General Council of British Shipping, and representatives of the National Association for the Employment of Regular Sailors, Soldiers, and Airmen, at various ports.

G

ENGAGEMENT AND CREW AGREEMENTS

Crew Agreements. Section 1 requires that, with certain exceptions, an agreement in writing must be made between each person
employed as a seaman in a U.K. registered ship and the persons
employing him. The agreements made with the several persons
employed in a ship are to be contained in one document (referred to
as a crew agreement) except that in certain cases the D.o.T. may
approve (*a*) agreements being contained in more than one crew
agreement, and (*b*) one crew agreement to relate to more than one
ship. The agreement must be carried in the ship to which it relates
whenever the ship goes to sea. However, if the agreement relates
to more than one ship it is to be kept at an address ashore in the
U.K. and a copy must be carried in the ship. Such copy must bear
a certificate signed by the master certifying that it is a true copy
and must specify the address at which, and the name of the person
by whom, it is kept. Agreements relating to more than one ship
are referred to as "multiple ship agreements" and are normally
restricted to cross-Channel ferries, but an application can be made
to the D.o.T. to have them in respect of other ships.

Regulations as to Crew Agreements. Section 2 empowers the
D.o.T. to make regulations relating to crew agreements and these
are contained in Part I of S.I. 1972 No. 918 to which reference is
made below.

Regulation 1 defines "coastal voyage" to mean a voyage between
places in the British Islands (including the Republic of Ireland) or
from and returning to such a place during which, in either case, no
call is made at any place outside those islands. It defines "ship" to
mean a ship registered in the U.K. not including a fishing vessel,
and states that references to tonnage in the case of a ship with
alternative tonnages are references to the larger.

Regulation 2 defines "the appropriate superintendent or proper
officer" to mean a superintendent or proper officer for the place at
which a crew agreement, or an agreement with any person added to
those contained in a crew agreement, is or is to be made.

Regulation 3 rules that section 1 of the Act does not apply to:—

(*a*)   (i)   a ship belonging to a general lighthouse authority;

    (ii)   a ship of less than 80 register tons engaged solely on
coastal voyages;

    (iii)   a pleasure yacht which is (*a*) engaged on a coastal
voyage, or (*b*) engaged on any other voyage, provided
that not more than 4 of the crew receive wages;

    (iv)   a coastal voyage by any ship solely for the purpose of
trials of the ship, its machinery or equipment;

(*b*)   (i)   a person employed in a ship solely in connection with
the construction, alteration, repair or testing of the ship,
its machinery or equipment, and not engaged in the
navigation of the ship;

(ii) a person employed in a ship solely to provide goods personal services or entertainment on board, who is employed by a person other than the owner or the persons employing the master and who is not a member of the medical or catering staff in the ship;

(iii) a member of the naval, military or air forces of the Crown or of any service administered by the Defence Council, when acting as such a member.

It will be seen from the above—(b)(ii)—that persons like bank clerks, shop assistants, musicians, hairdressers, etc. are exempted from the requirement to enter into a crew agreement, but they must be included in the list of Exempted Seamen which forms part of the crew list.

Regulation 4 requires that before engaging seamen on a new crew agreement, and before adding seamen to an agreement which is already current, at least 24 hours' notice must be given to the appropriate superintendent or proper officer. This notice must contain the following information:—

(a) name of ship;
(b) port of registry;
(c) official number;
(d) whether a new crew agreement is to be made or whether a person is to be added to an agreement already current;
(e) date, place and time that the agreement is to be made or the person added;
(f) the capacity in which each person to be engaged is to be employed.

Forms for this purpose are obtainable from M.M. Offices. The notice will usually be given in writing on the proper form, but if this is not possible a verbal notification will be accepted. Such verbal notification should, however, be followed as soon as possible by confirmation in writing. A notice need not be given (a) if it is not practicable to give it without unreasonably delaying the ship, or (b) where there are reasonable grounds for believing that the total number of seamen to be added to a crew agreement relating to a single ship, while that ship remains at one place in the U.K., will not exceed two.

Regulation 5 deals with the carrying of a copy of the crew agreement in a ship in cases where the agreement relates to more than one ship. This has already been referred to.

Regulation 6 deals with the delivery of crew agreements and copies, as follows:—

(1) The employer shall, within 2 days of the date on which a crew agreement is made or any agreement is added to those contained in a crew agreement or, if it is not practicable within that period, as soon as practicable thereafter, deliver to the appropriate

ALC. 3¹

**NOTIFICATION TO A SUPERINTENDENT OR PROPER OFFICER OF INTENTION
TO MAKE A CREW AGREEMENT OR ADD TO AN EXISTING CREW AGREEMENT**
(The Merchant Shipping (Crew Agreements, Lists of Crew and Discharge of Seamen)
Regulations 1972)

Name of ship		Port of registry		Official number		
Indicate if a new crew agreement or an addition to an existing crew agreement (tick in appropriate box)	New		If an addition state date and place of making the existing crew agreement			
			date		place	
	Addition					
Number of persons with whom agreements are to be made			Capacities			
Date place and time agreements are to be made			deck	engine	catering	GP
date	place	time				

To the superintendent or
proper officer at :-

....

....

Signature of employer (or person authorised on his behalf)

Date :- ....

superintendent or proper officer a copy of the crew agreement and
of any agreement so added.

(2) The employer shall, within 7 days of the date when the
last person remaining employed under the crew agreement ceases to
be employed under that agreement, deliver the crew agreement to a
superintendent or proper officer for the place where the ship was
when that person ceased to be so employed.

Regulation 7 requires the master of a ship to cause (a) a copy
of any crew agreement relating to the ship; or (b) an extract containing the terms of that agreement applicable (i) to all seamen
employed under it, and (ii) to each description of seaman so employed: to be posted in some conspicuous place on board where it
can be read by the persons employed. It must be kept so posted and
legible throughout its currency. For this purpose copies of the
standard form of crew agreement are available at M.M. Offices.

Regulation 8 requires that the employer or the master shall, on
the demand of a seaman, cause to be supplied to him a copy of the
crew agreement or relevant extracts therefrom, and cause to be
made available to him a copy of any document referred to in the
agreement. (e.g. The National Maritime Board Summary of Agreements.)

Regulation 9 requires that the master shall, on demand by an
officer of customs and excise, produce to him (a) any crew agreement
or copy carried in the ship, and (b) any certificate evidencing an
exemption granted by the D.o.T. from the requirements of section 1
of the Act.

It should be noted that a surveyor of ships, a superintendent or proper officer may inspect any document carried in a ship in pursuance of the Act or Regulations and may require the holder of a certificate of competency or qualification to produce it to him.

Regulation 10 states that a person who fails to comply with an obligation imposed on him by regulation 4, 6 or 8 and a master who similarly fails to comply under regulation 7, 8 or 9 shall be guilty of an offence punishable on summary conviction with a fine not exceeding £200.

Running Agreements. The maximum period for running agreements, whether N.C., M.T., or Unlimited, is 12 months. Those for vessels engaged in frequent short voyages (e.g. cross-Channel ferries) are limited to a duration of 6 months.

Forms of Crew Agreements. The D.o.T. in consultation with the shipping and fishing industries have produced standard agreements which are available from M.M. Offices and proper officers abroad. These are:—

1. An agreement for use on ships operating under N.M.B. conditions (Form ALC/NMB 1).
2. An agreement for ships not operating under N.M.B. conditions (Form ALC/NFD 1).
3. An agreement for use on fishing vessels (Form ALC/FSG 1).

Near Continental (N.C.) and Middle Trade (M.T.) Trading Areas. From 1st September 1981 the areas defined by home trade and middle trade limits that applied to agreements made before that date have been replaced by the Near Continental Trading Area and the Middle Trade Trading Areas shown on the map on page 165. Agreements which were previously called foreign-going are now known as Unlimited Trading Agreements and they apply to vessels trading beyond the Middle Trade areas shown on the same map.

Proper Officer. Section 97 defines "proper officer" to mean a consular officer appointed by Her Majesty's Government in the United Kingdom and, in relation to a port in a country outside the United Kingdom which is not a foreign country, also any officer exercising in that port the functions similar to those of a superintendent. The latter is often referred to as the Shipping Master.

Engagement of Indian Seamen. Section 125 of the Principal Act which dealt with agreements with lascars is now repealed and the question of the terms and conditions under which Indian seamen are employed in U.K. registered ships is a matter for negotiation with the Government of India.

CREW AGREEMENT AND LIST OF CREW FOR A SHIP IN WHICH SEAMEN ARE EMPLOYED UNDER NATIONAL MARiTIME BOARD CONDITIONS OF EMPLOYMENT.   ALC (NMB) I

The form and provisions of this agreement are approved by the Department of Trade and Industry under section 1(3) of the Merchant Shipping Act 1970.

If the form and provisions of this agreement are amended or clauses are added without the prior approval of the Department it will not be regarded as approved under the said section of the Act.

Name of ship:		Port of registry	Official number	Register (net) tonnage
Name and address of registered owner			Description of the ship (e.g., whether passenger ship, tanker, ferry, general cargo, bulk carrier)	

Date and place of commencement of agreement and list of crew	Date and place of termination of agreement and list of crew
Date.............................. place............................	Date.............................. place............................
Signature of master..	Signature of master..

Crew's Knowledge of English. Section 48 states:—

(1) Where in the opinion of a superintendent or proper officer the crew of a ship to which this section applies consists of or includes persons who may not understand orders given to them in the course of their duty because of their insufficient knowledge of English and the absence of adequate arrangements for transmitting the orders in a language of which they have sufficient knowledge, then— (*a*) if the superintendent or proper officer has informed the master of that opinion the ship shall not go to sea; and (*b*) if the ship is in the U.K. it may be detained.

(2) If a ship goes to sea or attempts to go to sea in contravention of this section the owner or master shall be liable on summary conviction to a fine not exceeding £1000.

Application of Sections 43, 45, 47 and 48 of the Act. Section 49 states that the sections referred to apply to every ship registered in the U.K. and also to any ship registered elsewhere which carries passengers (a) between places in the U.K. or between the U.K. and the Isle of Man or any of the Channel Islands; or (b) on a voyage which begins and ends at the same place in the U.K. and on which the ship calls at no place outside the U.K.

CLAUSES IN CREW AGREEMENTS

Contractual Clauses. These are contained in form ALC 1(d) (79) and read as follows:—

THIS AGREEMENT is made between (name and address of employer) "the employer" and each of the seamen whose name is included in the list of crew incorporated in this Agreement.
It is agreed that

(i) the employer will employ each seaman and the seaman will serve in the capacity and at the rate of wages expressed against his name in the list of crew incorporated in this agreement:

(ii) and (iii) (Voyage and notice clauses are here inserted:)

(iv)–(a) Each N.M.B. Agreement specified in paragraph (b) of this clause shall have effect in relation to each seaman employed hereunder who is of a description to which such agreement relates as if it were incorporated herein: and each such agreement shall have effect as it is set out in the N.M.B. Year Book current at the date the seaman becomes employed hereunder, together with any amendments which are effective and any further amendments which may become effective during the seaman's employment:

(b) The N.M.B. Agreements referred to in paragraph (a) of this clause are those made by the Board or by a panel of the Board relating to

(i) pay, hours of work, leave and subsistence: and

(ii) the section of the Officers' Hours Agreements indicated against an Officer's name in the list of crew incorporated in this Agreement; and

(iii) the other N.M.B. Agreements set out in the current edition of the N.M.B. Year Book and which are not inconsistent with the terms of this Agreement or the M.S. Acts for the time being in force.

(c) (Appropriate clause inserted here.)

(d) (Appropriate clause inserted here.)

(v) wages will not accrue for any hours during which a seaman refuses or neglects to work when required or is absent without leave or for any period during which a seaman is incapable of performing his duties by reason of illness or injury which has been caused by his own wilful act or default;

(vi) (*a*) The Trust Deed and Rules constituting the "Merchant Navy Officers Pension Fund" shall be deemed to be incorporated herein to the effect and intent that each of the parties hereto (and the master) who is or is eligible to be a member of the said Fund hereby agrees for the purposes of this Agreement to be bound by all the provisions of the said Deed and Rules and to authorise the deduction from the wages payable to him hereunder of the contributions payable by him respectively to the said Fund: and the employer hereby undertakes that the contributions payable under the said Deed and Rules by the employer shall be paid to the Fund in respect of such member;

(*b*) the Trust Deed and Rules constituting the "Merchant Navy Ratings' Pension Fund" shall be deemed to be incorporated herein to the effect and intent that each of the parties hereto who is or is eligible to be a member of the said Fund hereby agrees for the purposes of this Agreement to be bound by all the provisions of the said Deed and Rules and to authorise the deduction from the wages payable to him hereunder of the contributions payable by him to the said Fund; and the employer hereby undertakes that the contributions so deducted and the contributions payable under the said Deed and Rules by the employer shall be paid to the Fund in respect of such member; any reference above to the Merchant Navy Ratings' Pension Fund shall be taken as a reference to an exempt private fund as defined by the said Rules where the rating is a member of such an exempt private fund;

(vii) in all cases of salvage awards the rating of the Chief Officer shall be deemed to be the same as that of the Chief Engineer, the rating of the Second Officer that of the Second Engineer and the Third Officer that of the Third Engineer. A cadet who has not completed 2 years' service shall be deemed of the rating of Ordinary Seaman and a cadet of 2 years' service or over the rating of an Able Seaman;

(viii) any seaman who incompetently performs his work in the capacity in which he was first employed under this Agreement may be re-rated by the master and transferred to other duties, but re-rating shall not affect his remuneration under this Agreement;

(ix) in relation to an individual seaman this Agreement may be terminated:

(*a*) by mutual consent;

(*b*) if medical evidence indicates that a seaman is incapable of continuing to perform his duties by reason of illness or injury;

(c) by appropriate notice in accordance with the terms of this Agreement;

(d) if, in the opinion of the master, the continued employment of the seaman would be likely to endanger the ship or any person on board;

(e) if a seaman, having been notified of the time the vessel is due to sail, is absent without leave at the time fixed for sailing and the vessel proceeds to sea without him or if substitutes have been engaged. Substitutes shall not, however, be engaged on a Crew Agreement more than 2 hours before the time fixed for sailing.

(f) if the master is satisfied that an appropriate breach of the Code of Conduct for the Merchant Navy for the time being in force has occurred;

(x) each seaman agrees:—

(a) to join the ship by the time specified by the master and subsequently during the period of his employment to rejoin the ship by the time specified by the master;

(b) to submit to inoculation, vaccination and any other health precautions as may be directed by the master;

(c) in the event of the employer becoming liable for any expenses under Section 26 of the Merchant Shipping Act 1970 to afford the employer every facility to prosecute in his name any claim in respect of such expenses and to allow the employer reasonable discretion in the conduct of any proceedings for the settlement of any claim in respect of such expenses;

(d) to take all steps within his power to preserve in good condition the equipment of the ship and all property on on board;

(e) to return in good condition (fair wear and tear excepted) before the termination of his engagement all articles provided for his personal use during the voyage by the employer;

(f) that all stores and provisions issued to the crew are only for use and consumption on board the ship and any unused or unconsumed stores or provisions remain the property of the employer;

(g) to comply with the Code of Conduct for the Merchant Navy for the time being in force;

(h) in the event of the Agreement being terminated outside the U.K. or Continent of Europe (within N.C. Trading Area) in accordance with clause (ix) (f) above, to the deduction from his wages of an amount being the actual expense of his repatriation. Such amount shall not exceed one week's pay at the begin at or base rate, specified by the National Maritime Board for his rank or rating. Where no such rate is specified the relevant amount shall be that specified against the seaman's name in the Crew Agreement;

(i) to keep his quarters clean and tidy and in readiness for inspection by the master or officer deputed by him; and

(j) at the time when a seaman finally leaves the ship at the termination of his employment under this Agreement, to leave his quarters in a clean and orderly condition to the satisfaction of the master (or his authorised deputy). When he is ready to leave the ship, the master (or his authorised deputy) shall, on request made by the seaman, issue to the seaman a certificate that the quarters are clean;

(xi) the employer agrees:—

(a) if a seaman shows to the satisfaction of the master or employer that he can obtain command of a vessel or an appointment as mate or engineer or to any post of a higher grade than he actually holds, or that any other circumstance has arisen since his engagement which renders it essential to his interests that he should be permitted to take his discharge, he may claim his discharge provided that without increased expense to the employer and to the satisfaction of the employer or his agent he furnishes a competent and reliable man in his place. In such case the seaman shall be entitled to his wages up to the time of his leaving his employment;

(b) if a seaman is discharged otherwise than according to the terms of this Agreement before the commencement of the voyage, or before one month's wages are earned by him hereunder, without fault on his part justifying his discharge or without his consent, then he shall be entitled to receive from the employer in addition to any wages he may have earned up to the time of his discharge if an officer one-thirtieth of his monthly wage or one-seventh of his weekly wage; if a rating one-fifth of his weekly wage for each day for which basic pay would have been paid under the Crew Agreement for each day until he shall have been offered suitable employment by the employer or (if the seaman be a Registered Seafarer as defined in the Established Service Scheme Agreement of the N.M.B.) by the Merchant Navy Establishment Administration, provided always that his maximum entitlement under this clause shall not exceed one month's wages under this Agreement;

(c) notwithstanding anything contained in regulations made under Section 9(a) of the Merchant Shipping Act 1970, no deduction shall be made from wages due to a seaman under this Agreement in respect of any breach by him of his obligations except in respect of breach of clauses (x)(*a*), (x)(*d*), (x)(*e*) and (x)(*g*), but nothing in this clause shall in any way affect any other rights of the parties to this Agreement in relation to such breach;

(*d*) that the provisions of the M.S. (Disciplinary Offences) Regulations 1972; (as amended), including the master's power to impose fines, shall not be applied to any seaman employed under this Agreement;

(*e*) where there is a dispute relating to the amount payable to a seaman employed under this Agreement, the master will, if the seaman desires, agree to the dispute being referred to the Superintendent or proper officer for decision under Section 10 of the Act.

ADD ANY ADDITIONAL CLAUSES BELOW
(*Important*:—All such clauses must have been approved by the Department of Trade.

Signature of employer, master or any other person authorised by the employer

....*Date*.................*Place*...

Voyage Clauses. The standard crew agreements contain appropriate voyage clauses in which the geographical limits of the voyage and the maximum period of validity must be inserted. It is suggested that for voyage agreements the maximum period inserted should not exceed 24 months.

The voyage clause in an Unlimited voyage agreement reads:—
". . . of not exceeding . . . calendar months' duration to any ports or places within the limits of 75 degrees north and 60 degrees south latitude, commencing at . . . proceeding thence to . . . and/or any other ports within the above limits, trading in any rotation, and to end at such port in the United Kingdom as may be required by the Master. The Master shall, however, have power in his sole discretion to end the voyage at such port on the Continent of Europe (within N.C. Trading Area) as may be required by him."

In a N.C. area agreement the voyage clause reads:—"the employment will be in respect of a voyage or voyages within N.C. Trading Area for a period not to extend beyond the . . . (here state date of termination—not more than twelve months hence or six months in the case of cross channel ferries) next unless on that date the ship is engaged on a voyage to a port in the United Kingdom, in which case this Agreement shall end on the first return of the ship to a port in the United Kingdom after that date or the final discharge of cargo consequent upon that return."

In the case of a "run agreement" the voyage clause simply says "the employment shall be in respect of a voyage from . . . to . . ."

In a Near Continental and Middle Trade running agreement the voyage clause reads:—

"the employment shall be in respect of a voyage or voyages from . . . to . . . and/or any other ports or places on the Continent of Europe between Vest Fjord and Oporto, including the Baltic Sea under a Running Agreement which shall not extend beyond the . . . (here state date of termination—not more than twelve months hence) next unless on that date the ship is engaged on a voyage to a port in the United Kingdom in which case this Agreement shall end on the first return of the ship to a port in the United Kingdom after that date or the final discharge of cargo consequent upon that return."

Notice Clauses. Each of the standard crew agreements contains appropriate notice clauses which have been agreed by the National Maritime Board. These are set out below.

1. Notice Clause in Unlimited Voyage Agreement.

"Any member of the crew who has served under this Agreement for a minimum period of three calendar months may give notice to the Master, in writing or verbally before a witness, not later than seven days before the ship is due to arrive at any port on the Continent of Europe (within N.C. Trading Area), to terminate his engagement after the expiry of the notice at a port within these limits which shall be nominated by the Master. Provided that any such notice shall not take effect (a) if the ship is due to proceed to a port in the United Kingdom without leaving N.C. Trading Area, or (b) if the ship is due to reach a port in the United Kingdom within seven days of leaving the N.C. Trading Area.

The Master may give the like notice to terminate the engagement of any member of the crew who has served under this Agreement for the minimum period aforesaid.

If the voyage is not ended within seven days after the ship has arrived at the first port of call in the United Kingdom, then after the expiry of that period any member of the crew who has served under this Agreement for a minimum period of six calendar months may give not less than forty-eight hours' notice to the Master, in writing or verbally before a witness, to terminate his engagement at that port or a subsequent port of call before the final port.

If the voyage is not ended within fourteen days after the ship has arrived at the first port of call in the United Kingdom, then after the expiry of that period any member of the crew who has served under this Agreement for a minimum period of three calendar months may give the like notice as aforesaid.

The Master may give the like notice to terminate the engagement of any member of the crew who has served under this Agreement for the minimum period of six or (as the case may be) three calendar months aforesaid.

If the voyage is ended at a port on the Continent of Europe (within N.C. Trading Area), it is agreed that wages will continue until the arrival of the crew members in the United Kingdom, provided that no wages shall be due to any such crew member for any period of delay caused through his act or default.''

2. Duration of Service on Unlimited Voyage Agreements.

Any member of the crew who has served under this Agreement for a minimum period of 12 calendar months may (subject to the proviso hereinafter mentioned) at any time after the expiry of that period give not less than 28 days' notice to the Master, in writing or verbally before a witness, to terminate his engagement at the expiry of that notice or, if the ship is then at sea, at the next port of call thereafter, unless the ship is then bound for a port in the United Kingdom or Continent of Europe (within N.C. Trading Area). Provided that, if at any time any member of the crew is offered the opportunity, on not less than seven days' notice, of repatriation (by sea, air or other reasonable means at the sole discretion of the Master) and refuses that offer, he shall be required to serve for a further minimum period of seven calendar months from the date of that refusal (if the voyage shall last so long) before being able to give 28 days' notice as aforesaid.

A member of the crew shall not be entitled thus to terminate his engagement under this Agreement at a port which is only a bunkering port or a port of refuge.

The Master may give the like notice to terminate the engagement of any member of the crew who has served under this Agreement for the minimum period aforesaid.

3. U.K. Notice Clause in Unlimited Running Agreements (and N.C. and M.T.). This reads:—

''After one voyage outside N.C. area or . . .* days' service has been completed (whichever first occurs) by any member of the crew his engagement may be terminated in the United Kingdom by not less than . . . hours'/days'† notice (such period of notice not to include Saturdays, Sundays or public holidays) given in writing or verbally before a witness by either party before the ship is due to arrive at/sail from* a port in the United Kingdom.

Provided that, if after arrival at a port in the United Kingdom the ship is due to proceed to another port or ports in the United Kingdom, then notwithstanding any such notice as aforesaid the engagement shall automatically continue either until the ship's arrival at that other port or (as the case may be) the last such port or until the expiry of seven days from the date of her arrival at the first said port (whichever first occurs).

* The period to be inserted shall not exceed 28 days.
† Delete whichever is inapplicable.

4. Notice Clause in Unlimited Running Agreements (and Near Continental and Middle Trade). This reads:—

"Any member of the crew who has served under this Agreement for a minimum period of three calendar months may give notice to the Master, in writing or verbally before a witness, not later than seven days before the ship is due to arrive at any port on the Continent of Europe (within N.C. Trading Area), to terminate his engagement after the expiry of the notice at a port within these limits which shall be nominated by the Master. Provided that, if at any time the ship has returned to the United Kingdom and sailed therefrom again, any member of the crew who has not given due notice to terminate his engagement in the United Kingdom shall be required to serve for a further minimum period of 42 days (28 days in the case of N.C. and M.T. Agreements) from the date of the ship's departure from the United Kingdom before being able to give notice as aforesaid, and always provided that the minimum period of three calendar months has expired.

Provided furthermore that any such notice shall not take effect (a) if the ship is due to proceed to a port in the United Kingdom without leaving N.C. Trading Area, or (b) if the ship is due to reach a port in the United Kingdom within seven days of leaving N.C. Trading Area.

The Master may give the like notice to terminate the engagement of any member of the crew who has served under this Agreement for the minimum period aforesaid."

5. Notice Clause in N.C. Agreements. This reads:—

"After one voyage or seven days' service has been completed (whichever first occurs) by any member of the crew his engagement may be terminated in the United Kingdom by not less than . . . hours' notice (such period of notice not to include Saturdays, Sundays or public holidays) given in writing or verbally before a witness by either party before the ship is due to arrive at/sail from* a port in the United Kingdom."

Non-Federated Ships. For vessels in this category, which include salvage vessels, cable steamers, tugs and other specialised craft, there is a set of Contractual Clauses for insertion in agreements. The substance of these clauses is as follows:—

(i) The employer will employ each seaman and the seaman will serve in the capacity and at the rate of wages expressed against his name in the list of crew.

(ii) This agreement shall be for a voyage or voyages within (limits stated) and is not to extend beyond the expiration of six months from date of first signature or the time at which the ship first arrives at the port of final destination.

* Delete whichever is inapplicable.

(iii) After one voyage has been completed or seven days have elapsed since employment commenced either party may give notice to terminate the employment. The notice is to take effect at a U.K. port and be given not less than (period stated) either before the ship is due to arrive at that port or, if employment is to end at the port where the ship is when the notice is given, before it is due to sail. In relation to an individual seaman the agreement may be terminated by mutual consent, if the seaman is ill or injured, by appropriate notice, if the seaman is absent without leave at a fixed sailing time, or if (in the opinion of the master) continued employment would be likely to endanger the vessel or any person on board.

(iv) If a seaman shows to the satisfaction of the master or employer that he can obtain command of a ship or an appointment as mate or engineer or to any post of higher grade than he holds (and in certain other circumstances) he may claim his discharge provided that without increased expense to the employer, and to the employer's satisfaction, he furnishes a reliable substitute. In such case the seaman is entitled to wages up to the time of leaving his employment.

(v) Space is left for the insertion of further provisions about pay, hours of work, leave and subsistence. These additional clauses, if any, must have D.o.T. approval.

LIST OF CREW

Section 69 states that, except as provided by regulations, the master of every ship registered in the United Kingdom shall make and maintain a list of the crew containing such particulars as may be required by the regulations. The regulations that have been made form Part II of S.I. 1972 No. 918 and provide as follows:—

11. Interpretation of Part II. In this Part "seaman" includes the master of a ship and, except where the context otherwise requires, references to employment include references to engagement and references to discharge include references to termination of engagement.

12. Exemptions. The duty imposed by section 69 to make and maintain a list of crew shall not apply in relation to a pleasure yacht which is (a) engaged on a coastal voyage, or (b) engaged on any other voyage provided that not more than 4 crew members receive wages.

13. Lists of Crew Contained in Crew Agreements. A list of crew may be contained in the same document as a crew agreement relating to one ship only and any particulars entered in the crew agreement shall be treated as forming part of the particulars entered in the list.

14. Particulars to be Specified.

(1) Subject to paragraphs (2) and (3) of this regulation, a list of crew shall contain the following particulars—

(a) (i) name of ship, port of registry and official number;
   (ii) name of owner and his address; and
   (iii) the number of the certificate evidencing an exemption granted by the D.o.T. with respect to the ship or any person in it; and

(b) subject to paragraph (4) of this regulation, in respect of every seaman from time to time on board the ship, whether or not he is employed under a crew agreement—
   (i) his name;
   (ii) his address;
   (iii) the number of his current discharge book (if any) or the date and place of his birth;

ALC 1(a)

LIST OF CREW AND SIGNATURES OF SEAMEN WHO ARE PARTIES TO THE CREW AGREEMENT

ALC 1(b)

LIST OF CREW RELATING TO SEAMEN EXEMPTED UNDER SECTION 1(5) OF THE MERCHANT SHIPPING ACT, 1970, FROM THE REQUIREMENT TO SIGN A CREW AGREEMENT

(iv) name of ship in which last employed and, if discharged therefrom more than 12 months before, year of discharge;
(v) capacity in which employed;
(vi) grade and number of any certificate of competency held;
(vii) date on which he went on board to commence employment;
(viii) date on and place at which he left ship and, if he left on discharge, reason for discharge;

(ix) if left behind otherwise than on discharge, date and place of and reason for (if known) this being done; and

(x) name and relationship of next of kin and address if different from that of seaman.

(2) A list of crew which relates to a ship belonging to a general lighthouse authority need contain only particulars referred to in (1)(*a*)(i) and in (i), (ii), (vii) and (viii) of paragraph (1)(*b*) of this regulation.

(3) A list of crew which relates to seamen employed under a crew agreement need contain only the particulars referred to in paragraph (1)(*a*)(i) of this regulation and, in respect of each seaman, those referred to in (i), (ii), (iii), (v), (vii) and (viii) of paragraph (1)(*b*).

(4) In respect of a member of the naval, military or air forces of the Crown or of any service administered by the Defence Council when acting as such a member, a list of crew need contain only the particulars referred to in (i), (ii), (vii) and (viii) of paragraph (1)(*b*).

N.B.—In the List of Crew forms ALC 1(a) and ALC 1(b) there is provision for recording the name of the MNEA office at which the seaman is registered and, in respect of a seaman who is party to the crew agreement, his signature on engagement, signature on discharge, and the signature of the person before whom he is discharged. In the case of a seaman exempted from the requirement to sign a crew agreement only his signature on discharge and that of the person before whom he is discharged are required.

15. Delivery of Copies of Lists of Crew and Notification of Changes (Forms ALC 2 and ALC 2A).

(1) When (*a*) a new list of crew is made relating to a ship of 25 gross tons or more, or (*b*) any change (including the addition of any particulars) is made in a list of crew relating to a ship of 200 gross tons or more, the master shall, within 2 days thereafter or, if not then practicable as soon as possible, deliver to a superintendent or proper officer a copy of the list of crew or notification of change.

(2) The master shall endorse the copy of a list of crew or the notification of any change with a certificate that it is a true copy.

16. Copies of List of Crew. A copy of every list of crew, including all changes in it notified to the owner, must be maintained by him at an address in the U.K. The master must, as soon as practicable and in any event within 3 days of any change being made, notify it to the owner.

17. When any person having in his possession the copy of a list of crew has reason to believe that the ship to which it relates has been lost or abandoned, he must immediately deliver the copy to a superintendent, and must produce it on demand to a superintendent.

18. A person in possession of a copy of a list of crew relating to a ship of less than 25 gross tons or to a ship belonging to a general

lighthouse authority he shall deliver it on demand to a superintendent.

19. **Duration of Lists of Crew.** A list of crew shall remain in force (*a*) if any person is employed under a crew agreement, until all such persons in that ship have been discharged; and (*b*) in any other case, until the ship first calls at a port more than six months after the first entry relating to a seaman is made in the list.

20. **Delivery of Lists of Crew.** The master shall within 2 days after a list of crew has ceased to be in force, or if not then practicable as soon as possible, deliver the list to a superintendent or proper officer for the place where the ship is when the list ceases to be in force.

21. **Production of Lists of Crew.** A master shall, on demand, produce to the Registrar General of Shipping and Seamen, a superintendent or proper officer or an officer of customs and excise the list of crew required to be maintained in the ship.

22. **Offences.** A master or other person who fails to comply with an obligation imposed on him by the relevant regulations in Part II shall be guilty of an offence punishable on summary conviction with a fine not exceeding £50.

SPECIAL CREW LISTS

When a ship is bound to Canada, U.S.A. or certain South American countries, a special crew list has to be prepared (usually in triplicate) before the ship leaves the United Kingdom. These lists are taken by the master or ship's agent to the consulate or office of the authority concerned with the immigration regulations of the country to which the ship is bound. One copy is returned after endorsement, and the others are sent to the appropriate authority abroad. On the ship's arrival at her destination the local immigration officer will muster the crew and check particulars against the list in his possession. If not satisfied with the reason given for any discrepancies further inquiry will be made, and it is therefore important that the master should be in a position to account satisfactorily for any crew changes that may have taken place. Whilst in the country abroad any crew changes made there will have to be duly reported on a proper form, and that will be in addition to the formalities required under M.S. Acts and supporting Regulations. Any breach of immigration laws is a serious matter which may lead to the ship being heavily fined. If the crew contains persons who, by local law, are not permitted to land, or stowaways, a strict gangway watch is essential, and if local watchmen are not provided the master would be under a duty to appoint suitable watchmen from the crew. Cases do occur where persons who are potential illegal immigrants are kept in custody by the local authorities during the ship's stay in port, and returned to the ship under escort immediately before she sails. In U.S.A. ports the master may be served with an order to detain one or more of his crew and a heavy fine on the ship would almost certainly follow on the desertion of a "detainee". Those not under detention should be provided by the master with passes to reduce the risk of a detainee slipping ashore with, or being smuggled ashore by, his shipmates. No crew member should be allowed to land unless he has first been inspected and passed by the Immigration Inspector.

Ships bound to Australia are required to submit special crew lists on arrival in that country, but such lists can be prepared during the voyage as advance copies and endorsements are not demanded. A similar system may apply in respect of some other countries. On arrival at any unfamiliar place it is always very important to find out what landing restrictions, if any, there are, especially if the ship has a crew of mixed nationalities.

DISCHARGE OF SEAMEN

Section 3 empowers the D.o.T. to make regulations prescribing the procedure to be followed in connection with the discharge of seamen from ships registered in the U.K. These regulations form Part III of S.I. 1972 No. 918 and the substance of them is given below. Contravention of any provision of the regulations is an offence punishable on summary conviction with a fine not exceeding £200 or such less amount as is specified. In the case of an offence committed by a seaman the maximum fine is £10 whilst offences committed by the master or other person discharging a seaman can result in a maximum fine of £50 in some instances but £200 in respect of more serious offences.

Seamen Left Behind Abroad otherwise than on Discharge. Section 4 provides that regulations made under section 3 may apply any provision thereof, with appropriate modifications, to cases where a seaman employed in a U.K. registered ship is left behind outside the U.K. otherwise than on being discharged.

Discharge of Seamen when Ship ceases to be Registered in U.K. Section 5 provides that in such case any seaman employed in the ship shall be discharged unless he consents in writing to continue his employment in the ship, and that sections 7 to 10 shall apply in relation to his wages as if the ship had remained registered in the U.K.

REGULATIONS RELATING TO DISCHARGE

Notice of Discharge. Except in those cases where it is not required, before a seaman is discharged the master must give not less than 48 hours' notice in writing to a superintendent or proper officer for the place where the seaman is to be discharged, or if not then practicable as soon as possible thereafter. Forms for this purpose are obtainable at M.M. Offices.

Particulars to be included in the Notice of Discharge. The notice must contain the following:—

(*a*) name of ship, port of registry and official number;
(*b*) place, date and time of discharge;
(*c*) capacity in which seaman employed;

ALC.5

NOTIFICATION OF INTENTION TO DISCHARGE A SEAMAN OR SEAMEN
(The Merchant Shipping (Crew Agreements, Lists of Crew and
Discharge of Seamen) Regulations 1972)

Name of ship	Port of registry	Official Number

Date and place of making the agreement		Place and berth of ship
date	place	

Names or number of seamen (see note below)	Capacities			
	deck	engine	catering	GP

Date place and time of discharge			If outside United Kingdom is consent of proper officer required; if not, give reasons (see Note overleaf)
date	place	time	

To the superintendent or
proper officer at :-
....
Signature of master (or person authorised on his behalf)
Date :-
Note: The name of the seaman need only be entered when there is a wages submission (section 10 MSA 1970) or an appeal against a fine (section 35 MSA 1970). If there is insufficient space in the box additional names may be entered overleaf

(*d*) if to be discharged outside U.K. whether or not consent of proper officer is required;
(*e*) if outside U.K. and consent of proper officer is not required, which of the specified reasons is the one applicable;
(*f*) seaman's name if, at time of discharge, a dispute about wages is to be submitted to a superintendent or proper officer.

If a notice of discharge relates to more than one seaman it must also state the number being discharged.

Discharge in the United Kingdom. A notice of discharge is not required in the U.K.—

(*a*) if no dispute or appeal is to be submitted or made, and the master has reasonable grounds for believing that the total number of seamen (other than those exempted from the requirement to sign a crew agreement) who will be discharged will not exceed two; or

(b) if the seaman is to be discharged from a ship exempted from the requirements of section 1 of the Act; or

(c) if the seaman is exempted from the requirements of section 1 of the Act.

Discharge Outside the United Kingdom. A seaman must not be discharged outside the U.K. without the consent of a proper officer except where—

(a) he is employed for one or more voyages and is to be discharged either at the end of that voyage or of the last of such voyages; or

(b) he is employed for a specified period and is to be discharged at the end of that period; or

(c) seaman and master agree that he should be discharged at the place and at the time when he is discharged; or

(d) it appears to the master that it is not practicable without unreasonably delaying the ship to obtain the consent and that either—

   (i) in the interests of safety or for preservation of good order and discipline on board the discharge is necessary; or

   (ii) the seaman is incapable of performing his duties by reason of illness or injury and is in urgent need of medical or surgical attention which cannot be provided on board.

(e) the seaman is employed under an approved crew agreement to which the N.M.B. agreed disciplinary procedures apply and which requires compliance with the Code of Conduct, and the master is satisfied that the seaman has committed one of the acts of misconduct set out in paragraph 9 of the Code.

Where a proper officer consents to the discharge he must, if practicable, make and sign an entry in the official log book recording his consent, but if he does not the master must make and sign an entry recording that such consent has been given.

Procedure on Discharge.

(1) Where a seaman is present when he is discharged—

(a) the master or an officer authorised by him must—

   (i) if the seaman produces his discharge book, record in it:—
       name of ship and port of registry,
       gross or register tonnage and official number,
       description of voyage,
       capacity in which employed,
       date employment began, and
       date and place of discharge; or

   (ii) if discharge book not produced, give seaman a certificate of discharge containing the above particulars:

(b) the master must ensure the discharge is in the presence of the master himself, or the seaman's employer, or a person authorised by the master or employer.

(c) the person in whose presence the seaman is discharged must:—

   (i) make and sign an entry in the official log book recording place, time and date of discharge; and

   (ii) make and sign an entry in the crew agreement or, if there is a separate list of crew, in that, recording place and date of, and reason for, seaman's discharge;

(d) the seaman must also sign the entry in the crew agreement and list of crew.

(2) Where a seaman is not present when he is discharged, the master or a person authorised by him must make the entries referred to in paragraph (1)(c) above.

(3) The above-mentioned official log book entries must also be signed by a member of the crew.

(4) If a seaman so requests, the master or an officer authorised by him must give the seaman a certificate (separate from any other document) either as to the quality of his work or indicating whether he has fully discharged his obligations under his contract of employment. Forms for this purpose are obtainable at M.M. Offices.

WAGES

Payment of Wages. The provisions of section 7 are:—

(1) Except as provided by enactment, wages due to a seaman under a crew agreement must be paid in full at the time when he leaves the ship on being discharged.

(2) If the amount shown in the account delivered to a seaman as being the amount payable to him is replaced by an increased amount shown in a further account delivered, the balance must be paid within seven days of the time of discharge. If the amount shown in the account exceeds £50 and it is not practicable to pay the whole of it at the time of discharge, not less than £50 nor less than one-quarter of the amount shown must be paid at that time and the balance within seven days.

(3) If the amount due is not paid at the time specified the seaman is entitled to wages, at the last rate payable, for every day on which it remains unpaid during the 56 days following the time of discharge. Any amount remaining unpaid at the end of that period is to carry interest at the rate of 20 per cent per annum.

(4) Subsection (3) does not apply if failure to pay was due to a mistake, to a reasonable dispute as to liability, to act or default of the seaman, or to other cause not being the wrongful act or default of those liable to pay the wages. The reference to interest does not apply if a court in proceedings for recovery of wages so directs.

(5) Where a seaman is employed under a crew agreement relating to more than one ship, the termination of his employment under the agreement is regarded as the time of discharge.

(6) Where a seaman is discharged outside the U.K. from a ship which has ceased to be registered in the U.K. but returns to the U.K. under arrangements made by his employer, the time of his return to the U.K. is regarded as the time of discharge.

Account of Seaman's Wages. Section 8 provides that:—

(1) Subject to subsection (4) of this section and to regulations made under section 9 or 62 of the Act, the master of every U.K. registered ship must deliver to every seaman employed in the ship under a crew agreement an account of the wages due to him and of the deductions subject to which the wages are payable.

(2) The account must indicate that the amounts stated therein are subject to any later adjustment that may be found necessary and must be delivered not later than 24 hours before the time of discharge or, if the seaman is discharged without notice or at less than 24 hours' notice at the time of discharge.

(3) If the amounts require adjustment the employer must deliver a further account not later than the time at which the balance of wages is payable.

(4) Where a seaman is employed under a crew agreement relating to more than one ship the account must be delivered by the employer on or before the termination of the seaman's employment.

(5) If a person fails without reasonable cause to comply with the above provisions he will be liable on summary conviction to a fine not exceeding £20.

Regulations relating to Wages and Accounts. Section 9 empowers the D.o.T. to make regulations—

(a) authorising deductions to be made from wages (in addition to any authorised by enactment) in cases where a seaman's breach of his obligations is alleged against him and specified conditions are complied with;

(b) regulating the manner in which deductions are to be dealt with;

(c) prescribing the manner in which wages are to be or may be paid;

(d) regulating the manner in which wages are to be dealt with where a seaman leaves his ship in the U.K. otherwise than on being discharged;

(e) prescribing the form and manner in which any account is to be prepared and the particulars to be contained in it (which may include estimated amounts).

The regulations referred to in section 9 requires that wages due to a seaman under a crew agreement must be paid in cash unless the seaman has agreed to payment of the whole or part of his wages being made by cheque, money order or directly to a bank or giro account. It is recommended that the seaman's written agreement to such methods of payment should be obtained.

Accordingly the following additional clauses have been added to the basic Contractual Clauses to make up an approved agreement designated GCBS Form CAG 1 (Rev'd. 1.1.79) for use on GCBS ships where required:—

(x) each seaman agrees:—

    (*k*) to settle on-board accounts in respect of cash advances or goods or services received, by means of cheques made payable to the Company, at intervals to be determined by the employer;

    (*l*) to receive a monthly pay advice giving details of earnings and deductions at the end of each month to be sent to an address provided by the seaman.

(xi) the employer agrees:—

    (*f*) to investigate fully any disputes raised in respect of the time, method or amount of salary payment whether raised by the seafarer's organisation or the master, and to consult fully with the seafarer's organisation when so requested and to make full restitution for any under-payment of salary which may have been made;

    (*g*) to supply, on request, to each seaman who is a signatory to this agreement, any details he may require concerning his salary, leave and deductions and the calculations relative thereto;

    (*h*) to provide a system of monthly credit transfer, together with a monthly pay advice, for each seaman who is signatory to this agreement.

(xii) Payment of wages.

It is further mutually agreed that:—

    (*a*) payments on account of the wages of each seaman employed under this agreement (or numbered in the Schedule attached hereto) will be made at monthly intervals by credit transfer to a bank account nominated by the seaman (each such payment being not less than   ); and

    (*b*) if the seaman so requests, the amount of his wages required to be paid to him at the time of his discharge will be transmitted on his behalf (but at the expense of the employer) to a bank account nominated by the seaman.

(Reproduced by kind permission of The General Council of British Shipping.)

Accounts of Seamen's Wages. The account of wages delivered to a seaman must contain the particulars prescribed in the Schedule to the regulations and must indicate which amounts (if any) are estimated amounts. A further account delivered must contain the same particulars as the original, adjusted as circumstances require, must indicate adjusted amounts, state amount of wages already paid, and state the balance remaining to be paid.

The schedule referred to lists the same items as those shown on the Account of Wages form ASW 1 and the Final Account form ASW 2.

Account of Wages Forms. Official forms are obtainable from M.M. Offices but there is no objection to shipping companies making use of their own forms so long as they include all the particulars prescribed by the regulations.

Deductions from Wages. Deductions may be made from wages as authorised by M.S. Acts and supporting Regulations, or by other legislation such as that relating to Income Tax and National Insurance contributions. (See also reference to section 11 below.)

Masters have the authority to make a deduction of up to £50 in respect of actual expenses or pecuniary loss incurred by the employer resulting from the seaman's absence without leave, but if the seaman proves that his absence was due to an accident or mistake or other cause beyond his control, and that he took all reasonable precautions to avoid being absent, no deduction can be made.

Where a seaman employed under an approved crew agreement to which the N.M.B. agreement on disciplinary procedures applies and which requires him to comply with the 'Code of Conduct for the Merchant Navy' has been dismissed from the ship because he has committed one of the breaches of the Code specified in paragraph 9, the master is authorised to deduct an amount provided for in the crew agreement towards the seaman's repatriation expenses. This is normally an amount not exceeding one week's pay.

Masters have power to make deductions of up to £50 for wilful damage to ship's equipment and also in respect of a seaman's failure to return in good condition (fair wear and tear excepted) articles provided by the employer for the seaman's personal use on board. With respect to the latter two deductions, the amount deducted must not in total exceed £50 in relation to the period during which the seaman was serving under the crew agreement.

Where it is possible in each of the above situations, a notice of deduction must be given to the seaman involved, not less than 24 hours before his wages fall due to be paid and he must be given an opportunity to make representations about the deduction to the employer or master. The notice of deduction must specify each provision of the crew agreement which has been breached and the amount of the deduction it is proposed shall be made. If the seaman has not been given such notice and opportunity, it shall be sent to his last known address by registered post. In the case of deductions for wilful damage or non-return of articles, a deduction can be made only if the master is able to show that the employer has suffered loss to the extent of the proposed deduction.

The N.M.B. have agreed that before a deduction is made in respect of wilful damage an agreed procedure should be followed. The procedure, when the seafarer is on board, is as follows:—

ACCOUNT OF A SEAMAN'S WAGES
MERCHANT SHIPPING ACT 1970, Section 8　　ASW 1

Name of seaman	Reference number in crew agreement	Capacity in which employed	Number of discharge book (if any)	Income Tax code	National Insurance
					No. ...../...../...../...../.....
Name of ship and official number		Allotments			Date contributions commenced:-
	Amounts	Date of 1st payment	Intervals of payment		Contributions paid to:-

SECTION A — Months / Days / Part Days — **SECTION B**

SECTION A				SECTION B	
BOX 1 — Total period of employment in which wages were earned. From:-　To:-				Foreign Income Deduction (where appropriate)	No. of days
BOX 2 — Less any days or part days within the above period during which wages were NOT earned. Dates				Qualifying days	
BOX 3 — (Deduct total of Box 2 from Box 1)　Total of Box 2. Period for which wages are payable				Attributable leave if different from N.M.B. entitlement	

SECTION C — EARNINGS

Col 1	Col 2 £
Total period for which wages at the rate specified in the crew agreement are payable taken from Section A.	
..........months @ £...................per month	
..........weeks @ £...................per week	
..........days @ £...................per day	
Increases in wages (promotion, etc.)	
..........months @ £...................per month	
..........weeks @ £...................per week	
..........days @ £...................per day	
..........months @ £...................per month	
..........weeks @ £...................per week	
..........days @ £...................per day	
Overtime	
..........hours @ ....per hour	
..........hours @ ....per hour	
Leave and subsistence	
brought forward ....days	
Voyage leave ....days	
Sundays at sea ....days	
Total ....days	
Less leave taken ....days	
Balance due ....days	
Carried forward to next voyage ....days	
Balance paid under this account ....days	
..........days @ £................... £	
..........days @ £...................	
Subsistence...................days	
..........days @ £...................	
..........days @ £...................	
Total carried forward or if paid show also in earnings column	
Any other earnings during period of employment Give full details	
Gross earnings	
Less total deductions	
Total net earnings	
Less:- Amount paid on leaving the ship or at the time of the delivery of this account	
Balance remaining payable ....£	

SECTION D — DEDUCTIONS

Col 3	Col 4 £
Superannuation (MNOPF/MNRPF/Co.) £	
Taxable income (after Superannuation)	
Less any interim tax relief for period in Section B above	
net taxable earnings	
Income Tax	
Cash advances	
Allotments	
Fines deducted pursuant to section 38 MSA 1970	
Earnings Related National Insurance Contributions contracted out/not contracted out (delete as appropriate)	
..........weeks (include leave) @...........................	
..........weeks (include leave) @...........................	
Union, society or association contributions (specify which)	
Canteen bills	
Goods supplied	
Radio or telephone calls	
Postage expenses	
Amount (if any) retained under Section 17 MSA 1970; and Name of authority:-	
Other deductions (Full details must be given)	
Total deductions	
Ship's/Employer's stamp	

If any amount shown in columns 2 or 4 is an estimated amount, the amount so estimated should be denoted by an asterisk (*) in column 1 for earnings or column 3 for deductions.
A further account is not required unless any amounts stated in the above account require adjustment.

1. Where, in the opinion of the master, there has been a breach of the obligation in the crew agreement to preserve in good condition the equipment of the ship and all property on board, the master of the ship may, subject to the Regulation under section 9 of the M.S. Act 1970, impose a deduction from the wages of a seaman if he is satisfied that the seaman has been in breach of his obligation under the agreement.

2. The powers of the master in relation to such a deduction may be exercised by any officer authorised for the purpose by the master. The name and rank of any officer so authorised shall be entered by the master in the official log book.

3. When a master or his deputy proposes to make a deduction from a seaman's wages, in the circumstances in which he is authorised to make a deduction, he shall inform the seaman within 24 hours and make a log entry.

4. If at the time that the breach of the terms of the agreement is reported to the master it is not possible to identify the seaman or seamen responsible for the breach and the master intends to investigate the matter, a log entry shall be made within 72 hours of the matter being reported to the master. The log entry shall indicate that the master may take action by way of a deduction from the wages of the person or persons eventually established as being responsible for the breach.

5. Before imposing a deduction from a seaman's wages for a breach of the crew agreement, the following procedure, upon request by the seaman, shall be followed:—

   (a) The seaman shall, if he so requests, appear before the master accompanied by a friend for the purpose of advising him and the friend may speak on behalf of the seaman;

   (b) the alleged breach shall be entered in the official log book and shall be read to the seaman by the master, who shall record therein that it has been so read;

   (c) the seaman shall then be asked whether or not he admits responsibility. If he does, the admission shall be recorded in the official log book. In all other cases an entry to the effect that the seaman does not admit responsibility shall be recorded therein;

   (d) the evidence of any witness called by the master shall be heard in the presence of the seaman, who shall be afforded reasonable opportunity to question the witness on his evidence;

   (e) the seaman shall be given an opportunity to make a statement in answer to the allegation, including any comments on the evidence produced against him. Particulars of the statement (or a record that the seaman declined to make one, if such should be the case) shall be entered in the official log book or contained in a separate document annexed to, and referred to in an entry in the official log book;

(f) the seaman shall be permitted to call any witness to give evidence on his behalf, and any such witness may be questioned by the master on his evidence;

(g) the master shall give his decision in the presence of the seaman as to whether or not he finds that the seaman is responsible for the breach;

(h) if the master finds that the seaman is responsible, he shall inform him, in the presence of his friend, of the amount of the deduction, as soon as documentary evidence in support of the deduction is available;

(j) the master shall:—

  (i) inform a seaman on whom a deduction has been imposed, at the time the deduction is imposed, of his right of appeal under section 10 of the Act;

  (ii) if the seaman so requests, supply to him copies of extracts from the official log book of all entries therein (including any annexes thereto) referring to the breach to which the deduction relates;

(k) if an alleged breach occurs within 24 hours of the seaman's discharge from the vessel, the foregoing procedure is not applicable, but the seaman must be given the opportunity of making representations to the master if it is the master's intention to make a deduction.

Power of Superintendent or Proper Officer to decide Disputes about Wages. Section 10 provides that:—

(1) Any dispute relating to the amount payable to a seaman employed under a crew agreement may be submitted by the parties to a superintendent or proper officer for decision; but the superintendent or proper officer shall not be bound to accept the submission or, if he has accepted it, to decide the dispute, if he is of the opinion that the dispute, whether by reason of the amount involved or for any other reason, ought not to be decided by him.

(2) The decision of a superintendent or proper officer on a dispute submitted to him under this section shall be final.

Restriction on Assignment of and Charge upon Wages. Section 11 provides that:—

(1) Subject to subsections (2) and (3) the following provisions shall have effect with respect to wages due or accruing to a seaman employed in a U.K. registered ship—

  (a) wages shall not be subject to attachment or arrestment except when made for the purpose of securing payments due under a maintenance order made by a magistrate's court;

(b) an assignment thereof before they have accrued shall not bind the seaman and payment to the seaman shall be valid notwithstanding any previous assignment or charge; and

(c) a power of attorney or authority for the receipt of the wages shall not be irrevocable.

(2) Nothing in this section shall affect the provisions of this act with respect to allotment notes.

(3) Nothing in this section applies to any disposition relating to the application of wages—

(a) in payment of contributions to a fund declared by regulations to be a fund to which this section applies; or

(b) in payment of contributions in respect of membership of a body declared by regulations to be a body to which this section applies;

or to anything done or to be done for giving effect to such a disposition.

It has been declared that section 11 applies—

(a) in relation to contributions to a fund, to any pension fund, any charity; and

(b) in relation to contributions in respect of membership of a body, to any trade union and any friendly society.

Protection of Certain Rights and Remedies. Section 16 provides that a seaman's lien, his remedies for the recovery of his wages, his right to wages in case of the wreck or loss of the ship, and any right he may have or obtain in the nature of salvage shall not be capable of being renounced by any agreement. But this does not affect such of the terms of any agreement made with seamen belonging to a ship which, in accordance with the agreement, is to be employed on salvage service, as provide for the remuneration to be paid to them for salvage services rendered by that ship.

Recovery of Wages. If a wages dispute has not been submitted to a superintendent or proper officer for decision, or if it has and the officer has declined to give a decision, a seaman can always bring an action at court to recover unpaid wages. If the amount claimed does not exceed £50 he may sue before a summary court (with no right of appeal), or in a county court. Whatever the amount of the claim there is a right of action in the High Court. Arising out of his lien on the ship for wages, a seaman has a right to bring an action "in rem". It has been mentioned previously that a seaman's lien is independent of statute, whereas a master's lien for wages and disbursements is a statutory lien.

Remedies of Master for Remuneration, etc. Section 18 states that the master of a ship shall have the same lien for his remuneration, and all disbursements or liabilities properly made or incurred by him on account of the ship, as a seaman has for his wages.

Advance Notes. Section 140 of the 1894 Act ruled that an agreement could contain a stipulation for payment to or on behalf of the seaman, conditionally on his going to sea in pursuance of the agreement, of a sum not exceeding one month's wages. This is now repealed and has not been re-enacted. The 1970 Act makes no reference to such an advance of wages, conditional or otherwise. It is presumably left open to seamen's employers to use their own discretion in the matter. There is an N.M.B. recommendation to the effect that "except in the case of men leaving shore employment and coming back to sea, advance notes should be restricted to one week's pay (two weeks if an allotment is made)".

Advance of Wages already Accrued. Cash advances to crew members abroad are purely at the discretion of the master. Masters should transmit to the shipowner from every port of call a statement of the amounts chargeable against the wages of each crew member in respect of cash advances, canteen bills, goods supplied, etc., authenticated by the signatures of the seamen receiving the advances or goods. In the absence of such statements or vouchers difficulties could arise in respect of deductions of this kind from the wage accounts of crews of lost or missing ships.

Advances made in foreign currency should be at the rate of exchange current at the time when the advance is made and the master should retain documents obtained from a bank at a port where advances are granted to show the prevailing rate of exchange. It is a good practice to show on a cash advance statement, both in words and figures, the amount of the advance in local currency and the sterling equivalent at the official rate of exchange.

The N.M.B. have recommended that masters should comply with requests for advances of wages already accrued, provided they are satisfied that (*a*) allotments and statutory deductions can be met from the remaining balance, and (*b*) there is no evidence that the seaman concerned is likely to inconvenience the ship if the advance is made.

Allotments. Section 13 provides that a seaman may, by means of an allotment note issued in accordance with D.o.T. regulations, allot to any person or persons part of the wages to which he will become entitled in the course of his employment in a ship or ships registered in the U.K. This right is subject to such limitations as are imposed by regulations.

The regulations may prescribe the form of allotment notes and

(*a*) may limit the circumstances in which allotments may be made;

(*b*) may limit the part of wages that may be allotted and the number of persons to whom it may be allotted;

(*c*) may limit the persons to whom allotments may be made;

(*d*) may prescribe the times and intervals at which payments are to be made.

```
┌─────────────────────────────────────────────────────────────────────────────┐
│                      MERCHANT  SHIPPING  ACT, 1970                    ASW3    │
│          The Merchant Shipping (Seaman's Allotments) Regulations 1972         │
│                      SEAMAN'S  ALLOTMENT  NOTE                                │
│                                                                               │
│  I.......................................................employed in         │
│           (Name of seaman)              ┌──────────────────────────────────┐ │
│                                         │  Name of ship, port of registry  │ │
│                                         │           official Number         │ │
│                                         │                                   │ │
│      Name and address of employer       │                                   │ │
│  require you                            │           to pay to               │ │
│                                         └──────────────────────────────────┘ │
│  ┌──────────────────────────────────────────────────────────────┐           │
│  │   Name and address of person to whom the allotment is made    │           │
│  │                                                                │ the sum of│
│  │                                                                │           │
│  └──────────────────────────────────────────────────────────────┘           │
│  ┌──────────────────────────┐            ┌─────────────────────┐             │
│  │        Amount            │            │  Date of 1st payment │             │
│  │ Words....................│     en     │                      │ and at      │
│  │ Figures..................│            │                      │ intervals of│
│  └──────────────────────────┘            └─────────────────────┘             │
│  ┌──────────────────────────┐            ┌─────────────────────┐             │
│  │       Intervals          │            │  Number of payments *│             │
│  │                          │ thereafter │                      │             │
│  │                          │  until     │                      │             │
│  └──────────────────────────┘            └─────────────────────┘             │
│  have been made or until the agreement under which I am now employed is       │
│  terminated or until 7 days after I have given notice in writing of revocation│
│  of this allotment note to you or to the Master of my ship, whichever shall   │
│  be the earlier.                                                              │
│                                                                               │
│  Signed...........................................  Date.................     │
│              (Signature of seaman)                                            │
└─────────────────────────────────────────────────────────────────────────────┘
```
*Leave this box blank if the number of payments is NOT to be restricted.
  Note:— A separate form must be used for each allotment.

Right of Person Named in Allotment to Sue in Own Name. Section 14 provides that a person to whom part of a seaman's wages has been allotted shall have the right to recover that part in his own name and for that purpose shall have the same remedies as the seaman has for the recovery of his wages. In any proceedings brought by such a person it shall be presumed, unless the contrary is shown, that the seaman is entitled to the wages specified and that the allotment has not been varied or cancelled.

Seamen's Allotments Regulations. The main provisions of these regulations are:—

1. "ship" means a ship (including a fishing vessel) registered in the U.K.
2. A seaman employed under an agreement relating to one or more ships (apart from exemptions) may at any time while he is so employed, by means of an allotment note, allot part of his wages to any person or persons.
3. Unless the seaman's employer or the master otherwise agrees, a seaman shall not (*a*) allot more than one half of his wages; or (*b*) allot that part to more than 2 persons.

For this purpose the wages of a seaman shall be taken to be wages calculated at the rate stipulated in the agreement without any addition (including overtime payments) or deduction whatsoever.

4. Unless the employer or master otherwise agrees (a) the first sum payable shall be payable not less than one month from the date on which the allotment note is issued and subsequent sums shall become payable at regular intervals of not less than one month reckoned from the date when the first sum is payable; and (b) no sum shall be payable under an allotment note before the seaman has earned any of the wages allotted by it.

5. An allotment note must be in the form prescribed in the Schedule to the Regulations.

Since allotments may now be made to *any* person they can, of course, be made to a bank, savings bank or giro account. It will be noted that it is at the discretion of the master or employer whether the minimum requirements are exceeded, but consideration should be given to the N.M.B. agreement set out in the Summary of Agreements which reads:—

"It is agreed that any member of the crew, if he so desires, and the state of his indebtedness to the ship permits, shall be granted an allotment note payable at weekly, twice monthly or monthly intervals. A second allotment payable once monthly may be may be made direct to a bank. The total amount allotted shall not exceed 90% of his wages after allowance for statutory deductions (Income Tax, Pension Fund, and National Insurance contributions)."

RELIEF AND REPATRIATION OF SEAMEN LEFT BEHIND

Section 62 requires that where—

(a) a person employed as a seaman in a U.K. registered ship is left behind in any country outside the U.K. or is taken to such country on being shipwrecked; or

(b) a person who became so employed under an agreement entered into outside the U.K. is left behind in the U.K. or is taken to the U.K. on being shipwrecked;

the persons who last employed him as a seaman shall make such provision for his return and for his relief and maintenance until his return and such other provisions as may be required by D.o.T. regulations. Such provisions may include the repayment of expenses incurred in bringing a shipwrecked seaman ashore and maintaining him until he is brought ashore and payment of the expenses of burial or cremation of a seaman who dies before he can be returned·

The M.S. (Repatriation) Regulations 1979. The main provisions of these regulations are given below.

1. "employer" means the person who last employed a seaman before he was left behind or shipwrecked.

"master" means (except in regulations 8, 9 and 10) the master of the ship in which a seaman was last employed before he was left behind or shipwrecked.

"seaman" (except in regulations 11 to 14) includes the master of a ship.

"ship" means a ship (including a fishing vessel) registered in in the U.K.

2. The regulations apply to (a) any seaman employed in a U.K. registered ship and left behind in a country outside the U.K. or taken to such country on being shipwrecked; (b) any seaman who became so employed under an agreement entered into outside the U.K. who is left behind in or taken to the U.K. on being shipwrecked.

3. **Return and relief of seamen left behind or shipwrecked.** As soon as practicable after a seaman is left behind or brought ashore after shipwreck an employer must make provision for his return to a 'place for return' defined in regulation 6.

If the seaman is not immediately available the employer's obligation to return him being:—

(a) as soon as the seaman is available for return; or

(b) as soon as the seaman informs his employer, his employer's agent, a superintendent or a proper officer of his whereabouts and asks to be returned; or

(c) if the seaman is unable because of illness, incapacity or other cause beyond his control to inform the persons mentioned in (b), as soon as one of those persons obtains from him confirmation that he wishes to be returned by his employer.

Further, from the time when the seaman is left behind or brought ashore after shipwreck, until he is returned or until the employer's obligation to return him ceases, the employer must make such provision for the seaman's food and lodging and such other relief and maintenance as may be necessary having regard to the personal circumstances of the seaman and any special requirements. However the employer is not under any obligation to return or make provision for any seaman who is absent for a period of more than three months, from the date when he was left behind if, during that period, the employer did not know and could not reasonably have known of the seaman's whereabouts.

The employer's obligation to return a seaman defined above shall cease if the seaman:—

(a) being fit and able to undertake employment in a ship, fails to comply with a reasonable request made of him that he should enter into an agreement for employment in any ship (including any ship conveying him under a conveyance order) in which he is to be carried in the course of his return; or

H

(*b*) without reasonable cause fails to comply with any other reasonable arrangement made for him by his employer in relation to the provision for his return; or

(*c*) informs his employer in writing that he does not wish to be returned by him.

Without prejudice to the generality of the above, relief and maintenance shall include provision of clothing, toilet and other personal necessaries, surgical or medical treatment and such dental or optical treatment which is urgently required, and sufficient money to meet minor expenses. Also included is reasonable costs for the defence of the seaman in any criminal proceedings in respect of any act or omission within the scope of his employment, being proceedings where neither the employer nor the employer's agent is a party to the prosecution, and the seaman is not entitled to legal aid or legal aid is insufficient.

Other provisions to be made by an employer include the repayment of expenses incurred in bringing a shipwrecked seaman ashore and maintaining him until he is brought ashore; and the payment of the expenses of the burial or cremation of a seaman who dies before he can be returned to a place for return.

In deciding whether a seaman is to be returned by land, sea or air, or any combination of those means, an employer shall have regard to the personal circumstances of the seaman and of any requirement special to him.

4. **Other provisions relating to seamen left behind and shipwrecked seamen.**

(1) Except where a seaman has been discharged and notice of discharge has been given to a superintendent or proper officer, the employer must, within 48 hours after a seaman has been left behind or he learns that a shipwrecked seaman has been brought ashore (or if not then practicable as soon as possible), make provision to ensure that the superintendent or proper officer for the place where the seaman is left behind or brought ashore is informed of the particulars specified in paragraph (2).

(2) The particulars referred to are:—

(*a*) name of seaman;

(*b*) his home address as stated in the list of crew;

(*c*) name and address of his next of kin as stated in the list of crew;

(*d*) in the case of a seaman left behind—

(i) name of ship from which left behind;

(ii) date left behind;

(iii) place where left behind and, if known, present whereabouts of the seaman;

(iv) reason, if known, for being left behind;

(v) name and address of employer and those of agent, if any, at or nearest to place where seaman left behind;

(e) in the case of a shipwrecked seaman—

(i) name of ship from which shipwrecked;

(ii) dates on which shipwrecked and brought ashore;

(iii) place where brought ashore and, if known, name of person by whom brought ashore and present whereabouts of seaman;

(iv) name and address of employer and those of agent, if any, at or nearest to place where seaman brought ashore.

(3) In relation to seaman left behind the master must make entries recording (a) both in official log book and list of crew, date on and place at which seaman was left behind and reason (if known); and (b) in official log book, any provision he made on employer's behalf to ensure that the superintendent or proper officer is informed of the matters referred to above.

5. The employer must ensure that the superintendent or proper officer is kept informed of arrangements made in pursuance of his obligation to make provision for the seaman's return, relief and maintenance, including any changes in those arrangements. This means the superintendent or proper officer for the place where the seaman is at the time when arrangements are made.

6. **Place for Return.** A seaman to be returned in pursuance of these regulations must be returned—

(a) in the case of a seaman who is resident in the U.K., either to his home in the U.K. or to the place where the M.N.E.A. Office at which he is registered is situated, whichever is nearer to the place at which he first arrives in the U.K.; or

(b) in the case of a seaman not resident in the U.K., to a place in the country in which he is resident being—

(i) if he joined the ship from which he was left behind or shipwrecked in that country, the place where he joined; or

(ii) if he did not join the ship in that country, the place in that country at which he was engaged to join the ship; or

(c) to any other place which may be agreed between the seaman and his employer.

7. **Provision for Return, etc. by Superintendents and Proper Officers.**

(1) Where it appears to a superintendent or proper officer for any place where a seaman is that the employer has failed to make or to continue to make sufficient provision for a seaman's return,

relief and maintenance, the superintendent or proper officer must make that provision.

(2) Where a citizen of the U.K. and colonies is found in distress in any country outside the U.K. within 3 months after ceasing to be employed in ships registered in, or belonging to the government of, such a country, the proper officer for the place where that person is found must, as soon as practicable, make the like provision for return, relief and maintenance as the employer is required to make under these regulations.

8. Conveyance Orders and Directions.

(1) Where a superintendent or proper officer is requested by an employer to make provision for a seaman's return, he shall or, where he himself is under an obligation to make such provision, he may—

(*a*) by means of a conveyance order in writing require the master of a ship (which, where the order is made at the request of the employer, shall be specified by the employer) to convey the seaman or the citizen of the U.K. and colonies from any place specified in the order to such other place so specified as lies on a reasonable route between the specified place and the place ascertained under regulation 6 to which he is to be returned; and

(*b*) give the master of that ship such directions as may be necessary;

and more than one such order may be made in the course of the seaman's return.

(2) A master is not required to convey a person in his ship or to obey any direction given—

(*a*) if his ship is a fishing vessel;

(*b*) if any provision of an enactment or instrument would be infringed by reason of that person being conveyed in the ship in addition to the other persons carried in the ship;

(*c*) if his ship would be required to go to any place to which it would not otherwise go in the course of the voyage then being undertaken or about to be undertaken;

(*d*) if, by reason of compliance, his ship would be unreasonably delayed; or

(*e*) if the master has other reasonable cause for objecting to the requirement or direction.

9. A master must make entries in the official log book recording particulars of any requirement made of him under regulation 8 and of any directions given him by a superintendent or proper officer for the purpose of that requirement.

10. Payment for Conveyance. A master of a ship in which a person is conveyed in accordance with regulation 8 is entitled to payment at a rate not exceeding £2 per day for every day (including

part of a day) on which that person is on board. On presentation of the conveyance order and an account showing the total claimed and how that amount is calculated, payment must be made to the master or to his order by the seaman's employer. But where the conveyance is required by a superintendent or proper officer under regulation 7 the account should be submitted to the D.o.T. (Accounts Branch).

11. **Wages of seamen, employed in ships, who are left behind.** The wages of a seaman discharged abroad must be paid to him at the time of his discharge in accordance with sections 7 and 8 of the Act. The wages due to a seaman who is left behind other than on discharge shall be paid to him in full and an account shall be delivered by the person employing him (or the master acting in that behalf) within 28 days from the time when he was returned to his place for return. When the employer's obligation to return a seaman ceases because the seaman refuses reasonable employment or arrangements, or asks not to be returned, his wages shall be paid and an account delivered within 28 days from the date the obligation ceased. If the employer does not know of the seaman's current address, an account thereof and notice that his wages may be had on application to the employer shall be sent to the seaman's last known address.

12. Concerns wages of seamen employed in fishing vessels.

13. Wages due under an agreement other than a crew agreement, shall be dealt with under the provisions of the agreement under which the seaman is employed.

14. Where the wages cannot be paid in accordance with regulations 11 and 12 and the seaman is not known to be dead, then notwithstanding anything contained in sections 7 and 8 of the Act or those regulations, the wages shall be paid and accounts thereof delivered to the person named in the list of crew as the seaman's next of kin, as soon as practicable after the expiration of four months from the time for payment specified in regulations 11 and 12.

15. **Other records and accounts.** The seaman's employer, a superintendent and a proper officer are to keep records of all expenses incurred and sums paid by him in the discharge of his obligations under these regulations. Where, in respect of any expense incurred or sum paid by him in discharge of his obligations, the employer makes a deduction from the seaman's wages authorised by section 9 of the Act, the employer shall render an account of all such expenses and sums to the seaman, or to his next of kin if the money is paid under regulation 14.

16. **Property of Seamen Left Behind or Shipwrecked.**

(1) This regulation applies to any property, including money, left on board a ship by a seaman to whom the regulations apply.

RR1

ORDER

FOR THE CONVEYANCE OF A SEAMAN

Merchant Shipping Act 1970

Merchant Shipping (Repatriation) Regulations 1972

Under the Regulations it is the responsibility of the employer to make provision for the return of a seaman left behind. Proper officers and mercantile marine superintendents may be requested to issue an order for the conveyance of a seaman by a United Kingdom registered ship from any place specified in the order to such other place so specified as lies on a reasonable route between the place specified in the order and the place for return.

PART 1   **To the master of the conveying ship**

Name of the ship ....   Port of registry ....

Official number ....

Pursuant to Section 62 of the Merchant Shipping Act 1970 and Regulations made thereunder you are hereby required to receive on board your ship and convey to .... the seaman named below. For his conveyance you will be entitled to payment at the rate authorised by the Regulations.

Name of seaman	Capacity and discharge book number	Name of last ship

Dated at .... this ....day of ....,.........197

Seal

Signature..

Designation ....

Port..

Important information for the master of the conveying ship

The master should make entries in the ship's official log book recording the particulars of any requirements and any directions given to him by a superintendent or proper officer. If the seaman is transferred to any other ship the particulars with the date of transfer and the ship's name, port of registry and official number should be entered at the time of transfer in the official log book.

Payment for conveyance

The owner of a ship in which a seaman is conveyed under this order is entitled to payment at a rate not exceeding £2 per day for every day (including part of a day) on which the seaman is on board. Claims for reimbursement of conveyance expenses should be made to the seaman's employer (Noted in Part 2(b)) on completion of the certificate in Part 3 of this form.

(2) In the case of property left on board by a shipwrecked seaman (*a*) if the ship is lost this regulation has no effect; and (*b*) if the ship is not lost, but, as a result of shipwreck no person is master of the ship, the duties and powers of the master are transferred to the employer, except with respect to log entries.

(3) The master's duties are to (*a*) take charge of the property; and (*b*) enter in the official log book (i) a list of the property, (ii) a description of and sum received for any articles sold, (iii) a description of any article destroyed or disposed of and name of person to whom disposal was made.

(4) The master has power to (a) sell, by public auction or otherwise, property of a perishable or deteriorating nature, in which case the proceeds form part of the property; and (b) destroy or dispose of property likely to endanger health or safety.

(5) Unless the seaman requests the property to be delivered at an address stated by him, (a) the master must, when directed by the employer, cause the property to be delivered to the employer at an address in the country to which the seaman is to be returned; and (b) the employer must deliver it to the seaman's last known address, or, if wages are payable to the seaman's next of kin, to that next of kin at the address stated in the list of crew. The expense of delivery is to be borne by the person taking delivery.

(6) If the seaman so requests, the master must cause the property to be delivered, at the seaman's expense, to an address stated by the seaman.

(7) The seaman or next of kin to whom property is delivered must be given a record of all the property with particulars of any sold, destroyed or disposed of.

17. Official log book entries relating to (a) seamen left behind, (b) conveyance orders, and (c) property taken charge of by the master, must be signed by the master and by a member of the crew.

18. **Offences.** Failure by the master or employer to comply with obligations imposed by, or requirements made under, these regulations is punishable on summary conviction by maximum fines of £50 in some cases and £200 in others.

PROPERTY OF DECEASED SEAMEN

Section 65 empowers the D.o.T. to make regulations providing for the custody of and dealing with—

(a) property left on board a U.K. registered ship by a seaman dying while or after being employed in the ship;

(b) property left in a country outside the U.K. by a seaman dying while or within 6 months after being employed in such a ship; and

(c) property left in a country outside the U.K. by a citizen of the U.K. and colonies dying while or within 6 months after being employed as a seaman in a ship registered outside the U.K.;

until it is disposed of by the D.o.T.; and for recovery of any wages due at time of seaman's death in respect of employment in a U.K. registered ship.

Section 66 gives the D.o.T. the right to satisfy any expenses incurred by them in respect of a seaman or his property out of any assets which come into their hands. If the value of the residue of the assets does not exceed £500 they may, unless a grant of representation or confirmation (of which they know) has been made, deliver it to, or distribute it among, the following persons:—

(a) the next of kin named in the crew agreement or list of crew

(b) the seaman's widow or child;

(c) a beneficially entitled person under a will or, on intestacy, to the seaman's estate;

(d) a creditor of the seaman.

Property Regulations.

(1) In these regulations "seaman" includes the master, and "ship" includes a fishing vessel.

(2) **Property, including Money, Left on Board.** The master must (a) take charge of the property; (b) make an official log book entry of (i) a list of the property; (ii) in the case of a sale, a description of each article sold and the sum received; (iii) a description of any article destroyed or disposed of, and the name of the person to whom disposal was made. The entry must be signed by the master and a member of the crew.

(3) The master may (a) sell by public auction or otherwise any part of the property he considers to have perished or deteriorated so as to be unusable or valueless, and the proceeds shall form part of the property; and (b) destroy or dispose of property he considers likely to endanger health or safety.

(4) The master must deliver the property or what remains of it (a) if he so requests, to the superintendent or proper officer for (i) the port at which the ship is at the time of the death, or (ii) any port at which the ship calls and remains more than 48 hours; or (b) if no request made—

(i) in the case of a seaman who was resident in the U.K., to a superintendent at a U.K. port or, if the ship does not call at a U.K. port, to the proper officer for the place where the voyage ends; or

(ii) in the case of a seaman who was not so resident, to the superintendent or proper officer for the place where the seaman would have been discharged had he survived, or for the place where the voyage ends;

within 48 hours after the ship first arrives at such port or place.

(5) The master, when delivering the proprety to a superintendent or proper officer must also deliver a record of it, including particulars of any articles sold, destroyed or disposed of.

(6) **Property Left Abroad.** When property is left in a country outside the U.K. by a seaman who dies while or within 6 months after being employed in a ship (wherever registered) the proper officer for the place where it is must, if possible, take charge of it. Any person having custody of it must, if the proper officer so requests, forthwith deliver it to him.

(7) A superintendent or proper officer to whom property has been delivered must, if so directed, deliver to the D.o.T. or to

such person as they may direct. He may, on the directions of the D.o.T., sell the property by public auction or otherwise, in which case the proceeds form part of the property.

(8) **Wages of Deceased Seaman.** Wages of a seaman who dies outside the U.K. must be paid by the employer to the superintendent or proper officer to whom the property of the deceased seaman is delivered. Wages due to a seaman who dies in the U.K. must be paid by the employer to the D.o.T. within 7 days after the seaman's death. Any wages not so paid are recoverable from the employer by the D.o.T.

(9) **Accounts of Wages of Deceased Seamen.** The employer must deliver to the person to whom the deceased seaman's wages are payable such an account of those wages as he would have been required to deliver to the seaman had the seaman left the ship on being discharged therefrom at the time of his death.

(10) **Records.** A superintendent, proper officer or other person (other than a master) who takes property into his charge in accordance with these regulations must keep a record showing (*a*) date on which and person by whom it was delivered; (*b*) date of sale and sum received for any article sold; (*c*) date of disposal of any article and name of person to whom disposed.

(11) **Offences.** Failure to comply with certain of these regulations is an offence punishable on summary conviction by a maximum fine of £50 in some cases, £200 in others.

BIRTHS AND DEATHS

Section 72 provides that the D.o.T. may make regulations—

(*a*) requiring the master of a U.K. registered ship to make a return to a superintendent or proper officer for transmission to the Registrar General of Shipping and Seamen of any birth or death occurring in the ship and of the death, wherever occurring outside the U.K., of any person employed in the ship, and to notify a death to the deceased's next of kin; and

(*b*) requiring the master of a ship not registered in the U.K. which calls at a U.K. port to make a similar return of any birth or death of a citizen of the U.K. and colonies which has occurred during the voyage.

(*c*) requiring the Registrar General of Shipping and Seamen to record such information as may be specified in the regulations about such a death as is specified in paragraph (*a*) above, where it appears to him that the master of the ship cannot make the return required of him because he has himself died or is incapacitated or missing.

The regulations made are contained in S.I. 1979 No. 1577 and are summarised as follows:—

Where a child is born in a U.K. registered ship the master must make a return of the birth in accordance with regulations.

Where (a) any person dies in a U.K. registered ship, or (b) any person employed in any such ship dies outside the U.K., the master must make a return of the death in accordance with regulations and, as soon as practicable but not more than 3 days after the death, notify the death to such person (if any) as the deceased may have named to him as his next of kin.

Where a citizen of the U.K. and colonies is born or dies in a ship not registered in the U.K., and the ship thereafter calls at a U.K. port during or at the end of the voyage, the master must make a return of the birth or death in accordance with regulations.

Returns. The return of a birth in a U.K. registered ship and the return of the death of a person in a U.K. registered ship or a person employed in such a ship who dies outside the U.K. must be made by the master as soon as practicable after (but within 6 months after) the event. If the event occurs in the ship the return must be made to a superintendent or proper officer for the place where the ship is at the time or at the next port of call. In the case of a death occurring elsewhere than in the ship, it must be made to a superintendent or proper officer for the place where the ship is when the master first becomes aware of the death or at the next port of call. The return of a birth or death of a citizen of the U.K. and colonies in a ship not registered in the U.K. must be made to a superintendent at the next U.K. port of call, or the port where the voyage ends, before the ship leaves that port.

Contents of Returns. A return must be in writing, be signed by the master as informant, and must contain as many of the particulars as the master may reasonably be able to obtain as are specified in the Schedules to the regulations.

Schedule 1, which relates to births, calls for:—

(a) name of ship in which birth occurred,
(b) port of registry and official number (letters and number if fishing vessel),
(c) if not registered in U.K., name and address of owner,
(d) particulars of child, father and mother as indicated in the Official Log Books Regulations (see Chapter 5),
(e) name and surname of master or, if birth authorised to be recorded in the marine register, (i) name and surname, (ii) usual address, and (iii) qualification of informant.

Schedule 2, which relates to deaths, calls for:—

(a) name of ship in which death occurred or in which deceased was employed,

(b) port of registry and official number (letters and number if fishing vessel),

(c) particulars of deceased as indicated in the Official Log Books Regulations (see Chapter 5),

(d) particulars of informant as for Schedule 1.

Records of deaths where master unable to act. Where it appears to the Registrar General of Shipping and Seamen that the master cannot make a return because he has himself died or is incapacitated or missing, and the death has been the subject of an inquest or an inquiry or a post mortem examination, or preliminary investigation, then the Registrar General shall record such of the information specified in Schedule 2 as he may be able to obtain in the circumstances of the death.

Certified Copies of Returns. When a return has been transmitted to him or a record has been made by him, the Registrar General of Shipping and Seamen is required to send a copy, certified by him or a person authorised by him to be a true copy, to the appropriate Registrar General.

Other Births and Deaths outside the U.K. Where (i) any birth or death of a citizen of the U.K. and colonies occurs in a ship not registered in the U.K., (ii) any death of a citizen of the U.K. and colonies who has been employed in such a ship occurs elsewhere than in the ship, or (iii) any death of a person who has been employed in a U.K. registered ship occurs elsewhere than in the ship, the appropriate Registrar General may record in the marine register the relevant particulars specified in Schedule 1 or 2 as he thinks fit.

Appropriate Registrar General. The appropriate Registrar General for the above-mentioned purposes is:—

(a) (i) in the case of the birth of a child the father of whom or, if the child is illegitimate, the mother of whom was at the time of the birth usually resident in Scotland or Northern Ireland; or

(ii) in the case of the death of a person who at the date of his death was usually resident in Scotland or Northern Ireland;
the Registrar General of Births, Deaths and Marriages for Scotland or the Registrar General for Northern Ireland, as the case may require; and

(b) in any other case, the Registrar General for England and Wales.

Unregistered British Ships. Section 72 and the Regulations extend to unregistered British ships which are sea-going ships owned by persons resident in, or by bodies corporate having a principal place of business in, the U.K., and to masters and seamen employed in them.

Offences. The master of a ship who fails to comply with provisions of the Regulations will be guilty of an offence punishable on summary conviction with a fine not exceeding £50.

Forms for Making Returns. The following forms are obtainable from M.M. Offices:—

RBD 1/72   Return of births and deaths occurring on board.
RBD 2/72   Report of death ashore.
RBD 3/72   Report of a birth or death in a foreign ship.
RBD 4/72   Return of births or deaths on Commonwealth ships

The form RBD 1/72 has four pages. On page 1 there is provision for entering the particulars of the ship and a set of instructions to masters. Pages 2 and 3 are for entering particulars of births and/or deaths. The certificate to be signed by the master is on page 3, and that to be signed by the proper officer to whom the return is delivered is on page 2. Page 4 provides for entering additional particulars in respect of deceased members of crew, including name, relationship and address of next of kin and Discharge Book number. Copies of entries relating to death which appear in the narrative section of the official log book are also recorded on page 4.

The British Nationality Act 1948. This Act provides that a person born on a British ship is deemed to be born at the place where the ship is registered. Under our law a child born on board a British registered ship becomes a citizen of the United Kingdom irrespective of what other nationality he or she may have under the law of another country. But the same Act provides that a United Kingdom citizen of full age and capacity may renounce United Kingdom citizenship. The Act further provides that a child born on a foreign ship is deemed to have been born at the place where the ship is registered. But if the child's father was born in the United Kingdom or in a British colony, the child automatically becomes a United Kingdom citizen and, therefore, a British subject. In addition, the child might acquire the nationality of the country where the ship is registered, but that is a matter of foreign law.

Seamen's Wills. As seamen are regarded as persons who may meet with sudden emergencies, the law extends to them special privileges for disposing of their property by will. Normally, a testator must make a formal will, having his signature attested by two witnesses present at the time of signing, who must sign in the presence of the testator and of each other. Moreover, only a person who has reached the age of 18 can make a formal will. Under the Wills Acts 1837 and the Wills (Soldiers and Sailors) Act 1917, wills made by seaman being at sea need not be attested. They need not even be in writing but can be made verbally, and by a seaman under 18 years of age. Such wills remain valid until revoked, even though the testator returns home and dies ashore. But the testator must be

RBD 1/72
(for Masters U.K. ships
& for other ships at
U.K. ports)

RETURN OF BIRTHS AND DEATHS

FOR THE PURPOSES OF SECTION 72 1a & b OF THE MERCHANT SHIPPING ACT 1970

IMPORTANT: The Consul or other Officer abroad or the Superintendent in the United Kingdom to whom this Return is rendered should forward it without delay, BY AIR, wherever possible, direct to:-

THE REGISTRAR GENERAL OF SHIPPING AND SEAMEN
LLANTRISANT ROAD
CARDIFF CF5 2YS

Name of Ship	Official Number and, if a Fishing Vessel, Letters and Number	PORT OF REGISTRY If the ship is registered outside the U.K. or is unregistered state also name and address of owners

A Return of Birth or Death is to be delivered to a Superintendent, Consul or Shipping Master at the earliest opportunity. The Master should bring the Return together with his Official Log Book which records the occurrence.

INSTRUCTIONS TO MASTERS*

U.K. REGISTERED AND UNREGISTERED SHIPS

The Master is required to make a Return of any birth of a child and of any death in the ship ∤, and of the death, wherever occurring outside the U.K., of any person employed in the ship.

OTHER SHIPS

If the ship calls at a U.K. port the Master is required to make a Return of any birth or death of a citizen of the U.K. or Colonies which has occurred in the ship ∤ during the voyage.

INSTRUCTIONS TO CONSULS, SHIPPING MASTERS AND SUPERINTENDENTS

It is important that the Officer receiving a Return from a Master be satisfied that it is correctly completed in all particulars. Any omission or ambiguity — such as stating the cause of death simply as "missing" — will only lead to delay in registration., The Officer should also satisfy himself that the person making the Return is the Master of the ship and that the vessel is a sea-going ship. He should confirm that the entry in this Return and in the Official Log Book (where carried) are consistent with one another.

If a death occurred ashore it will be helpful if a copy of the Post Mortem findings or other medical or police reports with a translation into English if in a foreign language is attached to this Return. The Officer should also refer to the appropriate Instructions or Notes for Guidance in order to find out whether he is to hold an inquiry into the cause of death.

* Master includes every person (except a pilot) having command or charge of any ship.

∤ in the ship includes in a ship's boat or ship's life-raft and being lost from a ship, a ship's boat or ship's life-raft.

"actually at sea" when the will is made. If he is discharged from a ship and makes the will while in hospital ashore, an informal will is invalid. It has been held that a seaman was "actually at sea" while being a crew member of a ship stationed permanently in a harbour. For the purpose of the Acts relating to seamen's wills, the term "seaman" includes the master of a ship.

TERMINATION OF SERVICE

Termination of Service owing to sickness or injury. Employers have agreed on the N.M.B. in respect of tonnage entered in P. and I. Associations to extend their obligations under s. 62 of the M.S. Act 1970, by making a Special Payment to persons whose employment is terminated by reason of their being signed off abroad owing to sickness or injury. The payment shall be for the duration of the employer's obligation under the Section above referred to but subject to a maximum of 12 weeks in any case. The Special Payment shall be at the rate of wages shown in the Crew Agreement (less any benefit payable under the National Insurance Scheme).

The following rules shall be observed:

(*a*) The Special Payment shall not be made in cases of illness due to a seafarer's wilful act or default or own misbehaviour (venereal disease excepted).

(*b*) On arrival at a "Place of Return" as defined in the Regulations made under Section 62 of the M.S.A. 1970, the seafarer must report at once to his employer.

It shall be a condition of the Special Payment that any seafarer on discharge from hospital abroad shall report at once to the employer or the employer's local representative. When he becomes fit Special Payment ceases.

The Special Payment is also conditional on satisfactory medical evidence being provided that unfitness continues. The obligation to produce this evidence rests upon the seafarer. It is recommended that medical certificates issued overseas should, whenever possible, be authenticated by a Proper Officer.

Termination of Service by Wreck. Section 15 provides that where a U.K. registered ship is wrecked or lost a seaman whose employment is terminated before the date contemplated in the agreement shall be entitled to wages at the rate payable under the agreement for every day on which he is unemployed in the two months following the date of the wreck or loss.

Termination of Service by Sale or Change of Registry of Ship. Section 15 further provides that where a U.K. registered ship is sold outside the U.K. or ceases to be registered in the U.K. and a seaman's employment is thereby terminated before the date contemplated in the agreement, then, unless the agreement provides otherwise, he shall be entitled to wages at the rate payable under the agreement for every day on which he is unemployed in the two months following the date of termination.

Non-entitlement to Wages. A seaman is not entitled to wages for a day on which he was unemployed if it is shown that the unemployment was not due to the wreck, loss, sale or change of registry of the ship, or if he was able to obtain suitable employment for that day but unreasonably refused or failed to take it.

RE-RATING

The 1970 Act, unlike the 1906 Act (section 59 now repealed), does not mention the term "disrating", but one of the contractual clauses for insertion in the crew agreement does state that any seaman who incompetently performs his work may be re-rated by the master and transferred to other duties, but adding that re-rating shall not affect his remuneration. The term "re-rating" includes promotion, and a record of any re-rating with the date on which it takes effect must be entered in the official log book and be signed by the master and a member of the crew.

LOSS OF SEAMEN'S EFFECTS

One of the general decisions of the N.M.B. is that a master, officer or rating who suffers total or partial loss of or damage to personal effects arising from a marine peril (fire, flooding, collision, etc.), shall receive compensation up to a maximum not exceeding the scale agreed upon by the N.M.B. Additional compensation is payable in like circumstances for the loss of or damage to instruments, technical books and tools owned by certain officers and ratings. Payment is made conditional on the production of a certificate signed by the master or chief engineer that the loss was not occasioned by the claimant's own fault. Should a seafarer lose his life at the time, the compensation will be paid to his widow, child or other person entitled to his personal estate.

MAINTENANCE OF SEAMEN'S DEPENDANTS

Section 17 provides that where, during a seaman's employment in a ship, expenses are incurred by a responsible authority for the benefit of any dependant of his, the authority may by notice in writing require the seaman's employer (a) to retain for a stated period such proportion of his net wages as may be specified, and (b) to give the authority notice in writing of the seaman's discharge from the ship. The employer must comply with the notice and give written notice of its contents to the seaman.

A seaman's dependants include his spouse, any person under 16 whom he is liable to maintain or in respect of whom he is liable to make contributions to a local authority.

Not more than the following proportions of net wages may be retained, i.e. one-half if the notice relates to one dependant only; two-thirds if it relates to two or more.

The Maintenance of Seamen's Dependants Regulations include the following:—

1. The term "retention notice" means a notice by a responsible authority to a seaman's employer which relates to a claim against a seaman's wages for the maintenance, etc., of his dependants.

2. **Conditions for Service of Retention Notice.** A responsible authority may serve a retention notice on a seaman's employer if (a) it has incurred expenses of the kind specified in Regulation 4, (b) if the employer has a residence or registered or principal office in the U.K.

3. **Form and Contents of Retention Notice.** The notice must state that it is served under section 17 of the M.S. Act 1970 and that the responsible authority has incurred expenses of one or more of the descriptions specified in regulation 4, and also that the employer is required—

(i) to retain, for the period beginning with the service of the notice and ending 28 days after the seaman's discharge from the ship, a proportion (to be specified) of the seaman's net wages not exceeding one-half if only one dependant or two-thirds if more; and

(ii) to give the authority written notice of such discharge.

The notice must contain (a) name and address of authority, (b) name of employer, (c) name of seaman, (d) name of ship (if known) in which seaman employed, (e) capacity in which employed (if known), (f) description of expenses, (g) name of person in respect of whom expenses are incurred, and (h) name of person to whom payment has been or is intended to be made.

4. **Expenses in Respect of which Notice May be Served.** These are (a) benefit awarded under the Ministry of Social Security Act to meet requirements of seaman's spouse or children, (b) expenses of the provision by a local authority of accommodation, or by a welfare authority for the seaman's spouse and children whom he is liable to maintain, and (c) expenses of provision made by a local or welfare authority in respect of a child received into or committed to their care.

5. **Rules for Ascertaining Net Wages.** For the purpose of a retention notice net wages are the full amount of wages due at the time of discharge subject only to deduction of—

(a) National Insurance contributions;

(b) Income tax;

(c) Any deduction required to be made from wages paid to a seaman by an attachment of earnings order;

(d) Contributions to a pension fund and any charity, and contributions in respect of membership of a trade union and any friendly society;

(e) Sums allotted by the seaman by allotment notes to (i) his spouse, (ii) any other person in respect of whom expenses are stated in a retention notice to be incurred by the responsible authority or to whom any payment forming part of those expenses is so stated to have been paid or to be payable, (iii) any other person known to the seaman's employer to have the custody or care of a child whom the seaman is liable to maintain, or (iv) any responsible authority in respect of expenses specified in regulation 4, whenever payable; and other sums allotted before the notice is served;

(f) Sums (excluding loans) paid by the employer on account of a seaman's wages to or to the order of the seaman before the notice is served; and

(g) The amount of any liability to the employer before the notice is served in respect of canteen bills, goods supplied, radio or telephone calls and postage expenses.

DISCIPLINE AT SEA

At the time the 1970 Act became law the Government gave an undertaking to review its disciplinary provisions and successive Governments accepted that undertaking. In 1974 a limited review was undertaken which resulted in sections 29 and 31 of the 1970 Act being repealed, and section 30 being amended, by the Merchant Shipping Act 1974. On the other hand that Act provided increased penalties for offences concerned with safety of life and of a ship whilst at sea. During the debates on the 1974 Act, the Secretary of State for Trade announced his intention to establish a Working Group to examine in depth the disciplinary needs for sea-going employment in merchant ships. In May 1974 a Working Group was appointed consisting of representatives from the D.o.T., the General Council of British Shipping representing the employers, and the Associations and Unions representing masters, officers and ratings. The terms of reference of the Group were:—

"To review the disciplinary requirements on board merchant ships with particular reference to the framework of authority required in modern conditions in the interests of safety, good shipboard relations and effective operation, and to make recommendations."

The Group's report to the Secretary of State which was published in November 1975 made the following principal recommendations:—

(a) The present system of shipboard fines should be abolished and a new system of discipline should be instituted consisting of recorded warnings, reprimands and dismissal from the ship after the offence and action by joint disciplinary committees.

(b) Persistent and serious offenders to be excluded from employment in the industry for as long as necessary.

(c) Masters should be provided with wider power of discharge abroad with a view to the repatriation of a serious offender.

(d) Contracts of employment should contain provision for up to one week's wages to be required in lieu of notice from a seafarer repatriated under the draft Code of Conduct subject to the right of appeal.

(e) The question raised by the fact that certificated officers and ratings are liable to the withdrawal of their certificates by the D.o.T. for "misconduct or any other reason" and might thus be subject to two systems of "discipline" should be further considered.

(f) Necessary legislation should be introduced as soon as possible and the new arrangements come into operation after a comprehensive programme of education and training. The Working Group to remain in being to co-ordinate the programme.

(g) A Code of Conduct should be published with the approval of the Secretary of State, and any subsequent changes approved by him, and issued to all seafarers serving on United Kingdom ships giving advice and guidance as to their behaviour and as to the consequences of breaches of the code.

The Secretary of State in a foreword to the Report commented that he was most impressed that, on a subject that had been widely recognised as highly contentious, the Report was unanimous, that findings had been well researched and backed by evidence and that these were factors which disposed the Government to accept and act upon the Report as soon as there was an opportunity to legislate.

In 1978 the N.M.B. published the "Code of Conduct for the Merchant Navy" drawn up by the employers, unions and approved by the Secretary of State D.o.T. The Code sets out the basic rules of reasonable behaviour expected of officers and ratings, and as well as describing expected conduct in various situations lays down disciplinary procedures to be followed and provides for penalties in the event of serious or other breaches of the Code. It has not yet been found possible to bring in the Code by law compulsorily, but from 1st January 1979 seamen signing crew agreements subject to N.M.B. conditions have agreed to comply with the Code of Conduct and its disciplinary provisions because of clauses (ix)(f), (x)(g) and (x)(h) contained in the approved agreements A.L.C. 1 (d) (79) or G.C.B.S. Form C.A.G. 1. Employers by signing these agreements have agreed in clause (xi)(d) that the provisions of the M.S. (Disciplinary Offences) Regulations 1972 (as amended), including the master's power to impose fines, shall not be applied to any seaman employed under such agreement.

The Government introduced a Merchant Shipping Bill in late 1978 which amongst other things proposed further modifications to the sections of the 1970 Act dealing with criminal offences affecting safety. The Bill became the M.S. Act 1979 on 4th April 1979 and sections 42–45 dealing with offences came into force on 1st January 1980.

The situation in 1981 described below is that the M.S. Act 1970, as amended by the M.S. Acts 1974 and 1979, provides for certain criminal offences related to safety matters which can be applied by successful prosecutions through the Courts, and in addition, in G.C.B.S. federated ships, forming the largest part of the British fleet, an agreed disciplinary procedure contained within the "Code of Conduct for the Merchant Navy" is operated by contractual agreement between the seamen and the employers with the approval of the Secretary of State. It would appear that masters of non-federated ships may still be able legally to continue to use the power given by the Disciplinary Regulations 1972 to fine seamen who commit offences, but they probably do not use the power. The following paragraphs describe the statutory criminal offences which apply to all ships, then the Code of Conduct for the Merchant Navy and the back-up shore-based Disciplinary Committees, and finally briefly mention the now irrelevant Disciplinary Regulations 1972 (as amended).

OFFENCES BY SEAMEN

Misconduct Endangering Ship or Persons on Board. Section 27 provides that if the master of or any seaman employed in a U.K. registered ship (*a*) does any act which causes or is likely to cause the loss or destruction of or serious damage to the ship or its machinery, navigational equipment or safety equipment or the death of or serious injury to a person on board, or (*b*) omits to do anything required to preserve the ship or its machinery, navigational equipment or safety equipment from loss, destruction or serious damage or to preserve any person on board from death or serious injury; and the act or omission is deliberate, or amounts to a breach or neglect of duty, or he is under the influence of drink or a drug at the time, he shall be liable, on conviction on indictment, to imprisonment for a term not exceeding two years and to a fine, and, on summary conviction, to a fine not exceeding £1000. In this section "breach or neglect of duty", except in relation to a master, includes any disobedience to a lawful command.

Drunkenness, etc. on Duty. (Section 28) If a seaman employed in a U.K. fishing vessel is, while on board the vessel, under the influence of drink or a drug to such an extent that his capacity to carry out the duties of his employment is impaired, he shall be liable on conviction on indictment to imprisonment for a term not exceeding two years and a fine and, on summary conviction, to a fine not exceeding £1000.

Wilful Disobedience to Certain Lawful Commands. Section 29 of the 1970 Act which enacted this offence was repealed by the M.S. Act 1974.

Continued or Concerted Disobedience, Neglect, etc. (Section 30) If a seaman employed in a U.K. registered ship (*a*) persistently and wilfully neglects his duty, or (*b*) persistently and wilfully disobeys lawful commands, or (*c*) combines with other seamen to disobey lawful commands or neglect duty or to impede the navigation of the ship or the progress of a voyage while the ship is at sea and not securely moored in a safe berth, he shall be liable on conviction on indictment, to imprisonment for a term not exceeding two years and a fine and, on summary conviction, to a fine not exceeding £1000. This section was amended by the M.S. Act 1974 to make the offences in (c) only applicable while the ship is at sea.

Absence without Leave at Time of Sailing. This offence, enacted by section 31, was repealed by the M.S. Act 1974 on 1st November 1974.

Offences by Certain Other Persons. (Section 32) Where a person goes to sea in a ship without the consent of the master or other person authorised to give it, or is conveyed in a ship under a conveyance order, the relevant sections of the Act relating to offences by seamen shall apply as if he were a seaman employed in the ship.

Defence of Drug taken for Medical Purposes. (Section 33) In proceedings for an offence under Section 27 or 28 of the M.S. Act 1970 it shall be a defence to prove that at the time of the act or omission alleged against the defendant he was under the influence of a drug taken by him for medical purposes and either that he took it on medical advice and complied with any directions given as part of that advice or that he had no reason to believe that the drug might have had the influence it had.

NEW DISCIPLINARY PROCEDURES
Code of Conduct for the Merchant Navy

1. Seafaring is a civilian occupation which places upon those who go to sea demands not found in industry ashore. Seafarers are called upon to spend not only their working hours but their leisure hours too in the confined environment of a ship and with the same individuals for company. It might be said that they are more susceptible to the stresses and strains of everyday life than their fellows ashore. In this environment, the need for discipline and behaviour assumes a particular importance. However, disciplinary procedures should not be viewed primarily as a means of imposing sanctions. They are also designed to emphasise and encourage improvements in individual conduct.

2. The most effective form of discipline is self-discipline, which in turn springs from a responsible attitude to the job, whatever it may be, and concern for the efficient operation of the ship and for the comfort and convenience of fellow crew members. Failures of self-discipline which occur will have to be dealt with by reference to an imposed framework of discipline or Code of Conduct. This document sets out such a Code, containing the basic rules of reasonable behaviour expected of all officers and ratings. It has been drawn up by the organisations representing the seafarers and the

employers and approved by the Secretary of State for Trade. Observance of it will make seafaring a better and more rewarding job for all those involved and will help to secure the safety of everybody aboard. Rules drawn up by shipping companies, and Masters' Standing Orders relating to conduct aboard ship, should not conflict with this Code.

3. Orders must be given and obeyed if a ship is to operate safely and efficiently. Co-operation cannot be imposed but will normally be readily forthcoming if it is immediately apparent to the recipient of an order that the order is a reasonable one or, if it is not so apparent, if a reasonable request for an explanation of the necessity for the order is acceded to. At the same time wilful or repeated refusal to comply with reasonable orders or other anti-social behaviour must be expected to have certain consequences.

4. An important factor in securing co-operation, which cannot be too strongly stressed, is good communications. This applies both to communications between a company's shore-based administration and the ship and to communications within the ship itself. If all concerned are kept as fully informed as possible about the company's policies and objectives and can be made to feel that they have a personal stake in the successful outcome of the voyage upon which they are engaged, co-operation and harmony will be much more readily assured than by a "theirs is not to reason why" attitude.

Conduct in emergencies

5. In any emergency or other situation in which the safety of the ship or of any person on board her, whether crew or passengers, is at stake the Master, Officers and Petty Officers are entitled to look for immediate and unquestioning obedience of orders. There can be no exception to this rule. Failure to comply will be treated as among the most serious of breaches of this Code and will be liable to lead to the offender's dismissal not only from the ship (at the first opportunity) and his Company, but also his exclusion from the Merchant Navy. It may also warrant prosecution under the provisions of the Merchant Shipping Acts.

Conduct in situations other than emergencies

6. Emergencies are fortunately rare and this document is primarily concerned with the day-to-day situation on board. It should be borne in mind, however, that certain acts of misconduct (e.g. absence from place of duty or heavy drinking) could have the effect of causing a state of emergency. The following paragraph sets out some broad general rules for everyday conduct.

7. (a) PUNCTUALITY is very important both for the efficient operation of the ship and to avoid putting extra work on shipmates. This is true of joining the vessel at the time appointed, returning from shore leave, reporting for watchkeeping duty and all other work. Absence at the time of

sailing, in particular, may seriously delay the ship or even prevent her sailing until a replacement is found.

(b) DRUGS. The unlawful possession or distribution of drugs by any person on board ship renders him liable to dismissal as well as possible legal proceedings and to exclusion from further employment in the shipping industry.

(c) DRINKING. There should be ships' rules about bringing intoxicating liquor on board and they should be understood and strictly observed. Facilities for drinking on board are there to be used but they should not be abused. Bar rules should be strictly adhered to.

(d) BRINGING UNAUTHORISED PERSONS ON BOARD The ship's rules or port authority's restrictions on bringing unauthorised persons on board must be strictly observed.

(e) OFFENSIVE WEAPONS. These must not be brought on board.

(f) SMOKING IN PROHIBITED AREAS is dangerous on any ship but particularly on tankers, liquid gas carriers and vessels carrying explosive or inflammable materials. The ship's rules controlling smoking and the use of naked lights or unapproved electric torches must be scrupulously obeyed.

(g) DUTIES. Every member of the crew should carry out his duties efficiently to the best of his ability. He is entitled to be informed clearly what his duties are and to whom he is responsible for carrying them out. If he is in doubt he should ask. Within the scope of his duties, reasonable commands and instructions must be obeyed.

(h) TREATMENT OF ACCOMMODATION. For the duration of the voyage the ship is not only the seafarer's place of work but also his home. Accommodation and other facilities, whether provided for his personal use or to be shared with others, should therefore be treated with respect.

(i) BEHAVIOUR TOWARDS OTHERS. Anti-social behaviour can cause a seafarer to become a nuisance to others on board and in extreme circumstances can hazard the ship and the crew. This can include not only excessive drinking but also such behaviour as causing excessive noise, abusive language, aggressive attitudes and offensive personal habits. The fact that some need to sleep whilst others are awake should also be borne in mind.

Dealing with breaches of the code

8. It is necessary to have a procedure for dealing with breaches of this Code of Conduct backed by appropriate sanctions. These may range, according to the seriousness of the breach, from informal warnings for the most minor breaches, through various grades of

formal warning including reprimands, to dismissal from the ship, with a possibility that this will lead also to the suspension or cancellation of any Certificate of Competency and/or surrender of a Discharge Book held by an offender and to exclusion from the Merchant Navy. Seafarers are subject to the general law of the United Kingdom and for certain offences, prejudicial to the safety of the ship or those on board, there remains a liability to prosecution in the Courts under the relevant sections of the Merchant Shipping Acts. These are, at present, Sections 27 and 30 of the Merchant Shipping Act, 1970, as amended by the Merchant Shipping Act, 1974 and 1979.

9. The following acts of misconduct, if proved to the reasonable satisfaction of the Master to have been committed, are those for which dismissal from the ship either immediately or at the end of the voyage will, according to the circumstances of the case, be considered appropriate apart from any legal action which may be called for:—

(i) assault;

(ii) wilful damage to ship or any property on board;

(iii) theft or possession of stolen property;

(iv) possession of offensive weapons;

(v) persistent or wilful failure to perform duty;

(vi) unlawful possession or distribution of drugs;

(vii) conduct endangering the ship or persons on board;

(viii) combination with others at sea to impede the progress of the voyage or navigation of the ship;

(ix) disobedience of orders relating to safety of the ship or any person on board;

(x) to be asleep on duty or fail to remain on duty if such conduct would prejudice the safety of the ship or any person on board;

(xi) incapacity through the influence of drink or drugs to carry out duty to the prejudice of the safety of the ship or of any person on board;

(xii) to smoke, use a naked light or an unapproved electric torch in any part of a ship carrying dangerous cargo or stores where smoking or the use of naked lights or unapproved torches is prohibited;

(xiii) intimidation, coercion and interference with the work of other employees;

(xiv) behaviour which seriously detracts from the safe and efficient working of the ship;

(xv) behaviour which seriously detracts from the social well-being of any other person on board;

(xvi) causing or permitting unauthorised persons to be on board the ship whilst it is at sea;

(xvii) repeated commission of breaches of a lesser degree listed in paragraph 11 after warnings have been given in accordance with the procedures in paragraph 10.

10. Breaches of a lesser degree of seriousness may be dealt with by:—

(a) Informal warning administered at an appropriate level lower than that of the Master;

(b) Formal warning by the head of department which will be suitably recorded;

(c) Formal warnings by the Master recorded in the ship's official logbook;

(d) Written reprimands administered by the Master and recorded in the ship's official logbook.

When a formal warning is given the seafarer should be advised of the likely consequences of further breaches of the Code.

11. Breaches of the Code, if proved to the reasonable satisfaction of the Master, Officer, or Petty Officer to have been committed, for which the procedure in paragraph 10 is considered appropriate, are:

(a) offences of the kind described at paragraph 9, which are not considered to justify dismissal in the particular circumstances of the case;

(b) minor acts of negligence, neglect of duty, disobedience and assault;

(c) unsatisfactory work performance;

(d) poor time keeping;

(e) stopping work before the authorised time;

(f) failure to report to work without satisfactory reason;

(g) absence from place of duty or from the ship without leave;

(h) offensive or disorderly behaviour.

NOTE: Whilst paragraph 11 has been made as comprehensive as possible, it is recognised that some companies may wish to propose additions related to their particular trading patterns. Proposals for such additions should be submitted, after agreement with the organisations representing the seafarers concerned, to the Department of Trade for approval.

Procedures for dealing with breaches of the code

12. (i) A seafarer who is alleged to have breached the Code will be seen in the first instance by a Petty Officer or Officer designated by the Master. If the Petty Officer or Officer is satisfied that no further action is called for or that the breach, although proved, calls for no more than an informal warning of the kind referred to at paragraph 10(a) above, he will proceed accordingly and the matter will thereafter be regarded as closed.

(ii) If the offence is of a more serious nature or is a repetition of a similar minor offence, a formal warning will be given and the fact suitably recorded. Alternatively, the case may be referred to the Master; any offence falling under paragraph 9 must be referred to him.

(iii) The Master will deal with cases referred to him with the minimum of delay. He will inform the seafarer of the alleged breach giving him the opportunity to say whether he admits it, to call any witnesses and to question them on their evidence and to make any statement he wishes in answer to the alleged breach including any comments on the evidence produced against him.

(iv) After a careful and thorough investigation and having considered all the evidence the Master will orally inform the seafarer whether or not he finds that the seafarer committed the alleged breach.

(v) If he finds that the seafarer did commit the alleged breach, he will impose a penalty which he considers to be reasonable in all the circumstances, taking into account the seafarer's record on the ship and any other relevant factors. He may announce:

(a) that he is giving a warning; or

(b) that he is giving a written reprimand; and/or

(c) that the seafarer will be dismissed from the ship, and that fact will be reported to a shore-based Disciplinary Committee. If the Master decides that the continued presence of the offender on board would be detrimental to the efficient and safe running of the ship or to the maintenance of harmonious personal relations on board, he may arrange for dismissal to take place at the next port of call for repatriation to the United Kingdom.

(vi) The Master will enter details of the breach and the action taken in the official log.

(vii) The seafarer shall be given a copy of all entries made in the logbook relating to his breach of this Code and shall acknowledge receipt.

(viii) The seafarer shall be given a copy of any report made to a shore-based Disciplinary Committee relating to his breaching the Code and shall acknowledge receipt.

(ix) On receipt of a report of dismissal for breach of this Code, a shore-based Disciplinary Committee, duly constituted in accordance with arrangements agreed by the Secretary of State for Trade, will consider and make appropriate recommendations about the offender's future employment in the shipping industry.

(x) A seafarer shall have the right to be accompanied by a friend, who may advise him and speak on his behalf, whenever an alleged breach of this Code is being considered against him.

Dismissals

13. In the event of dismissal the seafarer may contact an official

of the appropriate seafarers' organisation who may take up the matter with an appropriate manager of the shipping company concerned. In such event the two representatives shall meet within five days to discuss the issue.

14. Nothing in this Code of Conduct shall be read as negating any seafarer's right to bring an unfair dismissal claim before an Industrial Tribunal as provided in the Employment Protection (Consolidation) Act, 1978.

15. Failure to contact a seafarers' organisation or an Industrial Tribunal, or to take a case to an Industrial Tribunal should the union and employer representatives declare his dismissal fair, will be taken as prima facie evidence that the seafarer accepts his dismissal as fair and of his willingness to abide by the decision of a shore-based Disciplinary Committee as to eventual disciplinary action.

The National Maritime Board (N.M.B.) agreed Shipboard Disciplinary Procedures

These arrangements apply to all officers, cadets and ratings who are subject to N.M.B. conditions, whether or not they are domiciled in the U.K. and who are serving in a U.K. registered ship managed by a G.C.B.S. member company on a D.o.T. approved crew agreement, which contains the appropriate clauses and which was opened on or after 1st January 1979. The new arrangements also apply to those officers and ratings supplied for service in non-U.K. registered ships managed by G.C.B.S. member companies and approved for manning under the G.C.B.S. Manning Policy as if they were serving in U.K. registered ships. This is provided the law of the ship's flag country is not in direct conflict with the Code of Conduct and does not impose a mandatory contractual penalty for breach of obligations in the Code. The arrangements do *not* apply to those serving on agreements opened under the authority of other administrations outside the U.K. (e.g. seafarers engaged in India on an Indian crew agreement.)

As has already been stated, the new procedures have been introduced by including a clause, (xi)(d), wherein the employer agrees that the master's power to impose a fine will not be applied to any seaman who signs the agreement, and in further clauses, each seaman, by signing the agreement, agrees to comply with the Code of Conduct (clause (x)(g)), accepts that if he fails to do so his Agreement may be terminated (clause (ix)(f)), and agrees to the deduction from his wages of a contribution to his repatriation expenses (maximum one week's pay) if he is dismissed from the ship outside Home Trade limits for breach of the Code.

Each seaman must be issued with a copy of the Code of Conduct, and it should be made clear to him when he signs the agreement, by the master or an officer, that by signing the agreement he is agreeing to be bound by the Code.

The procedures for dealing with breaches of the Code are described in paragraph 12, which include entries in the official log book. Where the alleged breach of the Code is likely to lead to dismissal, and if there is conflict of evidence, notes of evidence given should be taken and formed into written statements, signed by witnesses and certified by the master before being annexed to the official log book by a suitable entry. Similar detailed statements will be required if the master intends to recommend that a seaman be prosecuted in the criminal courts.

Dismissal. All disciplinary cases which result in a seaman being discharged from the ship must be reported to the employing company and to the Central Secretariat of the Merchant Navy Discipline Organisation (M.N.D.O.) for reference to a shore-based Disciplinary Committee.

At the time when the seafarer is discharged from the ship, the master must send to his company:—

(a) form M.N.D. 1—Discipline Report (blue copy);

(b) copies of *all* relevant log extracts, including those relating to earlier formal warnings etc., each endorsed "We certify this to be a true copy of the entry in the official log book", signed by the master and another senior officer;

(c) copies of any written statements taken, endorsed and certified as above; and

(d) copies of any written warnings on the ship's file, endorsed and certified as above.

The top copy of the M.N.D. 1 only should be sent to the Central Secretariat, M.N.D.O., as notification of a possible pending case, and the third (yellow) copy of M.N.D. 1 and copies of all documents specified in (b) and (c) above must be given to the seaman who should sign part 5 of the form as a receipt, and a log book entry should be made that this has been done. If a deduction is being made from the seaman's pay to cover part or all of his repatriation expenses, a 'notice of deduction' must be given to him, and the amount deducted recorded in the official log book.

Prosecution. When a breach of the Code also appears to be an offence under either the general criminal law or the Merchant Shipping Acts (Section 27 or 30), a master must warn the seaman that he intends to recommend prosecution ashore, enter the log book that the warning has been given, and then forward all detailed written and certified statements from witnesses, with certified extracts from the log book, to his employer. The form M.N.D. 1 should be endorsed "Company to consider prosecution" and if possible all documents should be sent to arrive before the seaman's repatriation.

Prosecution may be appropriate in cases of serious assault, certainly when resulting in death or serious injury, when there has been substantial theft of cargo, ship's stores or other crew possessions, and deliberate, negligent or drunken acts or omissions that cause the loss, destruction or serious damage to the ship or death or serious injury of any person on board. The decision to prosecute for an offence under the Merchant Shipping Acts will normally be taken by the D.o.T. or the company, and for other criminal offences, by the company or the police.

Procedure when a seaman is absent. A seaman who fails to join or rejoin a ship has breached clause (x)(a) of the agreement. This is not a breach of the Code of Conduct, but if the seaman is absent without leave and fails to join or rejoin he is covered by the new procedures and the reasons for his absence should be investigated, written statements taken from witnesses and entries concerning the absence made in the official log book. A deduction of up to £50 can be made from the seaman's wages in respect of any expense caused to the ship on account of his absence. The breach should be reported to the company and to the M.N.D.O. using form M.N.D. 1. The third yellow copy and copies of supporting documents should be sent by post to the seaman's home address. Should the man later rejoin the ship, the company and M.N.D.O. must be notified.

When a seaman who has allegedly committed a breach of paragraph 9 of the Code discharges himself before the disciplinary procedures and investigation can take place, or frustrates the procedures by being absent by other means, the case should be investigated in his absence and a report made as described above. This is called Advance Discharge.

Merchant Navy Discipline Organisation (M.N.D.O.). This organisation consists of:—

(a) a Central Disciplinary Committee in London, consisting of not more than 3 seafarers' representatives and not more than 3 G.C.B.S. representatives;

(b) a number of Local Disciplinary Committees, at agreed places in the U.K., each consisting of, not more than 3 seafarers' representatives and not more than 3 G.C.B.S. representatives;

(c) an Appeals Tribunal, consisting of an independent person agreeable to both seafarers and G.C.B.S., a seafarers' representative and a G.C.B.S. representative; and

(d) a Secretariat provided by the Merchant Navy Establishment Administration (M.N.E.A.) to serve the Committees and Appeals Tribunal. The Central Secretariat is in London and local offices have been established.

Disciplinary Committees have been established with the agreement of the Secretary of State for Trade, to review a seafarer's possible future service in the shipping industry following his dismissal from a ship, and, if he was on a Company Service Contract, the consequent termination of such contract. The dismissal would have resulted from a breach of the Code of Conduct while the seaman was serving on board a U.K. registered ship and bound by an appropriate crew agreement to comply with such Code. Such Committees will also consider cases where a seafarer has breached the Code and would have been dismissed the ship, but for the fact that he frustrated procedures by advanced discharge. They will also consider cases where a seaman serving on a crew agreement was absent without leave and failed to join or rejoin the ship.

The Committees and Appeals Tribunal do *not* exercise the functions of an Industrial Tribunal, nor similar functions to determine the rights of the seafarer with respect to his employer.

Outline of procedure. After receiving the master's report form and other documents the employer must first decide whether to confirm the master's dismissal of the seaman from the ship by terminating the seaman's Company Service Contract (if he holds one) or by not re-engaging him (if he does not). If the seaman is not retained or re-engaged, the employer must forward the master's report and the documents to the Central Secretariat at once; if the seaman is retained or re-engaged the Central Secretariat must also be informed.

Arrangements are then made by the Secretariat for a Local Disciplinary Committee to hear the case, but the seaman is first told of his rights to pursue a claim for unfair dismissal before an Industrial Tribunal, and if he does the Local Committee will usually adjourn proceedings until that hearing has been completed, but may meanwhile temporarily suspend the seaman's registration if he is a Registered Seafarer.

The Central Committee will be told of the Tribunal's decision, and if they rule that the dismissal is unfair on substantive grounds (i.e. not on a technicality), no further action against the seaman will be taken, his suspension (if any) will be lifted and his former employer will be told to refund any amount deducted from his wages as repatriation expenses. If the Tribunal decides the dismissal is fair, or the Central Committee rules that the dismissal resulted from apparently serious or repeated misconduct, the case is relisted for hearing by the Local Committee and the date, time, place of hearing and a summary of the Committee's rules of procedure are sent to the seaman and to his former employer. The seaman is told he can be aided by a friend.

The Local Committee at the hearing must first, on the basis of the log book extracts and other documents, decide whether the conduct described there constitutes a breach of the Code of Conduct. If in its opinion it does not, it will dismiss the case. If it decides the conduct described is a breach of the Code, and the seaman when asked does not admit the conduct, he will be asked to explain why, in his view, the Committee should not accept that he conducted himself as recorded in the log book. The Local Committee, after

considering the documents, and the seaman's (or friend's) explanation (if any), may decide to dismiss the case, or to take no disciplinary
action, or may impose one or more of the following penalties:—

    (i) if a *Registered* seafarer, caution him as to his future conduct
       on board ship; and/or instruct the M.N.E.A. to, either
       suspend Establishment Benefit for a specified period, or,
       cancel the seaman's registration;

OR

   (ii) if a *Company Service Contract* seafarer whose contract has
       been terminated on grounds of indiscipline, caution him as
       to his future conduct on board ship; and/or instruct the
       M.N.E.A. not to re-register the seafarer for further employ-
       ment in the industry;

OR

  (iii) for any other seafarer, issue such instructions to the M.N.E.A.
       as it may consider appropriate in relation to a seaman's
       exclusion from re-employment in the industry; and/or in
       relation to all seafarers, to recommend that the Secretary of
       State withdraw the seafarer's Discharge Book for a specified
       period or permanently.

The Central Disciplinary Committee is required to confirm any
Local Committee's decision to recommend withdrawal of a Discharge
Book before action is taken, and is also required to review any final
decision of the organisation if an Industrial Tribunal subsequently
rules that the seafarer was unfairly dismissed on substantive grounds.

There is right of appeal to the Central Committee within 14 days
of receipt of the decision of a Local Committee, and the Central
Committee also considers a case when a Local Committee is unable
to reach a decision. If it is unable to reach a decision itself on any
matter, that matter will be referred to an Appeals Tribunal, which
with the independent person in the chair is required to reach a
decision on the matter by a simple majority, which decision is final.

Penalties shall be imposed after consideration of the seaman's
prior record in the industry, but such information shall *not* be made
available to a Committee or Appeals Tribunal *before reaching a
decision whether to impose a penalty.*

DISCIPLINARY OFFENCES

NOTE:—It appears that although the following sections 34, 35, 37
and 38, and the supporting regulations, have not been repealed, they
are not being applied on any United Kingdom registered British
ships.

Section 34 provides that for the purpose of maintaining discipline on board U.K. registered ships the D.o.T. may make regulations specifying any misconduct on board as a disciplinary offence
and enabling the master, or such officer as may be authorised to

exercise his powers, to impose fines on seamen committing disciplinary offences. The fine may be an amount of up to 5 days' pay or a specified amount, but may not in any case exceed £20. (The fine was increased from £10 to £20 by the M.S. Act 1974.)

Section 35 provides that a seaman may appeal against a fine to a superintendent or proper officer who may confirm or quash the decision and may remit all or part of the fine.

Section 37 lays down that where any conduct is both a disciplinary offence and an offence against any provision of M.S. Acts, if it has been dealt with as the former it shall not be dealt with as the latter.

Section 38 provides that, unless an appeal is pending, the amount of a fine may be deducted from wages or otherwise recovered by the employer who must then pay it to a superintendent or proper officer. If wages are paid by the master on behalf of the employer, the amount of the fine must be paid when the seaman leaves the ship at the end of the voyage or, if earlier, when his employment is terminated. In any other case the master must notify the amount to the employer who must pay it when the next payment in respect of the seaman's wages falls to be made. Where an appeal is pending at the time for payment of the fine, no amount may be deducted, recovered, paid or notified until the appeal has been disposed of, but the regulations permit a provisional deduction from wages to be made in these circumstances. Fines paid to a superintendent or proper officer are transmitted to the D.o.T. who, in turn, pass them into the Consolidated Fund.

Civil Liabilities

Absence without Leave. (Section 39) Unless he proves that his absence was due to accident, mistake, or other cause beyond his control, a seaman who is absent without leave at a time when he is required under his contract to be on board is liable to damages. If no special damages are claimed his liability is fixed at £10, but if they are claimed his liability shall not be more than £100.

Smuggling. (Section 40) If a seaman employed in a U.K. registered ship is found in civil proceedings in the U.K. to have committed an act of smuggling, whether within or outside the U.K., he is liable to make good any loss or expense the act has caused to any other person.

Breach of Immigration Laws. (Section 41) If a U.K. registered ship is in the national or territorial waters of a country outside the U.K. and a seaman employed in it is absent without leave and present in that country in contravention of its laws, the seaman's employer may incur a penalty. Unless the seaman proves that his absence was due to accident, mistake, or cause beyond his control, the penalty will be attributable to his absence without leave and may be recovered from him as special damages for breach of contract. If the penalty incurred by the employer exceeds £100, £100 may be recovered from the seaman.

COMPLAINTS

Section 23 provides that if a seaman employed in a U.K. registered ship considers he has cause to complain about the master or any other seaman on board, or about conditions on board, he may complain to the master. If dissatisfied with the action taken by the master on the complaint, or by his failure to take action, he may state his dissatisfaction and, if the ship is outside the U.K., he can claim to complain to a proper officer. The master must, thereupon, make adequate arrangements to enable the seaman to do so as soon as the service of the ship permits. Failure by the master to comply will make him liable on summary conviction to a fine not exceeding £200.

The N.M.B. Year Book contains a recommended "complaints procedure" which, if followed, would involve a seaman first making his complaint to his Head of Section, and only when that fails to give satisfaction would the complaint be referred to the master. It is to be understood that no-one making a complaint in good faith and in accordance with the recommended procedure will be penalised in any way for making the complaint.

STOWAWAYS

Section 77 states that if a person, without the consent of the master or other person authorised to give it, goes to sea or attempts to go to sea in a U.K. registered ship he shall be liable on summary conviction to a fine not exceeding £200. Nothing in section 686 of the M.S. Act 1894 (which deals with jurisdiction in case of offences on board ship—see Chapter 1) shall be taken to limit the jurisdiction of any court in the U.K. to deal with a stowing away offence committed outside the U.K. by a person who is not a British subject.

Aiding and Abetting Stowaways. Where there is reason to believe that a member of the crew has assisted a stowaway, any evidence that can be obtained should be submitted by the master or employer to the General Council of British Shipping who will then consider whether it is sufficient to warrant a prosecution.

Procedure when a Stowaway is Discovered. If a stowaway is discovered when the ship is at sea he should be reasonably maintained until such time as he can be properly disposed of, but there is no reason why he should not be given some suitable work to do in return for his upkeep. Unreasonably harsh treatment, of course, can never be justified and could lead to the prosecution of the master. The law has always appeared to take the view that the presence of a stowaway on board is due to the fault of the ship, so it is important that a diligent search should be made before leaving port. Masters should also take care to see that they do not infringe local immigration laws at ports of call by allowing stowaways to slip ashore, as the ship may be heavily fined in the event of their being caught. The shipowner is always responsible for the cost of returning a stowaway to the place where he embarked, and for that reason the procedure of transferring a stowaway at sea to another ship bound in the opposite direction is sometimes resorted to. This could prove to be highly dangerous for, should the ship subsequently meet with an accident giving rise to loss of or damage to cargo, the shipowner would not be able to escape liability if it were held—as it probably would be—that deviation to land or transfer a stowaway could not be regarded as a reasonable deviation. Moreover, if the ship were insured for the voyage only, deviation of this kind could result in the voiding of the policy by the underwriters. If the master has standing instructions from his owners relating to this matter he should, naturally, comply with them. If he has not it would be advisable, when practicable, to obtain advice from the owners by radio. In other circumstances a careful study of the deviation clause in the contract of affreightment should be made and all possible risks weighed before making a decision. It would also be advisable to radio to the ship's agents at the next port of call requesting them to make the best possible arrangements for the reception and disposal of the stowaway.

SEAMEN'S DOCUMENTS

British Seamen's Cards. Section 70 empowers the D.o.T. to make regulations for the issue to British seaman of cards in such form and containing such particulars as may be prescribed, and for requiring British seamen to apply for such cards. These cards must be (a) produced, and (b) surrendered in certain prescribed circumstances. The term "British seamen" in this section means persons who are not aliens within the meaning of the British Nationality Act 1948 and are employed, or ordinarily employed, as masters or seamen.

If a person knowingly makes a false statement for the purpose of obtaining for himself or another person a British seaman's card he shall be liable on summary conviction to a fine not exceeding £500.

The Seamen's Documents Regulations are contained in S.I. 1972 No. 1295 and set out in detail the rules governing application for and issue of B.S.C.'s, the form they shall take, and their period of validity. A card is valid for 5 years from the date of issue, and for a further period of 5 years if officially endorsed to that effect. If, at the end of either period, the holder is not in the U.K. his card remains valid until he first returns to the U.K. within 12 months

I

after the date of expiry. The holder is required to produce his card to a superintendent, proper officer, his employer or the master of his ship, on demand or within such period as the person requiring its production may allow. He is also required to surrender it to a superintendent (*a*) forthwith, upon his ceasing to be a British seaman or upon the card being defaced; and (*b*) on demand, after he has ceased to have the right of abode in the U.K. under the Immigration Act 1971. Any person who comes into possession of a B.S.C. of which he is not the holder must deliver it to the Registrar General of Shipping and Seamen or to a superintendent.

Form of British Seaman's Card. This must be as set out in Schedule 1 to the Regulations, which illustrates the six pages of the document. Page 1 contains a number of Notices to the holder, including a statement that the card is a seafarer's identity document for the purpose of the Seafarer's Identity Documents Convention 1958. Page 2 is for the Declaration and signature of the issuing officer. Pages 3 and 4 contain the holder's personal particulars, which are:—

On page 3   Surname
              Other names
              Date and place of birth
              Height in ft. and in.
              Colour of eyes
              Distinguishing marks (if any)
              Discharge Book No. (if any)
              Nationality
              Home address
              National Insurance No.

On page 4   Serial No.
              Photograph of holder
              Embossing stamp
              Signature (or thumbprint) of holder
              Signature of a witness

Page 5 shows the period of validity with provision for endorsement for a further period and the signature of the endorsing officer. Page 6 is initially blank and is headed "For Use of H.M. Government".

Discharge Books. Section 71 empowers the D.o.T. to make regulations for the issue to persons who are or have been employed in U.K. registered ships of discharge books in such form and containing such particulars as may be prescribed, and for requiring such persons to apply for such discharge books. These books must be (*a*) produced, and (*b*) surrendered in certain prescribed circumstances. For example, upon the recommendation of a shore-based disciplinary committee that the holder of a discharge book who was employed under an approved crew agreement to which the N.M.B. agreement on disciplinary procedures applied and which required him to comply with the Code of Conduct, is no longer entitled to be the holder because of the commission by him of one of the breaches of the Code specified in paragraph 9, the holder shall, on demand made by the Secretary of State, surrender the discharge book to him for a temporary period or permanently according to his demand. Such a person who has been required to surrender his discharge book cannot then make an application for another one.

The Seamen's Documents Regulations set out the rules relating to the application for and issue of discharge books, their form and content, the entries to be made in them (and by whom), and the rules governing production and delivery.

Form and Content of Discharge Books. Regulation 20 requires that a discharge book shall be in book form and must provide for the recording of the following particulars in relation to its holder:—

(a) Those specified in Schedule 2 (except paragraphs 4 and 15—see below);

(b) Name of each U.K. registered ship in which employed, its port of registry, official number and gross or register tonnage, capacity in which employed, date and place at which employment begins, description of each voyage and date and place of discharge;

(c) Dates of any period for which he is working or standing by, any period of paid leave, any period of unpaid leave, any period of sickness and any period of study leave, and the certificates for which the study is undertaken;

(d) Dates and nature of training courses (including pre-sea) attended and certificates or other qualifications obtained;

(e) Income tax code, year to which it applies and date on which it becomes effective;

(f) Inoculation and vaccination certificates; and

(g) Records of tests of his eyesight.

Entries in Discharge Books. Regulation 21 rules that entries in discharge books of the particulars—

(a) referred to in paragraphs (a), (b), (d), (e), (f) and (g) of regulation 20 may be made by a superintendent or the Registrar General of Shipping and Seamen;

(b) referred to in paragraphs (a), (b) and (f) of regulation 20 may be made by a proper officer;

(c) referred to in paragraphs (b) and (c) of regulation 20 may may be made by the master of the ship in which the holder is employed or by one of the ship's officers authorised by the master in that behalf;

(d) referred to in regulation 20(e) and in paragraphs 2 and 16 of Schedule 2 may be made by the master of the ship in which the holder is employed;

(e) referred to in paragraphs (c) and (e) of regulation 20 and in
     paragraph 16 of Schedule 2 may be made by the seaman's
     employer;

(f) referred to in regulation 20(c) and in paragraphs 10 and 13 of
     Schedule 2 may be made by an official of the M.N.E.
     Administration;

and by no other person. A superintendent, a proper officer or the
Registrar General of Shipping and Seamen may at any time correct
an entry in a discharge book.

Production of Discharge Books. The holder must produce his
discharge book on demand to (a) a superintendent, a proper officer,
the Registrar General of Shipping and Seamen or an M.N.E.A.
official; (b) his employer and to the master of his ship; and (c) any
person authorised to make an entry in it. Failure so to produce it is
an offence.

Delivery of Discharge Books. A master in possession of a discharge book issued to a person (a) who has died, must deliver it to
the superintendent or proper officer to whom he makes a return
of the death; (b) who is not present when he is discharged, must
deliver it to the superintendent or proper officer for the place of
discharge within 48 hours after the discharge or as soon as practicable thereafter; (c) who is left behind in any country, must deliver
it to a superintendent or proper officer within 48 hours or as soon
as practicable. A person other than a master having possession of
a discharge book must, when aware that the holder has died, been
discharged or left behind, deliver it to a superintendent or proper
officer or to the Registrar General of Shipping and Seaman. Failure
to comply with any of these requirements is an offence.

Loss, Destruction, etc. of Discharge Books. When (a) his discharge book is lost, destroyed or defaced, or (b) the space provided
in it for entries of particulars except those referred to in Schedule 2
is filled up, a person ceases to be regarded as the holder and must,
within 7 days of satisfying the conditions laid down for application,
apply for a new discharge book.

Notification of Errors in Seamen's Documents. If it appears to
the holder of a document that an entry in it is not correct, he must
forthwith inform a superintendent. Failure to do so is an offence.

Alterations. No other than an authorised person is permitted
to make any mark or entry upon, or erase, cancel or alter any mark
or entry made upon or otherwise deface or destroy a seaman's
document. Contravention of this rule is an offence.

Application for the Issue of Documents. Application must be
made in writing to a superintendent and must, as far as is necessary,
state particulars of the matters set out in Schedule 2. The applicant

must furnish to the superintendent such documents (including 3 copies of a recent head and shoulders black and white photograph of himself measuring 2 inches by 2 inches) and such other evidence as he may require for proper consideration of the application.

Offences. An offence under the Regulations is punishable on summary conviction with a fine not exceeding £50.

Schedule 2. The particulars to be furnished in application for seamen's documents are:—

1. name of person applying;
2. home address;
3. date and place of birth;
4. if a woman who is or has been married, maiden surname and date of marriage;
5. nationality;
6. colour of eyes;
7. distinguishing marks (if any);
8. height;
9. number of discharge book (if any);
10. M.N.E.A. number (if any);
11. grade, number and date of issue of any certificate of competency held;
12. national insurance number;
13. pension fund of which applicant is a member and registered number therein;
14. trade union or professional society of which applicant is a member and registered number therein;
15. in the case of a cadet, name of employer and whether deck or engineer cadet;
16. name, relationship and address of next of kin.

HANDING OVER DOCUMENTS
ON CHANGE OF MASTER

Section 74 states that if a person ceases to be the master of a ship registered in the United Kingdom during a voyage of the ship he shall deliver to his successor the documents relating to the ship or its crew which are in his custody; and if he fails without reasonable cause to do so he shall be liable on summary conviction to a fine not exceeding £200.

An entry to the effect that this delivery has been made must go in the official log book and be signed by the new master in person and by the former master in person.

The documents concerned would include the following, where carried:—

General documents—

Certificate of registry.
British tonnage certificate.

Load line certificate.
Passenger and safety certificate, if a passenger ship.
Safety certificates (Construction, Equipment and Radio), if not a passenger ship.
Deratting, or deratting exemption, certificate.
Gunpowder magazine certificate.
Wireless broadcasting licence.
Anchor and cables certificate.
Suez Canal tonnage certificate.
Panama Canal tonnage certificate.
Stability information.
Loading and ballasting information.
Register of Machinery and Chains.
Confidential papers.

Documents relating to current voyage—
Crew agreement and list of crew.
Official log book and supplements.
Last port clearance.
Conveyance orders.
Certificate of seaworthiness and similar documents.
Cargo manifest.
Passenger list, if carrying passengers.
Charter-party, if under charter.
Captain's copies of bills of lading.
Any certificate of competency in master's custody.
Any discharge books in master's custody.
National insurance tables.
Income tax schedules and tables.
Certificate of financial responsibility against oil pollution.
Account of wages forms and cash books.
Notification forms for engagements and discharges.
Disbursement sheets and vouchers.
Portage bill forms.
Notices to Mariners and D.o.T. M notices.
Copies of noted and extended protests.

Admissibility in Evidence and Inspection of Documents. Section 75 rules that the following documents shall be admissible in evidence and, when in the custody of the Registrar General of Shipping and Seaman, shall be open to public inspection, that is to say:—

(a) crew agreements, lists of crews and notices given of additions to or changes in crew agreements and lists of crews;

(b) the official log book of any ship and any document purporting to be a copy of an entry therein and to be certified as a true copy by the master of the ship;

(c) documents purporting to be submissions to or decisions by superintendents or proper officers under section 10.

(d) returns or reports under section 72 (births and deaths) or under regulations made under section 19 (safety, health and welfare).

A certificate issued under section 43 shall be admissible in evidence.

MERCHANT NAVY UNIFORM

Section 87 provides as follows:—

(1) The D.o.T. may make regulations prescribing a uniform for the use of persons serving in U.K. registered ships, and distinguishing marks to be worn, as part of the uniform, by persons so serving in different positions or in different circumstances. (Regulations have not yet been made.)

(2) Regulations may prescribe the person by whom and the circumstances in which the merchant navy uniform or any part of it may be worn.

(3) If a person wears the uniform or any part of it, or anything bearing the appearance thereof, when not authorised he shall be liable on summary conviction to a fine not exceeding £50.

(4) Where any design, within the meaning of the Registered Designs Act 1949, which forms part of the M.N. uniform has been registered under that Act and the D.o.T. are the registered proprietor thereof their copyright in the design shall continue so long as the design remains so registered.

(5) Nothing in this section shall prohibit or restrict the use of the M.N. uniform or any part of it for the purposes of any stage, film or television performance, unless the use is such as to bring the uniform into disrepute.

DESERTERS

Section 89 provides that where a seaman deserts in the U.K. from a ship registered in a country to which this section (by Order in Council) applies, a J.P. may, on the application of a consular officer of that country and on information on oath, issue a warrant for the arrest of the seaman. After such arrest a magistrates' court may, on proof of desertion, order him to be conveyed on board his ship. Where a seaman is liable to be arrested, any person who, knowing or believing that he has deserted, does without lawful authority or reasonable excuse any act with intent to impede his arrest shall be liable on summary conviction to a fine not exceeding £50.

Seamen employed in U.K. registered ships who are absent without leave at time of sailing or who are left behind outside the U.K. and whose whereabouts are unknown would, under the appropriate sections of the 1894 and 1906 Acts, be classed as deserters. This is no longer so. The former are considered to have breached the agreement and are dealt with, as are the latter, under sections 62–64.

RECOVERY OF WAGES DUE OTHERWISE THAN UNDER CREW AGREEMENT

Section 12 states that in any proceedings by the master of a ship or a person employed in a ship otherwise than under a crew agreement for the recovery of any sum due as wages the court, unless it appears to it that the delay in paying the sum was due to a mistake, to a reasonable dispute as to liability or to the act or default of the person claiming the amount or to any other cause, not being the wrongful act or default of the persons liable to make the payment or their servants or agents, may order them to pay, in addition to the sum due, interest on it at the rate of twenty per cent per annum or such lower rate as the court may specify, for the period beginning seven days after the sum became due and ending when the sum is paid.

REGISTRY OF SEAMEN AND RECORDS

From 1696 onwards attempts have been made from time to time to establish a national register of seamen. Sometimes these attempts have met with limited success but all were relatively short-lived until, in the latter part of the nineteenth century there came into being the organisation which deals so effectively today with registry of seamen and shipping records.

Sections 251–2 of the principal Act of 1894 (now repealed) provided for the maintenance of the General Register and Record Office for Seamen. Originally established in London, the Office was later transferred to Cardiff. Section 80 of the 1970 Act provides that the D.o.T. shall appoint, and may remove, an officer to be styled the Registrar General of Shipping and Seamen, who shall exercise such functions as are conferred on him by the Merchant Shipping Acts and keep such records and perform such other duties as the Department may direct. It also rules that the D.o.T. may appoint and remove persons to perform on behalf of the Registrar General such of his functions as he or the Department may direct.

Some of the many functions of the General Register and Record Office are given at the end of this chapter.

NATIONAL INSURANCE OF SEAFARERS

Two schemes of national insurance have been in operation since 1948. One scheme covers unemployment, health and pensions etc., the other industrial injuries received by employees at their place of work. Under the Social Security Pensions Act 1975, pensions for retirement, widowhood and invalidity became earnings related instead of flat rate. Pensions consist of two parts, a basic pension, and an additional pension related to an employee's reckonable earnings above a qualifying earnings level necessary for the basic pension. Employees who are members of occupational pension schemes which meet certain requirements can be contracted out by their employers of the additional part of retirement pension. Generally speaking, people over school leaving age are required to contribute to the national insurance scheme, but housewives and those with very low incomes are excused. Others, for example those receiving unemployment or sickness benefit, or fulltime students up to the age of 18, may be credited with contributions without having to pay anything towards them. An employee normally ceases to contribute on reaching the minimum pension age (65 for a man, 60 for a woman). Contributions are divided into four classes payable as follows:—

Class 1 paid by employer and employee and based on earnings.
Class 2 paid by self-employed people at a flat-rate.
Class 3 paid by non-employed people voluntarily at a flat rate.
Class 4 paid in addition to class 2 by self-employed people and based on profits or gains.

National insurance Class 1 contributions for employees are related to their earnings and are collected along with income tax under a PAYE procedure. No contribution is payable by and for those earning less than a lower limit fixed each year by the government.

Details of the arrangements for employees generally are dealt with in leaflet NP.15 "Employer's guide to national insurance contributions" obtainable at local Social Security offices, and the additional responsibilities of shipowners, ship's masters and other employers of people working on board ship are explained in leaflet NI 25 "National insurance guide for Masters and employers of mariners" which can be obtained from Mercantile Marine offices.

Liability for National Insurance Contributions. Class 1 contributions are payable if a mariner is employed in a British ship and he is domiciled or resident in Great Britain and his employer is resident or has a place of business in Great Britain. Where the employer is not liable because he neither lives in, nor has a place of business in Great Britain, the mariner is still liable for the employee's contribution if he is resident or domiciled in Great Britain.

A British ship is defined as a ship or vessel in Crown service, or registered at a port in Great Britain, or a hovercraft so registered; a mariner means a person who is, or has been, employed under a contract of service as a master, crew member or radio officer of any ship or vessel, and also includes a supernumerary (*e.g.* cattleman, shop assistant or hairdresser employed in the ship's service).

If a mariner is neither domiciled nor resident in Great Britain neither he nor his employer are liable to pay contributions. (This rule may be affected by a reciprocal agreement.)

A mariner who maintains that he is not liable for contributions because he is not domiciled or resident in Great Britain must apply to the Department of Health and Social Security for a certificate of mariner's non-liability, otherwise if he signs a crew agreement in

Great Britain under N.M.B. conditions without producing such a certificate he will be treated as having a place of residence in Great Britain and contributions will be payable by him and his employer.

Contributions are payable if a mariner domiciled or resident in Great Britain is employed in a ship other than a British ship if the contract is entered into in the United Kingdom with a view to its performance while the ship is on her voyage and the employer has a place of business in Great Britain, or, if the contract is not entered into in the United Kingdom, but the employer has his principal place of business in Great Britain. (Not if mariner is a supernumerary.)

Contribution Rates. These are fixed annually by the Government and are advised in leaflet NI 208 obtainable from local Social Security offices. Liability for contributions from both employees and employers is subject to lower and upper earnings limits expressed in weekly terms. Equivalent amounts apply where earnings are paid at longer intervals. There is no liability for contributions where earnings do not reach the lower earnings limit. If earnings reach or exceed the lower earnings limit, contributions are payable at the not-contracted-out rate on the whole of the earnings up to and including the upper earnings limit for not-contracted-out mariners. Those contracted-out (usual) will pay the normal standard rate on earnings up to and including the lower earnings limit, plus contributions at the contracted-out rate on earnings between the lower and upper earnings limits. For employers, the ordinary contribution rate is reduced where the mariner employed is covered by the Redundancy Payments (Merchant Seamen Exclusion) Order 1973, and/or he is employed on a foreign-going ship.

Earnings on which Contributions are calculated. In general "earnings" includes all payments made to a mariner. Contributions are calculated on the gross pay, which includes any payments which the mariner may make to a superannuation fund on which he is entitled to tax relief. Contributions are not payable on a "special payment" which a shipowner makes to a mariner who has been left behind abroad on account of illness or injury, nor on a payment made by the D.o.T. to a mariner who has failed to rejoin his ship.

Assessing Contributions. The employer may calculate contributions either exactly by applying the appropriate percentage, or by using the contribution tables supplied by the D.H.S.S. which are as follows:—

Volume 1, is for home-trade vessels.

Volume 2, is for foreign-going vessels where the crew are engaged on N.M.B. Crew Agreements.

Volume 3, is for other foreign-going vessels and deep-sea fishing vessels.

The ultimate responsibility for ensuring that contributions are properly paid rests on the shipowner as the employer although in practice the master may be responsible for actually paying the contributions. The shipowner is liable both for the mariner's and for the employer's contributions but is entitled to deduct the mariner's contribution from his earnings.

When wages are paid to a mariner who is discharged abroad, contributions should be deducted in the normal way. Similarly, when wages are paid to a mariner who has been left abroad other than on being discharged, contributions should be deducted from h gross wages before deducting any repatriation expenses.   is

Contributions for mariners whose income tax is collected throu the PAYE arrangements are assessed and collected in the same w as for persons in shore employment.

Reciprocal Agreements with Other Countries. Reciprocal agreements made with other countries sometimes modify the normal liability for contributions. Under EEC Regulations mariners are normally covered under the social security scheme of the country where the ship in which they are serving is registered or in which the owner has his principal place of business. The EEC Regulations apply to nationals of member states. The exceptions to this are:—

(a) A mariner sent by his normal employer to work in a ship of another Community country remains covered under the scheme of the first country provided his duration of duty is not expected to last more than 12 months and he has not been sent to replace another worker whose tour of duty has been completed.

(b) A worker who is not normally employed as a mariner on board a ship of one member state while that ship is in a port or territorial waters of another member state, shall be covered under the legislation of the latter state.

(c) A mariner residing in one Community country who is employed in a ship of a second Community country and who is paid by an employer who is resident, or has his registered office, in the first country, is covered under the scheme of the first country.

Bilateral Reciprocal Agreements Covering Mariners. Reciprocal agreements containing provisions relating to mariners have been made with the following countries:—Austria, Belgium, Bermuda, the Channel Islands, Cyprus, Denmark, Finland, France, the Federal Republic of Germany, the Irish Republic, Italy, Jamaica, Malta, the Netherlands, Norway, Spain, Sweden, Switzerland, Turkey and Yugoslavia.

Multilateral Agreements Covering Mariners. Greek or Icelandic mariners not covered by the above two paragraphs who are ordinarily resident in Belgium, France, Italy or the Netherlands are insured under the British national insurance scheme whilst employed in a British ship.

Northern Ireland and the Isle of Man. The National Insurance schemes in Northern Ireland and the Isle of Man are similar to that in Great Britain and are linked by special arrangements. A mariner domiciled or resident in Northern Ireland or the Isle of Man who is employed in a British ship will pay contributions and be covered as if he were domiciled or resident in Great Britain. Similarly a mariner domiciled or resident in Great Britain who is employed in a Northern Irish or Manx ship will pay contributions and be covered as if he were domiciled or resident in those countries.

Radio Officers. Radio officers employed by someone other than the shipowner are normally covered under the scheme of the country in which they are ordinarily resident and in which the employer has his principal place of business.

Claims for Benefit. At Home

General. Shipowners and masters will not, as a rule, be concerned with claims for benefit by seafarers in the United Kingdom. The seafarer should claim unemployment benefit at the nearest Unemployment Benefit office or, if he is a Registered seafarer, the Local Establishment Office. Claims for any other benefit should be made at the nearest local Social Security office.

Reporting Accidents. When an industrial injuries claim is made in the United Kingdom the Department will communicate with the owners of the ship and ask them to supply particulars. Masters should accordingly report to their shipowners full details of all accidents.

Claims for Benefit. Abroad.
Sickness and Injury Benefit

Certification of Claims. When a mariner (including a radio officer, or crew member but not a supernumerary) is left behind abroad owing to illness or injury and is taken off crew agreement, a form BF19 must be completed. A supply of the form should always be carried on board. They can be obtained from Mercantile Marine Offices in the United Kingdom, from Shipping Masters or Consular Officers abroad, or from the Department of Health and Social Security Overseas Group, Newcastle upon Tyne. The form provides for:

(a) a claim by the mariner for sickness, invalidity or industrial injury benefit and his instructions as to disposal of benefit, and

(b) a report by the master, or in certain circumstances, by a Shipping Master or Consular Officer.

The appropriate portion of the form should be signed by the seafarer if he is able to do so, or, if he is not, by a responsible person on his behalf. The master of the ship, the Shipping Master or Consular Officer should send the completed form by airmail to the Department of Health and Social Security, Overseas Group (Mariners' Benefits), Newcastle upon Tyne NE98 1YX and will send continuation reports on forms BF19A.

Payment of Benefit. Sickness, invalidity or injury benefit can be paid to a dependant or someone else in the United Kingdom nominated by the seafarer to receive it on his behalf. Alternatively it can be kept until he returns to the United Kingdom. Where currency restrictions do not prevent the transfer of sterling, the benefit may be paid direct to the seafarer abroad, but in this event there would be some delay before he receives payment. If the seafarer nominates someone in this country to receive benefit on his behalf payment will begin as soon as possible after the form reaches Newcastle. The shipowner will be told the amount being paid and the date of the first payment. and will be informed if the benefit is stopped. The amount of benefit being paid, or the estimated amount of benefit payable will be deducted by the shipowner in calculating the amount payable in accordance with the special pay arrangements under National Maritime Board agreements. Any allotment can only continue at the previous rate if the mariner's special pay entitlement is sufficient. This should be carefully explained to the mariner before he decides whether to receive benefit abroad or to nominate a payee in the U.K.

Notification of Changes in Circumstances. The arrangement for the certification and forwarding of forms by the Shipping Master or Consular Officer does not affect the master's responsibility for making arrangements for the care of a mariner left behind because of sickness or injury. Ships' agents who act for the master in this respect should advise the proper officer immediately the mariner:

(*a*) is certified fit for work or travel; or
(*b*) fails to maintain contact; or
(*c*) obtains employment, or
(*d*) dies.

Notification from a Place where there is no Shipping Master or Consular Officer

If a mariner has to be left behind at a place where there is no Shipping Master or Consular Officer, the master should ask his agents or another responsible person in whose care the mariner is placed, to forward the form BF19 to Newcastle at the earliest possible moment and by airmail wherever this can be done, and to send monthly continuation reports on form BF19A.

Continuation of Benefit after Seafarer is Fit for Work

When a mariner who has been left ashore sick or injured is certified to be fit for work, benefit will continue for the days between his recovery and his arrival at a home port, or his obtaining or being offered suitable employment in another ship, provided that he returns or takes up the new employment at the earliest possible opportunity. The shipowner responsible for arranging his passage should notify his arrival in the United Kingdom to the Department of Health and Social Security, Overseas Group (Mariners' Benefits), Newcastle upon Tyne, NE98 1YX.

Unemployment Benefit. In certain circumstances a mariner left outside the United Kingdom, otherwise than on account of sickness or injury, will qualify for unemployment benefit until he returns to a home port or obtains fresh employment, provided he puts himself in the charge of the British Consul or Shipping Master within 14 days of the time when he was left behind, or if he was in custody at that time, immediately after his release. The payment of benefit will be subject to the usual conditions and there may be disqualification for up to six weeks if he was discharged through misconduct or left without good cause. The benefit can be paid in the same way as sickness benefit.

Benefit Rates. Weekly rates are fixed, and for parts of a week the daily rate applies, which is one-sixth of the weekly rate.

Unemployment and sickness benefit are the same for men, single women, and widows. Rates for married women are somewhat less. All are subject to reduction if contributions are short. Increases are allowed in respect of each dependent adult and each dependent child. Married women receive the same rate as single women if entitled to increase of benefit for husband, or if living apart from husband without financial help from him.

Injury Benefit. This consists of the temporary payment of a fixed amount while the seafarer is unable to work if the accident arises out of and in the course of his employment. The maximum "injury benefit period" is 26 weeks from the date of the accident. Adult rates are fixed with increases allowed for an adult and child dependant respectively. Young persons receive lower rates, but the adult rate is paid to a young person with one or more dependants. If incapacity exists after 26 weeks, Disablement Benefit is then paid at a rate depending upon the extent of disablement.

N.B.—(1) A person is "resident" in a country if he actually has a place of residence therein. It is not so easy to define the term "domiciled", as a state of mind is involved. Very broadly speaking, a person is domiciled in a country if he regards his home as being there. Hence, it is possible for a person to be resident in one country while domiciled in another.

(2) Accident reports made on B.F. 19 forms do not do away with the necessity for the master to make the required entries in the official log book, to report to his owners, and (when necessary) report to the D.o.T.

SEAMAN'S INCOME TAX

General

Introduction. The Pay As You Earn method of deducting income tax from pay applies to all income from offices or employments. It is the employer's duty to deduct income tax from the pay of his employees whether or not he has been directed to do so by the Tax Office. If he fails to do this he may be required to pay over to the Revenue the tax which he should have deducted, and, in addition, may incur liability to penalties.

To operate PAYE an employer needs deduction-cards, Codes for employees which reflect the tax allowances to which the employees are entitled, and tax tables. Broadly the amount of tax an employer has to deduct on any pay day is calculated as follows:—

(a) The pay due to the employee is determined and added to the total of all previous payments made to the employee from 6th April to date.

(b) Using the employee's code and Free Pay Tables the proportion of the employee's allowances from 6th April up to date is ascertained and subtracted from the total pay to date. The balance left is the taxable pay to date.

(c) The tax due to date is determined by looking up the taxable pay to date in the Taxable Pay Tables.

(d) From the figure of tax due to date, the total tax already paid is deducted, leaving the tax due to be deducted from the employee's pay on the pay day in question.

General instructions on the operation of Pay As You Earn accompany the documents sent to employers before 6th April each year and these should be referred to for further detailed information. A Guide is also available giving general information and procedures to be followed.

UNFAIR DISMISSAL

This section was prepared with the assistance of the "Manual on the law concerning Unfair Dismissal as it applies to Seafarers" prepared by the General Council of British Shipping, to whom grateful acknowledgement is made.

Masters must remember that, as well as complying with the various Merchant Shipping Acts which concern the employment of seamen, they must comply also with recent industrial legislation such as the Employment Protection (Consolidation) Act 1978 (as modified by the Employment Act 1980), which brought together in

one enactment provisions on individual employment rights previous-
ly contained in statutes such as the Redundancy Payments Act 1965,
Contracts of Employment Act 1972, Trade Union and Labour
Relations Act 1974, Employment Protection Act 1975 and the Trade
Union and Labour Relations (Amendment) Act 1976.

For many years a seaman has had a common law right to sue
his employer for damages for *wrongful dismissal*, if, for example, he
has not been given the proper notice of dismissal contained in his
contract of employment, or if he has been sacked on the spot when
his conduct did not justify it. These rights still apply, but the
legislation mentioned above introduced additionally a new statutory
wrong of "Unfair Dismissal". An unfair dismissal situation arises
when an employer dismisses an employee for an unfair reason and/or
in an unfair manner.

An *employee* is a person who works, or worked, under a contract
of employment; a contract of employment is a contract of service
or of apprenticeship which is implied, or made orally or in writing.
All seafarers, including masters and apprentices, are employees,
except those employed under contracts *for* service (e.g. persons
engaged on concessionaire contracts on passenger ships to provide
banking, casino, photographic services etc., or radio officers employed by a wireless company). In the case of persons on Company
Service contracts, the Company Service contract is the contract
of employment, supplemented by the Crew Agreement when the
person is signed on. Dismissal takes place only when the Company
Service contract is terminated, and will not normally be made by
the master. For Registered seafarers, the contract of employment
is the Crew Agreement, and here the master may be involved when
a seaman is dismissed.

Remedies for Unfair Dismissal. A seafarer who considers he has
been unfairly dismissed, or dismissed for an *inadmissible reason,*
may complain to an Industrial Tribunal. It will then be up to the
employer to show that he had a fair reason for dismissing the seaman, *and* that he acted reasonably in all the circumstances, and up
to the employee to show that he was dismissed and qualified for the
protection given by the Act. If the employer fails to defend such a
case successfully, he may have to pay substantial compensation to
the seaman, in an extreme case amounting to more than £16,000.

Who can claim? Any seafarer (unless excluded, see below) can
claim a remedy for unfair dismissal. A seafarer who claims to have
been dismissed because of pregnancy, or engaging in trade union
activity, or having and not disclosing a spent conviction, can claim
to have been dismissed for an *inadmissible reason*, which if proved
is automatically unfair. Persons excluded are:

(a) seafarers employed under contracts *for* service (for example, persons engaged on passenger ships on concessionaire contracts to provide banking, catering, casino or other such services);

(b) part-time seafarers normally working for less than 16 hours a week (with certain exceptions);

(c) seafarers who have not completed 52 calendar weeks or part weeks continuous employment with their employers at the "effective date of termination";

(d) seafarers who have reached normal retirement age for going to sea (males 62 years of age, females 60 years of age, or earlier where some company schemes apply), but this exclusion does not apply to dismissals for an inadmissible reason;

(e) seafarers engaged to work ordinarily outside Great Britain (this exclusion does not usually apply to a seaman employed on ships registered in the U.K., or, depending on all the terms of the seaman's contract of employment, where the seaman's operational base is considered to be in the U.K.);

(f) seafarers ordinarily resident outside the U.K.; and

(g) seafarers who have not complained within 3 months of the effective date of termination (but Tribunal can extend this period in extenuating circumstances).

Note to (e) above:—Seamen engaged to work on a ship registered in the U.K. will normally be covered, unless the employment is wholly outside the U.K. (or the seaman is not ordinarily resident in the U.K.). The Court of Appeal has ruled that where seafarers employed in ships registered outside the U.K. are claiming, the terms of their contracts of employment are likely to be decisive. All contractual terms will be examined in detail, and the decision will be based on a number of factors such as where the man is based, what currency he is paid in, where his home is, and whether he is required to pay U.K. National Insurance contributions, etc.

Effective Date of Termination. This term means either:—

(a) the date on which notice of dismissal expires where the contract is terminated by notice given by either side; or

(b) the date on which termination of the contract takes effect where it is terminated without notice by either side; or

(c) the date on which a fixed term contract (e.g. a Crew Agreement) expires and is not renewed.

If a seafarer is given notice of dismissal, and agrees to accept wages in place of part or all of the notice period, his effective termination date will be regarded as the date on which he last worked for that company, except for the purpose of calculating the 52 week period of continuous employment which will be regarded as ending on the last day of the notice period.

Continuous Employment. A seafarer's period of employment will be presumed to have been continuous unless the employer proves otherwise. The Tribunal hearing a case will decide whether the 52 week qualifying period has been exceeded. Periods of paid leave, sick leave, and study leave would not be considered as 'employment' in the case of a registered seafarer where they follow termination of employment, but it will be wise when considering the dismissal of a seaman to bear these periods in mind as well as the period of engagement when there is some evidence that the company and the seafarer had intended to continue the employment relationship. All periods on Company Service contracts or Cadets' Contract of employment count as employment.

Where a person is employed on a voyage-to-voyage basis, no action should be taken which implies permanent employment in case it becomes necessary to dismiss at a later date.

An officer serving under a Section A agreement is to be regarded as in the continuous employment of his company at all times irrespective of whether or not he is signed on a crew agreement, or holds a Company Service Contract, from the time he is taken on pay until employment has been terminated following the giving of appropriate notice in writing by either employer or officer. If such an officer is engaged on a probationary basis, or for a certain period only, this should be clearly stated in the letter of employment given to him, which should also clearly state the date his employment begins and the conditions upon which he is employed.

Dismissal. This occurs where:

(a) if a seafarer is employed on a Company Service contract, or is a cadet on a contract, the contract is terminated by the Company with or without notice; or

(b) a registered seafarer is not offered further employment after the Crew Agreement, being a fixed term contract, is closed; or

(c) the seafarer terminates his contract without notice because of the company's, or its officers', behaviour (i.e. constructive dismissal).

Expiry of Crew Agreement. A crew agreement constitutes a fixed term agreement that expires on closure of the agreement, irrespective of whether closure occurs at the end of the voyage or at the expiry of the twelve months or two year period usually contained therein, or whether an individual seafarer is signed off under a notice clause. A registered seafarer will therefore be considered to have been dismissed unless re-engagement is offered, and such dismissal would be held to be unfair unless there are good grounds for dismissal and a fair procedure has been followed, with careful records kept during the voyage of warnings, loggings, etc.

It would therefore be unwise for a master or company to continue the once common practice of refusing re-engagement to registered seafarers who are considered to be unsatisfactory unless the circumstances justify dismissal and a fair procedure has been followed, or, the seafarer does not have a remedy for unfair dismissal (e.g. he had not completed 52 weeks service.)

Constructive Dismissal. If a seaman leaves a vessel without notice and later complains to a tribunal alleging dismissal because of unfair treatment or coercion, the Tribunal would carefully examine the circumstances which caused the seaman to leave, and if the Tribunal decides that the behaviour of the company or its officers justified the man in walking off, this will be regarded as constructive dismissal. It is therefore good practice to ask, if possible, all seafarers who terminate their contracts, with or without notice, for their reasons, and to record any explanation for future reference.

Some possible reasons for a seaman to claim constructive dismissal are:—

(a) he had been treated in a discriminatory manner because of his race, colour or sex;

(b) he had been denied his rights under his contract of employment or crew agreement;

(c) an attempt had been made to coerce him into signing off, or to terminate his Company Service Contract;

(d) he had been publicly treated with marked discourtesy;

(e) steps had been taken to replace him without informing him;

(f) being a petty officer or officer his authority had been consistently undermined;

(g) he had been reduced in rank without his agreement.

Fair Reasons for Dismissal. Provided a fair dismissal procedure is followed, a dismissal will be regarded as fair if a company acts for one of the following reasons:

(a) The seafarer is not capable of carrying out his work due to incompetence, inadequate qualifications, or sickness.

(b) The seafarer's misconduct.

(c) To avoid contravening a statutory requirement.

(d) For taking part in a strike or other industrial action, or by way of a lock-out, as long as all involved are dismissed.

(e) Redundancy, but subject to a fair method of selection of those dismissed.

(f) For "some other substantial reason" (e.g. a seaman employed temporarily, to replace a sick person, with a clear understanding that employment is temporary.

However, a dismissal would be unfair, even if it fitted one of the above categories, if it is for an "inadmissible reason" and therefore automatically unfair. When a seafarer is dismissed he is entitled to ask for a written statement of the reason for his dismissal. It is important that it should be one of the above reasons.

Unfair dismissal for not becoming a member of a union. It is unfair to dismiss an employee for not complying with a requirement to be or become a member of a union in the following circumstances:-

(a) where the employee genuinely objects on the grounds of conscience or other deeply held personal convictions to being a member of any trade union whatsoever, or of a particular trade union; or

(b) the employee belonged to the class of employee covered by the closed shop agreement before it took effect, and has not been a member of a union specified in the agreement since; or

(c) the closed shop agreement came into effect for the first time on or after 15th August 1980 and has not been approved by a secret ballot of all employees affected, showing that at least 80% of those entitled to vote supported the agreement.

By the Employment Act 1980, an employee so dismissed has a right of complaint against an employer to an industrial tribunal.

Fair Dismissal Procedure. If the employer is unable to establish that the dismissal was fair, it will be held to be unfair. Even if the reason is held to be fair, the dismissal may still be considered unfair. The employer must then show that it was reasonable in all the circumstances for him to dismiss the person for that reason. Normally the company would have to show that:

(a) the decision to dismiss had been carefully considered;

(b) where lack of capability is the reason due to poor performance, the seaman must have been warned, if possible given further training and more supervision, given every chance to improve, and if necessary and possible, offered an alternative job; where lack of capability due to misconduct (not amounting to gross misconduct) is the reason; the employee must have been given at least one formal warning, given a chance to improve his conduct, and the latest incident investigated and the person given an opportunity to explain;

(c) where redundancy was the reason, or lack of qualification, suitable other employment was not available, or was rejected;

(d) taking all considerations into account the decision to dismiss was fair and reasonable. The test would be not whether the Tribunal considers the dismissal fair, but rather whether an experienced and reasonable personnel officer would consider the dismissal reasonable under the prevailing circumstances.

Note: Dismissal by one's immediate superior would probably not be considered reasonable unless reference was made to more senior management. A person on a Company Service contract should not normally be dismissed except on the authority of shore based management.

Penalties for Unfair Dismissal. A seafarer who has been continuously employed by a company for 52 weeks and who is dismissed, is entitled to ask for a written statement of the reasons for his dismissal to be given to him within 14 days of his request. An employee who is entitled to ask for such a statement, whether or not he is being fairly dismissed, or states that he will not complain to a tribunal, or resigns after his employer has given him notice, must be given one if he asks. Failure to comply can lead to an award of 2 weeks wages against the employer. As written statements are admissible in evidence, it is important for the statement to be accurate, specific and adequate.

A person who considers he has been unfairly dismissed can complain to an Industrial Tribunal and should do so within 3 months. There is then an opportunity for conciliation at the request of either side, or of an ACAS conciliation officer, to try to reach a voluntary settlement.

Reinstatement or Re-engagement. If no voluntary settlement can be arranged, the Tribunal will first consider then whether an order for reinstatement (meaning re-employment in the identical job) should be made, bearing in mind whether the complainant wants it and whether it is practicable, or even just to reinstate. In the shipping industry reinstatement will rarely be appropriate. If the decision is against reinstatement, then a re-engagement order (meaning return to work with the same employer, but not in the original job) will be considered, together with possible terms. The employer's financial liability to a reinstated or re-engaged seafarer will be assessed, taking account of the time between dismissal and reinstatement or re-engagement, any pay in lieu of notice or ex-gratia payments already made by the employer to the seaman, and any other remuneration paid for other employment taken by the seaman in the meanwhile. The seaman should have actively sought other work to mitigate his loss.

Where a reinstatement or re-engagement order has been made but not complied with by the employer, the Tribunal must make a compensation award to the seaman subject to a maximum amount of £6,250. The award is calculated on the same basis as that for unfair dismissal. In addition, a further compensation award will be made specifically on account of non-compliance with the order.

Compensation for Unfair Dismissal. If a Tribunal decides that reinstatement or re-engagement is not appropriate, monetary compensation may be awarded based on two concepts:

(a) a basic award related to the employee's service, and
(b) a compensatory award to reflect his loss.

The basic award provides for a payment to all unfairly dismissed of an amount based on the current statutory maximum pay of £130 per week. The basic award is calculated from the effective date of termination of continuous employment and allows:

(a) 1½ week's pay for each complete year of employment in which the employee is not below the age of 41;

(b) 1 week's pay for each complete year of employment in which the employee was below 41 and not below the age of 22; and

(c) half a week's pay for each complete year below 22.

No account is taken of service in excess of 20 years, so that the maximum for an employee of 61 or over for example, would be 20 × 1½ × £130 equals £3,900, but this is subject to deduction where there has been contributory fault.

The compensatory award is assessed by the Tribunal taking account of the loss that has been suffered by the employee, and expenses incurred by him, but again subject to deduction for contributory fault. The amount is limited to £6,250.

The maximum limits for compensation for unfair dismissal therefore are:

Basic award	£3,900
Compensatory award	£6,250
Additional award for not complying with a reinstatement or re-gagement order	£3,380
Total	£13,530

However, if the failure to reinstate or re-engage followed an unfair dismissal finding which was an inadmissible reason for dismissal, or dismissal contravened the Race Relations Act, or the Sex Discrimination Act, the upper limit for the additional award is £6,760 and the total liability becomes £16,910.

Employers' Liability (Compulsory Insurance) Act 1969. This Act requires every employer, unless exempt, to insure and maintain insurance, against liability for bodily injury or disease sustained by his employees in the course of their employment. Nationalised Industries, Local Authorities and Police Authorities are exempt from the provisions of the Act, and in addition, employers whose only employees are close relatives do not require compulsory insurance, but a limited liability company must arrange insurance if any person is employed.

The Act requires insurers to issue the insured employer with a Certificate of Insurance, and sufficient copies for display at each place of business so that one may be easily seen and read by any employee. The Certificate must not be displayed after expiry, or the policy has been cancelled.

Shipowners are included in respect of employment within territorial waters, subject to the following exception. Shipowners who are insured with a mutual insurance association of shipowners, i.e. a Protecting and Indemnity Club (P & I Club) are not required to take out further insurance, as insurance with such an association is an alternative under the Act. It is not necessary for such owners to display a Certificate of Insurance on board their ships. Such insurance covers a shipowner against liability to his employees while they are in port or at sea, whether inside, or outside territorial waters.

The Act does not apply in Northern Ireland, the Isle of Man or the Channel Islands, and it does not apply outside Great Britain, except to employment on offshore installations. The maximum penalty on summary conviction for non-insurance is £200 for any day on which the employer is not insured, and £200 for failure to display a certificate.

GENERAL REGISTER AND RECORD OFFICE OF SHIPPING AND SEAMEN

The General Register and Record Office, which was originally established in London and later transferred to Cardiff, is under the superintendence of the Registrar General of Shipping and Seamen.

Formerly, an important function of the Office was the maintenance of a Central Register of Seamen, but as this is not required under the Merchant Shipping Act 1970 the keeping of this service record has been discontinued.

Matters for which the Office remains responsible include:—

(a) The issue of war service medals.

(b) The maintenance of a record of the issue of certificates of competency of all types and grades. (A card index of all certificate holders is kept which shows all subsequent certificates issued to each holder. The duplicates of certificates are filed, and a record made of all suspensions and cancellations. Details of Commonwealth certificates issued outside the United Kingdom are recorded.)

(c) The circulation of particulars of lost certificates of competency to M.M. Offices throughout the country.

(d) The circulation to examiners at the various examination centres of lists of examinees who fail the D.o.T. sight test.

(e) Assistance to next of kin in the matter of proving death from the returns made on RBD forms, and the making of annual returns of shipping casualties and deaths.

(f) The sending of copies of returns of births and deaths received by the Registrar General of Shipping and Seamen to the appropriate Registrar General of Births and Deaths.

(g) Answering any questions that may be asked in relation to the Roll of Honour for Merchant Seamen and Fishermen which was compiled by the Office.

The Ships Record branch was at one time solely responsible for the preservation of official log books, crew lists, crew agreements, and other documents associated with agreements. The rule was that agreements would be kept in perpetuity, whilst log books would be destroyed after seven years unless they contained entries of births and deaths or were in respect of periods when the country was at war. The documents were regarded as public documents open to inspection on payment of fee or otherwise. Owing to the vast accumulation of these documents, it was later arranged that documents relating to voyages completed before 1857 would be preserved. Those relating to voyages completed in 1857 and later were to be retained for 50 years after which documents of specially notable ships, shown on a selective list provided by the National Maritime Museum, would be preserved. Of the remainder a sample of approximately 5 per cent covering all ships were to be preserved and the residue either (a) disposed of by presentation to shipping companies or other interested bodies, or (b) destroyed. It is still the intention to retain documents covering the periods of the two world wars. The latest move is that all crew lists, agreements and official log books, up to and including 1860, have been taken into the custody of the Public Record Office, together with a sample of those relating to the years 1861 to 1913. In addition, the Public Record Office have those documents relating to notable ships in that latter period. The General Register and Record Office is at present engaged in preparing a sample of crew lists, agreements and log books relating to the years 1914 to 1938 for handing over to the Public Record Office custody.

Other matters dealt with by the Ships Record branch include:—

(a) Keeping copies of ships' registers from which (i) information can be passed on to Lloyd's, (ii) details are available for publication in the "Merchant Navy List".

(b) The allocation of Official Numbers to ships. (These together with Signal Letters are listed in the official publication entitled "Signal Letters of British Ships".)

(c) Approval or otherwise of proposed names for ships including yachts, and proposed changes of name.

(d) The maintaining of a Fishing Boat Register.

N.B.—Transcripts of ships whose registries were closed up to and including 1955 have been handed over to the Public Record Office.

CHAPTER 5

LOG BOOKS, PROTESTS, AND OTHER RECORDS.

OFFICIAL LOG BOOKS

SECTION 68 of the M.S.A. 1970 requires that, except as provided by the M.S. (Official Log Books) Regulations 1981, an official log book shall be kept in a form approved by the D.o.T. in every ship registered in the United Kingdom. Ships exempted by the Regulations are (*a*) a ship belonging to a general lighthouse authority, (*b*) a ship of less than 25 gross tons, and (*c*) a pleasure yacht. The same Regulations prescribe the particulars to be entered in official log books, the persons by whom such entries are to be made, signed, or witnessed, and the procedure to be followed in the making of such entries and their amendment or cancellation. Section 68 of the 1970 Act also provides that if a person wilfully destroys or mutilates or renders illegible any entry in an official log book he shall be liable on summary conviction to a fine not exceeding £500.

The approved official log book is known as form LOG 1/72, the contents of which are as follows:—

The Log Book is enclosed in a thin paper cover which has printed on it "A Guide for Masters about keeping Official Log Books."

Page 1. This is the front cover page on which are entered—

> Name of ship.   Port of registry.   Official number.
> Gross tonnage.   Register (net) tonnage.
> Names of masters and numbers of certificates of competency.
> Name and address of the registered owner or of the registered managing owner; or of the ship's husband or manager.
> Date and place at which log book opened.
> Date and place at which log book closed.
> Where and when delivered to the superintendent or proper officer.
> Date when received by the Registrar General of Shipping and Seamen.

Pages 2 to 5. These are headed Record of Seamen employed in the ship, the column headings being:—

> Reference number in list of crew.
> Name of seaman.
> Capacity.
> If entry made in narrative section give relevant page.

Pages 8 and 9. Here are entered the Returns and Entries of Births and Deaths. It is pointed out that the duties of a master to make returns of births and deaths on board ship and returns of the death of any person employed in the ship who dies outside the United Kingdom are set out in the M.S. (Returns of Births and Deaths) Regulations 1972. These Regulations provide for a return to be made at the first opportunity of any (*a*) birth of a child in the ship; or (*b*) death in the ship, including death in the ship's boat or liferaft; or (*c*) a person being lost from the ship, a ship's boat or liferaft; or (*d*) of a death wherever occurring outside the United Kingdom of any person employed in the ship. This return should be made on form RBD 1. When making a return of the death of a seaman on form RBD 1 the master should also, if required at that time, give an account of (*a*) any moneys due to the deceased seaman, (*b*) any deductions from his wages and (*c*) any property left on board on the relevant form PDS 1. In addition to completing form RBD 1 the master is required to record substantially the same information in the official log book. He should therefore, as soon as practicable after the occurrence, make the necessary entries. The master is also required to enter in the narrative section of the log the circumstances of the death and if death occurred as a result of any person being lost from a ship, or the ship's boat or liferaft, the efforts which were made to rescue the deceased person as well as other particulars required by the regulations, including a statement that the next-of-kin of the deceased (giving name and address) has been notified. When completing form RBD 1 or making entries in the log book as to "cause of death", terms such as "suicide" or "missing" should be avoided and more specific terms such as "gunshot wound in the head" or "missing at sea believed killed or drowned", used instead. If the master is in any doubt about the completion of the forms required to be submitted by him or about any entries in the official log book he should get in touch with the appropriate mercantile marine superintendent or proper officer (*i.e.* the superintendent or proper officer for the place where the ship is at the time of delivery of the official log book).

The required log entries with respect to births are:—

Date of birth.

Place of birth (latitude and longitude if at sea).

Names (if any) and surname of child.

Sex.

Name, surname and nationality and (in separate column) occupation, rank or profession and usual residence of the father.

Name, surname and nationality and (in separate columns) maiden surname or surname at marriage if different, and usual residence of the mother.

Signature of father and/or mother.

Port at which return is made and date.

Record of the making of a return of birth, identifying the person to whom the return was made.

If the child is illegitimate, particulars relating to the father must *not* be given unless it is at the joint request, given in writing, of the mother and the person acknowledging himself to be the father. The written request must be attached to the return form RBD 1.

The required log entries with respect to deaths are:—

Date of death or loss.

Place of death or loss (latitude and longitude if at sea).

Name and surname of deceased (and, if married woman, maiden surname if known).

Sex.

Date of birth (if known) or age.

Occupation, rank or profession.

Usual residence at time of death or loss.

Nationality.

Cause of death or loss (certified by the ship's doctor or other medical practitioner where possible).

Signature of master in person.

Signature of a member of the crew.

Port at which return is made and date.

A record of the making of the return of the death, identifying the person to whom the return was made.

Pages 10 to 14. These pages are for the Record of Musters, Boat Drills and Fire Drills and Inspections of Life-Saving Appliances and Fire Appliances as required by the M.S. Acts. It is pointed out that the requirements for holding musters, etc. in various classes of ships are set out in the M.S. (Musters) Regulations 1980 (as amended by S.I. 1981 No. 578), and that if a muster etc. is not held as required a statement of the reasons must be recorded. Attention is also drawn to D.o.T. Notice No. M 694 (see reference in Chapter 7).

The column headings of these pages are:—

Date of muster or drill and inspections.

Nature of muster or drill.

Nature of the inspection of the life-saving appliances and fire appliances and the condition in which they were found.

Date of entry.

Signatures of master and member of crew.

Pages 15 to 19. These are headed Record of Inspections of Crew Accommodation carried out under Regulations made under Section 20 of the Merchant Shipping Act, 1970.

The column headings are:—

Time and date of inspection.

Names and ranks of persons making the inspection.

Particulars of any respects in which crew accommodation is found not to comply with the Regulations.

Date of entry.

Signatures of master and member of crew.

Pages 20 to 24. These are applicable only to foreign-going ships of 1,000 gross tons and over which go to sea from any port within home-trade limits, and are for a Record of Inspections carried out in accordance with the Food and Catering Convention 1946 of supplies of Food and Water provided for the Crew.

The column headings are:—

Date of inspection.

Name and ranks of persons making the inspection.

Result of inspection of supplies of food and water.

Date of entry.

Signatures of persons making the inspection.

Page 25. On this page are entered the particulars taken from the Load Line Certificate as to positions of the deck line and load lines and the maximum draught of water in summer in mm. The latter is the draught which would be shown on the scale of feet, or metres and decimetres, or decimetres on the stem and stern post of the ship if she were so loaded that the upper edge of the summer load line were on the surface of the water and the ship were upright on an even keel.

The following notes also appear on this page:—

1. The above particulars and particulars of depth of loading as detailed on the following pages, are to be recorded before the ship leaves any dock, wharf, harbour, or other place for the purpose of proceeding to sea.

2. The actual freeboard amidships on each side of the ship is to be measured from the upper edge of the deck line to the surface of the water, when the ship is loaded and ready to leave. The actual "mean" freeboard is the mean of the actual freeboards, port and starboard, measured as indicated above.

3. For any conversion from Imperial to metric units, or vice-versa, an equivalent of 25.4 millimetres to one inch is to be used.

4. Unless the ship is a home trade ship, a Notice on form FRE 13 is to be posted up in some conspicuous place on board the ship before she leaves any dock, wharf, harbour, or other place for the purpose of proceeding to sea, and the Notice is to be kept so posted up and legible until the ship arrives at some other dock, wharf, harbour or place. The date and time of posting the Notice is to be entered in column 15.

5. In the case of a home trade ship or a ship trading in the Near Continental trading area, columns 10 and 11 need not be filled in.

6. No entries are required in columns 8-14 when the actual draughts and freeboards when ready to sail are such that the load

line indicating the maximum depth to which the ship could then be loaded in salt water was not submerged.

7. If, in determining density of water use is made of a hydrometer on which the reading at the top of the scale is 1000 or 00 meaning "full fresh water", the hydrometer reading gives the density to be entered, *e.g.*, a reading of 15 on such hydrometers means a density of 1015. If the hydrometer used has the scale reversed, *i.e.*, if the reading 00 is at the bottom of the scale and means "full salt water", the density must be obtained by subtracting the hydrometer reading from 1025, *e.g.*, if the reading is at 15, the density to be entered will be 1010.

8. The periods during which the other seasonal load lines apply in different parts of the world are as indicated in the Merchant Shipping (Load Line) Rules 1968 and shown on the chart annexed to those rules.

Pages 26 to 29. Here are entered the dates of departure from and arrival at each dock, wharf, harbour or other place with the draught of water and freeboard upon every occasion of the ship proceeding to sea.

The columns which are numbered, are arranged as shown:—

(1) Date and hour of departure.
(2) Dock, wharf, harbour or other place.
(3) Actual draught of water forward in ft. or m. or dm.
(4) Actual draught of water aft in ft. or m. or dm.
(5) Actual freeboard amidships, port, in mm.
(6) Actual freeboard amidships, starboard, in mm.
(7) Actual freeboard amidships, mean, in mm.
(8) Density of water.
(9) Allowance for density of water in mm.
(10) For ashes and rubbish—weight and allowance in mm.
(11) For fuel, etc., to be consumed on stretch of inland water — distance and allowance in mm.
(12) Total allowances in mm.
(13) Mean draught in salt water as calculated after making the appropriate allowances in ft. or m. or dm.
(14) Mean freeboard amidships in salt water as calculated after making the appropriate allowances in mm.
(15) Date and time of posting the Notice (Notice FRE 13).
(16) Signature of master.
(17) Signature of an officer.
(18) Date and hour of arrival.
(19) Arrivals—dock, wharf, harbour or other place.

Pages 30 to 40. These pages constitute the narrative section of the Official Log. A note at the top of each page says that the entries regarding watertight doors, etc., as required under Part IV of the schedule to the Official Log Book Regulations, are to be made in a special supplementary log book. Another note at the foot of each page says, with respect to entries about disciplinary offences, the master's attention is called to the requirements of Part II of the schedule to the Official Log Book Regulations, made under Section 68 of the Merchant Shipping Act 1970.

The column headings of the narrative section are:—

> Date and hour of the occurrence.
> Place of the occurrence or situation by latitude and longi tude at sea.
> Date of entry.
> Entries required by Regulations made under Section 68, Merchant Shipping Act, 1970.

The last page of the narrative section (page 40) forms the back cover of the log book.

M.S. (Official Log Books) Regulations 1981

1. **Definitions.** This lists a number of definitions of which the following should be specially noted.

"Code of Conduct" means the N.M.B. publication entitled "Code of Conduct for the Merchant Navy" published in 1978 by the Board.

"Seaman" in paragraphs 18, 20 and 36 of the Schedule includes the master of a ship.

"Ship" means a ship registered in the United Kingdom but does not include a fishing vessel. (There are special Official Log Books Regulations for fishing vessels.)

"The Steering Gear Regulations" means the M.S. (Automatic Pilot and Testing of Steering Gear) Regulations 1981.

References to the gross or register tonnage of a ship are, in the case of a ship having alternative gross or alternative register tonnages, references to the larger of its gross tonnages or to the larger of its register tonnages, as the case may require.

2. **Exemptions.** The regulations do not apply to:—
   (a) a ship belonging to a general lighthouse authority;
   (b) a ship of less than 25 gross tons; or
   (c) a pleasure yacht.

3. **Entries in official log books.** Subject to the provisions of the M.S. Acts and of rules and regulations made thereunder, entries of particulars specified—

   (a) in column 1 in each paragraph of Part 1 of the Schedule shall from time to time be made in the official log book kept in every ship not exempted by regulation 2;
   (b) in column 1 of each paragraph of Part II of the Schedule shall be so made in the official log book kept in any such ship to which the Disciplinary Offences Regulations apply;

(c) in column 1 in each paragraph of Part III of the Schedule shall be so made in the official log book kept in any such ship in respect of which a load line certificate has been issued, except a ship which is (i) a sludge carrier; (ii) a dredger; (iii) a hopper barge; or (iv) a tug or tender which, in either case, is on or is about to undertake a voyage of not more than 600 nautical miles in the course of which it is at no time more than 200 miles from a port or place in which the persons on board could be placed in safety and, if it carries passengers, does not carry more than 12; and

(d) in column 1 in each paragraph of Part IV of the Schedule shall be so made in the official log book kept in any such ship to which the M.S. (Closing of Openings in Hulls and in Watertight Bulkheads) Regulations 1980 apply.

4. Making, signing and witnessing of entries.

(1) Each entry shall be made by the person or by one of the persons (or by a person authorised by any such person for that purpose) specified in column 2 in each paragraph of the Schedule.

(2) Each entry:—

    (a) subject to paragraph (3) of this regulation, shall be signed by the person or by one of the persons specified in column 2 in each paragraph of the Schedule; and

    (b) subject to the provisions of each paragraph of the Schedule, shall be witnessed by the person, if any, specified in column 3 in each paragraph of the Schedule.

(3) An entry which is to be signed by the master may, except where the contrary intention appears, be signed by an officer authorised by the master for that purpose.

(4) Each entry shall include the date when it is made.

5. This provides that if an entry which is to be signed or witnessed by the master or by a person who is a member of the crew is not made, signed and witnessed in accordance with the Regulations and Schedule, the master of the ship at the time when the entry is or should have been made, signed and witnessed shall be guilty of an offence.

6. **Annexes to official log books.** If it is not practicable by reason of its length, the circumstances in which it is to be made or for any other reason for an entry to be contained in the official log book, it shall be contained in a separate document annexed to the official log book and referred to in an entry in the official log book; and references in these Regulations to an official log book include references to any documents annexed to an official log book in accordance with this regulation.

7. Time for making of entries.

(1) (*a*) Entries of particulars specified in paragraphs 1, 2, 3, 5 and 43 of the Schedule shall be made at the time when an official log book is opened; and

  (i) a further entry of particulars specified in paragraph 3 shall be made as soon as practicable after any change of master; and

  (ii) a further entry of particulars specified in paragraph 43 shall be made as soon as practicable after a new load line certificate is issued in respect of the ship under section 6 of the Act of 1967.

(*b*) The entry of particulars specified in paragraphs 7 and 25 of the Schedule shall be made as soon as practicable after the ship arrives at or leaves any dock, wharf, port or harbour as the case may require.

(*c*) The entry of particulars specified in paragraph 11 of the accordance with the Musters Regulations.

(*d*) The entries of particulars specified in sub-paragraphs (b) and (c) of paragraph 38 of the Schedule shall be made daily or at such other times during the continuance of the illness or injury as the person intending to make any such entry thinks fit.

(*e*) The entry of particulars specified in paragraph 44 of the Schedule shall be made before the ship leaves any dock, wharf, harbour or other place for the purpose of proceeding to sea.

(*f*) Every other entry shall be made as soon as practicable after the occurrence to which it relates or, if it amends or cancels an existing entry, as soon as practicable after the person intending to sign it becomes aware of the facts giving rise to the amendment or cancellation.

(2) Subject to the provisions of regulation 8, no entry shall be made in an official log book after the time referred to in regulation 10(1).

8. Amendment and cancellation of entries.

(1) Subject to the provisions of this regulation, an entry shall not be amended or cancelled.

(2) Where—

  (*a*) in the case of an entry which was required to be signed by the master, it appears to the person who for the time being is master of the ship that the entry is inaccurate or incomplete; or

  (*b*) in the case of any other entry, it appears to the person who signed the entry that it is inaccurate or incomplete; that person shall, if it is practicable to do so before the time referred to in regulation 10(1), make and sign a further entry referring to the entry and amending or cancelling it; and paragraphs (1) and 2(*b*) of regulation 4 and regulations 5 and 6 shall apply to the further entry.

(3) Where, after the time referred to in regulation 10(1), it appears to a superintendent or proper officer or to the Registrar General of Shipping and Seamen that an entry is inaccurate or incomplete, he—

   (*a*) may make and sign a further entry referring to the entry and amending or cancelling it; and

   (*b*) shall, if it is practicable to do so, inform any master or seaman, to whom any such further entry relates, of its contents.

(4) Any person who fails to comply with paragraph (2) of this regulation shall be guilty of an offence.

9. Production of the official log book.

(1) The master of a ship shall, on demand, produce to the Registrar General of Shipping and Seamen, a superintendent, a proper officer or an officer of customs the official log book required to be kept in the ship.

(2) A master who fails to comply with this regulation shall be guilty of an offence.

10. Delivery of an official log book.

(1) The master shall, within 48 hours after the time specified in paragraph (2) or in paragraph (3) (as the case may be) of this regulation, or, if it is not practicable within that time, as soon as practicable thereafter, deliver the official log book to the appropriate superintendent or proper officer.

(2) Subject to paragraph (3) of this regulation, the time referred to in paragraph (1) is either —

   (*a*) if any person is employed in the ship under a crew agreement, the time when the last person remaining so employed is discharged from the ship; or

   (*b*) in any other case, the time when the ship first calls at a port more than 6 months after the first entry (other than an entry specified in paragraph 1, 2, 3, 5 or 43 of the Schedule to these Regulations) is made in the official log book.

(3) If, at the time specified in paragraph (2) of this regulation—

   (*a*) there is pending a wages submission: or

   (*b*) (i) there is pending an appeal against a fine, or

       (ii) if no such appeal is pending, an entry relates to a fine, which has not been remitted, imposed for a disciplinary offence and in respect of which the time for giving of notice of appeal by the appellant to

K

the master (in accordance with regulation 12 of the Disciplinary Offences Regulations) has not expired;

the time referred to in paragraph (1) of this regulation is either the time when all such submissions or appeals have been determined by a superintendent or proper officer or withdrawn, or the expiration of 7 days after the time specified in paragraph (2) of this regulation, whichever shall be the earlier.

(4) A master who fails to comply with paragraph (1) of this regulation shall be guilty of an offence.

11. **Offences.** Any offence under these Regulations shall be punishable on summary conviction with a fine not exceeding £50.

The Schedule to the Official Log Book Regulations. This schedule consists of four parts and is arranged in three columns. Column 1 contains the particulars of entry, Column 2 the signatory and Column 3 the witness. The Act of 1894 means the Merchant Shipping Act 1894, the Act of 1949 means the Merchant Shipping (Safety Convention) Act 1949, the Act of 1967 means the Merchant Shipping (Load Lines) Act 1967 and the Act of 1970 means the Merchant Shipping Act 1970.

Entries required to be made in the Official Log Books kept in U.K. registered ships which are not exempted.

Part I Entries relating to every ship

1. The name of the ship, its port of registry, official number and gross or register tonnage.
   Signatory: The master. Witness: None:

2. The name and address of the registered owner or of the registered managing owner or of the ship's husband or manager.
   Signatory: The master. Witness: None.

3. The name of the master and the number of his certificate of competency.
   Signatory: The master. Witness: None.

4. Where a person ceases to be master of the ship during a voyage, a record that, in accordance with section 74 of the Act of 1970, he has delivered to his successor the documents relating to the ship or its crew which are in his custody.
   Signatory: The master in person and the former master in person. Witness: None.

5. The date on and place at which the official log book is opened.
   Signatory: The master. Witness: None.

6. The date on and place at which the official log book is closed.
   Signatory: The master. Witness: None.

7. A record of—the date and hour of departure for sea from, and arrival from sea at, any dock, wharf, port or harbour.
Signatory: The master in person. Witness: An officer.

8. A record of every notification required by Regulation 16 of the (Certification of Deck Officers) Regulations 1980 to be made to a proper officer whenever one qualified deck officer less than the number required by the regulations is carried.
Signatory: The master. Witness: None.

9. A record of every notification required by Regulation 12 of the (Certification of Marine Engineer Officers) Regulations 1980 to be made to a proper officer whenever one qualified marine engineer officer less than the number required by the regulations is carried.
Signatory: The master. Witness: None.

10. A record of each occasion on which, in accordance with Regulation 6 (7) of the Muster Regulations 1980 (amended by S.I. 1981 No. 578) a muster, drill or training of the crew in the use of lifesaving and fire appliances and equipment is held on board the ship or on which the appliances and equipment required by those Regulations to be carried are examined to see whether they are fit and ready for use.
Signatory: The master. Witness: A member of the crew.

11. Where a muster, drill, training or inspection is not held on board the ship when required by the Musters Regulations 1980 a record of why the muster, drill, training or inspection, as the case may be, was not carried out or carried out only in part.
Signatory: The master. Witness: A member of the crew.

12. Where any of the following casualties has occurred—(a) the loss or presumed loss, stranding, grounding, abandonment or of damage to the ship; or (b) a loss of life caused by fire on board or by any accident to the ship or a ship's boat, or by any accident occurring on board the ship or a ship's boat; or (c) any damage caused by the ship—a description of the casualty and the place where, or the position of the ship when it occurred.
Signatory: The master. Witness: A member of the crew.

13. A record of every signal of distress or a message that a vessel, aircraft or person is in distress at sea, observed or received.
Signatory: The master. Witness: A member of the crew.

14. Where the master, on receiving at sea a signal of distress or information from any source that a vessel or aircraft is in distress, is unable, or in the special circumstances of the case considers it unreasonable or unnecessary to go to the assistance of the persons in distress (in accordance with section 22(1) of the Act of 1949 which relates to a master's obligation to assist vessels etc. in distress)—a statement of his reasons for not going to the assistance of those persons.

Signatory: The master in person. Witness: A member of the crew.

15. Where a dispute relating to the amount payable to a seaman under a crew agreement is submitted to a superintendent or proper officer under section 10 of the Act of 1970—(a) a record of the identity of the superintendent or proper officer; (b) a statement of the dispute; (c) a record of whether he accepts the submission; and (d) if he accepts the submission; either—(i) a record of his decision; or (ii) a statement that he is of the opinion that the dispute ought not to be decided by him.

Signatory: With respect to (a) the master; with respect to (b), (c) and (d) the superintendent or proper officer. Witness: With respect to (a) a member of the crew; with respect to (b), (c) and (d) none.

16. A record of—(a) every seaman discharged from the ship; and (b) the place, date and time of his discharge.

Signatory: The person in whose presence the seaman is discharged or (if the seaman is not present at the time he is discharged), the master. Witness: A member of the crew.

17. Where a proper officer consents to the discharge of a seaman outside the United Kingdom, a record of his consent.

Signatory: The proper officer (if practicable) or the master in person. Witness: If the entry is signed by the master, a member of the crew.

18. Where a seaman is left behind in any country outside the United Kingdom or is taken to such a country on being shipwrecked, or a person who became employed in the ship under an agreement entered into outside the United Kingdom is left behind in the United Kingdom or is taken to the United Kingdom on being shipwrecked—a record of (a) the name of the seaman; (b) the date on which and the place at which the seaman was left behind; (c) the reason, if known to the master, for the seaman being left behind; (d) any provision made by the master on the seaman's employer's behalf to ensure that a superintendent or proper officer is informed that the seaman has been left behind and is given the information referred to in regulation 4(3) of the Repatriation Regulations, identifying the superintendent or proper officer; (e) the seaman's employer being informed that the seaman has been left behind and of the employer being given any particulars required by him.

Signatory: The master. Witness: A member of the crew.

19. Where, in pursuance of regulation 8 of the Repatriation Regulations, the master is required by a superintendent or proper officer to convey a person under a conveyance order— a record of (a) the conveyance order, identifying the person to whom it relates, and the superintendent or proper officer

by whom it was given; (*b*) any direction received by the master in respect of any such requirement, specifying the direction and the superintendent or proper officer by whom it was given; (*c*) whether the person is engaged as a member of the crew and if not, (*i*) the date on which and the place at which he came on board the ship; and (ii) the date on which and the place at which he left the ship.

Signatory: The master. Witness: A member of the crew.

20. In respect of a seaman referred to in an entry made pursuant to paragraph 18 of this Schedule—a record of—(*a*) whether he left any property (including money) on board the ship; (*b*) all such property of which the master has taken charge in pursuance of regulation 16 (3)(*a*) of the Repatriation Regulations specifying each item of such property; (*c*) each article forming part of such property sold in pursuance of regulation 16 (4)(*a*) of the Repatriation Regulations, and the price received for it; (*d*) each article forming part of such property destroyed or disposed of in pursuance of regulation 16 (4)(*b*) of the Repatriation Regulations and the name of the person to whom disposal was made; (*e*) each article forming part of such property delivered to any person in pursuance of paragraph (5) or (6) of regulation 16 of the Repatriation Regulations specifying the person (whether the seaman, his employer or his next of kin) to whom the delivery was made and the date, place and manner of delivery.

Signatory: The master. Witness: A member of the crew.

21. A record of any inspection of crew accommodation carried out under regulations 38 (2) and 31 (2) of Schedule 6 to the Crew Accommodation Regulations 1978, showing—(*a*) the date and time of the inspection; (*b*) the names and ranks of the persons making the inspection; and (*c*) particulars of any respects in which the crew accommodation or any part thereof was found by any of the persons making the inspection not to comply with those Regulations.

Signatory: The master. Witness: A member of the crew.

22. A record of any inspection of provisions and water to be supplied to seamen employed in the ship with the result of the inspection.

Signatory: The persons making the inspection. Witness: None.

23. A record of any inspection by a person appointed by the Secretary of State of any anchors and chain cables (as defined in section 1(7) of the Anchors and Chain Cables Act 1967) on board the ship as part of its equipment and the findings of that person.

Signatory: The person making the inspection. Witness: None.

24. A record of any testing and inspection carried out by the ship's personnel of the rigging of the hoist and a load test to at least 150 kg. under regulation 8 (6)(d) of the Pilot Ladders and Hoists Regulations 1980 (as amended by S.I. 1981/581). Signatory: The master. Witness: An officer.

25. A record of any drill, check and test carried out by the ship's crew of the ship's steering gear, under regulation 6 (6) of the Steering Gear Regulations.

26. Where three or more seamen employed in the ship complain to the master under section 22 of the Act of 1970 (which relates to complaints about provisions and water) about the provisions or water provided for the seamen employed in the ship—a record of—(a) the names of the seamen making the complaint; (b) the complaint, specifying—(i) the provisions or the water complained of; and (ii) the manner in which they are alleged not to be in accordance with regulations made under section 21 of the Act of 1970 (whether because of bad quality, unfitness for use or deficiency in quantity); (c) action taken by the master on the complaint; (d) whether the seamen state to the master their dissatisfaction with the action taken by the master on the complaint and whether they claim to complain to a superintendent or proper officer; (e) if the seamen claim to complain to a superintendent or proper officer, the arrangements made for the master to enable the seamen to do so; (f) the investigation of the complaint by a superintendent or proper officer; and (g) every examination of provisions and water made under section 22(3) of the Act of 1970.
    Signatory: In respect of (a), (b), (c), (d) and (e) the master. Witness: One of the seamen making the complaint.
    Signatory: In respect of (f) the superintendent or proper officer investigating the complaint. Witness: None
    Signatory: In respect of (g) the person making the inspection. Witness: None.

27. Where a seaman employed in the ship complains to the master under section 23 of the Act of 1970 (which relates to complaints other than complaints about provisions and water) about the master or any other seaman employed in the ship or about the conditions on board the ship—a record of—(a) the name of the seaman making the complaint; (b) the complaint, specifying the person or matter complained of and the nature of the complaint; (c) action taken by the master on the complaint; (d) whether the seaman states his dissatisfaction with the action taken by the master on the complaint and whether, if the ship is outside the United Kingdom, he claims to complain to a proper officer; (e) if the seaman claims to complain to a proper officer the arrangements made by the master to

enable the seaman to do so; and (*f*) the investigation of the complaint by a proper officer.

Signatory: In respect of (*a*), (*b*), (*c*), (*d*) and (*e*) the master. Witness: The seaman making the complaint.

Signatory: In respect of (*f*) the proper officer investigating the complaint. Witness: none.

28. Where by reason of any event it appears to the master that an officer—(*a*) may be unfit to discharge his duties, whether by reason of incompetency or misconduct or for any other reason; or (*b*) may have been seriously negligent in the discharge of his duties; or (*c*) may have failed to comply with the provisions of section 422 of the act of 1894 (duty to give assistance and information after collision); a record of—(i) the name of the officer and the grade and number of his certificate; (ii) any such event or a reference to any other entry relating to it; (iii) any statement made by the officer to the master in respect of that event or those events and which the officer wishes to be recorded; and (iv) that the entries made in pursuance of sub-paragraphs (i) to (iii) of this paragraph have been read over to the officer by the master, and if they are not read over, the reason for not doing so.

Signatory: The master in person.   Witness: An officer other than the officer referred to in an entry under subparagraph (i) of this paragraph.

29. A record of any re-rating (including promotion) of a seaman, with the date upon which the re-rating takes effect.

Signatory: The master. Witness: A member of the crew.

30. When a seaman employed under a crew agreement, approved by the Secretary of State, to which the N.M.B. agreement on disciplinary procedures applies and which requires him to comply with the Code of Conduct, is alleged, before the master, to have committed one of the breaches of the Code specified in paragraphs 9 and 11 thereof, a record of such of the following particulars as are relevant—(*a*) the nature of the allegation; (*b*) the name of the person against whom the allegation is made; (*c*) that the master has read the allegation to the seaman; (*d*) that the master has advised the seaman of his right to be accompanied by a friend who may advise him and speak on his behalf; (*e*)(i) if the seaman admits the allegation, a statement that he admits it; (*e*)(ii) in any other case, a statement that the seaman does not admit the allegation; (*f*)(i) any statement made by the seaman, or by his friend on behalf of the seaman, in answer to the allegation; (*f*)(ii) that he declines to make a statement in answer to the allegation; (*g*) that the master has given a formal warning to the seaman; (*h*) that the master has given a written reprimand to the seaman; (*i*) that the master has informed the seaman that he will be dismissed from the ship either at the first

opportunity or at the end of the voyage and that the matter will be referred to a shore-based disciplinary committee; (*j*) that the seaman has been given, and has acknowledged receipt of, a copy of all entries made in the official log book relating to his breach of the Code, together with a copy of any report made to a shore-based disciplinary committee.

Signatory: The master. Witness: A member of the crew other than the seaman named in an entry under sub-paragraph (*b*) of this paragraph.

31. Where a seaman is convicted by a legal tribunal of any offence committed in the ship during a voyage—a record of the conviction and of the punishment inflicted.

Signatory: The master. Witness: A member of the crew.

32. Where, in the opinion of the master, consideration should be given to the prosecution of any person in respect of any conduct in the ship during a voyage (whether under the Merchant Shipping Acts or otherwise)—a record—(*a*) of the event; (*b*) of the name of the person concerned; (*c*) of any statement made by the person concerned to the master in respect of that event which that person wishes to be recorded; and (*d*) that the entries made in pursuance of sub-paragraphs (*a*) to (*c*) of this paragraph have been read over by the master to the person concerned.

Signatory: The master in person. Witness: A member of the crew other than the person named in an entry under sub-paragraph (*b*) of this paragraph.

33. A record of any reduction in the scale of provisions or water to be provided for seamen employed in the ship specifying —(*a*) the reduction made; (*b*) the reason for the reduction; and (*c*) the duration of the reduction.

Signatory: The master. Witness: A member of the crew.

34. Where a child is born in the ship or in one of the ship's boats —a record in the form shown in the description of the contents of pages 8 and 9 of the official log book. (*See* earlier page)

Signatory: The master in person. Witness: The mother of the child.

35. Where any person dies in the ship or in a ship's boat or is lost from the ship or a ship's boat or where any person employed in the ship dies outside the United Kingdom—a record in the form shown in the description of the contents of pages 8 and 9 of the official log book. (*See* earlier page)

Signatory: The master in person, but, in respect of the cause of death or loss, the ship's doctor (if one). Witness: A member of the crew.

36. In respect of a seaman dying while or after being employed in the ship—a record of—(*a*) whether he left any property (including money) on board the ship; (*b*) all such property of which the master has taken charge in pursuance of

regulation 2(2)(*a*) of the Property Regulations, specifying each item of such property; (*c*) each item forming part of such property sold in pursuance of regulation 2(3)(*a*) of the Property Regulations, and the price received for it; (*d*) each article forming part of such property destroyed or disposed of in pursuance of regulation 2(3)(*b*) of the Property Regulations, and the name of the person to whom disposal was made; (*e*) each article forming part of such property delivered to any person in pursuance of regulation 2(4) of the Property Regulations, specifying the superintendent or proper officer to whom delivery was made, and the date, place and manner of delivery.
Signatory: The master in person.   Witness: A member of the crew.

37. Where an inquiry into the cause of death is required to be held under section 61 of the Act of 1970—a record—(*a*) of the name of the deceased and a reference to the relevant entry made under paragraph 35 of this Schedule; (*b*) of either—(i) the name of the superintendent or proper officer holding the inquiry and the date and place at which the inquiry is held; or (ii) that the inquiry was not held at the next port where the ship calls after the death and where there is a superintendent or proper officer.
Signatory: With respect to (*a*) and (*b*)(ii) the master.   With respect to (*b*)(i) the superintendent or proper officer holding the inquiry.   Witness: None.

38. Where a person employed in the ship falls ill or is injured —a record of—(*a*) the circumstances of the injury; (*b*) the nature of the illness or injury or the symptoms thereof; (*c*) the treatment adopted; and (*d*) the progress of the illness or injury.
Signatory: With respect to (*a*) the master; with respect to (*b*), (*c*) and (*d*) the ship's doctor or (if there is no ship's doctor) the master.   Witness: A member of the crew.

Part II Entries relating to ships to which the M.S. (Disciplinary Offences) Regulations 1972 apply (Not GCBS ships)

39. When a seaman is charged with a disciplinary offence under the Disciplinary Offences Regulations—a record—(*a*) if the offence is not to be dealt with by the master, of the name of the officer authorised under regulation 5(2) of the Disciplinary Offences Regulations to exercise the powers and duties of the master in respect of that offence; (*b*) of the name of the seaman charged; (*c*) of the charge; (*d*) that the master or the officer referred to in sub-paragraph (a) of this paragraph has read the charge to the seaman; (*e*)(i) if the seaman admits the charge, a statement that he admits it; or (ii) in any other case, a statement that the seaman does

not admit the charge; (*f*)(i) particulars of any statement made by the seaman in answer to the charge; or (ii) that he declines to make a statement in answer to the charge; (*g*) the decision of the master or of the officer referred to in sub-paragraph (*a*)—(i) as to whether or not he finds that the seaman has committed the offence charged; and (ii) if he finds that the seaman has committed the offence, as to the amount of the fine which he is imposing for that offence or that he is imposing no fine.

Signatory: The master or the officer named in an entry under sub-paragraph (*a*) of this paragraph. Witness: A member of the crew other than the seaman named in an entry under sub-paragraph (*b*) of this paragraph.

40. If the master remits the whole or a part of a fine in accordance with the Disciplinary Offences Regulations, a record of the remission, referring to the relevant entry under paragraph 39, and stating the amount remitted and the reason for the remission.

Signatory: The master. Witness: None.

41. Where a seaman makes an appeal against a fine—a record— (*a*) of the date of receipt by the master of (i) the seaman's notice of appeal; (ii) the seaman's withdrawal of the appeal (if any); (*b*) that the appeal is to be heard at an intermediate port as defined in regulation 1(2) of the Disciplinary Offences Regulations; (*c*)(i) the date of receipt by a superintendent or proper officer of notice of the appeal; (ii) the identity of the superintendent or proper officer receiving notice of the appeal; (iii) the receipt by the superintendent or proper officer of the seaman's withdrawal of the appeal (if any); (iv) the decision of the superintendent or proper officer stating whether he confirms or quashes the decision of the master and whether he remits the whole or what part of the fine.

Signatory: With respect to (*a*) and (*b*) the master. Witness: A member of the crew other than the seaman named in an entry under paragraph 39(*b*).

Signatory: With respect to (*c*) the superintendent or proper officer named in an entry under sub-paragraph (*c*)(ii) of this paragraph. Witness: None.

42. Where a fine has been imposed on a seaman for a disciplinary offence—a record—(*a*) that the amount of the fine so far as not remitted by the master or on appeal has been paid to a superintendent or proper officer—(i) identifying the seaman on whom the fine was imposed; (ii) specifying the amount paid; (iii) identifying the superintendent or proper officer to whom the amount is paid; (*b*) of the receipt by the superintendent or proper officer of the amount specified in the entry made in pursuance of sub-paragraph (*a*)(ii) of this paragraph.

Signatory: With respect to (*a*) the master in person. With

respect to (*b*) the superintendent or proper officer receiving the amount. Witness: None.

Part III Entries relating to ships in respect of which a certificate has been issued under section 6 of the M.S. (Load Lines) Act 1967 and which are not exempted by regulation 3(c)

43. A record of all the particulars stated in the Load Line Certificate and the maximum draught of water in summer as shown in the description of the contents of page 23 of the official log book.
Signatory: The master. Witness: None.
44. A record of the draught and freeboard, etc. when the ship is ready to leave any dock, wharf, harbour or other place for the purpose of proceeding to sea, as shown in the description of the contents of pages 26 to 29 of the official log book.
Signatory: The master. Witness: An officer.

Part IV Entries relating to ships to which the M.S. (Closing of Openings in Hulls and in Watertight Bulkheads) Regulations 1980 apply

45. A record of—(*a*) the times of the last closing, before the ship proceeds to sea, of the watertight doors and other contrivances referred to in Rule 2 of the M.S. (Closing of Openings in Hulls and in Watertight Bulkheads) Regulations 1980, and of the next subsequent opening of such doors and contrivances; (*b*) the times of the closing and opening, while the ship is at sea, of any watertight door which is fitted between bunkers in the between decks below the bulkhead deck as defined in those Regulations; (*c*) whether the portable plates referred to in Regulation 4 of those Regulations are in place when the ship proceeds to sea, and the times, if any, of the removal and replacements of such plates when the ship is at sea; and (*d*) the occasions on which drills are practised and inspections made in compliance with the provisions of those Regulations, and whether the contrivances to which such drills and inspections relate are in good working order.
Signatory: The master. Witness: An officer.

Supplementary Log Books. These consist of:—

(1) Form LOG 2/72 for passenger ships in which log entries are made relating to (*a*) the times of opening and closing of watertight doors, etc., (*b*) practices of opening and closing of watertight doors, etc., and (*c*) inspection of watertight doors and valves shown above in Part IV of the regulations.

(2) Radiotelegraph logs (Parts I and II). The former, issued *gratis*, is for recording the routine tests of equipment whilst the latter,

for which a charge is made, is for recording the duty periods of radio officers and particulars of messages transmitted and received, etc. (See Chapter 7 for details.)

(3) Radiotelephone logs. These are issued to ships fitted with radiotelephone installations and correspond to the radio-telegraph logs mentioned above.

All the above supplementary logs are subject to the same rules with regard to entries, signatures, and proper delivery as the general official log book itself.

Prescribed forms are available for (a) Oil Record Book for Tankers, (b) Oil Record Book for ships other than tankers. These are for recording particulars relating to the discharge of oil for safety or other purposes, escape of oil through damage or leakage, ballasting and cleaning of oil tanks, discharge of ballast, discharge of slop tanks, disposal of oil residues and the discharge of oily bilge water. Additionally, in the case of tankers, the loading, transfer and discharge of oil cargoes, and the ballasting and cleaning of cargo tanks must be recorded. Such records must be kept available for inspection for a period of two years following the last entry, either on board in the master's custody, or at the owner's principal place of business if that is in the United Kingdom. The requirement that a record be kept by all ships of any transfer of oil within the limits of U.K. territorial waters can be complied with by using any convenient form at the master's discretion.

DECK AND ENGINE ROOM LOGS

It is most important that all entries in these log books should be made carefully and precisely, and only after due consideration so that alterations and interlineations can be avoided. Log books should always give a faithful and accurate account of the voyage, and the master and his officers should not on any account write exaggerated reports of weather conditions or other circumstances. If a judge or other investigator is satisfied, or even has good reason to suspect, that a single statement is false or exaggerated, it is only natural to suppose that he will tend to be highly critical in his scrutiny of all other statements including those which have been honestly and accurately made.

Fair copies of log books may have their uses, but it should always be kept in mind that, should any collision, accident, or other incident give rise to litigation or inquiry, it will be the so-called "scrap logs" which will be of most interest to the court and which will come under the closest investigation for the reason that they will (or should) have been written up immediately after the described events have occurred.

When entering or leaving port or when navigating in pilotage waters it is generally impracticable to make contemporaneous log entries.   In these circumstances records of engine movements, changes of course, signals given, and so on are best kept in a "bridge book" which should be used to write up the log book as soon as possible afterwards. A corresponding "movements book" should be kept in the engine room for the same purpose, and in this connection it may be remarked that the bridge and engine room clocks should have been synchronised. These books should be preserved so that the evidence contained in them will be available for production at any time afterwards if required. The practice of writing up log books from information that has been jotted down on scraps of paper which are afterwards thrown away is a thoroughly bad one. If the original record cannot be produced in court if asked for, the fact may very well prejudice the shipowner's interests.

The "mate's log" where one is kept is a fair copy of the deck "scrap log" written up by the chief officer who should take every care to see that the statements in it are strictly accurate. He should sign his name at the foot of each daily page. The master should examine the log periodically (preferably daily) and should also sign each page. If a pencil is used to write up the "scrap log" it should be an indelible pencil, whilst the fair copy should be written in ink. Where a "mate's log" is not kept in addition to the scrap log," the latter should be kept in ink and should be signed daily by the master and chief officer after careful scrutiny.

Besides routine particulars of the navigation of the vessel, entries should be made of all extraordinary happenings and of all matters affecting the interests of the owners, particularly in circumstances where claims by or against the ship are likely to arise, where matters are likely to be disputed, or where log entries may be needed in support of protests noted and/or extended by the master. In particular where the circumstances require it, all relevant facts should be logged relating to the following:—

In general:—

    Attention to ventilation of cargo spaces.

    Loss or damage to the ship or cargo from any cause whatsoever.

    Strandings and groundings.

    Collisions with other vessels or fixed objects with particulars of apparent damage.

    Machinery breakdowns.

    Search of ship for contraband and stowaways.

    Giving or receiving salvage services.

    Times of commencing, suspending, and completing processes of loading, discharging, or bunkering.

    Times of taking in or off-loading mails.

    Investigation of unusual or unexpected soundings.

    Attention to moorings and clearing of hawse.

If under charter:—

    Delays during the preliminary voyage to the loading port.

    Times of berthing and serving notice of readiness.

    Particulars of delays in loading, discharging, or bunkering.

Quantity of cargo loaded or discharged each day.
Time of signing bills of lading on completion of loading.

PROTESTS

In any of the circumstances enumerated below it is advisable for the master to note a protest.

1. Whenever during the voyage the ship has encountered conditions of wind and sea which may result in damage to cargo.
2. When from any cause the ship is damaged, or there is reason to fear that damage may be sustained.
3. When through stress of weather it has not been practicable to adopt normal precautions in the matter of ventilation of perishable cargo.
4. When cargo is shipped in such condition that it is likely to suffer deterioration during the voyage. In this case, however, the protest will not be effective unless the bills of lading were endorsed to show the condition of the cargo at the time of shipment.
5. When any serious breach of C/P terms is committed by the charterer or his agent, such as refusal to load, unduly delaying loading, loading improper cargo, refusal to pay demurrage, refusal to accept B's/L in the form signed by the master, etc.
6. When consignees fail to discharge cargo or take delivery thereof, and pay freight in accordance with C/P or B/L terms.
7. In all cases of general average.

Protests should be noted as soon as possible, certainly within 24 hours of arrival in port, and in the case of cargo protests before breaking bulk.

A "note of protest" is simply a declaration by the master of circumstances beyond his control which may give, or may have given, rise to loss or damage. Such declaration must be made before a notary public, magistrate, British consular officer, or other authority. Usually, statements under oath will be taken from the master and other members of the crew and these statements will have to be supported by appropriate log book entries. At the time of noting protest the master should reserve the right to extend it.

Protests are admissible in evidence before legal tribunals and, in many cases, are essential to the establishment of a claim. In many countries, particularly on the Continent, protests are received in evidence as a matter of course. In the United Kingdom, however, they are not accepted as evidence in favour of the party making the protest unless both parties consent. The chief use of a protest in the United Kingdom is to support a claim by a cargo owner against his underwriters. There is no legal necessity for a protest in the United Kingdom and legal rights are in no way affected if a protest has not been noted. On the Continent the position is different; there the noting of a protest is a condition precedent to certain legal remedies. For example, consignees are debarred from making a claim for cargo damage unless they protest within 24 hours of taking delivery of the goods and follow this up by a court summons within one month. The master, if he delivers the cargo and accepts the freight, will be barred from claiming the cargo's contribution in general average unless he notes protest within 24 hours and notifies the consignee that he has done so.

It is not essential that a protest should be made on a special form, but it is advisable and usual in practice.

A typical protest form reads as follows:—

NOTE OF PROTEST

On this................ ....day of.....................in the year of our Lord One Thousand Nine Hundred and.....................p^ersonally appeared and presented himself before me...British Consul/Notary Public.................................., ...
Master of the British.....................the.................of...........................
Official Number..................................... and ....Tons Register, which sailed from.....................................on or about the ....day of.....................with a cargo of.....................
bound for.....................and arrived at.....................on the.....................
day of.....................and fearing loss or damage owing to.................
.....................during the voyage, he hereby notes his protest agains all losses, damages, &c., reserving right to extend the same at time and place convenient.

Signed before me..................... (signed) ....
British Consul ⎱ at .... (Master
Notary Public ⎰ (signed) ....
this.....................day of..................... (British Consul)
One Thousand, Nine Hundred and......... (Notary Public)

I certify the foregoing to be a true and correct copy of the original Note of Protest, entered in the Acts of this Consulate and copied therefrom.

British Consulate, ..., 19.........
...., Consul.

N.B.—If the master makes his protest before a consul, the words "Notary Public" will be deleted; if before a notary public, then the words "British Consul" will be deleted. Following the words "owing to" there will be inserted a very brief statement of the cause of the master's fearing loss or damage, such as "collision", "stranding", "heavy weather", etc. Only in the case of heavy weather is it permissible to give details at this stage. Many cases arise where a master feels justified in noting a protest but where he cannot truthfully declare that the ship has encountered heavy weather. In these circumstances it is customary to make use of the phrase "boisterous weather", thereby avoiding exaggeration.

The original protest is entered into a Register at the Consulate or office of the notary public or magistrate, and true and certified copies are supplied to the master on his paying the fee demanded. At least three copies should be obtained so that the master can retain one copy on board and send the others to his owners who may require them for their underwriters and/or average adjusters. If the vessel has cargo for several ports, protest should be noted at each one in turn as it may not be sufficient to protest only at the first port of call.

Extended Protests. It often happens that at the time when a protest is originally noted it has not been established definitely whether, in fact, loss or damage has occurred or not. Even where some loss or damage is certain, the full extent of it will not be known. Should it transpire that there is no loss or damage, then there will be no need to carry the matter any further. Otherwise it will be necessary to extend the protest. In places where a master's protest affirmed by the official seal of a notary or other authority is accepted as conclusive evidence of the facts stated, it is most important than an extended protest should be available to support claims.

If necessary, a protest may be noted at one port and extended at another. In some countries a time limit of six months is imposed but in others, for example in the U.S.A., protests may be extended within any reasonable time after noting. Usually, an extended protest consists of two parts. The first consists of a statement of all the material circumstances leading up to the event and based on log book extracts supported by other available documents, such as weather charts, giving official information on the matter at issue. This statement should be very carefully and accurately drawn up to contain all relevant facts and should not, of course, be at variance with any statement made in the original protest. It must be signed by the master and countersigned by one or more responsible officers and other members of the crew. In the second part the Appearers and the Notary protest against the accident and against losses or damages thereby caused. As the requirements differ from one place to another, the master on arrival at a foreign port in circumstances where it is necessary to note or extend protest should, unless he is already familiar with the local requirements, lose no time in consulting his owner's agents for advice and making certain that all the necessary steps are taken immediately.

In a case of general average a copy of the extended protest will be one of the various documents required by the average adjuster.

In the case of cargo damage, so long as the cause of the damage is within the exceptions in the C/P or B/L, it will be unnecessary to extend protest in the United Kingdom so far as the shipowner's interests are concerned. However, cargo owners may request the master to note and extend protest for their benefit, viz., to support their claim against their underwriters. There is no reason why the master should not accede to such a request so long as it is clearly understood that the cargo owners concerned will themselves pay any expenses involved.

Although protests are often extremely valuable, it must be stressed that noting a protest will never exonerate a master from any failure to endorse B's/L in respect of goods short loaded or goods shipped in a damaged or defective condition. In the same way an endorsement on a B/L of a claim for demurrage incurred at a port of loading will safeguard the shipowner's interest far more effectively than any protest.

MASTER'S LETTERS TO OWNERS

Radio and cable facilities are, of course, always available when the master needs to communicate with his owners in respect of very urgent matters. Such services being relatively expensive, it follows that the master will make use of the ordinary air mail to communicate all important information of a less urgent nature. He should always bear in mind when writing such letters that they are documents that may at some future time be read in court if they contain statements which may become of importance in any legal action. The nature of the information which owners will require from the master in the latter's report following an accident will be found in the section on accidents in Chapter 7.

DISBURSEMENT ACCOUNTS

The master should always keep a careful and accurate account of all monies disbursed on behalf of the ship together with all receipts or vouchers. Unless these matters are attended to by the owner's agents, the master should send an accurate copy of the disbursement sheet with copies of vouchers to the owners before the ship departs from any port abroad. At the same time the master should furnish the owners with full particulars of any crew changes that have been made abroad. If a seaman who had stipulated for an allotment has been discharged or left behind, or if a seaman has been engaged abroad and has stipulated for an allotment, the owners must be informed of all the details, so that they can make the necessary arrangements for terminating or adjusting the allotment, or making payments pursuant to the new allotment, according to circumstances.

CHAPTER 6

ACCOMMODATION, PROVISIONS AND WATER, HEALTH AND HYGIENE

CREW ACCOMMODATION

SECTION 20 of the M.S. Act 1970 states:

The D.o.T. may make regulations with respect to the crew accommodation to be provided in ships registered in the United Kingdom.

The section specifies that the regulations may prescribe detailed requirements for sleeping accommodation, the position in the ship of crew accommodation, and the standards to be observed in constructing, equipping and furnishing the accommodation; they may require plans and specifications of proposed accommodation to be submitted to a surveyor of ships, authorise the surveyor to inspect such work, and provide for maintenance and repair of any such accommodation. Regulations authorised by the section may exempt specified ships from any requirements of the regulations, and may require the master or other authorised officer to inspect accommodation at prescribed intervals.

If the provisions of any regulations made under section 20 are contravened in the case of a ship, the owner or master are liable on summary conviction to a fine not exceeding £1000, and the ship, if in the United Kingdom, may be detained.

In this section "crew accommodation" includes sleeping rooms, mess rooms, sanitary, hospital and recreation accommodation, store rooms and catering accommodation, provided for use by seamen, but does not include any accommodation which is used by, or provided for, the use of passengers.

Crew Accommodation Regulations

After consulting with organisations representing employers, masters, officers and seamen, the Secretary of State to the D.o.T. made the M.S. (Crew Accommodation) Regulations 1978 in June 1978. These regulations apply from 1 July 1979.

The regulations are in two parts. Part I contains requirements to be complied with by:

(a) every ship registered in the United Kingdom the keel of which is laid on or after 1 July 1979; and

294

(b)   any ship registered outside the United Kingdom before 1 July 1979 which is reregistered in the United Kingdom on or after that date; and

(c)   every ship registered in the United Kingdom before 1 July 1979 but which has been reconstructed or substantially altered.

It does not apply to fishing vessels, vessels primarily used for sport or recreation, ships belonging to a General Lighthouse Authority, or a ship to which Part II applies.

Part II applies to every ship registered in the United Kingdom whose keel was laid before 1 July 1979, unless or until she is reconstructed or substantially altered.   Fishing vessels, vessels primarily used for sport or recreation, and ships belonging to a General Lighthouse Authority are excepted from Part II.

Extension to Unregistered British Ships.   The provisions of section 20, and Part I of the regulations are extended to unregistered British ships and to masters and seamen employed in them.   This extension applies to every British ship which is wholly owned by a person resident in, or by a company having a principal place of business in, the United Kingdom and which is required to be registered under the M.S. Act 1894, but is not so registered in the United Kingdom or elsewhere.

Some of the more important requirements of the regulations are as follows:

Plans.   A plan of a new ship showing the disposition of the crew accommodation must be submitted to D.o.T. surveyor before construction begins, and detailed plans of the accommodation arrangements are required before construction of the accommodation begins. Similar plans are required when re-construction or alteration of accommodation takes place in an existing ship.

Siting.   Apart for storerooms, accommodation must be wholly situated above the summer loadline and be situated either amidships or aft so as to exclude noise from other parts of the ship.   In a passenger ship sleeping rooms may not be directly beneath a working passageway.

Height All parts of the crew accommodation, except cold store rooms, shall have a clear headroom of at least 1·98 metres at every point where full and free movement is necessary.

Bulkheads.   Those enclosing any part of the accommodation which are exposed to the weather must be of steel or other suitable material and must be watertight, with weathertight means of closure provided for openings, and where necessary insulated to prevent overheating or condensation. Bulkheads separating accommodation from cargo or machinery spaces, bunkers, store rooms, lamp or paint rooms, battery lockers etc. must be gastight, and watertight where necessary to protect the crew accommodation.

Interior Bulkheads. These must be constructed of steel or other suitable material. Bulkheads separating crew accommodation from sanitary accommodation, galley, laundry, cold store etc. must be gastight, and watertight to a sufficient height. (Not less than 100 mm. in doorways.)

Overhead Decks. These, in ships built of metal, if forming the crown of the accommodation and exposed to the weather, must be of metal. The upper side must be sheathed with wood, properly laid and caulked, or other approved material. Wood sheathing to be at least 57 mm. thick. Other material when used to provide equivalent thermal insulation. Alternatively a deck may be insulated on its underside to provide the equivalent of a wooden deck 57 mm. thick. In ships not built of metal, any wooden overhead deck shall be not less than 63 mm. thick.

Floor Decks. Decks forming floors are to be properly constructed and shall have a surface giving a good foothold and which can be easily kept clean. If directly over an oil tank, it shall be oiltight. Any floor covering must be impervious to water, and if over an oil tank impervious to oil. If of wood, they must be at least 63 mm. thick, properly laid and caulked. Decks made of metal shall be covered with approved material providing thermal insulation equivalent to 57 mm. of wood deck, except in sanitary accommodation, galleys, laundries etc., which shall be covered with terrazzo, tiles or other hard material impervious to liquids. Floor deck coverings in officers' sleeping and day rooms, and in ships of 25,000 tons gross and over, in ratings' sleeping rooms, shall be covered with a fitted carpet over all exposed parts of the floor deck.

General Protection. Entrances into crew accommodation, if from the open deck, to be protected against weather and sea, and situated so that access is possible at all times in all weathers. At least one means of access to a sleeping room, day room etc. shall be from an enclosed passageway. Two entirely separate escape routes are to be provided for each compartment; escape routes which are to lead to boats or liferafts are not to pass through machinery spaces, galleys or other spaces where there is a high risk of injury from fire or steam etc. Stairs or ladders are to be of steel.

Steam pipes to steering gear, winches etc. are not to pass through accommodation, but where no other arrangement is practicable, may pass through passageways when properly encased and constructed. Steam and hot water pipes serving accommodation must be lagged to protect the crew against injury and discomfort, and cold water pipes must be lagged to prevent condensation.

Hawse pipes shall not pass through crew accommodation. Ships regularly employed on voyages to the Tropics or Persian Gulf must have adequate awnings.

Heating. All ships, except those solely employed in the Tropics or Persian Gulf, are required to have permanently installed heating systems. When the ventilation system is working so as to supply at least 25 cu. m. of fresh air per hour per person the accommodation is designed to accommodate, the heating system must be capable of maintaining a temperature of 21°C against an outside temperature of −1°C. The system must be operated by steam, hot water, electricity, or be a system supplying warm air. Radiators etc. are to be shielded to prevent danger or discomfort. The heating must be capable of being turned on and off and varied, and the operation of heaters must not be affected by the use or non-use of other appliances. The system is required to be in operation at all times when crew members are living or working on board and the circumstances require it, unless, when in port, a safe and efficient temporary means of heating the parts of the crew accommodation then in use to the required standard is provided.

Lighting. All accommodation except galleys, pantries, laundries, drying rooms and store rooms etc. must be adequately lit by natural light. Adequately lit means bright enough in day time in clear weather for a person with normal sight to read an ordinary newspaper in any part of the space available for free movement. An adequate electric lighting system complying with Schedule 3 to the regulations must be installed. It must include an electric reading light, with switch, at the head of each bed.

Ventilation. Enclosed spaces in accommodation are to be ventilated by a system capable of maintaining the air in a state of purity sufficient for the health and comfort of the crew in all conditions of weather and climate the ship is likely to meet on its intended voyages. It must be controllable and additional to scuttles, skylights, doors etc. In foreign going ships of 1,000 tons gross and over, except those regularly employed in latitudes north of 50° North or south of 45° South, and in all ships under 1,000 tons gross regularly on voyages solely within the Tropics or the Persian Gulf, the ventilation system is to be an air conditioning system capable of maintaining a temperature of 29°C (dry bulb) with 50% relative humidity, when ambient temperature is 32°C (dry bulb) with 78% relative humidity. The minimum number of air changes is to be 8 per hour in mess or recreation rooms, and 6 per hour elsewhere. Sanitary accommodation, laundries, drying rooms, etc. are to be provided with a mechanical exhaust ventilation system. Ships not fitted with an air conditioning system are to be fitted with a trunked mechanical ventilation system unless they are under 500 tons gross and either

Home Trade ships, or ships regularly trading on New Zealand coast, or latitudes north of 50° North or south of 45° South. Every enclosed space not ventilated by air conditioning, or by a trunked mechanical ventilation system, must be provided with a natural system of inlet and exhaust ventilation.

Side Scuttles and Windows. Where these are necessary to provide the regulation standard of light, they must be of opening type unless required for reasons of safety to be of a non-opening type. In rooms served by an air conditioning system, only 50% of side scuttles or windows need be of opening type. In ships of 3,000 tons gross or over every side scuttle shall be at least 300 mm. in diameter.

Drainage. Pipes and channels are to be provided to clear water shipped from the sea. Soil and other waste drainage systems are to be fitted with water seals, air vents and storm valves to prevent siphonage or blow-back. Scuppers in sanitary accommodation and laundries are to be at least 50 mm. in diameter and serve only such spaces. There must be no drainage into sanitary accommodation from other sources except other sanitary accommodation.

Interior Finishes. Interior walls and ceilings are to be painted white or a light colour, or covered with a suitable material. Paints or other materials with a nitro-cellulose or other highly flammable base are forbidden. Wooden parts of furniture and fittings must be painted, varnished or finished by other suitable means. Surface finishes must be easily kept clean. Furniture and fittings shall be arranged so as not to harbour dirt and vermin.

Marking. Sleeping spaces must be marked inside the room, and other spaces either inside or over the entrance door, to indicate the use for which the space is certified. Marks are to be cut in the structure or otherwise made permanent.

Sleeping Rooms. These are to be provided unless no crew members are required to sleep on board.

The following groups of persons are to have rooms separate from those provided for other groups: (a) officers, (b) petty officers, (c) cadets, (d) other deck ratings, (e) other engine room ratings, (f) other catering department ratings. Where general purpose ratings are employed groups (d) and (e) shall count as one group.

The maximum number of persons per room is to be as follows:

(a) Officers—one person per room.
(b) Cadets—where practicable, one per room and never more than two per room.
(c) Petty officers—one person per room.
(d) Other ratings—
    (i) ships under 25,000 tons gross (not passenger ships), not more than two per room;

(ii) ships 25,000 tons gross or over (not passenger ships) one
per room, but boy ratings not more than two per room;
(iii) passenger ships, not more than four persons per room.

Where there is more than one rating per room, those ratings shall
be members of the same watch.

The minimum floor area per person is varied according to the
tonnage of the ship, whether passenger or not, and to the number of
berths the room is certified for. It varies from 2·35 sq. m. in a 3 or
4 berth room in ships under 3,000 tons gross, to 4·75 sq. m. in single
berth rooms in ships 10,000 tons gross or over. Day rooms, next to
sleeping rooms, shall be provided in ships of 3,000 tons gross or
over for the Chief Officer, Chief Engineer, Second Engineer and the
Purser/Catering Officer.

Spaces occupied by berths, lockers, seats or chests of drawers
and other furniture is to be included when measuring floor area
unless the space is of such small size or irregular shape that it does
not add to the space for free movement or cannot accommodate
furniture.

The room for the First or only Radio Officer shall be as near as
practicable to the Radio room.

Beds. In each room there must be one for each person accom‚
modated. The framework etc. must be of metal or other hard-
smooth material not likely to corrode or harbour vermin. Tubular
frames must be without perforations. Adjoining beds are to have
separating screens.

Beds are not to be within 100 mm. of hot air trunks, or except
in certain circumstances within 50 mm. of the ship's side or a bulkhead. Not more than two tiers are allowed. Other regulations
prescribe the length, breadth and spacing of beds. Spring under-
mattresses are demanded and other mattresses must be damp-proof
and vermin-proof.

Furniture and Fittings. Very detailed regulations set out what is
required to furnish the sleeping rooms of the various ratings and
officers, and there are further rules for the furnishing of mess rooms.

Mess Rooms. These are to be large enough to accommodate the
greatest number of persons likely to use them at any one time. No
mess rooms shall be combined with a sleeping room, except, with
certain exceptions, in ships under 300 tons gross where it is impracticable to provide a separate mess room.

In ships of 500 tons gross and over the ratings' mess room must
be separate from that for the master and officers. Unless officers'
accommodation is in widely separated parts of the ship, a single
mess room is to be provided for all officers.

In ships of 1,000 tons gross and over, the following are to have
separate mess rooms: (*a*) deck petty officers, (*b*) engine room petty

officers, (c) other deck ratings, (d) other engine room ratings. But combined mess rooms may be permitted for (i) deck and engine room petty officers, (ii) petty officers and ratings of the same department, (iii) deck and engine room ratings. A single mess room for use by all deck and engine room ratings is also permitted.

In Foreign going ships and certain Home Trade ships of 3,000 tons gross and over, separate mess rooms are to be provided for catering department ratings, except where a single mess room is provided for all ratings.

Cadets are to have a separate mess room unless they share the officers' mess room.

Recreation Spaces. In Home Trade ships of 8,000 tons gross or over and Foreign going ships of 3,000 tons gross or over, a recreation room furnished with tables, easy chairs and a bookcase is to be provided for the officers. A similar recreation room is to be provided for the ratings on every ship of 8,000 tons gross and over. For ships other than those described above, the mess room is to be kept available and furnished for use as a recreation room. Facilities for watching films and television, a separate hobbies and games room, and where practicable, a swimming pool are to be provided for the crew on every ship over 8,000 tons gross. A communal bookcase for a ship's library is to be provided and to be accessible to all crew members on ships of 500 tons gross and over.

Offices. In ships of 3,000 tons gross and over, two rooms are to be provided as offices; one for all the deck officers and one for all the engineer officers.

Sanitary Accommodation. The regulations specify the number of private and semi-private bathrooms to be provided for officers on ships over 5,000 tons gross, and in ships over 25,000 tons gross, other than passenger ships, the number of semi-private bathrooms to be provided for ratings. For those crew members not provided with private or semi-private accommodation, there is to be provided separate accommodation for officers and cadets, petty officers, other ratings and female staff, on the basis of one bath or shower, one wash basin, one mirror and one W.C. per group of 6 persons or less. The regulations describe in detail the access, facilities, fittings and arrangements to be provided in such accommodation. In ships of 1,600 tons gross and over, a room containing a W.C. and wash basin adjacent to the bridge, engine room control compartment and galley is to be provided.

Drinking Water Supply. Cold drinking water for drinking, cooking and dish washing is to be laid on to taps in galleys, bar and pantries, and supplied from tanks having a minimum capacity of at least 18 litres per person for each day likely to elapse between watering ports. If water supply to sanitary accommodation is of drinking water standard, the storage tanks may be combined, and then the total capacity is to be 90 litres per person. If drinking water is provided by a distilling or evaporating plant, the tank storage capacity must be at least two days supply. In every ship of 1,000 tons gross and over, a supply of cooled drinking water must be available to the crew.

Washing Water Supply. Fresh water must be laid on to wash basins, baths and showers from tanks having a minimum capacity of 72 litres per person for each day likely to elapse between watering ports, alternatively tanks for two days supply of fresh water if water is provided by a distilling or evaporating plant.

Laundry. In ships of 500 tons gross and over, washing machines or washing troughs are to be provided. Drying machines or a drying room must be provided and adequate facilities for ironing clothes.

Oilskin Lockers. Lockers, adequately ventilated, must be provided for hanging up oilskins and working clothes, separate compartments being required for officers and ratings. Such lockers must be outside sleeping rooms but readily accessible therefrom.

W.C.s. There must be a minimum of:
On ships 500 tons gross or over but under 800 tons—3.
On ships 800 tons gross or over but under 3,000 tons—4.
On ships 3,000 tons gross or over—6.

Galleys. A galley must be provided as close to mess rooms as possible to enable food to be served hot in all weathers, but placed so that dust from dry cargoes will not enter it. The arrangement and equipment of galleys is set down in detail in the regulations.

Dry Provision Store Rooms. One or more are to be provided; each must have sufficient shelves, cupboards and bins, and they must not be over or alongside a space subject to abnormal heat.

Cold Store Rooms and Refrigerator. Adequate cold store rooms or facilities are to be provided bearing in mind the number of crew and period likely to elapse between replenishments. Access must be from a passageway, galley, pantry or from another cold store room. Machinery making use of ammonia or methyl chloride as refrigerant is not permitted.

Hospitals. Every ship intended to be continuously at sea for more than 3 days and carrying a crew of 15 or more must have a space appropriated for use as a permanent hospital which may be used only for the treatment of the sick and injured, and provided with at least one bed for every 50 crew members, or fraction of 50. Unless all personnel have single berth sleeping rooms, in every other ship a suitable room is to be appropriated for use as a temporary hospital in case of need. An independent natural ventilation system shall be provided in addition to any other. The regulations with respect to furnishings and fittings, which go into considerable detail, require that the space shall be capable of admitting a stretcher, and provide that at least one bed therein shall be accessible from both sides.

Medical Cabinet. This must be suitable for storing the medicines and medical stores required to be carried by the ship, be well ventilated, fitted in the crew accommodation so that it is always dry, accessible from (but not in) the hospital, and not subject to abnormal heat. The cabinet is to have either interior electric light, or one immediately outside it. The outer door must be fitted with a lock, and within a lockable dangerous drugs cupboard must be provided.

Protection from Mosquitoes. Every ship engaged on voyages to:
(a) all ports on coast of Africa, and all ports in Asia, Central and South America between 30°N. and 35°S., or
(b) ports on the coast of the Malagasy Republic,
must have the crew accommodation protected by rust-proof wire screens, or screens of other suitable material, against the admission of mosquitoes. The screening must be fitted or provided for all side-scuttles, windows, and skylights which can be opened, all natural ventilators and all doors leading to the open deck, except that in accommodation with an air conditioning system where side scuttles or windows are locked and all doors to the open deck are self-closing type, screening need not be provided.

Maintenance and Inspection. All accommodation must be maintained in a clean and habitable condition, and the equipment and installations kept in good working order. All spaces other than store rooms must be kept free of stores, cargo, and property not belonging to or provided for the occupants.

The master, or an officer appointed by him, accompanied by one or more of the crew must inspect every part of the accommodation at intervals not exceeding 7 days. An official log book entry must be made showing the time and date, the names and ranks of the persons making the inspection, and particulars of any non-compliance with the regulations.

Existing Ships. Ships registered in the United Kingdom whose keel was laid before 1 July 1979 will continue to comply with the amended 1953 regulations, which are restated in Schedule 6 of the new regulations, until such time as they are reconstructed or substantially rebuilt.

Passengers. Accommodation provided in conformity with the Crew Accommodation Regulations may not be used by passengers.

Provisions and Water

Section 21 of the M.S. Act 1970 provides as follows:—

(1) The D.o.T. may make regulations requiring such provisions and water to be provided for seamen employed in ships registered in the United Kingdom or any description of such ships as may be specified in the regulations; and regulations under this section may make different provision for different circumstances and different descriptions of seamen.

(2) Regulations under this section may require a ship to carry such weighing and measuring equipment as may be necessary to ensure that the quantities of provisions and water supplied to seamen employed in the ship are in accordance with the regulations.

(3) The D.o.T. may exempt any ship from any requirement of the regulations made under this section, either generally or in respect of a particular voyage.

(4) If the provisions of any regulations made under this section are not complied with in the case of a ship the master or owner shall be liable on summary conviction to a fine not exceeding £100 unless he proves that the failure to comply was not due to his neglect or default.

(5) If a person empowered under this Act to inspect the provsions and water to be supplied to the seamen employed in a ship is not satisfied that they are in accordance with regulations made under this section the ship, if in the United Kingdom, may be detained.

Complaints about Provisions or Water

Section 22 of the 1970 Act states:—

(1) If three or more seamen employed in a ship registered in the United Kingdom consider that the provisions or water provided for the seamen employed in that ship are not in accordance with regulations made under section 21 of this Act (whether because of bad quality, unfitness for use or deficiency in quantity) they may complain to the master, who shall investigate the complaint.

(2) If the seamen are dissatisfied with the action taken by the master as a result of his investigation or by his failure to take any action they may state their dissatisfaction to him and may claim to complain to a superintendent or proper officer; and thereupon the master shall make adequate arrangements to enable the seamen to do so as soon as the service of the ship permits.

(3) The superintendent or proper officer to whom a complaint has been made under this section shall investigate the complaint and may examine the provisions or water or cause them to be examined.

(4) If the master fails without reasonable cause to comply with the provisions of subsection (2) of this section he shall be liable on summary conviction to a fine not exceeding £200, and if he has been

notified in writing by the person making an examination under subsection (3) of this section that any provisions or water are found to be unfit for use or not of the quality required by the regulations, then,—

    (a) if they are not replaced within a reasonable time the master or owner shall be liable on summary conviction to a fine not exceeding £500 unless he proves that the failure to replace them was not due to his neglect or default; and

    (b) if the master, without reasonable cause, permits them to be used he shall be liable on summary conviction to a fine not exceeding £500.

The Merchant Shipping (Provisions and Water) Regulations 1972

These are the regulations made under section 21(1) of the 1970 Act and amended in 1975 comments on which appear below.

In Regulation 1 it is stated that "ship" means a ship registered in the U.K. but does not include a fishing vessel. There are separate regulations for fishing vessels. It also states that "tons" means gross tonnage (the larger in the case of a ship having alternative gross tonnages).

Regulation 2 requires that there shall be provided for each seaman employed in a ship of not less than 80 tons other than (a) a ship in which the crew furnish their own provisions and water; (b) a ship belonging to a general lighthouse authority; or (c) a pleasure yacht; provisions and water in accordance with the scales referred to in Regulation 3.

Regulation 3 provides that Scale I of the Schedule applies to a seaman other than a seaman who is ordinarily resident in India, Pakistan, Bangladesh, Singapore or Hong Kong; that the appropriate scale for a seaman ordinarily resident in India is Scale II; in Pakistan Scale III; in Bangladesh Scale III; in Singapore or Hong Kong Scale IV.

Regulation 4 requires that provisions and water (a) shall be of fine, first, good or prime quality, as may, in the case of any particular provision, be appropriate; (b) shall not contain anything which is likely to cause sickness or injury to health or which renders any provision or water unpalatable; and (c) shall otherwise be fit for consumption.

Regulation 5 relates to cases where quantities of provisions are prescribed by reference to a week and requires that, in certain cases, they shall be provided daily in approximately equal amounts and in other cases reasonably distributed throughout each week. It also requires that proportionate amounts are to be provided in respect of part of a week.

Regulation 6 requires that where, in any paragraph in any scale, more than one provision is specified, subject to that paragraph, the prescribed quantity may be made up of one of, or of any combination of, those provisions.

Regulation 7 requires that except where otherwise prescribed in column 2 or column 3 in any paragraph in any scale, the quantity of provisions to be provided in accordance with regulations 8 and 9 shall be the same as that prescribed in column 1 in that paragraph.

Regulation 8, which relates to Scale I, states that where an equivalent provision is described it may be provided instead of the standard provision, but not on more than 3 days in any week unless on any day it is not practicable to provide the standard provision. If not possible to provide either the standard or equivalent provision, the prescribed substitute provision shall be provided.

Regulation 9, which relates to Scales II, III and IV, states that where it is not practicable to provide a provision, the substitute prescribed shall be provided.

Regulation 10, relating to Scales II and III, sets out special requirements for (a) the period beginning 1st October and ending 31st March when the ship is north of 30°N. in the Atlantic or elsewhere north of 24°N.; and (b) the period beginning 1st May and ending 30th September when the ship is south of 30°S.

Regulation 11 requires that there shall be carried in every ship to which Regulation 2 applies such weighing and measuring equipment as may be necessary to ensure that quantities of provisions and water supplied are in accordance with the Regulations.

The Schedule sets out the scales referred to above. The three columns of Scale I give, respectively, standard provisions, equivalent provisions and substitute provisions, setting out the quantities per week in each case. Scales II, III and IV each have two columns, for standard and substitute provisions respectively, and indicate whether particular quantities are weekly, daily, to be provided on each alternate day or three times a week.

Inspection of Provisions Ashore

Subsection (3) of section 76 of the M.S. Act 1970 provides that where a surveyor of ships, a superintendent or any person appointed by the D.o.T. to exercise powers under section 76 has reasonable grounds for believing that there are on any premises provisions or water intended for supply to a ship registered in the United Kingdom which, if provided on the ship, would not be in accordance with regulations under section 21 of the Act, he may enter the premises and inspect the provisions and water for the purpose of ascertaining whether they would be in accordance with those regulations. The penalty for obstructing such an inspector is a fine not exceeding £1000 on summary conviction.

Food and Catering Convention. By agreement with the National Maritime Board the terms of this Convention apply to every ship which is required to carry a certificated cook. (See Chapter 4.) The master of any such ship, or an officer deputed by him, must not less than once per week inspect the food and water provided for the crew and enter the result of the inspection in the official log book.

Tinned and Pickled Foodstuffs. Before the advent of refrigerators and cold storage, the effective preservation of food on long voyages was always a problem of considerable magnitude, and much reliance had to be placed on tinned and pickled products. These often became tainted when kept on board for a long time and great care was necessary to ensure that unfit provisions were not served to the crew. The "Ship Captain's Medical Guide" contained much good advice on applying suitable tests. Under modern conditions this problem ought not to arise, but it should be understood that it is still primarily the master's responsibility to make certain that only good wholesome food is served. Where tinned and pickled foods are used, therefore, they should be carefully inspected before being served.

Drinking Water. It is very seldom that water is found to be chemically impure. Danger usually arises through germ content, and from this point of view the mere appearance of water is nc guide. It is possible for clear sparkling water to contain cholera, typhoid, and other deadly organisms whilst, on the other hand, discoloured water may be absolutely harmless. When in doubt about the quality and condition of fresh water supplied at a port abroad, local agents or the British Consul should be able to give reliable information.

Fresh water storage tanks must be kept clean, and it is strongly recommended that they be lined with bitumastic or other approved material or cement wash. Men employed to clean tanks should wear clean clothing and footwear and should be free from disease. In many ports harbour water is polluted, and a delivery hose which has fallen in the water in the process of connecting up should be firmly refused. Delivery cocks are often sunk into a dock edge and these pits may contain foul water. Accordingly, it is important to make sure that such condition is rectified before filling hoses are connected.

If the master has reason to be suspicious of the quality of water supplied, he should take no chances, and should take immediate steps to have it purified by means of stabilised chloride of lime. This is supplied in powder form and when mixed with water in the proportion of 1 part in 250,000 has the effect of destroying all organisms in the water. Each tin of powder contains a measure which holds 60 grains (*i.e.*, $\frac{1}{8}$th oz.) and is enough to purify 200 gallons. (One ton of fresh-water $=36$ cu. ft. $=224$ gallons.) The recommended method is to measure out enough powder for the capacity of the tank, pouring each measureful on to a sheet of clean paper. This should be put into a clean jug and a small quantity of water added. After stirring it to a paste, and breaking up any lumps, more water should be added and the stirring continued.

When the tank is about one quarter full the mixture should be poured in, and after the tank is filled an hour or so should be allowed to elapse before any of its contents are used. By that time all taste and smell from the powder should have vanished. In the event of the drinking water supply running out so that boiler water has to be used for drinking, the above treatment should be adopted. The minute quantity of powder cannot possibly do any damage to the boilers.

MEDICAL STORES AND ANTI-SCORBUTICS

Section 24 of the M.S. Act 1970 states:—

(1) The D.o.T. may make regulations requiring ships registered in the United Kingdom, or such descriptions of ships registered in the United Kingdom as may be specified in the regulations, to carry such medicines and other medical stores (including books containing instructions and advice) as may be specified in the regulations; and the regulations may make different provision for different circumstances.

(2) If a ship goes to sea or attempts to go to sea without carrying the medical stores which it is required to carry by regulations under this section the master or owner shall be liable on summary conviction to a fine not exceeding £500 unless he proves that the failure to carry the stores was not due to his neglect or default.

(3) If a person empowered under this Act to inspect the medical stores carried in a ship is not satisfied that the ship carries the stores which it is required to carry by regulations under this section, the ship, if in the United Kingdom, may be detained.

The M.S. (Medical Scales) Regulations 1974 (S.I. 1974 No. 1193) have now been made under powers given by sections 24 and 92 of the M.S. Act 1970. The regulations, which came into force on 1st October 1974, provide for six scales and there were amendments to them in 1975 and 1980.

The new scales specify medicines and medical stores to be carried on ships registered in the United Kingdom, but they do not apply to pleasure yachts, fishing boats and general lighthouse authority ships.

Medicines and other medical stores shall be carried in every such ship **whenever the ship goes to sea** in accordance with the following scales:—

Scale I applies to ships which are required by law to carry a qualified doctor. (F.G. ship with 100 persons or more on board.)

Scale II applies to ships which are not required by law to carry a qualified doctor and to which scales III, IV and V do not apply.

Scales III, IV, V and VI apply to ships which are not required by law to carry a qualified doctor and which are proceeding on voyages in the following areas:—

Scale III. (a) To or from any place in the United Kingdom
(except Northern Ireland) to or from any place in Northern
Ireland or in the Republic of Ireland, or (b) to or from any
place in the United Kingdom (including Northern Ireland)
or the Republic of Ireland to or from any place in the Isle
of Man, the Channel Islands, Iceland, the Faroe Islands or
Western Europe between Narvik and Corunna inclusive,
including any place in the Baltic Sea, the Gulf of Finland or
the Gulf of Bothnia.

Scale IV.   To or from any place on the mainland of Scotland
or the Inner Hebrides to or from any place in the Outer
Hebrides, the Isles of Shetland or the Isles of Orkney; or
to or from any place in the Isles of Shetland to or from any
place in the Isles of Orkney.

Scale V.   Not being a voyage to which scales III and IV apply,
between places in the United Kingdom (except Northern
Ireland) or from and returning to any such place, or between
places in Northern Ireland or between places in the Republic
of Ireland or between places in Northern Ireland and in the
Republic of Ireland or from and returning to any such place.

Scale VI applies to passenger ships (i.e. ships carrying more
than 12 passengers) which are proceeding on a voyage to
which Scale III, IV or V applies.

All medicines and other medical stores specified in the scales must
conform to the standards and requirements of the British Pharmaco-
poeia, or the British Pharmaceutical Codex or the British National
Formulary, and with the Schedules to the regulations.

Regulation 5 specifies the construction and labelling of any containers used to hold medicines or medical stores, and regulation 6
requires such containers to be marked with the latest date of use, or
the date of manufacture. The medicines in question are required to
have a shelf life of at least 3 months beginning when the ship goes to sea.

The quantities specified in the scales are based on the number
of persons carried on board and the length of voyage. The latest
edition of the Ships Captain's Medical Guide with any amendments
must be carried on all ships, together with a copy of the scales.

Section 24 of the M.S. Act 1970 and the regulations extend also to
unregistered British ships owned by persons resident in, or companies
having their principal place of business in, the United Kingdom and
which are required to be registered under the M.S. Act 1894 but are
not so registered, and to masters and seamen employed in them.

Maintenance of Medical Cabinets. Owners and masters are urged
to co-operate in the arrangements made to secure that medical
cabinets are properly maintained and equipped.

Medical Treatment on board Ship

Section 25 of the 1970 Act provides that where a ship registered in the United Kingdom does not carry a doctor among the seamen employed in it the master shall make arrangements for securing that any medical attention on board the ship is given either by him or under his supervision by a person appointed by him for the purpose.

Expenses of Medical Treatment, etc. during Voyage

Section 26 of the M.S. Act 1970 states:—

If a person, while employed in a ship registered in the United Kingdom, receives outside the United Kingdom any surgical or medical treatment or such dental or optical treatment (including the repair or replacement of any appliance) as cannot be postponed without impairing efficiency, the reasonable expenses thereof shall be borne by the persons employing him; and if he dies while so employed and is buried or cremated outside the United Kingdom, the expenses of his burial or cremation shall also be borne by those persons.

It should be noted that the employer's obligation to bear the cost of medical treatment is not restricted to illness, etc. "in the service of the ship", nor is illness due to the seaman's own wilful act, default or misbehaviour excluded.

There is an N.M.B. agreement to the effect that, if a seaman dies during employment, or after being left behind due to illness or injury, and if he would have been entitled to repatriation under the Merchant Shipping Acts, employers will make such arrangements as are practicable, at the request of the next of kin, to return the body of the deceased seaman to the next of kin at the employer's expense. It is recognised that lack of preservation facilities, the requirements of port health regulations, or foreign administrations, or the nature of the death, may mean that alternative arrangements for the disposal of the body may have to be made.

Anti-scorbutics. With the repeal of section 200 of the Principal Act and the Fifth Schedule thereto, the former rules as to anti-scorbutics no longer apply. It is interesting to note, however, that Scales II and III in the schedule to the Provisions and Water Regulations include a daily allowance of lime juice. It would seem, therefore, that our American friends will have to transfer the sobriquet "limey" from residents of the U.K. to residents of India, Pakistan and Bangladesh.

Ship's Doctor. *The repeal of section 209 of the Principal Act will not take effect until regulations under section 43 of the M.S.A. 1970 are made and brought into operation. In the meantime, therefore, it is still the rule that every foreign-going ship having 100 persons or upwards on board must carry a duly qualified medical practitioner.

* Now see S.I. 1981 No. 1065 from 1.9.81.

L

PUBLIC HEALTH (SHIPS) REGULATIONS

These regulations apply only to England and Wales, but there are also the Public Health (Ships) (Scotland) Regulations, and Public Health (Ships) Regulations (Northern Ireland). These are all very similar, and since there is a large measure of international co-operation in the matter of public health it will generally be found that regulations in force in practically all maritime countries will not vary very widely. The following extracts from the United Kingdom regulations are particularly important.

The term *Infectious Disease* used in these regulations means cholera, plague, smallpox and yellow fever, or any other infectious or contagious disease other than venereal disease or tuberculosis. An *Infected ship* means:

(a) a ship which has on board on arrival a case of cholera, plague, smallpox or yellow fever, or a case of lassa fever, rabies, viral haemorrhagic fever or marburg disease; or

(b) a ship on which a plague infected rodent is found on arrival; or

(c) a ship which has had on board during its voyage: (i) a case of plague develop more than 6 days after the embarkation of the affected person; or (ii) a case of cholera less than 5 days before arrival; or (iii) a case of yellow fever or smallpox; and on which no such case has been subjected to appropriate measures before the ship's arrival.

The term *Suspected ship* applies to:

(a) a ship not having a case of plague, but which had one which developed within 6 days of embarkation; or

(b) a ship on which there is abnormal mortality among rodents, the cause of which is unknown; or

(c) a ship which had a case of cholera more than 5 days before arrival; or

(d) a ship which left, within 6 days before arrival, an area infected with yellow fever; or

(e) a ship which has on board on arrival a person who the medical officer considers may have been exposed to infection from lassa fever, rabies, viral haemorrhagic fever or marburg disease.

In respect of (a) and (c) a ship will not be regarded as suspect if she has been subjected to appropriate measures equivalent to the additional measures specified in Schedule 4.

Additional Measures. The measures prescribed for infected or suspected ships will vary according to circumstances, but may include:

persons to be disinsected and placed under surveillance,

baggage to be disinsected and disinfected, also other articles and parts of the ship, deratting the ship and disinsecting,

isolation of persons,

disinfection and removal of water on board, and disinfection of tanks,

taking samples of food for culture examination,

vaccination of persons,

medical examination of persons,

supervision of unloading, and

control of communication with the shore.

An *Excepted Port* is any port in Belgium, France, Greece, the Republic of Ireland, Italy, Luxembourg, the Netherlands, Spain, and the United Kingdom, Channel Islands and the Isle of Man.

Incoming Ships. The master of a ship which has called at a port outside the U.K., or met with an offshore installation, or met with a ship which has proceeded from a foreign port, must ascertain the health of all persons on board before arrival at a U.K. port. If the vessel is healthy, the ship may proceed to its berth, although it may be stopped and its health checked at the boarding station. The master may if he wishes radio the state of health of his ship to the authorities, who may if satisfied transmit free pratique by radio or otherwise.

Illness on Board. The master must report by radio to the health authority not more than 12 hours, and not less than 4 hours, before the ship's E.T.A., or if that is not possible, then immediately on arrival:

(a) the occurrence on board before arrival of:

  (i) a person's death on board other than by accident; or

  (ii) illness on board where the patient's temperature was 38°C or more and which was accompanied by a rash, glandular swelling or jaundice, or where such temperature persisted for more than 48 hours; or

  (iii) an illness where a person has, or had, diarrhoea severe enough to interfere with work or normal activities;

(b) any case on board of infectious disease, or case with similar symptoms;

(c) any circumstances which might cause spread of infectious disease; and

(d) the presence of animals or captive birds (including poultry), and any death or sickness amongst them.

Coded radio messages must conform with part VIII of the International Code of Signals. On arrival within the district, the appropriate visual signal from the Code shall be shown until the ship is granted free pratique by an authorised officer.

The more important pratique messages in Part VIII of the International Code of Signals are:

ZS or Q My vessel is healthy and I request free pratique.

*QQ   I require health clearance.

ZT   My Maritime Declaration of Health has negative answers to the six health questions.

ZU   My Maritime Declaration of Health has a positive answer to question(s) . . . . . . (indicate number(s)).

ZV   I believe I have been in an infected area during the last 30 days.

ZW   I require Port Medical Officer.

*By night, a red light over a white light may be shown, where it can best be seen, by vessels requiring health clearance. These lights should be about 2 metres apart, should be exhibited within the precincts of a port, and should be visible all round the horizon as nearly as possible.

Maritime Declaration of Health. On arrival, a master who has had to report an infectious disease or a death, or is directed by the medical officer to do so, must complete a Maritime Declaration of Health and deliver it to an authorised officer. The Declaration requires details about the voyage, or the last four weeks of it, and requires answers to health questions, ports of call, passenger and crew numbers, etc. If within four weeks the ship calls at another district, the master must report any case or suspected case of infectious disease which has occurred since the Declaration was delivered. (The layout of the Declaration is shown in Chapter 10.)

Restrictions on Boarding or Leaving a Ship. Where the authorised officer directs, or where a master is required to report an infectious disease, no person other than the pilot, a customs officer or an immigration officer is to board or leave the vessel without permission until free pratique has been granted. The master must take steps to ensure compliance.

Supply of Information by Masters. On arrival a master is required to answer all questions about health conditions on board which may be put to him by a customs or authorised officer. He must notify any circumstances on board which are likely to cause the spread of infectious disease, and including the presence of animals or captive birds of any species, or mortality or sickness among such animals or birds.

Detention of Ships. Infected or suspected ships or any other ship on which there has been, during its current voyage and within the last four weeks, a case of disease subject to the International Health Regulations and which has not been subjected to appropriate additional measures shall be taken on arrival to a mooring station for medical inspection, unless an authorised officer allows or directs otherwise. The medical officer shall inspect the ship and persons as soon as possible, and may then require the ship to remain at the mooring station for further and additional measures.

Deratting, and Deratting Exemption Certificates. According to the regulations an "approved port" is one where deratting exemption certificates only are issued, whilst a "designated approved port" is one where both deratting and deratting exemption certificates are issued.

If a ship from a foreign port has no valid certificate, the medical officer for the district must either have the ship inspected to ascertain whether she is kept in such a condition that the number of rodents on board is negligible, or direct the ship to go to the nearest approved or designated approved port for the purpose. If, after such inspection, the medical officer is satisfied with the condition of the ship he is required to issue a Deratting Exemption Certificate. If not satisfied, he shall require the ship to be deratted, by fumigation or otherwise, or to proceed to a designated approved port for the purpose. In that case, when deratting is satisfactorily completed, a Deratting Certificate is issued.

If the master produces a Deratting or a Deratting Exemption Certificate but the authorised officer has evidence that the deratting was not satisfactorily completed, or that there is evidence of rodents on board, he may require the ship to be deratted.

Inspection, deratting if necessary, and the issue of the appropriate certificate can be obtained at any time, if desired, on a written application from the shipowner or master. The owner or master must pay the established charges for these services, and keep a copy of the certificate on board the ship. Certificates remain valid for 6 months; or 7 months if the ship is proceeding to an approved or designated approved port.

Outgoing Ships. Where a ship is due to depart for a port outside the U.K., the Medical Officer may where he has reasonable grounds for believing a person to be suffering from a disease subject to the International Health Regulations, examine such person who proposes to embark, prohibit embarkation, or place any person under surveillance. He must notify the master accordingly.

Ships unwilling to comply with the Regulations. The master of a ship on arrival in or already in a district who is unwilling to comply with the requirements of the Health Regulations must so notify the Medical Officer who may then require the master to remove the ship immediately from the district. But if before leaving the master wishes to discharge cargo or disembark passengers or take on board, fuel, water, or stores, the Medical Officer shall permit him to do so, but may impose such conditions as he considers necessary. When the Medical Officer has required the removal of a ship from his district, the ship shall not during the voyage call at any other district. (N.B.—Cases have occurred where the master has stated his unwillingness to comply and the authorities have permitted the ship to load or discharge alongside during daylight hours. The ship has been made to "lie off" during the night and return the following morning. While alongside severe restrictions have been placed on communication with the shore).

FUMIGATION

Fumigation of Ship by Hydrogen Cyanide. It is highly important that all persons be removed to safety before this process begins, and that all parts of the ship are thoroughly gas freed before persons return to live on board. When accomodation has been treated, all pillows, mattresses, cushions and the like should be taken into the open air and there be well beaten to get rid of poisonous deposits which, otherwise, might remain dangerous for a long period.

Ratproofing. During recent years a new method of ratproofing ships has been used in the United Kingdom ports with conspicuous success. This involves the use of sodium fluoracetate, an anti-coagulant, which causes spontaneous internal haemorrhage in rats. The preparation is known by the number 1080 and its effectiveness is due to the fact that its rapid action prevents rats from breeding.

ISOLATION OF INFECTIOUS CASE

If during the voyage a person is suspected of being infectious he should be isolated at once. The ship's hospital, if there is one, may be used for this puropse if it is not already occupied by non-infectious cases. Otherwise a cabin, as far away as possible from busy parts of the ship, should be used instead. In the latter event, all unnecessary fittings, books, pictures, curtains, rugs, and other dust collectors should be removed. Whenever the suspect is isolated, all unnecessary communication with the rest of the crew should be strictly prohibited. A nursing attendant should be appointed who should, as far as possible, wear only washable clothing. He should have an overall, boiler suit, or oilskin coat which should not be taken outside the isolation quarters. He should scrub his hands both before and after attending the patient, make full use of proper disinfectants, and take every precaution to prevent the spread of infection. The patient should have his own feeding utensils which should be washed and disinfected after use. After the patient has left the quarters they must be fumigated and thoroughly washed and disinfected before being brought into use again.

MEDICAL ADVICE AND ASSISTANCE BY RADIO

Medical advice can be obtained by radiotelegraphy from any coast radio station in the United Kingdom or the Irish Republic other than the station at Oban, and from any coast radio station, including Oban, by radiotelephone. Where the request is made in the form of a message, the coast station passes it to the appropriate medical authority, whose reply is transmitted by the radio coast station to the ship.

If a doctor from the shore is wanted, the request for assistance should be addressed as a message to the Medical Officer of the most convenient port.

Where the radiotelephone "link" service is available, the master of a ship may be connected by telephone direct to the medical authority.

The radiotelegraph urgency signal XXX should be used to initiate radiotelegraph messages, and initial calls to the coast station should be made on the distress and calling frequency of 500 kHz. The radiotelephone urgency signal PAN, followed by the word MEDICO, should be used to initiate radiotelephone messages, and initial calls to the coast station should be made on the distress and calling frequency of 2,182 kHz.

There is no charge for these services.

Details of facilities available to ships at sea for obtaining medical advice through the medium of the radio services of other countries are given in the Admiralty List of Radio Signals, Volume 1, and the International List of Stations Performing Special services, published by the Bureau of the International Telecommunication Union, Geneva.

RABIES

The D.o.T. have published Merchant Shipping Notice No. 759 to draw the attention of all seamen to the provisions of the Rabies (Importation of Dogs, Cats and other Mammals) Order 1974 which, to prevent the introduction of rabies in Great Britain, controls the landing in this country of many animals listed in the Annex to the notice (e.g. cats, dogs, rabbits, hares, bushbabies, squirrel monkeys, gibbons and many others).

The Order prohibits the landing in Great Britain of such animals, except under the authority of, and in compliance with conditions imposed by, a licence previously granted by the Ministry of Agriculture, Fisheries and Food. Animals may be licensed to be landed only at certain ports, and then they must be moved as soon as practicable after landing to authorised quarantine premises.

A person who knowingly and with intent to evade the Order's provisions, or of a licence, or attempts to land, or causes or permits the landing or attempted landing, of an animal in contravention of the Order or a licence, or of quarantine requirements, is liable to prosecution on indictment, and possible imprisonment for a maximum of 12 months or to an unlimited fine or to both.

Attention is drawn to the fact that shipboard pets acquired overseas are a possible source of dangerous infection to all on board ship, and, if landed other than in compliance with the quarantine regulations, or if they escape, may be the cause of isolated outbreaks of rabies in this country. The National Maritime Board has agreed that from 31 March 1977, animals which are potential carriers of rabies will not be permitted to be carried on board ship as ships' or crew members' pets.

CHAPTER 7

SAFETY, SEAWORTHINESS AND PUBLIC WELFARE

COLLISION

Regulations for the Prevention of Collisions at Sea. Section 418 of the principal Act provides that Her Majesty may, on the joint recommendation of the Admiralty and the Department of Trade by Order-in-Council, make regulations for the prevention of collisions at sea so as to regulate the lights to be carried and exhibited, the fog signals to be carried and used, and the steering and sailing rules to be observed. Such regulations have effect as if enacted in the Act. These regulations with other provisions of the Act relating thereto, or otherwise relating to collisions, must be observed by all foreign ships within British jurisdiction.

Centuries before any legislation appeared governing the prevention of collisions at sea there existed customary rules of good seamanship which were evolved and observed by seafaring peoples in different parts of the world. There was thus built up what might be called a common law of seamanship and this was given effect to in this country by the Court of Admiralty with the assistance and advice of the Trinity Masters. In 1840 Trinity House promulgated a set of rules which were given statutory force by a section of the Steam Navigation Act of 1846, since when a number of new laws have extended the power of the Executive to make regulations governing the "rule of the road" at sea and providing for the imposition of penalties for non-observance.

Collision regulations were made by an Order-in-Council in 1896 and rules as to steam pilot vessels by Orders dated 1892 and 1897. All these were repealed and reproduced without alteration as regards British vessels by the Order of 1910. The Regulations for Preventing Collisions at Sea made by that Order remained in force until 1st January, 1954, when they were replaced by the Regulations which were approved by the International Conference on Safety of Life at Sea held in London during 1948. In 1960 another International Conference on Safety of Life at Sea was held in London, this time under the auspices of the Inter-Governmental Maritime Consultative Organization, to consider and approve, amongst other things, proposed changes in the International Collision Regulations. The revised Regulations came into force on 1st September, 1965. By March, 1965, some thirty-six countries had agreed to apply the new Regulations and it was expected that many others would do so in due course. Upon the invitation of the Inter-Governmental Maritime Consultative Organisation a conference was held in London in October 1972 for the purpose of revising the Collision Regulations 1960. As a result of its deliberations the conference adopted and opened for signature the Convention on the International Regulations for Preventing Collisions at Sea, 1972, to which were attached the Rules and Annexes which constitute the regulations. The Convention was to enter into force 12 months after the date on which at least 15 States, the aggregate of whose merchant fleets constitutes not less than 65 per cent by number or by tonnage of the world fleet of vessels of 100 gross tons and over have become parties to it, whichever is achieved first. The necessary acceptances having been achieved by July 1976, the International Regulations for Preventing Collisions at Sea, 1972, came into force on 15 July 1977.

Observance of Regulations.   Section 419 of the principal Act provides as follows.

1. All owners and masters of ships shall obey the collision regulations, and shall not carry or exhibit any other lights, or use any other fog signals, than such as are required by those regulations.

2. The owner or master of a ship will be guilty of an offence in respect of an infringement of the regulations caused by his own wilful default and liable, on conviction on indictment, to a fine and imprisonment for a term not exceeding two years or, on summary conviction:—

(a) to a fine not exceeding £50,000 and imprisonment for a term not exceeding six months in the case of an infringement of Rule 10 (b)(i) of the Collision Regulations which requires a vessel using an I.M.C.O. adopted traffic separation scheme to proceed in the appropriate traffic lane in the general direction of traffic flow, for that lane; and

(b) to a fine not exceeding £1000 in any other case.

3. If damage to person or property arises from the non-observance of any of the regulations, such damage will be deemed to have been occasioned by the wilful default of the person in charge of the deck of the ship at the time, unless it is shown to the satisfaction of the court that the circumstances of the case made a departure from the regulation necessary.

4. The D.o.T. must furnish a copy of the collision regulations to any master or owner of a ship who applies for it.

Section 741 of the principal Act states that, except where specially provided, that Act shall not apply to ships belonging to Her Majesty. Hence the Collision Regulations do not apply to such ships. However, that is a fact of no practical significance because the "Queen's Regulations" bind Her Majesty's ships to rules of navigation which are precisely the same as the Collision Regulations.

In the case of a ship belonging to the Crown, but which had not been commissioned at the time when she was involved in a collision it was held by the Court that although neither the Collision Regulations nor the Queen's Regulations applied to her, the former contained a standard of care to which those in charge of her navigation should have conformed.

Application of Regulations. It will be noted that section 419 (1894 Act) refers to owners and masters of "ships" and it may be pertinent to consider what the expression "ship" means. Section 742 of the same Act defines "vessel" as including any ship or boat, or any other description of vessel used in navigation. Further, "ship" is defined to include every description of vessel used in navigation not propelled by oars.

The Collision Regulations themselves do not refer to "ships" but use the term "vessel" throughout. Rule 1 (a), for instance, commences "These Rules shall apply to all vessels upon the high seas and in all waters connected therewith navigable by seagoing vessels."

By section 421 (1894 Act) any rules made under the authority of any local Act concerning lights, signals, and steps to be taken for avoiding collision, have full effect. Where any such rules are not or cannot be made, Her Majesty in Council may, on the application of proper persons, make such rules which shall be of the same force as if they were part of the Collision Regulations. The Regulations, however, do not apply to artificial waterways locked off from the sea.

The application of the Regulations to vessels sailing in convoy has sometimes given rise to difficulty. The general position appears to be that such vessels must obey lawful convoy orders. But as soon as there is a definite risk of collision they must obey the Regulations if they can do so with safety. In particular, rules concerned with sound signals and conduct in restricted visibility must be obeyed in the absence of convoy orders inconsistent therewith, and a ship which relies on a convoy order to justify a breach of the Regulations must prove that she was bound by such order at the time when she took whatever action she did in fact take.

If it is impossible to conform with a regulation because some appliance (a fog horn, for example) has ceased to exist or ceased to function, the ship will not be held responsible for breach of rule provided that no fault or negligence attaches to the owner or those for whom he is responsible.

Dangers of navigation and collision require that due regard shall be had to (amongst other things) special circumstances which may render a departure from the Rules necessary in order to avoid immediate danger. Where, for instance, the only possible chance of averting an otherwise inevitable collision is to depart from the Rules, that procedure would be justified. If strict obedience to the Rules would result in the vessel taking the rocks or suffering some other serious casualty, departure from the Rules, again, would be justifiable.

Precisely at what stage in the approach of vessels to one another the Rules commence to have application is extremely difficult to define, as all the circumstances have to be taken into account. One legal ruling has suggested that "they only apply at a time when, if either of them does anything contrary to the regulations it will cause danger of collision".

The Use of Radar. From the moment when risk of collision is about to exist vessels, even when using radar, are bound to comply with the regulations. It is imperative that radar and any other scientific aids to navigation should be used intelligently and the information they supply must be correctly interpreted. Because the "echo" of another vessel has been sighted on the P.P.I. screen it cannot be assumed that her position has been ascertained; several successive observations should be taken as accurately as possible and plotted in order to determine whether risk of collision exists. Thus, in circumstances where a rule requires that a vessel should stop her engines, she should stop them. All the same, in conditions of bad visibility or in traffic, a ship fitted with radar should keep a continuous radar watch.

It should be especially noted that a vessel is not "stopped and making no way through the water" merely because she has stopped her engines. It must be established that she has run her way off before she is justified in sounding at intervals of not more than two minutes two prolonged blasts, with an interval of about two seconds between them.

The Maritime Conventions Act, 1911. This Act introduced two very important changes in the law relating to collision liability, viz.:—

1. It abolished what was known as the "statutory presumption of fault". Before the passing of that Act, if one of two colliding vessels had infringed a regulation that applied at the material time before the collision, the collision was deemed in the absence of proof to the contrary to have been caused by the wrongful act, neglect, or default of the master or person in charge of that vessel. Such presumption no longer exists, and an injured vessel must prove that the other's breach of a regulation was at least a contributory cause, if not the sole cause, of the collision.

2. Formerly, when a collision occurred which was held to be due to the fault of both vessels, they were held equally to blame, and each ship was held liable for half the damages resulting from the collision. Under present law the rule is that where, by the fault of two or more vessels, damage or loss is caused to one or more of those vessels, to their cargoes or freight, or to any property on board, the liability to make good the damage or loss shall be in proportion to the degree in which each vessel was at fault. Thus, for example, if A and B collide and both are held to blame, A may be, say 75%

to blame and B 25%. In such a case B's liability would be limited to 25% of the damages.

If, having regard to all the circumstances of the case, it is not possible to establish different degrees of fault, the liability is apportioned equally.

Statutory or contractual rights to limit liability are not affected by the provisions of the Maritime Conventions Act.

Time Limit. Another provision of the Maritime Conventions Act is that no action for damages or in respect of loss of life or personal injury, or in respect of salvage services, can be maintained unless it is brought within two years of the date when the damage or loss or injury was caused, or the salvage services were rendered, unless the Court sees fit to extend that period.

Collision Liabilities. Following a collision between two vessels the findings of the Admiralty Court may be (i) that one of the vessels was solely to blame, (ii) that both vessels were in some degree to blame so that the blame is apportionable, (iii) that both vessels were to blame but it is impossible to establish the relative degrees of fault, or (iv) that neither vessel is to blame, *i.e.*, that the collision was the result of "inevitable accident". The onus of proving inevitable accident will lie on the ship which alleges it if a *prima facie* case of negligence is made against her, and it will generally be found extremely difficult to establish such proof except, perhaps, in a case where there has been, say, a sudden breakdown of the steering gear which was the sole cause of the collision in circumstances where any other avoiding action could not have prevented it.

The Admiralty Court will not find a ship liable if in the "agony of the moment" different action could have been taken which, after reflection in the "comfort of the Court" is considered better than the action that was in fact taken, provided that the latter did not amount to negligence.

Although the subject of the settlement of collision claims is outside the scope of this book, a general idea of the situation in a straightforward case may be usefully presented by supposing that two vessels, A and B, collide, that both suffer damage, that damage is caused to the cargoes carried by both, and that A is held solely to blame. Questions which have to be settled include the liabilities of the owners of A to (i) the owners of B, (ii) the owners of the damaged cargo in A, (iii) the owners of the damaged cargo in B.

Briefly, the position may be stated as follows:—

1. The owners of A will be liable to the owners of B for the cost of making good the damage to B.

2. The owners of A will not be liable to the owners of the cargo damaged in A on account of the negligence clause in the contract of affreightment or the corresponding rule of the Carriage of Goods by Sea Act (or similar legislation) to the effect that the carrier shall

not be liable for loss or damage arising from errors or faults in the navigation or management of the ship.

3. The owners of A will be liable for the damage to cargo in the innocent carrier B.

In more detail:—

1. If B was under charter the owners can claim loss of chartered freight less disbursements that would have been incurred to earn the freight. They will also be able to claim something for being deprived of the use of their ship during the period of repairs. If they were obliged to hire another ship to meet their commitments and so incurred further loss, that would not be recoverable from A's owners as it would be considered too remote.

The owners of B are entitled to a ship as fully efficient as B was immediately before the collision, and should it be necessary to replace old materials by new (thereby increasing the value of B) no "new for old" deductions will be allowed. This is not simply a matter of indemnity as in a contract of marine insurance, but is a claim for "damages", namely the refund of the direct and natural expenses incurred by the owners of B to put them in the same position as they were before the collision.

2. The owners of the cargo damaged in A will, if normal practice is followed, have insured it, and will be able to recover their loss from their underwriters (subject, of course, to any franchise provided by the policy). These underwriters, after indemnifying the cargo owners, will not have a right to bring a claim against the owners of A, as those cargo owners had no such right themselves.

3. The owners of the cargo damaged in B will likewise be able to recover their loss from their underwriters but, in this case, the underwriters will in turn be able to recover from the owners of ship A, as they are subrogated to the rights which the cargo owners had themselves.

The owners of A, of course, on proving that they had not been personally at fault in any way, could bring an action to limit their liability. This they would do if the total amount of claims against them exceeded their maximum liability under the current Limitation of Liability Convention in respect of damaged property. If the owners of A have insured the vessel and have the usual R.D.C. (running down clause) attached to the policy, they will be able to recover from their hull underwriters three quarters of the damages they have had to pay in respect of ship B and her cargo, but this cover does not extend to the cargo carried in A.

Master's Duty in Case of Collision. By section 422 of the principal Act, in every case of collision between two vessels, it is the duty of the master of each vessel if and so far as he can do so without danger to his own vessel, crew, and passengers (if any):—

(a) to render to the other vessel, her master, crew, and pass-
    engers (if any) such assistance as may be practicable and

necessary to save them from danger caused by the collision, and to stay by the other vessel until he has ascertained that she has no need of further assistance, and

(b) to give the master or person in charge of the other vessel the name of his own vessel and of the port to which she belongs, and the names of the ports from which she has come and to which she is bound.

If the master or person in charge fails without reasonable cause to comply with the above he is guilty of an offence and,

(a) in the case of a failure to render assistance etc., liable on conviction on indictment to a fine and imprisonment for a term not exceeding two years and on summary conviction to a fine not exceeding £50,000 and imprisonment for a term not exceeding six months; and

(b) in the case of failure to exchange names, ports etc., liable on conviction on indictment to a fine and on summary conviction to a fine not exceeding £1000,

and in either case if he is a certificated officer, an inquiry into his conduct may be held, and his certificate cancelled or suspended.

It should be emphasised that the masters' statutory duties in case of collision must be carried out whatever the circumstances of the collision may be. Even if one of the colliding ships is at anchor or moored to a wharf, pier, jetty, etc., the provisions of the Act still apply. If more than two ships are involved in a collision the master of each one is under an obligation to comply with the rules relating to giving necessary assistance, exchanging information, and making the required official log book entries.

Jurisdiction in Collision Cases. Generally, an action to recover collision damages may be brought in the state whose flag the defendant vessel flies. If proceedings in that state appear likely to put the plaintiff to unreasonable expense, or if for any other reason he prefers to do so, he can sue in a court in his own country or in some other country whose law permits such actions to be brought. The courts in the United Kingdom will allow an action to be brought if the defendant ship is in a British port at the time. This holds good whatever may be the nationality of the defendant ship and irrespective of where the collision occurred. The same facilities are granted by U.S.A. courts, but such hospitality is not universal. French courts will entertain actions when neither of the colliding ship is French only when both consent. If, however, the damaged ship is French they will claim jurisdiction, as in French law a French ship is regarded as part of French territory so that the wrongful act is deemed to have been committed in France although the negligent conduct which caused the collision took place on board a ship of some other nationality. The courts of Italy will decide collision cases between other than Italian ships if an Italian port is the port nearest the scene of the collision or if one of the ships is forced to remain in an Italian port on account of collision damage.

Steps advisable in Owners' Interest after Collision. In accordance with the advice usually given by shipowners' Protecting and Indemnity Associations, the master of a ship which has suffered damage in a collision should, so far as he is able and justified, serve a written notice on the master of the other ship in the following terms:—

To the master and owners of s.s. "....................."

Gentlemen,

On behalf of my owners and their underwriters I give you formal notice holding you and your owners solely responsible for all loss or damage whatsoever sustained by my owners in consequence of the collision between my ship and your s.s. "....................." which occurred on (date given).

I also give you notice that a survey will be held on board my vessel at (place stated) on (date stated). You are invited to send a representative without prejudice,

(Signed)

Master, s.s. "................................."

If the master knows that his owners will themselves make all necessary arrangements for holding a survey, there will, of course, be no need for the second paragraph. The owners or their agents, or the master on their behalf, should also take steps to have the other vessel placed under arrest pending payment of bail up to the limit of liability. The owners may, of course, decide to enter into an arbitration agreement using Lloyd's Standard Form referred to below. The master, presumably, would be informed accordingly. In order to give owners' solicitors the information they require a full report should be drawn up by the master describing all the events which led to the collision including an estimate of the speeds of both vessels at the time of impact and the angle of impact. The surveyors who inspect the damage should also prepare detailed reports.

Should the master receive notice holding him and his owners responsible for the damage done to another ship he should, as far as he is justified, reply by denying liability, but should accept any invitation to attend the survey on the other ship without prejudice.

In all these matters the master should, whenever possible, consult his owners or their agents before acting on their behalf, and in any case he should inform them promptly of all steps taken and all developments.

Lloyd's Standard Form of Arbitration Agreement in Cases of Collision. This form of agreement may be used following a collision between two ships. It should be signed only by principals, viz., either the owners of the colliding ships or agents who have been given special authority for the purpose. Immediately after it is signed it should be lodged with the Committee of Lloyd's and each party should appoint an agent in London to represent their interests in regard to the arbitration and notify the name of the agent to the other party. As soon as possible each party should inform the other as to the amount of security they require as the Committee of Lloyd's will not appoint an arbitrator until satisfied that the required security has been given. By the terms of the agreement, as soon as security has been given the parties are bound to release all arrests of the opposing vessels and discontinue any legal proceedings they may have started. The security given will be available for payment into court should the party providing the security desire to limit liability under the M.S. Acts. Nothing in the agreement prejudices the right of a party to commence High Court proceedings to limit liability.

ACCIDENTS TO SHIPS

Notice of Accident to Ship to be sent to Underwriters or their Representatives. The "Tender Clause" of the Institute Clauses usually attached to a hull policy requires that, in the event of any accident giving rise to a claim, notice shall be given to underwriters before survey or, if the ship is abroad, to the nearest Lloyd's agent so that an underwriters' surveyor can be appointed if desired. If the ship is in the United Kingdom, owners will normally deal with this matter themselves, but if she is abroad, although there is no legal necessity to do so, it is most important in the owners' interests that the agent or master should make the necessary report as failure to do so will result in underwriters deducting 15% from the cost of repairs claim. (See Chapter 14 for further details of this clause.)

Accident Reports. In the United Kingdom reports of casualties should be made on the proper WRE forms obtainable from any Custom House or M.M. Office.

Form WRE 1 is headed *Report of a Shipping Casualty*. This report runs to four pages. On page 1 there is first entered the Type of Casualty, *i.e.* "Collision", "Foundering", "Missing", "Fire "etc. followed by the year. Then the following numbered entries are made:—

1. Name of ship.
2. Official number or nationality.
3. Port of registry.
4. Gross tonnage.
5. Length overall.
6. Iron steel or wood.
7. Year of build.
8. Speed.
9. No. of crew.
10. No. of passengers.

11. Nature of employment.
12. Name of master and number of his certificate.
13. Name of pilot (if any) and by whom licensed.
14. Name and rank of officer in charge at time of casualty.
15. Original port of departure and date of sailing.
16. Port last sailed from and date of sailing.
17. Port of destination.
18. Name and address of owners.
19. (a) Name of place and of country or sea, (b) latitude and longitude, (c) true bearing and distance of point of land or light, when in sight.
20. Date and hour, stating whether G.M.T., B.S.T., or local time.
21. State of tide.
22. State of weather and atmosphere.
23. Direction and force of wind.
24. State of sea and swell.
25. Number of lives lost (crew).
26. Number of lives lost (passengers).
27. Number of lives saved and by what means.
28. If salvage services rendered, by whom and whether paid for at salvage or ordinary rates.
29. Account of casualty, with remarks as to cause and whether it could have been avoided. (This entry can be extended on page 4, if necessary).
30. Extent of damage to ship and cargo.
31. (Space is left here for the use of the D.o.T. only).

Page 2 calls for particulars of vessel and cargo, and is to be completed in all cases irrespective of the type of casualty. The questions are:—

32. What was the vessel's draught of water forward and aft?
33. Title, number, date and publishers of the charts in use at the time of the casualty and number of last large and small correction.
34. Number of compasses. Were they in good order? (a) Gyro, (b) Magnetic.
35. Could any part of the cargo affect any compass?
36. Were the life-saving appliances on board in accordance with the statutory requirements?
37. Number of watertight compartments.
38. Did they prove of use in this case?
39. Were the fire appliances on board in accordance with the statutory requirements?
40. Was the vessel well found in all respects?
41. If coal was carried as boiler fuel how were the bunkers ventilated?
42. Cargo and/or ballast:— (a) what kind and quantity of cargo and/or ballast was carried? (b) where was it carried?

43. Had vessel a deck load?
44. If of timber, was it in accordance with the statutory require-
    ments?
45. Was she overladen?
46. Was the cargo properly stowed?
47. If vessel had a grain cargo, was it stowed in accordance with
    the statutory requirements?
48. If a coal cargo, were all holds completely full, if not state
    capacity of empty space left in each hold? How were the
    holds ventilated?
49. State weather at time of shipment.
50. What navigational and communication aids were carried and
    which were in use prior to the casualty?
50a. State radar range scale in use prior to the casualty.

On page 3 are listed the particulars required for strandings and
collisions.

In a case of stranding these are:—

51. If Decca Navigator fix obtained, state decometer reading.
52. What, and at what time, were the last land-marks, beacons,
    or buoys visible? State whether G.M.T., B.S.T. or local
    time.
53. Were these marks seen directly or by radar? Give visual
    bearings or radar ranges and bearings.
54. Were bearings obtained from any beacon or direction-
    finding station? If so, state bearings obtained. (State
    whether bearings are true, compass or relative).
55. How long before stranding were these bearings obtained?
56. Were soundings taken? How long before stranding?
57. What was the depth at first and last sounding?
58. Course steering when casualty happened.
59. Speed at time of stranding.
60. Direction of ship's head after stranding.
61. Was the casualty due to an uncharted obstruction?

In the case of a collision they are:—

62. Course of own vessel when other was first observed.
63. Speed of own vessel when other was first observed.
64. What was (a) bearing of other vessel when first seen? (b)
    bearing and range of other vessel when first observed by
    radar?
65. Colour of light or lights of other vessel first seen, and how
    long before the collision?
66. Course of other vessel when first observed? State how
    obtained, visually, or by radar plot.
67. Direction of own vessel's head at time of collision.
68. Direction of other vessel's head at time of collision.
69. Were the engines of own vessel slowed or stopped? Give
    particulars.

70. Own speed when collision took place.
71. Were lights properly fitted and shown and fog signals made in accordance with regulations?
72. Did the other vessel give her name and stand by after collision, in accordance with the statutory requirements?

On page 4 are listed the particulars required for founderings. These are:—

74. Had the main engines broken down or become inoperative before foundering?
75. Had the steering gear broken down or become inoperative before foundering?
76. Had any of the ship's pumps broken down or become inoperative before foundering?
77. Date and hour of springing leak or of vessel shipping heavy seas.
78. Course steered prior to vessel foundering?
79. Circumstances of the voyage immediately preceding the foundering.
80. Details of measures taken to prevent the foundering.

Space is also provided on page 4 for the signature and title of the person providing the above information together with the date. According to which of the following officers has been requested to submit the report, it should bear the signature or stamp of the Receiver of Wreck, Consular Officer, Proper Officer or D.o.T. Surveyor, with the date, and is sent to the Assistant Secretary, Marine Division 1, Department of Trade.

Further reference to these reports will be found in Chapter 1 in the section dealing with preliminary inquiries into shipping casualties.

Certificates of Seaworthiness. If during her voyage a ship sustains an accident to hull or machinery, or if she grounds and refloats, even though the damage is so slight that there appears to be no reason why she should not continue on her voyage, the master should on arrival at the next port arrange for a survey and obtain a "certificate of seaworthiness". An official log book entry should have been made to record the occurrence and a protest should be noted at the first opportunity.

The local Lloyd's agent may be consulted for advice and recommendation as to the surveyor to be employed or, in the absence of a Lloyd's agent, a British consular officer or British merchant. If the surveyor appointed is satisfied that there is no damage affecting the safety of the ship or persons on board, he can grant a certificate stating that in his opinion the vessel is fit, safe, and efficient to carry on her customary employment (*e.g.*, to carry a dry cargo) or he may give a qualified certificate recommending that the vessel be dry-docked for further examination on arrival at a named subsequent port. In all such cases it is advisable to call in the

surveyor to the classification society with which the ship is registered, and that is the usual procedure. The certificate issued by
him is known as an "Interim Certificate of Class". The surveyor
will acquaint his society with all the particulars of the case and so
long as there is no special reason why they should do otherwise,
the society will accept the recommendation of their own surveyor
for the continuance of the vessel's class. If the services of a classification society surveyor are unobtainable a private surveyor, preferably
one recommended by Lloyd's agent or the agent of the shipowner's
P. & I. Club, may be employed instead or, if no one else is available
two British shipmasters may be called upon. In the case of machinery damage, a joint survey by a shipmaster and a chief engineer
would be appropriate. Should the ship be in such an out-of-the-way
port that none of the persons mentioned is present, the master
should request survey by the most suitably qualified person he can
find. Failure to obtain either an interim certificate of class or a
certificate of seaworthiness may have serious consequences should
anything go wrong at a later stage of the voyage which could be
traced back to the incident giving rise to the need for survey. Not
only would insurance rights be jeopardised, but the shipowner may
be reduced to his common law status as a carrier and thereby be
unable to claim the benefit of any exceptions clauses in his contract of
affreightment.

Where the master of a classed ship has been obliged to proceed
on the voyage on the authority of a privately issued certificate of
seaworthiness, he should at the first possible opportunity call in a
society surveyor to confirm the position and issue an official provisional certificate.

Request for survey in the United Kingdom may be made either
to a Lloyd's agent or to the Salvage Association.

Putting into a Port of Refuge after Accident. Putting into a port
of refuge, or putting back to the port of loading, for the purpose of
effecting *necessary* repairs always constitutes a justifiable deviation
so that insurance and other contractual rights remain unaffected.
This applies also to putting into a bunkering port when short of
fuel provided that it can be proved that the vessel left her last port
with a normally adequate reserve of bunkers. Such action, since it is
taken reasonably and voluntarily to preserve the common adventure
from a peril that beyond doubt exists, is at the same time a general
average act.

The following is an outline of the procedure that will generally
be found necessary.

The owners should be informed by radio of the master's decision
to put into the port selected by him and be given the reasons for
such action. If there is an agent of the owner at the selected port
he should be informed as well, and be given the expected time

of arrival and sufficient information to enable him to make such preparations as he deems advisable in advance.

On arrival at the port the master should obtain pratique in the usual way, enter the ship at the Customs or Harbour Office, appear before the Consul, notary public, or magistrate and note protest reserving the right to extend it. The fact of the ship's safe arrival should be communicated to the owners. Underwriters or the nearest Lloyd's agent should be notified of the accident in accordance with the terms of the "Tender Clause".

If cargo damage has occurred or is merely suspected, or should it be necessary to discharge cargo in order to effect the repairs, a hatch survey should be arranged. As far as possible only officially registered cargo surveyors should be employed.

Arrangements will have to be made for a survey of the damage to the ship. If she is classed the local or nearest surveyor to the classification society should be called in. He will decide what repairs must be done to enable the vessel to continue in her class and he will render a report to the master or agent accordingly. If no society surveyor is available the master should take similar steps to those suggested in the section above.

On receipt of the surveyor's report and recommendations tenders should be invited from suitable repairing firms, bearing in mind the "Tender Clause" and the underwriters' power of veto (see Chapter 14). When advertising for tenders, it is advisable to include in the advertisement a statement that "the lowest or any tender will not necessarily be accepted".

All tenders received should be scrutinised very carefully, in consultation with Lloyd's agent or a merchant with an extensive knowledge of local facilities and customs and, subject to owners' and underwriters' approval where that can be obtained, the lowest tender of a reputable firm should be accepted unless there are sound reasons for preferring another. The time factor, of course, is most important in this connection. Good work done quickly at relatively high cost may prove in the long run more economical than similar work at a lower cost which takes much longer to complete. Any contract drawn up should contain a demurrage clause providing that if the work is not finished by some stipulated date demurrage will be payable at an agreed daily rate until the work is completed.

The repairs will be carried out under the supervision of the surveyor (and underwriters' surveyor if they decide to appoint one). On completion, if the repairs satisfy the classification society surveyor, he will issue an interim certificate of class and, assuming the society accept the surveyor's recommendation, the vessel will continue in class. If a private surveyor has been employed he should be requested to issue a certificate of seaworthiness. Such documents should be obtained in triplicate so that one copy can be retained on board and two sent to the owners. Both hull and cargo underwriters invariably accept an interim certificate of class or a certificate of seaworthiness as evidence that due diligence has been used to make the vessel seaworthy.

The note of protest should be extended, giving full details of damage and repairs, and copies of the extended protest should be obtained. Arrangements will have to be made for paying the repair bill and other port disbursements (see note below), and all necessary documents should be sent to the owners. The ship having been entered outwards can then be finally cleared to continue on her voyage.

N.B.—In connection with the above the master must at all times bear in mind that he is wholly responsible for both the ship and her cargo and should act as though both were his own uninsured property. It is his duty to make every effort to continue the voyage with respect to both ship and cargo with the minimum of expense and the least possible delay. However valuable the advice and recommendations of agents, consignees, surveyors, and other persons may be, they cannot give the master direct orders. Only the shipowners can do that. The master must, of course, comply with the law and follow the official instructions of local authorities. If the master has good reason to suppose that the surveyors' recommendations as to repairs are unreasonable, he should lose no time in communicating his opinion to the owners so that they can, if necessary, send their own superintendent to the scene.

By the terms of the "sue and labour" and "waiver" clauses in the policy of marine insurance the master is always justified in incurring reasonable expenditure in the attempt to prevent the ship or her cargo from becoming a total loss or in the attempt to minimise losses from perils insured against, even at the risk of failure, and underwriters are bound to pay their proportion of such expenses whether the property is saved or not.

In the report of survey of damage and repairs sent to owners all costs should be clearly stated, differentiating between ordinary wear and tear and actual damage. In respect of damage it will be necessary to distinguish between items caused by accident (particular average losses) and items caused voluntarily for the common benefit (general average losses). The owners will have the duty of appointing the average adjuster who will require to be supplied with all the evidence necessary to enable him to assess the various claims.

Money for Repairs and Disbursements. In these days of possible currency restrictions when it may be essential to observe exchange control regulations, it will be necessary for disbursements for repairs and other expenditures abroad to be made on behalf of the shipowner by his agents, either those he regularly employs at the port or, if none, agents appointed specially for the purpose, the agents being reimbursed by the shipowner through a banking arrangement. However, it will not be out of place to describe methods formerly used and which, even today, may have some application in certain cases.

When a pre-arranged advance from owners or their local agents was impracticable it was usual for the master to offer to draw bills on the owners. If these turned out to be unacceptable, the master might cable the owners with a request for money to be sent by telegraphic transfer. If that method failed, or as an alternative, he could consult Lloyd's agent as to the best way of borrowing money from a bank or a merchant (or from Lloyd's agent himself) at the most attractive rate of interest. If that proved unsuccessful he would then have to resort to "bottomry" or "respondentia", or both, according to circumstances. For such loans a bond is given on the understanding that if the security pledged is totally lost the sum advanced will not be repayable. Under a bottomry bond the ship alone may be pledged or the ship together with the freight she is in the process of earning. (Lloyd's form of Bottomry Bond makes provision for pledging the cargo as well.) A respondentia bond is in respect of cargo alone. The master would be acting as an agent of necessity of the shipowner in pledging the ship and freight, but of the cargo owner in pledging the cargo. Any number of bonds can be taken out in the course of completing the adventure, and they take priority in the reverse order of their execution on the grounds that it would be the last one which brought about the successful

Mortgage.

Only the owner may mortgage the ship or a share therein.

Every mortgage should be registered, although this is not compulsory.

The owner does not have to be without funds in order to raise a mortgage loan.

Money raised by mortgage may be used for any purpose so long as the terms of the mortgage agreement are adhered to.

If the ship is lost the mortgagee usually has a claim on the insurance indemnity.

A mortgage is a relatively long term arrangement with a moderate interest rate.

If the mortgagor fails to repay the loan and/or interest the property passes to the mortgagee.

Bottomry.

Only the master may borrow money under bottomry bond.

A bottomry loan does not require to be registered.

The master must have exhausted all the less drastic measures for raising money before he is entitled to pledge the ship, etc.

Money raised by bottomry may be used for one purpose only, viz., the continuance of the voyage.

If the ship is lost the bond is voided.

Bottomry is a short-term arrangement carrying a high rate of interest.

If the loan is not repaid together with interest the bondholder can exercise his right of maritime lien and have the ship arrested, but the property does not pass to him.

Mortgages rank in priority in accordance with their dates of registration.

Bottomry loans rank in priority in the reverse order of their being made.

completion of the voyage and thereby preserved the security out of which the earlier loans can be discharged. Money borrowed in this way would naturally carry a much higher interest rate than ordinary commercial loans.

It is interesting to contrast bottomry against mortgage. These two devices have one thing in common, viz., using the ship as security for a loan. In all other respects they are diametrically opposed to one another as the above remarks will indicate.

If the ship, freight, and cargo, collectively, do not provide sufficient security there is one last resource available to the master, and that is to sell sufficient of the cargo to meet his needs. It will be evident that the situation would have to be desperate indeed for such a step to be justified. In taking such action the master would, again, be an agent of necessity of the cargo owner.

N.B.—A Lloyd's Respondentia Bond (as distinct from ordinary respondentia) is designed to be used if necessary in cases where the ship has become a constructive total loss and the cargo has not. Under the terms of the bond the cargo is pledged as security for money borrowed to cover the cost of discharging the cargo, storing it, reloading it into another ship, and conveying it to its destination to enable the freight to be earned.

Lloyd's Agents. The Corporation of Lloyd's have agents in numerous ports in all parts of the world. Their business in the capacity of Lloyd's Agents is to act in the interests of underwriters generally, and this will require of them a very thorough knowledge of local facilities and customs. The agency is a much coveted one and is usually held by a merchant or a firm of merchants many of whom are shipbrokers, insurance brokers, ships' agents, shipping and forwarding agents, importers and exporters, and so on. Included in their duties is the rendering of assistance to masters of ships in cases of shipwreck, damage to ship or cargo, and difficulties arising in connection with the payment of port disbursements. Lloyd's agent is empowered to appoint a surveyor to survey damage to vessels and their cargoes on behalf of underwriting interests and to issue certificates of sea damage. Any such certificate should be signed by the surveyor appointed as "Surveyor to Lloyd's Agent" and Lloyd's agent should himself sign his authentication. In his capacity as such, a Lloyd's agent does not underwrite marine risks, but it is an important part of his general duty to keep Lloyd's posted with the latest information concerning the movements of ships and cargoes and all other matters of special interest to underwriters.

Damage caused or sustained by Ships in Docks, Harbours, Rivers, Etc. A vessel moored to a jetty in a river or narrow channel may suffer damage through ranging caused by some other vessel passing at such a speed as to set up a considerable wash. To recover damages for broken mooring lines or other losses the vessel must be able to prove that the other vessel was in breach of a local regulation providing for speed restriction or was in some other way negligent, and also that she herself was sufficiently secured by sound mooring lines all of which were bearing an even stress. If the passing ship is held to blame, and provided there was no actual contact of the two ships, her owners will not be able to recover their loss under the running down clause attached to the hull policy. They may, however, be protected by their P. & I. Association.

If the owner of a ship contracts for the repair or dry-docking of the vessel in a private dockyard, or contracts to have the vessel loaded or discharged at a private wharf, the ordinary law of contract applies and, unless the contract otherwise provides, there is no absolute duty on the dock owner or wharfinger to make the dock or wharf safe. The law, however, does require him to use all reasonable care and skill to make the premises safe for the purpose contemplated. On the other hand, where there is no contract, a ship entering any private waterway or dock does so in the capacity of an "invitee" who cannot demand that the premises be made safe. It would, nevertheless, be incumbent on the occupier of the premises to protect the invitee against traps and to give adequate warning of any hidden dangers that are known to him.

In the case of docks and waterways owned by statutory authorities, the statutes by which those authorities are constituted require that all reasonable care must be taken to make navigation safe. If it is proved that such reasonable care has been taken the authority will not be liable for loss or damage arising from any accident happening to a ship within the area over which they have control. On the other hand, if the negligence of the authority is proved they will be liable. (See Chapter 15 for references to Dock Owners' limitation of liability.)

Ships which damage privately owned docks, piers, etc., will be liable if negligence is proved. Where, however, damage is done to publicly owned property the owner of the ship which causes the damage will be liable whether his servants were negligent or not so long as they were actually in control of the vessel. The ship-owner can escape liability only when the damage has resulted from Act of God or Queen's enemies, or where the ship has been reasonably abandoned and left derelict or, although the master and crew or any of them remain on board, control of the ship has become impossible owing to the severe state of wind and sea. Damage done to public property not only affects an owner of property but also the entire community who make use of it, and for this reason liabilities are correspondingly heavier than when private property is damaged.

Removal of Wreck. Section 530 of the principal Act provides that where any vessel is sunk, stranded, or abandoned in a harbour or tidal water under the control of a harbour or conservancy authority, or in or near the approach thereto, so as to be an obstruction or danger to navigation, that authority may (a) take possession of, and raise, remove, or destroy the whole or any part of the vessel, (b) light or buoy the vessel or part until the raising, removal, or destruction thereof, and (c) sell any vessel or part so raised or removed and other property recovered and out of the proceeds of the sale reimburse themselves for expenses incurred, holding any surplus in trust for the person entitled thereto.

Apart from perishable property, however, a sale may not be made until 7 clear days' notice has been given by local newspaper advertisement. At any time before property is sold the owner is entitled to have it delivered to him on payment to the authority of its fair market value ascertained by agreement between the parties, or failing agreement by a person nominated by the D.o.T. Any sum paid under this provision is deemed to be the proceeds of the sale.

Section 531 extends the rights enjoyed by harbour and conservancy authorities under the provisions of the previous section to the general lighthouse authority where a vessel is sunk, stranded, or abandoned so as to become an obstruction or danger to navigation in a fairway, on the shore, or elsewhere in the British Islands where the place is not under the control of a harbour or conservancy authority. All expenses incurred by the general lighthouse authority which are not reimbursed in the manner provided in the Act are payable out of the General Lighthouse Fund.

By section 532 the term "vessel" as used in the preceding section includes every article or thing or collection of things forming part of the tackle, equipment, cargo, stores, or ballast of the vessel. Proceeds of sale arising from a vessel, her cargo, and other property recovered therefrom are regarded as a common fund.

Section 533 provides that if any question arises between a harbour or conservancy authority and a general lighthouse authority as to their respective powers for removal of wrecks, that question shall on the application of either authority be referred to the Board of Trade (now D.o.T.) whose decision shall be final.

Section 534 provides that the powers conferred on an authority by the M.S. Act for removal of wrecks are additional to and not in derogation of other powers for a like object. The Thames Conservancy Act, for instance, gives the Thames Conservators a personal remedy against the shipowner. If that authority, therefore, raises and removes a wreck they will be taken to have acted under the statute which gives them the greater advantage.

Fires in Ships. As masters of ships are personally responsible for seeing that all proper precautions are taken to prevent fires on board it is most important that they should comply strictly with regulations relating to drills, musters, and inspections of fire-fighting equipment. The contents of all D.o.T. "M" notices on the subject of shipboard fires should be studied and the recommendations they put forward should be taken seriously. Notices dealing with fire prevention and fire-fighting on ships in port and during welding and flamecutting operations are especially important in view of the fact that a large proportion of serious ship fires do occur in port, frequently at night, and during repair work. The substance of such notices is briefly as follows:—

Responsibility for fire prevention and fire-fighting in ships under construction rests on the builder, and in ships under repair on the owner unless, in either case, there is a written agreement to the contrary. Where major repairs are being carried out the D.o.T. recommend that where the ship-repairer has accepted responsibility for taking precautions against fire, testing and certification of spaces for "hot work" etc., the ship-repairer should provide the shipowner or the master with a clear written agreement confirming that responsibility has passed to the ship-repairer.

Patrolmen should be carefully selected, physically and mentally suitable, reliable, well-trained, and should be provided with whistles or other means of giving alarm. Realistic exercises should be arranged, and patrols organised to ensure every part of the ship being visited at least once an hour. Patrols should report at a point manned at all times and the bells of sprinklers and other alarms should ring at that point. Equipment maintained there should include breathing apparatus, lifelines, large axes, and spare hydrant keys. There should also be kept there all information about the ship relevant to fire-fighting.

Ship to shore communications should ensure the quickest possible contact with the public fire brigade at all times. Facilities available to a particular ship should be well known to all concerned and liaison between them should embrace training and fire-fighting arrangements generally.

The need for care and caution in smoking in places where it is not prohibited should be the subject of extensive and continuous propaganda. Cargo tanks, cargo holds or other tanks or spaces that have contained flammable substances must be certified as being free of flammable gases before any repair work is commenced.

Water supplies of adequate pressure should always be immediately available, as should extra apparatus such as adapters for hose couplings, boosters, etc., and appliances moved for repair or recharging should be immediately replaced.

When operations endanger a ship's stability and it is necessary to decide whether fire-fighting should cease, the decision of the harbour master or responsible port authority officer, after consultation with all interested parties, should prevail. But this does not relieve the master or officer in charge from bringing to the notice of the fire brigade special circumstances affecting the ship's safety or stability or the conduct of operations.

The need for port authorities to provide local fire brigades with daily lists of ships in their areas and other useful information. The use of ejector pumps for freeing ships of water during fire-fighting.

The D.o.T. strongly advise all concerned to apply these recommendations as fully as possible.

The Fire and Explosion Risks of Particular Cargoes. There are obviously special risks associated with the carriage of oil cargoes, liquid gases and liquid chemicals, for which reason owners will lay down special rules for the guidance of masters and others in the matter of the precautions to be taken to prevent fires and explosions. Strict enforcement of such rules is essential in the interests of the safety of the ship and all on board or in the vicinity.

Whenever inflammable or easily combustible goods are on board, or are being loaded or discharged, proper precautions should be taken whatever the type of ship, and familiarity should not be allowed to breed contempt. When goods of an unfamiliar kind are offered for shipment, the master and his officers should make diligent inquiries into the nature of such goods from the point of view of fire and explosion risk, arrange stowage accordingly, and take all the necessary precautions. Further reference is made to this matter in the section dealing with dangerous goods.

ACCIDENTS TO PERSONS

A Code of Safe Working Practices recommended for adoption on merchant ships was produced in 1978 under the supervision of an expert committee comprising representatives of all sides of the shipping industry.

The purpose of the Code is to provide guidance on procedures to be followed in operations aboard ship to ensure the safety of those concerned and to reduce the number of accidents and injuries affecting seafarers. Among the subjects dealt with are general precautions, mooring, gangways, ladders, working with winches, derricks and cranes and other aspects of cargo handling, rigging of stages, painting, entry into confined spaces and tanks, servicing of electronic equipment, work in machinery spaces and workshops and catering.

The M.S. (Code of Safe Working Practices) Regulations 1980, (S.I. 1980 No. 686) require not less than two copies of the Code to be carried in United Kingdom ships. On such ships where the master and seamen employed exceed 15 persons in all, there shall be carried not less than one copy of the Code in the custody of each of the following persons:—(a) the master; (b) the chief officer; (c) the chief engineer; (d) the purser or catering officer; (e) the safety officer; (f) a safety representative; and (g) any member of an accident prevention committee who requests a copy; and in addition, in different places, readily accessible to seamen, not less than one reference copy for every 25 seamen employed in the ship.

Where reference copies are required to be carried, the master must cause to be displayed at places accessible to the seamen, three legible notices specifying the places where the reference copies are kept.

Maximum penalties on summary conviction:—for not ensuring ship has sufficient copies £1000; for not making a copy temporarily available to a seaman who requests it £1000; for not displaying notices as required £50; and for removing a copy of the Code from the ship without consent £50.

The right of an employee, including a seaman, to sue his employer is in no way affected by the former's right to compensation under the industrial injuries insurance scheme of the National Insurance Acts. Benefits payable under those Acts depend on the nature of the injury suffered and the extent of disablement, not on loss of earnings. Additional allowances are made, however, for unemployability, family responsibilities, and so on, and in the case of a fatal accident a pension may be given to the widow of the employee supplemented by allowances for children. Claims under the Acts are settled by officers of the Department of Health and Social Security subject to right of appeal. Where an employee has the right to sue his employer or a third party for damages arising out of a breach of statute or negligence, the situation is governed by the Law Reform (Personal Injuries) Act, 1948.

Under present law, when an employed person suffers injury arising out of or in the course of his employment it would seem that the employer is always liable either through (1) common negligence, or (2) being in breach of some statutory requirement, so that an "accident" in the dictionary sense of being an event proceeding from an unknown cause is something which for this purpose has ceased to exist. The case quoted below will serve to emphasise how important it is to do everything possible to prevent injuries.

On board a ship crossing the Atlantic to load grain at a Canadian port holds were being prepared so that loading could commence immediately on arrival. Hatch covers had been removed but no guard rails were considered necessary as there was ample room for persons to move about the deck without the necessity to go near the open hatch, nor had it ever been the custom to fit guard rails in these circumstances. In some manner that was never explained a seaman carrying some timber along the deck fell down the hatch and was badly injured. No evidence of insufficient light or of any sudden motion of the ship was forthcoming. The seaman brought an action against the shipowner to recover damages for negligence and was awarded £10,000 by the trial judge and, following appeal, the House of Lords confirmed the award. It was held that the owner should have foreseen the risk although the risk was admittedly a small one and it was no defence to say that the accident, even going back over a period of 40 years, was the first of its kind.

It should always be borne in mind that the provision of "legal aid" nowadays enables employees to bring High Court actions against their employers even when, as may happen sometimes, their trade unions decline to assist them. Damages obtained for common law negligence are generally much higher than insurance benefits under the N.I. (I.I.) Act. Where the employee is unable to prove that anyone other than himself is at fault he will have to be satisfied with national insurance benefit, but in view of the possible advantage to him it is only natural that an employee will sue his employer whenever possible in addition to claiming insurance benefit. When the court takes into account loss of earnings, etc., in assessing the total damages of a claim based on negligence they will set against that item one half of the insurance benefits likely to be received by the injured person during the next five years following the date of the accident. Even so the injured person will be left much better off than if he relied on insurance benefits alone.

It seems to be considered that the relatively heavy damages awarded for negligence have had the effect of making employers take greater care and provide improved safety measures. While it is generally the case that the employer is insured against the risk of having to meet these heavy claims it also follows that, where repeated claims are experienced, insurers will either raise their rates or even decline the insurance. Hence it is argued that employers' liability for negligence serves a useful social purpose in reducing the accident rate. In other words, prevention is better than cure.

Many statutes and regulations provide elaborate codes of safety rules (including the Docks Regulations outlined below) for the benefit of persons employed in "dangerous trades". These laws and rules must be obeyed by employers under penalties, including liability to injured employees, when rules are broken. The tendency is to hold that these statutory duties are absolute and an employer in breach of a regulation will always be liable even though he did maintain a reasonable standard of safety. Further, it is not sufficient merely to comply with a regulation which demands a safety device to be provided; employees must be constantly persuaded, encouraged and directed to make proper use of it. In a case, for instance, where an employee removes a guard rail in order to do his work more conveniently, that will amount to contributory negligence if he is injured as a result. Although the amount of damages may be considerably reduced, he will still be able to claim against the employer unless the latter can show that he has persistently and repeatedly instructed the employee to use the guard provided.

If an employee injures himself entirely through his own fault by disregarding instructions relating to safety he will have no right of action against his employer or any third party for loss due to his own negligence. But the position is different where two persons in common employment commit a joint act of negligence. Each will be in a position to sue the employer for the negligence of his fellow servant. This, perhaps, does seem a bit hard on the employer who would have been liable to neither if they had acted separately.

Whenever an accident occurs on board ship first-aid should be administered and medical attention summoned without delay. (See section on "masters' duties" in Chapter 4). A report of the accident should be made as soon as possible after the event, and witnesses questioned, photographs taken, parts of broken wires or machinery etc. saved so that an assessment as to the cause of the accident can be made to perhaps prevent it happening again, and also to assist later in the settlement of claims that might arise. The accident should be reported to the appropriate authority and a written medical report obtained whenever possible. Where difficulties arise the master should not hesitate to seek the assistance of the representative of the General Council of British Shipping or the agent of the owner's P. & I. Club.

Accidents to stevedores' men and other shore personnel in ports abroad, especially in the U.S.A., have often given rise to exceptionally high claims so that it becomes especially important to take every possible step to avoid these incidents and, if they should occur, to do everything possible to protect the shipowner's interests.

Newly Opened Ballast Tanks. By means of a published notice the D.o.T. state that they wish to stress upon masters the need to ventilate adequately newly opened ballast tanks. For this purpose all doors and covers should be removed to allow fresh air to circulate freely throughout the compartment. Other aids to ventilation include the use of windsails and ballast pumps. In all cases when tanks are entered, someone should be standing by in case of emergency.

The Health and Safety at Work Act etc., 1974. This enabling Act has been superimposed over the existing Factory Act 1961, the Docks Regulations 1934, and other existing Acts and regulations, some of which concern shipping. The new legislation is administered by two new bodies known as the Health and Safety Commission which decides policy, and the Health and Safety Executive which provides an advisory service and controls the health and safety inspectors who are no longer scattered and working independently within several government departments.

The Act applies general duties to employers, occupiers of premises, suppliers of equipment, employees and others. For example it is the duty of every employer to ensure, so far as is reasonably practicable, the health, safety and welfare at work of all of his employees. Employers are required to publish a written safety policy and bring it to the attention of their employees. Employees have the duty to take reasonable care of themselves and others while working. These general duties apply to ships while in port in the U.K., and under the Health and Safety at Work Act 1974 (Application outside Great Britain) Order 1977 the provisions of sections 1 to 59 and 80 to 82 of the Act apply to the loading, unloading, fuelling or provisioning of a vessel within territorial waters. The above sections of the Act apply also to vessels within U.K. territorial waters or any area outside Great Britain designated by order under section 1 (7) of the Continental Shelf Act 1964, when work such as inspection, testing, loading, unloading, fuelling, provisioning, construction etc. of offshore installations is carried out from such vessels, or where the loading, unloading, fuelling or provisioning of vessels engaged in pipeline works is involved. For the above purposes a vessel includes a hovercraft and any floating structure capable of being manned.

Generally, safety matters while a ship is at sea are to be covered by the M.S. Act 1979, section 21, and safety regulations made in pursuance of that section.

Until such time as new regulations under the 1974 Act are made to cover loading and unloading in docks, harbours etc. in the U.K., the Docks Regulations 1934 continue to apply.

Enforcement of duties under the Health and Safety at Work Act and its regulations is in the hands of Inspectors who may, where a breach of the law is observed, issue an Improvement Notice requiring the breach to be remedied by a specified date. There is right of appeal against such notice to an Industrial Tribunal, but meanwhile work may continue. Where activities are seen "involving a risk of serious personal injury", whether a breach of the law is involved or not, a Prohibition Notice may be issued. Such activities must stop, either immediately or by a stated date, but having ceased the dangerous activity, there is right of appeal to a tribunal. Inspectors may prosecute for non-compliance leading on conviction to a fine.

The Docks Regulations 1934. These regulations consist of six parts and a schedule.

In a preamble various terms are defined, and under the general heading of "Duties" it is provided amongst other things that the ship is responsible for any hatch not taken over by stevedores. Further, when the stevedore has completed work at any hatch he must give written notice to that effect to the owner, master, or officer in charge of the ship who must in turn give written acknowledgement of such notice in prescribed form.

Part I applies to dock owners and managers and deals with the adequate lighting and fencing of premises, provision of first-aid equipment, and means of conveying casualties to hospital without delay.

Part II applies to owners, masters, and officers of ships. Important provisions include the following:—

To provide safe access from ship to shore and *vice versa*, where practicable there must be available the ship's accommodation ladder or a gangway not less than 22″ wide, properly secured and fenced on each side to a height of 2′ 9″ by upper and lower rails, taut ropes or chains or other safe means. Fencing on one side only is needed if the other side is protected by the ship's side. Otherwise, a sound ladder of adequate length must be provided properly secured against slipping. Certain small vessels are excluded from this regulation if it is possible to pass to and from the ship without risk in the absence of special appliances.

If a ship is alongside any other ship, vessel or boat, safe means of access from one to the other must be provided unless it is possible to pass to and fro safely without the aid of a special appliance. If one of the vessels is a barge or other vessel of low freeboard, means of access is to be provided by the ship which has the higher freeboard.

Where the depth from deck level to the bottom of the hold exceeds 5 feet there must be access by ladder with cleats or cups on the coamings. Ladders must be in line and must provide at least $4\frac{1}{2}$″ foothold for a width of 10″, and a firm handhold. Cargo must be stowed so as to leave $4\frac{1}{2}$″ minimum clearance behind any ladder. There must be room to pass between a winch or other obstruction and the coaming at the ladder head.

Shaft tunnels are to have adequate handhold and foothold on each side.

Holds, gangways, ladders, decks and all parts of the ship to which persons employed may require to proceed must be efficiently lighted.

Hatch beams are to have suitable gear for lifting them on and off without the need for any person to go out on them to adjust such gear.

Hatch coverings must be plainly marked to indicate the deck and hatch to which they belong and their position therein, unless they are interchangeable. Beams must be likewise marked, and hatch covers must have adequate hand grips.

The working space round a hatch is to be not less than 2 feet wide or some other provision must be made for the safe handling of beams and covers.

Part III applies to owners of shore machinery and plant, and to masters of ships in respect of ships' machinery and plant, as follows.

All lifting machinery is to be tested and examined by a competent person before being taken into use.

M

Derricks and their attachments must be inspected once in every 12 months and be thoroughly examined once at least every 4 years. All other lifting machinery must be thoroughly examined every 12 months. (A thorough examination means a visual examination, supplemented if necessary by other means such as hammer test, carried out carefully, with machines and gear dismantled as necessary.)

No chain, ring, hook, shackle, swivel, or pulley block is to be used unless tested and examined by a competent person.

Chains, rings, etc., *in general use* are to be annealed every 6 months if $\frac{1}{2}''$ or under, or every 12 months if over $\frac{1}{2}''$, unless they are subjected to some other prescribed treatment. (In respect of handworked gear the intervals stated are doubled.) In practice, most chains, hooks etc. supplied to ships are made of steel and will therefore be thoroughly examined at the intervals stated after heat treatment, but not annealing.

All chains, etc., must be inspected immediately before being used unless they have been inspected within the previous 3 months. Any which have been lengthened, altered, or repaired by welding are to be tested and examined before being taken into use again. No rope may be used unless of suitable quality and free from defect, and no wire rope may be used without examination and test by a competent person.

Wire rope *in general use* must be inspected every 3 months and, after any wire in it has broken, every month. Wire rope may not be used if in any length of 8 diameters the number of visible broken wires exceeds 10% of the total number, or if the wire shows signs of excessive wear, corrosion, or other defect.

A thimble or loop splice in a wire rope must have at least three tucks with a whole strand and two tucks with one half of the wires cut out of each strand. The tucks are to be against the lay. But this need not operate to prevent the use of another form of splice shown to be as efficient as the Regulation splice.

Certificates in prescribed forms containing particulars of tests, examinations, inspections, annealings, etc., are to be obtained and entered in the Register of Machinery, Chains, etc., and kept on the premises, or on board ship, or in some other approved place.

No pulley block may be used unless the safe working load is clearly stamped upon it. Means are to be provided to enable any person using a chain or wire rope sling to ascertain its safe working load, for which purpose chain slings are to have the S.W.L. stamped on the sling or on an attached ring or tablet of durable material. Wire rope slings must be similarly marked or a notice must be exhibited showing the S.W.L.'s of slings of various sizes used.

Chains are not to be shortened by tying knots in them, and packing must be used to prevent links coming into contact with the sharp edges of heavy loads.

Motors, cog-wheels, shafting, live wires, steam pipes, etc., must be securely fenced where necessary.

Cranes and winches must be provided with a means of reducing the risk of an accidental descent of the load; in particular, a reversing lever must have a suitable locking arrangement.

Measures must be taken to prevent exhaust steam from obscuring decks, gangways, stages, etc., and also to prevent the foot of a derrick from being accidentally lifted out of its socket.

Part IV has a general application to all employers, agents, and employees, as follows.

Precautions must be taken to facilitate the escape of workers employed in a hold or 'tween-deck dealing with coal or other bulk cargo.

No lifting machinery may be loaded beyond its S.W.L., except that a crane may be loaded beyond its S.W.L. in exceptional cases to such extent and subject to such conditions as may be approved by the engineer in charge or other competent person, if on each occasion (i) written permission of the owner or his agent has been obtained, (ii) a record of the overload is kept. Further, where the load on a single sheave block is attached to the block instead of to the chain or rope passing round the sheave, the load on the block shall be deemed to be half the actual load.

No load may be left suspended without a competent person remaining in charge of the machine.

No person under 16, and no person who is not competent and reliable, may be employed to drive a winch or crane, attend falls, or give signals.

No stage may be used unless it is substantial and secure, and no truck may be used on a stage so steep as to be unsafe. Slippery stages must be sanded or otherwise made safe.

In respect of hatches more than 5 feet deep from deck level to bottom of hold, if coamings are less than 2' 6" high, the hatch must be fenced to a height of 3 feet or be securely covered. Certain exceptions are made in the case of very small vessels and during brief interruptions of work.

No cargo may be worked at an intermediate deck unless the hatch at that deck is securely covered, or a landing platform of width not less than one section of hatch covers is placed across.

Unremoved beams must be adequately secured.

When working space is confined to the square of the hatch, hooks may not be made fast to the bands of bales, nor may can hooks be used to raise or lower barrels if that is likely to be unsafe.

Work on a skeleton deck is not permissible without adequate staging unless the space below is filled to within 2 feet of such deck.

With certain exceptions hatch signallers must be employed when cargo is being loaded by falls.

Safe transport must be provided over water to and from a ship. Any vessel used for this purpose must be in the charge of a competent person, must not be over-crowded, must be properly equipped, and must be kept in good condition.

Part V also has a general application, as follows.

No person, unless duly authorised, is to remove or interfere with things required by the Regulations. If any are removed they must be restored by the persons last engaged in the work necessitating removal.

Persons employed must use the means of access provided in accordance with the Regulations, and no person may authorise or order otherwise. No person is to go, or be ordered to go, out on to beams to adjust lifting gear.

Part VI, amongst other things, requires that the prescribed Register (of Machinery, etc.) shall on the application of any Inspector, be produced by the person in charge thereof. If it relates to a ship's gear and is kept on board, it must be produced together with the certificate of the ship's register by the person for the time being in charge of the ship.

The Schedule sets forth the manner of conducting tests, viz.

Every winch with all accessory gear must be tested with a proof load which is to exceed the S.W.L. as follows:—

S.W.L.	Proof Load.
Up to 20 tons.	25% in excess.
20 to 50 tons.	5 tons in excess.
Over 50 tons.	10% in excess.

The above test may be made (i) by hoisting moveable weights and swinging the derrick as far as possible in both directions, (ii) by means of a spring or hydraulic balance with the derrick swung as far as practicable first in one direction and then in the other. The angle which the derrick makes with the horizontal must be stated in the certificate of the test.

Similar tests are required in respect of cranes and other hoisting machines. The test of a variable radius jib crane must be made at both maximum and minimum radius. Where a proof load of 25% in excess of the S.W.L. is impossible in the case of a hydraulic crane, it is sufficient to hoist the greatest possible load.

Loose gear must be tested with proof loads as shown below:—

Chains, rings, hooks, etc.	Twice the S.W.L.
Single sheave blocks	4 times the S.W.L.
Multiple sheave blocks of S.W.L.:—	
up to 20 tons	Twice the S.W.L.
20 to 40 tons	20 tons in excess.
over 40 tons	1½ times S.W.L.

In the case of wire ropes, a sample must be tested to destruction and the S.W.L. must not exceed one-fifth of the breaking load of the sample tested.

THE SAFETY ASPECT OF THE CARRIAGE
OF CERTAIN CARGOES

Carriage of Grain. The safe carriage of grain is governed by the M.S. (Grain) Regulations 1980 which repealed Section 24 of the 1949 Safety Convention Act. The regulations apply to sea-going United Kingdom ships, and to other sea-going ships while they are within the United Kingdom or its territorial waters, when loaded with grain in bulk.

Where grain in bulk is loaded on board any U.K. ship or is loaded in any U.K. port on board any other sea-going ship it shall be loaded in accordance with the loading arrangements prescribed in the Schedule to the regulations, or with arrangements recognised by the Secretary of State as being equivalent. If such loading arrangements are not complied with, the owner, master or charterer of the ship, or any agent of the owner or charterer who was charged with the loading or with sending the ship to sea laden with grain, shall each be guilty of an offence and liable on summary conviction to a fine not exceeding £1000 or, on conviction on indictment, to imprisonment for a term not exceeding two years and a fine. A similar penalty applies when a ship loaded with grain outside the U.K. without complying with the Grain Regulations enters any port in the U.K. so laden.

Power to Detain. In any case where a ship does not comply with these regulations, the ship is liable to be detained; but the above will not apply if the ship would not have entered port but for stress of weather or other circumstances that neither owner, master or charterer (if any) could have prevented.

Document of Authorisation. Every ship loaded with grain shall have on board a valid document of authorisation, which must be produced on demand to a surveyor. In the case of a new U.K. ship the document shall be issued by a Certifying Authority and shall state that the ship is capable of complying with these regulations and with Chapter VI of the 1974 Safety Convention, and shall also incorporate the grain loading information required by that Convention. In the case of a U.K. ship whose keel was laid before 25th May 1980, the authorisation document shall include a statement by the Certifying Authority that the ship is capable of complying with the requirements of:—

    (a) Regulation 12 of Chapter VI of the 1960 Safety Convention; or

    (b) I.M.C.O. Resolution A 184 (vi); or

    (c) I.M.C.O. Resolution A 264 (viii).

A "Certifying Authority" means the Secretary of State or an authorised classification society such as Lloyd's Register of Shipping.

"Grain" includes wheat, maize, oats, rye, barley, rice, pulses and seeds, whether in natural form or in such a processed form that its characteristics resemble those of its natural form with regard to liability to shift when loaded.

Those ships which do not have a document of authorisation will need to satisfy the Secretary of State as to the intended method of loading. The Secretary of State can grant exemptions from the loading requirements and can approve equivalent fittings and provisions.

The requirements contained in the Schedule to the regulations concern the trimming of grain, specified minimum intact stability characteristics to be met throughout the voyage, longitudinal or transverse divisions either to reduce the adverse heeling effect of grain shift or to limit the depth of grain, used for securing the grain surface, the securing of grain surface in partly filled compartments, feeders and trunks and the loading of holds and 'tween decks as common compartments.

Timber Deck Cargoes. The Merchant Shipping (Load Lines) (Deck Cargo) Regulations 1968, which came into operation on 29 July 1968, provide in Part I the general requirements applicable to all deck cargo. Part II specifies the additional requirements to be complied with in the case of timber deck cargo. Those specified in Section A apply where such cargo is carried by ships which are either not marked with timber load lines or are so marked but are loaded within the limits of their ordinary load lines. Section B gives effect to requirements of the International Convention on Load Lines 1966 applicable where timber deck cargo is carried in a ship which is marked with timber load lines and is loaded accordingly to a depth exceeding that indicated by its ordinary load lines. The Schedule to the Regulations gives details of Winter Seasonal Zones or Areas and the dates of the winter period in each case. Further information and advice to masters is given in Merchant Shipping Notices Nos. M.687 and 886 which also draw attention to the I.M.C.O. publication "The Code of Safe Practice for Ships Carrying Timber Deck Cargoes", as amended by a Supplement published in 1979.

Dangerous Goods. The carriage of dangerous goods is regulated by certain sections of the principal Act and by Section 23 of the M.S. (Safety Convention) Act, 1949, together with the M.S. (Dangerous Goods) Rules, 1978 (as amended).* In these rules, "dangerous goods" means goods classified in the Blue Book or the I.M.D.G. Code as dangerous for carriage by sea and any other goods the properties of which might be dangerous if those goods were carried by sea.

"The Blue Book" is the 1978 Report of the Department of Trade's Standing Advisory Committee on the Carriage of Dangerous Goods in Ships amended by the latest Amendments published by H.M.S.O.

"The I.M.D.G. Code" means the 1977 edition of the International Maritime Dangerous Goods Code, as amended by the latest Amendments published by I.M.C.O. It is highly important that before

---

* Revoked and replaced by S.I. 1981 No. 1747 from 1.1.82.

proceeding with the loading and stowage of dangerous goods the master of a ship should study the relevant portions of the documents referred to and carry out the recommendations contained therein. Moreover, if he has reason to fear that goods offered for shipment will constitute a danger to the lives of persons on board or to the ship or other cargo, he should refuse them either absolutely or pending expert advice. In the United Kingdom advice can be sought from the D.o.T. or from the owners' P. & I. Association.

By Section 446 of the principal Act it is made an offence to send, carry, or attempt to send or carry, dangerous goods by any vessel (British or foreign) without distinctly marking their nature on the outside of the containing package and giving written notice to the owner or master of the vessel. The penalty for non-compliance on conviction on indictment, a fine, or on summary conviction a fine not exceeding £1000, but it shall be a defence to show that the accused was unaware or had no reason to suspect that the goods were dangerous. The expression "dangerous goods" for this purpose means aquafortis, vitriol, naphtha, benzine, gunpowder, lucifer matches, nitroglycerine, petroleum, any explosives within the meaning of the Explosives Act, 1875, and any other goods which are of a dangerous nature.

By Section 447 a person, under a penalty on conviction on indictment of a fine, or on summary conviction of a £1000 fine (maximum) in contravention, must not send, carry, or attempt to send or carry, in any vessel dangerous goods under a false description or falsely describe the sender or carrier.

Section 448 provides that the master or owner of a vessel may refuse to take on board any package he suspects to contain dangerous goods, and may require it to be opened to ascertain the fact. Further, where dangerous or suspected goods have been sent or brought on board without being properly marked or without proper notice being given, the master or owner may cause them to be thrown overboard together with their container, and this shall not subject the master or owner to any liability, civil or criminal.

By Section 449, where dangerous goods have been shipped without proper marking, without proper notice, under a false description, or with a false description of sender or carrier, any court having Admiralty jurisdiction may declare such goods to be forfeited and disposed of as the court directs.

It should also be noted that Article IV, Rule 6, in the Schedule to the Carriage of Goods by Sea Act, 1971 (see Appendix I), provides that "Goods of an inflammable, explosive or dangerous nature to the shipment whereof the carrier, master or agent of the carrier, has not consented, with knowledge of their nature and character, may at any time before discharge be landed at any place or destroyed or rendered innocuous by the carrier without compensation, and the shipper of such goods shall be liable for all damages and expenses directly or indirectly arising out of or resulting from such shipment.

If any such goods shipped with such knowledge and consent shall become a danger to the ship or cargo, they may in like manner be landed at any place or destroyed or rendered innocuous by the carrier without liability on the part of the carrier except to general average, if any."

Section 23 of the 1949 Safety Convention Act provides that the Minister may make rules for regulating in the interests of safety the carriage of dangerous goods in ships to which the section applies, viz.:

(a) British ships registered in the United Kingdom;

(b) other ships while they are within any port in the United Kingdom, or are embarking or disembarking passengers within the territorial waters of the United Kingdom, or are loading or discharging cargo or fuel within those waters.

The M.S. (Dangerous Goods) Rules, 1978* have been made pursuant to the Act and if any of them are not complied with in relation to any ship, the owner or master thereof will be liable on conviction on indictment to a fine, or on summary conviction to a fine not exceeding £1000, and the ship will be deemed unsafe by reason of improper loading. Goods declared by the above Rules to be dangerous in their nature are deemed to be dangerous goods for the purpose of Part V of the principal Act also.

Rule 1 deals with interpretation and repeal. Rules 2 to 8 apply to (a) British ships registered in the United Kingdom; (b) other ships while they are loading cargo within any port in the United Kingdom or within the territorial waters of the United Kingdom. Rule 9 applies to all ships to which Rules 2 to 8 do not apply as aforesaid while they are within any port in the United Kingdom or are embarking or disembarking passengers within the territorial waters of the United Kingdom or are loading fuel or discharging cargo or fuel within these waters.

Rule 9 makes it unlawful for dangerous goods to be carried in any ship to which that Rule applies unless (a) in the case of a 1960 Convention ship the goods are being carried in accordance with the law of the country in which the ship is registered; or (b) in the case of any other ship the provisions of the United Kingdom Rules are complied with, but it is provided that the D.o.T. may exempt such a ship from any of the requirements of the Rules if satisfied that the law of the country in which the ship is registered is complied with and its requirements are no less effective than those of the United Kingdom Rules.

Important provisions of the Rules are as follows:—

The expression "dangerous goods" shall include empty receptacles which have previously been used for the carriage of dangerous goods unless such receptacles have been cleaned and dried or, when

* See page 346

the nature of the former contents permits with safety, have been adequately closed, or in the case of radioactive substances have been both cleaned and adequately closed, but the expression shall not include (a) goods forming part of the equipment or stores of the ship in which they are carried; (b) goods which neither the owner of the ship nor any of his servants or agents knew or ought to have known or had reasonable grounds for suspecting to be dangerous goods.

It is unlawful for dangerous goods to be taken on board unless the shipper has furnished the owner or master of the ship with a certificate or declaration in writing that the shipment offered for carriage is properly marked and labelled in accordance with the provisions of the Rules and is packed in a manner adequate to withstand the ordinary risks of handling and transport by sea having regard to their nature.   Such certificate or declaration is required to indicate with the correct technical name the identity of the goods and to which of the following classes they belong, viz.:—

Class 1—Explosives.

Class 2—Flammable gases, poisonous gases, or compressed, liquefied or dissolved gases which are neither flammable nor
poisonous.

Class 3—Flammable liquids subdivided into 3 categories:—

    3.1—Low flashpoint group of liquids having a flashpoint
below $-18°C$; closed cup test;

    3.2—Intermediate flashpoint group of liquids having a
flashpoint of $-18°C$ up to, but not including 23°C;
closed cup test;

    3.3—High flashpoint group of liquids having a flashpoint
of 23°C up to and including 61°C, closed cup test.

Class 4.1—Flammable solids.

Class 4.2—Flammable solids or substances liable to spontaneous
combustion.

Class 4.3—Flammable solids or substances which in contact with
water emit flammable gases.

Class 5.1—Oxidising substances.

Class 5.2—Organic peroxides.

Class 6.1—Poisonous (toxic) substances.

Class 6.2—Infectious substances.

Class 7—Radioactive substances.

Class 8—Corrosives.

Class 9—Miscellaneous dangerous substances, that is any other
substance which experience has shown, or may show, to be
of such a dangerous character that these Rules should apply
to it.

Where goods have been packed into a freight container, the person responsible for packing the goods must furnish the owner or master of the ship with a certificate or declaration in writing that the goods are contained in sound packages, and have been properly packed and secured in a freight container suitable for the goods. Freight container includes a container carried on a chassis.

The master must cause a list, manifest or stowage plan to be carried in the ship setting forth in accordance with the above, details of the dangerous goods carried on the current voyage and the places in the ship where they are stowed.

It is unlawful for dangerous goods contained in any vehicle, freight container, portable tank, tank container or road tank vehicle, or receptacle or package to be taken on board unless such container is clearly marked with a distinctive label or stencil indicating the correct technical name of the goods and the nature of the danger. If loaded in the United Kingdom the label or stencil required to indicate the identity of the goods shall be the I.M.D.G. Code class label appropriate to the goods.

It is unlawful to ship dangerous goods **not loaded in bulk** if the owner or his servant knows or ought to know that the goods are not packed adequately to withstand the ordinary risks of handling and sea transport. But it is a good defence for the owner to prove that he or the master was furnished with a written statement by the shipper that the goods were packed in accordance with requirements and that neither the owner nor his servants or agents knew the goods were not so packed.

It is unlawful for goods to be **loaded in bulk** if the owner or his servant knows or ought to know that they cannot be safely carried in bulk to their destination.

Provided that where goods listed in the latest editions of the I.M.C.O. Codes for Ships carrying Dangerous Chemicals in Bulk, or for Ships carrying Liquefied Gases in Bulk, as appropriate, have been loaded in bulk in accordance with recommendations in those Codes, the requirements of this rule shall be deemed to have been complied with.

Dangerous goods and any containers holding dangerous goods must be stowed and kept stowed in a safe and proper manner having regard to their identity and dangerous nature as indicated by their markings. Dangerous goods of a different kind which the owner of the ship or his servants or agent knows or ought to know are liable to interact dangerously must be effectively separated and kept effectively separated from one another. There must be adequate ventilation.

It is unlawful to take on board any explosives (other than Safety Class Ammunition) which the owner or any of his servants knows or ought to know present a serious risk when carried in a ship unless such explosives are stowed in an electrically safe compartment, and where Category II stowage is required they are stowed in a closed magazine, and unless detonators are effectively separate from all other Class I goods.

It is unlawful for any explosives to be taken on board any ship which carries more than 12 passengers for carriage in that ship except:—

(a) Explosives set forth in Schedule 2 to the Rules. (This is a long list including certain types of percussion caps, cartridges and fuses.)

(b) Any explosives the total weight of which does not exceed 10 kilogrammes net weight.

(c) Distress signals for use in ships and aircraft if the total weight of such signals does not exceed 1000 kilogrammes.

(d) Shop goods fireworks (except in ships carrying unberthed passengers).

Items (c) and (d) must be stowed under the supervision of a person appointed by the master or owner of the ship.

It is unlawful for any dangerous goods to be taken on board any ship which carries more than 25 passengers, or more than one passenger per three metres of overall length, whichever is the greater, for carriage in that ship, if those goods are classified in the Blue Book as prohibited for carriage in a passenger ship or are specified in the I.M.D.G. Code or the Blue Book for on deck stowage only and such stowage cannot be provided.

Schedule 1 to the Rules stipulates what is necessary with respect to the packaging of dangerous goods which are not loaded in bulk, and Schedule 2 lists the explosives which may be taken on board ships carrying more than 12 passengers.

Marine Pollution. When the 1973 MARPOL Convention comes into force, a ship's master will have an obligation to report an incident involving actual or likely loss into the sea of a harmful substance. In the light of recent incidents where packaged dangerous goods have been washed ashore on the U.K. coast, the Department of Trade in Merchant Shipping Notice M.953 urge masters and shipowners now to report incidents involving packaged dangerous goods to allow an early and effective response to be made if they are washed ashore. Masters of all ships within 200 miles of the U.K. which have lost overboard (or are likely to lose overboard) packaged dangerous goods, are asked to make a short first report of the incident immediately either directly, or through the nearest U.K. coast radio station to H.M. Coastguard.

The first report should indicate:—

(i) the name and position of the ship and time of incident;

(ii) the correct technical name and the U.N. No. (if available) of the goods lost or jettisoned, or likely to be lost or jettisoned, indicating the I.M.C.O. Class(es) of the hazard(s), the name of the manufacturers of the goods (when known);

(iii) the type of package and whether or not the goods are packed in a freight container or vehicle;

(iv) an estimate of the quantities of substances and likely condition of the packages of dangerous cargo lost or jettisoned, or likely to be.

Further information concerning the loss can be sent later. Where, following a stranding, collision, or sinking, the loss of packaged dangerous goods seems imminent, the fact that dangerous goods are on board should be included in the first report of the incident. Should such a vessel be salved, or be proceeding into port after an incident, the presence of dangerous goods on board should be reported to the Port Authority in the proper way.

Other Hazardous Cargoes. In various notices the D.o.T. draw attention to the special dangers associated with the carriage of such cargoes as coal, slurry, steel billets, etc., and make recommendations in the interests of safety. A list of current M. notices concerned with cargoes having special hazards is given in notice M.722, and a "Code of Safe Practice for Bulk Cargoes" is published by I.M.C.O. Responsibility for the seaworthiness of a ship rests on the owner or master, largely on the latter in practice, and it will generally be the case that the standards of seaworthiness suggested by these official notices will be regarded as standards that ought to be observed.

The following Codes have been published by I.M.C.O. for the guidance of owners, masters, builders and repairers. The D.o.T. recommend the Codes as minimum requirements, and although for the time being they are not statutory requirements it is possible that ports here and abroad will require vessels to hold certificates of fitness before they can enter port. The Codes are:—

(1) The Code for the Construction and Equipment of Ships Carrying Liquefied Gases in Bulk (for ships delivered after 30th June 1978, or contracted after 31st October 1976).

(2) The Code for Existing Ships Carrying Liquefied Gases in Bulk (for ships delivered before 31st October 1976).

(3) The Code for the Construction and Equipment of Ships Carrying Dangerous Chemicals in Bulk (with amendments).

DISTRESS AND RESCUE AT SEA

From time to time various official notices have been published which contain advice to masters of ships on the action they should take if their vessels are in distress or when they go to the assistance of another vessel or an aircraft casualty. Copies of these notices are obtainable from H.M. Offices and Custom Houses in the United Kingdom, and copies may be inspected at Shipping Offices and British Consulates abroad.

It is pointed out that the radio watch on the international distress frequencies is one of the most important factors in the arrangements for the rescue of people in distress at sea, and it is urged that every ship fitted with suitable radio equipment should make its contribution to safety by guarding one or other of these distress frequencies for as long as is practicable whether or not required to do so by regulation. To supplement the efforts of ships at sea most maritime countries maintain a life-saving service round their coasts, and although the organisation of search and rescue may vary from country to country coast radio stations always play an important part by alerting ships in the vicinity and notifying the proper shore authorities. Off the coasts of the United Kingdom assistance may be given not only by ships in the vicinity but also by the following authorities:—

(i) **Coast Radio Stations.**

(ii) **H.M. Coastguard** is the authority responsible for initiating and co-ordinating the search and rescue measures for all vessels in distress off the coast of the United Kingdom, and in an area bounded by latitude 45° and 61° North, by longitude 30° West and by the adjacent European S.R.Rs.

(iii) **The Royal National Life-boat Institution** which is a private organisation supported by voluntary contributions. Each of the Institute's lifeboats is equipped with MF and VHF/FM radio, and when launched maintains listening watch on 2182kHz and VHF Ch. 16.

(iv) **The Royal Navy** which assists by means of surface craft and aircraft, including helicopters.

(v) **The Royal Air Force** which, operating through the Rescue Co-ordination Centres, provides rescue facilities for aircraft in and around the United Kingdom and, as far as service conditions permit, assists ships in distress by means of aircraft.

(vi) **Air Traffic Control Centres** which are often the first to receive information about aircraft in distress. Aircraft are able to communicate with these centres by radio and may be requested to assist in the search for a casualty.

(vii) **Lloyd's** who are informed of casualties by Coast Radio Stations and are responsible for notifying ocean-going tugs.

(viii) **Local Officers of the Fishery Departments** who liaise with the Coastguard when reports are received of missing or overdue fishing vessels.

Statutory Duty of Master to assist Persons in Distress. Section 6 of the Maritime Conventions Act, 1911, provides that the master or person in charge of a vessel shall, so far as he can do so without serious danger to his own vessel, her crew, and passengers (if any), render assistance to every person, even if such person be a subject of a foreign state at war with Her Majesty, who is found at sea in danger of being lost, and, if he fails to do so, he shall be guilty of an offence. Compliance with the provision shall not affect the right of the master or person in charge to salvage.

Statutory Distress Signals. These are the signals prescribed in the International Regulations for Preventing Collisions at Sea.

It is pointed out that two of the statutory signals, namely, "a continuous sounding with any fog-signal apparatus" and "flames on the vessel" could on occasions be misunderstood. It is recommended that distress signals should be as distinctive as possible so that they may be recognised at once and assistance despatched without delay. The best distress signals, it is suggested, are red parachute flares or rockets emitting red stars or hand flares showing red lights.

Disposal of Obsolete Fireworks. Line throwing rockets, distress rockets, red flares, etc., are liable to deteriorate if kept for a long period, and should be condemned and immediately replaced after the date of expiry marked on them. Special care should be taken regarding disposal, and on no account should obsolete fireworks be used for testing or practice purposes, or landed for any purpose. They should be kept in a safe place until opportunity occurs for throwing them overboard in deep water well away from land. They should be adequately weighted and removed from any protective plastic envelope packing before disposal.

Provided they remain in good condition, buoyant smoke signals should be serviceable for 3 years, but they should be examined for corrosion and other defects and replaced if necessary earlier than the date of expiry marked on them.

Misuse of Distress Signals. Section 21 of the 1949 Safety Convention Act has the effect that if prescribed signals are used in wrong circumstances, or if a private signal (whether registered or not) liable to be mistaken for a distress signal is used or displayed, the master who offends or permits any person under his authority to offend shall be liable on conviction on indictment to a fine, and on summary conviction to a fine not exceeding £1000 and shall be further liable to pay compensation for any labour undertaken, risk incurred, or loss sustained in consequence. Such compensation is recoverable in the same manner as salvage. (It is not to be implied, however, that there is any right to compensation for labour undertaken, etc., in going out in response to signals properly displayed, even though on arrival it is found that the proffered services are not required.)

Nothing in the M.S. (Safety Convention) Act, 1949, requiring persons in charge of wireless stations to give facilities for the reception of reports relating to dangers to navigation shall interfere with the transmission of distress signals.

Authority to use Distress Signals. By Rule 3 of the M.S. (Signals of Distress) Rules, 1977:—

1. No signal of distress shall be used by any ship to which these Rules apply unless the master of the ship so orders.

2. The master of the vessel shall not order any signal of distress to be used by his vessel unless he is satisfied:—

(a) that his vessel is in serious and imminent danger, or that another vessel or an aircraft is in serious and imminent danger and cannot of itself send that signal; and

(b) that the vessel in danger (whether his own vessel or another vessel) or the aircraft in danger, as the case may be, requires immediate assistance in addition to any assistance then available to her.

3. The master of a vessel which has sent any signal of distress by means of radio or other means shall cause that signal to be revoked by all appropriate means as soon as he is satisfied that the vessel or aircraft to which the signal relates is no longer in need of assistance as aforesaid.

N.B.—Failure to cancel a distress call when danger no longer exists may result in serious loss of time to other ships, or needless anxiety to relatives and friends of those on board because failure to find or establish communication with the ship sending the signal has led to a belief that she has foundered.

Obligation to assist Vessels or Aircraft in Distress. This is the subject of Section 22 of the M.S. (Safety Convention) Act, 1949, of which the following is a summary.

If a signal or other information from any source is received that a vessel or aircraft is in distress, the master of a British ship shall proceed with all speed to the persons in distress and, if possible, inform them that he is doing so, unless:—

(a) he is unable, or

(b) in special circumstances he considers it unreasonable or unnecessary, or

(c) he is released from the obligation.

Where the master of a ship in distress has requisitioned a British ship which has answered his call, it is the duty of the requisitioned ship to comply with the requisition and proceed with all speed.

The master shall be released from the obligation to go to the assistance of the persons in distress as soon as he is informed of the requisition of one or more ships other than his own and that such requisition is being complied with.

The master of a ship which has been requisitioned shall be released from the obligation to proceed to the assistance of persons in distress if he is informed by those persons or by the master of any ship which has reached the persons in distress that assistance is no longer required.

If a master fails to comply with the above provisions he shall be guilty of an indictable offence.

The Official Log Book Regulations require the Master of a U.K. registered ship to record every signal of distress, or a message that a vessel, aircraft or person is in distress at sea, observed or received. Further, where the master on receiving a signal of distress or information from any source that a vessel or aircraft is in distress, is unable or in the special circumstances of the case considers it unreasonable or unnecessary to go to the assistance of the persons in distress, he must enter a statement of his reasons for not going to the assistance of those persons.

Nothing in the above affects the provisions of Section 6 of the Maritime Conventions Act (dealing with the general duty of masters to render assistance to persons in danger at sea), and compliance with Section 22 of the Safety Convention Act does not affect salvage rights.

N.B.—Nor are insurance rights or the benefits of exceptions clauses in contracts of affreightment affected by deviation to save life.

Aircraft Casualties at Sea. One notice contains a section on aircraft casualties in which full details are given in relation to distress communications and action taken to render assistance. The following matters are singled out for special mention here as, in addition to their vital importance in practice, they may be of particular interest to students preparing for examinations.

Action when Survivors are picked up. A survivor from an aircraft casualty who is picked up by a ship may be able to give information which will assist in the rescue of others. Masters are therefore asked to put the following questions to rescued survivors and communicate the answers to a coast radio station, giving the position of the rescuing vessel and the time when the survivor was picked up.

1. Did you bale out or was the aircraft "ditched"? Time and date?
2. If you baled out, at what altitude?
3. How many others did you see leave the aircraft by parachute?
4. How many "ditched" with the aircraft?
5. How many did you see leave the aircraft after "ditching"?
6. How many survivors did you see in the water?
7. What flotation gear had they?
8. What was the total number of persons aboard the aircraft prior to the accident?
9. What caused the emergency?

Action when Aircraft is forced to "ditch". The captain of a distressed aircraft will be materially assisted in locating a ship if the latter:—

1. Transmits homing bearings, or (if so requested) transmits signals enabling the aircraft to take its own bearings;
2. By day makes black smoke;
3. By night directs a searchlight vertically.

Ditching an aircraft is difficult and usually dangerous. A ship which knows that an aircraft intends to ditch should, if practicable, try to provide a lee of calm water. This may be achieved by any means at the master's discretion, such as steering on a circular course through 360°, with the addition, if possible, of an oil "slick".

The captain of an aircraft normally sits on the port side of the cockpit, and thus has better visibility on that side. An aircraft will therefore usually ditch on the starboard side of a ship and heading into the wind, although, when seas are running high, it may be expected to attempt to land along the trough of the seas. In the absence of a pre-arranged plan, the ship should steam into the wind and assume that the aircraft will ditch on her starboard side. Helicopter captains sit on the starboard side of the aircraft and would, therefore, normally ditch on the port side of a ship heading into wind.

If it is dark, the ship should illuminate the sea as much as possible by searchlight on the side upon which the aircraft is expected to ditch. Care should be taken not to dazzle the pilot who might otherwise lose control of his aircraft at a critical moment. If battery operated floats are available, it will help the pilot considerably if they are laid in line astern to indicate the direction of the suggested alighting area. Six floats should be laid at 200-yard intervals.

The ship's master should if possible tell the captain of an aircraft which is going to ditch the general weather conditions, including wind speed and direction, visibility, state of sea and swell, approximate cloud base, and barometric pressure.

A land plane may break up immediately on striking the water, and life rafts may be damaged. The ship should therefore have a lifeboat ready for launching, and if possible boarding nets should be lowered from the ship and heaving lines made ready in the ship and the lifeboat. Survivors of the aircraft may have bright yellow life-jackets, water torches and whistles.

It should be borne in mind that military aircraft are often fitted with ejection seat mechanism, the position of which is indicated.

REMOVING PERSONS IN DANGER

Where the D.o.T., to enable persons to be removed from any place in consequence of a threat to their lives, has permitted more persons to be carried on board a ship than the Act permits, carriage of excess persons is not an offence.

The D.o.T. has power to exempt any ships or classes of ships from the requirements of the safety regulations either absolutely or subject to such conditions as it thinks fit.

URGENCY SIGNALS AND REPORTS OF DANGERS TO NAVIGATION

Urgency. A ship which is not in serious or imminent danger but which urgently requires assistance of some kind (*e.g.*, medical advice) should prefix any radio call for assistance with the Urgency Signal XXX or SECURITE repeated 3 times.

Navigational Warnings. The master of every United Kingdom ship, on meeting with dangerous ice, a dangerous derelict or any other direct danger to navigation, or a tropical storm, or on encountering, subfreezing air temperatures associated with gale force winds causing severe ice accretion on the superstructure of ships or winds of force 10 or above on the Beaufort Scale for which no storm warning has been received, shall send information about those matters by all means of communication at his disposal to all ships in the vicinity and to the nearest coast radio station or signal station. The information must be sent in English or by means of the International Code of Signals, and if sent to a signal station, it shall be requested to forward the information to the nearest coast radio station. The M.S. (Navigational Warnings) Regulations 1980 require the information that follows to be sent:—

(a) in case of ice, derelicts, and other dangers (except a tropical storm or winds of force 10 or above:—

1. The kind of ice, derelict or other danger observed;
2. The position of the danger when last observed;
3. The G.M.T. and date when danger last observed;

(b) in case of tropical storms (hurricanes, typhoons, cyclones, etc. and winds of force 10 or above):—

1. Position of storm as far as can be ascertained, with G.M.T. and date when the storm was encountered.
2. Position, true course, and speed of ship when observation was made.
3. Barometric pressure, stating units and whether corrected.
4. Change in pressure during previous 3 hours.
5. True direction of wind.
6. Wind force (Beaufort scale).
7. State of sea (smooth, moderate, rough or high).
8. State of swell and direction from which it comes (slight, moderate or heavy).
9. Period or length of swell (short, average, or long).
10. True course and speed of ship.

Items 1 and 2, above, are essential and the additional information should be sent as far as is practicable. The obligation to report a storm should be interpreted in a broad spirit and information transmitted whenever the master has good reason to believe that a tropical storm exists in his neighbourhood. When a storm has been reported it is desirable, but not obligatory, that other observations be made and transmitted as long as the ship remains under the influence of the storm.

(c) in the case of subfreezing air temperatures associated with gale force winds causing ice accretion:—

1. the G.M.T. and date when encounter was made.
2. the air temperature and (if practicable) the sea temperature at the time.
3. the force of the wind (Beaufort Scale) and its true direction.

Under the rules, a report of a danger to navigation if made by radiotelegraphy must be preceded by an indication of the nature of the danger and by the safety signal TTT repeated 3 times, or if by radiotelephony, by the safety signal consisting of the spoken word "SECURITE" (pronounced "SAYCURITAY") repeated 3 times. A master who fails to report a danger to navigation is guilty of an offence and liable on summary conviction to a fine not exceeding £500.

UNSEAWORTHY AND UNSAFE SHIPS

Section 457 of the M.S.A. 1894, under which it was an offence to send an unseaworthy ship to sea, has been repealed by section 44 of the M.S.A. 1979. This section creates instead an offence in respect of a dangerously unsafe ship. The offence is committed if any ship in a U.K. port, or any ship registered in the U.K. which is in any other port, is, having regard to the nature of the service for which the ship is intended, unfit, by reason of the condition of the ship's hull, equipment, or machinery, or by reason of undermanning, or overloading or improper loading, to go to sea without serious danger to human life. The master and owner of the ship are each guilty of the offence and liable on conviction on indictment to a fine, and on summary conviction to a fine not exceeding £50,000, but it is a defence in proceedings for the offence to prove that at the time of the alleged offence arrangements had been made to ensure that before the ship went to sea it was made fit to do so without serious danger to human life, or it was reasonable not to have made such arrangements.

No proceedings for the above offence shall be begun except by or with the consent of the Secretary of State or the Director of Public Prosecutions.

In every contract of service, express or implied, between the owner of a ship and the master or any seaman thereof, there shall be implied, notwithstanding any agreement to the contrary, an obligation on the owner that he, and the master, and every agent charged with loading or preparing the ship for sea, or sending the ship to sea, shall use all reasonable means to insure the seaworthiness of the ship for the voyage at the time when the voyage commences, and to keep her in a seaworthy condition for the voyage during the voyage. But this does not subject the owner to any liability by reason of the ship being sent to sea in an unseaworthy state where, in special circumstances, the sending of her to sea in such a state was reasonable or justifiable.

In respect of the above, the term "seaworthiness" relates to the degree of fitness of the ship as to structure, equipment; and manning. For marine insurance purposes a ship is "seaworthy" when she is reasonably fit in all respects to encounter the ordinary perils of the sea of the adventure insured. For the purpose of contracts of affreightment the term may have an even wider application and will include "cargoworthiness". It is important to distinguish between "statutory seaworthiness" and the implied or express warranty of seaworthiness contained in a contract of marine insurance or a contract of affreightment. A breach of statute is a criminal offence, whereas a breach of warranty is not. The latter may, however, be actionable if it gives rise to loss or damage, and may deprive a carrier of goods by sea of the benefits of "exceptions clauses" and reduce his status to that of a common carrier. Further reference to this will be found in Chapter 9.

Two striking examples of the wide application of the term "seaworthiness" are afforded by consideration of the following court cases.

In one case cargo owners sought to recover prepaid freight after the vessel concerned in the adventure had been seized for debts before completing her voyage. The court ruled that the ship was unseaworthy in that there was a multiplicity of creditors any of whom might arrest the ship. The court took the view that the term "seaworthiness" cannot be limited to physical matters and that the law imposed an obligation on the owners to exercise due diligence to make the ship seaworthy. It was held that the owners lacked the resources to free the ship from arrest and there could not, therefore, be any certainty of the ship completing her voyage.

The other case concerned a ship which had been time-chartered with a delivery date agreed. Shortly before this date it was discovered that the ship's deratting certificate had expired but it was expected that a new one would be available immediately after the ship had been inspected. As it turned out the port health authorities were not satisfied with the condition of the ship and insisted on fumigation. The time required for this to be arranged and effected was so long that the cancelling date was reached before a new certificate could be issued. Meanwhile the charterer decided to cancel the charter and engage another vessel. The owners brought an action to recover damages, but this failed on the grounds that the vessel was unseaworthy and unable to obtain a port clearance at the time when delivery was due under the terms of the contract.

If a ship is "unsafe" while in a United Kingdom port she may be detained for the purpose of holding a survey or for ascertaining the sufficiency of her crew. A ship is deemed unsafe when by reason of defective condition of hull, equipment, or machinery, or by overloading or improper loading, or by undermanning, she is unfit to go to sea without serious danger to human life. The provisions of the M.S.A. in respect of detention are broadly as follows.

If the D.o.T. have reason to believe, on complaint or otherwise, that the ship is unsafe they may order provisional detention and, after serving on the master a written notice of the grounds of detention, may appoint a surveyor to survey the ship and make a report to the D.o.T. On receipt of the report the Department may either order the ship to be released or, if in their opinion she is unsafe, order her to be finally detained either absolutely or until any defects have been remedied.

Before the order for final detention is made a copy of the surveyor's report must be served on the master of the ship, and within 7 days after that service the owner or master may appeal to the court of survey for the district where the ship is detained.

Where a ship has been provisionally detained, the owner or master, at any time before the appointed person makes his survey, may require that he be accompanied by such person as the owner or master may select out of the list of assessors for the court of survey. If the surveyor and the assessor are in agreement, the D.o.T. shall cause the ship to be detained or released accordingly, but if they differ, the Department may act as if the requisition had not been made, and the owner or master will retain the right of appeal to the court of survey.

On provisional detention the D.o.T. may at any time, if they think it expedient, refer the matter to the court of survey. If satisfied that the detained ship is not unsafe, the Department may order her to be released either upon or without any conditions.

A person appointed as a detaining officer has the same power as the D.o.T. have to order provisional detention, appoint surveyors, or release a ship he thinks is not unsafe. Any order made by him must be forthwith reported to the D.o.T.

An order for detention, provisional or final, and an order varying the same, must be served as soon as may be on the master of the ship.

Costs of detention and survey follow the event, that is they are payable by the shipowner if the ship is found to be unsafe, but by the D.o.T. otherwise. However, in the case, for instance, where a ship is provisionally detained pending the rectification of some breach of the Load Line Rules, liability for costs would still rest with the shipowner although the ship is not "finally detained". In some cases the D.o.T. may be liable to pay compensation for loss or damage sustained by the owner by reason of the detention of the ship in addition to costs, but that would not extend to general damages in respect of injury to the owner's reputation.

Security for Costs. Where a complaint is made to the D.o.T. or a detaining officer that a British ship is unsafe, the complainant may be required to give satisfaction for the costs and compensation which he may become liable to pay. But security shall not be required where the complaint is made by one-fourth, being not less than 3, of the seamen belonging to the ship, and is not considered frivolous or vexatious, if the complaint is made in sufficient time before the sailing of the ship for ascertaining whether the ship ought to be detained. If the ship is detained in consequence of the complaint and the D.o.T. become liable to the owner for costs or compensation, the former may recover the amount from the complainants.

Detention of Foreign Ships. Where a foreign ship at a port in the United Kingdom is unsafe, the provisions of the Act with respect to the detention of ships apply as if the ship were British, but with the following modifications:—

1. A copy of the order for provisional detention shall be forthwith served on the consular officer for the country to which the ship belongs at or nearest to the said port;
2. where a ship has been provisionally detained, the consular officer, on the request of the owner or master, may require the surveyor to be accompanied by such person as he may select;
3. where the owner or master appeals to the court of survey, the consular officer, on his request, may appoint a competent person as assessor in lieu of the assessor who, if the ship were British, would be appointed otherwise than by the D.o.T.

Survey of Ships alleged by Seamen to be Unseaworthy. If a seaman is being proceeded against for the offence of desertion or absence without leave, and it is alleged by one-fourth, or, if their number exceeds 20, by not less than 5 of the seamen belonging to the ship, that the ship is not in a fit condition to go to sea, or that the accommodation in the ship is insufficient, the court having cognisance of the case shall take such means as may be in their power to satisfy themselves concerning the truth or untruth of the allegation. For that purpose they shall receive the evidence of the persons making the allegation and summon other witnesses whose evidence they may think it desirable to hear. If satisfied that the allegation is groundless, the court shall adjudicate, but otherwise before adjudication they shall cause the ship to be surveyed.

A seaman charged with desertion or quitting his ship without leave shall not have the right to apply for survey unless before quitting his ship he has complained to the master of the circumstances so alleged in justification.

If necessary, the court shall require a surveyor of ships, or some other impartial surveyor appointed by the court, to survey the ship and answer such questions concerning her as the court think fit to put. After survey the surveyor must make his written report to the court, and the court shall cause the report to be communicated to the parties. Unless the opinions expressed in the report are proved erroneous, the court shall determine the questions before them in accordance with these opinions.   The surveyor appointed has, for the purpose of his survey, all powers of a D.o.T. inspector.

Here, again, costs follow the event and may, in appropriate circumstances, be deducted from wages due or to become due to the complainant.   In the reverse circumstances the owner or master of the ship may be liable to pay compensation for the seaman's detention as the court may award.

Enforcement of Detention. The procedure for the enforcement of the detention of a ship and the penalty for breaking detention are described in Chapter 1.

Safety Regulations. Section 19 of the M.S. Act 1970 gives power to the D.o.T. to make regulations for securing, as far as practicable, safe working conditions and safe means of access for masters and seamen employed in U.K. registered ships and for requiring the reporting of injuries sustained by them.   Such regulations may:—

(a) require the maintenance, inspection and testing of any equipment and impose conditions on its use;

(b) require, prohibit or regulate the use of any material or process;

(c) require the provision and use of any protective clothing or equipment;

(d) limit the hours of employment of seamen in any specified operation or in any specified circumstances;

(e) make provision for the discharge, by persons appointed from among the persons employed in a ship, of functions in connection with the arrangements to be made under the regulations.

The regulations may make different provisions for different descriptions of ship and for ships of the same description in different circumstances.   The D.o.T. may grant exemptions from any requirement of the regulations in respect of any ship, and the regulations may make a contravention of any provision an offence punishable on conviction on indictment with a fine and on summary conviction with a fine not exceeding £1000.

In December 1981, the M.S. (Means of Access) Regulations 1981 (S.I. 1981 No. 1729) covering gangways, ladders etc. were made.

MISCELLANEOUS PROVISIONS RELATING TO SAFETY

On 1st November 1974 in London, an International Conference adopted the International Convention for the Safety of Life at Sea, 1974. It was agreed that the Convention would enter into force 12 months after the date on which not less than 25 states, with combined total merchant fleets exceeding fifty per cent of the gross tonnage of the world's merchant shipping, had ratified the Convention. Sufficient ratifications had been received at I.M.C.O. by May

1979, and the Convention entered into force on 25th May 1980 for Convention countries.

Meanwhile in Parliament the Merchant Shipping Act 1979 received the Royal Assent and many sections of this Act came into operation during 1979 and 1980. Amongst such sections were sections 21 and 22 which gave the Secretary of State wide powers to make regulations concerning safety and health on ships, and the regulations which came into operation on 25th May 1980 to bring in the measures required by the SOLAS Convention 1974 were made under those sections. In 1978, to further improve matters concerning safety of life at sea, the states party to the 1974 Convention signed a Protocol relating to that Convention which included an Annex providing for modifications and additions to the 1974 Convention. The requisite number of states having become Parties to it, the Protocol entered into force on 1st May 1981, resulting in some amendments to the 1980 Regulations, and some additional new regulations. The references to regulations which follow are those in force from 1st May 1981 for United Kingdom ships, and for other ships while within the United Kingdom or its territorial waters.

For the purpose of the regulations a "United Kingdom ship" is defined in section 21 of the M.S. Act 1979 as meaning a ship which:—

(a) is registered in the United Kingdom; or

(b) is not registered under the law of any country but is wholly owned by persons each of whom is either a citizen of the United Kingdom and Colonies or a company which is established under the law of a part of the United Kingdom and has its principal place of business in a part of the United Kingdom.

References are made hereunder and elsewhere in this chapter and in Chapter 8 to the following sets of Regulations:—

The M.S. (Cargo Ship Construction and Survey) Regulations 1981.

The M.S. (Passenger Ship Construction) Regulations 1980 (as amended by S.I. 1981/580).

The M.S. (Radio Installations) Regulations 1980 (as amended by S.I. 1981/582).

The M.S. (Navigational Equipment) Regulations 1980 (as amended by S.I. 1981/579).

The M.S. (Navigational Warnings) Regulations 1980.

The M.S. (Grain) Regulations 1980 (as amended by S.I. 1981/576).

The M.S. (Life-saving Appliances) Regulations 1980 (as amended by S.I. 1981/577).

The M.S. (Closing of Openings in Hulls and in Watertight Bulkheads) Regulations 1980.

The M.S. (Fire Appliances) (Amendment) Rules 1980 (as amended by S.I. 1981/575).

The M.S. (Musters) Regulations 1980 (as amended by S.I. 1981/578).

The M.S. (Pilot Ladders and Hoists) Regulations 1980 (as amended by S.I. 1981/581).

The M.S. (Fire Appliances) Regulations 1980 (as amended by S.I. 1981/574).

The M.S. (Modification of Merchant Shipping (Safety Convention) Act 1949 and Merchant Shipping Act 1964) Regulations 1980.

The M.S. (Modification of Enactments) Regulations 1981.

The M.S. (Signals of Distress) Rules, 1977.

The M.S. (Dangerous Goods) Regulations 1981.

The M.S. (Automatic Pilot and Testing of Steering Gear) Regulations 1981.

The Deck Cargo Regulations 1968.

The M.S. (Carriage of Nautical Publications) Rules 1975.

The M.S. (Cargo Ship Safety Equipment Survey) Regulations 1981.

The M.S. (Radio Installations Survey) Regulations 1981.

Classification of Ships for the Purpose of Certain Regulations. For the purpose of the Life-saving Appliances, Fire Appliances, Musters, and Pilot Ladders and Hoists Regulations, ships are arranged in special classes arranged as shown below.

Passenger Ships:—

Class I.	Passenger ships engaged on voyages (not being short international voyages) any of which are long international voyages.
Class II.	Passenger ships engaged on voyages (not being long international voyages) any of which are short international voyages.
Class II(A).	Passenger ships in respect of which there is or should be in force a certificate entitled "Passenger Certificate Class II(A)" being a certificate for ships engaged on voyages of any kind other than international voyages.
Class III.	Passenger ships in respect of which there is or should be in force a certificate entitled "Passenger Certificate Class III" being a certificate for ships engaged only on voyages in the course of which they are at no time more than 70 miles by sea from their point of departure and not more than 18 miles from the coast of the United Kingdom, and which are at sea only in fine weather and during restricted periods.
Class IV.	Passenger ships in respect of which there is or should be in force a certificate entitled "Passenger Certificate Class IV" being a certificate for ships engaged only on voyages

	in partially smooth waters, or in smooth and partially smooth waters.
Class V.	Passenger ships in respect of which there is or should be in force a certificate entitled "Passenger Certificate Class V" being a certificate for ships engaged only on voyages in smooth waters.
Class VI.	Passenger ships in respect of which there is or should be in force a certificate entitled "Passenger Certificate Class VI" being a certificate for ships engaged only on voyages with not more than 250 passengers on board, to sea, in smooth or in partially smooth waters, in all cases in fine weather and during restricted periods, in the course of which the ships are at no time more than 15 miles, exclusive of any smooth waters, from their point of departure nor more than 3 miles from land.
Class VI(A).	Passenger ships in respect of which there is or should be in force a certificate entitled "Passenger Certificate Class VI(A)" being a certificate for ships carrying not more than 50 passengers for a distance of not more than 6 miles on voyages to or from isolated communities on the islands or coast of Scotland, and which do not proceed for a distance of more than 3 miles from land.

Ships other than Passenger Ships:—

Class VII.	Ships (other than ships of Classes I, VII(A), VII(T), X, XI, and XII) engaged on voyages any of which are long international voyages.
Class VII(A).	Ships engaged in the whaling industry or employed as fish processing or canning factory ships, and ships engaged in the carriage of persons employed in the whaling, fish processing or canning industries.
Class VII(T).	Tankers engaged on voyages any of which are long international voyages.
Class VIII.	Ships (other than ships of Classes II, VIII(T), IX, X, XI, and XII) engaged on voyages (not being long international voyages) any of which are short international voyages.
Class VIII(T).	Tankers engaged on voyages (not being long international voyages) any of which are short international voyages.

Class VIII(A).   Ships (other than ships of Classes II(A) to VI(A) inclusive, VIII(A)(T), IX, IX(A), IX(A)(T), X, XI and XII) engaged only on voyages which are not international voyages.

Class VIII(A)(T). Tankers engaged only on voyages which are not international voyages.

Class IX.   Tugs and tenders (other than ships of Classes II, II(A), III, VI, and VI(A)) which proceed to sea but are not engaged on long international voyages.

Class IX(A).   Ships (other than ships of Classes IV to VI inclusive) which do not proceed to sea.

Class IX(A)(T). Tankers which do not proceed to sea.

Class X.   Fishing vessels other than ships of Classes I to VI(A) inclusive.

Class XI.   Sailing ships (other than fishing vessels and ships of Class XII) which proceed to sea.

Class XII.   Pleasure craft (other than ships of Classes I to VI(A) inclusive) of 13·7 metres in length or over.

For the purpose of the Passenger Ship Construction Rules British passenger ships registered in the United Kingdom are arranged in Classes as indicated above for Classes I to VI(A) inclusive.

Cargo Ship Construction Regulations 1981. These regulations apply to seagoing United Kingdom ships of 500 tons gross or over; and to other seagoing ships of 500 tons gross or over while they are within the United Kingdom or its territorial waters. They do not apply to passenger ships, troopships, pleasure craft and fishing vessels and ships not propelled by mechanical means. The requirements specified in the regulations were introduced over a period and may not have to be complied with in their entirety by ships built before 1981. In order to decide exactly which regulations need to be complied with, it is necessary to know:—

(*a*) the date of signing the building contract for the ship or the contract for major alterations to it;

(*b*) the date on which the keel was laid or the ship was at a similar stage of construction, or alterations commenced;

(*c*) the date of completion of building or of major alterations.

With this information, an examination of regulation 1 paragraphs 3 to 6 inclusive will enable a decision to be made, but it should be noted that paragraph 7 allows the Secretary of State to grant exemptions from all or any of the provisions of the regulations for classes of cases or individual cases on such terms as he may specify, and he may alter or cancel any such exemptions, subject to reasonable notice.

Parts I, II (Section I), and IV of the regulations apply to all ships and contain provisions relating to the hull, equipment and machinery, and in particular to the watertight doors, bilge pumping arrangements, electrical equipment, steering gear, fire protection, boilers and machinery, compasses, anchors and cables; in Part II, Section II specifies additional special provisions for the steering gear of tankers of 10,000 tons gross or over, and Section III describes additional requirements for ships with machinery spaces which are periodically unattended.

Surveys. Before a Cargo Ship Construction certificate can be issued Part IV requires the ship's owner to arrange for the ship to be surveyed on its completion, and thereafter at intervals not exceeding five years, by a Certifying Authority's surveyor, who, if satisfied will forward to that Authority a declaration of survey containing such particulars of the ship as are required to enable a certificate to be issued. The expression 'Certifying Authority' means the Secretary of State or any person authorised by him and includes Lloyd's Register of Shipping, the British Committees of Bureau Veritas, Det Norske Veritas and Germanischer Lloyd, and the British Technical Committee of the American Bureau of Shipping.

For the purpose of seeing whether the certificate should remain in force, **intermediate surveys** are to be carried out as follows:—

(a) the hull and sea connection fastenings, overboard discharge valves and other ship-side fittings are to be examined in dry dock on a date within six months before or after the half-way date of the period of validity of the certificate. The sea connections, overboard discharge valves and other ship-side fittings shall be thoroughly examined in dry dock at intervals not exceeding five years.

(b) steam heated steam generators in any ship and water-tube boilers supplying main propulsion steam in ships fitted with either, more than one water-tube boiler, or with a single such water-tube boiler plus adequate auxiliary means of maintaining power in the event of boiler failure, shall be examined internally and externally at intervals not exceeding two years.

(c) all other boilers, including exhaust gas boilers, superheaters, economisers and domestic boilers (other than domestic boilers having a heating surface of not more than five square metres and a working pressure not more than 3·5 bar gauge) shall be examined internally and externally at intervals not exceeding two years until they are eight years old and thereafter annually.

(d) screw propeller shafts fitted with continuous liners or running in oil shall be withdrawn and surveyed at intervals not exceeding five years where the ship has more than one propeller, or for single screw ships the shaft and propeller attachment are specially designed. Other screw propeller shafts shall be withdrawn and surveyed at intervals not exceeding two years.

(e) tube shafts driving screw propellers shall, if fitted with continuous liners or running in oil, be surveyed at intervals not exceeding five years. Other tube shafts shall be withdrawn and surveyed at intervals not exceeding two years.

Application for a survey must be made by or on behalf of the ship's owner to the Certifying Authority by whom the certificate was issued.

The owner of every tanker of ten years of age and over, so long as the certificate remains in force, must arrange for an intermediate survey to be carried out in accordance with procedures specified in Merchant Shipping Notice M.694 and on a date within six months before or after the halfway date of the period of validity of the certificate. In no case shall the period between such surveys exceed three years. On satisfactory completion of the survey the surveyor must endorse the supplement to the cargo ship construction certificate.

In addition to the intermediate survey above mentioned and during the time that the certificate remains in force, the owner of a cargo ship must arrange for the ship to be subjected to an **annual survey**. Application must be made to the Certifying Authority who issued the certificate and the survey carried out within three months before or after the anniversary date of the certificate. The surveyor must satisfy himself that specified parts of the ship and its equipment remain efficient and that no alterations have been made in the hull, machinery or equipment without approval. When the surveyor is satisfied after survey, he shall endorse the attachment to the cargo ship safety construction certificate to that effect. If the ship is not so surveyed the Secretary of State may cancel the certificate.

Tankers. In addition to the parts already mentioned which apply to all cargo ships, Parts III and V apply additionally to sea-going tankers specified in regulation 1(5). The regulations in Part III describe the construction of accommodation, superstructures, separation of pump rooms and machinery spaces, separation of accommodation and service spaces from machinery spaces, bulkhead construction, restriction of combustible materials and other matters concerned with fire protection and insulation to restrict the spread of fire. In addition to the surveys required by Part IV, a tanker owner must cause the ship to be surveyed on completion and thereafter at intervals of five years by a marine surveyor of the Department of Trade who must satisfy himself that the ship complies with the requirements of Part III and is in all respect satisfactory for the service intended. The marine surveyor, if satisfied after the survey, must forward to the Certifying Authority a declaration of survey containing such particulars necessary to enable the Authority to issue a cargo ship safety construction certificate in respect of the ship. In addition, the owner of a ship to which Part III applies must arrange for an intermediate survey by a marine surveyor of the D.o.T. not more than six months before, nor later than six months after, the halfway date of the period of validity of the cargo ship construction certificate. The surveyor must establish that the insulation and integrity of fire protection divisions has been maintained, that doors in such divisions fitted with self-closing devices and remote release fittings operate properly and that the arrangement and insulation of ventilation ducts has been maintained. On satisfactory completion of the survey the surveyor shall send a declaration of the survey to the Certifying Authority.

For the purpose of the regulations, a "tanker" means a cargo ship constructed or adapted for the carriage in bulk of liquid cargoes of a flammable nature; Part III applies to tankers carrying crude oil and petroleum products having a closed flashpoint not exceeding 60°C, and the Reid vapour pressure of which is below that of atmospheric pressure, or other liquids having a similar fire hazard.

Responsibilities of owner or master. The owner or master is required in Part VI to ensure that the ship is maintained so as to comply with the requirements of the regulations, and after any survey has been held, no changes are to be made in the structural arrangements, machinery, equipment, etc., subject to survey, without the approval of the Certifying Authority.

Whenever an accident occurs to a ship, or a defect is discovered which affects the safety of the ship, or the efficiency or completeness of its equipment, it must be reported at the earliest opportunity to the Secretary of State or a proper officer and to the Certifying Authority who issued the certificate, any one of whom is to investigate whether a survey is necessary, and if it is, to require one to be carried out. If the ship is in a port outside the U.K., the master or owner shall, in addition, make such a report to the appropriate authorities of the country in which the port is situated. The Certifying Authority is required to check with those authorities that such report has been made.

Procedure when repairs or renewals are necessary. In any case where the Certifying Authority decides that the condition of the ship or its equipment does not agree with the particulars of the certificate or is such that the ship is not fit to proceed to sea without danger to the ship or persons on board, the authority is to advise the owner or master what corrective action in its opinion is required, and then notify the Secretary of State. If such corrective action is not taken within a specified time, the Certifying Authority will notify the Secretary of State, who may suspend the validity of the certificate and will give notice of the suspension to the owner and the Certifying Authority. The master must then deliver the certificate to the Authority on demand, and the owner, on receiving notice of suspension, must deliver the duplicate certificate to the Secretary of State.

When the Certifying Authority is satisfied that corrective action has been taken and the Secretary of State notified, the certificate's validity can be restored by him and returned to the master and the duplicate returned to the owner. Where the ship is not within a United Kingdom port and the advised corrective action has not been taken, the Certifying Authority shall in addition immediately notify the appropriate authorities of the country in which the port is situated.

Penalties and power to detain. If a ship proceeds or attempts to proceed to sea without complying with the requirements of the regulations, the owner or master of the ship shall each be guilty of an offence and liable on summary conviction to a fine not exceeding £1000 or, on conviction on indictment, to imprisonment for a term not exceeding two years or a fine or both. In any case where a ship does not comply with the requirements of the regulations, the ship is liable to be detained and the provisions of section 692 of the M.S. Act 1894 shall apply. (See page 35)

Passenger Ship Construction Regulations. These are extremely comprehensive and cover in great detail in the Regulations such matters as structural strength, watertight sub-division, bilge pumping arrangements, electrical equipment and installations, fire protection, boilers and machinery (including steering gear), and miscellaneous equipment including compasses, depth-sounding devices, anchors and chain cables, and hawsers and warps. The Regulations also require adequate provision to be made for persons to escape from enclosed spaces to the lifeboat embarkation deck, and regulate what is required by way of guard rails, stanchions and bulwarks for the proper protection of persons on board.

The four Schedules deal with calculations for deciding the maximum length of watertight compartments, stability information, stability in damaged condition and the construction of watertight bulkheads, etc.

These Regulations apply to United Kingdom passenger ships and to other sea-going passenger ships while they are within the United Kingdom or its territorial waters. They revoke the Passenger Ship Construction Rules 1965, but the new regulations go on to provide that in the case of an existing ship which undergoes repairs, alterations or modifications, it shall, as a minimum, comply with the 1965 Rules as if they had not been revoked; but, if the Secretary of State is of the opinion that it is reasonable and practicable in the circumstances, any major repairs, alterations or modifications to such a ship must comply with the 1980 Regulations (as amended by S.I. 1981 No. 580).

The Secretary of State may exempt certain classes of ships or individual ships from the provisions of any of the regulations, subject to specified conditions, and he may alter or cancel any exemption that is granted.

The regulations are divided into eight parts, of which parts IV, V, VI and VII concerning electrical equipment, fire protection, boilers and machinery and miscellaneous matters, respectively, make different provisions for new and existing ships. A new passenger ship is defined as a passenger ship which has its keel laid on or after 25th May 1980, (or is at a similar stage of construction), or which is a cargo ship converted to a passenger ship after that date; an existing ship is said to be not a new one.

Compasses. The Passenger Ship Construction Regulations require ships of Class I to be provided with three efficient magnetic compasses sited on the ship's centre line. One is to be provided as a steering compass sited at the normal steering position, and another as a standard compass sited near the normal steering position so that the view of the horizon is least obstructed. A third, at the after steering position, with its gimbal units is to be interchangeable with the steering compass. But a magnetic steering compass is not required if (i) the standard compass is of the reflector or projector type and has a device by which it may be read from the normal steering position; (ii) the standard compass is interchangeable with the after steering compass; and (iii) a card of a gyro-compass or repeater can be read from the normal steering position. Each such magnetic compass must be mounted on a binnacle, except that the after steering compass may be mounted on a pedestal.

Ships of Classes II, II(A), and III require two magnetic compasses sited on the centre line; one steering and one standard, each mounted on a binnacle. Other passenger ships require one magnetic compass readily available at the normal steering position.

The provision of compasses in cargo ships is now governed by Rule 34 of the M.S. (Cargo Ship Construction and Survey) Regulations 1981, which is as follows:—

(1) Subject to the provisions of paragraph (2) of this Rule, every ship to which these Rules apply shall be provided with two efficient magnetic compasses which shall be mounted on binnacles and sited on the ship's centre line. One of such compasses shall be provided for use as a standard compass and shall be sited near to the normal steering position and in a position from which the view of the horizon is least obstructed. The other of such compasses shall be provided for use as a steering compass and shall be sited at the normal steering position unless the projected or reflected image of the standard magnetic compass is provided for this purpose or a gyro-compass or a repeater from a gyro- or transmitting magnetic compass is positioned near the normal steering position, in which case the second

magnetic compass, mounted in a binnacle or on a pedestal, may be fitted at the emergency steering position.

(2) Where there is no emergency steering position, two magnetic compasses and binnacles shall not be required provided that the ship is equipped with a standard projector magnetic compass and a gyro-compass with repeaters and provided also that a spare magnetic compass bowl with its gimbal units is carried on board so that it may be interchanged with the standard compass if that compass should become unserviceable.

Depth-sounding devices. Every ship of Classes I, II and II(A) must be provided with an efficient mechanical depth-sounding device operated by means of a line, and with sufficient spare parts to enable it to be kept in working order while the ship is at sea. (Such a device is not required in Class II and II(A) ships which are less than 1600 tons gross). Every ship of Classes I to III inclusive is to be provided with two hand lead lines, each at least 45 metres long and each with a lead weighing at least three kilogrammes.

Nautical Publications. The M.S. (Carriage of Nautical Publications) Rules 1975, made under powers given by section 86 of the M.S. Act 1970, came into operation on 1st June 1975. These rules require ships registered in the United Kingdom (other than those less than 12 metres in length and fishing vessels) which go or attempt to go to sea, to carry at least one copy of the latest obtainable edition of each chart appropriate for each part of the intended voyage and published by the Hydrographer of the Navy or by an equivalent other authority. Charts are to be of such a scale that they show clearly with sufficient detail all navigational marks which may be used by a ship navigating the waters shown on the chart, all known dangers affecting those waters and information concerning any traffic separation schemes, two-way routes, recommended tracks etc., and areas which are to be avoided; they must have been corrected and kept up to date from the latest Notices to Mariners and Radio Navigational Warnings, or otherwise adequately corrected. In addition ships intending to go to sea beyond a distance of 5 nautical miles from any coastline must carry one copy of each of the following publications as is appropriate for that voyage, namely, International Code of Signals, Merchant Shipping Notices, Mariners Handbook, Notices to Mariners, Nautical Almanac, Navigational Tables, Lists of Radio Signals, Lists of Lights, Sailing Directions, Tide Tables, Tidal Stream Atlases, and Operating and Maintenance instructions for navigational aids carried by the ship. If a ship goes to sea or attempts to go to sea without carrying such publications, the master or owner will be liable on summary conviction to a fine not exceeding £500.

Safety Certificates and Associated Documents. The principal

N

Form P. & S. 1.
(SUR 286)

PASSENGER CERTIFICATE

For an international voyage

Issued under the provisions of the
MERCHANT SHIPPING ACTS.

Name of Ship _____

Owner or Agent _____

I, the undersigned (Name:

certify that the provisions of the Merchant Shipping Acts relating to the survey of passenger ships have been complied with, and that the above-mentioned ship is fit to ply on an international voyage with the number of passengers stated below.

Number of Passengers	Number of Crew	Total—Passengers and Crew

(a)—If any of the space measured for passengers is used for other purposes, one passenger is to be deducted from the numbers stated above for every 1.115 square metres so occupied.

(b)—All passengers are to have the use of sufficient promenade space on deck, and no deck passengers are to be carried in addition to the number of passengers stated above.

NOTES

1.- One of these duplicate certificates is to be put up in a conspicuous place on board the ship so as to be legible to all persons on board, and to be kept so put up and legible while the certificate remains in force and the ship is in use.

2.—If the number of passengers carried exceeds the number allowed by this certificate, the master or owner will be liable to a penalty not exceeding £50,000; and on conviction or indictment, a fine.

3.—In case of any accident occasioning loss of life or serious injury to any person, or any material damage affecting the seaworthiness or efficiency of the ship either in the hull or in any part of the machinery, a written report signed by the owner or master is to be forwarded to the Department of Trade as soon as possible after the happening of the accident or damage. A similar report is to be forwarded as soon as possible after any alteration or renewal in the ship's hull, equipments or machinery which affects the efficiency thereof or the seaworthiness of the ship.

4. The Department of Trade may cancel this certificate if they have reason to believe that since its issue the hull, equipments or machinery of the ship have sustained any injury or are otherwise insufficient.

5.—It will be sufficient to indicate the year in which the keel was laid or when the ship was at a similar stage of construction except for 1952, 1965 and 1980 in which cases the actual date should be given

In the case of a ship which is converted as provided in Regulation 1 (b)(i) of Chapter II-1 or Regulation 1(a)(i) of Chapter II-2 of the Convention, the date on which the work of conversion was begun should be given.

In duplicate **PASSENGER SHIP SAFETY CERTIFICATE**
For an international voyage

United Kingdom of Great Britain and Northern Ireland.

Issued under the provisions of the
INTERNATIONAL CONVENTION FOR THE SAFETY OF LIFE AT SEA, 1974

Name of Ship	Official Number	Port of Registry	Gross Tonnage	Date on which keel was laid (see Item 8)

I, the undersigned   (Name) certify

  I. That the above-mentioned ship has been duly surveyed in accordance with the provisions of the Convention referred to above.

  II. That the survey showed that the ship complied with the requirements of the Regulations annexed to the said Convention as regards—

    (1) the structure, main and auxiliary boilers and other pressure vessels and machinery;

    (2) the watertight subdivision arrangements and details;

    (3) the following subdivision loadlines—

Subdivision loadlines assigned and marked on the ship's side at amidships (Regulation 11 of Chapter II-1)	Freeboard	To apply when the spaces in which passengers are carried include the following alternative spaces.
C.1.		
C.2.		
C.3.		

  III. That the life-saving appliances provide for a total number of   persons and no more, viz.:—

    lifeboats (including   motor lifeboats) capable of accommodating   persons,

    and   motor lifeboats fitted with radiotelegraph installation and searchlight (included in the total lifeboats shown above),

    and   motor lifeboats fitted with searchlight only (also included in the total lifeboats shown above),

    requiring   certificated lifeboatmen;

    liferafts, for which approved launching devices are required, capable of accommodating ..   ..   persons; and

    liferafts, for which approved launching devices are not required, capable of accommodating ..   ..   persons;

    buoyant apparatus capable of supporting ..   ..   persons;

    lifebuoys   ..   ..

    lifejackets   ..   ..

  IV. That the lifeboats and liferafts were equipped in accordance with the provisions of the Regulations.

  V. That the ship was provided with a line-throwing appliance and portable radio apparatus for survival craft in accordance with the provisions of the Regulations.

  VI. That the ship complied with the requirements of the Regulations as regards radiotelegraph installations, viz.:—

	Requirements of Regulations	Actual provision
Hours of listening by operator		
Number of operators		
Whether auto-alarm fitted		
Whether main installation fitted		
Whether reserve installation fitted		
Whether main and reserve transmitters electrically separated or combined		
Whether direction-finder fitted		
Whether radio equipment for homing on the radio-telephone distress frequency fitted		
Whether radar fitted		
Number of passengers for which certificated.		

  VII. That the functioning of the radio-telegraph installations for motor lifeboats and/or the portable radio apparatus for survival craft, if provided, complied with the provisions of the Regulations.

  VIII. That the ship complied with the requirements of the Regulations, as regards fire-detecting and fire-extinguishing appliances, radar, echo-sounding device and gyro-compass and was provided with navigation lights and shapes, pilot ladder, and means of making sound signals and distress signals, in accordance with the provisions of the Regulations and also the International Collision Regulations.

  IX. That in all other respects the ship complied with the requirements of the Regulations, so far as these requirements apply thereto.

This combined Passenger and Safety Certificate is issued under the authority of the Government of the United Kingdom of Great Britain and Northern Ireland.   It will remain in force, unless previously cancelled, until the   day of   19 .

Issued at the DEPARTMENT OF TRADE,   the   day of   19

The undersigned declares that he is duly authorised by the said Government to issue this certificate.

Examined and Registered.

certificates issued under the provisions of the International Convention for the Safety of Life at Sea, 1974, as modified by the Protocol of 1978, after appropriate surveys are:—

Passenger Ship Certificate which term includes:—

1. A general safety certificate covering structure, main and auxiliary boilers and other pressure vessels and machinery, watertight subdivision, subdivision load lines, life-saving appliances (*i.e.*, lifeboats, motor lifeboats, lifeboat radio and searchlight, liferafts requiring launching devices and other liferafts, buoyant apparatus, lifebuoys and lifejackets, lifeboat and liferaft equipment), line-throwing appliance, portable radio for survival craft, radiotelegraph installation including D.F., radar, echo-sounder, gyrocompass, fire-detecting and fire-extinguishing appliances, navigation lights and shapes, pilot ladder, sound signals and distress signals.
2. A short voyage safety certificate, on similar lines to the above, but issued to a passenger ship engaged on short international voyages.
3. A qualified safety certificate issued to a ship which is exempt from certain of the requirements of the Regulations showing that she complies with those requirements from which she is not exempt.
4. A qualified short voyage safety certificate.

Cargo Ship Safety Construction Certificate covering the hull, machinery and equipment of a cargo ship and showing that the ship complies with the cargo ship construction and survey regulations applicable to the ship and the voyages she is to be engaged on.

Supplement to the Cargo Ship Safety Construction Certificate for endorsement after intermediate surveys have been held on certain tankers, as required by the Protocol of 1978.

Qualified Cargo Ship Safety Construction Certificate issued to a cargo ship which is exempt from certain of the requirements of the regulations and showing that she complies with the rest of those requirements.

Cargo Ship Safety Equipment Certificate covering life-saving appliances (*i.e.*, lifeboats, motor lifeboats, lifeboat radio and searchlight, liferafts requiring launching devices and other liferafts, lifebuoys and lifejackets, lifeboat and liferaft equipment), line-throwing apparatus, portable radio for survival craft, fire-extinguishing appliances and fire control plans, echo-sounder, gyro-compass, navigation lights and shapes, pilot ladder, sound signals and distress signals.

Supplement to the Cargo Ship Safety Equipment Certificate for endorsement after intermediate surveys have been held on certain tankers as required by the Protocol of 1978.

Cargo Ship Safety Radiotelegraphy Certificate issued to a cargo ship fitted with a radiotelegraph installation (including D.F.).

Cargo Ship Safety Radiotelephony Certificate issued to a cargo ship of under 1600 gross tons fitted with a radiotelephone installation.

Qualified Radio Certificate for special cases of cargo ships.

Exemption Certificate issued in conjunction with a qualified certificate stating which requirements of the Convention the ship is exempt from.

The owner or master of a ship in respect of which a certificate has been issued must notify the D.o.T. of any alterations to hull, equipment, etc., as soon as possible under £50 (max.) penalty. If the Department have reason to believe that alterations have been made since the last declaration of survey, they may cancel the certificate. If a ship attempts to proceed, or proceeds, to sea without the required certificate, penalties may be imposed as follows:—

On summary conviction to a fine not exceeding £1,000 and, on conviction on indictment, a fine, on owner, or master.

The required safety certificates must be produced to the officer of Customs from whom clearance is demanded or the ship may be detained. Non-compliance with the conditions of an Exemption Certificate is punishable by the penalty quoted above.

The periods of validity of the various certificates are as shown below.

Safety Certificate
Radio Certificate
Exemption Certificate stating that the ship is not wholly exempt from radio requirements.
> In force for 1 year (unless cancelled).

Safety Construction Certificate: In force for 5 years or such shorter period as may be specified in it (unless cancelled).

Safety Equipment Certificate: In force for 24 months (unless cancelled).

Other Exemption Certificates: In force for the same period as the corresponding Qualified Certificate.

The D.o.T. may extend the period of validity for 1 month, or if the ship is absent from the United Kingdom, for a period of 5 months from the date of expiry.

A general Safety Certificate, or a Short Voyage Safety Certificate

(Qualified or not), may be combined in one document with a Passenger Steamer's Certificate. This is the case, for instance, with a Passenger and Safety Certificate (Form P. & S.1).

All these certificates are admissible in evidence.

Before a Passenger and Safety Certificate can be issued, a Declaration of Survey of a Passenger Ship (of which further mention is made in Chapter 8) must be completed and signed by the surveyor, signed by the owner or his agent, and transmitted to the Assistant Secretary, Marine Safety Division, D.o.T. This document contains all the particulars of the ship pertinent to the circumstances and conditions under which a P. & S. Certificate may properly be issued, and provision is made thereon for separate declarations to be dated and signed by (i) a Ship Surveyor, (ii) a Ship (Nautical) Surveyor, and (iii) and Engineer and Ship Surveyor. Attached to it there will be a Form signed by a Radio Surveyor. Fraudulent alteration of a Declaration is an indictable offence.

Ships which carry a Safety Equipment Certificate have issued to them a document entitled a Record of Safety Equipment (Form Surveys 183). A copy of this is retained at the D.o.T. Surveyors' headquarters, another goes to the shipowner, and a third goes to the ship. The ship's copy must be kept on board and be available for inspection by D.o.T. Surveyors at all times.

Surveys for Cargo Ship Safety Certificates. The Protocol of 1978 relating to the 1974 SOLAS Convention introduced requirements concerning surveys which are additional to those set out in the M.S. (Safety Convention) Act 1949. Two statutory instruments which came into operation on 1st May 1981 give effect to these additional provisions for sea-going United Kingdom ships (except passenger ships, fishing vessels and pleasure craft) on international voyages. (i.e. from a port in one country to a port in another country.)

One of the statutory instruments, the **M.S. (Radio Installations Survey) Regulations 1981,** requires the owner of every such ship of 300 tons gross or over to arrange for the radio installation to be surveyed before the issue of the ship's first radio certificate and before each subsequent annual renewal by a surveyor nominated by the D.o.T. A survey held in a U.K. port or in U.K. territorial waters must be made by a D.o.T. radio surveyor. If the surveyor is satisfied after the survey that the radio installation is in all respects satisfactory for the ship's intended service, he will forward a Declaration of Survey to the Secretary of State, showing enough particulars of the ship and its radio equipment to enable a radio certificate to be issued.

The other is the **M.S. (Cargo Ship Safety Equipment Survey) Regulations** 1981 in which safety equipment "means life-saving appliances, fire appliances, lights, shapes, means of making sound signals, pilot ladders and associated equipment, mechanical pilot hoists, and echo-sounder, gyro compass, direction finder and radar installations, respectively. The owner of such a ship of 500 tons gross and over must arrange for all the above safety equipment to be surveyed before the issue of the ship's first safety equipment certificate, and before each subsequent occasion when it requires to be renewed. The survey must be carried out by a surveyor nominated by the D.o.T., and in the case of any such survey carried out in a U.K. port or in U.K. territorial waters, the surveyor must be a D.o.T. marine surveyor.

After the survey, if the surveyor is satisfied that the ship complies with the Safety Regulations applicable to her and is in all such respects satisfactory for her intended service, he must forward to the Secretary of State a Declaration of Survey showing sufficient particulars of the ship and its equipment to enable a cargo ship safety equipment certificate to be issued.

Annual and Intermediate Surveys. As long as the safety equipment certificate remains in force, the owner must arrange for the ship to be surveyed on a date which falls within three months before or after the anniversary date of the cargo ship safety equipment certificate to see whether the certificate should remain in force. The "anniversary date" is the date in each year corresponding to the date of expiry of the certificate.

The survey is to be termed an **intermediate survey** in respect of tankers of 10 years of age and over, and an **annual survey** in respect of other ships; the age of a ship shall be determined from the year of build shown on the ship's certificate of registry. The nominated surveyor must survey the ship in accordance with procedures specified in Merchant Shipping Notice M.693, and he must satisfy himself that the equipment specified in the notice remains efficient and that no alterations have been made to the equipment without the approval of the Secretary of State.

On completion of the survey, if satisfied, the nominated surveyor will endorse to that effect, the **supplement** to the cargo ship safety equipment certificate in the case of an intermediate survey of a tanker of 10 years of age and over, or in the case of an annual survey, the **attachment** to the cargo ship safety equipment certificate.

After the 1st May 1981, at least one survey required by the safety equipment survey regulations in any period of five years must be carried out by a marine surveyor of the D.o.T.

Responsibilities of owner and master. The owner or master must ensure that the condition of safety equipment and radio installations is maintained so as to comply with the relevant regulations and that after any survey required by these regulations has been completed no material change must be made in such equipment and installation without the approval of the Secretary of State. Whenever an accident occurs to a ship, or a defect is discovered, either of which affects the safety of the ship or the efficiency or completeness of its safety equipment or radio installation, it must be reported at the earliest opportunity to the Secretary of State or a proper officer, either of whom must initiate investigations to decide whether a survey is necessary, and in that event require a survey to be carried out by a nominated surveyor. If the ship is in a port outside the United Kingdom, the master or owner shall, in addition, make such a report immediately to the appropriate authorities of the country in which the port is situated; the nominated surveyor is required to ascertain from those authorities whether such report has been made.

Procedure when equipment etc. is deficient. In any case where the surveyor determines that the safety equipment or radio installation does not correspond substantially with the particulars of the relevant certificate, or is such that the ship is not fit to proceed to sea without danger to the ship or persons on board, the surveyor shall advise the owner of the corrective action which in his opinion is required, and shall notify the Secretary of State.

If such corrective action is not taken within a reasonable period specified by the surveyor, he must notify the Secretary of State, who may then suspend the validity of the appropriate certificate and give notice of the suspension to the owner and the surveyor. The surveyor must notify the master who on demand must deliver the certificate to the surveyor, the owner meanwhile delivering the duplicate to the Secretary of State. Where the ship is not within a U.K. port and corrective action specified by the surveyor has not been taken, he is required to notify immediately the appropriate authorities of the country in which the port is situated.

When the surveyor is satisfied that corrective action has been taken, he must notify the Secretary of State who will restore the validity of the certificate, give notice to the owner and return the duplicate certificate to him. The surveyor will return the ship's certificate to the master.

Penalties. If a ship to which these regulations apply proceeds or attempts to proceed to sea without complying with their requirements, the owner or master of the ship shall each be guilty of an offence and liable on summary conviction to a fine not exceeding £1,000 or, on conviction on indictment, to imprisonment for a term not exceeding two years or a fine or both. The ship is liable to be detained if it does not comply with the requirements of these regulations, and section 692 of the M.S. Act 1894 which relates to a ship's detention will have effect.

Radio Installations Regulations. These regulations apply to radiotelegraph and radiotelephone ships which are sea-going United Kingdom ships, also to other sea-going ships while they are within the United Kingdom and its territorial waters. They shall not apply to U.K. ships while being navigated in the North American Great Lakes and their tributary and connecting waters as far east as the lower exit of the St. Lambert Lock at Montreal, Canada. The regulations do not apply to troopships not registered in the U.K., ships not propelled by mechanical means, pleasure craft, fishing vessels and cargo ships of less tha 300 gross tons.

Radiotelephone Ships. Every cargo ship of 300 tons gross or more, but less than 1,600 tons gross, must be provided with a radiotelephone installation consisting of a transmitter, receiver, R.T. distress frequency watch receiver or R.T. auto-alarm, and R.T. alarm signal generating device. Alternatively such ships can be provided with a radiotelegraph installation.

Radiotelegraph Ships. Every cargo ship of 1,600 tons gross or more, and every passenger ship, must be provided with a radiotelegraph installation consisting of a main transmitter and receiver, radiotelegraph automatic alarm signal keying device, R.T. distress frequency watch receiver or R.T. auto-alarm, R.T. distress frequency transmitter, R.T. alarm signal generating device, and, when provided, a radiotelegraph auto-alarm. It must also have a reserve installation consisting of a transmitter and receiver. (A cargo ship of 300 tons gross or more with a radiotelegraph installation is also called a radiotelegraph ship.)

Further, every cargo ship of 300 tons gross or more and every passenger ship, shall in addition be provided with a VHF radiotelephone transmitter and receiver. Equipment to be provided must conform to IMCO performance standards, and in addition for U.K. ships, Home Office specifications, both standards being specified in Merchant Shipping Notice M.928.

Serviceability. Each radio installation must be in satisfactory working condition whenever the ship goes to sea, and when the ship is at sea, unless there is a defect at sea and maintenance is being carried out or is not practicable.

V.H.F. Radiotelephony. The installation shall be in the upper part of the ship and control of the VHF channels shall be immediately available on the bridge. A card of instructions giving a clear summary of the distress, urgency and safety procedures shall be displayed. A vertically polarised antenna suitable for use in the 156·025–162·025 MHz band shall be placed with an unobstructed all round view. Every radiotelephone operator using the VHF installation shall have a practical knowledge of operating it, and knowledge of the Radio Regulations concerning distress signals and traffic, alarm, urgency and safety signals.

V.H.F. Radio Watch. Each ship shall maintain a listening watch on the bridge on 156·8 MHz (VHF Channel 16). This listening watch may be discontinued:—

    (*a*) when the vessel is outside the VHF service area of shore stations;

(b) when the vessel is maintaining watch on a port operation or ship movement frequency;

(c) when receiver is being used on another frequency for traffic;

(d) when such watch is being maintained elsewhere on master's instructions;

(e) when, in the master's opinion, such watch is prejudicial to the ship's safety; in this case an entry is to be made in the ship's log of the times listening was discontinued and resumed, and of the circumstances.

A summary of all distress traffic received or transmitted is to be maintained.

Radiotelephony. The installation shall be in the upper part of the ship and sited so that it is protected from interference and noise. A reliable clock shall be provided with silence periods clearly marked, and emergency lighting. A card of instructions in English giving a clear summary of the distress, urgency and safety procedures shall be displayed. The normal range of transmitter shall be not less than 150 miles.

The number of radiotelephone operators required are:—

(a) ships of 300 GRT and more but less than 500 GRT—at least one;

(b) ships of 500 GRT and more but less than 1600 GRT—at least two, but if one is carried exclusively employed for R.T. duties, then only one need be carried.

The master, an officer or a member of the crew holding a valid certificate for radiotelephony may be a radiotelephone operator.

To be qualified as a radiotelephone operator a person must be the holder of (a) a valid certificate of competency in radiotelephony or radiotelegraphy issued by the Home Office, or by a Commonwealth authority or the Irish Republic, and recognised by the Home Office as equivalent; and (b) a valid Authority to Operate granted by the Home Office to operate a station in a ship licensed by the Home Office.

Radio Watch. A continuous watch must be maintained while at sea on the radiotelephone distress frequency (2182 kHz) by use of a distress frequency watch receiver or auto-alarm.

Radio Log. A radio log (diary of the radio service) is to be kept where the listening watch is maintained. It shall be inspected and signed each day by the operator and by the master, and produced to officials and delivered, in the same way as the official log book.

Radiotelegraphy. Main and reserve radiotelegraph apparatus is to be installed in an operating room placed as high in the ship as practicable, connected by an independent two-way communication system with the bridge. The room is to be provided with a reliable clock clearly marked with silence periods, and emergency lighting.

The minimum normal range of main and reserve transmitters when connected to the main antenna and transmitting signals ship to ship by day is to be:—

Passenger ships and cargo ships of 1600 GRT and upwards	(Main) 150 miles	(Reserve) 100 miles
Cargo ships below 1600 GRT	(Main) 100 miles	(Reserve) 75 miles

The sleeping accommodation of at least one radio officer shall be as near as practicable to the operating room.

Every radiotelegraph ship, provided with an auto-alarm, upon going to sea, must be provided with:—

(a) two radio officers on each passenger ship certificated to carry more than 250 passengers when engaged on a voyage exceeding 16 hours' duration; or

(b) one radio officer on all other such ships.

One further radio officer may be required on ships where no auto-alarm is fitted, depending on the period of time at sea between consecutive ports.

To be a chief radio officer on board a U.K. radiotelegraph ship a person must have served at sea as a radio officer for at least:—

(a) two years in the case of a U.K. radiotelegraph ship with a certificate in force that it is fit to carry 250 passengers;

(b) one year in the case of any other passenger ship; and

(c) six months in the case of a cargo ship.

To be qualified to be a radio officer on board a U.K. radiotelegraph ship, a person must be the holder of one of the following certificates issued by the Home Office:—

(i) a Maritime Radiocommunication General Certificate; or

(ii) a First or Second Class Certificate of Competency in Radiotelegraphy; or

(iii) a valid Certificate of Competency granted by a Commonwealth country or the Irish Republic and recognised by the Home Office as equivalent to the certificates in (i) and (ii) above.

Such radio officer must also hold a valid Authority to Operate granted by the Home Office to operate a station on a U.K. ship licensed by the Home Office. Further, the chief radio officer on a U.K. passenger ship must be the holder of either a Maritime Radiocommunication General Certificate or a First Class Certificate of Competency in Radiotelegraphy.

No certificate of competency is deemed to be valid on any date if granted more than two years before that date and either:—

(a) the holder's aggregate periods of experience on that date is less than three months, or

(b) the holder's experience was earlier than two years before that date, unless he can satisfy the Secretary of State, by re-examination or otherwise, that he possesses all the necessary qualifications and that his experience with modern equipment is adequate.

For the above purpose, experience means service, at sea as a radio officer, or on land as an operator at a Post Office radiotelegraph station communicating with ships.

Radio Watch. A continuous watch must be maintained on the bridge on 2182 kHz by use of a R.T. distress frequency watch receiver; and on 500 kHz by means of a radio officer using headphones or a loudspeaker during the working hours specified for that category of ship in the Radio Regulations, aided by a radiotelegraph auto-alarm, able to give an audible warning in the operating room, the radio officer's sleeping accommodation and on the bridge, when it is activated by an alarm signal, during off-duty hours and periods when the officer is handling traffic or carrying out essential maintenance to the equipment or navigational aids equipment. The listening watch by headphones or loudspeaker must always be maintained on 500 kHz during silence periods occurring within working hours.

The working hours of watchkeeping shall be those specified for the particular category of ship in the Radio Regulations which are annexed to the International Telecommunication Union Convention.

Radio Log. A radio log (diary of the radio service) shall be kept in the operating room during the voyage. The chief or only radio officer must sign it each day confirming that the requirements of the regulations have been met and the master must inspect and sign each day's entries. Logs must be available for inspection by officials and produced and delivered in the same way as the ship's official log book.

Radio Equipment for Lifeboats and Survival Craft. The fixed and portable equipment provided for survival craft shall comply with performance specifications set out in these regulations and tested in accordance with them.

Penalties. If a VHF radiotelephone operator, radiotelephone operator or radio officer contravenes any provision of these regulations he is guilty of an offence and liable on summary conviction to a £100 fine (maximum). If the regulations are contravened in any other way the owner or master shall each be guilty of an offence and liable on summary conviction to a fine not exceeding £1,000 or, on conviction on indictment to imprisonment for a term not exceeding two years and a fine. It is a defence to prove in any proceedings that all reasonable steps had been taken to ensure that the ship complied with the regulations.

In any case where a ship does not comply with the requirements of the regulations, the ship shall be liable to be detained, and s. 692 of the M.S.A. 1894 shall have effect in relation to the ship.

Navigational Equipment Regulations. These regulations apply to ships (except pleasure craft and fishing vessels) which are sea-going United Kingdom ships of 500 tons gross or over, and to other sea-going ships of 500 tons gross or over while they are within the United Kingdom or its territorial waters.

Echo Sounder Installation. Every ship of 500 tons gross or over whose keel was laid on or after 25th May 1980 must be provided with an echo sounder installation when engaged on an international voyage. (An international voyage means a voyage from a port in one country to a port in another country.) Passenger ships, with Class I, II or II(A) passenger certificates in force (or should be), when provided with the above echo sounder installation are not required to be provided with the depth-sounding device required by the Passenger Ship Construction Regulations 1980.

The echo sounder provided must comply with the IMCO standard and for U.K. ships, the D.o.T. specification, specified in Merchant Shipping Notice No. M.927. The transducer unit or units shall be sited so as to avoid, where practicable, the vicinity of all underwater openings and plugs so that satisfactory overall performance is achieved; and the graphical display is to be sited on the bridge so that the effect of any lighting necessary does not interfere with the keeping of an effective lookout.

Direction-finder Installation. Every ship of 1600 tons gross or over shall, when engaged on an international voyage, be provided with a direction-finder installation complying with the IMCO standard, and for U.K. ships the Home Office specification, specified in Merchant Shipping Notice No. M.927. The above is not required on ships with installations, provided before 25th May 1980, which comply with the requirements specified in the M.S. (Direction-Finders) Rules 1965.

Interference. Radio antennae which rise above the base of, and are within 17 metres horizontal distance of, the loop antennae are to be isolated whenever bearings are being taken, unless they do not cause significant errors in the accuracy of the bearings obtained. Any ship with an installation provided after 25th May 1980 is to be provided with a communal antennae system for all broadcast receivers, if it is impracticable to erect efficient antennae which (a) are outside a 17 metre radius from the D.F. antennae; or (b) do not rise above the base of the D.F. antennae; or (c) can be lowered quickly and stowed easily when the D.F. is in use.

The direction-finder shall be so sited that the taking of radio bearings will not be affected by extraneous noises and the antennae system shall be mounted so that the radio bearings obtained will be affected as little as possible by the proximity of antennae, derricks, wire halyards and other large metal objects.

Communication. An efficient two-way means of calling and voice communication is to be provided between the D.F. receiver and the bridge. An efficient means of signalling is to be provided for use, when calibrating or taking check bearings, between the D.F. receiver and the place from which visual bearings are taken.

Calibration. The master of every ship must cause the D.F. installation to be calibrated by two persons, one experienced in taking radio bearings, and the other in taking visual bearings, as soon as practicable after it has been installed, and whenever any change is made in the D.F. antenna system. The calibration is to be carried out by taking simultaneous radio and visual bearings of a transmitter at 5° intervals on a frequency between 285 kHz and 315 kHz. Calibration tables and curves are to be prepared to enable radio bearings, when adjusted, to be within two degrees of the correct bearing, and a Certificate of Calibration of Direction-Finder is to be completed. Check bearings are to be taken whenever the arrangement of deck cargo is different significantly from that when the D.F. was calibrated. The master is to cause the calibration curves to be verified by taking not less than 4 check bearings in each quadrant at intervals not exceeding 12 months, and whenever any change is made in any structure, rigging or antennae above deck likely to affect the accuracy of the D.F. The D.F. shall be recalibrated if such check bearings show the calibration curves or tables to be substantially inaccurate. In addition, check bearings shall be taken in each quadrant, at intervals not exceeding 12 months, on a frequency of about 500 kHz.

Records. The master must cause the following records to be available for a user of the D.F. and for inspection by a surveyor:—

(a) a list or diagram showing the position of the antennae and all moveable structures on board when the D.F. was last calibrated and which might affect its accuracy;

(b) the calibration tables and curves prepared on the last occasion the D.F. was calibrated;

(c) a certificate of calibration signed by persons making the calibration on the last occasion;

(d) a record of check-bearings taken to verify the calibration.

Gyro Compass Installation. Every ship of 1600 tons gross or over, when engaged on an international voyage, must be provided with a gyro-compass installation to comply with IMCO standards specified in Merchant Shipping Notice M.927. The master compass and visual bearing repeaters (where fitted) shall be installed with their fore-and-aft datum lines parallel to the ship's fore-and-aft datum line to within $\pm 0 \cdot 5°$, and the master, or a repeater shall be sited so that is clearly readable by the helmsman steering the ship.

Radar Installations. Every ship of 1600 tons gross or over, but less than 10,000 tons gross is to be provided with a radar installation. Every ship of 10,000 tons gross or over, is to be provided with two radar installations. Such installations shall comply with IMCO standards, and U.K. ships must also comply with the D.o.T. specifications contained in Merchant Shipping Notice M.927. Interswitching facilities may be provided where more than one radar is installed. Every ship shall be provided with facilities for plotting radar information.

Radar Watch. While a U.K. ship is at sea and a radar watch is being kept, the radar shall be under the control of a qualified radar observer, who may be assisted by unqualified personnel. A record shall be kept of the times a radar watch is commenced and discontinued.

Serviceability and Maintenance. The performance of the radar shall be checked before proceeding to sea, and at least once every four hours while the ship is at sea and radar watch is being maintained.

Every U.K. ship required to carry radar, going between the U.K. and locations in the unlimited trading area, or between locations in the unlimited trading area, shall from 25th May 1984 be provided with at least one officer or member of the crew qualified to carry out radar maintenance.

Where such officer is not available due to illness, incapacity or other unforeseen circumstances, after all reasonable steps have been taken to obtain such a qualified officer or crew member, the above regulation is not to apply for a period beginning when the ship goes to sea and ending either 14 days later or on the day when the ship sails from its next port of call whichever is the later, and providing that one such period without the officer is not to be followed immediately by another. Further the master must notify a proper office of his intention not to carry such qualified person; and make an entry of that notification in the ship's official log.

In U.K. ships, a record is to be kept of the approximate number of hours the radar is in operation and of the occasions when it becomes unserviceable and of brief details of all maintenance work carried out.

Siting. The antenna unit is to be sited so that satisfactory overall performance is obtained with respect to, avoidance of shadow sectors, avoidance of false echoes caused by reflection from the ship's structure, and to the effect of antenna height on the amplitude and extent of sea clutter. The display shall be sited on the bridge so that an observer faces forward when viewing, and so that two observers can view the display simultaneously. (Visor removed if necessary.)

The radar heading marker shall be accurately aligned with the ships fore-and-aft line, as soon as practicable after the equipment has been installed. The angular width and bearing of any shadow sectors displayed shall be determined and recorded and kept up to date.

General. Each navigational equipment installation required by these regulations shall be in satisfactory working condition whenever the ship goes to sea (but this does not apply in the case of a D.F. when going to sea from a place at which prompt maintenance is not available or practicable without delaying the ship). The equipment shall be in satisfactory working condition at all times when the ship is at sea, unless there is a defect and maintenance is being carried out or is not practicable.

Penalties. For proceeding to sea, (or attempting) without such radar installation(s) or direction-finder installation as she is required to carry, owner or master of ship are each guilty of an offence and liable on summary conviction to a fine not exceeding £1,000 or, on conviction on indictment, to imprisonment for a term not exceeding two years and a fine.

If a ship proceeds, or attempts to proceed, to sea without a required echo sounder installation, or gyro compass installation, the owner or master shall each be guilty of an offence and liable on summary conviction to a fine not exceeding £1,000.

If a ship proceeds, or attempts to proceed, to sea, without carrying a qualified radar observer, or after 25th May 1984, a qualified person able to carry out radar maintenance, the owner or master shall each be guilty of an offence and liable on summary conviction to a fine not exceeding £1,000.

It is a defence in proceedings, for an offence under these regulations, to prove that all reasonable steps had been taken to ensure that the ship complied with the Regulations.

Stability Information. The M.S. (Load Line) Rules 1968 now prescribe the particulars as to the information relating to stability, loading and ballasting to be supplied to the masters of ships to which those Rules apply.

Reference to this will be found in the section on load lines.

Stability Information for Passenger Ships. The requirements of the Safety of Life at Sea Convention 1974 as to stability of passenger ships is contained in regulations 9 and 10, and Schedule 2 of the Passenger Ship Construction Regulations 1980. These specify that, on completion, every ship is to be inclined and the elements of her stability determined, and the master is to be supplied by the owner with reliable information relating to the ship's stability, the particulars required and the form of presentation being specified in Schedule 2. Intact stability requirements are stated in regulation 10 by specifying that in all probable loading conditions the ship shall satisfy the following stability criteria after due allowance for free surface in tanks.

(a) Area under the curve of righting levers (GZ curve) shall not be less than:—

    (i) 0·055 metre-radian up to an angle of 30;

    (ii) 0·09 metre-radian up to an angle of 40° or the angle at which the lower edges of any hull, superstructure or deckhouse openings which cannot be closed weathertight, are immersed if that angle be less;

    (iii) 0·03 metre-radian between the angles of heel 30° and 40° or such lesser angle mentioned in (ii).

(b) The righting lever (GZ) shall be at least 0·20 metre at an angle of heel equal to or greater than 30°.

(c) The maximum righting lever (GZ) shall occur at an angle of heel not less than 30°.

(d) The initial transverse metacentric height shall not be less than 0·15 metre.

Stability in Damaged Condition. In addition to the intact stability requirements above, regulation 11 specifies that every ship must be so constructed as to provide sufficient intact stability in all service conditions to enable the ship to withstand the final flooding of a specified number of main compartments, the number, o ne, two, or three, being dependent on the ship's factor of subdi vision. A decision as to whether the ship has a sufficiency of intact stability is to be determined in accordance with the provisions of Schedule 3 to the regulations. Regulation 11 further lays down requirements concerning construction to enable unsymmetrical flooding when the ship is damaged to be kept to a minimum consistent with efficient arrangements. If cross-flooding fittings are provided they shall be capable of reducing the heel within 15 minutes sufficiently to meet the requirements of Schedule 3. To assist the master in the event of damage to his ship, regulation 11 further states:—

(a) There shall be provided in every such ship a document for the use of the master of the ship containing information as to the use of any cross-flooding fittings provided in the ship.

(b) There shall be provided in every ship of Classes I, II and II(A) a document for the use of the master of the ship containing the following additional information:—

    (i) information necessary for the maintenance of sufficient intact stability under service conditions to enable the ship to withstand damage to the extent referred to in Schedule 3 to these Regulations, and

(ii) information as to the conditions of stability on which the calculations of heel have been based, together with a warning that excessive heeling might result should the ship sustain damage when in a less favourable condition.

Regulation 74 states that in every ship to which this Part of these regulations applies there shall be permanently exhibited, for the information of the officer in charge of the ship, plans showing clearly for each deck and hold the boundaries of the watertight compartments, the openings therein, the means of closing such openings, the position of the controls, and the arrangements for the correction of any list due to flooding. In addition, booklets containing such information shall be available for the use of the officers of the ship.

Openings in Passenger Ships· Hulls and Watertight Bulkheads. The Regulations, which apply to all United Kingdom Passenger ships, make frequent reference to what is termed the "margin line". This is defined as a line drawn at least 76mm below the upper surface of the bulkhead deck at the side of a ship, and assumed for the purpose of determining the floodable length of the ship.

A brief summary of the Regulations is given as follows:—

The following must, immediately before a ship proceeds to sea, be securely closed, and kept closed while at sea:—

(a) watertight doors below the margin line fitted in watertight bulkheads dividing 'tween-deck cargo spaces.

(b) side scuttles in 'tween-decks below the margin line if their sills are below a line parallel to the bulkhead deck having its lowest point $1·37$ metres$+2\frac{1}{2}\%$ of the breadth of the ship above the water when the ship is first afloat in sea water after proceeding to sea. ($1·07$ metres$+2\frac{1}{2}\%$ of breadth in fine weather in the tropical zone);

(c) side scuttles below the margin line which will not be accessible at sea, together with their deadlights;

(d) side scuttles below the margin line in alternate passenger and cargo spaces, with deadlights if spaces used for cargo;

(e) gangway, coaling, and cargo ports below the margin line.

N.B.—"Below the margin line" means having the sill below the margin line. Side scuttles are not deemed closed unless they are locked.

Every watertight door, other than (a) above, must be kept closed while at sea unless it is required to be kept open for the working of the ship. When open, such doors must be kept free from obstruction.

Every portable plate fitted in the internal structure required to be watertight, where the opening is wholly or partly below the margin line, must be in place when proceeding to sea and kept in place except in emergency. When a plate is replaced the joints are to be made watertight.

The cover and valve of every ash shoot, rubbish-shoot or similar contrivance with the inboard opening below the margin line must be kept closed when not in use.

Watertight doors and other contrivances, except those required to be kept closed, must be opened and closed for drill purposes:—

(a) at intervals of not more than 7 days; and

(b) immediately before sailing if the ship is intended to remain at sea for more than 7 days.

Watertight doors in watertight bulkheads (not being doors required to be kept closed when the ship is at sea) must be opened and closed for drill purposes every 24 hours while at sea if the doors are both (a) hinged or power operated, and (b) required to be kept open for the working of the ship. But it is not necessary to open and close any bunker door before it has been opened for the working of the ship during the voyage.

The following must be inspected at intervals of not more than 7 days by a person appointed by the master.

(a) all watertight doors;

(b) the mechanisms, indicators, and warning devices connected with watertight doors;

(c) valves the closing of which is necessary to make a compartment below the margin line watertight; and

(d) valves the operation of which is necessary for the efficient working of damage control cross connections.

A master who contravenes these regulations shall be guilty of an offence and liable on summary conviction to a fine not exceeding £1,000 or, on conviction on indictment, to imprisonment for a term not exceeding two years and a fine.

The official log book LOG 2/72, which is a supplementary log for passenger ships only, is provided for recording (a) Time of Opening and Closing Watertight Doors, etc., (b) Practices of Opening and Closing Watertight Doors, etc., and (c) Inspection of Watertight Doors and Valves. Part IV of the Schedule to the Official Log Books Regulations designates the master as signatory and an officer as witness. The particulars to be recorded are:—

(a) The times of the last closing of watertight doors, etc., before sailing and the next subsequent opening.

(b) The times of opening and closing while at sea of 'tween-deck bunker watertight doors below the bulkhead deck.

(c) Whether portable plates are in place when the ship sails, and the times of removal and replacement while at sea, and

(d) All occasions of drills, practices and inspections, and whether the contrivances are found in good order.

Lifesaving and Fire Appliances. The regulations which apply to these appliances are very extensive and detailed and it is not convenient to reproduce them in a book of this size and type. Their subject matter is more closely related to the seamanship content of the examinations and in all probability readers will have access to seamanship manuals and similar publications which cover these matters adequately. Owners, their superintendents and others concerned with the equipping of new tonnage will, no doubt, consult the regulations directly. Here it will be sufficient to point out to what ships the regulations apply.

The M.S. (Life Saving Appliances) Regulations 1980 (as amended by S.I. 1981 No. 577) revoke and re-enact the provisions of the 1965 Rules, with additional requirements to give effect to the SOLAS Convention 1974 and the Protocol of 1978 relating to it. Among the additions are descriptions of tankers included in the classification of ships.

The requirements for fire appliances depend on whether the ship is a "new ship" or otherwise. "New ship" means a ship the keel of which was laid, or which was at a similar stage of construction, on or after 25th May 1980, and for such ships the equipment supplied and fitted must comply with the M.S. (Fire Appliances) Regulations 1980 (as amended by S.I. 1981 No. 577), which give effect to the Safety Convention and Protocol mentioned above.

The above two sets of regulations apply to United Kingdom ships, and other ships while they are within the United Kingdom or its territorial waters, and if a ship to which the regulations apply proceeds or attempts to proceed to sea without complying with them, the owner or master of the ship shall each be guilty of an offence and liable on summary conviction to a fine not exceeding £1,000 or on conviction on indictment, to imprisonment for a term not exceeding two years and a fine. A ship is liable to be detained in any case where it does not comply with the requirements of the regulations.

A ship which is not a "new ship" is known as an "existing ship", defined in the regulations as being a ship whose keel was laid, (or which was at a similar stage of construction) before 25th May 1980.

Existing British ships, and other existing ships while they are within any United Kingdom port, must comply with the M.S. (Fire Appliances) (Amendment) Rules 1980 (as amended by S.I. 1981 No. 575). These Rules further amend the 1965 Rules to give effect to the requirements of the 1974 Safety Convention and the Protocol of 1978 which relates to it. Additional requirements are specified for such ships and a description of tankers is added to the classification of ships. For ships built before 1965, Schedule 2 of the 1980 Amendment Rules specifies exemptions from the requirements of the 1965 Rules.

The Regulations and Rules named above are not to apply to:—

(i) a ship by reason of her being within a United Kingdom port if she would not have been in any such port but for stress of weather or any other circumstance that neither the master

nor the owner nor the charterer (if any) could have prevented;
  (ii) pleasure craft which are not passenger ships and are of less than 13·7 metres in length;
  (iii) mechanically-propelled sea-going fishing vessels registered in the United Kingdom under the M.S. Act 1894.

Section 12 of the M.S. (Safety and Load Line Conventions) Act, 1932, provides that if, on any international voyage, a British passenger steamer registered in the United Kingdom in respect of which a safety certificate is in force has on board a total number of persons less than the number stated in that certificate to be the number for which the life-saving appliances on the steamer provide, the D.o.T. or any person authorised by the Department for the purpose, may, at the request of the master, issue a memorandum stating the total number of persons carried on the steamer on that voyage, and the consequent modifications which may be made for the purpose of that voyage in the particulars with respect to life-saving appliances stated in the certificate.

If, for instance, one or more lifeboats became unserviceable as the result of an accident, and there was no time to replace them, then, provided the ship still had sufficient boatage for all the persons to be carried on the voyage, the master's proper procedure would be to complete and sign a form SUR 208. This is an application by the master requesting that a Memorandum be issued in accordance with the Section quoted above. If the request is acceded to, a Form SUR 209, dated and signed by an authorised Senior Surveyor, will be issued indicating the name, official number, and port of registry of the ship. This is to state the total number of passengers to be carried on the ship on that voyage, and the consequent modifications which may be made for that voyage in the particulars of life-saving appliances stated in the certificate. The memorandum must be annexed to the certificate. It is valid for one voyage only and is to be returned to the Marine Survey Office of issue at the end of the voyage to which it relates, and if it is not so returned the master is liable to a fine not exceeding £50.

International Voyage. An "international voyage" means a voyage from a port in one country to a port in another country.

A "short international voyage" means an international voyage—
  (a) in the course of which a ship is not more than 200 nautical miles from a port or place in which the passengers and crew could be placed in safety and,
  (b) which does not exceed 600 nautical miles in length between the last port of call in the country in which the voyage begins and the final port of destination.

But no account need be taken of deviation due to stress of weather or other unpreventable circumstances. Colonies, protectorates, etc., and territories administered by the United Nations are deemed to be separate countries.

A "long international voyage" is any international voyage which is not a short international voyage.

Certificated Lifeboatmen. The crew of every ship of Class I, II II(A) or III must include, for each lifeboat carried as part of the statutory life-saving appliances, a number of certificated lifeboatmen not less than that specified in the following table:—

Lifeboat complement less than 41 persons 2
,, ,, from 41 to 61 persons 3
,, ,, from 62 to 85 persons 4
,, ,, above 85 persons 5

An applicant for a lifeboatman's certificate shall be at least 18 years of age and shall submit himself for examination at such time and place as may be directed by the Department who, on being satisfied that he has had sufficient service at sea and has been trained in all the operations connected with the launching and practical handling of lifeboats and other life-saving equipment and in the use of oars and propelling gear and, further, that he is capable of understanding and answering any orders relative to all kinds of life-saving appliances, may issue a certificate to him.

While certificated officers are not precluded from obtaining lifeboatmen's certificates, and while officers holding such certificates are also not precluded from being counted in the minimum number of certificated lifeboatmen required, it is not considered desirable as a general rule that officers who would be required in an emergency to exercise functions of command and organisation should be included in the quota.

Information about the examination is published in the notice No. M.579.

Musters Regulations 1980. These regulations vary to some extent in their application to different classes of ships.

The following is a summary, in note form for the sake of brevity, of the outline of uniform schemes for training crews in emergency duties as contained in Part I of the notice No. M.694 applying to passenger ships (Classes I, II, II(A), and III) and cargo ships (Classes VII, VII(A), VII(T), VIII and VIII(T)).

Muster List

1. Must show special duties allotted to each member in emergency (including fire) and indicate station to go to when emergency warning is given. (Special arrangements necessary for native crews unable to read English.) In respect of passenger ships, the muster list must be in a form approved by D.o.T.

2. Must assign sufficient men to duties of clearing passenger accommodation, closing ports, etc., and extinction of fire. Against possibility of collision or accident causing entry of water, men to be

assigned to duty of closing doors, scuttles, shoots, discharges, and valves, and to other duties for combating results of accidents.

3. In case emergency becomes serious enough to abandon ship, list must provide for specified members to prepare boats and L.S.A. for use, and to marshal passengers at assembly stations for drafting to boats. Such members must ensure that equipment of boats is complete.

4. As far as is practicable men to whom special duties are assigned should have no other emergency duties assigned.

5. List must contain full particulars of signals for "emergency stations" and "abandon ship".

6. Muster list (or a separate list) must show boat station of each crew member.

7. When making out list, master must consider:—

(a) **Passenger Ships**

(i) Each lifeboat crew to include at least the number of certificated lifeboatmen specified in Regulation. Allocation of other certificated lifeboatmen may be at master's discretion.

(ii) A deck officer or certificated lifeboatman to be in charge of each boat and second-in-command nominated. Person in charge must have list of boat's crew and see that men know their duties.

(iii) Man able to work radio and searchlight to be assigned to each boat carrying such.

(iv) Duty of marshalling passengers normally to be assigned to steward's department.

(v) On vessels with davit launched life-rafts, a crew member trained in the handling of life-rafts should be assigned to each one to ensure safe unhooking when the raft becomes waterborne.

(vi) A damage control investigation party which includes responsible members of each department is to be arranged.

(b) **Passenger and Cargo Ships**

(i) Man able to operate motor must be assigned to each motorboat.

(ii) Man able to work portable radio must be assigned to boat wherein carried.

8. Muster list may be supplemented by issuing each man with card showing his boat station, emergency station(s), and duties and signals connected therewith. In some ships it may be better for list to show bunk numbers instead of names, in which case the card should be fixed to each bunk.

9. Master is reponsible for preparing list and he should sign and date it. List should be prepared (or revised) before putting to

sea after signing of agreement. If crew changes occur, master should alter list accordingly or make new one.

10. List should be posted conspicuously in several parts of ship (especially crew's quarters) before going to sea and kept posted while at sea. Responsible officers should make sure persons under their supervision understand contents of list, meanings of signals, and to which boats they are assigned.

Signals

11. The general emergency signal must be a succession of seven or more short blasts followed by one long blast on whistle or siren. A Class I ship must be provided throughout ship with electrically operated signals controlled from the bridge.

12. General emergency signal to be used only on master's responsibility when necessary to collect **passengers** at assembly stations in case ship might be abandoned.

13. Signals for calling **crew** to emergency stations (other than general emergency) or to practices are at the master's discretion. Such signals may be any combination of the audible sound system and/or public address system. If the emergency signal is to be used for a practice drill, all persons on board must be notified immediately beforehand that it is for a practice drill. Suitable signal to summon crew to fire stations in event of fire would be rapid and continuous ringing of bell, bell bars, or triangle.

14. Arrangements should be made to warn **passengers and crew** that ship is to be abandoned. Crew must be familiar with arrangements and signals.

15. **Training.** To be held as follows:—

(*a*) **Passenger Ships**

   (i) Crew **muster** before ship leaves final port of departure on an international voyage.

  (ii) Muster passengers within 24 hours after leaving port.

 (iii) Crew musters at intervals of not more than 7 days when practicable.

 (iv) If more than 25 per cent of crew replaced at any port, a muster of crew to be held within 24 hours of leaving that port.

(*b*) **Cargo Ships**

Boat and fire drill at intervals of not more than 14 days including a drill within 24 hours of leaving any port where 25 per cent or more of the crew were changed. Boat equipment to be examined at intervals of not more than one month to ensure that it is complete and in good order.

16. Practices should include (*a*) fire drill, (*b*) drill in closing doors, scuttles, valves, etc., (*c*) boat drill and where applicable life-raft drill, (*d*) drill in marshalling passengers.

17. Practices **in port** should be combined in one comprehensive practice. **At sea** either comprehensive or separate drills, or partly

combined, as desired, are in order provided that all are practised weekly or fortnightly in passenger and cargo ships, respectively.

18. At practice all men concerned should muster (wearing lifejackets) to perform and be instructed in their duties. The person in charge of a particular section must have a list of persons under his orders and see that each knows his duties.

Boat Drill

19. Each boat's crew (less men on normal duty or on other emergency duties) should muster at boat stations wearing life-jackets. Person in charge of each boat to have list of crew and see that men understand their duties. Boats used should include some from each side of ship distributed so as to enable crews of other boats to watch operations. Different groups of boats should be used at successive drills.

20. **At sea** at least one quarter of the boats attached to davits should, when circumstances permit, be cleared and swung out.

21. Boats not used should be examined with their equipment. Motor boat engines, radio, and searchlights should be examined and tested, engine spares checked, and mechanical hand-propelling gear tested.

22. **In port.** Clear and swing out as many boats attached to davits as possible. As far as practicable lower into water and exercise crew in pulling and sailing. On passenger ships where two boats have same davits, when one is lowered the other should be prepared and swung out. If practicable each boat to be lowered into water at least once every 4 months.

23. At each boat drill inspect lifebuoys, lifejackets, line-throwing apparatus and other L.S.A. See they are in good condition and readily available. Instruct crew, when launching buoyant apparatus to avoid damage to apparatus, boats, and persons in the water. The 1980 Musters Regulations specifically require the master to take steps to ensure that the crews are properly instructed in the handling and operation of the liferafts on board. Plans should be made to enable the passengers and crew to disembark into liferafts instead of lifeboats. This might mean that muster and embarkation points might need to be in different places and that some personnel might have to be assigned to different duties to launch and control entry into liferafts. If practicable, where carried, one davit-launched life-raft to be inflated and lowered in port at least once every 4 months; where possible similar training exercises to be arranged for non-davit launched rafts.

Marshalling Passengers

24. Men assigned for this duty should take up places on stair-ways and in passageways leading to assembly stations and at such stations. Officers in charge must ensure that men understand duties which include:—

(a) Warning passengers, seeing them suitably clad with life-jackets on correctly.

(b) Keeping order on stairways, etc., and generally controlling movements.

(c) Impressing on passengers risk of injury from jumping overboard and importance of using side ladders to embark in boats.

(d) Supply of blankets to lifeboats.

Practice Muster of Passengers

25. In ships of Class I a muster of the passengers embarked at any port must be held within 24 hours after leaving such port.

26. Notify time of muster to passengers in advance.

27. Master is to see that crew assigned to duties of para. 24 understand them. At assembly stations passengers are to be instructed in putting on lifejackets and in the matters referred to in para. 24 (a) and (c). Officers are to explain "abandon ship" procedure and emphasise that emergency signal is **not** an "abandon ship" signal but is intended to secure the orderly marshalling and assembly of passengers in the event of serious accident.

28. Assembly stations are to be selected and arranged so that passengers can readily proceed to allotted positions on embarkation deck.

Notice to Passengers

29. The following must be shown conspicuously on cards in all spaces providing sleeping accommodation for passengers.

(a) Passenger assembly stations of occupants.

(b) Nature and meaning of general emergency signal.

(c) Illustrated instructions for putting on lifejackets.

(d) Precise instructions as to what to do in an emergency.

(b) and (c) to be posted in other suitable positions in passenger accommodation. Information to be in English and other language or languages as considered necessary.

Drill—Closing Doors, Scuttles, Etc.

30. These drills must be held so as to comply with the M.S. (Closing of Openings in Hulls and in Watertight Bulkheads) Regulations 1980, set out earlier in this chapter.

31. Crews of emergency boats should, weather permitting, be mustered frequently at sea and especially instructed in the procedure for sending boats away promptly in emergency. Accident boat crews to be mustered not more than 3 hours after sailing from port, and thereafter at intervals of not more than 7 days.

Fire Drill

32. Assume outbreak of fire in some part of ship and make mock attack. **One Officer only** to take charge of all operations, wherever

fire may be. Vary site of fire, *e.g.*, cargo in holds, etc., bunker fire, oil cargo fire, engine or boiler room fire, crew or passenger accommodation fire, fire in galley (burning oil or cooking fat).

33. When fire signal given, fire parties should assemble at appointed stations for orders. Engine-room staff should ensure that fire pumps in machinery spaces are prepared, and full water pressure is put on fire mains. If an emergency pump is outside machinery space, start it up. Some members of fire party should be sent to seat of assumed fire. Hoses in vicinity should be laid out and water played through them. A number of portable extinguishers should be available, and men then instructed in the use of the type appropriate to the kind of fire (water, foam, dry powder, or CO_2). On occasion, one extinguisher should be discharged.

Fire party members should practice closing of ports, doors, ventilator shafts, annular space round funnel, etc., to restrict air supply and isolate fire from other parts of ship, especially stairways and lifts. They should learn positions of remote controls for fan engines, oil fuel pumps, oil tank valves, and be instructed in operation of them. Fixed installations for extinguishing fire (CO_2, steam, foam in machinery space—CO_2, steam in cargo space—sprinkler and alarm systems in passenger accommodation) should be tested with reasonable and practicable realism. Fire party should be exercised in use of smoke helmets and breathing apparatus; portable drilling machines, axes, and safety lamps should be carried by appointed members of the party at all drills.

Appliances not used at a particular drill should be examined. Alarms and fire-detecting apparatus should be inspected either at each drill or at other times within the same intervals (7 days in passenger ships, 14 days in others).

Sprinkler Installations

34. Weekly tests when installation is fitted in passenger ship:—

(*a*) Automatic cutting in of sprinkler pump. Pressure drop in tank at which pump cuts in to be noted. See fresh water level in pressure tank brought up to correct height immediately after test.

(*b*) Test automatic alarms (i) by opening in rotation test valve at each sectional control station; (ii) by local switches at control station.

Examine sprinkler heads periodically for damage and loss of coloured liquid. Make renewals without delay.

Miscellaneous

35. To avoid delay in sending out ship's position should assistance be needed, record position in chart room every two hours.

36. Persons in charge of lifeboats should be warned that after ship is abandoned it is advisable for boats to remain, if possible, in vicinity of accident.

37. Motor and other mechanically propelled boats should cruise about shepherding oared boats.

38. It should be impressed upon all the ship's personnel that suitable clothing contributes much to survival in all but the warmest climatic conditions.

Official Log Book Entries

Master must record each occasion on which a muster or training and drills in fire fighting are held on board or on which appliances and equipment are examined to see whether they are fit and ready for use. Record the date on which musters are held, details of training and drills in fire-fighting carried out, occasions on which boats are swung out and lowered, and on cargo ships, a report of examination of boat's equipment. When a muster is not held, or only a part muster is held, record why muster was not held, or where part muster held, record extent of it.

The M.S. (Automatic Pilot and Testing of Steering Gear) Regulations 1981 apply to U.K. sea-going ships, and other sea-going ships while they are within the U.K. or its territorial waters, but nothing in the regulations relating to the use of an automatic pilot is to override special rules made by an appropriate authority for roadsteads, harbours, rivers, lakes or inland waterways connected with the high seas and navigable by sea-going ships.

Use of the Automatic Pilot. The master must ensure that an automatic pilot, where fitted, must not be used in areas of high traffic density, in conditions of restricted visibility nor in any other hazardous navigational situation unless it is possible to establish manual control of the ship's steering within 30 seconds. Before entering any area of high traffic density, and whenever visibility is likely to become restricted, the officer of the watch is to have available the services of a qualified helmsman who is to be ready at all times to take over the manual steering, the change over from automatic being supervised by the officer of the watch or the master. The master must ensure that the manual steering is tested (a) after continuous use of the automatic pilot for 24 hours, and (b) before entering any areas where navigation demands special caution. When navigating in areas where special caution is required the master must ensure that the ship has more than one steering power unit in operation when such units are available and capable of simultaneous operation.

Steering Gear—Testing and Drills. Within 12 hours before sailing the master is required to cause the steering gear to be checked and tested to make sure that it is working satisfactorily, but where the ship is regularly making more than one voyage a week from the same port, the required test and check need only be made once in that week unless a part of the steering gear or its control system has been dismantled or changed since the last test.

Where applicable the test procedure shall include the operation of the main and auxiliary steering gear, the remote steering gear control systems and their power failure alarms, the bridge steering positions, the emergency power supply, the rudder angle indicators, the steering gear power unit failure alarms, and the automatic isolating arrangements and other automatic equipment required for steering gear. The checks and tests are to include the full movement of the rudder, a visual inspection of the steering gear and its connecting linkage, and the operation of means of communication between the bridge and the steering gear compartment.

The owner is to provide simple operating instructions, with a block diagram showing the changeover procedures, for the remote steering gear control systems and steering gear power units, and they are to be permanently displayed on the bridge and in the steering gear compartment.

In addition to the routine tests and checks described above, the master must arrange that drills which practise emergency steering gear procedures take place at least once every three months. These drills are to include, where applicable, use of direct control from within the steering gear compartment, the communications link with the bridge and the operation of alternative power supplies.

The date, time and place that the routine checks and tests are carried out and details of emergency steering drills carried out must be recorded in the official logbook by the master. In ships not required to keep an official logbook, the master must keep a record of each such test and drill and retain it on board for six months, available for inspection on demand by a superintendent, proper officer or surveyor of ships. Penalty £50 maximum fine.

Penalties. A master who fails to comply with the regulations concerning use of automatic pilot, operation of steering gear and tests and drills of gear, and an owner who fails to supply instructions etc., are guilty of an offence and liable on summary conviction to a fine not exceeding £1,000 or, on conviction on indictment, to imprisonment for a term not exceeding two years or a fine or both. A person who is directed to do so but fails to carry out the checks and tests required by the regulations is guilty of an offence and liable on summary conviction to a fine not exceeding £500 or, on conviction on indictment, to imprisonment for a term not exceeding one year or a fine or both.

The M.S. (Pilot Ladders and Hoists) Regulations 1980. Ships of Classes I, II, II(A), VII, VII(T), VII(A), VIII, VIII(A) and VIII(A) (T) where the distance in normal operating conditions, from water to point of access to vessel exceeds 2·5 metres must be provided with pilot ladders which comply with the following requirements:—

Each pilot ladder shall be efficient for the purpose of enabling a pilot to embark and disembark safely and such ladder shall be used only by officials and other persons while a ship is arriving at or leaving a port and for the embarkation and disembarkation of pilots.

Every such pilot ladder shall be secured in a position clear of any possible discharges from the ship and clear of the finer lines and as far as possible at the mid-length of the ship and so that each step rests firmly against the ship's side and so that the pilot can gain convenient access to the ship after climbing not less than 1·5 metres and not more than 9 metres.

A single length of ladder shall be used capable of reaching the water from the point of access to the ship and due allowance shall be made for all conditions of loading and trim of the ship.

Whenever the distance from the water to the point of access to the ship exceeds 9 metres, access from the pilot ladder to the ship shall be by means of an accommodation ladder with its lower end resting firmly against the ship's side as near to mid-length of the ship as practicable and leading aft, and with the pilot ladder rigged adjacent to the lower platform so that the pilot ladder's upper end extends at least two metres above the lower platform of the accommodation ladder, or other equally safe and convenient means.

The steps of the ladder shall be in one piece of hardwood or other material of equivalent strength and durability not less than 480 millimetres long, 115 millimetres wide and 25 millimetres in depth, have an efficient non-slip surface, be equally spaced not less than 300 millimetres nor more than 380 milimetres apart, and be secured in such a manner that they will remain horizontal. No ladder shall have more than two replacement steps which are secured in position by a different method from that used in the original construction of the ladder and any grooves required in the sides of replacement steps shall be in the longer sides of the step. Such steps shall be replaced using the original method of construction of the ladder as soon as practicable.

The side ropes of the ladder shall consist of two manilla ropes not less than 18 millimetres in diameter on each side and each rope shall be left uncovered and be continuous with no joins below the top step. Two man-ropes of not less than 20 millimetres in diameter, properly secured to the ship, and a safety line and harness shall be kept at hand ready for use if required. A heaving line shall be kept at hand.

Spreaders between 1·8 and 2 metres long shall be provided to prevent the ladder from twisting with the lowest spreader on the fifth step from the bottom and then at intervals not exceeding 9 steps.

Means shall be provided to enable the pilot ladder to be used on either side of the ship and to ensure safe and convenient passage for the pilot on to, or into, and off the ship, between the head of the pilot ladder, or accommodation ladder or other appliance, and the ship's deck. Adequate hand-holds shall be provided where passage is by means of a gateway in the rails or bulwark. If such passage is by means of a bulwark ladder, it shall be securely attached to the bulwark rail or landing platform and two hand-hold stanchions shall be fitted at the point of boarding or leaving the ship between 0·7 metre and 0·8 metre apart, each rigidly secured to the ship's structure at or near its base and also at a higher point, and each not less than 40 millimetres in diameter and extending not less than 1·2 metres above the top of the bulwarks.

A light shall be provided at night so that the pilot ladder overside and also the position where the pilot boards the ship shall be adequately lit. A lifebuoy equipped with a self-igniting light shall be kept ready for use at that position.

The regulations further require that the rigging of pilot ladders and the embarkation and disembarkation of persons thereby shall be supervised by a responsible officer of the ship.

Hoists. The regulations do not require pilot hoists to be provided, but introduce requirements for them if they are provided. A hoist is to consist of a mechanically powered winch, two separate falls and a ladder consisting of a rigid upper part to carry a person upwards or downwards, plus a flexible lower part consisting of a short length of pilot ladder to enable a person to climb from the pilot launch to the rigid upper part or vice versa. Hoists of other equally efficient construction may be allowed. Such a hoist is to be located, if practicable, at or about the ship's mid-length, and it should be arranged in such a way that the operator standing at the control point is able to see the hoist at any point between its highest and lowest positions. A copy of the manufacturer's approved maintenance manual, containing a log book, should be on board and the officer responsible for maintenance of the hoist is required to keep a record in that log book of all maintenance and repairs carried out. The hoist must be clearly marked with the maximum complement the hoist is permitted to carry.

Operation of the Hoist. The master must ensure that rigging and testing of the hoist before use and the embarkation and disembarkation of any person are to be supervised by a responsible ship's officer. Lighting is to be provided so that the hoist overside, its controls and the embarkation point are adequately lit. A safety line and harness, lifebuoy and light and a heaving line are to be kept at hand ready for use if required, and an approved pilot ladder is to be rigged adjacent to the hoist, available for immediate use so that access to it is available from the hoist at any point of its travel.

Testing. Every new hoist is to be subjected to an overload test of 2·2 times the working load, and after installation an operating test of 10 per cent overload is to be carried out on board ship.

Examinations of the hoist under working conditions are to be made at each renewal survey of the vessel's safety equipment certificate. In addition, the master must ensure that regular test rigging and inspection, including a load test to at least 150 kg., is carried out by the ship's personnel at intervals of not more than six months. A record to that effect must be made by the master in the ship's official log book. (In ships not required to keep an official log book, a record to that effect must be made by the master and retained on board for a period of not less than 12 months.) Penalty £50 fine.

Penalties. The master and the owner of a ship who contravene any provisions of the regulations that apply to them are guilty of an offence and liable on summary conviction to a fine not exceeding £1,000 or, on conviction on indictment, to imprisonment for a term not exceeding two years and a fine.

An officer who fails to supervise embarkation and disembarkation of any person as instructed by the master is guilty of an offence and liable on summary conviction to a fine not exceeding £500 or on conviction on indictment to imprisonment for a term not exceeding one year.

An officer responsible for the maintenance of the hoist who fails to keep a record as required by the regulations is guilty of an offence and liable on summary conviction to a fine not exceeding £500.

If a ship to which these regulations apply carries a pilot ladder or hoist which does not conform to the specified requirements of these regulations, the ship is liable to be detained.

North Atlantic Ice Service. The Act provides that sums required for the United Kingdom's contribution towards maintaining a service in the North Atlantic for the study and observation of ice, and for ice patrol, shall be paid by the Department of Trade out of moneys provided by Parliament.

N.B.—This service, which is contributed to on an international basis, is managed by the Government of the United States of America. Observations nowadays are made mainly from aircraft. The destruction of dangerous derelicts is within the scope of this service.

Navigation near Ice to be Careful. The Act requires the master of a British ship, when ice is reported on or near his course, **at night** either to proceed at a moderate speed or to change his course so as to keep amply clear of the ice reported and the area of danger. The penalty for failure to comply is on conviction on indictment a fine, on summary conviction a fine not exceeding £1,000. (The obligation of a master to report ice sighted from his ship has been referred to earlier in this chapter.)

Signalling Lamps. No British ship over 150 gross tons registered in the United Kingdom shall proceed to sea on an international voyage unless she is provided with a signalling lamp of approved type. If any ship proceeds, or attempts to proceed, to sea without being so provided, the owner or master is liable to a fine not exceeding £200.

The publication "Survey of Lights and Sound Signals" gives a specification of the type of lamp that will be approved.

The D.o.T. recommend that fishing vessels over 150 gross tons, although not actually engaged on international voyages should be, similarly equipped.

Subdivision Load Lines. Regulation 23 of the Passenger Ship Construction Regulations 1980 states that:—

(1) Every ship shall be marked on its sides amidships with the subdivision load lines assigned to it by the D.o.T. The marks shall consist of horizontal lines 25 mm. in breadth, and 230 mm. in length for any ship to which the M.S. (Load Lines) Act 1967 applies and 305 mm. in length for any other ship. The marks shall be painted in white or yellow if the background is dark or in black if the background is light and, if the sides of the ship are of metal, they shall be cut in, centre punched or indicated by welded beads; if the sides of the ship are of wood, the marks shall be cut into the planking to a depth of not less than 3 mm.; if the sides are of other materials to which the foregoing methods of marking cannot effectively be applied, the marks shall be permanently affixed to the sides of the ship by bonding or some other effective method.

(2) The subdivision load lines shall be identified with the letter C, and, in the case of ships of Classes I and II, with consecutive numbers beginning from the deepest subdivision load line which shall be marked C_1. In the case of ships of Classes II(A) to VI, inclusive:—

(a) if there is only one subdivision load line it shall be identified with the letter C;

(b) if there is more than one subdivision load line the subdivision load lines shall be identified by the letter C and with consecutive letters beginning from the deepest subdivision load line, which shall be marked C_A.

The identifying letters and numerals shall in every case be painted and cut or centre-punched or indicated by welded beads, or otherwise marked as appropriate, on the sides of the ship in the same manner as the lines to which they relate.

(3) Ships which are assigned freeboards and are required to be marked with load lines under the M.S. Load Lines Rules 1968 shall be marked as follows:—

(a) where the lowest of the ordinary load lines is higher on the ship's side than the deepest subdivision load line the latter

O

shall form part of the same marking, the vertical line of the grid being extended downwards as necessary to reach the lowest subdivision load line. The subdivision load line or lines shall appear on the after side of the vertical line;

(b) where the deepest subdivision load line coincides or nearly coincides with the fresh water line, the subdivision marking C, may be indicated on the forward side of the grid;

(c) where an "all seasons" freeboard is assigned and the deepest subdivision load line coincides with the horizontal line intersecting the load line mark, a vertical line shall be marked extending downwards from the fresh water load line to reach the subdivision load line marked C, on the after side of the vertical line.

The ships referred to in this Section are passenger ships having spaces which are sometimes used as cargo spaces, and at other times used to accommodate passengers. The subdivision load lines indicate the maximum depth to which the ship may be loaded having regard to the extent to which she is subdivided and which, if any, of the alternative spaces are actually being used for passengers. The ship's Safety Certificate will indicate the freeboard to be associated with each subdivision load line together with the circumstances in which it applies.

Section 23 of the 1967 Load Lines Act requires that a passenger ship to which that Act applies and which is marked with subdivision load lines, the lowest of which is lower than the ordinary load lines, shall not be loaded so as to submerge in salt water the appropriate subdivision load line on each side when the ship has no list. The penalty for non-compliance is the same as the penalty for unlawfully submerging the ordinary load lines. Details will be found in the section of this chapter which now follows.

LOAD LINES

An International Convention on Load Lines has been accepted by the United Kingdom and was signed in London on 5th April, 1966. To give effect to this Convention the Merchant Shipping (Load Lines) Act, 1967, was passed and came into operation on 21st July, 1968. This Act gave powers to the then Board of Trade to make the Rules known as the Merchant Shipping (Load Line) Rules, 1968, which were laid before Parliament on 15th July and came into operation on 21st July, 1968.

The following are some of the salient features of the Act:—

Application. The Act applies to all ships except (a) ships of war, (b) ships solely engaged in fishing, and (c) pleasure yachts.

Load Line Rules. The Board of Trade made rules in accordance with the provisions of the Act having regard in particular to the Convention of 1966.

Compliance with Load Line Rules. Subject to any exemption conferred, no United Kingdom registered ship shall proceed or attempt to proceed to sea unless the ship has been surveyed in accordance with the rules, is marked with a deck line and load lines, complies with the conditions of assignment, and is provided with information relating to stability, loading and ballasting for the guidance of the master.

If any ship proceeds or attempts to proceed to sea in contravention of the above, the owner or master shall be guilty of an offence and liable on summary conviction to a fine not exceeding £1,000, or on conviction on indictment to a fine.

Any ship which attempts to proceed to sea without being surveyed and marked may be detained, and a ship which does not comply with the conditions of assignment shall be deemed to be unsafe.

Submersion of Load Lines. Where a ship to which the Act applies is marked with load lines, the ship shall not be so loaded that (a) if the ship is in salt water and has no list, the appropriate load line on each side of the ship is submerged, or (b) in any other case, the appropriate load line on each side would be submerged if the ship were in salt water and had no list.

If any ship is loaded in contravention of the above the owner or master shall be guilty of an offence and liable:—(a) on conviction on indictment to a fine; (b) on summary conviction to a fine not exceeding £1,000 and to such additional fine as the court thinks fit to impose, having regard to the extent to which the earning capacity of the ship was increased by reason of the contravention. Such additional fine shall not exceed £1,000 for each complete centimetre by which the appropriate load line on each side was or would have been submerged.

If the master of a ship takes the ship to sea when she is overloaded, or if any other person, having reason to believe that the ship is overloaded, sends or is party to sending her to sea overloaded, then (without prejudice to any fine to which he may be liable in respect of the offence mentioned above) he shall be guilty of an offence and liable (a) on conviction on indictment, to a fine; (b) on summary conviction, to a fine not exceeding £1,000.

Where a person is charged with an offence relating to a ship being overloaded or taken or sent to sea in an overloaded condition it shall be a defence to prove that the contravention was due solely to deviation or delay caused solely by stress of weather or other circumstances which neither owner, master or charterer could have prevented or forestalled.

Without prejudice to any of the proceedings referred to above, any overloaded ship may be detained until she ceases to be overloaded.

Vessels more than 100 metres (328 ft.) in length

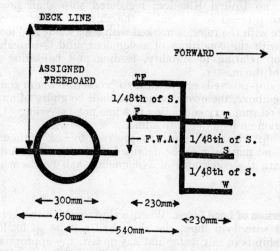

All lines are 25 mm thick.   S. means Summer Draught.

F.W.A. is Fresh Water Allowance equal to $\dfrac{\Delta}{4T}$ mm where Δ is the Summer salt.

water displacement in metric tons and T is the metric tons per centimetre immersion at the summer draught.

Vessels 100 metres (328 ft.) or less in length

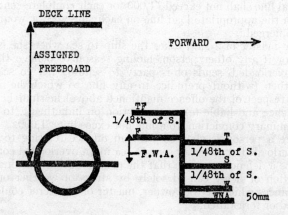

All lines are 25 mm thick.   S. means Summer Draught.

F.W.A. is the Fresh Water Allowance; see definition above.

Timber Load Lines—Vessels more than 100 metres in length

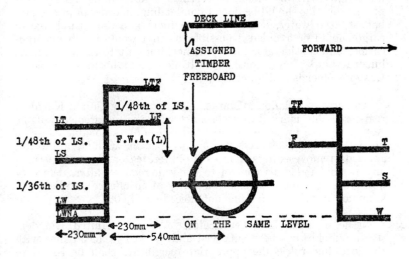

All lines are 25 mm thick.   LS. means Summer Timber Draught.

F.W.A.(L) is Fresh Water Allowance equal to $\frac{\Delta}{4T}$ mm where Δ is the LS salt water displacement in metric tons and T is the metric tons per centimetre immersion at the LS draught.

Timber Load Lines—Vessels 100 metres or less in length

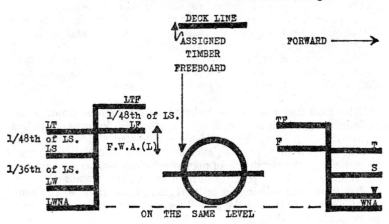

All lines are 25 mm thick.   LS means Summer Timber Draught.
F.W.A.(L) is Fresh Water Allowance, see definition above.

N.B.—If a ship is inadvertently overloaded slightly it is most important that this should be rectified before sailing. As far as is practicable this should be done by unloading, in order of preference, ballast, feed water, domestic water, fuel, or cargo. Discharge of cargo should be avoided if possible, as that would involve complications and considerable inconvenience, not only to the shipowners, but to shippers and consignees, bankers and insurance brokers, Customs officials and others.

Offences in Relation to Marks. In the case of a United Kingdom registered ship marked in accordance with the requirements of the Act, if (*a*) the owner or master fails without reasonable cause to keep the ship so marked, or (*b*) any person, without authority, conceals, removes, alters, defaces or obliterates, or causes, or permits any person under his control to conceal, remove, alter, deface or obliterate any mark, he shall be guilty of an offence and liable on summary conviction to a fine not exceeding £1,000.

Issue of Load Line Certificates. Where a United Kingdom registered ship has been surveyed and marked in accordance with the load line rules, the appropriate certificate shall be issued to the owner on his application. This is an "International Load Line Certificate (1966)" in the case of an existing ship of not less than 150 tons gross tonnage, and in the case of a new ship of not less than 24 metres in length. It is a "United Kingdom Load Line certificate" in the case of any other ship.

Except where the Dep't. of Trade request a Contracting Government, other than Her Majesty's Government in the United Kingdom, to issue an International Load Line Certificate (1966), any certificate required to be issued (*a*) shall be issued by the Dep't. of Trade or by a person authorised by the Dep't. (e.g. an authorised Classification Society), and (*b*) shall be in such form and be issued in such manner as prescribed by the load line rules.

When a certificate properly issued and for the time being in force is produced in respect of the ship to which it relates, the ship shall be deemed to have been surveyed and marked as required by the load line rules.

The load line rules shall make provision for determining the period during which any certificate is to remain in force, including (*a*) provision enabling the period to be extended within such limits and in such circumstances as may be prescribed, and (*b*) provision for cancelling the certificate in prescribed circumstances.

While a certificate remains in force there shall be endorsed on it such information relating to (*a*) periodical inspections of the ship, and (*b*) any extension of the period for which it was issued, as may be prescribed by the rules.

Subject to any exemption conferred, no United Kingdom registered ship shall proceed or attempt to proceed to sea unless the appropriate certificate is in force. Before any such ship proceeds to sea the master shall produce the appropriate certificate to the officer of customs from whom a clearance is demanded and a clearance shall not be granted, and the ship may be detained, until the certificate is so produced. Proceeding or attempting to proceed to sea in contravention of this requirement renders the master guilty of an offence and liable on summary conviction to a fine not exceeding £1,000, or on conviction on indictment, to a fine.

Posting up of Load Line Certificate. Where a certificate is issued in respect of a ship (*a*) the owner shall forthwith on receipt of it cause it to be framed and posted up in some conspicuous place on board, and cause it to be kept so framed and posted up and legible so long as it remains in force and the ship is in use.

Before any United Kingdom registered ship leaves any dock, wharf, harbour or other place for the purpose of proceeding to sea, the master shall, except in the case of a home trade ship exempted from the requirements of the regulations, cause a notice of particulars of loading to be posted up in some conspicuous place on board. Where such notice has been posted up, the master shall cause it to be kept so posted up and legible until the ship arrives at some other dock, wharf, harbour or place.

If the owner or master fails to comply with any of the above requirements he shall be guilty of an offence and liable on summary conviction to a fine not exceeding £50.

Inspection. A ship surveyor or engineer surveyor may inspect any ship to which the Act applies, being a ship registered in the United Kingdom, for the purpose of seeing that the provisions of the Act have been complied with.

Ships Not Registered in the United Kingdom. With respect to existing ships of not less than 150 tons gross and new ships of not less than 24 metres in length registered in or flying the flag of a Convention country, the Act provides that the Dep't. of Trade may, at the request of the Government of the parent country of the ship, issue International Load Line Certificates (1966) if satisfied that they could properly issue a certificate in respect of the ship if she were registered in the United Kingdom. Whilst such ships are in United Kingdom ports they will be under the same obligations as British ships with respect to compliance with load line rules, maximum depth of loading, and the production of the appropriate certificate to the officer of customs from whom clearance is demanded. Provision is made for the inspection of such ships by a surveyor, and there are powers of detention in cases where such ships are deemed to be unsafe.

The Act also provides for the issue of a United Kingdom load line certificate to a ship not registered in the United Kingdom, and which is not plying on international voyages, on the application of the owner.

Exemptions.   The Act gives the Dep't. of Trade powers to exempt certain ships from all the provisions of the Act and of the load line rules, and certain other ships from some of those provisions. In such cases the Dep't. shall issue the appropriate exemption certificate.

Subdivision Load Lines.   Where a passenger steamer is marked with subdivision load lines, and the lowest of those lines is lower than the line which otherwise would be the appropriate load line, that subdivision load line shall be regarded as the appropriate load line for the purposes of that section of the Act dealing with submersion of load lines.

Deck Cargo.   The Dep't. of Trade shall make regulations prescribing requirements to be complied with where cargo is carried in any uncovered space on the deck of a ship to which this Act applies; and different requirements may be so prescribed in relation to different descriptions of ships, different descriptions of cargo, different voyages or classes of voyages, different seasons of the year or any other different circumstances.

If the load line rules provide for assigning special freeboards for ships which are to have effect only where a cargo of timber is so carried, then the deck cargo regulations may prescribe special requirements to be complied with in circumstances where any such special freeboard has effect.

If any provisions of the deck cargo regulations are contravened the master of the ship shall be guilty of an offence and liable on summary conviction to a fine not exceeding £1,000, or on conviction on indictment to a fine.   But where a person is charged with an offence it shall be a defence to prove that the contravention was due solely to deviation or delay caused solely by stress of weather or other circumstances which neither the master nor owner nor charterer could have prevented or forestalled.

Any person authorised by the Dep't. of Trade may inspect any ship to which the Act applies which is carrying cargo in any uncovered space on her deck.

International Voyage.   In this Act the expression "international voyage" means a voyage between (*a*) a port in the United Kingdom and a port outside the United Kingdom, or (*b*) a port in a Convention country (other than the United Kingdom) and a port in any other country or territory (whether a Convention country or not (which is outside the United Kingdom.   For this purpose no account shall be taken of unpreventable deviation.

Gross Tonnage.   Where, in accordance with the tonnage regulations, alternative tonnages are assigned to a ship, the gross tonnage

SPECIMEN

No. 23456

LLOYD'S REGISTER OF SHIPPING

INTERNATIONAL LOAD LINE CERTIFICATE (1966)

Issued under the provisions of the International Convention on Load Lines, 1966,
under the authority of the .GOVERNMENT. OF...
by Lloyd's Register of Shipping.

Name of Ship	Distinctive number or letters	Port of Registry	Length (L) XX defined in XXXXXXXX
"TRANQUILLITY"			48,400 m.

Freeboard assigned as: XXXXXXXX *An existing ship

Type of Ship: *XXXXXXXXXXXXXXXXXXXXXXXXXXXXXXXXXX   *Delete whatever is inapplicable

	Freeboard from Deck Line			Load Line	
Tropical	950	mm (Inches) (T)		50 mm (XXXX) above (S)	
Summer	1000	mm (Inches) (S)		Upper edge of line through centre of ring	
Winter	1070	mm (Inches) (W)		70 mm (Inches) below (S)	
Winter North Atlantic	1120	mm (XXXX) (WNA)		120 mm (XXXX) below (S)	
Timber Tropical		mm (Inches) (LT)		mm (Inches) above (LS)	
Timber Summer		mm (Inches) (LS)		mm (Inches) above (S)	
Timber Winter		mm (Inches) (LW)		mm (Inches) below (LS)	
Timber Winter North Atlantic		mm (Inches) (LWNA)		mm (Inches) below (LS)	

Note : Freeboards and Load Lines which are not applicable need not be entered on the certificate.

Allowance for Fresh Water for all freeboards other than timber............ 80 ....mm (XXXX)

Allowance for Fresh Water for timber freeboards...mm (Inches)

The upper edge of the deck line from which these freeboards are measured is................ Nil ....mm (XXXX) ....
below top of steel upper deck at side.

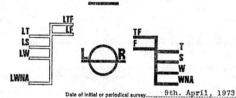

Date of initial or periodical survey................ 9th. April, 1973 ....

This is to certify that this ship has been surveyed and that the freeboards have been assigned and load lines shown above have been marked in accordance with the International Convention on Load Lines, 1966.

This certificate is valid until.... 8th. April, 1978 ...., subject to periodical inspections in accordance with Article 14 (1)(c) of the Convention.

Issued at........ London ....   on............ 15th. May, ... 73 ......19........

The undersigned declares that Lloyd's Register of Shipping is duly authorised by the said..... Government ....to issue this certificate.

(signed) T.R. Wilson
....
Lloyd's Register of Shipping,
71, Fenchurch Street, London, EC3M 4BS

ILLC 110

This is to certify that at a periodical inspection required by Article 14 (1) (c) of the Convention, this ship was found to comply with the relevant provisions of the Convention.

Place..   Date..

....
Surveyor to Lloyd's Register of Shipping

Place..   Date..

....
Surveyor to Lloyd's Register of Shipping

Place..   Date..

....
Surveyor to Lloyd's Register of Shipping

Place..   Date..

....
Surveyor to Lloyd's Register of Shipping

The provisions of the Convention being fully complied with by this ship, the validity of this certificate is, in accordance with Article 19 (2) of the Convention, extended until..

Place..   Date..

....
Lloyd's Register of Shipping

Notes:

1. When a ship departs from a port situated on a river or inland waters, deeper loading shall be permitted corresponding to the weight of fuel and all other materials required for consumption between the point of departure and the sea.

2. When a ship is in fresh water of unit density the appropriate load line may be submerged by the amount of the fresh water allowance shown above. Where the density is other than unity, an allowance shall be made proportional to the difference between 1·025 and the actual density.

3. This certificate is to be framed and posted up in some conspicuous place on board the ship, so long as the certificate remains in force and the ship is in use.

4. Article 14 (1) (c):
   A periodical inspection within three months either way of each annual anniversary date of the certificate, to ensure that alterations have not been made to the hull or superstructure which would affect the calculations determining the position of the load line and so as to ensure the maintenance in an effective condition of fittings and appliances for:
       (i)   protection of openings;
       (ii)   guard rails;
       (iii)   freeing ports; and
       (iv)   means of access to crew's quarters.

of the ship shall, for the purposes of this Act, be taken to be the larger of those tonnages.

COMMENTS ON THE LOAD LINE RULES

Ships to which the Rules Apply. These are all ships except (*a*) ships of war, (*b*) ships solely engaged in fishing, and (*c*) pleasure yachts.

Assigning Authorities. For the assignment of freeboards and the issue of load line certificates the Assigning Authorities in the United Kingdom are the Department of Trade, Lloyd's Register of Shipping, the British Committee of Bureau Veritas, the British Technical Committee of the American Bureau of Shipping, the British Committee of Det norske Veritas and the British Committee of Germanischer Lloyd. In a colony the authority is the Governor or such corporation or association as may be appointed by him.

Applications to Authority. Applications for assignment of freeboards and issue of load line certificate must be made to an Authority by or on behalf of the shipowner who is required to furnish such plans, drawings, specifications and other documents and information relating to design and construction as the Authority may require.

Load Line Survey. After receipt of the application and documents, etc., mentioned above the Authority must cause the ship to be surveyed by a Surveyor in order to ascertain whether the ship complies with such of the requirements relating to freeboard as are applicable to the ship and to enable information to be supplied to the master pursuant to the rules relating to stability and the loading and ballasting of ships. In the course of this survey the ship and any of her fittings or equipment are submitted to such tests as in the opinion of the Authority may be necessary. The owner must afford all necessary facilities for the survey and, if requested, furnish the Authority with such further documents and information as the Authority may require. On completion of the survey the Surveyor must furnish to the Authority a report giving the results of the survey and his findings in relation to certain specified matters.

Assignment of Freeboards. The Assigning Authority shall (*a*) if satisfied from the Surveyor's report that the ship complies with the relevant requirements, and (*b*) on receipt from the D.o.T. of notification that they are satisfied that the ship complies with the requirements relating to stability (1) assign freeboards to the ship, and (2) furnish the owner with particulars of the freeboards assigned, directions specifying which load lines are to be marked on the sides of the ship, the position in which the load lines, deck-line and load line mark are to be so marked, and two copies of the Surveyor's report.

Load Line Certificate. On being satisfied that the ship has been duly marked the Assigning Authority is required to issue to the shipowner either an International Load Line Certificate (1966) or a United Kingdom Load Line Certificate as may be appropriate, unless the ship is one which is exempt from some or all of the provisions of the Act and Rules in which case the appropriate Exemption Certificate is issued.

Duration of Validity of Certificate. Unless it is cancelled a load line certificate remains valid until a date to be determined by the Assigning Authority, not being a date more than five years after the date of completion of the load line survey mentioned above. (See reference to periodical inspections.)

Extension of Period of Validity. Where an application has been made to an Authority by the owner of a ship in respect of which a load line certificate is in force for the issue of a certificate to take effect on the expiry of the current certificate and, following such application, the ship has been duly surveyed, the Authority may, when satisfied with the surveyor's report and notified by the D.o.T. that the ship complies with the requirements relating to stability, if it considers that it will not be practicable to issue the new certificate before the date of expiry of the current one, extend the period of validity of the current one for a period not exceeding 5 months. However, such extension will have no effect unless particulars of the date to which the period of validity is extended together with particulars of the place at and the date on which such extension was given are endorsed by the Authority on the current certificate. The period of validity of any load line certificate coming into effect immediately on the expiry of a certificate extended as above may not exceed a period of 5 years commencing on the date of completion of the survey referred to.

Cancellation of Certificate. The D.o.T. may cancel a load line certificate:—

(*a*) if satisfied (by a report from an Assigning Authority or otherwise) that—

    (i) the ship concerned does not comply with the conditions of assignment; or

    (ii) the structural strength of the ship is lowered to such an extent that the ship is unsafe; or

    (iii) information on the basis of which freeboards were assigned was incorrect in a material particular;

(*b*) if the certificate is not endorsed in accordance with the requirements relating to periodical inspections;

(*c*) if a new certificate is issued in respect of the ship;

(*d*) if the ship was registered in the U.K. when the certificate was issued and has since ceased to be so registered.

In every such case the D.o.T. is required to notify the shipowner in writing specifying the grounds therefor and the date on which it is to take effect.

Periodical Inspections. Every ship in respect of which a load line certificate is in force must be periodically inspected by a Surveyor to ensure that (*a*) the fittings and appliances for the protection of openings, guard rails, freeing ports and means of access to crew's quarters are in an effective condition, and (*b*) no changes have occurred in hull or superstructures such as to render no longer accurate data on the basis of which freeboards were assigned. Application for inspection must be made by or on behalf of the owner to an Authority who will appoint a Surveyor to carry out the inspection. The Surveyor may require the carrying out of any tests considered by him to be necessary. Such inspection must be carried out on or within 3 months before or after each anniversary of the date of completion of the survey leading to the issue of the certificate. Unless the Authority otherwise consents the intervals between inspections must be not less than 9 or more than 15 months. The Surveyor, if satisfied that the ship complies with the requirements mentioned above, must endorse in the space provided on the load line certificate a record of his inspection and of the fact that the ship was found to comply with the relevant provisions of the Convention (in the case of an International Load Line Certificate) or with the relevant provisions of the Rules (in the case of a United Kingdom Load Line Certificate). He must also specify the Authority by which he was appointed to carry out the inspection.

LOAD LINES AND MARKS

Deck-line. This consists of a horizontal line 300 millimetres in length and 25 millimetres in width marked amidships on each side of the ship so as to indicate the position of the freeboard deck. Generally, the deck-line is marked so that its upper edge passes through the point amidships where the continuation outwards of the upper surface of the freeboard deck, or of any sheathing of that deck, intersects the outer surface of the shell. Where, however, the design of the ship or other circumstances render that impracticable, the Authority may direct that it be marked by reference to another fixed point in the ship as near as practicable to the position described.

Load Line Mark. This consists of a ring 300 millimetres in outside diameter and 25 millimetres wide, intersected by a horizontal line 450 millimetres long and 25 millimetres wide the upper edge of which passes through the centre of the ring. The centre of the ring is marked amidships vertically below the deck-line, so that, except in the case of a ship with "greater than minimum freeboard", the distance from the centre of the ring to the upper edge of the deck-line is equal to the Summer freeboard assigned to the ship.

Load Lines. These indicate the maximum depth to which a ship may be loaded in the prevailing circumstances in respect of Zones, Areas and Seasonal Periods. Except in the cases of sailing ships and ships with greater than minimum freeboards, load lines consist of horizontal lines each 230 millimetres in length and 25 millimetres in width extending forward or abaft of a vertical line 25 millimetres in width marked 540 millimetres forward of the centre of the ring of the load line mark and at right angles to that line. Individual load lines are:—

the **Summer load line,** which shall extend forward of the said vertical line and be marked S, and shall correspond horizontally with the line passing through the centre of the ring of the load line mark;

the **Winter load line,** which shall extend forward of the said vertical line and be marked W;

the **Winter North Atlantic load line,** which shall extend forward of the said vertical line and be marked WNA;

the **Tropical load line,** which shall extend forward of the said vertical line and be marked T;

the **Fresh Water load line,** which shall extend abaft the said vertical line and be marked F;

the **Tropical Fresh Water load line,** which shall extend abaft the said vertical line and be marked TF.

The maximum depth of loading referred to shall be the depth indicated by the upper edge of the appropriate load line.

In the case of a sailing ship the Summer load line consists of a line passing through the centre of the ring of the load line mark. Only the Winter North Atlantic and Fresh Water load lines appear and these are marked WNA and F, respectively.

Timber Load Lines. These consist of horizontal lines of the dimensions specified above extending abaft or forward of a vertical line 25 millimetres in width marked 540 millimetres abaft the centre of the ring and at right angles to that line. Individual Timber load lines are:—

the **Summer Timber load line,** which shall extend abaft the said vertical line and be marked LS;

the **Winter Timber load line,** which shall extend abaft the said vertical line and be marked LW;

the **Winter North Atlantic Timber load line,** which shall extend abaft the said vertical line and be marked LWNA;

the **Tropical Timber load line,** which shall extend abaft the said vertical line and be marked LT;

the **Fresh Water Timber load line,** which shall extend forward of the said vertical line and be marked LF;

the **Tropical Fresh Water Timber load line,** which shall extend forward of the said vertical line and be marked LTF.

Appropriate Load Line. This in respect of a ship at any particular place and time is ascertained in accordance with the provisions of Schedule 2 of the Rules which gives the full details of Zones, Areas and Seasonal Periods.

Position of Load Lines. Each required load line must be marked in such a position on each side of the ship that the distance measured vertically downwards from the upper edge of the deck-line to the upper edge of the load line is equal to the freeboard assigned which is appropriate to that load line.

Method of Marking. The appropriate marks must be marked on each side of the ship in accordance with the following requirements so as to be plainly visible. If the sides are of metal the marks are to be cut in, centre punched or welded; if they are of wood the marks are to be cut into the planking to a depth of not less than 3 millimetres. If of other materials to which the foregoing methods cannot effectively be applied, the marks are to be permanently affixed to the sides by bonding or other effective method. The marks must be painted in white or yellow if the background is dark, and in black if the background is light. Marks may not be concealed, removed, altered, defaced or obliterated except under the authority of an Assigning Authority.

Mark of Assigning Authority. Such a mark must consist of not more than four initials to identify the Authority's name, each measuring approximately 115 millimetres in height and 75 millimetres in width. It may be marked on each side of the ship in a position alongside the load line mark either above the horizontal line forming part of that mark, or above and below it.

Types of Freeboard. The freeboards assignable under the Rules are:—

Summer freeboard,
Tropical freeboard,
Winter freeboard,
Winter North Atlantic freeboard,
Fresh Water freeboard, and
Tropical Fresh Water freeboard.

In the case of ships to which Timber freeboards are assigned they are:—

Summer Timber freeboard,
Winter Timber freeboard,
Winter North Atlantic Timber freeboard,
Tropical Timber freeboard,
Fresh Water Timber freeboard, and
Tropical Fresh Water Timber freeboard.
Each of the above is referred to as a minimum freeboard.

Greater than Minimum Freeboards. The owner of a ship may, when making application for assignment, request the assignment of freeboards greater than the minimum freeboards. In any such case the Authority may, if satisfied after survey that the ship complies with the relevant requirements and has received notification from the D.o.T. that the ship complies with the requirements relating to stability, assign freeboards (other than timber freeboards) exceeding the minimum freeboards appropriate to the ship as they may determine, and furnish to the owner particulars thereof. Timber freeboards may not be assigned in such a case.

In any case in which the greater than minimum Summer freeboard assigned is such that the position on the sides of the ship of the load line appropriate to that freeboard would correspond to, or be lower than, the position at which the lowest of the load lines appropriate to minimum freeboards for the ship would be marked:—

(a) the following load lines only shall be marked, that is to say, those appropriate to the greater than minimum Summer freeboard and Fresh Water freeboard;

(b) the load line appropriate to the greater than minimum Summer freeboard shall be known as the "All Seasons load line" and shall consist of the horizontal line intersecting the load line mark and such mark shall be placed accordingly;

(c) the vertical line (described above) shall be omitted;

(d) subject to the provisions of sub-paragraph (c), the Fresh Water load line shall be as described and be marked accordingly.

Determination of Freeboards. The Summer freeboard is determined in accordance with the provisions set out in Schedule 5 of the Rules.

The Tropical freeboard is obtained by deducting from the Summer freeboard one forty-eighth (1/48th) of the summer draught. The freeboard so obtained by omitting any correction made for deck-line (for which a Table is provided) shall not be less than 50 millimetres except in certain special cases when it shall not be less than 150 millimetres.

The Winter freeboard shall be obtained by adding to the Summer freeboard one forty-eighth (1/48th) of the summer draught.

The Winter North Atlantic freeboard shall be obtained by adding to the Winter freeboard a distance of 50 millimetres.

The Fresh Water freeboard shall be obtained by deducting from the Summer freeboard the quantity:—

$$\frac{\Delta}{4T} \text{ millimetres}$$

where Δ is the displacement in salt water in metric tons at the Summer load waterline, and T represents metric tons per centimetre immersion in salt water at that waterline. If the displacement at that waterline cannot be ascertained the deduction shall be one forty-eighth of the summer draught.

The Summer Timber freeboard is determined in accordance with the provisions set out in Schedule 5 of the Rules.

The Winter Timber freeboard shall be obtained by adding to the Summer Timber freeboard one thirty-sixth (1/36th) of the summer timber draught.

The Winter North Atlantic Timber freeboard shall be the same as the Winter North Atlantic freeboard assigned to the ship.

The Tropical Timber freeboard shall be obtained by deducting from the Summer Timber freeboard one forty-eighth (1/48th) of the Summer Timber draught.

The Fresh Water Timber freeboard shall be obtained by deducting from the Summer Timber freeboard the quantity:—

$$\frac{\Delta}{4T} \text{ millimetres}$$

where Δ is the displacement in salt water in metric tons at the waterline which will when load lines have been marked correspond to the Summer Timber load line, and T represents metric tons per centimetre immersion in salt water at that waterline. If the displacement at that waterline cannot be ascertained the deduction shall be one forty-eighth of the Summer Timber draught.

Appropriate Load Lines. The following is Part 1 of Schedule 2 of the Rules.

1. Subject to paragraphs 3–6 of this Part, the load line appropriate to a ship shall be:—

    (1) the Summer load line when the ship is in a summer zone (excluding any part of such a zone which is to be regarded as a seasonal area in relation to the ship);

    (2) the Tropical load line when the ship is in the tropical zone;

    (3) when the ship is in a seasonal zone or area (including any part of a summer zone which is to be regarded as a seasonal area in relation to the ship) the Summer load line, the Winter load line or the Tropical load line according to whether the seasonal period applicable in that zone or area to that ship is respectively summer, winter or tropical.

2. (1) The zones,

    (2) the seasonal zones, seasonal areas and seasonal periods applicable to a ship, shall be those set out in Part II of this Schedule and shown by way of illustration on the Chart annexed to these Rules.

3. In the case of a ship of 100 metres or less in length, the appropriate load line shall be the Winter North Atlantic load line in:—

(1) the North Atlantic Seasonal Zone I as described in paragraph 1(1) of Part II of this Schedule;

(2) so much of North Atlantic Winter Seasonal Zone II, as so described, as lies between the meridians of longitude of 15°W and 50°W

during the winter seasonal periods respectively applicable in those zones.

4. In the case of a sailing ship the appropriate load line shall except in circumstances in which paragraph 3 applies, be the Summer load line.

5. In the case of a ship marked with an All Seasons load line in accordance with Rule 28 that load line shall be the appropriate load line in all circumstances.

6. In the case of a ship marked with Timber load lines and carrying timber deck cargo in accordance with the requirements of the deck cargo regulations, the load line to be observed in any particular circumstance shall be the Timber load line corresponding to the load line which would be applicable in those circumstances under paragraphs 1 to 5 of the Schedule if the ship were not so marked.

N.B.—Paragraphs 1 to 5 cover all the zones and areas except the Enclosed Seas (Baltic Sea, Black Sea, Mediterranean and Sea of Japan).

The Zone Chart. This indicates (1) **Permanent Zones,** (2) **Seasonal Zones and Areas.** There are two permanent zones, viz., the **Tropical Zone** which is coloured **Green** and, on each side of it, the **Summer Zone** which is coloured **Pink.**

So long as a ship *remains* within a permanent zone she may lawfully be loaded to the depth of the appropriate load line, tropical or summer as the case may be, unless her draught is restricted by the operation of a "Sub-division load line" which might be the case in a passenger ship. This holds good all the year round.

In both hemispheres there is a **Seasonal Winter Zone** which is coloured **Blue.** In the Northern one the **Winter Season** extends from 16th October to 15th April and the **Summer Season** extends from 16th April to 15th October. The reverse holds good in the Southern one. The **North Atlantic** has two Winter Seasonal Zones, I and II. In Zone I the Winter and Summer seasons are as stated above, but in Zone II, which is coloured **Light Blue,** Winter extends from 1st November to 31st March and Summer from 1st April to 31st October.

During the Winter Season it is unlawful for the winter load line to be submerged, but during the Summer Season a ship may be loaded to summer draught so long as that will not cause her to *become* overloaded as the voyage proceeds.

In the case of a ship with Timber load lines, when carrying a deckload of timber in accordance with the Deck Cargo Regulations, the Timber Winter and Timber Summer load lines, respectively, would govern the situation instead.

The Winter North Atlantic load line applies in the whole of Zone I and in that part of Zone II between the meridians of 15°W and 50°W during the winter season in those zones.

Special Areas. In the Northern Hemisphere certain areas are indicated by **Blue** or **Red Diagonal Bands.** The **Blue** diagonals denote a North Atlantic Winter Seasonal Area off Nova Scotia wherein for ships of 100 metres (328 ft.) or less in length the winter season is from 1st November to 31st March and summer from 1st April to 31st October. For ships over 100 metres in length winter is from 16th December to 15th February and summer from 16th February to 15th December. The **Red** diagonals denote areas which are Summer for ships which are over 100 metres in length and Seasonal Winter (between specified dates) for ships of 100 metres or less in length. These areas marked by Red diagonals are to be found off the East coast of U.S.A., the Baltic Sea, parts of the Northern Mediterranean and Black Seas and the Northern part of the Sea of Japan.

In the belt of low latitudes other areas are shown as **Light Green.** These are **Seasonal Tropical Areas** which have been designated in accordance with the frequency of gales and storms within their boundaries. Each of these areas is allotted dates during which the area is to be treated as part of the Tropical Zone and dates during which it is to be treated as part of the Summer Zone.

Ports on Boundary Lines. For the purposes of the application of the provisions of Schedule 2 to a ship at a port which stands on the boundary line between two zones or areas or between a zone and an area, the port is deemed to be within the zone or area into which the ship is about to proceed or from which she has arrived as the case may be.

Use of Timber Load Lines. The general principle involved is that if a vessel of adequate structural strength to warrant the deeper immersion is carrying a deckload of timber, stowed and secured in accordance with the Deck Cargo Regulations, there is the threefold effect that (i) the reserve buoyancy is increased by the compact mass of buoyant material above the freeboard deck, (ii) the effective freeboard is increased with beneficial effect on the range of positive stability, and (iii) the weather deck hatches are protected. On this account the vessel is justified in loading to a deeper draught than would be allowed if she had no deck cargo at all.

The Deck Cargo Regulations (S.I. 1968 No. 1089) require that timber deck cargo carried by a ship in a winter zone or area during the winter season shall be so stowed that at no point throughout its length does the height of the cargo above the level of the weather deck at side exceed one-third of the extreme breadth of the ship. This applies whether the ship is loading to timber load lines or not.

To take advantage of the deeper loading effected by submerging the ship to the depth of the appropriate timber load line it is necessary that the deckload should be built up to a certain *minimum* height. This is the height of the adjacent superstructure, but is standardised at 1.8 metres for a ship of 75 metres in length or less, 2.3 metres for a ship of 125 metres in length or more, and *pro rata* for lengths between 75 and 125 metres. These heights are measured from the well on which the timber is stowed.

In summer conditions no maximum height of deckload is prescribed but, of course, the height must be limited by practical considerations and to comply with the requirements of the Deck Cargo Regulations relating to adequate stability, proper lashings, proper access to crew's quarters, availability of emergency steering gear, and in all other respects so as not to interfere with the navigation or working of the ship.

Stability Information. The Rules require that the owner of any ship to which freeboards are assigned shall provide for the guidance of the master information relating to the stability of the ship. With certain exceptions such information must include particulars appropriate to the ship in respect of all matters specified in Schedule 7 to the Rules and be in the form required by that Schedule. This schedule is very comprehensive. The information, when first supplied, must be based on the determination of stability by means of an inclining test carried out in the presence of a surveyor (unless the D.o.T. permits otherwise) or on the test of a sister ship. The information provided must be furnished by the owner of the ship to the master in the form of a book which is to be kept on the ship at all times in the master's custody.

Information as to Loading and Ballasting. The Rules further require the owner of any ship to which freeboards are assigned, being a ship of more than 150 metres in length specially designed for the carriage of liquids or ore in bulk, to provide for the information of the master information relating to the loading and ballasting of the ship. Such information is to consist of working instructions specifying in detail the manner in which the ship is to be loaded and ballasted so as to avoid the creation of unacceptable stresses in her structure and must indicate the maximum stresses permissible for the ship. This information is to be contained in the book mentioned in the previous paragraph.

Submission of Stability Information. Stability information and information as to loading and ballasting, and any fresh information to replace the same, shall before issue to the master, if it relates to a ship which is an oil tanker over 100 metres, a bulk or ore carrier over 150 metres, a single deck bulk carrier between 100 and 150 metres, a single deck dry cargo ship over 100 metres, or a purpose built container ship over 125 metres, in length respectively, be submitted by or on behalf of the owner of the ship either to the D.o.T. or to the Assigning Authority which assigned the ship's freeboards for approval. Information relating to any other ship shall be submitted in duplicate to the D.o.T.

Definitions, Types of Ships and Special Rules.   In the Rules:—

"amidships" means the middle of the ship's length.

"freeboard" means the distance measured vertically downwards amidships from the upper edge of the deck-line to the position at which the upper edge of the load line appropriate to the freeboard is to be marked.

"freeboard deck" means the deck from which the freeboards assigned to the ship are calculated, being either:—

(a) the uppermost complete deck exposed to weather and sea, which has permanent means of closing all openings in its weather portions, and below which all openings in the sides of the ship are fitted with permanent means of watertight closing; or

(b) at the request of the owner and subject to the approval of the D.o.T., a deck lower than that described in paragraph (a), subject to its being a complete and permanent deck which is continuous both (i) in a fore and aft direction at least between the machinery space and peak bulkheads of the ship and (ii) athwartships,

a deck which is stepped being taken to consist for this purpose of the lowest line of the deck and the continuation of that line parallel to the upper part of the deck.

"sailing ship" means a ship designed to carry sail, whether as the sole means of propulsion or as a supplementary means.

"Surveyor" means a surveyor of ships appointed either by the D.o.T. under the Merchant Shipping Acts or by any other Assigning Authority.

"watertight" means capable of preventing the passage of water in any direction.

For the purpose of applying certain of the Rules ships are divided into two types, "A" and "B". A Type "A" ship is a ship designed to carry only liquid cargoes in bulk and which has certain characteristics set out in a schedule to the Rules. A Type "B" ship is either a new ship other than a Type "A" ship, or an existing ship constructed or modified to comply with all the conditions of assignment.

There are special rules laid down for the assignment of freeboards to (i) sailing ships and tugs, (ii) ships of wood or composite construction and ships having unusual constructional features, and (iii) unmanned barges.

OIL POLLUTION

Prevention of Oil Pollution. Of recent years the problem of oil pollution has become more and more serious and since 1920 has engaged the attention of authorities in the United Kingdom and in many other countries. The effects of oil pollution are (a) the spoiling of beaches and coastal resort amenities, (b) the destruction and injury of birds, (c) the fouling of boats, fishing gear, piers, quays, etc., (d) damage to fish, shellfish and larvae, and (e) some fire risk in enclosed waters, although the last mentioned is not considered very serious.

A Board of Trade Conference in 1921 gave rise to the Oil in Navigable Waters Act, 1922, which among other things provided penalties of up to £100 for the unlawful discharge of oil into United Kingdom territorial waters and harbours. In 1936 an international conference was held at Washington to consider the compulsory fitting of oily water separators in ships and the establishment of zones within which no oil should be discharged. In spite of failure on that occasion to secure international agreement, British ship-owners agreed to adopt voluntarily an obligation not to discharge oil within 50 miles of any coastline. Later this was extended to 100 miles in respect of the coasts of the United States of America. In 1954 another international conference was convened and the International Convention for the Prevention of Pollution of the Sea by Oil was signed on behalf of the United Kingdom Government in the same year. To give effect to this Convention the Oil in Navigable Waters Act, 1955, was passed and gradually brought into force. In 1959 the Inter-Governmental Maritime Consultative Organization (IMCO) was set up with headquarters in London to consider matters of common interest to all maritime states. This body, since renamed International Maritime Organisation (IMO), held an international conference on oil pollution at Copenhagen in July, 1959, on which occasion the American Committees recommended the United States to ratify the 1954 Convention. In April, 1962, the Conference of Contracting Governments to the International Convention for the Prevention of Pollution of the Sea by Oil, 1954, adopted amendments to that Convention. To enable effect to be given to those amendments and otherwise extend the 1955 Act, the Oil in Navigable Waters Act, 1963, was passed in July of that year. The ultimate aim at that time was that all governments should bind their ships not to discharge oil anywhere at sea. In 1971 another Oil in Navigable Waters Act appeared but that, like the 1955 and 1963 Acts, was repealed and replaced by the Prevention of Oil Pollution Act 1971 which consolidates the Oil in Navigable Waters Acts 1955 to 1971.

The subject of marine pollution generally is constantly being considered by the governments of countries having coastlines bordering the seas of the world, or whose nationals own and operate ships, particularly tankers and other bulk carriers. As a result of this interest, in 1973 IMCO (now IMO) convened an international conference in London which adopted the International Convention for the Prevention of Pollution from Ships 1973 (MARPOL 1973). This wide ranging convention contained five annexes defining regulations designed to prevent and control pollution of the sea by oil, noxious liquids in bulk, harmful substances in containers etc., and sewage and garbage from ships. It was hoped to bring in the regulations relating to oil and noxious liquids at the same time, but owing to the technical difficulties involved this has not been possible, and at a further conference in 1978 it was decided to concentrate on bringing in the regulations contained in Annex 1 relating to oil pollution for which a target date of June 1981 was set. To this end and to amend certain regulations the Protocol of 1978 relating to MARPOL 1973 was adopted.

At the time of writing in June 1981 the required conditions for bringing the convention and protocol into force have not been reached, and although many shipping companies have voluntarily implemented parts of the convention and section 20 of the M.S.A. 1979 provides for it to be given effect by Order in Council, the statutory requirements for U.K. registered ships, and foreign ships in U.K. territorial waters are still prescribed by the Prevention of Oil Pollution Act 1971 (as amended). The main provisions affecting ships are:—

General Provisions for Preventing Oil Pollution
1. Discharge of Certain Oils into Sea outside Territorial Waters

(1) If any oil to which this section applies or any mixture containing such oil is discharged from a ship registered in the United Kingdom into any part of the sea outside the territorial waters of the United Kingdom, the owner or master of the ship shall, subject to the provisions of this Act, be guilty of an offence.

(2) This section applies (a) to crude oil, fuel oil and lubricating oil; and (b) to heavy diesel oil as defined by regulations. It also applies to any other description of oil which may be specified by regulations or having regard to its persistent character and the likelihood that it would cause pollution.

(3) Regulations may make exceptions from the operation of subsection (1) either generally or with respect to particular classes of ships, particular descriptions of oil or mixtures, discharge in particular circumstances or into particular sea areas, and may do so either absolutely or subject to specified conditions.

(4) A person guilty of an offence under this section shall be liable on summary conviction to a fine not exceeding £50,000 or on conviction on indictment to a fine.

Notes:—(1) In March 1974 the House of Lords, by a majority of three to two, held that the phrase "owner or master of the ship" in subsection (1) above, meant that both the owner and the master should be liable for discharge of oil or mixture into the sea and could both be prosecuted for the offence of such pollution.

(2) "Heavy Diesel Oil" is defined as marine diesel oil, other than those distillates of which more than half the volume distils at a temperature not exceeding 340°C when tested by the ASTM Standard Method D.86.66. (SI 1967 No. 710).

(3) The regulations which apply under subsection (3) above are the **Oil in Navigable Waters (Exceptions) Regulations** 1972 which permit discharges to be made from ships other than tankers, and from the machinery space bilges of tankers, if the ship is proceeding on a voyage, and the instantaneous rate of discharge of oil content does not exceed 60 litres per mile, the oil content of the discharge is less than 100 parts per 1,000,000 parts of the mixture, and the discharge is made as far as practicable from the nearest land. All the above conditions must be satisfied.

The discharge of oil or oily mixture from the cargo spaces of tankers is totally prohibited within 50 miles of the nearest land. Clean ballast may be discharged from a tanker within 50 miles from the nearest land, if the ballast is from a cargo tank which has been so cleaned that any discharge into clean calm water on a clear day, with the tanker stationary, would produce no visible traces of oil on the surface of the water.

If all the following conditions are satisfied, the regulations permit oil or oily mixture to be discharged from a tanker when it is more than 50 miles from the nearest land. The conditions are that the tanker must be proceeding on a ballast voyage, or a cargo voyage immediately following a ballast voyage with oil residues still on board from a cargo of oil in bulk previously carried, the instantaneous rate of discharge of oil content must not exceed 60 litres per mile, and the total quantity of oil discharged during the voyage, or that cargo voyage and the immediately preceding ballast voyage taken together, must not exceed 1/15,000 of the total oil cargo carrying capacity of the tanker. **Instantaneous rate of discharge of oil content** when expressed in litres per mile means the rate of discharge of oil in litres per hour at any instant divided by the speed of the ship in knots at the same instant. **From the nearest land** means from the nearest base line defining the territorial sea of any territory in accordance with the Geneva Convention on the Territorial Sea and the Contiguous Zone 1958, except along the North-eastern coast of Australia, where the limit is defined by a series of straight lines along the edge of the Great Barrier Reef.

(4) Many countries have not accepted the 1969 amendments to the International Convention for the Prevention of Pollution of the Sea by Oil 1954, as amended 1962, on which the above regulations are based. The laws of such countries will, therefore, still be based on the concept of sea areas within which all discharges of oil or mixtures containing 100 parts or more per 1,000,000 are prohibited.

Where those areas extend only 50 miles from the nearest land no conflict is likely to arise because the requirements of the new regulations are at least as stringent as those of the 1954 Convention. Where such countries have more extensive prohibited sea areas, however, there is a possibility that some discharges from oil tankers within those areas may still be illegal under the law of the country concerned although conforming to the criteria set out in the United Kingdom law. Special care should therefore be exercised by United Kingdom registered oil tankers when operating more than 50 miles from the land in those circumstances, not to infringe the laws of the coastal state pertaining to allowable discharges.

2. Discharge of Oil into United Kingdom Waters

(1) If **any oil or mixture containing oil** is discharged as mentioned in the following paragraphs into waters to which this section applies, then, subject to the provisions of this Act, the following shall be guilty of an offence, that is to say:—

(a) if the discharge is from a vessel, the owner or master, unless he proves that the discharge took place and was caused as mentioned in paragraph (b);

(b) if the discharge is from a vessel but takes place in the course of a transfer of oil to or from another vessel or a place on land and is caused by the act or omission of any person in charge of any apparatus in that other vessel or that place, the owner or master of that other vessel or occupier of that place;

(c) if the discharge is from a place on land, the occupier of that place, unless he proves that the discharge was caused as mentioned in paragraph (d);

(d) if the discharge is from a place on land and is caused by the act of a person who is in that place without the permission (express or implied) of the occupier, that person;

(e) if the discharge takes place otherwise than is mentioned in the preceding paragraphs and is the result of any operations for the exploration of the sea-bed and subsoil or the exploitation of their natural resources, the person carrying on the operations.

(2) This section applies to (a) the whole of the sea within the seaward limits of the territorial waters of the United Kingdom; and (b) all other waters (including inland waters) which are within those limits and are navigable by sea-going ships.

(3) In this Act "place on land" includes anything resting on the bed or shore of the sea, or of any other waters to which this section applies, and also includes anything afloat (other than a vessel) if it is anchored or attached to the bed or the shore of the sea or of any such waters; and "occupier", in relation to any such thing as is mentioned in the preceding provisions of this subsection, if it has no occupier, means the owner thereof, and, in relation to a railway

wagon or road vehicle, means the person in charge and not the occupier of the land on which it stands.

(4) A person guilty of an offence under this section shall be liable on summary conviction to a fine not exceeding £50,000 or on conviction on indictment to a fine.

Note:—The Act states in section 29(1) that "oil" means oil of any description and includes spirit produced from oil of any description and also includes coal tar. A mixture containing oil is a mixture of oil with water or with any other substance. The prohibition therefore applies to oil of any description, whether animal, vegetable or mineral, and to any mixture containing oil. In order to establish that an offence has been committed under this section it is only necessary, in the case of discharge into United Kingdom territorial waters, to establish that there has been a discharge of any quantity of oil or oily mixture, however small. If follows that the contents of bilges which contain any quantity of oil of any type, including lubricating oil, should not be pumped into the sea while the ship is in United Kingdom territorial waters. Pumping of oil from below oil in tanks should not be undertaken while a vessel is in United Kingdom territorial waters, since it is not possible to guarantee that the water discharged will be entirely free from oil. As an oily water separator does not completely remove the oil content of the effluent it follows that the pumping of either oily bilge water, or water settled out in a tank, through a separator may not prevent a breach of the law. Only one exemption from the provisions of section 2 has been granted. This allows vessels of less than 80 tons gross tonnage to discharge from their bilges while they are in United Kingdom territorial waters a mixture in which the only oil is lubricating oil which has drained or leaked from machinery spaces.

3. Discharge of Certain Oils from Pipe-lines, etc.

This section applies to owners of pipelines and persons exploring the sea-bed. It makes it an offence for oil or oily mixture to be discharged into the sea from a pipeline or as the result of any operation for the exploration of the sea-bed and subsoil or the exploitation of their natural resources in a designated area.

4. Equipment in Ships to Prevent Oil Pollution

(1) For the purpose of preventing or reducing discharges of oil and mixtures containing oil into the sea, the Secretary of State may make regulations requiring ships registered in the United Kingdom to be fitted with such equipment and to comply with such other requirements as may be specified in the regulations.

(2) Without prejudice to the generality of subsection (1) of this section, where any regulations made thereunder require ships to be fitted with equipment of a specified description, the regulations may provide that equipment of that description:—

(a) shall not be installed in a ship to which the regulations apply unless it is of a type tested and approved by a person appointed by the Secretary of State;

(b) while installed in such a ship, shall not be treated as satisfying the requirements of the regulations unless, at such times as may be specified in the regulations, it is submitted for testing and approval by a person so appointed.

(3) The Secretary of State may appoint persons to carry out tests for the purposes of any regulations made under this section, and, in respect of the carrying out of such tests, may charge such fees as, with the approval of the Treasury, may be prescribed by the regulations.

(4) Every surveyor of ships shall be taken to be a person appointed by the Secretary of State to carry out tests for the purposes of any regulations made under this section, in so far as they relate to tests required in accordance with paragraph (b) of subsection (2) of this section.

(5) If, in the case of any ship, the provisions of any regulations made under this section which apply to that ship are contravened, the owner or master shall be guilty of an offence.

(6) A person guilty of an offence under this section shall be liable on summary conviction to a fine not exceeding £1,000 or on conviction on indictment to a fine.

Note:—The regulations referred to in this section are The Oil in Navigable Waters (Ships' Equipment) (No. 1) Regulations 1956 (SI 1956 No. 1423) and The Oil in Navigable Waters (Ships' Equipment) Regulations 1957 (SI 1957 No. 1424) which continue to apply under this Act.

Merchant Shipping Notice M.846 draws the attention of owners and masters of oil tankers of 150 gross tons and above, and other ships of 500 gross tons and above, to an IMO recommendation concerning oily-water separating equipment under the 1969 amendments to the 1954 Oil Pollution Convention. This recommended that such vessels be fitted with an approved separator or oil content meter which complied with the terms of IMO Resolution A.393(X), or a nationally approved equivalent. A later notice, M.933, urges owners and masters of ships of 400 gross tons and above to commence implementation of IMO Resolution A.444(XI) in order to bring their oily-water separating equipment up to the standard which will be required by Regulation 16 of Annex 1 to the MARPOL 1973 Convention, as modified by the 1978 Protocol, when it is brought into force.

5. Defences of Owner or Master charged with Offences under s.1 or s.2

(1) Where a person is charged with an offence under section 1 of this Act, or under section 2 as the owner or master, it shall be a defence to prove that the oil or mixture was discharged for the

purpose of securing the safety of any vessel, or of preventing damage to any vessel or cargo, or of saving life, unless the court is satisfied that the discharge was not necessary for that purpose or was not a reasonable step to take in the circumstances.

(2) Where a person is charged as above, it shall also be a defence to prove:—

(a) that the oil or mixture escaped in consequence of damage to the vessel, and that as soon as practicable all reasonable steps were taken for preventing, or (if it could not be prevented) for stopping or reducing, the escape of the oil or mixture, or

(b) that the oil or mixture escaped by reason of leakage, that neither the leakage nor any delay in discovering it was due to any want of reasonable care, and that as soon as practicable all reasonable steps were taken for stopping or reducing it.

6. Defences of Other Persons charged with Offences under s. 2 or s. 3

This section applies to occupiers of places on land, or persons carrying on operations for the exploration of the sea-bed and subsoil or the exploitation of their natural resources, or to the owners of a pipeline, who are charged in respect of the escape of oil or oily mixture.

7. Protection of Acts done in Exercise of Certain Powers of Harbour Authorities etc.

This section gives protection to harbour and other authorities who exercise their powers to remove wrecks, or to dispose of sunk, stranded or abandoned vessels to prevent them becoming obstructions or dangers to navigation, and which result in oil or oily mixture being discharged into the sea. Such authority, or person employed by or acting on behalf of the authority, will not be convicted of an offence under section 1 or 2 unless it is shown that they or he failed to take such steps (if any) as were reasonable in the circumstances for preventing, stopping, or reducing the discharge.

8. Discharge of Certain Ballast Water into Harbours

(1) A harbour authority may appoint a place within their jurisdiction where the ballast water of vessels in which a cargo of petroleum-spirit has been carried may be discharged into the waters of the harbour, at such times, and subject to such conditions, as the authority may determine; and, where a place is so appointed, the discharge of ballast water from such a vessel shall not constitute an offence under section 2 of this Act, if the ballast water is discharged at that place, and at a time and in accordance with the conditions so determined, and the ballast water contains no oil other than petroleum-spirit.

(2) In this Act:—

"harbour authority" means a person or body of persons empowered by an enactment to make charges in respect of vessels entering a harbour in the United Kingdom or using facilities therein;

"harbour in the United Kingdom" means a port, estuary, haven, dock, or other place which fulfils the following conditions, that is, to say:—

(a) that it contains waters to which section 2 of this Act applies, and

(b) that a person or body of persons is empowered by an enactment to make charges in respect of vessels entering that place or using facilities therein.

In this subsection "enactment" includes a local enactment, and "charges" means any charges with the exception of light dues, local light dues and any other charges payable in respect of lighthouses, buoys or beacons, and of charges in respect of pilotage.

8A. Cases excluded from sections 4 to 8

Sections 4 to 8 of this Act do not apply to a ship which at the time of the discharge or escape was registered in a country which was not a Convention country, and which was a country in respect of which the Liability of Owners of Seagoing Ships Convention 1957 was in force.

9. Facilities in Harbour for Disposal of Oil Residues

(1) The powers exercisable by a harbour authority in respect of any harbour in the United Kingdom shall include power to provide facilities for enabling vessels using the harbour to discharge or deposit oil residues (in this Act referred to as "oil reception facilities").

(2) Any power of a harbour authority to provide oil reception facilities shall include power to join with any other person in providing them, and references in this section to the provision of oil reception facilities by a harbour authority shall be construed accordingly; and any such power shall also include power to arrange for the provision of such facilities by any other person.

(3) A harbour authority providing oil reception facilities, or a person providing such facilities by arrangement with a harbour authority, may make reasonable charges for the use of the facilities, and may impose reasonable conditions in respect of the use thereof.

(4) Subject to the following provisions of this section, any oil reception facilities provided by, or by arrangement with, a harbour authority shall be open to all vessels using the harbour on payment of any charges, and subject to compliance with any conditions, imposed in accordance with subsection (3) of this section.

(5) Where in the case of any harbour in the United Kingdom it appears to the Secretary of State, after consultation with the harbour

authority and with any organisation appearing to the Secretary of State to be representative of owners of ships registered in the United Kingdom:—

  (a) if the harbour has oil reception facilities, that those facilities are inadequate, or

  (b) if the harbour has no such facilities, that the harbour has need of such facilities,

the Secretary of State may direct the harbour authority to provide, or arrange for the provision of, such oil reception facilities as may be specified in the direction.

(6) Notwithstanding the provisions of subsection (4) of this section, a harbour authority providing oil reception facilities, or a person providing such facilities by arrangement with a harbour authority, shall not be obliged to make those facilities available for use by tankers, or for the reception of oil residues discharged for the purpose of enabling a vessel to undergo repairs; and the requirements of tankers, and the reception of oil residues so discharged, shall be disregarded by the Secretary of State in exercising his powers under subsection (5) of this section.

(7) Nothing in this section shall be construed as requiring a harbour authority to allow untreated water ballast (that is to say, ballast water which contains oil and has not been subjected to an effective process for separating the oil from the water) to be discharged into any oil reception facilities provided by, or by arrangement with, the authority; and the Secretary of State shall exercise his powers under subsection (5) of this section accordingly.

(8) Any harbour authority failing to comply with any direction given under subsection (5) of this section within the period specified in the direction, or within any extended period allowed by the Secretary of State (whether before or after the end of the period so specified), shall be guilty of an offence, and liable on summary conviction to a fine not exceeding £500 and to a further fine not exceeding £50 for each day after the end of the period specified in the direction, or any extended period allowed by the Secretary of State, until the last day before that on which the facilities are provided in accordance with the direction.

(9) Subsections (1), (2), (5) and (8) of this section shall have effect in relation to arrangements for disposing of oil residues discharged or deposited by vessels using a harbour's oil reception facilities, and to the making of such arrangements, as those subsections have effect in relation to oil reception facilities and the provision of such facilities.

Note:—A vital factor in reducing oil pollution at sea is the availability of adequate oily waste reception facilities in ports. Merchant Shipping Notice M.877 draws attention to and shows a specimen of a two-part report form, approved by IMO, which enables a master of a ship faced with inadequate reception facilities to report on any special problems encountered. For British ships, a report should be submitted to the D.o.T. through the ship's owner.

10. Restrictions on Transfer of Oil at Night

(1) No oil shall be transferred between sunset and sunrise to or from a vessel in any harbour in the United Kingdom unless the requisite notice has been given in accordance with this section or the transfer is for the purposes of a fire brigade.

(2) A general notice may be given to the harbour master of a harbour that transfers of oil between sunset and sunrise will be frequently carried out at a place in the harbour within such period, not ending later than twelve months after the date on which the notice is given, as is specified in the notice; and if such a notice is given it shall be the requisite notice for the purposes of this section as regards transfers of oil at that place within the period specified in the notice.

(3) Subject to subsection (2) of this section, the requisite notice for the purposes of this section shall be a notice given to the harbour master not less than three hours nor more than ninety-six hours before the transfer of oil begins.

(4) In the case of a harbour which has no harbour master, references in this section to the harbour master shall be references to the harbour authority.

(5) If any oil is transferred to or from a vessel in contravention of this section, the master of the vessel, and, if the oil is transferred from or to a place on land, the occupier of that place, shall be liable on summary conviction to a fine not exceeding £200.

11. Duty to Report Discharge of Oil into Waters of Harbours

(1) If any oil or mixture containing oil:—

(a) is discharged from a vessel into the waters of a harbour in the United Kingdom; or

(b) is found to be escaping or to have escaped from a vessel into any such waters; or

(c) is found to be escaping or to have escaped into any such waters from a place on land;

the owner or master of the vessel, or the occupier of the place on land, shall forthwith report the occurrence to the harbour master, or, if none, to the harbour authority.

(2) A report made under subsection (1) by the owner or master of a vessel shall state whether the occurrence falls within paragraph (a) or paragraph (b) of that subsection.

(3) If a person fails to make a report as required by this section he shall be liable on summary conviction to a fine not exceeding £1000.

Shipping Casualties

12. Shipping Casualties

(1) The powers conferred by this section shall be exercisable where:—

(a) an accident has occurred to or in a ship; and

(b) in the opinion of the Secretary of State oil or substances other than oil from the ship will or may cause pollution on a large scale in the United Kingdom or in the waters in or adjacent to the United Kingdom up to the seaward limits of territorial waters; and

(c) in the opinion of the Secretary of State the use of the powers conferred by this section is urgently needed.

(2) For the purpose of preventing or reducing oil pollution or pollution by substances other than oil, or the risk of such pollution, the Secretary of State may give directions as respects the ship or its cargo:—

(a) to the owner of the ship, or to any person in possession of the ship; or

(b) to the master of the ship; or

(c) to any salvor in possession of the ship, or to any person who is the servant or agent of any salvor in possession of the ship, and who is in charge of the salvage operation.

(3) Directions under subsection (2) of this section may require the person to whom they are given to take, or refrain from taking, any action of any kind whatsoever, and without prejudice to the generality of the preceding provisions of this subsection the directions may require:—

(a) that the ship is to be, or is not to be, moved, or is to be moved to a specified place, or is to be removed from a specified area or locality; or

(b) that the ship is not to be moved to a specified place or area, or over a specified route; or

(c) that any oil, substances other than oil, or other cargo is to be, or is not to be, unloaded or discharged; or

(d) that specified salvage measures are to be, or are not to be, taken.

(4) If in the opinion of the Secretary of State the powers conferred by subsection (2) of this section are, or have proved to be, inadequate for the purpose, the Secretary of State may, for the purpose of preventing or reducing oil pollution, or pollution by substances other than oil, or the risk of such pollution, take, as respects the ship or its cargo, any action of any kind whatsoever, and without prejudice to the generality of the preceding provisions of this subsection the Secretary of State may:—

(a) take any such action as he has power to require to be taken by a direction under this section;

(b) undertake operations for the sinking or destruction of the ship, or any part of it, of a kind which is not within the means of any person to whom he can give directions;

(c) undertake operations which involve the taking over of control of the ship.

(5) The powers of the Secretary of State under subsection (4) of this section shall also be exercisable by such persons as may be authorised in that behalf by the Secretary of State.

(6) Every person concerned with compliance with directions given, or with action taken, under this section shall use his best endeavours to avoid any risk to human life.

(7) The provisions of this section and of section 16 of this Act are without prejudice to any rights or powers of Her Majesty's Government in the United Kingdom exercisable apart from those sections whether under international law or otherwise.

(8) It is hereby declared that any action taken as respects a ship which is under arrest or as respects the cargo of such a ship, being action duly taken in pursuance of a direction given under this section, or being any action taken under subsection (4) or (5) of this section:—

(a) does not constitute contempt of court; and

(b) does not in any circumstances make the Admiralty Marshal liable in any civil proceedings.

(9) In this section, unless the context otherwise requires:—

"accident" includes the loss, stranding, abandonment of or damage to a ship; and

"specified", in relation to a direction under this section, means specified by the direction;

and the reference in subsection (8) to the Admiralty Marshal includes a reference to the Admiralty Marshal of the Supreme Court of Northern Ireland.

Note:—"Substances other than oil" means those substances listed in the Schedule to the M.S. (Prevention of Pollution) (Intervention) Order 1980 (S.I. 1980 No. 1093), and those other substances which are liable to create hazards to human health, to harm living resources and marine life, to damage amenities or to interfere with other legitimate uses of the sea.

13. Right to Recover in Respect of Unreasonable Loss or Damage

(1) If any action duly taken by a person in pursuance of a direction given to him under section 12 of this Act, or any action taken under subsection (4) or (5) of that section:—

(a) was not reasonably necessary to prevent or reduce oil pollution, or the risk of oil pollution; or pollution by substances other than oil; or

P

(*b*) was such that the good it did or was likely to do was disproportionately less than the expense incurred, or damage suffered, as a result of the action,

a person incurring expense or suffering damage as a result of, or by himself taking, the action shall be entitled to recover compensation from the Secretary of State.

(2) In considering whether subsection (1) of this section applies, account shall be taken of:—

(*a*) the extent and risk of oil pollution or pollution by substances other than oil if the action had not been taken;

(*b*) the likelihood of the action being effective; and

(*c*) the extent of the damage which has been caused by the action.

(3) Any reference in this section to the taking of any action includes a reference to a compliance with a direction not to take some specified action.

(4) The Admiralty jurisdiction of the High Court, of the Court of Session and of the Supreme Court of Northern Ireland shall include jurisdiction to hear and determine any claim arising under this section.

14. Offences in Relation to s. 12

(1) If the person to whom a direction is duly given under section 12 of this Act contravenes, or fails to comply with, any requirement of the direction, he shall be guilty of an offence.

(2) If a person wilfully obstructs any person who is:—

(*a*) acting on behalf of the Secretary of State in connection with the giving or service of a direction under section 12 of this Act;

(*b*) acting in compliance with a direction under that section; or

(*c*) acting under subsection (4) or (5) of that section;

he shall be guilty of an offence.

(3) In proceedings for an offence under subsection (1) of this section, it shall be a defence for the accused to prove that he has used all due diligence to ensure compliance with the direction, or that he had reasonable cause for believing that compliance with the direction would have involved a serious risk to human life.

(4) A person guilty of an offence under this section shall be liable on summary conviction to a fine not exceeding £50,000, or on conviction on indictment to a fine.

15. Service of Directions under s. 12

(1) If the Secretary of State is satisfied that a company or other body is not one to whom section 412 or section 437 of the Companies Act 1948 (service of notices) applies so as to authorise the service of a direction on that body under either of those sections, he may give a direction under section 12 of this Act:—

(a) to that body, as the owner of, or the person in possession of, a ship, by serving the direction on the master of the ship; or

(b) to that body, as a salvor, by serving the direction on the person in charge of the salvage operations.

(2) For the purpose of giving or serving a direction under section 12 of this Act to or on any person on a ship, a person acting on behalf of the Secretary of State shall have the right to go on board the ship.

(3) In the application of subsection (1) of this section to Northern Ireland, for references to the Companies Act 1948 there shall be substituted references to sections 361 and 385 of the Companies Act (Northern Ireland) 1960.

16. Applications of ss. 12 to 15 to Certain Foreign and Other Ships

(1) Her Majesty may by Order in Council provide that sections 12 to 15 of this Act, together with any other provisions of this Act, shall apply to a ship:—

(a) which is not a ship registered in the United Kingdom; and

(b) which is for the time being outside the territorial waters of the United Kingdom;

in such cases and circumstances as may be specified in the Order; and subject to such exceptions, adaptations and modifications, if any, as may be so specified.

(2) An Order in Council under subsection (1) of this section may contain such transitional and other consequential provisions as appear to Her Majesty to be expedient.

(3) Except as provided by an Order in Council under subsection (1) of this section, no direction under section 12 of this Act shall apply to a ship which is not registered in the United Kingdom and which is for the time being outside the territorial waters of the United Kingdom, and no action shall be taken under subsection (4) or (5) of section 12 of this Act as respects any such ship.

(4) No direction under section 12 of this Act shall apply to any vessel of Her Majesty's navy or to any Government ship (within the meaning of section 80 of the M.S. Act 1906) and no action shall be taken under subsection (4) or (5) of that section as respects any such vessel or ship.

Note:—The M.S. (Prevention of Pollution) (Intervention) Order 1980, which came into operation on 26th August 1980 applies, in Part I of the Order, the provisions of sections 12, 13, 14, 15 and 16(4) to all ships (whether or not U.K. registered) when within the territorial waters of the United Kingdom. Part II of the Order applies the same sections 12–15, and 16(4) to all U.K. registered ships when outside the seaward limits of U.K. territorial waters, and further, extends the application of those sections to ships not registered in the United Kingdom and which are outside the territorial waters of the United Kingdom in any case in which the Secretary of State is satisfied that there is a need to protect the coast of the United Kingdom and its territorial waters up to the seaward limits, against grave and imminent danger of oil pollution or pollution by substances other than oil. The powers conferred on the Secretary of State by section 12 to give directions shall only be exercisable in relation to an individual who is a citizen of the United Kingdom and Colonies, or a body corporate which is established under the laws of a part of the United Kingdom, and the offence of obstruction shall only apply to such an individual or body corporate.

Enforcement
7. Oil Records

(1) The Secretary of State may make regulations requiring oil record books to be carried in ships registered in the United Kingdom and requiring the master of any such ship to record in the oil record book carried by it the carrying out, on board or in connection with the ship, of any operations such as loading, transfer and discharge of oil cargoes, ballasting of and discharge of ballast from oil tanks, separation of oil from water in oily mixtures, and disposal of oil residues; also any occasions on which oil or oily mixture is discharged from the ship for the purpose of securing the safety of any vessels, preventing damage to vessels or cargo, or of saving life; and any occasion on which oil or oily mixture is found to have escaped from the ship because of damage to the ship or by reason of leakage. The regulations may prescribe the form of oil record book to be carried and nature of entries to be made in such book, and provide for the custody of the records for a prescribed period. Regulations may also be made requiring the keeping of records relating to the transfer of oil to and from any vessels while they are within United Kingdom territorial waters.

(2) If any ship fails to carry such an oil record book as it is required to carry under this section the owner or master shall be liable on summary conviction to a fine not exceeding £500; if any person fails to comply with any requirements imposed on him by or under this section, he shall be liable on summary conviction to a fine not exceeding £500; and if any person makes an entry in any oil record book carried or record kept under this section which is to his knowledge false or misleading in any material particular, he shall be liable on summary conviction to a fine not exceeding £1000, or imprisonment for a term not exceeding six months, or both, or on conviction on indictment to a fine or to imprisonment for a term not exceeding two years or both.

(3) In any proceedings under this Act:—

(a) any oil record book carried or record kept in pursuance of regulations made under this section shall be admissible as evidence, and in Scotland shall be sufficient evidence, of the facts stated in it;

(b) any copy of an entry in such an oil record book or record which is certified by the master of the ship in which the book is carried or by the person by whom the record is required to be kept to be a true copy of the entry shall be admissible as evidence, and in Scotland shall be sufficient evidence, of the facts stated in the entry;

(c) any document purporting to be an oil record book carried or record kept in pursuance of regulations made under this section, or purporting to be such a certified copy as is mentioned in the preceding paragraph, shall, unless the contrary is proved, be presumed to be such a book, record or copy, as the case may be.

Note:—The following regulations apply under powers given by the above section.

The Oil in Navigable Waters (Transfer Records) Regulations 1957 apply to every vessel, whether registered or not, and of whatever nationality, which is capable of carrying in bulk, whether for cargo or bunker purposes, more than 25 tons of oil, or which, though not so capable is constructed or fitted to carry in bulk more than 5 tons of oil in any one space or container. The master of every vessel to which the regulations apply shall, when oil has been transferred to or from the vessel while it is within United Kingdom territorial waters, record the name and port of registry (if any) of the vessel or barge, the date, time and place or transfer, the amount and description of oil transferred, and from what vessel, barge or place on land, and to what vessel, barge or place, the oil was transferred. In the case of a transfer to or from a barge the record shall be kept by the person supplying the oil or to whom the oil is delivered respectively. The record of each operation shall be separately signed and dated by the master. Records may be kept in the deck or engine room log book, or other convenient form.

The Oil in Navigable Waters (Records) Regulations 1972 apply to ships registered in the United Kingdom. The word "tanker" means a vessel the greater part of the cargo space of which is constructed or adapted for the carriage of liquid cargoes in bulk and which is either carrying a cargo of oil in bulk in that part of its cargo space or has on board oil residues from a cargo of oil in bulk previously carried.

Tankers. The master of every tanker shall carry on board ship an oil record book, and shall record in such book details of any of the following operations carried out on board, namely—

   (i) loading of oil cargo;
  (ii) transfer of oil cargo during a voyage;
 (iii) discharge of oil cargo;
 (iv) ballasting of cargo tanks;
  (v) cleaning of cargo tanks;
 (vi) discharge of dirty ballast;
(vii) discharge of water from slop tanks;

(viii) disposal of oil residues;
  (ix) discharge overboard of oily bilge water which has accumulated in machinery spaces including pump rooms whilst in port;
   (x) the routine discharge at sea of oily bilge water, unless such discharge is from machinery spaces, including pump rooms, and has been entered in the engine room log book or deck log book.

Ships other than tankers. The master of every ship of 80 tons gross tonnage or more which uses oil fuel, not being a tanker, shall carry on board ship an oil record book, and shall record in such book details of any of the following operations carried out on board, namely—

   (i) ballasting or cleaning of bunker fuel tanks;
  (ii) discharge of dirty ballast or cleaning water from bunker fuel tanks;
 (iii) disposal of oil residues;
  (iv) discharge overboard of oily bilge water which has accumulated in machinery spaces including pump rooms whilst in port;
   (v) the routine discharge at sea of oily bilge water, unless such discharge is from machinery spaces, including pump rooms, and has been entered in the engine room log book or deck log book.

All ships. The master of every ship required to carry an oil record book shall record in such book (*a*) any occasion on which oil or a mixture containing oil is discharged from a ship for the purpose of securing the safety of any vessel or of preventing damage to any vessel or cargo, or of saving life; and, (*b*) any occasion on which oil or a mixture containing oil is found to be escaping, or to have escaped, from the ship in consequence of damage to the ship, or by reason of leakage. Any entry relating to the discharge of oily bilge water from machinery spaces, including pump rooms, whether made in the oil record book or in the engine room log book or deck log book, shall state whether the discharge was made through a separator. Where the pump discharging such bilge water starts automatically and discharges through a separator at all times it will be sufficient to enter each day "Automatic discharge from bilges through a separator". The record books specified in these regulations are obtainable from Mercantile Marine Offices, separate books being supplied for tankers and ships other than tankers.

Retention, custody and disposal of records. Every master of a ship in respect of which records are required to be kept shall retain the records in his custody in the ship for a period of two years following the date of the last entry, or alternatively if the principal place of business of the owners of the ship is in the United Kingdom, he may at any time within that period transmit the records to the owners at that place of business, and the records shall be retained there until the end of a period of two years following the date of the last entry.

18. Powers of Inspection

(1) The Secretary of State may appoint any person as an inspector to report to him (a) whether the prohibitions, restrictions and obligations imposed by virtue of this Act have been complied with; (b) what measures have been taken to prevent the escape of oil and mixtures containing oil; (c) whether the oil reception facilities provided in harbours are adequate.

(2) Every surveyor of ships shall be taken to be a person appointed generally under the preceding subsection to report to the Secretary of State in every kind of case falling within that subsection.

(3), (4), (5) and (6). These subsections deal with the powers of inspectors in relation to such matters as the inspection of premises and apparatus, inspection of vessels and their equipment, requiring the production of record books and records, requiring copies of entries in record books and records, and requiring masters to certify copies as true.

(7) A person exercising any powers conferred by subsection (6) of this section shall not unnecessarily detain or delay the vessel from proceeding on any voyage. (Subsection (6), which relates to a vessel for the time being in a United Kingdom harbour, gives powers of inspection to the harbour master as well as persons appointed by the Secretary of State.)

(8) This subsection provides for fines of up to £200 for certain offences, and up to £500 for wilfully obstructing a person acting in the exercise of powers conferred by virtue of this section.

19. Prosecutions

This section states by whom, or with whose consent, proceedings may be brought for various offences under this Act in England and Wales and also in Northern Ireland.

20. Enforcement and Applications of Fines

(1) Where a fine imposed by a court in proceedings against the owner or master of a vessel for an offence under this Act is not paid at the time ordered by the court, the court shall, in addition to any other powers for enforcing payment, have power to direct the amount remaining unpaid to be levied by distress or poinding and sale of the vessel, her tackle, furniture and apparel.

(2) Where a person is convicted of an offence under section 1 or section 2 of this Act, and the court imposes a fine in respect of the

offence, then, if it appears to the court that any person has incurred, or will incur, expenses in removing any pollution, or making good any damage, which is attributable to the offence, the court may order the whole or part of the fine to be paid to that person for or towards defraying those expenses.

21. This section deals with the enforcement of Conventions relating to oil pollution.

22. This section relates to the power to apply certain provisions of this Act to ships registered outside the United Kingdom.

23. This section gives the Secretary of State power to exempt any vessels or classes of vessels from the provisions of this Act.

24. Application of Act to Government Ships

(1) The provisions of this Act do not apply to vessels of Her Majesty's navy, nor to Government ships in the service of the Secretary of State while employed for the purposes of Her Majesty's navy.

(2) Subject to subsection (1) of this section and subsection (4) of section 16 of this Act:—

(a) provisions of this Act which are expressed to apply only to ships registered in the United Kingdom apply to Government ships so registered and also to Government ships not so registered but held for the purposes of Her Majesty's Government in the United Kingdom;

(b) provisions of this Act which are expressed to apply to vessels generally apply to Government ships.

(3) In this section "Government ships" has the same meaning as in section 80 of the M.S. Act 1906.

25. This section contains the provisions as to the Isle of Man, Channel Islands, colonies and dependencies.

26. This section provides for the Secretary of State to make an annual report on the exercise and performance of his functions under this Act, and for a copy of the report to be laid before each House of Parliament.

27. This section deals with the general provisions as to Orders in Council, regulations and orders.

28. This deals with financial provisions.

29. This is the Interpretation section which gives, amongst other things, the definitions of numerous terms. It may be noted that **oil** means oil of any description and includes spirit produced from oil of any description, and also includes coal tar.

30. This section covers the provisions as to Northern Ireland, to which this Act extends.

31. Application to Hovercraft

The enactments and instruments with respect to which provision may be made by an Order in Council under section 1(1)(h) of the

Hovercraft Act 1968 shall include this Act and any instrument made under it.

32. This section concerns saving for other restrictions and rights of action etc.

33. Three earlier Acts and sections of others are repealed by this section and it enables certain regulations made under powers given by those Acts to continue in operation, e.g. The Oil in Navigable Waters (Transfer Records) Regulations 1957.

34. States the short title of the Act.

The International Convention for the Prevention of Pollution from Ships, 1973 (**MARPOL**) 1973) **and the Protocol of** 1978. When it enters into force, this international convention, as modified by the 1978 Protocol, will supersede the amended 1954 Convention. The 1973 Convention contains five annexes defining regulations for the prevention of pollution by oil, noxious liquid substances in bulk, harmful substances in packaged forms or containers etc., sewage and garbage.

Originally it was intended that ratification of Annexes I and II together was to be compulsory, but due to serious technical difficulties in connection with treatment and disposal of chemical tank washings required by Annex II, acceptance by states has been slow and the 1978 Protocol now requires Annex I regulations for the prevention of oil pollution to be accepted as soon as possible, while delaying the Annex II requirements for a period of three years after the Protocol and Annex I enter into force, or for such longer period as may be decided by the Marine Environment Protection Committee (MEPC) of IMO. Many shipping companies are meanwhile already voluntarily implementing parts of Annex I requirements.

The Annex I regulations as amended by the 1978 Protocol requirements are:—

Survey and Issue of Certificate

Oil tankers of 150 gross tons and above, and every ship of 400 gross tons and above other than an oil tanker, are to have their structure and pollution prevention equipment surveyed initially before the issue of an International Oil Pollution Prevention Certificate which is to be valid for five years, but subject to one intermediate survey during that period.

Control of Discharge of Oil

Discharge of oil or oily mixture into the sea is to be prohibited for oil tankers except that when a tanker is not within a special area, is more than 50 nautical miles from the nearest land and is proceeding en route, mixture may be discharged from slop tanks as long as the instantaneous rate of discharge of oil content does not exceed 60 litres per mile and the total quantity of oil discharged into the sea does not exceed 1/15,000 (1/30,000 for new tankers) of the previous oil cargo while operating an oil discharge monitoring and control system (unless excepted). All of the above conditions are to be complied with.

For other ships of 400 gross tons or above, and for the machinery space bilges of tankers (not pump room bilges) the discharge of oil or oily mixture is to be prohibited except when the ship is not within a special area, is more than 12 miles from the nearest land proceeding en route, the oil content is less than 100 parts per million and the ship is operating an oil discharge monitoring and control system, oily water separating equipment, oil filtering system or other installation.

Special Areas

The special areas mentioned above are the Mediterranean, Baltic, Black and Red Seas, and the Persian Gulf area. In these areas adequate reception facilities for oily mixtures are to be provided.

Segregated Ballast Tanks, Dedicated Clean Ballast Tanks, and Crude Oil Washing.

Other measures which will be required when Annex I is brought into force concern the construction and operation of tankers. Existing crude oil tankers of 40,000 tons deadweight and above are to be provided with segregated ballast tanks (SBT), but may as an alternative, if the oil is suitable, operate a cargo tank cleaning procedure during discharge known as crude oil washing (COW). As a further alternative, such ships may operate for a limited period (2 years for ships of 70,000 tons deadweight and above, 4 years for ships 40,000 tons but under 70,000 tons deadweight), with adequate dedicated clean ballast tanks (CBT), together with an approved oil content meter to enable the oil content to be supervised during discharge of ballast water. The capacity of segregated or clean ballast tanks to be provided must ensure that at the ship's light weight condition plus segregated or clean ballast only, the ship's draught amidships is not to be less than $2 \cdot 0 + 0 \cdot 02L$ metres, with a trim by the stern not exceeding $0 \cdot 015L$, and in any case, such that the propeller is fully immersed. The capacity of ballast tanks provided is to be designed to ensure that ballast water will not be needed in cargo tanks except on those rare voyages when weather conditions are so severe that in the master's opinion it is necessary to carry extra ballast in cargo tanks for the safety of the ship. Existing product carriers of 40,000 tons deadweight and above are to be provided with segregated ballast tanks or operate with dedicated clean ballast tanks to produce the draught conditions described above.

New crude oil tankers of 20,000 tons deadweight and above, and new product carriers of 30,000 tons deadweight and above, are to be provided with "protectively located" segregated ballast tanks to comply with the draught conditions described above, plus crude oil washing facilities in the case of crude oil carriers. "Protectively located" means that such tanks are located within the cargo tank length and arranged in such a way that a measure of protection against oil outflow is provided in the event of grounding or collision damage. All new tankers of 20,000 tons deadweight and above are to have an approved inert gas system (IGS) in every cargo tank.

Restriction on Ballast in Fuel Tanks. Except where abnormal conditions apply or the need to carry large quantities of oil fuel make it necessary to carry ballast water in such tanks, no ballast water is to be carried in any oil fuel tank in new oil tankers of 150 gross tons and above, nor in other new ships of 4000 gross tons and above. If it is necessary to carry ballast in such tanks it is to be discharged, if not clean, to reception facilities or into the sea as described above using a separator and monitoring and control systems. All other ships are to comply with these requirements as far as reasonable and practicable.

Retention of Oil on Board. Except for oil tankers exclusively engaged on short voyages within 50 miles of land, all oil tankers of 150 gross tons and above are to be provided with means whereby cargo tanks can be cleaned and tank washings and dirty ballast residue can be transferred into a slop tank or tanks having a capacity of not less than 3 per cent of the oil carrying capacity of the ship, except where segregated ballast tanks are provided, when 2 per cent of carrying capacity may be accepted. New oil tankers over 70,000 gross tons deadweight are to have at least two slop tanks.

The arrangements shall be designed so that any effluent discharged into the sea can be monitored by an approved oil discharge monitoring and control system fitted with a recording device to provide a continuous record of discharge rate in litres per nautical mile and total quantity discharged, or, the oil content and rate of discharge. Such record must be identifiable as to time and date and kept for three years. The oil discharge monitor and control system shall be such that any discharge of oily mixture is automatically stopped when the instantaneous rate of discharge of oil exceeds that permitted by the regulations. An approved effective oil/water interface detector is to be provided for use in slop tanks, and available for use in other tanks where separation of oil and water is effected and effluent discharged directly into the sea.

Oil Discharge Monitoring and Oily-Water Separating Equipment. Any ship of 400 gross tons and above is to be fitted with an approved oily water separating equipment or filtering system such that any oily mixture discharged into the sea after passing through it shall have an oil content of less than 100 parts per million. In addition, any ship of 10,000 gross tons and above is to be fitted with an oil discharge monitoring and control system.

Alternatively, ships of 10,000 gross tons and above are to be fitted with an oily water separating system with output of oil content not exceeding 100 parts per million, and an oil filtering system accepting the discharge from the separator to produce an effluent with an oil content not exceeding 15 parts per million. It must be fitted with an alarm to indicate when this level cannot be maintained.

Tanks for Oil Residues (Sludge). Every ship of 400 gross tons and above is to be provided with a tank or tanks of adequate capacity to receive oily residues and sludge which result from purification of fuel and lubricating oils and from oil leakages in machinery spaces.

Oil Record Book. Every oil tanker of 150 gross tons and above, and every ship of 400 gross tons and above other than an oil tanker, is to be provided with an Oil Record Book in which a comprehensive record of various operations in connection with the handling of cargo, opening and closing of ship's side valves, ballasting and discharge of ballast and residues, cleaning of tanks, etc., is to be recorded and preserved for three years after the last entry has been made.

Minimizing Oil Pollution After Damage to the Ship. Requirements are specified for minimizing oil pollution from oil tankers which have received side and bottom damage. For this purpose, assumptions of the extent of damage are defined in order to compute hypothetical outflows of oil in the event of damage, such hypothetical outflows being used by the designer to determine the maximum size of cargo tanks permitted and their arrangement. The regulations further specify the subdivision and damage stability requirements that must be complied with in the event of damage.

New Ships. For the purpose of the regulations above dealing with segregated ballast tanks,* dedicated clean ballast tanks and crude oil washing, "new oil tanker" means an oil tanker:—

(a) for which the building contract was placed after 1 June 1979; or

(b) if no building contract, the keel was laid after 1 January 1980, or was at a similar stage of construction; or

(c) the delivery of which is after 1 June 1982; or

(d) which has undergone a major conversion, the contract for which, commencement or completion respectively came after the above dates.

*Note:—For the purpose of the requirement to provide segregated ballast tanks in oil tankers of 70,000 tons deadweight and above, the relevant dates for new tankers are (a) 31 December 1975, (b) 30 June 1976, (c) 31 December 1979, and these dates also apply to a major conversion, for placing the contract, commencing work and completion respectively.

Liability for Oil Pollution. The oil pollution legislation passed in 1955 and 1963 which culminated in the Prevention of Oil Pollution Act 1971 sought to reduce pollution by making it a criminal offence to discharge oil or oily mixtures into the sea, and by requiring ports to provide facilities for reception of oily ballast and residues. This was, and is still, backed up by the adoption by many large tanker owning companies of the "load on top" method whereby the oily water resulting from tank washing is transferred to a "slop" tank. Here the mixture is allowed to settle so that the clean water can be pumped out at sea leaving any oil residue to be pumped ashore at destination, or a fresh oil cargo to be loaded on top if the two are compatible. Nevertheless such methods do nothing to lessen the ever present risk of large oil spills resulting from collisions, strandings, carelessness etc. which could produce large scale pollution of a coastline causing damage to innocent owners of property, fishing and other industries, and expense to governments and others for cleaning up such pollution. Over the years, certain companies in the oil and shipping industries have accepted a good measure of responsibility for damage resulting from oil pollution through such schemes as the Tanker Owners Voluntary Agreement Concerning Liability for Oil Pollution (TOVALOP) and Contract Regarding an Interim Supplement to Tanker Liability for Oil Pollution (CRISTAL), whereby they agree to re-imburse national governments for expenses reasonably incurred by them to prevent or clean up oil pollution of coastlines as the result of a negligent discharge of oil from a tanker. The "Torrey Canyon" loss off Cornwall in 1967 which caused serious pollution on the coasts of England and France, made it clear that something more than voluntary action was required. After meetings in Brussels in 1969, the International Convention on Civil Liability for Oil Pollution Damage 1969 was signed by 29 states who agreed, subject to ratification by their respective governments, to adopt uniform international rules and procedures for determining questions of liability and providing adequate compensation to persons who suffer damage caused by pollution resulting from the escape of oil from ships.

Following the convention, Parliament passed the Merchant Shipping (Oil Pollution) Act 1971 which is the enabling act for the United Kingdom, and this Act and the Convention entered into force on 19 June 1975 after ratification by the requisite eight states. In addition to Great Britain and Northern Ireland, the Convention is in force in respect of over forty other states.

The Act provides that where, as a result of any occurrence (e.g. collision or stranding, etc.) taking place while a ship is carrying a cargo of persistent oil in bulk, any persistent oil carried by the ship, (cargo or otherwise) is discharged or escapes from the ship, the owner of the ship is liable, apart from three exceptions, for (a) any damage or loss caused within the territorial waters of the United Kingdom or any other Convention country by the resulting contamination; and (b) the cost of any measures reasonably taken afterwards to prevent or reduce the damage in those waters; and (c) any damage caused within such waters by the measures so taken. Where two or more ships are involved, owners are to be jointly liable for the total damage or cost if it is impossible to separate the individual damages. The only exceptions are where an owner is able to prove that the discharge or escape was due (a) to an act of war, hostilities, civil war, insurrection, or an exceptional, inevitable and irresistible natural phenomenon, or (b) wholly to a person (not a servant or agent) who has done, or left undone, anything with intent to do damage, or (c) to the negligence of a government or lighthouse authority responsible for maintaining lights or other navigational aids. A tanker owner's liability for damage or cost is restricted to that due to contamination, and no servant or agent of the owner, nor salvors employed with his agreement, shall be liable for any such damage or cost. The Act also provides in section 15 that the cost of clean-up measures may be recovered in some other cases, for example where fuel oil has escaped from a dry tanker or from a general cargo ship while in United Kingdom territorial waters. Claims shall be within the Admiralty jurisdiction of the High Court, but no court in the United Kingdom shall entertain any action to enforce a claim unless the action is commenced not later than 3 years after the claim arose or not later than 6 years after the occurrence which gave rise to the liability.

Where a shipowner, without his actual fault, incurs a liability under this Act, he may apply to the High Court to limit his liability to an amount not exceeding 133 special drawing rights (SDR) per ton of ship's tonnage with a maximum total not exceeding 14 million special drawing rights. Ship's tonnage for this purpose means registered tonnage plus the amount of any engine room space deduction. If limitation is granted, the limited amount determined by the court must be paid into court in sterling. For the purpose of converting an amount in special drawing rights into sterling, one special drawing right shall be treated as being equal to such sum in sterling as the International Monetary Fund (IMF) have fixed as being the equivalent of one SDR for the day on which the determination is made, or if no sum has been fixed for that day, the last day before that day for which a sum has been fixed. (The amount fixed by the IMF as being the equivalent in sterling to one SDR is published daily in the *Financial Times*. In July 1981 the approximate value of one SDR was £0·6.)

The court will then distribute it to the claimants in proportion to their claims in accordance with the provisions of section 5 of the Act.

Compulsory insurance against liability for oil pollution. Section 10 of the Act applies to any ship, wherever registered, carrying a bulk cargo of more than 2,000 tons of persistent oil. Such a ship shall not enter, arrive at, or leave a port or off-shore terminal within the territorial waters of the United Kingdom, nor, if the ship is registered in the United Kingdom, a port or off-shore terminal within the territorial waters of any other country, unless the ship carries a certificate certifying that there is in force in respect of that ship a contract of insurance or other security providing cover against the owner's liability for oil pollution damage up to an amount fixed by applying the section of the Act which allows the owner to limit his liability. If a ship enters, arrives at, or leaves, or attempts to enter or leave, a port or terminal without a certificate, the master or owner on conviction on indictment are liable to a fine; or on summary conviction to a fine not exceeding £35,000. A ship which attempts to leave a port in the United Kingdom without a certificate may be detained.

Oil Pollution Insurance Certificate. For a ship registered in the United Kingdom the certificate is issued by the Secretary of State, D.o.T. after the owner has produced satisfactory evidence that a policy of insurance or other financial security is in force for the ship (e.g. from a mutual assurance association). The certificate must contain the following information:—

(a) name of ship, distinctive number or letters and port of registry;
(b) name and address of owner;
(c) type of security and its duration;
(d) name and address of insurer or other person giving security;
(e) period of validity of certificate, which shall not be longer than the period of validity of the insurance or other security.

A state owned ship employed on commercial service is required to carry a certificate showing that the ship is owned by the state and that liability for oil pollution damage will be met up to the limit prescribed by the Act.

The certificate must be produced by the master on demand to any officer of customs or of the D.o.T., and if the ship is registered in the United Kingdom, to any proper officer. If a ship fails to carry, or the master fails to produce, a certificate when required, the master is liable on summary conviction to a fine not exceeding £500.

When he ceases to be the owner, regulations made under the Act, require the person to whom the certificate was issued to deliver it for cancellation to the D.o.T. or to a proper officer. Where, at any time while the certificate is in force, it is established that the contract of insurance is invalid, or there is a doubt whether the insurer can meet his obligations, the Secretary of State may cancel the certificate, and it shall then be delivered up to him by the person to whom it was issued. On summary conviction, the penalty for failing to deliver a certificate as required is a fine not exceeding £200.

The Act does not apply to any warship or any ship for the time being used by the government of any state for other than commercial purposes.

Other oil pollution legislation. Not all governments have ratified and brought into operation the 1969 Convention. A number of governments, and in some areas local governments within countries, have introduced and brought into operation their own oil pollution legislation which make an owner liable for any oil pollution damage caused and the cost of cleaning up such pollution. For example, the United States Government has passed a number of acts since 1970 to try and deal with the problem. Such acts, which may be more strict than the 1969 Convention, usually require evidence in the form of a Certificate of Financial Responsibility against oil pollution to be obtained before or on the ship's arrival in port, and require the reporting of any oil spill that occurs while within territorial waters. Masters of ships trading to non-convention countries must obtain details of local requirements if delays and possible fines are to be avoided.

The International Compensation Fund. It was recognised by the then Inter-Governmental Maritime Consultative Organisation (IMCO) at the 1969 Liability Convention that even if the Convention was implemented by all States, it might still be difficult for an authority which had spent large sums of money cleaning up a contaminated coastline to recover all or part of the sums expended. The spillage might have resulted from an Act of God, or was not the owner's fault; the guarantor might not be able to meet his obligations in full, or the damage might exceed the owner's liability as limited by the Convention. A conference was therefore held in Brussels in 1971 which adopted the International Convention on the Establishment of an International Fund for Compensation for Oil Pollution Damage 1971. The United Kingdom Government introduced and Parliament approved the Merchant Shipping Act 1974, Part I of which enacts in the United Kingdom the main provisions of the above Convention.

The Act provides for the setting up of an International Oil Pollution Compensation Fund financed by levying contributions from importers of oil into the United Kingdom. The Fund is liable for pollution damage in the United Kingdom if the person suffering damage has been unable to obtain full compensation under the M.S. (Oil Pollution) 1971 Act because of the exceptions or limitations of that Act. The Fund also indemnifies shipowners and their guarantors for a portion of their liability under the 1971 Act, provided the owner has complied with certain conditions concerning safety at sea. The 1971 Fund Convention came into force on 16 October 1978 and on that day Part I of the M.S. Act 1974 came into operation to enact the requirements of the Convention as far as the U.K. was concerned. The Fund provides compensation over and above the Civil Liability Convention limits up to a maximum of 675 million gold francs, but there is provision for the maximum to be raised to 900 million gold francs in the future. (When the 1976 Protocol to the Fund Convention is brought into force, these amounts will be changed to 45 million SDR's and 60 million SDR's respectively.)

The Fund is not liable, if it proves that the pollution damage resulted from an act of war, hostilities, civil war or insurrection, or the claimant cannot prove that the damage resulted from an incident involving one or more ships, or that the damage resulted from an intentional or negligent act of the claimant.

It appears that it will still be necessary for the voluntary schemes TOVALOP and CRISTAL to continue to give protection against damage not covered by the Civil Liability Convention and the Fund Convention. For example the costs of taking measures to remove the threat of a discharge of oil may be covered by the above schemes.

CLEAN AIR ACT

This Act makes provision for abating the pollution of the air and for that purpose prohibits the emission of dark smoke (with certain exceptions) from chimneys. The Act became effective from 1st June, 1958.

Section 20 of the Act provides that Sections 1 and 2 shall apply in relation to vessels in (a) all waters not navigable by sea-going ships, and (b) all waters navigable by sea-going ships within the seaward limits of United Kingdom territorial waters and contained within any port, harbour, etc., so long as a person or a body of persons is legally empowered to make charges in respect of vessels entering it or using its facilities. ("Charges" excludes light dues and pilotage dues.)

Section 1, in its application to vessels, provides that:—

(1) Dark smoke shall not be emitted from a vessel, and if, on any day, dark smoke is so emitted, the owner, master, or person in charge of the vessel shall be guilty of an offence. (Section 27 makes such offence punishable by a fine not exceeding £100.)

(2) Emissions lasting for not longer than such periods as may be specified by the Minister (i.e., Minister of the Environment) by regulations shall be left out of account for the purpose of this Section. (Regulations in respect of vessels have been made and are referred to below.)

(3) In any proceedings for an offence it shall be a defence to prove that the contravention complained of was due (a) solely to the lighting up of a boiler which was cold and that all practical steps had been taken to prevent or minimise the emission, (b) solely to a failure of apparatus which could not reasonably have been foreseen or provided against, and that contravention could not reasonably have been prevented after the failure occurred, (c) solely to the use of unsuitable fuel, that suitable fuel was unobtainable, that the least unsuitable fuel available was used, and all practicable steps had

been taken to prevent or minimise the emission, (*d*) to a combination of two or more of the above causes.

Section 2 provides for certain temporary exceptions from the provisions of Section 1.

It is realised that emissions of dark smoke are sometimes unavoidable as, for instance, in lighting up a boiler when cold, while soot blowing, cleaning fires, and so on. For that reason the Minister has arranged for separate regulations to apply to shore premises and shipping, respectively.

Those which apply to ships are the Dark Smoke (Permitted Periods) (Vessels) Regulations, 1958.

Important extracts from these regulations are:—

1. Emission from forced draught oil-fired boiler furnace or an oil engine: permitted for 10 minutes in the aggregate in any period of 2 hours.

2. Emission from natural draught oil-fired boiler furnace (except in cases mentioned in 4 below): permitted for 10 minutes in the aggregate in any 1 hour.

3. Emission from coal-fired boiler furnace:—

   (*a*) when not under way (except as in 4 below): permitted for 10 minutes in the aggregate in any 1 hour;

   (*b*) when under way: permitted for 20 minutes in the aggregate in any 1 hour.

   Note: For the purpose of the above, a vessel is not under way when she is at anchor or is made fast to the shore or the bottom. A vessel aground **is** under way for this purpose.

4. Emission from natural draught oil-fired boiler furnace or coal-fired boiler furnace in the following cases:—

   (*a*) a vessel with funnels shortened for the purpose of navigating the Manchester Ship Canal;

   (*b*) a tug not under way but preparing to get under way or supplying power to other vessels or to shore installations;

   (*c*) a vessel not under way but using her main power for the purpose of dredging, lifting, pumping, or performing any other special operation for which the vessel was designed: permitted for 20 minutes in the aggregate in any 1 hour.

5. Emissions from any other source are permitted for 5 minutes in the aggregate in any 1 hour, provided that:—

   (*a*) **continous** emissions of dark smoke caused otherwise than by soot blowing of a water-tube boiler shall not exceed (i) in cases 1 and 2, 4 minutes; and (ii) from a natural draught oil-fired boiler furnace in case 4, 10 minutes;

   (*b*) in no case shall **black** smoke be emitted for more than 3 minutes in the aggregate in any period of 30 minutes.

N.B.—"Dark smoke" means smoke which, if compared in the appropriate manner with a chart of the type known as the Ringelmann Chart, would appear to be as dark as or darker than shade 2 on the chart. "Black smoke" is smoke as dark as or darker than shade 4 on the chart.

FOULING OF SUBMARINE CABLES AND PIPELINES

The following matters, which are the subject of a D.o.T. notice, are of great importance from the point of view of both safety and public welfare.

Every care should be taken to avoid anchoring in areas where there are telegraph cables or submarine cables. Even though there may be no specific prohibition against doing so, it may result in damage to cables and serious interference with communications. Under provisions of the Submarine Telegraph Act, 1885, a penalty of imprisonment or fine, or both, may be imposed on any person who by culpable negligence breaks or injures a submarine cable. Such cables are easily injured and even when not actually broken may be rendered useless by being scraped, pierced or strained. In all cases of a cable being fouled great caution should be exercised in attempting to clear it. It is advisable to sacrifice gear entangled in a cable rather than to exert force in freeing it.

In the event of any vessel fouling a submarine cable, every effort should be made to clear the anchor or gear by normal methods; but should these efforts fail, the anchor or gear should be slipped and abandoned **without attempting to cut the cable.** High voltages are, or may be, fed into certain submarine cables. Hence, serious risk exists of loss of life to due electric shock, or at least of severe burns, if any attempt to cut the cable is made. No claim in respect of injury or damage sustained through such interference with a submarine cable will be entertained. On the other hand the Act provides that "Owners of ships or vessels who can prove that they have sacrificed an anchor, a net, or other fishing gear, in order to avoid injuring a submarine cable shall receive compensation from the owner of the cable."

In the event of any vessel fouling a pipeline the anchor or gear should be slipped or abandoned without attempting to get it clear. Any excessive force applied to a pipeline could result in a rupture; in the case of a gas pipeline the consequential release of gas at high pressure—somewhat like an explosion—could cause serious damage or loss of the vessel, and there would be an accompanying severe and immediate fire hazard.

To claim compensation a statement supported by the evidence of the crew should, whenever possible, be drawn up immediately after the occurrence, and the master must within 24 hours after his return to, or next putting into, port make a declaration to the proper authorities. The declaration on Form S.10 should set forth full particulars of the occurrence, including the exact hour, the position of the vessel (fixed, if possible, by at least three bearings), the depth of water and the nature of the bottom. This declaration should be made to a M.M. Superintendent, Chief Officer of Customs, Coastguard Officer, or Fishery Officer. An official log book entry should also be made of the facts of the case.

CHAPTER 8

CARRIAGE OF PASSENGERS

The Contract of Passage. A contract of carriage of passengers by sea is an ordinary contract for the conveyance by ship from one port to another of persons who are included within the definition of the term "passenger" as set forth in Part III of the principal Act and amended by the 1949 Safety Convention Act. Such conveyance may be by liner, a vessel engaged on a so-called pleasure cruise, a tramp, tanker, or excursion steamer, or any other type of ship. Any shipowner, so long as he complies with the statutory safety provisions which apply to the kind of ship he employs for the purpose, is free to enter into such a contract, unless he has given an undertaking under some other contract, *e.g.*, a charter-party, not to carry passengers.

Much of the law governing carriage of passengers is based on the common law that applies to all contracts. A proper contract must be made showing that real consent was reached between the shipowner and the intending passenger and where special terms are inserted to protect the shipowner it must be shown that those terms are reasonable, must have been known to the passenger and that he must have consented to them. The type of exemption clause that until recently was included in passengers' tickets to give the shipowner protection against liability for loss or damage from perils of the sea and from neglect or default of servants have become less relevant because of changes made by statute.

For contracts made on or after 1st January 1981, The Carriage of Passengers and their Luggage by Sea (Interim Provisions) Order 1980 (S.I. 1980 No. 1092) provides, under powers given by section 16 of the M.S. Act 1979, that pending the coming into force internationally of the Athens Convention relating to the Carriage of Passengers and their Luggage by Sea 1974, the Convention (which is set out in Schedule 3 to the M.S. Act 1979) shall, subject to certain modifications, have the force of law in the United Kingdom. The Order applies to the following contracts for the carriage of passengers, or of passengers and their luggage:—

(*a*) any contract for international carriage made in the U.K.;
(*b*) any contract for international carriage where a place in the U.K. is the place of departure or destination;
(*c*) any contract for carriage between places in the area consisting of the United Kingdom, the Channel Islands and the Isle of Man and where there is no intermediate port of call outside that area.

Contracts of carriage which are not for reward are excluded.

A **passenger** means any person carried in a ship under a contract of carriage and includes any person carried, who with the carrier's consent, is accompanying a vehicle or live animals covered by a contract for carriage of goods not covered by this Convention. **Luggage** means any article or vehicle carried under a contract of carriage, but excludes articles and vehicles carried under a charter party or bill of lading, and live animals. **International carriage** means carriage in which according to the contract, the places of departure and destination are situated in two different states, or in a single state if, according to the contract or scheduled itinerary, there is an intermediate call in another state.

Liability of the Carrier. The carrier, being a person by or on behalf of whom a contract for the carriage by sea of a passenger, or of a passenger and his luggage has been made, is liable for the damage suffered as a result of the death of or personal injury to a passenger and the loss of or damage to luggage if the incident which caused the damage occurred in the course of carriage and was due to the fault or neglect of the carrier or of his servants or agents acting within the scope of their employment.

The burden of proof that the incident occurred in the course of carriage and the extent of the loss or damage lies with the claimant.

Fault or neglect of the carrier or his servants or agents acting within the scope of their employment will be presumed, unless the contrary is proved, if the death or personal injury to a passenger or loss of or damage to cabin luggage or luggage in his possession, custody or control, arose from or in connection with the shipwreck, collision, stranding, explosion or fire, or defect in the ship.

Luggage loss or damage includes pecuniary loss due to it not being re-delivered to the passenger within a reasonable time after the ship's arrival, but does not include delay caused by labour disputes. In respect of loss or damage to other luggage, such fault or neglect will be presumed unless the contrary is proved irrespective of the nature of the incident which caused the loss or damage. In all other cases the burden of proving fault or neglect lies with the claimant. (e.g. He must prove that he got food poisoning on board, or that his baggage was tampered with on board).

The term **carriage** covers the passenger and his cabin luggage from the moment of embarkation, including the period of carriage by tender to or from the ship if included in the fare, to the moment of disembarkation, but so far as the passenger is concerned, does not include the period when he is in a marine terminal or station or on a quay or other port installation. The term covers luggage as soon as the carrier has taken it into his charge, which will be usually when the passenger hands it over on his arrival at the terminal, and it continues until re-delivered to him.

Valuables. The carrier is not liable for the loss of or damage to monies, negotiable securities, gold, silverware, jewellery or other valuables unless they have been deposited with him for safe keeping. Even when deposited, liability is limited to 18,000 gold francs per passenger per carriage unless a higher limit is agreed to in writing.

Limits of Liability. The carrier's limits of liability are per carriage, for death or personal injury 700,000 gold francs; for loss or damage to cabin baggage 12,500 gold francs per passenger; for vehicles, including luggage in or on them 50,000 gold francs per vehicle; and for other luggage 18,000 gold francs per passenger. The carrier and the passenger may agree that the carrier's liability is to be subject to a deductible not exceeding 1,750 gold francs for vehicle damage, and not exceeding 200 gold francs per passenger for damage to luggage.

Note:—The Secretary of State is authorised to specify by order from time to time the amounts in sterling represented by the above amounts in gold francs. By S.I. 1980 No. 1872 the values specified from 1st January 1981 were £25,147·67, £449·07, £1,796·26, £646·65, £62·87 and £7·19 respectively.

Loss of right to limit liability. The carrier loses the right to limit his liability if it is proved that the damage resulted from his act or omission done with the intent to cause such damage, or recklessly and with knowledge that such damage would probably result.

Defences and Limits for Carriers' Servants. Servants or agents of carriers, if sued for damages when acting within the scope of their employment, can invoke their employer's defences and limits of liability, unless it is proved that the damage resulted from an intentional or reckless act or omission with knowledge that damage would probably result.

Contributory Fault. If the carrier proves that death or personal injury to a passenger or luggage damage was caused or contributed to by the passenger's fault or neglect, the court may exonerate the carrier wholly or partly from liability.

Loss or Damage Claims. Passengers finding apparent damage to their luggage must give notice of such damage to the carrier or his agent, and if this is disputed must sue within two years. In the case of cabin luggage, notice must be given before or at the time of disembarkation and for other luggage before or at the time of its re-delivery. Where damage is not apparent, or luggage is lost, notice must be given within 15 days of the date of disembarkation or re-delivery or time when re-delivery should have taken place.

Time Bar and Jurisdiction. Any action for damages arising out of death or personal injury to a passenger will be time-barred after a period of two years from the date of disembarkation, or date the passenger should have disembarked. A claimant can bring his action in one of the following courts being a court:—

(a) at the place of the defendant's principal place of business, or

(b) at the place of the departure or destination according to the contract of carriage, or

(c) of the State of the claimant's domicile or permanent residence, if the defendant has a place of business in that State, or

(d) of the State where the contract was made, also provided the defendant has a place of business in that State.

After the incident which caused the damage has occurred, the parties may agree that the claim shall be submitted to any court or to arbitration.

The shipowner cannot contract out of the terms of the Convention, but is still entitled to avail himself of the limits of liability provided by section 503 of the M.S. Act 1894 as amended.

Notice to Passengers. The Carriage of Passengers and their Luggage by Sea (Interim Provisions) (Notice) Order 1980 (S.I. 1980 No. 1125) requires a carrier, in relation to any contract of carriage to which the principal order (S.I. 1980 No. 1092) described above applies, to give to passengers notice that the provisions of the Athens Convention may be applicable, and notice of the provisions of that Convention that relate to valuables, the limit of the carrier's liability for death or personal injury and for loss of or damage to luggage (including a vehicle), and of the notice to be given by the passenger in respect of loss or damage to his luggage. Notice must be given by the carrier before departure and, where practicable, on the ticket itself. A carrier who fails to comply is guilty of an offence and liable on summary conviction to a fine not exceeding £500.

Hovercraft. Many thousands of passengers and vehicles are carried across the English Channel by hovercraft each year, but the Athens Convention does not apply to such passengers and their baggage, as the definition of ship in the Athens Convention excludes "air-cushion vehicles". Such passengers are covered by the provisions of the Carriage by Air Act 1961.

Note:—When the Athens Convention has been accepted by the requisite number of States and has been brought into force for them, it will then apply to ships flying the flag of States party to the Convention, to contracts of carriage made in States party to the Convention, and, where the port of departure or destination is in a State party to the Convention.

Further, when the 1976 Protocol to the Convention is brought into force, the limits of liability expressed above as 700,000, 12,500,

50,000, 18,000, 1,750 and 200 gold francs respectively will be substituted by 46,666, 833, 3,333, 1,200, 117 and 13 Units of Account respectively, where the Unit of Account is the Special Drawing Right as defined by the International Monetary Fund, the value of which in sterling is to be that fixed for the day on which judgement is given, or that fixed for the last previous day. Such value is published each day in the *Financial Times*.

Other Breaches of Contract. As we have seen in the U.K. a shipowner cannot now exclude or restrict his liability to a passenger for death, injury or damage to luggage, caused by negligence, to less than that provided by the Athens Convention. However the Convention does not have anything to say about other obligations of the shipowner relating to a passenger's contract of carriage. A shipowner wishing to protect himself against claims for breach of contract, for example not delivering the passenger to the agreed destination, or not completing the passage, or providing a cabin not up to the standard envisaged by the fare paid, or changing a cruise itinerary by missing out a promised port of call, may include a clause in the contract giving him the right to make such changes at his discretion, but by the terms of the Unfair Contract Terms Act 1977 such a clause would only be effective if shown to the Court to be reasonable. The Court or arbitrator would have to determine whether the clause was reasonable bearing in mind the strength of the bargaining positions of the parties relative to each other, and if the clause seeks to restrict liability to a specified sum of money, regard must be had to the resources which the shipowner could expect to be available to him for the purpose of meeting the liability should it arise, and how far it was open to him to cover himself by insurance. It is for those claiming that a contract term is reasonable to show that it is.

For contracts not covered by the Athens Convention, the law of the country where the contract is made will probably apply and such law may or may not permit exemption clauses to be included in the contract of carriage. Under American law, a shipowner is not allowed to contract out of his obligations to passengers.

Definitions. The expression "passenger" means any person carried in a ship except:—

(*a*) a person employed or engaged in any capacity on board on the business of the ship;

(*b*) a person on board in pursuance of the master's obligation to carry shipwrecked, distressed, or other persons, or by reason of circumstances that neither the master, nor the owner, nor the charterer could have prevented or forestalled.

(*c*) a child under one year of age.

The expression "passenger steamer" for the purposes of the M.S.

(Safety Convention) Act means a steamer carrying more than twelve passengers.

N.B.—By Section 16 of the M.S.A., 1906, it is provided that a ship shall not carry passengers on more than one deck below the water line.

Annual Survey of Passenger Steamers. Section 271 (1) of the principal Act, which prohibits passenger steamers carrying more than twelve passengers from sailing without a certificate of survey, has been amended by Section 17 of the M.S. Act, 1964, and now provides that every passenger steamer which carries more than twelve passengers shall be surveyed once at least in each year in the manner provided by the Act; and no ship (other than a steam ferry boat working in chains) shall proceed to sea or on any voyage or excursion with more than twelve passengers on board, unless there is in force in respect of the ship a certificate as to survey under Part III of the Act, applicable to the voyage or excursion on which the ship is about to proceed, or that voyage or excursion is one in respect of which the Minister (now Secretary of State, D.o.T.) has exempted the ship from the requirements of this subsection.

A passenger steamer attempting to ply or go to sea may be detained until such certificate as aforesaid is produced to the proper officer of Customs, unless the voyage or excursion on which she is about to proceed is one in respect of which she has been exempted as aforesaid.

If a ship proceeds to sea or on any voyage or excursion when it is prohibited from doing so by section 271(1) above, the owner and the master of the ship shall each be guilty of an offence and liable on conviction on indictment to a fine or on summary conviction to a fine not exceeding £1,000.

The owner of every passenger steamer must cause the steamer to be surveyed by a ship surveyor, a nautical surveyor, an engineer surveyor, and a radio surveyor. On receipt of a declaration of survey the owner must, within 14 days, transmit it to the D.o.T. (see Chapter 7), and if he fails to do so without reasonable cause he shall forfeit a prescribed sum of money for every day during which the transmission is delayed. Such forfeit is payable on the granting of a passenger steamer's certificate in addition to the normal fee. (In practice the certificate is usually issued without the declaration having to pass through the owner's hands).

Issue of Passenger Steamer's Certificate. On receipt of the declaration of survey the D.o.T., when satisfied that all the requirements of the Act have been complied with, issue in duplicate a passenger steamer's certificate stating such compliance and, according to the declarations:—

(a) the limits (if any) beyond which the steamer is not fit to ply; and

(b) the number of passengers which the steamer is fit to carry, distinguishing, if necessary, the number to be carried in each part of the steamer, and any conditions and variations to which the number is subject.

If the owner is aggrieved by a surveyor's declaration or by a refusal to give one, he may appeal to a court of survey. On such appeal the judge of the court shall report to the D.o.T. on the question raised, and the Department, when satisfied that the requirements of the court's report and the provisions of the Act have been complied with, may grant a certificate. Subject to any order made by the judge the costs of and incidental to appeal shall follow the event. A surveyor in making a survey for the purpose of a declaration of survey shall, if the owner so requires, be accompanied by some person appointed by the owner, in which case if the two are in agreement there shall be no appeal to a court of survey.

Transmission of Certificate. The D.o.T. shall transmit the passenger steamer's certificate in duplicate to a superintendent or other public officer at the port nominated by the owner, and shall cause a notice of the transmission to be given to the master or owner or his agent who, on making application and paying the proper fee (plus forfeit, if any) shall have both copies of the certificate delivered to him by the officer.

Duration. A passenger steamer's certificate shall not be in force for more than 1 year from the date of issue, or such shorter time as may be specified in it, nor after due notice has been given that the D.o.T. have cancelled it. If the steamer is absent from the United Kingdom when her certificate expires, a fine shall not be incurred for want of a certificate until she first begins to ply with passengers after her next return to the United Kingdom.

Cancellation. The D.o.T. may cancel a certificate where any declaration on which the certificate was founded was in any particular fraudulently or erroneously made, where the certificate was issued on false or erroneous information, or where since the making of the declaration the hull, equipments, or machinery have sustained injury or are otherwise insufficient.

In every such case the Department may require the owner to have the steamer re-surveyed, and to transmit further declarations, before they re-issue or replace the certificate.

An expired or cancelled certificate must be delivered up as the D.o.T. direct, in default of which the owner or master will be liable to a fine not exceeding £50.

Posting up of Certificate. The owner or master of every passenger steamer shall, forthwith on receipt of the certificate, cause one of the duplicates to be put up in some conspicuous place on board so as to be legible to all persons on board, and kept so put up and legible while it remains in force, and the steamer is in use. Failure without reasonable cause is an offence punishable by a fine not exceeding £50 on summary conviction.

If a passenger steamer plies or goes to sea with passengers on board without the certificate being displayed as above, the owner is liable to a fine not exceeding £200, and the master a further fine not exceeding £200.

Penalty for Forgery, Etc. The forgery or fraudulent alteration of a passenger steamer's certificate or a declaration of survey, and similar offences, are indictable offences.

Colonial Certificate for Passenger Steamers. Where the legislature of a British possession provides for the survey of, and grant of certificates for, passenger steamers, and the D.o.T. report to Her Majesty that they are satisfied that the certificates are to the like effect, etc., as those issued in the United Kingdom, Her Majesty in Council may declare the certificates to be of the same force as if granted under the Act.

Excess Passengers. If a ship carries passengers in excess of the number allowed by her certificate, the owner or master is liable, irrespective of the number of passengers, on summary conviction, to a fine not exceeding £50,000; and, on indictment, a fine.

The penalty in respect of non-compliance with the provisions as to passenger steamers, and also in respect of the offence of going to. sea without the appropriate certificates, is on summary conviction a fine not exceeding £1,000, and on conviction on indictment, a fine

General Equipment. Part III of the principal Act lays down what equipment a passenger ship must have in the matter of compasses, fire-fighting and safety appliances, as well as shelter for the protection of deck passengers, but most of these requirements are now superseded by the requirements of the various regulations made pursuant to the M.S. (Safety Convention) Act, 1949, and the revised Merchant Shipping Regulations brought into force in May, 1980, and amended in May 1981, to give effect, so far as British ships are concerned (and foreign ships when in United Kingdom ports), to the provisions of the International Convention for the Safety of Life at Sea, 1974 and the Protocol of 1978. These are referred to in Chapter 7.

The principal Act provides that each boiler shall be provided with a safety valve constructed as to be out of control of the engineer when steam is up, and, if the safety valve is in addition to the ordinary valve, constructed as to have an area not less, and a pressure not greater, than the area of and pressure on the ordinary valve. On summary conviction a £1,000 (max.) fine, and on indictment a fine may be imposed on a person who increases the weight on a boiler safety valve beyond that fixed by the surveyor.

Keeping Order in Passenger Steamers. The principal Act provides for the imposition of fines on passengers who commit any of a variety of offences such as insisting on admission or refusing to leave when drunk, travelling without paying a fare, refusing to leave the ship at her destination, and so on. In practice, however, this provision appears to apply mainly to keeping order in excursion steamers. Further, the master of a home trade passenger steamer has a statutory right to refuse to receive on board any person who by reason of drunkeness or otherwise is in such a state, or mis-conducts himself in such a manner, as to cause annoyance or injury to passengers on board. If any such person is on board the master may put him ashore at any convenient place without returning any fare he has paid.

The Acts seem to give very little guidance to masters of deep sea passenger ships in the matter of keeping passengers in order, but it is recognised that a master is always entitled to exact obedience to any order he gives in the interests of the safety of the ship and of persons on board. Various court rulings given from time to time indicate that (a) the master is never justified in placing a passenger under restraint merely because he constitutes a nuisance, but (b) once a passenger becomes a positive danger, either to himself or the ship or other persons, the master should not hesitate to put him under restraint. It is provided by the principal Act that a person may be fined up to £50 for injuring any part of the ship, molesting the crew, or in any way impeding the navigation of the ship. If an offender, on the application of the master or other employee of the owner, refuses to give his name and address or gives false particulars thereof, he is liable to a fine not exceeding £50.

Section 79 of the M.S. Act 1970 provides that the master of any ship registered in the United Kingdom may cause any person on board the ship to be put under restraint if and for so long as it appears to him necessary or expedient in the interest of safety or for the preservation of good order or discipline on board the ship. This power of arrest should be used with care, as a master runs the risk of being sued for damages for the tort of false imprisonment if he continues to confine a passenger or other person or restrict his freedom of movement after the need for restraint no longer applies.

Passenger Tenders. Section 15 of the M.S. Act, 1906, provides that where a passenger steamer takes on board passengers from a tender, or lands passengers by means of a tender, she shall be deemed to be taking the passengers on board from, or landing the passengers at, the port from or to which the tender comes or goes, and passengers conveyed in a tender to or from a ship from or to a place in the United Kingdom shall for the purposes of Part III of the principal Act and for the purposes of any returns to be made under the M.S. Acts, be deemed to be passengers carried from or to a place in the United Kingdom.

It is pointed out in Chapter 7 that the owner or master of a tender taking passengers to a ship which attempts to proceed to sea without having an appropriate Safety Certificate is liable to be fined.

CHAPTER 9

THE SHIPMENT, CARRIAGE AND DELIVERY OF GOODS

CONTRACTS OF AFFREIGHTMENT AND SIMILAR ARRANGEMENTS

WHEREAS a "contract of passage" is a contract for the carriage of passengers by sea, a "contract of affreightment" is a contract for the carriage of inanimate things and livestock. A contract of affreightment can, and sometimes may, in the preliminary stages of negotiation, be made by word of mouth, but it is of course customary for the contract eventually to be embodied in some convenient form of document. The forms employed for this purpose may, according to circumstances, be (1) charter-parties, (2) bills of lading, (3) waybills, (4) special agreements, or (5) parcel tickets.

Charter-Parties. A charter-party is an agreement between a shipowner and a charterer for the use or hire of a ship for a particular voyage or series of voyages, or for a stipulated period of time. In some cases a charter-party may be for the hire of part of a ship for the carriage of goods on a particular voyage, or during a particular period. Some mention has already been made of this in the section of Chapter 3 dealing with the employment of ships, and further details of chartering are given in this Chapter. Some charter-party forms are reproduced in the Appendix. The term is derived from the Spanish "carta partita" and French "carte partie" meaning "divided document (card)". Originally the shipowner's and merchant's copies of the contract were both written side by side on the same sheet of material which was then divided down the middle to form "indentures".

Bills of Lading. Bills of lading may be issued, and commonly are, even where there is a charter-party in existence as well. This would be the case where a ship has been time-chartered to be employed on the berth so that the charterer is under an obligation to issue his own bills to the shippers of various parcels of cargo. Under a voyage charter also bills of lading may be issued, in the first instance as mere receipts for goods received on board, but where such goods are sold while they are still in transit the bills of lading transferred to third parties become much more than receipts.

Bills of lading are used in respect of goods carried on "liner" terms. Further references are made to bills of lading in this Chapter and a specimen form is shown in the Appendix.

Waybills. Up until the early 1960's when most cargo was shipped on conventional vessels, documentary delays were not a serious problem as there was usually time for negotiable bills of lading to catch up with the cargo. Since then, containerisation, faster vessels, fewer ports of call and improved handling facilities at loading and discharging berths have greatly reduced transit time but often the processing of bills of lading has failed to match this with the result that many consignments arrived at their destinations before the necessary documents, which was inefficient and costly for all concerned. To avoid this gap between the movement times of goods and essential documents, a new form, the waybill has been developed.

A waybill is a non-negotiable document which does not have to be presented at destination. The named consignee or his authorised agent takes delivery of the goods subject to proof of identity and authority, although in certain countries, national law still demands presentation of a bill of lading.

Special Agreements. Article VI of the Schedule to the Carriage of Goods by Sea Act (see Appendix I) gives a carrier freedom of contract in respect of particular goods carried under special conditions provided that no bill of lading is issued and provided that the terms of agreement are embodied in a non-negotiable document marked as such.

Parcel Tickets. Valuable goods of small bulk which are normally carried in the strong room or other kind of lock-up compartment and, very often, passengers' excess baggage are shipped under parcel tickets which are not generally regarded as contracts of affreightment. Such goods usually pay an *ad valorem* freight which may be subject to a minimum charge.

COMMON LAW WARRANTIES

In contracts of affreightment the following undertakings on the part of the shipowner are implied at common law, viz.:—

1. An absolute undertaking that the ship shall be seaworthy for the purposes of the contract at the time when the contract is made.

2. An undertaking that the ship shall be ready to commence the voyage and load the cargo and proceed on the voyage with reasonable despatch.

3. An undertaking that the ship shall not deviate from the contract route or the usual route except for some good reason or as provided for in the contract.

Of the above warranties, 1 and 3 apply equally to charter-parties and bills of lading. The despatch warranty generally applies only to voyage charter-parties and bills of lading issued pursuant thereto.

Although these undertakings have been referred to as warranties it would probably be more truthful to regard them as conditions precedent to the contract. Breach of any of them would result in the shipowner no longer being able to rely on any of the exceptions clauses in the contract and he would find himself reduced to the status of a common carrier with no protection against liability for loss of or damage to goods carried, other than the few common law exceptions. Moreover, he would have to prove that the loss would inevitably have occurred even if the undertaking complained of had not been broken. In the case of a deviation the same burden falls on the shipowner whether the loss or damage occurred before, during or after the deviation. The situation of the ship at the time when the contract is made is a condition the breach of which would entitle the charterer to rescind the charter-party. The seaworthiness of the ship and the fact that she is in every way fitted for the voyage is a condition at the beginning of the voyage, but there is no implied condition of warranty that the ship will continue to be seaworthy during the voyage. However, in accordance with what is called the "doctrine of stages", it is implied that the vessel must be seaworthy for each stage at the beginning of that stage where the voyage is divided into several distinct parts.

MODIFICATIONS OF THE COMMON LAW POSITION

In a charter-party it is customary to describe the vessel as being "tight, staunch, strong, and in every way fitted for the voyage," and in a bill of lading it was at one time usual to declare that the ship was seaworthy by describing her as a "good" ship. As long ago as 1830 the Carriers Act of that date gave carriers the right to contract out of certain of their common law obligations and, in practice, this was effected by inserting various exceptions clauses in contracts of affreightment. There are also certain Merchant Shipping Act provisions which have the effect of enabling a shipowner to escape liability completely in some circumstances and to limit his liability in others (see Chapter 15). Section 3 of the Carriage of Goods by Sea Act, 1971, does away with the common law absolute warranty of seaworthiness by stating that there shall not be implied in any contract for the carriage of goods by sea to which the Rules apply any absolute undertaking by the carrier of the goods to provide a seaworthy ship. Article III of the Rules referred to, however, does state that the carrier shall be bound, before and at the beginning of the voyage, to exercise due diligence to (a) make the ship seaworthy; (b) properly man, equip, and supply the ship; (c) make the holds, refrigerating and cool chambers, and all other parts of the ship in which goods are carried, fit and safe for their reception,

Q

carriage and preservation. To give an absolute undertaking to supply a seaworthy ship is one thing, to use due diligence to make a ship seaworthy is quite another. Where the Rules apply, the latter is as far as the carrier is expected to go, and even that is quite onerous, those responsible for framing the rules evidently considering that it would be unfair to expect an owner or charterer to be technically fully competent to know whether a modern complex ship fitted with all kinds of complicated equipment was in every detail seaworthy or not.

The Rules contained in the Schedule to the Carriage of Goods by Sea Act, generally known as the Hague-Visby Rules, do not apply to charter-parties as such, though they do apply to bills of lading issued pursuant to charter-parties.

There is an important difference between the common law position and that under the Hague-Visby Rules with regard to deviation. At common law deviation to save life has always been justifiable, but not so deviation to save property at sea. Any delay due to rendering salvage services to another vessel in circumstances where lives were not in danger would, at common law, constitute a breach of the non-deviation warranty. By contrast, Article IV (4) of the Rules provides that any deviation in saving or attempting to save life or property at sea, or any reasonable deviation shall not be deemed to be an infringement or breach of these Rules or of the contract of carriage, and the carrier shall not be liable for any loss or damage resulting therefrom.

COMMON AND PRIVATE (OR SPECIAL) CARRIERS

Common Carrier. A common carrier is a carrier who, for hire or reward, holds himself ready to carry from one terminus to another the goods of any person who chooses to employ him for the purpose. Such a carrier, therefore, cannot pick and choose his customers. He is bound to charge a reasonable price for his services, but is not bound to charge a uniform price. He must accept and carry whatever goods are offered for carriage unless:—

(a) his carriage is already full;
(b) the goods offered are not of a kind he is accustomed to carry;
(c) the destination of the goods is not on his accustomed route;
(d) the goods are of a specially dangerous nature so that the carriage of them would involve extraordinary risk;
(e) the goods would be harmful to others he has already accepted.

The customer must deliver the goods to be carried to the carrier or to the latter's representative, and the carrier has a possessory lien on the goods carried for his charge for carriage (e.g., shipowner's lien for freight).

A common carrier is absolutely responsible for the safe carriage of the goods and for delivery without unreasonable delay at the proper destination in the same apparent order and condition as when received, but he is not liable at common law for any loss or injury arising from:—

(a) Act of God.

(b) Restraint of Rulers, Princes, and Peoples.

(c) Queen's enemies.

(d) Jettison for the common benefit (general average sacrifices).

(e) Negligence of the consignor (e.g., insufficient packing which is not obvious to the carrier).

(f) Inherent vice or defect of the goods.

The above exceptions apart, a common carrier is liable for any loss of or damage to the goods he carries even though he has not been negligent.

Private Carriers. Where a carrier declines to accept the status of a common carrier, or refuses to carry goods other than those of a particular kind, and makes a special contract of carriage with each consignor in turn, he is a private carrier or special carrier. Although even he is bound by certain of the common law obligations, he is permitted to include an exceptions clause in his contracts relieving him from specified liabilities. He is, in addition, entitled to the same exceptions from liability as a common carrier.

Shipowners and Charterers as Carriers. It was held many years ago that the owner or master of a general ship is a common carrier. A "general ship" is a ship placed on the berth with an intimation by the owner or charterer thereof that he is willing to carry without special conditions the goods of anyone who offers them for carriage. In the same way the owner of a barge or lighter is a common carrier if he hires out his craft for the carriage of goods to any person applying for the use of it where the customer has the right to decide the places of arrival and departure of the vessel. However, from what has already been said about modern modifications of the common law position, it will be evident that a shipowner will very rarely, if ever, be nowadays regarded at law as a common carrier completely.

In respect of a ship under voyage charter, the owner is a private carrier carrying goods under the terms of a special contract, namely the charter-party. In respect of a time charter, when as is usual the master (or the ship's agent acting for the master) signs the bills of lading on the owner's behalf, the shipowner is the carrier, but if exceptionally the master has signed the bills of lading as the charterer's agent or the charterer has signed the bills of lading in his own name, the charterer is the carrier. To what extent (if any) he is a common carrier will depend on the manner in which he employs the ship. In respect of a ship placed on the berth, the owner or charterer acting as carrier will be a common carrier to a very limited extent, that is to say, he will be a common carrier except in so far as the goods are carried under the terms of a special contract (e.g., a bill of lading), and in so far as the carriage is governed by statute law (*e.g.*, certain sections of the M.S. Acts, the Carriage of Goods by Sea Act and the corresponding legislation of countries other than the United Kingdom). The modern position of lightermen and barge owners is referred to in Chapter 12.

CHARTER-PARTIES AND SOME CHARTERING TERMS

Negotiation of Charters. In fixing a ship for a voyage charter and in negotiating a time charter it is almost invariably the case that the services of a shipbroker are engaged on a commission basis to act as an intermediary between the shipowner and the charterer. Shipbroking is a highly skilled occupation, and it will be convenient at this juncture to mention briefly the different categories of brokers who specialise in one or other of the several branches of the business.

There are:—

1. Sale and purchase brokers whose speciality is the buying and selling of vessels on behalf of their principals as described in Chapter 3, and the arranging of contracts for the construction of new tonnage.
2. Shipowners' brokers whose business it is to find cargoes for vessels to carry.
3. Charterers' agents who specialise in finding ships to carry merchants' cargoes.
4. Coasting brokers who act both as shipowners' brokers and as charterers' agents in the coasting trades.
5. Cabling agents whose function is to keep a particular chartering market constantly advised of the requirements of markets elsewhere, and to inform owners and charterers abroad of the state of the market in the agent's own district.
6. Ships' agents who act on behalf of owners and masters of ships while in ports of call to make arrangements for loading and discharging cargo, embarking and disembarking passengers, bunkering, obtaining supplies, having repairs effected, and other details of ships' husbandry. In addition to making advance arrangements for docking or berthing, they collect freight due to the shipowner, assist with Customs requirements and attend to crew formalities. Agency fees for these services are charged according to a fixed scale.

In many cases the same firm of shipbrokers is concerned with more than one of the brokers' activities listed above. British shipbrokers both at home and overseas are usually members of the Institute of Chartered Shipbrokers.

A broker who negotiates a charter-party is entitled to com-mission or "brokerage", as it is usually called, in respect of his services, and the rate at which this is payable, though varying from case to case, is generally something like $1\frac{1}{4}$ to $1\frac{3}{4}$ per cent. of the freight or charter hire. A typical "brokerage clause" reads "A commission of .... per cent. on all freight, deadfreight and demurrage, and the customary freight brokerage is due to................................ on shipment of the cargo, vessel lost or not lost". If due on shipment of the cargo it will be based on the B/L weight, otherwise it will be calculated on the amount of freight actually received. In the "Transitime" form of time C/P the clause relating to commission reads "The Owners to pay a commission of...to ....on any hire paid under the Charter, but in no case less than is necessary to cover the actual expenses of the brokers and a reasonable fee for their work. If the full hire is not paid owing to breach of charter by either of the parties the party liable therefore to indemnify the brokers against their loss of commission. Should the parties agree to cancel the Charter, the Owners to indemnify the Brokers against any loss of commission, but in such case the commission is not to exceed the brokerage on one year's hire." There are, of course, many other forms of brokerage clause. The expression "lost or not lost" refers only to losses by expected perils.

Usually the broker retains the original charter-party and supplies the parties thereto with as many true and certified copies as they may require.

Charter-parties issued in the United Kingdom are exempt from stamp duty.

Signing of Charter-Parties. A C/P must be signed by or on behalf of the shipowner, by or on behalf of the charterer, and by a witness or witnesses. If the two principals or their agents sign the agree-ment on the same occasion, a single witness suffices for both, but if the contract is executed partly at one place and partly at another, or on different occasions at the same place, each principal signature must be individually witnessed. That is, four signatures would be required.

Captain's Copy of C/P. If it is the intention of the owners of a voyage-chartered ship that the master, with or without the assist-ance of agents, is to be solely or jointly responsible on their behalf for the conduct of business with the charterer and consignee (or their respective agents) at ports of loading and unloading it will be essential for him to be supplied with a copy of the charter-party. Should this be inadvertently overlooked the master should not hesi-tate to ask for a copy as without one he would be severely handi-capped, being directly concerned with all such matters as the con-duct of preliminary voyage, berthing arrangements at loading and discharging ports, the serving of notice of readiness, the kind and quantity of cargo to be shipped, the form in which bills of lading are to be signed, the obligations of the parties in the matter of demurrage or despatch money and, possibly in some cases, the collection of freight.

On the other hand, if it is the owners' policy to rely entirely on the skill and judgement of their agents to look after their interests in general matters relating to the performance of the contract, they will then consider the master to have fulfilled his part by attending properly to the navigation, stowage and stability of the ship. In that case they will probably regard it as unnecessary for the master to have a copy of the charter-party.

Charter-Party Forms. There are certain standard forms of both time and voyage charter-parties officially recognised by the General Council of British Shipping and/or the Baltic Conference for use in particular trades, and other standard forms which, although not officially recognised, are regularly used. In addition, there are a number of so-called "Private C/P forms" drawn up to meet the requirements of special trades wherein the volume of business is limited. The use of a standard form is often enforced by the rules of shipowners' Protecting and Indemnity Associations with the object of reducing to a minimum the possibility of disputes arising from different interpretations of ambiguous clauses. The official forms are known by Code Names such as:—

Austral	Australian Grain Charter-Party,
Baltime	Uniform Time Charter,
Centrocon	River Plate Charter-Party (Grain, etc.),
Gencon	Uniform General Charter,
Medcon	East Coast Coal Charter-Party,
Linertime	BIMCO Deep Sea Time Charter.

The coal, grain, rice, timber, stone, ore, fertiliser, and other trades all have their own forms of charter-party.

Preliminary Voyage and Cancelling Date. In the case of a voyage charter it is usual for the C/P to provide either that the ship is to proceed immediately to a named loading port, or that she is to be there by a certain date. If the former, she must proceed to the port with all reasonable speed, but should the voyage be delayed by one of the excepted perils the shipowner will not be held responsible for the delay. However, if the ship is delayed for so long that she cannot reach the port within a time that is reasonable having regard to the nature of the contemplated adventure, the charterer may cancel the C/P. If the latter, it may not be essential to proceed to the port at once. If time permits she may be employed in the interval under an intermediate charter. But if the ship cannot reach the agreed loading port by the date stipulated because the performance of the intermediate charter is delayed by perils of the sea, the owner will not be protected by the exceptions clause in the original C/P. Where the charterer has the express right of cancelling in the event of the ship failing to arrive by the agreed date, that option may be exercised even though the ship did proceed directly but was prevented from reaching the port in time by an excepted peril. Sometimes, instead of fixing a precise date, it is represented that the ship is " expected ready to load" by a given date. That means that there are reasonable grounds for representing that the ship will be ready to load on or about the date mentioned, and implies that the ship shall proceed from wherever she happens to be at such time as will enable her, by proceeding with reasonable despatch, to arrive at the loading port by the expected date. In a case where a vessel was "expected ready to load about 15th/18th November", the judge held that this meant not earlier than the 15th nor later than the 18th though he was prepared to accept that the word "about" gave the shipowner two or three days' grace either way.

A typical time charter clause provides that should the vessel not be delivered by the date agreed the charterers are to have the option of cancelling and, further, if the vessel cannot be delivered by the cancelling date, the charterers, if required, are to declare within 48 hours after receiving notice thereof whether they will cancel or take delivery.

In a voyage charter the "cancelling date" is the date fixed by the C/P as the latest on which the ship must be ready to load. If the ship is not arrived and ready by that date, the charterer has the option of cancelling the C/P. If it appears probable that the ship cannot arrive before the cancelling date through circumstances beyond the shipowner's control, the master should at the first opportunity note a protest to that effect. The ship must continue the voyage to the loading port however late she may be, unless the contract has become frustrated, as the charterer is under no obligation to decide whether he will accept the ship or cancel the C/P until notice of readiness to load has been tendered to him. What a charterer will do in such circumstances usually depends on the trend of the freight market. If the market has risen since the vessel was first fixed he will find it to his advantage to maintain the contract. On the other hand, if freight rates have fallen, and he can charter another ship for prompt loading, he will probably decide to cancel. The master should keep the owners fully and promptly informed of all developments, especially where the charterer delays his decision unreasonably. Meanwhile, the owners will no doubt make efforts to have the cancelling date extended, even agreeing to accept a lower rate of freight, and will instruct the master accordingly.

Notice of Readiness. Under a voyage charter, before the charterer or shipper is under an obligation to commence loading, three conditions must be satisfied, viz.:—

    1. The ship must be an "arrived ship".

2. The ship must be in all respects ready to load.
3. Notice of readiness to load must be served on the charterer or his agent.

If the ship has merely been ordered to a named port, she is an "arrived ship" as soon as she has arrived within the limits of the port and is at the charterer's disposal and ready to load in a place where ships waiting for a berth usually lie, even though she is not yet in that part of the port where cargo of the kind contemplated is customarily loaded. Although the charterer has the right to nominate the loading berth, it is not necessary for the ship to be in that berth in order to claim that she is an "arrived ship". It is different, however, if C/P terms require the ship to proceed to "berth as ordered" or to a named berth. In that case she is not an arrived ship until she is in the berth.

For the ship to be "ready", her loading appliances, if they are to be used, must be ready, rigged and in good order; holds and other cargo compartments to be used must be clean, dry, dunnaged and completely ready to receive the cargo and, if shifting boards or other special appliances are needed, they must be in place. Any necessary permits to load and surveyors' certificates, if needed, must have been obtained and must be produced when serving notice.

The notice of readiness must be in writing and must be tendered during normal office hours. The master should prepare the notice in duplicate and insist on the charterer signing his acceptance on one copy which the master should retain as a receipt, and this should state the date and precise time of acceptance. If the weight or volume of cargo to be loaded is limited by the ship's deadweight or cubic capacity, as the case may be, the master should include in the notice a declaration of the maximum deadweight of cargo the ship will be able to lift in accordance with season, bunkering requirements, etc., or the maximum cubic capacity that will be at the charterer's disposal, bearing in mind that the C/P will in all probability provide that the charterer is to have the "full reach and burthen of the ship". It is never sufficient to tender notice stating that the ship will be ready at some stated future time. The charterer is not bound to accept a notice in such form. The ship must actually be ready at the time when notice is served.

When the charterer has accepted the notice of readiness, or at some stipulated time thereafter if the C/P so provides, the time for loading commences to count, although this may be varied by other C/P terms or by a custom of the port.

If the ship is to load at two or more ports, notice of readiness need be given only at the first loading port unless the C/P provides to the contrary. If no notice is given, but the charterer actually begins to load, the absence of notice is immaterial.

Lay Days. This expression describes the number of days allowed by a charter-party for loading and for discharging the cargo or, if so-called "reversible" lay days are provided for, for both processes. Lay days may be "fixed" or "indeterminate", although the latter would be very unusual nowadays. Where lay days are fixed, the C/P will either state the number directly or state it indirectly by quoting the average rate per day at which the vessel is to be loaded or discharged. For instance, a C/P may use the phrase "to load in 10 working days", whilst another may provide for a ship with 9500 tons of cargo "to discharge at 1000 tons per running day" thereby fixing the time allowed for the discharge at $9\frac{1}{2}$ days. Unless the C/P or an established custom of the port otherwise provides, every day of the week is a lay day whether work is normally done on any particular day or not, but in general practice it is usual to agree that certain days shall not count, and that makes it necessary to consider the meanings of the various terms in common use, which are as follows.

Days and Running Days. Both of these expressions mean consecutive calendar days counting from midnight to midnight and, unless contract or custom dictate otherwise, include Sundays and holidays whether work is actually done, or normally done at the port or not.

Sundays and Holidays Excepted. Where a C/P provides that Sundays and holidays are not to count as lay days, those days still do not count even if they have been used for working by agreement between the master and the charterer. However, if the agreement in the C/P is that Sundays and holidays are not to count *unless used*, then the position is different. The term "holidays" applies only to official public or local holidays, and not to time arbitrarily taken off by workmen. It does not include Saturday afternoons unless there is a legal provision to the contrary in the country where the ship is loading or discharging. If there is an intention that Saturday afternoons should not count as lay time, they should be specifically excepted in the C/P.

Working Days. Unless a custom of the port not inconsistent with the provisions of the C/P gives the expression a different meaning, a working day is a day on which work is normally done at the port concerned, and is a 24-hour day from midnight to midnight even if work does not continue throughout the whole period. Hence, when lay days are described as working days they exclude Sundays and officially recognised holidays.

There is a custom of the port of Iquique that so-called "surf days" on which loading and discharging are commercially impracticable do not count as working days even though they may be days on which work would normally be done in the absence of the impediment. The courts have given effect to this custom.

Some C/P's stipulate "time from noon on Saturday or the day previous to any holiday to 7 a.m. on Monday or the day after such holiday not to count as lay days, unless used". In the absence of such a condition Saturdays and Mondays count as full days. If a C/P provides "time to count on Mondays from 8 a.m." without adding the words, "unless used", a Monday will count only as $\frac{16}{24}$ of a lay day.

Working Day of 24 Hours. Each period of 24 hours in which work is normally done counts as one lay day, even though the 24 hours are spread over two or more calendar days. Where, for example, the ordinary working hours of the port are from 6 a.m. to 6 p.m., a working day of 24 hours would occupy two calendar days.

Working Day of 24 Consecutive Hours. This is a day of 24 hours during some part of which work is ordinarily done at the port. The expression has the same meaning as "working day".

Weather Working Day. A weather working day is a working day of 24 hours on which work is not prevented by bad weather, whether work is intended or not. When inclement weather prevents work from being done during only part of a working day (whether work is intended or not), how much of the day counts as laytime is decided by comparing the working time when loading or discharging is prevented with the actual time normally worked each day at the port. For example, if the working day is continuous for 24 hours and four hours are lost due to bad weather, then 20 hours will count as laytime used. But if the normal working day there is from 0600 to 1200 and 1300 to 1900, a total of 12 hours, and bad weather preventing work occurs from say 0400 to 1000 (whether work intended or not), the part from 0600 to 1000, a total of four hours or $\frac{4}{12}$ of available working time is lost. Hence $\frac{4}{12}$ of a weather working day is considered lost, which means $\frac{4}{12}$ of 24 hours equal to eight hours. Therefore 24—8 equal to sixteen hours of laytime is to count for that day. There is sometimes a custom at a port, with the object of avoiding disputes, to declare what time has been lost due to bad weather on a particular day. Generally, however, it is a question of fact, if work was done the time counts; if no work was done, or work could not have been done, the time does not count.

Weather Working Day of 24 Consecutive Hours. This is a working day where any time in which bad weather halts cargo operations, or would have if work was intended or contemplated, is not to count as laytime, whether the bad weather occurs in normal working time at the port or not. Therefore in the example quoted above, if weather working days of 24 consecutive hours had been allowed, the period from 0400 to 1000, a total of six hours would have been considered lost and 18 hours on that day would have counted as laytime used.

Working Day, Weather Permitting. For time to be lost with this type of day, loading or discharging must actually be interrupted or prevented by bad weather. If, after laytime starts to count, no work was intended or contemplated on a particular day because of shortage of cargo for example, but bad weather would have prevented work, the laytime for that day would still count as lay-time used. When loading or discharging is prevented, the time lost has to be proportionally adjusted as in the example for weather working days above.

Working Hatch. Sometimes a C/P has stated "Cargo to be loaded/discharged at the average rate of ...... tons per working hatch per day". In the case of a loading ship a working hatch is a hatch which is still not fully loaded; in a discharging ship one which is not yet empty. Obviously, as soon as a hatch ceases to be a "working hatch" the loading or discharging rate is automatically reduced.

In order to avoid complication in calculating the laytime allowed it is usual to take the capacity of the largest hold and divide it by the rate per day quoted to provide the number of laydays allowed. If the largest hold can be served by two gangs then the rate per day must be doubled before dividing it into the hold capacity.

Colliery Working Days. These are days on which the colliery normally works.

Reporting day. This is the day on which the master's notice of readiness is tendered to the charterer or consignee. If the work of loading or discharging starts immediately the reporting day will count as a lay day, unless the C/P or a binding custom of the port provides otherwise.

Indeterminate Lay Days. Lay days are said to be indeterminate when a C/P provides for a ship to be loaded or discharged "as customary", or "according to the custom of the port", or "with all despatch", or "as fast as steamer can receive/deliver". This is a most unsatisfactory arrangement as it would always be very difficult to determine whether a vessel has in fact loaded or discharged "as fast as she can".

Reversible Lay Days. A C/P may provide that a ship is to load and discharge a cargo at a given average rate per day, in which case lay days are said to be "reversible". Time lost at the loading port may be made up by a faster rate of discharge and, conversely, time gained at the loading port makes more time available for discharge. For instance, if a ship has 12,000 tons to load and discharge at 1000 tons per day, and the average rate of loading turns out to be only 800 tons per day, the rate of discharge would have to be increased to 1333 tons per day to avoid demurrage. This arrangement is common in the case of tanker charters and is frequently made in the case of other bulk cargoes. Where reversible lay days are agreed it is important that bills of lading should be endorsed to show the time used for loading, so that the consignees will be in no doubt as to the time available for discharging the cargo.

In some C/P's it is agreed that lay days shall be reversible at loading ports only, in which case time lost at the first loading port can be made up for by an increased rate of loading at subsequent ports, or time gained at the first port can be made available at other ports.

Most tanker charters provide for a fixed number of "running hours" to be available for loading and discharging. Running hours, like running days, imply that once the time begins to count it runs continuously apart from any stipulated exceptions.

If reversible lay days are agreed for loading and discharging, it follows that the settlement of demurrage or despatch money, as the case may be, cannot be effected until after the discharge of cargo is completed and the total time used in both loading and discharging has been computed.

The Right to Average Lay Days. Some C/P's give the charterer the "right to average the days allowed for loading and discharging". This not very clearly worded clause has given rise to dispute and a fairly recent court decision has indicated that it should be interpreted to mean that time used in loading and time used in discharging must be considered separately, and the one should be set off against the other. The correct method of drawing up time sheets in accordance with this ruling is shown in Chapter 18.

Surf Days. C/P's for Chile nitrates provide that surf days, *i.e.*, days on which loading operations in the roads cannot be carried on because of heavy swell, shall not count as lay days. This is in accord with the custom of the port of Iquique previously mentioned.

Coal Charters. C/Ps' for coal cargoes, particularly, introduce many variations in lay day arrangements. For example, the rate of loading may be fixed according to "colliery scale", say 344 hours for 7600 tons, 360 hours for 8000 tons, and so on. A C/P may require a ship to load (*a*) in colliery turn, (*b*) in regular turn, or (*c*) free of turn. Of these (*a*) implies that loading is to commence when the particular kind of coal to be loaded becomes available; (*b*) implies that the ship will take her turn in order of arrival with other ships, and that time will not count until the ship has berthed; (*c*) implies that lay days are to begin as soon as the vessel is arrived and ready and the master has served notice of readiness, whether a berth is available or not.

When Lay Days Commence. Unless the C/P or a custom provides differently, the time for loading or discharging begins to count as soon as notice of readiness is accepted by the charterer or consignee.

In general practice, however, it will usually be the case that the C/P does provide otherwise. A fairly common C/P term is that "notice is to be given during business hours, 9 a.m. to 5 p.m. Monday to Friday or 9 a.m. to 1 p.m. on Saturday, and lay days to begin 24 hours after notice of readiness is accepted". In tanker charters 6 hours after notice is accepted is more usual. If this is unqualified, time will commence to count at the moment when the notice matures, neither sooner nor later, irrespective of whether the actual work or loading or discharging has begun earlier or has not begun at all. In other cases the clause may be qualified by the additional words "unless commenced earlier". In that case, obviously, time counts from the maturing of the notice or when work begins, whichever happens first. If the notice matures on a day which is not a lay day, time does not begin to count until the customary time of commencing work at the port on the next following lay day. (If, for instance, notice is accepted at 10 a.m. on a Saturday, the lay days being working days, although such notice will have matured at 10 a.m. on the Sunday the lay time will not commence to count until 7 a.m., or whatever is the usual time of commencing work at the port, on Monday.)

Demurrage. If the charterer or consignee detains the ship beyond the agreed number of lay days or, where the lay days are indeterminate, detains her for an unreasonable time, he will be in breach of the charter-party so that the shipowner will be entitled to either "damages for detention" or "demurrage".

Unless the C/P makes some other specific provision, the shipowner will be able to recover all the damages resulting from the detention, and in this respect the charterer's or consignee's liability is unlimited.

However, the usual practice is for the charterer's liability to be expressly limited to an agreed sum in respect of each day and/or fraction of a day of the delay. Days during which the ship is delayed are referred to as "demurrage days", and the sum payable to the shipowner in respect of the delay is commonly known as "demurrage" but, strictly speaking, demurrage in the proper sense of the term does not arise unless the C/P expressly provides for an agreed number of demurrage days over and above the agreed lay days. Demurrage is then a sum named in the charter-party to be paid by the charterer as liquidated damages for delay beyond the lay days. A C/P might, for instance, provide "vessel to be loaded in 12 working days, and 10 running days at £1200 per day and *pro rata* for part of a day to be allowed for demurrage". In that case, as soon as the 12 working days have expired the vessel will come on to demurrage, and the charterer's liability will be limited to £1200 for each day of delay thereafter up to 10 days. No breach of contract is involved in the charterer making use of agreed demurrage days. If the ship is still further detained after the demurrage days have passed then, in respect of such extra detention, the liability of the charterer, who then is in breach of contract, will be unlimited. In this connection it is important to note that if the C/P provides that the ship is to have a lien on the cargo for demurrage, that does not imply that she automatically has a lien for extra detention as well; such a lien must be contracted for separately.

The charterer or shipper is obliged to supply the cargo in sufficient time for it to be stowed before the lay days expire, in default of which he will be liable for the delay caused, as the ship is not deemed to be completely loaded until the cargo is stowed.

Payment of Demurrage. C/P's generally specify the rate at which demurrage is to be paid when incurred, quoting so much per day, or so much per registered ton per day, and adding the words "and *pro rata* for part of a day". In some charters, however, demurrage may be made payable at a fixed sum per running hour. If the contract does not provide for a fraction of a day to be allowed for on a proportionate basis, the common law ruling would prevail. At common law, demurrage days are indivisible, meaning that a fraction of a day counts as a whole day. In practice, however, it is most unusual for the "*pro rata*" term to be omitted.

Unless there is a contrary term in the contract, the principle of "once on demurrage, always on demurrage" applies. That is to say that demurrage days are always running days, and that is so irrespective of the kind of lay days contracted for. Similarly, unless the contrary is expressly agreed, exception clauses do not apply when the ship is on demurrage. However, days which follow the lay days can count as demurrage days only when the ship remains at the charterer's disposal, and if the shipowner removes the ship from the charterer's disposal, say for bunkering or other purposes, demurrage cannot be claimed for any time while she is so removed. If a C/P provides that a ship is to load in a stated number of working days, Sundays and holidays excepted, and that demurrage is to be paid at a fixed sum "per like day", then demurrage would not be payable in respect of Sundays or holidays falling during the period of detention. Such an arrangement is rare, and unsatisfactory to the shipowner.

Demurrage is payable daily and should be collected daily (except where lay days are reversible), and if the ship is to be detained over a week-end, Sunday's demurrage should be collected on Saturday together with Saturday's.

Damages for Detention. If the lay days have expired and demurrage has not been provided for, or the time for loading or discharge has not been agreed and a reasonable time for these processes has expired, or the demurrage is to be paid for an agreed number of days and a further delay occurs, the shipowner is entitled to sue for "damages for detention". In the case of such a claim, the damages are unliquidated and therefore the Court must assess what loss has been suffered by the shipowner due to his ship being detained in port. As a rule, if a demurrage rate has been fixed, any damages for detention will be assessed at the same rate, but where a breach of some other term of the contract has also been caused, such as not loading a full cargo, it may be possible to recover any additional damage due to such breach.

Cesser Clause. Under a voyage charter it often occurs that the charterer is not the shipper of the cargo but is a person who transfers that right to someone else. In such case the charterer, as soon as his profit is assured, will have no further interest in the ship and voyage and will be quite satisfied to leave the work of carrying and delivering the cargo to the ship owner on behalf of whom the master will have signed the bills of lading which, at this stage, constitute the contract of carriage. In order to let the charterer out, it is customary for the C/P to contain what is known as a "cesser clause", of which the following is a typical example—"The Charterers' liability shall cease as soon as the Cargo is shipped, and the advance of Freight, Deadfreight and Demurrage in loading (if any) are paid, the Owners having a lien on the Cargo for Freight, Demurrage and Average".

If the charterer refuses to pay demurrage incurred at the loading port, the master should note a protest and endorse the bills of lading with the amount due and remaining unpaid so that, at the discharging port, the lien can be enforced. If, however, a C/P containing a cesser clause also has a clause inserted to the effect that the master is to sign "clean" bills of lading, endorsement of unpaid demurrage could not be made. In that event the master should attempt to obtain a letter of guarantee from the charterer, countersigned by a bank, for payment of outstanding demurrage. If unsuccessful, he should then note a protest and inform the shipowner without delay. The shipowner will then have a right of action to recover the amount from the original charterer as the Court will, if necessary, set aside the cesser clause on the grounds that it can operate only to the extent that the shipowner's right of lien is preserved. There would, of course, be a resort to arbitration if the C/P so provides.

Despatch Money. Provided the C/P is claused to that effect, the shipowner becomes liable to pay despatch money to the charterer or receiver when the loading or discharging process is completed before the lay days have expired. If the charterer undertakes to give reasonable despatch and incurs extra expenditure in order to do so, such compensation is reasonable, but cases have occurred where the agreed rate of loading or discharging has been put at such a low figure that the charterer, without any special effort or expenditure, has succeeded easily in despatching the ship well within the period of the lay days, so that despatch money has been tantamount to a reduction in the freight rate.

Demurrage and despatch are sometimes dealt with in the same clause in the C/P; in other cases the despatch clause is separate from the demurrage clause. In either case the question of whether despatch money is payable in respect of all time saved to the ship, or merely for lay days that have not been used, is an important one to be determined by the particular form of words used. Where the C/P states that despatch money is to be paid "for all time saved" there is no doubt that the intention is that it must be paid in respect of Sundays and holidays saved as well as lay days saved. On the other hand, where despatch money is to be paid "for all laytime saved", this means it is payable only for lay days saved. Where the phrase "for all time saved in loading" has been used, and the meaning of this has been disputed, it has been ruled that despatch money is due only for lay days saved.

As with demurrage, it is usual to contract for despatch money to be paid at a fixed rate per day and *pro rata* for part of a day. If not so contracted for, the common law ruling would prevail whereby despatch money can be claimed only in respect of "clear" days saved. By clear day is meant any period of 24 consecutive hours. Hence, from 3 p.m. Monday to 3 p.m. Thursday of the same week constitutes three clear days. Sometimes the rate at which despatch money is to be paid is stated directly (*e.g.*, £100 per day and *pro rata*), or it may be related to the demurrage rate. It is fairly common for despatch money to be payable "at half the demurrage rate". Tanker charters either do not contain a despatch clause, or stipulate "No despatch money payable".

Unlike demurrage, despatch money is payable in a lump sum.

Port of Call. In spite of modern facilities for communicating with the master of a ship by radio it is still not unknown for a C/P to stipulate that a chartered ship shall, after loading, proceed to some named port "for orders". The C/P will have provided that the cargo is to be discharged at one or more safe ports within a named range, and at the time of sailing from the loading port the merchant shipper will not have decided which one the vessel is to proceed to. Unless the contrary has been agreed to, the master is not bound to inform the charterer of the ship's arrival at the port of call, but the ship must remain there for a reasonable time to receive orders, or for such time as may be specified in the C/P. If at the end of that reasonable or agreed time no orders are forthcoming, the master will be justified in proceeding to one of the several alternative ports of discharge named in the C/P and discharging the cargo there. The master should, of course, keep in touch with the shipowner, and carry out any instructions the owner may send him.

Deadfreight. This term is applied to the sum payable to the shipowner when the charterer has failed to load "a full and complete cargo" in accordance with the provisions of the contract. The rate per ton which should be, and usually is, stated in the C/P may or may not be the same as the rate for cargo that has been shipped. A lien on shipped cargo for deadfreight must be specially contracted for. (See Chapter 2.)

Where a ship has been fixed to carry, say, "8,000 tons, 5% more or less at steamer's option", the charterer will not have fulfilled his obligation by merely supplying 7,600 tons. He must ship more if the vessel can take more, but he is not obliged to supply more than 8,400 tons whether the ship can lift more than that quantity or not. If the master has declared in writing at the time of serving notice of readiness that the ship could take, say, 8,300 tons and the charterer supplied only 8,100 tons, he would be liable for deadfreight on 200 tons short-shipped.

There is a legal ruling that a charterer who is liable for dead-freight may deduct from it any additional expense that the ship-owner would have incurred if a full cargo had been loaded. In the case quoted, for example, the shipowner would save the stevedoring costs of loading and discharging an extra 200 tons, and there may be other savings. It is a matter of principle that the shipowner should not be better off as a result of carrying a part cargo than he would have been had he carried a full one.

It has been ruled that there is an implied term in any C/P also to the effect that, if the charterer fails to load a full cargo, the shipowner may load a substitute cargo provided that by doing so he is acting reasonably. The test of reasonableness is whether the shipowner's action in so doing will mitigate the damages to which the charterer has made himself liable. (See Chapter 2 on the duty of an injured party to minimise his loss.) It must also be implied that the ship is entitled, reasonably, to delay the charter voyage in order to obtain and load the substitute cargo. Calling at another port for this purpose would be deemed a reasonable deviation so long as the port chosen is on the route of the charter voyage.

Charterer's Agent. A C/P may contain a "consignment clause" consigning the ship to the charterer's agents at the port of loading and/or the port of discharge. Such agents automatically become the ship's agents when the ship arrives at the port and, in accordance with the law of agency, the shipowner as principal will be responsible for their acts on his behalf. Further mention is made of this in the section on Agency in Chapter 2.

Procedure where Charterer has no Cargo. If on arrival at the loading port it transpires that the charterer has no cargo ready for the vessel, the master should communicate the fact to the owners without delay. Without waiting for owners' instructions, however, the master should serve the usual notice of readiness on the charterer, bearing in mind that the latter's breach in failing to load is not complete until the lay days have expired. If, when that time comes, there is still no cargo forthcoming the master should note a protest, stating therein that he has complied with all the terms of the charterparty on the shipowner's behalf. Meanwhile the owners will probably try to effect another charter at the same or a nearby port, and will instruct the master accordingly. The remedy against the original charterer will lie in the deadfreight clause, if the C/P contains one, or in the penalty clause.

A typical penalty clause reads "The penalty for non-performance of this agreement shall be proved damages not exceeding the estimated amount of freight". This can be availed of by either party in the event of non-fulfilment of the contract by the other.

Charterparty Laytime Definitions 1980. In December 1980, the Baltic and International Maritime Conference (BIMCO), the Comite Maritime International (CMI), the Federation of National Associations of Ship Brokers and Agents (FONASBA) and the General Council of British Shipping (GCBS) after consultation with other shipping interests and with cargo interests sponsored the publication of "The Charterparty Laytime Definitions 1980" for voluntary adoption in charterparties by shipowners and charterers. In a joint announcement these organisations pointed out that over the years there have been an increasing number of disputes over the meaning of words and phrases used in charterparties and that very often these disputes have given rise to different interpretations of the same word or phrase within and between different jurisdictions. This has meant that the charterparty, a document of international character, has become subject to uncertainty, lack of clarity and lack of uniformity. It is the view of the sponsoring organisations that the availability to the parties at the time of negotiation of a list of definitions for voluntary adoption will limit and therefore reduce the scope for dispute.

If a shipowner or charterer wish to incorporate some or all of the Definitions, they may do so by attaching them to the charterparty after deleting any definitions which they do not want to apply and then inserting an incorporation clause in the charterparty itself such as:—

"The 'CHARTERPARTY LAYTIME DEFINITIONS 1980'
as attached are incorporated into this charterparty."

1. **Port**—means an area within which ships are loaded with and/ or discharged of cargo and includes the usual places where ships wait for their turn or are ordered or obliged to wait for their turn no matter the distance from that area.

If the word **Port** is not used, but the port is (or is to be) identified by its name, this definition shall still apply.

2. **Safe Port**—means a port which, during the relevant period of time, the ship can reach, enter, remain at and depart from without,

in the absence of some abnormal occurrence, being exposed to danger which cannot be avoided by good navigation and seamanship.

3. **Berth**—means the specific place where the ship is to load and/or discharge.

If the word **Berth** is not used, but the specific place is (or is to be) identified by its name, this definition shall still apply.

4. **Safe Berth**—means a berth which, during the relevant period of time, the ship can reach, remain at and depart from without, in the absence of some abnormal occurrence, being exposed to danger which cannot be avoided by good navigation and seamanship.

5. **Reachable on Arrival** or **Always Accessible**—means that the charterer undertakes that when the ship arrives at the port there will be a loading/discharging berth for her to which she can proceed without delay.

6. **Laytime**—means the period of time agreed between the parties during which the owner will make and keep the ship available for loading/discharging without payment additional to the freight.

7. **Customary Despatch**—means that the charterer must load and/or discharge as fast as is possible in the circumstances prevailing at the time of loading or discharging.

8. **Per Hatch per Day**—means that laytime is to be calculated by multiplying the agreed daily rate per hatch of loading/discharging the cargo by the number of the ship's hatches and dividing the quantity of cargo by the resulting sum. Thus:

$$\text{Laytime} = \frac{\text{Quantity of Cargo}}{\text{Daily Rate} \times \text{Number of Hatches}} = \text{Days}.$$

A hatch that is capable of being worked by two gangs simultaneously shall be counted as two hatches.

9. **Per Working Hatch per Day** or **Per Workable Hatch per Day**—means that laytime is to be calculated by dividing the quantity of cargo in the hold with the largest quantity by the result of multiplying the agreed daily rate per working or workable hatch by the number of hatches serving that hold. Thus:

$$\text{Laytime} = \frac{\text{Largest Quantity in one hold}}{\text{Daily rate per hatch} \times \text{Number of Hatches serving that hold}} = \text{Days}.$$

A hatch that is capable of being worked by two gangs simultaneously shall be counted as two hatches.

10. **As Fast as the Vessel can Receive/Deliver**—means that the laytime is a period of time to be calculated by reference to the maximum rate at which the ship in full working order is capable of loading/discharging the cargo.

11. **Day**—means a continuous period of 24 hours which, unless the context otherwise requires, runs from midnight to midnight.

12. **Clear Day** or **Clear Days**—means that the day on which the notice is given and the day on which the notice expires are not included in the notice period.

13. **Holiday**—means a day of the week or part(s) thereof on which cargo work on the ship would normally take place but is suspended at the place of loading/discharging by reason of:

   (i) the local law; or

   (ii) the local practice.

14. **Working Days**—means days or part(s) thereof which are not expressly excluded from laytime by the charterparty and which are not holidays.

15. **Running Days** or **Consecutive Days**—means days which follow one immediately after the other.

16. **Weather Working Day**—means a working day or part of a working day during which it is or, if the vessel is still waiting for her turn, it would be possible to load/discharge the cargo without interference due to the weather. If such interference occurs (or would have occurred if work had been in progress), there shall be excluded from the laytime a period calculated by reference to the ratio which the duration of the interference bears to the time which would have or could have been worked but for the interference.

17. **Weather Working Day of 24 Consecutive Hours**—means a working day or part of a working day of 24 hours during which it is or, if the ship is still waiting for her turn, it would be possible to load/discharge the cargo without interference due to the weather. If such interference occurs (or would have occurred if work had been in progress) there shall be excluded from the laytime the period during which the weather interfered or would have interfered with the work.

18. **Weather Permitting**—means that time during which weather prevents working shall not count as laytime.

19. **Excepted**—means that the specified days do not count as laytime even if loading or discharging is done on them.

20. **Unless Used**—means that if work is carried out during the excepted days the actual hours of work only count as laytime.

21. **To Average**—means that separate calculations are to be made for loading and discharging and any time saved in one operation is to be set against any excess time used in the other.

22. **Reversible**—means an option given to the charterer to add together the time allowed for loading and discharging. Where the option is exercised the effect is the same as a total time being specified to cover both operations.

23. **Notice of Readiness**—means notice to the charterer, shipper, receiver or other person as required by the charter that the ship has arrived at the port or berth as the case may be and is ready to load/discharge.

24. **In Writing**—means, in relation to a notice of readiness, a notice visibly expressed in any mode of reproducing words and includes cable, telegram and telex.

25. Time Lost Waiting for Berth to Count as Loading/Discharging Time or As Laytime—means that if the main reason why a notice of readiness cannot be given is that there is no loading/discharging berth available to the ship the laytime will commence to run when the ship starts to wait for a berth and will continue to run, unless previously exhausted, until the ship stops waiting. The laytime exceptions apply to the waiting time as if the ship was at the loading/discharging berth provided the ship is not already on demurrage. When the waiting time ends time ceases to count and restarts when the ship reaches the loading/discharging berth subject to the giving of a notice of readiness if one is required by the charterparty and to any notice time if provided for in the charterparty, unless the ship is by then on demurrage.

26. Whether In Berth or Not or Berth No Berth—means that if the location named for loading/discharging is a berth and if the berth is not immediately accessible to the ship a notice of readiness can be given when the ship has arrived at the port in which the berth is situated.

27. Demurrage—means the money payable to the owner for delay for which the owner is not responsible in loading and/or discharging after the laytime has expired.

28. On Demurrage—means that the laytime has expired. Unless the charterparty expressly provides to the contrary the time on demurrage will not be subject to the laytime exceptions.

29. Despatch Money or Despatch—means the money payable by the owner if the ship completes loading or discharging before the laytime has expired.

30. All Time Saved—means the time saved to the ship from the completion of loading/discharging to the expiry of the laytime including periods excepted from the laytime.

31. All Working Time Saved or All Laytime Saved—means the time saved to the ship from the completion of loading/discharging to the expiry of the laytime excluding any notice time and periods excepted from the laytime.

FREIGHT

Freight is the remuneration to which the carrier of goods by sea is entitled on the performance of his contractual obligations or otherwise, depending on the terms of the contract. According to the nature of the goods carried and/or the custom of the trade, freight may be payable at an agreed rate per ton deadweight, per measurement ton, per freight ton or other unit, or on an *ad valorem* basis. Heavy goods of relatively small bulk are normally charged for on a deadweight basis, *i.e.*, at so much per long ton of 2,240 lbs., per short ton of 2,000 lb., or per metric ton of 1,000 kg. By contrast, light bulky goods are charged for on a lightweight or measurement basis, *i.e.*, at so much per "ton" of 40 cubic feet. In some trades a freight unit may be, say, a "ton" of 50 cu. ft. For sawn timber the customary freight unit is the Petrograd Standard of 165 cu. ft. and for pulpwood or pit props the Piled Fathom of 216 cu. ft.

Primarily the liability to pay freight rests on the shipper of the goods, but by the terms of the contract the shipper's liability may be transferred to the person who takes delivery of the cargo under a B/L. Even so, the liability of a charterer to pay freight due under a C/P continues to attach to him in spite of the liability of B/L holders, unless he has been freed by a cesser clause or similar device.

If cargo is landed at some place short of its proper destination no freight can be claimed, but if the consignee agrees to accept goods at an intermediate port he will be liable for a *pro rata* freight. The shipowner can, of course, earn the full freight by transhipping or forwarding the goods to the agreed place of discharge.

Freight on Damaged Goods is due in full but will be subject to a counterclaim for damages unless the carrier is protected by exceptions clauses in the contract of affreightment or by common law exceptions. However, if goods are so badly damaged that they have ceased to be goods of the kind shipped then no freight can be claimed.

Back Freight can be claimed if goods cannot be discharged at the port of destination owing to circumstances beyond the control of the owner or master and, in consequence, have to be returned to the original port of shipment. It does not follow that it is always in the shipowner's best interests to enforce this right.

Lump Sum Freight. A ship may be chartered on a lump sum basis implying that a fixed amount of freight is payable by the charterer regardless of whether a full cargo is shipped or not. So long as some cargo is by some means delivered at the proper destination, the lump sum is payable in full, though it may be subject to counterclaim where goods have been stolen, jettisoned, or lost and the shipowner is not protected by "exceptions". Charters of this kind are usually for mixed cargoes such as "timber and generals". Liner owners occasionally resort to chartering a tramp on a lump sum basis when they are temporarily short of space to meet their berth commitments.

Advance Freight and Charges thereon. At one time it was common for a voyage C/P to contain a freight clause of which the following is typical. "Freight to be paid at £... per ton, ...% in advance at the port of loading to supply master with cash for steamer's disbursements less ...% for insurance and ...% interest; the balance to be paid at the port of discharge concurrently with discharge, sufficient in cash to meet steamer's disbursements and the remainder in good and approved 3 months Bills of Exchange on London".

In law no freight is considered to be earned until the cargo is finally delivered at its proper destination, but freight which is paid in advance is not recoverable from the shipowner in the event of the ship being lost. Therefore, at the loading port, as the freight is not yet earned, the advance ranks as a loan on which interest is payable. Also, as the money is advanced by the shipper at the risk of losing it should ship and cargo be lost, the shipper has an insurable interest in the advance. He is the proper person to effect the insurance and, in practice, will do so. But as the money is advanced to the ship for the ship's convenience, the shipowner will be charged with the cost of the insurance. It is usual for both of these charges to be levied by the shipper deducting a certain percentage from the gross amount of the advance. For instance, out of a total advance of £1,000, if the insurance and interest charges are fixed at 2½ per cent. and 1½ per cent., respectively, the shipper would retain £40. Sometimes the clause reads "less ...% for insurance and interest", giving no indication of how the total charge is divided.

If, as has sometimes occurred, the C/P merely provides that "the master is to be supplied with cash for disbursements at the loading port", without any specific mention of an advance of freight, the loan will be repayable in any case, even if the ship is lost, so that the shipowner will be the proper person to insure the money. Cases have been decided, when there has been doubt whether the advance was intended to be part payment of freight or merely an ordinary loan, on the fact of who it was who insured the money.

The object of paying the balance of the chartered freight concurrently with discharge is to keep sufficient cargo in the ship's possession to be able to enforce lien if necessary. In some cases freight has been collected twice daily during discharge, or even hourly, but a more common arrangement nowadays is for, say, 90 per cent. of the balance to be paid before discharge begins and final settlement made on the last day of discharge. Obviously, if freight is payable on out-turn weight, the exact amount cannot be determined until discharge is completed.

Where part of the balance of freight is paid in the form of bills of exchange, these will be drawn by the consignee on his London banker or agent in favour of the shipowner and will be delivered to the master or agent of the ship. They will be foreign bills in sets of two or three, all of the same tenor and date, and payable at some stated period "after sight". The master or agent should remit them to the shipowner by various routes, arranging for at least one part of each set to arrive as soon as possible.

When part of the balance of freight has been paid in cash in circumstances where the shipowner has had no agent at the discharging port, it has often been convenient for the master to remit the amount to the shipowner by going through the process known as "buying a bill of exchange". This involves depositing the cash at a bank and requesting the bank, on the strength of such credit, to draw its own bills on London in favour of the shipowner. Such bills should be made payable "on demand" and remitted to the owner as described above.

In present-day circumstances the somewhat cumbersome method of paying freight described in the preceding paragraphs is probably very rarely used, and a modern voyage C/P freight clause might read "The freight to be paid in...............on signing Bills of Lading, discountless and non-returnable, ship and/or cargo lost or not lost." Another fairly common arrangement is for the freight to be due within an agreed period of time "after final sailing". This means when the ship has finally departed from the commercial limits of the loading port in all respects ready to proceed on the contract voyage and with no intention of returning.

Distance Freight. In certain circumstances when it is impossible for the cargo to be discharged at the agreed port of discharge, delivery may be given at some other port which is the nearest safe port. If the distance to such safe port is substantially in excess of the distance to the port originally contemplated, extra freight, known as "distance freight," may become payable by the terms of the C/P. (See reference to the General Ice Clause.)

Distress Freight. At times when the chartering market is abnormally quiet, the owners of a tramp ship which might otherwise have to be laid up may, having been promised a tempting "starting parcel", decide to place the ship on the berth as a general ship and advertise accordingly. If they subsequently find difficulty in obtaining completion cargo at normal or near normal rates, they may in preference to despatching the ship with excessive vacant space resort to booking shipments at rates very far below those generally prevailing. Such low rates are referred to as "distress rates".

Bill of Lading Freight, or Aggregate B/L Freight. This is the freight due to the ship by the terms of the Bills of Lading as distinct from the freight due in accordance with the terms of the charter party. Where the charterer has himself supplied a full cargo, the balance of freight due from the B/L holders together with any advance freight paid by the shipper at the loading port should amount to the same as the chartered freight. But it may happen that the charterer has been unable to fill the ship and, to avoid being in breach of the C/P, has in accordance with the terms of that contract sublet the remaining space in the ship to other shippers at freight rates different from those stipulated in the C/P. If such rates are lower than the C/P rate, the master or ship's agent should collect the difference from the charterer before the B's/L are signed. Otherwise there may be difficulty in recovering it owing to the operation of the Cesser Clause, and when the ship reaches the port of discharge consignees will be liable only for the B/L freight and will not be bound by C/P terms unless the B's/L have been endorsed clearly to that effect. Some C/P's have a clause providing that if the freight on the substitute cargo is payable at a rate higher than the chartered rate, the difference is to be shared between the shipowner and the charterer in some agreed proportion (usually 50-50). In the absence of such a clause the excess freight could be claimed by the charterer.

Some C/P's contain a clause reading "The Captain to sign clean Bills of Lading for his cargo, also for portions of cargo shipped (if required to do so) at any rate of freight without prejudice to this charter, but not at lower than chartered rates, unless the difference is paid to him in cash before signing Bills of Lading". The phrase "without prejudice to this charter" implies that should the B's/L contain terms inconsistent with those of the C/P the master, by signing such bills, does not abandon the shipowner's rights under the C/P. Moreover, such rights are not affected by the master's obligation to sign "clean" bills.

Variation in Weight or Measurement, and Weighing Charges. Unless there is a special agreement to the contrary, freight is payable only on the quantity of cargo shipped, carried and delivered. Owing to expansion or contraction, increase or decrease of moisture content, or other factors, the weight or measurement of goods delivered may differ from the weight or measurement shipped. The general rule in such a case is that freight is payable only on the lesser quantity, whether that is the quantity shipped or the quantity delivered.

In one form of C/P for phosphate cargoes the following provision is made. "No freight to be payable on any excess moisture at the discharging port as compared with the loading port. A sample taken from the whole cargo is to be placed in two sealed bottles, one for the Captain and one to be retained by shippers for analysis. The Captain to have the option of having his analysed at the discharging port .... and the mean of the two results to be taken as final".

If by the contract freight is payable "on quantity delivered", the shipowner is responsible for the cost of weighing or measuring. Otherwise weighing charges must be borne by whichever party requires the cargo to be weighed, unless there is an agreement or binding custom to the contrary.

Where a C/P provides that freight is payable "at receiver's option on quantity delivered or on B/L quantity less 2% in lieu of weighing" such option need not be exercised until the time for payment arrives. If the receiver opts not to weigh, the 2 per cent. deduction is based on the whole chartered freight, not merely on the balance due at the discharging port.

If the receiver insists on having the cargo weighed or measured and the ship employs a check-weigher or measurer, the latter will be at the ship's expense.

In some ports there is a custom that weighing charges are to be shared equally by the ship and consignees.

DISCHARGE OF VOYAGE CHARTER CARGO

Although it may be expedient to do so, the master is not legally bound to notify the consignees of the ship's arrival at the discharging port, but a public announcement must be made by entering the ship at the Custom House or Harbour Office. Also a C/P term requiring notice of readiness to be tendered must be complied with.

If the ship has a general cargo she may discharge at any place within the commercial area of the port convenient to the consignees of the majority of the cargo. If not a general cargo, the proper place of discharge is usually that selected by the charterer, his agent, or the receiver.

Where a bulk cargo is to be discharged at two or more ports it is usual for the C/P to provide that "the vessel is to be left in seaworthy trim between ports of discharge". If the master is not informed of the intention to discharge at more than one port at the time of loading and, as a result, additional expenditure has to be incurred to comply with the "safe trim" requirement, that expense will be recoverable from the charterer.

Shifting from one berth to another in the same port of discharge, even when the berths are in different docks, does not amount to discharge at two ports, and the cost of shifting is for the shipowner's account.

Cargo must be discharged in the manner required by port regulations and customs unless the C/P or B/L stipulates a particular method. The contract may give the receiver the right to select one of several alternative methods, but if it does not, the choice lies with the shipowner subject to the receiver's right to require the least expensive method to be used. The shipowner may employ an alternative method if the one selected by the receiver becomes impossible.

If the contract provides that cargo is to be "taken from alongside", that means that the consignee must provide appliances to take delivery from the ship's tackles or from the quay at the ship's side. Where the shipowner is by contract entitled to require delivery in the river, the consignee has a duty to provide lighters to take the cargo from alongside. If that method is used when the shipowner is not so entitled, the "exceptions" in the contract will not apply while the goods are on their way from ship to shore. However, where the contract reserves "liberty to tranship", contractual exceptions will apply while the goods are in lighters.

The consignee must take steps to secure a berth and proceed with the discharge without unreasonable delay. Generally, however, lay time for discharge is fixed and commences from the moment when the vessel becomes an "arrived ship", and if delay occurs the shipowner has a remedy in the demurrage clause except where the consignee is protected by the exceptions clause.

As goods which have been shipped under a B/L must be delivered in accordance with B/L terms, it is important that the master should have a "Captain's copy" of every B/L. The question of the proper person to whom the master is entitled to give delivery is extremely important, and this is discussed further on in this Chapter in the section on Bills of Landing.

It is usual for a voyage-chartered ship to be ordered to discharge at some named port "or so near thereto as she can safely get". This means that the ship must discharge at a place sufficiently near to the named place which must be the nearest practical port or place of discharge *and* be within the so-called "ambit" of the named port in the sense of being in an area or zone within a range of proximity not beyond the reasonable contemplation of the parties as fair and reasonable men in the light of all the circumstances of the adventure. Only in an exceptional case could a port 250 miles from the named port be considered as within its "ambit" in this sense. In a particular case a vessel was chartered to carry cement from Sika to Saigon and discharge part of her cargo there and the remainder at Pnom Penh, some 250 miles farther on involving the navigation of two rivers. The pilotage authority refused to accept the ship for the passage to Pnom Penh on the grounds that she was not adequately powered to negotiate the river in its then state and conditions would not be suitable for the ship to reach Pnom Penh until some five months had elapsed. In the event the entire cargo was discharged at Saigon. In the ensuing dispute arbitrators found that the "ambit" of Pnom Penh included Saigon and that the discharge of her Pnom Penh cargo there was reasonable from a commercial point of view, but they also found that they were bound by authority to hold that the vessel was obliged to wait the five months at Saigon. The Court of Appeal, however, held that Saigon ought to be treated as a good port of discharge for the Pnom Penh cargo within the meaning of the words "so near thereto as she may safely get".

MISCELLANEOUS VOYAGE CHARTER-PARTY CLAUSES AND PHRASES, AND OTHER CHARTERING TERMS

From what has been said earlier in this Chapter it will be evident that every voyage C/P will indicate the names of the contracting parties or their agents, the kind and quantity of cargo to be carried, the loading and discharging ports, agreements as to lay days, demurrage and despatch, the rate of freight and method of payment. Other clauses in common use, and which have not been previously explained, are included in the summary which follows.

Address Commission. Some C/P's provide that a commission of 2 per cent. (or thereabouts) of the freight shall be paid to the charterers on signing bills of lading. As the charterers do not perform any particular services in return for this so-called "address commission", it amounts virtually to a reduction in the freight rate. Where the ship has no such liability she is said to be "free of address". One form of commission clause reads "The Vessel to be free of address at Port of Discharge, but to pay the usual Commission of two per cent. on the amount of freight on signing Bills of Lading". This address commission should not be confused with agency fees or brokerage which are payable in return for specific services rendered.

Always Afloat. A clause frequently inserted is: "Ship to proceed to .... and there load, always afloat, in the customary manner, ... a full and complete cargo of ...., and being so loaded, shall therewith proceed with all possible despatch (or with all reasonable despatch) to .... or so near thereunto as she can safely get, and there deliver her cargo alongside ...., always afloat, etc."

This relieves the ship of any obligation to wait until the tide is suitable for her to proceed to her appointed berth. The place named must be suitable in any tide, and if it is not suitable at the time when the ship arrives she is entitled to load or discharge at the nearest safe place. With respect to some ports where the nature of the bottom is suitable there may be a special agreement that the ship may lie aground at low water.

Arbitration Clause. With the object of avoiding expensive litigation, many C/P's contain a clause requiring that any disputes arising under the contract shall be referred to arbitration. (See Chapter 2 for further details.)

Berth Terms. Where shipments are made on a chartered ship on "berth terms" or "liner terms" the principal terms of the C/P will correspond with customary terms for shipment of the commodity concerned by regular liner. Special conditions relating to rates of loading or discharging are, however, not excluded. Loading and discharging expenses under berth terms will be for the account of the shipowner. An example of a loading clause which introduces this feature reads "Steamer to be loaded according to berth terms, with customary berth despatch, and if detained longer than five days, Sundays and holidays excepted, Charterers to pay demurrage at the rate of 2p British Sterling or its equivalent per net register ton per day, or *pro rata*, payable day by day, provided such detention shall occur by default of Charterers or their agents."

Bill of Lading Clause. This clause, to which reference has already been made, varies considerably from one C/P form to another. Sometimes clean bills are demanded, sometimes not. Frequently, a specimen of the B/L form to be used is printed in the C/P which then requires "The Master to sign Bills of Lading in the form endorsed hereon ....".

Both to Blame Collision Clause. Great Britain and practically all other maritime countries with the exception of the United States of America have ratified and given legal effect to the Brussels Collision Convention, 1910, whereby, when two colliding vessels are both held to blame, their liabilities are in proportion to their respective degrees of fault. Until 19 May 1975, in American law, when both ships were at fault, they were held to be equally at fault. On that date the U.S. Supreme Court overturned the previous rule and held:— "that when two or more parties have contributed by their fault to cause property damage in a maritime collision or stranding, liability for such damage is to be allocated among the parties proportionately to the comparative degree of their fault, and that liability for such damage is to be allocated equally only when the parties are equally at fault or when it is not possible fairly to measure the comparative degree of their fault." The Supreme Court's decision may not affect the rule that under American jurisdiction, cargo interests are entitled to recover 100 per cent of their losses from the non-carrying ship in spite of the fact that each ship is only partly to blame. The owners of the non-carrying ship, in turn, are entitled to recover from the owners of the carrying ship their proportion of the amount they have been called upon to pay to the owners of the cargo in the other vessel. The object of the "Both to blame collision clause" is to enable the owners of the carrying ship to recover the amount of the damage indirectly paid to their shippers.

The clause reads "If the ship comes into collision with another ship as a result of the negligence of the other ship and/or the negligence of any ship or ships other than or in addition to the colliding ship and any act, neglect or default of the Master, Mariner, Pilot or servants of the carrier in the navigation or in the management of the ship the owners of the goods carried hereunder will indemnify the carrier against all loss or liability to the non-carrying ship and/or any other ship or ships as aforesaid of her or their owners in so far as such loss or liability represents loss of or damage to or any claim whatsoever of the owners of the said goods paid or payable by the non-carrying ship and/or any other ship or ships as aforesaid or her or their owners to the owners of the said goods and set off recouped or recovered by the non-carrying ship and/or any other ship or ships as aforesaid or her or their owners as part of their claim against the carrying ship or carrier."

For a number of years it has been a recommendation of the General Council of British Shipping that the above clause should be inserted in all B's/L and charter-parties, and this recommendation still stands in spite of the fact that the Supreme Court in the United States declared the clause invalid and contrary to American public policy which prohibits a "common carrier" from contracting out of his liability for his own negligence or that of his servants. There appear to be two reasons for this, as follows:—

1. Even where collision liability has been decided in the United States there may be claims for indemnity under the clause in countries other than the United States, and it is considered unlikely that the clause would be held to be unenforceable and contrary to public policy in such countries.

2. Where the owner of the carrying ship is a "private carrier" in the sense that the ship is chartered to a single charterer, owner and charterer are considered to have contracted on equal terms, and if they have both agreed to the inclusion of the clause in the C/P and in B's/L issued pursuant thereto; the clause may be held to be enforceable even in the United States.

The example which follows gives a simple illustration of the effect the clause is intended to have, and for this purpose it has been assumed that both ships have been found equally to blame.

The ship "Carrier" collides with the ship "Non-carrier", and both are held 50 per cent. to blame by the American courts. Suppose the damage to the cargo in "Carrier" amounts to £12,000 and the damage to the ship "Non-carrier" herself amounts to £6,000.

The owners of the cargo in "Carrier" have no claims for damages from the owner of that ship, who is relieved from liability "for loss or damage arising from errors or faults in the navigation or management of the ship" by the terms of the B's/L.

In American law the owners of "Carrier's" cargo can claim their full £12,000 loss from the owners of "Non-carrier". In turn, those owners will include in their claim against the owners of "Carrier" 50 per cent. of that amount, namely £6,000. Over and above that they will claim £3,000 as 50 per cent. of the damage to their own ship. Thus, "Non-carrier's" total claim against "Carrier" will amount to £9,000. Finally, if the Both to Blame Collision Clause proves to be effective, the owners of "Carrier" will be indemnified by the owners of the cargo carried therein to the extent of £6,000 representing that part of the damages paid to "Non-carrier" relating to the goods carried by "Carrier".

In charter-parties which formerly contained the Both to Blame Collision Clause in the form reproduced above the word "New" has now been added, and bills of lading issued pursuant to such charter-parties are claused as shown below.

New Both to Blame Collision Clause. If the liability for any collision in which the vessel is involved while performing this Bill of Lading falls to be determined in accordance with the laws of the United States of America, the following clause shall apply:—

"If the ship comes into collision with another ship as a result of the negligence of the other ship and any act, neglect or default of the master, mariner, pilot or the servants of the Carrier in the navigation or in the management of the ship, the owners of the goods carried here-under will indemnify the Carrier against all loss or liability to the other or non-carrying ship or her owners in so far as such loss or liability represents loss of, or damage to, or any claim whatsoever of the owners of the said goods, paid or payable by the other or non-carrying ship or her owners to the owners of said goods and set off, recouped or recovered by the other or non-carrying ship or her owners as part of their claim against the carrying ship or Carrier.'

The foregoing provisions shall also apply where the owners, operators, or those in charge of any ship or ships or objects other than, or in addition to, the colliding ships or objects are at fault in respect to a collision or contact.

Calling for Orders. In certain grain charters there is a clause to the effect that "Orders for the first discharging port, unless given when signing bills of lading, to be given at .... within 12 running hours of arrival, or demurrage to accrue, but charterers to have the right to order the vessel to Falmouth for final orders to discharge at a safe port in the United Kingdom or on the Continent between Havre and Hamburg, both inclusive, etc." If the ship is ordered to Falmouth, there is provision for the freight rate to be slightly increased.

Deviation Clause. The ship must comply with the common law non-deviation warranty requiring her not to depart from the contract or usual route except where authorised by statute law or by the terms of the contract. The "deviation clause" states precisely for what purpose the vessel has liberty to deviate. A typical form of wording is "With liberty to sail without pilots, to call at any port or ports on the way for fuel, supplies, or any reasonable purpose, to tow and be towed and assist vessels in distress, all as part of the contract voyage". Sometimes liberty to deviate to adjust compasses is included.

Draftage. The "Austral" form of grain C/P provides for payment of freight "per ton of 2,240 lb. or 1,016 kilos net weight delivered, less a deduction for draftage of 2 lb. per 2,000 lb. of wheat discharged at a port in Great Britain or Ireland and weighed at the time of discharge by approved hopper scale in drafts of 2,000 lb. or over".

Dreading Clause. This is found in the "Centrocon" C/P (grain from the River Plate) and gives the charterer the option of shipping other lawful merchandise subject to an agreed minimum. If the option is exercised freight must be paid on the ship's deadweight capacity for wheat in bags at the rate agreed for heavy grain. Additional loading and discharging expenses must be paid by the charterer.

Exceptions Clause. Where the C/P includes a "Clause Para-mount" incorporating the Hague Rules, an "exceptions clause" is superfluous and may be omitted, as the Rules themselves contain the usual "exceptions" from liability. Otherwise, an "exceptions clause" will be included to relieve the shipowner from liability for loss or damage arising from:—

(a) **Act of God.** To prove loss from this cause it must be shown that the accident arose from natural causes, but without any human intervention, and could not have been prevented by any amount of care and foresight. Natural causes in them-selves are not enough. Fog is a natural cause, but if a ship goes aground in foggy weather that is not an Act of God as careful navigation could have prevented it.

(b) **Quarantine Restrictions.** If the ship is put in quarantine on arrival she is not a "ready ship" so that lay days will not begin until the quarantine period has ended. Otherwise, quarantine restrictions do not excuse a default on the part of the charterer in loading or the consignee in discharging. The position would be different, of course, if the C/P made an exception in favour of the charterer/consignee. Where there is an exception of "quarantine expenses" in the shipowner's favour, lighterage costs will be for the charterer's account if, because of quarantine, the ship is obliged to load in the roads instead of alongside.

(c) **Perils of the Sea.** This refers to accidents of an unforeseeable nature which can happen only at sea. Foundering, stranding, springing a leak in heavy weather, are examples. The inevitable action of wind and waves resulting in ordinary wear and tear is excluded. Sometimes the exception is extended to "Dangers and accidents of the seas, rivers, and navigation, of whatever nature and kind".

(d) **Fire.** As explained in Chapter 15, the owner of a registered British ship is given protection by statute against liability for loss caused by fire on board happening without his fault or privity, and this holds good even where fire results from a breach of the warranty of seaworthiness so long as the latter is not attributable to the owner. A contractual exception of "fire", which is considered a waiver of the statutory right does not protect the shipowner where the vessel was initially unseaworthy. Hence, owners entitled to the benefit of the statute should not include this exception in their contract. If goods are covered by a "received for ship-ment B/L" or a "through B/L" the statutory protection should be extended by using the clause "fire whether on board, in craft, or on quays or wharves (without prejudice to the operation of Section 502 of the Merchant Shipping Act, 1894)".

(e) **Inherent Vice or Defect of Goods.** This refers to the natural tendency of certain goods to deteriorate. Difficulty is often experienced in deciding whether damage to a perishable cargo is due to inherent vice, perils of the sea, or want of adequate precautions in stowage. Hence it is most unwise to place too much reliance on this exception.

(f) **Leakage, Breakage, Heat, Rust, and Sweat.** These exceptions cover only the damage caused to the goods which themselves suffer leakage, breakage, etc., and not damage to other goods stowed nearby. In any case none of these can be relied upon to give protection when there has been negligence on the part of the shipowner or his servants.

(g) **Jettison.** This covers jettison rendered necessary by a peril of the seas and, also, jettison rendered necessary by the neglect of master or crew in the navigation of the ship so long as the vessel was initially seaworthy and the goods were not carried in a manner contrary to the terms of the contract of carriage.

(h) **Contact with Other Goods.** The shipowner will not escape liability if damage from this cause is proved to be due to negligent or improper stowage but the onus of proving negligence rests on the party alleging it. If, say, parcels of different quality of the same commodity are stowed one on top of the other without adequate separation, and the owner or his servants did not know, and had no reason to know, that more effective separation was required, this exception will relieve the ship from liability for any resulting deterioration of one or other of the parcels.

(i) **Barratry.** This includes (i) any wilful act of violence to the ship or her cargo, (ii) any wrongful appropriation of the ship or her cargo, and (iii) any fraudulent or consciously illegal act which exposes the ship or cargo to damage or confiscation, done by the master or any of the crew without the consent of the shipowner. (Further reference to barratry will be found in Chapter 14 where it is mentioned in relation to insurance.)

(j) **Queen's enemies.** This refers to the actions of nationals of a country with which this country is in a state of war. The term "act of war" is wider than "Queen's enemies" since it includes acts of war where the carrying ship is neutral. An expression used more often in insurance policies than in C/P's is "consequences of hostilities or warlike operations" and this includes only the direct consequences of war, not accidents merely indirectly connected therewith.

(k) **Pirates.** Piracy is an act of violence done by individuals for their own profit on the high seas. The probably unimportant

R

distinction between "pirates" and "rovers" is that the former confine their activities within a limited area whilst the latter roam at large. Passengers in a ship who mutiny have been held to be pirates. Cases have occurred from time to time in Far Eastern waters where persons have embarked as fare-paying passengers and have at time and place of their own choosing made an armed attack on the master and crew with the intention of robbing the ship of the more valuable parts of her cargo. Rioters who attack a ship from the shore are also classed as pirates.

(*l*) **Thieves.** This exception covers robbery, *i.e.*, theft by violence, and theft in the sense of premeditated thieving by outside parties. It does not include "pilferage", *i.e.*, petty theft by passengers, crew or other servants of the shipowner.

(*m*) **Arrests or Restraints of Rulers, Princes, or Peoples.** This includes political or executive acts only, and does not cover loss caused by riot or by ordinary judicial process. By "People" is meant the "*de facto*" ruling or governing power as distinct from uncontrolled mobs or rioters. The exception covers acts that do not amount to act of war.

(*n*) **Embargo.** This is the name given to any government prohibition on the movement of ships or goods in particular circumstances.

(*o*) **Blockade.** This refers only to an effective blockade. Knowledge of an announcement of the intention to establish a blockade in the area containing the loading port or discharging port apparently does not excuse the ship from proceeding to the port. If, on arrival in the vicinity, it is found that the blockade is effective, the master will be entitled to go to the nearest safe port.

(*p*) **Riots, Strikes, or Stoppages of Labour.** A "strike" exception in itself can be relied on only when there is a general concerted refusal by workmen to work in consequence of an alleged grievance. It does not extend to the case where men refuse to work through fear of disease. The wider exception here quoted gives the ship far greater protection, and the addition of the words "from whatever cause" would be better still.

(*q*) **Explosions and Bursting of Boilers, Breakage of Shafts, and Latent Defects.** To claim the advantage of this exception there must, as usual, be no negligence on the part of the shipowner or his servants. A latent defect is one which is not apparent to the eye or the senses and which is not discoverable by "such an examination as a reasonably careful man skilled in the matter would make". Where there is an absolute obligation to provide a seaworthy ship, the exception of "latent defects" is of no avail if the ship is initially unseaworthy. The warranty of seaworthiness is qualified by express agreement only, so words such as "latent defects even existing at the time of shipment" must be used to give more adequate protection.. Where the Hague Rules apply, the carrier is not responsible for loss or damage arising from latent defects "not discoverable by due diligence". To rely on this the carrier does not have to prove that he failed to discover the defect in spite of using due diligence. If he used no diligence at all, he will still be protected if it can be proved that he would not have discovered the defect even if he had used all due diligence.

(*r*) **Negligence.** A typical form of "negligence clause" within the exceptions clause excepts the ship from liability for loss or damage due to "Collision, stranding or other accidents arising in the navigation of the steamer, even when occasioned by the negligence, default or error of judgment of the Pilot, Master, Mariners or other Servants of the Shipowners or persons for whom they may be responsible (not resulting, however, in any case from want of due diligence by the Owners of the Steamer, or by the Ship's Husband or Manager)". The exception "collision", standing by itself, does not cover loss due to collision caused by the negligence of the shipowner's servants, even compulsory pilots, but loss by collision due to the negligence of those in charge of another vessel is covered.

(*s*) **Strike of Seamen.** Another exception may be loss arising from delay in the commencement or prosecution of the voyage due to a general strike or lock-out of seamen or other persons necessary for the movement or navigation of the vessel.

An exceptions clause may include such words as "Nothing herein contained shall exempt the shipowners from liability for damage to or loss of cargo occasioned by bad stowage, by improper or insufficient dunnage, by absence of efficient ventilation, or by improper opening of valves, sluices, or ports".

In connection with "exceptions" it is necessary to bear in mind what is called the *ejusdem generis* (of a like kind) rule. Frequently a clause provides for one party or the other (or both) to be exempt from liability for loss arising from any one of a list of particular causes, such list then being followed by words of a general nature. Disputes often arise over the question of the scope of these general words. Unless such words are sufficiently all-embracing, the matter will be subject to the application of the *ejusdem generis* rule so that the general words will be given a limited meaning to cover only items or events of a like kind to those specifically mentioned. For instance, if a C/P is claused "Charterers not to be responsible for delays caused by frosts, floods, and other causes beyond their control", that would probably be taken to include delays caused by heavy snowfall, but it would not include, say, delay due to a strike. In the same way the phrase "strikes, lock-outs, civil commotions, and other causes or accidents beyond the control of the Charterers" would not cover a delay due to an epidemic, though it should include delay caused by a trade union ban on overtime working. Even the addition of the word "etc." after a list of specific events has been proved to have given considerable extension to the meaning of an exceptions clause. But to avoid altogether the application of the *ejusdem generis* rule, where it is the intention of the parties to give the clause unrestricted scope, use should be made of such words as "and all other delays howsoever, whensoever, and wheresoever caused".

Extra Work. One form of C/P makes provision for the steamer to work at night if required by the charterers, they paying all extra expenses for such work.

Freight in Full of .... Where this expression is used it means that the freight paid includes the charges specified, which will then be for the shipowner's account. Where the cargo needs to be trimmed, and the C/P quotes "freight in full of trimming" the ship will have to pay the trimming charges, but will earn a correspondingly higher freight than she would if those charges were paid directly by the charterer. Other charges which may be dealt with in this way include port charges, pilotage dues, light dues, consular fees, and lighterage at the port of discharge.

Full Reach and Burden. Where the contract gives the charterer the full reach and burden of the ship that applies to holds, 'tween-decks, and other underdeck compartments normally available for the carriage of cargo and, in addition, any lawful deck capacity. This provision is sometimes expressed more fully by the words ". . . not exceeding what the vessel can reasonably stow and carry, in the judgment of the master, over and above the space and burden necessary for the vessel's officers and crew, her cabins, tackle, apparel, furniture, provisions, fresh water, stores, necessary ballast, and fuel." Under a voyage charter the charterers are not entitled to stow cargo in passenger cabins or to carry passengers for their own gain. Any passenger accommodation the vessel may have remains at the free disposal of the shipowner. (Under a time charter that may not be so, and this is referred to in the section dealing with time C/P clauses.) "Reach" is concerned with the vessel's cubic capacity, and "burden" with her deadweight capacity.

The ship is not entitled to carry bunkers in excess of the amount necessary for the charter voyage. Where liberty to call at intermediate bunkering posts is given, the proper allowance for bunkers is the quantity required for the longest stretch between bunkering ports plus a reasonable amount for contingencies. If the charterer insists on the ship taking fuel for a longer run and thereby fails to load a full and complete cargo, the shipowner will have a remedy in deadfreight. On the other hand, it has been ruled that the charterer is not obliged to supply cargo to fill a cross bunker used alternatively for cargo or coal fuel.

Freight-paying Ballast. In the absence of any agreement otherwise, the shipowner must provide all necessary dunnage and ballast to comply with his obligation to provide a seaworthy ship or use due diligence to make the ship seaworthy, and he is not entitled to require the charterer to provide cargo of a kind which renders ballast unnecessary. Although this is probably of a significance only in the case of a sailing ship, it is a rule that even where the charterer has to provide the ballast it must be in place before the cancelling date, or the charterer will be entitled to exercise his option to cancel the contract. The shipowner is entitled to carry freight-paying merchandise as ballast so long as it occupies no more space or deadweight capacity than ordinary ballast would, and does not interfere with the C/P cargo.

General Average Clause. This invariably provides for G/A to be settled by the latest York-Antwerp Rules either with or without reservations. A typical example is "Average, if any, shall be settled according to the York-Antwerp Rules, 1974. Should the vessel put into any port or ports leaky or with damage, the Captain or Owners shall without delay inform the Charterers thereof."

Grab Damage. In C/P's for carriage of coal, metallic ores, and other cargoes where it is customary to discharge by means of grabs, there will usually be a clause governing the method of survey of grab damage and how payment for repair shall be made.

Ice Clauses. These are important features of some C/P's. They vary considerably according to the nature of the trade with which the C/P is concerned, but a good idea of their usual provisions will be evident from the following references to three of them.

1. "Centrocon" C/P ice clause: The main provision is that if the agreed port of discharge on the Continent is ice-bound the master has the option of waiting until it is open or going to the nearest safe port for fresh orders and telegraphing the consignees on arrival. If kept waiting more than 24 hours, lay days are to count. If ordered to a United Kingdom or open Continental

port and the extra distance exceeds 100 miles, the ship is to receive additional freight at some stated rate per ton (or tonne).

2. "Gencon" C/P ice clause:—

   With respect to the port of loading—

   (*a*) If the port is inaccessible when the vessel is ready to proceed, or during the voyage, or on arrival, or if frost sets in after arrival, the Captain is at liberty to leave without cargo and the charter shall be null and void.

   (*b*) If during loading the Captain, through fear of being frozen in, deems it advisable to leave, he has liberty to do so with what cargo is on board, and proceed to some other port or ports with the option of completing cargo for owner's benefit. The cargo loaded under charter is to be forwarded to destination at the vessel's expense against payment of freight.

   (*c*) If there is more than one loading port, and one or more are ice-bound, the Captain is at liberty either to load part cargo at the open port and fill up elsewhere for owner's benefit, or declare the charter void, unless the charterer agrees to load a full cargo at the open port.

   (*d*) This Ice Clause is not to apply in the spring.

   With respect to the port of discharge—

   (*a*) Should ice (except in spring) prevent the vessel from reaching the port, receivers have the option of keeping the vessel waiting on demurrage or ordering her to a safe port to discharge. Orders are to be given within 48 hours after the charterer is notified of the impossibility of reaching the port of destination.

   (*b*) If during discharge the Captain deems it advisable to leave, he has liberty to do so with what cargo is on board and proceed to the nearest accessible port.

   (*c*) On delivery of the cargo at such port all B/L conditions apply and the vessel shall receive the same freight as if she had discharged at the original destination, but if the distance of the substituted port exceeds 100 nautical miles the freight is to be increased in proportion.

3. North Russian Timber Charter ice clause. The main provisions are: (i) If the loading port is inaccessible by reason of ice on the vessel's arrival at the edge of the ice, or if frost sets in after the vessel's arrival in port, the charterer is to provide icebreaker assistance free of expense to the steamer. (ii) Time lost in waiting for icebreaker assistance in excess of 48 hours is to count as lay days when the vessel is arriving and to count as time on demurrage (or to be set off against despatch) when the vessel is leaving. (iii) The Captain is to follow official instructions issued by the authorities for vessels convoyed by icebreaker through the ice.

Lien Clause. This is an alternative name for the Cesser Clause already described.

Lighterage Clause. This clause in the "Centrocon" C/P reads "Owners to have liberty to lighten if required to cross bars and/or shoals in the River Parana at the Steamer's expense and the Merchant's risk, provided Steamer has not the option to complete at Buenos Aires or La Plata, but the Master to give notice before lightening to enable the Charterers to send their representatives on board". Other lighterage clauses may provide that if the vessel's draught exceeds a stated figure she shall reduce the draught by discharging part of the cargo into lighters in some "safe anchorage", which need not be within the commercial limits of the port. Lighterage expenses are, under such clauses, for the receivers' account, any custom of the port to the contrary notwithstanding.

Negligence Clause. This has already been described under "Exceptions Clause" of which it is usually a part.

New Jason Clause. Like the "Both to blame collision clause", this clause is one recommended by the General Council of British Shipping for insertion in all B's/L and C/P's. It is not usual to reproduce either clause in full in a C/P, but simply to incorporate them by reference. Details of the New Jason Clause will be found in the section on Bills of Lading.

Options. These usually refer to alternative loading and/or discharging ports and corresponding adjustments of freight rates. Options are sometimes given, too, for the shipment of different kinds of cargo.

Paramount Clause. This, being a B/L clause, is explained in detail in the section on B's/L. Where a C/P itself contains a specimen form of the B/L to be used, such B/L may contain the Paramount Clause to incorporate into the contract all the terms, provisions, and conditions of the Carriage of Goods by Sea Act or corresponding legislation.

P and I Bunkering Clause. The purpose of this clause, which appears to give liberty to deviate, is to allow the shipowner to take as much bunkers as possible at ports near the centre of oil production where bunker prices are usually lower than at ports away from such centres, and if necessary to proceed to any port or ports whether on or off the customary route or routes to the ports of loading or discharge named in the charter. It allows the owner to take bunkers to the full capacity of fuel tanks, whether such amount is or is not required for the chartered voyage. This clause appears to be realistic in accepting that by allowing the owner to take cheaper bunkers when he can, it may be to the benefit of all and result in lower freight rates than might otherwise apply. This clause is sometimes called the Bunker Deviation Clause.

Ready Berth Clause. Cases have occurred where a chartered ship on reaching the port of discharge has been ordered by the port authority to anchor outside the official port limits because no berth was immediately available for her. The ship, therefore, not being strictly an "arrived ship" has suffered serious loss through difficulties in tendering notice of readiness. To give the owners adequate protection in such circumstances, the following clause has been recommended by the Baltic Conference for insertion in C/P's.

"If a suitable discharging berth be not available on vessel's arrival at or off the port, whether entered at customs or not, the Charterer shall pay to Owners compensation at the demurrage rate stipulated in the charter for all time, counting from 24 hours after the first high water upon which the vessel could have berthed, until the vessel is in a suitable discharging berth. The Master or Owners shall have an absolute lien on the cargo for such compensation."

Rechartering. One version of this clause reads: "Charterers to have the right to transfer this Charter-party, but in such case the original Charterers shall remain responsible for the right and true fulfilment of the same."

Sailing Telegram. In some charters it is provided that a sailing telegram be sent to the charterers on the vessel leaving her last port (on the way to the first or only loading port), or in default 24 hours more shall be allowed for loading. This is necessary to give the charterers full opportunity to have the cargo ready on the vessel's arrival.

Safe Port. Many C/P clauses make reference to safe ports. To qualify for this description a port must be "safe" in the following respects.

1. There must be a safe access to the port free from any permanent obstruction. However safe a port may be in other respects, it is not a safe port if the ship cannot reach it without serious risk of damage by ice. A temporary obstruction, neap tides for instance, does not make an otherwise safe port unsafe.

2. The port must be one where the ship can lie safely afloat at all states of the tide, unless where it is customary and safe to load or discharge aground there is a special agreement to do so.

3. There must be adequate facilities for trade including a safe shore for the landing of goods, proper wharves, warehouses, and other establishments for dealing with the kind of cargo contemplated.

4. The port must be politically safe in the sense of being free from any state of war or embargo.

5. For any particular ship a port is not safe if the ship, having reached the port, cannot return from it without cutting her masts.

The safety of a port should be looked at in respect of a vessel which is properly manned and equipped, navigated and handled without negligence and in accordance with good seamanship.

If the master, when ordered to a port, knows it to be unsafe, he may refuse to proceed and may require the charterer to nominate another port. If he proceeds to a port as ordered and finds it unsafe when he arrives in the vicinity, he may refuse to enter or, if that is possible, he may incur expenditure (tug hire, for instance) to make the port safe and charge the amount to the charterer. Unless there is a specific agreement otherwise, the master is always entitled to refuse to enter a port which his vessel cannot safely reach without first lightening in a roadstead or another port even if that is a customary method of discharge at the port.

Safe Berth. A berth, to qualify as a "safe berth" must be safe in all the same respects as a safe port. In a number of cases in the past where the master, in obedience to charterer's orders, has taken his ship to a berth which has proved to be unsafe, and the ship and/or wharf have suffered damage in consequence, it has been held that it was the duty of the master to make certain that the berth was safe and to refuse to go there if he deemed it unsafe. Failure to do that has resulted in the shipowner having to bear the cost of repairing the damage. More recently, however, in a similar case (on final appeal to the Judicial Committee of the Privy Council, the case being first heard in Australia) the decision was given the other way. It was held that by the words "safe wharves as ordered" the charterers had given an undertaking that the nominated berth would be safe, that it was not safe for the particular ship concerned, and that the master even though aware of the defects of the berth had acted reasonably in taking the ship there.

Strikes Clause. The following will serve as one illustration. "If the cargo cannot be loaded by reason of Riots, Civil Commotions or of a Strike or Lock-out of any class of workmen essential to the loading of the cargo, or by reason of obstruction or stoppages beyond the control of the Charterers on the Railways, or in the Docks, or other loading places, or if the cargo cannot be discharged (for similar reasons), the time for loading or discharging, as the case may be, shall not count during the continuance of such causes, provided that a Strike or Lock-out of the Shippers' and/or Receivers men shall not prevent demurrage accruing if by the use of reasonable diligence they could have obtained other suitable labour at rates current before the Strike or Lock-out. In case of any delay by reason of the before-mentioned causes, no claim for damages or demurrage shall be made by the Charterers, Receivers of the Cargo, or Owners of the Steamer. For the purpose, however, of settling despatch money accounts, any time lost by the Steamer through any of the above causes shall be counted as time used in loading." Another clause recommended in the shipowner's interests is "Ship not to be responsible for any loss, damage, or delay directly or indirectly caused by or arising out of strikes, lock-outs, labour disturbances, trade disputes, or anything done in contemplation or furtherance thereof, whether the owners be parties thereto or not."

Stevedores. C/P's often provide that the charterers have liberty to appoint a stevedore to load the ship at a fixed rate per ton, not exceeding the current rate. Where this is agreed, legal relations between shipowner and stevedore remain unaffected so that the latter remains the servant of the former. Not only is the shipowner responsible for the default or negligence of the stevedore, but the master retains the duty of supervising and controlling the loading and stowage. On the other hand, if the C/P provides that the stevedore is to be both nominated and employed by the charterer, then it is the charterer who is liable for the faults of the stevedore. In a case where the C/P provided that charterers were to "load, stow, and trim the cargo at their expense under the supervision of the captain", charterers contended that the shipowner was responsible for damage to cargo through negligent stowage. It was held in the House of Lords that to the extent that the master exercises supervision and limits the charterers' control of the stowage, the charterers' liability is limited in a corresponding degree. As, in that case, there was no evidence that the master had interfered with the stowage, the charterers were held to be responsible.

Where the C/P provides for delivery of cargo "free alongside", the shipper's duty is complete when he has delivered the goods within reach of the ship's tackles. Further costs of loading, stowing, and trimming are then for the shipowner's account. This more or less traditional arrangement is aften associated with a similar arrangement at the port of discharge where the ship pays the stevedoring charges for unloading the cargo and the consignee takes delivery from the ship's tackles. Frequently, however, the charter provides for "free discharge" which means that the consignee bears the whole cost of discharging the cargo and taking delivery. Where the charter is on a "free in and out" basis, it becomes the responsibility of the charterer to load the ship at his expense and for the consignee to pay the complete costs of discharge. Freight rates, of course, take into account whichever method is contracted for. The advantage of "free discharge" is that disputes over the division of discharging and delivery costs are avoided. Where both loading and discharging operations take place alongside the charterer's own establishments, it is usual to contract "free in and out". To avoid doubt about the liability for other charges it is advisable to extend the phrase "free in and out" to "f.i.o., stowed and trimmed", or "Loaded, stowed, trimmed and discharged free of expense to the vessel". Cases have occurred where under an f.i.o.

contract charterers have contended that stowing and trimming charges were for the shipowner's account.

Ventilation and Dunnage. In charters for the carriage of rice, soya beans, and similar commodities, there is often a clause to the effect that the charterer is to provide and pay for ventilating appliances and dunnage, that mats are to be at the ship's expense and that rush or soft mats are not to be used, and that the ship is to be responsible for damage due to insufficient dunnage and mats. The clause may also stipulate that hatchways are to be opened during the voyage as often as weather permits, and that all ventilation cowls are to be trimmed from the wind.

War. Sometimes a C/P will contain a "war clause". The "Centrocon" form, for example, provides that "If the nation under whose flag the Steamer sails shall be at War, whereby the free navigation of the Steamer is endangered, or in a case of blockade or prohibition of export of grain and seed from the loading port, this charter shall be null and void at the last outward port of delivery or at any subsequent period when the difficulty may arise, previous to cargo being shipped".

The following War Risk Clauses are designed to clarify the positions of the two parties involved and to agree what action should be taken in the event of a war such as the Israel/Egypt or Iraq/Iran conflict starting during the voyage.

1. No bills of lading to be signed for any blockaded port and if the port of discharge be declared blockaded after bills of lading have been signed, or if the port to which the ship has been ordered to discharge either on signing bills of lading or thereafter be one to which the ship is or shall be prohibited from going by the Government of the Nation under whose flag the ship sails or by any other Government, the owner shall discharge the cargo at any other port covered by this charterparty as ordered by the charterers (provided such other port is not a blockaded or prohibited port as above mentioned) and shall be entitled to freight as if the ship had discharged at the port or ports of discharge to which she was originally ordered.

2. The ship shall have liberty to comply with any orders or directions as to departure, arrival, routes, ports of call, stoppages, destination, delivery or otherwise howsoever given by the Government of the Nation under whose flag the vessel sails or any department thereof, or by any Government or any department thereof, or any person acting or purporting to act with the authority of such Government or of any department thereof, or by any committee or person having, under the terms of the War Risks Insurance on the ship, the right to give such orders or directions and if by reason of and in

compliance with any such orders or directions anything is done or is not done, the same shall not be deemed a deviation, and delivery in accordance with such orders or directions shall be a fulfilment of the contract voyage and the freight shall be payable accordingly.

Weighing Charges (Coal C/P's). The following provision is sometimes made. "If receiver elects to weigh the cost is at his expense, and if the owner provides a check weigher it is at the owner's expense. Any deficiency alleged on the authority of such weighing is to affect freight only, provided that a statutory declaration is made by the master and officers that all cargo received has been delivered."

TIME CHARTER-PARTY CLAUSES AND TERMS

Different forms of time charter-parties, like voyage charters, vary considerably, although they have many features in common. The following paragraphs are intended to give a general idea of the substance of the more important clauses frequently used, with notes on performance of the contract.

Contracting Parties. The C/P will indicate the names of the owner and charterer, or those of their respective agents, and will be signed and witnessed in the same manner as a voyage charter.

Description of Ship. The name of the vessel and her position at the time of executing the contract will be shown together with her deadweight and cubic capacity, the latter in terms of grain space and bale space, and in some cases the deadweight capacity will be guaranteed. Where the deadweight is guaranteed to be "about .... tons", that is held to mean within a small percentage either way. The vessel's capabilities in the matter of speed and fuel consumption will be given, and a statement of the type of fuel to which such consumption refers. It is highly important that there should be no misrepresentation in respect of any of these particulars.

Delivery and Redelivery. There is usually a very precise agreement as to when and where the ship is to be delivered to the charterer, and when and where she is to be redelivered back to the owner at the end of the period of hire. On delivery a "certificate of delivery" will be drawn up and signed by the master, the owner's agents and the charterer's agents to show (i) the date and hour of delivery, (ii) the quantity of bunkers on board at the time, and (iii) the quantity of boiler water and galley fuel on board. On redelivery a similar "certificate of redelivery" will be made out and signed. What is called an "on survey" is held immediately prior to delivery and an "off survey" prior to redelivery. Both parties are represented on these surveys by comparison of which any excess damage can be assessed. Such damage must be made good at the charterer's expense, but "fair wear and tear" is always excepted. If the C/P requires the ship to be "redelivered in the same good order as when delivered" and there is damage for which the charterer is responsible, the owner is not entitled to refuse to accept redelivery, but the charterer will be liable not only for repair costs but also for detention during repairs. If the time for redelivery is fixed irrespective of where the vessel may be, and the owner resumes control while the ship is on the high seas, the time at which he does so is deemed to be the time of redelivery.

Final Voyage. It is seldom likely that the completion of the last voyage will coincide exactly with the termination of the period of hire. Unless the contract provides otherwise there is no breach on the part of the charterer if he redelivers within a reasonable time after the ending of the charter period so long as he acted reasonably in sending the ship on the final voyage. But if the contract shows clearly that the charter must not be extended beyond a fixed date the charterer will be in breach in failing to redeliver by that date, unless he can prove that he had good reason to suppose that the voyage would be finished in time. Hire for any such extended period will be payable at the charter rate, not at the market rate if that is different. Where the C/P makes special provision for the final voyage, it usually takes the form that the period of hire may be extended at the rate agreed in the C/P (which may be the market rate if higher than the charter rate) and under the conditions of the C/P for as long as may be necessary to complete the last voyage. This entitles the charterer to send the ship on a voyage which cannot possibly be completed before the end of the term of hire, but does not entitle him to send her on a new voyage after the term of hire has expired. If the last voyage ends at a port other than the agreed port of redelivery, the owner is entitled to resume control of the ship there and then, and the charterer has no right to send her on a new voyage to the agreed port. Where a vessel is chartered for a fixed period and is redelivered before the end of that period, the charterer is liable for hire at the agreed rate in respect of the unused portion of the term.

Cancelling Date. There will usually be a clause to the effect that if the ship is not delivered by a certain date the charterer has the option of cancelling the contract. As a general rule an option to cancel must be exercised within a reasonable time or it cannot be exercised at all, except by mutual consent. In one form of C/P it is provided that, if the ship cannot be delivered in time, the owner shall require the charterer to declare whether he will exercise his option to cancel and the charterer must answer this within 48 hours.

Trading Limits and Other Restrictions. These vary widely from one case to another. A ship may, for instance, be let on time charter for a voyage or for a number of consecutive voyages on a particular route. On the other hand, a charter may be for world wide trading, with or without restrictions regarding particular areas. Sometimes the charterer's powers are restricted to sending the vessel only to "good and safe ports". A reference to an "ice-bound place" as distinct from an "ice-bound port" covers not only a port but also the approaches to that port. Provision may be made for the master to have liberty to leave a port if he fears that the vessel may become frozen in or damaged by ice. In some cases, too, the owners may put a ban on the carriage of certain kinds of dangerous goods.

Hire Money. Every time C/P will, of course, contain a clause stating the rate of hire agreed and the method of payment. The most common arrangement is for hire to be paid monthly in advance and *pro rata* for part of a month. Unless agreed otherwise, "month" means calendar month, but where a fraction of a month is involved that month would be treated as a period of 30 days. Some charters do provide for hire to be payable "per month of 30 days". The liability to pay is continuous from the moment of delivery to the moment of redelivery unless some event occurs to take the ship off hire under the "off-hire clause". However, if by some breach of contract on the part of the shipowner the vessel is delayed in performing the service required by the charterer, hire paid during the period of delay would be taken into account in assessing the measure of damages due to the charterer.

Off-hire Clause. This clause, sometimes referred to as the "breakdown clause", usually provides that in the event of time being lost in certain specified circumstances which prevent the vessel from working for more than 24 hours, payment of hire shall cease until she is again efficient to resume the service required of her. If the time lost does exceed 24 hours, hire is not payable in respect of the first 24 hours of the breakdown. If the C/P uses the words "hindering or preventing the working of the vessel", that brings partial breakdowns within the scope of the clause as well as total breakdowns, say, for instance, where an accident has put some (but not all) of the winches out of service. However, even without this extended wording, it has been held that partial interference with working has been a sufficient prevention to take the ship off hire. The clause comes into operation only when time is lost in rendering the particular service required by the charterer at the time. In a case where a ship's main engines broke down so that she had to be towed for a considerable part of the voyage, it was held that hire was not payable during the period on tow but that she came on hire again while discharging with the aid of her own appliances which were efficient for that purpose. If the working of the ship is prevented by "deficiency of men" the clause does not operate unless the ship is undermanned in the ordinary sense of that term; a case where the whole crew go on strike is not covered. Where an accident to cargo has caused damage to the ship which necessitated putting into port to repair the ship, it has been held that the ship was off hire during the detention. On the other hand, where it was the condition of the cargo and not the condition of the ship which made it necessary to put into port, the off-hire clause did not operate. Unless the C/P provides otherwise, the term of hire is not extended by the length of periods off hire during the term.

This clause is anything but simple, and has produced much litigation. It is, therefore, very important that the master should never sign his agreement to an off-hire period without precise instructions from the owners who should be informed by the master of all the facts of the case of which he is certain.

Withdrawal of Ship if Hire Not Paid When Due. Time charters are frequently claused to the effect that if hire money is not paid on the due date the owners are entitled to withdraw the ship from the charterer's service, but this does not mean that the owner may withdraw the ship merely because hire is not *received* on the date agreed for payment. If hire is payable on a deadweight basis, the charterer is not obliged to make any payment until the vessel's deadweight has been disclosed to him. If withdrawal is made, payment of hire money ceases at the time of such withdrawal which is deemed to be redelivery, but if the owners are forced under protest to take back the ship on account of the charterer wrongfully repudiating the contract after hire has become due, the whole of the overdue hire is recoverable. Suppose, for example, that hire is payable every 90 days in advance and, say, one week after a payment has fallen due the charterer repudiates the C/P and during the following week the owners are compelled to take the ship back into their own service. They will in those or similar circumstances be entitled to hire for the full 90 days.

Indemnity Clause. An important clause in many time C/P's is to the effect that "The master shall be under the orders and direction of the charterer as regards employment (*i.e.*, employment of the ship, not of persons), agency, or other arrangements and the charterer hereby agrees to indemnify the owners for the consequences or liabilities that may arise from the master or officers signing B's/L or other documents or complying with such orders, as well as any irregularity consequent thereon in the ship's papers." Apart from the provisions of any "prohibition clause", this gives the charterer freedom of choice as to the manner in which the ship is to be employed during the charter period, and safeguards the position of the owners by giving them the right of indemnity against the consequences or liabilities which may arise from the master's compliance with the charterer's orders. The term "employment" as used in this clause does not embrace navigation or the incidents thereof.

Unlike the situation under a demise charter, the master remains responsible to the shipowner for the safety of the ship and cargo, and must himself decide, amongst other things, whether it is safe to leave port, to proceed on the voyage, or to enter a port he fears unsafe. One effect of the clause is to make the charterer's agents the ship's agents for such purposes as attending to customs, but it does not authorise them to hire appliances for discharging cargo, if that is the work of the ship, without the consent of the owner or master.

Even without this clause, an indemnity may be implied by law if the owners incur liability to a B/L holder which they would not have incurred under the terms of the C/P. There is an implied undertaking by the charterers to present B's/L which conform with the C/P and which do not expose the owners to liability in excess of that to which they are exposed under the C/P.

The indemnity clause may regulate the situation with regard to claims due to bad stowage and claims for short delivery of cargo, relieving owners from responsibility where charterer's stevedores are employed. If the charterers order a method of stowage which will adversely affect the seaworthiness of the ship, the master should intervene whether the C/P expressly makes him responsible for good stowage or not. Whenever his attention is drawn to anything likely to cause a claim, he should notify the charterers' representatives in writing holding them responsible, keeping in mind that in the first instance the claim may be brought against the owners under the terms of the B/L.

The clause usually gives charterers the right to require changes in the appointments of masters, officers, or engineers if dissatisfied with the conduct of any of them.

Time Charterers' Liabilities. Where a time-chartered ship is damaged as a result of the negligence of the charterers or their servants, the owners are entitled to recover the full amount of the loss, unless the C/P expressly makes an "exception" of such negligence.

Seaworthiness. In the law of Scotland, and most probably in English law although it appears not to have been put to the test, there is an implied warranty that a time-chartered ship shall be seaworthy at the time when she is delivered to the charterer. This does not extend to an obligation that she shall be seaworthy at the commencement of each voyage made under the charter, but if the ship starts on a subsequent voyage in an unseaworthy state through the negligence of the master, the owners will be liable for the consequences unless they are expressly excepted therefrom. It is usual for the C/P to provide that owners are to maintain the ship in a thoroughly efficient state in hull and machinery throughout the period of hire. If, therefore, accidents occur or events arise which cause the ship to be inefficient, the owners must take all reasonable and proper steps promptly to restore her efficiency.

Liens. It is usual for a time C/P to give the owners a lien on all cargoes, sub-freights for hire, and G/A contributions, and to give the charterer a lien on the ship for hire paid in advance and not earned. Reference is made to this in the section on "Liens" in Chapter 2.

Where there is a *bona fide* dispute as to liability, the exercising of a lien may be fraught with all manner of difficulties. If the master thinks he has good and sufficient reason to exercise lien on cargo, he should keep in his possession no more than is sufficient for the purpose and apply to the owners or their agents for instructions without delay.

Loss of Ship. If the ship is lost payment of hire will cease from the time of the loss. It would appear that "loss" includes constructive total loss. Unearned hire paid in advance is returnable.

Commission. There will be a clause providing for payment of commission to the broker who negotiated the charter. One form has been quoted in the section on "negotiation of charters".

The broker is not a party to the contract but, should it be necessary, the charterer can be compelled to sue as a trustee for him to recover commisssion due to him under the clause.

General Average. The usual provision is made for G/A to be settled according to York-Antwerp Rules, 1974, but the clause may provide that hire money is not to contribute to general average.

Owners' and Charterers' Responsibilities and Exemptions. A clause makes the owners responsible only for delays, losses, and damages caused by want of due diligence or other personal act or omission or default of themselves or their manager, and expressly relieves them of responsibility for damage or delay whatsoever and howsoever caused even if caused by the neglect or default of their servants. (This, however, should be read in the light of other clauses which impose express obligations on the owners.) Charterers are made responsible for loss or damage caused to steamer or owners by goods being loaded contrary to the terms of the charter, improper or careless loading or stowage, or other improper or careless acts on their part or that of their servants.

Cargo and Passengers. Another clause places the whole reach and burden of the ship, including lawful deck-capacity, at charterers' disposal, reserving the usual spaces for ship's use. Sometimes the C/P provides that all passenger accommodation shall be at charterers' disposal, but the following clause may be used, viz., "The owners shall (subject to charterers paying them in addition to the hire 70 per cent. of the gross amount of passage money in accordance with rates prevailing in the trades concerned) provide and pay for all provisions, subsistence, and other requisites normally required for passengers and for any additional personnel normally required on board by their carriage."

Sailing Directions and Logs. A common provision is "Charterers to furnish Captain with all instructions and sailing directions and Captain and Engineer to keep full and correct logs accessible to Charterers or their Agents."

Advance. There may be an agreement for charterers or their agents to advance to the master, if required, necessary funds for ordinary disbursements for the ship's account at any port, at an agreed rate of interest, such advances to be deducted from hire.

Bunkers on Delivery and Redelivery. A typical arrangement is for "Charterers at port of delivery and Owners at port of redelivery to take over and pay for all coal or oil fuel remaining in Steamer's bunkers at current price of the respective ports. Steamer to be redelivered with not less than .... tons and not exceeding .... tons coal or oil fuel in steamer's bunkers". (Current price means the price generally in force and charged at the particular port without any contract discount.)

Overtime. A usual provision is for the steamer to work day and night if required, and for the charterers to refund owners their outlays for all overtime paid to officers and crew according to the law of the steamer's flag.

Dry Docking. In time charters for long periods, the owners undertake to dry dock the vessel at the usual intervals in order to keep her in an efficient condition, hire ceasing during the period in dock.

Boiler Cleaning. The usual arrangement is for cleaning of boilers, if necessary, to be done during service, but if that is impossible the charterers are to give owners necessary time for cleaning. Should the steamer be delayed beyond 48 hours, hire ceases until she is ready again.

Division of Expenses. The usual apportionment of expenses between owners and charterers has been outlined in Chapter 3 under "Employment of ships". Further to what has been said there, it may be noted that one form of C/P makes it incumbent on the charterers to provide amongst other things "dunnage and shifting boards, except whatever are already on board". Another form simply requires the ship to be "in every way fitted for ordinary cargo service". In a case where the latter form was used, and the question of who should pay the cost of providing and erecting shifting boards was in dispute, it was held that the charterers were liable. It was pointed out that the charterers knew the nature of the cargo to be carried and that, under another clause, they were to pay "all other charges and expenses whatsoever". It would seem that what applies to shifting boards applies equally to bins and feeders.

Subletting. As in the case of a voyage charter, there is generally a clause giving charterers the option of subletting the vessel, but holding them responsible to the owners for due performance of the original charter.

Prolongation Clause. This gives the charterer the option of continuing the charter for a further period (or periods) beyond that originally agreed, subject to the owners being given due notice in writing.

War. By one form of C/P the following special provisions apply in case of war, viz., "Steamer not to be sent on any voyage before owners have been able to cover her full value against war-risk. Charterers to refund owners any war premium, and if same is not paid promptly on production of receipt this to be considered as non-payment of hire. No passengers to be carried unless charterers procure guarantees, satisfactory to owners, that the passengers do not expose steamer to the risk of being sunk or captured or to any other war risk. Steamer not to be sent on any voyage exposing her to attacks of submarines or aircraft or to the risk of being sunk by mines or otherwise. Charterers not to load goods which appear on the contraband list of any of the belligerent powers unless they procure guarantees .... that such goods will not be considered as contraband".

Supercargo. Sometimes charterers reserve the right to keep on board at any time and for any length of time during the charter term, and at their expense, one of their experienced officers to act as "supercargo". The C/P may require owners to provide him free of charge with officer's accommodation and to victual him at an agreed charge per day. Where a liner company charters a tramp to be employed on one of their regular routes, they may consider it essential to have on board an officer who knows the "run" and who is familiar with prevailing conditions in the various ports of call. He will be expected to do all he can to protect the charterers' interests without presuming to interfere with the management of the vessel. In no way does his presence lessen the master's responsibility for stowage, and it hardly needs to be said that, unless he is capable of displaying the utmost tact, his post will not be an enviable one.

Salvage. Should a time-chartered vessel succeed in earning a salvage award the question arises as to how it should be apportioned. Therefore there is usually a C/P clause to indicate what the parties have agreed. A typical form is "All salvage and assistance to other vessels to be for Owner's and Charterers' equal benefit after deducting Master's and Crew's proportion and all legal and other expenses including hire paid under this Charter for the time lost by salvage, also repairs of damage and fuel consumed. Charterers to be bound by all measures taken by the Owners in order to secure payment of salvage and of fixing the amount of same."

Arbitration. The "arbitration clause" in a time C/P may provide for the nomination of a single arbitrator in case of disputes arising under the charter, or it may require each party to appoint its own arbitrator and for the two to appoint an umpire in the event of their disagreement. (See Chapter 2 for further information.)

Indemnity for Non-performance. A clause sometimes called (or, strictly speaking, miscalled) a penalty clause usually provides that the indemnity (or "penalty") for non-performance of the charter shall be proved damages.

MATE'S RECEIPTS

A mate's receipt is a receipt, given and signed by the mate for goods actually received on board the ship, which should be drawn up carefully to show the identification marks and numbers from tally books (not copied from boat notes or shipper's notes). The ship's own receipt forms should be used in preference to signing amended boat notes as is sometimes done. Ship's receipt books normally provide triplicate forms. One copy goes to the lighterman or other person delivering the cargo to the ship, another to the ship's agents, and the third is kept in the book for use on board (*e.g.*, for preparing manifests and cargo plans).

Until he issues a B/L the shipowner will usually hold the goods on the terms of his usual B/L, and this may be expressly provided for in the M/R. If ownership of the goods is to be transferred before the B/L is issued, due notice of the transaction should be given by the shipper to the shipowner or his agent as the property does not pass from vendor to purchaser merely by indorsement and delivery of the M/R. The latter is not legally recognised as a document of title, and the shipowner is entitled to issue the B/L to the person who presents the M/R unless he has had prior notice that such person has no right to its possession.

As B's/L are subsequently signed by the master or agent (more often the latter) on production of M/R's, the mate must be sure that the particulars shown on the receipt truthfully describe the apparent order and condition of the goods. Where justified, the mate should add appropriate qualifying remarks such as "stained cases", "cases second-hand and renailed", "bags torn and resewn", and so on. He should sign only for the actual numbers checked by the tally on the ship's behalf, adding where necessary ". . . more in dispute, if on board to be delivered." Where it is not possible to check weights, the receipt should be claused "said to weigh . . .", or "shipper's weight only", or with some other appropriate remark. Similarly, when it is impossible to verify the contents of cases and other packages, the receipt should describe them as "said to contain . . .". The mate should also add any other clauses or remarks necessary to protect the ship against claims for loss or damage that may arise from causes beyond the ship's control.

TIME SHEETS

A time sheet is a document drawn up in respect of a voyage-chartered ship to assess the amount of demurrage due to the ship or the amount of despatch money due to the charterer or consignee, as the case may be. Usually separate time sheets are required at the port of loading and port of discharge, respectively, but where lay days for loading and discharging are reversible a single time sheet at the port of discharge only will be needed.

A well drawn up time sheet would show the following particulars:—

1. The date and time of the ship's arrival in port.
2. „ „ „ „ „ „ „ her berth.
3. „ „ „ when the ship is ready to load or discharge
4. „ „ „ of tendering notice of readiness.
5. „ „ „ „ notice being accepted.
6. The date and time when work begins.
7. „ „ „ „ lay days begin to count.
8. The number of hours on each day when work is done.
9. The rate of loading or discharging as agreed to in the C/P.
10. A statement of times when work could not be done, or was not done, with the reason therefor.
11. The quantity of cargo loaded or discharged each day.
12. The total quantity loaded or discharged.
13. The date and time when loading or discharging is completed.
14. „ „ „ „ bills of lading are presented and signed at the loading port.

The document should be signed by the master and by the charterer or consignee or their respective agents. If the parties fail to reach agreement, the master should sign "under protest" and note a protest. Alternatively, he may sign "subject to owners' approval", acquaint the owners with all the relevant facts, and leave it to them to re-open the matter in respect of matters in dispute.

Several examples of demurrage and despatch calculations are given in Chapter 18.

BILLS OF LADING

Functions of a B/L. In respect of goods shipped in a general ship a bill of lading fulfils three separate functions, as follows:—

1. It is a receipt signed by the master or the agent on behalf of the shipowner, for goods received on board or elsewhere into the shipowner's custody.

2. It is evidence of a contract between a shipper and a carrier for the carriage of goods by sea. In itself it is not a contract in the sense of being a document signed and witnessed by or on behalf of both parties. It is signed only by the shipowner's representative whose signature is not customarily witnessed. The orignal contract may be made by word of mouth or in some other way, but the fact that a B/L has been issued provides evidence that a contract does exist. It may evidence the whole contract or only part thereof.

3. It is a document of title to the goods described in it. That is, in the absence of proof of fraud, or in the absence of an intention that the B/L holder should not acquire ownership of goods, the holder of a B/L for the time being is regarded as the rightful owner of the property described in the bill.

When a B/L is issued by a ship trading under charter, it may occur that the terms of the B/L are different from those of the C/P and doubts may arise as to which apply. Briefly, the rules are:—

1. A B/L in the hands of a shipper, who is also the charterer, is a mere receipt and not a contractual document at all. So long as the B/L remains in his hands the goods are carried on C/P terms. This may be qualified if it appears from the wording of the two documents that shipowner and charterer intended the C/P to be varied by the B/L, in which case the B/L terms apply.

2. Between a shipper, who is not the charterer, and the shipowner the goods are carried on B/L terms unless the shipper proves that the B/L inaccurately records their agreement in some particular.

3. In the hands of an indorsee or consignee from a shipper who is also the charterer the B/L is conclusive evidence of the terms of carriage in accordance with Section 1 of the Bills of Lading Act, 1855. (This Section is reproduced later on in this Chapter.)

4. In the hands of an indorsee who is also the charterer the goods are carried on B/L terms, provided that the charterer acquired his title to the goods under and on the terms of the B/L.

Parts and Copies. B's/L are usually issued in sets of two or more negotiable "parts", together with one or more non-negotiable "copies", including the "Captain's Copy". The reason for issuing the bill in parts is to make it possible for the different parts to be sent by different routes, so increasing the likelihood of at least one part arriving at the port of destination of the goods before the goods themselves. Arrangements for taking delivery can then be made in good time and inconvenient delays are avoided. This system has from time to time come under criticism from the legal profession on account of the risk of fraud being practiced. Commercial interests, however, have long seemed satisfied that the advantages of the system far outweigh the disadvantages. The number of negotiable parts issued is made clear by the inclusion of a clause stating "In witness whereof the master or agent of the said ship hath affirmed . . . Bills of Lading all of the same tenor and date, any one of which being accomplished the others to stand void." Non-negotiable coipies are usually distinguished by the words "COPY—NOT NEGOTIABLE" being conspicuously overprinted, sometimes in large red lettering. The mere word "copy" would be sufficient though less expedient as it is very important not to mistake a copy for a part.

Dating. As goods are often sold while in transit by indorsement and delivery of the B/L for value, it is important that the B/L should be correctly dated with the actual date of shipment. Post-dating or ante-dating could lead to prosecution for fraud. The date of shipment is often of extreme importance in the contract between shipper and consignee.

Stamp Duty. B's/L issued in the United Kingdom have been, since 1949, exempt from stamp duty. Those issued abroad may or may not require to be stamped according to the revenue laws of the country of issue.

Duty to Supply B/L Forms. Basically it is the shipper's duty to supply B's/L, but in practice the carrier, for a small charge, makes them out on his own forms from invoices and instructions received from the shipper. Obviously, in the case of a general ship carrying a mixed cargo it would be most inconvenient if each shipper produced a B/L differing in form and content from all the others.

Clean B/L. A B/L is said to be "clean" when it bears no superimposed clauses expressly declaring a defective condition of the goods or packaging.

Foul B/L. A B/L which is not clean in the above sense is described as "foul", "dirty", "unclean", or "claused".

In accordance with a resolution accepted by the International Chamber of Shipping in 1951, a B/L should not be considered foul, and therefore unacceptable, merely because it contains:—

(a) Clauses which do not expressly state that the goods or the packaging are unsatisfactory, e.g., second-hand cases, used drums, etc.

(b) Clauses which emphasise the carrier's non-liability for risks arising through the nature of the goods or packaging.

(c) Clauses which disclaim on the part of the carrier knowledge of contents, weight, measurement, quality, or technical specification of the goods.

Received for Shipment B/L. This is a B/L issued to a shipper when he delivers goods into the custody of the shipowner or the latter's agent (*e.g.*, a wharfinger or dock authority) before the carrying ship has arrived or is ready to receive the goods. It is sometimes called a "custody bill of lading". The rules appended to the Carriage of Goods by Sea Act require that, after receiving the goods into his charge the carrier shall, on demand of the shipper, issue a B/L showing the marks, numbers (or weight) and apparent order and condition of the goods.

Shipped B/L. A B/L issued after the goods have actually been loaded into the ship is described as a "shipped bill". The rules just referred to require that after the goods are loaded, the B/L, if demanded, is to be a Shipped B/L. If a Received for Shipment B/L has previously been given, however, it must be surrendered in exchange for, or converted into, a Shipped B/L by endorsing upon it the name of the ship into which the goods are loaded and the date of shipment.

Direct B/L. This is a B/L covering the carriage of goods in one ship direct from one port to another.

Through B/L. A B/L used for multi-transport which provides evidence of a contract of carriage from one place to another in separate stages of which at least one stage is sea transit and by which the issuing sea carrier accepts responsibility for the sea carriage and acts as agent for the shipper in arranging carriage from the place of acceptance to the final place of delivery. It should be noted that more than one carrier is used, hence the term multi-transport, and that the issuer only accepts responsibility for his own segment of the carriage which would be limited to that contained in the Hague or Hague-Visby Rules. He then casts himself in the role of agent as between the shipper and the other carriers if the loss or damage was caused while in their hands. It is usual for the issuer of the B/L to agree that if it cannot be proved where the goods were when the loss or damage occurred, it shall be deemed to have occurred at sea and the carrier shall be liable to the extent prescribed by the Hague or Hague-Visby Rules. Sea carriers frequently undertake the responsibility of arranging through transit. For instance, a shipment consigned from London to Bangkok may be carried from London to Singapore and there transhipped for conveyance by local vessel to Bangkok. Freight for the entire journey would be prepaid to the principal sea carrier in London who, through his agents in Singapore, would arrange the transhipment and pay the freight for carriage from Singapore to Bangkok. It has been held that where freight for the whole transit has been paid in advance, and loss occurs on one stage of the journey, no freight is recoverable in respect of the unperformed stages.

A Railway Receipt or other similar document issued by a land carrier when goods are first conveyed overland prior to being shipped overseas may be referred to as a "through bill of lading", but in law such a document is not a bill of lading at all.

Combined Transport B/L. A negotiable document which evidences a combined transport contract, the taking in charge of the goods described by the combined transport operator (CTO) at a place of acceptance, and an undertaking by him to deliver the goods at a place of delivery against surrender of the document. A provision in the document that the goods are to be delivered to the order of a named person, or to the bearer, constitutes such an undertaking. In this case the issuer accepts responsibility for the entire movement, and acts as principal with respect to the shipper and other carriers. More than one type of carriage is generally involved. When the stage of transport where loss or damage occurred is known, the CTO's liability to the shipper or consignee is decided by the international convention or domestic law applicable. (i.e. Road, rail, air, sea). Where the stage is not known, the CTO's liability is limited to a stated amount, but he is not liable where loss is due to act or neglect of shipper or consignee, defective packing, inherent vice, labour disputes, inadequacy of marks and numbers, inevitable accident.

Open B/L. A B/L giving no indication whatsoever of whom the goods are consigned to would be described as "open". A holder presenting an open bill would be entitled to take delivery of the goods but would have no right to hold them against the rightful owner if there were a defect in the holder's title. The master giving delivery in such circumstances, however, would be protected.

Straight B/L. This is an American term for a B/L issued solely in favour of a named consignee. Unless it has been assigned to him by the indorsement of that consignee, no holder of such a bill other than the named consignee himself would be entitled to take delivery of the goods. Such bills are rarely issued by shipowners except, occasionally, in respect of parcels of very high value.

Bearer B/L. A B/L making goods deliverable "to bearer" does not require endorsement. The property passes by mere delivery.

Order B/L. The vast majority of B's/L are of this type and are negotiable documents. One part of the set must be surrendered, duly indorsed, in exchange for the goods or a delivery order. Indorsement may be effected in either of two ways, viz., (1) by "blank indorsement" where the person to whose order the goods are made deliverable simply writes his name on the back of the bill, converting it in effect from an "order" bill into a "bearer" bill, so that any further transfer may be effected by mere delivery; (2) by "special indorsement" which is an indorsement to some named person or persons, thus converting it in effect into what has been described above as a "straight" bill.

By way of illustration, if a B/L shows that goods are consigned to "Williams & Co. or order", that will require indorsement if Williams & Co. wish to transfer it to a buyer of the goods. If they simply indorse it "Williams & Co." without mentioning the name of the buyer, that buyer can in turn pass the goods on to someone else by mere delivery of the B/L which has now become a bearer bill. On the other hand, if they indorse it "Deliver to J. Green, Ltd., or order. (Signed) Williams & Co." it would require further indorsement should J. Green, Ltd., wish to pass the goods on to someone else. It may be noted that, according to the manner of indorsement, an order bill can be converted into a bearer bill at one stage and be reconverted back by a transferee into an order bill.

If an order bill is drawn up to the order of the shippers, they must indorse the full set either in blank or to a named consignee or order. Without indorsement only the shippers themselves could take delivery of the goods.

Outward B/L. As far as this country is concerned an "outward" B/L is one issued in respect of goods being exported from this country to a destination abroad. The Carriage of Goods by Sea Act 1971 does not require a B/L issued in Great Britain or Northern Ireland to have an express statement that it should have effect subject to the provisions of the Act, but it does provide that the Hague-Visby Rules shall have the force of law in connection with the carriage of goods by sea in ships under certain circumstances. It is usual therefore to include a Clause Paramount to make it quite clear to shippers etc., the circumstances when the Hague-Visby Rules (or Hague Rules where appropriate) are to apply to the contract evidenced by the B/L. An example of such a clause included in the GCBS Common Short Form Bill of Lading reads:—

"The contract evidenced by this Short Form Bill of Lading is subject to the exceptions, limitations, conditions and liberties (including those relating to pre-carriage and on-carriage) set out in the Carrier's Standard Conditions applicable to the voyage covered by this Short Form Bill of Lading and operative on its date of issue.

If the carriage is one where the provisions of the Hague Rules contained in the International Convention for unification of certain rules relating to Bills of Lading dated Brussels on 25th August, 1924, as amended by the Protocol signed at Brussels on 23rd February, 1968 (the Hague-Visby Rules) are compulsorily applicable under Article X, the said Standard Conditions contain or shall be deemed to contain a Clause giving effect to the Hague-Visby Rules. Otherwise, except as provided below, the said

Standard Conditions contain or shall be deemed to contain a Clause giving effect to the provisions of the Hague Rules.

The Carrier hereby agrees that to the extent of any inconsistency the said Clause shall prevail over the exceptions, limitations, conditions and liberties set out in the Standard Conditions in respect of any period to which the Hague Rules or the Hague Visby Rules by their terms apply. Unless the Standard Conditions expressly provide otherwise, neither the Hague Rules nor the Hague-Visby Rules shall apply to this contract where the goods carried hereunder consist of live animals or cargo which by this contract is stated as being carried on deck and is so carried.

Notwithstanding anything contained in the said Standard Conditions, the term Carrier in this Short Form Bill of Lading shall mean the Carrier named on the front thereof.

A copy of the Carrier's said Standard Conditions applicable hereto may be inspected or will be supplied on request at the office of the Carrier or the Carrier's Principal Agents''.

It appears that the "Himalaya Clause", extending to servants and agents of the carrier the same defences and limits of liability to which the carrier himself is entitled, continues to be inserted in B's/L. This may be because although the Hague-Visby Rules provide this extension to the carrier's servants or agents, they do not extend protection to his independent contractors (which the clause attempts to do) and also inclusion of such a clause would cover the situation where the Hague Rules still apply, but not the Hague-Visby Rules.

Homeward B/L. A "homeward" bill is one issued abroad to cover a shipment of goods being imported into the United Kingdom. Such a B/L may contain a Clause Paramount similar to the one shown above, although the Hague Rules seem to be accepted as being international in their application.

Common Short Form Bill of Lading. This is a Common document because it has a standard layout and bears no shipping company "logo" but upon which the shipper or agent adds the name of the actual carrier to be used for the shipment. The term Short Form means that the conditions of carriage which in a full B/L appear in small print on the back are referred to by an Incorporation Clause on the front which states that the contract is subject to the Carrier's Standard Conditions applicable to the voyage which may be inspected or will be supplied on request to the Carrier's or their agents' offices. An example of the form of wording used is shown above under Outward B/L.

Liner B/L. This is a B/L issued by the owner or charterer of a general ship and, so far as the shipper and consignee are concerned, is in no way related to any charter-party. The detailed contents of such bills vary widely according to the nature of the trade in which the company's ships are engaged, but the following may be considered more or less common features:—

1. The name of the ship and the names of the ports of loading and destination of the goods.
2. A description of the goods with their weight and/or measurement, and the marks and numbers of the packages.
3. The name of the consignee or, more frequently, "consigned to order", or "consigned to .... or order".
4. The freight payable, based on weight or measurement as the case may be, except in special cases, and the discount allowed (if any). (If the shipper has given an undertaking to confine all his shipments to vessels of the Liner Conference, of which the shipping company is a member, the contract rate of freight will be subject to a discount which may amount to some 9% or 10%.)
5. The remark "freight paid" will be added at the time when the freight has in fact been paid.
6. An instruction to the shipowner's agents at the port of destination of the goods to notify the fact of the ship's arrival to the consignee but without any liability.
7. A "deviation clause" reserving liberty to deviate for various purposes. This clause is often very elaborate and, in almost all cases, will include liberty to tow and be towed, assist vessels in all situations, save life and property, bunker, adjust compasses, drydock with or without cargo on board, and comply with orders given by Government and other authorities. Liberty is also reserved to sail with or without pilots, to call at any port or ports in any order (even in the contrary order to the advertised route) for the purpose of taking in or setting down cargo, mails or passengers, and there is usually added "to deviate for any purpose whatsoever whether connected with the contract voyage or otherwise". (Such wide clauses are not of much value unless it can be shown that the deviation was reasonable. To deviate purely for the carrier's convenience is not reasonable.)
8. The general "exceptions clause" wherein the carrier disclaims liability for loss or damage arising from Act of God, Enemies, Restraint, Barratry, Capture, Riots, Strikes, etc. (Similar to the list of exceptions in a voyage C/P.)
9. A clause whereby the carrier disclaims liability for loss or damage arising from rust, sweat, chemical or climatic action, rain, spray, etc., and insufficient marking, inadequate packing, and so forth. (This is of no avail unless the ship is proved to have exercised all reasonable care to

prevent loss or damage. With regard to goods inadequately packed, see separate paragraph on "marginal clauses").

10. A "negligence clause" ruling out liability for loss or damage arising from the negligence of the carrier's servants (master, officers, pilots and crew).

11. A "general average" clause to the effect that, either with or without reservations, G/A is to be settled according to Y-A Rules, 1974.

12. A clause whereby the carrier disclaims responsibility for overcarriage or short landing. (The carrier is, of course, fully responsible for eventual delivery, and short landed or overcarried goods must be forwarded to their proper destination at the carrier's expense. Liner Conference members usually have an arrangement for carrying each other's overcarried and short landed goods freight free.)

13. Special clauses as required by the particular nature of the goods, *e.g.*, for refrigerated cargo "Carrier not responsible for breakdown of refrigerating machinery". (Here, also, to be protected by the clause the carrier would have to show that first-class machinery and spares were installed, and that properly qualified maintenance personnel were engaged).

14. The "Paramount clause" if required by statute or if agreed to by the parties when not required by law. This clause renders the exceptions and negligence clauses redundant, and they may therefore be omitted.

15. Both to blame collision clause and New Jason clause (described elsewhere in this Chapter).

Note:—By the Unfair Contract Terms Act 1977, if a contract for carriage of goods by sea is made with a person who "deals as consumer", the carrier will not be permitted to rely on a clause excluding or restricting his liability for breaking the contract, or entitling him to render any performance other than that which was reasonably expected of him, unless the court considers it to be reasonable to do so. A person "deals as consumer" when he does not make the contract in the course of a business and the other party does, and such a person might be involved in this way when he sends personal property, such as furniture or personal belongings, as cargo to a place abroad. By the same Act (s.2(1)) a carrier cannot by a contract term exclude or restrict liability for death or personal injury resulting from negligence, but this is unlikely to apply to carriage of goods by sea.

Marginal Clauses in B's/L. The master or agent who signs a B/L has the right and the duty to insert any marginal clause he considers necessary to protect the interests of the carrier, so long as such clause is not repugnant to or inconsistent with the Hague Visby or Hague Rules where those rules apply. The right, however, is one that should not be abused. It should be remembered that most exports are financed by credits in some form or another, the "documentary credit" system being a method commonly employed. Usually the negotiating bank will not permit the exporter to draw on a letter of credit unless he supplies, amongst other documents, a "clean" set of B's/L, or unless he undertakes to indemnify the bank against any liability it may incur through accepting a "claused" bill. For that reason, if for no other, marginal clauses should not be inserted unless they are really necessary. If, for instance, goods are described in the body of the B/L as "unprotected", there is no need to add a marginal clause stating that the goods are not adequately packed, or are unpacked. That does no-one any good and may cause the shipper unnecessary difficulties.

The exception "inadequate packing" protects the carrier when it is not obvious on a reasonable inspection that the goods are not suitably packed to withstand the ordinary hazards of the voyage. On the other hand, if it is quite evident to those receiving the goods for shipment that they are improperly packed, or are not packed at all, then they should either be rejected in that condition, or given the extra care in the matter of handling and stowage that their special condition warrants.

Clauses framed to describe the pre-shipment condition of goods must be valid in law. For example, such a clause as "Ship not responsible for bursting of bags or for loss of contents" is not valid in a B/L subject to the Hague Rules, as it disclaims a responsibility imposed by those Rules and, accordingly, affords the carrier no protection whatever. A clause recommended for use when it is considered that packing is inadequate reads:—

"Attention is drawn to the packing of these goods, which in the opinion of the Carrier is insufficient. All the Carrier's rights and immunities in the event of loss of or damage to the goods arising by reason of the nature or quality of that packing and/or its insufficiency are hereby expressly reserved."

In the case of goods completely unpacked (*e.g.*, uncrated motor cars) which have not been described in the body of the B/L as "unprotected" or "unpacked", the clause recommended for insertion in the margin reads:—

"The goods hereby acknowledged are unprotected, and all the Carrier's rights and immunities in the event of loss of or damage to the goods by reason of that fact are hereby expressly reserved."

Cargo may sustain damage of various kinds prior to shipment, and it is not possible to draft a general clause to cover all cases. Therefore, whenever goods are offered for shipment in a damaged or defective state, the B/L should be claused with a factual statement particularising, in clear and unambiguous terms, the nature of the damage or defect, *e.g.*, "patches of rust showing where paint chipped off".

Waybill or Sea Waybill. This is a non-negotiable document which provides a receipt for the goods by the carrier and evidence of the contract of carriage for the goods described on it. It is not a document of title to the goods. It is a "received for carriage" document which can be converted into a "shipped" or "loaded on board" document by appropriate notation, signed and dated, by the carrier. The waybill is not intended to replace the B/L where it is necessary for an exporter to retain a clear title to the goods until security of payment has been assured. It is very suitable for use where there is a possibility of documents arriving at destination after the goods and therefore can be used in trade between multinational and associated companies, (e.g. Ford's), open account sales and transactions in which goods can be consigned to a trusted third party in the country of destination, such as a local agent or, by prior arrangement, an overseas bank. It may also be used when there are no payment requirements for goods such as household/personal effects, samples, documents, etc.

A waybill, when used, is usually in Short Form with a short Incorporation Clause on the front referring to the carrier's detailed conditions of carriage, which are available separately from the carrier's, or his agents', offices. Because the waybill is not a document of title, the consignee does not usually need it to take possession of his goods. Release of cargo is given to the consignee or his agent on the basis of conditions laid down by the carrier at destination, which include proof of identity and authority. This should normally mean that there is no need to wait for documents such as the B/L to arrive before delivery can be taken and should therefore reduce, in appropriate cases, the possibility of liability for demurrage charges at the terminal.

Waybills can be used with documentary credits if the documentary credit specifically authorises their acceptance. They can also be used when documents, or bills of exchange, are transmitted through a bank for collection, but if the U.K. bank is required to advance finance on the strength of the documents, it will normally be necessary to supply a shipped B/L.

B/L issued pursuant to a voyage C/P. As stated previously the C/P itself frequently contains a specimen of the form of B/L to be used but, in any case, where goods are being carried under two contracts of affreightment it is important that those contracts should be consistent with one another. Where charterer and shipper are one and the same person, the B/L issued is a mere receipt for the cargo received on board, the contract of carriage being embodied in the C/P. But should the charterer assign his interest in the goods to some third party by indorsement and delivery of the B's/L, he assigns not only the goods but the whole contract of carriage as well. At that stage the B/L acquires the full status of a receipt, plus evidence of contract, plus document of title. Therefore, if the B/L does not already make clear that the terms, etc., of the C/P apply, an incorporating clause should be added to the effect that "Freight and all other terms, conditions, exceptions and exemptions, including the negligence clause, as per charter-party".

Usually a B/L issued pursuant to a C/P is a much shorter and more simple document than a liner B/L because the detailed provisions of the contract contained in the C/P are incorporated into the B/L by reference.

A problem which may arise in respect of a B/L issued by a chartered ship is whether the shipper (when he is not the charterer) has contracted with the shipowner or with the charterer, that is to say, whether the master has signed the B/L as agent of the owner or as agent of the charterer. As it is a general rule that the master has a legal authority to sign B's/L on behalf of the shipowner who employs him, anybody who ships goods in the vessel, and who is unaware that the ship is chartered, is warranted in assuming that the master is acting under his ordinary authority and is signing the bill on behalf of the owners of the ship. Even where there is an agreement that the master should sign B's/L on behalf of the charterer, that does not appear to affect the liability of the shipowner unless the fact that the master is acting as agent of the charterer is brought to the knowledge of the shipper. It has been held in one particular case that "In the case of a voyage charter with a cesser clause the B/L contract is generally between the shipowner and the shipper, and this is so even though the C/P provides that the master shall sign B's/L as the agent of the charterer, if the shipper is ignorant of this provision".

B/L issued by a time-chartered ship. The position may be summed up briefly as follows:—

1. In the case of a demise charter the B/L contract is always between the charterer and the shipper.

2. In the case of a simple time charter where the master is to sign B's/L without prejudice to the C/P, the B/L contract is usually between shipowner and shipper, but, as against the charterer, the shipowner remains bound by the unaltered terms of the C/P. But where the charterer presents bills to the master for signature, and they impose on the shipowner an obligation greater than that imposed by the C/P, the charterer must indemnify the shipowner for all losses he suffers by reason of such increased obligation. Where, as sometimes happens, the charterer makes a freight agreement with the shipper and issues and signs B's/L headed with his name, the contract will be between charterer and shipper.

Signing of Bills of Lading. Except in connection with bulk oil and similar cargoes and, very often, other homogeneous cargoes carried in tramp vessels, it is not usual nowadays for B's/L to be signed by the master of the ship. Liner owners at their principal offices, and their agents at outports and abroad, maintain special departments where B's/L are signed by persons authorised for the purpose. Whoever signs, however, it is important that all precautions should be taken to ensure:—

1. That the B/L is in proper form, *i.e.*, usually the shipowner's own form, or the form prescribed by the C/P.
2. That it is correctly dated with the date of shipment.
3. That mate's receipts showing (*a*) that the goods are actually on board, and (*b*) the apparent order and condition of the goods and details of any shortage, have been surrendered.
4. That marginal clauses as required, but only those really necessary and lawful, have been duly inserted to show the apparent order and condition, and quantity.
5. That freight, if pre-payable, has been paid.
6. That, if the ship is under charter, that the owners' rights under the C/P are preserved. (See below).

When the master signs B's/L for goods received on board a voyage-chartered ship he should endorse on them the number of the lay day on which the goods were loaded or, if the ship is already on demurrage, the number of the demurrage day together with a statement as to whether the demurrage has been paid or not and, if not, the amount outstanding. This will then transfer the liability to subsequent B/L holders and enable the master to enforce the lien for demurrage (assuming such lien has been contracted for) at the port of discharge. In the same way, and for the same reason, any other charges against the cargo such as unpaid freight, advance freight or deadfreight should be likewise endorsed on the B's/L.

Finally, the person signing B's/L should note carefully how many parts there are to the set and sign them all.

Signing for Bulk Cargoes. A master cannot be made to sign a B/L stating that goods have been received on board which he knows have not been loaded. When loading bulk cargoes it is often difficult to know with certainty exactly what quantity has been loaded, and therefore to avoid the possibility of claims for short delivery the ship should endeavour to check shore figures by whatever means are available, say by draught check or volume calculations, before signing for the quantity shown on a B/L presented for signature. Whether there is a discrepancy or not will probably depend on the nature of the cargo, the port and its facilities, the size of ship, and perhaps other factors, such as the accuracy of calibration of the ship's tanks and the difficulties involved in taking draught readings at some berths. Experience suggests that if the B/L figure *differs* from the ship's figure by more than one half of one per cent (0·5%),

S

then the master has good grounds for questioning the accuracy of the B/L figures.

If the difference between the ship's and B/L figures exceeds 0·5%, every effort should be made to discover the reason for the difference. If this is not possible then the master should take one of the following courses of action to protect the ship's owners:—

(a) delete the B/L figure, insert the ship's figure and initial the alteration; or

(b) endorse the B/L with the remark "x tonnes in dispute"; or

(c) refuse to sign it, but then pass it to the agents with clear instructions in writing about signing on his behalf; or

(d) tear up the B/L presented and issue his own B/L using the company's or a well recognised form.

Note:—If action (c) is adopted the agents should be informed:—

(i) of the quantity and description of cargo they are authorised to sign for;

(ii) that they are not authorised to sign any B/L unless the terms, conditions and exceptions of the current C/P dated .... and/or the Hague or Hague-Visby Rules or equivalent legislation are specifically incorporated in the B/L;

(iii) that the destination shown in the B/L should be consistent with the C/P provisions which should then be stated;

(iv) that all the B's/L must be correctly dated; and

(v) that on no account should B's/L marked "freight prepaid" be issued without the authority of the ship's owners, to whom reference should be made on any other matter concerning signing and issuing of B's/L.

If the B/L figure is within ±0·5% of the ship's figure it is probably in order to sign it, but if the B/L figure *exceeds* the ship figure by more than one tenth of one per cent (0·1%), the master should note the difference in letters addressed to charterers and shippers, notifying the ship's owner what has been done.

Unless the C/P provides otherwise, a shipper cannot demand the master's signature to more than one set of bills for a bulk cargo shipped without separations. The practice of giving B's/L for separate parcels loaded in different holds may be to the owners' detriment unless the B/L is claused to the effect that excess of out-turn in one hold shall be set off against shortage in another, in which case each bill should be claused "weight and quantity unknown".

B's/L must be signed within a reasonable time of being presented. It is not reasonable to delay signing for a particular parcel until bills for the whole cargo are tendered.

Master's Authority to sign B's/L. If the ship is not under charter, the owner is bound by any term in a B/L signed by the master which is (a) within the master's ordinary authority, (b) outside his ordinary authority but within special authority given him, (c) within his ordinary authority but contrary to special instructions, if the shipper did not know of such instructions, and (d) outside ordinary or special authority known of by the shipper if the shipowner, by word or deed, subsequently ratifies the B/L.

If the ship is chartered, the master has no authority to sign a B/L in terms different from the C/P without special instructions from the owner, or unless the C/P provides that he may.

Letters of Indemnity. In the interests of honest trade it is essential that a B/L should never contain a false description of the condition or quantity of the goods. A person who buys goods he has never seen on the strength of their B/L description is entitled to a square deal, and if he fails to get one, has a remedy in prosecution for fraud. Cases do arise where a shipper, to avoid difficulties over the financing of a shipment (and sometimes for even less worthy reasons), offers the master or agent of the shipowner a "letter of indemnity" or "back letter" in return for clean bills of lading in circumstances where a qualified bill would appear to be justified. In such letter the shipper gives an undertaking to indemnify the shipowner in respect of any loss or liability the latter may be faced with as a result of issuing clean bills. No master should ever lend himself to this practice, which could possibly result in his being found guilty of conniving at fraud. In any case, a letter of indemnity has no legal standing whatever. It is binding in honour only, and cannot be sued upon should the shipper who issues it go back on his word. In certain trades, however, it appears that some shipowners and their agents are prepared to issue clean B's/L in exchange for letters of indemnity but, it should be said in all fairness, only in special circumstances in accordance with a resolution adopted by the International Chamber of Commerce. This resolution includes the following principle, viz., that in cases which involve *bona fide* and substantial grounds for dispute as to condition, number or amount of the goods, the Chamber is of opinion that a solution involving the elimination of letters of indemnity should be sought on the line of an understanding between buyer and seller, but that in the meantime the safeguards at present existing provide valuable assistance in eliminating certain malpractices and represent a very earnest effort, especially on the part of the carriers, although there is a difference of opinion as to their efficacy. The safeguards referred to are (1) that the acceptance of letters of indemnity should be communicated to the shipowners or their agents at the port of discharge, and (2) that the shipowners should, on application by the underwriters concerned, disclose to them the existence of such letters of indemnity should a claim arise. It will be evident that the issue of clean B's/L in respect of a shipment which is in some way defective is very much against the interests of cargo underwriters.

The Harter Act and New Jason Clause. In English law, as under the laws of most other maritime countries, a shipowner cannot escape liability for loss caused through his own personal negligence or default. Neither can he for loss caused through the fault or negligence of his servants, unless he is freed from such liability by the terms of the contract of carriage. But where he is freed by the terms of the contract, he can claim a general average contribution from cargo owners where a G/A sacrifice or expenditure has followed an accident of navigation.

In the United States of America the position is not the same. By their Harter Act (see Appendix) it is made illegal to insert any clause in a B/L exonerating the ship from liability for loss through negligence, but the same Act goes on to say that if the vessel is properly manned and equipped, etc., the owner shall not be responsible for losses arising from faults or errors in the navigation or management of the vessel, Act of God, public enemies, inherent fault or defect of cargo, or loss through attempting to save life or property at sea.

In spite of this, however, it is a ruling of American common law that even though the ship is freed from liability in that way, it still does not entitle the shipowner to claim G/A contribution from cargo in a case where there has been a fault or error in navigation or management of the vessel. For that reason it became a custom to insert a clause in B's/L covering goods carried to or from the U.S.A. entitling the shipowner to claim a G/A contribution from cargo by the terms of the contract of carriage.

In 1904 the validity of this clause came under test in the case of a ship named *Jason* and after a very lengthy period of litigation the U.S. Supreme Court finally, in 1911, upheld its validity. Following that case, the clause became known as the "Jason Clause". More recently, the clause has been redrafted and extended to include salvage charges, and is now known as the "New Jason Clause", and it is recommended that it should be inserted in all B's/L and all C/P's whether the ship is going to or from the United States or not. The present clause reads:—

"In the event of accident, danger, damage or disaster before or after the commencement of the voyage, resulting from any cause whatsoever, whether due to negligence or not, for which, or for the consequences of which, the carrier is not responsible, by statute, contract or otherwise, the goods, shippers, consignees or owners of the goods shall contribute with the carrier in general average to the payment of any sacrifices, losses or expenses of a general average nature that may be made or incurred in respect of the goods.

"If a salving ship is owned or operated by the carrier, salvage shall be paid for as fully as if the said salving ship or ships belonged to strangers. Such deposit as the carrier or his agents may deem sufficient to cover the estimated contribution of the goods and any salvage and special charges thereon shall, if required, be made by the goods, shippers, consignees or owners of the goods to the carrier before delivery."

Although to some extent superseded by the U.S. Carriage of Goods by Sea Act, 1936, the Harter Act is still on the U.S.A. Statute Book, and because it has proved beneficial to shipowners generally, it is recommended that all contracts of carriage to or from the U.S.A. should be claused (in addition to the N.J.C.) in the following way:—

"It is mutually agreed that this contract is subject to all terms and provisions of, and all exemptions from liability contained in, the Act of Congress approved on the 13th day of February, 1893."

The "ejusdem generis" Rule. This rule (explained in the section on C/P exceptions clauses) does not extend to bills of lading on account of the negotiability of those documents. B/L exceptions, in order to be effective, must be particularised.

The Bills of Lading Act, 1855. This Act provides:—

1. Every consignee of goods named in a bill of lading, and every endorsee of a bill of lading to whom the property in the goods therein mentioned shall pass, upon or by reason of such consignment or endorsement, shall have transferred to and vested in him all rights of suit, and be subject to the same liabilities in respect of such goods as if the contract contained in the bill of lading had been made with himself.

2. Nothing herein contained shall prejudice or affect any right of stoppage in transitu, or any right to claim freight against the original shipper or owner, or any liability of the consignee or endorsee by reason or in consequence of his being such consignee or endorsee, or of his receipt of the goods by reason or in consequence of such consignment or endorsement.

3. Every bill of lading in the hands of a consignee or indorsee for valuable consideration representing goods to have been shipped on board a vessel shall be conclusive evidence of such shipment against the master or other person signing the same, notwithstanding that the goods may not have been shipped, unless such holder of the bill of lading shall have had actual notice at the time of receiving the same that the goods had not been in fact laden on board.

It has long been a custom to treat a B/L as a negotiable instrument by which title to the goods described in it may be transferred and upon which money may be advanced. It will be seen that Section 1 of the above Act gives statutory effect to this custom, and provides that the person who assigns the B/L to another does not merely transfer the property in the goods represented in the bill, but assigns to him the whole contract of carriage. Section 2, however, protects the carrier of the goods by its provision that liability to pay freight remains with the original shipper until such time as the consignee or indorsee has performed his part. Although it is usual to speak of a B/L as a negotiable instrument, it would be truer to refer to it as a transferable instrument, as it is not fully negotiable in the same sense that a bill of exchange is. The essential features of negotiability are that the holder of the instrument for the time being (i) possesses a right of action in his own name, and (ii) is unaffected by equities, and can obtain a good title (though there are some exceptions) despite any defect in the title of the person from whom he received the instrument. The holder of a B/L acquires no better title than that of the person from whom he took it. Even if he is a *bona fide* holder for valuable consideration, he will still be affected by any previous defect in title.

A merchant who buys goods by having a B/L transferred to him will naturally want the best guarantee that can be given that the goods have in fact been shipped. For that reason, Section 3 of the Act, with the exception stated therein, makes the B/L conclusive evidence of shipment against the master or other person signing it. Since masters of ships are not usually men of very substantial means, the right of action against the master may not be of very much value. As far as the shipowner is concerned, the B/L constitutes only *prima facie* evidence, but even in his case such evidence can be displaced only by clear unambiguous notice in the B/L that the goods were defective or short in quantity at the time of shipment.

Stoppage in Transitu. Section 2 of the Bills of Lading Act, besides confirming the shipowner's lien on the goods for freight, allows the seller of the goods to retain the right conferred on him by the Sale of Goods Act, 1979, to stop the goods while they are in transit on their way to the buyer, if it comes to his knowledge that the latter has become insolvent. The right of "stoppage in transitu" may be exercised by taking possession either of the goods themselves or of the documents of title thereto. It may also be exercised by giving notice to the carrier who, within a reasonable time, must pass the notice on to his servant. The notice will be of no effect if it is addressed to the consignee only, and not to the owner or master of the ship carrying the goods. If part delivery has already been made, the right may still be exercised on the remainder of the goods unless the circumstances show an agreement to waive the right. A carrier who receives notice of stoppage must re-deliver the goods in accordance with the seller's directions, and the seller is under an obligation to pay the freight and incidental expenses of the stoppage.

The right of stoppage, which in any case is inferior to the shipowner's lien for freight and other charges (if any), will be defeated once the goods come into the actual or constructive possession of the buyer or his agent. In other words, the right exists only while the goods are "in transit", *i.e.*, in the hands of a middleman. For this purpose goods are deemed to be in transit "from the time when they are delivered to a carrier by land or water, or other bailee or custodier for the purpose of transmission to the buyer, until the buyer or his agent in that behalf takes delivery of them from such carrier or other bailee or custodier". The precise point at which transit ceases has to be determined by the facts of the case, and much will depend on the nature of the contract of sale. If, when goods have reached their appointed destination, the carrier acknowledges to the buyer or his agent that he holds the goods as bailee for the buyer or his agent, the transit is at an end. If the carrier remains in position after the buyer has rejected the goods, even if the seller has refused to take them back, transit is not at an end. If goods are delivered to a ship chartered by the buyer, it is a question depending on the circumstances whether they are in the possession of the master as a carrier, or as the buyer's agent. Delivery to the buyer's own ship is a delivery to the buyer. If the carrier wrongfully refuses to deliver the goods to the buyer, transit is at an end. So it is when (*a*) the buyer or his agent obtains possession before the goods have arrived at their appointed destination, or (*b*) when the goods reach the hands of an agent who is to keep them pending further instructions from the buyer. Where a document of title (*e.g.*, a B/L) has been transferred to any person as buyer or owner of the goods, and that person by way of sale transfers the document to a person who takes it in good faith and for valuable consideration, the unpaid seller's right of "stoppage in transitu" is defeated.

Purpose of the Hague Rules. Until well into the eighteenth century Parliament did not introduce any legislation governing the sea carriage of goods, and even then the few Acts which made their appearance were in favour of shipowners, exempting them from or limiting their liability in various circumstances. With the rapid growth of international sea transport it became the fashion to insert all manner of far-reaching exceptions in C/P's and B's/L. With regard to C/P's that was not considered to be a particularly serious matter since shipowners and charterers are able to contract with one another on more or less equal terms. But in the case of B's/L there were ever increasing complaints that carriers were by contract evading their obligations to a most unfair extent. It has already been pointed out that B's/L affect not only the original parties thereto, namely shipper and shipowner, but also consignees and indorsees and, to some extent, insurance interests as well as bankers who accept the documents as security for money advanced to their customers. Shipowners, for their part, defended their many devices to protect themselves on the grounds that, once a ship has left her home port to start a voyage, ship and cargo are beyond the personal control of the shipowner who has to place complete reliance on what is done by the master and crew, agents, stevedores, port authorities, and others. Shippers and consignees, on their side, complained amongst other things that an unfair burden of proof was thrust on them whenever thay had cause to try and establish the carrier's liability for loss of or damage to goods during transit. Some means, therefore, had to be found to regulate the situation and provide for the balance being held fairly between the two sides. As sea carriage is largely international, it was obvious that little good would result from isolated action by one country alone. The eventual outcome was that a meeting of the International Law Association was held at The Hague in 1921, at which representative bodies of interested parties attended with the object of agreeing what the rules relating to bills of lading should be. A set of rules, thereafter known as the Hague Rules, was agreed, and it was hoped that such rules would be adopted by the various maritime nations and given the force of law through the media of suitable statutes. With the passage of time some 68 countries have passed legislation giving statutory effect to the Hague Rules either with or without modifications. In Great Britain and Northern Ireland such effect was given by the passing and bringing into force of the Carriage of Goods by Sea Act, 1924.

The Carriage of Goods by Sea Act 1971. Application. With the introduction of new modes of carriage, particularly the advent of the container and change in the value of money, the Hague Rules needed amending, and in 1968, after meetings by interested parties, the Hague Rules 1924 were amended by Protocol signed at Brussels on 23 February 1968, the amended version being called the Hague-Visby Rules. The U.K. was a signatory to this Protocol, and the Carriage of Goods by Sea Act 1971 was passed to give effect to it. The requisite number of states having accepted the Protocol by the end of 1976, it came into force internationally on 23 June 1977. On that date the Carriage of Goods by Sea Act 1971 was brought into force, and this Act repealed the Carriage of Goods by Sea Act 1924 but it should be noted that for the time being the Hague Rules provisions will continue to apply in countries which have not enacted the Hague-Visby Rules. The Act and Schedule are reproduced as Appendix I.

The Act applies to:

(a) any contract for the carriage of goods by sea in ships where the port of shipment is a port in the U.K., and the contract provides for the issue of a bill of lading or similar document of title;

(b) any bill of lading if the contract in or evidenced by it expressly provides that the amended Hague Rules shall govern the contract;

(c) any non-negotiable receipt, marked as such, if it expressly provides that the Rules are to govern the contract as if the receipt were a bill of lading. (But Art. III, para. 4, second sentence, and para. 7 are not to apply.)

Where a bill of lading expressly provides that the Hague-Visby Rules shall govern the contract for carriage of live animals or deck cargo, or a non-negotiable receipt provides that the Rules are to govern the contract as if it were a bill of lading, the Act applies even though the cargo consists of live animals or deck cargo. "Deck cargo" means cargo which by the contract of carriage is stated as being carried on deck and is so carried.

Where the Act applies, the absolute warranty of seaworthiness implied in contracts for the carriage of goods by sea is abolished. Instead the carrier must exercise due diligence to make the ship seaworthy.

Nothing in the Act is to affect the operation of any sections of the M.S.A. 1894 or later enactments which give the carrier the right to limit his liability in appropriate circumstances.

Schedule:—Rules relating to Bills of Lading.

Art. I. Definitions.

(a) "Carrier" includes the owner or the charterer who enters into a contract of carriage with a shipper.

(b) "Contract of carriage" applies to contracts covered by a bill of lading or similar document of title, but only for that part of the contract which relates to the carriage of goods by sea. It includes any bill of lading or similar document issued under the terms of a charter-party, but only from the moment at which such bill of lading regulates the relations between a carrier and a holder of the same.

(c) The term "goods" includes goods and articles of every kind, except live animals and cargo which by the contract of carriage is stated as being carried on deck and is so carried.

(d) A "ship" means any vessel used for the carriage of goods by sea.

(e) "Carriage of goods" covers the period from the time when goods are loaded on to the time they are discharged from the ship.

Art. II. Risks.

Subject to the provisions of Article VI, under every contract of carriage of goods by sea the carrier, in relation to the loading, handling, stowage, carriage, custody, care and discharge of such goods, shall be subject to the responsibilities and liabilities, and entitled to the rights and immunities hereinafter set forth.

Art. III. Responsibilities and Liabilities.

1. The carrier is bound, before and at the beginning of the voyage, to exercise due diligence to (*a*) make the ship seaworthy; (*b*) properly man, equip, and supply the ship; and (*c*) make the holds, refrigerating and cool chambers, and all other parts of the ship in which goods are carried, fit and safe for their reception, carriage and preservation. *Note*:—The words "before and at the beginning of the voyage" mean the period from at least the beginning of the loading until the vessel starts on her voyage.

2. Subject to the provisions of Article IV, the carrier is to properly and carefully load, handle, stow, carry, keep, care for and discharge the goods carried.

3. After receiving the goods into his charge, the carrier, master or carrier's agent, is, on the shipper's demand, required to issue to the shipper a bill of lading showing among other things (*a*) the leading marks necessary for identification of the goods, (*b*) either the number of packages or pieces, or the quantity or weight, as the case may be, as furnished in writing by the shipper, and (*c*) the apparent order and condition of the goods. The master or agent can refuse to show marks in the bill of lading if the marks on the goods or containers will not ordinarily remain legible until the end of the voyage, and he need not show information which he has reasonable grounds for suspecting is inaccurate for the goods actually received, or which he has had no reasonable means of checking.

4. Such a bill of lading is *prima facie* evidence of the receipt by the carrier of the goods described therein.

5. The shipper is deemed to have guaranteed to the carrier the accuracy at the time of shipment of marks, number, quantity and weight, furnished by him, and the shipper is required to indemnify the carrier against all loss or damage and expenses which arise as a result of inaccuracies in such information. *Note*:—The carrier still remains liable to any person other than the shipper, but if as a result of inaccurate information received from the shipper and incorporated in a bill of lading the carrier settles a claim, he then has right of action against the shipper.

6. Unless notice of loss or damage is given in writing to the carrier or his agent at the port of discharge before or at the time of the removal of the goods into the custody of the person entitled to delivery of them, or, if the loss or damage is not apparent, within three days, such removal is prima facie evidence of the delivery by the carrier of the goods described

in the bill of lading. The notice in writing need not be given if the state of the goods has been the subject of a joint survey at the time of their receipt. In any event the carrier and the ship is discharged from all liability in respect of loss or damage unless suit is brought within one year after delivery of the goods, or the date when the goods should have been delivered. In the case of any actual loss or damage the carrier and the receiver shall give all reasonable facilities to each other for inspecting and tallying the goods.

6 *bis*. Action for indemnity against a third person may be brought even after one year if brought within the time allowed by the law of the Court seized of the case.

7. After the goods are loaded the carrier, master or carrier's agent must, if the shipper so demands, issue a "shipped" bill of lading. Alternatively at the carrier's option, if the shipper has already taken a "received for shipment" bill, it may be converted into a "shipped" bill by the carrier, master or carrier's agent noting on it at the port of shipment the name or names of the ship or ships upon which the goods have been shipped and the date or dates of shipment.

8. Any clause, covenant or agreement in a contract of carriage relieving the carrier or the ship from liability for loss or damage to or in connection with goods arising from negligence, fault or failure in the duties and obligation provided in this Article or lessening such liability otherwise than as provided in these Rules, is null and void and of no effect.

Art. IV. Rights and Immunities.

1. Neither the carrier nor the ship is liable for loss or damage arising or resulting from unseaworthiness unless caused by want of due diligence on the part of the carrier to make the ship seaworthy as required by Article III. Whenever loss or damage has resulted from unseaworthiness, the carrier has the burden of proving that he exercised due diligence to make the ship seaworthy.

2. Neither the carrier nor the ship is responsible for loss or damage arising or resulting from:—

    (*a*) act, neglect or default of the master, mariner, pilot, or the servants of the carrier in the navigation or in the management of the ship;

    (*b*) fire, unless caused by the actual fault or privity of the carrier;

    (*c*) perils, dangers and accidents of the sea or other navigable waters;

    (*d*) act of God;

    (*e*) act of war;

    (*f*) act of public enemies;

(g) **arrest** or restraint of princes, rulers or people, or seizure under legal process;

(h) quarantine restrictions;

(i) act or omission of the shipper or owner of the goods, his agent or representative;

(j) strikes or lock-outs or stoppage or restraint of labour from whatever cause, whether partial or general;

(k) riots and civil commotions;

(l) saving or attempting to save life or property at sea;

(m) wastage in bulk or weight or any other loss or damage arising from inherent defect, quality or vice of the goods;

(n) insufficiency of packing;

(o) insufficiency or inadequacy of marks;

(p) latent defects not discoverable by due diligence;

(q) any other cause arising without the actual fault or privity of the carrier, or without the fault or neglect of the agents or servants of the carrier, but the burden of proof is on the person claiming the benefit of this exception to show that neither the actual fault or privity of the carrier nor the fault or neglect of the agents or servants of the carrier contributed to the loss or damage.

Note:—The shipowner cannot rely on the "excepted perils" listed above, if he has not carried out his obligation to exercise due diligence to make the ship seaworthy and the fact that he has not is the cause of the damage, nor can he do so if the vessel makes a deviation not permitted by the Act.

3. The shipper is not responsible for loss or damage sustained by the carrier or the ship unless due to the act, fault or neglect of the shipper, his agents or his servants.

4. Any deviation in saving or attempting to save life or property at sea, or any reasonable deviation is not an infringement or breach of these Rules or of the contract of carriage, and the carrier is not liable for any loss or damage resulting therefrom. *Note*:—Whether a particular deviation is reasonable or not is a question of fact in each case.

5. The maximum liability of carrier or ship for any loss or damage to goods is an amount equivalent to 10,000 gold francs per package or unit or 30 gold francs per kilo of gross weight of goods lost or damaged whichever is higher, unless the nature and value of the goods declared before shipment and inserted in the B/L. The total amount recoverable is based on the value of the goods at the place and time the goods were discharged, or should have been. The value of gold francs is to be declared by Statutory Instrument from time to time. (On 1st January 1981, 10,000 gold francs were valued at £359·25, and 30 gold francs at £1·08. When the

provisions of the Protocol signed at Brussels on 21st December 1979 come into force 10,000 gold francs and 30 gold francs per kilo will be replaced by 666·67 units of account and 2 units of account per kilogramme respectively, where the unit of account is the special drawing right defined by the IMF. The value of one special drawing right on a day shall be the sum in sterling fixed by the IMF as being equivalent to one special drawing right on that day. This value is publicised each day in the *Financial Times*).

Where goods are stowed in a container or on a pallet or similar article of transport, the number of packages or units enumerated in the B/L as packed in such article of transport shall determine the liability of carrier; otherwise the container or pallet is to be considered the package or unit. By agreement the carrier and shipper may fix another maximum amount provided such maximum is not less than the amounts above named.

The carrier is not entitled to limit liability as above if it is proved that the damage resulted from the act or omission of the carrier done with intent to cause damage, or recklessly and with knowledge that damage would probably result.

6. Goods of an inflammable, explosive or dangerous nature to whose shipment the carrier, master or carrier's agent has not consented with knowledge of their nature and character, may at any time before discharge, be landed at any place or destroyed or rendered innocuous by the carrier without compensation, and the shipper of such goods shall be liable for all damages and expenses directly or indirectly arising out of or resulting from such shipment. If any such goods shipped with such knowledge and consent become a danger to the ship or cargo, they may be dealt with in like manner by the carrier without liability on the part of the carrier except to general average, if any.

Art. IV bis. The defences and liability limits provided for in the Rules apply in any action against the carrier in respect of loss or damage to the goods whether the action be founded in contract or in tort.

If an action is brought against a servant or agent of the carrier (such servant or agent not being an independent contractor) such servant or agent is entitled to avail himself of the defences and liability limits which the carrier is entitled to invoke under the Rules. The above is not to apply if it is proved that the damage resulted from act or omission of the servant done with intent to cause damage or recklessly and with knowledge that damage would result.

Art. V. Surrender of Rights and Immunities and Increases of Responsibilities and Liabilities.

A carrier is at liberty to surrender in whole or in part, all, or any of his rights and immunities, or to increase any of his responsibilities and liabilities under the Rules, provided such surrender or increase is embodied in the bill of lading issued to the shipper.

The Rules are not applicable to charter-parties, but if bills of lading are issued in the case of a ship under a charter-party, they are to comply with the terms of these Rules. Nothing in these Rules is to be held to prevent the insertion in a bill of lading of any lawful provision regarding general average.

Note:—If a charterer and shipper are one and the same person it would seem that the shipowner is not bound to issue a B/L in the form required by the Act, as a B/L in such hands is merely a receipt. But if such bill is issued and subsequently indorsed to a third party, it would upon such indorsement become a contract within the meaning of Art. 1 (*b*), as between shipowner and indorsee the goods would be carried on B/L terms, and the B/L would be construed as being subject to the provisions of the Act.

Art. VI. Special Conditions.

This article permits a carrier, master or carrier's agent to enter into any agreement in any terms with a shipper of any particular goods, with respect to responsibility and liability of the carrier for such goods, or his obligation as to seaworthiness, provided the terms are not contrary to public policy, that the carrier's servants or agents carefully load, handle, stow, carry, care for and discharge the goods, that no bill of lading is issued, and that the terms agreed are embodied in a receipt which is non-negotiable and marked as such.

Any such agreement is to have full legal effect.

The above is not to apply to ordinary commercial shipments made in the ordinary course of trade, but only to shipments where the character or condition of the property carried or the terms and conditions of carriage reasonably justify a special agreement.

Note:—From time to time it becomes necessary to carry special cargoes, or to carry cargoes in a special manner, by way of experiment. Once the trade has got beyond the experimental stage, the cargo concerned will come into the category of an ordinary commercial shipment and the special conditions will no longer apply.

Art. VII. Limitations on the Application of the Rules.

Nothing in these Rules is to prevent a carrier or a shipper entering into any agreement as to the responsibility and

liability of the carrier or the ship for loss or damage caused to
the goods during custody, care and handling prior to loading
on, and following discharge from, the ship which carried the
goods by sea.

Art. VIII. Limitation of Liability.

These Rules are not to affect the rights and obligations
of the carrier under any statute for the time being in force
relating to a shipowner's right to limit his liability.

The United States Carriage of Goods by Sea Act, 1936. In most
respects the American Act closely resembles our 1924 Act, but there
are some differences the most important of which are as follows:

1. The American Act seems to require from the carrier an absolute undertaking to provide a seaworthy ship, inasmuch that
   what was the substance of sect. 2 of the British Act is omitted.
   Yet both Acts bind the carrier before and at the beginning of
   the voyage to exercise due diligence to make the ship seaworthy.
2. Unlike our own Act which applied only to outward B's/L, the
   American Act applies to shipments to or from ports in the
   United States in foreign trade.
3. Deviation for the purpose of loading or discharging cargo, or
   embarking or disembarking passengers is *prima facie* regarded
   as unreasonable under the American Act.
4. The carrier's maximum liability is fixed at $500 per package
   lawful money of the United States, or in the case of goods not
   shipped in packages, per customary freight unit, or the equivalent of that sum in other currency.

It appears that there is no legislation pending in the U.S.A. to
embody the provisions of the 1968 Brussels Protocol to the Hague
Rules. Indeed there seems to be no reasonable possibility of the
United States ratifying that Protocol. Instead, the State Department
has backed "UNCITRAL" (United Nations Commission on International Trade Law) in its efforts to produce an entirely new International Convention on ocean bills of lading.

The Hamburg Rules 1978. For many years shippers and importers in the developing countries have complained that the Hague
Rules unfairly protected the shipowner, and placed too heavy a
burden on the shipper and consignee. The United Nations Commission for International Trade Law (UNCITRAL) worked for several
years on a new convention to try to remedy this alleged complaint
and in March 1978 at a conference in Hamburg attended by representatives from 78 states and observers from shipping, trade and
insurance interests the results of their labours were adopted as the
United Nations Convention on the Carriage of Goods by Sea, 1978,

to be known as the Hamburg Rules. The Convention is to be brought into force one year from the date of deposit of the twentieth instrument of ratification.

There is no required minimum proportion of the tonnage of the world fleet specified before the Convention can come into force, as with other Conventions.

The intention of the Rules is to bring carriage of goods by sea more into line with the rules that apply for carriage of goods by air, rail and road. To this end they attempt to make definite changes regarding liabilities of carriers, which are summed up in the "Common Understanding" contained in Annex II of the Conference's Final Act which, although not a legal provision, reads:—

"It is the common understanding that the liability of the carrier under this Convention is based on the principle of presumed fault or neglect. This means that, as a rule, the burden of proof rests on the carrier but, with respect to certain cases, the provisions of the Convention modify this rule."

The main provisions of the Rules are:—

Denunciation of the Hague Rules. When the Convention comes into force, any state party to it will have to denounce the Hague Rules, whether amended or not, and apply the new Rules.

In the definitions, "goods" includes live animals, and where goods are consolidated in a container or pallet etc., "goods" includes such article of transport, or packaging, if supplied by the shipper.

Scope of application. The provisions apply to all contracts of carriage by sea between two different states if:—

(a) the port of loading or port of discharge in the contract is in a Contracting State; or

(b) one of the optional ports of discharge in the contract is the actual port of discharge and is located in a Contracting State; or

(c) the B/L or other document evidencing the contract is issued in a Contracting State; or

(d) the B/L or other document evidencing the contract provides that the provisions of the Convention, or the legislation of any State giving effect to them are to apply.

The provisions of the Convention are not to apply to charter parties, but where a B/L is issued pursuant to a charter party, the provisions of the Convention are to apply to that B/L if it governs the relations between the carrier and the holder of the B/L, not being the charterer.

Liability of the Carrier. The carrier is responsible for the goods during the period when the carrier is in charge of them, that is from when he takes over the goods from the shipper, during the carriage, and until he has delivered the goods by handing them over to the consignee.

The carrier is liable for loss resulting from loss or damage to the goods, as well as from delay in delivery, if the occurrence which caused the loss or delay occurred while they were in the carrier's charge, unless he can prove that he, and his servants and agents took all measures that could reasonably be required to avoid the occurrence and its consequences. A person entitled to make a claim for loss of goods, may do so if the goods have not been delivered within 60 consecutive days of the agreed delivery date, or of a reasonable delivery date.

The carrier is liable for loss of or damage to the goods, or delay in delivery, caused by fire, if the fire is proved to be due to fault or neglect on the carrier's part, or his servants or agents, or fault or neglect on their part in taking all measures that could reasonably be required to put out the fire and avoid or mitigate its consequences.

With respect to live animals, the carrier is not liable for loss, damage or delay in delivery resulting from any special risks inherent in that kind of carriage.

Limitation of Liability. The liability of the carrier for loss or damage is limited to an amount equivalent to 835 units of account per package or other shipping unit, or 2·5 units of account per kilogramme of gross weight of the goods lost or damaged, whichever is the higher. The liability for delay in delivery is limited to an amount equivalent to two and a half times the freight payable for the goods delayed, but not exceeding the total freight payable under the contract of carriage. Where a container, pallet or similar articles of transport is used to consolidate goods, the package or other shipping units enumerated in the B/L or other document, as packed in such article of transport, are deemed packages or shipping units for the purpose of calculating the limit of liability. Except as aforesaid, the goods in such container are deemed one shipping unit. The carrier is not entitled to limit his liability if it is proved that the loss, damage, or delay resulted from an act or omission of the carrier done with intent to cause such loss, or recklessly and with knowledge that such loss, damage or delay would probably result.

Deck Cargo. The carrier is entitled to carry the goods on deck only if such carriage is agreed to with the shipper, or with the usage of a particular trade, or is required by statutory rules or regulations. If the carrier and the shipper have agreed that the goods shall or may be carried on deck, the carrier must insert in the B/L, or other document, a statement to that effect. In the absence of such a statement, the carrier has the burden of proving that an agreement for carriage on deck has been entered into; however, the carrier is not entitled to invoke such an agreement against a third party, including a consignee, who has acquired the B/L in good faith.

Carriage on deck contrary to the above provisions makes the carrier liable for loss or damage, and carriage of goods on deck contrary to express agreement for carriage under deck, is deemed an act or omission of the carrier and loss of his right to limit liability.

Liability of the Shipper. The shipper is not liable for loss sustained by the carrier, or for damage sustained by the ship, unless such loss or damage was caused by the fault or neglect of the shipper, his servants or agents, nor is any servant or agent of the shipper liable, unless caused by fault or neglect on his part. The shipper must mark or label in a suitable manner, dangerous goods as dangerous, and inform the carrier of the dangerous character of the goods, and if necessary, the precautions to be taken.

Transport Documents. When the carrier takes charge of the goods, he must, on demand of the shipper, issue to him a B/L. The B/L must include particulars such as the general nature of the goods, leading marks, dangerous character (if any), number of packages or pieces, and the weight of the goods or their quantity otherwise expressed, all as furnished by the shipper. Also the apparent condition of the goods, carrier's name and address, name of the shipper and consignee, the port of loading and date taken over, the port of discharge, number of original B's/L, the place where the B/L issued, the signature of the carrier or a person acting on his behalf; a statement that the goods shall, or may be carried on deck (if applicable), the freight payable by the consignee.

After the goods have been loaded on board, the carrier must issue to the shipper a "shipped" B/L stating that the goods are on board a named ship(s) and the date(s) of loading, or amend any such previously issued B/L to show the same information.

Where a shipped B/L is issued it is *prima facie* evidence of the loading by the carrier of the goods described therein, and proof to the contrary by the carrier is not admissable if the B/L has been transferred to a third party, including a consignee, who in good faith has acted in reliance on the description of the goods therein.

Claims and Actions. Unless notice of loss or damage, stating the general nature of the loss or damage, is given in writing by the consignee to the carrier not later than the working day after the day when the goods were handed over to the consignee, such handing over is *prima facie* evidence of the delivery by the carrier of the goods as described in the document of transport.

Where the loss or damage is not apparent, the above provisions apply if notice in writing is not given within 15 consecutive days after the day when the goods were handed over to the consignee.

If the state of the goods at the time they were handed over to the consignee has been the subject of a joint survey by the parties, notice in writing need not be given of loss or damage ascertained during such survey.

No compensation shall be payable for loss resulting from delay in delivery unless a notice has been given in writing to the carrier within 60 consecutive days after the day when the goods were handed over to the consignee.

Any action is time-barred if judicial or arbitral proceedings have not been instituted within a period of two years commencing on the day on which the carrier delivered the goods, or where no goods were delivered, on the last day on which the goods should have been delivered.

In judicial proceedings, the plaintiff, at his option, may institute an action in a court which, according to the law of the State where the court is situated, is competent, and within the jurisdiction of which is situated one of the following places:—

(*a*) the principal place of business of the defendant; or
(*b*) the place where the contract was made provided that the defendant has there a place of business, branch or agency through which the contract was made; or
(*c*) the port of loading or the port of discharge; or
(*d*) any additional place designated for that purpose in the contract of carriage by sea.

By August 1981 the Convention had been ratified and acceded to by four States, and therefore had not yet been brought into force. The Convention has not been ratified by the U.K. government.

Miscellaneous Words and Phrases used in B's/L. It is not uncommon for a C/P to contain the clause "B's/L shall be **conclusive evidence** against the shipowners of the quantity of cargo received on board". In the absence of any such clause it is open to the shipowner to show that a person assuming to sign a B/L on his behalf had, in fact, no authority to do so. Further, no master or agent has the owners' implied authority to sign for goods which have not been shipped. But where the "conclusive evidence" clause is used, the shipowner will be bound even by an unauthorised acknowledgement of the shipment of a greater quantity than has actually been shipped. Even without the clause the shipowner is placed in the extremely difficult position of having to prove that the quantity stated in the B/L is inaccurate. However, if the B/L statement is qualified by the words **"weight unknown"**, then the bill is not even *prima facie* evidence against the shipowner of the actual quantity shipped.

Where a B/L setting out the weight and description of goods also contains the words **"weight, contents, and value unknown"**, the original statements of weight and description will be taken to have been made by the shipper and not verified by the master or agent who signed and issued the bill, in which case the shipowner is not estopped from proving the actual weight of the goods at the time of shipment.

If a B/L describes, in error, goods of one kind as goods of some other kind, the shipowner cannot escape liability for loss of the package on the grounds that the B/L does not truly represent the actual goods shipped. The endorsement "weight, contents, and value unknown" in that case would make the B/L a contract for the carriage of the package and its contents, no matter what those contents may be.

In accordance with Art. III (3) of the Carriage of Goods by Sea Act the shipowner must declare in B's/L subject to the Act, should the shipper so demand, the quantity **or** weight **or** number of packages as furnished by the shipper in writing, unless (i) he has reasonable grounds to suspect inaccuracy of the shipper's figures, or (ii) he has no reasonable means of checking these figures. This statement, together with the required declaration as to leading marks and the apparent order and condition of the goods on shipment, are by Art. III (4) *prima facie* evidence of the facts represented, and the onus of proving them inaccurate will rest on the shipowner. If he chooses to declare the weight only, a qualification "weight unknown" will be of no effect. If weight and number of packages are both declared, the qualification "weight unknown" makes the B/L *prima facie* evidence of the number but not of the weight. If a declaration of both weight and number is qualified by the words "weight and number unknown," the B/L will be *prima facie* evidence of both, as such a qualification is contrary to the requirements of the Act.

Whether statements in a B/L are conclusive evidence of the facts they represent or not, the shipowner is estopped from proving them false if (i) the person who signed the bill had the shipowner's authority so to represent, and (ii) the indorsee acted on the representation in the belief that it was true and sustained damage by reason of its not being true. With regard to (i), statements by a master in a B/L as to weight, measure, or quantity do not estop the shipowner from denying their accuracy because, as already stated, the master has no implied authority to sign for goods which have not in fact been shipped. The master likewise has no authority to represent the particular quality of goods shipped. With regard to (ii), the fact that a B/L holder took up the bill without objection is usually evidence enough that he relied on the representations contained in it. But the position may be different if the indorsee or consignee named in the B/L receives notice of a sufficiently conclusive nature that a material representation in the bill is inaccurate at the time when it is still in his power to refuse to take up the bill.

The words **"quality unknown"** do not qualify the representation that goods have been shipped in "apparent good order and condition". Such representation refers only to the external condition of the goods, while "quality" refers to their internal condition or to something which is not usually apparent except to a specially skilled person. Accordingly, a shipowner is not estopped from proving the bad quality of goods on shipment, unless the defect is apparent from the external condition of the goods.

The words **"condition unknown"** are not a sufficient qualification of the statement "shipped in apparent good order and condition" to convey to the indorsee of a B/L that damage to the goods was apparent on shipment. The shipowner, in such case, is therefore estopped from denying their good condition at the time of shipment.

Where a statement in a B/L is qualified by words such as "said to be", "said to contain", or "said to weigh" the shipowner is not estopped from proving the true facts, as he is deemed merely to be repeating what was represented to him by the shipper.

If a B/L containing a conclusive evidence clause specifies the respective quantities of different kinds of goods (*e.g.*, deals, battens, and boards), the carrier is bound by the amount of each kind as specified. A shortage of one kind cannot be set off against an excess of another kind, The consignee is not bound to accept an excess of any particular kind. but if he does, he will be liable for freight on the excess. He will not, however, be bound to credit the shipowner with the value of the surplus amount.

Where in a "received for shipment B/L" the representation that the goods are in apparent good order and condition is qualified by a stamped endorsement "signed under guarantee to produce ship's clean receipt", that is regarded as an effective qualification should the mate's receipt show, that at the time of the actual shipment, the goods were in some way defective. In such case the shipowner is not estopped from proving the true condition of the goods on shipment.

Presentation of B/L in Foreign Language. If the master of a ship is presented with a B/L for signature which is printed in a language he does not understand, he should have it translated by some competent but disinterested person, and add any necessary qualifying clauses before signing it. If unable to find a translator, he should have his own form of B/L made out and sign that. Should it be refused, the master should deposit it with the British Consul and note protest. A protest may, of course, prove to be useless if the bill is later indorsed to a third party. In such a case, and in cases where similar difficulties arise, the master should in addition inform his owners without delay of all the relevant facts. If possible, he should report the matter to the agents of the owners' P. & I. Association.

Refusal to accept qualified B/L. If a charterer or shipper objects to the insertion of a qualifying clause in a B/L, the master may sign it "under protest". The words "signed under protest" following the master's signature will have the effect that the B/L will not be conclusive evidence against the master. Further steps, as suggested in the previous paragraph, should be taken in the shipowner's interests.

Where the master is under a contractual obligation to sign "clean" B's/L, he must do so. In that case it is most important to reject goods which cannot truthfully be described as being in apparent good order and condition. (Note what has been said earlier about letters of indemnity.)

STOWAGE

Deck Cargo. It is not permissible to stow goods on deck unless there is either a binding custom of the trade, or an express agreement with the shipper, to do so. Where goods are improperly carried on deck the shipowner, in relation to the owners of such goods, is reduced to the status of a common carrier. He loses the benefit of all but common law exceptions, and is placed in the same position as if the ship had unjustifiably deviated from the contract route.

If deck cargo is jettisoned for the safety of the ship, that will not amount to a general average act unless there is a binding custom to carry such goods on deck. If carried on deck by agreement, and properly jettisoned, the act will not give rise to a G/A claim against other cargo owners, but if there are no other cargo owners the owners of the jettisoned goods may have a claim against the ship.

The Hague-Visby Rules do not apply to deck cargo, but if goods in respect of which there is an agreement to stow on deck are, in fact, given underdeck stowage, the Rules will apply. Also, if deck cargo is covered by a B/L or non-negotiable receipt which expressly provides that the Rules are to apply, they will have effect as if Article I(c) did not exclude deck cargo.

Goods carried in a shelter deck or other approved covered space which does not form part of the ship's registered tonnage are not classed as deck cargo for commercial purposes, but are for the purpose of the payment of light and other dues.

Use is often made of the clause "on deck at shipper's risk". Following the rule that courts always adopt that construction of a doubtful clause which is adverse to the party for whose benefit it was inserted, it was held that a C/P clause "ship to be provided with a deck load, if required, at full freight but at merchant risk" did not exonerate the shipowner from a G/A contribution occasioned by a jettison of part of the cargo.

In a case a United States court gave a ruling which renders somewhat mythical the benefit enjoyed by a carrier under the Hague Rules whereby he is exempted from liability for loss or damage in respect of goods carried on deck provided the goods are stated in the B/L to be on deck and are in fact so carried. In the case reported a cargo of timber was loaded on deck and to facilitate further loading of deck cargo at the next port of call some fork lift trucks were stowed on deck with the timber. Bad weather during the voyage caused the trucks to move with the result that the timber lashings carried away and the deck load was lost. In the ordinary way the terms and conditions of the B/L would have given the carrier immunity from liability, but the Harter Act (superseded but not abolished by the United States Carriage of Goods by Sea Act) was brought into play. The Harter Act, it was ruled, not only applies prior to loading and subsequent to discharge, but it also applies to deck cargoes.

Bad Stowage. Where the contract of affreightment is subject to the Hague or Hague-Visby Rules, the carrier cannot avoid liability for loss or damage arising from negligent or improper stowage. Even where those Rules do not apply, such liability remains unless there is a specific agreement otherwise. In many countries legislation prohibits shipowners from contracting out of their liability for losses due to bad stowage, but no such restriction is recognised in Great Britain except where the Hague or Hague-Visby Rules operate. To enable the carrier to avoid such liability, the exceptions clause should include: "Any loss or damage occasioned by the negligence, default, or error in judgement of the pilot, master, mariners, engineers, stevedores, or other servants of the shipowner, in relation to the navigation, management and/or stowage of the ship or otherwise." However, not even this exception will give protection if the bad stowage is such as to render the ship unseaworthy. In giving judgement in favour of the shipowner in one particular case, it was remarked that "Bad stowage which endangers the safety of the ship may amount to unseaworthiness, but bad stowage which affects nothing but the cargo damaged by it is bad stowage and nothing more, and still leaves the ship seaworthy for the adventure, even though the adventure be the carrying of that cargo". This was a case where the shipowner was lawfully protected by an adequate exceptions clause.

DELIVERY OF GOODS

In the liner trades it is usual for the consignee to present his B/L, or where goods are carried under a waybill to provide evidence of identification, to the carrier or his agent and receive in exchange a delivery order. This is the consignee's authority to take delivery of the goods from the ship, wharf or terminal. In other cases the B/L itself may be presented to the ship when delivery is claimed.

If a B/L is presented to the master, he should see that it is properly indorsed and that freight and other charges, if any, have been paid or secured. He can then "sight" the bill by dating and signing it, and give delivery in exchange for a proper receipt. The original bill, or the master's copy, may be signed by the consignee as a form of receipt for retention by the master. A delivery order may be dealt with in the same way.

The fact that the person with a proper title to the goods usually holds the B/L generally ensures that delivery is made to the right person, but as B's/L are normally issued in sets of two or more parts it could happen, through mistake or fraud, that the separate parts are not all indorsed to the same person. The master, however, is always entitled to give delivery to the first claimant who presents a B/L which is in order, provided he has no grounds to suspect fraud and has no notice of any other claim. If it should happen that delivery is made to a person who has no proper title, the indorsee who is the rightful owner has no remedy against the shipowner or master. His right of action is against the person who assigned the B/L to him. In the most unlikely event of two persons presenting simultaneous claims for delivery, the master should, in the first instance, refuse delivery to either of them. What are called "interpleader proceedings" can then be taken in a court of law. In effect, the master declares to the court that he has the goods in his possession and is willing to deliver them to the rightful owner, but does not know who the rightful owner is. He leaves it to the court to decide and grants delivery of the goods accordingly. Meanwhile, to avoid delay to the ship, the goods may be placed in a warehouse under the control of the shipowner or his agent so that the lien for freight and/or other charges is preserved. If the correct procedure is not followed, the master could find himself in a very difficult position. By withholding goods from a person who is entitled to them, or giving delivery to one who is not, he may be considered guilty of the offence of "unlawful conversion".

M.S. Act dealing with Delivery of Goods. Part VII of the principal Act (Sections 492-500) contains the law relating to delivery of goods imported into the United Kingdom. The following is a brief summary of the provisions thereof.

Customs Entry, etc. Where the owner of goods imported from foreign parts into the United Kingdom fails to make entry of them or fails to land or take delivery of them, the shipowner may enter them (at the Customs) and land or unship them as follows:—

(a) At any time after the time for delivery agreed in B/L or C/P.

(b) If no time is agreed, then at any time after the expiration of 72 hours (S. & H.E.) from the time of the report of the ship.

Where the shipowner lands goods as provided above, he must cause them to be placed:—

(a) In the wharf or warehouse named in the B/L or C/P, if they can conveniently be received there.

(b) Otherwise in a wharf or warehouse where goods of a like nature are customarily placed, or (if dutiable) in a bonded warehouse.

If, before the goods are so landed, the owner of them offers to take delivery, he must be allowed to do so, and his entry will be preferred to the shipowner's.

If, for convenience in assorting, goods are landed at the wharf where the ship is discharging, and the owner has entered them and offered to take delivery, and convey them to some other wharf, the goods shall be assorted and, if demanded, delivered to the owner within 24 hours. The expense of landing and assortment is to be borne by the shipowner.

If, before the goods are landed, the owner has entered them for landing at a wharf other than that at which the ship is discharging, and has offered to take delivery, and the shipowner has failed to make that delivery and also failed at the time of the offer to notify the goods owner when the goods can be delivered, then the shipowner must before landing the goods give the owner of them (or the owner of the wharf) 24 hours' written notice of his readiness to deliver the goods. If the shipowner lands the goods without giving such notice, he does so at his own risk and expense.

Shipowner's Lien. If, when goods are landed and placed in the custody of a warehouseman, the shipowner gives the warehouseman written notice that they are to remain subject to a lien for freight and/or other charges to an amount mentioned, they will in the hands of the warehouseman continue to be subject to that lien, and the warehouseman must retain them until the lien is discharged.

The lien will be discharged:—

(1) On production to the warehouseman (by the goods owner) of a receipt for the amount claimed and delivery of a copy thereof, or on production of a release of freight from the shipowner.

(2) On deposit (by the goods owner) with the warehouseman of a sum of money equal in amount to the sum claimed (without prejudice to any other remedy the shipowner may have to recover freight, etc.).

The person making the deposit may, within 15 days, give the warehouseman written notice to retain it, stating in such notice the amount he admits to be payable (or that he does not admit any sum to be payable).

If such notice is given, the warehouseman must notify the shipowner and, according to circumstances, pay him the amount admitted to be payable and retain the balance, or retain the whole deposit. After 30 days from the date of the notice, unless the ship-owner has instituted legal proceedings against the goods owner and notified the warehouseman to that effect, the warehouseman must pay back the balance or deposit retained to the goods owner. The warehouseman will then be discharged from all liability.

If the lien is not discharged and no deposit is made as above, then the warehouseman may, and if required by the shipowner must, after 90 days from the time when the goods were placed in his custody (or earlier, at his discretion, if the goods are perishable) sell the goods by public auction for either home use or export or, alternatively, sell sufficient of them to satisfy the charges against the goods.

Before selling them, however, the warehouseman is obliged to give notice by advertisement either in two local papers or in one local paper and one London paper, and if the goods owner's address is known send him notice by post. The title of a purchaser is not affected by omission to send this notice, and the purchaser is not bound to inquire whether notice has been sent.

The proceeds of sale are applied as follows, in the order of priority stated:—

1. If sold for home use, payment of customs or excise duties.
2. The expenses of sale.
3. The warehouseman's charges and shipowner's charges in priority as agreed between them, or failing agreement as follows:—
   (a) rent, rates and charges due to the warehouseman.
   (b) shipowner's claims for freight and other charges.

The warehouseman is legally entitled to rent and has power to do, at the goods owner's expense, whatever is reasonably necessary for the proper custody and preservation of the goods. He has a lien on the goods for such rent and expenses.

Delivery Abroad. If, at a port of discharge abroad, the consignee fails to appear and take delivery of the cargo the master should, subject to instructions from the shipowner or his agent, after the lapse of a reasonable time, himself attend to the matter of customs entry and other formalities and discharge the goods to a warehouse where they can remain subject to lien. This may be difficult if there is no suitable warehouse under the control of the shipowner's agent, or if the warehouseman is not prepared to act as the master's agent. It is important that the right of lien should not be lost through parting with actual or constructive possession of the goods. It may be possible in some cases to arrange for a bank to pay the freight and accept delivery on behalf of the absent consignee. Although it would be prudent to advertise for the consignee, there is no legal necessity to do so. As stated earlier, it is the consignee's duty to look out for the public announcement of the ship's arrival.

Failure of B/L to arrive. Where the consignee claims delivery of goods, but cannot produce the B/L because that document has been lost or has failed to arrive before the ship has reached the port of discharge, the master may deliver the goods to him against adequate security. This usually takes the form of a letter of indemnity from a banker. Here again, owner's or agent's instructions should first be obtained, if possible.

The "London Clause". As it is important that liners should maintain their schedules, and that chartered ships should be free to take up new fixtures as soon as possible, shipowners are naturally concerned that discharging operations should commence with the minimum of delay. For this reason, and to obtain the quickest relief from their responsibility for the cargo, it is frequently the case that their B's/L will contain the so-called "London Clause". This reads, "The shipowner shall be entitled to land these goods on the quays of the dock where the steamer discharges immediately on her arrival, and upon the goods being so landed the shipowner's liability shall cease. This clause is to form part of this bill of lading, and any words at variance with it are hereby cancelled." Where this clause is used, the Sections of the M.S. Act dealing with delivery of goods will not apply.

DISCHARGE OF CONTRACTS OF AFFREIGHTMENT

As explained in some detail in Chapter 2, contracts may be discharged by agreement, by performance, by breach, by subsequent impossibility of performance amounting to frustration, or by operation of law. Contracts embodied in charter-parties and bills of lading are not exceptions, and all that has been said in the earlier Chapter relating to contracts in general applies to those particular forms of contract as well.

Discharge of C/P by Agreement. If the shipowner and the charterer agree to release one another from the obligations they have contracted to perform, the contract is thereby discharged. But an agreement of that kind can be enforced only so long as neither party has performed any of his duties under the C/P. Another form of discharge by agreement may arise where each party agrees to replace the original C/P by a new one. Such an agreement need not necessarily be expressed, but may be inferred by the conduct of the parties. Suppose, for example, that the charterer offers goods for shipment which are of a different kind from those described in the C/P. If the shipowner learns of this offer in time he may, of course, refuse to carry such goods. But more often than not he will have no knowledge of the offer until the goods have already been shipped and the vessel has sailed from the loading port. The question then arises as to what action the shipowner can take. There are two actions available to him, viz. (1) he can elect to treat the original C/P as subsisting, or (2) he can elect to treat the original contract as having been discharged and replaced by a new one. If he chooses (1) he will be entitled to freight on the non-contract goods at the charter rate, and in that case, all the other terms of the C/P, including the demurrage clause, will continue to be enforceable. On the other hand, if he chooses (2), he will be entitled to freight on the non-contract goods at the market rate instead of the charter rate, and such terms of the original C/P as are not inconsistent with the carriage of the non-contract goods will, by implication, become incorporated in the substituted contract. The original demurrage clause will not be considered consistent with the carriage of the non-contract goods. It may in some cases be difficult for a court or an arbitrator to decide which of the two alternatives the shipowner has, in fact, chosen. If he accepts freight at the C/P rate, that will be strong evidence that his intention was to affirm the original contract. On the other hand, if the master has permitted the loading of the non-contract cargo without protest, that is no evidence that the owner has affirmed the contract because, as has been stated elsewhere in this book, (i) the master has no ordinary authority to contract on behalf of the shipowner, and (ii) he has not authority to vary by agreement with the charterer the terms of a contract to which he himself, is not a party.

Repudiation. If A and B enter into a C/P contract and, before the time for performance arrives, A informs B of his intention not to perform his obligations thereunder, the contract is discharged by agreement if B accepts the repudiation. In such case B is excused from performing his part when the time comes, and he has a right to any damages he may suffer as a result of A's repudiation.

Should B, however, decide to hold A to the latter's obligations, the C/P is not discharged. It continues to subsist for the benefit of, and at the risk of, both parties. Moreover, if the contract is subsequently discharged by some cause for which A is not responsible, B will have no claim against him, because an unaccepted repudiation is of no legal effect. This situation arose in one particular case where, on arrival of the vessel at the loading port, the charterer refused to load her. The master, who presumably in those days (over one hundred years ago) had the owners' authority so to act, instead of accepting the repudiation and seeking a cargo elsewhere, continued to demand a cargo from the charterer. Before the lay days had expired war broke out between England and the country where the ship was lying, whereupon the C/P was discharged by operation of law. The shipowner, therefore, had no claim against the charterer in damages for non-performance of the contract.

It is not necessary that the party who decides not to perform his obligations when the time comes should expressly inform the other party of his intention. Such an intention can be inferred from the conduct of the first mentioned party. X chartered his ship to Y on condition that the ship would be placed at Y's disposal as soon as she was released from a government requisition. Later, whilst the ship was still under requisition, X sold her to Z "free from charter engagements". It was held that Y had a right of action for damages for non-performance of the C/P before the agreed date of delivery, as it was not reasonable to suppose that X would have re-purchased the ship in the meantime.

Frustration. The topic of discharge by "subsequent impossibility of performance amounting to frustration" having been adequately dealt with in Chapter 2, there is no need to say more about it here.

SHIPMENT OF GOODS

The exporting and marketing of goods are obviously in themselves extremely wide subjects, any detailed treatment of which could not be attempted in a book of this kind. It may, nevertheless, be useful to include a few brief remarks indicating something of what goes on in connection with goods which must come under the direct care of masters and officers of ships during the major part of the journey from seller to buyer.

Contracts of Sale. No doubt it would be ideal from his point of view, if, say, a manufacturer in the United Kingdom with goods to sell abroad could quote an **Ex-Works** price in sterling and leave the overseas buyer to take delivery from the factory and attend himself, or through his own agent, to all the troublesome procedures involved in getting the goods to their destination. Equally, it would suit the buyer ideally to have the goods delivered to his own premises free of all charges and at an inclusive price quoted in the currency of his own country. Naturally, neither of these methods will suit both parties, and it becomes necessary to arrange a contract of sale which will be mutually acceptable to both seller and buyer.

There are several different types of quotations in everyday use, but in respect of goods carried by sea the most common are the F.O.B. quotation and the C.I.F. quotation.

Under an **F.O.B.** (free on board) contract:—
the seller's duties are:—

1. To supply the goods in conformity with the contract of sale.
2. To deliver the goods on board the vessel named by the buyer, at the named port of shipment, in the manner customary at

the port, at the date or within the period stipulated, and notify the buyer without delay of such delivery.

3. To obtain at his own risk and expense any necessary export licence or other authorisation for the export of goods.

4. To bear all costs and risks of the goods until they have effectively passed the ship's rail (*e.g.*, dock dues and loading charges—but not necessarily stowage costs, which are normally borne by the ship. Whether the seller is legally responsible for port rates seems to be doubtful, but for convenience and because the rates are relatively small, it is customary to charge them to the seller).

5. To provide at his own expense the customary packing unless by custom the goods are shipped unpacked.

6. To pay any lighterage charges, and to bear the cost of clearing the goods through the customs.

7. To pay for any checking operations (weighing, measuring, counting, checking quality, etc.).

8. To provide, at the buyer's request and expense, a certificate of origin.

9. To produce to the buyer or his agent evidence that the goods have in fact been shipped. (What form this takes depends on the custom of the port. In some ports signed bills of lading are required; in others a mate's receipt or dock receipt provides sufficient evidence to fulfil the contract.)

the buyer's duties are:—

1. To charter a vessel or reserve space in a general ship at his own expense, and notify the seller of the name of the ship, the loading berth, and delivery dates.

2. To bear all costs and risks of the goods from the time when they have effectively passed the ship's rail at the port of shipment.

3. To pay the price for the goods as quoted in the contract.

4. To pay any additional costs arising from the failure of the named ship to arrive in time or arising from the ship being unable to take the goods.

5. To arrange, if necessary, for the shipment of the goods in a substituted vessel at the earliest possible moment.

6. To pay the costs and charges of obtaining bills of lading, certificates or origin and/or consular invoices.

To give a brief recapitulation, an F.O.B. contract of sale is a contract under which the seller delivers the goods free on board a ship, paying all the expenses up to the time of actual shipment. From then on the buyer takes responsibility, pays the freight, insurance during transit, and all subsequent expenses including import duties and landing charges at the port of destination.

Under a **C.I.F.** (cost, insurance, and freight) contract:—

the seller's duties are:—

1. To supply goods in conformity with the contract of sale.

2. To contract on usual terms at his own expense for the carriage of the goods to the agreed port of destination by the usual route in a vessel normally used for the transport of goods of the contract description.

3. To pay freight charges, and to pay any unloading charges at the port of discharge which may be levied by the carrier at the time and port of shipment.

4. To obtain at his own risk and expense any export licence or other authorisation for the export of the goods that may be required.

5. To load the goods at his own expense on board the vessel at the port of shipment at the date or within the period specified, and notify the buyers without delay that the goods have been in fact loaded.

6. To obtain at his own cost, and in a transferable form, a policy of marine insurance against the risks involved in the carriage. (It is customary to provide warehouse to warehouse cover, and the seller's obligation is fulfilled if he insures for a value equivalent to the invoice price of the goods plus all charges payable by him under the C.I.F. contract).

7. To provide, at the buyer's expense if the buyer requests it war risk insurance in the currency of the contract, if procurable.

(*N.B.*—Insurance protection must be customary. To avoid any misunderstanding, the contract should state whether insurance is to be W.A., *i.e.*, "with average", or F.P.A., *i.e.*, "free from particular average". If complete cover is required by the buyer under an A.A.R. policy, *i.e.*, "against all risks", that should be made clear to the seller to enable him to adjust his price to take into account the additional premium involved.)

8. To bear with certain exceptions should the buyer fail to give shipping instructions in time, all risks of the goods until they have effectively passed the ship's rail at the port of shipment.

9. To furnish the buyer, at his own expense and without delay, a clean negotiable bill of lading for the agreed destination, as well as the invoice of the goods shipped, and the policy or certificate of insurance. (A full set of "shipped" B's/L is required, which should be dated within the period agreed for shipment, and be endorsed for delivery to the order of the buyer or buyer's agreed representative. If the B/L refers to a C/P, a copy of the latter document must also be provided.)

10. To provide at his own expense customary packing unless by custom the goods are shipped unpacked.

11. To pay dues and taxes incurred in respect of the goods up to the time of their loading (*e.g.*, port dues and costs of clearing the goods through the Customs).

12. To provide the buyer, at the buyer's request and expense, with a certificate of origin and consular invoice.

13. To give the buyer, at the buyer's request, risk, and expense, all assistance he may need in obtaining documents required for the importation of the goods into the country of destination.

the buyer's duties are:—

1. To accept the documents tendered by the seller, so long as they conform with the contract, and pay the price as provided in the contract of sale.

2. To receive the goods at the agreed port of destination and bear with the exception of freight and marine insurance, all costs and charges incurred in respect of the goods during transit (e.g., general average or salvage charges) as well as unloading costs, including lighterage and wharfage charges unless such costs and charges have been included in the freight or collected by the carrier at the time when freight was paid.

3. To bear the expense of war risk insurance if provided.

4. To bear all risks of the goods from the time when they have effectively passed the ship's rail at the port of shipment.

5. To pay additional costs arising fom his failure to give shipping instructions in time.

6. To pay the costs and charges incurred in obtaining the certificate of origin and consular documents.

7. To pay costs and charges incurred in obtaining the documents referred to in item 13 above.

8. To pay all import duties and other landing charges at the port of destination, and procure at his own risk and expense any import licence or other permit required for the importation of the goods at the destination.

In brief, then, a C.I.F. contract is one under which the seller must ship the goods and pay the freight together with all charges up to the point where the goods are loaded on board, and insure them while they are in transit. He must also supply the buyer with all the documents required to enable the goods to be imported. The buyer is responsible for any loss of or damage to the goods after they have been delivered to the carrier, and must pay all expenses and customs duties, etc., on the arrival of the goods at the port of destination.

It will be noted that the choice of the carrying ship is the buyer's responsibility under an F.O.B. contract, but the seller's under a C.I.F. contract.

Goods shipped on either of these terms may be bought and sold, perhaps more than once, while they are in transit. The transfer of title when this takes place is effected by delivery of the documents of title duly assigned by endorsement, or in some other customary manner.

Shipping and Forwarding Agents, and Loading Brokers. Many manufacturers, instead of attending to the shipping of their products themselves, employ a firm of shipping and forwarding agents to look after that side of their business on their behalf. Such agents will be specialists in the kind of work they undertake to perform, and will have, in particular, full knowledge of the requirements of the country to which they despatch the goods. On behalf of their principals, they book the shipping space, prepare all the documents needed, clear the goods through the Customs and, if required to, arrange the insurance cover. These agents may collect the goods direct from the place of manufacture, or from some other place to which the exporter has delivered them, in either case at an agreed time.

Shippers, or their shipping and forwarding agents, do not always negotiate directly with the shipping company in whose vessel the goods are to be carried, as the company themselves may delegate that side of their business to their own special agents who are usually known as "loading brokers".

Packing and marking of Goods. This highly specialised work is of paramount importance, as the goods must not only be adequately protected against the handling and other risks incidental to sea transport, but packing must comply with the requirements of the shipping company and the Customs authorities. Moreover, if goods are not packed and marked in accordance with the terms of the contract of sale, the buyer may refuse to take delivery of them. Identification marks must be such that they will remain easily legible throughout the voyage.

Invoices. The exporter's bill of costs in accordance with the contract of sale is called an "invoice". This must contain a full description of the goods with details of the number of packages, indicating how they are marked. Suppliers of goods generally use their own special form of invoice which will be certified correct by some person authorised for the purpose. The document will show such things as the sizes of cases, their gross and net weight, and appropriate references to any import licence and/or exchange control form that may be required. To comply with Customs requirements the seller's invoice usually shows the actual value of the goods as a separate item, whilst other amounts charged to the buyer are entered elsewhere on the document.

Consular Invoices. In respect of goods exported to many foreign countries, a "consular invoice" must be prepared on an official form. Usually they must be sworn before the Consul of the importing country, or before an authorised official. The document must contain a declaration that no other invoice has been forwarded direct. Some of these documents are printed both in English and in the language of the importing country. Their purpose is partly

T

connected with the control of imports into the country concerned (to ensure, for instance, that an imposed quota is not exceeded), and partly to ensure that the goods are charged with the appropriate duty on entry at the port of discharge. For similar reasons some countries require, in addition, a "certificate of value" and/or a "certificate of origin".

Customs Declarations. For statistical purposes, exporters are required to lodge with H.M. Customs specifications of all goods sent out of the country, whether outside the sterling area or not. Suitable forms are obtainable from the Custom House at the port of shipment.

Insurance of Goods. Although the subject of marine insurance is given fairly full treatment in Chapter 14, a brief reference here is necessary to complete the overall picture of exporting procedure.

Goods insurance may be effected through an Insurance Company or by obtaining cover at Lloyd's through an Insurance Broker. Frequently an exporter will arrange his insurance through the Insurance Department of his bank.

An exporter who has repeated need for insurance cover usually finds it most convenient to effect a "Floating Policy" or an "Open Cover" (see Chapter 14 for details), and such a twelve months' contract gives automatic cover immediately the goods come on risk whether, at that moment, the shipment has been declared or not. As soon as details of the shipment are fully known, they are declared to the underwriters, who then issue policies or certificates as required, together with debit notes for the relative premiums. Such policies and certificates, unless made out to the order of the consignee or to bearer, must be endorsed by the assured.

In circumstances where serious loss would not be likely to occur unless the whole shipment were damaged, it is usual to insure F.P.A., as that is somewhat cheaper than the more comprehensive cover obtainable under a W.A. policy. The latter covers partial loss through marine risks as well as total loss. In addition to the normal marine risks, however, the shipper may require cover against such special risks as theft, pilferage, and non-delivery, in which case an A.A.R. policy would be taken out. British policies normally have the "warehouse to warehouse" clause attached, giving cover from the time when the goods leave the exporter's warehouse in the United Kingdom to the time when they are placed in the importer's warehouse abroad and, if required, for a specified number of days thereafter.

Documentary Credits. An exporter's method of obtaining payment for the goods he has sent abroad will depend, in the first place, on the form of contract of sale he has made with his customer overseas. There are various methods available to the seller to obtain payment from the buyer, but here it will suffice to mention, only, the method known as the "documentary credit" system, a system commonly used.

Under this system the importer at the request of the exporter makes an application to his banker to open a documentary credit through the bank's Correspondents (*i.e.*, another bank or a branch of the same bank in the exporting country), in favour of the exporter for a sum representing the value of the shipment, such credit to be available by drafts (bills of exchange) at sight, or at a fixed number of days after sight. Any such draft must be accompanied by certain specified documents, usually some or all of the following:—

Invoices (in duplicate or more),
Marine and war risk insurance policy or certificate covering 10 per cent. above the c.i.f. value of the goods (and possibly including Institute Cargo Clauses),
A full set of "clean" on board steamship company's bills of lading through to the port of destination,
Consular invoice (in duplicate),
Certificate of quality,
Certificate of origin.

The above must be strictly correct and, with the Bill of Exchange drawn on the bank, must be presented not later than the expiry date of the credit.

The bank issues a letter of credit (revocable or irrevocable, preferably the latter) authorising the exporter to draw on the correspondent bank for the account of the importer, a bill or bills of exchange for the amount authorised in the letter.

The documentary B/E is deposited by the beneficiary (*i.e.*, the exporter) with the correspondent bank for examination and, later, assuming the documents to be in order, a banker's draft is issued to him for the amount of the bill.

When the documents arrive in the country of destination, the issuing bank will release them to the importer on the latter's payment to the bank of the price of the goods. Armed with these documents, the importer is then in a position to obtain a delivery order from the shipowner's agents and take delivery of the goods from the ship or warehouse. (*N.B.*—Of the two negotiating banks, the one from whom the credit originates is the "issuing" bank; the one which advances money to the exporter against the credit is the "correspondent" bank.)

Under a somewhat similar arrangement, a documentary bill may be drawn on the importer himself, in which case the exporter sends the documents through his bank to be delivered to the importer against the latter's payment or acceptance of the accompanying bill of exchange. If this is drawn to be payable "at sight" the documents will not be handed to the drawee except against payment of the bill. Meanwhile, the goods will not be released by the shipowner or warehouseman until a "Bank Release" in proper form has been lodged. Where the consignee's credit is known to be good, the issuing bank may have issued the credit on the basis of "documents against acceptance". In that case, as soon as the consignee has "accepted" the bill by writing his name across the face of the bill, he will be entitled to have the documents delivered to him. The bill may have been drawn, say, at 30 days' sight, and in that case it becomes due for payment 30 days after the drawee has accepted it (plus the usual 3 days of grace, if any).

BILLS OF EXCHANGE

Exporters and other creditors can, of course, arrange for the amounts due to them to be paid by cheque or by banker's draft, but in many cases there are disadvantages associated with such methods of payment and, therefore, most commercial transactions are financed by the use of bills of exchange.

The primary object of a bill of exchange is to enable a creditor to obtain from his debtor an instrument which is an acknowledgement of the latter's liability, and which affords a method of obtaining funds immediately, or of discharging a liability of the creditor himself by his negotiating the bill to a third party. B's/E make possible the settlement of debts of a number of persons by means of the transfer of a single piece of paper, thereby increasing the credit facilities necessary to trade and limiting the demand for actual currency.

A bill of exchange is defined as an unconditional order in writing addressed by one person to another, signed by the person giving it, requiring the person to whom it is addressed to pay on demand or at a fixed or determinable future time, a sum certain in money, to, or to the order of, a specified person, or to bearer.

An order which does not comply with this definition, or one which requires some act to be done in addition to the payment of money, is not a bill of exchange. With regard to the words "fixed or determinable future time", it would, for instance, be in order to draw a bill to be payable 60 days after the death of a named person, as the death is something which is certain to happen sooner or later. On the other hand, a bill made payable three months after a named person's marriage would not be in order, as there is no absolute certainty that the event will take place. The phrase "sum certain" implies that the bill must provide for the payment of a fixed amount of money expressed in some definite currency. A bill drawn, for example, for the "value of my gold and diamond ring" is not in order, as the article referred to may have a different value at different times or in the opinions of different valuers. It is in order, however, to make the sum payable by stated instalments, or to be paid with interest at a stated rate.

A cheque drawn in the normal way is a bill of exchange, since it complies with the definition given, but a cheque drawn "pay cash" is not a bill of exchange. "Cash" is not a specified person.

The following terms may be noted:—

The person who draws the bill is the "drawer".

The person on whom the bill is drawn is the "drawee".

The person to whom the amount of the bill is made payable is the "payee".

When the drawee has accepted the bill, he becomes the "acceptor".

A person who indorses a bill is the "indorser".

The person to whom the bill is indorsed is the "indorsee".

A bill both drawn and payable in the British Islands is an "inland bill".

Any bill other than an inward bill is a "foreign bill".

Stamping of B's/E. Prior to 1961 bills drawn in the United Kingdom were subject to stamp duty which, with certain exceptions, varied accordingly to the amount for which the bill was drawn. The Finance Act of that year, however, changed that system and any bill then, irrespective of the amount, required only a 2d. stamp. More recently, however, stamp duties on bills of exchange have been abolished altogether.

Days of Grace. Provided the bill is not drawn to be payable on demand, or at sight, three days of grace are, if the bill is payable in the United Kingdom, added to the time of payment as fixed by the bill, and the bill is due and payable on the last day of grace. Where a fixed or certain time is stated in the bill, no days of grace are added. In the case of a B/E payable abroad, the question of days of grace is a matter for the law of the country concerned. If the last day of grace falls on a Sunday, Christmas Day, Good Friday, or a day appointed by Royal Proclamation as a public feast day, the bill is due and payable on the preceding business day. If it falls on a statutory Bank Holiday (other than Christmas Day or Good Friday) the bill is due and payable on the succeeding business day, and the same applies should the last day of grace be a Sunday when the second day of grace is a Bank Holiday.

Forms of B's/E.

Form of inland bill:—

Exchange for £100   London, 24th September, 1981.

   Three months after date pay this sole Bill of Exchange to
the order of C. K. Williams & Co.

ONE HUNDRED POUNDS

   Value received.

                                        For
   To H. Thompson & Co. Ltd.,   / Perkins & Son, Ltd.
          Birmingham.
                                           G. King, Director.

   With respect to the above bill, Perkins & Son, Ltd., are the
drawers, H. Thompson & Co. Ltd., are the drawees, and C. K.
Williams & Co. are the payees.
   If, for example, there are three parts to the set, the first will
contain the words "second and third unpaid", the second "first and
third unpaid", and the third "first and second unpaid". In this
way it will be obvious, on sighting any one part, how many parts
there are.

Form of foreign bill:—

Exchange for £357.50.   London, 28th January, 1981.

   At 30 days' sight pay this first Bill of Exchange (second
and third unpaid) to the Order of

                    L. G. Briggs & Co.

   Three hundred and fifty-seven pounds and fifty pence.

   Value received.

   To K. S. Providers,   p.p. L. G. Briggs & Co.
         Karachi,
         Pakistan.   W. Bolt (Secretary).
                                          P. Hill (Director).

Discounting a B/E. The holder of a B/E drawn at some stated period after sight, or after date, who wishes to obtain funds immediately, may have it discounted by a banker. If satisfied that all parties to the bill are persons of integrity whose credit is sound, the bankers will pay cash for the face value of the bill less discount at the prevailing rate per cent. When the bill ultimately matures, the banker will present it for payment, and will himself receive the full face value of the instrument.

Dishonoured Bills. A bill may be dishonoured by (a) non-acceptance when it has been duly presented for acceptance and it is not accepted within the customary time (usually 24 hours); or (b) non-payment when it is duly presented for payment and payment is refused or cannot be obtained. To enforce his rights under the bill, the holder of a bill dishonoured by non-acceptance could take action against the drawer or indorsers. The holders of a bill dishonoured by non-payment has an additional right against the acceptor. To provide evidence that he has complied with the provisions of the Bill of Exchange Act relating to due presentment, the holder should have the bill "noted" by a notary public as a preliminary to a formal "protest". Protest is essential in the case of a dishonoured foreign bill. If the services of a notary are unobtainable at the place where the bill is dishonoured, protest may be made by any householder in the presences of two witnesses.

LINER CONFERENCES

The advantages claimed for the Conference system may be stated as follows:—

1. Regular and efficient cargo services are maintained with up-to-date and well-designed vessels at all times, good or bad.
2. Because the Conferences take measures to avoid sudden fluctuations in freight rates, shippers are able to plan for a considerable time ahead confident in the knowledge that rates will remain stable.
3. Shippers of all kinds enjoy equality of treatment with regard to freight rates and conditions of carriage. There is no discrimination against those whose shipments are of relatively small volume.

The competition of "outsiders" is met by encouraging shippers to confine all their shipments to Conference ships. This may be effected in either of two ways. Under one scheme basic freight rates are fixed which apply to shippers in general, but those who enter into a contract with the Conference undertaking to ship only by Conference vessels are allowed a discount concession, usually a discount of 9 per cent. on scale freights. Under an alternative scheme the Conferences offer a "deferred rebate" of (usually) 10 per cent. of the aggregate amount of freight paid over a period of

6 months (or in some cases 12 months) to those shippers who are in a position to declare that, during the period referred to, they have not shipped goods on the routes served by the Conference by any other than Conference vessels.

The shipowner members of a particular Conference may enter into a pooling agreement designed to prevent unlimited competition between them, but not going so far as to exclude competition altogether. Under such an agreement the total freight revenue may be divided between the participating companies in some agreed proportion. An alternative scheme is for member lines to share the freight-tons of cargo carried. Should one line carry more than its permitted share, thereby becoming an "overcarrier", that line will be required to indemnify any "undercarriers", provided that the latter have properly fulfilled their obligations to continue to employ sufficient tonnage to carry their normal shares. There are other types of agreements, also, to prevent any one Conference member from gaining an unfair advantage over the others.

To facilitate negotiations with shippers and their forwarding agents, a Conference may establish a "booking office". It would obviously defeat the objects of the Conference to grant shippers the indisputable right to choose which ship or line their goods shall be carried by, but as far as may be practicable a booking office will endeavour to accede to shippers' requests in this respect.

Primage. At one time it was customary to add to the freight charged to a shipper a surcharge of 10 per cent. (or other proportion) which was known as "primage". Originally, primage was a reward to the master of the ship for his taking care of the cargo. At a later period of mercantile history masters gave up their right to this form of remuneration, but primage was still collected in addition to freight for the benefit of the shipowner on the principle that it represented the cargo's contribution to the payment of light dues, harbour dues, and similar expenses. With the formation and operation of Liner Conferences the practice became common of rebating primage to regular shippers at 6 months' intervals. More recently, however, the custom of adding primage to freight accounts has been generally given up and replaced by either the "discount" system, or the "deferred rebate" system, as described above.

CHARTERING MARKET REPORTS

The examples given below are typical of the reports which appear every day in the shipping press in relation to the chartering of ships.

Example 1.   Voyage charter fixture.
Gdynia and Szczecin to Madras and Calcutta.—"E............",
9,500 t.d.w. for cargo (465,000 cu. ft. bale), sulphate of ammonia

and/or soda ash in bags, lump sum based on £3·25 per ton, f.i.o. and stowed, Aug. 1–15.

This means that the vessel named has been chartered to load at Gdynia and Szczecin a cargo consisting of bagged sulphate of ammonia or bagged soda ash, or both, for discharge at Madras and Calcutta. She has a deadweight capacity of 9,500 tons for cargo, *i.e.*, exclusive of the deadweight required for fuel, water and stores. A lump sum freight is payable amounting to £3·25 per ton on the 9,500 tons. The cost of loading and stowing the cargo is for the shipper's account, and the cost of discharging for the receiver's account; *i.e.*, free of expense to the ship. The charterer is not under obligation to commence loading before 1st August, but the vessel must be arrived and ready at the first loading port by 15th August. The bale-space available to the charterer is also quoted.

Example 2.   Voyage charter fixture.
Gamlakarleby to East Coast U.K.—"K................." (Sw.), 1,400 fathoms, 10 p.c., pit props, £7·50 per fathom, Aug. 31-Sept. 15 (subject stem).

In this case the named vessel, which is Swedish, has been chartered to load, 1,400 fathoms of pit props, 10 per cent. more or less at the vessel's option. The freight rate and dates quoted need no further explanation. The fixture is "subject to stem", which means that the charterers and the suppliers of the pit props have yet to arrange delivery of the cargo at the loading berth within the agreed lay days. As soon as a "stem" (*i.e.*, some proportion of the cargo) has been arranged, the date on which loading is to commence is agreed and is known as the "stem date". Provided that the vessel is arrived and ready by that time, lay days will begin to count from the stem date. The term "free stem" (if used) implies that loading operations can start immediately upon the vessel's arrival at the loading port.

Example 3.   Voyage charter fixture.
West Australia to U.K.—"V................ C................" (m.s.), 9,500 t., 5 p.c. bulk wheat ex-silo, £3·25 per ton, option Antwerp-Hamburg range £3·00, London direct £3·12½, Antwerp-Hamburg range direct £2·87½, option ldg. South Australia/Victoria/New South Wales 50p extra, Oct. 10-Nov. 5.

Points for particular notice in this example are (1) as the wheat is to be shipped in bulk ex-silo it will be the charterer's responsibility to bring the cargo to alongside at his risk and expense, whilst all costs from alongside to the ship's holds will be for the ship's account; (2) £3·25 per ton is the freight rate if the cargo is discharged at two or more ports in the United Kingdom, £3·00 if discharge is at two or more ports within the Antwerp-Hamburg range, £3·12½ if the whole cargo is discharged in London, £2·87½ if the whole cargo is discharged at

one port in the Antwerp-Hamburg range: (3) if the charterers opt
to load in South Australia or New South Wales instead of West
Australia, the freight rate will be increased by an extra 50p per ton.

Example 4.   Voyage charter fixture.

Igarka to Hull—"W..............", 2,300 stds., d.b.b., £15.50
per std., Russwood charter, Aug. 7-20.

In this case the vessel named is to carry from Igarka to Hull
2,300 standards of deals, battens, and boards at a freight rate of
£15.50 per standard under the terms of the White Sea wood
Charter, 1933 (Code name "Russwood"). The dates have their
usual significance.

Example 5.   Time charter.

"R.............." (m.s.), 4,475 t.d.w. (253,000 cu. ft. bale) (14 knots
on 15-15½ t. diesel oil). $20,000 per month, delivery U.S. North
of Hatteras, six months' trading, Sept. 8-22.

The above is typical of the report of an arranged time charter in
which the name and type of vessel are indicated, together with
deadweight and cubic capacities, and particulars of performance.
The rate at which hire money is payable per calendar month is
shown, and the period of hire. The ship is to be delivered to the
charterers at a port on the East Coast of the United States north of
Cape Hatteras. Charterers are not obliged to take delivery before
8th September, but if the vessel is not delivered by 22nd September
they will have the option of cancelling.

In some reports the port or region of redelivery is given as well,
and sometimes the name or nationality of the charterers. There
may also be an indication of an option to prolong the period of hire.

Example 6.   Tanker charter for single voyage.
DIRTY.

Persian Gulf to Corunna.—"Raphael", 48,000 t., Worldscale
137½, Feb. 24. (Petrolibre.)

This is a charter for the carriage of dirty oils (see Chapter 3).
The code name "Worldscale" refers to a tanker freight scale which is
nowadays used universally. Worldscale 100 would represent a basic
rate to which differentials are applied according to circumstances
such as the number and situation of loading and discharging ports,
whether a canal transit is involved or not, and other considerations.
Worldscale 137½, quoted in this report, means Worldscale 100 plus
37½ per cent.

Reference to Chapter 3 will remind readers that there is a very
wide variety of tanker charters.

Loading and Discharging Costs. The vast majority of chartering
market reports in respect of voyage charters for dry cargoes indicate

which party is liable to pay loading and/or discharging expenses in one or other of the following ways, viz.:—

Gross terms: Ship pays both.

F.i.o.: Shipper pays for loading and receiver pays for discharging.

F.o.b.: Shipper pays for loading and ship pays for discharging.

Discharge free: Ship pays for loading and receiver pays for discharging.

CHAPTER 10

PROCEDURES ON ARRIVAL AT AND ON DEPARTURE FROM A PORT

THE number of commercial ports in the world runs into several thousands, and it is not to be expected that procedures are absolutely standardised in all of them. Nevertheless, at all places, there will be appropriate measures for the protection of public health and for the protection of public revenue, and the necessary formalities will follow on much the same lines everywhere.

At some British ports abroad which are wholly, or to a great extent, "free ports", entries and clearances will not be made at a Custom House. Instead there will be an Entry and Clearance Department in the local Harbour Office. In the same neighbourhood, possibly in the same building, there will be a "Shipping Office" where the proper authority for dealing with the engagement and discharge of seamen will be known as the "Shipping Master". The duties, powers, etc., of this officer will be the same as those of a M.M. Superintendent in the United Kingdom.

In foreign ports where there is a British consular officer, that officer attends to all crew formalities. In the larger ports he will usually be a person who has had considerable training and experience in shipping affairs, but in some of the smaller ports the Consul may be less experienced and may require some guidance from the master of the ship in the matter of observing the required formalities.

For the sake of convenience, what follows relates principally to arrivals at and departures from United Kingdom ports.

ARRIVAL

Signals on Approach. The master of a ship which has called at a port outside the U.K., or which has met with an off-shore installation or with a ship which last called at a foreign port and where any person boarded the ship or installation from the other, must ascertain the state of health of all persons on board. If the ship is healthy he can proceed to his berth, but may as a courtesy notify the situation by radio to the port health authority. A proportion of ships will be boarded and checked. In foreign ports it may still be a requirement to fly or flash Q on arrival when the ship is healthy.

If there has been a death on board (other than by accident) or if there has been illness on board where the patient had a high temperature or severe diarrhoea, or suffered from an infectious disease, or there are any circumstances on board likely to cause spread of infectious diseases, or there are animals or captive birds on board, and there has been death or sickness amongst them, the master must report the facts by radio to the health authority not more than 12 hours and not less than 4 hours before the ship's E.T.A. If this is not possible then notify on arrival, displaying the visual signals QQ or red light over white light where they can best be seen, until free pratique is granted or other measures put into force.

Bringing to. Where the master has to notify an infectious disease as above, or is directed to by a medical officer, he must complete a Maritime Declaration of Health, countersigned by the ship's surgeon (if one), and deliver it to the authorised officer on arrival at the boarding station. He should also have ready a valid Deratting Certificate or Deratting Exemption Certificate. Under such circumstances only the pilot, a customs officer or an immigration officer is permitted to board the ship until free pratique is granted.

PUBLIC HEALTH (SHIPS) REGULATIONS 1970

CERTIFICATE OF FREE PRATIQUE

Port	FALMOUTH	Date of arrival	12th April 1976
Ship	FORESTER	From	LISBON

I have examined _J. A. GREENWOOD_ Master of the above ship and under the above Regulations
_____(Name)_____

I hereby grant the vessel free pratique.

Stamp of Issuing Authority	.... (Signature)	Authorised Officer of the Port Health Authority
	a Williamson	or
	(Signature)	Customs Officer
	Time __1142__	Date __12th April 1976__

C304 Gp3642 (147382) 908829. 500M. 12/71 S(P&D)L

Reproduced by kind permission of the Controller of H.M. Stationery Office

"Certificate of Free Pratique"

Granting Pratique. Where the ship is infected or suspected an authorised officer will board, take delivery of the signed Maritime

Declaration of Health, ask questions regarding the health of persons on board, and if satisfied grant a Certificate of Free Pratique. If not satisfied, the officer may order the ship to be taken to a mooring station for further inspection, and if necessary, prescribed measures will be taken before pratique is granted and the ship may be detained.

Protection of Revenue. Although the Customs co-operate with the authorities for health purposes and, thereby, avoid much duplication of effort, the primary purpose of their boarding is for the protection of revenue, *i.e.*, to prevent the landing of uncustomed goods. Nevertheless, from 1 April 1978 the practice of boarding all commercial vessels from abroad which has applied in the past, is replaced by a selective system which places more responsibility on the master or his agent for the completion and lodging of customs forms.

For presentation on arrival, the following forms must be completed and signed by the master:

General Declaration, C.13, in triplicate.
Ship's Stores Declaration, C.14, in triplicate.
Crew Declaration, C.142, in duplicate.
Small Parcels List, C.143 (if appropriate), in duplicate.
Declaration of Deck Cargo, DCI C.1320 (if appropriate), in duplicate.

On arrival, *if the vessel is boarded*, the master must make a preliminary report and answer questions on matters relating to the voyage, and produce for inspection the ship's surplus dutiable stores, any livestock on board, and the crew's dutiable effects. In practice only high duty goods are required to be produced. The requisite duty will be collected there and then. All articles obtained abroad or during the voyage, and all United Kingdom banknotes howsoever obtained must be declared. Any articles found, which have not been declared, are liable to forfeiture, and the person concerned will be liable to prosecution. No livestock may be landed without a permit from the Ministry of Agriculture, Fisheries and Food. No document is required in connection with ship's stores. Strictly, the master is required to muster the crew for questioning, but in practice the list C.142, often called the "Tobacco Sheet", is prepared beforehand. The master must declare that he has no further goods on board not listed on the Report, if that is, in fact, the case. If he has such goods, list C.143 (commonly known as the "Parcel List") will have been completed to declare these "address packages".

The master will then be asked about the disposal of the surplus stores. If he is prepared to accept the responsibility (which is generally the case) these stores will be placed in a special locker or lockers, and will be sealed up. Such sealed goods are not protected by bond; the master is held entirely responsible for their safekeeping, and if a seal is broken he will be liable to a fine plus the duty chargeable on any goods which are missing. (Even if the seal remains intact and the locker is broken into, that will amount to a technical breakage of seal, and the master's liability is in no way affected). In the event of the master declining the responsibility, the goods will be removed from the ship and placed in bond ashore. The shipowner could then recover them (a) by paying the requisite duty, or (b) by re-shipping them for export. After dutiable goods have been sealed up on board the preventive officer signs the Ship's Stores Declaration, form C.14.

If the vessel is *not boarded* on arrival, to make the preliminary report one copy of each form must be lodged at the "designated Customs Office" by the master or agent within three hours of arrival at the place of discharge. The "designated Customs Office" will in most cases be the existing boarding officers' office, but might be a specially installed "post box". Requests for Customs attendance for the landing of persons or goods must be made to the same office. The ship will be boarded later, but it appears that stores left on board are the master's responsibility whether sealed up or not.

Passengers. If the ship arrives from outside the "common travel area" (i.e. the United Kingdom, Channel Islands, Isle of Man and the Republic of Ireland) the master must submit a passenger list to an Immigration Officer showing names and nationalities of all passengers. Each passenger, aged 16 years or over, who disembarks in the United Kingdom, must be supplied with a landing card by the ship's owner or agents which must be duly completed and produced to the Immigration Officer if required. All passengers, which for this purpose includes passage workers, supernumaries, distressed British seamen, stowaways and other persons not actually employed in the working or service of the ship, must be seen by an Immigration Officer, and may be examined by a Medical Inspector, before disembarking.

The master must also complete, sign and deliver Home Office Form IS 6 to an Immigration Officer within 12 hours of arrival. This form must show particulars of all members of the crew who were engaged outside the United Kingdom, and all those subject to United Kingdom Immigration control who were engaged in the United Kingdom. A crew member is subject to immigration control unless he holds a British Seaman's Card, a United Kingdom passport showing him to be born in the United Kingdom or otherwise exempt from immigration control, or a passport of the Republic of Ireland.

As soon as practicable after the arrival of the ship at its final port of destination in the United Kingdom, a Passenger Returns form (PAS 15) showing the numbers of passengers for each port of disembarkation in the United Kingdom, from each port of embarkation outside the United Kingdom, must be given to a Customs officer.

Entering inwards. When the ship is berthed the master must make the final report of her arrival at the Custom House. Under a

£100 (max.) penalty, the ship must be reported within 24 hours of arrival (Sundays and holidays excepted) and before breaking bulk.

If the vessel arrives outside working hours and immediate discharge is desired, the ship's agents should request the Collector of Customs to allow this. If permission is granted an "interim report" will be made on board immediately on arrival. This procedure is often adopted even during working hours, especially in the case of passenger ships, to save time.

Should the master be unable to attend in person at the Custom House, he can complete form C.74 on which he appoints an agent to make the report on his behalf. Both the master and his nominee are required to sign this form in the presence of an officer of Customs and Excise or, failing such officer, the broker of the ship or his usual and known representative. If the agent is unable to answer any of the questions put to him regarding the ship, crew or voyage, the master himself must make the report in person if so required by the customs officer.

H M Customs and Excise

APPOINTMENT BY MASTER OF AN AGENT TO MAKE REPORT AND CLEAR OUTWARDS

NOTE — *Unless this appointment is given for a single voyage only, this form must be produced to the Customs on each occasion that report is made or clearance sought.*

I, ... ARTHUR CLARK ...... appoint
(name of Master in BLOCK LETTERS)

WATERSIDE AGENTS CO. LTD. of ...... THAMES STREET
(name of agent)   (address of agent)

LONDON

      *(i) to make report on my behalf as required by the Customs and Excise Management Act, 1979, section 35; and
as my agent
      *(ii) to obtain clearance as required by the Customs and Excise Management Act, 1979, section 64
* of any ship of which for the time being I am Master

or

* of the ship .... *which arrived

* at .... *outward bound

     * from
.... on .... 19.........
     * to
* from

I accept responsibility for my agent's acts.

Date... 13 August ... 19.81   A. Clark   Master's signature
* Delete as necessary
C 74

F 2016 (September 1979)

96/00753 G4S 8028420 80m 8/79 A.G. 3640/4

Form C.74

It often occurs that a ship is berthed in an isolated district far removed from the nearest Custom House, so that it would be unreasonable to expect the master to report in the normal way, particularly if the ship is due to remain in port for only a few hours. In those circumstances the agents can arrange for the ship to be "reported on the station". Instead of the master going to the Custom House, an officer of Customs goes to the ship and the "entering in" formalities are conducted on board.

When reporting at the Custom House the first call in the "long room" is at the lights counter where inward light dues are paid and a receipted light bill is obtained. The certificate of registry and deck cargo certificate will be required to assess the amount due. The master then goes to the Reporting Officer with the necessary papers and swears the correctness of the information contained therein.

The papers required are:

Register, tonnage certificate and deck cargo certificate (if one).
Pratique certificate (if one).
All previously receipted light bills for the current financial year.
General Declaration, C.13 (in duplicate).
Cargo Declaration, C.16, or Cargo Manifest (in duplicate).
Parcel list (if any), C.143.
Tonnage dues slip.
Ship's Stores Declaration, C.14.
Passenger list (if any) stamped by Immigration Officer.
Passenger Return, PAS 15 (arrival) (if final destination port).
Oil Pollution Insurance Certificate (OPIC), if appropriate.
Details of certain of the above papers are given as follows:

General Declaration. This is an important document in which particulars are given of the ship and voyage, crew, passengers, and brief description of the cargo, together with subsequent ports of call with an indication where remaining cargo will be discharged. It must also show the ship's berth in the port and the name and address of the ship's agent. The declaration must be signed by the ship's master or his authorised agent in the presence of the reporting officer who, in turn, must countersign it, and it must be completed in duplicate. At the bottom of the form are spaces for the reporting officer to allocate a rotation number to the ship, and to indicate that he has sighted the various documents that must be presented to him.

Cargo Declaration (Arrival). A detailed cargo declaration is required in duplicate, showing B/L numbers, marks and numbers, number and kind of packages, description of goods and weights or measurements. The official form, C.16, is only normally used to declare a bulk cargo, or one where there are only a few bills of lading. Where a general cargo has to be declared, this can be done by submitting the ship's manifest in duplicate. One copy of the declaration

GENERAL DECLARATION

H.M. CUSTOMS AND EXCISE

Waterside Agents Co.Ltd.

Name of shipping line, agent, etc.

✓ Arrival †   ☐ Departure †

(1) Name and description of ship
m.v. Aston Grove

(2) * Port of arrival / departure
London

(3) * Date and time of arrival / dep.
7.7.76   1100

(4) Nationality of ship
British

(5) Name of master
A.Clark

(6) * Port arrived from / Port of destination
Baltimore

(7) Certificate of registry (Port; date; number)
London 29.7.75   344017

(8) Name and address of ship's agent
Waterside Agents Co.Ltd.
Thames Street,
London.

(9)   (10) Net register tons
16,300.39

(11) Position of the ship in the port (berth or station)
Tilbury Grain Terminal

(12) Brief particulars of voyage (previous and subsequent ports of call; underline where remaining cargo will be discharged)
Baltimore, London,

(13) Brief description of the cargo
Bulk wheat.

(14) Number of crew (incl. master)
36

(15) Number of passengers
4

(16) Remarks

(17) Attached documents (indicate number of pages)
2

(18) Cargo Declaration / Manifest   (19) Ship's Stores Declaration

(20)   (21)   (22) Date and signature by * master / authorised agent
A. Clark.   7/7/76.

(23)   (24)

NOTE: The general declaration must be completed in duplicate. For arrivals, each copy must be supported by a copy of the cargo manifest or, in the case of bulk goods or single commodity cargoes, by a copy of the cargo declaration. For departures, a copy of the cargo manifest must be delivered within 14 days after the clearance outwards of the ship.

† Tick in box as necessary.   * Delete as necessary.

FOR OFFICIAL USE

ARRIVAL

(36) Date stamp

(25) ROTATION NUMBER   (26) SURVEYS 107
(27) PASSENGER RETURNS
(28) AUTHORITY VERIFIED   (29) STORES DECLARATION
(30) CERTIFICATE OF REGISTRY   (31) TRANSIRE
(32) LIGHT DUES   (33)
(34) OTHER DUES   (35)

FOR COLLECTOR

DEPARTURE

(54) Date stamp

(37) ROTATION NUMBER   (38) LOAD LINE CERTIFICATE
(39) SAFETY EQUIPMENT CERTIFICATE
(40) AUTHORITY VERIFIED   (41) SAFETY RADIO CERTIFICATE
(42) CERTIFICATE OF REGISTRY   (43) CARGO SHIP SAFETY CONSTRUCTION CERTIFICATE
(44) LIGHT DUES   (45) PASSENGER SHIP SAFETY CERT. PASSENGER (NUMBER) CERT.
(46) OTHER DUES   (47) TRANSIRE
(48) PASSENGER RETURNS   (49)
(50) STORES DECLARATION   (51)
(52) INWARD CLEARING BILL   (53)

* TRANSIRE ISSUED
CLEARANCE GRANTED

FOR COLLECTOR

(55) REMARKS

* Delete as necessary.

C.13   Sec. F. 3984 (March 1973)   6226/3049(H) S4S 356074 500M 4/75 A.G. 3640/4.

IMCO Convention on Facilitation of International Maritime Traffic

Reproduced by kind permission of the Controller of H.M. Stationery Office

General Declaration, C.13

H.M. CUSTOMS AND EXCISE

Waterside Agents Co. Ltd.
(Name of shipping line, agent, etc.)

CARGO DECLARATION (Arrival)

Page number
1

1. Name of ship	Aston Grove	2. Port where report is made	London
3. Nationality of ship Br	4. Name of Master A. Clark	5. Port of loading	Baltimore

6. *B/L number	7. Marks and numbers	8. Number and kind of packages; description of goods	9. Gross weights	10. Measurements
1	None	Bulk wheat	26,420 tonnes	

11. Signature by Master
† Authorised agent ...... *A. Clark.* ...... Date 7/7/76

*Also state original ports of shipment in respect of goods shipped on through bills of lading.

C. 16   † *Delete as necessary*   F. 4011 (Mar. 1973)   RM 75166/1/335189 100m 8/74 CL

Cargo Declaration, C.16

goes to the preventive officer who checks the landing of goods destined for the port and the other goes to the landing officer to enable him to make comparisons with importer's entries.

In the case of a ship with a homogeneous cargo it is not unduly difficult for the master himself to make out the declaration in its entirety, but where the ship has a complicated mixed cargo it would be impracticable. In such cases, therefore, it is customary for the ship's manifest, in duplicate, to be submitted instead.

If discrepancies arise between what is entered in the report and what is actually found in the ship, the master will have to satisfy the Customs authorities concerning them. Where goods shown on the declaration are found not to be on board, as may happen when cargo has been shut out at the loading port and the agents have not been informed in time, the necessary amendments to the form are allowed to be made.

When the report shows that a significant quantity of highly dutiable goods is being imported (e.g., a large shipment of raw tobacco) the Customs will institute special controls.

The use to which the various information contained in the declaration is put may now be considered, as follows:

The information regarding the ship, i.e., name, net tonnage and name of master, is checked against the corresponding items in the certificate of registry.

Details of the cargo are needed to assess import duties, arrange controls, and check against importers' entries.

Details of surplus stores on board are needed to assess the maximum permissible quantities in respect of the next voyage when the "stores authority" is presented.

The information concerning passengers is required for statistical purposes.

The agent's name and address are required so that the Customs will know with whom to get in touch should difficulties arise over payments of various dues.

Tonnage Dues Slip. This is issued by the port authority and gives details of the amount of tonnage dues paid or payable. In some ports Customs collect these dues on behalf of the port authority; in others they inspect receipts. In either case they will stamp the ship's report when satisfied that the dues have been paid. A shipping company may have a deposit account with the port authority out of which tonnage dues are paid in respect of the company's ships using the port.

In addition to Customs formalities, other business that the master will have to attend to on arrival, when necessary, includes the following:

Notice of Readiness. If the ship is carrying cargo under a voyage charter-party the master should, as soon as the ship is an "arrived ship", serve notice of readiness on the receiver or his agent.

Hatch Survey and Protest. If the cargo is a perishable one or if, for any other reason, the master has grounds to fear that cargo may be damaged, he should (unless this has been done by radio beforehand) arrange a hatch survey and notify the consignees accordingly. That gives them an opportunity to appoint a surveyor to act on their behalf if they so wish. When cargo damage is suspected a protest should be noted before a notary public and the right to extend it reserved. In the United Kingdom rights are not affected by the fact of a protest not having been noted but, as stated in Chapter 5, protests may be of the utmost importance in ports abroad. When a hatch survey has been arranged, the hatches should be opened in the presence of both surveyors who should report what, in their opinion, was the cause of the damage and particularly, in the case of moisture damage, whether it was the result of fresh water or salt water. If, during discharge, damaged cargo is discovered, the surveyors should be recalled to make a survey and report. Generally, if the surveyors find that the hatches had been properly covered and secured, that the top stowage was in order, that ventilation and dunnaging arrangements were satisfactory, and that any water damage was not due to salt water, that will be sufficient to defeat claims against the ship. It is never advisable to disturb damaged cargo until the surveyors have inspected it and agreed to its removal. If, in ports abroad, the services of a registered cargo surveyor cannot be obtained, the master should request the services of two other shipmasters. In any case the surveyors should be completely independent and disinterested parties. Certificates of hold surveys prior to loading and certificates of stowage on completion of loading are often of great value in resisting claims and, in respect of certain cargoes (chilled and frozen cargoes, for example) such certificates are obtained as a matter of course.

Paying-off Procedure. Unless the circumstances are such that it is not required, the master should give 48 hours' notice in writing (on the appropriate form) to a superintendent of the intention to discharge members of the crew. It is also his responsibility to deliver an account of wages to every seaman employed under a crew agreement not later than 24 hours before the time of discharge or, if discharged without notice or at less than 24 hours' notice, at the time of discharge. In principle wages must be paid in full at the time of discharge but, if the amount due to a seaman exceeds £50, and it is not practicable to pay the whole amount at the time of discharge, then a sum not less than £50 nor less than one quarter of the amount due, must be paid. Any remaining balance is then payable within seven days.

Whether the master is making the remittances himself, or whether his owners or their agents are to do so, he will have to have ready the necessary documents in respect of national insurance contributions as

HM Customs and Excise

DISCHARGE OF CARGO CERTIFICATE

Port .... *London* ....   Date ....

Vessel .... *Forester* ....   Master .... *A. Clark* ....

All inward foreign cargo intended for this port has now been discharged. My next port of

call is .... *Leith* ....

*For UK coastwise voyages only.

I have inward foreign cargo for discharge at ...... *Leith* ....,

I request permission to retain on board the stores listed on Form C 14 and undertake to produce them to the proper officer of Customs and Excise at that, or any other port in the United Kingdom and, on demand, to pay duty on any deficiency.

.... *A. Clark* ....
Master or other responsible officer

FOR OFFICIAL USE

Office stamp

Officer ....

Form C 1321

**Delete as necessary*
F4863   (April 1978)

Dd 528888 200m 1/78 BTP

well as those pertaining to income tax to be sent to the Collector of Taxes.

Discharge of Cargo Certificate. Customs officers will attend the ship as considered necessary during the discharge of cargo. When all the inward cargo for the port has been discharged, the master must notify this fact and his next port of call, on a Discharge of Cargo Certificate, C.1321, by lodging it at the designated Customs office. He must also notify the Customs on this form if he has further inward foreign cargo to discharge at another port. He also requests permission to retain on board stores listed on form C.14, promises to produce them to a Customs officer at the next or any other U.K. port, and on demand to pay duty on any deficiency. This form is issued to the master or agent when making report.

DEPARTURE

Entry Outwards. The master or his agent authorised on form C.74 must go to the Custom House and enter the ship outwards on the General Declaration, form C.13. Unless the ship after being cleared inwards is going to be laid up or put under repair, it is most convenient to enter outwards as soon as possible, as the ship cannot commence to load her outward cargo until this has been done.

If it is required to commence loading outwards before all the inward cargo has been discharged, a special permit must be applied for and obtained. This permit is not a "stiffening order" which, as its name implies, is a permit to take on board material as ballast. Special permission is also necessary to load coastwise cargo before all inward cargo is discharged, and the request to do this should be made out on form X.S.40.

The General Declaration form must have the Departure box ticked. It calls for the name of ship, name of master, port, date and time of departure, port of destination, port of registry and official number, net tonnage, position of the ship in port, brief particulars of voyage and cargo, number of crew and passengers, and the name and address of the ship's agent. It must be signed by the master or his authorised agent.

The master or agent (usually the latter) will have to attend to the shipment of stores for the new voyage, and this will require another Customs form called the Stores Authority, X.S.17., to be completed and lodged at the designated Customs office. This form must be signed by the master or owner in the presence of an officer of Customs and Excise, or in the presence of the storekeeper giving bond or his authorised clerk. In the latter case, the storekeeper or clerk is required to sign a declaration before a Customs or Excise officer that the signature is a genuine one. Besides showing the name and net tonnage of the ship, the name of the master, and the name of the stores dealer, the form must show the number of crew and passengers and the estimated duration of the round voyage in days. The quantity of stores allowed is based on this information, the scale applied being 1 oz. tobacco and $\frac{1}{4}$ pint of spirits per person per day. When the stores are ordered the ship's agent and stores dealer prepare the Shipping Bills. It is the responsibility of the shipper to notify Customs when stores are delivered to a vessel.

HM Customs and Excise

(Name of shipping line, agent, etc.)
Waterside Agents Co. Ltd.

SHIP'S STORES DECLARATION

*ARRIVALS
*DEPARTURES

1. Name of ship *Aston Grove*	2. *Port of arrival/departure *London* 3. *Date of arrival/departure 7/7/78
4. Nationality of ship *British.*	5. *Port arrived from/Ports of destination *Baltimore*
6. Number of crew *36* 7.	8. Places where stores are secured *Bonded stores locker.*

9. Name of article		10. Quantity
Tobacco .. .. (lbs/grammes)	3
Cigarettes .. .. (No.)	1700
Cigars .. .. (No.)	50
Cigarillos .. .. (No.)	—

11. British currency in ship's funds *£32*

Spirits *(including liqueurs)*

Litre bottles (.22 liquid gallons) .. (No.)	
Standard bottles (.16 liquid gallons) .. (No.)	12
Other size bottles .. .. .. (No.)	

12. Gaming machines on board *(number and location)*

Wine

Litre bottles (.22 liquid gallons) .. (No.)	
Standard bottles (.16 liquid gallons) .. (No.)	10.
Other size bottles .. .. .. (No.)	

13. FOR USE BY CUSTOMS OFFICER

Livestock and birds *(include description)*

.... (No.)

.... (No.)

.... (No.)

Goods in shops, kiosks, etc., *(e.g. cameras, watches radios, mechanical lighters, clocks)*

ARRIVALS ONLY

*a) All stores checked

*b) The articles ticked have been checked

.... Signature and grade

.... Station

WARNING

Any person who makes or signs or causes to be made or signed any declaration relating to the Customs which is untrue in any material particular is liable to heavy penalties.

14.

I DECLARE the particulars on this form to be a true account of all stores, livestock, currency and gaming machines on board this ship. I understand that the unauthorised consumption, landing or disposal of the listed articles, or of any new stores placed on board, is an offence and may render me liable to heavy penalties.

Signature by Master authorised agent or officer *A. Clark* Date *7/7/78*

*Delete as necessary   F 3501 (April 1978)   528889 1/78 AP Ltd

Reproduced by kind permission of the Controller of H.M. Stationery Office

Ship's Stores Declaration Outwards, C.14

Having placed the goods on board, he must obtain the master's receipt on two copies of the shipping bill, and deliver them to the designated Customs office. Customs officers will check a percentage of shipments and place them under seal. All shipments on vessels proceeding coastwise will be verified and placed under seal.

When a ship leaves the United Kingdom bound for a foreign destination, the seals may be broken as soon as she is beyond territorial waters (three-mile limit), but it is not a good practice to make an immediate issue of large quantities of tobacco, cigarettes, etc. Should the vessel, through breakdown or other reason, be obliged to put back into a United Kingdom port, the master might well find it exceedingly difficult to recover excessive amounts of issued stores in order to have them sealed up again and, thereby, may find himself liable for a large sum by way of duty.

Engagement of Crew and Preparation for Voyage. An agreement may be opened on board the ship, in the shipping company's office, or in a Merchant Navy Establishment Office, whichever is most convenient. Where the company does not have an "approved" office within the meaning of clause 14 of the N.M.B. Established Service Scheme Agreement, it may be convenient to arrange for the signing on to take place in an Establishment Office, preferably at the same time as the crew are being selected.

Before engaging seamen on a new agreement, and before adding seamen to an agreement which is already current, at least 24 hours' notice must be given to the appropriate superintendent. This is done on form ALC 3 in which the following information is required:

(a) name of ship;
(b) port of registry;
(c) official number;
(d) whether a new crew agreement is to be made or whether a person is to be added to a current agreement;
(e) date, place and time that the agreement is to be made or the person added;
(f) the capacity in which each person engaged is to be employed.

Forms for this purpose are obtainable from Mercantile Marine Offices. If it is impossible to give notice in writing, a verbal notification will be accepted though this should be followed, as soon as possible, by confirmation in writing. A notice need not be given (a) if it is not practicable to do so without unreasonably delaying the ship, or (b) where not more than two seamen are to be added to an agreement relating to a single ship.

It is important that those signing on should have all the necessary documents such as certificates of competency or certificates of qualification, British Seamen's Cards, and Discharge Books. To conform with trade union requirements it is usual for a seaman to produce the N.M.B. Employment Form (P.C.5), and with a view to avoiding quarantine delays he should have an effective vaccination certificate.

Section 1 of the M.S.A. 1970 provides that, with certain exceptions, an agreement in writing shall be made between each person employed as a seaman and the person employing him. The agreements with the individual persons employed in a ship must be contained in one document (known as the crew agreement). The D.o.T. may, however, approve (a) the agreements being contained in more than one document, and (b) a crew agreement relating to more than one ship. The form of agreement and the clauses inserted in it must be approved by the D.o.T. Standard forms of agreement which do comply with D.o.T. requirements are available at M.M. Offices. Employers who wish to use non-standard forms or modified standard forms must submit them to the D.o.T. at least 14 days before the agreement is used as the D.o.T. will require to know the views of seafarers' organisations on the proposed provisions.

When a crew agreement relates to a single ship it must be carried in the ship. An agreement relating to more than one ship must be kept at an address in the U.K. A copy of the agreement should be delivered to the superintendent within two days of its being opened or, if that is not practicable, as soon as possible. A copy, or an extract of its terms, must be displayed in the ship in a conspicuous place, and for this purpose copies of standard forms can be obtained from M.M. Offices.

The master must maintain a List of the Crew with a separate list of Young Persons (under 18) and a list of Exempted Seamen (if any). The details required in these lists are set out in Chapter 4. A copy of the crew list must also be delivered to a superintendent within two days of it being made.

Now that the agreement is between a seaman and his employer it is no longer a requirement for the master to sign first. The definition of "seaman" in Section 742 of M.S.A. 1894 does not include a master and consequently he is excluded from the requirement of Section 1 of M.S.A. 1970 to enter into a crew agreement. However, he must enter his details in the List of Crew (Section 69, M.S.A. 1970) because the definition of "seaman" in the Regulation pertaining to Lists of Crew includes the master of a ship.

(See Chapter 4 for details of cases where persons do not have to be employed under a crew agreement, and also details of voyage clauses).

The master should see that he has an Official Log Book for the voyage together with the necessary supplementary logs (Radio 1 and 2, Watertight doors, etc., for passenger ship), Oil Record Books, and a supply of the following:

Account of wages forms.

RBD 1 forms.

Forms FRE 13 (draught and freeboard particulars for posting up).

National Insurance forms BF 19 and 19A.

Income Tax forms 46M.

Admiralty Notices to Mariners up to date.

Latest M notices of importance to masters.

Latest notices relating to dangers to navigation.

He should also make sure that the ship's medical stores have been adequately replenished.

Clearance Outwards. The master, or the agent must go to the Custom House and first pay the outward light dues, unless in respect of the ship dues for the current financial year are already fully paid. If the ship is a foreign-going ship and has deck cargo, the owner, agent, or master must complete form DCO C.1319 to declare the space occupied by the deck cargo, and this form must be produced with the certificate of registry when dues are demanded. A note on this form emphasises that the certificate given for dues paid on the amount of deck cargo is not to be regarded as a certificate that the ship is fit to carry deck cargo. Should any allegation of unseaworthiness arise, the D.o.T. will deal with the case on its merits entirely unprejudiced by the existence of the deck cargo certificate. The form must be shown to the Customs Officer who is last on board at the commencement of the voyage so that he can check the statement in it against the actual amount of deck cargo on board. It will be the duty of that officer to report any discrepancy.

Having settled the matter of light dues, the master or agent must then go to the Inspector with the following papers, viz.:

Certificate of registry, with deck cargo certificate (if one).

Safety Certificate (or certificates).

Outward light bill receipted.

Load line certificate.

General Declaration, C.13.

Ship's Stores Declaration, C.14.

Manifest (or declaration that one will be delivered within 14 days of vessel's departure).

Passenger Return, PAS 15 (departure) (within 4 days of sailing from final port).

Oil Pollution Insurance Certificate (OPIC), if appropriate.

When the inspector is satisfied with the above documents he will date stamp and sign the General Declaration and hand it to the master.

Formerly it was the practice to issue, at this stage, a Bill of Health on payment of the appropriate fee, but this is no longer done. However, if the ship is to call at a port in a country which is not bound by the International Sanitary Regulations, or a country in which the position with regard to health regulations is not defined, the master should, with a view to avoiding vexatious delays, apply to the Customs clearing officer for a form C.220, which is worded as follows:

PORT OF ....

Whereas the ship named the ....

SCHEDULE 1

(Name of shipping line, agent, etc.)

PASSENGER RETURN

PAS 15 (ARRIVAL)

Page No   1

Waterside Agents Co. Ltd.

1 Name of ship		2 Port of arrival in the UK Southampton	3 Date of arrival in the UK 5/9/78

| 4 Nationality of ship   British | | | |

5 Numbers of Passengers.	6	7	8 Port of embarkation	9 Port of disembarkation in the UK
Note:				
(1) These figures should show for each port of disembarkation in the UK, the number of passengers travelling from each port of embarkation outside the UK.				
(2) Passengers on round-trip cruises (from the UK and back) should be included on this list.				
874			NEW YORK	SOUTHAMPTON
42			CHERBOURG	SOUTHAMPTON

10 Date and signature of master, authorised agent or officer

Signature .... J. Tait ....

Date .... 5/9/78 ....

Passenger Return, PAS 15

of (port of registry) is about to depart from the above-named Port and the Master of the ship has asked to be supplied with a certificate concerning the health conditions of the said Port:

I, the undersigned Customs officer at the said Port, hereby certify that, at the date of issuing this document, no case of plague, cholera, yellow fever, smallpox, typhus or relapsing fever exists in the said port or its immediate neighbourhood.

| Office Stamp | (Signed) .... |

Once the port clearance has been issued the ship is, as far as the Customs authority is concerned, free to sail from the port.

REMARKS ON SOME OF THE DOCUMENTS REQUIRED FOR CLEARING OUTWARDS

General Declaration. The form is designed for use either inwards or outwards. The Departure box at the top must be ticked and information about the ship, master, voyage, cargo, crew and passengers declared. It is signed by the master or his authorised agent. At the bottom are spaces for the Collector to indicate that he has sighted the documents that must be presented to him, which include the certificate of registry, load line certificate, safety certificates and Oil Pollution Insurance Certificate (if appropriate). When he is satisfied the Collector signs the form and date stamps it to grant clearance.

Ship's Stores Declaration (Departure). This form lists the total quantities of dutiable stores carried in the ship on departure such as tobacco, cigarettes, cigars, spirits, wine and any goods in shops or store for sale such as cameras, lighters, clocks etc.

Manifest. There is no official form for this, which may be in ordinary manuscript form written or typed, though some shipping companies may have their own special forms for the purpose. It should contain a detailed description of the ship's cargo showing, with respect to each consignment, marks and numbers of packages or other units, weights or quantities, name of shipper, name of consignee (or "to order"), port of shipment, intended port of discharge, reference number of the B/L for each package or unit, name and particulars of the vessel, and the name of the master. In the case of a general cargo liner it is rarely the case that the manifest is ready at the time when the vessel clears. Accordingly, the clearing officer accepts a declaration that a manifest will be delivered within 14 days.

This document is of value to H.M. Customs to enable them to supply statistics to the Government Departments and other bodies interested in the country's exports. A copy taken to sea, or a manifest compiled on board from the ship's copies of M/R's and/or B's/L, would in time of war supply *prima facie* evidence of the contents of the ship to a contraband control boarding officer, though it would not necessarily prevent a belligerent from exercising a right of search. Advance copies sent to agents of the ship abroad are useful to enable them to make preparations for berthing and unloading, particularly if the manifest specifies which holds the various shipments are stowed in, and enables them to assure consignees that their particular goods are, in fact, due to arrive.

OTHER ASPECTS OF CUSTOMS BUSINESS

Issue of duty free wines, tobaccos, etc. While the ship is engaged in foreign trade *bona fide* members of the crew are permitted to have a duty free issue of reasonable quantities of wines, spirits, tobacco, etc. But once the cargo has been discharged the crew cease to be entitled to duty free goods until the ship commences to load for a foreign destination again. If the ship is to sail in ballast, no issue is allowed until after the ship has cleared outwards and has left territorial waters. In its strict application the concession made to the crew of a ship in foreign trade does not extend to crew reliefs on board during the vessel's stay in port.

Smuggling Offences. The master of a ship is legally responsible for seeing that the ship is periodically rummaged. A good practice, which some shipping companies insist upon, is to enter in the official log book the result of the search on every occasion when the ship is rummaged. If an offender is caught smuggling, both he personally and the ship may be fined. If a responsible officer is found guilty, it invariably follows that the ship will be fined. The personal fine will generally depend on the status of the officer, and may be as much as double the amount of duty involved. Fines on the ship can be imposed by H.M. Customs, but fines on persons must be recovered by court procedure. Where an officer is not involved, the ship's record will be taken into account, and although the ship may be fined as well as the guilty person this does not follow automatically. In this connection log entries of searches for contraband may assume considerable importance.

Night Work. If a ship is required to load or discharge cargo outside ordinary working hours, the owners or their agents must make an application to H.M. Customs who will then be in a position to make their staffing arrangements accordingly. The ship will be required to pay some part of the charges for this Customs attendance.

Transires. The General Transire, C.197 (XS42), is granted by H.M. Customs to the owner of coasting vessels in respect of each ship and each port to which the ship operates. On the back of the form an alphabetical list of the ports to which the Transire applies must be written in. Due notice of loading and discharge for respective voyages must be lodged on approved forms with the Collectors of Customs at the various ports. Form X.S.97 is the Notice of Loading, and X.S.98 the Notice of Unloading under General Transire. This system facilitates entry and clearance and relieves the master of any necessity to attend in person at the Custom House. General control over such coastal traffic is maintained by Preventive Officers hailing or boarding ships as necessary, and making occasional inspections of the ship's "Cargo Book" which must be kept up to date. This book serves as a kind of running manifest, inspection of which should reveal what has been put in and taken out of the ship at different ports, and should correspond to the contents of the Notices of Loading and Unloading.

The Transire (Original), C.196 (XS18), is issued together with the Transire (Duplicate), C.196 (XS19), in respect of an occasional coastwise voyage, and gives an account of the goods loaded. Both forms are delivered to the Collector before departure. The "original", signed by the Collector, is returned to the master and serves as clearance from the port as well as entry at the next port. At the port of unloading it must be delivered to H.M. Customs with an indorsement, signed by the master or agent, to show the name of the dock, wharf, or other station where the cargo listed in the transire will be discharged.

Another document sometimes required in the coasting trade is form X.S.61, which is a Notice to Load Explosives Coastwise. This is completed and signed by the shipper or his agent and shows the name of the carrying ship, her port of registry, the name of the master, where the ship is bound, and a description of the explosives the shipper intends to load. The reverse side of the form is the "Sufferance to load explosives coastwise" which is signed by the Collector of Customs directing the officer of Customs and Excise at the place of loading to allow the goods to be shipped. Such goods are not held to have been duly cleared unless they are entered in the Cargo Book and on the Transire.

Drawback. This is the sum paid back by the Government on certain classes of goods on which duty has already been paid, Drawback goods consist of (1) goods manufactured in the United Kingdom on which Excise Duty is paid, such as spirits, malt liquors, etc., and (2) goods composed of raw materials on which Customs Duty was paid at the time of their importation into the country, e.g., snuff, manufactured tobacco, cigarettes and cigars.

Since neither Customs nor Excise Duty is payable on goods which are not consumed in the United Kingdom, provision has to be made for the refunding of duty which has been paid. To secure drawback notice must be given to a Revenue Officer of the intention to export the goods, which are then placed in charge of the customs officer in attendance on the exporting ship. A Shipping Bill is

H M Customs and Excise

GENERAL TRANSIRE – APPLICATION AND GRANT FORM

Sections A, C and D are to be completed by the applicant. An additional copy, similarly completed, is required in respect of each port listed overleaf. Carbon copies must be legible.

A

PORT OF _LONDON_

To the Collector or other proper officer of Customs and Excise

I/We hereby request the issue of a † General Transire in respect of the vessel specified in Section C (overleaf) for † the period

from _22 MARCH_ 19...... to _21 MARCH_ 19...... both dates inclusive
to cover the ports specified in Section D.

~~A General Transire has not previously been held~~

The previous General Transire was granted at the Port of _LONDON_

Signature of Applicant _P.W Stansfield_   Date _17 March_ 19.....

*Delete as necessary
†See Notes below

(*Owner/Agent)

Address _95 Tower Street, London_

B

Office date stamp

A General Transire is hereby granted to the ship described in Section C overleaf to trade between the ports mentioned in Section D during the period requested above upon condition that due notice of loading and discharge for the respective voyages be lodged on the approved forms with the Collectors of those Ports.

With the authority of the Commissioners of Customs and Excise

Signed ....
(Collector or other proper officer of Customs and Excise)

NOTES

1. Under the Customs and Excise Acts 1979, the Commissioners of Customs and Excise may, subject to such conditions as they see fit to impose, grant a general transire in respect of any coasting ship and any goods carried therein. Any such general transire may be revoked by the proper officer by notice in writing delivered to the master or the owner of the ship or any member of the crew on board the ship.

2. General Transires are granted for periods not exceeding twelve months and only in respect of ports to which the vessel trades regularly and frequently.

C 197 (XS 42)   F 2003 (March 1979)   *continued overleaf*

54088 [22178] DD 0586235 10M 3/79 GWB LTD. GP. 870

C

Particulars of the vessel in respect of which the application is made

Date of expiry ...21 March...

Nationality	Port of Registry	Official Number	Net Tonnage	Steam, sail or motor	Name of vessel (BLOCK LETTERS)
BRITISH	LONDON	143627	849	MoTor	"JOAN APPLETON"

Owner's Name and address ...Appleton Shipping Co. Ltd. 95, Tower Street, London.

D

List of ports in alphabetical order, including the Port of Application

AVON·MOUTH		
CARDIFF		
FELIXSTOWE		
LIVERPOOL		
LONDON		
PLYMOUTH		
PORTSMOUTH		
SHOREHAM		
SOUTHAMPTON		
SWANSEA		

Further supplies of this form can be obtained from any Collector of Customs and Excise

FOR OFFICIAL USE

LOAD LINE CERTIFICATE:— Authority .... Date of expiry ....

Valid M.M Clearance Certificate-Form .... produced .... Light Dues ....

Cargo Book inspected .... Notices of loading and unloading ....

C 197 (XS 42)

Reproduced by kind permission of the Controller of H.M. Stationery Office

U

TRANSIRE (ORIGINAL)

C 196

PORT OF .... LONDON ....

Official number of ship ....

HM Customs
and Excise

Sailing vessel/Steamer/Motor vessel   *Delete as necessary*

Name of ship	Net tonnage	If British, Port of Registry If foreign, the country	Master's name	Whither bound	Date of sailing
HILBURY	792	LONDON	JAMES HYDE	LIVERPOOL	23/8

I .... James Hyde .... Master of the .... m.v. Hilbury .... do hereby declare the particulars stated on this form to be true, and that all the requirements of the Merchant Shipping Acts have been duly complied with.

Dated .... 21st August .... 19....

Cleared out .... 23rd August .... 19....

.... J. Hyde .... Master

....
Collector or other proper officer

Agent .... Adams and Brown Ltd. ....

Address .... 24–28, Block Street, London ....

THIS DOCUMENT IS TO ACCOMPANY THE VESSEL AND TO BE DELIVERED AT THE PORT OF UNLOADING WITH THE NAME OF THE WHARF OR PLACE OF DISCHARGE INSERTED ON THE BACK.

Further supplies of this form may be obtained from any Collector of Customs and Excise

C 196 (ORIGINAL)
(XS 18)

F1965 (July 1979)

continued overleaf

Foreign goods, listing separately warehoused goods removed under Bond	Goods liable to Excise Duty OR entitled to Drawback thereof	Other British goods
NIL	NIL	325 tonnes General cargo

State whether carrying passengers   *YES/NO

Last from .... Rotterdam .... *Light/In ballast/With cargo

Vessel loading at .... Tilbury ....
*Delete as necessary

To be filled in at place of discharge

Date of arrival ...... 26 August .... The above cargo (or portion thereof, stating particulars) will be discharged at

.... Gladstone Dock, Liverpool .... Date ...... 27 August ....
Name of Dock, Wharf, or Station

Signature of Master or Agent .... J. Hyde .... Date ....

Name and address of Agent ...... J. R. Dunn & Co. Ltd., 1370 Water Street, Liverpool ......

Reproduced by kind permission of the Controller of H. M. Stationery Office

prepared and signed, as in the case of bonded goods, and on production of this to the proper officer of Customs or Excise an export certificate, known as a "debenture" is handed to the exporter. This document serves as the latter's authority to receive repayment of the amount of the duty.

OUTWARD PILOT

If the ship is departing from a port in a compulsory pilotage district, or in the case of a ship carrying passengers even from a port in a non-compulsory district, she must be under the pilotage of a pilot licensed for the district. The master or agent should, in such circumstances, make arrangements well in advance to obtain the services of a pilot so that the vessel is not delayed.

MARITIME DECLARATION OF HEALTH

Mention has already been made of this document in Chapter 6. The form which the declaration takes is as follows:

PUBLIC HEALTH (SHIPS) REGULATIONS, 1979
MARITIME DECLARATION OF HEALTH

Port of Arrival.. Date..............................

Name of Ship.............................. From................. To....................

Nationality of Ship.............................. Master's Name........................

Net Registered Tonnage..............................

Deratting Certificate
Deratting Exemption Certificate } issued at.................. Dated..............

No. of {Cabin.............................. No. of Crew..................
Passengers {Deck..............................

List of ports of call from commencement of voyage with dates of departure.

....

....

Health Questions	Answer Yes or No
1. Has there been on board during the voyage* any case or suspected case of plague, cholera, yellow fever, or smallpox? Give particulars in the Schedule ...	....
2. Has plague occurred or been suspected amongst the rats or mice on board during the voyage,* or has there been an abnormal mortality among them? ...	....
3. Has any person died on board during the voyage* otherwise than as a result of accident? Give particulars in Schedule	....
4. Is there on board or has there been during the voyage* any case of disease which you suspect to be of an infectious nature? Give particulars in Schedule	....
5. Is there any sick person on board now? Give particulars in Schedule	....
Note.—In the absence of a surgeon, the Master should regard the following symptoms as ground for suspecting the existence of disease of an infectious nature; fever accompanied by prostration or persisting for several days, or attended with glandular swelling; or any acute skin rash or eruption with or without fever; severe diarrhoea with symptoms of collapse; jaundice accompanied by fever.	
6. Are you aware of any other condition on board which may lead to infection or the spread of disease?	....

* If more than four weeks have elapsed since the voyage began, it will suffice to give particulars for the last four weeks.

I hereby declare that the particulars and answers to the questions given in this Declaration of Health (including the Schedule) are true and correct to the best of my knowledge and belief.

Signed..
(Master)

Countersigned..
Date....................................... (Ship's Surgeon)

The reverse side of the form comprises the "Schedule to the Declaration" on which are to be entered particulars of every case of illness or death occurring on board. The several columns are headed as follows:

Names
Class or rating
Age
Sex
Nationality
Port of embarkation
Date of embarkation
Nature of illness
Date of its onset
Result of illness (whether recovered, still ill, or died)
Disposal of case (whether still on board, landed—port to be
      named—or buried at sea).

N.B.: In the United Kingdom the Maritime Declaration of Health
(when required) is delivered to the Customs Officer or the Authorised
Officer, whoever is the first to board. In some ports abroad the
inward pilots are authorised to take delivery of the document on
behalf of the Health Authority.

VACCINATION CERTIFICATES

These are usually only for vaccination against smallpox and will
probably not now be required, but where a vessel arrives from a
country declared by the World Health Authority to have one or
more of the scheduled diseases, either endemic or epidemic, a full
vaccination/inoculation certificate may be required.

BILLS OF HEALTH

By Article 95 of the International Sanitary Regulations it is
laid down that health administrations are not to demand bills of
health with or without consular visas. In spite of this it appears
that these documents have been issued by the authorities of some
countries which are bound by the Regulations, and in some cases
masters of ships have requested to be supplied with bills of health
even when their ships have been proceeding to countries bound by
the Regulations. It is reported, however, that the practice seems
to be declining.

WORLD HEALTH ORGANISATION AND POSITION TAKEN BY VARIOUS COUNTRIES WITH RESPECT TO THE INTERNATIONAL REGULATIONS

Of all the countries of the world, some are active members of
the W.H.O., some inactive members, some associate members, and
others non-members. But because a particular country is a non-
member, it does not follow that that country has refused to be
bound by the International Health Regulations.

CHAPTER II

WRECK AND SALVAGE

WRECK

THE main purpose of the law relating to wreck is to ensure the preservation of property rights. The D.o.T. have the general super-intendence of all matters relating to wreck in the United Kingdom and may, with the consent of the Treasury, appoint any officer of Customs, Coastguard, or Inland Revenue, or any other person to be a "Receiver of Wreck". They must give due notice of such appointment.

The United Kingdom coast is divided into a number of "wreck areas", each in the charge of a receiver of wreck who is generally, though not invariably, an officer of Customs holding the appointment as receiver from the D.o.T. on a part-time basis. Such officer will carry out receiver's duties in addition to his routine Customs work.

Any person who finds wreck within the limits of the United Kingdom must, (a) if he is the owner of the wreck, notify the receiver of wreck for the district, (b) if he is not the owner, deliver the wreck to the receiver. Failure to comply involves a fine of up to £500, forfeiture of any claim to salvage, and liability to pay double the value of the wreck.

The law requires all reports of wreck made to a receiver to be posted up in the nearest Custom House within 48 hours. The notice must give a description of the property, a statement of when and where it was found, its estimated value, and its present position. If the estimated value exceeds £20, a copy of the notice must be sent to the Secretary at Lloyd's with the object of attracting the attention of the owner.

Normally wreck is kept up to twelve months awaiting claim, but goods of low value which are not worth storing may be sold within that period. (Several thousands of wreck reports may be handed in during the course of a year, and it is not unknown for sales of unclaimed wreck to reach as much as £30,000 or more in the same period.)

In Part IX of the principal Act the expression "wreck" is defined to include jetsam, flotsam, lagan, and derelict found in or on the shores of the sea or any tidal water. These terms may be explained as follows:

Jetsam: goods cast or lost overboard from a ship which are recoverable through being eventually washed ashore, or remaining submerged in relatively shallow water.

Flotsam: goods cast or lost overboard which are recoverable by reason of their remaining afloat.

Lagan (or Ligan): goods cast overboard and buoyed so as to render them recoverable.

Derelict: a vessel remaining afloat but completely abandoned.

Nominally, the duties of a receiver of wreck include not only the taking of wreck into his custody pending claim, but the organisation of assistance to casualties, for which latter purpose the M.S. Act provides that where a British or foreign vessel is wrecked, stranded, or in distress at any place on or near the coasts of the United Kingdom or any tidal water within the limits of the United Kingdom the receiver of wreck for the district shall, on being made acquainted with the circumstances, forthwith proceed there, and upon his arrival take command of all persons present and assign such duties and give such directions to each person as he thinks fit for the preservation of the vessel and of the lives of the persons belonging to the vessel and of the cargo and apparel of the vessel. Moreover, if any person wilfully disobeys the direction of the receiver he shall, for each offence, be liable to a fine not exceeding £50; but the receiver shall not interfere between the master and the crew of the vessel in reference to the management thereof unless he is requested to do so by the master. For the purpose of preserving shipwrecked persons, vessels, and other property, powers vested in a receiver include power to require such persons as he thinks necessary to assist him, to require the master of a vessel near at hand to give aid with his men or vessel, and to demand the use of transport. He is also given the right to pass over adjoining lands unless there is some public road equally convenient in order to give assistance. He may cause plunderers to be apprehended and use force to suppress plundering, with the right to command all Her Majesty's subjects to assist him. If any person is killed, maimed, or hurt through resisting the receiver or anyone acting under his orders, neither the receiver nor his assistant will be liable to punishment or to pay damages. A person who refuses without reasonable cause to comply with a receiver's requisition or demand, or who hinders or impedes the endeavours of a receiver in any way, is liable to a fine not exceeding £100.

Owners of wrecked or stranded vessels and owners of cargo are entitled to compensation if they suffer loss at the hands of rioters or plunderers. (In England such compensation is to be made in the same manner, by the same authority, and out of the same rate, as if the plundering, damage, etc., were an injury in respect of which compensation is payable under the provisions of the Riot (Damages) Act, 1886. If the scene of the plundering is not in any police district, the compensation is payable as though the plundering had taken place in the nearest police district. There are corresponding measures which apply in Scotland and Northern Ireland.)

Where a receiver is not present, the following officers or persons (each in the absence of the other, in the order named) may do what is authorised to be done by the receiver, viz., chief officer of customs, principal officer of coastguard, officer of inland revenue, sheriff, justice of the peace, commissioned officer on full pay in H.M. naval service, or commissioned officer on full pay in H.M. military service.

In practice, nowadays, the statutory duties of a receiver of wreck in the matter of organising assistance to casualties are usually undertaken by the Coastguard and Lifeboat services and by private salvors.

Except in some areas where certain landowners and other persons hold prior rights, unclaimed wreck goes to the Crown in accordance with Section 525 of the principal Act, although in practice it appears that the proceeds of unclaimed wreck are paid into the Exchequer.

The master of a ship may repel by force anyone who, without his leave, boards or attempts to board his vessel when wrecked, stranded, or in distress, unless the person is a receiver of wreck or his representative. The penalty for unlawful boarding is a fine not exceeding £200.

Any person who hinders the saving of a vessel or who wrongfully carries away wreck is liable to a fine not exceeding £500 in addition to any other penalty he may incur.

Any wreck which is found outside United Kingdom limits and afterwards brought within such limits must be delivered to the receiver of wreck. If any person takes into a foreign port any vessel, stranded, derelict, or otherwise in distress, found on or near the coasts of the United Kingdom, or any part of the cargo or apparel thereof, or anything belonging thereto, or any wreck found within those limits, and there sells the same, that person shall be guilty of an offence and liable to imprisonment for a term not less than 3 years and not exceeding 5 years.

Where any ship is or has been in distress **on** the coasts of the United Kingdom (note that this does not apply to ships in distress **near** the coasts of the United Kingdom), a receiver of wreck or at the request of the D.o.T., a wreck commissioner or approved deputy, or a J.P., shall, as soon as conveniently may be, examine on oath (and the Act empowers such persons to administer the oath) any person belonging to the ship, or any other person who may be able to give any account thereof or of the cargo or stores thereof, as to the following matters:

(a) name and description of ship;
(b) name of master and of owners;

(c) names of owners of cargo;
(d) ports from and to which ship was bound;
(e) the occasion of the distress of the ship;
(f) the services rendered;
(g) such other matters or circumstances relating to ship or cargo as the person holding the examination thinks necessary.

The person holding the examination, who for the purpose has all the powers of a D.o.T. inspector, must take down the particulars in writing and send one copy each to the D.o.T. and the secretary of Lloyd's. The latter is required to place it in a conspicuous position for inspection.

Removal of Wreck. The powers of harbour or conservancy authorities and lighthouse authorities to remove wrecks which become obstructions or dangers to navigation are dealt with in Chapter 7.

Marking of Anchors. So that anchors may be easily identifiable, it is provided by a section of the Act that every manufacturer of anchors shall mark on every anchor manufactured by him in legible characters and both on the crown and also on the shank under the stock his name or initials, and shall in addition mark on the anchor a progressive number and the weight of the anchor. The penalty for failure to comply is a fine not exceeding £5.

Duties on Wreck. It is provided by the Customs and Excise Management Act 1979, that "Any goods brought or coming into the United Kingdom by sea otherwise than as cargo, stores or baggage carried in a ship shall be chargeable with the like duty, if any, as would be applicable to those goods if they had been imported as merchandise; and if any question arises as to the origin of the goods, unless that question is determined under s.120 below, s.14 of Customs and Excise Duties (General Reliefs) Act 1979 or under a Community regulation or other instrument having the force of law, they shall be deemed to be the produce of such country as the Commissioners may on investigation determine".

In accordance with the principal M.S. Act, "The Commissioners of Customs and Inland Revenue shall permit all goods, wares and merchandise saved from any ship stranded or wrecked on her homeward voyage to be forwarded to the port of her original destination, and all goods, wares and merchandise saved from any ship stranded or wrecked on her outward voyage to be returned to the port at which the same were shipped; but those Commissioners shall take security for the due protection of the revenue in respect of those goods".

SALVAGE

The term "salvage" applies to (a) the service performed by a salvor, and (*b*) the reward paid to a salvor in respect of his success-ful services.

The right to salvage can arise only in respect of "maritime property", which term does not include every kind of property found in tidal waters. Vessels used in navigation, whether registered or not, their apparel, cargo and wreckage thereof do constitute maritime property, and so do rafts, but not such things as light-vessels, buoys or other floating seamarks.

Three conditions must be fulfilled before the rescue of maritime property can give rise to a valid claim for a salvage award. These are (1) the property must be in danger, (2) the service rendered must be of a voluntary character, *i.e.*, the salvor must not be under any contractual or official duty to render assistance, and (3) the service must be successful.

With regard to danger, the rule is that the danger must be a real one. It is not sufficient that some vague or fancied danger may subsequently arise. The degree of danger is a matter on which it is not in the public interest to lay down too strict rules. Over-strictness might tend to discourage salvors in a genuine case whilst, on the other hand, too little strictness might have the effect that unscrupulous persons would be tempted to impose services on ships that are in no real need of them. The danger does not have to be absolute or immediate, but it must be of such a kind that a prudent master would not hesitate to accept a salvor's help. Indeed the test to be applied is whether the master on being asked "Are you in need of assistance?" would reply "Yes" or "No". For instance, a single-screw vessel disabled in mid-ocean in fine weather through the loss of her propeller, in circumstances where it is not practicable to ship a spare one, would not be in any immediate danger. The later onset of bad weather, however, would obviously leave her at the mercy of the elements, so that a prudent master in such case would accept the offer of, or arrange for, a tow to port.

With regard to the voluntary character of the service, it is true that nowadays very few salvage services are absolutely voluntary. Colliding vessels are under a statutory obligation to stand by one another and to give necessary assistance, life salvage is a statutory duty, and vessels are required by statute to respond to distress calls. Nevertheless, none of these statutory duties affect salvage rights. Persons who obey them retain their volunteer status for the purpose of the law of salvage, and they may claim their due reward.

Salvage work undertaken in accordance with a salvage agree-ment is not of a voluntary nature, but the existence of some other kind of agreement may still allow a valid claim to salvage to exist in a proper case. This may occur, for instance, where there is a contract of towage or pilotage and salvage services are rendered by the tug or pilot, as the case may be. Except in special cases, there is a tendency for the courts to look with disfavour on salvage claims put forward by tugs or pilots, but a good claim can be established provided that:

(1) the vessel being towed or piloted is really in danger;

(2) the tug or pilot has in no way contributed towards her being in danger;

(3) the tug was well equipped for the services contemplated in the towage contract;

(4) the tug or pilot has rendered services substantially in excess of those normally to be expected in return for their customary remuneration;

(5) the tug or pilot successfully saves, or materially contributes towards saving, the vessel in danger.

Ships' agents and passengers are not normally allowed to share in a salvage award, but a passenger who could escape from a ship in danger but who voluntarily remains on board to assist with salvage work will rank as a salvor and earn a share.

The crew of a salved ship cannot be classed as salvors as their contract of service binds them to do their utmost for the preservation of the ship and her cargo. However, if the master gives a definite order to abandon the ship **with the intention of not returning** and any of the crew do subsequently return and render successful salvage services, they will be considered to have returned as strangers and may claim an award.

Officers and men of the Royal Navy at one time could not claim salvage as they were considered to be under an official duty to assist British vessels in distress. Later they were given the right to claim, provided they obtained the consent of the Admiralty. During the First World War the Admiralty were granted the right to salvage in cases where services were performed with their specially equipped salvage craft. The M.S. (Salvage) Act, 1940, however, repealed the Act of 1916, and today the Ministry of Defence have the same right to salvage as any other shipowner. If a salvage service is given by a privately owned ship which the M.O.D. have requisitioned, salvage rights belong to the M.O.D. unless they have previously agreed for them to be reserved for the shipowner.

In the event of salvage assistance being needed by one of Her Majesty's ships, outside assistance is to be accepted only in emergency. The officer in command must, where possible, make use of the nearest available M.O.D. resources, and he is not permitted to enter into any agreement binding the M.O.D. to pay a definite salvage award. Nor is he allowed to agree to submit to an agreed procedure for ascertainment of reward. It is his duty to instruct the salvor to deal direct with the M.O.D. who will consider the circumstances with a view to reasonable payment and he should notify the M.O.D. by signal. There is no fixed scale of remuneration. Each case is treated on its merits.

Coastguards have no salvage rights unless they do substantially more than their office demands, and lifeboat crews remunerated by the Royal National Life-boat Institution are in a similar position. But if the latter on finding their services are not needed for life-saving undertake the salvage of property, they will in that respect rank as volunteers. In such case they would be deemed to have borrowed the lifeboat and would be personally responsible to the R.N.L.I. for any damage it suffered.

If, in wartime, the master of a ship in convoy is ordered by the naval officer in charge of the convoy to go to the assistance of a vessel in danger, the master in obeying the order still retains the status of a volunteer as he has no contractual or official duty to-wards the salved property.

With regard to the fulfilment of the third condition, it is only necessary to say that, as the reward is payable out of the salved property, success is essential to entitlement. Where there are several salvors, each is entitled to a share provided that his services materially contributed to the ultimate success. No matter how meritorious a service may be, it cannot give title to a reward if it has not contributed to the eventual success.

The Parties to a Salvage Operation. The two parties to the trans-action are (1) the salvors who are entitled to the reward, and they are in most cases the owner, master and crew of the salving ship, and (2) the owners of the salved property who are liable to pay salvage, namely, the owners of the ship, cargo and freight salved.

Master's Right of Decision where several Salvors appear. If several would-be salvors appear on the scene, the master of the ship needing assistance has the absolute right to decide which of them shall be employed. If he decides that he needs more help than can be given by the first salvors on the spot, the latter have no right to exclude others who appear later with offers of assistance. On the other hand, latecomers who interfere against the wishes of the master will not only earn no reward, but they may be proceeded against if their interference impedes the efforts of legitimate salvors.

Derelicts. In the case of a derelict vessel the position is different. The first salvor to take possession has absolute right and control, and no one may interfere with him except in the face of manifest incompetence.

Lien for Salvage. There is a maritime lien on property saved, giving the right to arrest the property even if it has changed hands, in order to have it sold so that claims can be satisfied. This lien ranks in priority over all previous liens on the property, and is considered to be such good protection that salvors are not normally allowed to retain possession of salved property and thereby prevent the owners of it from making use of it. Apart from this remedy *in rem* the salvor may also proceed *in personam* against the owners of the salved property, which would be a very valuable right in the event of the lien becoming lost.

The Reward. Wilful or criminal misconduct will result in the salvor forfeiting his reward, but misconduct which is not wilful or criminal does not give rise to forfeiture though it will lead to the amount of the reward being reduced. Where one ship negligently collides with another and afterwards renders successful salvage services, the question arises as to whether she can claim a reward. In the past courts have decided against such a claim, but more recent statements in the House of Lords suggest that these cases were wrongly decided. One thing has been made clear in a recent case, and that is that where a ship belonging to the same owner as the wrongdoing ship has performed salvage services following a collision, there is a right to salvage (subject, of course, to a counter-claim for damages). Salvage awards are usually on a fairly generous scale, with a view to encouraging salvage services, but the award cannot in any event exceed the value of the property saved. Factors taken into account in assessing the award are:

(1) the degree of danger from which the property was salved;
(2) the enterprise of the salvors and the degree of risk to their own lives;
(3) the extent of the labour incurred and skill displayed by the salvors;
(4) the degree of risk to which the salvor's property was exposed, and the value of the property risked;
(5) the value of the property salved;
(6) the loss, if any, suffered by the salvor.

Freight will be called upon to contribute to the award if, but for the salvage services, it would not have been earned.

The assessment of the award is based on the values of the several interests saved at the place where the salvage services terminate, and each interest must contribute its proportion. Unlike the position with regard to general average contributions, liability for salvage is not affected by a subsequent total loss of the ship and cargo. (General average contributions are based on the net arrived values of the interests at the place where the adventure ends, and total loss before arrival at that place puts an end to liability to contribute.)

The apportionment of the award will depend on circumstances. If the ship, as such, has performed the main task, as in a towage service, the major part will go to the shipowner But if the success is mainly due to the efforts and skill of the master and crew, then they will earn the major part. The usual apportionment in a towage case provides for something in the order of two-thirds to three-quarters of the award to go to the shipowner and the rest to be divided between master and crew. The master's share is usually stated separately and the crew's share is divided according to rank or according to the nature of individual services. Where there are several salvors much depends on who performed the most important service but, other things being equal, the courts are inclined to favour those first on the scene. Salvage not exceeding £200 may be apportioned by a receiver of wreck in respect of services rendered in the United Kingdom. Where the amount finally ascertained exceeds £200 or, in any case, in respect of services rendered elsewhere than in the United Kingdom, apportionment may be made by any court having Admiralty jurisdiction. Apportionment may, of course, be settled privately, and so long as it is equitable the courts will not disturb such procedure.

Salvage Agreements. Under such an agreement the salvor can bargain for a reward beforehand, but it is not necessary to do so. Where a specific amount is not fixed the agreement is called an "open" agreement. All the usual conditions of salvage are implied in a salvage agreement, hence they are entered into on a "No cure— No pay" basis, and the salvors have a lien on the salved property. The form of agreement almost universally employed nowadays is the Lloyd's Standard Form of Salvage Agreement with which a number of advantages are associated. These are as follows:

The owner of the property in danger benefits from the "No cure —No pay" principle.

The salvor benefits by having an agreement which can be obtained in a few moments and which is not likely to be contested. He also retains his right of lien.

All parties benefit from the provision of the agreement that the salvor's remuneration shall be referred to arbitration (unless the parties agree otherwise).

Underwriters of the property in danger benefit because their liability cannot be increased beyond liability for total loss. That is to say they will not, under the "No cure—No pay" principle, become liable for suing and labouring charges as well in the event of total loss occurring.

In May 1980 a new version of Lloyd's Standard Form of Salvage Agreement was introduced which, with the object of trying to reduce oil pollution following an accident, provides for the payment of expenses to a salvor even when he has not been successful.

In paragraph 1(a) (see Appendix), as well as attempting to salve the ship, cargo, etc., and take her to a place of safety, the salvor agrees to use his best endeavours to prevent the escape of oil from the vessel while performing the services. Further the "no cure–no pay" principle is accepted except that, where the property being salved is a laden or partly laden oil tanker, if without negligence on the part of the salvor (or his servants or agents) the services are not successful, or only partially successful, or the salvor is prevented from completing the services, the agreement provides for the salvor to be awarded, solely against the owners of the tanker, his reasonably incurred expenses and an increment not exceeding 15 per cent of such expenses, but only if such amount is greater than any amount otherwise recoverable under the agreement. Expenses, in addition to actual out of pocket expenses, are to include a fair rate for all tugs, craft, personnel and equipment used. Oil is to mean crude oil, fuel oil, heavy diesel oil and lubricating oil.

Signing of Agreement. It is not necessary, nor is it usual, to sign Lloyd's form of agreement until the salvage has been successfully performed so long as there is good evidence that the parties have agreed to carry out the salvage under this form of agreement. When the time comes for signing, it should be signed on the one part either by the contractor personally or by the master of the salving vessel for and on behalf of the contractor. On the other part it should be signed, preferably by the master of the vessel to be salved, for and on behalf of the owners.

Advice to Masters. The following advice to masters on the use of Lloyd's Standard Form of Salvage Agreement was published in *Lloyd's Calendar* for many years.

Where a vessel finds herself in need of assistance and it is not possible or desirable to accept assistance on fixed terms, the Master should do his best to arrange for help to be rendered under the terms of Lloyd's Form of Salvage Agreement—"no cure–no pay"; it is also desirable that the Master should, with as little delay as possible, request the advice and assistance of the nearest Lloyd's Agent. A large number of cases are dealt with each year under the terms of this Agreement, which has become increasingly popular as the medium of deciding the remuneration to be paid for salvage services all over the world.

The Master of the vessel to be salved will normally sign an agreement on the printed Lloyd's Agreement at the time the services are rendered, but provision is made in the Agreement for it to be signed after the termination of the services; it may be noted that it is sufficient for a simple agreement on a sheet of paper to be signed stating that the services are to be rendered under the terms of Lloyd's Form of Salvage Agreement; in such simple agreement the name of the Salvor should be clearly stated.

It may be of interest to state that Lloyd's Form of Salvage Agreement first came into being in the year 1890, when a Salvor in the Dardanelles agreed to use a form of agreement in which his remuneration was left to the decision of the Committee of Lloyd's or that of an Arbitrator appointed by them; during the next two years slightly different forms were used by other Salvage Contractors. The first Standard Form was published in November 1892 and since that time various amendments have been made, perhaps the most noteworthy being the introduction in 1926 of a clause providing for appeal, should the award not be satisfactory to one or other of the parties. Prior to 1926 the Arbitrator's decision had been final and binding.

The Advantages of Lloyd's Form of Agreement

Under normal circumstances when Lloyd's Form of Salvage Agreement has been signed, the Owners of the salved property obtain early release of their property and the Salvor an early deposit of security for his claim, without the necessity of having recourse to the Courts of the country in which the services terminate. In most cases this is a definite advantage, as the procedure for arresting and releasing a vessel is in some countries a slow process. It also avoids the possibility of the Award having to be decided in a Court with little experience of salvage cases. The panel from which the Committee of Lloyd's select their Arbitrators consists of persons with long experience of salvage matters, and without doubt one of the greatest advantages of the Form is that Lloyd's have a tribunal such as this to decide the amount of Awards, which decision can be obtained at a reasonable cost.

Circumstances in which Agreement may become unenforceable. This is perhaps best illustrated by quoting a particular case. One ship agreed to tow another to Gibraltar on a "No cure—No pay" basis for the sum of £600. During the towage a gale was encountered and the towing hawser parted repeatedly. Eventually, with only one sound rope left, the salving vessel decided to tow only as far as Cartagena. Accordingly, no remuneration could be claimed under the agreement. However, the salvor still had the right to make a claim under the general law of salvage. This he did, and the Court actually fixed the award at £900.

The Parties bound by an Agreement. In signing an agreement the master of the salving ship binds his owners as far as he acts under necessity and for their benefit. He also binds the crew so long as the reward is reasonable, but the crew retain the right to have their salvage awarded by the Court. The master may not exercise his power to bargain away vested rights. If the owner himself signs the agreement, it binds the master and crew so long as it is fair. The master of the vessel to be salved likewise binds his owners, and they alone are liable to the salvors who have no direct claim against cargo owners. The shipowner must, in the first instance, pay the entire award and afterwards recover the cargo's contribution under the law of general average.

Salvage Agreements other than between Shipowners. Cases occur from time to time where a ship has become a constructive total loss and the underwriters, having indemnified the shipowner and become subrogated to the rights remaining in the property, themselves enter into an agreement with salvors to raise the wreck so that they can recover some part of their loss by selling what is salved. An agreement of this kind is not a salvage agreement in the proper sense of the term as it is made long after the essential danger has passed. It is simply a contract of employment and the salvors have no maritime lien on the property.

Life Salvage. Originally the law of salvage did not provide for rewarding salvors of human life, as the reward is payable out of property saved. Something more than life must be saved in order to form a fund out of which salvage can be paid. Nowadays the principle applies that if property is saved as well as life, then life salvage is payable. The ship, cargo and freight saved must all contribute. It is further provided that if salvage services are rendered to a British ship, or to a foreign ship in British waters, and no property, or insufficient property is saved, the D.o.T. may in their discretion award a sum to life salvors payable out of public funds.

Deviation. To deviate from the contract route to save life is always justifiable, but deviation to save property is justifiable only when the contract of affreightment reserves the right to deviate for that purpose. By Art. IV of the schedule to the Carriage of Goods by Sea Act the carrier is relieved of responsibility for loss or damage resulting from saving or attempting to save life or property at sea, and even in bills of lading and charter-parties which are not subject to the Hague Rules it is customary to include a similar exception.

Disputes as to Salvage. Proceedings may be started in any County Court having Admiralty jurisdiction, unless the value of the property saved exceeds £15,000, or the salvage claimed exceeds £5000. If the parties agree in writing such court can determine claims where these values are exceeded. In all cases the High Court in England or the Court of Session in Scotland has jurisdiction, but costs will be disallowed if a case within the jurisdiction of an inferior court is brought before a higher court.

When salvage is due a receiver of wreck may detain property until the claim is satisfied or the property is arrested by court process. If adequate security is given the receiver may release the property.

If a salvor abandons his lien in exchange for an agreement to abide by the decision of the Court, coupled with security, such an agreement binds ship, cargo and freight.

The M.S. Act provides that a seaman shall not abandon any right that he may have or obtain in the nature of salvage, and any stipulation in an agreement inconsistent with this provision shall be void. Masters are expected to look after their own interests in this respect but, even so, the Court will set aside any agreement between owner and master if it is not honestly made.

Much salvage work is nowadays undertaken by specialist firms who operate specially fitted salvage vessels and carry out salvage work as a business. Agreements for service in these special salvage vessels are not affected by the provisions of the Act which is designed to protect the rights of seamen serving in ordinary trading vessels.

The Salvage Association. In former times, before systems of rapid communication came into being, the full responsibility for minimising losses following marine casualties rested on the master of the ship, who was expected to make all the necessary arrangements to safeguard insured property. Moreover, when a casualty was reported, there would generally be a number of underwriters separately interested which could well create difficulty in reaching a quick decision as to the proper steps to be taken. Hence, there arose the need for some co-ordinating body to act on behalf of underwriters in general in respect of casualties, salvage, repairs, the best method of dealing with various commodities, investigation of doubtful losses, frauds, and so on. To this end the Salvage Association was formed in 1856 since when it has developed extensively. Although today it is largely an underwriters' organisation, very close co-operation exists with shipowners and their average adjusters and with cargo interests. The Association has established surveying staffs at ports in the United Kingdom, on the Continent, and in Canada and U.S.A. It is non-profit making and is financed entirely out of the fees charged for the cases it deals with. As soon as a broker is notified of a casualty by the assured or by report at Lloyd's, underwriters will request the broker to instruct the Salvage Association who will then take immediate steps to see that the best possible arrangements are made to minimise the loss. Nowadays the Association deals with aircraft casualties as well as marine.

Taking a Vessel in tow. A vessel requiring a tow into port is not necessarily in distress, so that before accepting the offer the master of a vessel able to tow should make certain that a clause giving liberty to tow is included in the C/P and/or B's/L. In addition, the following points also require careful consideration.

1. Sufficiency of bunkers, including an adequate reserve.
2. Notifying the owners so that they can ratify the master's decision and inform their underwriters in case additional premiums are required.
3. In the case of a vessel under charter, notifying the charterer.
4. The possibility, when under charter, of reaching the loading port or port of delivery before the cancelling date.
5. The nature of the cargo, if any, being carried, and in the case of a perishable cargo the possible effect of delay thereon.

6. The power and condition of main propelling machinery and any deck machinery that may have to be used.

7. The probable value of the vessel needing the tow, including the value of her cargo, and whether it is sufficient to hold promise of an adequate salvage award.

8. Coming to an agreement with the master of the vessel needing the tow as to the destination. Where practicable it is preferable to take her to a British port rather than to a foreign port.

9. The obtaining of a Lloyd's form of salvage agreement.

It is important to keep in mind that final success is vital to the earning of a reward. From this point of view the master should not hesitate to engage tug assistance where that is really necessary to navigate safely the approaches to the agreed port of destination and to berth the tow in a safe position on arrival. Such tugs, however, should not be allowed to take over the tow as principals, but should be employed by the master or owner of the salving vessel under an ordinary contract of towage. Otherwise, the towage contractor will be in a position to make salvage claims on his own account which may have the effect of reducing the amount awarded to the salving vessel. If it is possible to manage without tugs, then so much the better, but it is not advisable to take undue risks.

If it is necessary to take in tow a vessel which actually is in distress, i.e., where lives are in danger, there is a statutory duty which overrides any clause in any contract of affreightment or policy of insurance. But once such vessel is in a position of safety and lives are no longer in danger, the master of the towing vessel has no right to continue the towage merely for the purpose of earning an increased salvage award unless the towage clause is included in the contract of affreightment.

CHAPTER 12

LIGHTERAGE, TOWAGE AND PILOTAGE

LIGHTERAGE

Very frequently lighters and barges are operated, not by the owners or by demise charterers, but by simple hirers who are not the servants of the lighter owner or charterer. Therefore, when such a lighter has caused damage to the property of a third party the wrongdoers are the servants of the hirer and not the servants of the owner. At one time hirers of lighters were placed at a disadvantage by not being covered by the law permitting owners and demise charterers to limit their liability. Since 1921, however, the privilege has been extended to any hirer of a barge or lighter who has contracted to take over sole charge and management thereof and is responsible for navigation, manning and equipment thereof. The words "sole charge" are given a reasonably wide interpretation, so that where the owner of a barge or lighter reserves to himself repairs of a particular kind, that does not affect the status of the hirer with respect to the latter's right to limit his liability.

The law relating to the taking or sending of a ship to sea in such an unseaworthy state that life is likely to be endangered does not apply in the case of a ship employed in rivers and inland waters, but the use in navigation of lighters or barges or similar vessels which are so unsafe as to be likely to endanger life is an offence punishable on conviction on indictment to a fine or on summary conviction to a fine not exceeding £1000.

TOWAGE

Towage by a trading vessel for the purpose of earning a salvage award has been dealt with in Chapter 11. This section is concerned only with contracts made for the services of tugs.

The master of a ship always has authority to engage the services of tugs whenever they are reasonably required for the proper performance of the voyage, and any contract he makes in those circumstances will be binding on the shipowner so long as the terms of the contract are reasonable. Such contracts may be agreed verbally or they may be expressed in writing but, in either case, except where there are express agreements to the contrary, certain obligations will be imposed on the owner of the tug. A towage contract is a contract of service, that is to say a contract to tow a vessel from one named place to another, and failure to perform that service will bar

617

the tug owner's claim for remuneration. Not only must the tug be fit to perform the particular service contracted for, but her crew, tackle and equipment must be adequate to the task in the weather and circumstances reasonably to be expected. The extent of this implied warranty of fitness will depend to a great degree on whether the choice of tug is made by the tug owner or the owner of the tow. In the latter case the owner of the tow will be considered to have prejudged the efficiency and suitability of the tug without relying entirely on the skill of the tug owner who, therefore, will not be deemed to have warranted that the tug is able to perform the required service, certainly not that she is able to perform it in all circumstances and at all hazards. The tug owner will, however, be deemed to warrant that the service will be performed with all reasonable care and skill and that the crew, tackle and equipment of the tug are such as may reasonably be expected in vessels of her class. If the service is not to be performed at once, the tug owner must use all reasonable care to keep the tug as efficient for the service as she was at the time of making the contract. Where the owner of the tow does not contract for a particular named tug to be supplied, the tug owner must provide one which is fit for the contemplated service, but that is not to say that he is deemed to give an absolute warranty that the tug will be free from defects "which no skill could have detected and the effects of which no care or foresight could have averted".

There is an implied term in every towage contract that if in the course of the towage the tow is placed in danger due to some extraordinary and unforeseen peril, the tug must render all necessary assistance. In doing so, as explained in Chapter 11, the tug may become entitled to salvage.

Obligations of the Tow. In the absence of express agreement to the contrary, it will be implied that the tow is under an obligation to play her proper part in the joint operation, that those on board the tow will use all reasonable skill and diligence and will not increase the risk incidental to the service by any kind of negligence or misconduct, and that any material fact affecting the nature of the service required will be disclosed.

Concealment of material facts may result in the tug owner becoming entitled to recover damages in respect of additional expenses incurred. It may also, in some cases, give the tug owner the right to repudiate the towage contract and claim a salvage award. In one case a sailing vessel had lost an anchor, damaged her sails and windlass, and failed to disclose these facts to the tug engaged to tow her from the mouth of the Thames to London. The tug owners did repudiate the contract on learning the truth and received by way of salvage a sum four times as great as the contract price of the towage. The fact that the crew on board the tow are insufficient to handle the tow ropes is a matter that should be disclosed to the tug.

Liability of Tug. Except in special cases, as for instance where the tow is a wreck or an unmanned vessel or raft, the tow has control of the towage operations, and if there is a pilot in charge of the navigation of the tow the tug will be under the directions of that pilot. Although the tow has a duty to give such orders to the tug as are necessary for the control of both vessels, the tow is not obliged to be continually giving directions to the tug in respect of matters which are by common usage within the scope of the tug-master's duties. Moreover, where the tug-master by reason of local circumstances or knowledge has special facilities for judging what proper action should be taken, he has a duty to take such action without waiting for orders from the tow. The tug-master must, of course, obey specific orders from the tow and if, as a result of such directions, the tow is placed in danger or meets with disaster, the tug will not be liable and may earn salvage in respect of successful services subsequently rendered. Where the tow is assisting the operations by using her own propelling power, the tug has a duty to look out for such movements. When the tug is making fast to the tow both vessels are obliged to take due care, but on account of the tug's greater handiness in manœuvring the main responsibility in making fast will rest with her.

Where the tow has control of operations her owners will be liable for any damage which the tug may inflict on a third party. In addition, the tug will be liable as well, and the person whose property has sustained damage may recover the whole of such damage from either tug or tow. In fact, where the tug is owned by a substantial contracting firm, it may be a considerable advantage for the owner of the damaged ship or other property to sue both tug owners and tow owners.

Indemnity Clauses in Towage Contracts. For many years towage contracts have included indemnity clauses which sought to exempt the tug owner from loss or damage caused as a result of the negligence of the tug owner's servants while towing or rendering other services, and sometimes for his own default in not supplying an efficient tug. Whether such clauses achieved what was required of them often depended on whether they were against public policy, whether they were reasonable and had been agreed to by the contracting parties, and whether they were worded clearly with no ambiguities. Where there is ambiguity in a clause it is generally construed against the person in whose favour it is included. Also an exemption clause protects a contracting party only if he commits no fundamental breach of the contract himself. A person who is not party to the towage contract, e.g. the owner of cargo in the ship being towed, cannot be made to indemnify a tug owner by an exemption clause in the same way as the owner of the vessel carrying the cargo might be required to when his ship is being towed.

A Law Commission report in 1975 recommended that contractual terms which excluded or limited the liability of a party for breach of contract, or which limit rights or remedies available against him, or which enable a party to render no performance or a substantially different performance from that envisaged in the contract, should be subject to control where the party was acting in the course of business and the contract was either a consumer contract or a standard form contract. The two Bills annexed to the report were enacted and became the Unfair Contract Terms Act 1977 which came into force in 1978. In the U.K. the provisions of this Act must be considered when reading contractual terms in such Standard Conditions as are shown below.

The Act expressly extends section 2(1) to any contract of marine salvage or towage and this sub-section makes illegal clauses in such contracts which exclude or restrict liability for negligently causing death or personal injury. The rest of the Act, with one exception, does not apply to towage and salvage contracts, and it would appear that, as between businessmen, other indemnity clauses would be enforceable. The one exception is where the towage contractor or salvor has to deal with a consumer such as the owner of a yacht in need of a tow or assistance, when any such term in a contract restricting or excluding liability for loss or damage, or for breach of contract, or for lack of contractual performance, must be shown by the contractor to be reasonable.

Whether contracts for "other services" provided by tugs are affected by the Act is not certain, but it would seem that any clause excluding liability for death or personal injury due to negligence would not be legally enforceable, and if the Act applied, other exemption and indemnity clauses would have to be shown to be reasonable.

If, during the towage, the tow is damaged by the tug, the tug owner will avoid liability if the contract contains an indemnity clause excluding his liability. In respect of damages to third parties, however, avoidance of liability by the tug owner is possible only in a roundabout way. Since no contract exists with the third party the tug, in the first instance, will be liable. But it is generally the case that the towage contract will contain a further indemnity clause to the effect that should the tug, whilst towing, become liable to pay damages to a third party the tow shall indemnify the tug in respect of such payment.

Both of these indemnity clauses operate only during the towage, that is to say after the towage operation has commenced and before it has ended, and should the operation be interrupted at any stage the tug owner cannot rely on the indemnity clauses during the period of the interruption. Such clauses do not indemnify the tug owner against damage done to his own property by his own servants unless they make such provision in clear and unambiguous language. Tug owners cannot claim to be indemnified by the owners of the tow in respect of liability to a third party which has arisen from a breach of the towage contract by the tug owners if such breach of contract is not covered by the exceptions clause.

Since indemnity and exceptions clauses operate only during the towage, it is extremely important that there should be a clear understanding of precisely when the towage service commences and when it ends. A decision was given in one case that the service does not commence until the tow ropes have been passed. Such a ruling, naturally, does not meet with the approval of tug owners who, therefore, will clause their contracts to provide for the towage service to begin at some earlier stage.

Typical of the sort of standard conditions that might be met are the U.K. Standard Conditions which follow, but these should be taken as an example only as the British Tugowners' Association state that they are not to be taken as a recommendation of that Association. Other forms of General Conditions might be met which have been drawn up for individual tug owners, and there are Conditions drawn up for use by Dutch and Scandinavian tug owners.

UNITED KINGDOM STANDARD CONDITIONS FOR TOWAGE AND OTHER SERVICES (REVISED 1974)

1. (a) The agreement between the Tugowner and the Hirer is and shall at all times be subject to and include each and all of the conditions hereinafter set out.

   (b) For the purpose of these conditions:—

   (i) "towing" is any operation in connection with the holding, pushing, pulling, moving, escorting or guiding of the Hirer's vessel, and the expressions "to tow", "being towed" and "towage" shall be defined likewise.

   (ii) "vessel" shall include any vessel, craft or object of whatsoever nature (whether or not coming within the usual meaning of the word "vessel") which the Tugowner agrees to tow or to which the Tugowner agrees at the request, express or implied, of the Hirer, to render any service of whatsoever nature other than towing.

   (iii) "tender" shall include any vessel, craft or object of whatsoever nature which is not a tug but which is provided by the Tugowner for the performance of any towage or other service.

   (iv) The expression "whilst towing" shall cover the period commencing when the tug or tender is in a position to receive orders direct from the Hirer's vessel to commence pushing, holding, moving, escorting, or guiding the vessel or to pick up ropes or lines, or when the tow rope has been passed to or by the tug or tender, whichever is the sooner, and ending when the final orders from the Hirer's vessel to cease pushing, holding, moving, escorting or guiding the vessel or to cast off ropes or lines has been carried out, or the tow rope has been finally slipped, whichever is the later, and the tug or tender is safely clear of the vessel.

(v) Any service of whatsoever nature to be performed by the Tugowner other than towing shall be deemed to cover the period commencing when the tug or tender is placed physically at the disposal of the Hirer at the place designated by the Hirer, or, if such be at a vessel, when the tug or tender is in a position to receive and forthwith carry out orders to come alongside and shall continue until the employment for which the tug or tender has been engaged is ended. If the service is to be ended at or off a vessel the period of service shall end when the tug or tender is safely clear of the vessel or, if it is to be ended elsewhere, then when any persons, baggage, goods, mails, specie, ship or engine parts or gear or articles of whatsoever description have been landed or discharged from the tug or tender and/or the service for which the tug or tender has been required is ended.

(vi) The word "tug" shall include "tugs", the word "tender" shall include "tenders", the word "vessel" shall include "vessels", the word "Tugowner" shall include "Tugowners", and the word "Hirer" shall include "Hirers".

(vii) The expression "Tugowner" shall include any person or body (other than the Hirer or the owner of the vessel on whose behalf the Hirer contracts as provided in Clause 2 hereof) who is a party to this agreement whether or not he in fact owns any tug or tender, and the expression "other Tugowner" contained in Clause 5 hereof shall be construed likewise.

2. If at the time of making this agreement or of performing the towage or of rendering any service other than towing at the request, express or implied, of the Hirer, the Hirer is not the owner of the vessel referred to herein as "the Hirer's vessel", the Hirer expressly represents that he is authorised to make and does make this agreement for and on behalf of the owner of the said vessel subject to each and all of these conditions and agrees that both the Hirer and the Owner are bound jointly and severally by these conditions.

3. Whilst towing or whilst at the request, express or implied, of the Hirer, rendering any service other than towing, the master and crew of the tug or tender shall be deemed to be the servants of the Hirer and under the control of the Hirer and/or his servants and/or

his agents, and anyone on board the Hirer's vessel who may be employed and/or paid by the Tugowner shall likewise be deemed to be the servant of the Hirer and the Hirer shall accordingly be vicariously liable for any act or omission by any such person so deemed to be the servant of the Hirer.

4. Whilst towing, or whilst at the request, either express or implied of the Hirer, rendering any service of whatsoever nature other than towing:—

(a) The Tugowner shall not be responsible for or be liable

   (i) for damage of any description done by or to the tug or tender, or done by or to the Hirer's vessel or done by or to any cargo or other thing on board or being loaded on board or intended to be loaded on board the Hirer's vessel or the tug or tender or by or to any other object or property; or

   (ii) for loss of the tug or tender or the Hirer's vessel or of any cargo or other thing on board or being loaded on board or intended to be loaded on board the Hirer's vessel or the tug or tender or any other object or property; or

   (iii) for any personal injury or loss of life howsoever and wheresoever caused including personal injury or loss of life of the master and/or crew of and/or any person on board the tug or tender; or

   (iv) for any claim by a person not a party to this agreement for loss or damage of any description whatsoever,

   arising from any cause, including (without prejudice to the generality of the foregoing) negligence at any time of the Tugowner's servants or agents, unseaworthiness, unfitness or breakdown of the tug or tender, its machinery, boilers, towing gear, equipment, lines, ropes or hawsers, lack of fuel, stores, speed or otherwise, and

(b) The Hirer shall be responsible for, pay for and indemnify the Tugowner against and in respect of any loss or damage and any claims of whatsoever nature or howsoever arising or caused whether covered by the provisions of Clause 4(a) hereof or not (including any arising from or caused by the negligence of the Tugowner or his servants or agents) including the loss of or damage to the tug or tender, provided that the Hirer shall not be liable to the Tugowner for or in respect of loss, damage or claims which the Hirer proves (the burden of proof being on the Hirer) to have been solely caused by the failure of the Tugowner, and due to the actual fault or privity of the Tugowner, to make his tug or tender seaworthy for the towage or service other than towage.

Provided however, notwithstanding anything hereinbefore contained, the Tugowner shall under no circumstances be responsible for or be liable for any loss or damage caused or contributed to, by or arising out of any delay or detention of the Hirer's vessel or of the cargo on board or being loaded on board or intended to be loaded on board the Hirer's vessel or of any other object or property or of any person, or any consequences thereof, whether or not the same shall be caused or arise whilst towing or whilst at the request, either express or implied of the Hirer, rendering any service of whatsoever nature other than towing or at any other time whether before, during or after the making of this agreement.

5. The Tugowner shall at any time be entitled to substitute one or more tugs or tenders for any other tug or tender or tugs or tenders. The Tugowner shall at any time (whether before or after the making of this agreement between him and the Hirer) be entitled to contract with any other Tugowner (hereinafter referred to as "the other Tugowner") to hire the other Tugowner's tug or tender and in any such event it is hereby agreed that the Tugowner is acting (or is deemed to have acted) as the agent for the Hirer, notwithstanding that the Tugowner may in addition, if authorised whether expressly or impliedly by or on behalf of the other Tugowner, act as agent for the other Tugowner at any time and for any purpose including the making of any agreement with the Hirer. In any event should the Tugowner as agent for the Hirer contract with the other Tugowner for any purpose as aforesaid it is hereby agreed that such contract is and shall at all times be subject to the provisions of these conditions so that the other Tugowner is bound by the same and may as a principal sue the Hirer thereon and shall have the full benefit of these conditions in every respect expressed or implied therein.

6. Nothing contained in these conditions shall limit, prejudice or preclude in any way any legal rights which the Tugowner may have against the Hirer including, but not limited to, any rights which the Tugowner or his servants or agents may have to claim salvage remuneration or special compensation for any extraordinary services rendered to vessels or anything aboard the vessels by any tug or tender. Furthermore, nothing contained in these conditions shall limit, prejudice or preclude in any way any right which the Tugowner may have to limit his liability.

7. The Tugowner will not in any event be responsible or liable for the consequences of war, riots, civil commotions, acts of terrorism or sabotage, strikes, lockouts, disputes, stoppages or labour disturbances (whether he be a party thereto or not) or anything done in contemplation or furtherance thereof or delays of any description, howsoever caused or arising, including by the negligence of the Tugowner or his servants or agents.

8. The Hirer of the tug or tender engaged subject to these conditions undertakes not to take or cause to be taken any proceedings against any servant or agent of the Tugowner or other Tugowner

whether or not the tug or tender be substituted or hired or the contract or any part thereof has been sublet to the owner of the tug or tender, in respect of any negligence or breach of duty or other wrongful act on the part of such servant or agent which, but for this present provision, it would be competent for the Hirer so to do and the owners of such tug or tender shall hold this undertaking for the benefit of their servants and agents.

A towage contract signed by the master of a ship under time charter and stamped with the words "for time charterer's account" is a contract between the tug owner and the time charterer. The owners of the tow, therefore, will not be liable under an indemnity clause in the contract for damage sustained by the tug whilst towing.

PILOTAGE

The Pilotage Commission. As a result of the passing of the M.S.A. 1979, a Pilotage Commission has been set up which consists of not less than 10 and not more than 15 persons appointed by the Secretary of State D.o.T. with at least one person drawn from among the following categories of persons interested in the matter, namely, licensed pilots, ship managers, administrators of pilotage services and dock and harbour managers. He may also appoint other persons with special knowledge or experience likely to be of value to the Commission. The Commission is not to be regarded as a servant or agent of the Crown or as enjoying any status, privilege or immunity of the Crown.

Functions of Commission. It is the duty of the Commission to give to the Secretary of State and to pilotage authorities, dock and harbour authorities, pilots and shipowners, such advice as the Commission considers appropriate for any of the following purposes, namely:—

(a) securing by means of pilotage the safety of navigation in ports and waters of the U.K. coasts;

(b) ensuring that efficient pilotage services, with suitable equipment, are provided for those ports and waters;

(c) ensuring that the terms of service of pilots providing those services are fair; and

(d) promoting standards, in the qualifications required for those applying for pilots' licences and in the training of pilots, which are uniform for areas which the Commission considers are of the same kind.

Additional functions may be conferred on the Commission by Order made by the Secretary of State.

Review of Pilotage Services. It is the duty of the Commission to keep under consideration the organisation of pilotage services at ports and waters off the U.K. coasts, to consider what number of pilots are needed and to carry out investigations as appropriate in order to ascertain whether pilotage should be made compulsory at places where it is not compulsory and to make proposals for compulsory pilotage as a result of those investigations.

Pilotage Districts. The British Islands are divided up into a number of pilotage districts, each under the control of a pilotage authority set up by the Department of Trade. The four classes of existing pilotage authorities are:—

1. Trinity Houses, as at London, Hull, Newcastle and Leith. (The Southampton pilots are licensed by the London Trinity House.)
2. Municipal authorities, as at Bristol and Avonmouth.
3. Harbour Authorities, such as the Mersey Docks and Harbour Board.
4. Pilotage Boards, Trusts, etc., such as the Clyde Navigation Trust.

Compulsory Pilotage. Every ship, unless excepted, while navigating in a pilotage district in which pilotage is compulsory for the purpose of entering, leaving, or making use of any port in the district, and every ship carrying passengers (other than an excepted ship) while navigating for any such purpose in any district, whether compulsory or not, must be under the pilotage of a licensed pilot of the district, or under the pilotage of a master or mate possessing a pilotage certificate for the district who is *bona fide* acting as master or mate of the ship.

If any ship, other than an excepted ship, is not under pilotage as required by the above after a pilot licensed for the district has offered to take charge of the ship, the master will be liable on summary conviction to a fine not exceeding double the amount of the pilotage dues that would have been payable in respect of the ship if it had been under pilotage as so required. (Disregarding any increase in dues for failure to comply with the requirements of bye-laws about requests for pilots).

Excepted Ships. For the purpose of the Pilotage Act the following are excepted ships.

(a) Ships belonging to Her Majesty;
(b) Fishing vessels, of registered length less than 47·5 metres;
(c) Ferry boats plying as such exclusively within the limits of a harbour authority;
(d) Ships of less than 50 tons gross tonnage;
(e) Ships exempted from compulsory pilotage by bye-laws made before 4th July 1980 which continue in force until revoked. The power given to pilotage authorities by the Pilotage Act 1913 (s.11(4)) to make such bye-laws was repealed on 4th July 1980.

These include:—

(i) Ships trading coastwise if not carrying passengers;
(ii) Home trade ships trading other than coastwise if not carrying passengers;
(iii) Ships whose ordinary course of navigation does not extend beyond the seaward limits of a harbour authority, whilst navigating within those limits or within such parts thereof as may be specified in the bye-law.

For this purpose a ship which habitually trades to or from any port or ports outside the British Islands shall not be deemed to be trading coastwise, and a ship which habitually trades to or from any port outside the home trade limits shall not be deemed to be a home trade ship, by reason only that she is for the time being engaged on a voyage between ports in the British Islands, or within the home trade limits, as the case may be. For instance, a ship which has loaded a cargo at a port abroad for discharge at two ports in the British Islands cannot claim to be "trading coastwise" whilst she is proceeding from the first discharging port to the second one.

It should be noted that:

(a) A foreign-going ship making an occasional coastwise voyage is not an excepted ship.
(b) A passenger ship when not carrying passengers does not require to have a pilot if she is in other respects an excepted ship, but any ship carrying passengers (even one passenger) is not a ship which is exempted from compulsory pilotage by bye-law.
(c) The Pilotage Act does not apply to tugs, dredgers, sludge vessels, barges, and similar craft.
(d) A ship calling at a port in one district to embark or land a pilot licensed for another district is not deemed to be navigating for the purpose of entering, leaving, or making use of the port.

Pilot regarded as Servant of Shipowner. It has always been the case that where pilotage is voluntary the pilot is the servant of the shipowner who is responsible to third parties for any loss or damage arising from the pilot's negligence. At one time, however, where pilotage was compulsory shipowners were not liable for compulsory pilot's negligence. This was altered by the provisions of the Pilotage Act, 1913, which brought about the abolition of the defence of compulsory pilotage after a suspensory period of five years. Since 1918, therefore, the section of the Act quoted below has had full effect.

"Notwithstanding anything in any public or local Act, the owner or master of a vessel navigating under circumstances in which pilotage is compulsory shall be answerable for any loss or damage caused by the vessel or by any fault of the navigation of the vessel in the same manner as he would if pilotage were not compulsory."

The defence of compulsory pilotage will still be available to a shipowner in respect of areas to which the Pilotage Act does not apply unless, of course, local law provides otherwise. Where a shipowner is answerable (*i.e.*, responsible) for loss or damage in circumstances where pilotage is compulsory, he is responsible for the damage to his own ship as well as for injury to the property of a third party. Even in an area where the shipowner is not liable for the negligence of a compulsory pilot, he would in an action brought in England be held liable for loss or damage if the negligence of the master or crew was shown to be the sole or a contributory cause of the accident or if the accident was due to some defect in the equipment of the ship.

The laws of most foreign countries provide that a pilot whose employment is compulsory is not regarded as having control of the navigation of the ship, but has his duties restricted to advising the master of local conditions which affect safe navigation. The master of the ship, accordingly, retains full responsibility for directing the course of and manœuvring the ship, and the shipowner retains liability for the consequences of negligent navigation.

Division of Control between Master and Pilot. Generally speaking the rights and duties of a pilot are the same whether the pilotage is compulsory or voluntary, and whether the pilot is licensed or unlicensed. Although he is charged with the safety of the ship and is bound to use all reasonable diligence, care, and skill, he is charged with "pilot's duties" only. He does not supersede the master in command but acts as his "adviser". He is, nevertheless, entitled to the same assistance from the crew as the master is entitled to when no pilot is on board, and the master has a duty to see that officers and crew duly attend to the pilot's orders. The courts always tend to take the view that the "advice" of a pilot is advice that the master should follow on account of the pilot's specialised local knowledge and special skill, but that is not to say that the master is bound to follow the pilot's advice implicitly if it would appear in the master's deliberate judgment to involve danger to the ship. The master must watch carefully every move in the navigation of the ship, urge the pilot to use every precaution and insist on such being taken. When and to what extent the master should interfere with the pilot will always be a difficult matter to resolve. It is impossible to formulate a general rule, and each case has to be treated on its merits. There is no doubt, however, that the master should always state his opinion in matters of importance and warn the pilot if the latter is taking or proposing to take some action of which the master disapproves. Obviously, the master must interfere in such exceptional circumstances as, for example, the pilot being manifestly incapable through illness or drunkenness, or where the pilot's orders infringe the International Collision Regulations or local bye-laws. As previously stated, it generally makes no difference, as far as the shipowner's liability to third parties is concerned, whether loss or damage arises from the negligence of the master or from the negligence of the pilot, as both are in law (except in places where the Pilotage Act does not apply and local law does not make similar provisions) regarded as the servants of the shipowner who is vicariously responsible for the wrongful acts of either.

The master of a ship entering a foreign port is not expected to have detailed information of all the local lights, signals, etc., nor is he under a duty to check the pilot's knowledge of such matters. It has been held, accordingly, that a master who is part owner of a ship is not prevented from limiting his liability under the M.S. Acts when damage has resulted from the failure of a pilot to obey a local signal.

Masters' and First Mates' Pilotage Certificates. These are issued by a Pilotage Authority to a person acting as *bona fide* master or first mate of a ship, on that person's application and after examination. They are issued only to British subjects, or to nationals of a member State of the Economic Community other than the U.K. and where the ship is registered under the law of a member State of the Economic Community. The certificate shows the name and draught of the ship in respect of which it is issued, the name of the person to whom it is granted, and the date of issue. It is valid for one year but may if held by the master or first mate of a ship be renewed annually, by re-examination if the bye-laws require it. A certificate may be granted so as to extend to more than one ship belonging to the same owner, but the ships must be of substantially the same class and registered under the law of a member State of the Economic Community. On application by the holder the certificate may be altered to relate to other ships of not substantially greater draught and tonnage. A pilotage authority may treat ships under the management of the same person as ships being owned by that person (*e.g.*, time-chartered ships). A ship navigating in a pilotage district with a master or first mate on board holding a pilotage certificate must fly the pilot flag.

Note:—Nothing in the above paragraph affects the validity or prevents the renewal of any such pilotage certificate which before 4th July 1980 was in force in respect of a ship which was not registered under the law of a member State of the Economic Community.

Licensed and Unlicensed Pilots. A licensed pilot may supersede a pilot who is not licensed for the district in which the ship is being navigated, but the master must pay the latter an appropriate proportion of the pilotage dues payable in respect of the ship. Any

V

question as to the proportion must be referred to the pilotage authority whose decision is final.

If an unlicensed pilot continues pilotage, or attempts to, when he knows that a licensed pilot has offered to pilot the ship the former is liable to a fine not exceeding £500. The master of the ship is similarly liable if he knowingly continues to employ an unlicensed pilot after a licensed pilot has offered his services or, in the case of an outward bound ship, he fails to take all reasonable steps to obtain the services of a licensed pilot.

If any person other than the master or a seaman being one of the crew is on the ship's bridge, or in some other position from which the ship is navigated, he shall be deemed to be piloting the ship unless the contrary is proved. Whether a person on board a tug is in a position from which the tow is navigated is a question of fact.

The phrase "employ an unlicensed pilot" means employ in fact, whether for a remuneration or otherwise.

Declaration of Draught, Etc.

A licensed pilot may require the master to declare to him the ship's length, draught, and beam, and to provide him with such other information relating to the ship or its cargo as the pilot specifies and is necessary to enable him to carry out his duties as pilot of the ship, and the master must comply. It is the duty of a ship's master to bring to the notice of each licensed pilot who pilots the ship any defects in, and any matter peculiar to, the ship and its machinery and equipment of which the master knows and which might affect the navigation of the ship.

A master who refuses to provide the information required above, or fails in his duty above is guilty of an offence and liable to a fine not exceeding £500. For knowingly or recklessly making a false statement in answer to a request for information, or being privy to another person making a known false statement, a master is liable to a fine not exceeding £1000.

Moving Ship in Harbour or Dock.

A ship being moved within a harbour forming part of a pilotage district is deemed to be navigating in a pilotage district except as far as may be provided by bye-law in the case of a ship changing from one mooring to another, or being taken into or out of dock.

A ship being navigated within a closed dock or lock in a pilotage district is deemed to be navigating in a district in which pilotage is not compulsory.

Pilot's Documents.

A pilot must be furnished with a copy of the Pilotage Act and copies of Pilotage Orders and bye-laws in force for the time being. He must also be provided with his licence which he must produce when required under penalty of a fine not exceeding £200.

Taking a Pilot out of his District. Except in circumstances of unavoidable necessity, a master may not take a licensed pilot without the latter's consent out of his district or beyond the point up to which he has been engaged to pilot the ship. The penalty for non-compliance is a fine not exceeding £1000.

Limitation of Liability. A licensed pilot, an assistant to a licensed pilot and the pilotage authority who employ them shall not be liable:—

(a) in the case of the pilot or assistant, for neglect or want of skill; and

(b) in the case of a pilotage authority, for neglect or want of skill by the pilot, or assistant or by the authority in employing the pilot or assistant,

beyond the amount of £100 and the amount of the pilotage dues in respect of the voyage during which the liability arose.

Where without their actual fault or privity any loss or damage is caused to any vessel or vessels or to any goods, merchandise or other things on board any vessel, a pilotage authority is not liable beyond the amount of £100 multiplied by the number of pilots it has licensed.

Pilot Flag. When a ship navigating in a pilotage district has on board a pilot licensed for that district, or a master or mate holding a pilotage certificate for that district, the master must cause the pilot flag to be exhibited, the penalty for failure to do so being a fine not exceeding £500. (The pilot flag required by the Act is a square flag divided horizontally white over red. It seems to be a common practice to display the International Code Flag H, meaning "I have a pilot on board").

Pilot Signal. The master of a ship, other than an excepted ship, navigating in a district in which pilotage is compulsory must display a pilot signal and keep it displayed until a licensed pilot boards.

The master of a ship navigating in any district (except in a dockyard port), whether pilotage is compulsory or not, which is being piloted by a pilot who is not licensed for that district must display a pilot signal and keep it displayed until a licensed pilot boards.

Failure to comply without reasonable excuse in either case is an offence punishable by a fine not exceeding £50.

Note: In a non-compulsory district, of course, it is not essential to employ a pilot at all, but the intention of the Act is that, if the master does employ a pilot he must use every endeavour to employ a properly qualified pilot, *i.e.*, a pilot licensed for the district. If, however, a licensed pilot is not forthcoming, there is no reason why the master should not proceed with the unlicensed pilot so long as he keeps the pilot signal displayed. There is an implied obligation on the master to keep a good lookout for offers of pilotage, but it seems that he is not obliged to go out of his way to find the pilot boat.

The Act does not specifically provide for the case where a pilot is not forthcoming in a compulsory district. The results of various court cases, however, seem to indicate that the master is not justified in proceeding without a pilot unless to do otherwise would be dangerous.

The Authorised Pilot Signals and Improper Use Thereof. The signals to be used or displayed where the services of a pilot are required on any vessel shall be the single-letter signal G made by one of the methods set out in Chapter III of the International Code of Signals 1969 and indicated as appropriate below.

(i) In fog, mist, falling snow, heavy rainstorms or any other condition similarly restricting visibility, whether by day or night:—

Any method except (a) flag signalling, (b) flashing light signalling or (g) signalling by hand flags or arms.

(ii) In conditions not restricting visibility, by day:—

Any method.

(iii) In conditions not restricting visibility, by night:—

Any method except (a) flag signalling or (g) signalling by hand flags or arms.

If any of the above are used for a wrong purpose, or if other signals are used to summon a pilot, the master of the ship concerned will be liable to a fine not exceeding £50.

Indictable Offence by Pilot. If a pilot by wilful breach or neglect of duty, or through drunkenness, does any act tending to the loss, destruction or serious damage of a ship, or tending to endanger the life or limb of a person on board, he will be guilty of an offence and liable on summary conviction to (max.) three months imprisonment or a fine not exceeding £1000 or both; on conviction on indictment to imprisonment for a term not exceeding two years or a fine or both. He will be equally guilty if he omits to do any lawful act proper to be done by him to preserve the ship from loss, etc., or to preserve a person on board from danger to life or limb.

Other Offences by a Pilot. There are a number of offences in respect of which a licensed pilot may be punished by fine under the provisions of the Pilotage Act. The maximum fines vary according to the nature of the offence, but may in some cases be as much as £500. The specified offences include:—

1. Lending his licence.
2. Acting as pilot when suspended or when intoxicated.
3. Being concerned with corrupt practices relating to ships, etc.

4. Wilfully delaying a ship or refusing to pilot a ship without reasonable cause.
5. Quitting a ship before completing his services and without the consent of the master.

Pilotage Dues. The liability to pay pilotage dues in respect of the services of a licensed pilot rests on the owner, master, or consignee of the ship. Unpaid dues are recoverable by proceedings in a summary court. A licensed pilot may not demand or receive, and a master may not offer or pay, dues at rates other than the lawful rates, under penalty of a fine not exceeding £200.

No maritime lien attaches for pilotage dues on the principle that such liens should not be granted in respect of ordinary commercial transactions into which category a pilotage contract comes. However, should a pilotage service become merged in or superseded by a salvage service, then a pilot would have a maritime lien on the property salved for his award. The question of when a pilot may have a claim to salvage has been dealt with in Chapter 11.

In the case where an unlicensed pilot has been employed, the master will have contracted in his capacity as agent of the shipowner. The latter will therefore have a sole liability for the pilot's remuneration and the pilot, if unpaid, would have a common law right of action to recover the debt in a county court. The right to have the case dealt with summarily, enjoyed by a licensed pilot under the Pilotage Act, does not extend to an unlicensed pilot's claim.

Leading Ships. If a boat or a ship having a licensed pilot on board leads a ship having no pilot because the latter cannot, from particular circumstances, be boarded, the pilot is entitled to the same dues as if he had been actually on board and had charge.

Dues where Service is Interrupted. Where a pilot is under contract to take a ship from the seaward limit of a pilotage district to a berth in a port in the district, and the service is temporarily interrupted by a normal risk of navigation, say where the ship is obliged to anchor in the roads until a berth becomes available, the pilotage from sea to anchorage and from anchorage to berth is still one service, and the pilot—even if he leaves the ship in the meantime—is not entitled to charge for two separate services.

Boarding Facilities. The Pilotage Act provides as follows:—
1. The master of a non-excepted ship in a compulsory pilotage district which is not under pilotage shall, if a licensed pilot makes a signal offering his services, by any practical means consistent with the safety of the ship, facilitate the pilot getting on board and shall give charge of piloting to that pilot.

2. Where the master accepts the services of a licensed pilot in any district, whether compulsory or not, he shall likewise facilitate the pilot and any assistant of his getting on board and subsequently leaving.

3. The penalty for failure, without reasonable excuse, to comply, on summary conviction, a fine not exceeding double the pilotage dues that are payable or would have been payable in respect of the ship or £500, whichever is the greater.

This means, amongst other things, that the master must comply with the statutory requirements in relation to pilot ladders, the details of which are given in Chapter 7.

Pilotage Abroad. Except where the context clearly indicates otherwise, all that has been said above relates only to pilotage in the British Islands. Elsewhere, of course, local laws and bye-laws will prevail and masters should inquire what they are. In some pilotage areas it is customary for the master of a ship on arrival to be issued with a book of the local regulations. Such documents are well worth studying. It would appear that in American law a shipowner who has been compelled to accept the services of the first pilot who offers them is not liable *in personam* for the negligence of such a pilot, but the ship is liable *in rem*.

Qualified Pilot. A pilot is entitled to this description only when he holds a valid licence for the particular district in which he is piloting a ship. A pilot who is licensed for one district could not claim to be qualified to pilot ships in some other district for which he does not hold a licence.

CHAPTER 13

LIGHTHOUSES AND LIGHT DUES

IN many maritime countries the cost of installing and maintaining lighthouses and other coastal navigation marks is a national charge, but in the United Kingdom such cost is borne by the owners and charterers of ships which make use of United Kingdom ports. This is provided for by Part XI of the principal Act.

General Lighthouse Authorities. The superintendence and management of lighthouses, buoys, and beacons is vested in the following authorities, viz.—

1. The London Trinity House in England, Wales, the Channel Islands, and Gibraltar.
2. The Commissioners of Northern Lights in Scotland and the Isle of Man.
3. The Commissioners of Irish Lights in Ireland.

These authorities are known collectively as the General Lighthouse Authorities, and they are obliged by the provisions of the Act to make such returns and explanations to the Department of Trade as that Department may require. The London Trinity House have powers superior to those of the other authorities and have the right to make inspections in any of the lighthouse areas. With respect to the construction, alteration, or removal of any lighthouse or other mark, it is the function of Trinity House to report the proposals of other authorities to the D.o.T. and, with the sanction of the Department, to give directions to the other authorities. The D.o.T. may, on receipt of a complaint that any lighthouse or other work is inefficient or improperly managed or unnecessary, appoint a person to make an inspection.

Tables of Light Dues. These together with copies of regulations in force respecting light dues are required to be posted up in all United Kingdom custom houses. All dues collected are carried to the General Lighthouse Fund. Dues are payable in the first place to H.M. Customs.

Liability for Payment. The liability to pay light dues in respect of any ship rests upon the following persons:

(a) the owner or master of the ship;
(b) such consignees or agents as have paid, or made themselves liable to pay, other charges on account of the ship at the port of arrival or discharge.

635

(**N.B.:** If a charter-party provides that "charterers shall pay port charges", this will include light dues payable at the port concerned.)

Recovery of Unpaid Dues. If dues are not paid on the demand of the authorised collector, that collector may, in addition to any other remedy he may have, enter upon the ship and distrain goods

---

LIGHT CERTIFICATE
OWNERS OR AGENTS COPY

IMPORTANT. All Light Certificates for this vessel for the current year must be produced to the Collector at the Customs House when Light Dues are being paid or exemption claimed. Exemption will not be granted without the production of these certificates.

CERTIFICATE No. C 16278

1st April   31st March
1980 / 1981

Customs Stamp Received the sum detailed below

Name and address of Owner or Agent paying Light Dues

No Certificate valid unless stamped

Vessel Details	Vessel Name.	BLOCK CAPITALS THROUGHOUT				Gross Tonnage
						·00

Previous Certificates	Voyages Paid on Previous Certificates for 1980/81 produced at time of payment.			
	Home Trade		Foreign Trade	

Vessel Category	03 Oil Tanker	04 Ore Carrier	05 General Cargo	06 Bulk Carrier	07 Container	08 Passenger	09 Visiting Cruise
	10 Ferry	11 Sailing/Towed	12 Pleasure Boat	13 Yacht	14 Tug	15 Other:-	

Country of Registry	Quote Number as Shown on Reverse

Source of Tonnage Details	18 British Tonnage Certificate	19 National Certificate of Registry	20 Others Specify:-

Voyage(s)	From	To	Via	No.of Voyages covered by this payment

Tonnage Details	NRT		·00 Tons	● If Dual Tonnage Vessel Indicate whether tonnage mark
	Uplift @ %		·00 Tons	Submerged
	Deck Cargo		·00 Tons	Not Submerged

Type of Rate	35 Annual	36 Full Home Trade	37 Full Foreign Trade	38 Home Cruise/ Sail Rate	39 Foreign Cruise/ Sail Rate	40 Balance	41 Supplementary

Payment	Total Paid	£	D	Endorsement No.	Now Applies

If deck cargo only, payment relates to NRT payment on Certificate No.   at

If supplementary payment only, payment relates to Certificate No.   at

C.A.1.	Serial No. of last Certificate issued	at	Dated

ENDORSEMENTS

1. Payment accepted on deposit. Consideration will be given to adjusting the charge on production of an acceptable tonnage certificate within two years of the date shown on this light dues certificate but unless a valid certificate of British tonnage is produced for inspection within two years

of that date the transaction will be regarded as closed and no refund in respect of it will be paid.

2. This certificate has been issued without production by the holder of a certificate or duplicate thereof relating to a former voyage within the current year shown on the face of this certificate. The benefit of limitation of charges under the rules cannot be allowed until the directions of Trinity House have been received.

3. The advance payment made in respect of this certificate is in excess of the legal liability at the date when it was made and is accepted without prejudice.

4. Exempt from further payment of light dues for the year shown on the face of this certificate on the net registered tonnage but not in respect of deck cargo.

5. Exempt from further payment of light dues for the current year shown on the face of this certificate in respect of home trade voyages only.

6. The vessel named on this certificate is entirely exempt from further payment of light dues during the year ending 31st March, 1981.

7. Exempt from further payment of Light Dues for the month of . . . . 19 . . . . in respect of home trade voyages only.

Against Country of Registry on reverse, please quote number shown below:
     1.   United Kingdom/Republic of Ireland

Countries to which uplift is not applicable providing Vessel holds Certificate of Registry of the country which issued the Tonnage Certificate:—

2.	Australia	29.	Japan
3.	Austria	30.	Kenya
4.	Bahamas	31.	Kuwait
5.	Bangladesh	32.	Lebanon
55.	Belgium	33.	Malaysia
6.	Bermuda	34.	Malta
7.	Burma	35.	Netherlands
8.	Canada	36.	New Zealand
56.	Cayman Islands	37.	Nigeria
9.	Ceylon	38.	Norway
10.	Channel Islands	39.	Pakistan
11.	China (Peoples Republic)	40.	Poland
12.	Cyprus	41.	Portugal
13.	Denmark	42.	Sierra Leone
14.	Egypt	43.	Singapore
15.	Faroe Islands	44.	Somali
16.	Finland	45.	S. Africa
17.	France	46.	Spain
57.	Gambia	47.	Sudan
18.	E. Germany (G.D.R.)	48.	Sweden
19.	W. Germany (G.F.R.)	49.	Tanzania
20.	Ghana	50.	Uganda
21.	Greece	51.	U.S.S.R. (Russia)
22.	Guyana	52.	U.S.A.
23.	Hong Kong	53.	Venezuela
24.	Iceland	54.	Yugoslavia
25.	India	55.	Belgium
26.	Israel	56.	Cayman Islands
27.	Italy	57.	Gambia
28.	Jamaica		

Countries to which uplift is applicable:-
    70.   Argentina
    71.   Liberia
    72.   Any other country

or other articles belonging to or on board the ship, and detain that distress until the dues are paid. If payment is then not made within three days, the collector may have the goods valued and sold, retain the dues and expenses of collecting them out of the proceeds, and return any surplus to the owner or master on demand.

Official Receipt. A receipt for light dues must be given by the collector, and a ship may be detained at any port where light dues are payable until the receipt is produced to the proper office of Customs when demanding clearance. A blank Light Certificate form is reproduced.

Local Lights, Etc. These may be installed by local authorities with D.o.T. sanction. Dues may be fixed and these are payable and recoverable in the same manner as general light dues. Such dues may be applied only to the maintaining or improving of the lights or other works in respect of which they are levied. The local authority must keep a separate account of the receipt and expenditure of dues for submission to the Department of Trade. (This does not apply to local navigation marks erected for temporary purposes.)

Injury to Lighthouses, Etc. If a person wilfully or negligently injures, removes, alters, or destroys any light, buoy, or beacon; or rides by, makes fast to, or runs foul of any lightship or buoy, he is liable to a fine not exceeding £500 as well as to the expense of making good the damage.

Prevention of False Lights. In order to prevent the exhibition of a false or misleading light, the General Lighthouse Authorities have power to enforce the extinguishing or screening of fires or lights which are liable to be mistaken for a light from a lighthouse.

Colonial Lights. For many years light dues were levied, under the authority of Orders in Council made under Section 670 of the Merchant Shipping Act, 1894, on ships which passed and derived benefit from certain colonial lighthouses administered by the Government of the United Kingdom and constituting a charge on the General Lighthouse Fund. Such dues were payable in the United Kingdom and were collected in the same manner as general light dues.

Revocation of these Orders in Council became necessary to give effect to Article 18 of the Convention of the Territorial Sea and Contiguous Zone which was ratified in March, 1960, and which provides that no charge may be levied upon foreign ships by reason only of their passage through the territorial sea. Accordingly, an Order in Council was made on 16th March, 1960, providing for the collection of all colonial light dues to be terminated as from 25th March, 1960.

The lights concerned, administered by the D.o.T., continue to be a charge on the General Lighthouse Fund, but it appears that the only colonial lights maintained at the present time (1981) are Sombrero, one of the Leeward Islands and Cape Pembroke in the Falkland Islands. Contributions made by H.M. Government in respect of lights on the islands of Abu Ail and Jabal at Tair in the Red Sea are also paid out of the General Lighthouse Fund.

Scale of Light Dues. Light Dues are levied on the scale and in accordance with regulations made by statutory instrument under powers given the Secretary of State by section 5(2), as amended, of the Merchant Shipping (Mercantile Marine Fund) Act, 1898. Dues are payable per voyage in respect of all vessels arriving at or departing from ports in the United Kingdom, the Republic of Ireland or the Isle of Man, which load or discharge cargo, passengers or mails, unless they come within the scope of the exemptions laid down in Part III of the Schedule to the regulations.

The scale of charges varies according to whether the vessel is a sailing ship or steamer, also according to whether the voyage made is "Home Trade" or "Foreign Going".

In calculating any payment of light dues where the vessel's tonnage is not a multiple of 10 tons, any excess not exceeding 5 tons shall be rounded down and any excess over 5 tons shall be rounded up to the nearest such multiple.

Schedule to the M.S. (Light Dues) Regulations 1981
Part I—Scale of Payments

1. Home-trade sailing ships: 80p per 10 tons per voyage.
2. Foreign-going sailing ships: £1·60 per 10 tons per voyage.
3. Home-trade steamers:
   Full rate: £1·60 per 10 tons per voyage.
   Reduced rate (visiting cruise ships) 80p per 10 tons per voyage.
4. Foreign-going steamers:
   Full rate: £3·20 per 10 tons per voyage.
   Reduced rate (visiting cruise ships) £1·60 per 10 tons per voyage.
5. In the place of payments per voyage, the following payments:
   (*a*) for pleasure yachts which the general lighthouse authority is satisfied are ordinarily kept or used outside any of the following countries and territories (including the territorial waters adjacent thereof), namely the United Kingdom, Isle of Man, Republic of Ireland, a payment in respect of any visit of 80p per 10 tons for every period of 30 days or less comprised in such visit;

   (*b*) for tugs and pleasure yachts not included in sub-paragraph (*a*) of this paragraph an annual payment of £9·60 per 10 tons.

Part II—Rules

(1) A ship shall not in any year be required to make payments on account of light dues—

(a) if the ship is a home-trade ship, for more than 14 voyages; and

(b) if the ship is a foreign-going ship, for more than 7 voyages; and

(c) if the ship makes voyages during the year both as a home-trade and as a foreign-going ship, for more than 14 voyages, counting each voyage made as a foreign-going ship as two voyages.

Provided that in any year no steamer shall be required to pay more than £22·40 per 10 tons and that no sailing vessel shall be required to pay more than £11·20 per 10 tons.

(2) A ship shall not pay dues both as a home-trade ship and as a foreign-going ship for the same voyage, but a ship trading from a port outside home-trade limits, and discharging cargo or landing passengers or mails at any port within home-trade limits, shall be deemed to be on one voyage as a foreign-going ship, until she has arrived at the last port of discharge of cargo or passengers brought from beyond home-trade limits; and a ship trading to a port outside home-trade limits, and loading cargo or receiving passengers or mails at any port within home-trade limits, shall be deemed to be on one voyage as a foreign-going ship from the time she starts from the first port of loading of cargo or passengers destined for a port beyond home-trade limits.

(3) The voyage of a home-trade ship shall be reckoned from port to port, but a home-trade ship shall not be required to pay dues for more than three voyages in one month.

(4) The voyage of a foreign-going ship trading outwards shall be reckoned from the first port of lading in the U.K., Ireland or the Isle of Man of cargo destined for a port outside home-trade limits.

(5) The voyage of a foreign-going ship trading inwards shall be reckoned from her last port of lading outside home-trade limits to the last port in the U.K., Ireland or the Isle of Man at which any cargo laden outside those limits is discharged.

(6) A ship shall be treated as a visiting cruise ship if and only if it makes a call at one or more ports in the U.K., Isle of Man or Ireland for the purpose of disembarking passengers for a visit ashore and for subsequent re-embarkation (whether or not at the same port) and at no time during that cruise does the ship:—(a) embark or disembark any other passengers; or (b) load or discharge any cargo or mails,—at any such port.

Tonnage for Light Dues Purposes

The tonnage of a vessel on which light dues are calculated is the register tonnage reckoned in accordance with M.S. Act 1965 and denoted on the British Certificate of Registry or on the certificate or other national papers of a country which has adopted the British tonnage regulations, with an addition in the case of foreign-going voyages of deck cargo, i.e. stores, cargo, oil fuel or other goods stowed in spaces not included in the register tonnage. In the cases of ships registered in those countries with whom the United Kingdom has no reciprocal tonnage agreements, the General Lighthouse Fund is safeguarded by a surcharge on the ship's national net register tonnage unless they are in possession of a valid Certificate of British Tonnage. The dues thus collected can be adjusted on production of a Certificate of British Tonnage within two years of the date of payment.

In the case of an unregistered vessel dues are payable on "Thames Measurement" as obtained from the formula:

$$\frac{(L - B) \times B \times \dfrac{B}{2}}{94}$$

where L = length measured from fore part of stem to afterside of sternpost at deck level;

and B = extreme breadth over planking or plating, excluding rubbing strakes and beltings.

Carriage of Deck Cargo during a Year in respect of which Dues have been fully paid. Suppose, for instance, that a foreign-going ship has already paid light dues for 7 voyages in a particular year and then, subsequently, but during the same year, arrives at or departs from a United Kingdom port carrying deck cargo. The question arises as to whether she is liable for additional dues in respect of such deck cargo. The practice appears to be that if the full year's dues had been paid in advance on the 1st April (which is sometimes done) she would be charged the additional dues, but if the year's dues had been paid voyage by voyage she would not be charged additional dues in respect of deck cargo carried after the seventh and final payment.

Part III—Ships exempted from Payment of Light Dues

1. Ships belonging to Her Majesty or to a foreign Government unless carrying cargo or passengers for freight or fares.
2. Sailing ships (not being pleasure yachts) of less than one hundred tons, and all ships of less than twenty tons.
3. Vessels (other than tugs or pleasure yachts) when navigated wholly and bona fide in ballast on which no freight is earned and without any passenger.
4. Ships putting in for bunkers, stores or provisions for their own use on board.
5. Vessels for the time being employed in sea fishing or in sea fishing service, exclusive of vessels used for catching fish otherwise than for profit.

6. Ships putting in from stress of weather or for the purpose of repairing, or because of damage, provided they do not discharge or load cargo other than cargo discharged with a view to such repairs, and afterwards re-shipped.

7. Dredgers and hoppers for the time being employed solely in dredging channels or deepening water for or on behalf of a harbour or a conservancy authority, within the area in which that authority has jurisdiction, or in disposing within or without such area, otherwise than by way of sale or exchange, of the spoil from such operations.

8. Sailing yachts of and above 100 tons, which are not registered in the United Kingdom, Isle of Man, Channel Islands or the Republic of Ireland, and which come into the territorial waters of the United Kingdom or the Republic of Ireland with the sole object of taking part in yacht racing, so long as such yachts are coming into, remaining in, or leaving such territorial waters solely in connection with such object, and hold a certificate in a form approved by the Secretary of State.

9. Ships making voyages entirely performed in waters in respect of which no lighthouse, buoy or beacon is maintained by a General Lighthouse Authority at the expense of the General Lighthouse Fund.

10. Yachts in respect of any year ending 31st March during the whole of which they are laid up.

Fiscal Year

A year, for light dues purposes, means a fiscal year from 1st April to 31st March.

CHAPTER 14

MARINE INSURANCE AND AVERAGE

MARINE insurance is a branch of commerce with a history so long that it can be measured in terms of thousands of years rather than hundreds. When and where it began is not known with any certainty, but it is probable that in some form or another it was practised by the Phoenician traders a thousand years before the dawn of the Christian era. In the comparatively modern period of Queen Elizabeth I there existed an Act the preamble to which contained, the words ". . . by means of which policy of assurance it cometh to pass that upon the loss or perishing of any ship there followeth not the undoing of any man, but the loss alighteth rather easily upon many men than heavily upon few, and rather upon them that adventure not, than those that do adventure, whereby all merchants, especially the younger sort, are allured to venture more willingly and freely". Those words are as significant today as they were when they were first written, and point the conclusion that, without marine insurance facilities, the development of trade which the modern world has witnessed would have been quite impossible.

Even today no shipowner is under any legal obligation to insure his vessels, nor a merchant to insure his goods while in transit, but the enormous capital at risk, the frequent practice of mortgaging ships to bankers, the interests of bankers in the financing of shipments, and other considerations render marine insurance essential.

In this country the law relating to marine insurance is codified in the Marine Insurance Act, 1906, parts of which were amended in 1958. Section 1 of this Act defines a contract of marine insurance as a contract whereby the insurer undertakes to indemnify the assured, in manner and to the extent thereby agreed, against marine losses, that is to say, the losses incident to marine adventure. This contract of indemnity is usually based on values agreed in advance which may be greater or less than the values actually at risk.

In consideration of payment of "premium" the underwriter agrees to indemnify the assured against loss or damage caused by "maritime perils" defined by the Act as "Perils consequent on, or incidental to, the navigation of the sea, that is to say, perils of the seas, fire, war perils, pirates, rovers, thieves, captures, seizures, restraints and detainments of princes and peoples, jettisons barratry, and any other perils, either of the like kind or which may be designated by the policy."

The document which embodies the contract is called a "policy" and its wording covers only maritime perils on insurable property whilst afloat. But the Marine Insurance Act provides for the insurance to extend to protecting the assured against losses on inland waters or any land risk incidental to a sea voyage, also to a ship in the course of being built or to the launching of a ship.

Most marine risks are underwritten by Lloyd's underwriters who, in addition, underwrite other kinds of risks. But there is also a number of Insurance Companies each of which contains a marine department for the purpose of issuing marine policies.

Lloyd's Underwriters. The Corporation of Lloyd's, universally known as Lloyd's (to which further reference is made in Chapter 16), does not itself undertake insurance or issue policies, but provides facilities for its members to transact their underwriting business. The control and management of this famous Corporation is vested in the Committee, elected by the members from the members. The Committee, in turn, is responsible for the election of new members. A candidate for membership has to satisfy the Committee in respect of his status and financial responsibility and, in the event of his election, will be required to deposit with the Committee a substantial sum in approved investments as a form of security for his underwriting liabilities. A Lloyd's underwriter always has an individual liability under a Lloyd's policy bearing his subscription which is absolutely unlimited, he is required to submit his underwriting account annually to Lloyd's special audit to show that his assets are sufficient to meet his liabilities and that his premiums are placed in trust in accordance with Lloyd's Trust Deed, and must generally conduct his business in compliance with the rules laid down by the Committee. Although they all trade for their own account and carry on their business as individuals, it is customary for Lloyd's underwriters to form themselves into "syndicates" each under the leadership of a chairman. This, however, does not affect the liability of the syndicate members in severalty, and the syndicates are not in the legal sense of the term partnerships.

Insurance Companies. Those companies which engage in marine business house their marine departments in London in the vicinity of Lloyd's, which is of great convenience to brokers whose daily business is with both. Each company appoints a salaried official as underwriter with authority to accept marine risks on behalf of his company. It is frequently the case that a particular risk, especially if it is a large one, will be underwritten partly by Lloyd's underwriters and partly by one or more of the companies. This being so, it is natural to find the two sections of the marine insurance market working in close harmony, and for brokers to show no discrimination in accepting the security of either in placing their insurances.

KINDS OF POLICIES

Though commonly in one form, marine policies are known by different names according to their manner of execution and the nature of the risks covered.

Voyage Policy. This is a policy in which the limits of the risk are determined by places or termini as, for example, Liverpool to Rangoon, or Lagos to Hull. Such policies are always used for goods insurance, sometimes for freight insurance, but only rarely nowadays for hull insurance.

Time Policy. This is designed to give cover for some specified period of time, say, for instance, from noon, 1st January 1976 to noon, 1st January 1977. Time policies are usual in the case of hull insurance, though there may be cases where an owner prefers to insure his vessel for each separate voyage under a voyage policy.

Voyage and Time Policy (or Mixed Policy). Under such a policy the hull machinery, etc., of a vessel could be insured for a named voyage and by agreement for some stipulated period after arrival at her destination, for example, from Cardiff to Bahia Blanca and for sixty days after arrival at Bahia Blanca.

N.B.—For many years prior to 1959 time policies of marine insurance were, in the interests of Revenue, invalid in respect of periods exceeding 12 months. The Finance Act, 1959, abolished *ad valorem* stamp duties on marine policies and, accordingly, Section 25 (2) of the Marine Insurance Act, 1906, was repealed, thereby removing the ban on time policies for periods in excess of 12 months. Stamp duties on marine policies are now abolished.

Construction Policy, or Builder's Policy. This is designed to cover the risks incidental to the building of a vessel, usually giving cover from the time of laying the keel until completion of trials and handing over to owners. In the case of a very large vessel the period may extend over several years. While time policies for periods over 12 months were invalid, advantage was taken of the provision of the 1903 Revenue Act which allowed a construction policy to be stamped as a "voyage policy". On account of the changes introduced by the Finance Act, 1959, there would now seem to be no reason for keeping up the fiction that for insurance purposes a ship under construction is making her "first voyage".

Port Policy. This is to cover a vessel during a period in port against the risks peculiar to a port as distinguished from voyage risks. This kind of policy is probably very rarely used nowadays, except possibly in the case of a vessel laid up out of commission, as most vessels while employed are covered by time policies which during their currency attach whether the vessel is at sea or in port.

In any case, where a vessel insured for a period of time is laid up, the assured can take advantage of the "Returns Clause" to recover some proportion of the premiums if the vessel has not been exposed to all the risks insured against.

Valued Policy. This is one which specifies the agreed value of the subject matter insured, which is not necessarily the actual value. Such agreed value is referred to as the "insured value". A policy may be, say, for £100,000 on Hull and Machinery, etc., valued at £200,000, or for £7,000 on 100 Cases of Whisky valued at £7,000. Once a value has been agreed it cannot be reopened unless there is proof of fraudulent intention. It remains binding on both parties. Hull policies and goods policies are nowadays invariably valued policies.

Unvalued Policy. This is one which does not specify the value of the subject matter insured, but leaves what is called the "insurable value" to be subsequently ascertained in the manner provided for by Section 16 of the Marine Insurance Act. Unvalued policies are used in connection with freight insurance presumably because the insurable value would differ very little from the insured value if the latter were agreed. Section 16 of the Act states "In insurance on freight, whether paid in advance or otherwise, the insurable value is the gross amount of the freight at the risk of the assured, plus the charges of insurance."

Open Covers. In order to arrange their marine insurance in advance and to be assured of cover at all times, and also to avoid the effects of possibly rapidly fluctuating rates, it is the practice of regular importers and exporters to avail themselves of some kind of "blanket" insurance. One way, and the most popular one, of achieving this is by means of "open covers". An open cover is an agreement between the assured and his underwriters under which the former agrees to declare, and the latter to accept, all shipments coming within the scope of the open cover during some stipulated period of time. The open cover itself is simply an original slip with the disadvantage that, like any other slip, it is not legally enforceable but is binding in honour only. It is constructed so as to cover all the shipments of the assured during the stipulated period, but is naturally expressed only in general terms as the names of carrying vessels and the precise nature of the shipments will not be known at the time when the cover is effected. Whenever a shipment is made the assured notifies and gives the details to the underwriters who then issue a stamped policy. Although the underwriters' aggregate liability during the period of cover is unlimited, a stipulation is invariably made that no shipment shall exceed a specified sum in any one vessel. On this "limit per bottom" underwriters base the amount of their "lines" when accepting the insurance. In the case of a small limit, a single underwriter may accept the whole amount; if large, the broker will find it necessary to invite a number of underwriters to subscribe in order to place the full amount. The proportion that an underwriter's line bears to the limit per bottom is the proportion he will receive of all the shipments declared under the open cover.

Floating Policy. This provides another method of obtaining a long-term contract for goods insurance, which may be used instead of or in addition to an open cover. A floating or open policy describes the insurance in general terms. leaving the names of the ship or ships to be defined by subsequent declaration. Such a policy has the advantage of being a valid marine policy, in all respects fully complying with the requirements of the Marine Insurance Act. The declarations may be made by indorsement on the policy or in any other customary manner. Unless the policy otherwise provides, declarations must be made in the order of shipment. They must comprise all the consignments within the terms of the policy, and values must be honestly stated. Errors and omissions, however, may be rectified, even after a loss has occurred, if made in good faith. When the total amount declared exhausts the amount for which the policy was originally issued, it is said to be "run off" or "fully declared". The assured may then arrange for a new policy to be issued to succeed the one about to lapse; otherwise the cover terminates when the policy is fully declared. If a declaration has been omitted, that must be rectified by inserting it in its proper sequence. Meanwhile, if a loss has occurred in connection with a declaration subsequent to the one omitted, and it is found that as a result of the rectification the policy would have been fully declared before the subsequent declaration could have attached, the underwriter will not be liable.

It should be observed that the period of cover afforded by a floating policy depends entirely upon the amount of the sum insured and the frequency and value of shipments necessary to render the policy fully declared. By contrast, the voyages or risks insured under an open cover are generally in respect of sailings during an agreed period, commonly 12 months, but sometimes less.

As explained in Chapter 9, in connection with the financing of shipments, insurance policies are frequently lodged with a bank or despatched to the consignee. With open cover insurance this presents no difficulty, but with a floating policy designed to cover a number of shipments a policy relating to a particular shipment is not available. For this reason another insurance document has been introduced called a "certificate of insurance". This document takes the place of the policy in respect of the shipment to which it refers and, provided a valid policy is available, will be accepted by a banker as proof that the goods are adequately insured. The certificate has no legal value in the absence of a supporting policy.

Other Features of Floating Policy and Open Cover Insurance.
As most cargo policies contain the Warehouse to Warehouse clause,
the period during which a shipment is covered is not limited merely
to the time whilst the goods are in transit on board the carrying
ship. The insurance attaches from the time the goods leave the warehouse at the place named in the policy for the commencement of
the transit. It may happen, therefore, that a large quantity of
goods comprising several shipments declared under an open cover or
floating policy may accumulate in one particular place at a particular
time and there be heavily damaged or destroyed by a peril insured
against, such as fire or some other disaster. In such an event the
underwriters' liability may be vastly in excess of anything contemplated at the time of accepting the insurance. For this reason it
is usual to include in the contract a "Location Clause" to the effect
that, in the event of loss or damage to the insured goods before
shipment, the underwriter shall not be liable in respect of any one
accident for more than an agreed maximum figure. Normally the
"location limit" will be the same as the limit per bottom, but where
there is a likelihood of an accumulation of goods at the port of
shipment, the underwriters may, in return for an adequate increase
of premium, agree to a "200 per cent. Location Clause".

When negotiating an open cover or floating policy the assured,
although he will know the type of goods he will be shipping, will not
known the names of the vessels in which the goods will be carried.
The underwriter, on his part, will find difficulty in fixing suitable
rates without knowing what class and type of vessel will be employed to carry the goods. To resolve this difficulty it is usual for
the contract to contain a "Classification Clause" to the effect that
the rates of premium agreed refer only to shipments effected by
liners, or by vessels not more than 15 years old and in the highest
class of one of the recognised classification societies listed in the
clause. Shipments by vessels other than these are not excluded
from the protection of the cover, but are held covered at rates to
be arranged.

Floating policies may contain provisions for cancellation by a
clause such as "Either party shall be at liberty to cancel the policy
by giving . . . days' notice in writing to that effect without prejudice
to any risk outstanding at the termination of that period". An open
cover contract may also contain a provision for cancellation.

Gaming or Wagering Policy. This is a policy issued without there
being any insurable interest, or a policy bearing evidence that the
insurer is willing to dispense with any proof of interest. Such
policies have inserted in them the words "policy proof of interest",
or "interest or no interest", or some similar phrase.

By Section 4 of the Marine Insurance Act such policies are void
in law, but the Act distinguishes, in effect, between two different
classifications of gaming or wagering policies, viz.:

(a) those which are gaming and wagering contracts in fact, *i.e.*, where the assured not only has no insurable interest, but has no expectation of acquiring one, and,

(b) those which by their wording appear to be gaming or wagering policies.

With regard to category (a), a later Act of 1909 provides that a person procuring a contract of insurance without having a *bona fide* interest is guilty of an offence and is liable to a fine or to a term of imprisonment.

With regard to category (b), in spite of the fact that such contracts are void in law, and, therefore, binding in honour only, they continue to be executed as a customary commercial practice. These "Honour Policies", as they are often called, are regarded as a commercial necessity in innumerable cases, where it would be difficult or impossible to give actual proof of interest even though such interest exists. P.P.I. (Policy Proof of Interest) policies are frequently in use for the insurance of commissions and the increased value of commodities. They may also be useful to cover the risk of increased Government duty or the imposition of a duty on articles that were previously duty free. So-called "disbursements" (in effect, "excess value of hull") are normally issued on a P.P.I. basis.

A P.P.I. contract is often incorporated in an ordinary policy but is not affixed adhesively as other attached clauses usually are. Instead, it is pinned on. The original idea behind this practice was that when the need for the P.P.I. clause ceased to exist, it could be easily detached so that the policy would then acquire full legal effect. This, however, has been proved to be of no practical value, as it has been held that a policy which is invalid at the time when it is first issued remains invalid no matter what may be done to it later. Nevertheless, the practice of pinning on the P.P.I. clause seems to have become an established "custom".

In practice, P.P.I. policies are scrupulously honoured by underwriters although they are divested of all enforceable rights. A broker cannot be held liable for negligence in effecting such a void contract, neither can an underwriter sustain any right of subrogation.

THE INSURANCE BROKER

In general practice the assured does not deal directly with his underwriters, but negotiates through an insurance broker who will be a person specially trained in insurance law and practice. Shipowners always employ brokers to effect hull insurances, and any insurance at Lloyd's must be effected through the medium of a Lloyd's broker as no one other than a member of Lloyd's may do business there.

An agent or broker must make to the underwriters a full disclosure of all material facts both as regards his own knowledge and the information he receives from his principal. When a principal employs a broker, the former is entitled to rely on the exercise of reasonable care and skill on the part of the latter in carrying out the instructions given him. If such instructions are not properly given effect to, with the result that a loss occurs which is not recoverable under the policy, the broker will be liable for damages for breach of contract.

Section 53 of the Marine Insurance Act provides:

(1) Unless otherwise agreed, where a marine policy is effected on behalf of the assured by a broker, the broker is directly responsible to the insurer for the premium, and the insurer is directly responsible to the assured for the amount which may be payable in respect of losses, or in respect of returnable premium.

(2) Unless otherwise agreed, the broker has, as against the assured, a lien upon the policy for the amount of the premium and his charges in respect of effecting the policy; and, where he has dealt with the person who employs him as a principal, he has also a lien on the policy in respect of any balance on any insurance account which may be due to him from such person, unless when the debt was incurred he had reason to believe that such person was only an agent.

Section 54 provides:

Where a marine policy effected on behalf of the assured by a broker acknowledges the receipt of the premium, such acknowledgement is, in the absence of fraud, conclusive as between the insurer and the assured, but not as between the insurer and broker.

A Lloyd's form of policy includes a receipt for the premium by virtue of the words ". . . confessing ourselves paid the consideration due unto us for this assurance by the assured, at and after the rate of . . ."

THE SLIP

The slip is, in fact, merely a slip of paper on which the assured, or more generally his broker, sets forth the details of the risk in a skeleton and abbreviated form which will be intelligible only to an expert. This is submitted to an underwriter who, if willing to accept the risk, initials it. If he agrees to accept only a portion of the risk, he inserts the amount he is willing to underwrite and initials that. The customary procedure is for the broker to approach first an underwriter who is recognised as a "lead" in the particular type of insurance being sought. Having acquired a good lead on his slip, the broker will not normally experience difficulty in completing the slip, although he may meet with refusals from underwriters already interested in the same voyage or who, for other good reasons, prefer not to accept any part of the risk. As soon as an underwriter has inserted the amount of the risk he has agreed to accept and has initialled the slip, the contract with that underwriter is concluded, but that is not to say that the date of the conclusion of the contract is the date when the insurance commences or the date from which the underwriter becomes liable. If a time policy is to be issued the insurance will not commence until the date agreed, and in the case of a voyage policy the wording of the policy and/or the attached clauses will determine precisely when the risk attaches. Moreover, the contract concluded by the initialling of the slip is not a valid and enforceable contract until such time as it has been embodied in a proper marine policy. The slip is binding in honour only: it cannot itself be made into a policy, nor can it be enforced as a contract to issue a policy. However, it is not entirely devoid of legal value, for it can be produced in evidence to show the intention of the parties, to prove the date of the conclusion of the contract, or for the purpose of rectifying a mistake. It goes without saying that no underwriter, having initialled a slip, will take advantage of his legal position to refuse to subscribe his name to the policy, but should an underwriter go into liquidation it would be beyond the powers of the liquidator to issue policies in respect of insurances accepted but unclosed at the date of the liquidation.

COVER NOTES

Having obtained a completed slip the broker sends his client a cover note to advise him of the terms and conditions on which the insurance has been placed, and whether it has been placed at Lloyd's, or with one or more of the companies, or both. The cover note is simply an insurance memorandum which is usually accompanied by a request for closing instructions so that the policy can be prepared. A cover note issued by an insurance company direct to the assured in a case where a broker has not been employed takes the place of a slip and has a value similar to that of a slip.

DISCLOSURE

The Marine Insurance Act lays down that a contract of marine insurance is a contract based upon the utmost good faith (*uberrimae fidei*), and, if the utmost good faith be not observed by either party, the contract may be voided by the other party. Accordingly, the assured must disclose to the underwriter every material circumstance known to him, that is everything which would influence the judgement of a prudent insurer in fixing the premium or in deciding whether or not to accept the risk. But, in the absence of inquiry, the following need not be disclosed:

(a) Any circumstance which lessens the risk.
(b) Any circumstance known or presumed to be known by the insurer; that is anything which he ought to know in the ordinary course of his business.

(c) Any circumstance as to which information is waived by the insurer.

(d) Any circumstance which it is superfluous to disclose by reason of an express or implied warranty.

Excessive additional insurances by policies on freight and disbursements must be disclosed, also over-valuation of cargo, but not over-valuation of hull as the underwriter is assumed to be as well able as the assured to estimate the proper value of the hull.

If an underwriter accepted an insurance knowing it to be safely expired, that would constitute a breach of good faith on his part, and the assured would be able to avoid the policy and claim a return of the premium paid.

WARRANTIES

Although an underwriter is protected by the operation of the principle of the utmost good faith, as described above, it may often be extremely difficult to prove misrepresentation or non-disclosure of material facts and, for that reason, a more practical way of ensuring the honest character of an insurance contract is by the employment of so-called "warranties". It has been explained in Chapter 3 that the term "warranty" as used in connection with marine insurance has the same meaning as the term "condition" as used in respect of other contracts.

Section 33 (1) of the Marine Insurance Act defines a warranty as a promissory warranty, that is to say a warranty by which the assured undertakes that some particular thing shall or shall not be done, or that some condition shall be fulfilled, or whereby he affirms or negatives the existence of a particular state of facts.

A warranty may be expressed or implied, and two very important implied warranties are as follows:

(1) In every voyage policy it is implied that the vessel shall be seaworthy when the risk commences.

(2) In every policy (voyage, or time, or mixed) it is implied that the adventure shall be lawful.

With regard to the warranty of seaworthiness, where the risk attaches while the ship is in port it is implied that the ship is fit to encounter the perils of the port, and where a voyage is performed in stages it is implied that the ship is at the commencement of each stage seaworthy for that stage.

In a time policy there is no implied warranty that the ship is seaworthy at any stage of the adventure, but where, with the privity of the assured, the ship is sent to sea in an unseaworthy state the underwriter is not liable for loss attributable to unseaworthiness.

In a goods policy there is no implied warranty that the goods themselves are seaworthy. Such a warranty is not necessary as the insurance is only against the perils enumerated in the policy. Hence, in the absence of a special stipulation, the underwriter is not liable for losses arising from "inherent vice" of goods. But in a voyage policy on goods it is implied that the ship is seaworthy at the beginning of the voyage and is fit (*i.e.*, cargoworthy) to carry the goods to the destination contemplated by the policy. This warranty, however, does not extend to lighters if the policy includes "risk of craft to and from ship".

A shipper, obviously, is seldom in a position to know whether the vessel into which his goods are loaded is seaworthy or not. Therefore, in a voyage policy on cargo it is usual to insert the clause "seaworthiness of vessel hereby admitted". If the underwriter then pays a loss arising from unseaworthiness, he becomes subrogated to any rights which the cargo owner might have had against the shipowner. A similar clause will usually be found in a policy covering the sea voyage of a vessel or structure not normally employed at sea and in process of being delivered, say, a river steamer or a floating dock.

With regard to the warranty of legality, it is the law of England which determines the lawfulness of the adventure. Foreign laws are not recognised for this purpose. But if the existence of a foreign law affects the risk, and it is not common knowledge that the underwriter may be assumed to share, disclosure must be made to enable the underwriter to assess the premium accordingly.

The adventure may be lawful when the insurance is effected but become unlawful on account of altered conditions. For example, suppose a ship leaves a port in country A bound for a port in country B, and while the ship is at sea war breaks out between England and B so that there is a Government proclamation making it illegal for British subjects to trade with the enemy. Should the adventure be abandoned by the vessel proceeding to a British port by Government direction or otherwise, any loss arising is a loss caused by "Restraint of Princes, etc." which, being a peril insured against, renders the underwriter liable. On the other hand, if the assured in defiance of English law attempted to continue the adventure after it had become unlawful and his goods were seized, the policy would not protect him as he would have failed to comply with the implied warranty.

Express Warranties. The Act provides that an express warranty may be in any form of words from which the intention to warrant is to be inferred; that it must be included in or written upon the policy, or must be contained in some document incorporated by reference into the policy; and that an express warranty does not exclude implied warranty unless it is inconsistent therewith.

Suppose, for example, the policy contains the clause "Warranted not north of 70°N. latitude". If the ship in fact proceeds beyond that limit the warranty would be breached and the underwriters would have no further liability under the policy. If the shipowner requires the ship to go beyond the named limit his proper procedure is to notify the underwriters, directly or through his broker, and the underwriters may then, in return for additional premium, be prepared to waive the warranty.

Where, in time of war, a vessel is "warranted neutral", it is an implied condition that she shall be properly documented in the sense that she shall carry the necessary papers to establish her neutrality, and that she shall not falsify or suppress her papers, or use simulated papers. Any breach of this condition would enable the insurer to avoid the contract.

Institute Warranties. In policies on vessels of the "liner" class it is usual to include a warranty that such vessels will be employed only in their normal regular services, that is to say within well defined limits. Owners of vessels of the "tramp" class, however, will require freedom to trade within very much wider limits. Accordingly, the Institute Warranties are designed to fix the standard trading limits of vessels not engaged on regular services. These warranties are six in number, of which the first four put a ban on trading to certain icebound regions in the far north (in some cases all the year round, in others during the winter season only), the fifth prohibits trading to certain Antarctic regions, and the sixth prohibits the carriage of Indian coal between 1st March and 30th September except to near Asiatic ports between certain dates. Owners who wish to employ their vessels in the prohibited areas or in the prohibited trade may take advantage of Clause 5 of the Institute Time Clauses (Hulls) which reads "Held covered in case of any breach of warranty as to cargo, trade, locality, towage, salvage services or date of sailing, provided notice be given immediately after receipt of advices and any additional premium required be agreed".

When Breach of Warranty is Excused. It is an important provision of the Marine Insurance Act that a warranty is a condition which must be exactly complied with, whether it be material to the risk or not, and it will be noted that in this respect warranties differ from non-disclosure and misrepresentation. The Act, however, does provide that non-compliance with a warranty is excused (*a*) when, by reason of a change of circumstances, the warranty ceases to be applicable to the circumstances of the contract, or (*b*) when compliance with the warranty is rendered unlawful by any subsequent law.

It is always open to an underwriter to waive a breach of warranty, and a policy may make provision for a breach of warranty to be held covered at an additional premium. Breaches of Institute Warranties are naturally not uncommon, and underwriters have actually agreed scales of additional premiums to apply in such cases.

INSURABLE INTEREST

It has already been made clear that any person who effects or attempts to effect an insurance must have an insurable interest, or at least must have a reasonable expectation of acquiring such an interest.

The Act defines the term "insurable interest" in Section 5 as follows:

(1) Subject to the provisions of this Act, every person has an insurable interest who is interested in a marine adventure.

(2) In particular a person is interested in a marine adventure where he stands in any legal or equitable relation to the adventure or to any insurable property at risk therein, in consequence of which he may benefit by the safety or due arrival of insurable property, or may be prejudiced by its loss or by damage thereto, or by the detention thereof, or may incur liability in respect thereof.

Where a person is not interested in the adventure or property at risk, any insurance contract he may effect is nothing more than a mere wager. It is not a contract of indemnity, and it is legally void.

On the other hand, a person who has a reasonable expectation of acquiring an insurable interest need not actually have such an interest at the time of effecting the insurance, though he must have an interest at the time when a loss occurs to be entitled to be indemnified.

It may be remarked that it is not necessary to own property in order to have an insurable interest in it. For instance:

An underwriter has an insurable interest in his risk and may therefore re-insure it.

A bottomry bondholder has an interest in an adventure in respect of the bottomry loan.

The master and crew of a vessel have interests in respect of their wages.

A person who advances freight has an insurable interest in the advance in so far as it is not recoverable in the event of the ship and/or cargo being lost.

If the property is mortgaged, the mortgagee has an insurable interest in it.

The Act provides that a defeasible interest is insurable, as also is a contingent interest. An example of the former might arise during wartime in connection with the capture of an enemy ship. Whilst taking her to port for adjudication, the captor would have an insurable interest in her, and if the captured vessel were condemned as a prize of war such interest would be complete. If, however, the Prize Court ordered the vessel's release, the interest would be rendered defeasible. A contingent interest is one dependent upon a contingency. For instance, a purchaser of goods may, in the contract of sale, reserve the right to reject them if they do not come up to sample, or he may reserve the right to refuse goods which do not arrive by a specified date. Until such contingency occurs the purchaser has an insurable interest in the goods.

THE POLICY

Contract Embodied in Policy. Subject to the provision of any statute, a contract of marine insurance is inadmissible in evidence unless it is embodied in a marine policy which may be executed and issued either at the time when the contract is concluded, or afterwards.

The policy must specify the name of the assured, or of some person who effects the insurance on his behalf.

Signing of Policy. The policy must be signed by or on behalf of the insurer, though the Act provides that the corporate seal of a corporation is sufficient. Where a policy is subscribed by or on behalf of two or more insurers, each subscription, unless the contrary be expressed, constitutes a distinct contract with the assured.

In the case of insurances effected at Lloyd's one policy is sufficient for all the subscribing Lloyd's underwriters. When checked against the slip, the names of the several underwriters together with their respective proportions of the sum insured are impressed on the policy which is issued by Lloyd's Policy Signing Office bearing the seal of that Office.

Insurance companies who are members of the Institute of London Underwriters operate a similar scheme to that in use at Lloyd's by virtue of the Institute's policy department where policies prepared by brokers are signed by or on behalf of the Secretary of the Institute. The Institute sends daily returns of all policies signed to the individual companies interested. An insurance company's own form of policy may be used, if the broker so desires, where the whole insurance is underwritten by that company and would, of course, have to be used for an insurance placed with a company which is not a member of the Institute.

STAMP DUTIES

At one time all marine policies were required to be stamped with a Revenue stamp for an amount depending on the extent of the sum insured and a very large sum of money would then have had to be paid out annually out in stamp duties in connection with, for example, the fleet insurances of large shipping companies. The situation was altered by Section 30 of the Finance Act, 1959, under the provisions of which various sections of other Acts were wholly or partly repealed.

The general effect of Section 30 of the Finance Act, 1959, was to bring marine insurance into line with all other insurances (with the exception of life assurance) for the purposes of stamp duty. Some of the consequences of the changes have been mentioned elsewhere in this Chapter. Others, although possibly far reaching, are beyond the scope of this book, but it may be noted that the following are exempt from all stamp duties, viz.:

(a) cover notes, slips and other instruments usually made in anticipation of the issue of a formal policy, not being instruments relating to life insurance;

(b) instruments embodying alterations of the terms or conditions of any policy of insurance other than life insurance;

(c) policies of insurance on baggage or personal and household effects only, if made or executed out of Great Britain.

and an instrument exempted by virtue of paragraph (a) of this subsection shall not be taken for the purposes of the Stamp Act, 1891, to be a policy of insurance.

More recently still all marine policy stamp duties were abolished, and to ensure that a policy has full legal force it is necessary only that it conforms with the provisions of the Marine Insurance Act as amended.

ASSIGNMENT

Assignment of Interest. Where the assured assigns or otherwise parts with his interest in the subject matter insured, he does not thereby transfer to the assignee his rights under the contract of insurance, unless there be an express or implied agreement to that effect. But this does not affect transmission of interest by operation of law (in case of death or bankruptcy).

Assignment of Policy. A marine policy is assignable unless it contains terms expressly prohibiting assignment, and may be assigned either before or after a loss. The assignee who has acquired the beneficial interest in the policy is entitled to sue thereon in his own name, and the defendant is entitled to make any defence arising out of the contract which he would have been entitled to make if the action had been brought in the name of the person by or on behalf of whom the policy was effected. Assignment may be by endorsement or in other customary manner. Where the assured has parted with or lost his interest in the subject matter insured, and has not, before or at the time of so doing expressly or impliedly agreed to assign the policy, any subsequent assignment is inoperative. But this does not affect the assignment of a policy after a loss.

The opening words of Lloyd's form of policy are "Be it known that.................as well as in.................own name as for and in the name and names of all and every other person or persons to whom the same doth, may or shall appertain.................". It will be seen that provision for assignment is thereby made.

It is often the case that goods change hands whilst they are in transit, for which reason it is essential that cargo policies should be freely assignable, but it is important that the original assured should assign the policy before or at the time of his parting with the interest, as assignment at a later stage would be inoperative. It is not necessary to notify the underwriters of an assignment, but in the case of a hull policy continuance of the insurance should the vessel be sold or transferred to new management is dependent on the underwriters' written agreement. (See Clause 6 of the Institute Time Clauses in Appendix V).

Goods policies are usually assigned by blank endorsement, and hull policies by specific endorsement in accordance with Clause 22 of the Institute Time Clauses (Hulls).

LLOYD'S FORM OF POLICY

The standard form of marine policy is Lloyd's S.G. Policy, which is reproduced in Appendix IV. Opinion is divided as to the meaning of the letters S.G. Some favour "Ship and Goods", others take them to mean *Salutis Gratia* (for the sake of safety), and there are other suggested interpretations.

The policy in its present form dates from 1779 and is very antiquated in its wording, but the meaning which the courts attach to practically every word has long been ascertained, and on that account underwriters, merchants, shipowners and brokers have always been reluctant to accept suggestions that a new form is desirable. Under modern conditions, however, it is most unlikely that the standard form will ever express all the requirements of the parties to a marine insurance contract, so its defects are remedied by writing in or adhesively attaching additional clauses. Any superfluous or inapplicable words in the body of the policy itself are left undeleted, as it is a rule that attached or written-in words or clauses override the printed words of the policy with which they are at variance so long as they are initialled by or on behalf of the insurer. The wording of a policy is always deemed to be the language of the insurer, and if there are ambiguous words or phrases the Court in construing the contract will give the benefit of the doubt to the assured. Additional clauses are mainly those known as "Institute Clauses" to which reference is made further on.

TERMS USED IN THE STANDARD POLICY FORM

Section 30 of the Act provides (1) that a policy may be in Lloyd's S.G. Form, and (2) that unless the context of the policy otherwise requires, the terms and expressions mentioned in the First Schedule to the Act shall be construed as having the scope and meaning in that schedule assigned to them. The terms and expressions and their meaning are as follows:

Lost or Not Lost. Where the subject-matter is insured "lost or not lost" and the loss has occurred before the contract is concluded, the risk attaches unless, at such time the assured was aware of the loss, and the insurer was not. (In pre-telegraphic days this was of much more significance than it is under modern conditions.)

From. Where the subject-matter is insured "from" a particular place, the risk does not attach until the ship starts on the voyage insured. (This also is of little practical significance today, as hull insurances are generally on a time basis, and the cover provided by goods policies is defined by special clauses.)

At and From. (*a*) Where a ship is insured "at and from" a particular place, and she is at that place in good safety when the contract is concluded, the risk attaches immediately.

(*b*) If she be not at that place when the contract is concluded, the risk attaches as soon as she arrives there in good safety, and, unless the policy otherwise provides, it is immaterial that she is covered by another policy for a specified time after arrival. (To avoid overlapping of policies a clause may be inserted to the effect that the risk is not to attach until previous policies have expired.)

(*c*) Where chartered freight is insured "at and from" a particular place, and the ship is at that place in good safety when the contract is concluded, the risk attaches immediately. If she be not there when the contract is concluded, the risk attaches as soon as she arrives there in good safety.

(*d*) Where freight, other than chartered freight, is payable without special conditions and is insured "at and from" a particular place, the risk attaches *pro rata* as the goods or merchandise are shipped; provided that if there be cargo in readiness which belongs to the shipowner, or which some other person had contracted with him to the ship, the risk attaches as soon as the ship is ready to receive such cargo.

From the Loading thereof. Where goods or other moveables are insured "from the loading thereof", the risk does not attach until such goods or moveables are actually on board, and the insurer is not liable for them while in transit from the shore to the ship. (In modern practice a more extended cover is normally required and is provided for by special clauses.)

Safely Landed. Where the risk on goods or other moveables continues until they are "safely landed", they must be landed in the customary manner and within a reasonable time after arrival at the port of discharge, and if they are not so landed the risk ceases. (In this connection also the situation is governed by the provisions of the special clauses attached to policies nowadays.)

Touch and Stay. In the absence of any further licence or usage, the liberty to "touch and stay at any port or place whatsoever" does not authorise the ship to depart from the course of her voyage from the port of departure to the port of destination. (The Act does lay down in what circumstances deviation is excused, and this is referred to further on under the heading of "Deviation".)

Perils of the Seas. The term "perils of the seas" refers only to fortuitous accidents or casualties of the seas. It does not include the ordinary action of the winds and waves. (The object of the insurance is to indemnify the assured in respect of losses arising from accidents that may happen; not in respect of events which must happen.

Pirates. The term "pirates" includes passengers who mutiny and rioters who attack the ship from the shore.

Thieves. The term "thieves" does not cover clandestine theft or a theft committed by any one of the ship's company, whether crew or passengers. (If the assured requires cover against clandestine theft or pilferage, he must make a special arrangement with the underwriter.)

Restraint of Princes. The term "arrests, etc., of kings, princes, and people" refers to political or executive acts, and does not include a loss caused by riot or by ordinary judicial process. (The term "arrests, etc.", applies not only to authoritative or executive acts in time of war, but also to the operation of ordinary municipal law in times of peace. It could apply, for instance, in a case of Government prohibition of the importation of cattle coming from a country where a contagious cattle disease was prevalent. On the other hand, it would not apply, say, where a vessel is arrested and sold by court order in the process of satisfying claims through the exercise of a maritime lien on the vessel.)

Barratry. The term "barratry" includes every wrongful act wilfully committed by the master or crew to the prejudice of the owner, or, as the case may be, the charterer. (Acts of barratry include such things as wilfully casting away the vessel or wilfully running her ashore with fraudulent or malicious intent; fraudulently selling the ship, her equipment, or cargo; sailing in breach of an embargo; wilfully assisting illegal immigration; smuggling without the owner's consent. Obviously, if the owner himself engages in smuggling, that is not barratry. A shipowner cannot commit barratry against himself.)

All Other Perils. The term "all other perils" includes only perils similar in kind to the perils specifically mentioned in the policy. (This is another case of the application of the *ejusdem generis* rule mentioned in Chapter 9.)

Average Unless General. The term "average unless general" means a partial loss of the subject-matter insured other than a general average loss, and does not include "particular charges".

Stranded. Where the ship has stranded, the insurer is liable for the excepted losses, although the loss is not attributable to the stranding, provided that when the stranding takes place the risk has attached and, if the policy be on goods, that the damaged goods are on board. (Suppose a vessel is to load cargo at Glasgow and Liverpool for ports in South America, and the goods policies contain the clause "warranted free from particular average unless the ship be stranded". Further, suppose that (a) the ship strands whilst on passage from Glasgow to Liverpool, and (b) particular average damage is caused to cargo due to perils of the seas whilst on passage from Liverpool to South America. Underwriters will be liable for damage caused to cargo loaded in Glasgow, but not for damage to the cargo loaded at Liverpool which was not on board at the time of the stranding.)

Ship. The term "ship" includes the hull, materials and outfit, stores and provisions for the officers and crew, and in the case of vessels engaged in a special trade, the ordinary fittings requisite for the trade, and also, in the case of a steamship, the machinery, boilers, and coals and engine stores, if owned by the assured.

Freight. The term "freight" includes the profit derivable by a shipowner from the employment of his ship to carry his own goods or moveables, as well as freight payable by a third party, but does not include passage money.

Goods. The term "goods" means goods in the nature of merchandise, and does not include personal effects or provisions and stores for use on board.

In the absence of any usage to the contrary, deck cargo and living animals must be insured specifically, and not under the general denomination of goods.

THE MASTER'S NAME

By virtue of the clause "Whereof is master, under God, for this present voyage................or whosoever else shall go for master in the said ship", Lloyd's S.G. policy provides for the name of the master to be stated. It is not customary nowadays, however, for the name to be inserted. Nevertheless, if a well-known and experienced master is removed and replaced by one who is less experienced, that is a fact which must be disclosed to the underwriters.

DEVIATION

A voyage policy may enumerate ports of call, or it may give leave to call at "any ports or places whatsoever". This expression,

W

however, is very restricted in its meaning and the liberty given is only to call at the usual ports on the particular voyage. If the ship deviates without lawful excuse, the underwriters are discharged from liability from the time of the deviation, and it is immaterial that the ship may have regained her route before loss occurs.

There is a deviation whenever:

(a) the route designated by the policy is departed from;
(b) if no route is designated, the usual route is departed from.

Where ports of discharge in a given area are not named, or not mentioned in any special order, the ship must go to them in strict geographical order. Failure to do so amounts to deviation.

An intention to deviate will not void the policy if a loss occurs before the ship actually deviates.

In the case of a voyage policy, the voyage must be prosecuted with reasonable despatch. Any unreasonable delay will void the policy.

Section 49 of the Act provides that deviation or delay in prosecuting the voyage contemplated by the policy is excused:

(a) where authorised by any special term in the policy; or
(b) where caused by circumstances beyond the control of the master and his employer; or
(c) where reasonably necessary in order to comply with an express or implied warranty; or
(d) where reasonably necessary for the safety of the ship or subject-matter insured; or
(e) for the purpose of saving human life, or aiding a ship in distress where human life may be in danger; or
(f) where reasonably necessary for the purpose of obtaining medical or surgical aid for any person on board the ship; or
(g) where caused by the barratrous conduct of the master or crew, if barratry be one of the perils insured against.

When the cause excusing the deviation or delay ceases to operate, the ship must resume her course, and prosecute her voyage, with reasonable despatch.

THE PERILS ENUMERATED IN LLOYD'S
S.G. POLICY

This policy form contains the paragraph:

"Touching the adventures and perils which we the assurers are contented to bear and do take upon us in this voyage, they are of the seas, men-of-war, fire, enemies, pirates, rovers, thieves, jettisons, letters of mart and countermart, surprisals, takings at sea, arrests, restraints, and detainments of all kings, princes and people, of what nation, condition or quality soever, barratry of the master and mariners, and of all other perils, losses and misfortunes that have or shall come to the hurt, detriment or damage of the said goods and merchandises, and ship, etc., or any part thereof."

It will be noticed that some of the perils enumerated above are identical with some of the "maritime perils" listed in Section 3 of the Marine Insurance Act which also includes perils "which may be designated by the policy". The following are additional to the terms mentioned in the Rules for Construction of Policy.

Men-of-war. This term applies to warships generally, both hostile and friendly. If, for instance, a merchant ship were captured as prize by an enemy and then recaptured by a friendly warship whose gunfire caused damage to the merchant ship, that would be a loss recoverable as a loss by "man-of-war".

Fire. Losses by fire are normally recoverable under the policy. The policy does not, however, cover cargo fired by spontaneous combustion if the underwriter can prove that the cargo was shipped in a condition likely to give rise to spontaneous combustion. That would be a loss due to inherent vice of goods, which is not a peril insured against. Moreover, if the assured knew that the goods were shipped in an improper condition and he failed to disclose that fact to the underwriter, the latter would have the further reason for repudiating liability that there had been concealment of material fact. If spontaneous combustion of one parcel of cargo caused damage to another parcel of a different kind, the latter damage would be covered by the policy.

Enemies. This term includes all naval units and aircraft of the enemy in time of war. (See section headed "War Risks".)

Rovers. This means much the same as "pirates". The distinction probably was that, whereas pirates operated in a particular locality, rovers "roved" the seas with the object of intercepting and robbing merchant vessels carrying valuable cargoes.

Jettisons. Jettison usually means throwing overboard cargo or equipment to lighten or relieve a vessel in peril, or to refloat a stranded ship, or to right a ship badly listed or on her beam ends. It has been held to cover the throwing overboard of valuables to prevent them from falling into enemy hands. Jettison of cargo carried on deck is covered only when it is on deck in accordance with a well recognised custom of the trade or it has been specifically insured. If goods improperly carried on deck or improperly carried in any other insecure place are jettisoned, the underwriter will not be liable for the loss. If the voyage is so prolonged owing to bad weather that perishable goods have to be jettisoned on account of their becoming putrid, the loss is not recoverable under the policy unless an agreement that the underwriter shall be liable has been specifically included in the policy. A policy covering dangerous goods, such as acids, carried on deck will usually contain a special agreement that the insurance is to include the risk of jettison.

It was pointed out in Chapter 11 that jetsam is included in the term "wreck". Where jettisoned property is recovered, the original owner may claim it on paying the salvage and other charges in respect of it, or the underwriter who has already paid the loss may claim it by virtue of his right of subrogation.

Letters of Mart and Countermart. These perils are now of historical interest only. A letter of mart (or marque) was a state-authorised commission granted to an individual giving him power to assail and capture the merchant ships of an enemy state. Letters of countermart were similar commissions by which reprisals on an enemy's merchant shipping were given state sanction.

Surprisals and Takings at Sea. The former term has much the same meaning as "capture", whilst the latter appears to relate to the stopping of neutral merchant ships in wartime if they are suspected of carrying contraband, and taking them into port for examination and possible confiscation of contraband goods.

IMPORTANT CLAUSES IN LLOYD'S POLICY

Sue and Labour Clause. The wording of this clause is as follows:

"And in case of any loss or misfortune it shall be lawful to the assured, their factors, servants and assigns, to sue, labour, and travel for, in and about the defence, safeguards and recovery of the said goods and merchandises and ship, etc., or any part thereof, without prejudice to this insurance; to the charges whereof we, the assurers, will contribute each one according to the rate and quantity of his sum herein assured."

The clause makes it lawful for the assured and his servants, when there is a danger that the subject-matter insured may suffer loss or damage for which the underwriter would be liable, to take such steps as may be reasonable to avert or minimise the loss or damage, and at the same time it binds the underwriters to pay their share of the expenses incurred. Section 78 of the Marine Insurance Act provides that (1) the engagement entered into under a suing and labouring clause is deemed to be supplementary to the contract of insurance, so that sue and labour expenses properly and reasonably incurred are payable irrespective of percentage and even in addition to a total loss; (2) that general average losses and contributions and salvage charges are not recoverable under the sue and labour clause; (3) that expenses incurred to avert or diminish a loss not covered by the policy are not recoverable under the clause; and (4) it is the duty of the assured and his agents to take reasonable measures to avert or minimise a loss.

Expenses recoverable under the sue and labour clause are known as "particular charges" (not to be confused with particular average). Such expenses are recoverable only when:

(*a*) they are incurred for the benefit of the subject-matter insured. (Expenses incurred in time of peril for the common benefit are general average charges);

(*b*) they are reasonable;

(*c*) they are incurred by the assured himself, or by his factors, servants or assigns. (Expenses incurred by strangers to the adventure would be salvage charges);

(*d*) they are incurred to avert or minimise a loss covered by the policy.

On account of (*d*), expenses incurred to avert a particular average loss would not be recoverable under a Free from Particular Average policy. In practice this would give rise to considerable difficulty. This is avoided by the following provision of the F.P.A. clause in the Institute Cargo Clauses (F.P.A.), viz. "............................. also to pay special charges for landing, warehousing and forwarding if incurred at an intermediate port of call or refuge, for which Underwriters would be liable under the standard form of English Marine Policy with the Institute Cargo Clauses (W.A.) attached".

The value of the subject-matter for the purpose of general average contributions or salvage charges may differ from the insured value with the result that such charges may not be recoverable from underwriters in full. Sue and labour charges, on the other hand, when reasonably incurred, are recoverable in full. In the absence of any stipulation otherwise, that is still so even where there is an under-insurance. In respect of hull policies, however, Clause 9 of the Institute Time Clauses (Hulls) brings these charges into line with general average and salvage charges.

N.B.—Any expenditure incurred to save ship and cargo and to continue the voyage must come under the heading of salvage charges, particular charges, or general average charges. The following examples will serve as simple illustrations:

Case 1. The ship has a cargo on board and is earning freight. She strands, and the master hires the services of a tug to refloat the ship and continue the voyage after necessary repairs. The cost of the tug is a general average charge, as the expenditure is reasonably and voluntarily incurred for the benefit of the common adventure in time of peril.

Case 2. The circumstances are the same as in Case 1, except that the ship is in ballast and is earning no freight. As there is no "common" adventure, general average cannot arise and the cost of the tug is a "particular charge" recoverable from underwriters under the Sue and Labour clause.

Case 3. The ship, either with or without cargo, strands. Another ship arrives on the scene and volunteers to pull the stranded ship off and, if necessary, tow her to a place of repair. The master of the stranded ship accepts the offer. The salving ship is remunerated by a "salvage award" and the cargo owners (if any) will have to contribute their share, *i.e.*, the cargo will be liable for "salvage charges".

Waiver Clause. This has a twofold effect, as follows:

(1) If, in a case of constructive total loss, the assured has given notice of abandonment to the underwriters and they have declined to accept it, any measure taken by the assured to save the property, or any part of it, is not to be taken as a waiver or withdrawal of the notice of abandonment.

(2) Similarly, any action taken by the underwriters to save the property shall not be regarded as acceptance by them of the notice they had previously declined.

Any action taken by either party under this clause must be pursued diligently with a view to protecting the interests of both parties.

FRANCHISES

It has long been an established principle in marine insurance that if the assured undertakes to bear some portion of the risk himself, he is more likely to exercise greater care to avoid losses than he might be if the risk were entirely covered by insurance. The application of the principle, by eliminating small particular average claims, operates to the advantage of underwriters generally, and is provided for by the incorporation in most contracts of a clause introducing a so-called "franchise" which may be deductible or non-deductible. The former is more properly called an "excess".

A franchise is, simply, that proportion of the insured value of the subject-matter for which the underwriter is not liable.

An early form of franchise, still contained in present day policies, is that provided by the "Memorandum" which became a feature of the then form of Lloyd's policy in 1749. It reads:

"*N.B.*—Corn, fish, salt, fruit, flour and seed are warranted free from average unless general, or the ship be stranded— sugar, tobacco, hemp, flax, hides and skins are warranted free from average, under five pounds per cent., and all other goods, also the ship and freight, are warranted free from average, under three pounds per cent., unless general, or the ship be stranded."

(The Memorandum in a Company Policy adds the words "sunk or burnt" after "stranded" in each case.)

The intention of the Memorandum is briefly as follows. If articles specified in the first list are wetted by sea water during the voyage, they are likely to suffer more damage than those in the second list if exposed to the same degree, and they in turn would be more seriously damaged than "other goods", *e.g.*, manufactured articles. Hence the arrangement is that underwriters are not liable at all for particular average losses in the first case, not liable in the second case unless the loss amounts to 5 per cent. of the insured value, and not liable in the last case unless the loss reaches 3 per cent. of the insured value.

It will be noticed that, as the same form of policy is employed for different kinds of insurances, provision is made for a 3 per cent. franchise in the case of hull insurance, and the same for freight insurance.

If the vessel is stranded (or, in the case of a company policy, sunk or burnt) the warranty is said to be breached, and the franchise does not apply. Underwriters are then liable in full, irrespective of the franchise mentioned, and it is not necessary that the loss or damage should have occurred during the stranding.

For the purpose of the above, reasonable interpretations must be put on the terms "stranded", "sunk", and "burnt". For instance, a vessel which takes the ground in a tidal harbour and refloats on the rising tide has not stranded. On the other hand, a vessel intentionally run ashore to prevent her sinking in deep water has stranded. To constitute a stranding the voyage must be forcibly interrupted by the vessel remaining on the ground for an appreciable time. "Sinking" must generally be of such a nature that the vessel is completely covered with water, but it was admitted in one case that a timber-laden vessel had "sunk" sufficiently to break the warranty because it was only the nature of her cargo that prevented her from sinking completely. In the same way, a ship is not "burnt" if a relatively small fire has resulted merely in a little structural damage. The burning must be substantial. Sometimes the words "or in collision" are added as well. They refer only to a collision with another vessel, not to collision with stationary objects.

It has long been realised that the Memorandum is inadequate to be generally applicable to the insurances of the wide variety of goods that are carried by sea and, accordingly, other clauses have been introduced to provide for more convenient franchises. Such clauses are usually known as "F.P.A. clauses" or "Average clauses".

In the case of a time policy on a ship the attached Institute Time Clauses (Hulls) for many years included an F.P.A. warranty which freed underwriters from particular average under 3 per cent. although if the vessel had been stranded, sunk, on fire, or in collision with any other vessel they agreed to pay the damage occasioned thereby. This warranty has now been removed and replaced by an arrangement whereby it is provided that no claim arising from a peril insured against shall be payable unless the aggregate of all such claims arising out of each separate accident or occurrence exceeds a stipulated sum (as agreed and written in) in which case this sum shall be deducted. This sum is referred to as the "deductible". Further, in the event of a claim for loss of or damage to any boiler, shaft, machinery or associated equipment arising from certain causes and attributable wholly or partly to the negligence of master, officers or crew the assured is required to bear, in addition to the deductible, an amount equal to 10 per cent. of the balance of the claim. As a result of this revision of the Institute Time Clauses for Hulls the memorandum is now virtually not used in hull insurance.

Another clause sometimes found attractive by shipowners because it reduces premiums, and by underwriters because it lessens their liability, is the so-called "Jansen Clause". This was originally intended to relieve the underwriter for the first 3 per cent. of any claim in the case of particular average on the ship, *although* the vessel be stranded, sunk or burnt. A later version reads "In the event of a particular average claim the underwriters only to be liable for the excess of..............per cent. of the entire value". The agreed percentage is written in and may, of course, be more than 3 per cent. This is a deductible franchise or an "excess". Other things being equal, naturally the higher the limit agreed the smaller the premium will be. This clause may sometimes be used when insuring dangerous goods, or hulls in cases where particular average claims are expected to be frequent. (It is important that this clause should not be confused with the bill of lading Jason Clause through the similarity of name.)

Goods Policies and Franchises. According to the nature of the risks to be covered, goods insurances are usually effected "against all risks", or "with average", or "free from particular average".

In an A.R. policy claims recoverable thereunder are payable irrespective of percentage.

In a W.A. policy, in order to free the underwriter from trifling claims, it is usual to insert a franchise clause "to pay average *if amounting* to .... per cent.". The "Average Clause" of the Institute Cargo Clauses (W.A.) reads:

"Warranted free from average under the percentage specified in the policy, unless general, or the vessel or craft be stranded, sunk or burnt, but notwithstanding this warranty the Underwriters are to pay the insured value of any package which may be totally lost in loading, transhipment or discharge, also for any loss of or damage to the interest insured which may reasonably be attributed to fire, explosion, collision or contact of the vessel and/or craft and/or conveyance with any external substance (ice included) other than water, or to discharge of cargo at a port of distress.

This Clause shall operate during the whole period covered by the policy."

Sometimes a deductible franchise is agreed. This differs from the ordinary franchise as the underwriter is not liable for any loss below the franchise. Such an arrangement may be "To pay average **in excess** of 5 per cent.".

Average clauses are deemed to be inserted for the benefit of the assured with the intention of extending the underwriters' liability beyond the provision of the Memorandum. Hence, if the effect of a special average clause were to deprive the assured of some benefit he would receive under the terms of the Memorandum, he retains his right to base his claim on the latter.

Under F.P.A. policies claims for particular average damage are not recoverable at all unless the vessel be stranded, sunk, or burnt, or the damage be due to some cause specified in the F.P.A. Clause (see Clause 5 of the Institute Cargo Clauses, F.P.A.). For the assured to be able to recover partial losses from underwriters on the grounds that the free from particular average warranty has been broken it is essential that the goods should have been on board at the time of the stranding or other accident, although it is not necessary that the accident should be the cause of the damage. When a claim does arise it is payable irrespective of percentage, *i.e.*, no franchise is involved.

INSTITUTE CLAUSES

There are numerous sets of these Institute Clauses, so called because they are framed and sanctioned by the Technical and Clauses Committee of the Institute of London Underwriters for attachment to the standard form of marine policy. Which particular set, or sets, will be attached in any given case will depend upon the nature of the subject-matter insured and what risks it is intended to cover. Included amongst these clauses are the following, some of which have already been referred to:

Institute Time Clauses (Hulls).
Institute Time Clauses (Hulls) F.P.A.A.
Institute Time Clauses (Freight).
Institute Voyage Clauses (Hulls).
Institute Cargo Clauses (All risks).
Institute Cargo Clauses (W.A.).
Institute Cargo Clauses (F.P.A.).
Institute Port Risk Clauses.
Institute War Clauses.
Institute Strikes Riots and Civil Commotions Clauses.
Institute Dual Valuation Clause.
Institute Excess Clause (Hulls).

It is only to be expected that all Institute Clauses will be subject to revision from time to time to take into account changing circumstances. Revised clauses usually take effect from 1st January or 1st July following the revision.

Institute Time Clauses (Hulls). These are reproduced in full in Appendix to which reference should be made in respect of details.

Here it will be sufficient to make a few brief remarks on the individual clauses.

1. **Running Down Clause.** In an ordinary marine policy the assured is covered in respect of the damage sustained by his own ship in case of collision, but such cover does not extend to his liability for the damage done to the other ship. This clause provides a supplementary contract whereby the assured is given some protection against such third party damages. It provides that if the insured vessel collides with another vessel, the underwriters agree to pay three-quarters of the amount of damages to which the assured becomes liable up to a maximum of three-quarters of the sum insured. The remaining fourth remains uninsured so far as those underwriters are concerned, but in practice it is usually covered by mutual insurance through a Protecting and Indemnity Association (Small Damage Club). If the R.D.C. does make underwriters liable for the full amount of the damage, which may sometimes be arranged, it is known as "4/4ths. R.D.C.". The protection does not extend to liabilities in respect of removal of obstructions, damage to piers, oil pollution of beaches etc. Nor does it cover the cargo or engagements of the insured vessel, loss of life, or personal injury. Underwriters will, however, pay three-quarters of the costs incurred in contesting or limiting liability with their consent. It may be noted that if a ship which sinks and becomes a total loss as the result of collision is also held liable for the damage to the other ship, underwriters will have to pay both the total loss indemnity and the claim arising under the R.D.C. clause.

2. **Sister Ship Clause.** This provides that if the injured vessel collides with, or receives salvage services from another ship belonging to the same owner, the assured shall have the same rights under the policy as if the other vessel were owned by strangers. In such case the liability is to be referred to a sole arbitrator agreed between the assured and underwriters. Without this provision difficulties would arise out of the facts that where ships belong to the same owner there can be no legal liability for salvage, and in respect of collision the owner cannot sue himself.

3. **Towage Clause, etc.** This provides that the vessel is covered at all times subject to the provisions of the policy. She has to leave to sail with or without pilots, go on trial trips, and assist and tow vessels in distress, but it is warranted that the vessel shall not be towed except as is customary or when in need of assistance, or undertake towage or salvage under a previously arranged contract.

Should the vessel be employed in a trade which requires her to go alongside another vessel at sea in order to load or discharge, any damage to the insured ship or liability for damage to the other ship arising from ranging alongside at sea during such loading or discharging is excluded, unless previously agreed with underwriters.

4. Continuation Clause. Should the vessel when the policy expires be at sea or in distress or at a port of refuge or of call, she shall, provided previous notice is given to underwriters, be held covered at a *pro rata* monthly premium to her port of destination. This clause is seldom brought into operation as time policies in respect of the same ship are almost invariably taken out to follow one another immediately without any intervening gap.

5. Held Covered or Breach of Warranty Clause. In the event of any breach of warranty as to cargo, trade, locality, towage, salvage services or date of sailing, the vessel will be held covered provided that notice is given immediately after receipt of advices and any additional premium required be agreed.

6. Change of Ownership Clause. If the vessel is sold or transferred to new management then, unless underwriters agree in writing to continue the insurance, the policy is cancelled. But if the vessel has sailed from a loading port or is at sea in ballast, cancellation is suspended until she arrives at a port of discharge or port of destination. Obviously, change of ownership cannot much affect the risk whilst the vessel is at sea. In the event of cancellation a *pro rata* daily return of premium is made.

7. Inchmaree (or Negligence) Clause. This is designed to extend the underwriters' liability to cover risks of a kind which are not included within the ordinary meaning of maritime perils. It provides for the insurance to cover loss or damage to hull or machinery **directly caused by**:

(*a*) Accidents in loading, discharging or shifting cargo or fuel.
   Explosions on shipboard or elsewhere.
   Breakdown of or accident to nuclear installations or reactors on shipboard or elsewhere.
   Bursting of boilers, breakage of shafts, or any latent defect in the machinery or hull.
   Negligence of Master, Officers, Crew or Pilots.
   Negligence of repairers provided such repairers are not Assured(s) hereunder.

(*b*) Contact with aircraft.
   Contact with any land conveyance, dock or harbour equipment or installation.
   Earthquake, volcanic eruption or lightning.

provided such loss or damage is not due to want of diligence by the assured. Masters and other servants of the shipowner are not considered as part owners within the meaning of this clause should they hold shares in the vessel.

The words "directly caused by" are very important. It is not the intention that underwriters shall be liable for the cost of replacing, say, a burst boiler. They are liable only for the damage that the bursting of the boiler directly causes. A latent defect is something which, presumably, must reveal itself sooner or later and, as has so often been pointed out, insurance is meant to protect the assured against what may happen, not what must happen. Nevertheless, there is another form of "Additional Perils Clause", sometimes called the "Liner Negligence Clause", which does give a more comprehensive cover than the "Tramp" form of negligence Clause here being considered. The Liner form is by its different wording deliberately drafted with the intention that underwriters shall be liable for the cost of renewing a burst boiler, broken shaft, etc. Even so, if there has been no actual failure or accident, but merely the condemnation of a part owing to the presence of a latent defect or error in design or construction, there is no liability for the cost of replacement.

Claims under this clause are subject to the deductible expressed in clause 12, and in addition, where appropriate, to the 10% deductible imposed by clause 11.

8. **General Average Clause.** This provides that general average and salvage shall be adjusted according to the law of the place where the adventure ends, or according to York-Antwerp Rules if the contract of affreightment so provides. It is further stated that Y-A Rules shall apply (with certain reservations) when the vessel sails in ballast and not under charter. This gives the shipowner the right to treat as general average (which, strictly, it is not as only one interest is involved) any sacrifice or expenditure which would not be recoverable under the policy either as particular average or particular charges but which has been made or incurred for the preservation of the subject-matter insured.

9. **Sue and Labour Expenses.** This clause explains in detail the extent of underwriters' liability for such expenses. In particular it provides that the liability shall not exceed the proportion that the amount insured bears to the value of the vessel. It has been previously mentioned that in the absence of this provision underwriters would be liable for the full amount of sue and labour charges even where there was under-insurance.

10. **Average Clause.** This states that average, *i.e.*, partial loss, shall be payable on each valuation separately, or on the whole, without deduction "new for old," whether particular or general.

11. **Machinery Co-insurance Clause.** In the event of a claim for loss of or damage to any boiler, shaft, machinery or associated equipment, arising from any of the causes enumerated in Clause 7 (*a*), attributable in part or in whole to the negligence of Master, Officers or Crew and recoverable under this insurance only by reason of Clause 7, then the Assured shall, in addition to the deductible, also bear in

respect of each accident or occurrence an amount equal to 10% of the balance of such claim. This clause shall not apply to a claim for total or constructive total loss of the vessel.

e.g. Claim for machinery damage caused by negligence £6,000
      Policy deductible (Clause 12)   say £1,000
                                                            £5,000
      Machinery Co-insurance deductible 10%   £500
                                          Nett Claim   £4,500

12. **Deductible Average Clause.** No claim arising from a peril insured against shall be payable under this insurance unless the aggregate of all such claims arising out of each separate accident or occurrence (including claims under the Running Down and Suing and Labouring Clauses) exceeds (*the agreed sum is here written in*) in which case this sum shall be deducted. Nevertheless the expense of sighting the bottom after stranding, if reasonably incurred specially for that purpose, shall be paid even if no damage be found. This paragraph shall not apply to a claim for total or constructive total loss of the vessel.

Claims for damage by heavy weather occurring during a single sea passage between two successive ports shall be treated as being due to one accident. In the case of such heavy weather extending over a period not wholly covered by this insurance the deductible to be applied to the claim recoverable hereunder shall be the proportion of the above deductible that the number of days of such heavy weather falling within the period of this insurance bears to the number of days of heavy weather during the single sea passage.

The expression "heavy weather" in the preceding paragraph shall be deemed to include contact with floating ice.

Excluding any interest comprised therein, recoveries against any claim which is subject to the above deductible shall be credited to the Underwriters in full to the extent of the sum by which the aggregate of the claim unreduced by any recoveries exceeds the above deductible.

Interest comprised in recoveries shall be apportioned between the Assured and the Underwriters, taking into account the sums paid by Underwriters and the dates when such payments were made, notwithstanding that by the addition of interest the Underwriters may receive a larger sum than they have paid.

13. **Grounding Clause.** This provides that grounding in certain canals or in parts of certain rivers, etc., where minor strandings are fairly commonplace, shall not be deemed to be a stranding, and hence underwriters will not pay the cost of sighting the bottom following a grounding in such an area.

14. No claim shall in any case be allowed in respect of scraping or painting the vessel's bottom.

15. No claim shall be allowed in particular average for wages and maintenance of the Master, Officers and Crew, or any member thereof, except when incurred solely for the necessary removal of the vessel from one port to another for repairs, or for trial trips for average repairs, and then only for such wages and maintenance as are incurred whilst the vessel is under way.

However, this policy shall bear only that proportion of such wages and maintenance that the cost of repairs at the repair port recoverable under this policy bears to the total cost of work done at the repair port.

16. This clause states that underwriters will not be liable for unrepaired damage in addition to a subsequent total loss sustained during the period of cover.

17. **Valuation Clause.** The Marine Insurance Act provides that a ship becomes a constructive total loss when she is so damaged by a peril insured against that the cost of repairing the damage would exceed the value of the ship "when repaired". To avoid the difficulty that would arise in making an accurate assessment of the repaired value of a damaged ship, the "valuation clause" provides that in ascertaining whether a vessel is a constructive total loss the insured value shall be taken as the repaired value, and that nothing in respect of the break-up value shall be taken into account. No claim for C.T.L. based upon the cost of recovery and/or repair shall be recoverable unless such cost would exceed the insured value.

18. **Freight Abandonment Clause.** It has been known for hull underwriters, under their right of subrogation after paying a constructive loss total of the ship, to forward the cargo to its destination and collect the freight so earned. As the freight had been earned, the shipowner had no claim against his freight underwriters for a total loss of freight, which was not lost to the shipowner through a peril insured against. To avoid difficulties of this nature, Clause 18 provides that in the event of actual or constructive total loss no claim shall be made by underwriters for freight whether notice of abandonment has been given or not.

19. **Tender Clause.** This has been referred to in Chapter 17 in connection with accidents to ships and port of refuge procedure. The clause provides that in the event of an accident giving rise to a claim, notice shall be given to underwriters before survey, or to the nearest Lloyd's agent if the ship is abroad, so that an underwriters' surveyor can be appointed if desired. Underwriters have power to decide the repair port and to veto any port or repairing firm. They may take tenders or require them to be taken. Any additional expense incurred to comply with underwriters' requirements will be refunded to the assured. On the other hand, in the event of

failure to comply with the conditions of this clause, 15 per cent. will be deducted from the amount of the claim.

20. **Disbursements Clause.** This clause enumerates what additional insurances are permitted over and above the agreed value of hull and machinery, etc. Such additional insurances are in respect of (a) disbursements, managers' commissions, profits or excess or increased value of hull and machinery; (b) freight, chartered freight or anticipated freight, insured for time; (c) freight or hire under contracts for voyage; (d) anticipated freight if vessel sails in ballast not under charter; (e) charter hire for series of voyages; (f) premiums; (g) returns of premiums; (h) risks excluded by the F.C. & S. clause, and risks enumerated in the Institute War and Strike clauses. Item (a) is restricted to a sum not exceeding 10 per cent. of the hull, etc., valuation. Item (b) is restricted to a sum not exceeding 25 per cent. of that valuation less the sum insured under (a). Items (c), (d), (e), and (f) are also subject to certain restrictions, but item (h) allows insurance irrespective of amount. It is warranted that no other insurance on P.P.I. terms shall be effected by or on account of the assured during the currency of the policy. The object of this clause is to secure an adequate insured value in a hull policy. Without it an owner might be induced to insure his vessel on a low valuation thereby obtaining full cover against particular average losses up to the limit of the sum insured, and then obtain full protection against total loss by effecting a further insurance on limited conditions at a relatively low premium rate for the balance of the sum he wished to cover.

21. **Returns Clause.** This clause, sometimes known as the "lying up clause", stipulates what percentage of the premium is returnable (a) if the policy be cancelled by agreement, (b) if the vessel be laid up in a port or lay-up area approved by the underwriters, and thereby not exposed to certain of the perils insured against. The percentage returnable in the case of a laid up vessel will vary according to whether she is under repair or not. Reference to the clause will show that some of its provisions are qualified by the phrase "and arrival". The meaning of this phrase is "subject to the vessel not having become a total loss during the period covered by the policy". In other words, if a total loss indemnity is paid during the currency of the policy no return of premium can be claimed in respect of either (a) the period between the time of the loss and the date of expiration of the policy, or (b) any period during which the vessel may have been laid up before the loss occurred. It is the practice that cancellation and lying up returns are not collected until after the normal expiry of the policy.

22. This provides that underwriters will not recognise any assignment of the policy unless such assignment is endorsed on the policy and is signed by the assured. But this does not affect the terms of Clause 6.

Clauses 23, 24 and 25 are preceded by the statement "Unless deleted by the Underwriters the following clauses shall be paramount and shall override anything contained in this insurance inconsistent therewith."

23. Free of Capture and Seizure clause (F.C. & S. clause).

This reads: Warranted free of capture, seizure, arrest, restraint or detainment, and the consequences thereof or of any attempt thereat; also from the consequences of hostilities or warlike operation, whether there be a declaration of war or not; but this warranty shall not exclude collision, contact with any fixed or floating object (other than a mine or torpedo), stranding, heavy weather or fire unless caused directly (and independently of the nature of the voyage or service which the vessel concerned or, in the case of a collision, any other vessel involved therein, is performing) by a hostile act by or against a belligerent power; and for the purpose of this warranty "power" includes any authority maintaining naval, military or air forces in association with a power.

Further warranted free from the consequences of civil war, revolution, rebellion, insurrection, or civil strife arising therefrom, or piracy.

It will be recalled that the Marine Insurance Act includes war perils within the meaning of the term "maritime perils", and the S.G. policy includes amongst the perils insured against men of war, enemies, arrests, etc., of kings, princes and people. At one time it was the custom for war risks to be covered by the ordinary marine policy, but in more recent times such risks have generally been excluded. Whilst the F.C. & S. clause is designed to remove war risks from the scope of the policy, it will be obvious from the wording above that the assured remains covered against the ordinary marine perils during wartime. The subject of war risk insurance is dealt with in a separate section at the end of this Chapter.

24. This clause reads: Warranted free from loss damage liability or expense arising from (a) the detonation of an explosive, (b) any weapon of war, and caused by any person acting maliciously or from a political motive.

25. Reads: Warranted free from loss damage liability or expense arising from any weapon of war employing atomic or nuclear fission and/or fusion or other like reaction of radioactive force or matter.

Institute Cargo Clauses. These will be found in Appendix where it will be seen that the three sets (All risks, F.P.A., and W.A.) are almost identical except for Clause 5. The individual clauses are commented on briefly, as follows:

1. Transit Clause (incorporating Warehouse to Warehouse Clause). Lloyd's S.G. policy provides, with respect to goods, for the risk to attach "from the loading thereof aboard the said ship" and for the insurance to continue until the goods are discharged and safely landed at the port of discharge. Modern trading conditions call for a policy which provides cover during the entire period of transit, for which reason this clause is designed to extend the period of cover from the time the goods leave the exporter's warehouse until they are delivered to the importer's warehouse at the named destination, or to any other warehouse, whether prior to or at the named destination, which the assured elect to use either for storage or for allocation or distribution, or on the expiry of 60 days after discharge from the oversea vessel at the final port of discharge, whichever first occurs. If, after discharge at the final port but prior to the termination of the insurance, the goods are to be forwarded to a destination other than the one named, the insurance, whilst subject to termination as above, does not extend beyond the commencement of transit to such other destination. However, the insurance will remain in force, subject to termination as above and the provisions of Clause 2, during delay beyond the control of the assured, deviation, forced discharge, re-shipment, transhipment, and during any other variation of the adventure arising from the exercise of a liberty granted by the contract of affreightment.

2. **Termination of Adventure Clause.** This describes in what circumstances the insurance shall remain in force, subject to notice being given and additional premium being paid if required, should the contract of affreightment be terminated elsewhere than at the destination named in the policy or otherwise terminated before delivery of the goods into the consignee's warehouse, owing to circumstances beyond the control of the assured.

3. **Craft, Etc., Clause.** It is normal for lighters to attempt to contract out of their liability for loss of or damage to goods arising from negligence. Ordinarily, where a goods owner makes such a contract with a lighterman, that is a material circumstance that he should disclose to his underwriter who, in the event of a loss, may be seriously prejudiced by having no right of recovery from the lighter owner. As such contracts are so general, however, disclosure is waived and the practice is formally recognised by virtue of this clause which provides for the insurance to include transit by craft, raft and/or lighter to and from the vessel. Moreover, each craft, etc., is deemed a separate insurance. Hence, if part of a shipment of goods is completely lost through the sinking of a lighter, the assured would have a claim for the total loss of that part.

4. **Change of Voyage Clause.** Section 45 of the Marine Insurance Act provides that where there is a change of voyage then, unless the policy otherwise provides, the insurer is discharged from liability as from the time of the change. Through this clause the policy does provide otherwise, and the event is held covered at a premium to

be arranged. The same provision is made in the case of any omission or error in the description of the interest, vessel or voyage.

5. **All Risks Clause.** (For the All Risks policy.) This provides that the insurance is against all risks of loss of or damage to the subject-matter insured (excluding only loss, etc., proximately caused by delay or inherent vice) and that claims are payable irrespective of percentage.

F.P.A. Clause. (For the F.P.A. Policy.) Previously referred to.

Average Clause. (For the W.A. policy.)

6. **Constructive Total Loss Clause.** This provides that damaged goods cannot be the subject of a claim for C.T.L. unless they are reasonably abandoned on account of their actual total loss appearing unavoidable, or the cost of recovering, reconditioning, and forwarding would exceed the value of the goods on arrival at the named destination.

7. **General Average Clause.** This provides that G/A and salvage charges are payable according to Foreign Statement or to York-Antwerp Rules if in accordance with the contract of affreightment.

8. **Seaworthiness Admitted Clause.** The reason for this clause has been given in the section on implied warranties.

9. **Bailee Clause.** This places the duty on the assured to take reasonable measures to avert or minimise losses and ensure that rights against third parties are properly preserved and exercised.

10. **Not to Inure Clause.** This states that the insurance shall not inure (*i.e.*, take effect) to the benefit of the carrier or other bailee.

11. **"Both to Blame Collision" Clause.** This extends the policy to indemnifying the assured against such proportion of liability under the bill of lading "Both to Blame Collision" Clause as is, in respect of a loss, recoverable under the policy. In the event of a claim by shipowners under the "Both to Blame Collision" Clause, the assured agree to notify underwriters who retain the right at their own expense to defend the assured against such claim.

12. **F.C. & S. Clause.** This is the same as the F.C. & S. Clause in a hull policy. A goods owner, however, may require to insure against war risks. It is therefore provided that should Clause No. 12 be deleted, the current Institute War Clauses shall be deemed to form part of the contract.

13. **F.S.R. & C.C. Clause.** This relieves the underwriters from liability for loss or damage (*a*) caused by strikers, locked-out workmen, or persons taking part in labour disturbances, riots or

civil commotions; (*b*) resulting from strikes, lock-outs, labour disturbances, riots or civil commotions. As the assured may wish to have cover against such risks, it is provided that should Clause No. 13 be deleted the current Institute Strikes Clauses shall be deemed to form part of the contract.

14. Reasonable Despatch Clause. This makes it a condition of the insurance that the assured shall act with reasonable despatch in all circumstances within their control.

MARINE LOSSES

Marine losses may be classified as follows:

Total loss	Actual Presumed Constructive
Partial loss	Particular Average General Average

Actual Total Loss occurs when the subject-matter is destroyed, or is so damaged as to cease to be a thing of the kind insured, or when the assured is irretrievably deprived of it.

Presumed Total Loss. When the ship concerned in the adventure is missing her total loss may, after the lapse of a reasonable time, be presumed. Ordinarily, it will be presumed that the loss arose from "peril of the sea" which is an ordinary marine risk. But if the ship was last known to have been in a war-infested area then, in the absence of other evidence, the presumption will be that she was lost through war risk.

Constructive Total Loss. This occurs when the subject-matter is reasonably abandoned on account of its actual total loss appearing to be unavoidable, or because it could not be preserved from actual total loss without an expenditure that would exceed its value after the expenditure had been incurred.

In case of constructive total loss the assured may either treat the loss as a partial loss, or abandon the subject-matter to the underwriters and claim for total loss. If he elects to abandon he must serve notice of abandonment on the underwriters, otherwise the loss can be treated only as a partial loss.

Notice may be given in any manner, but it must indicate the intention of the assured to abandon his interest in the subject-matter to the insurer unconditionally. It must be given with reasonable diligence after receipt of reliable information of the loss but the assured is entitled to a reasonable time to make inquiry if his information is of a doubtful character.

The acceptance of an abandonment may be either expressed or implied from the conduct of the insurer (but see "Waiver" clause).

The mere silence of the insurer after notice is not an acceptance.

Notice of abandonment is not necessary:

(a) if it would be of no possible benefit to underwriters at the time when the assured receives information of the loss;

(b) if underwriters waive the notice;

(c) in respect of re-insurance.

Once the notice is accepted it cannot be revoked, and acceptance admits both liability and the sufficiency of the notice.

Where there is a valid abandonment the insurer is entitled to take over all the interests of the assured in whatever remains of the subject-matter and all propriety rights incidental thereto. By the Marine Insurance Act this right of subrogation extends to the freight in course of being earned by a ship abandoned to underwriters, but in practice underwriters relinquish this right in accordance with Clause 18 of the Institute Hull Clauses.

Where underwriters decline to accept abandonment the assured, to legalise his abandonment and enforce his claim, is obliged to issue a writ against the underwriters, and the circumstances prevailing at the time when the writ is issued are those which determine whether or not there is a constructive total loss. In practice underwriters always decline, in the first instance, to accept the abandonment, and to save the assured the costs and trouble of taking legal proceedings an undertaking is given by underwriters that the assured will be placed in the same position as if a writ had been issued on the day when the abandonment was declined.

Whilst the underwriter is entitled to take over the abandoned property, it does not follow that he must, and in some cases it would not be in his best interests to do so. For instance, if a ship became a constructive total loss in a place where she is a menace to navigation, it would obviously be better for the underwriter to admit the loss and pay the claim for total loss, but at the same time to refuse acceptance of the abandonment and leave the assured to bear the cost of removing the wreck. It follows that if the underwriter takes over the rights remaining in and attached to the abandoned property he must take over the liabilities as well.

Particular Average Loss. This is defined by the Marine Insurance Act as a partial loss of the subject-matter insured caused by a peril insured against which is not a general average loss. It may, perhaps, be more directly described as a partial loss arising from any kind of accident. General average sacrifices and expenditures, particular charges, and salvage charges do not arise by accident and, therefore, are not included in particular average. A particular average loss falls directly upon the party interested in the subject-matter. In the case of accidental or fortuitous damage to the ship it is the shipowner or, to the extent that he is insured against such loss, his underwriters who must bear the loss. Similarly, in the case of accidental damage to cargo, the loss rests with the cargo owner or his underwriters.

There are innumerable varieties of particular average, including, such things as:

straining of ship in bad weather,

loss of masts or spars through heavy weather,

damage to hull, machinery, or cargo due to heavy weather or fire,

damage to ship or cargo due to collision or stranding.

If a particular average loss arises in respect of ship or cargo protest should be noted and the damage should be surveyed on the ship's behalf. The surveyor's report should give full details of the damage.

Where the ship is damaged the underwriters or the nearest Lloyd's agent should be informed without delay to conform with the requirements of the "Tender" clause.

In the case of P/A damage to cargo, the surveyor's report should indicate:

the cause and nature of the damage;

the gross sound market value of the goods duty paid at port of destination;

the gross proceeds of any damaged goods sold;

the agreed amount of depreciation of damaged goods not sold;

the costs of sale, if any;

the charges incurred in survey.

Sections 69, 70 and 71 of the Marine Insurance Act define the measure of indemnity in the case of partial loss of ship, freight, and goods, respectively. In particular, the following provisions are made:

Ship: Where the ship has been repaired, the assured is entitled to the reasonable cost of the repairs, less the customary deductions, but not exceeding the sum insured in respect of any one casualty. (This is modified, however, by Clause 10 of the Institute Hulls Clauses providing that average, whether particular or general, shall be paid without deductions "new for old".)

Where the ship has been only partially repaired, the assured is entitled to the reasonable cost of such repairs, computed as above, and also to be indemnified for the reasonable depreciation, if any, arising from the unrepaired damage, provided that the aggregate amount shall not exceed the cost of repairing the whole damage, computed as above.

Where the ship has not been repaired, and has not been sold in her damaged state during the risk, the assured is entitled to be indemnified for the reasonable depreciation arising from the unrepaired damage, but not exceeding the reasonable cost of repairing such damage, computed as above.

Freight: Subject to any express provision in the policy, where there is a partial loss of freight, the measure of indemnity is such proportion of the sum fixed by the policy in the case of a valued policy, or of the insurable value in the case of an unvalued policy, as the proportion of freight lost by the assured bears to the whole freight at the risk of the assured under the policy.

Goods: Where there is a partial loss of goods, merchandise, or other moveables, the measure of indemnity, subject to any express provision in the policy, is as follows:—

(1) Where part of the goods, etc., insured by a valued policy is totally lost, the measure of indemnity is such proportion of the sum fixed by the policy as the insurable value of the part lost bears to the insurable value of the whole, ascertained as in the case of an unvalued policy.

(2) Where part of the goods, etc., insured by an unvalued policy is totally lost, the measure of indemnity is the insurable value of the part lost, ascertained as in case of total loss.

(3) Where the whole or any part of the goods, etc., insured has been delivered damaged at its destination, the measure of indemnity is such proportion of the sum fixed by the policy in the case of a valued policy, or of the insurable value in the case of an unvalued policy, as the difference between the gross sound and damaged values at the place of arrival bears to the gross sound value.

(4) "Gross value" means the wholesale price, or, if there be no such price, the estimated value, with, in either case, freight, landing charges, and duty paid beforehand; provided that, in the case of goods or merchandise customarily sold in bond, the bonded price is deemed to be the gross value. 'Gross proceeds" means the actual price obtained at a sale where all charges on sale are paid by the sellers.

Adjustment of particular average by comparing *gross* sound and damaged values is a long-established principle to which the Act gives statutory effect. By adhering to that principle underwriters avoid additional losses due to fluctuations in market values because prices realised by both sound and damaged goods rise and fall in sympathy. If net values, obtained by deducting freight and other fixed charges, were made the basis of comparison, not only would the underwriter's liability be increased, but it would vary according to whether the goods arrived on a steady, rising, or falling market.

As already mentioned in the section on "franchises" it is, of course, essential that the damage should have reached any franchise stipulated in the policy in order to substantiate a claim for any particular average loss.

General Average Loss. This is defined as a partial loss caused by, or following as a direct consequence of, a general average act.

The statutory definition of the term general average act is, of course, the one contained in section 66 of the Marine Insurance Act, viz.: There is a general average act where any extraordinary sacrifice or expenditure is voluntarily and reasonably made or incurred in time of peril for the purpose of preserving the property imperilled in the common adventure.

The definition which constitutes Rule A of the York-Antwerp Rules is as follows:

"There is a general average act when, and only when, any extraordinary sacrifice or expenditure is intentionally and reasonably made or incurred for the common safety for the purpose of preserving from peril the property involved in a common maritime adventure."

It is important to bear in mind that before any question of general average can arise:

1. The sacrifice or expenditure must be of an extraordinary nature. Damage to a ship, her machinery, or equipment whilst being used for the purpose for which they are intended would not amount to general average. On the other hand, using a ship's engines in an effort to refloat when stranded would, if the engines were damaged as a result, be an extraordinary sacrifice.

2. There must be a **common** adventure. That is to say, the ship, freight and cargo must all be involved. In any case, there must be more than one interest.

3. The common adventure must be in **peril**. That is, all interests must be imperilled.

4. There must be a **sacrifice** (of property) or an **expenditure** (of money).

5. The sacrifice or expenditure must be made or incurred **reasonably** and **intentionally** for the **sole** purpose of preserving the adventure from the immediate peril.

General average acts include such things as:

Putting into a port of refuge to effect necessary repairs.

Voluntary stranding to avoid sinking.

Working of engines when a steamship is ashore in a position of peril.

General average sacrifices include:

Jettison, for the common safety, of cargo from under deck.

Jettison of cargo from the deck if carried on deck by virtue of a well recognised custom of the trade.

Slipping of anchor and cable to avert fire or other imminent peril.

Cutting away of masts and spars to right a ship dangerously listed or on her beam ends.

General average expenditures include:

Cost of discharging cargo to refloat a stranded ship or to carry out necessary repairs at a port of refuge.

Hire of tug to assist refloating a stranded ship with cargo.

Wages and provisions of crew during period of delay at a port of refuge if York-Antwerp Rules apply.

It should be noted that a general average act embraces both a general average sacrifice and a general average expenditure.

When there is a general average loss the party on whom it falls is entitled to a rateable contribution from the other interested parties. The parties benefiting by the sacrifice or expenditure may be (1) the shipowner, for the value of the ship saved; (2) cargo owners, for the value of their cargo saved; (3) the shipowner, in respect of freight payable by charter-party or bills of lading or charter hire money; and (4) the charterer, under a time charter, for freight payable under bills of lading. Each will be called upon to contribute according to the value of his interest saved as a result of the sacrifice or expenditure. The main contributing interests are, therefore, ship, freight, and cargo. Broadly speaking, all these contribute on their net values at the place where the voyage ends or is abandoned. Such values are called "contributory values". The sum necessary to reimburse the interest which has suffered the general average loss is called the "amount made good" or "general average allowance".

It is important that the amount made good should itself contribute to the loss. Otherwise the interest making the sacrifice or incurring the expenditure would be relatively better off by being fully reimbursed for a loss which other interests are helping to bear.

Contributory values are:

Ship: Her value to her owners in the arrived condition at the place where the voyage ends. If damaged, her sound value is first assessed. The cost of repairs is then deducted and the G/A allowance is added.

Freight: The gross amount at risk and earned, less the expenses of earning it from the date of the G/A act, plus the G/A allowance. (Any freight paid in advance is not at risk and is merged in the value of the cargo. If the ship is in ballast but under charter, the chartered freight contributes.)

Cargo: The market value, sound or damaged, on arrival at the place where the voyage ends, less freight and other charges payable on delivery which would not have been incurred had the adventure been a total loss, plus the G/A allowance.

Amounts made good are:

Ship: The reasonable cost of repairing the damage, less deductions "'new for old".

Freight: The gross freight lost by the sacrifice of goods, less any charges saved. Any additional freight earned by carrying other goods in place of those sacrificed must be credited.

Cargo: For goods lost the allowance is the net value they would have had on the day of discharge at the place where the voyage ends, less freight and other charges that would have been payable had the goods not been sacrificed. If the remaining cargo arrives damaged from causes that would equally have affected the sacrificed goods, the probable extent of such damage must be taken into account.

For goods arriving damaged through general average sacrifice the allowance is the difference between the net sound and damaged values.

Where claims for general average contribution have arisen the amounts of such contribution are usually ascertained at the port of first discharge. The shipowner has the duty of appointing the Average Adjuster and of collecting the contributions due from the various cargo owners. As explained in Chapter 2, the ship has a common law lien on cargo for G/A contributions.

An average adjuster is a kind of arbitrator, with an expert knowledge of the law and practice relating to insurance and average whose task it is to decide what is and what is not by law or contract allowable in general average, and to assess the various contributory values and general average allowances. The outcome of his findings, is called the "Average Statement" and in a complex case may take many months to prepare. Professional adjusters will be found in all the major ports of the world, but it is not essential for the shipowner to appoint an adjuster practising in the port where the adventure ends. To enable the adjuster to carry out his task he will require to be supplied with all the relevant documents. Precisely what he will need in this respect will, of course, depend upon the nature of the case, but the following items will generally be necessary

1. A manifest of the cargo on board at the time of the occurrence giving rise to the general average act.
2. Copies of the bill of lading forms used for the cargo.
3. The signed average bonds.
4. Counterfoils of general average deposit receipts. These should indicate the identification marks and numbers of the cargo and the numbers of the bills of lading to which the deposits apply.
5. Copies of general average guarantees, if any, signed by bankers or underwriters.
6. The deck and engine room log books in respect of the voyage during which the general average act occurred, or adequate and duly certified extracts therefrom.
7. Copies of extended protests.
8. Original vouchers in respect of an additional expenses incurred, such as port of refuge expenses, extra bunkers, and so on.
9. The portage account for the voyage, or other details of the wages and maintenance of master and crew, and an account of stores consumed during the voyage.

10. Damage survey reports in respect of any hull and/or machinery damage. Such reports should differentiate carefully between G/A sacrifices, P/A damage, and ordinary wear and tear.
11. The original accounts for any hull and/or machinery repairs and expenses incidental thereto.
12. Survey reports giving details of any cargo lost or damaged by G/A sacrifice, stating how the cargo was disposed of and what allowances for loss or damage, if any, were agreed.
13. The account sales of any cargo sold on the recommendation of a surveyor.
14. Copies of shipping invoices.

Owing to the time required for general average adjustment in order to avoid delay in delivering the cargo and consequent loss, it is usual for cargo owners (or their underwriters) to provide some form of security in order to obtain release of their cargo. The shipowner or average adjuster will advise the master or agents of the form the security is to take. It will usually consist of an **average bond** signed by each receiver of cargo, and in addition, a **cash deposit** calculated at a certain percentage of the goods' value, or an **underwriter's guarantee**, or a **bank guarantee**. If the shipowner so decides, in some instances the additional security may be dispensed with and cargo delivered upon the signature on the average bond only. The form of bond in general use is Lloyd's Average Bond, the form of which is shown in Appendix IX and is in two parts. The top part is the average bond which should be signed and returned to the ship's agent to obtain release of the cargo. After he has received the cargo and ascertained its condition, the receiver of the cargo should complete the bottom page which is a Valuation Form and return it to the agents or average adjuster with a copy of the commercial invoice sent to him. Where a cash deposit is required, it will be placed in a separate account, bearing interest where possible, generally in the joint names of the shipowner or their agents representing their own interests, and Lloyd's Agents, representing cargo interests. Receipts for deposits must only be issued on Lloyd's form (see Appendix X) and a separate receipt (if practicable) should be given by the cargo covered by each B/L. When the average statement is eventually produced and settlement is made, any excess of contribution deposited is returned to the cargo owner (or underwriter) concerned together with its share of the accrued interest.

The master of a ship should never deliver cargo which is liable for a general average contribution until he is satisfied that such contribution is adequately secured by bond or deposit or both. In foreign ports especially, and in all cases where the ship has suffered a G/A loss the extent of which is difficult to assess (for instance, when a hold has been flooded for the common safety, say, to extinguish a fire), the master should insist on a deposit which he would judge to be more than the consignee will ultimately be called upon to pay. The consignee will not lose by it in the long run, but once the cargo has been parted with the shipowner's right of lien is lost.

Settlement of General Average. Unless the contract of carriage provides otherwise, the rule is that general average is settled in accordance with the law and practice of the place where the adventure ends, that is to say, the place where the cargo is discharged. Evidently, if a ship had a mixed cargo for discharge in ports in several different countries, the case would be affected by several different national law systems, and adjustment and settlement would become excessively complicated. To avoid such a state of affairs it is usual for charter-parties and bills of lading to be claused to the effect that "General average is to be settled according to York-Antwerp Rules, 1974". These rules, briefly referred to below, are reproduced fully in Appendix III.

In modern practice, when insured property suffers a general average loss, it is customary for underwriters to make good the loss as particular average in the first place. They then, being subrogated to all rights and remedies of the assured so far as the latter have been indemnified, are afterwards reimbursed out of the general average fund. In effect, all general average settlements are in the long run made between underwriters.

York-Antwerp Rules. The basic principle of general average is that a person whose property is sacrificed for the general benefit should have his loss made good by all those who have benefited, and this principle has been put into practice for many centuries. It was recognised by the merchants of Tyre and Sidon and probably by all the early Mediterranean maritime communities. Long before marine insurance was known Roman law contained provisions for settling general average claims, and since the days of the Roman Empire the principles of the law relating to general average have been common to all maritime countries. However, certain differences of detail exist in the laws of various countries and these differences can give rise to uncertainty and complication when adjustments take place in more than one country. For this reason shipowners, merchants, underwriters, and adjusters have collaborated to produce a standard set of rules which can be incorporated by agreement into any contract of affreightment. Even now, if these rules are not so incorporated, the general law still prevails. The rules originally drawn up in 1860 were known as the Glasgow Resolutions, but they were followed in 1864 by what were then called the York Rules. Modifications to the York Rules were approved at a meeting held at Antwerp in 1877, and the amended rules became the York-Antwerp Rules. This title still holds good although changing circumstances have necessitated further amendments being made as a result of conferences held at Liverpool in 1890, Stockholm in 1924, Amsterdam in 1950, and Hamburg in 1974.

These 1974 rules consist of seven rules lettered A to G covering general principles, and twenty-two numbered rules covering special circumstances.

Comparison of Y-A Rules and English Law on G/A. The main difference is that the Y-A Rules provide a set code of rules, whereas English law on G/A never has been codified but is part of the common law. There is also an important difference in principle. The view taken by the constructors of the Y-A Rules is that any sacrifice or expenditure is allowable as general average so long as it follows as a direct consequence of a G/A act. By contrast, the common law of England has always held that G/A ceases to apply once the adventure is no longer in peril. This affects the treatment of port of refuge expenses. By the Y-A Rules the costs of reloading and stowing cargo and stores discharged for the purpose of effecting necessary repairs, and all outward expenses from the port up to the time of the vessel regaining her contract route, are allowed as G/A. By English law this is not so, because as soon as the necessary repairs are completed the adventure is deemed to be no longer in peril. In spite of this, however, it appears that it has long been the practice of average adjusters in England to allow such expenses as G/A although their doing so has, of course, been challengeable at law.

Suggestions to Abolish G/A. It has been mentioned that in modern practice the long-term settlement of G/A is usually settlement between underwriters who have previously made good the losses involved as P/A. From time to time the suggestion has been put forward that, such being the case, the principle of G/A has outlived its usefulness and, with all its complications, might well be abolished. There would seem to be, however, at least two grave objections to the idea. One is the difficulty of reaching international agreement on such a drastic proposition. If some countries agreed to abolish G/A whilst others insisted on retaining it, the situation would be even more complicated than it is now. The other objection is the invidious position in which the master of a ship would be placed in, in the "agony of the moment", he had to stop to consider whose interests he should sacrifice. As it is, he is free to take whatever steps he, as the man in charge and on the spot, feels to be best for the preservation of the adventure as a whole.

MISCELLANEOUS MARINE INSURANCE TOPICS

Burning Cargo as Fuel. Rule IX of the Y-A Rules provides that ship's materials and stores burnt as fuel for the common safety are admitted as G/A so long as an ample fuel supply had been provided. But the cost of the extra fuel that would have been consumed must be credited. No specific mention of cargo is made in this rule, but the burning of cargo in similar circumstances is considered to be a G/A act, and is covered by the general Rule A.

Claims Documents. In order to substantiate a claim on under-writers various documents will be required, as the onus of proving loss or damage sustained rests on the assured. The documents needed will depend upon the type of claim and whether the insurance is on ship, freight, or cargo.

In the case of a hull claim there would generally be required:

The hull policy.

The average statement, even where there are P/A claims only, incorporating deck and engine room log extracts, surveyors' reports (owner's, underwriters', and classification society's), repair specifications, details of any tenders taken, receipted accounts for repairs, and other disbursement vouchers.

Copies of extended protests, if any.

In the case of cargo P/A claims there would be required:

The cargo policy.

The bill (or bills) of lading showing the terms and conditions of the contract of carriage and the apparent order and condition of the goods at time of shipment.

The surveyor's certificate showing the cause of the loss or damage, the gross sound and damaged values of the goods, and other details.

The account sales showing the proceeds of any damaged goods sold.

A letter of subrogation signed by the assured giving under-writers authority to sue in the name of the assured if there is a possibility of recovery from the shipowner or other third party.

The assured must supply all the necessary evidence to prove that the proximate cause of the loss or damage is one or other of the perils insured against. If underwriters disclaim liability on the grounds that the vessel was unseaworthy, the onus rests on them to prove such allegation. In the case of a cargo claim where the policy has the "seaworthiness admitted" clause, underwriters must first indemnify the assured before they can themselves claim against the shipowner under their right of subrogation.

Deck Cargo. As stated in Chapter 9, loss by jettison of cargo carried on deck is not made good by G/A contributions unless it is so carried by established custom. Where the entire cargo is the property of one owner who has expressly agreed to part of it being on deck, jettison of the deck cargo will give rise to a G/A claim against the ship. Cargo carried on deck by agreement between the shipper and the shipowner and jettisoned for the common safety will give rise to a G/A contribution from the shipowner, but not from the owners of other cargo carried under deck unless they have consented to the jettisoned cargo being on deck. It may be that such consent could be implied if all B's/L reserved the liberty to carry goods on deck.   No jettison of deck cargo is allowed in G/A if the goods are on deck "at shipper's risk".

Different Voyage.   If a vessel sails on a voyage different from that described in the policy, the risk does not attach and the premium paid is returnable on the grounds that there has been failure of consideration.   This, it should be noted, is quite distinct from either "deviation" or "change of voyage".   Deviation has already been defined, and there is a change of voyage where, after the commencement of the risk, the destination of the ship is voluntarily changed from the destination contemplated by the policy.   Unless the policy otherwise provides, where there is a change of voyage, the insurer is discharged from liability as from the time of the change, i.e. as from the time when the determination to change it is manifested; and it is immaterial that the ship may not in fact have left the course of the voyage contemplated by the policy when the loss occurs.

Double Insurance.   An assured is said to be over-insured by double insurance when two or more policies are effected by him, or on his behalf, on the same adventure and interest so that the total sums insured exceed the measure of indemnity.   Unless the policy provides otherwise, he may claim from insurers in such order as he thinks fit, but is not entitled to receive any sum in excess of the measure of indemnity.   In the case of a valued policy he must give credit as against the valuation for any sum received under any other policy without regard to the actual value of the subject-matter insured.   Where he receives any sum in excess of the measure of indemnity, he is deemed to hold such sum in trust for the insurers according to their right of contribution among themselves.

It is not common for double insurance to occur except through inadvertence, say, where shipper and consignee unknown to each other insure the same shipment of goods, and the former assigns his policy to the latter.   When this is discovered it is the custom for each underwriter to reduce his policy by half and return half the premium to the assured.   If an assured, because he has reason to doubt the security of his underwriters, insures the same risk with other underwriters, no return of premium can be recovered in respect of the double insurance.

Dry Dock Expenses.   If a ship is dry docked for repairs which are for the underwriters' account, the shipowner is entitled to avail himself of the opportunity to have other repairs executed for his own account provided such repairs are not immediately necessary for maintaining the seaworthiness of the vessel.   Repairs which are necessary to make the vessel seaworthy come under a Rule of Practice of the Association of Average Adjusters.   The rule is:

(a) "Where repairs on Owner's account which are immediately necessary to make the vessel seaworthy and which can only be effected in dry-dock are executed concurrently with other repairs, for the cost of which the underwriters are liable, and which also can only be effected in dry-dock,

(b) Where the repairs, for the cost of which the underwriters are liable, are deferred until a routine drydocking and are then executed concurrently with repairs on Owner's account which require the use of the drydock, whether or not such owners' repairs affect the seaworthiness of the vessel. The cost of entering and leaving the dry-dock, in addition to so much of the dock dues as is common to both repairs, shall be divided equally between the Shipowner and the Underwriters, irrespective of the fact that the repairs for which Underwriters are liable may relate to more than one voyage or accident or may be payable by more than one set of Underwriters."

Dual Valuation Clause. If the insured value of a ship is agreed at a very low figure, underwriters may find themselves liable for a constructive total loss which, had a higher agreed value been fixed, would have been merely a substantial partial loss. On the other hand, where a high figure is agreed underwriters have to face a heavy liability if a total loss does occur. To counter these disadvantages it is frequently the case that a hull policy will include a "dual valuation" clause providing for two valuations, viz., a relatively low one more or less consistent with the actual market value of the ship and to be used as the basis of liability for total loss, and a higher one on which all claims other than total loss claims are to be based. The higher value has the effect of maintaining the franchise for particular average purposes at a reasonable level.

Fleet Insurances. When an entire fleet of vessels in the same ownership is insured on an original slip, the fleet is usually covered for a period of twelve months. It is not necessarily the case, however, that policies on individual vessels will all commence on the same date. Separate slips are required for placing additional risks such as disbursements, freight, charter hire, premiums, etc., which run concurrently with the hull insurances. An insured value is first agreed between the owners and underwriters for each vessel in the fleet, also the premium rate which will depend upon the underwriters' assessment of the quality of management, past claims experience, the manner of employment of the ships, and other considerations. The broker will approach a leading underwriter who may be expected to write a "line" on the highest valued vessel on the slip and a *pro rata* line on each of the other vessels. Following underwriters do likewise with the result that liability is graded from a maximum on the most valuable units of the fleet down to a minimum on the older and less highly valued vessels.

Foreign General Average Clause. (See Clause 8 of the Institute Hull Clauses and Clause 7 of the Institute Cargo Clauses.)

Although underwriters are liable for general average, it does not follow that they will agree to be bound by an adjustment secured by a B/L clause which is particularly favourable to the shipowner. Hence, in a hull policy it is provided that G/A is to be adjusted according to the law and practice at the place where the voyage ends, as if the contract of affreightment contained no reference thereto; but where the contract of affreightment so provides, the York-Antwerp Rules shall apply.

Whereas the shipowner is himself responsible for the G/A clause in his contract of affreightment, it is recognised that a cargo owner has little control over such a matter. Accordingly, the G/A clause in a cargo policy gives the assured more extensive cover by making underwriters liable to G/A and salvage charges according to foreign statement, or to York-Antwerp Rules if in accordance with the contract of affreightment.

Frustration Clause. This reads "Warranted free of any claim based upon loss of, or frustration of, the insured voyage, or adventure, caused by arrests, restraints or detainments of kings, princes or peoples".

The clause was first introduced following a case which occurred in the early days of the 1914–1918 war. Two grain-laden British vessels had left a South American port for a port in Germany and, by the terms of a Proclamation forbidding trade with the enemy, were unable to deliver their cargoes at the destination originally contemplated. They were diverted to the United Kingdom where the grain was discharged and sold. Although the goods themselves were not actually lost, underwriters were held liable for a constructive total loss on the grounds that the insured *adventure* was lost by a peril insured against. The object of the Frustration Clause was to enable underwriters to escape such liabilities in similar cases in the future.

It should be noted that the Frustration Clause comes into operation only when the F.C. & S. Clause is deleted. Where the latter clause remains operative there is no need for the former. Obviously, no claim can be based upon the frustration of the adventure by the perils of arrests, restraints, or detainments if those perils are themselves excluded from the insurance. If, on the other hand, the policy does include war risks, loss of or damage to the *goods* arising directly from war risks is fully covered by the policy.

The current Institute Cargo Clauses provide that, should the F.C. & S. Clause be deleted, the Institute War Clauses (which include the Frustration Clause) shall be deemed to form part of the contract.

The Institute Voyage Clauses for hulls and freight also provide for the Frustration Clause to operate in the event of the F.C. & S. Clause being deleted.

General Average Disbursements. As stated elsewhere, G/A contributions are levied on arrived values, and in the event of the ship and cargo being subsequently lost on the voyage during which G/A expenditures have been incurred there will be no arrived values and no adjustment of general average. In respect of G/A sacrifices this is of no consequence as any property sacrificed would inevitably have been totally lost with ship and cargo. In respect of G/A expenditures, however, the problem is more serious for the shipowner who has been obliged to make G/A disbursements at a port of refuge or elsewhere. In practice, therefore, a prudent shipowner who has incurred such G/A expenditure will effect a special insurance on "Average Disbursements" so that in the event of total loss he would be able to claim the amount from underwriters. The premium for such a policy will itself be allowed in general average. (See Rule XX of Y-A Rules).

G.M.T. In the case of a time policy it is essential that the commencement and termination of the risk should be exactly specified. It is usual to mention the hour of commencement and termination, but in the absence of a specific provision the days will be deemed to begin from and end at midnight. Also, in the absence of a special provision, the contract is governed by Greenwich mean time and not by the local time of the place where the ship may happen to be.

Label Clause. This provides that in a case of damage from perils insured against affecting labels only, the loss is to be limited to an amount sufficient to pay the cost of reconditioning, the cost of new labels and re-labelling the goods, provided that the damage will have amounted to a claim under the terms of the policy (*i.e.*, reached any franchise limit there may be).

Mutual Insurance (P. & I. Clubs). To secure cover against third party risks which are normally outside the scope of an ordinary marine policy, groups of shipowners form what are known as Protecting and Indemnity Associations, sometimes referred to as P. & I. Clubs or "Small Damage Clubs". These are maintained by way of a levy on the amount of tonnage owned by members and entered into the Club, each making his proportionate payment to the Club funds. Calls are made periodically by the Club Secretaries to replenish funds, only enough being asked to cover losses sustained by members and costs of management. Naturally, when severe losses have to be met the subscriptions become correspondingly heavy. The distinction between "protection and indemnity" seems to be that the former relates to liabilities incurred by the

X

employment of the ship as a ship, whilst the latter is concerned
with liabilities incurred by the employment of the ship as a carrier
of cargo.

Risks coming under the heading of Protection include:

Loss of life and personal injury claims.

Hospital, medical, and funeral expenses arising from injury
claims.

Sickness and repatriation of distressed seamen.

Third party collision damages not covered by the Running
Down Clause.

Cargo damage due to improper navigation.

Damage to piers, wharves, and other stationary objects.

Cost of D.o.T. inquiries.

Cost of raising wreck.

Oil pollution.

Quarantine expenses.

Legal costs of defending claims if incurred with the consent
of the Club directors.*

Cargo's irrecoverable proportion of general average.

Risks under the heading of Indemnity include:

Claims in respect of wrong delivery of cargo.

Ship's liability to cargo after collision not covered by
insurance.

Fines or penalties imposed as a result of innocent breaches of
Customs Laws, Public Health Regulations, Immigration
Laws, or arising from barratrous acts, including smug-
gling, of the servants of the shipowner.

Cost of resisting cargo claims with the consent of the directors.*

The vast experience of these Associations in dealing with claims
on shipowners enables them to suggest methods by which future
claims may be kept down to a minimum, and since this tends to
ensure that cargoes are delivered in sound condition there is no
doubt that the activities of the Clubs are of great value to the
mercantile community as a whole.

Open Slip. This is an agreement whereby an underwriter agrees
to insure, up to a specified amount, an interest in respect of which
shipping arrangements have still to be made. A merchant might,
for instance, purchase a large quantity of grain to be shipped
eventually from U.S. Gulf ports to Europe but without knowing by
what vessels the grain is to be carried. His broker would prepare the
necessary "slip" for submission to an underwriter who, if he decides
to accept the risk, would agree at a fixed premium, or at rates of
premium to be arranged in due course, to insure the grain up to,
but not in the aggregate beyond, the amount specified, by whatever

---

* These do not include ordinary commercial claims, but only those in the
nature of "test cases" of interest to shipowners in general.

vessels are subsequently engaged to carry it. A stipulated "limit per bottom" would probably be arranged. As shipments are made from time to time the underwriter will be notified. Each notification, referred to as an insurance "off slip" will call for the necessary policy to be issued.

Proximate Cause. Section 55 of the Marine Insurance Act states that, unless the policy otherwise provides, the insurer is not liable for any loss which is not proximately caused by a peril insured against. The principle adopted is *causa proxima non remota spectator*, which means that it is the proximate cause, and not the remote cause, which shall be regarded. In a case where a ship was scuttled with the connivance of the owner, a mortgagee suing under a policy taken out to cover his interest in the ship contended that the ship was lost through the entry of sea water, a "peril of the sea" which was a peril insured against. It was ruled that the proximate cause was the actual act of scuttling for which the underwriters were not liable, the loss arising from the misconduct of the assured. It is not necessarily the case that the proximate cause should be the cause nearest in time. During the 1914-1918 war a torpedoed vessel managed to reach a French port where she was berthed. While attempts were being made to pump the water out of her a gale sprang up, pumping operations were discontinued, and the ship was shifted to an outer berth on the instructions of the port authority for fear of her sinking at the inner berth. She took the ground at successive low waters and eventually broke her back and sank, becoming a total loss. She was insured against marine perils but warranted free of ". . . all consequences of hostilities". It was held that the proximate cause of the loss was a consequence of hostilities, as she had never been out of danger from the time of the torpedoing. There was, therefore, no right of recovery under the marine policy.

Re-insurance. There are various reasons why an underwriter may deem it prudent to re-insure part or all of a risk for which he has accepted liability. For instance, he may find that his commitments on any one vessel or in any locality have become too burdensome. Declarations under open covers or floating policies and acceptances by his agents in other markets may give him an accumulated liability considerably in excess of his usual retention. He may have accepted a line on "all risk" terms and then desire to re-insure in respect of total loss only. Further, there may be a possibility of placing the risk in some other market at a profit, or he may ultimately decide after due consideration that his acceptance of a particular risk was an error of judgement.

By section 9 of the Marine Insurance Act, the insurer has an insurable interest in his risk, and may re-insure in respect of it. However unless the policy otherwise provides, the original assured has no right or interest in respect of such re-insurance.

An underwriter may re-insure (1) facultatively, (2) by means of an open cover, or (3) by means of a re-insurance treaty.

Facultative re-insurance is the direct re-insurance of individual risks through the medium of a broker in precisely the same way as original insurances are placed. The re-insuring underwriter may fix the rate of premium or, if the re-insurance is effected on the identical conditions of the original policy, he may be content to accept the original premium of the re-insured. The speculative re-insurance of an overdue vessel or a vessel which is known to have met with some casualty may be effected in this way. In the early stages the original underwriter may be able to re-insure at a reasonably commensurate premium, but if with the passage of time no good news is received then re-insurance rates would increase and should the vessel eventually be posted as "missing" she may well become uninsurable.

Open cover re-insurance is often used by underwriters in respect of their cargo business, say, to re-insure their interest on particular voyages, commodities, or types of vessels. Such open covers may be effected on free from particular average conditions at lower rates of premium than the original insurances effected on more comprehensive terms.

Re-insurance treaties can be used for either hull or cargo re-insurance. They are generally very elaborate contracts between insurance companies providing for the cession of some proportion of the whole of the re-assured's business to the re-insuring company at the original premiums less an over-riding commission.

Whichever of these three methods of re-insurance is employed, the original underwriter has a choice of re-insuring on a first interest basis, a quota-share basis, or an excess basis. If an underwriter accepts £2,000 on a vessel and re-insures £1,000 on a first interest basis, and only £1,600 is finally "closed" to the underwriter, the re-insurer's line would still remain at £1,000. On the other hand, if the re-insurance is placed on a quota-share basis the re-insurer's line would be reduced to £800. If the same re-insurance were arranged "excess of £1,000," the re-insurer's liability would be £600 whilst the re-assured would retain £1,000.

Re-insurance policies are in virtually the same form as original policies but with the addition of the Re-insurance Clause. The usual wording of this clause is "Being a re-insurance and subject to the same clauses and conditions as the original policy, and to pay as may be paid thereon". In the frequent instances where re-insurances are effected on restricted conditions it becomes necessary to qualify the clause by adding suitable words. For example, in respect of hull re-insurance there may be added "but against Total and/or Constructive and/or Arranged Total Loss Only". Similarly, in respect of cargo re-insurance the appended words might be "but Free from Particular Average as per the Institute Cargo Clauses".

Replacement Clause. So long as the assured is prepared to pay any additional premium required a cargo policy can usually be extended to cover all kinds of extraneous cargo risks, but underwriters require that all such additional risks should be specifically mentioned in the policy. The replacement clause is an instance of this, and is frequently inserted in a policy covering machinery. Its purpose is to limit the underwriters' liability to the cost of replacing, forwarding, and refitting any broken part of a machine, and to free the underwriters from any claim for total loss.

Self Insurance. This name is sometimes applied to a system whereby a shipowner, instead of paying insurance premiums to underwriters, forms a special fund out of which he can reimburse himself for marine losses sustained.

Sentimental Damage. It may happen that cargo discharged in a sound condition from a ship which has sustained damage during the voyage, or from which other cargo has been landed in a damaged condition, loses some of its market value and has to be sold at a lower price than it would otherwise have fetched. Such a loss is called "sentimental damage" and as such damage is merely suspected and not actual, the loss is one for which underwriters are not liable. Depreciation not accompanied by any physical damage cannot possibly be traced to insured perils.

Subrogation and Abandonment. The term subrogation means the substituting of one creditor for another. The extent of the insurer's right of subrogation depends upon whether he pays for a total loss or a partial loss. Where he pays for a total loss either of the whole subject-matter or, in the case of goods, a total loss of an apportionable part thereof, he is entitled to take over whatever may remain of the subject-matter and is subrogated to all rights and remedies of the assured in respect of that subject-matter. On the other hand, where he pays for a partial loss only, the insurer is not entitled to what remains of the subject-matter but is subrogated only to the rights and remedies of the assured so far as the latter has been indemnified.

For example, if a parcel of cargo is jettisoned for the common benefit, and the underwriter indemnifies the owner of that parcel by paying him the full insured value, the former then takes over the right to claim the amount made good in general average from other contributing interests. Were this not so, the assured would make a profit out of a loss by recovering both the insurance indemnity and the G/A allowance.

Where a vessel becomes a constructive total loss the underwriters, after paying a total loss indemnity, are entitled to take over the wreck though, as previously stated, it may not always be in their interests to avail themselves of the right.

When settling a cargo claim for partial loss, if there is any possibility of recovering from the carrier or other bailee of the goods, underwriters will require a "letter of subrogation" from the assured authorising them to institute proceedings to effect such recovery in the name of the assured but at their expense. Such a measure, although convenient, is not legally necessary as the right of subrogation is a statutory right.

The Bailee Clause of the Institute Cargo Clauses requires the assured to undertake to cause appropriate measures to be taken to prevent any remedy against the carrier or other bailee becoming barred by non-compliance with terms and conditions governing the bailee's liability, but provides that any expenses incurred by so doing will be reimbursed by the underwriters.

Substituted Expenses. When a damaged vessel has entered a port of refuge it may be possible to adopt some alternative course to avoid an expense which could not be avoided by having the vessel repaired at that port. To effect the repairs there it might, for instance, be essential to discharge all or most of the cargo, store it, and afterwards reload it, and it may turn out to be much cheaper to have ship and cargo towed to the port of destination. The cost of towage would be classed as a "substituted expense". However, the alternative must be a genuine one. Towage to destination would not count as a substituted expense if the reason for it was the impracticability of getting the repairs done at the port of refuge. Moreover if, by having the ship towed to her destination, the shipowner is able to effect a saving on the cost of the particular average repairs, he would be debited with his proportion of the substituted expense.

Superintendents' and Surveyors' Fees and Overtime. When hull or machinery repairs are to be effected, both the shipowner and the underwriters usually appoint surveyors to survey the damage, decide the extent of the repairs considered necessary, and agree the price to be paid for the work. In addition, the owner will generally engage a surveyor, superintendent, or other qualified person to supervise the repair work. In any event underwriters will be liable for the fee of their own surveyor. They will also be liable to reimburse the fees paid by the shipowner for superintending and surveying the repairs, provided such fees are reasonable, and the cost of repairs, having reached the franchise (if any), is recoverable as a claim under the policy. In deciding whether the required percentage has been reached, the cost of superintendence, being part of the cost of repairs, may be included. The cost of surveying the damage, on the other hand, may not. The latter is not part of the cost of repairs, but is merely the cost of ascertaining and proving the loss.

In order to expedite repairs it may be decided to incur overtime. The question then arises as to whether underwriters will be liable for the cost thereof. Each case, it would seem, must be treated on its merits. For instance, if as a result of an expenditure on overtime other charges in excess of that expenditure have been saved, the overtime cost would be considered part of the reasonable cost of repairs and, as such, recoverable from underwriters.

Sympathetic Damage. In ships carrying general cargoes there is often a danger of one commodity causing taint damage to another. Unless this risk is specifically insured underwriters are not liable for the resulting loss, except in circumstances where a marine peril has operated to damage one commodity and the other has suffered as a direct consequence. In such case the damage to the second commodity is known as sympathetic damage.

Transhipment. Section 59 of the Marine Insurance Act provides as follows:

"Where, by a peril insured against, the voyage is interrupted at an intermediate port or place, under such circumstances as, apart from any special stipulation in the contract of affreightment, to justify the master in landing and re-shipping the goods or other moveables, or in transhipping them, and sending them on to their destination, the liability of the insurer continues, notwithstanding the landing or transhipment."

From the above it will be seen that, in the absence of a special agreement with the underwriters, transhipment of cargo during an insured voyage, is covered only when it is necessitated by a peril insured against. Transhipment may arise as a result of a peril not insured against, *e.g.*, a war peril, in which case both the insured voyage and the insurance would be terminated as the Act makes no provision for this contingency. In present day practice, however, insurance remains in force during transhipment by virtue of the Transit Clause of the Institute Cargo Clauses.

Unrepaired Damage. If damage to a ship from a peril insured against remains unrepaired and, during the currency of the policy, the vessel becomes a total loss, underwriters are liable only for the total loss. The position is the same whether the total loss is caused by a peril insured against or not. Where the ship is not totally lost before the expiry of the policy, underwriters are liable for the reasonable depreciation to the ship if there is unrepaired damage. If damage sustained during the currency of one policy is left unrepaired, and the ship is lost during the currency of the succeeding policy, underwriters on the former policy are liable for the unrepaired damage, but it does not follow that the assured will enjoy an undeserved gain thereby, as the insured value on the succeeding policy would almost certainly have been agreed at a figure which took into account the fact of the unrepaired damage.

War Risk Insurance. With respect to hull insurance, in order to cover war risks it was at one time customary to delete the F.C. & S.

Clause. Later, the same effect was accomplished by adding the clause "This policy covers the risks excluded by the following clause" and this was then followed by the F.C. & S. Clause. When the ordinary marine insurance market found itself unable to give adequate cover on account of the enormous losses suffered during the sustained submarine attacks on shipping and other large scale hostilities, the necessary cover was obtained by mutual insurance through P. & I. Associations. During the First World War a scheme was brought into operation under which vessels could be covered 80% by the Government and 20% by the Clubs. At a later stage the Government accepted the full risk but continued to use the machinery of the Clubs to administer the scheme. At the end of that war the Government dropped out. During the Second World War a similar scheme was instituted whereby the Government re-insured the Associations to the extent of 80%. Premiums varied, of course, according to the degree of risk. Under this scheme the Clubs received 20% of the premiums and paid 20% of the claims. After the war the State again, naturally, stepped out.

With regard to cargo insurance, goods are still insurable against war risks in any part of the world by the simple expedient of deleting the F.C. & S. Clause in the cargo policy whereupon the Institute War Clauses are deemed to be part of the contract of insurance. Premiums will, of course, be adjusted accordingly. There are also special War Clauses drafted to suit the requirements of particular trades.

CHAPTER 15

LIMITATION OF LIABILITY OF SHIPOWNERS
AND OTHERS

SECTION 502 of the principal M.S. Act provides that the owner of a British sea-going ship, or any share therein, shall not be liable to make good to any extent whatever any loss or damage happening without his actual fault or privity in the following cases:

(i) where any goods, merchandise, or other things whatsoever taken in or put on board his ship are lost or damaged by reason of fire on board the ship; or

(ii) where any gold, silver, diamonds, watches, jewels, or precious stones taken in or put on board his ship, the true nature and value of which have not at the time of shipment been declared by the owner or shipper thereof to the owner or master of the ship in the bills of lading or otherwise in writing, are lost or damaged by reason of any robbery, embezzlement, making away with, or secreting thereof.

The operation of the above section is not affected by anything contained in the Carriage of Goods by Sea Act, 1971. The latter Act provides that neither the carrier nor the ship shall be responsible for loss or damage arising or resulting from (among other things) fire, unless caused by the actual fault or privity of the carrier, "carrier" being defined as including the owner or the charterer who enters into a contract of carriage with a shipper.

It is realised that ship operating is a very hazardous occupation in the sense that, arising out of negligent navigation, even a relatively small ship may place a huge liability on the shoulders of the person responsible for her operation, especially in the case where an accident of navigation results in heavy loss of life. For this reason it is provided by Section 503 M.S.A. 1894 that the owners of a ship, British or foreign, shall not be liable to damages beyond certain fixed amounts where all or any of the following occurrences take place without their actual fault or privity, viz.:

(a) Where loss of life or personal injury is caused to any person carried in the ship.

(b) Where damage or loss is caused to goods, merchandise, or other things on board the ship.

(c) Where any loss of life or personal injury is caused to any person not carried in the ship through the act or omission of any person (whether on board or not) in the navigation or management of the ship or in the loading, carriage or discharge of its cargo or in the embarkation, carriage or disembarkation of its passengers, or through any other act or omission of any person on board.

(d) Where loss or damage is caused to any property (other than that mentioned in (b) above), or any rights are infringed through the act or omission of any person (whether on board or not) in the navigation or management of the ship or in the loading, carriage or discharge of its cargo or in the embarkation, carriage or disembarkation of its passengers, or through any other act or omission of any person on board.

The provisions above in s.503 have been amended by s.35, M.S.A. 1979 so that, for an occurrence which takes place after 1st August 1979, a shipowner will not be able to limit his liability for loss of life, personal injury or damage to property claims made by an employee employed on board the ship under a contract of service governed by U.K. law.

The maximum liability fixed by the M.S. (Liability of Shipowners and Others) Act 1958, based on the 1957 Brussels Convention on Limitation of Liability of Shipowners, is an amount equivalent to 3,100 gold francs per ton of the ship's tonnage where there are life or injury claims alone, or where there are both life or injury claims and property claims together. In respect of property claims alone the limit is an amount equivalent to 1,000 gold francs per ton.

Where there are claims of both kinds it would appear that, if the former practice of the courts is maintained, life claimants will have a prior claim to 2,100 gold francs per ton in advance, and will then share the remaining 1,000 gold francs per ton with property claimants.

Tonnage for limitation of liability purposes is net registered tonnage plus the engine room space deducted for ascertaining the net registered tonnage. For a sailing ship it is net registered tonnage without any addition.

In respect of life or injury claims, where the tonnage concerned is less than 300 tons, the amount per ton mentioned above is to be multiplied by 300 to fix the maximum liability. In respect of property claims the actual tonnage would apply.

The Act provides that a gold franc shall be taken to be a unit consisting of 65½ milligrams of gold of millesimal fineness 900.

The Secretary of State (D.o.T.) may from time to time, by order made by statutory instrument, specify the amounts which are to be taken as equivalent to 3,100 and 1,000 gold francs, respectively. In 1981 the equivalent of 3,100 gold francs was approximately £111 and that of 1,000 gold francs about £36

Note:—The M.S. Act 1981* enacts the 1979 Protocol to the 1957 Brussels Convention mentioned above. The Protocol changes the

* Not yet in force August, 1981

amounts 3,100 and 1,000 gold francs per ton shown above to 206·67 and 66·67 special drawing rights (SDR) per ton respectively. The SDR's referred to are defined by the International Monetary Fund (IMF) and the value in sterling of one SDR is fixed by the IMF on most days and published in the *Financial Times*. If a limitation action is brought, the equivalent of the above amounts in sterling shall be that for the day on which the limitation fund is constituted and in any other case, on the date of judgement of the case.

In order to limit liability in accordance with the Acts a separate action must be brought, the shipowner or other persons seeking to limit liability having to bear the costs of the Limitation Suit. If the Admiralty court hearing the case is satisfied that the occurrence has taken place without the actual fault or privity of the applicant, the action will succeed. A sum based on the figures quoted above will then have to be paid into court. If this fund is sufficient to cover all claims they will have to be met in full. If it is not, the fund will be divided rateably amongst the various claimants in proportion to their individual and approved claims. The example given below will serve as a simple illustration of the apportionment in a case where the amount paid into court is insufficient to meet all claims in full.

Net registered tonnage of ship	.. ..	.. 1,800 tons
Deduction from gross tonnage on account of propelling space	..	400 tons
Special tonnage for limitation purposes	.. .. ..	.. 2,200 tons
Paid into court @ £111 (3,100 gold francs) per ton	..	.. £244,200

Life and injury claims amount to, say, £310,000	
Property claims amount to, say,	£140,000
Total claims are therefore	£450,000

Apportionment:

Life and/or injury claimants receive the first £75 (2,100 gold francs) per ton in advance, *i.e.*, £165,000, leaving £79,200 of the fund to be apportioned as follows:—

Balance of life and injury claims £145,000 receive £40,295	
Property claims	£140,000 receive £38,905
i.e., total outstanding claims	£285,000 receive £79,200

Thus, altogether, life and injury claimants receive £165,000 + £40,295, *i.e.*, £205,295. Adding the £38,905 which goes to property claimants, that accounts for the entire fund of £244,200.

Hence each life and injury claimant gets $\dfrac{205,295}{310,000}$ or approximately 2/3 of his actual claim, and each property claimant gets $\dfrac{38,905}{140,000}$ or approximately 1/4 of his actual claim.

By an Act of 1906 demise charters were granted the same rights as shipowners with respect to limitation of liability, but the 1958 Act goes further by providing that persons whose liability in connection with a ship is excluded or limited shall include **any** charterer and any person interested in or in possession of the ship, and—in particular—any manager or operator of the ship.

By an Act of 1900, dock owners, canal owners, harbour and conservancy authorities enjoy certain limitation rights. Their maximum liability where, without their fault or privity, loss or damage is caused to any vessel or vessels or goods or other things thereon, is fixed (as amended by the 1958 Act) at the equivalent of 1,000 gold francs per ton of the tonnage of the largest British registrated ship which is—or within five years previous to the occurrence has been—within the area over which they have control.

Note:—The M.S. Act 1981* changes this to 66·67 SDR's of the IMF, see previous note.

Another important provision of the 1958 Act is as follows:

In relation to a claim arising from the act or omission of any person in his capacity as master or member of the crew or, otherwise than in that capacity, in the course of his employment as a servant of the owners, charterers, etc., (*a*) the person whose liability is excluded or limited shall also include the master, crew member, or servant; (*b*) the liability of the master, crew member, or servant shall be excluded or limited notwithstanding his actual fault or privity in that capacity, except in connection with stolen valuables.

The sections of the principal Act dealing with liability of shipowners apply to any structure, whether completed or in course of completion, launched and intended for use in navigation as a ship or part of a ship. The same sections also apply to any British ship notwithstanding that it has not yet been registered. It should be noted that owners of ships which are not required by law to be registered are privileged to limit their liability. On the other hand, an owner who has failed to register a ship which ought to be registered is thereby deprived of the privilege. But this does not affect the owner of a new ship, or part of a ship, who intends to have the ship registered when the appropriate time for taking that action arrives.

The Acts make provision for a special procedure to ascertain, when necessary, the tonnage of a foreign ship, an unregistered British ship, or a structure, for limitation of liability purposes.

Limitation of shipowners' liability under the Carriage of Goods by Sea Act is dealt with in Chapter 9, and in Chapter 12 there will be found references to the limitation of liability of pilots and pilotage authorities. Limitation of liability as provided for in the Prevention of Oil Pollution Act is referred to in Chapter 7, and for passengers in Chapter 8.

Convention on Limitation of Liability for Maritime Claims 1976.

The conference that agreed on this Convention was held in London in 1976. The text of the Convention forms Part I of Schedule 4 of

* Not yet in force August, 1981

the M.S. Act 1979, and sections 17 and 18 of that Act also deal with the subject. When the Convention has been ratified by 12 states, it will be brought into force for the U.K. 12 months later by statutory instrument. (In August 1981, four states, including the U.K. had ratified the Convention). When it comes into force the Convention will apply to accepting countries, but others, signatories of the 1957 Convention, will continue to apply the terms of that Convention until they in turn ratify the later one.

The Convention defines the right of limitation and states that a shipowner, meaning an owner, charterer, manager or operator of a sea-going ship, also salvors, and also employees of shipowners and salvors, may limit their liability for claims listed in Article 2. Claims subject to limitation specified in that article include those in respect of loss of life or personal injury, or loss of or damage to property (including damage to harbour works and aids to navigation), occurring on board or in direct connection with ship or salvage operations and consequential loss therefrom; loss resulting from delay in carriage by sea of cargo, passengers and luggage; raising, removal, destruction or the rendering harmless of a ship which is sunk, wrecked, stranded or abandoned and similarly in respect of the cargo of the ship.

Claims Excepted from Limitation. The Rules of this Convention do not apply to claims for salvage or general average contributions, for oil pollution damage within the meaning of the 1969 Civil Liability Convention as amended, for nuclear damage covered by other Conventions or arrangements, and claims by employees of the shipowner or salvor whose duties are connected with the ship or the salvage operation, if under the employment law governing the contract of service, the employer cannot limit his liability, or is restricted in his right to limit. (Art. 3).

Conduct Barring Limitation. (Art. 4) Limitation is barred for a person if it is proved that the loss resulted from his personal act or omission, committed with intent to cause such loss, or recklessly with knowledge that such loss would probably result. This will probably be more difficult for a claimant to prove than the provisions of the present 1957 Convention.

General Limits. The general limits provided (Arts. 6 and 8) are based on a sliding scale per ton for ships over 500 tons and are to be calculated as follows:—

(a) **Claims for loss of life or personal injury**

    (i) For ships with tonnage not exceeding 500 tons—333,000 Units of Account;

(ii) In addition, for ships over 500 tons, for each ton:—
from   501 to 3,000 tons,   500 Units of Account;
from 3,001 to 30,000 tons,   333 Units of Account;
from 30,001 to 70,000 tons, 250 Units of Account;
in excess of 70,000 tons,   167 Units of Account.

(b) **In respect of any other claims**

(i) For ships with tonnage not exceeding 500 tons—167,000 Units of Account;

(ii) In addition, for ships over 500 tons, for each ton:—
from   501 to 30,000 tons, 167 Units of Account;
from 30,001 to 70,000 tons, 125 Units of Account;
in excess of 70,000 tons,   83 Units of Account.

The Unit of Account is the Special Drawing Right defined by the International Monetary Fund, which shall be converted into the national currency of the State in which limitation is sought, according to the value of such currency at the date the limitation fund is constituted, payment is made or security is given.

Limit for Passenger Claims. (Art. 7) In respect of claims by or on behalf of passengers for loss of life or personal injury while being carried in the ship, the limit of liability of the shipowner is 46,666 Units of Account multiplied by the number of passengers the ship is certified to carry, but not exceeding 25 million Units of Account.

Provisions having effect in connection with the Convention. Part II of Schedule 4 of the M.S.A. 1979 states provisions that will have effect as far as British law is concerned when the Convention is brought into force. These include the right for owners of non-sea-going ships to limit their liability, the general limits for ships of less than 300 tons to be 166,667 and 83,333 Units of Account under (a) and (b) above respectively, and for the ship's tonnage used in the calculations to be its gross tonnage calculated in such manner as may be prescribed by the Secretary of State by order. Any such order shall give effect to the regulations in Annex I of the International Convention on Tonnage Measurement of Ships, 1969 (as far as is practicable).

CHAPTER 16

SOME GOVERNMENT DEPARTMENTS AND OTHER INSTITUTIONS CONCERNED WITH SHIPPING AND SEAFARERS

DEPARTMENT OF TRADE

THE Government department mainly responsible for shipping affairs is the Department of Trade (D.o.T.) which has its shipping responsibilities organised into two divisions, viz.:

Shipping Policy Division,
Marine Division, including the Marine Survey Service.

The Shipping Policy Division is concerned with shipping interests in shipbuilding, U.K. ports, cargo handling, taxation and investment incentives, coastal and short sea trades and related developments in the E.E.C. It also deals with shipments of Government cargoes, sales of Governments ships and gives advice on charter, purchase and use of shipping for Government purposes. International legal questions affecting shipping including Law of the Sea, shipowners' liability, U.K. planning in relation to N.A.T.O. planning for merchant shipping and also War Risk insurance are other matters dealt with by this division. It also deals with matters concerning shipping relations with developed and developing countries, E.E.C. Shipping policy, shipping conferences, shipping councils, flags of convenience, shipping questions in U.N.C.T.A.D. and O.E.C.D., and policy on flag discrimination.

In one of its branches the Marine Division deals with ship registration, prevention of marine pollution, wreck and salvage, and hovercraft legislation and regulations. Fishing vessels' safety, prevention of accidents to seamen and safety in private pleasure craft are the responsibility of a second branch, while a third deals with navigational aids, radio, search and rescue, lights and pilotage, safety of navigation and traffic systems, and also includes amongst its responsibilities H.M. Coastguard Service. A further branch deals with matters concerning merchant seamen and fishermen including qualifications and certification, safe manning, crew accommodation, welfare, inquiries into deaths, conditions of service and repatriation; this branch also has responsibility for M.M. Offices and the General Register and Record Office of Shipping and Seamen.

The Marine Survey Service carries out survey and examination work, including the setting and enforcement of appropriate standards of construction, equipment and navigation of ships. It is also responsible for professional work on marine pollution and hazardous cargoes, carries out inquiries into ship casualties, and represents the department in professional matters at the I.M.O.

The Department is required by the M.S. Act 1970 to appoint an officer who is to be called the Registrar General of Shipping and Seamen. This officer is required to exercise functions conferred on him by the Merchant Shipping Acts and he is also required to keep records and perform other duties under the direction of the Department. Mercantile marine superintendents are appointed by the Department to carry out duties conferred on them by the Merchant Shipping Acts. Since the coming into operation of the Merchant Shipping Act, 1970, M.M. Superintendents are no longer required to witness the engagement and discharge of seamen, but they may do so on occasions in an inspectorial capacity. Furthermore, the Department's surveyors make spot checks from time to time to see that ships are properly manned and equipped and that they comply with the requirements of M.S. Acts and associated Regulations.

H.M. CUSTOMS AND EXCISE

H.M. Customs and Excise is one of the two main tax collecting departments of the Government and is one of the oldest Departments of State. The present system of collection of duties by civil servants responsible directly to the Crown dates from 1671 when the first Board of Customs was appointed. The Commissioners of Customs and Excise forming successive Boards are still individually appointed by the Sovereign. Parliamentary responsibility for the Board's work is exercised by Treasury ministers.

The Department manages and collects the bulk of the taxes on consumer expenditure. These include customs duties on imported goods, excise duties on some goods produced in, or imported into, the United Kingdom, betting and gaming duties, car tax, and Value Added Tax which is levied on goods and services supplied in the course of a business and on imported goods (but not on imported services). The other taxes on expenditure such as vehicle licence duties, stamp duties etc., are not the responsibility of the Department. It also performs many non-revenue functions which include compiling external trade statistics and aspects of import and export controls, as well as maintaining the Register of British ships.

Customs and Excise receipts in 1978-9 totalled £13,763·6 million which was one third of total revenue from central government taxation. Most of the revenue comes from the duties on hydrocarbon oil, tobacco, alcoholic drinks, car tax and value added tax.

For the purpose of revenue control and collection, the United Kingdom is divided into 29 areas, known as Collections, each in the charge of a Collector. Collections are divided into Divisions, each managed by an Assistant Collector, and each Division contains "Districts" headed by Surveyors of Customs and Excise.

The main functions of the staff in various grades are:—

(i) to control the landing and shipping of import and export cargoes, control of the crews of ships, aircraft and hovercraft and their passengers entering and leaving the country, to detect and prevent smuggling, and to prevent evasion of prohibitions and restrictions of many kinds;

(ii) to control and assess duty on the production of exciseable goods, control traders concerned with the supply of goods and services liable to Value Added Tax, and check for duty transactions liable to betting or gaming duties; and

(iii) to perform clerical and executive work arising from the control functions, such as the examination and clearance of goods against merchants' import and export declarations, and the receipt of tax and duty payments.

Work at Port and Airports. It is illegal to import or export goods other than through Customs approved ports and airports or by approved routes across the Irish Land Boundary. To prevent illicit import and export, regular controls of sea approaches and land boundaries are maintained.

On arrival at a port from abroad the first duty in the control of ships may be to ensure that certain specified infectious diseases are not brought into this country. The Customs Boarding Officer will not permit a ship to enter port if there is a case having an infectious disease on board. Other important controls are the detection and seizure of prohibited dangerous drugs and enforcement of rabies control regulations which prohibit importation of some kinds of animals unless they are put into quarantine. To achieve this Customs Officers search arriving ships for undeclared dutiable goods or prohibited items. This searching, or rummaging as it is known in the Customs service, is done at unspecified times before, during and after unloading.

Ships' Reports. The ship's master, or his authorised agent, must submit a report of the ship, voyage, cargo etc. to Customs at the port of arrival. This report includes a list of cargo or a manifest, port of loading and a statement of unused dutiable ship's stores. Until the report has been submitted the ship cannot begin to discharge cargo or other goods, unless special permission has been obtained. A copy of the report is sent to the Customs Officer at the docks responsible for controlling, landing and custody of cargo until it is released to the importer. The further required procedures for entering and clearing the ship inwards, and entering and clearing the ship outwards are described in Chapter 10.

Cargo Landing and Examination. As soon as the arrival of a ship is reported to the Custom House, or earlier by special arrangement, the cargo may be unloaded under the control of the Customs officer at the ship's side. This Customs "Landing Officer" ensures that all goods landed remain under official control until released or removed elsewhere under Customs control.

Importers' Entries. Importers must prepare "entries" on the appropriate forms for all imported goods. An "entry" is a Customs form on which an importer declares the description, value, quantity, rate of duty and various other details about the goods. The importer presents the entry to the appropriate Customs office (usually the Custom House but in certain cases it may be presented to the Customs officer at the docks) and pays any duty chargeable unless the goods are subject to deferred payment arrangements or are being forwarded to a bonded warehouse. After scrutiny of the entry in the Customs House and the collection of any duty, the entry is sent to the Customs Officer at the docks, who may decide to examine the goods. In certain instances the entry may be presented direct to this Customs Officer, not at the Custom House. If the entry is found correct it serves as a warrant for clearance of goods from Customs control, or for removal of them if still under Customs control to a bonded warehouse. An additional copy is required for compilation of trade figures. Importers offering an approved form of guarantee may defer payment of duty for about one month. Tobacco is excluded from this arrangement and any Excise duty payable on imported goods is also ineligible for deferment. Payment of the amount deferred is effected by means of bank direct debit. Importers who are registered for V.A.T. may postpone V.A.T. upon imported goods until their periodic V.A.T. "return" becomes due.

Examination of imported goods is selective and the importer or the agent must open any of his packages which the Landing Officer wishes to examine. If the officer is satisfied that the goods are those declared on the entry, and the proper duty has been paid or secured, the officer clears them from Customs charge or releases them for removal elsewhere, after repacking by the importer or his agent. If an entry declaration is incorrect the goods will be detained until it has been corrected and any additional duty and tax has been paid. Any unentered goods concealed with intent to evade payment of duty are liable to seizure, as are goods packed with them and their container. If the importer has deliberately made a false declaration he is liable to prosecution.

Exporters' Declaration. Exporters are required to declare their goods for export. The accepted declarations after checking at the Customs House, are sent to the docks if the export is of a type which demands Customs control at the ship's side.

Export Controls. Although there are no export duties (except, sometimes, payments arising under the Common Agricultural Policy) control is necessary for various reasons, such as the production of Overseas Trade Statistics for the D.o.T. Export of arms, military equipment, strategic goods and certain other goods, may be totally prohibited, or subject to licence control.

Goods which would be dutiable for home use, may be exported duty-free under bond. Arrangements can be made for the temporary importation of foreign goods into the U.K. free of duty for re-exportation after process or repair, or for use at exhibitions etc.

The Export Officer ensures that goods subject to export licensing control are not shipped unless covered by a valid licence. He examines goods for export to ensure that all items are duly shipped. Dutiable goods for use as ship's stores, or for sale in shops on passenger vessels, are placed in a sealed store-room on board to prevent their use before the ship leaves U.K. territorial waters.

Container Traffic. Facilities are available for goods imported or exported in secure transport containers and in "roll-on", "roll-off" traffic. Such goods may be dealt with either at ports or at specially approved inland depots. Customs procedures at these places have been developed to meet the requirements of the traffic, but containers and their contents may be selected for Customs examination and it may be necessary for a container to be completely emptied at the ship's side.

Effect of U.K. Membership of the E.E.C. U.K. membership of the E.E.C. has required numerous changes in Customs procedures for dealing with overseas trade. These include the progressive alignment of rates of duty with the Common External Tariff of the Community leading to eventual abolition of duty on trade within the Community, procedures for facilitating the movement of goods within the Community, the implementation of the Common Agricultural Policy (C.A.P.) under which certain goods may at import or export be either liable to a charge or eligible for a payment, and the operation of tariff quotas and other means of regulating admission of certain goods at a reduced or nil rate of duty.

Excise Duty. The law requires most manufacturers of exciseable goods in the U.K. to be licensed. These manufacturers, which include brewers, distillers, producers of wine and made-wine, makers of matches and mechanical lighters, etc., must pay duty on all such goods produced for home consumption, and they are subject to strict control and survey by Customs Officers who may be resident at manufacturers' premises or make frequent visits. As from 1 January 1976 due to a technical restructuring of revenue duties, the term "excise duty" applies to a new fiscal duty charged alike on imported and home produced goods at the same rate, and "customs duty" means the protective duty charged on certain imports.

Bonded Warehouses. A bonded warehouse is a secure place approved by Customs and Excise for the safe-keeping of dutiable goods on which the duty has not been paid. Warehouses are not owned by the Crown; they are operated by warehousing companies, dock and harbour authorities and similar bodies. Each warehouse-keeper is required to enter into a bond with approved sureties as a guarantee that duty will be paid on any goods not accounted for to the Commissioners' satisfaction. Most goods liable to duty or other Customs charges (except those solely liable to V.A.T.) may be deposited in a bonded warehouse. Duty is normally charged on delivery of goods from a warehouse for home use, but not on export or removal to another bonded warehouse, or on delivery for duty free use. Various operations such as blending, bottling or repacking, are allowed in a bonded warehouse. Home produced goods may also be warehoused free of excise duty in certain circumstances.

The stringency of revenue control varies according to the nature of goods and operations for which a warehouse has been approved. Some are under constant supervision when open and are "Crown locked" by the Customs, as well as by the warehouse keeper, when closed. Others are not Crown locked but are controlled by visiting officers. The responsible officer ensures that an accurate stock account is set up when goods enter the warehouse and that it is properly maintained. An officer will permit removal of goods only on presentation of the proper documents and after payment of the appropriate duties. Natural losses such as evaporation are taken into account but all losses are subject to close scrutiny and duty is charged if deficiencies cannot be satisfactorily explained.

THE CORPORATION OF TRINITY HOUSE

The Corporation is an association of English mariners which originally had its headquarters at Deptford in Kent. It received its first Royal Charter from Henry VIII in 1514 although the Trinity brethren had existed in a corporate capacity before then. The charter described the Corporation as "The Guild or Fraternity of the most Glorious and Undivided Trinity of St. Clement in the parish of Deptford Strond". The first master appointed was the founder of the Corporation, Sir Thomas Spent, Comptroller of the Navy.

Deptford was made a Royal Dockyard by Henry VIII, and being a station where outgoing ships were supplied with pilots, the Corporation rapidly extended its influence and usefulness. By Henry VIII it was entrusted with the direction of the then new dockyard. From Elizabeth I, who conferred on it a grant of arms in 1573, the Corporation received authority to erect beacons and other marks for the guidance of navigators along the coasts of England.

In 1604 a select class was constituted called Elder Brethren, the other members being called Younger Brethren. By a charter of 1609 the sole management of the Corporation's affairs was conferred on the Elder Brethren but Younger Brethren, however, were given a vote in the election of the Master and Wardens.

The practical duties of the fraternity are discharged by the Elder Brethren, usually about 13 in number, of whom 2 may be elected from the Royal Navy and the others from the Merchant Navy. As a mark of honour, a number of persons of rank and eminence are admitted as Hon. Elder Brethren, and the Master is always a person of eminence.

In 1647 the Corporation was dissolved by Parliament, but was reconstructed in 1660, and its charter was renewed by James II in 1685. In 1687 a bye-law of Trinity House for the first time required an agreement in writing between the master and crew of a ship.

A new hall and almshouses were erected at Deptford in 1765, but for some time the offices of the Corporation had been transferred to London where they had a house in Water Lane, Lower Thames Street. In 1795 the headquarters were removed to Trinity House, Tower Hill. The Tower Hill headquarters were practically destroyed by enemy action in the Second World War, but have since been reconstructed.

By an Act of 1836 the Corporation received powers to purchase from the Crown, as well as from private proprietors, all interest in coast lights. For the maintenance of lights, buoys, beacons, etc., they had power to raise money by tolls, any surplus being devoted to the charitable relief of old and indigent mariners or their near relatives.

In 1853 the control of funds collected was transferred to the Mercantile Marine Department of the Board of Trade and moneys over which the Brethren were allowed independent control were eventually reduced to the income derived from funded and trust properties. The practical duties of the Corporation in the erection and maintenance of lighthouses, buoys, etc., still remains as important as ever. Similar functions are carried out by the Commissioners of Northern Lights in Scotland and by the Commissioners of Irish Lights in Ireland. Trinity House still remains the pilotage authority for the London district extending from Felixstowe to Dungeness and also for a number of outports including Southampton.

Other Trinity Houses established under Charter or Act of Parliament for the appointment and control of pilots are at Hull, Newcastle and Leith.

The Elder Brethren of Trinity House act, when required to do so, as nautical assessors in the Admiralty Court.

The Corporation has a large wharf and repair shop at the mouth of the River Lea where most of the work in connection with buoying the Thames is carried out. Other depots are at Harwich and Yarmouth.

LLOYD'S

The world famous institution known as the Corporation of Lloyd's, or more generally simply as "Lloyd's" (its renown is such that any further qualification is really superfluous), owes its origin, as everybody is aware, to the enterprise of Edward Lloyd, the 17th-century coffee-house keeper, under whose roof merchants, ship-owners, and underwriters of the day found it convenient to meet to carry on their business with each other, and to take advantage of Lloyd's special flair for collecting shipping information from ship-masters and others from all parts of the world.

The present-day activities of Lloyd's, which cover a wide range of shipping and marine insurance affairs, still include the collection and dissemination of information by Lloyd's Intelligence Depart-ment. The daily publication of *Lloyd's List & Shipping Gazette* and the annual appearance of *Lloyd's Nautical Yearbook* are of great value to the shipping community which also has the benefit of such agree-ments as Lloyd's Average Bond, Arbitration Agreement in Collision Cases, Salvage Agreement, and so on. Special facilities are available for masters of ships to report direct to Lloyd's casualties and ac-cidents to their own and other vessels, whilst shipowners, salvage contractors and others can be supplied with casualty reports at all hours of the day or night. The Corporation has facilities for com-mercial maritime signalling at stations in many parts of the world whereby owners and others can, at small cost, obtain information of vessels in which they are interested.

To enable Lloyd's to acquire without delay the latest information in respect of all shipping matters there exists the organisation of Lloyd's Agents to which reference has been made in Chapter 7. Those shipping firms in various parts of the world who have been appointed as Lloyd's Agents consider themselves specially honoured to act in such capacity and are not remunerated otherwise than by the fees and charges payable by those to whom their particular services are rendered.

Members of Lloyd's are underwriting members and subscribing members. Marine insurance companies which subscribe to Lloyd's have the benefit of many of the services of the Corporation but have no part in its direction or control. As far as underwriting is con-cerned, the Corporation serves as a kind of umbrella under the shelter of which underwriters are provided with facilities to trans-act their business. As stated previously, the Corporation does not itself underwrite risks or accept liability under policies. That is left to the underwriting members. Nevertheless, the control exercised by the Committee of Lloyd's over the election and conduct of under-writing members is to a large extent responsible for the high degree of public confidence all the world over in "insurance at Lloyds".

THE BALTIC MERCANTILE AND SHIPPING EXCHANGE

This is another London shipping organisation which, in certain respects, has much in common with Lloyd's. The elected committee which controls the Exchange does not itself engage in commercial activities, but provides accommodation and facilities for the members to do so. Membership is open to shipowners and shipbrokers of accepted standing who, in addition to paying the entrance fee and annual subscription, are required to own a share in the Baltic Exchange. Many kinds of activities take place on The Baltic, including auctions of primary products, but the Exchange is probably best known as the place where very many chartering fixtures are negotiated and, not infrequently, ship sale and purchase contracts.

THE GENERAL COUNCIL OF BRITISH SHIPPING (G.C.B.S.)

The general Council of British Shipping became operative on the 1st March 1975 when it took over the roles of the Chamber of Shipping of the United Kingdom and the British Shipping Federation. Members are persons resident in, or companies registered in, the United Kingdom who own or manage United Kingdom registered ships, and they cover almost the entire merchant fleet consisting of some 200 or so shipping companies owning or managing about 33 million tons deadweight of shipping. Associations of shipowners established in the United Kingdom who represent the interests of shipowners in a particular area or in respect of a particular type of ship, and also Protection and Indemnity Associations having United Kingdom shipowners as members may join the Council as Associate Members.

The primary object of the Council is to promote and protect the interests of the owners and managers of British ships and to take appropriate action, nationally and internationally, to achieve that end. Because of its comprehensive membership it is able to speak for the whole industry. It is not directly involved in the commercial affairs of individual companies but tries to set the climate in which shipping can best serve trade and operate as a free enterprise competitive industry.

The Council is closely concerned with legislation which affects or could affect shipping and it advises, consults, negotiates and, where necessary, takes issue with the Government of the day on policies which directly or indirectly can affect the interests of the shipping industry. There is also liaison with members of all parties of both Houses of Parliament to ensure that they are kept well informed of developments within the shipping industry.

On matters concerning sea-going personnel the Council represents British shipowners and managers on bodies such as the National Maritime Board, the Merchant Navy Training Board, the Seafarers' Pension Funds and the Merchant Navy Welfare Board.

It is responsible for the recruitment, selection, and shore training of most of the rating personnel employed in the Merchant Navy. It also plays an important part in the recruitment of deck and engineer cadets, and in the formulation and co-ordination of policy on the training of officers.

The Council administers the Merchant Navy Established Service

Scheme which has two aims: to offer seafarers a stable and an attractive career and regularity of employment and income, and to provide shipping companies with efficient and reliable personnel to man and maintain their ships. The Scheme is geared to the special needs of seafarers and is operated through offices situated at the main seaports. All seafarers are registered under the Scheme which entitles them to financial provision while they are ashore awaiting voyages, under training, or ill. The Scheme also provides medical facilities.

Shipping being an international business effective working relationships are important with the many organisations concerned with trade and shipping throughout the world. The Council is therefore linked with the work of the International Maritime Organisation (I.M.O.), the International Labour Organisation (I.L.O.), the United Nations Conference on Trade and Development (U.N.C.T.A.D.), the United Nations Commission on International Trade Law (U.N.C.I.T.R.A.L.), the International Chamber of Shipping (I.C.S.) and many others of direct concern to the industry.

The work at headquarters is administered on a divisional basis under the following headings:—Industrial Relations, Manning, Training, Marine Safety, Foreign Shipping Policy, Legal and General and Economics and Statistics. The District Offices in ports give day to day advice to shipowners and other services concerned with crew matters, interpreting agreements etc.

THE NATIONAL MARITIME BOARD

This Board was constituted for the purpose of:

1. The prevention and adjustment of differences between owners masters, seamen, and cadets.
2. The establishment, revision and maintenance of standard rates of wages and approved conditions of employment in the Mercantile Marine.
3. The establishment of a single source of supply of sailors and firemen jointly controlled by employers and employed on the principle that:
   (a) The shipowner shall have the right to select his own crew through the jointly controlled supply office.
   (b) All seamen are to have equal rights of registration and employment. Raw recruits to be registered as such.
   (c) Seamen to have the right of selecting their ship.

Those members of the Board who represent the employers are elected by the General Council of British Shipping.

Those who represent the employed are the constituent Panels consisting of the Shipmasters' Panel, Navigating Officers' Panel, Engineer Officers' Panel, Radio Officers' Panel, Sailors' and Firemen's Panel and Catering Department Panel. The Shipmasters' Panel consists of representatives nominated by the representative organisations (Mercantile Marine Service Association and Merchant Navy and Airline Officers' Association). Representatives on the other Panels are nominated by the appropriate Unions. There are District Panels and Port Consultants at the major United Kingdom ports.

The Board publishes a Summary containing the current agreements and issues amendments from time to time as necessary.

The Summary gives details of the Established Service Scheme Agreement and states, amongst other things, that the object of the Agreement is to enable seafarers to look to the Merchant Navy to offer them a suitable and attractive career and greater regularity of employment and income, and give Shipping Companies efficient and reliable personnel to man and maintain their ships at sea and in port. The number of seafarers who can be covered by the Agreement must depend upon the employment requirements of the industry. Estimates will have to be made from time to time of prospective employment over as long a period as possible.

The Agreement applies to Shipping Companies represented by the General Council of British Shipping and to seafarers, being Registered Seafarers, Registered Seafarers (Seasonal) and Company Service Contract Seafarers, who are engaged for service in, or working by, U.K. registered vessels to which N.M.B. Agreements apply and such other vessels as may be approved by the Merchant Navy Establishment Administration. It does not apply to those Radio Officers who have a direct contract of employment with any recognised Marine Radio Company which is party to N.M.B. Agreements or to certain ranks and ratings listed in Appendix 1 who are normally employed only in passenger ships (e.g. Purser, Surgeon, Nurse, Master at Arms, Hairdresser, Shop Attendant etc.). The Registered Seafarers, Registered Seafarers (Seasonal) and Company Service Contract Seafarers together form and are known collectively as the Merchant Navy Establishment.

The General Council of British Shipping is responsible, after consultation with the Seafarers Organisations, for the administration and control of the Merchant Navy Establishment. The administration keeps and maintains Registers of the seafarers to whom the Agreement applies. Selection of crews by Shipping Companies may take place only at offices of the administration or at shipping company offices approved by the administration. At any such selection a representative of the shipping company shall be present with authority to engage.

THE MERCHANT NAVY TRAINING BOARD

The Merchant Navy Training Board had its origins in the Central Board for The Training of Officers in the Merchant Service which was set up in 1935 with the main purpose of organising schemes of study and examinations for navigating cadets at sea.

Since that time there has been a growing awareness in the industry of the value of systematic progressive training, the need for agreed policies and a degree of uniformity, coupled with flexibility, essential to the progress in training demanded by changing conditions. It was consequently decided that the surveillance and advancement of training in the Merchant Navy could be best achieved through a formal organisation representative of the industry and the other bodies mainly responsible for nautical training and education.

The Board has been reconstituted from time to time as necessity demanded but has maintained throughout its voluntary nature and its twofold aim of ensuring firstly, that the training and associated education required by seafarers to perform their various duties adequately is available and, secondly, that the opportunities exist for those making their career in the Merchant Navy to develop their abilities as fully as possible. Following a major reorganisation in 1964 it was agreed that specialist sections should be set up covering the training of deck officers, engineer officers, engineroom ratings, deck ratings and catering personnel. Later a radio officers' section was added.

By early 1971 changes and developments prompted further reorganisation under which the Board, still retaining its voluntary nature, was constituted in a similar way to the Statutory Training Boards. A Qualifications Panel and a section covering management and supervisory training were added.

As part of the reconstitution an independent Chairman was elected. A Director (who also serves as Chief Training Executive to the G.C.B.S.) and a full-time Secretary were appointed. The G.C.B.S. assumed administrative responsibility for the Board and the Council training advisory staff serve both the Council and the M.N.T.B.

During recent years the Board has directed increasing attention to the development of courses leading towards nationally recognised educational qualifications as well as Department of Trade and Home Office examinations for certificates of competency. In this respect the Board was interested in the Ordinary National Certificate and Ordinary National Diploma courses forming part of the cadet training scheme and which enable successful candidates to gain certain exemptions from the 2nd Mate and 1st Mate Certificate examinations, the B.Sc. (Nautical Science) courses now offered at a number of Universities, Polytechnics, etc., and the Higher National Diploma in Nautical Science. Certain Marine Engineering and Electrical qualifications are included as well as those concerned with Radio Communications and marine electronics maintenance. Revised arrangements for the medical training of deck officers, which claim a further share of the Board's interest, include a "First Aid at Sea" course taken at the 2nd Mate stage and a further course at a later stage leading to the award of a "Ship Captain's Medical Training Certificate".

Every aspect of Deck and Engineroom Rating Training receives its share of the Board's attention, in particular courses leading to Lifeboatman and Efficient Deck-hand Certificates. Catering training comes in for further attention and the surveillance of Management and Supervisory courses which formerly rested with a Joint Committee set up by the G.C.B.S. will in future fall to the Management and Supervisory sections of the M.N.T.B.

In addition to training specific to one or other of the departments on board ship, the Board is interested in a number of training schemes available to seafarers generally. These include Accident Prevention, Fire-Fighting and Training for Seafarers in Ships Carrying Hazardous Cargoes in Bulk.

THE MARINE SOCIETY

The Marine Society is the oldest marine charity in the world having been founded in 1756 to help poor boys to make a career at sea. It established the first training ship, thus establishing a pattern of training for the sea which lasted for 150 years. Since the Second World War the society has continued to help young men and women to start a sea career, mainly by way of grants and loans for uniform but also, in case of need, for college fees. It also helped greatly to establish the Nautical Institute.

In 1976 the Marine Society's powers were enlarged by Parliament to incorporate those of the Seafarers Education Service and the two organisations then amalgamated. The S.E.S. had been founded in 1919 to provide a first-class library service to merchant ships and to provide educational facilities for British seafarers. Libraries are supplied to some 1,600 ships, each library being changed three times a year. At each exchange the ship's company can ask for any book to be incorporated. In addition all books are lent on personal loan to British seafarers, a hire charge being made for nautical textbooks and new fiction. Books can also be bought from the Service. The reputation of the S.E.S. has been established by prompt, efficient and courteous service. Free advice is given on anything to do with books, careers and education, including the education of children. Through its department, the College of the Sea, the society teaches all general subjects by correspondence. Its role is complementary to that of the nautical colleges and it aims to provide seafarers with a complete adult education service. It arranges G.C.E. and other examinations on board ship and cooperates with the Open University in making the University's facilities available to seafarers. The College of the Sea has pioneered the provision of language tapes and programmed books in certain fields, and the society runs a documentary film library. All hobbies come within the society's range, and hobby kits of many varieties are supplied to ships and seafarers. Each year the society organises competitions for short stories, essays, photographs, poetry, paintings and handicrafts.

The Marine Society has a particular interest in helping seafarers to make the most of their talents and, in addition to helping officers with their studies, it offers scholarships to those ratings who aspire to officer status, together with special coaching in English, mathematics and physics. The society also teaches by correspondence for its own diploma in Merchant Navy studies. It has power to initiate research in subjects connected with the welfare and education of seafarers. In recent years it has also run pre-retirement courses for seafarers, and has sponsored books in its own field: "Introduction to the Merchant Navy", "Spare Time at Sea", "The Shoregoers's Guide to World Ports" and "Retirement from the Sea", as well as collections of seafarers' poems and stories.

In 1975, when the British Ship Adoption Society ceased to be viable as an independent organisation, the S.E.S. took over this work, now operated as Ship Adoption. The purpose is to put seafarers in touch with schools "to bring a breath of sea air into the classroom". Seafaring volunteers are in demand; a correspondence between school and seafarer is fostered and visits are encouraged.

Officially approved in its work by the Department of Trade, the Department of Education and Science, the education authorities and all branches of the shipping industry, the Marine Society is nevertheless a charity dependent in part upon voluntary donations and subscriptions. Shipboard collections can help, and individuals can subscribe for the society's magazine "The Seafarer". Those associated with the work may wear Marine Society tie which displays the society's emblem, an heraldic sea-dog bearing the torch of learning.

THE INTERNATIONAL MARITIME ORGANISATION (I.M.O.)

Before the Second World War all problems relating to shipping which required international agreement were dealt with by conferences set up for the purpose, although as long ago as 1889 at a conference in Washington, the establishment of a permanent international maritime commission to deal with questions of safety of life and property at sea was proposed but postponed. Two short lived inter-governmental organisations were set up in 1944 and 1946, the second of which prepared a draft convention for the setting up of a permanent organisation which became the basis for discussion at a conference held at Geneva in 1948. This conference successfully prepared and opened for signature a Convention on the Inter-Governmental Maritime Consultative Organisation (I.M.C.O.) which was to enter into force when 21 States, including seven having at least one million gross tons of shipping, became parties to it. In March 1958, Japan became the twenty-first State to accept the Convention and the organisation came into being in January 1959 as the 12th specialised agency of the United Nations. Its members include not only the traditional maritime countries but also those which rely largely on the shipping services of other countries. I.M.C.O. changed its name to the International Maritime Organisation (I.M.O.) on 22nd May 1982.

The first objective of the I.M.O. is to facilitate cooperation among governments in technical matters of all kinds affecting shipping. Its aim is to achieve the highest practicable standards of maritime safety and efficient navigation. It has a special responsibility for the safety of life at sea. It also provides for the wide exchange of information between nations on all technical maritime matters.

A further purpose of the I.M.O. is to promote the freest possible availability of shipping services to meet the world wide need for overseas transport by discouraging discriminating, unfair and restrictive practices affecting ships in international trade. The I.M.O. is also required to give advice to other international bodies on shipping matters, including agencies of the United Nations. In the legal field, the Legal Committee of I.M.C.O. was involved in the work which resulted in the two Conventions on oil pollution which came into force in 1975, and in the setting up of the International Compensation Fund. It is further involved in work on the international combined transport of goods, the status of ocean data acquisition systems and the maritime carriage of nuclear substances.

The organisation consists of an Assembly, a Council, a Maritime Safety Committee, other subsidiary organs as necessary and a Secretariat. Membership is open to all States and in May 1981 there were 121 members and one associate member. The Assembly is composed of all members and normally meets once every two years. The Council, consisting of 24 members elected by the Assembly to represent suppliers and users of shipping services of all major geographic areas of the world, meets as often as maybe necessary; it receives the recommendations and reports of the Maritime Safety Committee and transmits them to the Assembly, and to the members for information, together with its comments and its recommendations. It also appoints the Secretary-General.

The Maritime Safety Committee consists of members from all States. It deals with the technical work of the I.M.O. The Committee is elected for a four year term and has the duty of considering any matter concerned with aids to navigation, construction and equipment of vessels, manning from a safety standpoint, collision prevention rules, handling dangerous cargoes, maritime safety procedures, hydrographic information, log books and navigational records, casualty investigation, salvage and rescue and any other matters directly affecting maritime safety. The Committee meets once a year and submits to the Assembly through the Council, its proposals for safety regulations and for amendments to existing safety regulations, together with its comments or recommendations.

The Secretariat consists of the Secretary-General, a Secretary of the Maritime Safety Committee and such staff as the organisation may require. It must maintain records necessary for the functioning of the I.M.O., and prepare, collect, and circulate papers, documents, agenda, minutes etc. that may be required for the work of the Assembly, Council and Maritime Safety Committee. The headquarters of the I.M.O. is in London.

THE UNITED NATIONS CONFERENCE ON TRADE AND DEVELOPMENT (U.N.C.T.A.D.)

This is an organisation, established in 1964, in which all members of the United Nations are entitled to participate. Its origin lies in the demands of the developing countries for a greater share in the industrial world's riches. It is an organ of the General Assembly, meeting at three year intervals, and has a permanent elected Trade and Development Board and a permanent Secretariat.

At its first conference held in Geneva in 1964 the following special principle was agreed to:—

"All countries should cooperate in devising measures to help developing countries to build up maritime and other means of transport for their economic development, to ensure the unhindered use of international transport facilities, the improvement of terms of freight and insurance for the developing countries, and to promote tourism in these countries in order to increase their earnings and reduce their expenditure on invisible trade."

The Board has established three committees—on commodities, on manufactures and on invisible trade which includes shipping, insurance charges, interest on debt and tourist spending. The Shipping Committee has since discussed a wide variety of subjects ranging from freight rates, discriminatory practices, improvement of port facilities and the expansion of the mercantile marines of developing states, to the complicated legal issues raised when considering revision of present international conventions on merchant shipping. The Shipping Committee, following the Second Conference, appointed a working sub-committee to deal with international shipping legislation whose first work was a study of bills of lading and possible modification of the Hague Rules, which was completed in 1971. The study raised legal problems and as the sub-committee did not have the expertise to draft new, or to amend existing legislation, it referred the matter to the United Nations Commission on International Trade Law (U.N.C.I.T.R.A.L.), while continuing studies on other shipping matters such as liner conferences, combined transport of goods, and legal and economic questions in charter parties, marine insurance and general average, which may later be referred to U.N.C.I.T.R.A.L.

THE UNITED NATIONS COMMISSION ON INTERNATIONAL TRADE LAW (U.N.C.I.T.R.A.L.)

This commission, which meets annually, is an organ of the General Assembly, and consists of representatives of 36 states elected to membership by the Assembly on a regional basis. It was established in 1966 and had its first session in 1968. It owes its origin to the need for cooperation in the field of East-West trade, but also fulfils the U.N. Charter mandate for progressive changes to harmonise and unify international trade law.

From its beginning U.N.C.I.T.R.A.L. concentrated on international sales of goods, international payments and commercial arbitration, and it was not until its fourth session in 1971 that a regular working committee on international shipping legislation was set up, consisting of 21 members.

From 1972 to 1975 this committee has examined the three main problems raised by U.N.C.T.A.D. in its study of bills of lading and the Hague Rules. These are (1) the responsibility for loss or damage to cargo during the period after delivery to the carrier but before shipment, and during the period after discharge of cargo and before delivery to the consignee; (2) the effect of clauses in bills of lading which require claims to be presented to a tribunal at a location that is inconvenient to the claimant; and (3) the exclusion of goods carried on deck from the Brussels Convention of 1924 (based on the Hague Rules). The Committee produced a Draft Convention on Bills of Lading in 1975 for consideration by U.N.C.T.A.D. Eventually after discussions these were adopted at a Convention as the Hamburg Rules 1978.

CHAPTER 17

GLOSSARY OF TERMS AND LIST OF ABBREVIATIONS
OF SHIPPING TERMS

GLOSSARY

THE list of terms which follows is intentionally limited to those terms which have not been mentioned in the preceding Chapters but which the author has thought fit to include with a view to making the book a more complete work of reference. Terms and phrases which have been treated elsewhere will, of course, be easily located by consulting the index.

Accostage. The charge customarily made in certain North African ports for the use of a jetty and usually levied on the net registered tonnage of the ship.

Agency Fee. The remuneration for agents who have attended to the business of the ship during her stay in port. In most places there are fixed scales of charges for agency work. In some cases a specific fee may be agreed to in the C/P, in other cases the fee may vary according to the tonnage of the ship or to the kind and quantity of cargo being loaded and/or discharged.

All Told. If the deadweight capacity quoted in a C/P is qualified by the phrase "all told" this means that the stated figure includes not only cargo capacity, but fuel, stores, and water as well.

Bar Bound. This describes a vessel which is unable to cross a bar at the port approaches because her draught exceeds the maximum depth of water on the bar.

Bar Draught. The maximum draught to which a vessel can load in order to cross a bar safely.

Bar Port. A river port which cannot be reached without crossing a bar. Obviously, a vessel committed to loading a full cargo at a bar port would, after loading to her bar draught above the bar, be obliged to complete loading below the bar. Lighterage incurred in such circumstances is usually, by a term of the C/P, for the account of the charterers.

Benefit of Fall. In the liner trades exporters frequently make forward bookings at current rates of freight. If, during the agreed booking period (which may be, say, for the current and two following

724

months), freight rates should rise, shipments already booked will still be accepted to the exporter's advantage at the original rates. On the other hand, it will be to the exporter's disadvantage should freight rates fall during the same period. Sometimes, however, it is agreed that the exporter shall have the "benefit of fall", in which case the reduced rates will apply to cargo booked in advance but not shipped until after the fall in rates has taken place.

Berthage. The charge made for use of a berth.

Berth Note. Sometimes called a Booking note, this is a form of chartering contract used when it is desired to ship a large parcel of cargo (usually in bulk) for carriage by a ship trading on the berth. It may take the form of a letter addressed to the charterers and signed by an agent or broker on behalf of the shipowner to confirm the booking of a part cargo in the vessel named. The charterers will sign their own confirmation of the contents of the note on the same document. The contents will generally include the following:—

The kind and quantity of cargo to be loaded.
The port, or range of ports, where the cargo is to be loaded.
The port, or ports, where the cargo is to be discharged.
Lay days and cancelling date.
The rate of freight and place and method of payment thereof.
Rates of loading and discharging.
Form of B/L to be used. (Usually Owners' B/L.)
Vessel to have liberty of loading other cargo before and/or after loading the charterer's cargo.
Option, if any, for charterer to load additional cargo.
When, and to whom, orders for first loading port are to be given.

Bill of Store. A form of Customs entry required when goods exported from the United Kingdom are to be re-imported within a named period. This entry frees such goods from the conditions which apply to the importation of foreign goods.

Board Measurement Foot. A timber trade term meaning the cubic measurement of a piece of lumber $1' \times 1' \times 1''$. Hence, 1,000 board feet occupy a space of $\frac{1,000}{12} = 83\frac{1}{3}$ cubic feet excluding broken stowage.

Coefficient of Loading. The relationship between the ship's deadweight cargo carrying capacity and her cubic capacity for cargo. As an example:

Summer displacement	...	...	...	...	...	16,000 tons
Light displacement	...	...	...	...	...	5,800 ,,
Summer deadweight	...	...	...	...	...	10,200 ,,
Fuel, stores, water, spares, etc.		...	...	...	...	1,200 ,,
Deadweight cargo capacity	...	...	...	...	9,000 ,,
Bale-space ...	...	...	...	...	...	576,000 cu, ft.

Y

The coefficient (average number of cubic feet per ton) is therefore $\frac{576,000}{9,000} = 64$ cu. ft. per ton. If, under the conditions suggested this vessel could load a cargo averaging 64 cu. ft per ton, she would if loaded to her summer marks be cubically full, *i.e.*, "full and down". Needless to say, this would be extremely difficult to achieve in practice, if not impossible.

Cranage. The charge made for the hire of a crane to load or discharge goods too heavy to be lifted by the ship's own gear.

Danger Money. Additional payment made to persons engaged on work which exposes them to more than the normal risk of personal injury or contraction of disease.

Dirty Money. Additional payment made to persons engaged on work involving the handling of goods of a dirty or objectionable nature.

Dock Dues. Charges levied on shipping for the use of docks and generally calculated on the net registered tonnage of the ship plus the tonnage of any deck cargo loaded or discharged.

Dock Warrant. The receipt given for goods received into a dock warehouse. Warehoused goods represent dormant capital, hence a dock warrant is treated as a negotiable document of title. Where the dock authority has no statutory power to issue negotiable warrants any warrant given is not at law negotiable, but there may be a custom to treat it as such. It may therefore be pledged as security for an advance against the goods described in it, though evidence of value would have to be forthcoming.

Duration Clause. The clause in a marine insurance time policy which defines the commencement and termination of the risk.

Entrepôt. An intermediate warehouse for the temporary deposit of goods in transit; a port where foreign merchandise is kept in bond or in store whilst awaiting re-exportation; or a commercial centre to which goods are sent for distribution.

Fighting Ship. If a tramp ship is put on the berth in competition with Conference liners, the Conference may decide to berth one of its own liners to load simultaneously but offering freight rates substantially below the normal rates. Once the intervening tramp has been withdrawn, or has sailed, freight rates would be restored to normal. Any loss incurred by the owner of the liner would be borne by Conference as a whole. A liner employed in this manner is described as a "fighting ship".

Fittage. A term used in the coal trade meaning the margin of profit which a merchant puts on his cost selling price.

Fixing Letter. When the negotiations for the chartering of a vessel have resulted in a definite fixture, the broker may draw up what is called a fixing letter in which are summarised the principal conditions of the charter. This will be accepted by the shipowner and charterer as a provisional confirmation of the contract pending the signing of the actual charter-party.

Flat Rate. A vessel may be fixed to carry various kinds of cargo, the exact nature of which is not known at the time of fixing, or she may be fixed to carry cargo to be discharged at any one of the ports within a specified range and, in either case, an invariable rate of freight may be agreed. For instance, a fixture may be:

Prince Rupert to picked ports U.K.—m.v. "..........................", 9,000 t., 10 p.c., barley, flat rate £2.95 per ton, Aug. 10-31.

Irrespective of whether the vessel is ordered to discharge at Hull, Liverpool, or any other U.K. port, whereby distance and despatch may vary considerably, the freight rate will still be £2.95 per ton.

Franco. This means prepaid and free of all charges, in other words, the price quoted includes all charges up to and including delivery to the buyer.

Freight Release. An official document given by a shipbroker, or an endorsement on a bill of lading, giving the officer in charge of a ship authority to deliver goods the freight on which has been paid.

Full Out Rye Terms. Where rye or other grain is purchased on these terms the price is paid on the full out-turn weight from the carrying ship at the port of discharge. (See also Rye Terms).

Full Terms. An expression used on the chartering market to imply that the freight rate quoted includes all commissions and other deductions recognised as customary in the particular trade in which the ship is being engaged. It implies further that despatch money will be payable for time saved in loading or discharging. As, in these circumstances, the effective freight rate may be considerably less than the rate quoted, it is important to ascertain in advance just what deductions will be made.

Groundage. A charge made for permission to anchor in a particular place.

Guaranteed Deadweight and Bale-space. Some C/P's provide for freight to be paid at an agreed rate per ton on the vessel's deadweight cargo capacity as mutually agreed between the captain and charterers' agents before the vessel commences to load, but subject to a *pro rata* reduction if the guaranteed deadweight cargo capacity and the guaranteed bale-space are not placed at the disposal of the charterers. The effects of such an agreement may be illustrated as follows.

Suppose the guaranteed capacities are deadweight 12,000 tons, and balespace 600,000 cu. ft., and the freight rate is fixed at £4 per ton. Then:

(a) If both capacities are placed at the charterers' disposal, the lump sum freight is calculated by multiplying together the agreed rate and the guaranteed deadweight capacity, in this case £4 × 12,000 or £48,000.

(b) If the master and charterers' agent agree only 11,800 tons deadweight, but the full guaranteed bale capacity, the lump sum freight is calculated by multiplying together the agreed rate and the agreed deadweight capacity, in this case £4 × 11,800 or £47,200.

(c) If they agree only, say, 11,400 tons and 540,000 cu. ft., the lump sum is calculated by multiplying together the agreed rate, the agreed deadweight and the agreed cubic capacity, and dividing the product by the guaranteed bale-space. In this case that would amount to:

$$\frac{£4 \times 11,400 \times 540,000}{600,000} = £41,040.$$

Held Covered. A marine insurance term to denote that the underwriters have accepted the risk although no formal marine policy has yet been issued. Such a contract is binding in honour only, being legally unenforcable. The same term is often incorporated into the policy itself to provide that, should the risk be not exactly as insured, the underwriters will agree to the assured remaining covered by the policy subject to their being notified and to any additional premium being paid.

Leadage. The cost of transporting coal from the colliery to the port of loading.

Levelling Charges. Charges which may arise in connection with the carriage of sulphur in bulk. The appropriate form of C/P generally stipulates that levelling, if required, will be for the ship's account, as distinct from loading and trimming expenses, which are for the account of the shipper. The extent of levelling required will depend on the kind of cargo, if any, by which the bulk sulphur is to be overstowed.

Loco Price. A term used in connection with contracts of sale. In quoting a price for goods it is always important that the place of purchase should be stated, that is the particular location where the goods are to be delivered by the seller to the buyer. Common quotations are Ex-farm, Ex-silo, Ex-works, Ex-warehouse, Ex-ship, Ex-quay, and so on. Ex-quay, for instance, implies that the purchaser will be responsible for all charges after delivery of the goods on the quay. Cost "ex-warehouse" implies that the buyer takes delivery from the seller's warehouse and pays all subsequent charges such as freight and insurance during transit. On the other hand, where a price is quoted "ex-ship", the seller will pay the freight to the port of destination. F.o.b. and C.i.f. contracts are described in Chapter 9.

Net (or Nett) Weight. The weight of goods excluding the container (case, carton, cask, drum, etc.).

Nett nett weight. The weight of goods excluding both outer packing and individual container. Biscuits, for example, might be packed in tins a number of which are then cased. The nett nett weight is the weight of the actual biscuits.

Open Charter. Where a C/P specifies neither the kind of cargo to be carried nor the port or ports of destination, the contract is described as an "open charter".

Open Indent. This is an order to a supplier for goods which does not specify the name of the manufacturer. This leaves it open to the supplier to obtain the most suitable goods at competitive prices. By contrast, a closed indent does specify the name of the manufacturer and gives the supplier no opportunity to take advantage of competitive offers.

Peage Dues. The name given to dues payable by ships loading bulk phosphate cargoes in North African ports and applied to the cost of maintaining and improving the facilities of the port.

Picked Ports. Those ports within a given range where reasonably quick despatch may be expected. In the grain trades especially, where a chartered ship is ordered to discharge at a port which is not classed as a "picked port" a higher rate of freight is usually agreed to offset the effect of slow despatch.

Post Entry. In respect of the inward Customs clearance of dutiable goods it may happen that the importer's "Prime Entry" inadvertently shows an incorrect amount of duty payable. When this is discovered, unless the discrepancy is trifling, a "Post entry" must be made and the additional duty paid if the prime entry is too small. If there has been an over-payment of duty, an "Over entry" must be certified and the excess duty paid will be refunded.

Pro Forma. As a matter of form.

Prompt Ship. A chartering term implying that the vessel so described can be ready to load at a very short notice.

Riggers. Seamen engaged on a temporary basis to man a ship which has to be shifted from one part of a port to another part of the same port.

Runners. Seamen engaged to man a ship for a coastal "run" from, say, a discharging port to a loading port. By employing runners for this purpose the engagement of the full crew for the next voyage can be postponed until nearer the time when the ship will have completed loading. The same method may be used to transfer a ship from a discharging port to a port of repair. Besides paying the men's wages for the run, the shipowner will have to defray the cost of returning the runners to the port where they were engaged.

Rye Terms. When grain is bought on these terms the seller guarantees the condition on arrival, hence sea water damage *en route* is at his risk.

Salvage Loss. A marine insurance term for the loss settled by underwriters when goods which have been damaged by a peril insured against are sold at a port of refuge because carrying them on farther would result in them losing still more of their value. The measure of indemnity in such cases is the difference between the insured value of the goods and the net proceeds from their sale.

Scale Discharge. C/P's for bulk cargoes, especially coal, sometimes stipulate that the cargo shall be discharged according to a scale ranging from, say, 800 tons per day to 2,000 tons per day, the rate per ton charged to the ship increasing from a minimum for the slowest rate to a maximum at the fastest rate. Before breaking bulk the consignee is required to declare at which rate he elects to discharge, and on this declaration the lay days allowed for discharging will be based. If he chooses a high rate he will do so at the risk of having to pay demurrage, though that may be compensated by the higher cost per ton charged to the ship. Conversely, the choice of a lower rate of discharge may result in despatch money being earned which would compensate for the lower discharging tariff.

Sea-Damaged Terms. A contract for the sale and purchase of grain on these terms gives the buyer the right either to reject goods delivered damaged by sea water, or to claim from the seller the proved amount of sea water damage. Sweat damage is also at the risk of the seller.

Short Ton. A ton of 2,000 lb., as distinct from the ton avoirdupois (long ton) of 2,240 lb.

Sous-Palan Clause. The French name for the "Overside delivery clause" giving consignees the option, provided certain conditions are complied with, of taking delivery of their parcels by their own lighters. It is provided that, should consignees avail themselves of the option and fail to provide the necessary lighters, the master or agents have the right to discharge the goods into other craft or on the wharf at the consignees' expense.

Spot. If a vessel is fixed to load a cargo at the port where she is already lying and the ship is ready for immediate loading, the term "spot charter" would apply. The term "spot" can also apply to goods which are ready for immediate loading.

Subject to Stem. Coal charters are sometimes reported as being "subject to stem" which means subject to the coal suppliers being able to arrange delivery of a parcel of coal within the agreed lay days. When a "stem" has been arranged, the date on which loading is to begin is called the "stem date" and, provided that the chartered ship is arrived, ready and tendered, that will be the date on which the lay days will commence. The term "free stem" implies that loading can be started immediately on the ship's arrival at the loading port.

Tale Quale. A grain trade term implying that the buyer of a parcel must accept it in whatever condition it is at the time of delivery, the seller having given an undertaking that the goods were in good condition on shipment. Sea water damage *en route* is therefore at the risk of the buyer who must pay for the goods "as sound". (Compare this with "Sea-damaged terms".)

Tariff. In general, a table of charges. In particular, a list of duties chargeable on goods. Also the list of current freight rates issued by a Liner Conference.

Tret. The allowance made to purchasers of goods for certain kinds of damage or deterioration during transit.

Ullage. Originally the quantity that a cask lacks of being full, possibly due to abstraction, evaporation, contraction due to change of temperature, or seepage. Now also used to describe the empty space intentionally left in tanks after loading oils or other liquids in bulk to allow for expansion due to increase of temperature during transit. The ullage of a tank may be expressed as the vertical distance between the surface of the liquid and the crown of the tank, or as a percentage of the total capacity of the tank. From $1\frac{1}{2}$ per cent. to $2\frac{1}{2}$ per cent. is fairly common.

Vice Propre. Means the same as inherent vice.

Way Bill. This term, basically, can apply to any carrier's receipt for goods received for carriage, but until recently has probably best been known in shipping circles in connection with the carriage of Post Office mails. When mails are delivered to the carrying ship way bills are presented in triplicate which indicate the numbers and descriptions of all mail bags and postal packets shipped. If the ship loads mails for several ports of destination there will be several sets of way bills accordingly. With respect to each set one copy is signed as a form of receipt and returned to the Post Office at the port of shipment. Another is delivered with the mails and is retained by the postal authorities at the port of destination, whilst the third is retained by the ship after being receipted by the person taking delivery of the mails. See further notes in Chapter 9.

Wharfage. The charge made for the use of a wharf.

ABBREVIATIONS

a.a.	Always afloat	B.O.T.	Board of trade
a.a.r.	Against all risks	B/P.	Bills payable
A.B.	Able-bodied seaman	B.R.	Builder's risks. Bordeaux or Rouen (grain trade)
A/C.	Account current		
a/c.	Account	B/R.	Bills receivable
Acc.	Accepted. Acceptance	Brl.	Barrel
A.& C.P.	Anchors and chains proved	B.S.	Balance sheet. Boiler survey
Ad. val.	*Ad valorem*		
a/d	After date	B/S.	Bill of sale. Bill of store
Add.	Addressed	B/s.	Bags. Bales
adv.	Advice	B.S.F.	British Shipping Federation
A.F.	Advanced freight	B/St.	Bill of sight
Agt.	Agent. Against	B.S.T.	British Summer Time
a.h.	After hatch	b.t.	Berth terms
amt.	Amount	B.T.U.	(B.Th.U.) British thermal unit
a/o	Account of		
A/P	Additional premium	B.V.	Bureau Veritas
A.P.	Average payable	bxs.	Boxes
appro.	Approval		
approx.	Approximately	C.	Collected. Currency. Centigrade
A/R.	All risks		
A/S.	After sight. Account sales. Alongside	c/-	Case
		cancl.	Cancelled
A.T.	American terms (grain trade)	C.B.	Cash book
		C. B. & H.	Continent between Bordeaux and Hamburg
At. wt.	Atomic weight		
aux.	Sailing vessel with auxiliary engine	C.C.	Civil commotions. Current cost. Continuation clause
Av.	Average	C.Cl.	Continuation clause
avdp.	Avoirdupois	c.d.	country damage
		C. &. D.	Collected and delivered
B/-	Bale. Bag	c. & f.	Cost and freight
bal.	Balance	c.f.(cu.ft.)	Cubic feet. Carried forward
bar.	Barrel		
B.B.	Below bridges	c/f	Carried forward
B.C.	Bristol Channel	c.f.o.	Coast (or Channel) for orders
B.D.	Banker's draft. Bar draught	C.G.A.	Cargo's proportion of general average
b/d	Brought down	C. H. & H.	Continent between Havre and Hamburg
b.d.i.	Both dates inclusive		
Bdls.	Bundles	C.H.	Custom House
Bds.	Boards	chq.	Cheque
B/E.	Bill of exchange. Bill of entry	c. & i.	Cost and insurance
		C.I.	Consular invoice. Channel Islands
b/f.	Brought forward		
B/G.	Bonded goods	c/i	Certificate of insurance
Bg.	Bag	C.I.E.	Captain's imperfect (Customs) entry
B/H.	Bill of health. Bordeaux-Hamburg (range)		
		c.i.f.	Cost, insurance, and freight
B.H.P.	Brake horse power	c.i.f.& c.	Cost, insurance, freight, and commission
Bk.	Bank. Backwardation. Book		
		c.i.f.c.& e.	Cost, insurance, freight, commission and exchange
B/L.	Bill of Lading		
Bls.	Bales. Barrels	c.i.f.c.& i.	Cost, insurance, freight, commission, and interest,
b.m.	Board measure (timber)		
B.O.	Buyer's option	c.i.f.L.t.	Cost, insurance, and freight, London terms
B/O.	Brought over		

C/k.	Cask
c./l.	Craft loss
cld.	Cleared
C.N.	Cover note. Consignment note. Credit note.
C/O	Certificate of origin. Cash order. Case oil
c/o	Carried over. Care of
C.O.D.	Cash on delivery
Com.	Commission
Consgt.	Consignment
Cont.	Continent (of Europe)
Cont.B/H.	Continent, Bordeaux-Hamburg range
Cont.H/H.	Continent, Havre-Hamburg range
convs.	Conveyances
C/P.	Charter-party
c.p.d.	Charterers pay dues
C.R.	Current rate. Carrier's risk. Company's risk
Cr.	Credit. Creditor
C.S.	Colliery screened. Cotton seed
c/s	Cases
C.T.C.	Corn trade clauses
C.T.L.	Constructive total loss
C.T.L.O.	Constructive total loss only
cum	With
cum.	Cumulative
Cur.(Curt.)	Current
c.v.	Chief value
cwt.	Hundredweight
C.W.	Commercial weight
c.w.o.	Cash with order
D/A.	Documents against acceptance
D/a.	Discharge afloat
d.a.a.	Discharge always afloat
d.b.	Deals and battens (timber)
d.b.b.	Deals, battens, and boards (timber)
D.B.	Day book
Dbk.	Drawback
D.C.(D.Cl.)	Deviation clause. Detention clause
D.D.	Damage done
d.d.	due date
D/D.	Demand draft. Delivered at docks
D/d.	Days after date
dd.	Delivered
dd/s.	Delivered sound
D.D.& Shpg.	Dock dues and shipping
d.d.o.	Despatch discharging only
d.f.	Dead freight
dft.	Draft
Dis.	Discount

d.l.o.	Despatch loading only
dely. & re-dely.	Delivery and re-delivery
D/N.	Debit note.
D/O.	Delivery Order
D.o.T.	Department of Trade
D/P.	Documents against payment
d.p.	Direct port
D/R.	Deposit receipt
Dr.	Debit. Debtor. Drawer
D/s.	Days after sight
D.T.I.	Department of Trade and Industry
D/W.	Dock warrant
d.w.	Deadweight
d.w.c.	Deadweight capacity
dwt.	Pennyweight
dy.	Delivery
E.C.	East coast
E.C.A.	East coast of Africa
E.C.C.P.	East coast coal port (Great Britain)
E.C.G.B.	East coast of Great Britain
E.C.I.	East coast of Ireland
E.C.U.K.	East coast of the United Kingdom
E.D.H.	Efficient deck hand
E.E.	Errors excepted
e.g.	*Exempli gratia* (for example). *Ejusdem generis* (of a like kind)
E.I.	East Indies
E. & O.E.	Errors and omissions excepted
e.o.h.p.	Except otherwise herein provided
eq.	Equivalent
est.	Estimated
E.T.A.	Estimated time of arrival
et. al.	And others
et seq.	And the following (singular)
et seqq.	And the following (plural)
Ex.	Excluded. Out of. Without. Examined. Exchange. Executed
Exd.	Examined
Exs.	Expenses
f.a.	Free alongside
F.A.A.	Free of all average
f.a.c.	Fast as can
F. & D.	Freight and demmurrage
f.a.q.	Fair average quality
f.a.s.	Free alongside ship (steamer)
F.C. & S.	Free of capture and seizure
Fco.	Franco
f.c.s.r.c.c.	Free of capture, seizure, riots, and civil commotions

f.d.	Free Discharge. Free delivery. Free despatch. Free docks	G.F.	Government Form (chartering)
f.f.a.	Free from alongside. Free foreign agency	g.f.a.	Good fair average
		G.M.	Good middling
f.g.	Fully good	g.m.b.	Good merchantable brand
F.G.A.	Foreign general average	g.m.q.	Good merchantable quality
f.g.f.	Fully good, fair	G.M.T.	Greenwich mean time
f.h.	Fore hatch	g.o.b.	Good ordinary brand
f.i.a.	Full interest admitted	gr.	Grain. Gross
f.i.b.	Free into bunkers. Free into barge	g r.t.	Gross register tonnage
		g.s.	Good safety
f.i.o.	Free in and out	g.s.m.	Good sound merchantable
f.i.o.s.	Free in and out and stowed	G.T.	Gross tonnage
f.i.o.t.	Free in and out trimmed	G.V.	Grand vitesse (fast goods train)
f.i.t.	Free of income tax		
f.i.w.	Free into wagon		
fl.	Florin (Netherlands)	H.A. or D.	Havre, Antwerp, or Dunkirk
f.l.n.	Following landing numbers	H.&M.	Hull and materials
f.o.	For orders. Firm offer. Full out (terms)	H/C	Held covered
		h.& o.	Hook and oil (damage)
f.o.b.	Free on board	hf.	Half
f.o.c.	Free on car. Free of charge	H/H.	Havre to Hamburg
f.o.d.	Free of damage	hhd.	Hogshead
f.o.q.	Free on quay	h.h.d.w.	Heavy handy deadweight scrap
F.O.R.	Free on rail		
f.o.r.t.	Full out rye terms	H.M.etc.	Hull, machinery, etc.
forwd.	Forward	H.P.	Horse power
f.o.s.	Free on ship (steamer)	H.P.N.	Horse power nominal
f.o.t.	Free on truck (train)	hr. hrs.	Hour. Hours.
f.o.w.	Free on wagon. First open water	H.T.	Half time (survey)
		H.W.	High water
F.P.	Floating policy. Fully paid	H.W.M.	High water mark
F.P.A.	Free from particular average		
F.P.A.A.	Free from particular average absolutely	I.A.T.A.	International Air Transport Association
		I.B.	Invoice book
F.P.A.u.c.b.	Free from particular average unless caused by (stranding, etc.)	I.C.A.O.	International Civil Aviation Organisation
		I.C.&C.	Invoice cost and charges
f.p.i.l.	Full premium if lost	I.C.C.	Institute cargo clauses
F/R	Freight release	I.H.P.	Indicated horse power
f.r. & c.c.	Free of riots and civil commotions	I.M.C.O.	Inter-Governmental Maritime Consultative Organization
F.R.C.	Free Carrier		
f.r.o.f.	Fire risk on freight	I.M.O.	International Maritime Organisation
Frt.	Freight		
Frt.fwd.	Freight forward	inc.	Increase. Inclusive
Frt.ppd.	Freight paid	int.	Interest
f.t.	Full terms	ince.	Insurance
F.T.W.	Free trade wharf	i/o.	In and/or over (stowage under or on deck)
fwd.	Forward		
f.w.d.	Fresh water damage	I.O.M.	Isle of Man
		i.o.p.	Irrespective of percentage
G/A	General average	I.O.W.	Isle of Wight
G/A con.	General average contribution	i.p.f.	Intake piled fathom
		i.v.	Invoice value. Increased value
G/A dep.	General average deposit		
GB.	Great Britain		
g.b.o.	Goods in bad order	J/A	Joint Account

j. & w.o.	Jettison and washing overboard
K.D.	Knocked down
K.I.D.	Key industry duty
£E.	Pounds Egyptian
£T.	Pounds Turkish
L/A.	Letter of authority. Landing account. Lloyd's agent
lat.	Latitude
L.A.T.	Linseed Association Terms
L.C.	London clause
L/C.	Letter of credit
L. cl.	Label clause
L.C.T.A.	London Corn Trade Association
Ld.	Load
ldg.	Loading. Landing
Ldg. & Dely.	Landing and delivery
lds.	Loads
L.H.A.R.	London, Hull, Antwerp, or Rotterdam
L.I.P.	Life insurance policy
Lkg. & Bkg.	Leakage and breakage
L.L.T.	London landed terms
Ll. & Co's.	Lloyd's and Companies
L.M.C.	Lloyd's Machinery Certificate
l.m.c.	Low middling clause (cotton)
long.	Longitude
loc. cit.	In the place stated
loco.	On the spot
L.Q.T.	Liverpool Quay Terms
L.R.M.C.	Lloyd's Refrigerating Machinery Certificate
L.S.	*Locus sigilli* (place of the seal)
l.s.	Lump sum
ltg. tge.)	Lighterage
Lt.-V.	Light vessel
ltr.	Lighter
L/U.	Laid up
l.w.l.	Load water line
L.W.	Low water
M.	Nautical mile
m.	Mile. Minute. Metre
M/A	My account
M.C.	Machinery certificate
M/C.	Metalling clause
m/c.	Metallic currency
M/d.	Months after date
M/D.	Memorandum of deposit
m.d.	Malicious damage
M.D.H.B.	Mersey Docks and Harbour Board
mfrs.	Manufacturers
m.h.	Main hatch
M.H.W.S.	Mean high water springs

Min. B/L.	Minimum bill of lading
Min. wt.	Minumum weight
M.I.P.	Marine Insurance policy
mkt.	Market
M.L.W.S.	Mean low water springs
M.M.	Mercantile Marine
m.m.	Made merchantable
M.M.A.	Merchandise Marks Act
M.M.O.	Mercantile Marine Office
M.N.E.A.	Merchant Navy Establish ment Administration
M.N.T.B.	Merchant Navy Training Board
mo.	Month
M.O.H.	Medical officer of health
M/R.	Mate's receipt
M.S.	Motor ship. Machinery survey
M/s.	Months after sight
M.S.A.	Merchant Shipping Act
M.S.C.	Manchester Ship Canal
mst.	Measurement
M.T.	Mean time
mt.	Empty
M.T.L.	Mean tide level
M.V.	Motor vessel
N/a.	No advice. No account
N.A.	North America. Not absolutely
n.a.a.	Not always afloat
N/C	New charter. New crop. No charge.
N.C.V.	No commercial value
N.D.	No discount
n.d.	non-delivery
n.d.w.	Net deadweight
n.e.	Not exceeding
N.E.	No effects
n.e.p.	Not elsewhere provided
n.e.s.	Not elsewhere specified
N/f.	No funds
N.F. (Nfld.)	Newfoundland
N.H.P.	Nominal horse power
N.M.B.	National Maritime Board
N/m.	No mark
N/o.	No orders (banking)
nom. std.	Nominal standard
n.n.	Not north of
n/n.	No number
n.o.p.	Not otherwise provided
n.o.r.	Not otherwise rated
n.p.	Net proceeds
N.R.	Northern Range (of ports)— includes Norfolk, Newport News, Baltimore, Philadelphia, New York, Boston and Portland
N/R.	Not reported
n.r.	Net register. No risk

n.r.a.d.	No risk after discharge
n.r.a.l.	No risk after landing
n.r.a.s.	No risk after shipment
n.r.t.	Net register tons
n.r.t.o.r.	No risk till on rail
n.r.t.w.b.	No risk till waterborne
N.S.	Nova Scotia
n/s.	Not sufficient
n.s.p.f.	Not specially provided for
N.S.W.	New South Wales
N.T.	Net tonnage
N/t.	New terms (grain trade)
Nt. wt.	Net weight
N.Y.T.	New York mean time
o/a.	On account of
o.a.	Over all
O/C.	Open charter. Old charter. Old crop. Open cover.
o/c.	Overcharge
Oc. B/L	Ocean bill of lading
o/c.d.	Other cargo damage
o/d.	On demand. On deck.
O.E.E.C.	Organisation for European Economic Co-operation
O/o.	Order of
O.P.	Open policy
O.R.	Owner's risk
O.R.B.	Owner's risk of breakage
O.R.C.	Owner's risk of chafage
O.R.D.	Owner's risk of damage
O.R.F.	Owner's risk of fire
O/S.	Off slip. Open slip.
O/s.	On sale. On sample. Out of stock
O/t.	Old terms (grain trade)
o.t.	On truck
oz.	Ounce
p.a.	Per annum
P/A.	Particular average. Power of attorney. Private account
P.B.	Permanent bunkers
P/C.	Price current. Petty cash. Per cent.
P. chgs.	Particular charges
pcl.	Parcel
pcs.	Pieces
P.D.	Port dues
pd.	Paid. Passed
P. & I.	Protection and indemnity
Pkge.	Package
P/L.	Partial loss
P. & L.	Profit and loss
P.L.A.	Port of London Authority
pm.	Premium
P/N.	Promissory note
p.o.c.	Port of call
P.O.D.	Pay on delivery
p.o.r.	Port of refuge

p.p.	Picked ports. Per procuration
ppd.	Prepaid
p.p.i.	Policy proof of interest
ppt.	Prompt (loading)
P.R.	Port risks. Parcel receipt
P/R.	Provisional release
pr.	Pair
P/S.	Public sale
P.T.	Parcel ticket. Perte totale (total loss)
p.t.	Private terms
Ptg.Std.	Petrograd Standard (timber)
P.V.	Petite vitesse (slow goods train)
qlty.	Quality
Qn.	Quotation
qrs.	Quarters
qty.	Quantity
q.v.	*Quod vide* (which see)
R/A.	Refer to acceptor
R.A.T.	Rapeseed Association Terms
R. & C.C.	Riots and Civil commotions
R.C.C. & S.	Riots, civil commotions, and strikes
R/D.	Refer to drawer
r.d.	Running days
R.D.C.	Running down clause
reg. (regd.)	Registered
res.	Residue
R.I.	Re-insurance
R.N.L.I.	Royal National Life-Boat Institution
r.o.b.	Remain(ing) on board
Rotn. no.	Rotation number
R/p.	Return of post
R.P.	Return premium. Reply paid
r.p.m.	Revolutions per minute
R.S.	Revised statutes (U.S.A.)
R.T.	Rye terms
r.t.b.a.	Rate to be arranged
S.A.	South America. South Africa. South Australia
s/a.	Safe arrival. Subject to approval
s.a.n.r.	Subject to approval, no risk (to attach until confirmation)
S.B.	Short bill
s.b.s.	Surveyed before shipment
S.C.	Salvage charges
S.D.	Sea damaged
S.d.	Short delivery
s.d.	Small damage
S. & F.A.	Shipping and forwarding agent

S. & H.E. Sundays and holidays excepted
S.H.P.   Shaft horse power
S.H.E.X. Sundays and holidays excepted
S.H.I.N.C. Sundays and holidays inclusive
shpt.   Shipment
S.I.   Short interest
sk.   Sack
S.L.   Salvage loss
S/L.C. (Cl.) Sue and labour clause
sld.   Sailed
S/N.   Shipping note
S.O.   Seller's option
S.O.L.   Shipowner's liability
Soton.   Southampton
S.P.   Supra protest
s.p.d.   Steamer pays dues
S.R. & C.C. Strikes, riots and civil commotions
S.R.L.   Ship repairer's liability
S.R. ports. U.S.A. Atlantic ports south of Norfolk, Va. (Southern range)
s.s.   Steamship
s.s. & c. Same sea and country
s.s. or b. Stranded, sunk, or burnt
s.t.   Short ton
Std.   Standard (of timber)
stg.   Sterling
stk.   Stock
Str.   Steamer
S. to S. Station to station
s.v.   Sailing vessel
S.W.   Shipper's weight
S. W.G.   Standard wire guage
S/Y   Steam Yacht

t.   tons, tonnes
T.   Tare. Ton
T. & G.   Tongued and grooved (timber)
t. & p.   (Petty) theft and pilferage
t. & s.   Touch and stay
T.B.   Trial balance
T/C   Till countermanded
T.E.   Trade expenses
T.G.B.   Tongued, grooved, and beaded (timber)
T.I.B.   Trimmed in bunkers
T.L.   Total loss
T.L.O.   Total loss only
T/O.   Transfer order
Tonn.   Tonnage
T.P.C.   Tonnes per centimetre (immersion)
T.Q.   Tale quale (As found)
Tr.   Trustee
T.R.   Tons registered

t.s.s.   Twin screw steamer
T.T.   Telegraphic transfer

U/A.   Underwriting account
u.c.b.   Unless caused by
u.d.   Under deck
U.K.   United Kingdom
U.K./Cont. United Kingdom or Continent
U.K./Cont.(B.H.) United Kingdom or Continent (Bordeaux-Hamburg range)
U.K./Cont.(G.H.) United Kingdom or Continent (Gibraltar-Hamburg range)
U.K./Cont.(H.H.) United Kingdom or Continent (Havre-Hamburg range)
U.K.f.o. United Kingdom for orders
U.K.H.A.D. United Kingdom, Havre, Antwerp or Dunkirk
u.p.   Under proof
u.s.   Under seal (Customs)
u/w.   Underwriter
v.   Versus (against). Via
V.C.   Valuation clause
v.o.p.   Value as in original policy
vsl.   Vessel
v.v.   Vice versa

W.A.   With average
W.B.   Water ballast. Warehouse book. Way bill
W.B./E.I. West Britain/East Ireland
w.b.s.   Without benefit of salvage
W.C.A.   West coast of Africa
W.C.N.A. West coast of North America
W.C.S.A. West coast of South America
Wd. (W/d) Warranted
W.F.T.U. World Federation of Trade Unions
w.g.   Weight guaranteed
whf.   Wharf
W.H.O.   World Health Organisation
whse.   Warehouse
W.I.   West Indies
W.I.B.O.N. Whether in berth or not
W.I.F.P.O.N. Whether in free pratique or not
W.I.P.O.N. Whether in port or not
wkg.   Working
W/M.   Weight and/or measurement
W.N.A.   Winter North Atlantic
w.o.b.   washed overboard
W.O.L.   Wharfowner's liability
w.p.   Without prejudice. Weather permitting
W.P.A.   With particular average
w.p.p.   Waterproof paper packing

W.R.	Warehouse receipt	x.in.	Ex interest
w.r.o.	War risk only	x.new.	Ex new
wt.	Weight		
Wtd.	Warranted		
W/W.	Warehouse warrant		
W.W.D.	Weather working days	Y-A. R.	York-Antwerp Rules
		yd.	Yard
x.c.	Ex coupon	yday.	Yesterday
x.d.	Ex dividend	yr. yrs.	Year. Years.

CHAPTER 18

CALCULATIONS

THIS Chapter is included primarily for the benefit of officers preparing themselves for examination for a Class I (Master Mariner) certificate of competency. The examination paper in "Business and Law" sometimes includes a calculation which may consist of an owner's account current with the master, a loading or discharging time sheet for the assessment of demurrage or despatch money payable, or a loading or bunkering problem.

Many shipping companies have their own systems of rendering accounts on their own specially drawn up forms which may differ in many respects from the specimen accounts shown in this Chapter, but those given here are based on sound principles and should be acceptable for examination purposes. Moreover, the methods here adopted could be safely followed by a master who is not bound to a particular company's system.

The lay-out of time sheets is not by any means standardised, but the method adopted here has the advantage of simplicity and is, for that reason, recommended as being suitable for examination candidates.

Since wage rates, insurance contributions, etc., are frequently adjusted to meet changing circumstances, it may well be that figures used in the following calculations are not always realistic. This, however, does not affect the principles involved and, therefore, makes no difference to the methods to be employed.

CALCULATION OF SEAMEN'S WAGES

The period of engagement will have to be expressed in calendar months and days (if the rate of pay is monthly), or in weeks and days (if the rate of pay is weekly). A calendar month may be the period from the first day of any month to the last day of the same month, or it may be the period from any day in any month to that day of the following month whose number is one less (in either case, both dates inclusive). Where more than one complete month is involved, the period from any day of a month to the day in any subsequent month whose number is one less constitutes an exact number of calendar months. The following illustrations should make this clear.

From 1st August to 31st August is one month.
From 25th October to 24th November is one month.
From 19th June to 18th September (in same year) is 3 months.
From 11th February to 10th November (in same year) is 9 months.

The month of February, of course, introduces a variation of the general rule. Obviously, it is impossible to reckon a month, for instance, from 31st January to 30th February because the latter date does not exist. Hence:

From 31st January to 29th February in a leap year is one month.
From 31st January to 28th February in a non-leap year is one month.
From 30th January to 29th February in a leap year is one month.
From 30th January to 28th February in a non-leap year is one month.

Leap Years are those whose numbers are exactly divisible by 4, unless the year marks the end of a century, in which case the year is not a leap year unless the number of the century is also divisible by 4.

For example:

1976, 1980, 1984, 1988, etc., are leap years.
1900 was not a leap year, as 19 is not a multiple of 4.
2000 will be a leap year (assuming the present calendar system still prevails then).

When expressing any period in months and days, both dates are inclusive; *e.g.*, the period from 27th April to 14th July is 2 months and 18 days made up as follows:

27th April to 26th June = 2 months
27th June to 14th July = 18 days*

* Note that from 27th June to 30th June, both dates inclusive, is 4 days to which 14 days of July are added to make 18 days in all.

Rule for Calculating Wages for Part of a Month. The daily rate of pay is always one-thirtieth of the monthly rate, irrespective of what month it is. It should be noted that a period such as 1st July to 30th July is not a complete calendar month; but it is a period of 30 days for which a seaman is entitled to 30/30th of a month's pay.

Worked Example 1. Calculate wages for the period 5th February 1981 to 13th May 1981 at £948·60 per month.

5th February to 4th May:	3 months	@ £948·60	=	£2845·80
5th May to 13th May:	9 days	@ £31·62	=	£284·58
			Total =	£3130·38

N.B.—It is advisable to show the daily rate, as above, in the same way as it is shown on an Account of Wages Form (ASW 1 or ASW 2).

If the rate of pay is weekly, the period of engagement must be expressed in weeks and days. If no calendar is available, the period of engagement in weeks and days can be calculated by dividing the total number of days by seven, any remainder being the odd days to be paid at the daily rate which is taken to be one seventh of the weekly rate.

Worked Example 2. Calculate wages at £89·60 per week from 30th January 1980 to 9th March 1980.

$$
\begin{array}{rcl}
\text{30th January to 31st January} &=& \text{2 days} \\
\text{Days in February (leap year)} &=& \text{29 days} \\
\text{1st March to 9th March} &=& \text{9 days} \\
\text{Total} &=& 7\overline{)\text{40 days}}
\end{array}
$$

5 wks + 5 remainder.

Period of engagement **5 weeks 5 days.**

$$
\begin{array}{rcl}
 & & £ \\
\text{5 weeks @ } £89·60 &=& 448·00 \\
\text{5 days @ } £12·80 &=& 64·00 \\
\text{Total} &=& \overline{512·00}
\end{array}
$$

Promotions. When a seamen's rate of pay changes during the voyage by reason of his being promoted, or through N.M.B. rates being changed with the consequent operation of the "Retrospective Clause", or through increments of Efficient Service Pay becoming due, the master must not calculate wages for the two parts of the voyage separately at the different rates and then add the amounts together, but must initially calculate wages for the whole period at the rate originally agreed to, and then make an addition based on the difference of rate from the date on which the new rate takes effect. The following examples will serve to illustrate the correct method.

Worked Example 3. Calculate an officer's wages for the period 17th March 1981 to 21st September 1981. He is engaged at £952·50 per month, but becomes eligible for the higher rate of £972·00 as from 6th June.

17th March to 16th September:	6 months @ £952·50 = 5,715·00	
17th September to 21st September:	5 days @ £31·75 = 158·75	
	Total at original rate =	5,873·75
6th June to 5th September:	3 months @ £19·50 = 58·50	
6th September to 21st September:	16 days @ 65p = 10·40	
	Increment	68·90
	Total wages	5,942·65

CONVERSION OF FOREIGN MONEY INTO STERLING

In connection with cash advances of wages given abroad and other transactions made in foreign currency it will be necessary to convert the amounts involved into sterling. If a calculator is not available the following method can be used.

Worked Example 4. Convert $436 (U.S.A.) into sterling at 1·82 to £1.

Method: Make the divisor a whole number by shifting the decimal point 2 places to the right and adding a corresponding number of noughts to the dividend. Then by long division obtain the quotient expressed to at least three places of decimals. Thus:

```
182)43600(239·5604
    364
    ---
    720
    546
    ---
   1740
   1638
   ----
   1020
    910
   ----
   1100
   1092
   ----
    800
    728
```

The sterling equivalent is £239·56

ACCOUNT OF WAGES AND BALANCE DUE AT PAY-OFF

A master should be prepared to draw up a statement of the balance of wages due to a seaman. The calculation of total wages should be made as shown previously and other earnings, if any, added. The various deductions when totalled up are subtracted from the total earnings to give the balance due at pay-off.

The amounts of some of the deductions will be in sterling but others, such as cash advances abroad, may be in a foreign currency and will require to be converted into sterling. Other deductions may be a little more troublesome as it may be necessary to work out the number of allotments due to be paid during the period of the engagement. Pension fund contributions may also introduce a complication.

NATIONAL INSURANCE CONTRIBUTIONS

Since April 1975 national insurance contributions payable by seafarers and others have been related to wages. In practice a seaman's contribution for a voyage can be calculated by multiplying the total wages, overtime and leave pay by the appropriate percentage for the current year, or by inspection from tables supplied to the master by the Department of Health and Social Security.

Allotments. A stipulation in an agreement for an allotment may be for a sum allotted to any person or persons to be payable monthly, half-monthly, fortnightly, or weekly. It is most important to distinguish between a half-monthly allotment and a fortnightly allotment. In the absence of any information to the contary, the following should be assumed.

Monthly Allotment. The first one is due to be paid on the last day of the calendar month commencing on the date when wages commence. For example:

If wages begin on 1st June, the first allotment is payable on 30th June.

If wages begin on 1st July, the first allotment is payable on 31st July.

If wages begin on 12th August, the first allotment is payable on 11th September.

If wages begin on 30th November, the first allotment is payable on 29th December.

Subsequent ones are payable on the last day of each succeeding calendar month.

Worked Example 5. A seaman engaged on 12th March, is discharged on 18th December (same year). What deduction should be made from his wages in respect of allotments if he has arranged for a monthly allotment of £45?

Allotments will fall due as follows:—11th April, 11th May, 11th June, 11th July, 11th August, 11th September, 11th October, 11th November and 11th December. That is to say, 9 in all. Hence the deduction will be £9 × 45 = £405·00.

Half-Monthly Allotment. The date of payment of the first allotment is found either by going forward 15 days from the date when wages commence, or by working back 15 days from the last day of the first complete calendar month. For instance, if wages begin on 23rd July, the first allotment is payable on 7th August, *i.e.*, 15 days on from 23rd July, or 15 days back from 22nd August. Subsequent allotments will then be paid at the rate of two per calendar month. It should be observed that over a full year only 24 allotments would be payable under this system.

Worked Example 6. What sum should be deducted from wages on account of £20 half-monthly allotments if the engagement commences on 28th April and ends on 10th November (same year)?

Allotments will fall due on 13th May, 28th May, 13th June, 28th June, 13th July, 28th July, 13th August, 28th August, 13th September, 28th September, 13th October and 28th October. That is to say, 12 in all. Hence, the deduction will be 12 × £20 = £240.

N.B. In this case, if 15 days are counted back from 27th May, instead of 15 days on from 28th April, the first allotment is payable on 12th May and others on 27th May, 12th June, etc. But it makes no difference to the total number payable.

Fortnightly Allotment. With this system all allotments will become payable on the same day of the week. The first one will be paid on the last day of the first completed fortnight of the engagement. For example, if the seaman is engaged on Wednesday, 10th June, the first allotment is due to be paid on Tuesday, 23rd June, and subsequent ones on Tuesday, 7th July; Tuesday, 21st July; and so on. It should be noted that in a complete year 26 fortnightly allotments would be payable (27 if the first fell due on 1st January, or on either 1st or 2nd January in a leap year) as compared with only 24 half-monthly allotments.

Worked Example 7. A seaman engaged on Wednesday, 9th September, has a £12 fortnightly allotment. What should be deducted from his wages on this account if the voyage ends on 17th December (same year)?

Allotments will fall due on Tuesdays as follows:—22nd September, 6th October, 20th October, 3rd November, 17th November, 1st December and 15th December. That is 7 in all. Hence the deduction is $7 \times £12 = £84.00$.

Weekly Allotment. In this case, too, all are payable on the same day of the week, but commencing on the last day of the first completed week and thereafter at weekly intervals.

Worked Example 8. A seaman engaged on Thursday, 7th May, has a £7.50 weekly allotment. What should be deducted by way of allotments if he is paid off on 21st July (same year)?

Allotments will fall due on Wednesdays as follows:—13th, 20th, and 27th May; 3rd, 10th, 17th and 24th June; 1st, 8th and 15th July. That is 10 in all. Hence the deduction is $10 \times £7.50 = £75.00$.

N.B. In all of the above cases it has been assumed that the seaman concerned has not been given an advance on joining as well as an allotment. If he has, he can be made to work off such advance before the first allotment is made, but in practice this may not be insisted upon if it is shown that he would have sufficient funds to his credit to meet the allotment in spite of the advance. If, for instance, an advance of half a month's pay is given, the first allotment will become payable 15 days later than it would if no advance had been made.

It may happen that an allotment falls due for payment on or shortly before the last day on the agreement, and the question then arises as to whether it is in fact paid to the allotment holder or not. The master can check this from the "Returns List" supplied to him by the owners.

Merchant Navy Officers' Pension Fund. Rates of contribution are 7·5% of that part of earnings described as pensionable earnings from the officer, and a further larger contribution is paid by the employer. "Pensionable earnings" means all earnings in excess of $1\frac{1}{2}$ times the annual amount of the lower earnings' limit for the purpose of the payment of Class 1 contributions in respect of non-contracted out employment current at the time of payment. In calculating earnings for contribution purposes, all emoluments paid for work or for conditions under which work is performed attract liability for contributions, but the following payments or bonuses do not:—

(i) all sums paid as reimbursement of expenses such as travelling expenses, lodging allowances, subsistence allowances, leave food allowances (not consolidated), examination and course fees, Australian leave allowance and North and Central American Coastal Trade Bonus;

(ii) all fringe benefits such as wives' air fares and uniform allowances;

(iii) discretionary bonuses such as those related to company profits or for examination successes;

(iv) terminal and redundancy payments; and

(v) cash payments in lieu of leave where they have been agreed.

Merchant Navy Ratings' Pension Fund. A scheme for ratings has been set up based on seamen contributing 5% of "pensionable earnings" (as defined above) plus a further larger contribution from employers. Earnings for this purpose are to be calculated as described above.

Worked Example 9. An officer's total wages for a voyage amount to £3420. What deduction should be made in respect of pension fund contributions if lower earnings limit is £1404?

Total contributions are $7\frac{1}{2}\%$ of $(3420 - 1\frac{1}{2} \times 1404) = \underline{£98 \cdot 55}$.

Worked Example 10. An officer is engaged on Thursday 9th April 1981 and is discharged on Monday 21st September 1981. His rate of pay is £835·50 per month. Given the following information calculate the balance due to this officer on his being discharged.

Leave 88 days.

Allotment £300 per month.

National Insurance contributions from tables £391·32.

M.N.O.P.F. contributions at $7\frac{1}{2}\%$ of pensionable earnings, the lower earnings limit being £1,404.

Income Tax, from tables £1,537·88.

Wines and Tobacco etc. £79·80.

Radio messages £10·70.

Cash advances:—Vancouver 200 dollars at 2·22 to £1; Osaka 50,000 yen at 421 yen to £1; Rotterdam 250 guilders at 5·20 guilders to £1.

Postage £10·42.

Preliminary Calculations.

Allotments: fall due on 8th May/June/July/August and September. That is
5 at £300 = £1500.

$$\begin{array}{ll} & 200 \\ \textit{Advances}: \text{Vancouver} & \dfrac{£2 \cdot 22}{50000} \end{array}$$ .. .. £90·09

$$\text{Osaka} \quad \dfrac{£\,421}{250}$$ .. .. £118·76

$$\text{Rotterdam} \quad \dfrac{£5 \cdot 20}{} $$ .. .. £48·08

Total advances .. £256·93

Wages: 9 Apr. to 8 Sept.: 5 mo. @ £835·50 .. .. .. £4177·50
9 Sept. to 21 Sept.: 13 d. @ £27·85 .. .. .. 362·05

Total wages .. 4539·55

Leave pay: 88 days at £27·85 .. .. 2450·80

Pension Fund: Wages £4539·55 + leave pay £2450·80 = £6990·35.
$7\frac{1}{2}\%$ of $(6990 \cdot 35 - 1\frac{1}{2} \times 1404) = £366 \cdot 33$.

Account of Wages

	£	£
Total wages	4539·55	
Leave pay	2450·80	
Total earnings	6990·35	6990·35
Deductions:		
Allotments	1500·00	
Nat. Ins. contributions	391·32	
Pension Fund	366·33	
Income Tax	1537·88	
Wines etc.	79·80	
Radio messages	10·70	
Cash advances	256·93	
Postage	10·42	
Total deductions	4153·38	4153·38
Balance due on discharge		£2836·97

PORTAGE BILLS

At the end of a voyage a "Portage Bill" and an "Owners' Account
Current with the Master" may have to be rendered by the master to
the owners. In the latter he debits the amount of the portage bill and
other disbursements to the owners, and credits them with (*a*) all
moneys received, (*b*) payments made by them on behalf of the crew,
and (*c*) the amounts of any bills drawn on them during the voyage.
In the portage bill itself the master analyses the accounts of wages,
and by giving the totals of each kind of deduction as well as the
total wages he has a check on wage slips and ready information for

drawing up the account current. A cash book is kept to record all transactions in connection with the accounts as they occur. The account current is compiled from particulars shown in the cash book, portage bill, radio officer's account, chief steward's account, and receipts (vouchers) supporting sundry disbursements.

Frequently, the master's portage bill and the account current (which is sometimes known as the owners' portage bill) are prepared on opposite sides of the same sheet of paper, in which case the complete document may be referred to simply as "The Portage Bill".

Masters' examination papers sometimes include a question which requires the candidate to draw up a simple account current showing the balance and stating to whom it is due. As with a seaman's wage account, certain items may be expressed in foreign currency so that some preliminary arithmetic will be necessary to find the sterling equivalent, using the given rate of exchange. Occasionally, one or more items may be included in the given data which, not being relevant to the account current, are intended to be ignored. The following list of items and explanations of how they should be dealt with should be sufficient to cover examination requirements.

Crew's Wages. The amount given under this heading will be the gross wages without any deductions whatsoever and, in the absence of any statement to the contrary, may be taken to include the master's wages as well. The amount should be entered on the debit side of the account on the understanding that amounts paid directly by owners will be credited to them.

Allotments. Enter on the credit side. This offsets the effect of debiting them as part of the gross wage account, and is consistent with the fact that the master does not handle this money at all, allotments being paid direct from the shipowner's office to the allotment holders.

Advance Notes. Enter on the credit side. Like allotments, they are initially debited as part of the gross wage account but are paid directly by the owners. If the expression "advances on joining" is used, it should be assumed that advance notes were given unless it is specifically stated that the amounts were paid in cash.

National Insurance Contributions. If it is stated that the total contributions (employer's share and employees' share) are remitted by the master to the Collector of Taxes, the two amounts should be added together and entered as a debit. Then, the amount recovered from the crew as a deduction from wages should be entered on the credit side. This, of course, has the same effect as simply debiting the owners with their own share. On the other hand, if it is stated that payment was made by cheque drawn by the owners or their agents, nothing should go on the debit side, but the amount recovered from the crew should still be entered as a credit. If it is not stated how the amount was paid, it is probably best to assume that a remittance was made, adding an explanation to that effect, and to make the entries accordingly.

Income Tax. If stated to have been paid by the master direct to the Collector of Taxes, this item is of no interest to the owners and should be omitted from the account. But if it is stated to have been paid by owners' cheque, the owners must be credited with the amount deducted from wages under this heading. If no indication of the method of payment is given, an assumption one way or the other should be made, acted on and declared.

Cash Advances on Voyage. The amount under this heading, if given, should be omitted from the account as it will already have been debited as part of the gross wages. If some or all of the cash drawn from agents has been applied to making advances of wages to crew members, the amount will be shown as a credit under the heading of "cash received from agents".

Port Wages. If this item is included in the given data it may be inferred that the intention is that it should be treated as a disbursement to be entered on the debit side. Normally, the proper place for this item to appear is the Harbour Portage Bill, which is quite separate from the voyage account covering the period on articles. However, if the harbour wages have been paid by the master and the sum has not already been recovered from the owners, the master would be entitled to debit the amount to his owners in his next voyage account.

Overtime. This should be entered on the debit side as a disbursement as it is not included in the gross wage account. Wages and overtime are kept in separate accounts, and will be given separately in the data for the account current in an examination question.

Crew's Expenses Joining Ship. When this item is included it is reasonable to assume that one or more of the crew have been sent by the owners from one place to another to join the ship, and have been instructed to claim their travelling expenses from the master. The master will pay these expenses or, more probably, credit them to the wage accounts of the seamen concerned, and will then be justified in placing the amount on the debit side of the account current.

Officers' Pension Fund Contributions. It is customary for the owners to pay direct to the Fund their own contributions and those of the officers concerned. Therefore, amounts deducted from officers' wages under this heading should be credited to the owners in the account current.

Seamen's Union Subscriptions. When these are included and there is no direct information to the contrary it may be assumed that the owners have undertaken to pay those subscriptions to the Union on behalf of the seamen while the ship is absent from the United Kingdom. Accordingly, the master will deduct the amounts from wages and reimburse the owners by placing the amount on the credit side of the account current.

Steward's Account. This item may appear under any one of a variety of headings such as "Bar Account", "Slops", "Tobacco and Postage", etc. In the absence of any statement to the contrary it should be assumed that an "Owners' Bond" arrangement is intended and the amount should therefore be placed on the credit side. (If the item were specifically qualified by the statement "Master's Bond", then it would be left out of the account as being of no interest to the owners.)

Master's Incidental Expenses. The master may be granted a fixed allowance to cover official entertainments and other sundry expenses, or he may claim to be reimbursed for the actual amount spent in this way during the voyage. In either case the amount should be classed as a disbursement to be placed on the debit side.

Drafts (or Bills) on Owners. Where goods or services are paid for by bills drawn on the shipowner the amount for which the bill is drawn should be credited to the owner provided that the disbursement has already been debited by being included in port disbursements. An examination question may indicate that a bill for some stated amount has been drawn without stating the reason for it. In those circumstances the candidate is justified in assuming that the disbursement has first been debited and should, accordingly, credit the owners with the amount of the bill.

Cash Drawn from Agents. Owners should be credited with the entire sum drawn irrespective of how much of it is subsequently disbursed.

Port Disbursements. These should be entered on the debit side of the account. For the purpose of the account current it is not necessary to give details of disbursements as it may be assumed that separate and detailed disbursement sheets will have been sent to the owners together with copies of all relevant vouchers.

Advance Freight Payable at Loading Port in Accordance with C/P Terms. In modern practice, if any part of the freight is to be payable in advance, it would be collected by owners' agents and remitted through a banking arrangement. However, if this item is mentioned in an examination question, it may be assumed that the master will collect the net amount of the advance after the agreed charges for interest and insurance have been deducted. The formal method of including this in the account current is to credit the owners with the gross amount of the advance and then debit them with the cost of interest and insurance, bearing in mind that it is the whole advance which is subject to both charges.

Freight or Balance of Freight Due Under C/P at Port of Discharge. Here again in modern practice it will be the owners' agents who will attend to the collection of freight. However, in the event of freight being paid to the master, he would include it in the account current for the voyage. Some C/P's made provision for sufficient of the freight to meet the steamer's disbursements (or a specified amount) to be paid in cash and the remainder to be paid in good and approved bills of exchange on London. Freight bills delivered to the master would be remitted by him to the owners without delay. Accordingly, having first credited the owners with the gross amount of freight collected (cash and bills), he would debit them with the amount of the freight bills of exchange previously sent to them.

Crew's Radio Messages. The amount deducted from crew's wages under this heading should be placed to the owners' credit.

Cash Radio Messages. Cash received from crew or passengers in respect of radio messages sent from the ship should also be placed to owners' credit.

Leave Pay. A seaman with leave pay due to him may receive the amount on being discharged together with his balance of wages etc., for the voyage. The master should debit to owners the amount of the leave pay.

Leave Subsistence. This should be dealt with in the same manner as leave pay.

To Balance the Account. If the sum of the items credited to owners exceeds the sum debited it will be evident that the balance is in favour of the owners. In this case the balance should be entered on the debit side of the account so that, when the two sides are finally totalled up, a balanced account results, showing the same total on both sides. The "debt" to the owners may be discharged by transferring the balance to the master's personal account in the manner shown in Worked Example 12. Alternatively, it may be carried over to the next voyage. In the latter event the master would begin his next voyage account on the credit side with the entry "Balance to owners from previous voyage account".

Conversely, if the debits exceed the credits the balance will be in favour of the master, in which case the balance should be entered on the credit side so that a balanced account is obtained. The entry may appear as "Balance to master" or "Cash drawn to balance account", as appropriate.

In practice, in order to reach a final settlement with the owners at the end of a voyage, it may be necessary for the master to draw up a "Master's Personal Account" to which the balance of the account current is transferred. This will provide a check on the whole accounting system, as the cash due to or from the owners should equal the amount required to balance the personal account.

Examination papers do not appear to include personal accounts, but simple specimens are given in Worked Examples 11 and 12 to show how the final balance of the account current may be disposed of.

Worked Example 11 (a). From the information given draw up an Owner's Account Current with the master showing the balance and to whom it is due.

Portage account (master's and crew's wages) £10,907·45.
Overtime £412·90.
National Insurance contributions paid by master: Owner's share £965·16, crew's share £706·96.
Leave pay and subsistence £974·65.
Officers' Pension Fund contributions £241·65.
Cash advances on voyage £946·89.
Cash bar sales £332·55.
Advance notes £243·00.
Allotments £6,990·00.
Master's bar allowance £25.
Master's bar account £22·50.
Cash drawn from agents at "A" £771·24.
Master's port expenses £34·33.
Disbursements at "A" £301·20.
Cash drawn from agents at "B" £475.

DR.	Owners of m.v.......... Voyage No... ..... in account current with............. Master		CR.
To:	£	By:	£
Master's and crew's		Nat. Ins. (crew)	706·96
wages	10,907·45	Officers' Pension Fund ..	241·65
Overtime	412·90	Cash bar sales	332·55
Leave pay & subsistence	974·65	Advance notes	243·00
Nat. Ins. (total) ..	1,672·12	Allotments	6,990·00
Master's bar allowance	25·00	Master's bar account ..	22·50
Master's port expenses	34·33	Cash from agents at "A"	771·24
Disbursements at "A"	301·20	Cash from agents at "B"	475·00
Disbursements at "B"	1,420·06	Crew radio messages ..	25·70
Freight B's/E remitted		Crew's postage	22·60
from "B"	13,790·00	Cash drawn to pay off	
		crew	4,000·00
		Freight collected at "B"	15,290·00
		Cash drawn to balance	
		a/c	416·51
	29,537·71		29,537·71

Balance due to master = £416·51.

Disbursements at "B" £1,4200·6.
Crew's radio messages £25·70.
Crew's postage £22·60.
Cash drawn to pay off crew £4,000.
Freight collected at "B" £15,290 of which £1,500 was in cash and the rest in
    B's/E on London.
Income Tax paid by master £2,459·62.

Personal Account. In the personal account the master credits to himself his wages for the voyage, expenses and allowances. He debits himself with all amounts the owners have paid on his behalf, including income tax if that is paid by owners, cheque, his bar account, postages and radio messages, cash drawn abroad for his own personal use, any cash in hand retained after balancing the cash book, and the amount drawn to balance the account current.

Worked Example 11 (b). From the account current of Worked Example 11 (a) and the additional information given below, draw up the master's personal account for the voyage period of 1 month 27 days.

Master's rate of pay £501 per month.
Leave pay £317·30.
Allotment £350.
Pension Fund contributions £63·46.
Radio messages £4·45.
Postage £4·12.
Cash drawn for personal use at "A" £26·85.
Cash drawn for personal use at "B" £30·00.
Income Tax £279·22.
Nat. Ins. contributions £60·08.
Balance of cash book (cash in hand) £71·34.

DR.			Master's Personal Account			CR.
To:			£	By:		£
Allotment	..	..	350·00	1 mo. 27 d. @ £501		
Pension Fund	..	..	63·46	per mo.		951·90
Radio messages	..	..	4·45	Leave pay		317·30
Postage	..	..	4·12	Port expenses..	..	34·33
Bar account ..	..	..	22·50	Bar allowance	..	25·00
Cash drawn for personal use:						
at "A"	..	..	26·85			
at "B"	....	..	30·00			
Income tax	..	..	279·22			
Nat. Ins. contr.	..	..	60·08			
Balance of cash book (cash in						
hand)	..	..	71·34			
Cash drawn to balance a/c						
current	..	..	416·51			
			£1328·53			£1328·53

Worked Example 12 (a). From the data below draw up an account current showing the balance and to whom it is due.

Crew's wages (including master) £14,025·75.
Overtime £2,244·80.
Nat. Ins. contributions paid by owner: owner's share £1,403·45, crew's share £1,015·90.
Income Tax paid by owner: £4,269·54.
Leave pay £3,136·72.
Leave subsistence £72·64.
Officers' Pension Fund contributions £439·96.
Cash advances on voyage £3,096·42.
Cash bar sales £446·74.
Crew's postage £11·12.
Advance notes £120.
Allotments £8,415.
Cash drawn from agents at "A" £1,900·68.
Disbursements at "A" £424·60.
Cash drawn from agents at "B" £2,314·14.
Disbursements at "B" £672·89.
Crew's radio messages £24·89.
Master's port expenses £34·16.
Master's bar allowance £30·00.
Master's bar account £28·94.
Cash drawn to pay off crew £1,650.
Balance due owner from previous a/c carried forward £94·86.

Owners of m.v......... Voyage No.........				
DR.	in account current with............. Master			CR.
To:	£	By:		£
Master's and crew's wages	14,025·75	Balance due owner from		
Overtime	2,244·80	previous a/c carried		
Leave pay	3,136·72	forward		94·86
Leave subsistence ..	72·64	Nat. Ins. (crew) ..		1,015·90
Disbursements at "A" ..	424·60	Income tax		4,269·54
Disbursements at "B" ..	672·89	Officers' Pension fund..		439·96
Master's port expenses ..	34·16	Cash bar sales		446·74
Master's bar allowance ..	30·00	Crew postage		11·12
		Advance notes ..		120·00
		Allotments		8,415·00
		Cash from agents at "A"		1,900·68
		Cash from agents at "B"		2,314·14
		Crew's radio messages		24·89
		Master's bar account ..		28·94
		Cash drawn to pay off		
Balance to owners ..	90·21	crew		1,650·00
	20,731·77			20,731·77

Balance due to owners £90·21.

Worked Example 12 (b). Making use of information from Worked Example 12 (a) and the following data, draw up the master's personal account assuming the voyage to have occupied 2 months and 15 days.

Master's rate of pay £504 per month.
Leave pay £403·20.
Allotments (2) at £300 per month.
Pension Fund £83·16.
Radio messages £5·75.
Postage £1·74.
Cash drawn for personal use: at "A" £68·42, at "B" £70·00.
Income Tax £365·90.
Nat. Ins. contributions £60·09.
Cash in hand after balancing cash book £562·51.

DR.			Master's Personal Account			CR.
To:		£	By:			£
Allotments 2 @ £300	..	600·00	2 mo. 15 d. at £504			
Pension Fund ..	..	83·16	per month. ..	..	1,260·00	
Radio messages ..	..	5·75	Leave pay ..	..	403·20	
Postage ..	..	1·74	Port expenses ..	..	34·16	
Cash drawn for personal			Bar allowance ..	..	30·00	
use: at "A" ..	..	68·42				
at "B" ..	..	70·00				
Income tax ..	..	365·90				
Nat. Ins. contribution	..	60·09				
Balance of cash book						
(cash in hand)	..	562·51				
		1,817·57				
Less balance of a/c current						
due to owner ..	..	90·21				
		£1,727·36				£1,727·36

TIME SHEETS

The sections of Chapter 9 dealing with voyage charter-parties and chartering terms should be carefully read before calculations of this type are attempted.

Master's examination questions may require the candidate to "give an account of the lay days and calculate the amount of demurrage or despatch money payable". To comply satisfactorily with the first requirement it is advisable to adopt a standard method of setting the work out, and the lay-out of the worked examples is recommended as being simple and straightforward.

The main points to consider are:

1. **The number of lay days allowed** for loading or discharging, or for both processes if reversible lay days are stipulated. Where the time allowed has to be calculated from the given weight of cargo and the daily rate of loading or discharging, it should be worked out to the nearest minute.

2. **The kind of lay days.** The various arrangements that arise in practice are fully dealt with in Chapter 9. Examination

questions are of necessity somewhat economically worded and it may sometimes be necessary to make certain assumptions. Where, for instance, lay days are described as "working days" or "weather working days", it should be assumed that Sundays and holidays are excepted unless it is specifically stated otherwise. With regard to holidays, however, a candidate should not treat any day as a holiday unless it is actually stated to be a holiday. If, for instance, the loading or discharging period includes 25th December, that day should not be assumed to be a holiday.

3. **When the lay time begins to count.** No difficulty arises over this if the question gives a direct statement such as "lay days to begin 24 hours after notice of readiness is accepted" and the time of acceptance is stated as well, or "lay days to begin when vessel is in berth" with the time of berthing also mentioned. If, however, no mention is made of the time when lay days are to commence, the candidate will be justified in assuming that lay days count from the moment when loading or discharging is said to begin.

4. **When the lay days expire.** If the recommended lay-out of the time sheet is employed, the moment when the time expires is very easily determined. It will be noticed that in the column headed "hours to count" the number of hours and minutes which are counted are entered for each day. In the adjacent column there is entered the total amount of lay time that has accumulated at the end of each day in succession. Entries in that column are continued until the whole period of time allowed has been accounted for, and that will make it quite clear at what hour on what day the lay days expire.

5. **When the loaded ship is ready to sail** or the discharged ship is again fully at the disposal of her owners. In the former case the ship is ready either when the loading is completed or when the B's/L are presented for signature, whichever occurs later. In the latter case she is ready as soon as the discharge of cargo is completed.

6. **Assessment of demurrage, if any, due to the ship.** If the ship is not loaded (which means with the cargo safely stowed), or discharged, until after the lay time has expired, the whole period of detention should, in the absence of a clear indication to the contrary, be used as the basis for assessing the amount of demurrage payable. Usually the demurrage rate given in the question will be expressed as so much "per day and *pro rata* for part of a day". However, if the *pro rata* phrase is missed out, it will be reasonable to assume that the intention

is nevertheless to treat any fraction of a day for what it is worth on the grounds that that will be consistent with customary practice. A doubtful situation could, of course, be dealt with by giving alternative answers. If, for example, the question merely says "demurrage, if incurred, to be paid at £2400 per day" and the period of detention is, say, 2 days 4 hrs. 30 min., the answer could be expressed as follows:

(a) demurrage payable is £7200 if the common law position is strictly adhered to;

(b) demurrage payable is £5250 if a *pro rata* basis is assumed.

7. **Assessment of despatch money** due to shipper or consignee. If the ship has been completely loaded or discharged and B's/L have been presented before the lay time has expired, there will, if such provision has been made in the C/P, be despatch money payable in respect of the time saved. Doubt may arise in deciding what is meant by time saved. In the absence of any direct indication otherwise, it will be reasonable to assume that despatch money is payable for *all* time saved, although if Sundays and holidays are not intended to be treated as despatch days the question ought to make that clear by stating "all laytime saved".

Despatch money may be expressed as being payable at "so much per day and *pro rata*", or it may be stated to be payable in respect of "clear days saved". In the former case any fraction of a day counts for what it is worth; in the latter case it does not count at all. If neither *pro rata* nor "clear days" is mentioned, alternative answers with an appropriate explanation would, again, seem the best way of dealing with a doubtful situation.

8. **Special points** arising in particular types of questions.

(a) Where a question includes a statement that a specified number of days is to be allowed for demurrage, no complication will arise if (i) the ship loads a full cargo, and (ii) loading is completed before the demurrage days expire. If, however, a full cargo is not loaded, the ship must remain at the loading port throughout the agreed demurrage days before she is entitled to sail with a part cargo, in which case the amount of demurrage due will be assessed on the full period of the demurrage days. If it is indicated that loading continued after the demurrage days had expired, the additional time at the loading port is "detention", not demurrage, but in the absence of any direction to the contrary "damages for detention" should be assessed for that extra period at the quoted demurrage rate.

(b) If the ship does have to sail with only a part cargo, dead-freight will be due to the ship. The net amount payable will be the amount calculated at the quoted rate on the quantity of cargo short-shipped, *less* any expenses saved to the ship as a result of not loading, carrying and dis-charging a full cargo (*e.g.*, additional stevedoring charges that would have been incurred if a full cargo had been loaded). For examination purposes a candidate should take into account only those expenses which are actually mentioned in the question.

(c) It should always be kept in mind that when a voyage-chartered ship is in a loading or discharging port any one of the following situations may apply according to particular circumstances and the provisions of the C/P:
    (1) cargo being worked; time counting as lay time;
    (2) cargo being worked; time not counting, or not counting in full;
    (3) no work being done; time counting as lay time;
    (4) no work being done; time not counting, or not counting in full.
In particular, even if the master has given permission for work to be done on Sundays or holidays that by the terms of the C/P are not lay days, such days still do not count as lay days unless there is clear evidence that the charterer and shipowner (*i.e.*, the principals to the contract) have specifically agreed otherwise.

(d) If the question brings in reversible lay days or reversible lay hours it will be necessary to construct a time sheet for both the loading port and the discharging port. Any time saved at the former will be available at the latter. Con-versely, if time is lost at the loading port it may be set off by a quicker rate of unloading at the port of discharge. Unless a contrary direction is given it should be assumed that "notice of readiness" terms apply at both ports. Obviously, in the case of lay days being reversible settle-ment of demurrage or despatch money cannot be effected until the discharge of cargo is completed, and so that consignees will know what time is left for discharging. B's/L should be endorsed to show the time used for loading.

(e) Some charter-parties have been claused to give the char-terer the right to "average the days allowed for loading and discharging". Different interpretations of this clause gave rise to dispute, but a definite ruling has now been given by the Court. It is hardly likely that examination questions involving this complication will appear in a master's examination paper, but a worked example is included to illustrate what is now ruled to be the proper method of computation.

z

(f) Time lost through winch breakdowns or other stoppages for which the ship is in default cannot be counted as part of the lay time. For instance, if the question states that in a 5-hatch ship work was held up for 3 hours on a particular day due to winch breakdown, then one-fifth of three hours, i.e., 36 minutes of that day would not count.

Worked Example 13 (a). A C/P provides for 8575 tonnes of cargo to be loaded at 1,250 tonnes per weather working day (S. & H.E.). Lay days are to commence 24 hours after written notice has been given by the master to the charterer's agents during office hours on any day (S. & H.E.) that the vessel is ready to receive cargo, whether in berth or not. Time is not to count between 1 p.m. Saturday and 7 a.m. Monday, or between 1 p.m. on the last working day preceding a holiday and 7 a.m. on the first working day after such holiday. Demurrage, if incurred, is to be paid at £2500 per day and *pro rata*, and despatch money at £1250 per day and *pro rata* for all time saved.

$$\text{Number of lay days allowed} = \frac{8575}{1250} = 6 \cdot 86 \text{ days} = 6\text{d. } 20\text{h. } 38\text{m.}$$

Day	Date	Remarks	Hours to count	Total time counted	Time on demurrage
			h. m.	d. h. m.	d. h. m.
W.	4 Nov.	1330 Notice served. 1500 loading commenced ..	nil	nil	nil
Th.	5 ,,	1330 Time begins to count	10 30	0 10 30	nil
F.	6 ,,	–	24 00	1 10 30	nil
S.	7 ,,	Time not counted after 1300	13 00	1 23 30	nil
Su.	8 ,,	Not counted ..	nil	1 23 30	nil
M.	9 ,,	Time not counted before 0700	17 00	2 16 30	nil
T.	10 ,,	0900 to 1130 work prevented by bad weather ..	21 30	3 14 00	nil
W.	11 ,,		24 00	4 14 00	nil
Th.	12 ,,	Time not counted after 1300 (day prior to holiday) ..	13 00	5 3 00	nil
F.	13 ,,	Public holiday—not counted	nil	5 3 00	nil
S.	14 ,,	0700 to 1300 only counted ..	6 00	5 9 00	nil
Su.	15 ,,	Not counted ..	nil	5 9 00	nil
M.	16 ,,	Time not counted before 0700	17 00	6 2 00	nil
T.	17 ,,	1838 lay time expires ..	18 38	6 20 38	0 5 22
W.	18 ,,	1400 to 1600 work prevented by bad weather			1 0 00
Th.	19 ,,	1110 Loading completed and B's/L signed			0 11 10

Total time on demurrage = 1 16 32

						£
Demurrage at £2500 p.d. for					1 day	2500·00
,,	,,	,,	,,	,,	12h.	1250·00
,,	,,	,,	,,	,,	4h.	416·6667
,,	,,	,,	,,	,,	30m.	52·0833
,,	,,	,,	,,	,,	2m.	3·4722
,,	,,	,,	,,	,,	1d. 16h. 32m.	£4222·2222

∴ Demurrage due to ship = £4,222·22

Notice was served at 1.30 p.m. on Wednesday, 4th November, and loading commenced at 3 p.m. on the same day. Friday, 13th November, was declared a public holiday. Bad weather prevented work being done from 9 a.m. to 11.30 a.m. on 10th November and again from 2 p.m. to 4 p.m. on 18th November. Loading was completed and B's/L were signed at 11.10 a.m. on 19th November.

Give a statement of the lay days and the amount of demurrage or despatch money payable.

N.B. The fact that work was prevented by bad weather for 2 hours on 18th November has no bearing on the amount of demurrage payable, as the lay days had already expired.

Worked Example 13 (b). Suppose Worked Example 13 (a) to be modified as follows:

   (i) Loading rate 1,000 tonnes per working day of 24 consecutive hours (S. & H.E.).

  (ii) 13th November not a holiday.

 (iii) Lay days to begin 24 hours after notice of readiness is given or when loading begins, whichever is earlier.

 (iv) Loading completed, etc., at noon on 13th November.

The time sheet would then appear as follows:

Number of lay days allowed $= \dfrac{8575}{1000} = 8 \cdot 575$ days $= 8$d. 13h. 48m.

Day	Date	Remarks	Hours to count	Total time counted	Time saved
			h. m.	d. h. m.	d. h. m.
W.	4 Nov.	1500 loading commenced. Time begins to count ..	9 00	0 9 00	
Th.	5 ,,		24 00	1 9 00	
F.	6 ,,		24 00	2 9 00	
S.	7 ,,	Time not counted after 1300	13 00	2 22 00	
Su.	8 ,,	Not counted	nil	2 22 00	
M.	9 ,,	Time not counted before 0700	17 00	3 15 00	
T.	10 ,,		24 00	4 15 00	
W.	11 ,,		24 00	5 15 00	
Th.	12 ,,		24 00	6 15 00	
F.	13 ,,	1200 loading completed and B's/L signed	24 00	7 15 00	0 12 00
S.	14 ,,	Time not counted after 1300	13 00	8 4 00	1 0 00
Su.	15 ,,	Not counted	nil	8 4 00	1 0 00
M.	16 ,,	Time not counted before 0700, 1648 time expired.. ..	9 48	8 13 48	0 16 48

Total time saved $=$ 3   4 48

Despatch money due to charterers
at £1250 per day for 3 days   £3750·00
,, ,, ,, ,, ,, 4 hours   208·3333
,, ,, ,, ,, ,, 48 mins.   41·6667

,, ,, ,, ,, ,, 3d. 4h. 48m. £4000·0000

Despatch money payable $=$ £4000.

Worked Example 14. A vessel of 3,348 n.r.t. is chartered for a full cargo to be loaded and discharged in 14 running days, bunkering time excepted. Lay days are to commence when the vessel is in the berth and ready to load and discharge, respectively. Demurrage, if incurred, is to be paid at 30p per net registered ton per day and *pro rata*, and despatch money at half the demurrage rate for all time saved.

The facts are as follows:

Thur. 27th Aug.	..	1030 vessel arrived at loading port.
		1200 in berth and ready to load.
		1345 loading commenced.
Mon. 31st Aug.	..	Declared a public holiday; no work done.
Wed. 2nd Sept.	..	0600 left loading berth to proceed to oiling berth.
		0830 commenced bunkering.
		1530 completed bunkering.
		1945 made fast in loading berth and resumed loading.
Thur. 3rd Sept.	..	1630 completed loading; B's/L signed.
		1800 sailed from loading port.

Sun. 20th Sept.   ..   1115 arrived at discharging port.
Mon. 21st Sept.   ..   0500 berthed and ready to discharge.
              ..   0800 commenced discharging.
Fri. 25th Sept.   ..   1345 completed discharging.
              ..   1445 sailed from discharging port.

Draw up a statement of the lay days and calculate the amount of demurrage or despatch money payable.

Total lay time (loading and discharging) = 14 days.

Loading port time sheet:

Day	Date	Remarks	Hours to count	Total time counted	Time saved
			h. m.	d. h. m.	d. h. m.
Th.	27 Aug.	1200 berthed; lay days begin	12 00	0 12 00	
F.	28 ,,		24 00	1 12 00	
S.	29 ,,		24 00	2 12 00	
Su.	30 ,,		24 00	3 12 00	
M.	31 ,,	Holiday; but still counts ..	24 00	4 12 00	
T.	1 Sept.		24 00	5 12 00	
W.	2 ,,	0600 to 1945 bunkering time not counted	10 15	5 22 15	
Th.	3 ,,	1630 completed loading ..	16 30	6 14 45	

Discharging port time sheet:

Su.	20 Sept.	1115 arrived at discharging port	nil	6 14 45	
M.	21 ,,	0500 berthed. Lay time resumed	19 00	7 9 45	
T.	22 ,,		24 00	8 9 45	
W.	23 ,,		24 00	9 9 45	
Th.	24 ,,		24 00	10 9 45	
F.	25 ,,	1345 completed discharging	24 00	11 9 45	0 10 15
S.	26 ,,		24 00	12 9 45	1 0 00
Su.	27 ,,		24 00	13 9 45	1 0 00
M.	28 ,,	1415 time expired	14 15	14 0 00	14 15

Total time saved = 3   0 30

Despatch money due to charterer's agents at 15p per n.r.t. per day

$$= \pounds \frac{3\frac{1}{48} \times 15 \times 3348}{100}$$

$$= \pounds \frac{145 \times 15 \times 3348}{48 \times 100}$$

$$= \pounds 1517 \cdot 06$$

Worked Example 15. A C/P provides for a vessel to load a full cargo of not less than 11,400 tons and not exceeding 12,600 tons at the rate of 1,500 tons per day, Sundays and holidays excepted. Lay days are to commence 24 hours after notice of readiness is handed in, and charterer's stevedores are to be employed at £1·75 per ton deadweight. Demurrage, if incurred, is to be paid at £1600 per day and *pro rata*, and 6 running days are to be allowed for demurrage. Deadfreight, if any, is to be paid at £16·25 per ton and the vessel is to have a lien on the cargo for freight, deadfreight, and demurrage.

Notice was accepted at 10.30 a.m. on Tuesday, 5th May, and the charterer's agent agreed with the master's declaration that the vessel's deadweight capacity was 12,200 tons. Monday, 11th May, was an official holiday. Loading commenced on Thursday, 7th May, and cargo was received on board as follows:

7th May 1,200 tons;	12th May 1,500 tons;	16th May 850 tons;
8th ,. 1,145 ,, ;	13th ,, 1,100 ,, ;	18th ,, 1,075 ,, ;
9th ,, 475 ,, ;	14th ,, 960 ,, ;	19th ,, 875 ,, ;
11th ,, 1,050 ,, ;	15th ,, 980 ,, ;	20th ,, 750 ,, ;

Thereafter no more cargo was forthcoming. Calculate the amounts due to the vessel by the way of demurrage and deadfreight, and state when the vessel is free to sail with the incomplete cargo

$$\text{Number of lay days allowed} = \frac{12250}{1500} = \frac{49}{6} = 8\tfrac{1}{6} \text{ days}$$
$$= 8\text{d. } 4\text{h. } 00\text{m.}$$

Day	Date	Remarks	Cargo loaded	Hours to count	Total time counted	Time on demurrage
			tons	h. m.	d. h. m.	d. h. m.
T.	5 May	1030 notice accepted	nil	nil	nil	
W.	6 ,,	1030 time begins to count	nil	13 30	0 13 30	
Th.	7 ,,		1,200	24 00	1 13 30	
F.	8 ,,		1,145	24 00	2 13 30	
S.	9 ,,		475	24 00	3 13 30	
Su.	10 ,,	Not counted ..	nil	nil	3 13 30	
M.	11 ,,		1,050	24 00	4 13 30	
T.	12 ,,		1,500	24 00	5 13 30	
W.	13 ,,		1,100	24 00	6 13 30	
Th.	14 ,,		960	24 00	7 13 30	
F.	15 ,,	1430 lay days expire	980	14 30	8 4 00	0 9 30
S.	16 ,,		850		———	1 0 00
Su.	17 ,,		nil			1 0 00
M.	18 ,,		1,075			1 0 00
T.	19 ,,		875			1 0 00
W.	20 ,,		750			1 0 00
Th.	21 ,,	1430 demurrage days expire	nil			0 14 30

Total time on demurrage = 6   0 00

Total cargo loaded	11,960 tons	
Full capacity	12,250 ,,	
Cargo short shipped	**290**	,,

Demurrage due to vessel for 6 days at £1600 p.d. ..	..	..	£9600·00

Gross deadfreight at £16·25 per ton on 290 tons ..	..	.. £4712·50
Less stevedoring charges saved at £1·75 per ton on 290 tons	..	507·50
Net deadfreight payable to vessel ..	.. .. ..	.. £4205·00

Vessel free to sail with incomplete cargo at **1430 on Thursday, 21st May.**

Mention has already been made of the C/P clause which gives the charterer the right to "average the days allowed for loading and discharging". It was pointed out that although this phrase can be interpreted in different ways a test case in court has now established which interpretation is regarded in law as the correct one.

Worked Example 16 will serve as an illustration of how different interpretations produce widely differing results.

Working Example 16. The C/P terms include the following:

Loading rate 500 tons per day, S. & H.E.

Discharging rate 1500 tons per day, S. & H.E.

Charterer to have the right to average the days allowed for loading and discharging.

Lay days to commence at loading and discharging ports at 8 a.m. after the ship has been reported ready and in free pratique whether in berth or not.

Vessel to be reported during customary office hours.

If shippers arrange to load, or consignees to discharge, on Sundays or on holidays or before lay days begin, the master is to allow work to be done and half of such time is to count, except that time between noon on Saturday and 8 a.m. on Monday or the day following a holiday is not to count whether used or not.

Demurrage, if incurred, is to be paid at £1200 per day and *pro rata* and despatch money at half the demurrage rate for all time saved at both ends.

The facts of the case are:

Notice of readiness accepted at loading port at 10.30 a.m. on Friday, 28th August.

Loading commenced at 1.30 p.m. on 28th August and went on for 6 hours on that day.

Loading was completed at 7.15 p.m. on 22nd September.

Notice of readiness accepted at discharging port at 3.20 p.m. on Thursday, 5th November.

Discharging commenced at 4 p.m. on 5th November and continued without interruption until 2 p.m. on 7th November when it was completed.

There were no holidays or non-working days other than periods between noon on Saturday and 8 a.m. on Monday.

The weight of cargo loaded was 7650 tons.

Method 1: Time sheet drawn up on the principle that time on demurrage at the loading port should de deducted from the lay days allowed for discharging, and that charterers will be liable for demurrage in respect of discharging time used in excess of the net lay days remaining.

Number of lay days allowed for loading $= \dfrac{7650}{500} = $ **15d. 7h. 12m.**

,, ,, ,, ,, ,, ,, discharging $= \dfrac{7650}{1500} = $ **5d. 2h. 24m.**

Loading port:

Day	Date	Remarks	Hours to count	Total time counted	Time on demurrage
			h. m.	d. h. m.	d. h. m.
F.	28 Aug.	1030 notice accepted. 1330 to 1930 half time counts	3 00	0 3 00	
S.	29 ,,	0800 lay days proper begin. Time not counted after 1200	4 00	0 7 00	
Su.	30 ,,	Not counted	nil	0 7 00	
M.	31 ,,	Time not counted before 0800	16 00	0 23 00	
T.	1 Sept.		24 00	1 23 00	
W.	2 ,,		24 00	2 23 00	
Th.	3 ,,		24 00	3 23 00	
F.	4 ,,		24 00	4 23 00	
S.	5 ,,	Time not counted after 1200	12 00	5 11 00	
Su.	6 ,,	Not counted	nil	5 11 00	
M.	7 ,,	Time not counted before 0800	16 00	6 3 00	
T.	8 ,,		24 00	7 3 00	
W.	9 ,,		24 00	8 3 00	
Th.	10 ,,		24 00	9 3 00	
F.	11 ,,		24 00	10 3 00	
S.	12 ,,	Time not counted after 1200	12 00	10 15 00	
Su.	13 ,,	Not counted	nil	10 15 00	
M.	14 ,,	Time not counted before 0800	16 00	11 7 00	
T.	15 ,,		24 00	12 7 00	
W.	16 ,,		24 00	13 7 00	
Th.	17 ,,		24 00	14 7 00	
F.	18 ,,		24 00	15 7 00	
S.	19 ,,	0012 Loading time expired	0 12	15 7 12	0 23 48
Su.	20 ,,				1 0 00
M.	21 ,,				1 0 00
T.	22 ,,	1915 Loading completed ..			0 19 15

Excess time at loading port = **3 19 03**

∴Time available for discharge = 5d. 2h. 24m.–3d. 19h. 03m. = **1d. 7h. 21m.**

Discharging port:

Day	Date	Remarks	Hours to count	Total time counted	Time on demurrage
			h. m.	d. h. m.	d. h. m.
Th	5 Nov.	1600 to 2400 half time counts	4 00	0 4 00	
F.	6 ,,	0000 to 0800 half time counts	4 00	0 8 00	
F.	6 ,,	0800 to 2400 full time counts	16 00	1 0 00	
S.	7 ,,	0721 time expired ..	7 21	1 7 21	
S.	7 ,,	1400 discharging completed			0 6 39

Demurrage at £1200 per day for 6h. 39m. = **£332·50**

Method 2: Time sheet drawn up on the principle that loading and discharging should be treated as a continuous process.

		d.	h.	m.
Time allowed for loading		15	7	12
,, ,, ,, discharging		5	2	24
Total time allowed for both processes		20	9	36

Loading:

Day	Date	Remarks	Hours to count	Total time counted	Time saved
			h. m.	d. h. m.	d. h. m.
F.	28 Aug.	1030 notice accepted. 1330 to 1930 half time counts	3 00	0 3 00	
S.	29 ,,	0800 lay days proper begin. Time not counted after 1200	4 00	0 7 00	
Su.	30 ,,	Not counted	nil	0 7 00	
M.	31 ,,	Time not counted before 0800	16 00	0 23 00	
T.	1 Sept.		24 00	1 23 00	
W.	2 ,,		24 00	2 23 00	
Th.	3 ,,		24 00	3 23 00	
F.	4 ,,		24 0	4 23 00	
S.	5 ,,	Time not counted after 1200	12 00	5 11 00	
Su.	6 ,,	Not counted	nil	5 11 00	
M.	7 ,,	Time not counted before 0800	16 00	6 3 00	
T.	8 ,,		24 00	7 3 00	
W.	9 ,,		24 00	8 3 00	
Th.	10 ,,		24 00	9 3 00	
F.	11 ,,		24 00	10 3 00	
S.	12 ,,	Time not counted after 1200	12 00	10 15 00	
Su.	13 ,,	Not counted	nil	10 15 00	
M.	14 ,,	Times not counted before 0800	16 00	11 7 00	
T.	15 ,,		24 00	12 7 00	
W.	16 ,,		24 00	13 7 00	
Th.	17 ,,		24 00	14 7 00	
F.	18 ,,		24 00	15 7 00	
S.	19 ,,	Time not counted after 1200	12 00	15 19 00	
Su.	20 ,,	Not counted	nil	15 19 00	
M.	21 ,,	Time not counted before 0800	16 00	16 11 00	
T.	22 ,,	1915 loading completed ..	19 15	17 6 15	

Discharging:

Day	Date	Remarks	Hours to count	Total time counted	Time saved
Th.	5 Nov.	1600 discharging commenced. Half time counts to 2400	4 00	17 10 15	
F.	6 ,,	0000 to 0800 half time counts	4 00	17 14 15	
F.	6 ,,	0800 to 2400 full time counts	16 00	18 6 15	
S.	7 ,,	Time not counted after 1200. 1400 discharge completed	12 00	18 18 15	0 10 00
Su.	8 ,,	Not counted	nil	18 18 15	1 0 00
M.	9 ,,	Time not counted before 0800	16 00	19 10 15	1 0 00
T.	10 ,,	2321 time expired	23 21	20 9 36	0 23 21

Total time saved = 3 9 21

Despatch money at £600 per day for 3d. 9h. 21m. = £2033·75.

Method 3: Time sheet drawn up on the principle that time used in loading and time used in discharging should be considered separately, and that the one should be set off against the other. Hence, in this case, the time saved at the discharging port should be set off against the excess time used at the loading port.

Time on demurrage as shown in Method 1 = 3d. 19h. 03m.
Time allowed for discharge   = 5d. 2h. 24m.

Day	Date	Remarks	Hours to count	Total time counted	Time saved
			h. m.	d. h. m.	d. h. m.
Th.	5 Nov.	1600 discharging commenced. Half time counts to 2400..	4 00	0 4 00	
F.	6 ,,	0000 to 0800 half time counts	4 00	0 8 00	
F.	6 ,,	0800 to 2400 full time counts	16 00	1 0 00	
S.	7 ,,	Time not counted after 1200. 1400 discharge completed	12 00	1 12 00	0 10 00
Su.	8 ,,	Not counted	nil	1 12 00	1 0 00
M.	9 ,,	Time not counted before 0800	16 00	2 4 00	1 0 00
T.	10 ,,		24 00	3 4 00	1 0 00
W.	11 ,,		24 00	4 4 00	1 0 00
Th.	12 ,,	2224 time expired	22 24	5 2 24	0 22 24

Total time saved = 5 8 24

                                     d. h. m.
Time saved in discharging   = 5 8 24
Excess time used at loading port = 3 19 03
Net time saved   = 1 13 21

Despatch money at £600 per day for 1d. 13h. 21m. = £933·75.

In giving judgement it was held that the word "averaging" implies a levelling, *i.e.*, a setting of good against bad, and does not mean that time allowed for loading and discharging can be pooled. Accordingly, the time sheet should be drawn up in the manner illustrated by Method 3 above.

LOADING CALCULATIONS

Masters' examination questions which come under this heading have been set in a variety of styles, so that a suitable standard method of setting out the work applicable to all cases, although one can be devised, would prove unnecessarily cumbersome in some cases. However, such questions should not give rise to undue difficulty so long as the candidate has acquired the necessary basic knowledge of the details of load lines, and adheres strictly to the principle that the vessel must be loaded in such a way that she will not become overloaded at any stage of the voyage. Simply because a ship is loading under tropical conditions it does not follow that she may load to her tropical load line, and a ship loading under summer conditions is not necessarily able to load to the depth of her summer load line. The maximum permissible depth of loading will depend upon the route she is to take and whether the increase of freeboard due to consumption of fuel, stores and water is more or less than the increase, if any, demanded by the change of circumstances *en route* (*i.e.*, change of zone or area, or change of season). In some cases, too, the maximum permissible deadweight at a first loading port will be partly governed by what additional deadweight is to be taken on at subsequent ports.

Before attempting calculations of this type it is essential to study what has been said in Chapter 7 about load line rules and the official chart of zones and seasonal areas.

Worked Example 17. A ship of deadweight capacities 8940 tonnes (winter), 9335 tonnes (summer), and 9738 tonnes (tropical) is to load a full cargo of heavy grain at Bahia Blanca for Kobe via Cape Town and Miri. After discharging at Kobe she is to proceed in ballast to Prince Rupert. From the information given below find the maximum amount of cargo she can load at Bahia Blanca and what bunkers should be taken there and at Cape Town and Miri, respectively, with the intention of leaving Kobe with the maximum possible amount.

Bahia Blanca to Cape Town 10½ days—summer zone throughout.
Cape Town to Miri 16 days—summer—tropical, in that order.
Miri to Kobe 8 days—tropical for the first 1½ days, then summer.
Daily consumption—diesel oil 16 tonnes, water 10 tonnes. (Port consumption to be ignored.)
Fuel prices per tonne are $340 Bahia Blanca, $335 Cape Town, $306 Miri, $329 Kobe.
Maximum diesel oil capacity 850 tonnes.
Reserves of fuel and water to be 5 days' supply at all times of sailing.
Allowances for stores, etc. consumed—Bahia Blanca to Cape Town 15 tonnes, Cape Town to Miri 22 tonnes.
Allowances for stores, etc. replenished—Cape Town 36 tonnes, Miri 24 tonnes.
Provisions and stores (not including water) on board at Bahia Blanca amount to 128 tonnes.

Fuel required at Bahia Blanca = 10½ + 5 days' supply @ 16 t.p.d.
                                       = 248 tonnes.
  ,,   ,,   ,,   Cape Town = 16 days' supply @ 16 t.p.d.
                                       = 256 tonnes.
  ,,   ,,   ,,   Miri   = Max. possible amount on account of low price as compared with Kobe.
Water required at Bahia Blanca = 10½ + 5 days' supply @ 10 t.p.d.
                                       = 155 tonnes.
  ,,   ,,   ,,   Cape Town = 16 days' supply @ 10 t.p.d.
                                       = 160 tonnes.
  ,,   ,,   ,,   Miri   = 8 days' supply @ 10 t.p.d.
                                       = 80 tonnes.

The dominant factors are that the ship can be loaded at Miri to summer deadweight plus the equivalent of $1\frac{1}{2}$ days' consumption, but may not leave Cape Town with more than her summer deadweight. Thus:

Deadweight leaving Miri $= 9335 + (1\frac{1}{2} \times 26)$ t.	=	9,374 t.
Total bunker capacity at Miri (850 t. less 80 t. already in reserve.	=	770 t.
		8,604 t.
Water and stores required at Miri	=	104 t.
Max. dwt. to arrive at Miri in order to use all fuel capacity	=	8,500 t.
Cape Town to Miri consumption—fuel 256, stores 22, water 160 t.	=	438 t.
Dwt. to leave Cape Town on this basis	=	8,938 t.
Summer deadweight	=	9,335 t.
Difference	=	397 t.

As shippers at Bahia Blanca are entitled to load a full cargo they should have the advantage of this 397 tonnes, so that the max. fuel that can be taken in at Miri will be 770-397 = 373 tonnes.

Deadweight leaving Cape Town	=	9,335 t.
To load at Cape Town—fuel 256, stores 36, water 160 t.	=	452 t.
Max. dwt. to arrive at Cape Town	=	8,883 t.
Bahia Blanca to Cape Town consumption—fuel 168, stores 15, water 105 t.	=	288 t.
Max. dwt. to leave Bahia Blanca	=	9,171 t.
Required at Bahia Blanca—fuel 248, stores 128, water 155 t.	=	531 t.
Cargo ship can lift at Bahia Blanca	=	8,640 t.

Hence:

Cargo to load at Bahia Blanca	..	..	8,640 tonnes
Fuel to take ,, ,, ,,	..	..	248 ,,
Fuel to take ,, Cape Town	..	..	256 ,,
Fuel to take ,, Miri ..	..	..	373 ,,

An alternative method of working example 17 would be to assume that the ship loads to the maximum permissible deadweight according to area and season at the first port and then "test" this figure by working through the voyage stage by stage to find at what stage (if any) she becomes overloaded. The place where the greatest overloading occurs will then indicate what "excess" should be deducted from the assumed deadweight at the first port to find the maximum permissible deadweight in the circumstances and thence the weight of cargo that can be lifted.

In cases where fuel can be taken at more than one port it will usually be an advantage to work first on the basis of taking only sufficient fuel at one port to reach the next so that the weight of cargo to take at the first port is established. Then consideration can be given to the possibility of taking in extra fuel at a place where bunkers are cheaper if lifting capacity proves to be available.

The alternative working shown below is based on the initial assumption that the ship loads to summer deadweight at Bahia

Blanca and takes only sufficient fuel, etc. at each port in order to reach the next.

Place or item	Assumed, Tonnes	Allowed, Tonnes	Excess Tonnes	Check and calculation of fuel at Miri Tonnes
Depart Bahia Blanca	9,335	9,335	—	9,171
Consumption to Cape Town (10½ × 26 + 15) t.	− 288			− 288
Arrive Cape Town	9,047	9,335	—	8,883
Fuel ,, ,,	+ 256			+ 256
Water ,, ,,	+ 160			+ 160
Stores ,, ,,	+ 36			+ 36
Depart Cape Town	9,499	9,335	164	9,335
Consumption to Miri (16 × 26 + 22) t.	− 438			− 438
Arrive Miri	9,061	9,738		8,897
Fuel ,,	128			+ 80 water
Water ,,	80			+ 24 stores
Stores ,,	24			9,001 before fuelling
Depart Miri	9,293	9,738		9,374 Max. after
Consumption to S. Zone	− 39			fuelling, *i.e.* 9,335 + 1½ × 26
				373 Available for
Arrive S. Zone	9,254	9,335		fuel
Consumption to Kobe	− 169			
Arrive Kobe	9,085	9,335		

Assumed leaving Bahia Blanca		9,335 t.
Excess (Cape Town)		− 164 t.
Permissible dwt. at Bahia Blanca ..		9,171 t.
Fuel, water & stores at Bahia Blanca ..		− 531 t.
Available for cargo at Bahia Blanca ..		8,640 t.

Hence:

Cargo Bahia Blanca	..	..	..	.. 8,640 tonnes
Fuel Bahia Blanca	..	..	..	.. 248 ,,
Fuel Cape Town ..	..	..	..	.. 256 ,,
Fuel Miri	..	..	..	.. 373 ,,

Worked Example 18. From the given data calculate the weight of cargo a vessel can load at Montreal if she is to sail for Glasgow at about midnight of the 9th/10th October.

Length 98·2 m., Breadth 12·3 m., Summer draught 6·24 m., Block coefficient 0·79, T.P.C. 10, Light displacement 1,727 tonnes. The vessel consumes 14 tonnes of fuel and 6 tonnes of water per day. On board at Montreal are 310 tonnes of fuel, 80 tonnes of water and

10 tonnes of stores. She will be in the North Atlantic Winter
Seasonal Zone 1 when the winter season commences at 0000, 16th
October. (Relative density of sea water = 1·025.)

Note:—Since the vessel is less than 100 metres in length, and will be in the
North Atlantic winter Seasonal Zone 1 when the winter season commences at
0000, 16th October, the minimum permitted freeboard then will be the
W.N.A. freeboard which is 50 mm. (5 cm.) greater than the winter freeboard.
The Winter freeboard is one forty-eighth of the summer draught greater than
the summer freeboard. The relevant displacements and deadweights are
shown below.

Summer displacement	=	$98·2 \times 12·3 \times 6·24 \times 0·79 \times 1·025$ tonnes	
	=	6,103 tonnes	
Light displacement	=	1,727 ,,	
Summer deadweight	=	4,376 ,,	
Winter reduction	=	130 ,,	(1/48 × 624cm × 10 TPC)
Winter deadweight	=:	4,246 ,,	
W N A reduction	=	50 ,,	(5 cm × 10 TPC)
W.N.A. deadweight	=	4,196 ,,	
6 days consumption @ 20 t.p.d.	=	+120 ,,	
Dwt. for leaving Montreal	=	4,316 ,,	
Fuel, stores & water on board	=	400 ,,	
Available for cargo	=	3,916 tonnes.	

Worked Example 19. A ship's tropical, summer and winter
deadweight capacities are respectively 10,286, 9,948 and 9,613
tonnes. She is to load at Vancouver for London via the Panama
Canal, calling at Los Angeles and Curaçao for fuel. On departure
she will have on board 370 tonnes of fuel, 180 tonnes of water and
12 tonnes of stores. She consumes 27 tonnes of fuel and 6 tonnes of
water and stores daily. Passages are estimated as follows:

Vancouver to Los Angeles: 4 days—all summer.
Los Angeles to Panama Canal: 9 days—summer—tropical—in that order.
Panama Canal to Curaçao: 3 days—all tropical.
Curaçao to London: 12 days—tropical for 2 days, then summer for 4 days,
    then winter for 6 days.

Find the maximum weight of cargo the ship can lift at Vancouver
if she is to maintain a reserve of 6 days' fuel at all times. What
quantities of fuel should she take in at Los Angeles and Curaçao,
respectively, if fuel prices are lower at the latter port?

Fuel on board at Vancouver	=	370 tonnes
,, consumed Vancouver to Los Angeles	=	108 ,,
,, on arrival at Los Angeles	=	262 ,,
,, (min.) req'd. at Los angeles to reach Curaçao with reserve (18 × 27) t.	=	486 ,,
,, to load at Los Angeles	=	224 ,,

Fuel on board leaving Los Angeles = 486 tonnes
,, consumed Los Angeles to Curaçao = 324 ,,
,, on arrival at Curaçao = 162 ,,
,, req'd. at Curaçao to reach London with reserve (18 × 27) = 486 ,,
,, to load at Curaçao = 324 ,,

Place or item	Assumed tonnes	Allowed Tonnes	Excess	Check
Depart Vancouver	9,948	9,948	—	9,791
Consumption to Los Angeles (4 × 33) t.	− 132			− 132
Arrive Los Angeles	9,816	9,948	—	9,659
Fuel at Los Angeles	+ 224			+ 224
Depart Los Angeles	10,040	9,948	92	9,883
Consumption to Curaçao (12 × 33) t.	− 396			− 396
Arrive Curaçao	9,644	10,286	—	9,487
Fuel at Curaçao	+ 324			+ 324
Depart Curaçao	9,968	10,286	—	9,811
Consumption to Winter Zone (6 × 33) t.	− 198			− 198
Arrive Winter Zone	9,770	9,613	157	9,613
Consumption to London (6 × 33) t.	− 198			− 198
Arrive London	9,572	9,613	—	9,415

Assumed leaving Vancouver   9,948 tonnes
Excess on arrival at W. Zone   − 157 ,,
Permitted dwt. leaving Vancouver   9,791 ,,
Fuel, stores and water on board   − 562 ,,
Available for cargo at Vancouver   9,229 ,,

N.B. Cheaper fuel at Curaçao is no advantage in this case as the minimum required at Los Angeles is only just sufficient to reach Curaçao with 162 tonnes (6 days' reserve).

Summary
{ Cargo to load at Vancouver .. .. 9,229 tonnes
{ Fuel to take at Los Angeles .. .. 224 ,,
{ Fuel to take at Curaçao .. .. .. 324 ,,

EXAMPLES FOR EXERCISE

Question 1. A seaman is engaged at £49·28 per week on Tuesday 20th April and is discharged on Friday 30th July the same year. He has a monthly allotment of £100 and other charges against his wages are:—Income tax £241·96; National insurance contributions £62·39; tobacco, etc. £27·16; cash advances £94·88. He is entitled to overtime payment for 206 hours at £1·20 per hour, and to payment for 17 days leave, with leave subsistence at 88p per day. Calculate the balance due to him on his discharge.

(*Answer:* £373·53)

Question 2. An officer is engaged on Wednesday 14th April for a voyage which terminates on Friday 6th August the same year. He is paid at the rate of £356·40 per month, but is eligible for an increase to £367·20 as from 24th May. Calculate the balance due to this officer at the time of his discharge given the following details:—

Monthly allotment £180.
Officers' Pension Fund contributions £92·30.
National Insurance contributions £106·15.
Income Tax £406·14.
Cash advances $300 at $1·82 to £1.
Radio Messages £2·94.
Wine account £22·89.
Leave 38 days, paid at final rate of pay.

(*Answer:* £510·82)

Question 3. From the items given below, draw up an account current for the voyage. Show the balance and state to whom it is due:—(a) if the owner pays National Insurance contributions and income tax to the Collector of Taxes, and Officers' Pension contributions to the Fund, and (b) if the master pays the National Insurance contributions and income tax to the Collector of Taxes, and the owner pays the Officers' Pension Fund contributions to the Fund.

Portage Account (crew's wages) £11,114·24.
Overtime £414·64.
Leave pay £894·62.
Leave subsistence £86·10.
National Insurance contributions: Owner £964·42.
　　　　　　　　　　　　　　　　　 Crew　£704·24.
Income Tax £2,466·72.
Officers Pension Fund contributions £244·33.
Master's bar allowance £26·00.
Master's port expenses £35·27.
Disbursements at port "A" £300·19.
Cash drawn from agents at port "A" £778·36.
Disbursements at port "B" £1,421·37.
Cash drawn from agents at port "B" £480·00.
Cash bar sales £340·60.
Advance notes £245·00.
Allotments £6,995·00.
Master's bar account £23·58.
Crew radio messages £28·94.
Crew's postage £23·48.
Cash drawn to pay off crew £500·00.
Freight collected at "B" £16,100 with £1,600 in cash and the remainder in B's/E on London.

(*Answers:* (a)　Balance to owner £137·82)
(　　　　　　(b)　Balance to master £3,997·56)

Note:—The amount shown in (b) would need to be drawn and added to remaining cash to enable the master to pay the Collector of Taxes.

Question 4. A C/P provides for 16 weather working days (S. & H.E.) to be allowed for loading and discharging. Stoppages due to machinery failures are not to count as part of the lay time, and

Saturday is to count as ¾ of a lay day. At the loading port the time used amounted to 10 days 4 hours 30 minutes.

At the discharging port lay time commenced at 0830 on Tuesday, 26th July, and discharging was completed at 1724 on 4th August. The first Monday in August was a public holiday. Rain prevented work being done during $5\frac{1}{2}$ hours on 28th July and work at No. 4 hatch was suspended for 2 hours on 29th July due to winch breakdown. The ship has 5 hatches.

Calculate the demurrage or despatch money payable if the demurrage rate is £250 per day and *pro rata*, and the despatch rate is half the demurrage rate.

(*Answer:* Demurrage payable is £265·62½)

Question 5. A tanker voyage C/P provides for the vessel to load and discharge in 120 running hours. Lay time is to begin at both loading and discharging ports 6 hours after notice of readiness is accepted, and any time used for bunkering through the loading lines is not to count as part of the lay hours

At the loading port notice was accepted at 10.30 a.m. on Friday, 9th September. Loading commenced at 11 a.m. on the same day and was completed at noon on 12th September. $4\frac{1}{2}$ hours were used for bunkering through loading lines on 10th September.

At the discharging port notice was accepted at 4 p.m. on 21st October and discharging finished at 9.45 a.m. on 25th October.

Calculate the demurrage payable by charterers at £500 per day and *pro rata* for part of a day.

(*Answer:* £557·29)

Question 6. A vessel is to discharge at the rate of 800 tons per running day, and freight is payable at the rate of £1·60 per ton on quantity delivered, or on B/L weight less 2 per cent. in lieu of weighing, at receiver's option. The consignee opts not to have the cargo weighed out, and B's/L were signed for a total of 6,750 tons. 25 per cent. of the chartered freight was paid in advance at the loading port. Demurrage, if incurred, is payable at £300 per day and *pro rata*, and despatch money is payable for all time saved at half the demurrage rate. Lay days are to commence 24 hours after notice of readiness is accepted or when discharging begins, whichever is the earlier.

Notice was accepted at 11.30 a.m. on Tuesday, 14th October, and discharging commenced at 4 p.m. on the same day. Work went on continuously day and night, except for the period from midnight on Saturday, 18th October, until 7 a.m. on Monday, 20th October, when no work was done. Discharging was completed at 5.45 p.m. on Tuesday, 21st October

Calculate the amount of cash due to the ship at the discharging port.

(*Answer:* £7,679·31)

Question 7. A ship of 12,500 tonnes deadweight on a summer draught of 8·66 m. and T.P.C. 23·2 is to sail from Osaka for London on 1st February via Singapore and Cape. Her daily consumption of fuel and water is 32 tonnes. She is to load 420 tonnes of fuel at Singapore, 250 tonnes at Dakar, and is to call at Colombo for 500 tonnes of cargo. Fuel, water and stores on board when leaving Osaka amount to 1,570 tonnes. Passages are estimated to be:

Osaka to Singapore: 7 days—summer, then tropical.
Singapore to Colombo: 4½ days—tropical throughout.
Colombo to Dakar: 22 days—4 days tropical, then 11½ summer, then 6½ tropical.
Dakar to London: 8 days—2½ days tropical, then 2 summer, then 3½ in winter seasonal zone in winter season.

Find the maximum amount of cargo that can be loaded at Osaka.

(*Answer:* Cargo to load at Osaka 10,506 tonnes.)

Question 8. A 10-knot steamer with a timber load line is to carry a full cargo of timber, including a deck load, from Georgetown, Prince Edward Island, to Cardiff, sailing at about noon on 11th October. The winter season in the North Atlantic Winter Seasonal Zone 1 through which her track passes begins at 0000 hours on 16th October.

Particulars are as follows:

Summer displacement 9,310 tonnes.
Light displacement 3,045 tonnes.
Summer draught 7·92 m.
Length 116 m., beam 15 m., T.P.C. 12.
Daily consumption: fuel 17 tonnes, water 5 tonnes.
On board leaving Georgetown: fuel 410 tonnes, water 190 tonnes, stores 95 tonnes.

Find the weight of cargo she can load and the maximum mean draught to which she can load. State the minimum and maximum permissible heights of the deckload.

(*Answers:* Cargo 5471 tonnes, mean draught 7·8375 m., Maximum height of deck load 5·0 m.)

Note:—Winter North Atlantic loadlines apply to appropriate vessels while in the North Atlantic Winter Seasonal Zone I in the winter season. This vessel has a LWNA loadline but because of the ship's length it is on the same level as the W loadline, and so the ship must not be deeper than the W loadline at 0000 16th October. Therefore no minimum height of deck load is involved as the vessel is not loaded beyond the depth to which she would be entitled to load if she had no timber loadline.

APPENDIX I

CARRIAGE OF GOODS BY SEA ACT, 1971

An Act to amend the law with respect to the carriage of goods by sea.

[8th April 1971]

BE IT enacted by the Queen's most Excellent Majesty, by and with the advice and consent of the Lords Spiritual and Temporal, and Commons, in this present Parliament assembled, and by the authority of the same, as follows:

1.—(1) In this Act, "the Rules" means the International Convention for the unification of certain rules of law relating to bills of lading signed at Brussels on 25th August 1924, as amended by the Protocol signed at Brussels on 23rd February 1968.

(2) The provisions of the Rules, as set out in the Schedule to this Act hall have the force of law.

(3) Without prejudice to subsection (2) above, the said provisions shall have effect (and have the force of law) in relation to and in connection with the carriage of goods by sea in ships where the port of shipment is a port in the United Kingdom, whether or not the carriage is between ports in two different States within the meaning of Article X of the Rules.

(4) Subject to subsection (6) below, nothing in this section shall be taken as applying anything in the Rules to any contract for the carriage of goods by sea, unless the contract expressly or by implication provides for the issue of a bill of lading or any similar document of title.

(5) The Secretary of State may from time to time by order made by statutory instrument specify the respective amounts which for the purposes of paragraph 5 of Article IV of the Rules and of Article IV bis of the Rules are to be taken as equivalent to the sums expressed in francs which are mentioned in sub-paragraph (a) of that paragraph.

(6) Without prejudice to Article X(c) of the Rules, the Rules shall have the force of law in relation to—

(a) any bill of lading if the contract contained in or evidenced by it expressly provides that the Rules shall govern the contract, and
any receipt which is a non-negotiable document marked as such if the contract contained in or evidenced by it is a contract for the carriage of goods by sea which expressly provides that the Rules are to govern the contract as if the receipt were a bill of lading,

but subject, where paragraph (b) applies, to any necessary modifications and in particular with the omission in Article III of the Rules of the second sentence of paragraph 4 and of paragraph 7.

(7) If and so far as the contract contained in or evidenced by a bill of lading or receipt within paragraph (a) or (b) of subsection (6) above applies to deck cargo or live animals, the Rules as given the force of law by that subsection shall have effect as if Article I(c) did not exclude deck cargo and life animals.

In this subsection "deck cargo" means cargo which by the contract of carriage is stated as being carried on deck and is so carried.

2.—(1) If Her Majesty by Order in Council certifies to the following effect, that is to say, that for the purposes of the Rules—

(a) a State specified in the Order is a contracting State, or is a contracting State in respect of any place or territory so specified; or

(b) any place or territory specified in the Order forms part of a State so specified (whether a contracting State or not),

the Order shall, except so far as it has been superseded by a subsequent Order, be conclusive evidence of the matters so certified.

(2) An order in Council under this section may be varied or revoked by a subsequent Order in Council.

3. There shall not be implied in any contract for the carriage of goods by sea to which the Rules apply by virtue of this Act any absolute undertaking by the carrier of the goods to provide a seaworthy ship.

4.—(1) Her Majesty may by Order in Council direct that this Act shall extend, subject to such exceptions, adaptations and modifications as may be specified in the Order, to all or any of the following territories, that is—

(a) any colony (not being a colony for whose external relations a country other than the United Kingdom is responsible),

(b) any country outside Her Majesty's dominions in which Her Majesty has jurisdiction in right of Her Majesty's Government of the United Kingdom.

(2) An Order in Council under this section may contain such transitional and other consequential and incidental provisions as appear to Her Majesty to be expedient, including provisions amending or repealing any legislation about the carriage of goods by sea forming part of the law of any of the territories mentioned in paragraphs (a) and (b) above.

(3) An Order in Council under this section may be varied or revoked by a subsequent Order in Council.

5.—(1) Her Majesty may by Order in Council provide that section 1(3) of this Act shall have effect as if the reference therein to the United Kingdom included a reference to all or any of the following territories, that is—

(a) The Isle of Man;

(b) any of the Channel Islands specified in the Order;

(c) any colony specified in the Order (not being a colony for whose external relations a country other than the United Kingdom is responsible);

(d) any associated state (as defined by section 1(3) of the West Indies Act 1967) specified in the Order;

(e) any country specified in the Order, being a country outside Her Majesty's dominions in which Her Majesty has jurisdiction in right of Her Majesty's Government of the United Kingdom.

(2) An Order in Council under this section may be varied or revoked by a subsequent Order in Council.

6.—(1) This Act may be cited as the Carriage of Goods by Sea Act 1971.

(2) It is hereby declared that this Act extends to Northern Ireland.

(3) The following enactments shall be repealed, that is—

(a) the Carriage of Goods by Sea Act 1924,

(b) section 12(4)(a) of the Nuclear Installations Act 1965,

and without prejudice to section 38(1) of the Interpretation Act 1889, the reference to the said Act of 1924 in section 1(1)(i)(ii) of the Hovercraft Act 1968 shall include a reference to this Act.

(4) It is hereby declared that for the purposes of Article VIII of the Rules section 502 of the Merchant Shipping Act 1894 (which, as amended by the

Merchant Shipping (Liability of Shipowners and Others) Act 1958, entirely exempts shipowners and others in certain circumstances from liability for loss of, or damage to, goods) is a provision relating to limitation of liability.

(5) This Act shall come into force on such day as Her Majesty may by Order in Council appoint, and, for the purposes of the transition from the law in force immediately before the day appointed under this subsection to the provisions of this Act, the Order appointing the day may provide that those provisions shall have effect subject to such transitional provisions as may be contained in the Order.

Schedule
The Hague Rules as amended by the Brussels Protocol 1968

Article I
In these Rules the following words are employed, with the meaning set out below:

(*a*) "Carrier" includes the owner or the charterer who enters into a contract with a shipper.

(*b*) "Contract of carriage" applies only to contracts of carriage covered by a bill of lading or any similar document of title, in so far as such document relates to the carriage of goods by sea, including any bill of lading or any similar document as aforesaid issued under or pursuant to a charter party from the moment at which such bill of lading or similar document of title regulates the relations between a carrier and a holder of the same.

(*c*) "Goods" includes goods, wares, merchandise, and articles of every kind whatsoever except live animals and cargo which by the contract of carriage is stated as being carried on deck and is so carried.

(*d*) "Ship" means any vessel used for the carriage of goods by sea.

(*e*) "Carriage of goods" covers the period from the time when the goods are loaded on to the time they are discharged from the ship.

Article II
Subject to the provisions of Article VI, under every contract of carriage of goods by sea the carrier, in relation to the loading, handling, stowage, carriage custody, care and discharge of such goods, shall be subject to the responsibilities and liabilities, and entitled to the rights and immunities hereinafter set forth.

Article III
1. The carrier shall be bound before and at the beginning of the voyage to exercise due diligence to—

(*a*) Make the ship seaworthy.

(*b*) Properly man, equip and supply the ship.

(*c*) Make the holds, refrigerating and cool chambers, and all other parts of the ship in which goods are carried, fit and safe for their reception, carriage and preservation.

2. Subject to the provisions of Article IV, the carrier shall properly and carefully load, handle, stow, carry, keep, care for, and discharge the goods carried.

3. After receiving the goods into his charge the carrier or the master or agent of the carrier shall, on demand of the shipper, issue to the shipper a bill of lading showing among other things—

(*a*) The leading marks necessary for identification of the goods as the same are furnished in writing by the shipper before the loading of such goods starts, provided such marks are stamped or otherwise shown clearly upon the goods if uncovered, or on the cases or coverings in which such goods are contained, in such a manner as should ordinarily remain legible until the end of the voyage.

(b) Either the number of packages or pieces, or the quantity, or weight, as the case may be, as furnished in writing by the shipper.

(c) The apparent order and condition of the goods.

Provided that no carrier, master or agent of the carrier shall be bound to state or show in the bill of lading any marks, number, quantity, or weight which he has reasonable ground for suspecting not accurately to represent the goods actually received, or which he has had no reasonable means of checking.

4. Such a bill of lading shall be primâ facie evidence of the receipt by the carrier of the goods as therein described in accordance with paragraph 3 (a), (b) and (c). However, proof to the contrary shall not be admissible when the bill of lading has been transferred to a third party acting in good faith.

5. The shipper shall be deemed to have guaranteed to the carrier the accuracy at the time of shipment of the marks, number, quantity and weight, as furnished by him, and the shipper shall indemnify the carrier against all loss, damages and expenses arising or resulting from inaccuracies in such particulars. The right of the carrier to such indemnity shall in no way limit his responsibility and liability under the contract of carriage to any person other than the shipper.

6. Unless notice of loss or damage and the general nature of such loss or damage be given in writing to the carrier or his agent at the port of discharge before or at the time of the removal of the goods into the custody of the person entitled to delivery thereof under the contract of carriage, or, if the loss or damage be not apparent, within three days, such removal shall be primâ facie evidence of the delivery by the carrier of the goods as described in the bill of lading.

The notice in writing need not be given if the state of the goods has, at the time of their receipt, been the subject of joint survey or inspection.

Subject to paragraph 6bis the carrier and the ship shall in any event be discharged from all liability whatsoever in respect of the goods, unless suit is brought within one year of their delivery or of the date when they should have been delivered. This period may, however, be extended if the parties so agree after the cause of action has arisen.

In the case of any actual or apprehended loss or damage the carrier and the receiver shall give all reasonable facilities to each other for inspecting and tallying the goods.

6bis. An action for indemnity against a third person may be brought even after the expiration of the year provided for in the preceding paragraph if brought within the time allowed by the law of the Court seized of the case. However, the time allowed shall be not less than three months, commencing from the day when the person bringing such action for indemnity has settled the claim or has been served with process in the action against himself.

7. After the goods are loaded the bill of lading to be issued by the carrier, master, or agent of the carrier, to the shipper shall, if the shipper so demands, be a "shipped" bill of lading, provided that if the shipper shall have previously taken up any document of title to such goods, he shall surrender the same as against the issue of the "shipped" bill of lading, but at the option of the carrier such document of title may be noted at the port of shipment by the carrier, master or agent with the name or names of the ship or ships upon which the goods have been shipped and the date or dates of shipment, and when so noted, if it shows the particulars mentioned in paragraph 3 of Article III, shall for the purpose of this article be deemed to constitute a "shipped" bill of lading.

8. Any clause, covenant, or agreement in a contract of carriage relieving the carrier or the ship from liability for loss or damage to, or in connection

with, goods arising from negligence, fault, or failure in the duties and obligations provided in this article or lessening such liability otherwise than as provided in these Rules, shall be null and void and of no effect. A benefit of insurance in favour of the carrier or similar clause shall be deemed to be a clause relieving the carrier from liability.

Article IV

1. Neither the carrier nor the ship shall be liable for loss or damage arising or resulting from unseaworthiness unless caused by want of due diligence on the part of the carrier to make the ship seaworthy, and to secure that the ship is properly manned, equipped and supplied, and to make the holds, refrigerating and cool chambers and all other parts of the ship in which goods are carried fit and safe for their reception, carriage and preservation in accordance with the provisions of paragraph 1 of Article III. Whenever loss or damage has resulted from unseaworthiness the burden of proving the exercise of due diligence shall be on the carrier or other person claiming exemption under this article.

2. Neither the carrier nor the ship shall be responsible for loss or damage arising or resulting from—

(*a*) Act, neglect, or default of the master, mariner, pilot, or the servants of the carrier in the navigation or in the management of the ship.
(*b*) Fire, unless caused by the actual fault or privity of the carrier.
(*c*) Perils, dangers and accidents of the sea or other navigable waters.
(*d*) Act of God.
(*e*) Act of war.
(*f*) Act of public enemies.
(*g*) Arrest or restraint of princes, rulers or people, or seizure under legal process.
(*h*) Quarantine restrictions.
(*i*) Act or omission of the shipper or owner of the goods, his agent or representative.
(*j*) Strikes or lockouts or stoppage or restraint of labour from whatever cause, whether partial or general.
(*k*) Riots and civil commotions.
(*l*) Saving or attempting to save life or property at sea.
(*m*) Wastage in bulk or weight or any other loss or damage arising from inherent defect, quality or vice of the goods.
(*n*) Insufficiency of packing.
(*o*) Insufficiency or inadequacy of marks.
(*p*) Latent defects not discoverable by due diligence.
(*q*) Any other cause arising without the actual fault or privity of the carrier, or without the fault or neglect of the agents or servants of the carrier, but the burden of proof shall be on the person claiming the benefit of this exception to show that neither the actual fault or privity of the carrier nor the fault or neglect of the agents or servants of the carrier contributed to the loss or damage.

3. The shipper shall not be responsible for loss or damage sustained by the carrier or the ship arising or resulting from any cause without the act, fault or neglect of the shipper, his agents or his servants.

4. Any deviation in saving or attempting to save life or property at sea or any reasonable deviation shall not be deemed to be an infringement or breach of these Rules or of the contract of carriage, and the carrier shall not be liable for any loss or damage resulting therefrom.

5. (*a*) Unless the nature and value of such goods have been declared by the shipper before shipment and inserted in the bill of lading, neither the carrier nor the ship shall in any event be or become liable for any loss or damage to or in connection with the goods in an amount exceeding the equivalent of

10,000 francs per package or unit or 30 francs per kilo of gross weight of the goods lost or damaged, which ever is the higher.

(b) The total amount recoverable shall be calculated by reference to the value of such goods at the place and time at which the goods are discharged from the ship in accordance with the contract or should have been so discharged.

The value of the goods shall be fixed according to the commodity exchange price, or, if there be no such price, according to the current market price, or, if there be no commodity exchange price or current market price, by reference to the normal value of goods of the same kind and quality.

(c) Where a container, pallet or similar article of transport is used to consolidate goods, the number of packages or units enumerated in the bill of lading as packed in such article of transport shall be deemed the number of packages or units for the purpose of this paragraph as far as these packages or units are concerned. Except as aforesaid such article of transport shall be considered the package or unit.

(d) A franc means a unit consisting of 65·5 milligrammes of gold of millesimal fineness 900. The date of conversion of the sum awarded into national currencies shall be governed by the law of the Court seized of the case.

(e) Neither the carrier nor the ship shall be entitled to the benefit of the limitation of liability provided for in this paragraph if it is proved that the damage resulted from an act or omission of the carrier done with intent to cause damage, or recklessly and with knowledge that damage would probably result.

(f) The declaration mentioned in sub-paragraph (a) of this paragraph, if embodied in the bill of lading, shall be primâ facie evidence, but shall not be binding or conclusive on the carrier.

(g) By agreement between the carrier, master or agent of the carrier and the shipper other maximum amounts than those mentioned in sub-paragraph (a) of this paragraph may be fixed, provided that no maximum amount so fixed shall be less than the appropriate maximum mentioned in that sub-paragraph.

(h) Neither the carrier nor the ship shall be responsible in any event for loss or damage to, or in connection with, goods if the nature or value thereof has been knowingly mis-stated by the shipper in the bill of lading.

6. Goods of an inflammable, explosive or dangerous nature to the shipment whereof the carrier, master or agent of the carrier has not consented with knowledge of their nature and character, may at any time before discharge be landed at any place, or destroyed or rendered innocuous by the carrier without compensation and the shipper of such goods shall be liable for all damages and expenses directly or indirectly arising out of or resulting from such shipment. If any such goods shipped with such knowledge and consent shall become a danger to the ship or cargo, they may in like manner be landed at any place, or destroyed or rendered innocuous by the carrier without liability on the part of the carrier except to general average, if any.

Article IV bis

1. The defences and limits of liability provided for in these Rules shall apply in any action against the carrier in respect of loss or damage to goods covered by a contract of carriage whether the action be founded in contract or in tort.

2. If such an action is brought against a servant or agent of the carrier (such servant or agent not being an independent contractor), such servant or agent shall be entitled to avail himself of the defences and limits of liability which the carrier is entitled to invoke under these Rules.

3. The aggregate of the amounts recoverable from the carrier, and such servants and agents, shall in no case exceed the limit provided for in these Rules.

4. Nevertheless, a servant or agent of the carrier shall not be entitled to avail himself of the provisions of this article, if it is proved that the damage resulted from an act or omission of the servant or agent done with intent to cause damage or recklessly and with knowledge that damage would probably result.

Article V

A carrier shall be at liberty to surrender in whole or in part all or any of his rights and immunities or to increase any of his responsibilities and obligations under these Rules, provided such surrender or increase shall be embodied in the bill of lading issued to the shipper. The provisions of these Rules shall not be applicable to charter parties, but if bills of lading are issued in the case of a ship under a charter party they shall comply with the terms of these Rules. Nothing in these Rules shall be held to prevent the insertion in a bill of lading of any lawful provision regarding general average.

Article VI

Notwithstanding the provisions of the preceding articles, a carrier, master or agent of the carrier and a shipper shall in regard to any particular goods be at liberty to enter into any agreement in any terms as to the responsibility and liability of the carrier for such goods, and as to the rights and immunities of the carrier in respect of such goods, or his obligation as to seaworthiness, so far as this stipulation is not contrary to public policy, or the care or diligence of his servants or agents in regard to the loading, handling, stowage, carriage, custody, care and discharge of the goods carried by sea, provided that in this case no bill of lading has been or shall be issued and that the terms agreed shall be embodied in a receipt which shall be a non-negotiable document and shall be marked as such.

Any agreement so entered into shall have full legal effect.

Provided that this article shall not apply to ordinary commercial shipments made in the ordinary course of trade, but only to other shipments where the character or condition of the property to be carried or the circumstances, terms and conditions under which the carriage is to be performed are such as reasonably to justify a special agreement.

Article VII

Nothing herein contained shall prevent a carrier or a shipper from entering into any agreement, stipulation, condition, reservation or exemption as to the responsibility and liability of the carrier or the ship for the loss or damage to, or in connection with, the custody and care and handling of goods prior to the loading on, and subsequent to the discharge from, the ship on which the goods are carried by sea.

Article VIII

The provisions of these Rules shall not affect the rights and obligations of the carrier under any statute for the time being in force relating to the limitation of the liability of owners of sea-going vessels.

Article IX

These Rules shall not affect the provisions of any international Convention or national law governing liability for nuclear damage.

Article X

The provisions of these Rules shall apply to every bill of lading relating to the carriage of goods between ports in two different States if:

    (a) the bill of lading is issued in a contracting State,
       or
    (b) the carriage is from a port in a contracting State,
       or

(c) the contract contained in or evidenced by the bill of lading provides that these Rules or legislation of any State giving effect to them are to govern the contract,

whatever may be the nationality of the ship, the carrier, the shipper, the consignee, or any other interested person.

[*The last two paragraphs of this article are not reproduced. They require contracting States to apply the Rules to bills of lading mentioned in the article and authorise them to apply the Rules to other bills of lading.*]

[*Articles 11 to 16 of the International Convention for the unification of certain rules of law relating to bills of lading signed at Brussels on 25th August are not reproduced. They deal with the coming into force of the Convention, procedure for ratification, accession and denunciation, and the right to call for a fresh conference to consider amendments to the Rules contained in the Convention.*]

APPENDIX II

HARTER ACT, 1893

U.S.A. Carrier's Act, February 13, 1893.—An Act relating to navigation of vessels, bills of lading, and to certain obligations, duties and rights in connection with the carriage of property.

Be it enacted by the Senate and House of Representatives of the United States of America in Congress assembled:

That it shall not be lawful for the manager, agent, master, or owner of any vessel transporting merchandise or property from or between ports of the United States and foreign ports to insert in any bill of lading or shipping document any clause, covenant, or agreement whereby it, he, or they shall be relieved from liability for loss or damage arising from negligence, fault, or failure in proper loading, stowage, custody, care, or proper delivery of any and all lawful merchandise or property committed to its or their charge. Any and all words or clauses of such import inserted in bills of lading or shipping receipts shall be null and void and of no effect.

Section 2. That it shall not be lawful for any vessel transporting merchandise or property from or between ports of the United States of America and foreign ports, her owner, master, agent, or manager, to insert in any bill of lading or shipping document any covenant or agreement whereby the obligation of the owner or owners of said vessel to exercise due diligence, to properly equip, man, provision, and outfit said vessel, and to make said vessel seaworthy and capable of performing her intended voyage, or whereby the obligations of the masters, officers, agents, or servants to carefully handle and stow her cargo and to care for and properly deliver same, shall in anywise be lessened, weakened, or avoided.

Section 3. That if the owner of any vessel transporting merchandise or property to or from any port in the United States of America shall exercise due diligence to make the said vessel in all respects seaworthy and properly manned, equipped and supplied, neither the vessel, her owner or owners, agent, or charterers shall become or be held responsible for damage or loss resulting from faults or errors in navigation or in the management of said vessel, nor shall the vessel, her owner or owners, charterers, agent, or master be held liable for losses arising from dangers of the sea or other navigable waters, acts of God, or public enemies, or the inherent defect, quality, or vice of the thing carried, or from insufficiency of package, or seizure under legal process, or for loss resulting from any act or omission of the shipper or owner of the goods, his agent or representative, or from saving or attempting to save life or property at sea, or from any deviation in rendering such service.

Section 4. That it shall be the duty of the owner or owners, master or agent of any vessel transporting merchandise or property from or between ports of the United States and foreign ports to issue to shippers of any lawful merchandise a bill of lading, or shipping document, stating, among other things, the marks necessary for identification, number of packages or quantity stating whether it be carrier's or shipper's weight, and apparent order or condition of such merchandise or property delivered to and received by the owner, master, or agent of the vessel for transportation, and such document shall be prima facie evidence of the receipt of the merchandise therein described.

Section 5. That for a violation of any of the provisions of this Act the agent, owner, or master of the vessel guilty of such violation, and who refuses to issue on demand the bill of lading herein provided for, shall be liable to a fine not exceeding two thousand dollars. The amount of the fine and costs for such violation shall be a lien upon the vessel, whose agent, owner, or master is guilty of such violation, and such vessel may be libelled therefore in any district court of the United States, within whose jurisdiction the vessel may be found. One-half of such penalty shall go to the party injured by such violation and the remainder to the Government of the United States.

Section 6. That this Act shall not be held to modify or repeal sections forty-two hundred and eighty-one, forty-two hundred and eighty-two, and forty-two hundred and eighty-three of the Revised Statutes of the United States, or any other statute defining the liability of vessels, their owners, or representatives.

Section 7. Sections one and four of this Act shall not apply to the transportation of live animals.

Section 8. That this Act shall take effect from and after the first day of July, eighteen hundred and ninety-three.

APPENDIX III

YORK-ANTWERP RULES, 1974

Rule of Interpretation

In the adjustment of general average the following lettered and numbered Rules shall apply to the exclusion of any Law and Practice inconsistent therewith.

Except as provided by the numbered Rules, general average shall be adjusted according to the lettered Rules.

Rule A. There is a general average act when, and only when, any extraordinary sacrifice or expenditure is intentionally and reasonably made or incurred for the common safety for the purpose of preserving from peril the property involved in a common maritime adventure.

Rule B. General average sacrifices and expenses shall be borne by the different contributing interests on the basis hereinafter provided.

Rule C. Only such losses, damages or expenses which are the direct consequence of the general average act shall be allowed as general average.

Loss or damage sustained by the ship or cargo through delay, whether on the voyage or subsequently, such as demurrage, and any indirect loss whatsoever, such as loss of market, shall not be admitted as general average.

Rule D. Rights to contribution in general average shall not be affected, though the event which gave rise to the sacrifice or expenditure may have been due to the fault of one of the parties to the adventure; but this shall not prejudice any remedies or defences which may be open against or to that party in respect of such fault.

Rule E. The onus of proof is upon the party claiming in general average to show that the loss or expense claimed is properly allowable as general average.

Rule F. Any extra expense incurred in place of another expense which would have been allowable as general average shall be deemed to be general average and so allowed without regard to the saving, if any, to other interests, but only up to the amount of the general average expense avoided.

Rule G. General average shall be adjusted as regards both loss and contribution upon the basis of values at the time and place when and where the adventure ends.

This rule shall not affect the determination of the place at which the average statement is to be made up.

Rule I   **Jettison of Cargo**

No jettison of cargo shall be made good as general average, unless such cargo is carried in accordance with the recognised custom of the trade.

Rule II   **Damage by Jettison and Sacrifice**
for the Common Safety

Damage done to a ship and cargo, or either of them, by or in consequence of a sacrifice made for the common safety, and by water which goes down a

785

ship's hatches opened or other opening made for the purpose of making a jettison for the common safety, shall be made good as general average.

RULE III **Extinguishing Fire on Shipboard**

Damage done to a ship and cargo, or either of them, by water or otherwise, including damage by beaching or scuttling a burning ship, in extinguishing a fire on board the ship, shall be made good as general average; except that no compensation shall be made for damage by smoke or heat however caused.

RULE IV **Cutting Away Wreck**

Loss or damage sustained by cutting away wreck or parts of the ship which have been previously carried away or are effectively lost by accident shall not be made good as general average.

RULE V **Voluntary Stranding**

When a ship is intentionally run on shore for the common safety, whether or not she might have been driven on shore, the consequent loss or damage shall be allowed in general average.

RULE VI **Salvage Remuneration**

Expenditure incurred by the parties to the adventure on account of salvage, whether under contract or otherwise, shall be allowed in general average to the extent that the salvage operations were undertaken for the purpose of preserving from peril the property involved in the common maritime adventure.

RULE VII **Damage to Machinery and Boilers**

Damage caused to any machinery and boilers of a ship which is ashore and in a position of peril, in endeavouring to refloat, shall be allowed in general average when shown to have arisen from an actual intention to float the ship for the common safety at the risk of such damage; but where a ship is afloat no loss or damage caused by working the propelling machinery and boilers, shall in any circumstances be made good as general average.

RULE VIII **Expenses Lightening a Ship when Ashore and Consequent Damage**

When a ship is ashore and cargo and ship's fuel and stores or any of them are discharged as a general average act, the extra cost of lightening, lighter hire and re-shipping (if incurred), and the loss or damage sustained thereby, shall be admitted as general average.

RULE IX **Ship's Materials and Stores Burnt for Fuel**

Ship's materials and stores, or any of them, necessarily burnt for fuel for the common safety at a time of peril, shall be admitted as general average, when and only when an ample supply of fuel had been provided; but the estimated quantity of fuel that would have been consumed, calculated at the price current at the ship's last port of departure at the date of her leaving, shall be credited to the general average.

RULE X **Expenses at Port of Refuge, etc.**

(a) When a ship shall have entered a port or place of refuge, or shall have returned to her port or place of loading in consequence of accident, sacrifice or other extraordinary circumstances, which render that necessary for the common safety, the expenses of entering such port or place shall be admitted as general average; and when she shall have sailed thence with her original cargo, or a part of it, the corresponding expenses of leaving such port or place consequent upon such entry or return shall likewise be admitted as general average.

When a ship is at any port or place of refuge and is necessarily removed to another port or place because repairs cannot be carried out in the first port or place, the provisions of this Rule shall be applied to the second port or place as if it were a port or place of refuge and the cost of such removal including temporary repairs and towage shall be admitted as general average. The provisions of Rule XI shall be applied to the prolongation of the voyage occasioned by such removal.

(b) The cost of handling on board or discharging cargo, fuel or stores whether at port or place of loading, call or refuge shall be admitted as general average when the handling or discharge was necessary for the common safety or to enable damage to the ship caused by sacrifice or accident to be repaired, if the repairs were necessary for the safe prosecution of the voyage, except in cases where the damage to the ship is discovered at a port or place of loading or call without any accident or other extraordinary circumstances connected with such damage having taken place during the voyage.

The cost of handling on board or discharging cargo, fuel or stores shall not be admissible as general average when incurred solely for the purpose of re-stowage due to shifting during the voyage unless such re-stowage is necessary for the common safety.

(c) Whenever the cost of handling or discharging cargo, fuel or stores is admissible as general average, the costs of storage, including insurance if reasonably incurred, reloading and stowing of such cargo, fuel or stores shall likewise be admitted as general average. But when the ship is condemned or does not proceed on her original voyage storage expenses shall be admitted as general average only up to the date of the ship's condemnation or of the abandonment of the voyage or up to the date of completion of dischergre of cargo if the condemnation or abandonment takes place before that date.

RULE XI **Wages and Maintenance of Crew and other Expenses bearing up for and in a port of Refuge, etc.**

(a) Wages and maintenance of master, officers and crew reasonably incurred and fuel and stores consumed during the prolongation of the voyage occasioned by a ship entering a port or place of refuge or returning to her port or place of loading shall be admitted as general average when the expenses of entering such port or place are allowable in general average in accordance with Rule X (a).

(b) When a ship shall have entered or been detained in any port or place in consequence of accident, sacrifice or other extraordinary circumstances which render that necessary for the common safety, or to enable damage to the ship caused by sacrifice or accident to be repaired, if the repairs were necessary for the safe prosecution of the voyage, the wages and maintenance of the master, officers and crew reasonably incurred during the extra period of detention in such port or place until the ship shall or should have been made ready to proceed upon her voyage, shall be admitted in general average. Provided that when damage to the ship is discovered at a port or place of loading or call without any accident or other extraordinary circumstances connected with such damage having taken place during the voyage, then the wages and maintenance of master, officers and crew and fuel and stores consumed during the extra detention for repairs to damages so discovered shall not be admissible as general average, even if the repairs are necessary for the safe prosecution of the voyage.

When the ship is condemned or does not proceed on her original voyage, wages and maintenance of the master, officers and crew and fuel and stores consumed shall be admitted as general average only up to the date of the ship's condemnation or of the abandonment of the voyage or up to the date of completion of discharge of cargo if the condemnation or abandonment takes place before that date.

Fuel and Stores consumed during the extra period of detention shall be admitted as general average, except such fuel and stores as are consumed in effecting repairs not allowable in general average.

Port charges incurred during the extra period of detention shall likewise be admitted as general average except such charges as are incurred solely by reason of repairs not allowable in general average.

(*c*) For the purpose of this and the other Rules, wages shall include all payments made to or for the benefit of the master, officers and crew, whether such payments be imposed by law upon the shipowners or be made under the terms or articles of employment.

(*d*) When overtime is paid to the master, officers or crew for maintenance of the ship or repairs, the cost of which is not allowable in general average, such overtime shall be allowed in general average only up to the saving in expense which would have been incurred and admitted as general average, had such overtime not been incurred.

RULE XII   **Damage to Cargo in Discharging, etc.**

Damage to or loss of cargo, fuel or stores caused in the act of handling, discharging, storing, reloading and stowing shall be made good as general average, when and only when the cost of those measures respectively is admitted as general average.

RULE XIII   **Deductions from Cost of Repairs**

Repairs to be allowed in general average shall not be subject to deductions in respect of "new for old" where old material or parts are replaced by new unless the ship is over fifteen years old in which case there shall be a deduction of one third. The deduction shall be regulated by the age of the ship from the 31st December of the year of completion of construction to the date of the general average act, except for insulation, life and similar boats, communications and navigational apparatus and equipment, machinery and boilers for which deductions shall be regulated by the age of the particular parts to which they apply. The deduction shall be made only from the cost of the new material or parts when finished and ready to be installed in the ship.

No deduction shall be made in respect of provisions, stores, anchors and chain cables.

Drydock and slipway dues and costs of shifting the ship shall be allowed in full.

The costs of cleaning, painting or coating of bottom shall not be allowed in general average unless the bottom has been painted or coated within the twelve months preceding the date of the general average act in which case one half of such costs shall be allowed.

RULE XIV   **Temporary Repairs**

Where temporary repairs are effected to a ship at a port of loading, call or refuge, for the common safety, or of damage caused by general average sacrifice, the cost of such repairs shall be admitted as general average.

Where temporary repairs of accidental damage are effected in order to enable the adventure to be completed, the cost of such repairs shall be admitted as general average without regard to the saving, if any, to other interests, but only up to the saving, in expense which would have been incurred and allowed in general average if such repairs had not been effected there.

No deductions "new for old" shall be made from the cost of temporary repairs allowable as general average.

RULE XV   **Loss of Freight**

Loss of freight arising from damage to or loss of cargo shall be made good as general average, either when caused by general average act, or when the damage to or loss of cargo is so made good.

Deduction shall be made from the amount of gross freight lost, of the charges which the owner thereof would have incurred to earn such freight, but has, in consequence of the sacrifice, not incurred.

RULE XVI   **Amount to be made good for Cargo lost or Damaged by Sacrifice**

The amount to be made good as general average for damage to or loss of cargo sacrificed shall be the loss which has been sustained thereby based on the value at the time of discharge, ascertained from the commercial invoice rendered to the receiver or if there is no such invoice from the shipped value. The value at the time of discharge shall include the cost of insurance and freight except insofar as such freight is at the risk of interests other than the cargo.

When cargo so damaged is sold and the amount of the damage has not been otherwise agreed, the loss to be made good in general average shall be the difference between the net proceeds of sale and the net sound value as computed in the first paragraph of this Rule.

RULE XVII   **Contributory Values**

The contribution to a general average shall be made upon the actual net values of the property at the termination of the adventure except that the value of cargo shall be the value at the time of discharge ascertained from the commercial invoice rendered to the receiver or if there is no such invoice from the shipped value. The value of the cargo shall include the cost of insurance and freight unless and insofar as such freight is at the risk of interests other than the cargo, deducting therefrom any loss or damage suffered by the cargo prior to or at the time of discharge. The value of the ship shall be assessed without taking into account the beneficial or detrimental effect of any demise shall be added the amount made good as general average for property sacrificed, if not already included, deduction being made from the freight and passage money at risk of such charges and crew's wages as would not have been incurred in earning the freight had the ship and cargo been totally lost at the date of the general average act and have not been allowed as general average; deduction being also made from the value of the property of all extra charges incurred in respect thereof subsequently to the general average act, except such charges as are allowed in general average. Where cargo is sold short of destination, however, it shall contribute upon the actual net proceeds of sale, with the addition of any amount made good as general average.

Passengers' luggage and personal effects not shipped under bill of lading shall not contribute in general average.

RULE XVIII   **Damage to Ship**

The amount to be allowed as general average for damage or loss to the ship her machinery and/or gear caused by a general average act shall be as follows:

(a) When repaired or replaced the actual reasonable cost of repairing or replacing such damage or loss subject to deduction in accordance with Rule XIII.

(b) When not repaired or replaced, the reasonable depreciation arising from such damage or loss, but not exceeding the estimated cost of repairs. But where the ship is an actual total loss or when the cost of repairs of the damage would exceed the value of the ship when repaired, the amount to be allowed as general average shall be the difference between the estimated sound value of the ship after deducting therefrom the estimated cost of repairing damage which is not general average and the value of the ship in her damaged state which may be measured by the net proceeds of sale, if any.

RULE XIX   **Undeclared or Wrongfully Declared Cargo**

Damage or loss caused to goods loaded without the knowledge of the shipowner or his agent or to goods wilfully misdescribed at time of shipment shall not be allowed as general average, but such goods shall remain liable to contribute, if saved.

Damage or loss caused to goods which have been wrongfully declared on shipment at a value which is lower than their real value shall be contributed for at the declared value, but such goods shall contribute upon their actual value.

RULE XX   **Provision of Funds**

A commission of 2 per cent. on general average disbursements, other than the wages and maintenance of master, officers and crew and fuel and stores

AA

not replaced during the voyage, shall be allowed in general average, but when the funds are not provided by any of the contributing interests, the necessary cost of obtaining the funds required by means of a bottomry bond or otherwise, or the loss sustained by owners of goods sold for the purpose, shall be allowed in general average.

The cost of insuring money advanced to pay for general average disbursements shall also be allowed in general average.

Rule XXI   **Interest on Losses made good
in General Average**

Interest shall be allowed on expenditure, sacrifices and allowances charged to general average at the rate of 7 per cent. per annum, until the date of the general average statement, due allowance being made for any interim reimbursement from the contributory interests or from the general average deposit fund.

Rule XXII   **Treatment of Cash Deposits**

Where cash deposits have been collected in respect of cargo's liability for general average, salvage or special charges, such deposits shall be paid without any delay into a special account in the joint names of a representative nominated on behalf of the shipowner and a representative nominated on behalf of the depositors in a bank to be approved by both. The sum so deposited, together with accrued interest, if any, shall be held as security for payment to the parties entitled thereto of the general average, salvage or special charges payable by cargo in respect to which the deposits have been collected. Payments on account or refunds of deposits may be made if certified to in writing by the average adjuster. Such deposits and payments or refunds shall be without prejudice to the ultimate liability of the parties.

APPENDIX IV

Reproduced by kind permission of "Lloyd's"

LLOYD'S MARINE INSURANCE POLICY (HULL FORM)

(No.   )

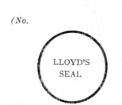

LLOYD'S
SEAL

Any person not an Underwriting Member of Lloyd's subscribing this Policy, or any subscribed, will be liable to be proceeded against under Lloyd's Acts.

S.G.

£

Printed at Lloyd's, London, England.

No Policy or other Contract dated on or after 1st Jan., 1924, will be recognised by the Committee of Lloyd's as entitling the holder to the benefit of the Funds and/or Guarantees lodged by the Underwriters of the Policy or Contract as security for their liabilities unless it bears at foot the Seal of Lloyd's Policy Signing Office.

Be it known that

as well in *their* own Name, as for and in the Name and Names of all, and every other Person or Persons to whom the same doth, may, or shall appertain, in part or in all, doth make Assurance, and cause *themselves* and them and every of them to be insured, lost or not lost, at and from
upon any kind of Goods and Merchandises, and also the Body, Tackle, Apparel, Ordnance, Munition, Artillery, Boat and other Furniture, of and in the good ship or Vessel called the

whereof is Master under God, for this present Voyage,   or whosoever else shall go for Master in the said Ship, or by whatsoever other Name or Names the same Ship, or the Master thereof, is or shall be named or called, beginning the Adventure upon the said Goods and Merchandises from the loading thereof aboard the said Ship *as above*   upon the said Ship, &c, *as above*   and shall so continue and endure during her Abode there, upon the said Ship, &c., and further, until the said Ship, with all her Ordnance, Tackle, Apparel, &c., and Goods and Merchandises whatsover, shall be arrived at *as above*
upon the said Ship, &c., until she hath moored at Anchor Twenty-four Hours in good Safety, and upon the Goods and Merchandises until the same be there discharged and safely landed; and it shall be lawful for the said Ship, &c., in this Voyage to proceed and sail to and touch and stay at any Ports or Places whatsoever, and *wheresoever for all purposes*
without Prejudice to this Insurance. The said Ship, &c., Goods and Merchandises, &c., for so much as concerns the Assured by Agreement between the Assured and Assurers in this Policy, are and shall be valued at
TOUCHING the Adventures and Perils which we the Assurers are contented to bear and do take upon us in this Voyage, they are of the Seas, Men-of-War, Fire, Enemies, Pirates, Rovers, Thieves, Jettisons, Letters of Mart and Countermart, Surprisals, Takings at Sea, Arrests, Restraints and Detainments of all Kings, Princes and People, of what Nation, condition, or Quality soever, Barratry of the Master and Mariners, and of all other Perils, Losses and Misfortunes that have or shall come to the Hurt, Detriment or Damage of the said Goods and Merchandises and Ship, &c., or any Part thereof; and

in case of any Loss or Misfortune, it shall be lawful to the Assured, their Factors, Servants and Assigns, to sue, labour, and travel for in and about the Defence, Safeguard and Recovery of the said Goods and Merchandises and Ship, &c.; or any Part thereof, without Prejudice to this Insurance; to the Charges whereof, we, the Assurers, will contribute, each one according to the Rate and Quantity of his Sum herein assured. And it is especially declared and agreed that no acts of the Insurer or Insured in recovering, saving, or preserving the property insured, shall be considered as a waiver or acceptance of abandonment. And it is agreed by us, the Insurers, that this Writing or Policy of Assurance shall be of as much Force and Effect as the surest Writing or Policy of Assurance heretofore made in Lombard Street, or in the Royal Exchange, or elsewhere in London.

Warranted free of capture, seizure, arrest, restraint or detainment, and the consequences thereof or of any attempt thereat; also from the consequences of hostilities or warlike operations, whether there be a declaration of war or not; but this warranty shall not exclude collision, contact with any fixed or floating object (other than a mine or torpedo), stranding, heavy weather or fire unless caused directly (and independently of the nature of the voyage or service which the vessel concerned or, in the case of a collision, any other vessel involved therein, is performing) by a hostile act by or against a belligerent power; and for the purposes of this warranty "power" includes any authority maintaining naval, military or air forces in association with a power.

Further warranted free from the consequences of civil war, revolution, rebellion, insurrection or civil strife arising therefrom, or piracy.

And so we, the Assurers, are contented, and do hereby promise and bind ourselves, each one for his own Part, our Heirs, Executors, and Goods, to the Assured, their Executors, Administrators, and Assigns, for the true Performance of the Premises, confessing ourselves paid the Consideration due to us for this Assurance by the Assured

at and after the Rate of

IN WITNESS whereof we, the Assurers, have subscribed our Names and Sums assured in *LONDON*,

as hereinafter appears.

N.B.—Corn, Fish, Salt, Fruit, Flour, and Seed are warranted free from Average, unless general, or the Ship be stranded; Sugar, Tobacco, Hemp, Flax, Hides, and Skins are warranted free from Average under Five Pounds per Cent.; and all other Goods, also the Ship and Freight, are warranted free from Average under Three Pounds per Cent., unless general, or the Ship be stranded.

NOW KNOW YE, that We the Assurers, members of the Syndicate(s) whose definitive number(s) in the attached list are set out in the Table overleaf, or attached overleaf, hereby bind Ourselves, each for his own part and not one for another, and in respect of his due proportion only, to pay or make good to the Assured all such Loss and/or Damage which he or they may sustain by any one or more of the aforesaid perils, and so that the due proportion for which each of Us the Assurers is liable shall be ascertained by reference to his proportion as ascertained according to the said List of the Amount, Percentage or Proportion of the total Sum assured which is in the said Table set opposite the definitive Number of the Syndicate of which such Assurer is a member.

IN WITNESS whereof the Manager of Lloyd's Policy Signing Office has subscribed his Name on behalf of each of Us.

LLOYD'S POLICY SIGNING OFFICE,

Manager

(In the event of accident whereby loss or damage result in a claim under this Policy, the settlement will be much facilitated if immediate notice be given to the nearest Lloyd's Agent.)
(15.6.43)

> Definitive Numbers of Syndicates and Amount, Percentage or Proportion of the Total Amount Assured shared between the Members of those Syndicates.

APPENDIX V

Reproduced by kind permission of the Institute of London Underwriters

INSTITUTE TIME CLAUSES
HULLS

1/10/70

1. It is further agreed that if the Vessel hereby insured shall come into collision with any other vessel and the Assured shall in consequence thereof become liable to pay and shall pay by way of damages to any other person or persons any sum or sums in respect of such collision for

    (i) loss of or damage to any other vessel or property on any other vessel,

    (ii) delay to or loss of use of any such other vessel or property thereon, or

    (iii) general average of, salvage of, or salvage under contract of, any such other vessel or property thereon,

the Underwriters will pay the Assured such proportion of three-fourths of such sum or sums so paid as their respective subscriptions hereto bear to the value of the Vessel hereby insured, provided always that their liability in respect of any one such collision shall not exceed their proportionate part of three-fourths of the value of the Vessel thereby insured, and in cases in which, with the prior consent in writing of the Underwriters, the liability of the Vessel has been contested or proceedings have been taken to limit liability, they will also pay a like proportion of three-fourths of the costs which the Assured shall thereby incur or be compelled to pay; but when both vessels are to blame, then unless the liability of the Owners of one or both of such vessels becomes limited by law, claims under this clause shall be settled on the principle of cross-liabilities as if the Owners of each vessel had been compelled to pay to the Owners of the other of such vessels such one-half or other proportion of the latter's damages as may have been properly allowed in ascertaining the balance or sum payable by or to the Assured in consequence of such collision.

Provided always that this clause shall in no case extend or be deemed to extend to any sum which the Assured may become liable to pay or shall pay for or in respect of:

    (a) removal or disposal, under statutory powers or otherwise, of obstructions, wrecks, cargoes or any other thing whatsoever,

    (b) any real or personal property or thing whatsoever except other vessels or property on other vessels,

    (c) the cargo or other property on or the engagements of the insured Vessel,

    (d) loss of life, personal injury or illness.

2. Should the Vessel hereby insured come into collision with or receive salvage services from another vessel belonging wholly or in part to the same Owners or under the same management, the Assured shall have the same rights under this Policy as they would have were the other vessel entirely the property of Owners not interested in the Vessel hereby insured; but in such cases the liability for the collision or the amount payable for the services rendered shall be referred to a sole arbitrator to be agreed upon between the Underwriters and the Assured.

3. (a) The Vessel is covered subject to the provisions of this Policy at all times and has leave to sail or navigate with or without pilots, to go on trial trips and to assist and tow vessels or craft in distress, but it is warranted that the Vessel shall not be towed, except as is customary or to the first safe port or place when in need of assistance, or undertake towage or salvage services under a contract previously arranged by the Assured and/or Owners and/or Managers and/or Charterers. This clause shall not exclude customary towage in connection with loading and discharging.

(b) In the event of the Vessel being employed in trading operations which entail cargo loading or discharging at sea from or into another vessel (not being a barge, lighter or similar harbour or inshore craft) no claim shall be recoverable under this insurance for loss of or damage to the Vessel or any other vessel arising from such loading or discharging operations, including whilst approaching, lying alongside and leaving, unless previous notice that the Vessel is to be employed in such operations has been given to the Underwriters and any amended terms of cover and any additional premium required by them have been agreed.

4. Should the Vessel at the expiration of this Policy be at sea or in distress or at a port of refuge or of call, she shall, provided previous notice be given to the Underwriters be held covered at a *pro rata* monthly premium to her port of destination.

5. Held covered in case of any breach of warranty as to cargo, trade, locality, towage, salvage services or date of sailing, provided notice be given to the Underwriters immediately after receipt of advices and any amended terms of cover and any additional premium required by them be agreed.

793

60 **6.** If the Vessel is sold or transferred to new management then unless the Under-
61 writers agree in writing to continue the insurance this Policy shall become cancelled
62 from the time of sale or transfer, unless the Vessel has cargo on board and has already
63 sailed from her loading port or is at sea in ballast, in either of which cases such can-
64 cellation shall, if required, be suspended until arrival at final port of discharge if with
65 cargo, or at port of destination if in ballast. A *pro rata* daily return of premium shall
66 be made.
67 This clause shall prevail notwithstanding any provision whether written, typed or
68 printed in the Policy inconsistent therewith.

69 **7.** This insurance includes loss of or damage to the subject matter insured directly
70 caused by:
71   (*a*) Accidents in loading discharging or shifting cargo or fuel
72   Explosions on shipboard or elsewhere
73   Breakdown of or accident to nuclear installations or reactors on shipboard or
74   elsewhere
75   Bursting of boilers breakage of shafts or any latent defect in the machinery
76   or hull
77   Negligence of Master Officers Crew or Pilots
78   Negligence of repairers provided such repairers are not Assured(s) hereunder
79   (*b*) Contact with aircraft
80   Contact with any land conveyance, dock or harbour equipment or installation
81   Earthquake, volcanic eruption or lightning
82 provided such loss or damage has not resulted from want of due diligence by the Assured,
83 Owners or Managers.
84 Masters Officers Crew or Pilots not to be considered as part Owners within the mean-
85 ing of this clause should they hold shares in the Vessel.

86 **8.** General average and salvage to be adjusted according to the law and practice
87 obtaining at the place where the adventure ends, as if the contract of affreightment
88 contained no special terms upon the subject; but where the contract of affreightment
89 so provides the adjustment shall be according to York-Antwerp Rules.
90 When the Vessel sails in ballast, not under charter, the provisions of the York-
91 Antwerp Rules, 1974 (excluding Rules XX and XXI) shall be applicable, and the
92 voyage for this purpose shall be deemed to continue from the port or place of departure
93 until the arrival of the Vessel at the first port or place thereafter other than a port
94 or place of refuge or a port or place of call for bunkering only. If at any such inter-
95 mediate port or place there is an abandonment of the adventure originally contemplated
96 the voyage shall thereupon be deemed to be terminated.

97 **9.** (*a*) In the event of expenses being incurred pursuant to the Suing and Labouring
98 Clause, the liability under this Policy shall not exceed the proportion of such expenses
99 that the amount insured hereunder bears to the value of the Vessel as stated herein,
100 or to the sound value of the Vessel at the time of the occurrence giving rise to the
101 expenditure if the sound value exceeds that value. Where the Underwriters have
102 admitted a claim for total loss and property insured by this Policy is saved, the fore-
103 going provisions shall not apply unless the expenses of suing and labouring exceed the
104 value of such property saved and then shall apply only to the amount of the expenses
105 which is in excess of such value.
106 (*b*) Where a claim for total loss of the Vessel is admitted under this Policy and
107 expenses have been reasonably incurred in salving or attempting to salve the Vessel
108 and other property and there are no proceeds, or the expenses exceed the proceeds,
109 then this Policy shall bear its *pro rata* share of such proportion of the expenses, or of
110 the expenses in excess of the proceeds, as the case may be, as may reasonably be regarded
111 as having been incurred in respect of the Vessel; but if the Vessel be insured for less
112 than its sound value at the time of the occurrence giving rise to the expenditure, the
113 amount recoverable under this clause shall be reduced in proportion to the under-
114 insurance.

115 **10.** Average payable without deduction new for old, whether the average be particular
116 or general.

117 **11.** In the event of a claim for loss of or damage to any boiler, shaft, machinery or
118 associated equipment, arising from any of the causes enumerated in Clause 7(a), attribut-
119 able in part or in whole to negligence of Master Officers or Crew and recoverable under
120 this insurance only by reason of Clause 7, then the Assured shall, in addition to the
121 deductible, also bear in respect of each accident or occurrence an amount equal to 10%
122 of the balance of such claim. This clause shall not apply to a claim for total or con-
123 structive total loss of the Vessel.

124 **12.** No claim arising from a peril insured against shall be payable under this insur-
125 ance unless the aggregate of all such claims arising out of each separate accident or
126 occurrence (including claims under the Running Down and Suing and Labouring
127 Clauses) exceeds..................................in which case this sum shall be
128 deducted. Nevertheless the expense of sighting the bottom after stranding, if reasonably
129 incurred specially for that purpose, shall be paid even if no damage be found. This
130 paragraph shall not apply to a claim for total or constructive total loss of the Vessel.
131 Claims for damage by heavy weather occurring during a single sea passage between
132 two successive ports shall be treated as being due to one accident. In the case of such
133 heavy weather extending over a period not wholly covered by this insurance the
134 deductible to be applied to the claim recoverable hereunder shall be the proportion of
135 the above deductible that the number of days of such heavy weather falling within the

136 period of this insurance bears to the number of days of heavy weather during the single
137 sea passage.
138 The expression "heavy weather" in the preceding paragraph shall be deemed to
139 include contact with floating ice.
140 Excluding any interest comprised therein, recoveries against any claim which is
141 subject to the above deductible shall be credited to the Underwriters in full to the
142 extent of the sum by which the aggregate of the claim unreduced by any recoveries
143 exceeds the above deductible.
144 Interest comprised in recoveries shall be apportioned between the Assured and the
145 Underwriters, taking into account the sums paid by Underwriters and the dates when
146 such payments were made, notwithstanding that by the addition of interest the Under-
147 writers may receive a larger sum than they have paid.

148 **13.** Grounding in the Panama Canal, Suez Canal, Manchester Ship Canal or its
149 connections, River Mersey above Rock Ferry Slip, River Plate (above a line drawn from
150 the North Basin Buenos Aires to the mouth of the San Pedro River) or its tributaries,
151 Danube or Demerara Rivers or on the Yenikale Bar, shall not be deemed to be a
152 stranding.

153 **14.** No claim shall in any case be allowed in respect of scraping or painting the
154 Vessel's bottom.

155 **15.** No claim shall be allowed in particular average for wages and maintenance of the
156 Master, Officers and Crew, or any member thereof, except when incurred solely for the
157 necessary removal of the Vessel from one port to another for repairs, or for trial trips for
158 average repairs, and then only for such wages and maintenance as are incurred whilst
159 the vessel is under way.
160 However, this Policy shall bear only that proportion of such wages and maintenance
161 that the cost of repairs at the repair port recoverable under this Policy bears to the total
162 cost of work done at the repair port.

163 **16.** In no case shall the Underwriters be liable for unrepaired damage in addition to a
164 subsequent total loss sustained during the period covered by this Policy or any extension
165 thereof under Clause 4.

166 **17.** In ascertaining whether the Vessel is a constructive total loss the insured value
167 shall be taken as the repaired value and nothing in respect of the damaged or break-up
168 value of the Vessel or wreck shall be taken into account.
169 No claim for constructive total loss based upon the cost of recovery and/or repair of
170 the Vessel shall be recoverable hereunder unless such cost would exceed the insured
171 value.

172 **18.** In the event of total or constructive total loss no claim to be made by the Under
173 writers for freight whether notice of abandonment has been given or not.

174 **19.** In the event of accident whereby loss or damage may result in a claim under this
175 Policy, notice shall be given to the Underwriters prior to survey and also, if the Vessel is
176 abroad, to the nearest Lloyd's Agent so that a surveyor may be appointed to represent
177 the Underwriters should they so desire. The Underwriters shall be entitled to decide the
178 port to which the Vessel shall proceed for docking or repair (the actual additional expense
179 of the voyage arising from compliance with the Underwriter's requirements being
180 refunded to the Assured) and shall have a right of veto concerning a place of repair or a
181 repairing firm. The Underwriters may also take tenders or may require further tenders
182 to be taken for the repair of the Vessel. Where a tender so taken is accepted with the
183 approval of the Underwriters an allowance shall be made at the rate of 30% per annum
184 on the insured value for time lost between the despatch of the invitations to tender and
185 the acceptance of a tender to the extent that such time is lost solely as the result of tenders
186 having been taken and provided that the tender is accepted without delay after receipt
187 of the Underwriters' approval.
188 Due credit shall be given against the allowance as above for any amount recovered:

189   (a) in respect of fuel and stores and wages and maintenance of the Master Officers and
190   Crew or any member thereof allowed in general or particular average,
191   (b) from third parties in respect of damages for detention and/or loss of profit and/or
192   running expenses,

193 for the period covered by the tender allowance or any part thereof.
194 Where a part of the cost of average repairs other than a fixed deductible is not
195 recoverable from the Underwriters the allowance shall be reduced by a similar propor-
196 tion.
197 In the event of failure to comply with the conditions of this clause, 15% shall be
198 deducted from the amount of the ascertained claim.

199 **20.** Additional insurances as follows are permitted:

100   (a) *Disbursements, Managers' Commissions, Profits or Excess or Increased Value of*
201 *Hull and Machinery.* A sum not exceeding 10% of the value stated herein.
202   (b) *Freight, Chartered Freight or Anticipated Freight, insured for time.* A sum not
203 exceeding 25% of the value as stated herein less any sum insured, however described,
204 under Section (a).
205   (c) *Freight or Hire, under contracts for voyage.* A sum not exceeding the gross freight
206 or hire for the current cargo passage and next succeeding cargo passage (such insurance
207 to include, if required, a preliminary and an intermediate ballast passage) plus the
208 charges of insurance. In the case of a voyage charter where payment is made on a time
209 basis, the sumpermitted for insurance shall be calculated on the estimated duration of

210 the voyage subject to the limitation of two cargo passages as laid down herein. Any
211 sum insured under Section (b) to be taken into account and only the excess thereof may
212 be insured, which excess shall be reduced as the freight or hire is advanced or earned by
213 the gross amount so advanced or earned.

214 (d) *Anticipated Freight if the Vessel sails in ballast and not under Charter.* A sum not
215 exceeding the anticipated gross freight on next cargo passage, such sum to be
216 reasonably estimated on the basis of the current rate of freight at time of insurance plus
217 the charges of insurance. Any sum insured under Section (b) to be taken into account
218 and only the excess thereof may be insured.

219 (e) *Time Charter Hire or Charter Hire for Series of Voyages.* A sum not exceeding 50%
220 of the gross hire which is to be earned under the charter in a period not exceeding 18
221 months. Any sum insured under Section (b) to be taken into account and only the excess
222 thereof may be insured, which excess shall be reduced as the hire is advanced or earned
223 under the charter by 50% of the gross amount so advanced or earned but the sum
224 insured need not be reduced while the total of the sums insured under Sections (b) and
225 (e) does not exceed 50% of the gross hire still to be earned under the charter. An
226 insurance under this Section may begin on the signing of the charter.

227 (f) *Premiums.* A sum not exceeding the actual premiums of all interests insured for a
228 period not exceeding 12 months (excluding premiums insured under the foregoing
229 sections but including, if required, the premium or estimated calls on any Club or War
230 etc. Risk insurance) reducing *pro rata* monthly.

231 (g) *Returns of Premium.* A sum not exceeding the actual returns which are recover-
232 able subject to "and arrival" under any policy of insurance.

233 (h) *Insurance irrespective of amount against:—*
234   Risks excluded by the Free of Capture etc. Clause and risks enumerated in the
235   Institute of War and Strike Clauses.

236 Warranted that no insurance on any interests enumerated in the foregoing Section
237 (a) to (g) in excess of the amounts permitted therein and no other insurance P.P.I.,
238 F.I.A. or subject to any other like term, is or shall be effected to operate during the
239 currency of this Policy by or for account of the Assured, Owners, Managers or Mort-
240 gagees. Provided always that a breach of this warranty shall not afford the Under-
241 writers any defence to a claim by a Mortgagee who has accepted this Policy without
242 knowledge of such breach.

243   **21.** To return as follows:—

244   per cent. net for each uncommenced month if this Policy be
245 cancelled by agreement.
246 and for each period of 30 consecutive days the Vessel may be laid up in a port or in a
247 lay-up area provided such port or lay-up area is approved by the Underwriters (with
248 special liberties as hereinafter allowed):

249   (a)   per cent. net not under repair.
250   (b)   per cent. net under repair.

251 If the Vessel is under repair during part only of a period for which a return is
252 claimable, the return payable shall be calculated pro-rata to the number of days
253 under (a) and (b) respectively.
254   Provided always that
255   (i) in no case shall a return be allowed when the Vessel is lying in exposed or
256   unprotected waters, or in a port or lay-up area not approved by the Under-
257   writers but, provided the Underwriters agree that such non-approved lay-up
258   area is deemed to be within the vicinity of the approved port or lay-up area,
259   days during which the Vessel is laid up in such non-approved lay-up area may
260   be added to days in the approved port or lay-up area to calculate a period of
261   30 consecutive days and a return shall be allowed for the proportion of such
262   period during which the Vessel is actually laid up in the approved port or
263   lay-up area.
264   (ii) loading or discharging operations or the presence of cargo on board shall not
265   debar returns but no return shall be allowed for any period during which the
266   Vessel is being used for the storage of cargo.
267   (iii) in the event of a return for special trade or any other reason being recover-
268   able, the above rates of return of premium shall be reduced accordingly.

and arrival

269 In the event of any return recoverable under this clause being based on 30 consecutive
270 days which fall on successive policies, effected for the same Assured, this Policy shall only
271 be liable for an amount calculated at pro-rata of the period rates (a) and/or (b) above for
272 the number of days which come within the period of this Policy and to which a return is
273 actually applicable. Such overlapping period shall run, at the option of the Assured,
274 either from the first day on which the Vessel is laid up or the first day of a period of 30
275 consecutive days as provided under (a) or (b) or (i) above.

276   **22.** No assignment of or interest in this Policy or in any moneys which may be or
277 become payable thereunder is to be binding on or recognised by the Underwriters unless
278 a dated notice of such assignment or interest signed by the Assured, and by the assignor
279 in the case of subsequent assignment, is endorsed on this Policy and the Policy with such
280 endorsement is produced before payment of any claim or return of premium thereunder;
281 but nothing in this clause is to have effect as an agreement by the Underwriters to a sale
282 or transfer to new management.

283 **Unless deleted by the Underwriters the following clauses shall be**
284 **paramount and shall override anything contained**
285 **in this insurance inconsistent therewith**

286 **23.** Warranted free of capture, seizure, arrest, restraint or detainment, and the
287 consequences thereof or of any attempt thereat; also from the consequences of hostilities
288 or warlike operations, whether there be a declaration of war or not; but this warranty
289 shall not exclude collision, contact with any fixed or floating object (other than a mine or
290 torpedo), stranding, heavy weather or fire unless caused directly (and independently of the
291 nature of the voyage or service which the Vessel concerned or, in the case of a collision,
292 any other vessel involved therein, is performing) by a hostile act by or against a belli-
293 gerent power; and for the purpose of this warranty "power" includes any authority
294 maintaining naval, military or air forces in association with a power.
295 Further warranted free from the consequences of civil war, revolution, rebellion,
296 insurrection, or civil strife arising therefrom, or piracy.

297 **24** Warranted free from loss damage liability or expense arising from:—

298 (a) the detonation of an explosive
299 (b) any weapon of war

300 and caused by any person acting maliciously or from a political motive.

301 **25.** Warranted free from loss damage liability or expense arising from any weapon of
302 war employing atomic or nuclear fission and/or fusion or other like reaction or radio-
303 active force or matter.

1/10/71

INSTITUTE AMENDED RUNNING DOWN CLAUSE

It is further agreed that if the Vessel hereby insured shall come into
collision with any other vessel and the Assured shall in consequence thereof
become liable to pay and shall pay by way of damages to any other person
or persons any sum or sums in respect of such collision for

(i) loss of or damage to any other vessel or property on any other vessel,
(ii) delay to or loss of use of any such other vessel or property thereon or
(iii) general average of, salvage of, or salvage under contract of, any such
other vessel or property thereon.

the Underwriters will pay the Assured such proportion of three-fourths of
such sum or sums so paid as their respective subscriptions hereto bear to the
value of the Vessel hereby insured, provided always that their liability in
respect of any one such collision shall not exceed their proportionate part of
three-fourths of the value of the Vessel hereby insured, and in cases in which,
with the prior consent in writing of the Underwriters, the liability of the
Vessel has been contested or proceedings have been taken to limit liability,
they will also pay a like proportion of three-fourths of the costs which the
Assured shall thereby incur or be compelled to pay; but when both vessels
are to blame, then unless the liability of the Owners of one or both of such
vessels becomes limited by law, claims under this clause shall be settled on
the principle of cross-liabilities as if the Owners of each vessel had been
compelled to pay to the Owners of the other of such vessels such one-half or
other proportion of the latter's damages as may have been properly allowed
in ascertaining the balance or sum payable by or to the Assured in consequence
of such collision.

*Provided always that this clause shall in no case extend or be deemed to
extend to any sum which the Assured may become liable to pay or shall pay
for or in respect of;—*

(a) *removal or disposal, under statutory powers or otherwise, of obstructions,
wrecks, cargoes or any other thing whatsoever,*
(b) *any real or personal property or thing whatsoever except other vessels
or property on other vessels,*
(c) *pollution or contamination of any real or personal property or thing
whatsoever (except other vessels with which the insured Vessel is in
collision or property on such other vessels),*
(d) *the cargo or other property on or the engagements of the insured Vessel,*
(e) *loss of life, personal injury or illness.*

APPENDIX VI

Reproduced by kind permission of the Institute of London Underwriters

INSTITUTE CARGO CLAUSES (ALL RISKS)

1/1/63

1. This insurance attaches from the time the goods leave the warehouse or place of storage at the place named in the policy for the commencement of the transit, continues during the ordinary course of transit and terminates either on delivery — **Transit Clause (incorporating Warehouse to Warehouse Clause)**

    (a) to the Consignees' or other final warehouse or place of storage at the destination named in the policy,

    (b) to any other warehouse or place of storage, whether prior to or at the destination named in the policy, which the Assured elect to use either

        (i) for storage other than in the ordinary course of transit

        or

        (ii) for allocation or distribution,

    or (c) on the expiry of 60 days after completion of discharge overside of the goods hereby insured from the oversea vessel at the final port of discharge.

whichever shall first occur.

If after discharge overside from the oversea vessel at the final port of discharge, but prior to termination of this insurance, the goods are to be forwarded to a destination other than that to which they are insured hereunder, this insurance whilst remaining subject to termination as provided for above, shall not extend beyond the commencement of transit to such other destination.

This insurance shall remain in force (subject to termination as provided for above, and to the provisions of Clause 2 below) during delay beyond the control of the Assured, any deviation, forced discharge, reshipment or transhipment and during any variation of the adventure arising from the exercise of a liberty granted to shipowners or charterers under the contract of affreightment.

2. If owing to circumstances beyond the control of the Assured either the contract of affreightment is terminated at a port or place other than the destination named therein or the adventure is otherwise terminated before delivery of the goods as provided for in Clause 1 above, then, subject to prompt notice being given to Underwriters and to an additional premium if required, this insurance shall remain in force until either — **Termination of Adventure Clause**

    (i) the goods are sold and delivered at such port or place, or, unless otherwise specially agreed, until the expiry of 60 days after completion of discharge overside of the goods hereby insured from the oversea vessel at such port or place, whichever shall first occur,

    or (ii) if the goods are forwarded within the said period of 60 days (or any agreed extension thereof) to the destination named in the policy or to any other destination, until terminated in accordance with the provisions of Clause 1 above.

3. Including transit by craft raft or lighter to or from the vessel. Each craft craft raft or lighter to be deemed a separate insurance. The Assured are not to be prejudiced by any agreement exempting lightermen from liability. — **Craft, &c. Clause**

4. Held covered at a premium to be arranged in case of change of voyage or of any omission or error in the description of the interest vessel or voyage. — **Change of Voyage Clause**

5. This insurance is against all risks of loss or damage to the subject-matter insured but shall in no case be deemed to extend to cover loss damage or expense proximately caused by delay or inherent vice or nature of the subject-matter insured. Claims recoverable hereunder shall be payable irrespective of percentage. — **All Risks Clause**

6. No claim for Constructive Total Loss shall be recoverable hereunder unless the goods are reasonably abandoned either on account of their actual total loss appearing to be unavoidable or because the cost of recovering, reconditioning and forwarding the goods to the destination to which they are insured would exceed their value on arrival. — **Constructive Total Loss Clause**

7. General average and salvage charges payable according to Foreign Statement or to York-Antwerp Rules if in accordance with the contract of affreightment. — **G. A. Clause**

8. The seaworthiness of the vessel as between the Assured and Underwriters is hereby admitted. In the event of loss the Assured's right of recovery hereunder shall not be prejudiced by the fact that the loss may have been attributable to the wrongful act or misconduct of the shipowners or their servants, committed without the privity of the Assured. — **Seaworthiness Admitted Clause**

9. It is the duty of the Assured and their Agents, in all cases, to take such measures as may be reasonable for the purpose of averting or minimising a loss and to ensure that all rights against carriers, bailees or other third parties are properly preserved and exercised. — **Bailee Clause**

10. This insurance shall not inure to the benefit of the carrier or other bailee. — **Not to Inure Clause**

11. This insurance is extended to indemnify the Assured against such proportion of liability under the contract of affreightment "Both to Blame Collision" Clause as is in respect of a loss recoverable hereunder.
In the event of any claim by shipowners under the said Clause the Assured agree to notify the Underwriters who shall have the right, at their own cost and expense, to defend the Assured against such claim. — **"Both to Blame Collision" Clause**

12. Warranted free of capture, seizure, arrest, restraint or detainment, and the consequences thereof or of any attempt thereat; also from the consequences of histilities or warlike operations, whether there be a declaration of war or not; but this warranty shall not exclude collision, contact with any fixed or floating object (other than a mine or torpedo), stranding, heavy weather or fire unless caused directly (and independently of the nature of the voyage or service which the vessel concerned or, in the case of a collision, any other vessel involved therein, is performing) by a hostile act by or against a belligerent power; and for the purpose of this warranty "power" includes any authority maintaining naval, military or air forces in association with a power.
Further warranted free from the consequences of civil war, revolution, rebellion, insurrection, or civil strife arising therefrom, or piracy.
Should Clause No. 12 be deleted, the relevant current Institute War Clauses shall be deemed to form part of this insurance. — **F.C. & S Clause**

13. Warranted free of loss or damage
(a) caused by strikers, locked-out workmen, or persons taking part in labour disturbances riots or civil commotions;
(b) resulting from strikes, lock-outs, labour disturbances, riots or civil commotions.
Should Clause No. 13 be deleted, the relevant current Institute Strikes Riots and Civil Commotions Clauses shall be deemed to form part of this insurance. — **F.S.R. & C.C. Clause**

14. It is a condition of this insurance that the Assured shall act with reasonable despatch in all circumstances within their control. — **Reasonable Despatch Clause**

NOTE. **It is necessary for the Assured when they become aware of an event which is "held covered" under this insurance to give prompt notice to Underwriters and the right to such cover is dependent upon compliance with this obligation.**

INSTITUTE CARGO CLAUSES (W.A.)

1/1/63

1. This insurance attaches from the time the goods leave the warehouse or place of storage at the place named in the policy for the commencement of the transit, continues during the ordinary course of transit and terminates either on delivery

    (a) to the Consignees' or other final warehouse or place of storage at the destination named in the policy

    (b) to any other warehouse or place of storage, whether prior to or at the destination named in the policy, which the Assured elect to use either

        (i) for storage other than in the ordinary course of transit

        or

        (ii) for allocation or distribution,

or (c on the expiry of 60 days after completion of discharge overside of the goods hereby insured from the oversea vessel at the final port of discharge, whichever shall first occur.

If, after discharge overside from the oversea vessel at the final port of discharge, but prior to termination of this insurance, the goods are to be forwarded to a destination other than that to which they are insured hereunder, this insurance whilst remaining subject to termination as provided for above, shall not extend beyond the commencement of transit to such other destination.

This insurance shall remain in force (subject to termination as provided for above and to the provisions of Clause 2 below) during delay beyond the control of the Assured, any deviation, forced discharge, reshipment or transhipment and during any variation of the adventure arising from the exercise of a liberty granted to shipowners or charterers under the contract of affreightment, but shall in no case be deemed to extend to cover loss damage or expense proximately caused by delay or inherent vice or nature of the subject matter insured.

2. If owing to circumstances beyond the control of the Assured either the contract of affreightment is terminated at a port or place other than the destination named therein or the adventure is otherwise terminated before delivery of the goods as provided for in Clause 1 above, then, subject to prompt notice being given to Underwriters and to an additional premium if required, this insurance shall remain in force until either

    (i) the goods are sold and delivered at such port or place, or, unless otherwise specially agreed, until the expiry of 60 days after completion of discharge overside of the goods hereby insured from the oversea vessel at such port or place, whichever shall first occur,

    or (ii) if the goods are forwarded within the said period of 60 days (or any agreed extension thereof) to the destination named in the policy or to any other destination, until terminated in accordance with the provisions of Clause 1 above.

3. Including transit by craft raft or lighter to or from the vessel. Each craft raft or lighter to be deemed a separate insurance. The Assured are not to be prejudiced by any agreement exempting lightermen from liability.

4. Held covered at a premium to be arranged in case of change of voyage or of any omission or error in the description of the interest vessel or voyage.

5. Warranted free from average under the percentage specified in the policy, unless general, or the vessel or craft be stranded, sunk or burnt, but notwithstanding this warranty the Underwriters are to pay the insured value of any package which may be totally lost in loading, transhipment or discharge, also for any loss of or damage to the interest insured which may reasonably be attributed to fire, explosion, collision or contact of the vessel and/or craft and/or conveyance with any external substance (ice included) other than water, or to discharge of cargo at a port of distress. This Clause shall operate during the whole period covered by the policy.

6. No claim for Constructive Total Loss shall be recoverable hereunder unless the goods are reasonably abandoned either on account of their actual total loss appearing to be unavoidable or because the cost of recovering, reconditioning and forwarding the goods to the destination to which they are insured would exceed their value on arrival.

Transit Clause (incorporating Warehouse to Warehouse Clause)

Termination of Adventure Clause

Craft, &c. Clause

Change of Voyage Clause

Average Clause

Constructive Total Loss Clause

Antwerp Rules if in accordance with the contract of affreightment.

8. The seaworthiness of the vessel as between the Assured and Underwriters is hereby admitted. Seaworthiness Admitted Clause

In the event of loss the Assured's right of recovery hereunder shall not be prejudiced by the fact that the loss may have been attributable to the wrongful act or misconduct of the shipowners or their servants, committed without the privity of the Assured.

9. It is the duty of the Assured and their Agents, in all cases, to take such measures as may be reasonable for the purpose of averting or minimising a loss and to ensure that all rights against carriers, bailees or other third parties are properly preserved and exercised. Bailee Clause

10. This insurance shall not inure to the benefit of the carrier or other bailee. Not to Inure Clause

11. This insurance is extended to indemnify the Assured against such proportion of liability under the contract of affreightment "Both to Blame Collision" Clause as is in respect of a loss recoverable hereunder. "Both to Blame Collision" Clause

In the event of any claim by shipowners under the said Clause the Assured agree to notify the Underwriters who shall have the right, at their own cost and expense, to defend the Assured against such claim.

12. Warranted free of capture, seizure, arrest, restraint or detainment, and the consequences thereof or of any attempt thereat; also from the consequences of hostilities or warlike operations, whether there be a declaration of war or not; but this warranty shall not exclude collision, contact with any fixed or floating object (other than a mine or a torpedo), stranding, heavy weather or fire unless caused directly (and independently of the nature of the voyage or service which the vessel concerned or, in the case of a collision, any other vessel involved therein, is performing) by a hostile act by or against a belligerent power; and for the purpose of this warranty "power" includes any authority maintaining naval, military or air forces in association with a power. F.C. & S. Clause

Further warranted free from the consequences of civil war, revolution, rebellion, insurrection, or civil strife arising therefrom, or piracy.

Should Clause No. 12 be deleted, the relevant current Institute War Clauses shall be deemed to form part of this insurance.

13. Warranted free of loss or damage F.S.R. & C.C. Clause
   (a) caused by strikers, locked-out workmen, or persons taking part in labour disturbances riots or civil commotions;
   (b) resulting from strikes, lock-outs, labour disturbances, riots or civil commotions.

Should Clause No. 13 be deleted, the relevant current Institute Strikes Riots and Civil Commotions Clauses shall be deemed to form part of this insurance.

14. It is a condition of this insurance that the Assured shall act with reasonable despatch in all circumstances within their control. Reasonable Despatch Clause

NOTE.—It is necessary for the Assured when they become aware of an event which is "held covered" under this insurance to give prompt notice to Underwriters and the right to such cover is dependent upon compliance with this obligation.

1/1/63

INSTITUTE CARGO CLAUSES (F.P.A.)

1. This insurance attaches from the time the goods leave the warehouse or place of storage at the place named in the policy for the commencement of the transit, continues during the ordinary course of transit and terminates either on delivery Transit Clause (incorporating Warehouse to Warehouse Clause)
   (a) to the Consignees' or other final warehouse or place of storage at the destination named in the policy
   (b) to any other warehouse or place of storage, whether prior to or at the

7　　destination named in the policy, which the assured elect to use either

8　　　　(i) for storage other than in the ordinary course of transit

9　　　　　or

10　　　　(ii) for allocation or distribution,

11　　or (c) on the expiry of 60 days after completion of discharge overside of the

12　　goods hereby insured from the oversea vessel at the final port of

13　　discharge,

14　　whichever shall first occur.

15　　　If, after discharge overside from the oversea vessel at the final port of discharge, but prior

16　　to termination of this insurance, the goods are to be forwarded to a destination other than that

17　　to which they are insured hereunder, this insurance whilst remaining subject to termination as

18　　provided for above, shall not extend beyond the commencement of transit to such other

19　　destination.

20　　　This insurance shall remain in force (subject to termination as provided for above and to the

21　　provisions of Clause 2 below) during delay beyond the control of the Assured, any deviation, forced

22　　discharge, reshipment or transhipment and during any variation of the adventure arising from the

23　　exercise of a liberty granted to shipowners or charterers under the contract of affreightment, but

24　　shall in no case be deemed to extend to cover loss damage or expense proximately caused by delay

25　　or inherent vice or nature of the subject matter insured.

26　　　2.　If owing to circumstances beyond the control of the Assured either the contract of affreight-

27　　ment is terminated at a port or place other than the destination named therein or the adventure is

28　　otherwise terminated before delivery of the goods as provided for in Clause 1 above, then, subject

29　　to prompt notice being given to Underwriters and to an additional premium if required, this

30　　insurance shall remain in force until either

31　　　(i) the goods are sold and delivered at such port or place, or, unless otherwise specially

32　　　　　agreed, until the expiry of 60 days after completion of discharge overside of the goods

33　　　　　hereby insured from the oversea vessel at such port or place, whichever shall first occur.

34　　or (ii) if the goods are forwarded within the said period of 60 days (or any agreed extension

35　　　　　thereof) to the destination named in the policy or to any other destination, until

36　　　　　terminated in accordance with the provisions of Clause 1 above.

37　　　3.　Including transit by craft raft or lighter to or from the vessel. Each craft raft or lighter to

38　　be deemed a separate insurance. The assured are not to be prejudiced by any agreement exempting

39　　lightermen from liability.

40　　　4.　Held covered at a premium to be arranged in case of change of voyage or of any omission

41　　or error in the description of the interest vessel or voyage.

42　　　5.　Warranted free from Particular Average unless the vessel or craft be stranded, sunk, or

43　　burnt, but notwithstanding this warranty the Underwriters are to pay the insured value of any

44　　package or packages which may be totally lost in loading, transhipment or discharge, also for any

45　　loss of or damage to the interest insured which may reasonably be attributed to fire, explosion,

46　　collision or contact of the vessel and/or craft and/or conveyance with any external substance

47　　(ice included) other than water, or to discharge of cargo at a port of distress, also to pay special

48　　charges for landing warehousing and forwarding if incurred at an intermediate port of call or refuge

49　　for which Underwriters would be liable under the standard form of English Marine Policy with the

50　　Institute Cargo Clauses (W.A.) attached.

51　　This Clause shall operate during the whole period covered by the policy.

52　　　6.　No claim for Constructive Total Loss shall be recoverable hereunder unless the goods are

53　　reasonably abandoned either on account of their actual total loss appearing to be unavoidable or

54　　because the cost of recovering, reconditioning and forwarding the goods to the destination to

55　　which they are insured would exceed their value on arrival.

56　　　7.　General Average and Salvage Charges payable according to Foreign Statement or to York-

57　　Antwerp Rules if in accordance with the contract of affreightment.

58　　　8.　The seaworthiness of the vessel as between the Assured and Underwriters is hereby admitted.

59　　In the event of loss the Assured's right of recovery hereunder shall not be prejudiced by the

60　　fact that the loss may have been attributable to the wrongful act or misconduct of the shipowners of their servants, continued without the privity of the Assured.

9. It is the duty of the Assured and their Agents, in all cases, to take such measures as may be reasonable for the purpose of averting or minimising a loss and to ensure that all rights against carriers, bailees or other third parties are properly preserved and exercised.

Bailee Clause

10. This insurance shall not inure to the benefit of the carrier or other bailee.

Not to Inure Clause

11. This insurance is extended to indemnify the Assured against such proportion of liability under the contract of affreightment "Both to Blame Collision" Clause as is in respect of a loss recoverable hereunder.

In the event of any claim by shipowners under the said Clause the Assured agree to notify the Underwriters who shall have the right, at their own cost and expense, to defend the Assured against such claim.

"Both to Blame Collision" Clause

12. Warranted free of capture, seizure, arrest, restraint or detainment, and the consequences thereof or of any attempt thereat; also from the consequences of hostilities or warlike operations, whether there be a declaration of war or not: but this warranty shall not exclude collision, contact with any fixed or floating object (other than a mine or torpedo), stranding, heavy weather or fire unless caused directly (and independently of the nature of the voyage or service which the vessel concerned or, in the case of a collision, any other vessel involved therein, is performing) by a hostile act by or against a belligerent power; and for the purpose of this warranty "power" includes any authority maintaining naval, military or air forces in association with a power.

Further warranted free from the consequences of civil war, revolution, rebellion, insurrection, or civil strife arising therefrom, or piracy.

F.C. & S Clause

Should Clause No. 12 be deleted, the relevant current Institute War Clauses shall be deemed to form part of this insurance.

13. Warranted free of loss or damage
  (a) caused by strikers, locked-out workmen, or persons taking part in labour disturbances, riots or civil commotions;
  (b) resulting from strikes, lock-outs, labour disturbances, riots or civil commotions.

F.S.R. & C.C. Clause

Should Clause No. 13 be deleted, the relevant current Institute Strikes Riots and Civil Commotions Clauses shall be deemed to form part of this insurance.

14. **It is a condition of this insurance that the Assured shall act with reasonable despatch in all circumstances within their control.**

Reasonable Clause Despatch

NOTE.—It is necessary for the Assured when they become aware of an event which is "held covered" under this insurance to give prompt notice to Underwriters and the right to such cover is dependent upon compliance with this obligation.

1/10/70

INSTITUTE WAR AND STRIKES CLAUSES
Hulls—Time

1. Subject always to the exclusions hereinafter referred to, this insurance covers only
  (1)(a) the risks excluded from the Standard Form of English Marine Policy by the clause:
  "Warranted free of capture, seizure, arrest, restraint or detainment, and the consequences thereof or of any attempt thereat: also from the consequences of hostilities or warlike operations, whether there be a declaration of war or not; but this warranty shall not exclude collision, contact with any fixed or floating object (other than a mine or torpedo), stranding, heavy weather or fire unless caused directly (and independently of the nature of the voyage or service which the vessel concerned or in the case of a collision, any

other vessel involved therein, is performing) by a hostile act by or against a belligerent power; and for the purpose of this warranty "power" includes any authority maintaining naval, military or air forces in association with a power.

Further warranted free from the consequences of civil war, revolution, rebellion, insurrection, or civil strife arising therefrom, or piracy";

(b) the cover excluded from the Standard Form of English Marine policy with the Institute Time Clauses—Hulls 1.10.70. (including 4/4ths Collision Clause) attached, by the clause:—

"Warranted free from loss damage liability or expense arising from:

(a) the detonation of an explosive
(b) any weapon of war

and caused by any person acting maliciously or from a political motive.";

(2) loss of or damage to the property hereby insured caused by:
(a) hostilities, warlike operations, civil war, revolution, rebellion, insurrection, or civil strife arising there-from;
(b) mines, torpedoes, bombs or other engines of war;

(3) loss of or damage to the property hereby insured caused by strikers, locked-out workmen or persons taking part in labour disturbances, riots or civil commotions;

(4) destruction of or damage to the property hereby insured caused by persons acting maliciously.

2. Average payable irrespective of percentage.

3. The Institute Time Clauses—Hulls 1.10.70. (including 4/4ths Collision Clause) except Clauses 3(b), 4, 5, 6, 11, 12, 20(h), 21, 23, 24 and 25 are deemed to be incorporated in this insurance in so far as they do not conflict with the provisions of these clauses.

Held covered in case of breach of warranty as to towage or salvage services provided notice be given to the Underwriters immediately after receipt of advices and any additional premium required by them be agreed.

4. This insurance excludes
(1) loss, damage or expense arising from
(a) any hostile detonation of any weapon of war employing atomic or nuclear fission and/or fusion or other like reaction or radioactive force or matter, hereinafter called a nuclear weapon of war;
(b) the outbreak of war (whether there be a declaration of war or not) between any of the following countries;
United Kingdom, United States of America, France,
The Union of Soviet Socialist Republics,
the People's Republic of China;
(c) requisition or pre-emption;
(d) capture, seizure, arrest, restraint, detainment or confiscation by the Government of the country in which the Vessel is owned or registered;
(e) arrest, restraint or detainment under quarantine regulations or by reason of infringement of any customs regulations;
(2)(a) loss, damage or expense covered by the Standard Form of English Marine Policy, with the Free of Capture etc. Clause (as quoted in Clause 1(1)(a) above) inserted therein and with the Institute Time Clauses—Hulls 1.10.70. (including 4/4ths Collision Clause) attached or which would be recoverable under such insurance but for Clauses 11 and 12 thereof;
(b) any claim for any sum recoverable under any other insurance on the property hereby insured or which would be recoverable under such insurance but for the existence of this insurance.
(3) any claim for expenses arising from delay except such expenses as would be recoverable in principle in English law and practice under the York-Antwerp Rules 1974.

5. NOTICE OF CANCELLATION AND
AUTOMATIC TERMINATION OF COVER CLAUSE

(a) This insurance may be cancelled by either the underwriters or the Assured giving 14 days notice (such cancellation becoming effective on the expiry of 14 days from midnight of the day on which notice of cancellation is issued by or to the Underwriters). The Underwriters agree however to reinstate this insur-ance subject to agreement between the Underwriters and the Assured prior to the expiry of

Whether or not such notice of cancellation has been given this insurance shall TERMINATE AUTO-
MATICALLY

   (i) upon the occurrence of any hostile detonation of any nuclear weapon of war as defined in Clause
      4(1)(a) wheresoever or whensoever such detonation may occur and whether or not the Vessel may
      be involved;

   (ii) upon the outbreak of war (whether there be a declaration of war or not) between any of the following
      countries:

          United Kingdom, United States of America, France,
          the Union of Soviet Socialist Republics,
          the People's Republic of China;

   (iii) in the event of the vessel being requisitioned, either for title or use.

  (b) In the event either of cancellation by notice or of automatic termination of this insurance by reason
     of the operation of section (a) of this clause, or of the sale of the Vessel, pro rata net return of premium
     shall be payable to the Assured.

This insurance shall not become effective if, prior to the intended time of its attachment there has occurred any event which
would have automatically terminated this insurance under the provision of Clause 5 above had this insurance attached
prior to such occurrence.

APPENDIX VII

Reproduced by kind permission of the Institute of London Underwriters

1/7/76

INSTITUTE WARRANTIES

1. Warranted no:
   - (a) Atlantic Coast of North America, its rivers or adjacent islands,
     - (i) north of 52° 10′ N. Lat. and west of 50° W. Long.;
     - (ii) south of 52° 10′ N. Lat. in the area bounded by lines drawn between Battle Harbour/Pistolet Bay; Cape Ray/Cape North; Port Hawkesbury/Port Mulgrave and Baie Comeau/Matane, between 21st December and 30th April b.d.i.
     - (iii) west of Baie Comeau/Matane (but not west of Montreal) between 1st December and 30th April b.d.i.
   - (b) Great Lakes or St. Lawrence Seaway west of Montreal.
   - (c) Greenland Waters.
   - (d) Pacific Coast of North America its rivers or adjacent islands north of 54° 30′ N. Lat., or west of 130° 50′ W. Long.

2. Warranted no Baltic Sea or adjacent waters east of 15° E. Long.
   - (a) North of a line between Mo (63° 24′ N. Lat.) and Vasa (63° 06′ N. Lat.) between 10th December and 25th May b.d.i.
   - (b) East of a line between Viipuri (Vyborg) (28° 47′ E. Long.) and Narva (28° 12′ E. Long.) between 15th December and 15th May b.d.i.
   - (c) North of a line between Stockholm (59° 20′ N. Lat.) and Tallinn (59° 24′ N. Lat.) between 8th January and 5th May b.d.i.
   - (d) East of 22° E. Long. and south of 59° N. Lat. between 28th December and 5th May b.d.i.

3. Warranted not North of 70° N. Lat. other than voyages direct to or from any port or place in Norway or Kola Bay.

4. Warranted no Behring Sea, no East Asian waters north of 46° N. Lat. and not to enter or sail from any port or place in Siberia except Nakhodka and/or Vladivostok.

5. Warranted not to proceed to Kerguelen and/or Croset Islands or south of 50° S. Lat., except to ports and/or places in Patagonia and/or Chile and/or Falkland Islands, but liberty is given to enter waters south of 50° S. Lat., if *en route* to or from ports and/or places not excluded by this warranty.

6. Warranted not to sail with Indian Coal as cargo:
   - (a) between 1st March and 30th June, both days inclusive.
   - (b) between 1st July and 30th September, both days inclusive, except to ports in Asia, not West of Aden or East of or beyond Singapore.

APPENDIX VIII

Reproduced by kind permission of "Lloyd's"

LLOYD'S STANDARD FORM OF SALVAGE AGREEMENT
(Approved and Published by the Committee of Lloyd's)

No Cure—No Pay

On board the   dated   19

It is hereby agreed between Captain†   for and on
behalf of the Owners of the "   " her cargo freight
bunkers and stores and   for and on behalf of
(hereinafter called "the Contractor"*):—

1. (*a*) The Contractor agrees to use his best endeavours to salve the
       and/or her cargo bunkers and stores and take
them to   or other place to be hereafter agreed or
if no place is named or agreed to a place of safety. The Contractor
further agrees to use his best endeavours to prevent the escape of
oil from the vessel while performing the services of salving the subject
vessel and/or her cargo bunkers and stores. The services shall be
rendered and accepted as salvage services upon the principle of
"no cure—no pay" except that where the property being salved is
a tanker laden or partly laden with a cargo of oil and without
negligence on the part of the Contractor and/or his Servants and/or
Agents (1) the services are not successful or (2) are only partially
successful or (3) the Contractor is prevented from completing the
services the Contractor shall nevertheless be awarded solely against
the Owners of such tanker has reasonably incurred expenses and an
increment not exceeding 15 per cent of such expenses but only if
and to the extent that such expenses together with the increment
are greater than any amount otherwise recoverable under this
Agreement. Within the meaning of the said exception to the
principle of "no cure—no pay" expenses shall in addition to actual
out of pocket expenses include a fair rate for all tugs craft personnel
and other equipment used by the Contractor in the services and oil
shall mean crude oil fuel oil heavy diesel oil and lubricating oil.

   (*b*) The Contractor's remuneration shall be fixed by arbitration in
London in the manner herein prescribed and any other difference
arising out of this Agreement or the operations thereunder shall be
referred to arbitration in the same way. In the event of the services
referred to in this Agreement or any part of such services having
been already rendered at the date of this Agreement by the Contractor to the said vessel and/or her cargo bunkers and stores the
provisions of this Agreement shall apply to such services.

   (*c*) It is hereby further agreed that the security to be provided to the
Committee of Lloyd's the Salved Values the Award and/or Interim
Award and/or Award on Appeal of the Arbitrator and/or Arbitrator(s)
on Appeal shall be in   currency. If this Clause is not

---

† See Note 1 below   * See Note 2 below

Notes.—(1) Insert name of person signing on behalf of Owners of property to be salved.
The Master should sign wherever possible.

(2) The Contractor's name should always be inserted in line 3 and whenever the Agreement
is signed by the Master of the Salving vessel or other person on behalf of the Contractor the name
of the Master or other person must also be inserted in line 3 before the words "for and on behalf
of". The words "for and on behalf of" should be deleted where a Contractor signs personally.

completed then the security to be provided and the Salved Values the Award and/or Interim Award and/or Award on Appeal of the Arbitrator and/or Arbitrator(s) on Appeal shall be in Pounds Sterling.

(d) This Agreement shall be governed by and arbitration thereunder shall be in accordance with English law.

2. The Owners their Servants and Agents shall co-operate fully with the Contractor in and about the salvage including obtaining entry to the place named in Clause 1 of this Agreement or such other place as may be agreed or if applicable the place of safety to which the salved property is taken. The Owners shall promptly accept redelivery of the salved property at such place. The Contractor may make reasonable use of the vessel's machinery gear equipment anchors chains stores and other appurtenances during and for the purpose of the operations free of expense but shall not unnecessarily damage abandon or sacrifice the same or any property the subject of this Agreement.

3. The Master or other person signing this Agreement on behalf of the property to be salved is not authorised to make or give and the Contractor shall not demand or take any payment draft or order as inducement to or remuneration for entering into this Agreement.

Provisions as to Security

4. The Contractor shall immediately after the termination of the services or sooner in appropriate cases notify the Committee of Lloyd's and where practicable the Owners of the amount for which he requires security (inclusive of costs expenses and interest). Unless otherwise agreed by the parties such security shall be given to the Committee of Lloyd's and security so given shall be in a form approved by the Committee and shall be given by persons firms or corporations resident in the United Kingdom either satisfactory to the Committee of Lloyd's or agreed by the Contractor. The Committee of Lloyd's shall not be responsible for the sufficiency (whether in amount or otherwise) of any security which shall be given nor for the default or insolvency of any person firm or corporation giving the same.

5. Pending the completion of the security as aforesaid the Contractor shall have a maritime lien on the property salved for his remuneration. Where the aforementioned exception to the principle of "no cure—no pay" becomes likely to be applicable the Owners of the vessel shall on demand of the Contractor provide security for the Contractor's remuneration under the aforementioned exception in accordance with Clause 4 hereof. The salved property shall not without the consent in writing of the Contractor be removed from the place (within the terms of Clause 1) to which the property is taken by the Contractor on the completion of the salvage services until security has been given as aforesaid. The Owners of the vessel their Servants and Agents shall use their best endeavours to ensure that the Cargo Owners provide security in accordance with the provisions of Clause 4 of this Agreement before the cargo is released. The Contractor agrees not to arrest or detain the property salved unless (a) the security be not given within 14 days (exclusive of Saturdays and Sundays or other days observed as general holidays at Lloyd's) after the date of the termination of the services (the Committee of Lloyd's not being responsible for the failure of the parties concerned to provide the required security within the said 14 days) or (b) the Contractor has reason to believe that the removal of the property is contemplated contrary to the above agreement. In the event of security not being provided or in the event of (1) any attempt being made to remove the property salved contrary to this agreement or (2) the Contractor having reasonable grounds to suppose that such an attempt will be made the Contractor may take steps to enforce his aforesaid lien. The Arbitrator appointed under Clause 6 or the person(s) appointed under Clause 13 hereof shall have power in their absolute discretion to include in the amount awarded to the Contractor the whole or such part of the expense incurred by the Contractor in enforcing or protecting by insurance

or otherwise or in taking reasonable steps to enforce or protect his lien as they shall think fit.

Provisions as to Arbitration

6. (a) Where security within the provisions of this Agreement is given to the Committee of Lloyd's in whole or in part the said Committee shall appoint an Arbitrator in respect of the interests covered by such security.

(b) Whether security has been given or not the Committee of Lloyd's shall appoint an Arbitrator upon receipt of a written or telex or telegraphic notice of a claim for arbitration from any of the parties entitled or authorised to make such a claim.

7. Where an Arbitrator has been appointed by the Committee of Lloyd's and the parties do not wish to proceed to arbitration the parties shall jointly notify the said Committee in writing or by telex or by telegram and the said Committee may thereupon terminate the appointment of such Arbitrator as they may have appointed in accordance with Clause 6 of this Agreement.

8. Any of the following parties may make a claim for arbitration viz.:— (1) The Owners of the ship. (2) The Owners of the cargo or any part thereof. (3) The Owners of any freight separately at risk or any part thereof. (4) The Contractor. (5) The Owners of the bunkers and/or stores. (6) Any other person who is a party to this Agreement.

9. If the parties to any such Arbitration or any of them desire to be heard or to adduce evidence at the Arbitration they shall give notice to that effect to the Committee of Lloyd's and shall respectively nominate a person in the United Kingdom to represent them for all the purposes of the Arbitration and failing such notice and nomination being given the Arbitrator or Arbitrator(s) on Appeal may proceed as if the parties failing to give the same had renounced their right to be heard or adduce evidence.

10. The remuneration for the services within the meaning of this Agreement shall be fixed by an Arbitrator to be appointed by the Committee of Lloyd's and he shall have power to make an Interim Award ordering such payment on account as may seem fair and just and on such terms as may be fair and just.

Conduct of the Arbitration

11. The Arbitrator shall have power to obtain call for receive and act upon any such oral or documentary evidence or information (whether the same be strictly admissible as evidence or not) as he may think fit and to conduct the Arbitration in such manner in all respects as he may think fit and shall if in his opinion the amount of the security demanded is excessive have power in his absolute discretion to condemn the Contractor in the whole or part of the expense of providing such security and to deduct the amount in which the Contractor is so condemned from the salvage remuneration. Unless the Arbitrator shall otherwise direct the parties shall be at liberty to adduce expert evidence at the Arbitration. Any Award of the Arbitrator shall (subject to appeal as provided in this Agreement) be final and binding on all the parties concerned. The Arbitrator and the Committee of Lloyd's may charge reasonable fees and expenses for their services in connection with the Arbitration whether it proceeds to a hearing or not and all such fees and expenses shall be treated as part of the costs of the Arbitration. Save as aforesaid the statutory provisions as to Arbitration for the time being in force in England shall apply.

12. Interest at a rate per annum to be fixed by the Arbitrator from the expiration of 21 days (exclusive of Saturdays and Sundays or other days observed as general holidays at Lloyd's) after the date of publication of the Award and/or Interim Award by the Committee of Lloyd's until the date payment is received by the Committee of Lloyd's both dates inclusive shall

(subject to appeal as provided in this Agreement) be payable upon any sum awarded after deduction of any sums paid on account.

Provisions as to Appeal

13. Any of the persons named under Clause 8 may appeal from the Award but not without leave of the Arbitrator(s) on Appeal from an Interim Award made pursuant to the provisions of Clause 10 hereof by giving written or telegraphic or telex Notice of Appeal to the Committee of Lloyd's within 14 days (exclusive of Saturdays and Sundays or other days observed as general holidays at Lloyd's) after the date of the publication by the Committee of Lloyd's of the Award and may (without prejudice to their right of appeal under the first part of this Clause) within 14 days (exclusive of Saturdays and Sundays or other days observed as general holidays at Lloyd's) after receipt by them from the Committee of Lloyd's of notice of such appeal (such notice if sent by post to be deemed to be received on the day following that on which the said notice was posted) give written or telegraphic or telex Notice of Cross-Appeal to the Committee of Lloyd's. As soon as practicable after receipt of such notice or notices the Committee of Lloyd's shall refer the Appeal to the hearing and determination of a person or persons selected by it. In the event of an Appellant or Cross-Appellant withdrawing his Notice of Appeal or Cross-Appeal the hearing shall nevertheless proceed in respect of such Notice of Appeal or Cross-Appeal as may remain. Any Award on Appeal shall be final and binding on all the parties concerned whether such parties were represented or not at either the Arbitration or at the Arbitration on Appeal.

Conduct of the Appeal

14. No evidence other than the documents put in on the Arbitration and the Arbitrator's notes of the proceedings and oral evidence if any at the Arbitration and the Arbitrator's Reasons for his Award and Interim Award if any and the transcript if any of any evidence given at the Arbitration shall be used on the Appeal unless the Arbitrator(s) on the Appeal shall in his or their discretion call for or allow other evidence. The Arbitrator(s) on Appeal may conduct the Arbitration on Appeal in such manner in all respects as he or they may think fit and may act upon any such evidence or information (whether the same be strictly admissible as evidence or not) as he or they may think fit and may maintain increase or reduce the sum awarded by the Arbitrator with the like power as is conferred by Clause 11 on the Arbitrator to condemn the Contractor in the whole or part of the expense of providing security and to deduct the amount disallowed from the salvage remuneration. And he or they shall also make such order as he or they shall think fit as to the payment of interest on the sum awarded to the Contractor. The Arbitrator(s) on the Appeal may direct in what manner the costs of the Arbitration and of the Arbitration on Appeal shall be borne and paid and he or they and the Committee of Lloyd's may charge reasonable fees and expenses for their services in connection with the Arbitration on Appeal whether it proceeds to a hearing or not and all such fees and expenses shall be treated as part of the costs of the Arbitration on Appeal. Save as aforesaid the statutory provisions as to Arbitration for the time being in force in England shall apply.

Provisions as to Payment

15. (a) In case of Arbitration if no Notice of Appeal be received by the Committee of Lloyd's within 14 days (exclusive of Saturdays and Sundays or other days observed as general holidays at Lloyd's) after the date of the publication by the Committee of the Award and/or Interim Award the Committee shall call upon the party or parties concerned to pay the amount awarded and in the event of non-payment shall realize or enforce the security and pay therefrom to the Contractor (whose receipt shall be a good discharge to it) the amount awarded to him together with interest as hereinbefore

provided but the Contractor shall reimburse the parties concerned to such extent as the final Award is less than the Interim Award.

(b) If Notice of Appeal be received by the Committee of Lloyds in accordance with the provisions of Clause 13 hereof it shall as soon as but not until the Award on Appeal has been published by it call upon the party or parties concerned to pay the amount awarded and in the event of non-payment shall realize or enforce the security and pay therefrom to the Contractor (whose receipt shall be a good discharge to it) the amount awarded to him together with interest if any in such manner as shall comply with the provisions of the Award on Appeal.

(c) If the Award and/or Interim Award and/or Award on Appeal provide that the costs of the Arbitration and/or of the Arbitration on Appeal or any part of such costs shall be borne by the Contractor such costs may be deducted from the amount awarded before payment is made to the Contractor by the Committee of Lloyd's unless satisfactory security is provided by the Contractor for the payment of such costs-

(d) If any sum shall become payable to the Contractor as remuneration for his services and/or interest and/or costs as the result of an agreement made between the Contractor and the parties interested in the property salved or any of them the Committee of Lloyd's in the event of non-payment shall realise or enforce the security and pay therefrom to the Contractor (whose receipt shall be a good discharge to it) the amount agreed upon between the parties.

(e) Without prejudice to the provisions of Clause 4 hereof the liability of the Committee of Lloyd's shall be limited in any event to the amount of security held by it.

General Provisions

16. Notwithstanding anything hereinbefore contained should the operations be only partially successful without any negligence or want of ordinary skill and care on the part of the Contractor his Servants or Agents and any portion of the vessel her appurtenances bunkers stores and cargo be salved by the Contractor he shall be entitled to reasonable remuneration and such reasonable remuneration shall be fixed in case of difference by Arbitration in manner hereinbefore prescribed.

17. The Master or other person signing this Agreement on behalf of the property to be salved enters into this Agreement as Agent for the vessel her cargo freight bunkers and stores and the respective owners thereof and binds each (but not the one for the other or himself personally) to the due performance thereof.

18. In considering what sums of money have been expended by the Contractor in rendering the services and/or in fixing the amount of the Award and/or Interim Award and/or Award on Appeal the Arbitrator or Arbitrator(s) on Appeal shall to such an extent and in so far as it may be fair and just in all the circumstances give effect to the consequences of any change or changes in the value of money or rates of exchange which may have occurred between the completion of the services and the date on which the Award and/or Interim Award and/or Award on Appeal is made.

19. Any Award notice authority order or other document signed by the Chairman of Lloyd's or any person authorised by the Committee of Lloyd's for the purpose shall be deemed to have been duly made or given by the Committee of Lloyd's and shall have the same force and effect in all respects as if it had been signed by every member of the Committee of Lloyd's.

20. The Contractor may claim salvage and enforce any Award or agreement made between the Contractor and the parties interested in the property salved against security provided under this Agreement if any in the name and on

behalf of any Sub-Contractors Servants or Agents including Masters and members of the Crews of vessels employed by him in the services rendered hereunder provided that he first indemnifies and holds harmless the Owners of the property salved against all claims by or liabilities incurred to the said persons. Any such indemnity shall be provided in a form satisfactory to such Owners.

21. The Contractor shall be entitled to limit any liability to the Owners of the subject vessel and/or her cargo bunkers and stores which he and/or his Servants and/or Agents may incur in and about the services in the manner and to the extent provided by English law and as if the provisions of the Convention on Limitation of Liability for Maritime Claims 1976 were part of the law of England.

For and on behalf of the Contractor

For and on behalf of the Owners of property to be salved

. . . .

(To be signed either by the Con-tractor personally or by the Master of the salving vessel or other person whose name is inserted in line 3 of this Agreement.)

. . . .

(To be signed by the Master or other person whose name is inserted in line 1 of this Agreement.)

APPENDIX IX

Reproduced by kind permission of "Lloyd's"

LLOYD'S AVERAGE BOND.

To

Owner(s) of the

Voyage and date

    Port of shipment

    Port of destination/discharge

    Bill of lading or waybill number(s)

Quantity and description of goods

In consideration of the delivery to us or to our order, on payment of the freight due, of the goods noted above we agree to pay the proper proportion of any salvage and/or general average and/or special charges which may hereafter be ascertained to be due from the goods or the shippers or owners thereof under an adjustment prepared in accordance with the provisions of the contract of affreightment governing the carriage of the goods or, failing any such provision, in accordance with the law and practice of the place where the common maritime adventure ended and which is payable in respect of the goods by the shippers or owners thereof.

We also agree to:

(i) furnish particulars of the value of the goods, supported by a copy of the commercial invoice rendered to us or, if there is no such invoice, details of the shipped value and

(ii) make a payment on account of such sum as is duly certified by the average adjusters to be due from the goods and which is payable in respect of the goods by the shippers or owners thereof.

Date   Signature of receiver of goods.

Full name and address

VALUATION FORM

To ....

Owner(s) of the ....

Voyage and date ....

       Port of shipment ....

       Port of destination/discharge ....

       Bill of lading or waybill number(s) ....

	Particulars of value	
	A	B
Quantity and description of goods	Invoice value	Shipped value
	(specify currency)	
Currency		

1. If the goods are insured please state the following details (if known):—

   Name and address of insurers or brokers ....

   Policy or certificate number and date .... Insured value ....

2. If the goods arrived subject to loss or damage, please state nature and extent thereof ....
....
....

   and ensure that copies of supporting documents are forwarded either direct or through the insurers to the average adjusters named below.

3. If a general average deposit has been paid, please state:—

      (a) Amount of the deposit .... (b) Deposit receipt number ....

      (c) Whether you have made any claim on your insurers

         for reimbursement ....

Date .... Signature ....

Full name and address ....
....
....

NOTES

1. If the goods form the subject of a commercial transaction, fill in column A with the amount of the commercial invoice rendered to you, *and attach a copy of this invoice hereto.*
2. If there is no commercial invoice covering the goods, state the shipped value, if known to you, in column B.
3. In either case, state the currency involved.
4. The shipowners have appointed as average adjusters ....

   to whom this form should be sent duly completed together with a copy of the commercial invoice.

APPENDIX X

Reproduced by kind permission of "Lloyd's"

GENERAL AVERAGE DEPOSIT RECEIPT

No. . . . .

LLOYD'S FORM

Dated at . . . . 19 . . . .

Vessel . . . . *from* . . . . *to* . . . .

Nature and date of Accident . . . .

. . . .

Received *from Messrs.* . . . .

the sum of . . . .

deposit on account of General Average and or Salvage and or Charges,

being . . . . *per cent. on* . . . .

provisionally adopted as the net arrived value of the following goods, viz.:

. . . . Marks and
. . . . Nos. and
Description
. . . . of Interest
to be in-
B/L *No.* . . . . serted here

£ }Trustees

N.B.— The refund, if any, will be made only to the bearer of, and in
exchange for, this Receipt, and will be the whole balance of the
deposit after satisfying the General Average and or Salvage
and or Charges, without deduction or set off of any other claims
of the Shipowner against the Shipper or Consignee.

The General Average will be adjusted in . . . . **and the Shipowners have given the necessary instructions to Messrs.** . . . .
. . . . **Average Adjusters.**

APPENDIX XI

THE CLAUSES OF THE UNIFORM GENERAL CHARTER (GENCON)

...........................19....

Owners.

1. IT IS THIS DAY MUTUALLY AGREED between
....
Owners of the steamer or motor vessel....................
of......tons $\frac{\text{gross}}{\text{net}}$ Register and carrying about............

Position.

tons of deadweight cargo, now...........................
and expected ready to load under this charter about........
....

Charterers.

and Messrs...
of..................................as Charterers.

Where to load.

That the said vessel shall proceed to..................
.....................or so near thereto as she may safely
get and lie always afloat, and there load a full and complete

Cargo.

cargo (if shipment of deck cargo agreed same to be at Charterers' risk) of..
....
....
....

(Charterers to provide all mats and/or wood for dunnage and
any separations required, the Owners allowing the use of any
dunnage wood on board if required) which the Charterers bind
themselves to ship, and being so loaded the vessel shall proceed
to ....

Destination.

....
....
....

as ordered on signing Bills of Lading or so near thereto as she
may safely get and lie always afloat and there deliver the cargo
on being paid freight—on $\frac{\text{delivered}}{\text{intaken}}$ quantity—as follows:

Rate of Freight.

....
....
....
....

Owners' Responsibility Clause.

2. Owners are to be responsible for loss of or damage to
the goods or for delay in delivery of the goods only in case
the loss, damage or delay has been caused by the improper
or negligent stowage of the goods (unless stowage performed
by shippers or their stevedores or servants) or by personal want
of due diligence on the part of the Owners or their Manager
to make the vessel in all respects seaworthy and to secure that
she is properly manned, equipped and supplied or by the personal act or default of the Owners or their Manager.

And the Owners are responsible for no loss or damage or
delay arising from any other cause whatsoever, even from the
neglect or default of the Captain or crew or some other person
employed by the Owners on board or ashore for whose acts

they would, but for this clause, be responsible, or from unseaworthiness of the vessel on loading or commencement of the voyage or at any time whatsoever.

Damage caused by contact with or leakage, smell or evaporation from other goods or by the inflammable or explosive nature or insufficient package of other goods not to be considered as caused by improper or negligent stowage, even if in fact so caused.

Deviation Clause.

3. The vessel has liberty to call at any port or ports in any order, for any purpose, to sail without pilots, to tow and/or assist vessels in all situations, and also to deviate for the purpose of saving life and/or property.

Payment of Freight.

4. The freight to be paid in cash without discount on delivery of the cargo at mean rate of exchange ruling on day or days of payment, the receivers of the cargo being bound to pay freight on account during delivery, if required, by Captain or Owners.

Cash for vessel's ordinary disbursements at port of loading to be advanced by Charterers if required at highest current rate of exchange, subject to two per cent. to cover insurance and other expenses.

Loading.

5. Cargo to be brought alongside in such a manner as to enable vessel to take the goods with her own tackle and to load the full cargo in.........running working days. Charterers to procure and pay the necessary men on shore or on board the lighters to do the work there, vessel only heaving the cargo on board.

If the loading takes place by elevator cargo to be put free in vessel's holds, Owners only paying trimming expenses.

Any pieces and/or packages of cargo over two tons weight, shall be loaded, stowed and discharged by Charterers at their risk and expense.

Time to commence at 1 p.m. if notice of readiness to load is given before noon and at 6 a.m. next working day if notice given during office hours after noon.

The notice to be given to the Shippers, Messrs.............
....
Time lost in waiting for berth to count as loading time.

Discharging.

6. Cargo to be received by Merchants at their risk and expense alongside the vessel not beyond the reach of her tackle and to be discharged in...................running working days. Time to commence at 1 p.m. if notice of readiness to discharge is given before noon, and at 6 a.m. next working day if notice given during office hours after noon.

Time lost in waiting for berth to count as discharging time.

Demurrage.

7. Ten running days on demurrage at the rate of......
............per day or pro rata for any part of a day, payable day by day, to be allowed Merchants altogether at ports of loading and discharging.

Lien Clause.

8. Owners shall have a lien on the cargo for freight, deadfreight, demurrage and damages for detention. Charterers shall remain responsible for dead - freight and demurrage (including damages for detention), incurred at port of loading. Charterers shall also remain responsible for freight and demurrage (including damages for detention) incurred at port of discharge, but only to such extent as the Owners have been unable to obtain payment thereof by exercising the lien on the cargo.

**Bill of
Lading.**

9. The Captain to sign Bills of Lading at such rate of freight as presented without prejudice to this Charter-party, but should the freight by Bills of Lading amount to less than the total chartered freight the difference to be paid to the Captain in cash on signing Bills of Lading.

**Strike, War
and Ice Clauses.**

10. *Strike Clause, War Clauses and Ice Clauses as below.*

**Cancelling
Clause.**

11. Should the vessel not be ready to load (whether in berth or not) on or before the............Charterers have the option of cancelling this contract, such option to be declared, if demanded, at least 48 hours before vessel's expected arrival at port of loading. Should the vessel be delayed on account of average or otherwise, Charterers to be informed as soon as possible, and if the vessel is delayed for more than 10 days after the day she is stated to be expected ready to load, Charterers have the option of cancelling this contract, unless a cancelling date has been agreed upon.

**General
Average.**

12. General average to be settled according to York-Antwerp Rules, 1974, Proprietors of cargo to pay the cargo's share in the general expenses even if same have been necessitated through neglect or default of the Owner's servants (see Clause 2).

Indemnity.

13. Indemnity for non - performance of this Charter-party, proved damages, not exceeding estimated amount of Freight.

Agency.

14. In every case the Owner shall appoint his own broker or Agent both at the port of loading and the port of discharge.

Brokerage.

15. ....% brokerage on the freight earned is due to ....
....
In case of non-execution at least ⅓ of the brokerage on the estimated amount of freight and dead-freight to be paid by the Owners to the Brokers as indemnity for the latter's expenses and work. In case of more voyages the amount of indemnity to be mutually agreed.

GENERAL STRIKE CLAUSE

Neither Charterers nor Owners shall be responsible for the consequences of any strikes or lock-outs preventing or delaying the fulfilment of any obligations under this contract.

If there is a strike or lock-out affecting the loading of the cargo, or any part of it, when vessel is ready to proceed from her last port or at any time during the voyage to the port or ports of loading or after her arrival there, Captain or Owners may ask Charterers to declare, that they agree to reckon the laydays as if there were no strike or lock-out. Unless Charterers have given such declaration in writing (by telegram, if necessary) within 24 hours, Owners shall have the option of cancelling this contract. If part cargo has already been loaded, Owners must proceed with same (freight, payable on loaded quantity only) having liberty to complete with other cargo on the way for their own account.

If there is a strike or lock-out affecting the discharge of the cargo on or after vessel's arrival at or off port of discharge and same has not been settled within 48 hours, Receivers shall have the option of keeping vessel waiting until such strike or lock-out is at an end against paying half demurrage after expiration of the time provided for discharging, or of ordering the vessel to a safe port, where she can safely discharge without risk of being detained by strike or lock-out. Such orders to be given within 48 hours after Captain or Owners have given notice to Charterers of the strike or lock-out affecting the discharge. On delivery of the cargo at such port, all conditions of this

Charter-party and of the Bill of Lading shall apply and vessel shall receive the same freight as if she had discharged at the original port of destination, except that if the distance of the substituted port exceeds 100 nautical miles, the freight on the cargo delivered at the substituted port to be increased in proportion.

GENERAL WAR CLAUSE

If the nation under whose flag the vessel sails should be engaged in war and the safe navigation of the vessel should thereby be endangered either party to have the option of cancelling this contract, and if so cancelled, cargo already shipped shall be discharged either at the port of loading, or, if the vessel has commenced the voyage, at the nearest safe place at the risk and expense of the Charterers or Cargo-Owners.

If owing to outbreak of hostilities the goods loaded or to be loaded under this contract or part of them become contraband of war whether absolute or conditional or liable to confiscation or detention according to international law or the proclamation of any of the belligerent powers each party to have the option of cancelling this contract as far as such goods are concerned, and contraband goods already loaded to be then discharged either at the port of loading, or if the voyage has already commenced, at the nearest safe place at the expense of the Cargo-Owners. Owners to have the right to fill up with other goods instead of the contraband.

Should any port where the vessel has to load under this Charter be block-aded the contract to be null and void with regard to the goods to be shipped at such port.

No Bills of Lading to be signed for any blockaded port, and if the port of destination be declared blockaded after Bills of Lading have been signed, Owners shall discharge the cargo either at the port of loading, against payment of the expenses of discharge, if the ship has not sailed thence, or, if sailed at any safe port on the way as ordered by Shippers or if no order is given at the nearest safe place against payment of full freight.

GENERAL ICE CLAUSE
PORT OF LOADING

(a) In the event of the loading port being inaccessible by reason of ice when vessel is ready to proceed from her last port or at any time during the voyage or on vessel's arrival or in case frost sets in after vessel's arrival, the Captain for fear of being frozen in is at liberty to leave without cargo, and this Charter shall be null and void

(b) If during loading the Captain, for fear of vessel being frozen in, deems it advisable to leave, he has liberty to do so with what cargo he has on board and to proceed to any other port or ports with option of completing cargo for Owner's benefit for any port or ports including port of discharge. Any part cargo thus loaded under this Charter to be forwarded to destination at vessel's expense but against payment of freight, provided that no extra expenses be thereby caused to the Receivers, freight being paid on quantity delivered (in proportion if lump sum) all other conditions as per Charter.

(c) In case of more than one loading port, and if one or more of the ports are closed by ice, the Captain or Owners to be at liberty either to load the part cargo at the open port and fill up elsewhere for their own account as under section (b) or to declare the Charter null and void unless Charterers agree to load full cargo at the open port.

(d) This Ice Clause not to apply in the Spring.

PORT OF DISCHARGE

(a) Should ice (except in the Spring) prevent vessel from reaching port of discharge Receivers shall have the option of keeping the vessel waiting until the re-opening of navigation and paying demurrage, or of ordering the vessel to a safe and immediately accessible port where she can safely discharge without risk of detention by ice. Such orders to be given within 48 hours after Captain or Owners have given notice to Charterers of the impossibility of reaching port of destination.

(b) If during discharging the Captain for fear of vessel being frozen in deems it advisable to leave, he has liberty to do so with what cargo he has on board and to proceed to the nearest accessible port where she can safely discharge.

(c) On delivery of the cargo at such port, all conditions of the Bill of Lading shall apply and vessel shall receive the same freight as if she had discharged at the original port of destination, except that if the distance of the substituted port exceeds 100 nautical miles, the freight on the cargo delivered at the substituted port to be increased in proportion.

APPENDIX XII

THE BALTIC AND INTERNATIONAL MARITIME CONFERENCE UNIFORM TIME-CHARTER
(Box Layout 1974)
CODE NAME: "BALTIME 1989"

PART I

1. Shipbroker

2. Place and date

3. Owners/Place of business

4. Charterers/Place of business

5. Vessel's name

6. GRT/NRT

7. Class

8. Indicated horse power

9. Total tons d.w. (abt.) on Board of Trade summer freeboard

10. Cubic feet grain/bale capacity

11. Permanent bunkers (abt.)

12. Speed capability in knots (abt.) on a consumption in tons (abt.) of

13. Present position

14. Period of hire (Cl. 1)

15. Port of delivery (Cl. 1)

16. Time of delivery (Cl. 1)

822

17. (a) Trade limits (Cl. 2)

(b) Cargo exclusions specially agreed

18. Bunkers on re-delivery (state min. and max. quantity) (Cl. 5)

19. Charter hire (Cl. 6)

20. Hire payment (state currency, method and place of payment; also beneficiary and bank account) (Cl. 6)

21. Place or range of re-delivery (Cl. 7)

22. War (only to be filled in if Section (C) agreed) (Cl. 21)

23. Cancelling date (Cl. 22)

24. Place of arbitration (only to be filled in if place other than London agreed) (Cl. 23)

25. Brokerage commission and to whom payable (Cl. 25)

26. Numbers of additional clauses covering special provisions, if agreed

It is mutually agreed that this Contract shall be performed subject to the conditions contained in this Charter which shall include Part I as well as Part II. In the event of a conflict of conditions, the provisions of Part I shall prevail over those of Part II to the extent of such conflict.

Signature (Owners)

Signature (Charterers)

PART II
"BALTIME 1939" Uniform Time-Charter (Box Layout 1974)

It is agreed between the party mentioned in Box 3 as Owners of the Vessel named in Box 5 of the gross/net Register tonnage indicated in Box 6, classed as stated in Box 7 and of indicated horse power as stated in Box 8, carrying about the number of tons deadweight indicated in Box 9 on Board of Trade summer freeboard inclusive of bunkers, stores, provisions and boiler water, having as per builder's plan a cubic-feet grain/bale capacity as stated in Box 10, exclusive of permanent bunkers, which contain about the number of tons stated in Box 11, and fully loaded capable of steaming about the number of knots indicated in Box 12 in good weather and smooth water on a consumption of about the number of tons best Welsh coal or oil-fuel stated in Box 12, now in position as stated in Box 13 and the party mentioned as Charterers in Box 4, as follows:—

1. Period/Port of Delivery/Time of Delivery

The Owners let, and the Charterers hire the Vessel for a period of the number of calendar months indicated in Box 14 from the time (not a Sunday or a legal Holiday unless taken over) the Vessel is delivered and placed at the disposal of the Charterers between 9 a.m. and 6 p.m., or between 9 a.m. and 2 p.m. if on Saturday, at the port stated in Box 15 in such available berth where she can safely lie always afloat, as the Charterers may direct, she being in every way fitted for ordinary cargo service.

The Vessel to be delivered at the time indicated in Box 16.

2. Trade

The Vessel to be employed in lawful trades for the carriage of lawful merchandise only between good and safe ports or places where she can safely lie always afloat within the limits stated in Box 17.

No live stock nor injurious, inflammable or dangerous goods (such as acids, explosives, calcium carbide, ferro silicon, naphtha, motor spirit, tar, or any of their products) to be shipped.

3. Owners to Provide

The Owners to provide and pay for all provisions and wages, for insurance of the Vessel, for all deck and engine-room stores and maintain her in a thoroughly efficient state in hull and machinery during service.

The Owners to provide one winchman per hatch. If further winchmen are required, or if the stevedores refuse or are not permitted to work with the Crew, the Charterers to provide and pay qualified shore-winchmen.

4. Charterers to Provide

The Charterers to provide and pay for all coals, including galley coal, oil-fuel, water for boilers, port charges, pilotages (whether compulsory or not), canal steersmen, boatage, lights, tug-assistance, consular charges (except those pertaining to the Master, Officers and Crew), canal, dock and other dues and charges, including any foreign general municipality or state taxes, also all dock, harbour and tonnage dues at the ports of delivery and re-delivery (unless incurred through cargo carried before delivery or after re-delivery), agencies, commissions, also to arrange and pay for loading, trimming, stowing (including dunnage and shifting boards, excepting any already on board), unloading, weighing, tallying and delivery of cargoes, surveys on hatches, meals supplied to officials and men in their service and all other charges and expenses whatsoever including detention and expenses through quarantine (including cost of fumigation and disinfection).

All ropes, slings and special runners actually used for loading and discharging and any special gear, including special ropes, hawsers and chains required by the custom of the port for mooring to be for the Charterers' account. The

Vessel to be fitted with winches, derricks, wheels and ordinary runners capable of handling lifts up to 2 tons.

5. Bunkers

The Charterers at port of delivery and the Owners at port of re-delivery to take over and pay for all coal or oil-fuel remaining in the Vessel's bunkers at current price at the respective ports.

The Vessel to be re-delivered with not less than the number of tons and not exceeding the number of tons of coal or oil-fuel in the Vessel's bunkers stated in Box 18.

6. Hire

The Charterers to pay as hire the rate stated in Box 19 per 30 days, commencing in accordance with Clause 1 until her re-delivery to the Owners.

Payment

Payment of hire to be made in cash, in the currency stated in Box 20, without discount, every 30 days, in advance, and in the manner prescribed in Box 20.

In default of payment the Owners to have the right of withdrawing the Vessel from the service of the Charterers, without noting any protest and without interference by any court or any other formality whatsoever and without prejudice to any claim the Owners may otherwise have on the Charterers under the Charter.

7. Re-delivery

The Vessel to be re-delivered on the expiration of the Charter in the same good order as when delivered to the Charterers (fair wear and tear excepted) at an ice-free port in the Charterers' option at the place or within the range stated in Box 21, between 9 a.m. and 6 p.m., and 9 a.m. and 2 p.m. on Saturday, but the day of re-delivery shall not be a Sunday or legal Holiday.

Notice

The Charterers to give the Owners not less than ten days' notice at which port and on about which day the Vessel will be re-delivered.

Should the Vessel be ordered on a voyage by which the Charter period will be exceeded the Charterers to have the use of the Vessel to enable them to complete the voyage, provided it could be reasonably calculated that the voyage would allow re-delivery about the time fixed for the termination of the Charter, but for any time exceeding the termination date the Charterers to pay the market rate if higher than the rate stipulated herein.

8. Cargo Space

The whole reach and burthen of the Vessel, including lawful deck-capacity to be at the Charterers' disposal, reserving proper and sufficient space for the Vessel's Master, Officers, Crew, tackle, apparel, furniture, provisions and stores.

9. Master

The Master to prosecute all voyages with the utmost despatch and to render customary assistance with the Vessel's Crew. The Master to be under the orders of the Charterers as regards employment, agency, or other arrangements. The Charterers to indemnify the Owners against all consequences or liabilities arising from the Master, Officers or Agents signing Bills of Lading or other documents or otherwise complying with such orders, as well as from any irregularity in the Vessel's papers or for overcarrying goods. The Owners not to be responsible for shortage, mixture, marks, nor for number of pieces or packages, nor for damage to or claims on cargo caused by bad stowage or otherwise.

If the Charterers have reason to be dissatisfied with the conduct of the Master, Officers, or Engineers, the Owners, on receiving particulars of the complaint, promptly to investigate the matter, and, if necessary and practicable, to make a change in the appointments.

10. Directions and Logs

The Charterers to furnish the Master with all instructions and sailing directions and the Master and Engineer to keep full and correct logs accessible to the Charterers or their Agents.

11. Suspension of Hire etc.

(a) In the event of drydocking or other necessary measures to maintain the efficiency of the Vessel, deficiency of men or Owners' stores, breakdown of machinery, damage to hull or other accident, either hindering or preventing the working of the Vessel and continuing for more than 24 consecutive hours, no hire to be paid in respect of any time lost thereby during the period in which the Vessel is unable to perform the service immediately required. Any hire paid in advance to be adjusted accordingly.

(b) In the event of the Vessel being driven into port or to anchorage through stress of weather, trading to shallow harbours or to rivers or ports with bars or suffering an accident to her cargo, any detention of the Vessel and/or expenses resulting from such detention to be for the Charterers' account even if such detention and/or expenses, or the cause by reason of which either is incurred, be due to, or be contributed to by, the negligence of the Owners' servants.

12. Cleaning Boilers

Cleaning of boilers whenever possible to be done during service, but if impossible the Charterers to give the Owners necessary time for cleaning. Should the Vessel be detained beyond 48 hours hire to cease until again ready.

13. Responsibility and Exemption

The Owners only to be responsible for delay in delivery of the Vessel or for delay during the currency of the Charter and for loss or damage to goods on board, if such delay or loss has been caused by want of due diligence on the part of the Owners or their Manager in making the Vessel seaworthy and fitted for the boyage or any other personal act or omission or default of the Owners or their Manager. The Owners not to be responsible in any other case nor for damage or delay whatsoever and howsoever caused even if caused by the neglect or default of their servants. The Owners not to be liable for loss or damage arising or resulting from strikes, lockouts or stoppage or restraint of labour (including the Master, Officers or Crew) whether partial or general.

The Charterers to be responsible for loss or damage caused to the Vessel or to the Owners by goods being loaded contrary to the terms of the Charter or by improper or careless bunkering or loading, stowing or discharging of goods or any other improper or negligent act on their part or that of their servants.

14. Advances

The Charterers or their Agents to advance to the Master, if required, necessary funds for ordinary disbursements for the Vessel's account at any port charging only interest at 6 per cent. p.a., such advances to be deducted from hire.

15. Excluded Parts

The Vessel not to be ordered to nor bound to enter:

(a) any place where fever or epidemics are prevalent or to which the Master, Officers and Crew by law are not bound to follow the Vessel.

Ice

(b) any ice-bound place or any place where lights, lightships, marks and buoys are or are likely to be withdrawn by reason of ice on the Vessel's arrival or where there is risk that ordinarily the Vessel will not be able on account of ice to reach the place or to get out after having completed loading or discharging. The Vessel not to be obliged to force ice. If **on**

account of ice the Master considers it dangerous to remain at the loading
or discharging place for fear of the Vessel being frozen in and/or damaged, he has liberty to sail to a convenient open place and await the
Charterers' fresh instructions.

Unforeseen detention through any of above causes to be for the Charterers'
account.

16. Loss of Vessel

Should the Vessel be lost or missing, hire to cease from the date when she
was lost. If the date of loss cannot be ascertained half hire to be paid from
the date the Vessel was last reported until the calculated date of arrival at the
destination. Any hire paid in advance to be adjusted accordingly.

17. Overtime

The Vessel to work day and night if required. The Charterers to refund
the Owners their outlays for all overtime paid to Officers and Crew according
to the hours and rates stated in the Vessel's articles.

18. Lien

The Owners to have a lien upon all cargoes and sub-freights belonging to
the Time-Charterers and any Bill of Lading freight for all claims under this
Charter, and the Charterers to have a lien on the Vessel for all moneys paid in
advance and not earned.

19. Salvage

All salvage and assistance to other vessels to be for the Owners' and the
Charterers' equal benefit after deducting the Master's and Crew's proportion
and all legal and other expenses including hire paid under the charter for time
lost in the salvage, also repairs of damage and coal or oil-fuel consumed. The
Charterers to be bound by all measures taken by the Owners in order to secure
payment of salvage and to fix its amount.

20. Sublet

The Charterers to have the option of subletting the Vessel, giving due
notice to the Owners, but the original Charterers always to remain responsible
to the Owners for due performance of the Charter.

21. War

(a) The Vessel unless the consent of the Owners be first obtained not to be
ordered nor continue to any place or on any voyage nor be used on any
service which will bring her within a zone which is dangerous as the
result of any actual or threatened act of war, war hostilities, warlike
operations, acts of piracy or of hostility or malicious damage against
this or any other vessel or its cargo by any person, body or State
whatsoever, revolution, civil war, civil commotion or the operation of
international law, nor be exposed in any way to any risks or penalties
whatsoever consequent upon the imposition of Sanctions, nor carry any
goods that may in any way expose her to any risks of seizure, capture,
penalties or any other interference of any kind whatsoever by the
beligerent or fighting powers or parties or by any Government or Ruler.

(b) Should the Vessel approach or be brought or ordered within such zone,
or be exposed in any way to the said risks, (1) the Owners to be entitled
from time to time to insure their interests in the Vessel and/or hire
against any of the risks likely to be involved thereby on such terms as
they shall think fit, the Charterers to make a refund to the Owners of
the premium on demand; and (2) notwithstanding the terms of Clause 11
hire to be paid for all time lost including any lost owing to loss of or
injury to the Master, Officers, or Crew or to the action of the Crew in
refusing to proceed to such zone or to be exposed to such risks.

(c) In the event of the wages of the Master, Officers and/or Crew or the cost of provisions and/or stores for deck and/or engine room and/or insurance premiums being increased by reason of or during the existence of any of the matters mentioned in section (a) the amount of any increase to be added to the hire and paid by the Charterers on production of the Owners' account therefor, such account being rendered monthly.

(d) The Vessel to have liberty to comply with any orders or directions as to departure, arrival, routes, ports of call, stoppages, destination, delivery or in any other wise whatsoever given by the Government of the nation under whose flag the Vessel sails or any other Government or any person (or body) acting or purporting to act with the authority of such Government or by any committee or person having under the terms of the war risks insurance on the Vessel the right to give any such orders or directions.

(e) In the event of the nation under whose flag the Vessel sails becoming involved in war, hostilities, warlike operations, revolution, or civil commotion, both the Owners and the Charterers may cancel the Charter and, unless otherwise agreed, the Vessel to be re-delivered to the Owners at the port of destination or, if prevented through the provisions of section (a) from reaching or entering it, then at a near open and safe port at the Owners' option, after discharge of any cargo on board.

(f) If in compliance with the provisions of this clause anything is done or is not done, such not to be deemed a deviation.

Section (c) is optional and should be considered deleted unless agreed according to Box 22.

22. Cancelling

Should the Vessel not be delivered by the date indicated in Box 23, the Charterers to have the option of cancelling.

If the Vessel cannot be delivered by the cancelling date, the Charterers, if required, to declare within 48 hours after receiving notice thereof whether they cancel or will take delivery of the Vessel.

23. Arbitration

Any dispute arising under the Charter to be referred to arbitration in London (or such other place as may be agreed according to Box 24), one Arbitrator to be nominated by the Owners and the other by the Charterers, and in case the Arbitrators shall not agree then to the decision of an Umpire to be appointed by them, the award of the Arbitrators or the Umpire to be final and binding upon both parties.

24. General Average

General Average to be settled according to York/Antwerp Rules, 1974. Hire not to contribute to General Average.

25. Commission

The Owners to pay a commission at the rate stated in Box 25 to the party mentioned in Box 25 on any hire paid under the Charter, but in no case less than is necessary to cover the actual expenses of the Brokers and a reasonable fee for their work. If the full hire is not paid owing to breach of Charter by either of the parties, the party liable therefor to indemnify the Brokers against their loss of commission.

Should the parties agree to cancel the Charter, the Owners to indemnify the Brokers against any loss of commission but in such case the commission not to exceed the brokerage on one year's hire.

APPENDIX XIII

" INTERTANKVOY 76 "

TANKER VOYAGE CHARTER PARTY

It is this day............, 19...... mutually agreed between........................
.... of ....
OWNERS/CHARTERED OWNERS/DISPONENT OWNERS (hereinafter
called "Owners") of the motor/turbine tank vessel called ....
(hereinafter called "the vessel") flying the .... flag and ....
.... of ....
(hereinafter called "Charterers") that the transportation(s) herein provided
for will be performed subject to the terms and conditions of this Charter Party
which includes Part I and Part II.

PART I

(a) Description of the vessel:
Classed ....
Deadweight ....metric/long tons (of 2240 lbs) on a saltwater draft
on summer marks of ....
Length overall .... m/ft. Beam extreme .... m/ft. Capacity
available for cargo ....metric/long tons, ... per cent more or less
at Owners' option.
Cubic capacity for cargo ....m³/cu.ft. (at 100%) including ....
slop tank(s) with a cubic capacity of ....m³/cu.ft. (at 100%).
Last cargo before commencement of this Charter Party:

....
Penultimate cargo: ....
Owners undertake that the vessel is:
Fitted with heating coils in good working order in .... cargo tanks
and capable of maintaining a temperature of the cargo when loaded not
in excess of .... degrees Fahrenheit/Centigrade.
Equipped with .... cargo pumps with an aggregate maximum
capacity of ....m³/tons fresh water per hour against a back-pressure
of .... at ship's rail.
Equipped with .... derricks with a maximum safe working load of
.... tons each for lifting submarine hoses to the vessel's port and
starboard manifolds.
Internal tank coating as follows ....
....

(b) Present position of the vessel ....
Expected readiness to load ....
Commitments prior to commencement of this Charter Party ....
....
Owners undertake to keep Charterers currently informed as to the vessel's
position and any change of the vessel's expected readiness to load.

(c) Description of cargo: ....
....
Unless otherwise stated above this Charter Party is for a full and complete
cargo having regard to the permissible freeboard for the voyage in
accordance with the International Loadline regulations currently in force

and *to* the limitations provided in (a) above.

No cargo shall be shipped which is injurious to the vessel.

No cargo shall be shipped having a Vapour Pressure at 100 degrees Fahrenheit in excess of **13·5**/ ....lbs/sq.in. as determined by the current A.S.T.M. Method (Reid) D. 323.

(d) Loading range ....
....
Discharging range ....
....

(e) Laydays shall not commence before .... unless with Charterers' consent.

(f) Cancelling date ....

(g) Laytime .... running hours Sundays and holidays included.

(h) Freight rate shall be ...... per cent of the applicable rate of Worldscale in force at the date of commencement of loading.

(i) Freight shall be due and payable:
(at the time of) ....
(place) ....
(payee) ....
....

(j) Demurrage rate based on the vessel's summer deadweight shall be ...... per cent of the Worldscale rate in force at the date of commencement of loading.

(k) All other terms and conditions of Worldscale in force at the date of commencement of loading shall apply.

(l) General average shall be adjusted in...

(m) Arbitration shall take place in London in accordance with Part II, Clause 32 and this Charter Party shall be governed by English Law.

(n) Special provisions:

" INTERTANKVOY 76 "

PART II

1. Condition of Vessel

The vessel's class as specified in Part I shall be maintained during the currency of this Charter Party.

The Owners shall

    (a) before and at the beginning of the loaded voyage exercise due diligence to make the vessel seaworthy and in every way fit for the voyage, with her tanks, valves, pumps and pipelines tight, staunch, strong and in good order and condition and with a full and efficient complement of master, officers and crew for a vessel of her type, tonnage and flag;

    (b) throughout the voyage have the responsibilities and immunities of the Hague Rules as incorporated in Clause 25 hereof.

2. Nomination/Renomination

The necessary loading orders shall be given by Charterers before the vessel sails from her previous port or place of call (or concurrently with the fixture of this Charter Party if the vessel has already sailed) but Charterers shall have the option of ordering the vessel to a safe port or place en route to loading or discharging ranges for orders.

If Charterers exercise such option they shall nominate actual loading or discharging port or place in sufficient time to avoid delay to or deviation of the vessel.

If after loading or discharging port or place have been nominated, Charterers desire to vary them, Owners agree to issue such revised instructions as are necessary to give effect to Charterers' revised orders.

Charterers shall reimburse Owners for any expenses resulting from any such revision of orders including additional bunkers consumed at cost price where and when bunkers are next taken. Charterers shall pay for loss of time caused by such revision at the rate of demurrage stipulated in Part I (j) less the value of the vessel's daily bunkers consumption in port at cost price. Charterers shall indemnify Owners for any claim brought against Owners by reason of such deviation, including all legal costs and expenses.

Charterers shall not be liable for any other loss resulting from Charterers revising their orders, unless upon receiving the new orders Owners promptly notify Charterers that such other loss may occur. Unless Charterers then give new orders which will avoid such other loss it shall when proved be recoverable from Charterers.

3. Voyage

The vessel shall proceed with all convenient despatch as soon as her prior commitments, as specified in Part I (b) are completed, to a berth, dock, anchorage, submarine line, alongside a lighter or lighters or any other place as ordered by Charterers within the limits specified in Part I (d), or so near thereto as she may safely get, lie and depart from, and there load, always afloat, the cargo as described in Part I (c) and being so loaded shall proceed as ordered on signing bills of lading direct to a berth, dock, anchorage, submarine line, alongside a lighter or lighters or any other place as ordered by Charterers within the limits specified in Part I (d) or so near thereto as she may safely get and lie, and there deliver the cargo always afloat. Should it appear that the aforesaid conditions for ship and cargo are not fulfilled, the ship shall not be obliged to proceed.

Charterers shall exercise due diligence to ascertain that any places to which they order the vessel are safe for the vessel and that she will lie there always afloat. Charterers shall, however, not be deemed to warrant the safety of any place and shall be under no liability in respect thereof except for loss or damage caused by their failure to exercise due diligence as aforesaid.

Transfer of oil from and to the vessel to and from another ocean-going ship made fast alongside or while under way shall be allowed in accordance with the ICS/OCIMF Ship to Ship Transfer Guide and under the conditions for lighterage in Clause 18, provided Owners have been given reasonable notice in advance and only to the extent such operation is safe. All extra equipment required for such transfer operation shall be provided by Charterers who undertake to reimburse Owners any additional insurance premiums.

4. Disposal of Residues

Owners shall ensure that the vessel's personnel will:

(a) During the ballast passage and before presenting for loading hereunder, retain on board all oil residues remaining in the vessel from her previous cargo;

(b) during tank washing collect the washings into a separate compartment and, after maximum separation of free water, discharge such water overboard;

(c) thereafter notify Charterers as soon as possible through Owners of the amounts of oil and water in the segregated tank washings.

On the vessel's arrival at or off loading port or place, Charterers shall provide facilities for the reception of any such tank washings, the cost of such facilities and the ultimate disposal of the tank washings being for Charterers' account. Any delay in the provision of the necessary facilities shall count as laytime.

Should Charterers fail to provide facilities for the reception of part or all of the tank washings remaining on board, freight shall be payable thereon as specified in Part I (h) up to a maximum tonnage equivalent to 1% (one per cent) of the vessel's deadweight on tropical marks, the water contained in such tank washings not to exceed $0 \cdot 15\%$ of such deadweight.

Should Charterers require segregation of the cargo to be loaded from the tank washings remaining on board they shall pay any deadfreight so incurred.

5. Cleaning

The Master is bound to keep the tanks, pipes and pumps of the vessel suitable for the cargo specified in Part I (c). For clean cargoes, cleaning shall be effected to Charterers' inspector's satisfaction.

The vessel shall not be responsible for any admixture if more than one quality of oil is shipped, nor for leakage, contamination or deterioration in quality of the cargo unless the admixture, leakage, contamination or deterioration results from (a) unseaworthiness existing at the time of loading or at the inception of the voyage which was discoverable by the exercise of due diligence, or (b) error or fault of the servants of Owners in the loading, care or discharge of the cargo.

6. Charterers' Option of Cancelling

If the vessel has not given a valid notice of readiness as provided in Clause 8 by 12 midnight (2400 hours) local time on the cancelling date specified in Part I (f), Charterers shall have the option of cancelling this Charter Party, unless the vessel has been delayed due to ice risks as mentioned in Clauses 21 and 22 or to Charterers' revision of orders under Clause 2, in which cases the cancelling date shall be extended by any time so lost. Whether or not Charterers exercise their option of cancelling no claim they may have on Owners shall be prejudiced thereby.

Nevertheless, if it clearly appears that despite due diligence on the part of Owners the vessel will be delayed beyond the cancelling date Owners may, at the earliest 72 hours before the vessel is to sail for the loading port or place and as soon as they are in a position to state—with reasonable certainty—a new readiness date, ask Charterers whether or not they will exercise their option of cancelling. The option must then be declared within 7 days thereafter but not later than one day after the cancelling date. If Charterers do not cancel the Charter Party within such time limit, the seventh day after the new readiness date stated shall be the new cancelling date unless otherwise agreed.

7. Owners' Option of Cancelling

If for reasons not attributable to the vessel and/or Owners
(a) Charterers fail in their duty to furnish voyage instructions or loading orders in accordance with Clause 2, and such failure has lasted for not less than 10 days,
    or
(b) loading has not commenced and 20 days have passed after valid notice of readiness has been tendered,
Owners shall have the option of cancelling this Charter Party.

If such option is exercised and the delay is attributable to Charterers, they shall be liable for loss of charter. Whether or not Owners exercise this option no claim they may have on Charterers for loss of time or otherwise shall be prejudiced thereby.

8. Notice of Readiness

When the vessel has arrived at a loading or discharging port or place, or at a usual waiting place off such port or place if vessel cannot enter or berth by reason of any cause beyond the control of Owners, and the vessel is ready to load or discharge, a notice of readiness, which may be tendered at any time on any day of the year, shall be given to Charterers or their agent. The vessel shall be deemed ready within the meaning of this clause whether or not she has ballast water or residues or washings in her tanks.

Subject to Part I (e) laytime shall commence at the first loading and discharging port or place at the expiration of six running hours after tendering such notice or upon connection of hoses, whichever first occurs.

At subsequent port or place laytime shall resume when notice of readiness is tendered.

9. Laytime

The running hours specified in Part I (g) shall be allowed Charterers for the loading and discharging of the cargo and other Charterers' purposes connected therewith.

If Charterers, suppliers, consignees or the regulations of the port authorities prohibit loading or discharging at night, time so lost shall count as laytime.

Laytime shall count until the hoses have been disconnected or until Charterers or their agents have fulfilled their obligation to produce any necessary documents, whichever is the later.

Time lost by any of the following causes shall not count for laytime or for demurrage even if the vessel is already on demurrage:

(a) waiting for pilot or tugs, or while moving from anchorage to place of loading or discharging;

(b) cleaning of tanks, discharging of ballast water, residues or washings;

(c) stoppages on the vessel's orders or breakdown or inefficiency of the vessel, or negligence or default on the part of Owners or their servants or agents or a strike of the crew.

10. Demurrage

Charterers shall pay demurrage at the rate specified in Part I (j).

If, however, demurrage is incurred due to any of the events set out below which commences or occurs before the expiry of the allowed laytime, the rate of demurrage shall be reduced to one-half until the said event ceases:

(a) fire, explosion or breakdown of machinery at shore installation not caused by negligence on the part of Charterers or the shippers or the receivers or their servants or agents;

(b) or any of the exceptions set out in the last sentence of Clause 25 (save for quarantine as provided in Clause 23).

11. Loading and Discharging

(a) The cargo shall be loaded into the vessel at the expense of and at the risk and peril of Charterers as far as the vessel's permanent hose connections only, and shall be pumped out of the vessel at the expense of and at the risk and peril of the vessel as far as the vessel's permanent hose connections only.

Hoses for loading and discharging shall be furnished by Charterers and shall be connected and disconnected by Charterers or, at the option of Charterers, by Owners at Charterers' risk and expense.

The vessel shall provide her pumps and the necessary motive power for discharging in all ports where regulations so permit, as well as the necessary personnel, but if shore regulations do not permit fire on board and steam is necessary for discharging purposes, Charterers shall supply such steam at their expense.

(b) Overtime: Loading and discharging may be carried out at any time on any day of the year, Charterers paying all extra expenses, including overtime, incurred ashore only.

12. Freight Payment

Freight shall be paid at the rate specified in Part I (h), and calculated on the intaken quantity of cargo, plus any residues or washings remaining on board as specified in Clause 4, no deduction being made for water and/or sediment contained in the cargo. Payment of freight as specified in Part I (i) shall be made by Charterers in cash without discount.

13. Deadfreight

Should Charterers or their agents fail to supply a cargo as specified in Part I (c), deadfreight shall be payable, but in no event shall Charterers be required to furnish cargo in excess of the quantity stated in Part I (a) as the vessel's capacity for cargo.

14. Slack Tanks

The vessel shall not be required to proceed to sea until such of her tanks are filled as will place her in a seaworthy condition.

15. Lien

Owners shall have a lien on the cargo for all claims under this Charter Party and costs of recovering same.

16. Dues and other Charges

Dues, taxes and other charges upon the vessel, including those assessed with reference to the quantity of cargo loaded or discharged shall be paid by Owners, and dues and other charges upon the cargo and taxes on the freight shall be paid by Charterers. However, irrespective of the foregoing, where under a provision of Worldscale any such dues and charges are expressly for the account of Owners or Charterers, then they shall be payable in accordance therewith.

17. Shifting

Charterers shall have the right to load and/or discharge at more than one berth at each port or place on payment of all expenses incurred in moving the vessel from the first to the second and any subsequent berth or place, including any extra bunkers consumed whilst shifting and any dues incurred in excess of those which would have been incurred if all the cargo had been loaded or discharged at the first berth or place only. Time used in shifting between berths or places shall count as laytime.

18. Lighterage

Any lighterage shall be at the expense, risk and peril of Charterers and any time lost to the vessel on account of lighterage shall count as laytime. Lighterage shall be effected only in port or place where the vessel can continuously lie safely always afloat, and Charterers shall indemnify Owners against the consequences of any spillage of cargo not due to the negligence of officers, master or crew of the vessel.

19. Heating

When heating of cargo is required by Charterers in accordance with Part I (a), Owners shall exercise due diligence to maintain the temperature requested on passage to and whilst at the discharging port or place.

20. Liberty

The vessel shall have liberty to sail with or without pilots to tow or go to the assistance of vessels in distress, to call at any port or place for oil fuel supplies, and to deviate for the purpose of saving life or property, or for any other reasonable purpose whatsoever.

21. Ice on Voyage

In case port or place of loading or discharge should be inaccessible owing to ice, the vessel shall direct her course according to Master's judgment, notifying by telegraph or radio, if available, Charterers, the shipper or consignee, who is bound to telegraph or radio orders for another port, which is free from ice and where there are facilities for the loading or reception of the cargo in bulk. The whole of the time occupied from the time the vessel is diverted by reason of the ice until her arrival at an ice-free port of loading or discharge, as the case may be, shall be paid for by Charterers at the demurrage rate stipulated in Part I (j) plus the cost of actual consumption of bunkers less normal bunker consumption in port.

22. Ice at Loading/Discharge Port or Place

If, on account of ice, the Master considers it dangerous to enter or remain at any loading or discharging port or place for fear of the vessel being frozen in or damaged, the Master shall communicate by telegraph or radio, if available, with Charterers, the shipper or consignee of the cargo, who shall telegraph or radio him in reply, giving orders to proceed to another port or place as per Clause 21 where there is no danger of ice and where there are the necessary facilities for the loading or reception of the cargo in bulk, or to remain at the original port or place at their risk, and in either case Charterers to pay for the time that the vessel may be delayed, at the demurrage rate stipulated in Part I (j) plus the cost of actual consumption of bunkers less normal bunker consumption in port.

23. Quarantine

If at the time of nomination quarantine is in force at the nominated port or place of loading or discharging any time thereby lost by the vessel to count as laytime. If, however, quarantine comes into force at such port or place after nomination, only half the time thereby lost by the vessel shall count as laytime except that full time shall count for demurrage after the expiry of the laytime.

24. Agency

The vessel shall be addressed to Owners' agents at port(s) or place(s) of loading and discharging.

25. Responsibility and Immunities

The provisions of Articles III (other than Rule 8), IV, VIII and IX of the Carriage of Goods by Sea Act, 1924 of the United Kingdom shall apply to this Charter Party and shall be deemed to be inserted in extenso herein. This Charter Party shall be deemed to be a contract for the carriage of cargo by sea to which the said articles apply and Owners shall be entitled to the protection of the said articles in respect of any claim made hereunder. Charterers shall not, save to the extent otherwise in this Charter Party expressly provided, be responsible for any loss or damage or delay or failure in performance hereunder arising or resulting from Act of God; act of war; seizure under legal process; quarantine restrictions; strikes; boycotts; lockouts; riots; civil commotions; and arrest or restraint of princes, rulers or peoples.

26. Both to Blame Clause

If the liability for any collision in which the vessel is involved while performing this Charter Party falls to be determined in accordance with the laws of the United States of America, the following clause shall apply:

"If the vessel comes into collision with another vessel as a result of the negligence of the other vessel and/or any act, neglect or default of the Master, mariner, pilot or the servants of Owners in the navigation or in the management of the vessel, the owners of the cargo hereunder will indemnify Owners against all loss or liability to the other or non-carrying vessel or her owners in so far as such loss or liability represents loss of, or damage to, or any claim whatsoever of the owners of the said cargo, paid or payable by the other or non-carrying vessel or her owners to the owners of the said cargo and set off, recouped or recovered by the other or non-carrying vessel or her owners as part of their claim against the carrying vessels or Owners.

The foregoing provisions shall also apply where the owners, operators or those in charge of any vessel or vessels or objects other than, or in addition to, the colliding vessels or objects are at fault in respect to a collision or contact."

and Charterers shall procure that all bills of lading issued under this Charter Party shall contain this clause.

27. General Average: New Jason Clause

General average shall be payable according to the York/Antwerp Rules, 1974, but if, notwithstanding the provisions specified in Part I (l), the adjustment is made in accordance with the law and practice of the United States of America, the following clause shall apply:

"In the event of accident, danger, damage or disaster before or after the commencement of the voyage, resulting from any cause whatsoever, whether due to negligence or not, for which, or for the consequence of which, Owners are not responsible, by statute, contract or otherwise, the cargo, shippers, consignees or owners of the cargo shall contribute with Owners in general average to the payment of any sacrifices, loss or expenses of a general average nature that may be made or incurred and shall pay salvage and special charges incurred in respect of the cargo.

If a salving vessel is owned or operated by Owners, salvage shall be paid for as fully as if the said salving vessel or vessels belonged to strangers. Such deposit as Owners, or their agents, may seem sufficient to cover the estimated contribution of the cargo and any salvage and special charges thereon shall, if required, be made by the cargo, shippers, consignees or owners of the cargo to Owners before delivery."

and Charterers shall procure that all bills of lading issued under this Charter Party shall contain this clause.

28. Paramount Clause

Charterers shall procure that all bills of lading issued pursuant to this Charter Party shall contain the following Paramount Clause:

"This bill of lading shall:

(a) in relation to the carriage of any cargo from any port in Great Britain or Northern Ireland to any other port whether in or outside Great Britain or Northern Ireland have effect subject to the provisions of the Carriage of Goods by Sea Act, 1924, of the United Kingdom (or any statutory modification or re-enactment thereof), and to the Rules contained in the Schedule thereto as applied by that Act and nothing herein contained shall be deemed a surrender by Owners of any of their rights or immunities or an increase of any of their responsibilities or liabilities under the said Act;

(b) in relation to the carriage of any cargo from any port of shipment in territory in which legislation similar in effect to the Carriage of Goods by Sea Act, 1924, of the United Kingdom (or any statutory modification or re-enactment thereof), is in force have effect subject to such legislation and to the Rules contained in the Schedule thereto as applied by such legislation and nothing herein contained shall be deemed to be a surrender by Owners of any of their rights or immunities under the said legislation or an increase of any of their responsibilities or liabilities under the said legislation; and

(c) in any other case have effect as if the contract of carriage herein contained were a contract of carriage to which the provisions of the Carriage of Goods by Sea Act, 1924, of the United Kingdom (or any statutory modification or re-enactment thereof) applied and Owners shall be entitled to the benefit of the privileges, rights and immunities conferred by the said Act and the Rules contained in the Schedule thereto as if the same were herein specifically set out.

If any terms of this bill of lading be repugnant to the provisions of the said Act or to the said legislation to any extent, such term shall be void to that extent but no further."

29. War Risks

(a) The Master shall not be required or bound to sign bills of lading for any blockaded port or for any port which the Master or Owners in his or their discretion consider dangerous or impossible to enter or reach.

(*b*) If any port of loading or of discharge named in this Charter Party or to which the vessel may properly be ordered pursuant to the terms of the bills of lading be blockaded, or

If owing to any war, hostilities, warlike operations, civil war, civil commotions, revolutions, or the operation of international law (1) entry to any such port of loading or of discharge or the loading or discharge of cargo at any such port be considered by the Master or Owners in his or their discretion dangerous or prohibited, or (2) it be considered by the Master or Owners in his or their discretion dangerous or impossible for the vessel to reach any such port of loading or of discharge Charterers shall have the right to order the cargo or such part of it as may be affected to be loaded or discharged at any other safe port of loading or of discharge within the range of loading or discharging ports respectively established under the provisions of the Charter Party (provided such other port is not blockaded or that entry thereto or loading or discharge of cargo thereat is not in the Master's or Owners' discretion dangerous or prohibited). If in respect of a port of discharge no orders be received from Charterers within 48 hours after they or their agents have received from Owners a request for the nomination of a substitute port, Owners shall then be at liberty to discharge the cargo at any safe port which they or the Master may in their or his discretion decide on (whether within the range of discharging ports established under the provisions of the Charter Party or not) and such discharge shall be deemed to be due fulfilment of the contract or contracts of affreightment so far as cargo so discharged is concerned. In the event of the cargo being loaded or discharged at any such other port within the respective range of loading or discharging ports established under the provisions of the Charter Party, the Charter Party shall be read in respect of freight and all other conditions whatsoever as if the voyage performed were that originally designated. In the event, however, that the vessel discharges the cargo at a port outside the range of discharging ports established under the provisions of the Charter Party, freight shall be paid as for the voyage originally designated and all extra expenses involved in reaching the actual port of discharge and/or discharging the cargo thereat shall be paid by Charterers or cargo owners. In this latter event Owners shall have a lien on the cargo for all such extra expenses.

(*c*) The vessel shall have liberty to comply with any directions or recommendations as to departure, arrival, routes, ports of call, stoppages, destinations, zones, waters, delivery or in any otherwise whatsoever given by the government of the nation under whose flag the vessel sails or any other government or local authority including any de facto government or local authority or by any person or body acting or purporting to act as or with the authority of any such government or authority or by any committee or person having under the terms of the war risks insurance on the vessel the right to give any such directions or recommendations. If by reason of or in compliance with any such directions or recommendations, anything is done or is not done such shall not be deemed a deviation.

If by reason of or in compliance with any such direction or recommendation the vessel does not proceed to the port or ports of discharge originally designated or to which she may have been ordered pursuant to the terms of the bills of lading, the vessel may proceed to any safe port of discharge which the Master or Owners in his or their discretion may decide on and there discharge the cargo. Such discharge shall be deemed to be due fulfilment of the contract or contracts of affreightment and Owners shall be entitled to freight as if discharge has been effected at the port or ports originally designated or to which the vessel may have been ordered pursuant to the terms of the bills of lading. All extra expenses involved in reaching and discharging the cargo at any such other port of discharge shall be paid by Charterers and/or cargo owners and Owners shall have a lien on the cargo for freight and all such expenses.

Charterers are to procure that all bills of lading issued under this Charter Party shall contain this clause.

30. TOVALOP

The vessel to be entered into TOVALOP and the current P. & I. Clubs' Recommended TOVALOP Clause shall be deemed to be incorporated unless any other TOVALOP clause is attached hereto.

31. Bills of Lading

Bills of lading are to be signed as presented without prejudice to this Charter Party, and Charterers hereby indemnify Owners against all liabilities and expenses including legal costs that may arise from the signing of bills of lading as presented to the extent that the terms of such bills of lading are more onerous to Owners than are the terms of this Charter Party.

Neither Owners nor their servants shall be required to sign or endorse bills of lading showing freight prepaid until the freight due to Owners has actually been paid.

32. Arbitration

Any dispute or difference arising out of this Charter Party shall be referred to arbitration in London to the arbitrament of three persons, one to be appointed by each of the parties hereto and the third by the two so appointed; their decision, or that of any two of them, shall be final and binding upon the parties, and for the purpose of enforcing any award this agreement and any such award may be made a rule or order or judgment of the Court without the merits of the dispute or difference being re-opened.

33. Subletting/Assigning

Charterers shall have the liberty of subletting or assigning this Charter Party to any individual or company, but Charterers shall always remain responsible for the due fulfilment of all the terms and conditions of this Charter Party and shall warrant that any such sublet or assignment will not result in the vessel being restricted in her future trading.

BILL OF LADING

Code name: "INTANKBILL 78"

(1) PARAMOUNT CLAUSE

(*a*) The Hague Rules contained in the International Convention for the Unification of certain rules relating to Bills of Lading, dated Brussels the 25th August 1924 as enacted in the country of shipment shall apply to this contract. When no such enactment is in force in the country of shipment, the corresponding legislation of the country of destination shall apply, but in respect of shipments to which no such enactments are compulsorily applicable, the terms of the said Convention shall apply.

(*b*) In trades where the International Brussels Convention 1924 as amended by the Protocol signed at Brussels on February 23rd, 1968— The Hague-Visby Rules—apply compulsorily, the provisions of the respective legislation shall be considered incorporated in this Bill of Lading.

(*c*) In any event, as regards the period before loading and after discharge and while the cargo is in the charge of another carrier, the Carrier makes all reservations possible under such legislation.

(2) GENERAL AVERAGE

(*a*) General Average, if any, shall be adjusted, stated and settled in accordance with York-Antwerp Rules 1974, at the place agreed in the Charter Party, otherwise in London.

(*b*) Cargo's contribution to General Average shall be paid to the Carrier even when such average is the result of a fault, neglect or error of the Master, Pilot or the Crew. The Charterer, Shipper and Consignee expressly renounce the Netherlands Commercial Code, Art. 700, and the Belgian Commercial Code, Part II, Art. 148.

(*c*) If the adjustment of General Average or the liability for any collision in which the vessel is involved while performing the carriage under this Bill of Lading falls to be determined in accordance with the law and practice of the United States of America, the following clauses shall apply:

New Jason Clause

In the event of accident, danger, damage or disaster before or after the commencement of the voyage, resulting from any cause whatsoever, whether due to negligence or not, for which, or for the consequence of which, the Carrier is not responsible, by statute, contract or otherwise, the cargo, Shippers, Consignees or owners of the cargo shall contribute with the Carrier in General Average to the payment of any sacrifices, losses or expenses of a General Average nature that may be made or incurred and shall pay salvage and special charges incurred in respect of the cargo.

If a salving ship is owned or operated by the Carrier, salvage shall be paid for as fully as if the said salving ship or ships belonged to strangers. Such deposit as the Carrier or his Agents may deem sufficient to cover the estimated contribution of the cargo and any salvage and special charges thereon shall, if required, be made by the cargo, Shippers, Consignees or owners of the cargo to the Carrier before delivery.

Both-to-Blame Collision Clause

If the Vessel comes into collision with another ship as a result of the negligence of the other ship and any act, neglect or default of the Master, Mariner, Pilot or the servants of the Carrier in the navigation or in the management of the Vessel, the owners of the cargo carried hereunder will indemnify the Carrier against all loss or liability to the other or non-carrying ship or her Owners in so far as such loss or liability represents loss of, or damage to, or any claim whatsoever of the owners of said cargo, paid or payable by the other or non-carrying ship or her Owners to the owners of said cargo and set-off, recouped or recovered by the other or non-carrying ship or her Owners as part of their claim against the carrying Vessel or Carrier. The foregoing provisions shall also apply where the Owners, Operators or those in charge of any ship or ships or objects other than, or in addition to, the colliding ships or objects are at fault in respect of a collision or contact.

For the purpose of this Bill of Lading: SHIPPER means the person consigning the cargo for the carriage on Charterer's behalf; CHARTERER means the person entering the Charter Party contract with the Carrier; CARRIER is equivalent to terms like Shipowner, Owner, Chartered Owner, Disponent Owner, whichever is used in the Charter Party referred to in this Bill of Lading to define a person undertaking the carriage.

APPENDIX XIV

TANKER TIME CHARTER PARTY

IT IS THIS DAY ....19......, agreed between ....
....
of...
as Owners/Chartered Owners (hereinafter called "Owners") of the motor/
turbine tank vessel called ....
(hereinafter called "the vessel") flying the .... flag and
....
of...
(hereinafter called "Charterers") that the Owners will let and the Charterers
will hire the vessel for the period and upon the terms and conditions herein
contained.

PART I

(a) General Description of the vessel:
Subject to the details set out in the Technical Specification referred to in
Part II Clause I and attached to this Charter Party the vessel's main
characteristics shall be:
Class: .... Year Built...............
Deadweight: .... metric/long tons ....
on a saltwater draught on summer marks of ....
Total cargo tank capacity (100%):........................... m³ /cu.ft. ....
Length overall: ....m/ ....ft. ......in.
Beam extreme: ....m/ ....ft. ......in.
Heating coils: the vessel shall be fully coiled and capable of maintaining
cargo at a temperature of ....°C/°F...
Cargo pumps: the vessel shall be fitted with .... main cargo pumps.
Rated capacity of each pump shall be .... metric/long tons fresh
water per hour against a back pressure of .... kg./sq. cm./lb./sq. in.
at the vessel's cargo manifold.
Speed/Consumption: the average speed of the vessel will not be less than
.... knots when loaded and .... knots in ballast on an average
daily consumption of no more than .... metric/long tons of fuel oil
having a maximum viscosity of .... seconds Redwood No. 1 at
100°F/Centistokes at 50°C and .... metric/long tons diesel oil for
main engine and auxiliaries respectively excluding heating of cargo and
tank cleaning. (See Clause 23)

(b) Cargo:
The vessel is chartered for the purpose of carrying exclusively
....
....
No cargo shall be shipped having a Vapour Pressure at 100°F in excess
of 13·5/ .... lb./sq. in., as determined by the A.S.T.M. Method (Reid)
D. 323. (See Clause 29)
Owners shall not be responsible for admixture of oil and leakage if more
than ....grades or qualities are carried simultaneously. (See
Clause 25)

(c) Quantities of fuel oil and diesel oil on board on delivery and redelivery shall not be less than, fuel oil .... metric/long tons, diesel oil .... metric/long tons and shall not exceed, fuel oil .... metric/long tons and diesel oil .... metric/long tons. (See Clause 15)

(d) The vessel shall be delivered and redelivered with cargo tanks in a proper state for the carriage of .... petroleum products. (See Clause 2A)

(e) Period:

....

14 days more or less at Charterers' option. (See Clause 17B)

(f) Range/Place of Delivery ....

....in Owners' option.

Notice(s) to be given...

....

Earliest delivery date ....

Cancelling date .... (See Clause 2A)

(g) Range/Place of Redelivery ....

....

.... in Charterers' option.

Notice(s) to be given...

....

.... (See Clause 2B)

(h) Rate of hire ....

.... per metric/long ton on the vessel's total summer deadweight. (See Clause 3)

(i) Hire shall be due and payable in ....(currency)

at ....(place)

to ....(bank)

Account No. ....

for the credit of...

....(See Clause 3)

(j) Late Payment of Hire:
Notify ....

....

at...

....

Interest rate .... per cent per ....

....(See Clause 4)

(k) Sum for:
Overtime ....

Cables ....

Victualling ....

(See Clause 10)

(l) War cancellation/outbreak of war between two or more of the following countries ....

....

....

.... (See Clause 33E)

(m) Requisition (See Clause 32) ....

....

.... government.

(n) Period between periodical dry-dockings shall not be more than ....

.... and not less than ....

Vessel last dry-docked .... (See Clause 21)

(o) Place of Arbitration/Governing Law:
Arbitration shall take place in ....
....
This Charter Party shall be governed by ....
.... Law. (See Clause 37)
(p) Commission ....per cent
to..
.... (See Clause 39)
(q) Names and addresses of parties for notices:
Owners: ....
....
(address) ....
....
(telegraphic address) .... (telex) ....
Charterers: ....
....
(address) ....
....
(telegraphic address) ....-(telex) ....
(r) Special Provisions:

Special Provisions continued:

OWNERS   CHARTERERS

The clauses referred to are contained in Part II

INTERTANKTIME 80

PART II

1. Condition of Vessel

Owners shall, before and at the date of delivery of the vessel under this
Charter Party, exercise due diligence to make the vessel
  (a) in every way fit to carry the commodities described in Part I (b); and
  (b) tight, staunch, strong, in good order and condition, in every way fit
     for the service, with her machinery, boilers and hull in a thoroughly
     efficient state and with a full and efficient complement of Master,
     officers and crew for a vessel of her tonnage.
Owners warrant that at the date of delivery under this Charter Party the
vessel shall be of the description set out in the Technical Specification
mentioned in Part I (a) hereof and attached hereto.
Owners further undertake that throughout the period of service under this
Charter Party they will, whenever the passage of time, wear and tear or any
event (whether falling within Clause 28 hereof or not) requires steps to be
taken to maintain the vessel as stipulated in Part I (a) hereof and in this clause
or to restore the vessel to such condition, exercise due diligence to maintain
or restore the vessel as aforesaid.

2. Delivery and Cancelling/Redelivery

(a) The vessel shall be delivered by Owners with cargo tanks as specified
in Part I (d) in accordance with Part I (f) at a safe port or place which is not
ice-bound and from where she can freely and safely depart without undue
delay.
If it clearly appears that despite the exercise of due diligence by Owners,
the vessel will not be ready for delivery by the cancelling date, and provided

Owners are able to state with reasonable certainty the date on which the vessel will be so ready, they may, at the earliest 7 days before the vessel is expected to sail for the port or place of delivery, require Charterers to declare whether or not they will cancel this Charter Party. Should Charterers elect not to cancel or should they fail to reply within 7 days or by the cancelling date, whichever shall first occur, then the 7th day after the expected date of readiness for delivery as notified by Owners shall replace the cancelling date contained in Part I (f). Should the vessel be further delayed, Owners shall be entitled to require further declarations of Charterers in accordance with this clause.

(b) The vessels shall be redelivered to Owners in accordance with Part I (g) at a safe port or place which is not ice-bound and from where she can freely and safely depart without undue delay.

3. Rate and Payment of Hire

Charterers shall pay for the use and hire of the vessel at the rate specified in Part I (h) on the vessel's total summer deadweight, as assigned at the date hereof or ascertained in the case of a newbuilding at the date of delivery to the Owners, per calendar month, and pro rata for any part of a month, commencing at and from the time and date of her delivery as aforesaid, and continuing until the time and date of her redelivery to Owners. The time to be paid for shall be based upon local time at ports of delivery and redelivery.

Payment of hire shall be made in accordance with Part I (i) monthly in advance less any expenses disbursed on Owners' behalf and less any hire paid or expenses incurred by Charterers as may reasonably be estimated by them to relate to off-hire periods, and less any amounts due for payment under the terms of Clause 23 hereof, any adjustment to be made at the due date for the next monthly payment after the facts have been ascertained.

4. Late Payment of Hire

In default of punctual payment Owners shall notify Charterers in accordance with Part I (j), whereupon Charterers shall make payment of the amount due within 144 hours of receipt of notification from Owners, failing which Owners shall have the right to withdraw the vessel from the service of Charterers without prejudice to any claim Owners may otherwise have against Charterers under this Charter Party.

Payment received in Owners' bank after the due date shall bear interest at the rate specified in Part I (j) which shall be payable by Charterers simultaneously with the next month's hire.

As long as a hire instalment is due but not yet paid the Owners shall not be obliged to commence or to continue loading, nor to release bills of lading in respect of any cargo received. In such event the vessel shall remain on hire, and Charterers shall hold Owners harmless for any extra expenditure and for any claim by third parties.

The provisions of Clause 13 notwithstanding, any express or implied authority given by Owners to Charterers or their Agents to issue bills of lading on Owners' behalf shall by such default in payment be automatically revoked.

5. Trade/Lightening at Sea

The vessel shall trade in any part of the world between such safe ports, berths or places where she can lie always safely afloat as Charterers shall direct subject to the limits of the current British Institute Warranties and any subsequent amendments thereto.

Transfer of oil from and to the vessel to and from another ocean-going vessel made fast alongside or while under way shall be allowed in accordance with the "ICS/OCIMF Ship to Ship Transfer Guide (Petroleum)", provided Owners have been given reasonable notice in advance and only to the extent that such operation is safe. All extra equipment required for such transfer operation shall be provided by Charterers at their expense, Charterers also reimbursing to Owners any additional insurance premiums. The vessel shall remain on hire for any time lost whether directly or indirectly as a result of such transfer operation.

6. Ice Clause

The vessel shall not be ordered to nor be bound to enter any ice-bound port or place or any port or place where lights, lightships, marks and buoys are or are likely to be withdrawn by reason of ice on the vessel's arrival or where there is risk that the vessel will not be able on account of ice to reach the port or place or to depart after completing loading or discharging. If on account of ice the Master considers it dangerous to remain at the loading or discharging port or place for fear of the vessel being frozen in and/or damaged, he has liberty to sail to a convenient open port or place and await Charterers' fresh instructions.

Any time lost through any of the foregoing causes or on account of the vessel being frozen in shall be for Charterers' account.

The vessel shall not be obliged to force ice, nor to follow ice-breakers.

7. Owners to Provide

Owners shall provide and pay for all provisions, wages, and shipping and discharging fees and all other expenses of the Master, officers and crew; also, except as provided in Clauses 5 and 33 or elsewhere in this Charter Party, to pay for all insurance on the vessel, for all deck, cabin and engine-room stores, and water, except water for the boilers which (unless the vessel is off-hire) is to be supplied and paid for by Charterers; and for all fumigation expenses and deratisation exemption certificates.

Owners' obligations under this clause shall extend to cover all liability for customs or import duties arising at any time during the performance of this Charter Party in relation to the personal effects of the Master, officers and crew, and in relation to the stores, provisions and other matters aforesaid which Owners are to provide and/or pay for and Owners shall refund to Charterers any sums they or their agents may have paid or been compelled to pay in respect of such liability. Any amounts allowable in General Average for wages and provisions and stores and bunkers shall be credited to Charterers insofar as such amounts are in respect of a period when the vessel is on hire.

8. Charterers to Provide

Charterers shall provide and pay for all bunkers, towage and pilotage and shall pay agency fees, port charges (including any charges relating to the period of this Charter Party retroactively imposed), commissions, expenses of loading and discharging cargoes, canal dues and all charges other than those payable by Owners in accordance with the preceding clause hereof (but including any foreign general municipality or state taxes), provided that all charges for the said items shall be paid by Owners when incurred solely for Owners' purposes, whether the vessel is on hire or off hire. Notwithstanding the foregoing provision Owners shall pay for any bunkers used in connection with the preparation for and the dry-docking or repair of the vessel over and above usual tank cleaning during a normal voyage. Owners shall give Charterers the use and benefit of any bunker contracts they may have in force, at home and/or abroad, if so required by Charterers, provided suppliers agree and so far as Owners' contracts of supply allow.

9. Space Available to Charterers

Subject to the International Loadline Convention and provided always that the distribution of cargo, ballast and bunkers is such as to ensure that hull stresses are kept within acceptable limits in accordance with Classification Society's Recommendations, the whole reach, burthen and decks of the vessel shall be at Charterers' disposal, reserving only proper and sufficient space for the vessel's Master, officers and crew, tackle, apparel, furniture, equipment, provisions and stores. The vessel shall load and discharge cargo as rapidly as possible by night as well as by day when required by Charterers or their agents to do so.

10. Duties of Master

The Master shall prosecute his voyages with the utmost despatch and shall render all reasonable assistance with the vessel's officers and crew and equipment. A sum in accordance with Part I (k) per calendar month (and pro rata for part of a month) shall be paid by Charterers covering overtime, cables and victualling, and this amount shall be paid simultaneously with hire.

11. Instructions and Logs

The Master shall be furnished by Charterers from time to time with all requisite instructions and sailing directions, and shall ensure that full and correct deck and engine logs for the voyage or voyages are kept which shall be open to inspection by Charterers or their agents as required. The Master shall furnish Charterers or their agents when required to do so with a true copy of such logs and with properly completed loading and discharging port sheets and voyage reports for each voyage and other returns as Charterers may reasonably require. Charterers shall be entitled to take copies at Owners' expense of any such documents as are not provided by the Master.

12. Conduct of the Vessel's Personnel

If Charterers shall complain of the conduct of the Master or any of the officers, Owners and Charterers jointly shall immediately investigate the complaint, and if the complaint proves to be well founded, Owners shall, without delay, make any appropriate changes in the appointments.

13. Bills of Lading/Employment and Indemnity

The Master (although appointed by Owners) shall be under the orders and directions of Charterers as regards employment of the vessel, agency and other arrangement. Bills of lading are to be signed at any rate of freight Charterers or their agents may direct, without prejudice to this Charter Party, the Master attending as necessary at the offices of Charterers or their agents to do so. Charterers hereby indemnify Owners against all consequences or liabilities that may arise from the Master, Charterers or their agents signing bills of lading or other documents, or from the Master otherwise complying with Charterers' or their agents' orders, as well as from any irregularities in papers supplied by Charterers or their agents.

14. Employment of Pilots and Tugboats

Owners hereby indemnify Charterers, their servants and agents, against all losses, claims, responsibilities and liabilities arising in any way whatsoever from the employment of pilots or tugboats who, although employed by Charterers shall be deemed to be the servants and in the service of Owners and under their instructions, but such indemnity shall not exceed the amount to which Owners would have been entitled to limit their liability if they had themselves employed such pilots or tugboats.

15. Bunkers at Delivery and Redelivery

Charterers shall accept and pay for all bunkers and boiler water on board at time of delivery, and Owners shall, on the expiry of this Charter Party, pay for all bunkers and boiler water then remaining on board. The price for the bunkers shall be lowest listed prices published by a major oil company prevailing at the times of delivery/redelivery at the respective ports. Quantities of bunkers on board on delivery and redelivery shall be in accordance with Part I (c) unless otherwise agreed. Should the vessel be delivered or redelivered at sea or should there be no such companies at the pertinent port, the party taking over bunkers from the other shall pay the net unit price of the vessel's last main bunkering.

16. Sub-let

Charterers may sub-let the vessel, but shall always remain responsible to Owners for the due fulfilment of this Charter Party.

17. Final Voyage

(a) PAYMENT: Should the vessel be on her voyage towards the port of redelivery at a time when a payment of hire is due, payment of hire shall be made for such length of time as may reasonably be required to complete the voyage, and when the vessel is redelivered any overpayment shall be refunded by Owners or any underpayment paid by Charterers.

(b) REDELIVERY: Charterers undertake to arrange the vessel's trading so as to permit redelivery within the period and area stipulated in Parts I (e) and I (g). However, should the vessel be sent on a final voyage reasonably calculated to allow redelivery within such period at a port of redelivery as provided by this Charter Party, and the voyage is prolonged for reasons outside Charterers' control, and which they could not reasonably have foreseen or guarded against, Charterers shall have the use of the vessel at the rate and on the conditions of this Charter Party for such extended time as may be required for completion of said voyage and redelivery as aforesaid. For the purposes of this clause, the expression "final voyage" shall be taken to include the ballast trip to the loading port.

18. Loss of Vessel

Should the vessel be lost, hire shall cease at noon on the day of her loss and, should the vessel be missing, hire shall cease at noon on the day on which she was last heard of, and any hire paid in advance and not earned shall be returned to Charterers.

19. Laying up

Charterers shall have the option of laying up the vessel at an agreed safe port or place for all or any portion of the charter period, in which case hire hereunder shall continue to be paid, but there shall be credited against such hire the whole amount which Owners shall save, or reasonably should save having regard *inter alia* to the envisaged length of the lay-up period and the time of re-entry into service indicated by Charterers, during such period of lay-up through reduction in expenses. Charterers shall reimburse Owners for any extra expenses incurred by them as a result of such lay-up.

Should Charterers, having exercised the option granted hereunder, desire the vessel again to be put into service, Owners shall, upon receipt of written notice from Charterers to such effect, immediately take steps to restore the vessel to service as promptly as possible. The option granted to Charterers hereunder may be exercised one or more times during the currency of this Charter Party.

20. Off-Hire

In the event of loss of time arising from interruption in the performance of the vessel's service or from reduction in the speed of the performance thereof or in any other manner due to deficiency of personnel or stores, repairs, breakdown (whether partial or otherwise) of machinery or boilers, collision or stranding or accident or damage to the vessel or any other cause preventing the efficient working of the vessel; or due to strikes or refusal to sail or breach of orders or neglect of duty on the part of the Master, officers or crew; or for the purposes of obtaining medical advice or treatment for or landing any sick, injured or dead person (other than a person carried at Charterers' request); no hire shall be due or payable in respect of any time lost during which the vessel is unable to perform the service immediately required of her.

In the event of the vessel deviating (which expression includes putting back, or putting into any port or place other than that to which she is bound under the instructions of Charterers) for any cause or purpose previously mentioned in this clause, hire shall cease to be payable from the commencement of such deviation until the time when the vessel is again ready to resume her service from a position not less favourable to Charterers than that at which the deviation commenced, provided always that due allowance shall be given for any distance made good towards the vessel's destination and any bunkers saved such allowance being calculated by reference to the vessel's description as per Part I (a). In the event of the vessel, for any cause or any purpose previously mentioned in this clause, putting into any port other than the port to which she is bound on the instructions of Charterers, the port charges, pilotage and other expenses at such port shall be borne by Owners. However, should the vessel be driven into port or anchorage by stress of weather, the vessel shall remain on hire and all costs thereby incurred shall be for Charterers' account.

In the event of detention of the vessel by authorities at home or abroad in consequence of legal action against Owners (unless brought about by the act or neglect of Charterers), whereby the vessel is rendered unavailable for Charterers' service, the vessel shall be off hire until the service can again be resumed.

Time lost by the vessel gas freeing for repairs and in and waiting her turn to enter drydock shall, irrespective of duration, count as off-hire, unless otherwise provided in this Charter Party.

Any time during which the vessel is off-hire under the terms of this Charter Party shall count as part of the charter period.

21. Periodical Dry-Docking

It is agreed that, within the period stipulated in Part I (n) since the vessel was last dry-docked, and at the expiry thereafter of similar periods of use under this Charter Party, Charterers shall, upon receiving 3 months notice from Owners, offer to place the vessel at Owners' disposal free of cargo for the purpose of dry-docking at a port having accommodation suitable and available for the purpose: and Owners shall then at their expense put the vessel into dry-dock for cleaning, painting, survey, routine repairs and maintenance.

Notwithstanding the provision in Clause 20 as to time lost by the vessel gas-freeing, time lost and expenses incurred in making tanks free of gas for the purpose of dry-docking as per this clause shall be for account of Charterers provided Owners shall have exercised due diligence to make the tanks free of gas before the arrival of the vessel at the dry-docking port or as soon as practicable thereafter. The vessel shall be off hire from the time of arrival at or off the dry-docking port or from arrival at the dry-docking yard if the vessel is loading, discharging or bunkering at that port, but provided due diligence is exercised as aforesaid any time lost thereafter in gas freeing for the purpose aforesaid shall be excluded from the off-hire period and shall count as on hire. (See Clause 38A). The vessel shall remain off hire until she is again in every way ready to resume Charterers' service at the position at which the off-hire period commenced, or at a position not less favourable to Charterers.

Owners shall be entitled to demand that dry-docking shall take place at a port in Owners' option instead of at the port named by Charterers. In such case, the above provisions shall apply, but Owners shall bear any additional expenses and loss of time caused thereby.

22. Repair and Maintenance

Notwithstanding the provisions of Clause 20 hereof, loss of time due to any of the reasons specified therein or to cleaning of boilers and/or opening up of pistons and/or overhauling of engines shall be allowed on hire between the commencement of the charter period and the first periodical dry-docking as provided for in Clause 21 hereof and thereafter between each consecutive periodical dry-docking up to a total calculated at the rate of 72 hours per year and pro rata for part of a year from the commencement of the charter period, it being understood that Owners shall be entitled to offset any unused portion of such allowance against off-hire time in dry-dock under this Charter Party.

23. Performance

Further to the warranties contained in this Charter Party, but always subject to the provisions of this clause, Owners guarantee that the speeds loaded and in ballast of the vessel and its bunker consumption will be as stated in Part I (a).

The vessel's speed and consumption of fuel and diesel oil will be reviewed at the end of each 12 months, or other lesser period as appropriate, by reference to the observed distance travelled from pilot station to pilot station on all sea passages and over the whole of the time when the vessel is on hire during such passages otherwise than as provided in Clause 22 hereof, and provided always that the following shall be excluded from all consideration for the purposes of this clause:

(a) any day on which winds of Beaufort force 7 or above are encountered for more than 6 hours.

(b) any time during which speed is deliberately reduced to comply with Charterers' requirements,

(c) any time during which the vessel's speed is deliberately reduced for reasons of safety while navigating within narrow waters, having due regard to the vessel's size and draught or when assisting a vessel in distress,

(d) any complete sea passage of less than 12 hours.

If in respect of any such review period it is found that the vessel's speeds have fallen below or improved upon the average speeds herein guaranteed, hire shall be reduced or increased as may be appropriate by an amount equivalent to the loss or gain in time involved, and if in respect of any such review period it is found that the vessel's fuel and/or diesel consumption has been greater or smaller than if the vessel had performed as guaranteed herein, hire shall be reduced or increased as may be appropriate by an amount equivalent to the cost or savings to Charterers resulting from such increase or reduction.

Reduction of hire under the foregoing provisions shall be without prejudice to any other remedy available to Charterers.

In the event that the vessel has in compliance with Charterers' instructions lain at or off one or more ports or places for more than 30 days within any 60-day period, then the provisions of this clause shall cease to apply until after the vessel returns to service following its next dry-docking. Should Charterers so wish they may require Owners to dry-dock the vessel prematurely for bottom cleaning and painting, and in such event all costs and charges thereby incurred shall be for Charterers' account and the vessel shall remain on hire.

24. Slow Speed Steaming

Charterers shall be entitled from time to time to instruct the vessel to proceed at reduced speed for economic or other reasons subject to prior consultation with Owners concerning the characteristics of the vessel and its machinery in this respect. Charterers shall always indemnify Owners and hold them harmless against all consequences or liabilities towards third parties resulting from such instructions. Further, the provisions of Clause 23 hereof shall cease to apply throughout the currency of such instructions, except that Owners shall be entitled to recover from Charterers any bonus which, but for such instructions, would otherwise have been earned by Owners under the provisions of the said Clause 23.

25. Tanks

Owners undertake to exercise due diligence to ensure that the tanks, valves and pipelines are oil-tight at the commencement of this Charter Party, and further Owners shall exercise due diligence to ensure that the tanks, valves and pipelines are maintained in this condition during the charter period, but subject to the above and always provided stowage is in accordance with the vessel's natural segregation, Owners are not to be responsible for admixture of oil and leakage if more qualities or grades are shipped than are specified in Part I (b).

26. Salvage

All salvage and all proceeds from derelicts shall be divided equally between Owners and Charterers after deducting the Master's, officers' and crew's share, hire of vessel for time lost and cost of bunkers consumed and all other expenses incurred. Subject as aforesaid, and subject to the provisions of Clause 20 hereof, all loss of time and all expenses (excluding any damage to or loss of the vessel) incurred in saving or attempting to save life or in standing by vessels in distress and in unsuccessful attempts at salvage shall be borne by Charterers, provided that Charterers shall not be liable to contribute towards any salvage payable by Owners arising in any way out of services rendered under this clause.

Delay or expenses solely for the purpose of saving property shall not be incurred by the Master before prior approval from Charterers has been obtained.

27. Lien

Owners shall have a lien upon all cargoes and all freights for any amounts due under this charter; and Charterers shall have a lien on the vessel for all monies paid in advance and not earned, and for all claims for damages arising from any breach by Owners of this Charter Party. Charterers will not suffer, nor permit to be continued, any lien or encumbrance incurred by them or their agents, which might have priority over the title and interest of Owners in the vessel.

28. Exceptions

Save that Part I (a), (b), (e) and Clauses 1 and 23 hereof shall be unaffected hereby, the vessel, the Master and Owners shall not, unless otherwise in this Charter Party expressly provided, be responsible for any loss or damage arising or resulting from any act, neglect or default of the Master, pilots, mariners or other servants of Owners in the navigation or management of the vessel; fire, unless caused by the actual fault or privity of Owners; collision or stranding; dangers and accidents of the sea; explosion, bursting of boilers, breakage of shafts or any latent defect in hull, equipment or machinery. And neither the vessel, the Master or Owners, nor Charterers shall, unless otherwise in this Charter Party expressly provided, be responsible for any loss or damage or delay or failure in performance hereunder arising or resulting from Act of God, act of war, seizure under legal process, quarantine restrictions, strikes, lock-outs, riots, civil commotions and arrest or restraint of princes, rulers or people. The vessel shall have liberty to sail with or without pilots, to tow or go to the assistance of vessels in distress or to stand by or to deviate for the purpose of saving life or property, always subject to Clause 26. This clause is not to be construed as in any way affecting the provisions for cessation of hire as provided in this Charter Party.

29. Injurious Cargoes

No acids, explosives or cargoes injurious to the vessel shall be shipped, nor shall any voyage be undertaken, nor goods or cargoes be loaded, that would involve risk of seizure or capture or penalty imposed by any rulers or governments, and without prejudice to the foregoing any damage to the vessel and/or loss of time caused by the shipment of any such cargo as aforesaid shall be at Charterers' risk and expense, and the time taken to repair such damage shall be for Charterers' account.

30. Grade of Bunkers

Charterers shall supply suitable bunkers for the vessel's requirements, the viscosity of which shall not exceed that stated in Part I (a). If Owners require the vessel to be supplied with more expensive bunkers, they shall be liable for the extra cost thereof. However, diesel oil may be used in the main engine for the purpose only of manoeuvring in narrow waters or within port limits or for reasons of safe navigation, and Owners warrant that in such circumstances the vessel's rate of consumption of diesel oil will not exceed that given in Part I (a) for fuel oil.

31. Disbursements

Should the Master require advances and commission thereon for ordinary disbursements at any port, Charterers or their agents shall make such advances to him, in consideration of which Owners shall pay a commission of $1 \cdot 5$ per cent, and all such advances shall be deducted from hire.

32. Requisition

Should the vessel be requisitioned by the government specified in Part I (m) during the period of this Charter Party, the vessel shall be deemed to be off-hire during the period of such requisition, and any hire paid by the said government in respect of such requisition period shall be retained by Owners. The period during which the vessel is under requisition to the said government shall count as part of the period provided for in Part I (e) of this Charter Party.

33. War

(a) Unless the consent of Owners be first obtained, the vessel shall not be ordered nor continue to any port or place or on any voyage nor be used on any service which will bring the vessel within a zone which is dangerous as a result of any actual or threatened act of war, war, hostilities, warlike operations' acts of piracy or of hostility or malicious damage against this or any other vessel or its cargo by any person, body or State whatsoever, revolution, civil war, civil commotion or the operation of international law, nor be exposed in any way to any risks or penalties whatsoever consequent upon the imposition of Sanctions, nor carry any goods that may in any way expose her to any risks of seizure, capture, penalties or any other interference of any kind whatsoever by the belligerent or fighting powers or parties or by any Government or Rulers.

(b) Should the vessel approach or be brought or ordered within such zone, or be exposed in any way to the said risks,

    (1) Owners to be entitled to insure their interest in the vessel for such terms as they deem fit up to its open market value and also in the hire against any of the risks likely to be involved thereby, and Charterers shall make a refund on demand of any additional premium thereby incurred, and

    (2) Notwithstanding the terms of Clause 20 hire shall be payable for all time lost including any loss owing to loss or injury to the Master, officers or crew or to refusal by the Master, officers or crew to proceed to such zone or to be exposed to such risks.

(c) In the event of the wages of the Master and/or officers and/or crew and/or the cost of provisions and/or stores for deck and/or engine room and/or insurance being increased by reason of or during the existence of any of the matters mentioned in Section (a) the amount of any increase shall be added to the hire and paid by Charterers on production of Owners' account therefor, such account being rendered monthly.

Furthermore, notwithstanding any other provision of this Charter Party, any war bonus payable to Master and/or officers and/or crew shall be for Charterers' account.

(*d*) The vessel shall have liberty to comply with any orders or directions as to departure, arrival, routes, ports of call, stoppages, destination, delivery or in any other way whatsoever given by the Government of the nation under whose flag the vessel sails or any other Government or any person (or body) acting or purporting to act with the authority of such Government or by any committee or person having under the terms of the war risks insurance on the vessel the right to give any such orders or directions.

(*e*) In the event of the outbreak of war (whether there be a declaration of war or not) between any of the countries mentioned in Part I (l) or in the event of the nation under whose flag the vessel sails becoming involved in war (whether there be a declaration of war or not) either Owners or Charterers may terminate this Charter Party, whereupon Charterers shall redeliver the vessel to Owners in accordance with Part I (d) if it has cargo on board after discharge thereof at destination or if debarred under this clause from reaching or entering it at a near open and safe port or place as directed by Owners, or if the vessel has no cargo on board, at the port or place at which it then is or if at sea at a near, open and safe port or place as directed by Owners. In all cases hire shall continue to be paid in accordance with Part I (h) and (i) and except as aforesaid all other provisions of this Charter Party shall apply until redelivery.

(*f*) If in compliance with the provisions of this clause anything is done or is not done, such shall not be deemed to be a deviation.

Charterers shall procure that all bills of lading issued under this Charter Party shall contain the stipulations contained in Sections (*a*), (*d*) and (*f*) in this clause.

34. Both to Blame

Charterers shall procure that all bills of lading issued under this Charter Party shall include the following clause:

"If the ship comes into collision with another vessel as a result of the negligence of the other vessel and/or any act, neglect or default of the Master, mariner, pilot or the servants of Owners in the navigation or in the management of the vessel, the owners of the cargo carried hereunder will indemnify Owners against all loss or liability to the other or non-carrying vessel or her owners in so far as such loss or liability represents loss of, or damage to, or any claim whatsoever of the owners of the said cargo, paid or payable by the other or non-carrying vessel or her owners to the owners of the said cargo and set off, recouped and recovered by the other or non-carrying vessel or her owners as part of their claim against the carrying vessels or Owners.

The foregoing provisions shall also apply where the owners, operators or those in charge of any vessel or vessels or objects other than, or in addition to, the colliding vessels or objects are at fault in respect of a collision or contact."

35. General Average/New Jason Clause

General Average shall be adjusted in London according to the York/Antwerp Rules, 1974.

Charterers shall procure that all bills of lading issued under this Charter Party shall contain a provision to this effect, together with the following:

"In the event of accident, danger, damage or disaster before or after the commencement of the voyage, resulting from any cause whatsoever, whether due to negligence or not, for which, or for the consequence of which, Owners are not responsible, by statute, contract or otherwise, the cargo, shippers, consignees or owners of the cargo shall contribute with Owners in General Average to the payment of any sacrifices, loss or expenses of a General Average nature that may be made or incurred and shall pay salvage and special charges incurred in respect of the cargo.

If a salving vessel is owned or operated by Owners, salvage shall be paid for as fully as if the said salving vessel or vessels belonged to strangers. Such deposit as Owners, or their agents, may deem sufficient to cover the estimated contribution of the cargo and any salvage and special charges thereon shall, if required, be made by the cargo, shippers, consignees or owners of the cargo to Owners before delivery.''

Hire shall not contribute to General Average and Charterers shall indemnify Owners for any General Average contribution levied on them in respect of freight and/or hire.

36. Paramount Clause

Charterers shall procure that all bills of lading issued under this Charter Party shall contain the following clause Paramount:

"(a) The Hague Rules contained in the International Convention for the Unification of certain Rules relating to Bills of Lading, dated Brussels the 25th August 1924 as enacted in the country of shipment shall apply to this contract. When no such enactment is in force in the country of shipment, the corresponding legislation of the country of destination shall apply, but in respect of shipments to which no such enactments are compulsorily applicable, the terms of the said Convention shall apply.

(b) In trades where the International Brussels Convention 1924 as amended by the Protocol signed at Brussels on February 23rd, 1968— The Hague-Visby Rules—apply compulsorily, the provisions of the respective legislation shall be considered incorporated in this Bill of Lading.

(c) In any event, as regards the period before loading and after discharge and while the cargo is in the charge of another carrier, the Carrier makes all reservations possible under such legislation.''

37. Arbitration and Governing Law

Any dispute or difference arising out of this Charter Party shall be referred to arbitration in London (unless otherwise specified in Part I (o)) to the arbitrament of three persons, one to be appointed by each of the parties hereto and the third by the two so appointed. Their decision, or that of any two of them, shall be final and binding upon the parties, and for the purpose of enforcing any award this agreement and any such award may be made a rule or order or judgment of the Court without the merits of the dispute or difference being re-opened. This Charter Party shall be governed by English Law unless otherwise specified in Part I (o).

38. Avoidance of Oil Pollution

(a) Clean Seas: Charterers agree to participate in Owners' oil pollution avoidance policy as set out below. Such policy aims to prevent the discharge into the sea of all oily water, oily ballast or oil in any form of a persistent nature, except under extreme circumstances whereby the safety of the vessel, cargo or life would be imperilled.

The Master will be instructed by Owners to retain on board the vessel after discharge all oily residues from consolidated tank washings, dirty ballast and the like in a compartment. All water settling out to be discharged overboard.

Charterers will instruct the Master to pump the remaining oil residues ashore at the loading or discharging terminal either as segregated oil or as dirty ballast or commingled with cargo whichever may be possible for Charterers to arrange in each case.

CC

The vessel to be on hire during such operations and any expenses incurred to be for Charterers' account.

Should it be determined by Charterers that the residues are to be commingled with cargo or segregated on board Owners agree to instruct the Master to furnish Charterers with a report giving details of the quantity of oil residues. Charterers shall in no case claim loss of deadweight if they determine that the residues are to be kept on board, whether segregated or not.

Any expenses or loss of time incurred by reason of carrying the residues on board including but not limited to canal transits shall be for Charterers' account.

Owners' oil pollution avoidance policy shall also apply during off-hire periods within the terms of this Charter Party including the preparing of cargo tanks for dry-docking and repairs. In the latter case, Charterers to bear the cost for the disposal of residues and the vessel to be on hire should delays/deviations occur in the disposal of cargo into a reception facility.

(b) **Tovalop:** Owners warrant that the vessel is a Participating Tanker in Tovalop and will so remain during this Charter, provided however that nothing herein shall prevent Owners, upon prior notice to Charterers, from withdrawing from Tovalop under Clauses III (b) or X thereof, and provided further that upon any withdrawal under Clause III (b) or under Clause X, following an amendment to Tovalop which does not materially increase the obligations of the Parties thereunder, Charterers shall have the option to terminate this Charter.

When an escape or discharge of Oil occurs from the vessel and causes or threatens to cause Pollution Damage, or when there is the threat of an escape or discharge of Oil (i.e. a grave and imminent danger of the escape or discharge of Oil which, if it occurred, would create a serious danger of Pollution Damage), then Charterers may, at their option, upon notice to Owners or Master, undertake such measures as are reasonably necessary to prevent or minimise such Damage or to remove the threat, unless Owners promptly undertake the same. Charterers shall keep Owners advised of the nature and result of any such measures taken by them, and if time permits, the nature of the measures intended to be taken by them. Any of the aforementioned measures taken by Charterers shall be deemed taken on Owners' authority and as Owners' agent, and shall be at Owners' expense except to the extent that:

(1) any such escape or discharge of threat was caused or contributed to by Charterers, or

(2) by reason of the exceptions set out in Article III, paragraph 2, of the 1969 International Convention on Civil Liability for Oil Pollution Damage, Owners are or, had the said Convention applied to such escape or discharge or to the threat, would have been exempt from liability for the same, or

(3) the cost of such measures together with all other liabilities, costs and expenses of Owners arising out of or in connection with such escape or discharge or threat removal exceeds One Hundred and Sixty U.S. Dollars per ton or Sixteen Million Eight Hundred Thousand U.S. Dollars, whichever is the lesser, save insofar as Owners shall be entitled to recover such excess under either the 1971 International Convention on the Establishment of an International Fund for Compensation for Oil Pollution Damage or under CRISTAL;

PROVIDED ALWAYS that if Owners in their absolute discretion consider said measures should be discontinued, Owners shall so notify Charters and thereafter Charterers shall have no right to continue said measures under the provisions of this Clause and all further liability to Charterers under this Clause shall thereupon cease.

(c) **Financial Responsibility:** Owners by production of a Certificate of Insurance or otherwise shall satisfy the requirements of:

(1) Section 311 (p) of the United States Federal Water Pollution Control Act Amendments of 1972 (Public Law 92–500) but only as regards oil; and

(2) Article VII of the International Convention on Civil Liability for Oil Pollution Damage, 1969, as far as applicable; and

the vessel shall at any time carry on board the necessary valid certificate(s) in compliance with the said legislation and convention and Charterers shall in no case be liable for loss of time as a result of Owners' failure to obtain and present such certificates to competent authorities.

Save as aforesaid Owners shall not be required to establish or maintain financial security or responsibility in respect of oil or other pollution damage unless and to the extent Owners are covered under their normal P & I insurance to enable the vessel lawfully to enter, remain in or leave any port, place, territorial or contiguous waters of any Country or State or territory in performance of this Charter Party and provided the vessel's P & I Club is willing and able to establish evidence of such financial security and/or responsibility; and further if the vessel is ordered to any such port, place, territorial or contiguous waters, it shall not be obliged to proceed thereto and Owners shall be entitled to require Charterers to give alternative orders unless Charterers themselves establish the required financial security or responsibility.

39. Commission

A commission as stated in Part I (p) is payable by the Owners on hire earned and paid under this Charter Party, and also upon any continuation or extension of this Charter Party.

Should the parties agree to cancel the Charter Party, Owners to indemnify the Brokers against any loss of commission but in such case the commission not to exceed the brokerage on one year's hire.

Commission shall be adjusted for bonus or penalty payments made in respect of speed under Clause 23 hereof. No such adjustment shall be made in respect of bonus or penalty payments in respect of bunkers.

APPENDIX XV

LINER BILL OF LADING

Reference No.

B/L No.

Consignee

Notify address

Pre-carriage by*	Place of receipt by pre-carrier*
Vessel	Port of loading
Port of discharge	Place of delivery by on-carrier*

Marks and Nos.	Number and kind of packages; description of goods	Gross weight	Measurement

Particulars furnished by the Merchant

Freight details, charges etc.	SHIPPED on board in apparent good order and condition, weight, measure, marks, numbers, quality, contents and value unknown, for carriage to the Port of Discharge or so near thereunto as the Vessel may safely get and lie always afloat, to be delivered in the like good order and condition at the aforesaid Port unto Consignees or their Assigns, they paying freight as indicated to the left plus other charges incurred in accordance with the provisions contained in this Bill of Lading. In accepting this Bill of Lading the Merchant expressly accepts and agrees to all its stipulations on both pages, whether written, printed, stamped or otherwise incorporated, as fully as if they were all signed by the Merchant. One original Bill of Lading must be surrendered duly endorsed in exchange for the goods or delivery order. IN WITNESS whereof the Master of the said Vessel has signed the number of original Bills of Lading stated below, all of this tenor and date, one of which being accomplished, the others to stand void.
Daily demurrage rate (additional Clause A)	

* Applicable only when document used as a Through Bill of Lading	Freight payable at	Place and date of issue
	Number of original Bs L	Signature

Printed and sold
by Fr. G. Knudtzon, Ltd., 57, Toldbodgade, Copenhagen.
by authority of The Baltic and International Maritime Conference,
openhagen.

LINER BILL OF LADING

(Liner terms approved by The Baltic and International Maritime Conference)
Code Name: "CONLINEBILL"

Amended January 1st, 1950, August 1st, 1952, January 1st, 1973, July 1st, 1974, August 1st, 1976, January 1st, 1978.

1. Definition

Wherever the term "Merchant" is used in this Bill of Lading, it shall be deemed to include the Shipper, the Receiver, the Consignee, the Holder of the Bill of Lading and the Owner of the cargo.

2. General Paramount Clause

The Hague Rules contained in the International Convention for the Unification of certain rules relating to Bills of Lading, dated Brussels the 25th August 1924 as enacted in the country of shipment shall apply to this contract. When no such enactment is in force in the country of shipment, the corresponding legislation of the country of destination shall apply, but in respect of shipments to which no such enactments are compulsorily applicable, the terms of the said Convention shall apply.
Trades where Hague-Visby Rules apply.
In trades where the International Brussels Convention 1924 as amended by the Protocol signed at Brussels on February 23rd 1968—The Hague-Visby Rules—apply compulsorily, the provisions of the respective legislation shall be considered incorporated in this Bill of Lading. The Carrier takes all reservations possible under such applicable legislation, relating to the period before loading and after discharging and while the goods are in the charge of another Carrier, and to deck cargo and live animals.

3. Jurisdiction

Any dispute arising under this Bill of Lading shall be decided in the country where the carrier has his principal place of business, and the law of such country shall apply except as provided elsewhere herein.

4. Period of Responsibility

The Carrier or his Agent shall not be liable for loss of or damage to the goods during the period before loading and after discharge from the vessel, howsoever such loss or damage arises.

5. The Scope of Voyage

As the vessel is engaged in liner service the intended voyage shall not be limited to the direct route but shall be deemed to include any proceeding or returning to or stopping or slowing down at or off any ports or places for any reasonable purpose connected with the service including maintenance of vessel and crew.

6. Substitution of Vessel, Transhipment and Forwarding

Whether expressly arranged beforehand or otherwise, the Carrier shall be at liberty to carry the goods to their port of destination by the said or other vessel or vessels either belonging to the Carrier or others, or by other means of transport, proceeding either directly or indirectly to such port and to carry the goods or part of them beyond their port of destination, and to tranship, land and store the goods either on shore or afloat and reship and forward the same at Carrier's expense but at Merchant's risk. When the ultimate destination at which the Carrier may have engaged to deliver the goods is other than the vessel's port of discharge, the Carrier acts as Forwarding Agent only.

The responsibility of the Carrier shall be limited to the part of the transport performed by him on vessels under his management and no claim will be acknowledged by the Carrier for damage or loss arising during any other part of the transport even though the freight for the whole transport has been collected by him.

7. Lighterage

Any lightering in or off ports of loading or ports of discharge to be for the account of the Merchant.

8. Loading, Discharging and Delivery

of the cargo shall be arranged by the Carrier's Agent unless otherwise agreed.

Landing, storing and delivery shall be for the Merchant's account.

Loading and discharging may commence without previous notice.

The Merchant or his Assign shall tender the goods when the vessel is ready to load and as fast as the vessel can receive and—but only if required by the Carrier—also outside ordinary working hours notwithstanding any custom of the port. Otherwise the Carrier shall be relieved of any obligation to load such cargo and the vessel may leave the port without further notice and deadfreight is to be paid.

The Merchant or his Assign shall take delivery of the goods and continue to receive the goods as fast as the vessel can deliver and—but only if required by the Carrier—also outside ordinary working hours notwithstanding any custom of the port. Otherwise the Carrier shall be at liberty to discharge the goods and any discharge to be deemed a true fulfilment of the contract, or alternatively to act under Clause 16.

The Merchant shall bear all overtime charges in connection with tendering and taking delivery of the goods as above.

If the goods are not applied for within a reasonable time, the Carrier may sell the same privately or by auction.

The Merchant shall accept his reasonable proportion of unidentified loose cargo.

9. Live Animals and Deck Cargo

shall be carried subject to the Hague Rules as referred to in Clause 2 hereof with the exception that notwithstanding anything contained in Clause 19 the Carrier shall not be liable for any loss or damage resulting from any act, neglect or default of his servants in the management of such animals and deck cargo.

10. Options

The port of discharge for optional cargo must be declared to the vessel's Agents at the first of the optional ports not later than 48 hours before the vessel's arrival there. In the absence of such declaration the Carrier may elect to discharge at the first or any other optional port and the contract of carriage shall then be considered as having been fulfilled. Any option can be exercised for the total quantity under this Bill of Lading only.

11. Freight and Charges

(a) Prepayable freight, whether actually paid or not, shall be considered as fully earned upon loading and non-returnable in any event. The Carrier's claim for any charges under this contract shall be considered definitely payable in like manner as soon as the charges have been incurred.

Interest at 5 per cent., shall run from the date when freight and charges are due.

(b) The Merchant shall be liable for expenses of fumigation and of gathering and sorting loose cargo and of weighing onboard and expenses incurred in repairing damage to and replacing of packing due to excepted causes and for all expenses caused by extra handling of the cargo for any of the aforementioned reasons.

(c) Any dues, duties, taxes and charges which under any denomination may be levied on any basis such as amount of freight, weight of cargo or tonnage of the vessel shall be paid by the Merchant.

(d) The Merchant shall be liable for all fines and/or losses which the Carrier, vessel or cargo may incur through non-observance of Custom House and/or import or export regulations.

(e) The Carrier is entitled in case of incorrect declaration of contents, weights, measurements or value of the goods to claim double the amount of freight which would have been due if such declaration had been correctly given. For the purpose of ascertaining the actual facts, the Carrier reserves the right to obtain from the Merchant the original invoice and to have the contents inspected and the weight, measurement or value verified.

12. Lien

The Carrier shall have a lien for any amount due under this contract and costs of recovering same and shall be entitled to sell the goods privately or by auction to cover any claims.

13. Delay

The Carrier shall not be responsible for any loss sustained by the Merchant through delay of the goods unless caused by the Carrier's personal gross negligence.

14. General Average and Salvage

General Average to be adjusted at any port or place at Carrier's option and to be settled according to the York-Antwerp Rules 1974. In the event of accident, danger, damage or disaster before or after commencement of the voyage resulting from any cause whatsoever, whether due to negligence or not, for which or for the consequence of which the Carrier is not responsible by statute, contract or otherwise, the Merchant shall contribute with the Carrier in General Average to the payment of any sacrifice, losses or expenses of a General Average nature that may be made or incurred, and shall pay salvage and special charges incurred in respect of the goods. If a salving vessel is owned or operated by the Carrier, salvage shall be paid for as fully as if the salving vessel or vessels belonged to strangers.

15. Both-to-Blame Collision Clause. (This clause to remain in effect even if unenforcible in the Courts of the United States of America).

If the vessel comes into collision with another vessel as a result of the negligence of the other vessel and any act, negligence or default of the Master, Mariner, Pilot or the servants of the Carrier in the navigation or in the management of the vessel, the Merchant will indemnify the Carrier against all loss or liability to the other or non-carrying vessel or her Owner in so far as such loss or liability represents loss of or damage to or any claim whatsoever of the owner of the said goods paid or payable by the other or non-carrying vessel or her Owner to the owner of said cargo and set-off, or recouped or recovered by the other or non-carrying vessel or her Owner as part of his claim against the carrying vessel or Carrier. The foregoing provisions shall also apply where the Owner, operator or those in charge of any vessel or vessels or objects other than, or in addition to, the colliding vessels or objects are at fault in respect of a collision or contact.

16. Government Directions, War, Epidemics, Ice, Strikes, etc.

(a) The Master and the Carrier shall have liberty to comply with any order or directions or recommendations in connection with the transport under this contract given by any Government or Authority, or anybody acting or purporting to act on behalf of such Government or Authority, or having under the terms of the insurance on the vessel the right to give such orders or directions or recommendations.

(b) Should it appear that the performance of the transport would expose the vessel or any goods onboard to risk of seizure or damage or delay, resulting from war, warlike operations, blockade, riots, civil commotions or piracy, or any person onboard to the risk of loss of life or freedom, or that any such risk has increased, the Master may discharge the cargo at port of loading or any other safe and convenient port.

(c) Should it appear that epidemics, quarantine, ice—labour troubles, labour obstructions, strikes, lockouts, any of which onboard or on shore—difficulties in loading or discharging would prevent the vessel from leaving the port of loading or reaching or entering the port of discharge or there discharging in the usual manner and leaving again, all of which safely and without delay, the Master may discharge the cargo at port of loading or any other safe and convenient port.

(d) The discharge under the provisions of this clause of any cargo for which a Bill of Lading has been issued shall be deemed due fulfilment of the contract. If in connection with the exercise of any liberty under this clause any extra expenses are incurred, they shall be paid by the Merchant in addition to the freight, together with return freight if any and a reasonable compensation for any extra services rendered to the goods.

(e) If any situation referred to in this clause may be anticipated, or if for any such reason the vessel cannot safely and without delay reach or enter the loading port or must undergo repairs, the Carrier may cancel the contract before the Bill of Lading is issued.

(f) The Merchant shall be informed if possible.

17. Identity of Carrier

The Contract evidenced by this Bill of Lading is between the Merchant and the Owner of the vessel named herein (or substitute) and it is therefore agreed that said Shipowner only shall be liable for any damage or loss due to any breach or non-performance of any obligation arising out of the contract of carriage, whether or not relating to the vessel's seaworthiness. If, despite the foregoing, it is adjudged that any other is the Carrier and/or bailee of the goods shipped hereunder, all limitations of, and exonerations from, liability provided for by law or by this Bill of Lading shall be available to such other.

It is further understood and agreed that as the Line, Company or Agents who has executed this Bill of Lading for and on behalf of the Master is not a principal in the transaction, said Line, Company or Agents shall not be under any liability arising out of the contract of carriage, nor as Carrier nor bailee of the goods.

18. Exemptions and Immunities of all servants and agents of the Carrier

It is hereby expressly agreed that no servant or agent of the Carrier (including every independent contractor from time to time employed by the Carrier) shall in any circumstances whatsoever be under any liability whatsoever to the Merchant for any loss, damage or delay arising or resulting directly or indirectly from any act, neglect or default on his part while acting in the course of or in connection with his employment and, but without prejudice to the generality of the foregoing provisions in this clause, every exemption, limitation, condition and liberty herein contained and every right, exemption from liability, defence and immunity of whatsoever nature applicable to the Carrier or to which the Carrier is entitled hereunder shall also be available and shall extend to protect every such servant or agent of the Carrier acting as aforesaid and for the purpose of all the foregoing provisions of this clause the Carrier is or shall be deemed to be acting as agent or trustee on behalf of and for the benefit of all persons who are or might be his servants or agents from time to time (including independent contractors as aforesaid) and all such persons shall to this extent be or be deemed to be parties to the contract evidenced by this Bill of Lading.

The Carrier shall be entitled to be paid by the Merchant on demand any sum recovered or recoverable by the Merchant or any other from such servant or agent of the Carrier for any such loss, damage or delay or otherwise.

19. Optional Stowage. Unitization

(a) Goods may be stowed by the Carrier as received, or, at Carrier's option, by means of containers or similar articles of transport used to consolidate goods.

(b) Containers, trailers and transportable tanks, whether stowed by the Carrier or received by him in a stowed condition from the Merchant, may be carried on or under deck without notice to the Merchant.

(c) The Carrier's liability for cargo stowed as aforesaid shall be governed by the Hague Rules as defined above notwithstanding the fact that the goods are being carried on deck and the goods shall contribute to general average and shall receive compensation in general average.

ADDITIONAL CLAUSES

(To be added if required in the contemplated trade).

A. Demurrage

The Carrier shall be paid demurrage at the daily rate per ton of the vessel's gross register tonnage as indicated on Page 2 if the vessel is not loaded or discharged with the dispatch set out in Clause 8, any delay in waiting for berth at or off port to count. Provided that if the delay is due to causes beyond the control of the Merchant, 24 hours shall be deducted from the time on demurrage.

Each Merchant shall be liable towards the Carrier for a proportionate part of the total demurrage due, based upon the total freight on the goods to be loaded or discharged at the port in question.

No Merchant shall be liable in demurrage for any delay arisen only in connection with goods belonging to other Merchants.

The demurrage in respect of each parcel shall not exceed its freight.

(This Clause shall only apply if the Demurrage Box on Page 2 is filled in).

B. U.S. Trade. Period of Responsibility

In case the Contract evidenced by this Bill of Lading is subject to the U.S. Carriage of Goods by Sea Act, then the provisions stated in said Act shall govern before loading and after discharge and throughout the entire time the goods are in the Carrier's custody.

Applicable only when document used as a Through Sea Waybill

Shipper

NON-NEGOTIABLE SEA WAYBILL

UK Customs Assigned No.   SWB No.

Shipper's Reference

F/Agent's Reference

Consignee

Name of Carrier

Notify Party and Address (leave blank if stated above)

The contract evidenced by this Waybill is subject to the exceptions, limitations, conditions and liberties (including those relating to pre-carriage and on-carriage) set out in the Carrier's Standard Conditions of Carriage applicable to the voyage covered by this Waybill and operative on its date of issue, if the carriage is one where by a Bill of Lading been issued the provisions of the Hague Rules contained in the International Convention for unification of certain rules relating to Bills of Lading dated Brussels 25th August, 1924, as amended by the Protocol signed at Brussels on the 23rd February, 1968 (the Hague Visby Rules) would have been compulsorily applicable under Article X, the said Standard Conditions contain or shall be deemed to contain a Clause giving effect to the Hague Visby Rules. Otherwise the said Standard Conditions contain or shall be deemed to contain a Clause giving effect to the provisions of the Hague Rules. In neither case shall the proviso to the first sentence of Article V of the Hague Rules or the Hague Visby Rules apply. The Carrier hereby agrees, to that to the extent of any indemnifications the said clause shall prevail over the said Standard Conditions in respect of any period to which the Hague Rules or the Hague Visby Rules by their terms apply, and on that for the purpose of this terms of this Contract of Carriage this Waybill falls within the definition of Article 1(b) of the Hague Rules and the Hague Visby Rules.
The Shipper accepts the said Standard Conditions on his own behalf and on behalf of the Consignee and the owner of the goods and warrants that he has authority to do so. The Consignee by presenting this Waybill and/or requesting delivery of the goods further undertakes all Liabilities of the Shipper hereunder, such undertaking being additional and without prejudice to the Shipper's own liability. The benefit of the contract, evidenced by this Waybill shall thereby be transferred to the Consignee or other persons presenting this Waybill.
Notwithstanding anything contained in the said Standard Conditions, the term Carrier in this Waybill shall mean the Carrier named on the front thereof.
A copy of the Carrier's said Standard Conditions applicable herein may be inspected or will be supplied on request at the office of the Carrier or the Carrier's Principal Agents.

Pre-Carriage by*	Place of Receipt by Pre-Carrier*
Vessel	Port of Loading
Port of Discharge	Place of Delivery by On-Carrier*

| Marks and Nos: | Container No. | Number and kind of packages: Description of Goods | Gross Weight | Measurement |

Particulars declared by Shipper

Freight Details; Charges etc.

RECEIVED FOR CARRIAGE as above in apparent good order and condition, unless otherwise stated hereon, the goods described in the above particulars.

Ocean Freight Payable at   Place and Date of Issue

Signature for Carrier; Carrier's Principal Place of Business

711

APPENDIX XVI

D.o.T. "BUSINESS AND LAW" SYLLABUSES

Class 1 Certificate of Competency Master Mariner
3 hours written examination

The legal knowledge required will not go beyond an understanding of the Acts and Statutory Instruments applicable to shipping and the mercantile law which a shipmaster must know in order to conduct the business of a ship.

(a) Registration of ships. The certificate of registry and its legal significance.

(b) Certificates and other documents or publications required to be carried aboard ship; their use, how they are obtained, and (if appropriate) the period of their validity.

(c) Engagement, discharge and management of crews. Manning scales and certificates. Contracts of employment, wages and other remuneration, allotments, money orders, payments into bank accounts, superannuation, national insurance, income tax. Deceased seamen, engagement of substitutes, repatriation.

(d) The Official Log Book and the law relating to entries. Offences relating to misconduct, to endangering ship and against persons on board. Discipline, and treatment of disciplinary offences. Civil liability for certain offences.

(e) Custom house procedure, entering and clearing ship. Function of ships' agents.

(f) Loadline marks; calculations involving their use. Entries and reports in respect of freeboard, draught and allowances.

(g) The safety of the ship, crew and passengers. Assistance of vessels in distress. Duties in the case of stranding, collision or other casualty. Towage and salvage.

(h) The law relating to navigation, including the prevention of collision, the reporting of dangers to navigation, and marine casualties. Compulsory and non-compulsory pilotage.

(i) A general knowledge of shipping practice and documents with particular reference to charter parties, bills of lading, and waybills. An understanding of the main clauses in a contract of affreightment. Lay days, demurrage and despatch (including calculations). The law relating to the carriage of cargo, and the ship-owner's liabilities and responsibilities. Protests, cargo surveys, certificates of seaworthiness.

(j) An outline knowledge of the expressed and implied conditions and statutory terms contained in a contract of marine insurance. Particular average, general average. Procedure at a port of refuge. Lloyd's agents.

(k) A background knowledge of U.K. and international organisations concerned with shipping.

Class 2 Certificate of Competency
2 hours written examination

This paper covers aspects of a Chief Officer's commercial duties not examined elsewhere, and also includes sufficient introduction to Shipmaster's

Business and Maritime Law to enable the Chief Officer to take temporary command of the vessel in the event of the Master's incapacity or death.

(a) A working knowledge of:
    (i) the action to be taken on assuming command;
    (ii) the Certificate of Registry and its legal significance;
    (iii) certificates and other documents required to be carried on board ship by U.K. Legislation or by International Conventions;
    (iv) the Official Log Book and entries to be made therein;
    (v) current legislation as it affects the day-to-day running of Merchant ships, in respect of safety of crew and discipline.

(b) Documentation of cargo, including mate's receipts, bills of lading, dangerous goods lists, waybills and cargo plans.

(c) The Master's duties and obligations with respect to:
    (i) stranding, collision or other casualty;
    (ii) the reporting of dangers to navigation;
    (iii) traffic separation schemes;
    (iv) navigation in port areas.

(d) Crew accommodation. Hygiene of the ship and welfare of the crew. Inspection and reports. Procedures in cases of illness or accident. The nature and source of medical assistance available to a ship at sea. Fumigation and pest control. U.K. and International Health Regulations.

(e) The prevention of pollution and the keeping of records.

Master (Middle Trade) Endorsement
2 hours written examination

(a) The certificate of registry and its legal significance.

(b) Certificates required to be carried by British ships. Procedure for obtaining certificates including periodical surveys and inspections and periods of validity.

(c) Engagement and discharge of crews. Manning scales. Agreement with crew. Discipline and the treatment of disciplinary offences.

(d) The official log book and the law relating to entries. Reports to be made in the event of injury to or death of crew or other personnel on board ship.

(e) Custom house procedure, entering or clearing a British ship.

(f) Documentation of cargo, including mate's receipts, bills of lading, dangerous cargo lists, waybills, and cargo plans.

(g) The tonnage mark; a general appreciation of the effect of submersion of the tonnage mark.

(h) The safety of the ship, crew and passengers. Assistance to vessels in distress. Duties in the case of stranding, collision or other casualty. Salvage.

(i) The law relating to the reporting of dangers to navigation.

(j) Pollution; the Master's duties, obligations and liabilities, including the keeping of records.

(k) An outline knowledge of the Master's obligations with respect to marine insurance and the contract of carriage of goods by sea. Protests, cargo surveys, certificates of seaworthiness.

(l) An outline knowledge of the Master's obligations with respect to pilotage.

(m) United Kingdom and International health regulations. Medical assistance available to a ship at sea.

Master (Near Continental) Endorsement
Oral examination

During the course of this examination the Examiner may require certain questions to be answered in writing by the candidate. Such written questions will be restricted to those deemed necessary to establish the competence of the candidate in this subject and will not detract from the basically oral nature of the examination.

(a) The certificate of registry and its legal significance.

(b) Certificates required to be carried by British ships. Procedure for obtaining certificates including periodical surveys and inspections and periods of validity.

(c) Engagement and discharge of crews. Manning scales. Agreement with crew. Discipline and the treatment of disciplinary offences.

(d) The official log book and the law relating to entries. Reports to be made in the event of injury to or death of crew or other personnel on board ship.

(e) Custom house procedure, entering or clearing a British ship.

(f) Loadline marks. Entries and reports in respect of freeboard, draught and allowances.

(g) The tonnage mark; a general appreciation of the effect of submersion of the tonnage mark.

(h) The safety of the ship, crew and passengers. Assistance to vessels in distress. Duties in the case of stranding, collision or other casualty. Salvage.

(i) The law relating to the reporting of dangers to navigation.

(j) Pollution; the Master's duties, obligations and liabilities, including the keeping of records.

(k) United Kingdom and International health regulations. Medical assistance available to a ship at sea.

(l) An outline knowledge of the Master's obligations with respect to marine insurance and the contract of carriage of goods by sea. Protests, cargo surveys, certificates of seaworthiness.

(m) An outline knowledge of the Master's obligations with respect to pilotage.

Test questions based on the above syllabuses

Registration

1. Describe the manner in which a ship must be marked prior to registry.
2. State (a) what persons are entitled to be registered as owners of British ships and (b) what British ships are exempted from the obligation to be registered.
3. State who acts as registrar of shipping (a) at a United Kingdom port of registry, (b) at a port of registry in a British possession abroad.
4. Describe the procedure of taking over command of a ship in a foreign port.
5. After leaving port the master discovers that the ship's certificate of registry is not on board. What should he do?
6. Give a brief summary of the information contained in a ship's certificate of registry.
7. State what national colours a British ship is allowed to wear and in what circumstances they must be hoisted.
8. State what must be done with the certificate of registry (a) when a British ship is sold to a qualified person (b) when sold to an unqualified person.

9. State briefly the procedure for transferring the registry of a ship from one port of registry to another.

Ship Certiffcates

10. What is the procedure for obtaining a Panama Canal Tonnage Certificate?

11. What information is given in a British Tonnage Certificate for a ship to which a tonnage mark has been assigned?

12. When and where are "Deratting" and "Deratting Exemption" certificates issued, and for how long do they remain valid?

13. What is the function of a Safety Certificate issued in respect of a passenger steamer (Class 1)? For how long is it valid?

14. State the period of validity and the function of a Safety Equipment Certificate issued in respect of a Class VII ship.

15. What document should be consulted to check the details of the fire appliances carried in a Class VII ship?

16. To what type of ship will there be issued a Safety Radiotelegraphy Certificate? State for how long this certificate remains valid and what installations are covered by it.

17. Give details of the law relating to the posting up on board of a passenger steamer's certificate.

18. What authorities issue Load Line Certificates, and for how long do such certificates remain valid? Why is it necessary for a ship to have more than one copy?

Crew matters

19. The requirements of the Act relating to crew agreements do not apply to certain descriptions of ships and voyages. State what these are.

20. To what descriptions of seamen do the requirements of the Act relating to crew agreements not apply?

21. With certain exceptions it is necessary to give to a superintendent or proper officer a notice of the intention to employ a seaman under a crew agreement. State what particulars such a notice should contain.

22. Where must a crew agreement be kept (a) if it relates to a single ship, (b) if it relates to more than one ship? In the latter case what is the master required to do in respect of the copy carried in the ship?

23. A seaman's employer is required to deliver to a superintendent or proper officer a copy of the crew agreement, and also the agreement itself when the last person on it has been discharged. State, in each case, within what period of time this must be done.

24. Give details of the requirements of the law relating to the display of a crew agreement on board the ship, and state what person can demand the production of a crew agreement to him.

25. What particulars should be included in the list of crew with respect to a non-exempted seaman?

26. A separate list containing particulars of young persons under 18 years of age is provided for in the standard form of crew agreement. State what particulars it must contain.

27. During what period does a list of crew remain in force? What is the master required to do when it ceases to be in force?

28. State what persons have the right to demand production of a list of crew.

29. When, and to whom, should a master give a notice of discharge before a seaman is discharged? In what circumstances is this notice not required in the United Kingdom?

30. Normally, the consent of the proper officer is required when a seaman is discharged outside the United Kingdom. What are the exceptions to this?

31. Describe the procedure on discharge (a) if the seaman to be discharged is present, (b) if he is not present.

32. What is the period of validity of a British Seaman's Card?

33. In what circumstances is the holder of a British Seaman's Card required to surrender it to a superintendent?

34. What information, etc. is required to be entered into the Personal Particulars section of a British Seaman's Card?

35. State what entries should be made, or may be made, in a Discharge Book by the master. Who should make them if they are not made by the master?

36. To whom is the holder of a Discharge Book required to produce it on demand at any time?

37. What is the master required to do with a Discharge Book in his possession (a) if it was issued to a person who has died, (b) if it was issued to a person who is not present when he is discharged, (c) if it was issued to a person who is left behind in any country?

38. What precautions should a master take before granting a seaman an advance of wages?

39. The Merchant Shipping Act 1970 restricts assignment of and charges upon the wages of seamen employed in U.K. registered ships, but this does not affect contributions to certain funds and contributions in respect of membership of certain bodies. State what these funds and bodies are.

40. Unless a seaman's employer or the master agrees otherwise, there is a statutory limitation on the issue of allotment notes and on the times and intervals of payment under allotment notes. State what these limitations are.

41. Before permitting a seaman to have an allotment note (or notes) in excess of the minimum requirements of the M.S. Act 1970 what factors should be taken into consideration?

42. In general, the wages due to a seaman must be paid to him in full at the time of his discharge. Give details of any exception to this general rule.

43. It is essential that a seaman's wages should be paid to him in cash unless he agrees otherwise. What alternative methods of payment are available to him?

44. What additional payment is a seaman entitled to if there is a failure to pay him his wages at the time of his discharge if the failure is not due to a mistake or to a reasonable dispute as to liability?

45. State the requirements of the law relating to the delivery of an account of wages to a seaman employed under a crew agreement.

46. In what circumstances and to what extent is a master authorised to make a deduction from a seaman's wages where the seaman's absence without leave has caused his employer pecuniary loss?

47. Give a brief account of the procedure to be adopted when it is proposed to make a deduction from a seaman's wages in respect of wilful damage done by the seaman to property on board the ship.

48. In what way, and to what extent, can a seaman's employer be compensated if the employer is fined on account of the seaman being absent without leave in some country in contravention of that country's immigration laws?

49. Explain briefly what is required of the master in respect of a deceased seaman's property left on board the ship.

50. What should be done with the wages of a seaman who dies outside the U.K. while being employed in a ship? State whether an account of wages will be required and, if so, by whom and to whom it should be delivered.

51. What should be done with the wages of a seaman who dies in the U.K. while or after being employed in a ship? Mention any time limit involved.
52. State who has the duty of holding an inquiry into the cause of death of a seaman employed in a ship who dies in a country outside the U.K. In what circumstances will an inquiry not be held?
53. State briefly what responsibilities rest on the employer of a seaman who is left behind abroad.
54. At what stage does an employer's liability for the maintenance and repatriation of a seaman left behind commence (a) if a seaman is absent without leave, (b) if the seaman is not absent without leave. For how long will this obligation continue?
55. Where no notice of discharge is given, what particulars should be supplied to the proper officer for the place where a seaman is left behind? State also what further obligation rests on the seaman's employer after arrangements for the seaman's maintenance and return have been made.
56. State what the proper place of return is in the case of a seaman left behind (a) if the seaman is a resident of the U.K., (b) if he is not.
57. Where a proper officer is requested by the employer of a seaman left behind to make provision for the seaman's return, what procedure is he required to follow?
58. In what circumstances is a master not required to convey a person in his ship when served with a conveyance order?
59. What is the proper time for the payment of the wages of a seaman (a) who is discharged abroad, (b) who is left behind without being discharged?
60. What are the duties of a master in respect of the property left on board by a seaman who is left behind abroad?
61. State what should be done by a seaman's employer in a case where the seaman has been left behind abroad and the seaman's property has been delivered to the employer by the master of the ship. Who will be responsible for any expenses involved?
62. What other items besides food and lodging are included in the provision for relief and maintenance of seamen left behind or shipwrecked?
63. State what national insurance documents a master should be supplied with and where they can be obtained.
64. Describe an effective method of preparing a national insurance schedule at the end of a voyage.
65. What categories of seafarer are exempted from the necessity to pay national insurance contributions?
66. What should be done in the case where a seaman, on joining a ship, fails to produce a national insurance number?
67. In connection with the national insurance of seafarers, explain what a seaman's contribution is based on.
68. What items are included in the total pay of a seaman for income tax purposes?
69. How, in normal circumstances, does the master of a ship decide what deduction should be made from a seaman's wages in respect of income tax?
70. From where can a master obtain a supply of Tax Tables and other income tax forms required by him?

Official Log Book, misconduct

71. The M.S. Act 1970 lays down that an official log book in an approved form must be kept in every U.K. registered ship except as provided by regulations. What are the exceptions made by the Official Log Book Regulations?

72. Certain Official log book entries are required to be signed by the master. Certain others are to be signed by the master in person. Explain the difference.

73. What entries must be made in the official log book at the time when it is opened?

74. State briefly the provisions of the Official Log Books Regulations with regard to the amendment and cancellation of entries.

75. State what persons have the right to demand the production by the master of the ship's official log book.

76. State briefly the requirements of the Official Log Books Regulations in respect of the delivery of the log by the master to the appropriate superintendent or proper officer.

77. When the record of seamen discharged from a ship is entered in the official log book, who is required (a) to sign the entry, (b) to witness it?

78. State what persons are required to sign and witness the official log book entry where a proper officer has given his consent to the discharge of a seaman outside the U.K.

79. What particulars should be recorded in the official log book when a proper officer has required the master of a ship to convey a person under a conveyance order? State who should sign and witness an entry of this kind.

80. State what particulars should be recorded in the official log book where three or more seamen employed in the ship complain to the master about the provisions or water provided for them. Who should sign and witness an entry of this kind?

81. State what particulars should be recorded in the official log book where a child is born in the ship whilst at sea. Who should sign and witness the entry?

82. When a person employed in the ship falls ill or is injured, what entries should be made in the official log book? Who should sign and witness such entries?

83. For what offences defined in the M.S. Act 1970 may a seaman be imprisoned if convicted on indictment?

84. What entries should be made in the official Log Book after a seaman has been formally warned by the master as to his future conduct?

85. What defence can a seaman put forward who has been taking drugs if it has resulted in him being prosecuted for misconduct endangering the ship or persons on board?

86. A seaman misses the ship when it sails and rejoins at the next port. The agent pays £22 for the man's rail ticket. How can the master recover this sum?

87. State briefly the procedure to be followed in dealing with a breach of the Code of Conduct for the Merchant Navy.

88. A seaman is dismissed the ship in a port abroad outside Home Trade limits for breach of the Code of Conduct for the Merchant Navy. What must the master do following the dismissal?

89. What procedure is followed after a seaman has been dismissed from his ship for breach of the Code of Conduct?

90. What redress, if any, has the employer of a seaman in a case where he has suffered loss or expense arising from an act of smuggling on the part of the seaman?

91. Under what obligations is a seaman who proposes to terminate his employment in a U.K. registered ship in contemplation of a trade dispute?

Crew Accommodation, health, hygiene

92. For the purposes of the Regulations, what parts of a ship are included within the meaning of the term "crew accommodation"?

93. State the principal rules governing the siting of crew accommodation on board ship.

94. State the principal requirements of the Crew Accommodation Regulations with respect to heating, lighting and ventilation.

95. Who is responsible for inspecting crew accommodation, and how frequently should inspections be made? What should be entered in the official log book following such inspections?

96. In what manner are sleeping spaces required to be marked?

97. State briefly the rules relating to the siting of galleys.

98. What ships are required to have a space appropriated for use as a permanent hospital?

99. In what circumstances is a D.o.T. ship surveyor required to inspect crew accommodation?

100. The contractual clauses of a crew agreement contain a clause setting out what each seaman agrees to. State what is agreed to with respect to living quarters.

101. What facilities are provided by the M.S. Act 1970 for members of the crew to complain about provisions and water which they allege are of bad quality or deficient in quantity?

102. If a master has been notified in writing by a superintendent that provisions inspected have been found to be unfit for use, and the master fails to have them replaced within a reasonable time, to what extent can the master be fined?

103. What steps should be taken to ensure a supply of wholesome drinking water on board a ship?

104. What should the master do if he has reason to suspect that drinking water shipped at a port abroad is not free from harmful germs?

105. What is the law governing the carriage of a doctor on board ship, and what is the penalty for non-compliance therewith?

106. What steps should be taken by the master (a) while at sea, (b) on approaching port, if there is a suspected case of infectious disease on board?

107. Describe a Maritime Declaration of Health and give details of the master's duties in respect of it.

108. What should a master do if he is unwilling to comply with the requirements of the Public Health (Ships) Regulations, and what may be required of him?

109. What steps shold be taken in the interests of safety after a ship has been fumigated with hydrogen cyanide gas?

110. How should a master deal with a seaman who reports sick but is suspected of malingering?

111. What precautions should be taken for the protection of the crew in a malarious port?

112. What can be done to prevent mosquitoes from breeding on board?

113. What persons, if any, could the master justifiably permit to board his ship prior to free pratique being granted?

114. What is the master of an infected ship required to do on arrival in a port health district?

115. A cabin on board a ship has been used to accommodate a person suffering from an infectious disease. What steps should be taken before bringing this cabin back into normal use?

116. A member of the crew of a ship which does not carry a doctor is taken seriously ill at sea. The master is uncertain as to the correct treatment of the patient. What should he do?

117. Whilst discharging cargo in a port abroad a stevedore's man is badly injured as the result of a sling breaking. State fully what procedure should be adopted (a) in the interests of the injured man, (b) in the interests of the shipowner.

118. What precautions should be taken to protect the crew of a ship bound to a port where it is known that cholera is endemic?

119. What arrangements are available to ensure that a ship's medical cabinet is properly maintained and equipped?

120. How can the master of a ship obtain information regarding the inoculations and vaccinations to which members of the crew have been subjected?

Entering port, Customs

121. For what purposes do customs officers board foreign-going ships on arrival at the outer boarding station of a United Kingdom port?

122. What documents will be required by the customs officer who boards a ship on her arrival at the outer boarding station of a United Kingdom port? What must the master do with customs forms if the Customs officer does not board?

123. Describe the process of entering inwards at a United Kingdom port and state what documents the master will be required to produce.

124. What information must be given in the report when entering inwards?

125. What is a "Parcel List"?

126. A vessel arriving from the Far East has cargo for discharge at Southampton, London and Hull, in that order. State what documents will be required to enter the ship, and what document will be needed to clear from Southampton for London.

127. A master is unable to attend in person to enter his ship inwards at the Customs House. What is he required to do?

128. If the master decides that his ship is healthy, what procedure must he follow when he arrives at a British port from abroad?

129. State when and to whom United Kingdom light dues are payable.

130. Describe the process of entering a ship outwards at a United Kingdom port.

131. What information must be given in the General Declaration form for vessels with cargo?

132. Explain what "transires" are used for?

133. Describe the process of clearing outwards from a United Kingdom port. State what documents must be taken to the clearing officer and what is then done by him before clearance is granted.

134. State the usual information given in a cargo manifest. What undertaking must be given if a ship's manifest is not ready at the time when outward clearance is demanded?

135. State the contents of the form known as the General Declaration.

136. Explain what is meant by "drawback" and state the procedure for collecting it.

137. Describe and state the purpose of a Dock Pass.

Loadlines

138. State by whom load lines are assigned in the United Kingdom. What is the penalty for proceeding to sea without having the ship surveyed and marked with load lines and a deck-line?

139. State the maximum period of validity of a load line certificate and in what circumstances the D.o.T. will cancel such a certificate.

140. What special duty falls to a shipowner on being issued with a load line certificate in respect of his ship?

141. What official log book entries are required in connection with load lines and depths of loading?

142. Describe the load line markings on a vessel 95 metres in length to which a timber load line has been assigned.

143. State what authorities in the United Kingdom can demand to sight a vessel's load line certificate and on what occasions.

144. What are the penalties for (a) overloading a ship, (b) taking or sending an overloaded ship to sea so that lives are endangered?

145. What factors decide the maximum depth to which a vessel may be loaded when she is about to depart from a river port?

146. How can one determine precisely whether a ship is overloaded or not if she is in a closed dock where the water has a density less than that of sea water?

147. What does an "All Seasons load line" consist of? In what circumstances can such a load line be assigned?

148. Enumerate the type of freeboard that are assignable under the Load Line Rules.

Safety

149. What are a master's statutory duties in case of collision? State the penalties for non-compliance.

150. Is the master of a ship under an obligation to report any accident to the ship to the nearest Lloyd's Agent? Explain fully.

151. What is the penalty for misuse of distress signals?

152. In what circumstances is the master of a ship justified in ordering a signal of distress to be used?

153. What are the duties of the master of a British ship on receiving a distress call from another ship or an aircraft?

154. When should crew emergency practice be held (a) in passenger ships (b) in cargo ships, in order to comply with the requirements of the Musters Rules?

155. What official log book entries are required in connection with drills and musters?

156. What are the principal rules governing the issue of lifeboatmen's certificates? How many certificated lifeboatmen would be required in a sea-going passenger ship equipped with four lifeboats each designed to accommodate fifty persons?

157. In what circumstances is a ship deeemed to be unsafe and thereby subject to detention?

158. What factors should a master take into account before deciding to accept the offer to tow a disabled vessel into port?

159. What circumstances are usually taken into account in assessing the amount of a salvage award?

160. What advantages are associated with the use of Lloyd's Standard Form of Salvage Agreement from the point of view of (a) the owner of the salving vessel, (b) the owner of the property to be salved, and (c) the underwriters of the vessel being salved?

161. State the principal duties of a Receiver of Wreck. What persons are usually appointed to this office?

162. Define the terms "flotsam", "jetsam", and "ligan".

163. If the master of a ship successfully tows into a United Kingdom port a vessel found derelict in mid-Atlantic, what action should he take on arrival?

164. In rescuing the crew of a sinking vessel a substantial quantity of vegetable oil is sacrificed. By whom will this loss be borne?

165. In what circumstances could a towage or pilotage contract become merged in or superseded by a salvage service?

166. Ship "A" is at anchor in a harbour when ship "B" arrives and anchors dangerously near so as to foul "A's" berth. What action should be taken by the master of "A"?

167. What action should be taken by the master of a ship when dangerous ice is sighted.

168. What action should be taken by the master of a ship when ice is reported to be on or near his course?

169. What action should a master take on realising that his ship is under the influence of a tropical revolving storm?

Pilotage

170. What is the penalty for proceeding without a licensed pilot in a United Kingdom pilotage district in which pilotage is compulsory?

171. State in what particular manner the Pilotage Act applies to ships which carry passengers?
172. What are the duties of the master of a ship navigating in a district in which pilotage is compulsory when there is no pilot on board? What are his further duties when a licensed pilot offers his services?
173. Under what obligation is the master of a ship being piloted by an unlicensed pilot in a district in which pilotage is not compulsory?
174. What information concerning the ship is the master obliged to declare to a licensed pilot on the latter's request, and what is the penalty for refusing to give such information or making a false statement?
175. What documents is a licensed pilot required to carry with him when on duty and produce to the master or person employing him when required to do so?

Carriage of cargo

176. What is meant by the expression "loading on the berth"?
177. To what extent, if any, may a shipowner be deemed to be a common carrier?
178. What is a charter-party?
179. Distinguish between a voyage charter-party, a simple time charter-party, and a demise charter-party.
180. What conditions must be satisfied before the charterer is under an obligation to commence loading a voyage-chartered ship?
181. What constitutes (a) an arrived ship, (b) a ready ship?
182. What is a "notice of readiness', and what are the master's duties in respect of it?
183. How can the master of a voyage-chartered ship be certain that the charterer or charterer's agent has accepted the notice of readiness?
184. What is usually provided for by the cancelling clause (a) in a voyage charter-party, (b) in a time charter-party?
185. What steps should be taken by the master of a voyage-chartered ship when he realises that, on account of delays, it has become impossible to reach the loading port before the agreed cancelling date?
186. Explain what is meant by the expression "lay days".
187. Distinguish between running days, working days, and weather working days.
188. What is implied by the statement that lay days are to be reversible?
189. How can the master of a voyage-chartered ship tell when the time allowed for loading commences to count?
190. Explain fully the meaning of the terms "demurrage", "despatch", and "deadfreight".
191. Explain the "Cesser Clause" in a voyage charter-party.
192. A ship is loading under charter, the lay days have expired, and further delay will keep the ship at the loading port over a weekend. What action should the master take?
193. A charter party provides for a ship to load 10,000 tonnes of cargo, 5% more or less at vessel's option. In what circumstances will the charterer or shipper be able to claim that he has fulfilled his obligation in loading a full and complete cargo?
194. When a ship has loaded all but 1,000 tons of the cargo the charterer has contracted to load, the master is informed that no more cargo is available. What action should he take?
195. On arrival at the loading port it is found that the charterer has no cargo for the vessel. What steps should the master take?
196. The Consignment Clause in a charter-party provides that the vessel is to be consigned to the charterer's agents at the port of loading. State what this implies, and what jurisdiction (if any) those agents have over the master of the vessel.

197. Explain the terms "lump sum freight", "back freight", "distance freight" and "distress freight".

198. Explain briefly the law relating to payment of freight when goods are delivered in a damaged condition.

199. Where a charter-party provides for a portion of the freight to be paid in advance at the loading port, such advance is usually made subject to charges for interest and insurance. Explain why this is so.

200. A charterer, unable to load a full cargo himself, sublets the remaining space in the ship to another shipper at a rate of freight less than the charter-party rate. What special duty falls on the master in these circumstances?

201. Explain briefly what is meant by (a) a safe port, (b) a safe berth.

202. Explain the meaning of the following abbreviations:

b.d.i.	c.i.f.
F.A.A.	f.o.r.t.
N.R.	T.L.O.

203. State what the following abbreviations stand for:

a.a.r.	d.b.b.
F.C. & S.	f.i.o.s.
S. & H.E.	W.W.D.

204. Explain the "always afloat" clause in a voyage charter-party.

205. The freight clause in a charter-party uses the phrase "freight in full of port charges, pilotage, and light dues". Explain what this means.

206. It is common for a charter-party to provide that the charterer is to have the full reach and burden of the ship. What is the significance of (a) "reach", and (b) "burden" in this context. State also how this provision affects the shipowner's position with regard to bunkers.

207. Give the substance of one of the more usual ice clauses in a voyage charter-party.

208. Explain the significance of the following charter-party clauses, viz. "Penalty Clause", "Deviation Clause". "Brokerage Clause".

209. Some charter-parties contain what is known as the "ready berth clause". What protection does this clause give to the shipowners?

210. In some voyage charters it is provided that a sailing telegram be sent to the charterer on the vessel leaving her last port at the start of the preliminary voyage to the loading port. State the purpose of this. How may the shipowner be affected by failure to comply?

211. What particulars are usually contained in the time-charter party clause designed to give a description of the vessel?

212. What is usually provided by the "off-hire" or "breakdown" clause in a time charter-party?

213. Explain the following clauses to be found in some time charter-parties, viz. Bunkers Clause, Dry Docking Clause, Boiler Cleaning Clause, and Prolongation Clause.

214. A bill of lading may be said to fulfil three different functions. State what these are.

215. Is a shipowner obliged to issue a bill of lading to a shipper on the demand of the latter? Explain fully.

216. Why is it considered necessary for bills of lading to be issued in sets of two or more?

217. How is it possible to tell how many negotiable parts of a set of bills of lading have been signed by the master or agent of the ship when only one part is presented?

218. If non-negotiable copies of bills of lading are issued, how are they distinguished from negotiable parts?

219. Explain what is meant by a clean bill of lading, and by a foul or dirty bill of lading.

220. A shipper who objects to qualifying clauses being inserted in a bill of lading offers the master a letter of indemnity in exchange for a clean bill. What action should the master take? Give reasons.

221. What should the master of a ship make certain of before signing a bill of lading?

222. Why is a liner bill of lading usually a far more elaborate document than a bill of lading issued pursuant to a voyage charter-party?

223. Explain the purpose of the New Jason Clause.

224. What steps should be taken by a master who is presented with a bill of lading printed in a foreign language which he does not understand, and which he is asked to sign?

225. Explain the "Deviation" and "Negligence" clauses in a bill of lading

226. What are the main provisions of an "Exceptions" clause in a bill of lading?

227. What is a Delivery Order?

228. What precautions should a master take before giving delivery of cargo to the person claiming delivery?

229. To whom is the master normally entitled to give delivery of cargo?

230. What should the master do if the consignee fails to appear and take delivery of his cargo?

231. What are the requirements of the Carriage of Goods by Sea Act 1971 with regard to seaworthiness?

232. When cargo is weighed on discharge from a chartered ship, who is responsible for the cost thereof?

233. What is the extent of the shipowner's liability in the event of cargo being damaged or destroyed by fire on board?

234. What notice, if any, must be given by consignees if they propose to bring a claim against the ship for damage to cargo? Is there any exception to the general rule?

235. Whose is the responsibility for damage to goods shipped with insufficient packing? Give details.

236. In what circumstances is it permissible to carry cargo on an open deck? How is the shipowner affected by the improper carriage of goods on deck?

237. What is a possessory lien, and how may it be exercised?

238. What action is available to the master if the consignee who claims delivery of the cargo cannot produce the bill of lading because that document has been lost or has failed to arrive at the discharging port before the ship?

239. Enumerate the circumstances in which a master should note a protest.

240. Explain what is meant by a note of protest.

241. What is the value of a protest?

242. Before whom should a master note a protest (a) in the United Kingdom, (b) in a British possession abroad, (c) in a foreign port?

243. What is meant by extending a protest? How soon should this be done if it becomes necessary?

244. Why is it particularly important to note protest in a case of general average?

245. If a master decides to note a protest, when should he do this, and what special right should he be careful to reserve?

246. In a port of refuge it is found necessary to discharge some cargo in order to effect repairs to the ship, and it is intended to reship this cargo when the repairs are completed. Whom should the master employ to conduct a hatch survey, and at what stage should such a survey be conducted?

247. In what circumstances would it be advisable for the master to obtain the services of a cargo surveyor on arrival at a discharging port?

248. During the voyage the ship takes the ground, but damage appears to be negligible and seaworthiness unaffected. What action should the master take?

249. What is an Interim Certificate of Class? In what circumstances is it issued?

250. A ship in a port without repair facilities has suffered minor damage which has been temporarily repaired by the ship's personnel. No qualified surveyor is available. What should the master do to obtain a certificate of seaworthiness? Would he be justified in relying on the efficacy of this document throughout the rest of the voyage?

251. A ship has undergone repairs in a port where no classification society surveyor is available. From whom could the master seek reliable advice with regard to the appointment of a surveyor competent to issue a certificate of seaworthiness?

Marine Insurance

252. Distinguish between voyage, time, and mixed policies of marine insurance.

253. What is a construction policy? Over what period of time is it usually arranged to be effective?

254. What is the purpose of a port policy?

255. Explain what is meant by (a) a valued policy, (b) an unvalued policy. In what circumstances might the latter type be used?

256. In what circumstances would a policy of marine insurance be regarded as a gaming or wagering policy?

257. Explain fully what is meant by P.P.I.

258. Any person who effects an insurance must either have an insurable interest or have a reasonable expectation of acquiring such an interest in the subject-matter of the insurance. Explain briefly what this means.

259. What are Institute Clauses, and why are they so called? Distinguish between Institute Time Clauses and Institute Voyage Clauses.

260. Define the term "deviation" as applied to marine insurance.

261. Explain the significance of the Sue and Labour Clause in a marine policy.

262. What is the effect of the Waiver Clause in a marine policy?

263. What is meant by the term "franchise" in connection with marine insurance?

264. Give a brief explanation of the "Memorandum" which forms part of Lloyd's standard form of marine policy.

265. A vessel insured under a time policy to which the Institute Time Clauses are attached suffers damage from a peril insured against. Will the underwriters be liable to make good the full cost of repairing the damage? What will be their liability in respect of the expense of sighting the bottom after stranding?

266. What is the advantage (a) to the assured, (b) to his underwriters, of inserting the Jansen Clause in a hull policy?

267. Explain the customary Running Down Clause and state what is meant by 4/4ths R.D.C.

268. State briefly the provisions and purpose of the Sister Ship Clause.

269. Explain the "Continuation" and "Change of Ownership" clauses.

270. Explain the purpose and provisions of the "Inchmaree" clause.

271. What is the effect of the Grounding Clause?

272. What is the reason for, and the effect of, the Valuation Clause?

273. State the provisions of the "Tender" Clause and explain why it is of special importance to the master of the insured vessel.

274. What is provided for by the "Lying Up" or "Returns" clause?

275. What is a marine insurance "slip"?

276. Distinguish between the actual and constructive total loss of a vessel.

277. State in what circumstances the owner of an insured vessel would serve a notice of abandonment on his underwriters and how he would be affected if the underwriters declined to accept it.

278. Define Particular Average and General Average and give examples of each.

279. State what constitutes a General Average Act.

280. Give two examples each of a general average sacrifice and a general average expenditure.

281. On account of fire breaking out in a forward hold a quantity of explosives is jettisoned from an after hold. How will the loss of the explosives be made good?

282. A parcel of cargo "A" in No. 1 hold is damaged by fire and another parcel "B" in the same hold is damaged by water used to extinguish the fire. Will the owners of parcel "C" in No. 2 hold be liable for a general average contribution in respect of either "A" or "B"? Give the reasons for your answer.

283. What parties are usually liable to contribute in general average to make good a loss sustained for the common benefit?

284. In order to extinguish a fire it has been necessary to flood a hold thereby causing some damage to the ship and considerable damage to the cargo in that hold. What precautions should the master take on arrival in port?

285. What is an Average Bond, and what are the master's duties regarding it?

286. What is an average adjuster, and who has the duty of appointing him?

287. What is the object of the York-Antwerp Rules?

288. Who would be responsible for making good the loss arising out of the burning of fittings or cargo as fuel in a case where a coal-burning ship runs short of bunkers?

289. Explain how shipowners usually obtain cover against third party risks which are normally outside the scope of an ordinary marine policy of insurance.

290. A vessel is badly damaged after encountering a tropical revolving storm so that it is necessary to put into port for repairs. Give an outline of the procedure and the duties of the master.

291. What documents should the master send to his owners after his ship has undergone repairs at a port of refuge? How should the various repairs be classified?

292. Give a brief summary of the duties of a Lloyd's Agent.

293. State in what ways a Lloyd's Agent could render very useful services to the master of a ship.

APPENDIX XVII

INTERNATIONAL MARITIME AGREEMENTS AND LEGAL KNOWLEDGE SYLLABUS

(Extra Masters' Examination)

SECTION A

1. IMO CONVENTIONS
    (a) Application
        (i) the functions of IMO and the implementation of Conventions.
        (ii) excepted and exempted ships.
        (iii) non convention ships.
    (b) Certificates—the certificates required to be carried by vessels on international voyages.
    (c) Safety of Navigation
        (i) arrangements for monitoring hazards and the duties of masters.
        (ii) traffic separation and control.
        (iii) search and rescue.
    (d) Cargoes
        (i) Code of Safe Practice for Bulk Cargoes.
        (ii) Dangerous Goods Code
        (iii) grain.
        (iv) other Codes relating to ships carrying specialised cargoes.
        (A detailed technical knowledge is not required).
    (e) (i) Reporting casualties and the findings of inquiries.
        (ii) Reporting of sub-standard ships.
    (f) Pollution—agreements on pollution.

2. HEALTH
    (a) International agreements and measures to prevent the spread of disease by shipping.
    (b) International organisation for medical advice at sea.
    (c) International arrangements for medical assistance at sea.

3. Other international agreements and conventions affecting shipping.

4. COMMERCIAL
    (a) (i) Marine Insurance Act—an understanding of the content and meaning.
        (ii) York-Antwerp Rules—a knowledge of the rules.
    (b) Hague Rules—a general knowledge of the rules relating to the carriage of goods by sea.

SECTION B

1. UK legislation resulting from the international agreements in section A.

878

2. MERCHANT SHIPPING ACTS and related legislation as applied to:

   (a) Crew

       (i) the engagement and discharge of seamen;
       (ii) the terms and conditions of their employment;
       (iii) offences and discipline;
       (iv) allotments and advances;
       (v) complaints' procedure;
       (vi) manning and certification.

   (b) General

       (i) investigations, inquiries and courts;
       (ii) prosecution of offences;
       (iii) detention of unseaworthy ships
       (iv) liens;
       (v) wreck and salvage.

3. UK legislation relating to

   (a) pollution of the atmosphere;
   (b) safe working conditions aboard ship.

APPENDIX XVIII

LIST OF FORMS

Prefix	Title or purpose
ALC(NMB)1	Crew agreement outer cover (Federated ships).
ALC(NFD)1	Crew agreement outer cover (non-Federated ships).
ALC(EX)1	List of crew outer cover for ship in which all seamen are exempt from signing a crew agreement.
ALC1(a)	List of crew signatures (crew agreement).
ALC1(b)	List of crew (exempt).
ALC1(d)	Contractual clauses (NMB).
ALC1(e)	Scale of provisions and water.
ALC1(e) India	Scale of provisions and water (Residents of India).
ALC1(e) Pakistan/ Bangladesh	Scale of provisions and water (Residents of Pakistan and Bangladesh).
ALC1(e) Hong Kong/ Singapore	Scale of provisions and water (Residents of Hong Kong and Singapore).
ALC(NFD)1(f)	Contractual clauses (non-Federated ships).
ALC1(d)(i)	Voyage and notice clause—Unlimited trading agreement.
ALC1(d)(ii)	Voyage and notice clause—running agreement (Unlimited).
ALC1(d)(iii)	Voyage and notice clause—running agreement (Near Continental).
ALC1(d)(iv)	Voyage and notice clause—run agreement.
ALC1(d)(v)	Voyage and notice clause—running agreement (Near Continental and Middle Trade).
ALC1(d)(vi)	Additional clause.
ALC2	Notification of crew changes in crew agreements and lists of crew.
ALC2A	ALC2 continuation sheet.
ALC3	Notification to make or add to a crew agreement.
ALC4	Notification of intention to make or add to a list of crew relating to exempted seamen.
ALC5	Notification of intention to discharge a seaman or seamen.
DIS 1/72	Certificate of discharge.
DIS 4/72	Certificate of employment (ILO Convention 22).
LOG 1/72	Official log book (merchant ships).
LOG 2/72	Official log book (passenger ships).
ASW 1/ASW 2	Account of wages (interim) (final).
ASW 3	Seaman's allotment note.
ALC(FSG)1	Fishing agreement—outer cover.
ALC(FSG)1(a)	List of crew signatures (fishing).
ALC(FSG)1(b)	List of crew (exempt) (fishing).
ALC(FSG)1(d)	Contractual clauses (fishing).
ALC(FSG)1(e)	Scale of provisions and water (fishing).
LOG 1(FSG)72	Official log book (fishing vessels).
ASW(FSG)4	Account of wages (fishing).
ALC1(c)	List of young persons.
ALC 6	Crew copy of agreement.
RR 1	Conveyance order.
RBD 1/72	Return of births and deaths.
RBD 2/72	Report of death ashore.

RBD 3/72	Report of birth or death in a foreign ship.
RBD 4/72	Return of births or deaths on Commonwealth ships other than U.K. registered ships.
PDS 1	Account of the property of a deceased seaman.
B.F.19	Seaman's claim for benefit and master's report on sickness or injury.
B.F.19A	Progress report on sick or injured seaman.
WRE 1	Report of shipping casualty.
WRE 1K	Report of deaths, injuries, etc. in respect of fishing vessels.
WRE 52	Casualty report for delivery to Lloyd's Agent.
INQ 1	Statement on oath about a casualty.
INQ 2	Summons to attend preliminary inquiry.
INQ 5	Notice to attend preliminary inquiry.
FSG 10	Application for compensation for lost gear after fouling telegraph cable.
FRE 14	Stability declaration.
FRE 13	Draught of water and freeboard (for posting up before sailing).
SLL 14B	Similar to SLL 14A but for ships to which timber load lines are assigned.
SUR 23	Compass certificate.
SUR 85A	Notice (to master) of detention of ship under M.S. Act 1894.
SUR 85B	Notice (to master) of detention of ship under M.S. (Load Lines) Act 1967.
DCI	Deck cargo declaration made by master, inwards.
DCO	Deck cargo declaration made by master, outwards.
SUR 183	Report of inspection of safety equipment.
SUR 190	Certificate of inspection of dangerous goods stowage compartments.
SUR 191	Certificate of inspection of dangerous goods magazines.
IS 6	List of aliens in crew, crew members engaged abroad, and stowaways.
Form No. 9	Certificate of British Registry.
Form No. 19	Transcript of Register.
C.348	Report to registrar of change of master.
C.355	Copy of transactions subsequent to registry (mortgages, transfers and transmissions).
C.1321	Discharge of Cargo Certificate.
C.13	General Declaration to Customs (Arrival or Departure).
C.14	Ship's Stores Declaration.
C.16	Cargo Declaration (Arrival).
C.74	Master's appointment of agent to act on his behalf in matters relating to clearance.
X.S.17	Stores Authority (for shipment of dutiable goods as stores).
C.196 (X.S.18)	Transire (Original) for occasional coastwise voyage, to accompany vessel and be delivered at port of unloading.
C.196 (X.S.19)	Transire (Duplicate)—Custom House copy of X.S.18.
X.S.40	Permit to load coastwise cargo before all inward foreign cargo is discharged.
C.197 (X.S.42)	General Transire. Form of Application and Grant. For period not exceeding 12 months in respect of ports to which vessel trades regularly.
X.S.50	Permit to commence loading outwards before discharge of inward cargo is completed.
X.S.53	Permit to land perishable goods.

X.S.61	Notice to Load Explosives Coastwise.
X.S.65	Shipping Bill for Goods as Stores other than those exported from bond or drawback goods.
X.S.97	Notice of Loading under General Transire.
X.S.98	Notice of Unloading under General Transire.
C.142	List of dutiable goods belonging to crew.
C.143	List of "address packages" not shown on Report as cargo (Parcel List).
812 TA	Ministry of Agriculture permit to land livestock.
P7(Master)	Master's Guide to the Marine Tax deduction Scheme.
Leaflet NI 25	Guide for Masters and Employers of Mariners.
P45	Tax certificate for seaman leaving M.N.
P46S(Marine)	Seaman's request for income tax code.
P6S(Marine)	Slip for recording tax codes in discharge books.
New Card P10	Seaman's Tax Tables.
46M	Return of Income Tax and N.I. contributions.
OPIC	Oil Pollution Insurance Certificate.

INDEX

DD*